Birnbaum

Caribbean

A BIRNBAUM TRAVEL GUIDE

Alexandra Mayes Birnbaum
EDITORIAL CONSULTANT

Lois Spritzer
Editorial Director

Laura L. Brengelman
Managing Editor

Mary Callahan
Beth Schlau
Senior Editors

Jill Kadetsky
Editor

Patricia Canole
Gene Gold
Susan McClung
Associate Editors

Marcy Pritchard
Map Coordinator

Susan Cutter Snyder
Editorial Assistant

▰ HarperPerennial
A *Division* of HarperCollins*Publishers*

For Perry Wachtel, who helped more than he knows.

FIRST EDITION

ISSN 0749-2561 (Birnbaum Travel Guides)
ISSN 0883-248X (Caribbean)
ISBN 0-06-278214-2 (pbk.)

95 96 97 98 ❖/RRD 5 4 3 2 1

Cover design © Drenttel Doyle Partners
Cover photograph © Bob Krist

Contents

Getting Ready to Go

Practical information for planning your trip.

The Islands

*Thorough, qualitative guides to all the islands and
the most popular Caribbean coastal destinations.
Each section offers a comprehensive report on the city's
most compelling attractions and amenities—
highlighting our top choices in every category.*

Diversions

A selective guide to a variety of unexpected pleasures, pinpointing the best places to pursue them.

Exceptional Pleasures and Treasures

Glossary

Foreword

My husband, Steve Birnbaum, was one of those people who occasionally went around the Caribbean clucking under his breath, pointing at new hotels and resort developments, sorrowfully describing them with paragraphs that began, "You should have seen how it used to be . . . ." The truth of the matter is that although even I do, in fact, treasure memories of beaches without high-rises on their periphery and remember inland trails before they became four lanes of macadam, the good old Caribbean days weren't always that wonderful for visitors.

But the extensive development of the Caribbean area during the past several decades—and its increasing appeal to US travelers—has made it one of the most important travel magnets on this planet. Although often referred to as a single destination, the Caribbean encompasses countless cultures, and the marvelous blending of all these influences has spawned an environment that is both unique and compelling. It has been our aim to produce a guide that accurately reflects the diversity and allure of this vast canvas, complete with the appropriate bouquets and blemishes. (Because the US government's ban on travel to Cuba for most US citizens was still in effect at press time, we do not cover this Caribbean country, nor do we cover Haiti, because of the continued political and economic crisis there.)

And, the broadening sophistication of island travelers and the (often wrenching) maturation of the islands themselves have made it essential that Caribbean guidebooks also evolve in very fundamental ways in order to keep pace with readers and their needs.

That's why we've tried to create a guide that's specifically organized, written, and edited for today's demanding modern traveler, one for whom qualitative information is infinitely more desirable than mere quantities of unappraised data. We realize that it's impossible for any single travel writer to visit hundreds of restaurants (and nearly as many hotels) in any given year and provide accurate appraisals of each. And even if it were physically possible for one human being to survive such an itinerary, it would of necessity have to be done at a dead sprint, and the perceptions derived therefrom would probably be less valid than those of any other intelligent individual visiting the same establishments. It is, therefore, both impractical and undesirable (especially in an annually revised and updated guidebook series such as we offer) to have only one person provide all the data on the entire world. Instead, we have chosen what we like to describe as the "thee and me" approach to restaurant and hotel evaluation and, to a more limited degree, to the sites and sights we have included in other sections of our text. What this really reflects is personal sampling tempered by intelligent counsel from informed local sources.

This guidebook is directed to the "visitor," and such elements as restaurants have been specifically picked to provide the visitor with a representative, enlightening, and, above all, pleasant experience. Our choices can in no way be construed as an exhaustive guide to island dining, but we think we've listed all the best places, in various price ranges, with a visitor's enjoyment in mind.

Other evidence of how we've tried to tailor our text to reflect modern travel habits is apparent in the section we call DIVERSIONS. Where once it was common for travelers to spend an island visit nailed to a single spot, seeing only the obvious sights, today's traveler is more likely to want to pursue a special interest or to venture off the beaten track. In response to this trend, we have collected a series of special experiences so that it is no longer necessary to wade through a pound or two of superfluous prose just to find exceptional pleasures and treasures.

Finally, I also should point out that every good travel guide is a living enterprise; that is, no part of this text is carved in stone. In our annual revisions, we refine, expand, and further hone all our material to serve your travel needs better. To this end, no contribution is of greater value to us than your personal reaction to what we have written, as well as information reflecting your own experiences while using the book. Please write to us at 10 E. 53rd St., New York, NY 10022.

We sincerely hope to hear from you.

Alexandra Mayes Birnbaum

ALEXANDRA MAYES BIRNBAUM, editorial consultant to the *Birnbaum Travel Guides*, worked with her late husband, Stephen Birnbaum, as co-editor of the series. She has been a world traveler since childhood and is known for her travel reports on radio on what's hot and what's not.

Caribbean

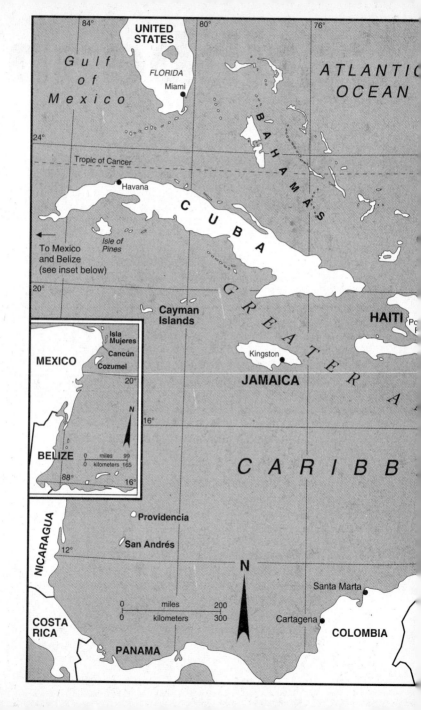

THE CARIBBEAN

DETAIL OF VIRGIN ISLANDS

N

miles 16
kilometers 25

64°40'

Anegada

18°40'

Tortola

St. Thomas

Virgin Gorda

18°20'

St. John

UK
US

64°20'

68°

64°

20°

DETAIL OF LEEWARD ISLANDS

Anguilla

St. Martin/
St. Maarten

miles 22
kilometers 33

N

18°

St. Barthélemy

Saba

St. Eustatius

St. Kitts

Nevis

17°

Montserrat

63°

60°

PUERTO RICO

San Juan

VIRGIN IS.

St. Croix

Santo Domingo

DOMINICAN REPUBLIC

LEEWARD ISLANDS

Barbuda

Antigua

Guadeloupe

16°

A N T I L L E S

L E S S E R   A N T I L L E S

Dominica

Martinique

St. Lucia

St. Vincent

Barbados

N   S E A

Grenadines

WINDWARD ISLANDS

L E S S E R

Grenada

12°

Aruba

Curaçao

Bonaire

A N T I L L E S

Margarita

Tobago

Trinidad

Caracas

VENEZUELA

How to Use This Guide

A great deal of care has gone into the organization of this guidebook, and we believe it represents a real breakthrough in the presentation of travel material.

Our text is divided into three basic sections, in order to present information in the best way on every possible aspect of a Caribbean vacation. We feel that our main job is to highlight what's where and to provide basic information—how, when, where, how much, and what's best—to assist you in making the most intelligent choices possible.

Here is a brief summary of what you can expect to find in each section. We believe that you will find both your travel planning and on-island enjoyment enhanced by having this book at your side.

GETTING READY TO GO

A mini-encyclopedia of practical travel facts with all the precise data necessary to create a successful trip to the Caribbean. Here you will find how to get where you're going, plus selected resources—including useful publications, and companies and organizations specializing in discount and special-interest travel—providing a wealth of information and assistance useful both before and during your trip.

THE ISLANDS

Individual reports on every island and Caribbean country offer short-stay guides with a consistent format: An essay introduces each subject island or nation as a historic entity and a contemporary place to live and visit; the *At-a-Glance* section is a site-by-site survey of the most important, interesting, and unique sights to see and things to do; *Sources and Resources* is a concise listing of pertinent tourist information, such as the address of the local tourist office, which sightseeing tours to take, and where the best nightlife, scuba diving, golf, tennis, fishing, and swimming are to be found; and *Best on the Island* is just that: our choice of each island's very best places to eat and sleep on a variety of budgets.

DIVERSIONS

This section is designed to help travelers find the best places in which to engage in a variety of exceptional experiences for the mind and body, without having to wade through endless pages of unrelated text. In every case, our particular suggestions are intended to guide you to that special place where the quality of experience is likely to be highest.

GLOSSARY

This section provides helpful information that you may need on your trip. A climate chart indicates seasonal temperatures throughout the Caribbean.

A weights and measures table will help you translate metric measurements and temperatures in Celsius to their US equivalents.

To use this book to full advantage, take a few minutes to read the table of contents and random entries in each section to get a firsthand feel for how it all fits together. You will find that the sections of this book are building blocks, designed to help you put together the best possible trip. Use them selectively as a tool; a source of ideas; a reference work for accurate facts; and a guidebook to the best buys, the most exciting sights, the most pleasant accommodations, the tastiest foods—*the best travel experience* that you can possibly have.

Getting Ready to Go

Getting Ready to Go

When to Go

For most of the Caribbean, the best weather—and the peak travel season—is from mid-December through mid-April. Toward the coast of South America, the peak season tends to start earlier, in November. Although summers on some Caribbean islands can be hot, travel during the off-season and shoulder seasons (the months immediately before and after the peak months) offers relatively fair weather and smaller crowds, and often is less expensive.

If you have a touch-tone phone, you can call *The Weather Channel Connection* (phone: 900-WEATHER) for current worldwide weather forecasts. This service, available from *The Weather Channel* (2600 Cumberland Pkwy., Atlanta, GA 30339), costs 95¢ per minute; the charge will appear on your phone bill.

Traveling by Plane

SCHEDULED FLIGHTS

Airlines offering flights between the US and the Caribbean include *Aeroméxico, Air Aruba, Air Jamaica, ALM, American, American Eagle, American Trans Air, Avensa, Avianca, British West Indian Airlines (BWIA), Carnival Air Lines, Cayman Airways, Continental, Delta, Dominicana, Kiwi, LACSA/TACA, LanChile, Mexicana, National Airlines, Northwest, Tower Air, TWA, United, USAir,* and *Viasa.*

FARES The great variety of airfares can be reduced to the following basic categories: first class, business class, coach (also called economy or tourist class), excursion or discount, and standby, as well as various promotional fares. For information on applicable fares and restrictions, contact the airlines listed above or ask your travel agent. Most airfares are offered for a limited time. Once you've found the lowest fare for which you can qualify, purchase your ticket as soon as possible.

RESERVATIONS Reconfirmation is strongly recommended for all international flights. It is essential that you confirm your round-trip reservations—*especially the return leg*—as well as any flights within the Caribbean.

SEATING Airline seats usually are assigned on a first-come, first-served basis at check-in, although you may be able to reserve a seat when purchasing your ticket. Seating charts may be available from airlines and are included in the *Desktop Flight Guide* (Official Airline Guides, 2000 Clearwater Dr., Oak Brook, IL 60521; phone: 800-342-5624 or 708-574-6000; fax: 708-574-6565).

SMOKING US law prohibits smoking on flights scheduled for six hours or less within the US and its territories (including Puerto Rico and the US Virgin Islands) on both US and foreign carriers. These restrictions do not apply to non-stop flights between the US and international destinations, although a number of US carriers have independently banned smoking on some of their flights. For example, at press time, *Northwest* and *USAir* did not permit smoking on flights to the Caribbean, and *Delta* had banned smoking on *all* of its flights. A free wallet-size guide that describes the rights of nonsmokers under current regulations is available from *ASH* (*Action on Smoking and Health;* DOT Card, 2013 H St. NW, Washington, DC 20006; phone: 202-659-4310).

SPECIAL MEALS When making your reservation, you can request one of the airline's alternate menu choices for no additional charge. Though it is not always required, it's a good idea to reconfirm your request the day before departure.

BAGGAGE On major international airlines, passengers usually are allowed to carry on board one bag that will fit under a seat or in an overhead bin and to check two bags in the cargo hold. Specific regulations regarding dimensions and weight restrictions vary among airlines, but a checked bag usually cannot exceed 62 inches in combined dimensions (length, width, and depth) or weigh more than 70 pounds. There may be charges for additional, oversize, or overweight luggage, and for special equipment or sporting gear. Note that baggage allowances may be more limited on flights within the Caribbean. Check that the tags the airline attaches are correctly coded for your destination.

CHARTER FLIGHTS

By booking a block of seats on a specially arranged flight, charter operators frequently can offer travelers bargain airfares. If you do fly on a charter, however, read the contract's fine print carefully. Federal regulations permit charter operators to cancel a flight or assess surcharges of as much as 10% of the airfare up to 10 days before departure. You usually must book in advance, and once booked, no changes are permitted, so buy trip cancellation insurance. Also, make your check out to the company's escrow account, which provides some protection for your investment in the event that the charter operator fails. For further information, consult the publication *Jax Fax* (397 Post Rd., Darien, CT 06820; phone: 203-655-8746; fax: 203-655-6257).

DISCOUNTS ON SCHEDULED FLIGHTS

COURIER TRAVEL In return for arranging to accompany some kind of freight, a traveler pays only a portion of the total airfare (and sometimes a small registration fee). One agency that matches would-be couriers with courier companies is *Now Voyager* (74 Varick St., Suite 307, New York, NY 10013; phone: 212-431-1616; fax: 212-219-1753).

Courier Companies

Discount Travel International (169 W. 81st St., New York, NY 10024; phone: 212-362-3636; fax: 212-362-3236).

F.B. On Board Courier Club (10225 Ryan Ave., Suite 103, Dorval, Quebec H9P 1A2, Canada; phone: 514-633-0740; fax: 514-633-0735).

Halbart Express (147-05 176th St., Jamaica, NY 11434; phone: 718-656-5000; fax: 718-917-0708).

Midnite Express (925 W. Hyde Park Blvd., Inglewood, CA 90302; phone: 310-672-1100; fax: 310-671-0107).

Way to Go Travel (6679 Sunset Blvd., Hollywood, CA 90028; phone: 213-466-1126; fax: 800-700-8359).

Publications

Insiders Guide to Air Courier Bargains, by Kelly Monaghan (The Intrepid Traveler, PO Box 438, New York, NY 10034; phone: 212-569-1081 for information; 800-356-9315 for orders; fax: 212-942-6687).

Travel Unlimited (PO Box 1058, Allston, MA 02134-1058; no phone).

CONSOLIDATORS AND BUCKET SHOPS These companies buy blocks of tickets from airlines and sell them at a discount to travel agents or directly to consumers. Since many bucket shops operate on a thin margin, be sure to check a company's record with the *Better Business Bureau*—before parting with any money.

Council Charter (205 E. 42nd St., New York, NY 10017; phone: 800-800-8222 or 212-661-0311; fax: 212-972-0194).

Fare Deals Travel (9350 E. Arapahoe Rd., Suite 330, Englewood, CO 80112; phone: 800-878-2929 or 303-792-2929; fax: 303-792-2954).

Omniglobe Travel (690 Market St., Suite 510, San Francisco, CA 94104; phone: 800-894-9942 or 415-433-9312; fax: 415-433-9315).

Southwest Travel Systems (1001 N. Central Ave., Suite 575, Phoenix, AZ 85004; phone: 800-STS-TRAVEL or 602-255-0234; fax: 602-255-0220).

STT Worldwide Travel (9880 SW Beaverton Hillsdale Hwy., Beaverton, OR 97005; phone: 800-348-0886 or 503-641-8866; fax: 503-641-2171).

Travac Tours and Charters (989 Ave. of the Americas, New York, NY 10018; phone: 800-872-8800 or 212-563-3303; fax: 212-563-3631).

Unitravel (1177 N. Warson Rd., St. Louis, MO 63132; phone: 800-325-2222 or 314-569-0900; fax: 314-569-2503).

LAST-MINUTE TRAVEL CLUBS Members of such clubs receive information on imminent trips and other bargain travel opportunities. Some clubs charge an annual fee; others offer free membership. Despite the names of some of the clubs listed below, you don't have to wait until literally the last minute to make travel plans.

> ***Discount Travel International*** (169 W. 81st St., New York, NY 10024; phone: 212-362-3636; fax: 212-362-3236).
>
> ***FLY ASAP*** (PO Box 9808, Scottsdale, AZ 85252-3808; phone: 800-FLY-ASAP or 602-956-1987; fax: 602-956-6414).
>
> ***Last Minute Travel*** (1249 Boylston St., Boston, MA 02215; phone: 800-LAST-MIN or 617-267-9800; fax: 617-424-1943).
>
> ***Moment's Notice*** (425 Madison Ave., New York, NY 10017; phone: 212-486-0500/1/2/3; fax: 212-486-0783).
>
> ***Spur of the Moment Cruises*** (411 N. Harbor Blvd., Suite 302, San Pedro, CA 90731; phone: 800-4-CRUISES or 310-521-1070 in California; 800-343-1991 elsewhere in the US; 24-hour hotline: 310-521-1060; fax: 310-521-1061).
>
> ***Traveler's Advantage*** (3033 S. Parker Rd., Suite 900, Aurora, CO 80014; phone: 800-548-1116 for membership services; 800-835-8747 for reservations; fax: 303-368-3985).
>
> ***Vacations to Go*** (1502 Augusta Dr., Suite 415, Houston, TX 77057; phone: 713-974-2121 in Texas; 800-338-4962 elsewhere in the US; fax: 713-974-0445).
>
> ***Worldwide Discount Travel Club*** (1674 Meridian Ave., Miami Beach, FL 33139; phone: 305-534-2082).

GENERIC AIR TRAVEL These organizations operate much like an ordinary airline standby service, except that they offer seats on not one but several scheduled and charter airlines. One pioneer of generic flights is *Airhitch* (2472 Broadway, Suite 200, New York, NY 10025; phone: 212-864-2000; fax: 212-864-5489).

BARTERED TRAVEL SOURCES Barter—the exchange of commodities or services in lieu of cash payment—is a common practice among travel suppliers. Companies that have obtained travel services through barter may sell these services at substantial discounts to travel clubs, who pass along the savings to members. One organization offering bartered travel opportunities is *Travel World Leisure Club* (225 W. 34th St., Suite 909, New York, NY 10122; phone: 800-444-TWLC or 212-239-4855; fax: 212-564-5158).

CONSUMER PROTECTION

Passengers whose complaints have not been satisfactorily addressed by the airline can contact the *US Department of Transportation* (*DOT;* Consumer Affairs Division, 400 Seventh St. SW, Room 10405, Washington, DC 20590; phone: 202-366-2220). Also see *Fly Rights* (*Consumer Information Center,* Dept. 133B, Pueblo, CO 81009; phone: 719-948-3334; fax: 719-948-9724). If you have safety-related questions or concerns, write to the *Federal Aviation Administration* (*FAA;* 800 Independence Ave. SW, Washington, DC 20591) or call the *FAA Consumer Hotline* (phone: 800-322-7873). If you have a complaint against a travel service in the Caribbean, contact the local tourist authorities.

Traveling by Ship

Your cruise fare usually includes all meals, recreational activities, and entertainment. Shore excursions are available at extra cost, and can be booked in advance or once you're on board. An important factor in the price of a cruise is the location (and sometimes the size) of your cabin. Charts issued by the *Cruise Lines International Association* (*CLIA;* 500 Fifth Ave., Suite 1407, New York, NY 10110; phone: 212-921-0066; fax: 212-921-0549) provide information on ship layouts and facilities, and are available at some *CLIA*-affiliated travel agencies.

The *US Public Health Service (PHS)* inspects all passenger vessels calling at US ports. For the most recent summary or a particular inspection report, write to the *National Center for Environmental Health* (Attention: Chief, Vessel Sanitation Program, 1015 N. America Way, Room 107, Miami, FL 33132; phone: 305-536-4307). Most cruise ships have a doctor on board, plus medical facilities.

For further information on cruises and cruise lines, consult *Ocean and Cruise News* (PO Box 92, Stamford, CT 06904; phone/fax: 203-329-2787). And for a free list of travel agencies specializing in cruises, contact the *National Association of Cruise Only Agencies* (*NACOA;* 3191 Coral Way, Suite 630, Miami, FL 33145; phone: 305-446-7732; fax: 305-446-9732).

Below is a list of companies that offer cruises or make arrangements for chartered yachts and other boats. For information on companies offering charters in specific Caribbean destinations, see *Sources and Resources* in THE ISLANDS chapters.

International Cruise Lines

American Canadian Caribbean Line (PO Box 368, Warren, RI 02885; phone: 401-247-0955 in Rhode Island; 800-556-7450 elsewhere in the US; fax: 401-245-8303).

Carnival Cruise Lines (3655 NW 87th Ave., Miami, FL 33178-2428; phone: 800-327-9501 or 305-599-2600; fax: 305-471-4740).

Celebrity Cruises and Fantasy Cruises (5200 Blue Lagoon Dr., Miami, FL 33126; phone: 800-437-3111 or 305-262-6677; fax: 800-437-9111 or 305-267-3505).

Clipper Cruises (7711 Bonhomme Ave., St. Louis, MO 63105-1956; phone: 800-325-0010 or 314-727-2929; fax: 314-727-6576).

Club Med (3 E. 54th St., New York, NY 10022; phone: 800-CLUB-MED; fax: 212-750-1697).

Commodore Cruise Line (800 Douglas Rd., Suite 600, Coral Gables, FL 33134; phone: 800-237-5361; fax: 800-654-9031).

Costa Cruises (80 SW Eighth St., Miami, FL 33130; phone: 800-462-6782 or 305-358-7330; fax: 305-375-0676).

Crystal Cruises (2121 Ave. of the Stars, Los Angeles, CA 90067; phone: 800-446-6620 or 310-785-9300; fax: 310-785-0011).

Cunard (555 Fifth Ave., New York, NY 10017; phone: 800-5-CUNARD, 800-221-4770, or 212-880-7300; fax: 718-786-2353).

Dolphin Cruise Line (901 South America Way, Miami, FL 33132-2073; phone: 800-222-1003 or 305-358-2111; fax: 305-358-4807).

Holland America Line/West Tours (300 Elliot Ave. W., Seattle, WA 98119; phone: 800-426-0327 or 206-281-3535; fax: 800-628-4855 or 206-281-7110).

INTRAV (7711 Bonhomme Ave., St. Louis, MO 63105-1961; phone: 800-456-8100 or 314-747-0500; fax: 314-727-0908).

Majesty Cruise Line (same address as *Dolphin Cruise Line,* above; phone: 800-532-7788 or 305-536-0000; fax: 305-358-4807).

Norwegian Cruise Line (95 Merrick Way, Coral Gables, FL 33134; phone: 800-327-7030 or 305-445-0866; fax: 305-448-6406).

OdessAmerica Cruise Company (170 Old Country Rd., Mineola, NY 11501; phone: 800-221-3254 or 516-747-8880; fax: 516-747-8367).

P&O Cruises (c/o *Golden Bear Travel,* 16 Digital Dr., Suite 100, Novato, CA 94948; phone: 800-551-1000 or 415-382-8900; fax: 415-382-9086).

Princess Cruises (10100 Santa Monica Blvd., Los Angeles, CA 90067; phone: 800-421-0522 or 310-553-1770; fax: 310-284-2844).

Radisson Seven Seas Cruises (11340 Blondo St., Omaha, NE 68164; phone: 800-333-3333 or 402-498-5072; fax: 402-498-5055).

Regency Cruises (260 Madison Ave., New York, NY 10016; phone: 212-972-4774 in New York State; 800-388-5500 elsewhere in the US; fax: 800-388-8833).

Renaissance Cruises (1800 Eller Dr., Suite 300, Ft. Lauderdale, FL 33316; phone: 800-525-2450; fax: 800-243-2987 or 305-463-8125; mailing address: PO Box 350307, Ft. Lauderdale, FL 33335-0307).

Royal Caribbean Cruise Lines (1050 Caribbean Way, Miami, FL 33132; phone: 800-327-6700 or 305-539-6000; fax: 800-722-5329).

Royal Cruise Line (1 Maritime Plaza, Suite 1400, San Francisco, CA 94111; phone: 800-792-2992 in California; 800-227-4534 elsewhere in the US; fax: 415-956-1656).

Seabourn Cruise Line (55 Francisco St., Suite 710, San Francisco, CA 94133; phone: 800-929-9595 or 415-391-7444; fax: 415-391-8518).

Special Expeditions (720 Fifth Ave., New York, NY 10019; phone: 800-762-0003 or 212-765-7740; fax: 212-265-3770).

Sun Line Cruises (1 Rockefeller Plaza, Suite 315, New York, NY 10020; phone: 800-872-6400 or 212-397-6400; fax: 212-765-9685).

Swan Hellenic Cruises (c/o *Esplanade Tours,* 581 Boylston St., Boston, MA 02116; phone: 800-426-5492 or 617-266-7465; fax: 617-262-9829).

Windjammer Barefoot Cruises, Ltd. (PO Box 190120, Miami, FL 33119-0120; phone: 800-327-2601 or 305-534-7447; fax: 305-674-1219).

Windstar Cruises (300 Elliott Ave. W., Seattle, WA 98119; phone: 800-258-7245; fax: 206-281-0627).

Chartered Boat Companies

Le Boat (215 Union St., Hackensack, NJ 07601; phone: 800-922-0291 or 201-342-1838; fax: 201-342-7498).

Charterboat Center (6300 Estate Smith Bay 16-3, St. Thomas, VI 00802-1304; phone: 800-866-5714 or 809-775-7990; fax: 809-779-6116).

Hideaways International (767 Islington St., Portsmouth, NH 03801; phone: 800-843-4433 or 603-430-4433; fax: 603-430-4444).

Lynn Jachney Charters (PO Box 302, Marblehead, MA 01945; phone: 617-639-0787 in Massachusetts; 800-223-2050 elsewhere in the US; fax: 617-639-0216).

SailAway Yacht Charter Consultants (15605 SW 92nd Ave., Miami, FL 33157; phone: 305-253-7245 in Dade County, Florida; 800-724-5292 elsewhere in the US; fax: 305-251-4408).

Sunsail (115 E. Broward Blvd., Ft. Lauderdale, FL 33301; phone: 800-327-2276 or 305-524-7553; fax: 305-524-6312).

Whitney Yacht Charters (4065 Crocker's Lake Blvd., Suite 2722, Sarasota, FL 34238; phone: 800-223-1426 or 813-927-0108; fax: 813-922-7819).

Touring by Car

Although it may seem that a car is unnecessary for an island stay, even where a car is not essential, driving still can be an enjoyable and flexible way to explore. **Note, however, that in some parts of the Caribbean, crime and/or civil strife make it unsafe to drive far afield after dark.** For sources of travel advisory information, see *Consular Services,* below.

Documents required for tourists to drive in the Caribbean vary throughout the islands. In some areas, a US driver's license is the only requirement. In others, an International Driver's Permit (IDP)—essentially a translation of your license into nine languages—is either required or strongly recommended. The IDP can be obtained from US branches or the main office of the *American Automobile Association* (*AAA;* 1000 AAA Dr., Heathrow, FL 32746-5080; phone: 407-444-7000; fax: 407-444-7380). Some islands also require that you apply for a local license or driving permit and/or purchase local car insurance. Contact the applicable tourist authorities in advance of your trip; car rental companies also should be able to provide this information.

On some islands, driving is on the left side of the road (steering wheels in rental cars may be on either side). And, depending on the country or island, distances may be stated in kilometers (km) or in miles (1 km =

approximately .62 mile; 1 mile = approximately 1.6 km), and speeds in kilometers per hour (kph) or miles per hour (mph).

MAPS

Detailed road maps are available from Caribbean tourist offices, travel and other bookstores, and specialists such as *Map Link* (25 E. Mason St., Suite 201, Santa Barbara, CA 93101; phone: 805-965-4402; fax: 800-MAP-SPOT or 805-962-0884). *Map Link* also offers geographical overview maps, such as the Greater and Lesser Antilles *Nelles Verlag* maps.

AUTOMOBILE CLUBS AND BREAKDOWNS

To protect yourself in case of breakdowns while driving in the Caribbean, and for travel information and other benefits, consider joining a reputable automobile club. The largest of these is the *American Automobile Association* (*AAA;* address above). Before joining this or any other automobile club, however, check whether it has reciprocity with clubs in the areas you plan to visit.

GASOLINE

On the many Caribbean islands that use the metric system of measurement, gasoline is sold by the liter (slightly more than 1 quart; approximately 3.8 liters = 1 US gallon). On other islands, gasoline may be sold by the US gallon or the British or "imperial" gallon, which is 20% larger than the US gallon (1 imperial gallon = approximately 1.2 US gallons). Leaded, unleaded, and diesel fuels usually are available.

RENTING A CAR

You can rent a car through a travel agent or international rental firm before leaving home, or from a local company once in the Caribbean. Reserve in advance.

Most car rental companies require a credit card, although some will accept a substantial cash deposit. The minimum age to rent a car is set by the company; some also may impose special conditions on drivers above a certain age. Electing to pay for collision damage waiver (CDW) protection will add to the cost of renting a car, but releases you from financial liability for the vehicle.

Below is a list of international car rental companies with offices in the Caribbean. For information on local car rental companies, see the individual chapters in THE ISLANDS.

International Car Rental Companies

Auto Europe (phone: 800-223-5555).
Avis (phone: 800-331-1084).
Budget (phone: 800-472-3325).
Dollar Rent A Car (phone: 800-800-4000).
European Car Reservations (phone: 800-535-3303).

Hertz (phone: 800-654-3001).
Holiday Autos (phone: 800-422-7737 or 909-949-1737).
Kemwel Group (phone: 800-678-0678).
National (phone: 800-227-7368).
Payless (phone: 800-PAYLESS).
Sears (phone: 800-527-0770).
Thrifty (phone: 800-367-2277).

Package Tours

A package is a collection of travel services that can be purchased in a single transaction. Its principal advantages are convenience and economy—the cost usually is lower than that of the same services purchased separately. Tour programs generally can be divided into two categories: escorted or locally hosted (with a set itinerary) and independent (which usually are more flexible).

When considering a package tour, read the brochure *carefully* to determine exactly what is included and any conditions that may apply, and check the company's record with the *Better Business Bureau.* The *United States Tour Operators Association (USTOA;* 211 E. 51st St., Suite 12B, New York, NY 10022; phone: 212-750-7371; fax: 212-421-1285) also can be helpful in determining a package tour operator's reliability. As with charter flights, to safeguard your funds, always make your check out to the company's escrow account.

Many tour operators offer packages focused on special interests such as the arts, nature study, or sports. *All Adventure Travel* (5589 Arapahoe, Suite 208, Boulder, CO 80303; phone: 800-537-4025 or 303-440-7924; fax: 303-440-4160) represents such specialized packagers. Many also are listed in the *Specialty Travel Index* (305 San Anselmo Ave., Suite 313, San Anselmo, CA 94960; phone: 415-459-4900 in California; 800-442-4922 elsewhere in the US; fax: 415-459-4974). In addition, a variety of package tours to the Caribbean are listed in the *Island Vacation Catalog,* issued by *TourScan* (PO Box 2367, Darien, CT 06820; phone: 800-962-2080 or 203-655-8091; fax: 203-655-6689).

Below is a list of companies offering package tours to the Caribbean. Note that those companies described as wholesalers accept bookings only through travel agents.

Package Tour Operators

Adventure Center (1311 63rd St., Suite 200, Emeryville, CA 94608; phone: 510-654-1879 in northern California; 800-227-8747 elsewhere in the US; fax: 510-654-4200).

Adventure Tours (10612 Beaver Dam Rd., Hunt Valley, MD 21030-2205; phone: 410-785-3500 in the Baltimore area; 800-638-9040 elsewhere in the US; fax: 410-584-2771). Wholesaler.

AIB Tours (2500 NW 79th Ave., Suite 211, Miami, FL 33122; phone: 305-715-0056 in Florida; 800-242-8687 elsewhere in the US; fax: 305-715-0055). Wholesaler.

American Airlines FlyAAway Vacations (offices throughout the US; phone: 800-321-2121).

American Museum of Natural History Discovery Tours (Central Park W. at 79th St., New York, NY 10024; phone: 212-769-5700).

American Wilderness Experience (PO Box 1486, Boulder, CO 80306; phone: 800-444-0099 or 303-444-2622; fax: 303-444-3999).

Angling Travel and Tours (c/o *John Eustice & Associates,* 1445 SW 84th Ave., Portland, OR 97225; phone: 800-288-0886 or 503-297-2468; fax: 503-297-3048).

Apple Vacations East (7 Campus Blvd., Newtown Square, PA 19073; phone: 800-727-3400 or 610-359-6500; fax: 610-359-6524). Wholesaler.

Backroads (1516 Fifth St., Berkeley, CA 94710; phone: 800-462-2848 or 510-527-1555; fax: 510-527-1444).

Barron Adventures (16501 Pacific Coast Hwy., Suite 100, Sunset Beach, CA 90742; phone: 310-592-2050; fax: 310-426-5664).

Bentley Tours (1649 Colorado Blvd., Los Angeles, CA 90041-1435; phone: 800-821-9726 or 213-258-8451; fax: 213-255-7204).

Biological Journeys (1696 Ocean Dr., McKinleyville, CA 95521; phone: 800-548-7555 or 707-839-0178; fax: 707-839-4656).

Butterfield & Robinson (70 Bond St., Suite 300, Toronto, Ontario M5B 1X3, Canada; phone: 800-387-1147 or 416-864-1354; fax: 416-864-0541).

Caiman Expeditions (3449 E. River Rd., Tucson, AZ 85718; phone: 602-299-1047; fax: 602-577-0208).

Caribbean Concepts (575 Underhill Blvd., Suite 140, Syosset, NY 11791; phone: 516-496-9800 in Nassau County; 800-423-4433 elsewhere in the US; fax: 516-496-9880).

Certified Vacations (110 E. Broward Blvd., Ft. Lauderdale, FL 33302; phone: 800-233-7260 or 305-522-1440; fax: 305-357-4687).

Continental Grand Destinations (offices throughout the US; phone: 800-634-5555).

Coral Way Tours (9745 Sunset Dr., Suite 104, Miami, FL 33173; phone: 800-882-4665 or 305-279-3252; fax: 305-279-3167).

Delta's Dream Vacations (PO Box 1525, Ft. Lauderdale, FL 33302; phone: 800-872-7786).

Earthwatch (680 Mt. Auburn St., PO Box 403BG, Watertown, MA 02272; phone: 800-776-0188 or 617-926-8200; fax: 617-926-8532).

Ecosummer Expeditions (main office: 1516 Duranleau St., Vancouver, British Columbia V6H 3S4, Canada; phone: 800-688-8605 in the US;

800-465-8884 or 604-669-7741 in Canada; fax: 604-669-3244; US mailing address: 936 Peace Portal Dr., PO Box 8014-240, Blaine, WA 98231).

Equitour (PO Box 807, Dubois, WY 82513; phone: 307-455-3363 in Wyoming; 800-545-0019 elsewhere in the US; fax: 307-455-2354).

Escapade Tours (9 W. Office Center, 2200 Fletcher Ave., Ft. Lee, NJ 07024; phone: 800-356-2405 or 201-346-9061; fax: 201-346-0511).

Fishing International (PO Box 2132, Santa Rosa, CA 95405; phone: 800-950-4242 or 707-539-3366; fax: 707-539-1320).

FITS Equestrian (685 Lateen Rd., Solvang, CA 93463; phone: 800-666-3487 or 805-688-9494; fax: 805-688-2943).

Forum Travel International (91 Gregory La., Suite 21, Pleasant Hill, CA 94523; phone: 510-671-2900; fax: 510-671-2993 or 510-946-1500).

4th Dimension Tours (1150 NW 72nd Ave., Suite 333, Miami, FL 33126; phone: 800-343-0020 or 305-477-1525; fax: 305-477-0731). Wholesaler.

Frontiers International (PO Box 959, Wexford, PA 15090-0959; phone: 412-935-1577 in Pennsylvania; 800-245-1950 elsewhere in the US; fax: 412-935-5388).

Funway Holidays Funjet (PO Box 1460, Milwaukee, WI 53201-1460; phone: 800-558-3050 for reservations; 800-558-3060 for customer service). Wholesaler.

GOGO Tours (69 Spring St., Ramsey, NJ 07446-0507; phone: 201-934-3759).

GWV International (300 First Ave., Needham, MA 02194; phone: 800-225-5498 or 617-449-5460; fax: 617-449-3473). Wholesaler.

International Expeditions (1 Environs Park, Helena, AL 35080; phone: 800-633-4734 or 205-428-1700; fax: 205-428-1714).

Journeys (4011 Jackson Rd., Ann Arbor, MI 48103; phone: 800-255-8735 or 313-665-4407; fax: 313-665-2945).

Kerrville Tours (PO Box 79, Shreveport, LA 71161-0079; phone: 800-442-8705 or 318-227-2882; fax: 318-227-2486).

Ladatco Tours (2220 Coral Way, Miami, FL 33145; phone: 800-327-6162 or 305-854-8422; fax: 305-285-0504). Wholesaler.

Latin America Reservation Center (*LARC*; PO Box 1435, Dundee, FL 33838; phone: 800-327-3573 or 813-439-1486; fax: 813-439-2118).

LATOUR (15-22 215th St., Bayside, NY 11360; phone: 800-825-0825 or 718-229-6500; fax: 718-229-6978).

Liberty Travel (for the nearest location, contact the central office: 69 Spring St., Ramsey, NJ 07446; phone: 201-934-3500; fax: 201-934-3888).

Marathon Tours (108 Main St., Boston, MA 02129; phone: 800-444-4097 or 617-242-7845; fax: 617-242-7686).

Marnella Tours (33 Walt Whitman Rd., Suite 233, Huntington Station, NY 11746; phone: 800-937-6999 or 516-271-6969; fax: 516-271-8593).

Maya Route Tours (PO Box 1948, Murray Hill Station, New York, NY 10156; phone: 212-683-2136; fax: 212-575-7730).

MTA International (1717 N. Highland Ave., Suite 1100, Los Angeles, CA 90028; phone: 800-876-4682 or 213-462-6444 for tours in Mexico; 800-876-6824 or 213-462-8643 for tours to all other destinations; fax: 213-461-7559). Wholesaler.

Nature Expeditions International (PO Box 11496, Eugene, OR 97440; phone: 800-869-0639 or 503-484-6529; fax: 503-484-6531).

New England Vacation Tours (PO Box 560, West Dover, VT 05356; phone: 800-742-7669 or 802-464-2076; fax: 802-464-2629). Wholesaler.

Northwest World Vacations (c/o *MLT*, 5130 Hwy. 101, Minnetonka, MN 55345; phone: 800-328-0025 or 612-989-5000; fax: 612-474-0725). Wholesaler.

Oceanic Society Expeditions (Ft. Mason Center, Building E, San Francisco, CA 94123; phone: 800-326-7491 or 415-441-1106; fax: 415-474-3395).

Outland Adventures (PO Box 16343, Seattle, WA 98116; phone/fax: 206-932-7012).

PanAngling Travel Service (180 N. Michigan Ave., Room 303, Chicago, IL 60601; phone: 800-533-4353 or 312-263-0328; fax: 312-263-5246).

Path Tours (PO Box 221300, Newhall, CA 91321-1300; phone: 800-843-0400 or 805-255-2740; fax: 805-255-1064). Wholesaler.

Petrabax Tours (97-45 Queens Blvd., Suite 600, Rego Park, NY 11374; phone: 800-367-6611 or 718-897-7272; fax: 718-275-3943).

Pleasant Holidays (2404 Townsgate Rd., Westlake Village, CA 91361; phone: 800-242-9244 or 818-991-3390; fax: 805-495-4972).

Pleasure Break (3701 Algonquin Rd., Suite 900, Rolling Meadows, IL 60008; phone: 708-670-6300 in Illinois; 800-777-1885 elsewhere in the US; fax: 708-670-7689). Wholesaler.

Quasar Tours (1523 W. Hillsborough Ave., Tampa, FL 33603; phone: 800-444-1770 or 813-237-4990; fax: 813-238-4175). Wholesaler.

See & Sea Travel (50 Francisco St., Suite 205, San Francisco, CA 94133; phone: 415-434-3400 in California; 800-348-9778 elsewhere in the US; fax: 415-434-3409).

Sierra Club Outings (730 Polk St., San Francisco, CA 94109; phone: 415-923-5630).

Slickrock Adventures (PO Box 1400, Moab, UT 84532; phone/fax: 801-259-6996).

Smithsonian Associates Study Tours and Seminars (1100 Jefferson Dr. SW, Room 3045, Washington, DC 20560; phone: 202-357-4700; fax: 202-786-2315).

Solar Tours (1629 K St. NW, Suite 502, Washington, DC 20006; phone: 800-388-7652 or 202-861-5864; fax: 202-452-0905). Wholesaler.

South American Fiesta (910 W. Mercury Blvd., Hampton, VA 23666; phone: 800-334-3782 or 804-825-9000; fax: 804-826-1747).

Steppingstone Environmental Education Tours (PO Box 373, Narberth, PA 19072; phone: 800-874-8784 or 610-649-3891; fax: 610-649-3428).

Steve Currey Expeditions (PO Box 1574, Provo, UT 84603; phone: 800-937-7238; phone/fax: 801-224-5715).

Sunmakers (S. Tower, 100 W. Harrison, Suite 350, Seattle, WA 98199; phone: 800-841-4321 or 206-216-2906; fax: 800-323-2231). Wholesaler.

Tara Tours (6595 NW 36th St., Suite 306-A, Miami, FL 33166; phone: 800-327-0080 or 305-871-1246; fax: 305-871-0417). Wholesaler.

Thomas Cook Vacations (headquarters: 45 Berkeley St., Piccadilly, London W1A 1EB, England; phone: 44-171-499-4000; fax: 44-171-408-4299; main US office: 100 Cambridge Park Dr., Cambridge, MA 02140; phone: 800-846-6272 or 617-868-2666; fax: 617-349-1094).

Tours and Travel Odyssey (230 E. McClellan Ave., Livingston, NJ 07039; phone: 800-527-2989 or 201-992-5459; fax: 201-994-1618).

Trans National Travel (2 Charlesgate W., Boston, MA 02215; phone: 800-262-0123 or 617-762-9200; fax: 617-638-3445). Wholesaler.

Travel Impressions (465 Smith St., Farmingdale, NY 11735; phone: 800-284-0077, 800-284-0044, or 516-845-8000; fax: 561-845-8095). Wholesaler.

Trek America (PO Box 470, Blairstown, NJ 07825; phone: 800-221-0596 or 908-362-9198; fax: 908-362-9313).

Tropical Adventures Travel (111 Second Ave. N., Seattle, WA 98109; phone: 800-247-3483 or 206-441-3483; fax: 206-441-5431).

TWA Getaway Vacations (Getaway Vacation Center, 10 E. Stow Rd., Marlton, NJ 08053; phone: 800-GETAWAY; fax: 609-985-4125).

United Airlines Vacations (PO Box 24580, Milwaukee, WI 53224-0580; phone: 800-328-6877; fax: 414-351-5256).

Uniworld (16000 Ventura Blvd., Suite 210, Encino, CA 91436; phone: 800-733-7820 or 818-382-7820; fax: 818-382-7829). Wholesaler.

Victor Emanuel Nature Tours (PO Box 33008, Austin, TX 78764; phone: 800-328-VENT or 512-328-5221; fax: 512-328-2919).

Wide World of Golf (PO Box 5217, Carmel, CA 93921; phone: 800-214-4653 or 408-624-6667; fax: 408-625-9671).

Wilderness: Alaska/Mexico (1231 Sundance Loop, Department BB, Fairbanks, AK 99709; phone/fax: 907-479-8203).

Wildland Adventures (3516 NE 155th St., Seattle, WA 98155; phone: 800-345-4453 or 206-365-0686; fax: 206-363-6615).

Insurance

The first person with whom you should discuss travel insurance is your own insurance broker. You may discover that the insurance you already carry protects you adequately while traveling and that you need little additional coverage. If you charge travel services, the credit card company also may provide some insurance coverage (and other safeguards). Below is a list of the basic types of travel insurance and companies that specialize in such policies.

Types of Travel Insurance

Automobile insurance: Provides collision, theft, property damage, and personal liability protection while driving. Note that US insurance policies are not accepted in some countries and travelers must purchase local insurance.

Baggage and personal effects insurance: Protects your bags and their contents in case of damage or theft at any point during your travels.

Default and/or bankruptcy insurance: Provides coverage in the event of default and/or bankruptcy on the part of the tour operator, airline, or other travel supplier.

Flight insurance: Covers accidental injury or death while flying.

Personal accident and sickness insurance: Covers cases of illness, injury, or death in an accident while traveling.

Trip cancellation and interruption insurance: Guarantees a refund if you must cancel a trip; may reimburse you for additional travel costs incurred in catching up with a tour or traveling home early.

Combination policies: Include any or all of the above.

Travel Insurance Providers

Access America International (PO Box 90315, Richmond, VA 23230; phone: 800-284-8300 or 804-285-3300; fax: 804-673-1491).

Carefree (c/o *Berkely Care,* Arm Coverage, PO Box 310, Mineola, NY 11501; phone: 800-645-2424 or 516-294-0220; fax: 516-294-0258).

NEAR Services (PO Box 1339, Calumet City, IL 60409; phone: 708-868-6700 in the Chicago area; 800-654-6700 elsewhere in the US; fax: 708-868-6706).

Tele-Trip (3201 Farnam St., Omaha, NE 68131; phone: 800-228-9792 or 402-345-2400; fax: 402-978-2456).

Travel Assistance International (c/o *Worldwide Assistance Services,* 1133 15th St. NW, Suite 400, Washington, DC 20005; phone: 800-821-2828 or 202-331-1609; fax: 202-331-1530).

Travel Guard International (1145 Clark St., Stevens Point, WI 54481; phone: 800-826-1300 or 715-345-0505; fax: 800-955-8785).

Travel Insurance PAK Worldwide Coverage (c/o *Travel Insured International,* PO Box 280568, East Hartford, CT 06128-0568; phone: 800-243-3174 or 203-528-7663; fax: 203-528-8005).

Disabled Travelers

Make travel arrangements well in advance. Specify to all services involved the nature of your disability to determine if there are accommodations and facilities that meet your needs.

International Organizations

ACCENT on Living (PO Box 700, Bloomington, IL 61702; phone: 800-787-8444 or 309-378-2961; fax: 309-378-4420).

Access: The Foundation for Accessibility by the Disabled (PO Box 356, Malverne, NY 11565; phone/fax: 516-568-2715).

American Foundation for the Blind (15 W. 16th St., New York, NY 10011; phone: 800-232-5463 or 212-620-2147; fax: 212-727-7418).

Information Center for Individuals with Disabilities (Ft. Point Pl., 27-43 Wormwood St., Boston, MA 02210; phone: 800-462-5015 in Massachusetts; 617-727-5540 elsewhere in the US; TDD: 617-345-9743; fax: 617-345-5318).

Mobility International (main office: 25 Rue de Manchester, Brussels B-1070, Belgium; phone: 32-2-410-6297; fax: 32-2-410-6874; US office: *MIUSA,* PO Box 10767, Eugene, OR 97440; phone/TDD: 503-343-1284; fax: 503-343-6812).

Moss Rehabilitation Hospital Travel Information Service (telephone referrals only; phone: 215-456-9600; TDD: 215-456-9602).

National Rehabilitation Information Center (8455 Colesville Rd., Suite 935, Silver Spring, MD 20910-3319; phone: 301-588-9284; fax: 301-587-1967).

Paralyzed Veterans of America (*PVA;* PVA/Access to the Skies Program, 801 18th St. NW, Washington, DC 20006-3585; phone: 202-872-1300 in Washington, DC; 800-424-8200 elsewhere in the US; fax: 202-785-4452).

Partners of the Americas (1424 K St. NW, Suite 700, Washington, DC 20005; phone: 800-322-7844 or 202-628-3300; fax: 202-628-3306).

Royal Association for Disability and Rehabilitation (*RADAR;* 12 City Forum, 250 City Rd., London EC1V 8AF, England; phone: 44-171-250-3222; fax: 44-171-250-0212).

Society for the Advancement of Travel for the Handicapped (*SATH;* 347 Fifth Ave., Suite 610, New York, NY 10016; phone: 212-447-7284; fax: 212-725-8253).

Travel Industry and Disabled Exchange (*TIDE;* Attention: Yvonne Nau, 5435 Donna Ave., Tarzana, CA 91356; phone: 818-344-3640; fax: 818-344-0078).

Publications

Access Travel: A Guide to the Accessibility of Airport Terminals (Consumer Information Center, Dept. 575A, Pueblo, CO 81009; phone: 719-948-3334; fax: 719-948-9724).

Air Transportation of Handicapped Persons (Publication #AC-120-32; *US Department of Transportation,* Distribution Unit, Utilization and Storage Section, M-45.3, 400 Seventh St. SW, Washington, DC 20590; phone: 202-366-0039; fax: 202-366-2795).

The Diabetic Traveler (PO Box 8223 RW, Stamford, CT 06905; phone: 203-327-5832; fax: 203-975-1748).

Directory of Travel Agencies for the Disabled and Travel for the Disabled, both by Helen Hecker (Twin Peaks Press, PO Box 129, Vancouver, WA 98666; phone: 800-637-CALM for orders; 206-694-2462 for information; fax: 206-696-3210).

Guide to Traveling with Arthritis (*Upjohn Company,* 7000 Portage Rd., Kalamazoo, MI 49001; phone: 800-253-9860).

The Disabled Driver's Mobility Guide (*American Automobile Association,* Traffic Safety Dept., 1000 AAA Dr., Heathrow, FL 32746-5063; phone: 407-444-7961; fax: 407-444-7956).

Handicapped Travel Newsletter (PO Box 269, Athens, TX 75751; phone/fax: 903-677-1260).

Handi-Travel: A Resource Book for Disabled and Elderly Travellers, by Cinnie Noble (*Canadian Rehabilitation Council for the Disabled,* 45 Sheppard Ave. E., Suite 801, Toronto, Ontario M2N 5W9, Canada; phone/TDD: 416-250-7490; fax: 416-229-1371).

Holidays and Travel Abroad, edited by John Stanford (*Royal Association for Disability and Rehabilitation,* address above).

On the Go, Go Safely, Plan Ahead (*American Diabetes Association,* 1660 Duke St., Alexandria, VA 22314; phone: 800-232-3472 or 703-549-1500; fax: 703-863-7439).

Travel for the Patient with Chronic Obstructive Pulmonary Disease (Dr. Harold Silver, 1601 18th St. NW, Washington, DC 20009; phone: 202-667-0134; fax: 202-667-0148).

Travel Tips for Hearing-Impaired People (*American Academy of Otolaryngology,* 1 Prince St., Alexandria, VA 22314; phone: 703-836-4444; fax: 703-683-5100).

Travel Tips for People with Arthritis (*Arthritis Foundation,* 1314 Spring St. NW, Atlanta, GA 30309; phone: 800-283-7800 or 404-872-7100; fax: 404-872-0457).

Traveling Like Everybody Else: A Practical Guide for Disabled Travelers, by Jacqueline Freedman and Susan Gersten (Modan Publishing, PO Box 1202, Bellmore, NY 11710; phone: 516-679-1380; fax: 516-679-1448).

Package Tour Operators

Accessible Journeys (35 W. Sellers Ave., Ridley Park, PA 19078; phone: 800-846-4537 or 610-521-0339; fax: 610-521-6959).

Accessible Tours/Directions Unlimited (Attention: Lois Bonanni, 720 N. Bedford Rd., Bedford Hills, NY 10507; phone: 800-533-5343 or 914-241-1700; fax: 914-241-0243).

Classic Travel Service (8 W. 40th St., New York, NY 10018; phone: 212-869-2560 in New York State; 800-247-0909 elsewhere in the US; fax: 212-944-4493).

CTM Beehive Travel (77 W. 200 S., Suite 500, Salt Lake City, UT 84101; phone: 800-777-5727 or 801-578-9000; fax: 801-297-2828).

Dahl's Good Neighbor Travel Service (124 S. Main St., Viroqua, WI 54665; phone: 800-338-3245 or 608-637-2128; fax: 608-637-3030).

Dialysis at Sea Cruises (PO Box 218, Indian Rocks Beach, FL 34635; phone: 800-544-7604 or 813-596-4614; fax: 813-596-0203).

Flying Wheels Travel (PO Box 382, Owatonna, MN 55060; phone: 800-535-6790 or 507-451-1966; fax: 507-451-1685).

The Guided Tour (7900 Old York Rd., Suite 114B, Elkins Park, PA 19027-2339; phone: 800-783-5841 or 215-782-1370; fax: 215-635-2637).

Hinsdale Travel (201 E. Ogden Ave., Hinsdale, IL 60521; phone: 708-325-1335 or 708-469-7349; fax: 708-325-1342).

MedEscort International (*Lehigh Valley International Airport*, PO Box 8766, Allentown, PA 18105-8766; phone: 800-255-7182 or 215-791-3111; fax: 215-791-9189).

Prestige World Travel (5710-X High Point Rd., Greensboro, NC 27407; phone: 800-476-7737 or 910-292-6690; fax: 910-632-9404).

Sprout (893 Amsterdam Ave., New York, NY 10025; phone: 212-222-9575; fax: 212-222-9768).

Weston Travel Agency (134 N. Cass Ave., Westmont, IL 60559; phone: 708-968-2513 in Illinois; 800-633-3725 elsewhere in the US; fax: 708-968-2539).

Single Travelers

The travel industry is not very fair to people who vacation by themselves—they often end up paying more than those traveling in pairs. There are services catering to single travelers, however, that match travel companions, offer travel arrangements with shared accommodations, and provide information and discounts. In addition, some resorts in the Caribbean cater specifically to single travelers.

Useful publications include *Going Solo* (Doerfer Communications, PO Box 123, Apalachicola, FL 32329; phone/fax: 904-653-8848) and *Traveling on Your Own,* by Eleanor Berman (Random House, Order Dept., 400 Hahn Rd., Westminster, MD 21157; phone: 800-733-3000; fax: 800-659-2436).

Organizations and Companies

Gallivanting (515 E. 79th St., Suite 20F, New York, NY 10021; phone: 800-933-9699 or 212-988-0617; fax: 212-988-0144).

Globus and Cosmos (5301 S. Federal Circle, Littleton, CO 80123; phone: 800-221-0090, 800-338-7092, or 303-797-2800; fax: 303-798-5441).

Jane's International Travel and Sophisticated Women Travelers (2603 Bath Ave., Brooklyn, NY 11214; phone: 800-613-9226 or 718-266-2045; fax: 718-266-4062).

Marion Smith Singles (611 Prescott Pl., N. Woodmere, NY 11581; phone: 800-698-TRIP, 516-791-4852, 516-791-4865, or 212-944-2112; fax: 516-791-4879).

Partners-in-Travel (11660 Chenault St., Suite 119, Los Angeles, CA 90049; phone: 310-476-4869).

Singleworld (401 Theodore Fremd Ave., Rye, NY 10580; phone: 800-223-6490 or 914-967-3334; fax: 914-967-7395).

Solo Flights (612 Penfield Rd., Fairfield, CT 06430; phone: 800-266-1566 or 203-256-1235).

Suddenly Singles Tours (161 Dreiser Loop, Bronx, NY 10475; phone: 718-379-8800 in New York City; 800-859-8396 elsewhere in the US; fax: 718-379-8858).

Travel Companion Exchange (PO Box 833, Amityville, NY 11701; phone: 516-454-0880; fax: 516-454-0170).

Travel Companions (Atrium Financial Center, 1515 N. Federal Hwy., Suite 300, Boca Raton, FL 33432; phone: 800-383-7211 or 407-393-6448; fax: 407-451-8560 or 407-393-6448).

Travel in Two's (239 N. Broadway, Suite 3, N. Tarrytown, NY 10591; phone: 914-631-8301 in New York State; 800-692-5252 elsewhere in the US).

Umbrella Singles (PO Box 157, Woodbourne, NY 12788; phone: 800-537-2797 or 914-434-6871; fax: 914-434-3532).

Older Travelers

Special discounts and more free time are just two factors that have given older travelers a chance to see the world at affordable prices. Many travel suppliers offer senior discounts—sometimes only to members of certain senior citizens organizations (which provide benefits of their own). When considering a particular package, make sure the facilities—and the pace of the tour—match your needs and physical condition.

Publications

Going Abroad: 101 Tips for Mature Travelers (*Grand Circle Travel,* 347 Congress St., Boston, MA 02210; phone: 800-221-2610 or 617-350-7500; fax: 617-423-0445).

The Mature Traveler (PO Box 50820, Reno, NV 89513-0820; phone: 702-786-7419).

Take a Camel to Lunch and Other Adventures for Mature Travelers, by Nancy O'Connell (Bristol Publishing Enterprises, PO Box 1737, San Leandro, CA 94577; phone: 510-895-4461 in California; 800-346-4889 elsewhere in the US; fax: 510-895-4459).

Unbelievably Good Deals & Great Adventures That You Absolutely Can't Get Unless You're Over 50, by Joan Rattner Heilman (Contemporary Books, 180 N. Stetson Ave., Suite 1200, Chicago, IL 60601; phone: 312-782-9181; fax: 312-540-4687).

Organizations

American Association of Retired Persons (*AARP;* 601 E St. NW, Washington, DC 20049; phone: 202-434-2277).

Golden Companions (PO Box 754, Pullman, WA 99163-0754; phone: 208-858-2183).

Mature Outlook (Customer Service Center, 6001 N. Clark St., Chicago, IL 60660; phone: 800-336-6330; fax: 312-764-5036).

National Council of Senior Citizens (1331 F St. NW, Washington, DC 20004; phone: 202-347-8800; fax: 202-624-9595).

Package Tour Operators

Elderhostel (75 Federal St., Boston, MA 02110-1941; phone: 617-426-7788; fax: 617-426-8351).

Gadabout Tours (700 E. Tahquitz Canyon Way, Palm Springs, CA 92262; phone: 800-952-5068 or 619-325-5556; fax: 619-325-5127).

Grand Circle Travel (347 Congress St., Boston, MA 02210; phone: 800-221-2610 or 617-350-7500; fax: 617-542-2887).

Grandtravel (6900 Wisconsin Ave., Suite 706, Chevy Chase, MD 20815; phone: 800-247-7651 or 301-986-0790; fax: 301-913-0166).

Interhostel (*University of New Hampshire,* Division of Continuing Education, 6 Garrison Ave., Durham, NH 03824; phone: 800-733-9753 or 603-862-1147; fax: 603-862-1113).

Mature Tours (c/o *Solo Flights,* 612 Penfield Rd., Fairfield, CT 06430; phone: 800-266-1566 or 203-256-1235).

OmniTours (104 Wilmot Rd., Deerfield, IL 60015; phone: 800-962-0060 or 708-374-0088; fax: 708-374-9515).

Saga International Holidays (222 Berkeley St., Boston, MA 02116; phone: 800-343-0273 or 617-262-2262; fax: 617-375-5950).

Money Matters

Although US currency is the official means of exchange on only a few islands, in areas where local currencies are used, US dollars also may be welcome—or even preferred. This is *not* the case in countries such as

Colombia, Mexico, and Venezuela, where using US currency means negotiating the exchange rate for every small purchase. For information about
the currencies of particular Caribbean islands and countries, and the rates
of exchange at press time, see *Sources and Resources* in THE ISLANDS.

Exchange rates are listed in international newspapers such as the
International Herald Tribune. Foreign currency information and related services are provided by banks and companies such as *Thomas Cook Foreign
Exchange* (for the nearest location, call 800-621-0666 or 312-236-0042; fax:
312-807-4895); *Harold Reuter and Company* (200 Park Ave., Suite 332E,
New York, NY 10166; phone: 800-258-0456 or 212-661-0826; fax: 212-557-
6622); and *Ruesch International* (for the nearest location, call 800-424-2923
or 202-408-1200; fax: 202-408-1211). In the Caribbean, you usually will find
the official rate of exchange posted in banks, airports, money exchange
houses, hotels, and some shops. Since you will get more local currency for
your US dollar at banks and money exchanges, don't change more than $10
at other commercial establishments. Ask how much commission you're
being charged and the exchange rate, and don't buy money on the black
market (it may be counterfeit). Estimate your needs carefully; if you over-
buy, you lose twice—buying and selling back.

CREDIT CARDS AND TRAVELER'S CHECKS

Most major credit cards enjoy wide domestic and international acceptance;
however, not every hotel, restaurant, or shop in the Caribbean accepts all
(or in some cases any) credit cards. When making purchases with a credit
card, note that the rate of exchange depends on when the charge is processed.
Most credit card companies charge a 1% fee for converting foreign currency charges. It's also wise to carry traveler's checks while on the road,
since they are widely accepted and replaceable if stolen or lost. You can
buy traveler's checks at banks and some are available by mail or phone.
Keep a separate list of all traveler's checks (noting those that you have
cashed) and the names and numbers of your credit cards. Both traveler's
check and credit card companies have international numbers to call for
information or in the event of loss or theft.

CASH MACHINES

Automated teller machines (ATMs) are increasingly common worldwide,
and most banks participate in international ATM networks such as
MasterCard/Cirrus (phone: 800-4-CIRRUS) and *Visa/PLUS* (phone: 800-
THE-PLUS). Using a card—with an assigned Personal Identification
Number (PIN)—from an affiliated bank or credit card company, you can
withdraw cash from any machine in the same network. The *MasterCard/Cirrus
ATM Travel Directory* and the *Visa/PLUS International ATM Locator Guide
1996* provide locations of network ATMs worldwide and are available from
banks and other financial institutions.

SENDING MONEY ABROAD

Should the need arise, you can have money sent to you in many areas of the Caribbean via the services provided by *American Express MoneyGram* (phone: 800-926-9400 for information; 800-866-8800 for money transfers) or *Western Union Financial Services* (phone: 800-325-6000 or 800-325-4176). In some cases, you also can have money wired to you via a direct bank-to-bank transfer from the US; arrangements can be made with the participating institutions. If you are down to your last cent and have no other way to obtain cash, the nearest *US Consulate* (see *Consular Services* for addresses) will let you call home to set matters in motion.

Accommodations

For specific information on hotels, resorts, and other accommodations, see *Checking In* in THE ISLANDS chapters; selected accommodations also are mentioned in DIVERSIONS. A particularly appealing option in the Caribbean is to stay at one of the all-inclusive resorts located throughout the region. These properties offer packages that include accommodations, meals, local transportation, recreational activities, entertainment, and other amenities.

RENTAL OPTIONS

An attractive accommodations alternative for the visitor content to stay in one spot is a vacation rental. For a family or group, the per-person cost can be reasonable. To have your pick of the properties available throughout the Caribbean, make inquiries at least six months in advance.

The *Worldwide Home Rental Guide* (3501 Indian School Rd. NE, Suite 303, Albuquerque, NM 87106; phone/fax: 505-255-4271) lists rental properties and managing agencies. In addition, *Rental Directories International* (*RDI;* 2044 Rittenhouse Sq., Philadelphia, PA 19103; phone: 215-985-4001; fax: 215-985-0323) publishes national and regional directories of vacation properties that can be rented directly from the owners—including a guide called *The Islands and Mexico,* which covers the Caribbean.

Rental Property Agents

At Home Abroad (405 E. 56th St., Suite 6H, New York, NY 10022-2466; phone: 212-421-9165; fax: 212-752-1591).

B & V Associates (140 E. 56th St., Suite 4C, New York, NY 10022; phone: 800-546-4777 or 212-688-9538; fax: 212-688-9467).

Barclay International Group (150 E. 52nd St., New York, NY 10022; phone: 212-832-3777 in New York City; 800-U4-LONDON elsewhere in the US; fax: 212-753-1139).

Condo World (4230 Orchard Lake Rd., Suite 3, Orchard Lake, MI 48323; phone: 800-521-2980 or 810-683-0202; fax: 810-683-5076).

Creative Leisure (951 Transport Way, Petaluma, CA 94954; phone: 800-4-CONDOS or 707-778-1800; fax: 707-763-7786).

Europa-Let (92 N. Main St., Ashland, OR 97520; phone: 800-462-4486 or 503-482-5806; fax: 503-482-0660).

Heart of the Caribbean, Ltd. (17485 Penbrook Dr., Brookfield, WI 53045; phone: 800-231-5303 or 414-783-5303; fax: 414-781-4026).

Hideaways International (767 Islington St., Portsmouth, NH 03801; phone: 800-843-4433 or 603-430-4433; fax: 603-430-4444).

La Cure Villas (11661 San Vicente Blvd., Suite 1010, Los Angeles, CA 90049; phone: 800-387-2726 or 416-968-2374; fax: 416-968-9435).

Orion (c/o *B & V Associates,* address above).

Property Rentals International (1 Park W. Circle, Suite 108, Midlothian, VA 23113; phone: 800-220-3332 or 804-378-6054; fax: 804-379-2073).

Rent a Home International (7200 34th Ave. NW, Seattle, WA 98117; phone: 206-789-9377; fax: 206-789-9379).

Rent a Vacation Everywhere (*RAVE;* 135 Meigs St., Rochester, NY 14607; phone: 716-256-0760; fax: 716-256-2676).

VHR Worldwide (235 Kensington Ave., Norwood, NJ 07648; phone: 201-767-9393 in New Jersey; 800-633-3284 elsewhere in the US; fax: 201-767-5510).

Villa Leisure (PO Box 30188, Palm Beach, FL 33420; phone: 800-526-4244 or 407-624-9000; fax: 407-622-9097).

Villas and Apartments Abroad (420 Madison Ave., Suite 1105, New York, NY 10017; phone: 212-759-1025 in New York State; 800-433-3020 elsewhere in the US; fax: 212-755-8316).

Villas International (605 Market St., Suite 510, San Francisco, CA 94105; phone: 800-221-2260 or 415-281-0910; fax: 415-281-0919).

Villas St. Lucia (28 Allegheny Ave., Suite 1307, Towson, MD 21204; phone: 800-823-2002 or 410-583-9600; fax: 410-825-0938).

HOME EXCHANGES

For comfortable, reasonable living quarters with amenities that no hotel could possibly offer, consider trading homes with someone abroad. The following companies provide information on exchanges:

Home Base Holidays (7 Park Ave., London N13 5PG, England; phone/fax: 44-181-886-8752).

Intervac US/International Home Exchange (PO Box 590504, San Francisco, CA 94159; phone: 800-756-HOME or 415-435-3497; fax: 415-435-7440).

Loan-A-Home (2 Park La., Apt. 6E, Mt. Vernon, NY 10552-3443; phone: 914-664-7640).

Vacation Exchange Club (PO Box 650, Key West, FL 33041; phone: 800-638-3841; phone/fax: 305-294-1448).

Worldwide Home Exchange Club (main office: 50 Hans Crescent, London SW1X 0NA, England; phone: 44-171-589-6055; US office: 806 Brantford Ave., Silver Spring, MD 20904; phone: 301-680-8950).

HOME STAYS

United States Servas (11 John St., Room 407, New York, NY 10038; phone: 212-267-0252; fax: 212-267-0292) maintains a list of hosts worldwide willing to accommodate visitors free of charge. The aim of this nonprofit cultural program is to promote international understanding and peace, and *Servas* emphasizes that member travelers should be interested mainly in their hosts, not in sightseeing, during their stays.

ACCOMMODATIONS DISCOUNTS

The following organizations offer discounts of up to 50% on accommodations throughout the Caribbean:

Carte Royale (131 N. State St., Suite J, Lake Oswego, OR 97034; phone: 800-847-7002 or 503-635-6300; fax: 503-635-4937).

Encore Marketing International (4501 Forbes Blvd., Lanham, MD 20706; phone: 800-638-0930 or 301-459-8020; fax: 301-731-0525).

Entertainment Publications (2125 Butterfield Rd., Troy, MI 48084; phone: 800-477-3234 or 810-637-8400; fax: 810-637-9779).

Great American Traveler (Access Development Corp., PO Box 27965, Salt Lake City, UT 84127; phone: 800-331-8867 or 801-262-2233; fax: 801-262-2311).

Hotel Express International (International Concepts Group, 707 E. Arapaho Rd., Richardson, TX 75081-2260; phone: 800-866-2015, 800-770-2015, or 214-497-9792; fax: 214-994-2298).

Impulse (6143 S. Willow Dr., Suite 410, Englewood, CO 80111; phone: 303-741-2457; fax: 303-721-6011).

International Travel Card (6001 N. Clark St., Chicago, IL 60660; phone: 800-342-0558 or 312-465-8891; fax: 312-764-8066).

Privilege Card (3391 Peachtree Rd. NE, Suite 110, Atlanta, GA 30326; phone: 800-236-9732 or 404-262-0255; fax: 404-262-0235).

Quest International (402 E. Yakima Ave., Suite 1200, Yakima, WA 98901; phone: 800-325-2400 or 509-248-7512; fax: 509-457-8399).

Mail

When sending mail between the Caribbean and the US, always use airmail and allow at least 10 days for delivery. If your correspondence is especially important, you may want to send it via an international courier service, such as *FedEx* (*Federal Express;* phone: 800-238-5355 in the US) or *DHL Worldwide Express* (phone: 800-225-5345 in the US); contact local offices when in the islands.

In the Caribbean, stamps are sold at post offices, hotel desks, and some shops. On many islands there are public mailboxes on street corners, and most hotels have mail drops.

You can have mail sent to you care of your hotel (marked "Guest Mail, Hold for Arrival") or to a post office (the address should include "c/o General Delivery"—*"a/c Poste Restante"* in French- and Dutch-speaking destinations; *"a/c Lista de Correos"* in Spanish-speaking destinations). Some *American Express* offices in the Caribbean also will hold mail for customers ("c/o Client Letter Service"); information is provided in their pamphlet *Travelers' Companion.* Note that *US Embassies* and *Consulates* abroad will hold mail for US citizens *only* in emergency situations.

Telephone

Most developed areas of the Caribbean have relatively efficient phone systems, although service may be less reliable on more remote islands and in rural areas of coastal countries. Public telephones are widely available, and can be found in restaurants, hotel lobbies, post offices, transportation and tourism centers, and booths on the street. There also may be telephone offices from which long-distance calls can be made.

The number of digits in phone numbers varies throughout the Caribbean. Much of the region lies within the 809 area code, and calls can be dialed like long-distance calls within the US. Outside of the 809 area, standard international calling procedures apply. General instructions for making calls to, from, and within the Caribbean are provided below. For information on calling procedures for specific Caribbean islands and countries, see *Sources and Resources* in the individual chapters in THE ISLANDS.

From the US

To call a number within the 809 area code, dial 1 + 809 + the local number.

To call a number outside the 809 area code, dial 011 (the international access code) + the island or country code + the city code (if applicable) + the local number.

To the US

When calling from within the 809 area code, dial 1 + the area code + the local number.

When calling from outside the 809 area code, dial the international access code (which varies) + 1 (the US country code) + the area code + the local number.

Between Islands

When calling from one location to another within the 809 area code, dial 1 + the local number.

When calling from a location *within* the 809 area code to a location *outside* the 809 coverage area, dial 011 (the international access code) + the country code + the city code (if applicable) + the local number.

When calling from a location *outside* the 809 area code to one *within* the 809 area code, dial the international access code (which varies) + 809 + the local number.

The procedure for reaching a local or international operator varies throughout the Caribbean. For operator-assisted calls between islands or countries in the Caribbean, usually you will dial a direct number or the international access code, which is followed by a number for an international operator.

Although you can use a telephone company calling card on any phone, pay phones that take major credit cards (*American Express, MasterCard, Visa*, and so on) are increasingly common. Also available are combined telephone calling/bank credit cards, such as the *AT&T Universal Card* (PO Box 44167, Jacksonville, FL 32231-4167; phone: 800-423-4343). Similarly, *Sprint* (8140 Ward Pkwy., Kansas City, MO 64114; phone: 800-669-8585) offers *VisaPhone*, through which you can add phone card privileges to your existing *Visa* card. Companies offering long-distance phone cards without additional credit card privileges include *AT&T* (phone: 800-CALL-ATT), *Executive Telecard International* (4260 E. Evans Ave., Suite 6, Denver, CO 80222; phone: 800-950-3800), *LDDS/Metromedia Communications* (1 International Center, 100 NE Loop 410, San Antonio, TX 78216; phone: 800-275-0200), *MCI* (323 Third St. SE, Cedar Rapids, IA 52401; phone: 800-444-4444; and 12790 Merit Dr., Dallas, TX 75251; phone: 800-444-3333), and *Sprint* (address above; phone: 800-THE-MOST). Note that you may not be able to use some of these cards for calls to or from particular Caribbean destinations; contact the issuing company for current information when planning your trip.

Hotels routinely add surcharges to the cost of phone calls made from their rooms. Long-distance telephone services that may help you avoid this added expense are provided by a number of companies, including *AT&T* (International Information Service, 635 Grant St., Pittsburgh, PA 15219; phone: 800-874-4000), *LDDS/Metromedia Communications, MCI,* and *Sprint* (addresses above). Note that some of these services may not be available from specific Caribbean destinations, and some can be accessed only with the companies' long-distance calling cards (see above). In addition, even when you use such long-distance services, hotels still may charge a fee for line usage.

AT&T's Language Line Service (phone: 800-752-6096) provides interpretive services for telephone communications in French, Spanish, and numerous other languages. Useful telephone directories for travelers include the *AT&T Toll-Free 800 National Shopper's Guide* and the *AT&T Toll-Free 800 National Business Guide* (phone: 800-426-8686 for orders), the *Toll-Free Travel & Vacation Information Directory* (Pilot Books, 103 Cooper St., Babylon, NY 11702; phone: 516-422-2225; fax: 516-422-2227), and *The*

Phone Booklet (Scott American Corporation, PO Box 88, W. Redding, CT 06896; no phone).

Electricity

Although 110-volt, 60-cycle, alternating current (AC) is used in some parts of the Caribbean, other islands and countries operate on either 220-volt, 50-cycle, alternating (AC) or 220-volt direct current (DC). Where 220-volt current is used, travelers from the US will need electrical converters to operate the appliances they use at home, or dual-voltage appliances, which can be switched from one voltage standard to another. To be fully prepared, pack a plug adapter set for the different plug configurations you may find in the Caribbean. For information on electrical standards for specific Caribbean destinations, see *Sources and Resources* in the individual chapters in THE ISLANDS.

Staying Healthy

For up-to-date information on current health conditions, call the Centers for Disease Control's *International Travelers' Hotline*: 404-332-4559. The Centers for Disease Control also publishes *Health Information for International Travel, 1996* which provides worldwide information on health risks and vaccination requirements. It can be ordered from the Superintendent of Documents (*US Government Printing Office,* PO Box 371954, Pittsburgh, PA 15250-7954; phone: 202-512-1800; fax: 202-512-2250).

Travelers to most of the destinations covered in this guide face few serious health risks. For those planning to visit Mexico and South America, however, the *US Public Health Service* recommends diphtheria and tetanus shots, and children should be inoculated against measles, mumps, rubella, and polio. In addition, in certain areas of the Caribbean, Chagas' disease, dengue fever, malaria, and yellow fever can be transmitted through insect bites. (At the time of this writing, for example, the *US State Department* had issued warnings about malaria in the Dominican Republic, particularly along its border with Haiti.) If traveling in such areas, a yellow fever inoculation, antimalarial tablets, and a strong insect repellent are advisable. Scorpion stings and bites from spiders, snakes, or any wild animal can be serious and must be treated immediately.

In Mexico, South America, and on some Caribbean islands, it also is not safe to drink the tap water—do not even brush your teeth with it. Stick to bottled water (if unavailable, boil the water or use water purification tablets) or other bottled or canned beverages. Stay away from fresh fruit juices and mixed alcoholic drinks (which may contain tap water) and any drinks served with ice. Similarly, do not eat salads, uncooked vegetables, and unpeeled fruit. Milk sold in stores usually is pasteurized and safe to drink, but beware of spoilage due to improper refrigeration. Also avoid unpasteurized or uncooked dairy products, and *never* buy food from street vendors.

One health problem frequently experienced by travelers to the Caribbean is sunburn. When spending any length of time outdoors, take appropriate precautions—including the use of a sunscreen with a Sun Protection Factor (SPF) of 15 or higher.

When swimming in the ocean, be careful of the undertow (the water running back down the beach after a wave has washed ashore), which can knock you off your feet, and riptides (currents running against the tide), which can pull you out to sea. Sharks are found in Caribbean waters, but usually do not come close to shore. Jellyfish—including Portuguese men-of-war—also are common, as are eels and sea urchins. And note that coral reefs, while beautiful, can be razor sharp.

Should you need non-emergency medical attention, ask at your hotel for the house physician or for help in reaching a doctor. Lists of English-speaking doctors and dentists also may be available from *US Embassies* and *Consulates* in the Caribbean. Island pharmacies usually are not open around the clock; if you need a prescription filled during off-hours, go directly to a local hospital. **In an emergency: Go to the emergency room of the nearest hospital, dial the local emergency number, or call an operator for assistance. (For the numbers to call in the event of an emergency in particular Caribbean islands and countries, see *Sources and Resources* in THE ISLANDS.)**

When traveling abroad, be extremely cautious about injections, because reusable syringes and needles may be used and sterilization procedures sometimes are inadequate. If you have a condition that requires periodic injections, bring a supply of syringes with you or buy disposable syringes at a local pharmacy—although in some areas, this may require a prescription from a local doctor. To avoid any potential problems with customs authorities when bringing such items to or from the Caribbean, contact the consular offices of the countries or islands you plan to visit for information about applicable regulations. In general, it's a good idea to bring along a note from your doctor stating that the syringes are required for treatment of a medical condition.

Additional Resources

    Global Emergency Services (2720 Enterprise Pkwy., Suite 106, Richmond, VA 23294; phone: 804-527-1094; fax: 804-527-1941).

    Health Care Abroad/Global (c/o *Wallach and Co.,* PO Box 480, Middleburg, VA 22117-0480; phone: 800-237-6615 or 703-687-3166; fax: 703-687-3172).

    International Association for Medical Assistance to Travelers (*IAMAT;* 417 Center St., Lewiston, NY 14092; phone: 716-754-4883; and 40 Regal Rd., Guelph, Ontario N1K 1B5, Canada; phone: 519-836-0102; fax: 519-836-3412).

International Health Care Service (440 E. 69th St., New York, NY 10021; phone: 212-746-1601).

International SOS Assistance (PO Box 11568, Philadelphia, PA 19116; phone: 800-523-8930 or 215-244-1500; fax: 215-244-2227).

Medic Alert Foundation (2323 Colorado Ave., Turlock, CA 95382; phone: 800-ID-ALERT or 209-668-3333; fax: 209-669-2495).

Travel Care International (*Eagle River Airport,* PO Box 846, Eagle River, WI 54521; phone: 800-5-AIR-MED or 715-479-8881; fax: 715-479-8178).

Traveler's Emergency Network (*TEN;* PO Box 238, Hyattsville, MD 20797-8108; phone: 800-ASK-4-TEN; fax: 301-559-5167).

TravMed (PO Box 10623, Baltimore, MD 21285-0623; phone: 800-732-5309 or 410-296-5225; fax: 410-825-7523).

Consular Services

The American Services section of the *US Consulate* is a vital source of assistance and advice for US citizens abroad. If you are injured or become seriously ill, the consulate can direct you to sources of medical attention and notify your relatives. If you become involved in a dispute that could lead to legal action, the consulate can provide a list of English-speaking attorneys. In cases of natural disasters or civil unrest, consulates handle the evacuation of US citizens if necessary.

The *US State Department* operates an automated 24-hour *Citizens' Emergency Center* travel advisory hotline (phone: 202-647-5225). You also can reach a duty officer at this number from 5:15 PM to 10 PM, eastern standard time, seven days a week; at other times, call 202-647-4000. For faxed travel advisories and other consular information, call 202-647-3000 using the handset on your fax machine; instructions will be provided. Using a personal computer with a modem, you can access the consular affairs electronic bulletin board (phone: 202-647-9225).

US Embassies and Consulates in the Caribbean

Serving Anguilla, Antigua, Barbados, Barbuda, the British Virgin Islands, Dominica, Grenada, Guadeloupe, Martinique, Montserrat, St. Barthélemy, St. Kitts and Nevis, St. Lucia, St. Martin, and St. Vincent and the Grenadines: *US Consulate,* Alico Bldg., Cheapside, Bridgetown, Barbados (phone: 809-431-0225; 24-hour emergency number: 809-436-4950; fax: 809-431-0179).

Serving Aruba, Bonaire, Curaçao, Saba, St. Eustatius, and St. Maarten: *US Consulate General,* walk-in address: Gorsiraweg JB 1, Willemstad, Curaçao; mailing address: PO Box 158, Willemstad, Curaçao (phone: 599-961-3066; 24-hour emergency number: 599-961-0579; fax: 599-961-6489).

Serving Belize: *US Embassy* and *Consulate,* Gabourel La. and Hutson St., PO Box 286, Belize City, Belize (phone: 501-2-77161; fax: 501-2-35321).

Serving the Cayman Islands and Jamaica: *US Embassy,* Jamaica Mutual Life Centre, 2 Oxford Rd., Third Floor, Kingston 5, Jamaica (phone: 809929-4850; 24-hour emergency number: 809-926-6440; fax: 809-926-6743); *US Consulate,* 16 Oxford Rd., PO Box 541, Kingston 5, Jamaica (phone: 809-929-4850; fax: 809-926-5833).

Serving Colombia: *US Embassy,* 8-61 Calle 38, Bogotá (phone: 57-1-320-1300; 24-hour emergency number: 57-1-232-9995; fax: 57-1-288-5687); *US Consulate,* Calle 77 and Carrero 68, 6815 Centro Comercial Mayorista, Barranquilla, Colombia (phone: 57-58-45-8480; 24-hour emergency number: 57-58-45-9467; fax: 57-58-45-5216).

Serving the Dominican Republic: *US Embassy,* Calle César Nicolás Penson, Esquina Calle Leopoldo Navarro, Santo Domingo, Dominican Republic (phone: 809-221-2171; 24-hour emergency number: 809-221-8100; fax: 809-686-7437); *US Consulate,* Calle César Nicolás Penson, Esquina Av. Máximo Gómez, Santo Domingo, Dominican Republic (phone: 809-474-3789; fax: 809-686-7437).

Serving Mexico (Cancún, Cozumel, Isla Mujeres, and the Yucatán Peninsula): *US Embassy,* 305 Paseo de la Reforma, Cuauhtémoc, México, DF 06500, México (phone: 52-5-211-0042; 24-hour emergency number: 52-5-560-3317; fax: 52-5-511-9980 or 52-5-208-3373); *US Consulate,* 453 Paseo de Montejo, Apdo. 130, Mérida, Yucatán 97000, Mexico (phone: 52-99-255409 or 52-99-255011; fax: 52-99-256219); *US Consular Agency* (40 Av. Nader, Marruecos Building, Third Floor, Room 31, Cancún, Quintana Roo 77500, México (phone: 52-98-842411; fax: 52-98-848222).

Serving Trinidad and Tobago: *US Embassy,* 15 Queen's Park W., Port of Spain, Trinidad, West Indies (phone: 809-622-6371; 24-hour emergency number: 809-628-4262; fax: 809-628-5462).

Serving Venezuela: *US Embassy* and *Consulate,* Avdas. Principal de la Floresta y Francisco de Miranda, Caracas, Venezuela (phone: 2-285-2222 or 2-285-3111; 24-hour emergency number: 2-285-2981; fax: 2-285-0336).

Entry Requirements and Customs Regulations

ENTERING THE ISLANDS

Most of the Caribbean destinations covered in this guide require visitors from the US to provide proof of US citizenship upon arrival. The exceptions are Puerto Rico (where no documentation is required) and the US

Virgin Islands (where you may be asked to show proof of US citizenship upon *departure*). Usually a birth certificate, affidavit of birth, voter's registration card, or valid passport will be accepted. Those forms of identification without a photograph must be accompanied by some form of official photo ID. Note, however, that a driver's license alone *will not* suffice as proof of citizenship. Officials at some destinations also may want to see that you have a return or ongoing ticket and may require proof of pre-arranged accommodations and/or sufficient funds for the duration of your stay.

Most Caribbean governments impose limits on the length of stay, and a few require tourist cards. Tourist cards usually must be obtained before departure from a consulate, government tourist office, airline, or travel agent, although in some cases, arrangements can be made upon arrival. For longer stays, or for work or study, visas (issued by consulates) generally are required. For information on entry requirements for specific Caribbean destinations, see *Sources and Resources* in THE ISLANDS.

Most Caribbean countries impose limitations on the quantities of specific items (such as tobacco products and liquor) that may be imported duty-free. For specific information on customs regulations, contact island tourist authorities in the US.

DUTY-FREE SHOPS

Located in international airports, duty-free shops provide bargains on the purchase of goods imported from other countries. But beware: Not all foreign goods are automatically less expensive. You *can* get a good deal on some items, but know what they cost elsewhere. Also note that although these goods are free of the duty that island customs authorities normally would assess, they will be subject to US import duty upon your return to the US (see below).

RETURNING TO THE US

US citizens returning from all Caribbean destinations except Puerto Rico must declare to *US Customs* officials at points of entry everything acquired in the islands. (Those returning from Puerto Rico do not have to pass through customs and no duty is assessed on goods purchased there.) The duty-free allowances are as follows:

$400 for Anguilla, the Cayman Islands, Colombia, Guadeloupe, Martinique, Mexico, St. Barthélemy, St. Martin, and Venezuela.

$600 for Antigua and Barbuda, Aruba, Barbados, Belize, Bonaire, the British Virgin Islands, Curaçao, Dominica, the Dominican Republic, Grenada, Jamaica, Montserrat, Saba, St. Eustatius, St. Kitts and Nevis, St. Lucia, St. Maarten, St. Vincent and the Grenadines, and Trinidad and Tobago.

$1,200 for the US Virgin Islands.

If your trip is shorter than 48 continuous hours, or if you have been out-side the US within 30 days of your current trip, the duty-free allowance is reduced to $25. (Again, there is no limit for goods purchased in Puerto Rico.) Families traveling together may make a joint customs declaration. To avoid paying duty unnecessarily on expensive items (such as computer equipment) that you plan to take with you on your trip, register these items with *US Customs* before you depart.

A flat 10% duty is assessed on the next $1,000 worth of merchandise; additional items are taxed at a variety of rates (see *Tariff Schedules of the United States* in a library or any *US Customs Service* office). Some articles are duty-free only up to certain limits. The $1200 allowance includes 1,000 cigarettes (five cartons), 100 cigars (not Cuban), and five liters of liquor or wine (for those over 21); the $600 and $400 allowances include 200 ciga-rettes (one carton), 100 cigars (not Cuban), and one liter of liquor or wine (for those over 21); the $25 allowance includes 10 cigars, 50 cigarettes, and four ounces of liquor or perfume. Note that the Generalized System of Preferences (GSP), which allows US citizens to bring certain goods into the US duty-free, applies to many of the Caribbean destinations covered in this guide. Each day you are abroad, you also can ship up to $200 in gifts (excluding alcohol, perfume, and tobacco) to the US duty-free.

Antiques (at least 100 years old) and paintings or drawings done entirely by hand are duty-free. However, certain Caribbean governments prohibit or restrict the export of archeological finds and other artifacts. If you are interested in bringing any such items back to the US, contact the local tourist authorities.

FORBIDDEN IMPORTS

Note that US regulations prohibit the import of some goods sold abroad, such as fresh fruits and vegetables, most meat products (except certain canned goods), and dairy products (except fully cured cheeses). Also pro-hibited are articles made from plants or animals on the endangered species list.

FOR ADDITIONAL INFORMATION Consult one of the following publications, avail-able from the *US Customs Service* (PO Box 7407, Washington, DC 20044): *Currency Reporting; International Mail Imports; Know Before You Go; Pets, Wildlife, US Customs;* and *Pocket Hints. Travelers' Tips on Bringing Food, Plant, and Animal Products into the United States* is available from the *United States Department of Agriculture, Animal and Plant Health Inspection Service* (*USDA-APHIS;* 6505 Belcrest Rd., Room 613-FB, Hyattsville, MD 20782; phone: 301-436-7799; fax: 301-436-5221). For tape-recorded information on customs-related topics, call 202-927-2095 from any touch-tone phone.

For Further Information

Caribbean tourist offices in the US are the best sources of travel information. Offices generally are open on weekdays, during normal business hours. In addition, the *Caribbean Tourism Organization* (20 E. 46th St., New York, NY 10017; phone: 212-682-0435; fax: 212-697-4258) serves as a central tourist information bureau for the region. The best sources of local tourist information in the Caribbean are listed in *Sources and Resources* in THE ISLANDS chapters. For information on entry requirements and customs regulations, contact each island's embassy or consulates in the US.

CARIBBEAN TOURIST OFFICES IN THE US

Anguilla

Anguilla Tourist Information and Reservation Office

New York: c/o *Medhurst & Associates,* 775 Park Ave., Huntington, NY 11743 (phone: 800-553-4939 or 516-271-2600; fax: 516-425-0903).

Antigua

Antigua Department of Tourism

Florida: 25 Second Ave., Suite 300, Miami, FL 33131 (phone: 305-381-6762; fax: 305-381-7908).

New York: 610 Fifth Ave., Suite 311, New York, NY 10020 (phone: 212-541-4117; fax: 212-757-1607).

Aruba

Aruba Tourism Authority

Florida: 2344 Salzedo St., Miami, FL 33134-5033 (phone: 305-567-2720; fax: 305-567-2721).

Georgia: 199 14th St. NE, Suite 1506, Atlanta, GA 30309 (phone: 404-892-7822; fax: 404-873-2193).

New Jersey: 1000 Harbor Blvd., Weehawken, NJ 07087 (phone: 800-TO-ARUBA or 201-330-0800; fax: 201-330-8757).

Barbados

Barbados Tourism Authority

California: 3440 Wilshire Blvd., Suite 1215, Los Angeles, CA 90010 (phone: 213-380-2198; fax: 213-384-2763).

New York: 800 Second Ave., New York, NY 10017 (phone: 212-986-6516; fax: 212-573-9850).

Belize

Belize Tourist Board

New York: 421 Seventh Ave., Suite 701, New York, NY 10001 (phone: 800-624-0686 or 212-563-6011; fax: 212-563-6033).

Bonaire

Tourism Corporation of Bonaire

New York: c/o *Adams Unlimited,* 10 Rockefeller Plaza, Suite 900, New York, NY 10020 (phone: 800-U-BONAIR or 212-956-5911; fax: 212-956-5913).

British Virgin Islands

British Virgin Islands Tourist Board

California: 1686 Union St., Suite 305, San Francisco, CA 94123 (phone: 800-835-8530 or 415-775-0344; fax: 415-775-2554).

New York: 370 Lexington Ave., Suite 313, New York, NY 10017 (phone: 212-696-0400; fax: 212-949-8254).

Cayman Islands

Cayman Islands Department of Tourism

California: 3440 Wilshire Blvd., Suite 1202, Los Angeles, CA 90010 (phone: 213-738-1968; fax: 213-738-1829).

Florida: 6100 Blue Lagoon Dr., Suite 150, Miami, FL 33126 (phone: 305-266-2300; fax: 305-267-2932).

Illinois: 9525 W. Bryn Mawr Ave., Rosemont, IL 60018 (phone: 708-678-6446; fax: 708-678-6675).

New York: 420 Lexington Ave., Suite 2733, New York, NY 10170 (phone: 212-682-5582; fax: 212-986-5123).

Texas: 2 Memorial City Plaza, 820 Gessner St., Suite 170, Houston, TX 77024 (phone: 713-461-1317; fax: 713-461-7409).

Colombia

At press time, the *Colombian Government Tourist Office* had no branches in the US. Some tourist information is available from the country's national airline, *Avianca* (6 W. 49th St., New York, NY 10020; phone: 800-AVIANCA or 212-399-0858; fax: 212-399-0811).

Curaçao

Curaçao Tourist Board

Florida: 330 Biscayne Blvd., Suite 808, Miami, FL 33132 (phone: 800-445-8266 or 305-374-5811; fax: 305-374-6741).

New York: 475 Park Ave. S., Suite 2000, New York, NY 10016 (phone: 800-270-3350 or 212-683-7660; fax: 212-683-9337).

Dominica

Dominica Tourist Board

New York: c/o *Caribbean Tourism Organization,* 20 E. 46th St., New York, NY 10017 (phone: 212-682-0435; fax: 212-697-4258).

Dominican Republic

Dominican Republic Tourist Information Center

New York: 1 Times Sq. Plaza, 11th Floor, New York, NY 10036 (phone: 212-768-2482; fax: 212-768-2677).

French West Indies (Guadeloupe, Martinique, St. Barthélemy, St. Martin)

French Government Tourist Office

California: 9454 Wilshire Blvd., Suite 715, Beverly Hills, CA 90212 (phone: 310-271-2358; fax: 310-276-2835).

Illinois: 645 N. Michigan Ave., Suite 630, Chicago, IL 60611-2836 (phone: 312-337-6301; fax: 312-337-6339).

New York: 444 Madison Ave., 16th Floor, New York, NY 10022 (phone: 212-838-1800; fax: 212-838-7855).

Texas: 750 N. St. Paul St., Suite 570, Dallas, TX 75201 (phone: 214-720-4011; fax: 214-720-0250).

Grenada

Grenada Tourist Office

New York: 820 Second Ave., Suite 900D, New York, NY 10017 (phone: 212-687-9554; fax: 212-573-9731).

Guadeloupe

See **French West Indies,** above.

Jamaica

Jamaica Tourist Board

California: 3440 Wilshire Blvd., Suite 1207, Los Angeles, CA 90010 (phone: 213-384-1123; fax: 213-384-1780).

Florida: 1320 S. Dixie Hwy., Suite 1100, Coral Gables, FL 33146 (phone: 305-665-0557; fax: 305-666-7239).

Georgia: 300 W. Wieuca Rd. NE, Suite 100A, Atlanta, GA 30342 (phone: 404-452-7799; fax: 404-452-0220). Phone and mail inquiries only; no walk-in office.

Illinois: 500 N. Michigan, Suite 1030, Chicago, IL 60611 (phone: 312-527-1296; fax: 312-527-1472).

New York: 801 Second Ave., 20th Floor, New York, NY 10017 (phone: 800-233-4582 or 212-856-9727; fax: 212-856-9730).

Texas: 8214 Westchester Dr., Suite 500, Dallas, TX 75225 (phone: 214-361-8778; fax: 214-361-7049).

Martinique

See **French West Indies,** above.

Mexico (Cancún, Cozumel)

Mexican Government Tourism Office

California: 10100 Santa Monica Blvd., Suite 224, Los Angeles, CA 90067 (phone: 310-203-8191; fax: 310-203-8316).

Florida: 128 Aragon Ave., Coral Gables, FL 33134 (phone: 305-443-9160; fax: 305-443-1186).

Illinois: 70 E. Lake St., Suite 1413, Chicago, IL 60601 (phone: 312-565-2786; fax: 312-606-9012).

New York: 405 Park Ave., Suite 1401, New York, NY 10022 (phone: 212-838-2949; fax: 212-753-2874).

Texas: 2707 N. Loop W., Suite 450, Houston, TX 77008 (phone: 713-880-5153; fax: 713-880-1833).

Washington, DC: 1911 Pennsylvania Ave. NW, Washington, DC 20006 (phone: 202-728-1750; fax: 202-728-1758).

Montserrat

Montserrat Tourist Board

New York: c/o *Caribbean Tourism Organization,* 20 E. 46th St., New York, NY 10017 (phone: 212-682-0435; fax: 212-697-4258).

Puerto Rico

Government of Puerto Rico Tourism Company

California: 3575 W. Cahuenga Blvd., Suite 560, Los Angeles, CA 90068 (phone: 800-874-1230 or 213-874-5991; fax: 213-874-7257).

Florida: 901 Ponce de Leon Blvd., Suite 604, Coral Gables, FL 33134 (phone: 800-815-7391 or 305-445-9112; fax: 305-445-9450).

New York: 575 Fifth Ave., 23rd Floor, New York, NY 10017 (phone: 800-223-6530 or 212-599-6262; fax: 212-818-1866).

Saba

Saba Tourist Office

Florida: c/o *Classic Communications International,* 10242 Northwest 47th St., Suite 31, Ft. Lauderdale, FL 33351 (phone: 800-SABA-DWI or 305-741-2681; fax: 305-741-1243).

St. Eustatius

St. Eustatius Tourist Information Office

Ontario, Canada (no US representative): c/o *New Concepts Canada,* 2455 Cawthra Rd., Suite 70, Mississauga, Ontario L5A 3P1, Canada (phone: 905-803-0131; fax: 905-803-0132).

St. Barthélemy

See **French West Indies,** above.

St. Kitts and Nevis

St. Kitts/Nevis Tourism Office

New York: 414 E. 75th St., Fifth Floor, New York, NY 10021 (phone: 800-582-6208 or 212-535-1234; fax: 212-734-6511).

St. Lucia

St. Lucia Tourist Board

New York: 820 Second Ave., Suite 900E, New York, NY 10017 (phone: 800-456-3984 or 212-867-2950; fax: 212-370-7867).

St. Maarten

St. Maarten Tourist Office

New York: 675 Third Ave., 23rd Floor, New York, NY 10017 (phone: 800-ST-MAARTEN or 212-953-2084; fax: 212-953-2145).

St. Martin

See **French West Indies,** above.

St. Vincent and the Grenadines

St. Vincent and the Grenadines Tourist Board

New York: 801 Second Ave., 21st Floor, New York, NY 10017 (phone: 212-687-4981; fax: 212-949-5946).

Texas: 6505 Cove Creek Pl., Dallas, TX 75240 (phone: 214-239-6451; fax: 214-239-1002).

Trinidad and Tobago

Trinidad and Tobago Tourist Board

New York: 25 W. 43rd St., Suite 1508, New York, NY 10036 (phone: 800-232-0082 or 212-719-0540; fax: 212-719-0988).

US Virgin Islands

US Virgin Islands Division of Tourism

California: 3460 Wilshire Blvd., Suite 412, Los Angeles, CA 90010 (phone: 213-739-0138; fax: 213-739-2005).

Florida: 2655 Le Jeune Rd., Suite 907, Coral Gables, FL 33134 (phone: 305-442-7200; fax: 305-445-9044).

Georgia: 225 Peachtree St. NE, Suite 760, Atlanta, GA 30303 (phone: 404-688-0906; fax: 404-525-1102).

Illinois: 500 N. Michigan Ave., Suite 2030, Chicago, IL 60611 (phone: 312-670-8784; fax: 312-670-8788).

New York: 1270 Ave. of the Americas, Suite 2108, New York, NY 10020 (phone: 212-332-2222; fax: 212-332-2223).

Washington, DC: 900 17th St. NW, Suite 500, Washington, DC 20006 (phone: 202-293-3707; fax: 202-785-2542).

Venezuela

New York: c/o *Consulate General of Venezuela,* 7 E. 51st St., New York, NY 10022 (phone: 212-826-1660; fax: 212-644-7471).

CARIBBEAN EMBASSIES AND CONSULATES IN THE US

Anguilla

Consular matters are handled by the *British Embassy* and *Consulates.*

British Embassy

Washington, DC: 3100 Massachusetts Ave. NW, Washington, DC 20008-3600 (phone: 202-462-1340; fax: 202-898-4255); *Consular Section:* 19 Observatory Circle, Washington, DC 20008-3600 (phone: 202-986-0205; fax: 202-797-2929).

British Consulates

California: *Consulate General,* 11766 Wilshire Blvd., Suite 400, Los Angeles, CA 90025 (phone: 310-477-3322; fax: 310-575-1450); *Consulate General,* 1 Sansome St., Suite 850, San Francisco, CA 94109 (phone: 415-981-3030; fax: 415-434-2018).

Georgia: *Consulate General,* Marquis One Tower, 245 Peachtree Center Ave., Suite 2700, Atlanta, GA 30303 (phone: 404-524-5856; fax: 404-524-3153).

Illinois: 33 N. Dearborn St., Ninth Floor, Chicago, IL 60602 (phone: 312-346-1810; fax: 312-346-7021).

Massachusetts: *Consulate General,* Federal Reserve Plaza, 600 Atlantic Ave., 25th Floor, Boston, MA 02210 (phone: 617-248-9555; fax: 617-248-9578).

New York: *Consulate General,* 845 Third Ave., Ninth Floor, New York, NY 10022 (phone: 212-745-0200; fax: 212-754-3062).

Texas: *Consulate General,* 1000 Louisiana St., Suite 1900, Houston, TX 77002 (phone: 713-659-6270; fax: 713-659-7094).

Antigua and Barbuda

Embassy

Washington, DC: 3216 New Mexico Ave. NW, Third Floor, Washington, DC 20016 (phone: 202-362-5122; fax: 202-362-5225).

Consulate General

New York: 25 SE Second Ave., Suite 300, Miami, FL 33131 (phone: 305-381-6762; fax: 305-381-7908).

Aruba

Consular matters are handled by the *Aruba Tourism Authority* (see list above).

Barbados

Embassy

Washington, DC: 2144 Wyoming Ave. NW, Washington, DC 20008 (phone: 202-939-9200; fax: 202-332-7467).

Consulate General

New York: 800 Second Ave., Second Floor, New York, NY 10017 (phone: 212-867-8435; fax: 212-986-1030).

Belize

Embassy

Washington, DC: 2535 Massachusetts Ave. NW, Washington, DC 20008 (phone: 202-332-9636; fax: 202-332-6888).

Bonaire

Consular matters are handled by the *Embassy of the Netherlands.*
Embassy of the Netherlands

Washington, DC: Attention: Harold Henriquez, Minister for the Netherlands Antilles, 4200 Wisconsin Ave. NW, Washington, DC 20016 (phone: 202-244-5300; fax: 202-362-5344).

British Virgin Islands

Consular matters are handled by the *British Embassy* and *Consulates* (see **Anguilla,** above).

Cayman Islands

Consular matters are handled by the *British Embassy* and *Consulates* (see **Anguilla,** above).

Colombia

Embassy

Washington, DC: 2118 Leroy Pl. NW, Washington, DC 20008 (phone: 202-387-8338; fax: 202-232-8643).
Consulates

California: *Consulate General,* 3580 Wilshire Blvd., Suite 1450, Los Angeles, CA 90010 (phone: 213-382-1136; fax: 213-383-2785); *Consulate General,* 595 Market St., Suite 2130, San Francisco, CA 94105 (phone: 415-495-7195; fax: 415-777-3731).

Florida: *Consulate General,* 280 Aragon Ave., Coral Gables, FL 33134 (phone: 305-448-5558; fax: 305-441-9537).

Georgia: *Consulate,* 3379 Peachtree Rd. NE, Room 555, Atlanta, GA 30326 (phone: 404-237-1045; fax: 404-237-7957).

Illinois: *Consulate General,* 500 N. Michigan Ave., Suite 2040, Chicago, IL 60625 (phone: 312-923-1196; fax: 312-923-1197).

Louisiana: *Consulate General,* 2 Canal St., Suite 1844, New Orleans, LA 70130 (phone: 504-525-5580; fax: 504-525-4903).

Massachusetts: *Consulate,* 535 Boylston St., 11th Floor, Boston, MA 02116 (phone: 617-536-6222; fax: 617-536-9372).

New York: *Consulate,* 10 E. 46th St., New York, NY 10017 (phone: 212-949-9898; fax: 212-972-1725).

Texas: *Consulate General,* 2990 Richmond Ave., Suite 544, Houston, TX 77098-3185 (phone: 713-527-8919 or 713-527-9093; fax: 713-529-3395).

Washington, DC: *Consulate General,* 1825 Connecticut Ave NW, Suite 218, Washington, DC 20009 (phone: 202-332-7476; fax: 202-332-7180).

Curaçao

Consular matters are handled by the *Embassy of the Netherlands* (see **Bonaire,** above).

Dominica

Consulate General

New York: 820 Second Ave., Ninth Floor, New York, NY 10017 (phone: 212-949-0853; fax: 212-808-4975).

Dominican Republic

Embassy

Washington, DC: 1715 22nd St. NW, Washington, DC 20008 (phone: 202-332-6280; fax: 202-265-8057).

Consulates

Alabama: *Consul,* María Teresa Diaz, 4009 Old Shell Rd., Apt. E-16, Mobile, AL 36608 (phone: 205-433-8894).

California: *Consul General,* Miguel Angel Jiménez, 870 Market St., Suite 915, San Francisco, CA 94102 (phone: 415-982-5144; fax: 415-391-6924).

Florida: *Consul,* Tabaré González, 1914 Beach Way Rd., Suite 1B, Jacksonville, FL 32207 (phone: 904-396-9131); *Consul General,* Manuel Guaroa Liranzo, 1038 Brickell Ave., Miami, FL 33131 (phone: 305-358-3221; fax: 305-358-2318).

Louisiana: *Consul General,* Joaquín Balaguer, World Trade Center, 2 Canal St., Suite 1647, New Orleans, LA 70130 (phone: 504-522-1843; fax: 504-522-1007).

Massachusetts: *Consul General,* Sabrina Marina Román, Statler Bldg., 20 Park Plaza, Suite 1124, Boston, MA 02116 (phone: 617-482-8121; fax: 617-482-8133).

New York: *Consul General,* José Casada, One Times Sq., 11th Floor, New York, NY 10036 (phone: 212-768-2480; fax: 212-768-2677).

Pennsylvania: *Consul,* Caperuza Díaz de Almonte, Lafayette Building, Fifth and Chestnut Sts., Suite 422, Philadelphia, PA 19106 (phone: 215-923-3006).

Texas: *Consul,* Modesto L. Díaz, 3300 S. Gessner Rd., Suite 113, Houston, TX 77063 (phone: 713-266-0165; fax: 713-974-2050).

Washington, DC: *Consul,* Germania Abatte de Gaskill, 1715 22nd St. NW, Washington, DC 20008 (phone: 202-332-6280; fax: 202-265-8057).

French West Indies (Guadeloupe, Martinique, St. Barthélemy, St. Martin)

Consular matters are handled by the *French Embassy* and *Consulates.*

French Embassy

Washington, DC: 4101 Reservoir Rd. NW, Washington, DC 20007 (phone: 202-944-6000; fax: 202-944-6212).

French Consulates General

California: 10990 Wilshire Blvd., Suite 300, Los Angeles, CA 90024 (phone: 310-479-4426; fax: 310-312-0704); 540 Bush St., San Francisco, CA 94108 (phone: 415-397-4330; fax: 415-433-8357).

Florida: 1 Biscayne Tower, 2 S. Biscayne Blvd., Suite 1710, Miami, FL 33131 (phone: 305-372-9798; fax: 305-372-9549).

Georgia: Marquis Tower Two, 285 Peachtree Center Ave., Suite 2800, Atlanta, GA 30303 (phone: 404-522-4226; fax: 404-880-9408).

Illinois: 737 N. Michigan Ave., Suite 2020, Chicago, IL 60611 (phone: 312-787-5359/60/61; recorded visa information: 312-787-7889; fax: 312-664-4196).

Louisiana: 300 Poydras St., Suite 2105, New Orleans, LA 70130 (phone: 504-523-5772; fax: 504-523-5725).

Massachusetts: visa applications: 20 Park Plaza, Suite 1123, Boston, MA 02116 (phone: 617-482-2864; fax: 617-426-9236); all other business: 3 Commonwealth Ave., Boston, MA 02116 (phone: 617-266-1680; fax: 617-437-1090).

New York: 934 Fifth Ave., New York, NY 10021 (phone: 212-606-3688; recorded visa information: 212-606-3644, 212-606-3652, or 212-606-3653; fax: 212-606-3670).

Texas: 2777 Allen Pkwy., Suite 650, Houston, TX 77019 (phone: 713-528-2181; fax: 713-528-1933).

Grenada

Embassy

Washington, DC: 1701 New Hampshire Ave. NW, Washington, DC 20009 (phone: 202-265-2561; fax: 202-265-2468).

Consulate General

New York: 820 Second Ave., Ninth Floor, New York, NY 10017 (phone: 212-599-0301; fax: 212-599-1540).

Guadeloupe

See **French West Indies,** above.

Jamaica

Embassy

Washington, DC: 1520 New Hampshire Ave. NW, Washington, DC 20036 (phone: 202-452-0660; fax: 202-452-0081).

Consulates General:

Florida: 842 Ingraham Bldg., 25 SE Second Ave., Miami, FL 33131 (phone: 305-374-8431/2; fax: 305-577-4970).

New York: 767 Third Ave., Third Floor, New York, NY 10017 (phone: 212-935-9000; fax: 212-935-7507).

Martinique

See **French West Indies,** above.

Mexico

Embassy

Washington, DC: 1911 Pennsylvania Ave. NW, Washington, DC 20006 (phone: 202-728-1600); *Consular Section:* 2827 16th St. NW, Washington, DC 20009 (phone: 212-736-1000/1/2; fax: 202-797-8458).

Consulates

Arizona: *Consulate,* 480 Grand Ave., Nogales, AZ 85621 (phone: 602-287-2521; fax: 602-287-3175); *Consulate,* 1990 W. Camelback Rd., Suite 110, Phoenix, AZ 85015 (phone: 602-242-7398/9; fax: 602-242-2957); *Consulate,* 553 S. Stone Ave., Tucson, AZ 85701 (phone: 602-882-5595; fax: 602-882-8959).

California: *Consulate,* 331 W. Second St., Calexico, CA 92231 (phone: 619-357-3863 or 619-357-4132; fax: 619-357-5284); *Consulate,* 905 N. Fulton St., Fresno, CA 93728 (phone: 209-233-3065; fax: 209-233-5638); *Consulate General,* 2401 W. Sixth St., Los Angeles, CA 90057 (phone: 213-351-6800 or 213-351-6807; fax: 213-389-9249); *Consulate,* Transportation Center, 201 E. Fourth St., Suite 209, Oxnard, CA 93030 (phone: 805-483-4684; fax: 805-486-9213); *Consulate,* 9812 Old Winery Pl., Suite 10, Sacramento, CA 95827 (phone: 916-363-3885; fax: 916-363-0625); *Consulate,* 532 N. D St., San Bernardino, CA 92401 (phone: 909-889-9836; fax: 909-889-8285); *Consulate General,* 1549 India St., San Diego, CA 92101 (phone: 619-231-8414; fax: 619-231-4802); *Consulate General,* 870 Market St., Suite 528, San Francisco, CA 94102 (phone: 415-392-5554; fax: 415-392-3233); *Consulate,* 380 N. First St., Suite 102, San Jose, CA 95112 (phone: 408-294-3414/5; fax: 408-294-4506); *Consulate,* 828 N. Broadway, Santa Ana, CA 92701 (phone: 714-835-3069; fax: 714-835-3472).

Colorado: *Consulate General,* 707 Washington St., Suite A, Denver, CO 80203 (phone: 303-830-0601 or 303-830-0607; fax: 303-830-0704).

Florida: *Consulate,* 1200 NW 68th Ave., Suite 200, Miami, FL 33126 (phone: 305-716-4977; fax: 305-441-7180); *Consulate,* 1717 W.

Cass St., Tampa, FL 33606 (phone: 813-254-5960; fax: 813-251-2032).

Georgia: *Consulate General,* 3220 Peachtree Rd. NE, Atlanta, GA 30305 (phone: 404-266-2233; fax: 404-266-2302).

Illinois: *Consulate General,* 300 N. Michigan Ave., Second Floor, Chicago, IL 60601 (phone: 312-855-1380; fax: 312-855-9257).

Louisiana: *Consulate General,* World Trade Center Building, 2 Canal St., Suite 840, New Orleans, LA 70130 (phone: 504-522-3596; fax: 504-525-2332).

Massachusetts: *Consulate,* 20 Park Plaza, Suite 506, Boston, MA 02116 (phone: 617-426-8782; fax: 617-426-5795).

Michigan: *Consulate,* 600 Renaissance Center, Suite 1510, Detroit, MI 48243 (phone: 313-567-7713; fax: 313-567-7543).

Missouri: *Consulate,* 1015 Locust St., Suite 922, St. Louis, MO 63101 (phone: 314-436-3233 or 314-436-3065; fax: 314-436-2695).

New Mexico: *Consulate,* Western Bank Building, 401 Fifth St. NW, Albuquerque, NM 87102 (phone: 505-247-2139; fax: 505-842-9490).

New York: *Consulate,* 1875 Harlem Rd., Buffalo, NY 01423 (phone: 716-895-9800; fax: 716-895-9947); *Consulate General,* 8 E. 41st St., New York, NY 10017 (phone: 212-689-0456/7/8/9; fax: 212-545-8197).

Pennsylvania: *Consulate,* Bourse Building, 111 S. Independence Way E., Suite 1010, Philadelphia, PA 19106 (phone: 215-922-4262; fax: 215-923-7281).

Texas: *Consulate,* 200 E. Sixth St., Suite 200, Austin, TX 78701 (phone: 512-478-2866; fax: 512-478-8008); *Consulate,* 724 E. Elizabeth St., Brownsville, TX 78520 (phone: 210-542-4431; fax: 210-542-7267); *Consulate,* N. Tower, 800 N. Shoreline Blvd., Fourth Floor, Corpus Christi, TX 78401 (phone: 512-882-3375; fax: 512-882-9324); *Consulate General,* 1349 Empire Central, Suite 100, Dallas, TX 75247 (phone: 214-630-7341/2/3; fax: 214-630-3511); *Consulate,* 300 E. Losoya St., Del Rio, TX 78840 (phone: 210-774-5031; fax: 210-774-6497); *Consulate,* 140 Adams St., Eagle Pass, TX 78852 (phone: 210-773-9255/6; fax: 210-773-9397); *Consulate General,* 910 E. San Antonio Ave., El Paso, TX 79901 (phone: 915-533-3644/5; fax: 915-532-7163); *Consulate General,* 3015 Richmond St., Suite 100, Houston, TX 77098 (phone: 713-524-2300; fax: 713-523-6244); *Consulate,* 1612 Farragut St., PO Box 659, Laredo, TX 78042 (phone: 210-723-6360 or 210-723-6369; fax: 210-723-1741); *Consulate,* 600 S. Broadway, McAllen, TX 78501 (phone: 210-686-0243, 210-686-0244, or 210-686-0554; fax: 210-686-4901); *Consulate,* 511 W. Ohio Ave., Suite 121, Midland, TX 79701 (phone: 915-687-2334; fax: 915-687-3952); *Consulate General,* 127

Navarro St., San Antonio, TX 78205 (phone: 210-227-9145/6; fax: 210-227-1817).

Utah: *Consulate,* 458 E. 200 S., Salt Lake City, UT 84111 (phone: 801-521-8502/3; fax: 801-521-0534).

Washington State: *Consulate General,* 2132 Third Ave., Seattle, WA 98121 (phone: 206-448-3526; fax: 206-448-4771).

Montserrat

Consular matters are handled by the *British Embassy* and *Consulates* (see **Anguilla,** above).

Saba/St. Eustatius

Consular matters are handled by the *Embassy of the Netherlands* (see **Bonaire,** above).

St. Barthélemy

See **French West Indies,** above.

St. Kitts and Nevis

Embassy

Washington, DC: OECS Building, 3216 New Mexico Ave. NW, Washington, DC 20016 (phone: 202-686-2636; fax: 202-686-5740).

St. Lucia

Consulate General

New York: 820 Second Ave., Suite 900E, New York, NY 10017 (phone: 212-697-9360; fax: 212-867-2795).

St. Maarten

Consular matters are handled by the *Embassy of the Netherlands* (see **Bonaire,** above).

St. Martin

See **French West Indies,** above.

St. Vincent and the Grenadines

Embassy

Washington, DC: 1717 Massachusetts Ave. NW, Suite 102, Washington, DC 20036 (phone: 202-462-7806; fax: 202-462-7807).

Consulate General

New York: 801 Second Ave., 21st Floor, New York, NY 10017 (phone: 212-687-4490; fax: 212-949-5946).

Trinidad and Tobago

Embassy

Washington, DC: 1708 Massachusetts Ave. NW, Washington, DC 20036 (phone: 202-467-6490; fax: 202-785-3130).

Consulate General

New York: 733 Third Ave., Suite 1716, New York, NY 10017 (phone: 212-682-7272; fax: 212-986-2146).

Venezuela

Embassy

Washington, DC: 1099 30th St. NW, Washington, DC 20007 (phone: 202-342-2214; fax: 202-342-6820).

Consulate General

New York: 7 E. 51st St., New York, NY 10022 (phone: 212-826-1660; fax: 212-644-7471).

The Islands

The Islands

Anguilla

For its first four and a half centuries Anguilla (pronounced An-*gwil*-la) lazed away its days in what seemed—to the outside world, at least—a content, nearly comatose, state. In fact, none of the islanders probably noticed when Columbus, sailing by in 1493, gave the island its name (the Spanish word for "eel," because of its long, narrow shape and serpentine shoreline).

The island's Arawak Indian residents continued their quiet existence until 1650, when the first British settlers arrived. In the 18th century Anguillans were stung twice by French attacks. Both times the invaders were forced to retreat, and the island continued to avoid interaction with the outside world.

For the next century and a half no one—except Anguillans—thought much about the island. Even the islanders failed to react at first when, in 1825, the British government made a single Crown Colony of St. Kitts, Nevis, and Anguilla.

But during the 1950s the Anguillans began to mutter; and in 1966, when Britain made an associated state of the three-island colony without giving Anguilla a say in its own government, the islanders objected loudly. Prodded by what they perceived as subjugation to a "foreign" power—the legislature in St. Kitts, some 70 miles away—Anguillans seceded from the alliance.

The cry of the "eel" brought international media attention, especially after neighboring islands talked of sending expeditionary forces. To forestall any precipitous local action, the Crown dispatched a "peacekeeping force" in 1969. To their surprise they were greeted warmly by the Anguillans, who were waving Union Jacks instead of submachine guns. When the dust had settled, no lives had been lost (the one barrage reported turned out to be photographers' flashbulbs rather than gunfire). In response to its subjects' wishes, in 1971 Britain once more took Anguilla under its colonial wing. In February 1976 a new and separate constitution providing a ministerial system of government, with elected representatives handling most island affairs, went into effect. Soon after that Anguilla, now wide awake, took its first look at tourism as a potential source of income, even prosperity.

There were two major drawbacks at the start: near total obscurity and a dearth of accommodations for comfort-craving (let alone luxury-seeking) guests. In the late 1970s the island had fewer than 150 rooms for visitors. On the other hand, Anguilla's bone-dry climate and isolation blessed the island with spectacular natural attractions: truly glorious beaches, incredibly clear water, and undisturbed reefs alive with fantastic fish.

Aware of others' mistakes, the government declared itself "committed to development of a *controlled* tourist industry" and began exploring pos-

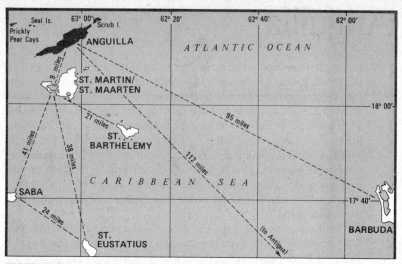

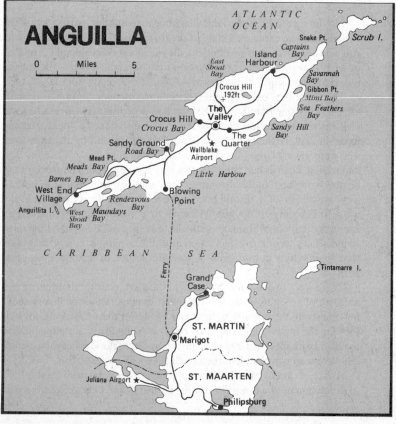

sibilities. Today, low-rise first class and luxury hotels, villas, and condominiums dot the island, and others are quietly popping up on a regular basis. While the government is sincerely determined "to preserve peace and tranquillity," the island is no longer "the Caribbean's best-kept secret." Anguilla's small, serene, and select hotels are among the most talked-about in the Caribbean, and its restaurants rival those of any metropolis. Tourism is becoming big business in every sense—yet the Anguillans remain genuinely warm and welcoming.

The rise in development on the island has been a mixed blessing. The good news is that there are now enough rooms to house almost all the visitors eager to enjoy Anguilla's unique blend of sophistication and unspoiled beaches. The bad news is that petty crime has made an appearance. But locals still feel secure enough to leave their homes and cars unlocked at night, and rooms at the elegant *Cap Juluca* have no keys.

Even the most fertile imagination could not describe Anguilla as bustling or exciting, but the quiet atmosphere is a large part of its appeal. Besides sunning, lazy snorkeling, sailing, or picnicking, there really isn't much to do. More comforts and diversions may be on the way, but for now, if the sun, the sand, the sea, and a stack of paperbacks are *really* all you need for a perfect vacation, have we got an island for you.

Anguilla At-a-Glance

FROM THE AIR

Anguilla, northernmost of the British Leeward Islands, stretches for 16 miles from southwest to northeast, with small Scrub Island off its northeastern end and minuscule Anguillita Island off its southwestern tip. The French/Dutch island of St. Martin/St. Maarten is 4 miles south; St. Kitts is 70 miles south and slightly east; Puerto Rico is 150 miles due west. Anguilla is only 3 miles across at its widest point, and the shining white coral beaches that notch its coasts make for an undulating shoreline. The island rises only 213 feet above sea level, and has no cities, no rivers, no streams or rushing waterfalls; the land is dry, with several salt ponds and a few palm trees, but mostly short, sparse vegetation. The island's inhabitants, numbering about 9,500, make their living lobstering, fishing, building hotels or the famed Anguillan boats, and working for the government or in the tourism industry.

Anguilla's main road leads from West End, a village in the southwest, to The Quarter, a small settlement at the island's midpoint; the road then loops northeast to Island Harbour and back again. At a number of places auxiliary roads branch off north and south toward beaches and fishing villages. The island's central area is called The Valley. It's the administrative center for Anguilla's elected ministerial government and the home of the *Anguilla Tourist Board* office. Sandy Ground at Road Bay, the island's principal port of entry, is on the north coast. Ferries to Marigot on St. Martin leave from Blowing Point on the south coast. *Wallblake Airport* is in the middle of the island, near The Quarter and The Valley.

SPECIAL PLACES

On Anguilla, beaches definitely get top billing: With more than 33 from which to choose, you probably won't even have time to see them all. But this one's a must.

DREAM BEACH

Shoal Bay Our vote for the island's most superb strand goes to this stunning, sweeping, silvery beach—literally one of the enormous beauties of this island. And much of the time it's enchantingly empty. The only crowds are offshore and underwater—clouds of iridescent fish that dart about the astonishing coral gardens. The drop-off and reef beyond lure experienced divers. There are shady trees to laze under when you've had enough sun and sea, but bring *everything* with you—snorkel gear, beach towels, cover-ups. Nearby beach bars provide drinks and food. On the Caribbean coast at the northeastern tip of the island.

But don't stop here. Many vacationers visit several beaches before settling on one or two favorites—you'll need a car or a mini-moke (an open-air jeep) to do this, although hitchhiking is perfectly acceptable. On the south shore, sweeping Rendezvous Bay is among the most beautiful. During the summer of 1986 some 3,000 pieces of ancient pottery, as well as some human remains from a large Amerindian settlement (possibly dating back to 100 BC), were found during excavations for a hotel on the beach here. Along the south coast to the west of Rendezvous Bay, facing the rolling hills of St. Martin, are the white shores of secluded Cove Bay (where you may share the clear water with only fishing boats) and Maunday's Bay. The latter is very good for shelling, and is the site of *Cap Juluca,* a sparkling white superluxury resort sprawling over 179 acres of land and water (see *Checking In*). At the northeastern edge of Anguilla is Captain's Bay, one of the most secluded beaches on the island, with coral outcrops bracketing a romantic stretch of white sand. You're unlikely to find another soul here. There also is good snorkeling at Shoal Bay West, Mimi Bay, Little Harbour, Limestone Bay, Sea Feather's Bay, and at Little Bay, on the northern end of Crocus Bay, which is accessible by boat or via steep cliffs from the road's edge. Framed by the island's largest hill, vast Crocus Bay is the departure point of many Anguillan boat races—the island's favorite sport—but otherwise is very peaceful. Sandy Ground, on Road Bay, between the Salt Pond and the sea, is a small harborside village that is one of the island's prettiest. While Sandy Ground and Shoal Bay (also known as Shoal Bay East—

not to be confused with West Shoal Bay) are the most commercial of Anguilla's many beaches, they are, by any standards, clean, uncrowded, and picturesque.

Still under way above Shoal Bay is the excavation of a cave known as The Fountain, which contains a large stalagmite and a number of interesting petroglyphs. Few people are aware of Anguilla's many archaeological digs: 23 aboriginal sites have been discovered so far, some dating from as early as the second millennium BC. Anguilla has established a 3½-acre national park around The Fountain. For additional information contact the *Anguilla Tourist Board* (phone: 2759 or 2451; 800-553-4939).

EXTRA SPECIAL

The most fun place on this most peaceful of islands is surely Scilly Cay (pronounced Silly Key), an acre or so of coral, sand, and exotic plants that's just a two-minute boat ride from Island Harbour Jetty. Quiet during the week, it becomes one big happy party on weekends. It's a perfect place to spend a day swimming, snorkeling, soaking up the sun, and feasting on the delicious barbecued lobster, crayfish, and chicken creations (the recipe for the curry sauce is a closely guarded secret) served at the *Gorgeous Scilly Cay* restaurant (see *Eating Out*). Just stand on the dock and wave— they'll send a boat for you.

Sources and Resources

TOURIST INFORMATION

Information about Anguilla can be obtained at the *Tourist Board* office in The Valley (phone: 2759 or 2451). You also can write to the director of tourism (The Valley, Anguilla, BWI). The office will reply immediately, but allow at least two weeks for mailed correspondence. Publications available from the *Tourist Board* include annually updated hotel and villa rate brochures and a sketchy map of the island. The better *Calabash Skyview* color maps are available free at the airport and at most hotels. For information on Anguilla tourist offices in the US, see GETTING READY TO GO.

LOCAL COVERAGE *The Chronicle,* published on St. Maarten, arrives daily except Sundays, and currently is the best local source of summarized world and local news. There's also a weekly Anguillan newspaper, *The Light.* Two other publications produced on Anguilla, *What We Do in Anguilla* and *Anguilla Life,* are useful sources of local news and events.

RADIO AND TELEVISION Anguilla has three radio stations: ZGF (105.5 FM), which programs primarily music; the government station, Radio Anguilla (KHZ 1505 AM), which broadcasts news and music; and the privately owned religious station Caribbean Beacon (1610 AM or 100.1 FM). Caribbean Television International is available islandwide; cable TV, beamed in 24 hours a day via US satellite, reaches most of Anguilla.

TELEPHONE When calling from the US dial 1 + 809 (area code) + 497 (country code) + (local four-digit number). To call from another Caribbean island the code may vary, so call the local operator. When dialing on Anguilla use only the local number unless otherwise indicated. Dial 911 for emergency assistance.

ENTRY REQUIREMENTS All visitors are required to show some sort of identification with a photo. Those staying overnight will be asked for proof of citizenship (a valid passport is preferred, although a birth certificate or voter's registration card, along with a government-approved photo ID such as a driver's license, is accepted) and a return or ongoing ticket. There is a $10 departure tax at the airport; the ferryboat departure tax is $3.

CLIMATE AND CLOTHES Anguilla is in the path of the easterly trade winds, which means cooling breezes and low humidity throughout the year. The year-round temperature ranges from 80 to 85F (27 to 29C). Rainfall is light but erratic, and may fall at any time of year. The wettest months are usually September through December and sometimes April and May. You'll need only light, casual sports clothes (lots of beachwear), unless you feel like dressing up for dinner at the *Malliouhana* hotel dining room or at *Cap Juluca's Pimms* restaurant (see *Eating Out* for both).

MONEY Anguilla's official currency is the Eastern Caribbean dollar (EC), at press time valued at about $2.70 EC to $1 US. Prices in shops usually are quoted in $EC, but hotels and restaurants more often use $US, and, if you pay in $US most can give US currency for change. Be sure to ask which "dollars" are meant. Traveler's checks, and often personal checks, are readily accepted, and credit cards are being accepted more in most hotels. Barclays Bank International has a branch in The Valley, and there are three other commercial banks: *Anguilla National, Caribbean Commercial,* and *Scotia Bank.* Banking hours are 8 AM to 3 PM Mondays through Thursdays and 8 AM to 5 PM Fridays; closed weekends and holidays. There is also an American Express office in The Valley. All prices in this chapter are quoted in US dollars.

LANGUAGE English.

TIME Atlantic standard time is maintained all year. It's one hour ahead of eastern standard time in winter (when it's noon on the US East Coast it's 1 PM on Anguilla), and the same as eastern daylight saving time in summer.

CURRENT In most places outlets are 110 AC, the same current used in the US. Check with your hotel ahead of time to be sure; if a converter is required for your American appliances, bring one along.

TIPPING The 10% or 15% service charge added to hotel bills takes care of everyone, although waiters/waitresses and bartenders do not object to a little something more; if you are pleased with the service, show it. Taxi drivers need not be tipped, either, but if they have given you special service or a good tour, a 10% to 15% tip is a nice way of showing your appreciation. Young boys help arriving visitors with baggage (in their wheelbarrows) at Blowing Point, and $1 will usually make them very happy. There are no official porters at *Wallblake Airport,* but you probably won't need one; your cab driver can always double as a porter. If someone else should help with your bag, a smile and a heartfelt thank you is probably all he or she expects.

GETTING AROUND

CAR RENTAL Varying vintages are available; if possible, get a newer model with air conditioning. With the island's many unpaved roads and grazing goats, you may want to opt for a jeep. *Apex Car Rental* (phone: 2642) offers automatic and stick-shift models. *Connor's Car Rental* (phone: 6433 or 6541) has the island's largest selection. Other car rental firms include *Bennie's* (phone: 6221, 2788, or 2360), which represents *Avis,* a short taxi ride from Blowing Point; *Budget* (phone: 2217; 800-472-3325); *Island Car Rentals* on the Airport Road (phone: 2723, days; 4330, after 5 PM); and *Triple "K"* (phone: 2934). The island's two full-service gas stations are in The Valley and on the way to Blowing Point. Driving is on the left, and there are no street signs (and only six traffic lights). Roads are entirely unmarked, so ask your hotel for landmarks before setting out (though Anguilla is so small that it's fairly hard to get lost). Visitors must obtain an Anguillan driver's license by presenting a home license and paying about $7 at the car rental agency. Mopeds, scooters, and motorbikes may be rented but are fairly expensive. Call *Boo's Cycle Rental* (phone: 2323) or *MultiScenic* (phone: 5810). Jeeps are available from *Triple "K"* and *Connor's. Note:* The police now use radar to check the speed of traffic, so be sure to keep within the posted speed limit (usually 30 mph) to avoid paying a $35 fine.

FERRY SERVICES Regular ferry service links Blowing Point, Anguilla, with Marigot, French St. Martin, from about 7 AM to 10:30 PM or so daily. These power-boats, most built by Anguilla's famed craftsmen, make the trip in about 20 minutes. During the day a ferryboat departs every 30 minutes or so, and the one-way fare is $9. At night service is less frequent and the fare is $11 one way. Day-trippers to St. Martin also pay a $3 departure tax at Blowing Point.

INTER-ISLAND FLIGHTS *American Eagle* (phone: 3500/1/3) runs two flights daily from its San Juan, Puerto Rico, hub direct to Anguilla. *Windward Island Airways (WINAIR;* phone: 2748), *Air Anguilla* (phone: 2643 or 2725), *Tyden Air* (phone: 2717; 800-842-0261) and *LIAT* (phone: 5000/1/2) schedule daily flights from St. Maarten's *Juliana Airport* to Anguilla. *LIAT* also offers regular service to Anguilla from Antigua, Nevis, St. Thomas, and St. Kitts. *Air*

Anguilla flies daily to St. Thomas, St. Croix, San Juan, and St. Kitts. *Tyden Air* and *Air Anguilla* also offer "flightseeing" excursions and charter service to most Caribbean islands. It's a good idea to check for last-minute schedule changes and to be flexible enough to accommodate the elasticity of island time. For airline reservations and travel arrangements, contact *Malliouhana Travel & Tours* (phone: 2431), *Bennie's* (see *Car Rental,* above), or *J. N. Gumbs Travel Agency* (phone: 2238, days; 2838, evenings).

SEA EXCURSIONS Pretty, palm-tufted Sandy Island and the even more remote Prickly Pear Cays used to be ideal escape sites, but have become crowded with day-trippers from St. Martin. However, both still offer good snorkeling and beach bars that grill lobster, chicken, and ribs for lunch. A boat making stops at both places leaves Sandy Ground at 10 AM and returns later in the day. Ask at the small jetty by *Johnno's Beach Bar* (see *Eating Out*) or contact Neville Connors at *Sandy Island Enterprises* (phone: 6395, 6433, or 5643). *Suntastic Cruises* (phone: 3400 days; 6847 or 3699 evenings) sails its 37-foot sloop *Skybird* and the power cruiser *Sunbird* on day trips to Prickly Pear, including lunch, drinks, and snorkeling gear; sunset cruises include drinks and snacks. Similar trips are available aboard *Ragtime* (phone: 6395 or 5643), a 28-foot sailboat. Other day, sunset, and overnight cruises are offered by *Princess Soya Catamaran Cruises* (phone: 2671), *Junior's Glass-Bottom Boat Cruises* (phone: 2051 or 4155), and *Smitty's* in Shoal Bay (phone: 4300). The *Madeariman Reef* beach bar on Shoal Bay arranges glass-bottom boat tours (phone: 3833).

TAXI Call *Bennie's Tours* (see *Car Rentals,* above), *Connor's Taxi* (phone: 6136), or *Malliouhana Travel & Tours* (see *Inter-Island Flights,* above).

TOURS Taxi touring is a sociable way to get acquainted with the island and to learn something of its lore. Drivers will show you every nook and cranny in a couple of hours. The typical around-the-island tour includes about 2½ hours of sightseeing, after which the driver will drop you at a lunch spot or beach of your choice; for an additional charge, the taxi will pick you up at an appointed time for the return trip. Local tour operators include *Bennie's Tours* and *MultiScenic* (see *Car Rentals,* above, for both); *Connor's Taxi* (see *Taxi,* above), and *Malliouhana Travel & Tours* (see *Inter-Island Flights,* above); as well as *Bertram's* (phone: 2256) and *Paradise Ventures* (phone: 2107). *Bennie's* and *MultiScenic* both offer a "transfer" service for visitors traveling to and from St. Martin, including taxis and boats.

SPECIAL EVENTS

Carnival is a week-long holiday climaxing on the first Monday in August and featuring boat races, sports events, costume parades, music competitions, and nonstop partying. The island's three national holidays are *Anguilla Day* (May 30), marking the commencement of its secession from its partnership with St. Kitts and Nevis; *Constitution Day* (August 7); and *Separation Day* (December 19). Other holidays include *New Year's Day, Good Friday*

(April 5 in 1996), *Easter Monday* (April 8 in 1996), *Labour Day* (May 1), *Whitmonday* (May 27 in 1996), the *Queen's Official Birthday* (early June), *August Monday* (the first Monday in August), *August Thursday* (the first Thursday in August), *Christmas,* and *Boxing Day* (December 26).

SHOPPING

Serious shoppers head for St. Martin, but a few spots on Anguilla offer clothing and handicrafts. For high fashion, the island's top shop is the *Malliouhana* hotel boutique, featuring Gottex swimsuits and leather fashions (see *Checking In*). The Valley post office's stamps appeal to collectors. If you're in the market for a traditional hand-built Anguillan racing boat, contact Ron Webster (phone: 4465); for a super-strong wooden craft made with the WEST (Wood Epoxy Saturated Technique) System (used on some small ferry boats), contact David Carty (phone: 2616). Small models and other souvenirs and local crafts are sold at *Bertram's* (see *Tours,* above) and *Bencraft* (no phone), both at Sandy Ground. Splendid shells are Anguilla's best souvenirs—yours for the finding on all island beaches, especially the north side of Rendezvous Bay and Maunday's Bay. Most shops are open Mondays through Saturdays from 9 AM to 6 PM. Here are some other places to explore:

Beach Stuff All the togs you'll need for sunning and swimming can be found in a hot pink and turquoise shop perched above the harbor at Sandy Ground. Road Bay (phone: 6814).

Caribbean Style A lively, extensive collection of Caribbean arts and crafts. At *Pineapple Beach Club,* Rendezous Bay (no phone).

Cheddie's Carving Studio Cheddie exhibits and sells his carvings in a white house trimmed in blue and green. Sculptures made from local mahogany and driftwood range in price from $50 to $2,000. The Cove (phone: 6027).

Devonish–Cotton Gin Art Gallery Features some fine oils and watercolors by owner Courtney Devonish and other local artists, plus ceramics. Historic cotton gin machinery is exhibited, too. Wallblake (phone: 2949).

SPORTS

BOATING Sailboat racing ranks as the island's "national" sport. The ad hoc races that set sail from Sandy Ground, Shoal Bay, or Crocus Bay are often accompanied by beachside barbecues, "jump-ups" (outdoor parties featuring barbecues, steel bands, and dancing), and betting. Scheduled races take place on *New Year's Day, Easter,* and *Anguilla Day.* For a closer look at the Anguillan boats made by the island's famed master builders, visit the fishing village of Island Harbour. *Enchanted Island Cruises* charters boats for up to 35 people, and *Sandy Island Enterprises* has sailboats for rent (see *Sea Excursions,* above, for both).

SNORKELING AND SCUBA DIVING The island offers 18 fine dive sites, including coral reefs both shallow and deep (up to 130 feet) and seven shipwrecks—island freighters deliberately sunk offshore to encourage coral growth and attract sea life. Some of the best sites are off Prickly Pear Cays, Dog Island, West and Mid Cays, Anguillita, and Scrub Island. Many hotels offer scuba packages. Or contact PADI-affiliated *Tamariain Water Sports* (phone: 2020; fax: 5125) at Sandy Ground for daily excursions on their comfortable dive boat. *Tamariain* offers resort and certification courses, plus scuba and snorkel gear rental and sales. On the northern tip of Anguilla at Island Harbour, *Anguilla Divers Ltd.* offers gear rentals, dive excursions, and resort and certification courses seven days a week (phone: 4750 or 4105).

Snorkel gear can be rented from *Sandy Island Enterprises* and *Smitty's* (see *Sea Excursions,* above, for both). Both these outfits, as well as the *Madeariman Reef* beach bar (see *Sea Excursions*), offer snorkel excursions to Sandy Island, Prickly Pear Cays, Scrub Island, and Little Bay. The off-shore reefs at Shoal Bay are easily reached without a boat.

SPORT FISHING Trips with local skippers and fishermen can be arranged through hotels. Or try *Junior's Glass-Bottom Boat Cruises* or the beach bar at the *Madeariman Reef* (see *Sea Excursions,* above, for both). Ask about bringing your own tackle. DuBois Webster (locally known as "Nature Boy") is a knowledgeable young man who can take you deep-sea fishing, water skiing, on snorkel trips to Prickly Pear Cays and Sandy Island, or on other custom sailing/water sports excursions. Contact him at the *Casablanca* resort (see *Checking In*).

SWIMMING AND SUNNING The beaches are absolutely superb (see *Special Places*). There is no organized lifeguard system, so observe commonsense safety rules: Don't swim out too far alone and beware of currents, especially near reefs (coral scratches take an annoyingly long time to heal in tropical climates). Generally, the waters here are calm, clear, and safe even for children. Note that topless and nude bathing are illegal on Anguilla.

TENNIS At the hotels, there are four courts (three lighted) at the *Malliouhana,* three at *Cap Juluca,* and two each at *Cinnamon Reef, Casablanca, Carimar, Rendezvous Bay,* and *Coccoloba; Mariners* and *Covecastles* have one court each (see *Checking In* for all). To book courts at the *Scouts Headquarters,* south of *St. Mary's Anglican Church,* contact the *Anguilla Drug Store* (across the street in The Valley; phone: 2738); while there's no charge to play, donations are accepted for court maintenance. Tennis matches with members of the *Anguilla Tennis Association* can be arranged through the tourist office (see *Tourist Information,* above).

WINDSURFING AND WATER SKIING Offered by *Sandy Island Enterprises* and the *Madeariman Reef* beach bar (see *Sea Excursions,* above, for both), as well as *Tamariain Water Sports* (see *Snorkeling and Scuba Diving,* above) and the major hotels.

NIGHTLIFE

Although this generally is a quiet island, there is usually live music some-where every night of the week. The best sources of local entertainment information are the "Day & Night" listings in *Anguilla Life* magazine and the "Weekly Music Menu" in *What We Do in Anguilla*. There is live music most nights at *Cap Juluca*'s *Pimms* restaurant, one night—which varies from week to week—at *Lucy's Harbour View,* Thursday and Saturday nights at the *Beach Terrace* restaurant at the *Mariners* hotel, and Fridays through Mondays at the *Coccoloba* resort. *Cinnamon Reef* frequently has music, particularly on Fridays at the manager's poolside cocktail party and West Indian barbecue. On Wednesday, Friday, and Saturday nights, and Sunday afternoons, *Johnno's Beach Bar* at Sandy Ground is *the* place to be; the music is good and loud, and the flavor decidedly local. Wednesday and Sunday afternoons, *Gorgeous Scilly Cay* and *Uncle Ernie's Shoal Bay Beach Bar* feature live music and a great party atmosphere. (See *Checking In* and *Eating Out* for details on the above hotels and restaurants.) Local bands include *North Sound, the Mussington Brothers, Spraka, Dumpa and the Angvibes, Sleepy and the All Stars,* and *Keith and the Mellow Tones.* One of the best local singers is Banky Banx, a musician who performs at his new beach bar, *Dune* (Lower Rendezvous Bay; no phone); his records and tapes, which are a big hit throughout the Caribbean, are sold in shops all over the island. In addition, several of the beach bars and small restaurants set up local string and scratch bands some afternoons and evenings, especially if there is an occasion, such as a small cruise ship anchored offshore. The one dance club in town, *Red Dragon Disco* (in South Hill; phone: 2687), gets going at about 9:30 PM on Fridays and after midnight on Saturdays. Makeshift clubs and dance halls often pop up overnight, and then fade away just as quickly. To find the latest hot spot, ask at your hotel or, better yet, consult your cab driver. Or take a late-afternoon ferry to Marigot for drinks and dinner, then return to Anguilla afterwards (but be sure to catch the last ferry at around 10:30 PM.) There have been some reports of crime in Marigot at night, so take appropriate precautions.

Best on the Island

CHECKING IN

In deference to both government wishes and owner preference, new prop-erties are low-rise and high-quality; traditional cottage and villa architec-ture—shaped to fit the land as well as the island's beach-oriented, outdoor-indoor vacation style—remains dominant.

Rates can run as high as $3,800 per day for a five-bedroom villa at *Cap Juluca,* $1,240 for a two-bedroom suite at the *Malliouhana,* or $990 for three bedrooms at *Covecastles.* We classify $400 or more per day for a double room without meals in winter as very expensive, $250 to $400 as expensive,

$150 to $250 as moderate, and less than $150 as inexpensive. Clearly, Anguilla is no bargain if you crave top-of-the-line digs. Nonetheless, there are some apartments that cost less than $100 a night, a list of which may be obtained from the tourist offices in New York and Anguilla. An 8% government tax is added to all hotel rates, plus a 10% service charge. Rates are reduced by 30% to 60% in summer, making this a great off-season bargain spot. Unless otherwise noted, all hotels listed below have air conditioning, telephones, TV sets, and private baths.

Many vacationers who stay at a hotel one season arrange to rent an apartment or cottage the following year. A reliable on-island rental agency for privately-owned villas and cottages is *Sunshine Villas,* run by David Yates (PO Box 142, Anguilla, BWI; phone: 6149; 800-ANGUILLA; fax: 6021). A rate list for apartments, villas, and cottages is also available from the *Department of Tourism* (see *Tourist Information,* above). Because they are so popular here, we have included choice villa properties in our list of available accommodations.

Reservations for inns can be made by contacting *Inns of Anguilla* (phone: 3180); some resorts may be booked through *International Travel Resorts* (phone: 800-223-9815; 212-251-1800 in New York City; fax: 212-251-1767). For information, call the *Anguilla Tourist Information Office* in New York (see GETTING READY TO GO). When on Anguilla, use only the local four-digit numbers listed below. For information about dialing from elsewhere, see *Telephone,* above.

We begin with our favorite havens, all of which fall in the "very expensive" category, followed by recommended hotels listed by price category.

A REGAL RESORT AND SOME SPECIAL HAVENS

Cap Juluca One of the Caribbean's superluxury resorts is spread over 179 acres of stunning southwestern coast and overlooks the smoky mountains of St. Martin. Named for the Arawak rainbow god, this property is exquisitely Moroccan in style, with white Moorish-style arches, domes, and courtyards awash in lush greenery. There are 78 luxury doubles; 14 one- and two-bedroom suites, which feature terraces and baths with sophisticated decor in neutral, understated tones, complete with huge tubs for two people; and six spacious and splendidly appointed private villas, each with three to five bedrooms and private pools. TV sets and VCRs are available for an extra charge, but you probably won't want them. The restaurant, *Pimms,* offers *the* most romantic dining on Anguilla (see *Eating Out*); breakfast and lunch are served at the less formal *Chattertons.* There are also three tennis courts, a pool, a fitness center, a croquet lawn, a full range of water sports, and a new 32-foot motor cruiser for excursions. A complimentary program, offered during school holidays in spring and summer, features lunch, games, and supervised activities for children ages three to nine. Maunday's Bay (phone: 6666; 800-323-0139; 212-425-4684 in New York City; fax: 6617).

Covecastles Designed by renowned New York architect Myron Goldfinger, this ultramodern complex features four one- to three-bedroom villas and eight one- and two-bedroom beach houses. The elegant appointments are the epitome of understated luxury: large rattan furniture upholstered with raw silk, hand-embroidered cotton sheets, flower arrangements, and ceiling fans (but no air conditioning). Each villa has two large baths and cable TV. Sports facilities include complimentary snorkeling equipment, a lighted tennis court, a lovely beach, windsurfing, Sunfish sailing, and a yacht that may be chartered for day trips. Its dining room, *The Café,* serves first-rate presentations of French, creole, and Italian dishes; meals also may be ordered and delivered to the villas. Closed from mid-August through mid-October. West Shoal Bay (phone: 6801; 800-348-4716; fax: 6011).

Malliouhana In a soaring white Mediterannean-style villa perched on a cliff overlooking Mead's Bay at the northwestern reaches of the island, this resort is one of the Caribbean's most elegant and distinguished. Here is an authentic tropical hideaway, with food and wine of the highest quality, and a luxurious landscape that more than makes up for an island that's otherwise rather flat and undistinguished. Owned and managed by the British magnate Leon Roydon and his son, Nigel, this oasis has 53 units and a fully outfitted exercise center. The doubles, suites, and two-bedroom villas are all stunningly furnished and decorated in white-on-white and rattan. (Three of the one-bedroom suites and six of the double rooms lack air conditioning; none of the units has a TV set.) There are two swimming pools plus a heated outdoor Jacuzzi; four Laykold tennis courts (three lighted) supervised by a *Peter Burwash International* pro; a water sports center whose complimentary activities include day trips on a 35-foot cruiser; an exercise facility overlooking the ocean; a spectacular children's playground with daily supervised activities; and a renowned restaurant created by the late Jo Rostang, former chef-owner of the first-rate *La Bonne Auberge* in Antibes (see *Eating Out*). It's perfect for the kind of traveler for whom escapism is an art; the price may be high, but then so is the quality of the experience. Closed September and October. No credit cards accepted, except in boutiques and for non-guest diners; personal checks accepted by prior arrangement. Mead's Bay (phone: 6111; 800-835-0796; fax: 6011).

Frangipani This beachfront condominium complex on the northwest coast of the island has eight luxury suites and 15 one-, two-, and three-bedroom suites. The guestrooms are set in a pink Spanish-Mediterranean–style villa on a 2-mile beach that looks out to the Prickly Pear Cays. Each has a large terrace, full kitchen, and washer/dryer. Private cooks are available to prepare West Indian dinners. Also on the premises are snorkeling facilities and a beach restaurant serving all meals. American Express accepted. Mead's Bay (phone: 6442 or 6444; 800-892-4564; fax: 6440).

Carimar Beach Club Trellises drip with fuschia and white bougainvillea on 23 well-appointed one-, two-, and three-bedroom units arranged in a horseshoe around gardens and lawns; all units feature full kitchens, dining rooms, ceiling fans (but no air conditioning), and patios or balconies. There's cable TV in the clubhouse, but not in the rooms. There are two tennis courts, plus complimentary snorkeling equipment; other water sports can be arranged. There is no restaurant, but several are nearby (including the posh *Malliouhana* next door and the excellent *Blanchard's* a short stroll away; see *Eating Out* for both). Mead's Bay (phone: 6881; 800-235-8667; fax: 6071).

Casablanca Facing a white sand beach, this pink Moroccan fantasy–style all-inclusive resort offers 72 guestrooms appointed in peach and mint green with genuine Moroccan rugs, separate lounge areas, cable TV, complimentary mini-bars, and private patios overlooking the sea. The rate covers all meals, including drinks, champagne, and vintage wines with lunch and dinner; also included are dining privileges with 15 of Anguilla's top restaurants and two days' free rental car service. Facilities include a health club with sea views, a large pool with a poolside grill, a beach bar, a "hammock garden," and two tennis courts with pro instruction available. The elegant, open-air *Casablanca* restaurant serves European fare (see *Eating Out*), and casual dining and complimentary afternoon tea are offered in the *Café Americain*. Rendezvous Bay West (phone: 6999; 800-231-1945 or 800-382-6309; fax: 6899).

Cinnamon Reef The main building of this complex, with its Moorish-style arch, is surrounded by 14 private luxury villas and four beachfront suites back-to-back with four garden suites; each beachfront suite has a connecting door with a garden suite, and the two may be joined to become a two-bedroom, two-bath accommodation. Each cottage has a sea view, oversize bedrooms, a sunken living room with ceiling fans, a dressing room with hair dryer, spacious bathrooms, and a breezy patio; none has air conditioning or a TV set. Sports facilities include a 60-by-40-foot freshwater swimming pool, two Deco Turf tennis courts, most water sports, and an eight-foot Jacuzzi.

Continental breakfast is complimentary, and one of the best restaurants around, the *Palm Court* (see *Eating Out*), is here as well. Closed September and October. Little Harbour (phone: 2727; 800-346-7084; fax: 3727).

Coccoloba Straddling the beautiful white sand beaches of Mead's and Barnes Bays, this comfortable resort has a handsome pool with a swim-up bar, as well as the *Pavilion* restaurant and live entertainment several nights a week. Management changes of late have meant uneven service and upkeep, but a new team seems to be bringing the resort back up to its previous high standards. Accommodations are in 51 charming one-bedroom beachfront cottages bedecked with greenery, featuring oceanview patios (but no TV sets). There is also an additional pool, water sports facilities, tennis on two lighted courts, and a refurbished exercise room. Barnes Bay (phone: 6871; 800-982-7729; fax: 6332).

Fountain Beach Down an unpaved road on the western end of lovely, secluded Shoal Bay East, it's worth the drive. The Mediterranean-style pink complex houses spacious and comfortable bi-level rooms, all with full kitchens, accented with neutral tones and Haitian art. Six of the 10 rooms have air conditioning and Jacuzzis; others have ceiling fans (all get lots of sea breezes). None of the rooms has a TV set. *La Fontana* restaurant serves breakfast and lunch alfresco. There's a lap pool in the garden and great offshore snorkeling; two colorful local beach bars are a short stroll away. Shoal Bay (phone: 3491).

Paradise Cove This resort has 14 elegantly appointed suites (eight two-bedroom and six one-bedroom), each with a living room and dining area, two private patios, and a fully equipped kitchen complete with microwave oven, toaster, and coffee maker. Features include beautifully landscaped gardens, an Olympic-size pool, a kiddie pool, a pool bar, a croquet court, and a children's play area. The *Garden Terrace Café* serves breakfast, light lunches, and snacks. The property is just a short walk from the Cove Bay and Rendezvous Bay beaches. The Cove (phone: 497-6603; fax: 497-6927).

MODERATE

Mariners On one of Anguilla's most picturesque beaches, this charming West Indian–style resort draws yachtspeople, local dignitaries, and expatriates to its friendly bar, breezy gazebo, and restaurant, the *Beach Terrace* (see *Eating Out*). The 67 units are distributed among 20 gingerbread cottages with cove ceilings and wide verandahs bearing handsome deck furniture; each cottage has two double rooms connected by a studio with kitchen facilities and a foldaway bed. Only six units have air conditioning; TV sets are available for an extra charge. Fishing charters, yacht cruises, lighted tennis courts, a pool, a Jacuzzi, and water sports also are offered. All-inclusive packages and diving programs are available. Sandy Ground (phone: 2671 or 2815; 800-848-7938; fax: 2901).

Pineapple Beach Club Formerly the *Anguilla Great House,* this is now an an all-inclusive property with 27 rooms in six pastel-colored, gingerbread-trimmed units set around a wide lawn on beautiful Rendezvous Bay. The simple white rooms have traditional mahogany furniture, ceiling fans, and huge tile showers (but only two have air conditioning). Besides meals and drinks, the single price includes all non-motorized water sports and snorkeling excursions. Dining is on a lovely outdoor terrace with live music. The atmosphere is generally quiet and relaxed, and the staff pleasant and helpful. Rendezvous Bay (phone: 6061; 800-345-0356; fax: 6019).

Rainbow Reef Villas Remote and secluded, these four very private and quiet two- and three-bedroom white villas overlook the sea. All have kitchens and verandahs, and are furnished with good-looking Haitian rattan; there are no TV sets or air conditioning (the villas have ceiling fans and there are nice sea breezes), and only one has a telephone. The beach, which has barbecue facilities and a gazebo, is better for snorkeling than for swimming because of an offshore coral reef. Six days' housekeeping service is included in the weekly rate. Sea Feather Bay (phone: 2817; 708-325-2299; fax: 3116).

Shoal Bay Resort Four white three-story buildings (though boxy and less than gorgeous) sit right on the beautiful beach here. Of the 26 units, those on the ground floor are the most appealing. All have small terraces, but no air conditioning or TV sets. Dining options include two inexpensive beach bars, *Uncle Ernie's Shoal Bay Beach Bar* and *Madeariman Reef* (see *Eating Out* for both), just next door. Shoal Bay (phone: 2011; 800-223-9815; 212-545-8469 in New York City; fax: 3355).

Shoal Bay Villas Charming white two-story buildings amid palm and sea grape trees are adorned with bougainvillea-laden trellises. The 13 well-appointed units have full kitchens, living areas, patios or terraces, and an extra fold-away bed (but no air conditioning or TV sets). There's a pool and water sports rentals, and next door is *Reefside,* a flower-bedecked beach restaurant with good local food at reasonable prices. Shoal Bay (phone: 2051; 800-223-9185; fax: 3531).

La Sirena This place has 20 attractively decorated, balconied rooms and five villas, all recently refurbished and most with ocean views. Some are air conditioned; only villas have TV sets, as well as kitchen facilities and living/dining room areas. The *Top of the Palms* restaurant serves French food; the poolside *Coconuts* serves Italian. Other facilities include two pools and a bar in the open-air lobby. Only 300 feet from Mead's Bay Beach (phone: 6827; 800-331-9358; fax: 6829).

INEXPENSIVE

Harbour Villas Overlooking Scilly Cay and Island Harbour, these four villas offer modern, comfortable accommodations amid plenty of local color. All of the four Mediterranean-style units have arched terraces, full kitchens, and spacious tiled living and sleeping areas (but no air conditioning or TV sets). Several excellent restaurants are within walking distance. Island Harbour (phone: 4393; 206-822-0589 in the US; fax: 4196).

Inter Island Here are 14 simple but clean rooms, with ceiling fans (no air conditioning), a family-style restaurant, and gracious West Indian hospitality. The rooms lack air conditioning, TV sets, phones, or frills in general, and the showers are tiny. There is, however, complimentary transportation to the beach, a half mile away, and in general it's a good value for the price. Lower South Hill (phone: 6259; fax: 5381).

EATING OUT

Anguilla's restaurants offer fine French dishes and wines as well as traditional local fare, both of which often feature the fresh fish and spiny lobster caught by Anguillan fishermen in handcrafted boats. Expect to pay $125 or more for a meal for two, not including wine, tip, or drinks, in the restaurant listed below as very expensive, $80 to $125 in those listed as expensive, $50 to $80 in those listed as moderate, and less than $50 at spots described as inexpensive. A 10% service charge is usually added to all food and beverage tabs. Some restaurants charge a fee for taking credit cards, and many close in September and October, so call ahead. Unless otherwise noted all restaurants listed below are open for lunch and dinner. When calling on Anguilla use only the local four-digit numbers listed below. For information about dialing from elsewhere, see *Telephone* earlier in this chapter.

VERY EXPENSIVE

Malliouhana The ambience of this hotel dining room is elegant and romantic—soft lights, sea breezes, Limoges china, and fresh flowers. The imaginative menu was created by the late Jo Rostang, former chef-owner of the very popular *La Bonne Auberge* in Antibes; currently, the kitchen is overseen by his son Michel Rostang (whose eponymous Paris restaurant has earned two Michelin stars). Here, Rostang serves a wide selection of fresh fish and meat dishes, most with delicate French-style sauces. Among the excellent offerings are snapper sushi with caviar, risotto with truffles and conch, the prized *volaille de Bresse* (duck or chicken roasted on a spit with mango chutney), and *tartes* with freshly made sorbet and ice cream. There is also a vast wine cellar, reported to hold some 25,000 bottles. The price for all this is rather dear (dinner for two will run from $125 to $200), but it's worth it. Open daily for breakfast, lunch, and dinner. Reservations necessary (and hard for non-guests to get in high season). Major credit cards accepted. Mead's Bay (phone: 6111).

Blanchard's One of Anguilla's newest and best restaurants, its unique and original fare, combining Southwestern, Cajun, and creole influences, is served in a beachfront house with a picket fence. Perfectly blending sophistication with island charm, the intimate, candlelit dining room looks out over greenery to the sea beyond. Offerings on the ever-evolving menu include chili-crusted sea scallop salad, gumbo *ya-ya* soup, lemon-glazed lobster dumplings, and seafood imaginatively prepared with local fruits and vegetables. The homemade cinnamon ice cream with peaches or mangoes is mouth-watering. Closed Sundays. Reservations required. MasterCard and Visa accepted. Mead's Bay (phone: 6100).

Casablanca Exquisite French fare with nouvelle touches is served indoors or alfresco, with a view of the sea and St. Martin. Recommended starters are smoked marlin carpaccio and warm lobster salad with hazelnut dressing; entrées include Moroccan-spiced barbecued swordfish and roast loin of lamb in a potato crust. For dessert, try pistachio *crème brûlée* with bitter chocolate sauce. A piano player performs nightly in the lounge. Open daily for breakfast, lunch, and dinner. Reservations advised. Major credit cards accepted. At the *Casablanca* resort, Rendezvous Bay West (phone: 6999).

Hibernia A popular French retreat with consistently superior food served in a setting that makes guests feel as if they're in a private, typically Anguillan home overlooking the water. Menu items are prepared with Asian influences. Entrées such as grilled crayfish served with thyme and lemongrass, Thai broth aswim with seafood, and Burmese coconut noodle casserole showcase the chef's skills. A fine finish is provided by homemade soursop sorbet or pastry swans with almond cream, topped with Burmese gold sauce (made with genuine gold leaf—said to be good for the heart). Post-prandial Cuban cigars are available as well. Closed Mondays and September through October. Reservations necessary. Major credit cards accepted. Island Harbour (phone: 4290).

Mango's One of the hottest spots on the island, this small eatery is great for people watching. The setting—an open-air 13-table structure on Barnes Bay—is spare yet charming. The fare is simple yet very good; it is prepared, the management says, "with the absolute minimum of added fats, salts, and calories—excepting the desserts." Menu highlights include grilled meat, chicken, and the freshest fish and lobster, as well as such creative starters as red chicken soup (chicken broth with tomatoes, curry, and *christophines*) and desserts like coconut cheesecake. Dinner only; closed Tuesdays and late July through early November. Reservations necessary a week in advance. Major credit cards accepted. Barnes Bay (phone: 6479).

Palm Court In a pretty and spacious gallery of the *Cinnamon Reef* hotel, this dining spot offers outstanding food. Chefs Zeff Bonsey and Vernon Hughes bring prize-winning techniques to contemporary American fare with Caribbean influences. Sautéed red snapper with a soy *beurre blanc* sauce is just one of the outstanding dinner entrées; steamed jumbo shrimp in a banana leaf papillote wins raves as an appetizer; while the fresh coconut blancmange makes a superb dessert. Monday night is a manager's cocktail party, and a steel band plays most nights. Open daily for breakfast, lunch, and dinner. Reservations advised. Major credit cards accepted. Little Harbour (phone: 2727 or 2781).

Pimms Diners at *Cap Juluca*'s breezy Moorish-style oasis overlooking Maunday's Bay can watch the sun set behind the resort's brilliant white Moroccan-style domed villas; this is the most dramatic and romantic restaurant on the island. The chef works Gallic wonders with seafood, grilled dishes with innovative sauces, and nouvelle-style desserts. There also is a pleasant bar area and live music five nights a week. Open daily. Reservations necessary for dinner. American Express accepted. Maunday's Bay (phone: 6914).

MODERATE

Arlo's At this Italian-American restaurant overlooking the bay, great pizza is a draw, along with hearty standard dishes such as lasagna, veal scallopine, and angel-hair pasta with seafood. Open for dinner only; closed Sundays. Reservations advised. MasterCard and Visa accepted. South Hill (phone: 6810).

Barrel Stay Local color abounds at this thatch-roofed beachside bar and restaurant, with barrel stays for tables and chairs made from barrels. The menu features French-creole food, including a good fish soup, fresh red snapper in "Portuguese" sauce (tomatoes, onions, green peppers), barbecued lobster, Hawaiian ham steaks, and a creamy chocolate mousse. Open daily. Reservations advised. Major credit cards accepted. Sandy Ground (phone: 2831).

Beach Terrace Meals on this breezy West Indian porch overlooking the very white sand beach at Sandy Ground are a memorable island experience. Lunches feature salads, soups, rotis, and hamburgers as well as fresh grilled fish of the day and lobster. Poached snapper or grouper in lemon-butter sauce, seafood salads, and chicken baked with coconut and ginger are regular dinner offerings, but don't miss the lobster grilled with fresh basil butter. Thursday is barbecue night, and Saturday offers a traditional West Indian dinner, both with live music. Open daily for breakfast, lunch, and dinner. Reservations unnecessary. Major credit cards accepted. At the *Mariners* resort, Sandy Ground (phone: 2671).

Cyril's Fish House A new branch in Island Harbour of the original in Montauk, on New York's Long Island, this indoor-outdoor eatery offers mostly seafood and local dishes, as well as a West Indian all-you-can-eat Sunday brunch with live music. Try the gorgonzola salad, Cajun fried fish, Buffalo squid with blue cheese dip, or mesquite-grilled chicken; or you can always stick with the selection of burgers, sandwiches, and pastas. Open daily. Reservations unnecessary. Major credit cards accepted. Island Harbour (phone: 4488).

Gorgeous Scilly Cay Don't miss this experience, especially on a Sunday, when locals, day-trippers from St. Martin, and half of Anguilla's restaurateurs gather at this eatery. It's on a private island reached via a two-minute boat ride from the Island Harbour dock (be prepared to get your feet wet). The menu is limited—grilled chicken, lobster, prawns, or a combination, all marinated in a dynamite secret curry sauce, accompanied by pasta salad and garlic bread. There's live music Wednesdays, Fridays, and Sundays. Wear a bathing suit and expect a fun time. The restaurant has added a landing pad to accommodate helicopters from St. Martin. Reservations advised. No credit cards accepted. Open from 11 AM to 5 PM; closed Mondays. Island Harbour (phone: 5123).

Koal Keel One of the island's newest—and best—dining rooms is in a restored house that dates from 1780. The owners set an elegant table (the decor includes antiques and a sleigh bed in the center of the room), and the service is as impressive as the menu. Among the many choices are smoked salmon sausage with caviar and basil sauce, as well as seared duck breast in ginger and lemongrass gravy. A featured specialty is the Anguilla dinner of homegrown ingredients—pigeon peas, conch fritters, potfish-and-sweet-corn dumplings, ginger-spiced barbecued lamb, and *fraico* (a kind of Italian ice). Open daily for lunch and dinner. Reservations advised. Major credit cards accepted. The Valley (phone: 2930).

Lucy's Harbour View Perched on a hill overlooking Road Bay and the lagoon, this place is best at dusk, when you can watch the glorious sunset. Vivacious Anguillan chef Lucy Connor creates dishes of kid and stewed mutton, conch soup, curried goat or chicken, and whole red snapper, all creole style, and all famous on the island. Service is not speedy, so come before your normal mealtime and enjoy a rum punch and the spectacular view. Live entertainment one night a week (see *Nightlife*). Closed Sundays. Reservations advised. Major credit cards accepted. South Hill (phone: 6253).

Old House Set in a charming West Indian–style house on George Hill, this popular place dispenses fine local and continental fare along with lively island gossip. The catch of the day here might include "old wife" or "hind" (yellowtail or grouper, respectively) prepared Anguillan style (with tomatoes, onions, lemon, butter, and fresh thyme). Barbecued chicken, pork, and beef also are featured, along with salads, sandwiches, and an excellent kids' menu. Open daily for breakfast, lunch, and dinner. Reservations advised. Major credit cards accepted. George Hill (phone: 2228).

Paradise Café This 10-table place serves Asian and French fare, including breast of duck with mandarin pancakes, Chinese stuffed ravioli, and Thai curry dishes, plus local dishes such as West Indian bouillabaisse. The quality is generally very good, though a bit uneven. Closed Mondays and September through October. Reservations necessary for dinner. Major credit cards accepted. Shoal Bay West, near *Covecastles* (phone: 3210 or 6010).

Tropical Penguin The casual hearty fare at this beachside spot includes red snapper, sautéed pork chops, and sliced curried chicken with local vegetables. Lunches are lighter, with salads, burgers, and pasta dishes. Open daily. Reservations advised. Major credit cards accepted. Road Bay (phone: 2253).

Riviera Another pretty beachside bistro, featuring seafood with a Japanese touch: sushi, sashimi, and oysters (when available) sautéed in soy sauce and sake, and the island's best fish soup, thick and chunky with a properly piquant rouille. The friendly bar attracts visiting yachtspeople and coin collectors. Happy hour is 6 to 7 PM. Open daily for lunch and dinner. Reservations advised. Major credit cards accepted. Sandy Ground (phone: 2833).

Roy's For a taste of English heaven and everything you ever wanted to know about Anguilla's goings-on, visit this eatery on quiet Crocus Bay, the only pub on the island. The fish and chips are fresh and cooked to perfection, the Sunday roast beef is rare and delectable, and the Yorkshire pudding is coveted by British expatriates. There's a lovely terrace, and you'll never be lonely at the bar. Closed Saturday lunch and Mondays. Reservations advised. MasterCard and Visa accepted. Crocus Bay (phone: 2470).

Smugglers This open-air spot with a nautical theme is perched over the water, with lights shining on the sea so diners can watch bobbing fishing boats and snapping fish. Besides steaks, chops, fresh fish, and the complimentary salad bar, there are 10 lobster dishes. The lobster *exotique,* from southeast Asia, is particularly notable—the tender meat is served in a sweet-and-sour sauce flavored with pineapple, ginger, and bamboo shoots. Save room for the apple pie made with custard and calvados. The prime attractions, though, may be charming French owner Marysa West and her 15-year-old daughter Maribelle, who works harder than most servers yet never stops smiling. Dinner only; closed Sundays. Reservations advised. Major credit cards accepted. The Forest (phone: 3728).

Madeariman Reef Formerly *Trader Vic's,* this large, casual, and very simple thatch-roofed beach bar and grill has now expanded across the road into a restaurant that dispenses proper meals and occasionally a good buffet with a live band. The à la carte menu features fish or conch soup, grilled lobster, crayfish, grouper, snapper, and barbecued chicken or ribs. Lunches are still served at the very pleasant beach bar (where Heinekens are just a dollar). Open daily. Reservations unnecessary. No credit cards accepted (phone: 3822).

Johnno's Beach Bar Everyone on the island, locals and visitors alike, seems to turn up at this large tin-roofed shack to dance or just to hang out with friends. The menu features barbecued chicken, fish, and ribs. Things get really busy around 8 PM Wednesday, Friday, Saturday, and Sunday nights, when a local band attracts a large crowd. Open for lunch and early dinner Tuesdays and Thursdays; closed Mondays. Reservations unnecessary. No credit cards accepted. Sandy Ground (phone: 2728).

Uncle Ernie's Shoal Bay Beach Bar With three tables on the terrace and another seven on the sand, this shack on the beach between *Shoal Bay Villas* and *Madeariman Reef* is one of the most popular places on booming Shoal Bay. You can get a beer and barbecued chicken, ribs, or catch of the day, all served with a smile. Live music adds to the flavor Sundays between 2 and 7 PM and sometimes on Wednesdays. Open daily. Reservations unnecessary. No credit cards accepted. The Valley (phone: 2452).

ISLAND EATS

Other restaurants/snack bars serving "local" food include three in the Valley: *Pepper Pot* (phone: 2328), which features rotis (a full West Indian meal wrapped burrito-style); *Cross Roads* (phone: 2581), near the government buildings (try the stewed conch); and *Brother's Cafeteria* (phone: 3550), with huge portions of great West Indian food. On Shoal Bay a good spot is the *Round Rock Bar* (phone: 2076), and on the main road near the airport is *Rôti Hut* (no phone), which serves giant Trinidad-style rotis. For picnics on the beach, as well as fancy take-out fare or catering (especially if you're staying in a villa), *Fat Cat Gourmet* (phone: 2307) offers pumpkin soup, quiche, chili, pasta salads, chicken or conch stew, and homemade pastries.

Antigua

Antiguans claim their island has a beach for every day of the year—a necklace of alluring pink and white coves lapped by the sparkling azure Caribbean. Not surprisingly, Antigua (An-*tee*-gah) is a prime destination for those who demand a gorgeous stretch of sand and a daily dose of sunshine—annual rainfall measures only 45 inches, and most of that arrives in ten-minute showers of what islanders refer to as "liquid sunshine." Formerly a British colony, Antigua still clings to colonial legacies such as afternoon tea and cricket—two fitting metaphors for a community that appreciates the need to do things in the fullness of time, with little rush but great enthusiasm.

Before the British arrived, Antigua was inhabited by Amerindians: first the Siboney, or "stone people"; then the pastoral Arawak; and finally the warlike Carib, who harassed European settlers as late as the 1700s. On his second voyage to the New World in 1493, Columbus christened the island in the heart of the Leewards after Santa María la Antigua of Seville.

About 130 years later, the English sailed from nearby St. Kitts to settle Antigua, and the island has remained British ever since, except for one brief year (1666) when the French took possession. Antigua, along with its tiny dependencies Barbuda and Redonda, became an Associated Member of the British Commonwealth in 1967, a status it retains to this day. In 1981, it declared itself an independent nation.

During the 17th and 18th centuries, the British built forts and established a major naval installation at English Harbour while awaiting the return of the French (who never came). In 1784 the dashing naval captain Horatio Nelson took command of the dockyard that now bears his name. In his service was the captain of the HMS *Pegasus,* Prince William Henry, Duke of Clarence (who later became King William IV). With the decline of the sugar trade and the abolition of slavery, Antigua's importance receded, and the dockyard that had once given England supremacy in the Caribbean was abandoned. Efforts to renovate *Nelson's Dockyard* and restore it to active service began in the 1930s. Today, the *Nelson's Dockyard National Park,* opened during the 1980s, preserves Antigua's historical heritage within a 15-square-mile perimeter encompassing the harbor, dockyard, Dow's Hill, and Shirley Heights.

Despite its placid appearance, Antigua is bubbling with daytime activities—from golfing and tennis on championship courses and courts, to diving, snorkeling, sailing, and windsurfing along some of the Caribbean's most spectacular shores. And at day's end, a peripatetic night bird may while away the evenings at Antigua's clubs and casinos—while the "little sister" isle of Barbuda sleeps on, lulled by the gentle surf.

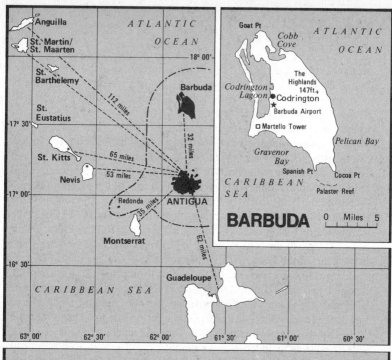

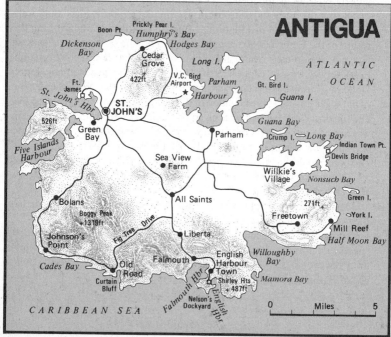

Antigua At-a-Glance

FROM THE AIR

Flying into the newly expanded and renovated *V. C. Bird International Airport* during the dry season (February through April), the visitor sees Antigua's hillsides faded to dusty brown, brightened by purple bougainvillea and sapphire seas. When the rains come, the landscape turns a soft green framed by the lush profiles of Guadeloupe, Montserrat, Nevis, and St. Kitts on the horizon. Antigua is small—a scant 108 square miles—as are the other two islands that make up this nation in the heart of the Leewards—Barbuda, which is 27 miles due north, is 62 square miles; and Redonda, 30 miles to the southwest, is only a half-mile square rock jutting from the sea with a single tree. There are about 65,000 people on Antigua, 1,400 on Barbuda, and only goats on Redonda. Flying time from New York is approximately four hours and 45 minutes; from Miami, the flight takes three hours and 15 minutes.

SPECIAL PLACES

Though island sightseeing centers around English Harbour, most visitors begin their tour in St. John's, the island's capital and foremost town.

ST. JOHN'S There's plenty of shopping and places to see in this 17th-century colonial town that still bears a few examples of Georgian architecture. The bustling outdoor *Public Market* between Valley Road and All Saints Road is best seen early on Saturday morning, when colorful vendors set up shop. It's closed Sundays. At the corner of Long and Market Streets, the *Old Courthouse,* which dates from 1747, is the town's oldest building still in use. It houses the *Museum of Antigua and Barbuda* (phone: 462-1469), with a modest collection of Amerindian artifacts, an archive/research center, plantation-era exhibits, and a gift shop. Closed Sundays; admission charge. Originally built of wood in 1681, the twin-spired Anglican *Cathedral of St. John the Divine* facing Church Lane was rebuilt in stone after a devastating 1745 earthquake, but this structure was then destroyed by another earthquake in 1843. The current edifice was consecrated in 1848. Its statues of St. John the Baptist and St. John the Divine are said to have been taken from one of Napoleon's ships. The *Museum of Marine and Living Art* at Gambles Terrace on the outskirts of town has an interesting selection of seashells, specimens of sand from beaches around the island, and shipwreck relics (no phone).

ELSEWHERE ON THE ISLAND

Just north of *Nelson's Dockyard,* the village of Falmouth is one of Antigua's earliest settlements, supported by a harbor that provides safe anchorage for beautiful yachts. *Fort Charles*, on Blake Island in the middle of the harbor, was begun in 1672. Visible from the road en route, stone sugar-mill towers have been converted into homes.

NELSON'S DOCKYARD The British Royal Navy used the dockyard continuously from 1707 until 1899. The impressive installation saw its finest moments from 1784 to 1787 under the command of Captain Horatio Nelson, who formed a fast friendship there with Prince William Henry, Duke of Clarence (later King William IV). *Clarence House,* visible across the harbor, was built for the prince; at press time it was undergoing restoration and was closed to the public indefinitely.

The main buildings include the wooden *Admiral's House,* now a museum; the *Officers' Quarters Building,* now an art gallery; the *Admiral's Inn,* a hostelry constructed of bricks once used as ballast; and the *Copper & Lumber Store,* now a charming inn (see *Checking In* for details on the latter two). A good guide to the history of the only remaining Georgian-era dockyard in the world is *The Story of English Harbour,* by Desmond Nicholson. Published by the *Museum of Antigua and Barbuda,* it's available at the museum or local bookstores for $6 (at press time). For additonal details, see *testaments in Stone: Historic Sites* in DIVERSIONS. Open daily. Admission charge for museum (phone: 460-1053, 460-1379, or 460-1380).

DOW'S HILL INTERPRETATION CENTRE Built among historic ruins just inside *Nelson's Dockyard National Park* along the road to Shirley Heights, it offers an informative multimedia journey through Antigua's history, as well as guided walking tours of historic sites within the park. There is a gift shop and cafeteria/bar. Open daily. Admission charge (phone: 460-2777).

SHIRLEY HEIGHTS Minutes from Dow's Hill, the fortifications erected by General William Henry Shirley in 1787, known as *Shirley Heights Lookout,* offer a panoramic view of English Harbour and the *Dockyard,* with Montserrat and Guadeloupe in the distance. An obelisk in the nearby cemetery salutes the 54th Regiment. The extensive fortifications, barracks, and powder magazines along the route to the summit protected the dockyard from invaders. The *Antigua Historical Society* has published a map of the ruins and facilities, available at the *Shirley Heights Museum,* as well as at the *Museum of Antigua and Barbuda.* The *Shirley Heights Museum* contains pre-Columbian and British-era artifacts. It's closed weekends; no admission charge (no phone). The *Lookout* restaurant (phone: 460-1785) provides refreshment and a stunning view.

FIG TREE DRIVE The most scenic drive in Antigua—starting near Swetes Village in the island's center and extending to the southwest coast—is along this 15-minute stretch of road that once encompassed the island's largest banana plantation ("fig" is the Antiguan name for "banana"). A lush retreat on an otherwise dry island, this twisting tunnel of foliage lined with mango and banana trees is the closest thing to a rain forest you'll find. It winds through the hilliest section of the island, rising and falling steeply around Fig Tree Hill before descending to Old Road and the Curtain Bluff area. The road begins opposite the pink coral *Tyrells Catholic Church* in Swetes.

PARHAM HARBOUR One of the island's older waterfront villages, east of St. John's near the airport, it is in the midst of a major restoration with plans to include a boardwalk, restaurants, and shops, but no projected completion date at press time.

Sources and Resources

TOURIST INFORMATION

The *Antigua & Barbuda Department of Tourism* is on Thames Street in St. John's (phone: 462-0480; fax: 462-2483). There also are information centers at *V. C. Bird International Airport* (phone: 462-3082, ext. 121), at Heritage Quay (no phone), and at the *Cruise Ship Terminal* in St. John's (no phone). All are closed weekends. For information about Antigua tourist offices in the US, see GETTING READY TO GO.

LOCAL COVERAGE The *Daily Observer* is the island's daily newspaper. Other good sources of island information include: *The Antiguan* magazine, updated annually; the annually published *Adventure Tourist Guide;* and the bimonthly *What's Happening* (the latter two are distributed free of charge). Stateside newspapers are flown in daily.

RADIO AND TELEVISION The ABS (Antigua-Barbuda Broadcasting Service) broadcasts on TV Channel 10 (13 if cable-ready) and 620 AM radio. Other radio stations are GEM Radio Network (93.9 FM) for news, marine weather, and music; Caribbean Relay (89.1 FM) for BBC programming; ZDK (1100 AM; 99 FM) for Caribbean music and international/local news and sports; and Radio Lighthouse (1165 AM) for Christian programming. The local cable TV company, CTV-2, carries 12 channels.

TELEPHONE When calling from the US, dial 1 + 809 (area code) + (local number). The access code may vary from other Caribbean islands; contact the local operator for assistance. When calling on Antigua, dial the five-digit local number only (all telephone numbers on the island begin with 46). Major credit cards can be used to call home by dialing 1-800-877-8000. Caribbean Phonecards (debit cards), good for local and long-distance calls, can be purchased and used in specially marked phones. Dial 999 or 911 for emergency assistance.

ENTRY REQUIREMENTS US, Canadian, and British citizens need a valid passport (or original birth certificate with raised seal, plus a government-approved photo ID such as a driver's license) and an ongoing or return ticket. There is a $9 departure tax at the airport.

CLIMATE AND CLOTHES Temperatures range from an average low of 73F (23C) in winter to a high of 85F (30C) in summer and fall. Except in September, there are steady, cooling trade winds (sometimes gusting to 30 miles per hour). Though the island is one of the driest in the Eastern Caribbean, the months of September, October, and November are relatively wet, with daily, 10-minute showers.

Swimwear is for the beach only. Sightseeing or shopping requires modest street clothes (Bermuda-length shorts are OK). British tradition requiring men to dress for dinner (jackets and ties or just jackets) survives in some deluxe hotels. Restaurants are casual to casually elegant. Dress for casinos runs the gamut from casual to glitzy. Clothing is optional only at the beach beyond Hawksbill.

MONEY The official currency is the Eastern Caribbean dollar, valued at about $2.70 EC to $1 US. Banks exchange currency at the day's exact rate; hotels and shops at a slightly lower rate. Banking hours are 8 AM to 2 PM Mondays through Thursdays, 8 AM to noon and 3 to 5:30 PM Fridays. US dollars are accepted everywhere, Canadian less frequently. Credit cards (principally American Express, Visa, and Mastercard) and traveler's checks are accepted at all major hotels and most shops and restaurants. All prices in this chapter are quoted in US dollars.

LANGUAGE The King's English arrived with the British in the 1630s and has dominated ever since. Sprinkled with colloquialisms and laced with a lilting accent, native speech is a pleasant (if sometimes confusing) variation. Listen and learn to say "Good mornin'" the Antiguan way.

TIME Antigua is on Atlantic standard time. In the winter, when it's noon in New York, it's 1 PM in Antigua. In summer, when daylight saving time is in effect in the US, the time is the same both places.

CURRENT Most hotels operate on 110 volts, 60 cycles—standard in the US and Canada. Those that have 220-volt outlets (but 110-volt shaver outlets) usually provide converters.

TIPPING A 10% service charge is usually added to the bill at hotels and restaurants. When a service charge is not included (if in doubt, ask), tip waiters 10% to 15%, maids $1 per room per day, and bellhops 50¢ per bag (greater generosity is in order if service is above standard). Tip taxi drivers 10% of the fare. Uniformed Red Caps at the airport are salaried and do not accept tips. Neither do employees at some all-inclusive resorts.

GETTING AROUND

BUS Public transport is available only on limited routes and on uncertain schedules, but it is inexpensive. The maximum fare anywhere on-island is under $2.

CAR RENTAL Renting a car is a good choice for visitors who want flexibility for sightseeing or dining—and don't mind driving on the left or along unposted roads. The required Antiguan driver's license can be obtained at the airport or any police station for about $12 by presenting a valid driver's license. Carry a spare and jack if you venture into the country on unpaved roads, and watch for stray sheep and goats. *M and M's* gas station on Old Parham Road is open 24 hours.

Rental firms on the island include international chains and independent operations. Most of the major firms have locations at *V. C. Bird International Airport*. Among the best: *Avis* (phone: 462-2840), *Budget* (phone: 462-3009), *Capital Rentals* (phone: 462-0863), *Carib Car Rentals* (phone: 462-2062), *Dollar* (phone: 462-0362), *Hertz* (phone: 462-4111), and *National* (phone: 462-2113). During certain holiday peak times—*Christmas, Easter, Antigua Sailing Week*—reserve well ahead.

INTER-ISLAND FLIGHTS *BWIA* (phone: 800-JET-BWIA; 462-0262/3 or 462-0934 in St. John's; 462-3101/2 at the airport) and *American* (phone: 462-0950) connect to Antigua via San Juan, Puerto Rico and St. Maarten; Antigua-based *LIAT* (phone: 462-0700) provides links to most Caribbean islands; *Air St. Kitts–Nevis* (phone: 465-8571), *Carib Aviation* (phone: 462-3147), and *Montserrat Airways* offer inter-island charters.

SEA EXCURSIONS The only thing more perfect than a lazy day on one of Antigua's 365 beaches is an exhilarating day afloat. A variety of power or sail sight-seeing cruises, including day sails, snorkeling trips, and dinner cruises, are available from the following operators: *Le Bistro,* a high-speed, island-hopping, 32-foot Scarab (Hodges Bay; phone: 462-3881); *Horatio Historic Cruises* (*Nelson's Dockyard;* phone: 460-1178); *Jolly Roger Pirate Cruises* (St. John's; phone: 462-2064); *Kokomo Cat* (Jolly Harbour; phone: 462-7245); *Lamarine* (Jolly Harbour; phone: 462-7686); *Lobster King,* a glass-bottom boat (Jolly Beach; phone: 462-4363); *Miguel's Holiday Adventure* (Hodges Bay; phone: 461-0361); *Obsession,* a 45-foot Hatteras (Falmouth; phone: 462-3174); *Paradise I,* offering day sails (at the *Spinnakers* restaurant, Dickenson Bay (phone: 462-4158; evenings, 461-9241); *Sagitoo Catamaran Cruise* (phone: 460-1244); *Sentio,* offering half- or full-day sails (phone: 464-7127); *Shorty's Glass-Bottom Boat* (Halcyon Cove; phone: 462-0271); *Titi I,* offering power-boat tours (phone: 460-1452 or 460-3336); or *Wadadli Watersports,* offering daily outings (phone: 462-2980).

TAXI Taxis (with license plate numbers beginning with "H") are available at the airport, at ports of entry, in St. John's, and through hotels. Standard fares are fixed by law (no meters), and rate schedules are available at the airport customs area or local tourist offices. To avoid confusion, ask for the fare and confirm in what currency it's being quoted—US or EC—in advance. Touring by taxi or mini-bus is a good value for groups. Drivers are generally friendly and informative, but they do tend to drive very fast! Taxi tours are easily arranged through hotels or the *United Taxi Association* (phone: 461-1876). *Estate Safari Adventure* offers interesting four-wheel-drive historical tours (phone: 463-4713).

SPECIAL EVENTS

In late April to early May, Antigua turns to the sea for *Antigua Sailing Week,* the largest warm-weather regatta (and arguably the longest beach party) in the Western Hemisphere. By day, yachts from around the globe battle it out in offshore races; by night, sailors on the party path shift from hotel to hotel. Landlubbers get their chance to frolic on *Lay Day,* which takes place midway through the regatta week and features a tug-of-war and a "boat"-building competition, and on *Dockyard Day* on the last day of the regatta, when awards are presented amid boisterous celebration. When the sun sets, the raucous, formal-dress Lord Nelson's Ball rounds out the festivities.

Barbuda's *Caribana Festival* is held in June; then for 10 days at the end of July and into August, *Summer Carnival,* the cultural explosion of the year, consumes Antigua. Held in downtown St. John's, festivities range from warm-up Calypso King competitions and steel drum contests, to the climactic *J'Ouvert* "street tramps," when rowdy crowds dance along the streets behind bands (August Monday), and the *Last Lap* masquerade parade (August Tuesday). October sees the revived *Antigua Jazz Festival,* organized by the Jazz Society to provide a platform for Caribbean and international artists (phone: 462-2672).

Official public holidays, when banks and stores are closed, include *New Year's Day* (celebrated on both January 1 and 2), *Good Friday* (April 5 in 1996), *Easter Monday* (April 8 in 1996), *Labour Day* (first Monday in May), *Whitmonday* (May 27 in 1996), *Caricom Day* (July 4), *Carnival Monday/Tuesday* (first Monday/Tuesday in August), *Independence Day* (November 1), *Christmas,* and *Boxing Day* (December 26).

SHOPPING

Local spirits, which include Cavalier and English Harbour Antigua Rum (about $5 for 26 ounces), are bargains in anyone's book. Other great buys include Sea Island cotton, local artwork, calypso and steel drum records, beautiful stamps, and handcarved *warri* boards (a strategy game of African origin). Major shopping districts include Heritage Quay, at the foot of St. Mary's Street, and the adjacent *Redcliffe Quay Shopping & Entertainment Plaza* (a restored 19th-century slave compound) in St. John's; *Jolly Harbour Marina & Shopping Centre* at Jolly Harbour; and the new *Woods Estate Shopping Centre,* north of St. John's. Shopping hours are from 8 AM to 4 PM Mondays through Saturdays. Non-tourist shops close early Thursdays. Some shops now open on Sundays if cruise ships are in port. Below are some of our favorites:

Galley Boutique Unusual clothing and gifts (many made on the premises), fashions by Caribbean designers John Warden and Ken Done, and hammocks. English Harbour (phone: 460-1525) and *St. James's Club Marina* (Mamora Bay; phone: 460-1333).

Goldsmitty Here you'll find the exclusive gold, diamond, and gemstone creations of jeweler Hans Smit, Antigua's "modern-day Fabergé." *Redcliffe Quay* (phone: 462-4601).

Harmony Hall Antigua's foremost arts and crafts gallery complex, featuring frequent exhibitions of original woodcarvings, silk paintings, and masks. Open daily. There's also a restaurant and the *Sugar Mill* bar overlooking Nonesuch Bay. Near Freetown (phone: 460-4120).

Jacaranda *The* place for batik fabric items by Bouboudima—from perky tops to elegant pareo wraps—plus Antiguan-designed clothing, prints by Barbadian Jill Walker, and Sunny Caribbee herbal and spice products. *Redcliffe Quay* (phone: 462-1888) and Jolly Harbour (phone: 462-7689).

Nelson's Dockyard Gift Shop Local crafts, pottery, scrimshaw, historical maps, and nautical memorabilia. Open daily. English Harbour (phone: 460-1525).

La Parfumerie A nose-pleasing place with a selection of more than 100 perfumes. Heritage Quay, St. John's (phone: 462-2601).

Sunseakers Wide selection of designer swimwear for adults and children, plus silk screen fashions. Heritage Quay, St. John's (phone: 462-3618).

West Indian Sea Island Cotton Home of sought-after Caribelle Batik and other craft items. St. Mary's St., St. John's (phone: 462-9272).

SPORTS

BOATING For day, overnight, or term charters (bareboat or crewed), contact *Sun Yacht Charters* (phone: 460-2615; 800-772-3500) or *Nicholson Yacht Charters* (phone: 460-1530; 800-662-6066), both in *Nelson's Dockyard.*

CRICKET Antigua is passionate about this sport (which also stands in as a social event) and has produced some of the world's top cricketers, such as batsman Viv Richards, who got their start on ovals (fields) ranging from vacant lots to exquisitely manicured greens. Check newspapers for matches from January through July, especially the *Red Stripe Tournament* in February and the *International Test Matches* in April.

CYCLING Rentals (with delivery and pick-up) are available from *Sun Cycles* in Hodges Bay (phone: 461-0324). *Island Bikes* (English Harbour; phone: 460-1484) has mountain bikes. Also try *Cycle Krazy* (St. John's; phone: 462-9253).

GOLF The new *Jolly Harbour Golf Club* at the *Jolly Harbour Villas* (see *Checking In*) is set to become one of the Caribbean's premier golfing venues, with an 18-hole, 6,300-yard, par 71 course designed by Karl Litton, complete with sculpted fairways planted with exotic trees. There's also a driving range, clubhouse, restaurant/bar, and locker room; lessons are available. *Cedar Valley Golf Club* (phone: 462-0161), outside St. John's, is a 6,077-yard, 18-hole, par 70 course that hosts the *Antigua Open* each March. The *Half Moon*

Bay Club (see *Checking In*) offers stunning views along a skillfully designed, nine-hole, par 34 course that stretches 2,140 yards. Veteran instructor Wentworth Brodie provides lessons and runs weekly tournaments.

HIKING A bit off the beaten path, the Pillars of Hercules, large rock formations south of Galleon Beach at the entrance to English Harbour, are fun to explore. A footpath along the west side of the harbor from *Nelson's Dockyard* leads south to *Fort Berkeley,* where there's a beautiul panorama of the harbor. On the eastern side of the harbor, the rugged 30-minute trek to Shirley Heights through the forest (the path begins at the turn in the road opposite the *Inn at English Harbour*) may require a taxi for the return trip. Another interesting hike is through the forests around 1,319-foot Boggy Peak in the southwest part of the island. *Warning*: Start early, take your time, and bring water, a map, a hat, and a snack. The *Historical and Archaeological Society* at the *Museum of Antigua and Barbuda* (see *Special Places*) occasionally arranges hikes and excursions.

HORSE RACING None of the thoroughbreds that parade to the post at the course by the airport would qualify for the *Kentucky Derby,* but that doesn't keep the betting from being fast and furious or make the action any less exciting. Races are held on all public holidays. For information, contact Kenny Sumwell (phone: 462-6000 or 462-4337).

HORSEBACK RIDING Excursions are available through the *Spring Hill Riding Club* at Falmouth (phone: 460-1333), the *St. James's Club* (see *Checking In*), or *Charlie's* at Half Moon Bay (no phone).

PARASAILING *Sea Sports Parasail* offers pick-up at Dickenson Bay Beach and Jolly Beach (phone: 462-3355).

SNORKELING AND SCUBA Most hotels provide snorkel equipment (a few have scuba gear) and arrange trips; also try *Miguel's Holiday Adventure* (see *Sea Excursions*). For scuba diving, the barrier reefs and wrecks a mile or two off Antigua's northeast, south, and west coasts and off Barbuda provide excellent day-trip destinations for shallow-water dives. Dive operations that can assist with instruction and trips include *Aquanaut Diving Centres* at the *St. James's Club* (see *Checking In*) and *Galleon Beach Club* (Freeman's Bay; phone: 460-1024); *Dive Antigua* at the *Rex Halcyon Cove* (Dickenson Bay; phone: 462-3483) and the *Royal Antiguan* (see *Checking In*); *Dive Runaway* at the *Runaway Beach Club* (Dickenson Bay; phone: 462-2626); *Dockyard Divers* at *Nelson's Dockyard* (phone: 460-1178); *Jolly Dive* at *Club Antigua* (Jolly Harbour; phone: 462-0061, ext. 149) and Jolly Harbour (phone: 462-8305); *Long Bay Dive Shop* at the *Long Bay* hotel (phone: 462-3094); *M/Y Nimrod* in Falmouth (phone: 464-0143); and *Pirate Divers* at the *Lord Nelson Beach* hotel (Dutchman's Bay; phone: 462-3094).

SPORT FISHING Charters are available through *Saltfish* (Dickenson Bay; phone: 462-4158), *Catamaran Marina* (Falmouth Harbour; phone: 460-1503), *Miss*

Ferdie (phone: 462-1440), Captain Nunes's *Overdraft* (phone: 462-0649), as well as *Lobster King* and *Obsession* (see *Sea Excursions* for the latter two). Tournaments are held in June and November.

SWIMMING AND SUNNING All beaches on Antigua are public, but with so many choices, it's not hard to find a secluded strand (a few still require a four-wheel-drive vehicle to reach them). The northern shore is home to the island's most popular beaches and many resorts; its bays and coves offer safe havens for swimmers and enticing marine life for beginning snorkelers. South shore beaches are the most secluded and have the best reefs for snorkeling. Western beaches offer breathtaking sunsets, sometimes displaying the elusive "green flash" phenomenon, when refracted light rays produce a brief emerald flare before the sun sinks below the horizon. Facing the Atlantic Ocean, eastern shores are a beachcomber's paradise; for calmer waters here, seek out places like Half Moon Bay, where one end is like a clear swimming pool (the other end is rougher and good only for experienced swimmers and body-surfers).

TENNIS Tennis ranks as one of the island's favorite land-based activities for tourists. A growing number of annual tournaments hosted by hotels around the island have popularized the sport among locals. Most hotels have courts (some reserved for guests only during peak season) and offer instruction.

CHOICE COURTS

Curtain Bluff The site of the *Curtain Bluff Hotel Pro-Am Tennis Classic* each May, which attracts pros and celebrity players from the US and Europe, *Curtain Bluff* established tennis programs for island youth during the 1960s and has been spawning its share of champions ever since. Facilities include four lighted Laykold championship courts, the expertise of resident pro John Maginley (former Davis Cup player for Commonwealth Caribbean), a pro shop, and teaching equipment (see *Checking In*).

Tennis facilities also can be found at the *Temo Sports Ltd.* complex (English Harbour; phone: 460-1781), with two lighted courts, plus glass-backed squash courts, showers, a bar/bistro, and training equipment, and at *BBR Sportive Ltd.* (Jolly Harbour; phone: 462-6260), with four lighted courts, plus an international squash court. Other hotels that have courts include the *Carlisle Bay Club* (10, including one lighted); *Club Antigua* (eight, including six lighted); *Galley Bay* (one); *Half Moon Bay Club* (five lighted); *Hodges Bay Club* (two); *Jumby Bay Island* (three courts, including two lighted); *Rex Halcyon Cove* (four lighted); the *Royal Antiguan* (eight, including four lighted); and *St. James's Club* (five lighted). See *Checking In* for details on these hotels.

WATER SKIING Several hotels offer water skiing, either included in their rates or at a nominal charge; if yours doesn't, a good place to try is *Halcyon Cove Watersports* (phone: 462-0256).

WINDSURFING Constant trade winds and placid coves make windsurfing a popular activity. The *Great Board Race* is held each January and July, with windsurfers racing from Antigua to Barbuda and back. Most hotels provide equipment and instruction, or try *Patrick's Windsurfing School* at the *Rex Halcyon Cove* hotel (see *Checking In*); the *Lord Nelson Beach* hotel (Dutchman's Bay; phone: 462-3094); *Paradise Watersports* at the *Spinnakers* restaurant in Dickenson Bay (phone: 462-4158); or *Wadadli Watersports* (see *Sea Excursions*).

NIGHTLIFE

In season, nightlife centers around hotels, which offer such island entertainment as steel bands, limbo dancers, dance bands, and fire-eaters. For example, the *Royal Antiguan* (see *Checking In*) offers live music in its *Lagoon Café* and floor shows nightly in the *Andes* restaurant.

Casino-goers can try their luck at the newly opened *Gabriela Casino* at Runaway Bay's *French Quarter* restaurant (see *Eating Out*); at the renovated casino with an adjoining lounge at the *Royal Antiguan* (see *Checking In*); at the European-style casino at the glitzy *St. James's Club* (see *Checking In*); and at the *King's Casino* at Heritage Quay (phone: 462-1727). At *Club Antigua* (see *Checking In*), non-guests can pay a special half-day rate that includes a night out at the newly renovated *Coral Reef Casino* and disco. Most casinos operate nightly until 4 or 5 AM and feature blackjack, craps, roulette, and one-armed bandits, as well as baccarat and backgammon.

Clubs and discos sometimes sprout during the winter season, then disappear, but a good time can usually be found at *The Deck* in English Harbour (phone: 460-1719), and in St. John's at *Lime Antigua* (*Redcliffe Quay* shopping center; phone: 461-4557); *Grasshopper* (Airport Rd.; phone: 462-1933); *Zone* (on the Roundabout at the *Deep Water Harbour Complex;* no phone); *Web* (Old Parham Rd., just east of town toward the airport; phone: 462-3186); and Friday nights (jazz night) at *Café Club* (Church St.; no phone). Restaurants are also a good bet for dancing to DJs or live music, afternoons or evenings: Check out *Spinnakers* (phone: 462-4158) or *Coconut Grove Beach* (see *Eating Out*), both at Dickenson Bay, or the *French Quarter* at Runaway Bay.

Best on the Island

CHECKING IN

Antigua and Barbuda offer a staggering diversity of accommodations, ranging from no-frills inns that charge about $75 a night to deluxe hotels, plush villas, and super-exclusive private resorts. For information on guesthouses and small hotels, contact the Antigua Hotels & Tourist Association (phone: 462-0374; fax: 462-3702). On Barbuda, contact George Burton (phone: 460-0103).

During "high season" (mid-December through mid-April), accommodations for two—with a MAP (breakfast and dinner) or all-inclusive option—will cost a minimum of $500 at properties listed as very expensive; from $350 to $500 at those we call expensive; and from $170 to $350 in the moderate category. In the inexpensive category, for a double room without meals (unless otherwise indicated), expect to pay from $75 to $160. Some hotels boost rates during holidays. Summer rates are 30% to 45% lower. Rates are subject to a 7% government tax and 10% service charge. Also keep in mind that what's "all-inclusive" at one resort may translate to "semi-inclusive" at another, so it's best to compare what's offered for the price. If you plan to leave your hotel frequently to explore the island or dine out, keep in mind when choosing your location that taxi fares can add up quickly. Unless otherwise stated, many guestrooms are not air conditioned, though most have ceiling fans and abundant breezes; some hotels can provide air conditioning on request, so if this is important to you, be sure to ask. In-room telephones, TV sets, and bathtubs (water is precious) are not standard. All hotels listed below feature ceiling fans and private baths with shower, unless otherwise noted.

We begin with our favorite haven, which falls in the "very expensive" category, followed by recommended hotels listed by price category.

A SPECIAL HAVEN

Curtain Bluff Most repeat guests (including Sophia Loren) at Curtain Bluff never really check out; they merely return home to tend to their affairs until their next holiday at this classic beachfront hotel, whose ambience has been likened to an English country estate where houseguests dress for tea and dinner. Run by owner Howard Hulford for nearly four decades, this all-inclusive haven has 58 rooms (including six suites) that are hidden away high on a headland above the sculpted sands on the island's south shore. Guests may reserve time with the resident pro on one of four lighted championship tennis courts, site of the hotel's annual *Pro-Am Tennis Classic* (see *Tennis*). Others may opt for a game on the racquetball/squash court, a workout at the fitness center, or a genteel round of croquet. The two beaches, which offer a choice of gently lapping Caribbean waves or wind-driven Atlantic surf, are perfect for whiling away a day just basking in the sun or taking advantage of an array of water sports—from scuba diving, sailing, and sport fishing to water skiing and windsurfing. The beautifully appointed rooms and suites have terraces overlooking the sea, marble bathrooms, living rooms, and telephones; TV is in the main lounge. Award-winning Swiss chef Ruedi Portmann presides over the breezy dining room (see *Eating Out*), where in winter protocol requires jacket and tie, and the informal palm-shaded *Beach Club*, where on Sundays the place loosens up with a Caribbean-theme dinner and dancing to live music. To accompany the perfect meal, the wine cellar offers a selection from over 25,000 bottles. Closed June to October 10. Old Road, about 9 miles south of St. John's (phone: 462-8400; 800-67-BLUFF; 212-289-8888; fax: 462-8409).

VERY EXPENSIVE

Jumby Bay Island This all-inclusive luxury resort on a 300-acre private island 2 miles off Antigua's north coast is a serene oasis with superb beaches (endangered turtles nest on one), nature trails, and a 200-year-old greathouse. Guests on this former plantation may choose from 24 junior suite–style cottages, 14 rooms in a Mediterranean-style villa, 12 two- and three-bedroom luxury villas, and three larger, private villas, all with ocean views and terraces; there are no telephones (except in the private homes) or TV sets. All the accommodations are stocked with thoughtful amenities, and the luxury villas have fully-equipped kitchens. In addition to elegant alfresco dining in the greathouse's courtyard, there's the *Beach Pavilion* restaurant and bar at Pond Bay. Tennis on three courts (two lighted), snorkeling, windsurfing, water skiing, bicycling, croquet, and use of day-sailers and a putting green are included in the rate. Sailing, sport fishing and diving charters can be arranged. No children under eight. Closed September and October. Long Island (phone: 462-6000; 800-421-9016; fax: 462-6020).

St. James's Club One of the world's finest resorts, "membership" in this exclusive club is well worth seeking out. There are 73 two-bedroom villas, 20 suites, 85 rooms, plus hillside homes and a marina on this lushly landscaped, private 100-acre peninsula on Antigua's southern coast, favored with balmy bayside and ocean-washed beaches. All units feature air conditioning, telephones, cable TV, mini-bars, and terraces with ocean views. Guests may unwind in the Jacuzzi, the four pools, the fitness center, or on the five lighted tennis courts or croquet lawn. Water sports such as snorkeling and windsurfing are included in the rate, and scuba, sport fishing, and horseback riding are available at an extra charge. Shoppers will enjoy the boutiques and the art gallery. Other amenities include four international restaurants, including the *Rainbow Garden* (see *Eating Out*), five bars, a nightclub, a beauty salon, a deli, and a casino. Mamora Bay, 12 miles from St. John's (phone: 460-5000; 800-274-0008; fax: 460-3015).

Sandals Designed for romance in the tradition of the all-inclusive, couples-only chain, this five-star luxury resort set along 1,400 feet of powdery beach boasts an indoor waterfall surrounded by exotic birds. Available in eight categories ranging from standard doubles to honeymoon suites right on the beach, all 163 units have air conditioning, telephones, satellite TV, hair dryers, and safes. Facilities include three restaurants, three bars, four swimming pools, four Jacuzzis, a spa, two lighted tennis courts, all water sports (including scuba and sailing), and nightly entertainment. Less than 2 miles from St. John's on Dickenson Bay (phone: 462-0267; 800-SANDALS; fax: 462-4135).

EXPENSIVE

Carlisle Bay Club Once a coconut plantation, this luxury condominium complex made its debut just last year with 32 beachfront suites (12 additional three-bedroom suites were scheduled for completion at press time). Each one-bedroom suite offers two bathrooms, a fully-equipped kitchen, a living room with pull-out sofa, a private terrace, air conditioning, and a convenient beach shower; the three-bedroom suites sleep six to eight. None of the accommodations has a telephone or TV set. The formal restaurant—with its vaulted ceiling, antique reproductions, murals, piano, and louvered wooden shutters—serves continental dishes overlooking a magnificent pool and Jacuzzi; or select lighter fare at the funky *Beach Bar,* one of three bars on the premises. Included in the room rate are daytime tennis on 10 all-weather courts (one lighted) with a pro shop, as well as croquet, Sunfish sailing, windsurfing, walking trails, and snorkeling. Available at additional charge are tennis instruction, water skiing, scuba, sport fishing, cruises, and health and beauty treatments. Frequent live entertainment is also featured. Old Road, Carlisle Bay (phone: 462-1377; 800-875-4999; fax: 462-1365).

Galley Bay From its lagoon lapping a half-mile expanse of beach to its bird sanctuary, this intimate all-inclusive resort on 40 lush acres offers an idyllic setting complete with hammocks. There are 31 beachfront rooms and 14 romantic, palm-thatched one- and two-bedroom "Gauguin" cottages, all with refrigerators, coffee makers, and hair dryers, but no air conditioning, telephones, or TV sets. Activities include tennis (there's one court), water sports, and biking, with golf and horseback riding nearby. Dine alfresco at the beachfront restaurant/bar, which features frequent live entertainment. Deep Bay, 4 miles west of St. John's (phone: 462-0302; 800-223-6510; fax: 462-4551).

Half Moon Bay Club With a superb location on the southeastern tip of the island, this all-inclusive Clubs International resort abuts a nine-hole golf course and hiking trails and is dominated by a three-quarter-mile-long crescent beach with complimentary Sunfish, windsurfers, canoes, and snorkel equipment. All 100 balconied rooms and two suites feature full or partial ocean views and telephones (no TV sets or air conditioning). Facilities include a pool, five lighted tennis courts (with a nominal charge for lessons), tennis and golf pro shops, a beauty salon, boutiques, and two restaurants and bars.

In addition, activities and entertainment are scheduled daily. Half Moon Bay, 20 miles from St. John's (phone: 460-4300; 800-223-6510; fax: 460-4306).

Long Bay This classic, family-run hideaway is set on a reef-protected bay along the northeastern shore. There are 20 oceanfront rooms with verandahs, five self-catering one-bedroom cottages, and one fully-equipped two-bedroom bayfront villa; none of the units has a telephone or TV set. Facilities include a championship tennis court, two restaurants and bars, a library/gameroom, and complimentary water sports. Sport fishing and scuba instruction and equipment are offered at an on-site dive shop. There's also frequent live entertainment. Closed June through mid-October. Long Bay, 10 miles from St. John's (phone: 463-2005; 800-448-8355; fax: 463-2439).

Pineapple Beach Club This relaxed, all-inclusive resort with a sparkling 2-mile beach on Antigua's southeastern shore has 133 air conditioned rooms; none has a telephone or TV set (there's TV in a main lounge), but all have terraces, and some have bathtubs. Guests enjoy complimentary afternoon tea, snorkeling, kayaking, windsurfing (including lessons), and sightseeing boat trips. Facilities include a pool, four championship tennis courts, boutiques, a fitness center, and the *Pirate's Den* mini-casino. There are also two restaurants and three bars, with nightly live entertainment, and a roster of scheduled daily activities. Rendezvous Bay, 15 miles from St. John's (phone: 463-2006; 800-345-0356; 407-994-5640 in Florida; fax: 463-2452).

Royal Antiguan This place offers all the comforts of a deluxe hotel, with a secluded half-mile stretch of beach and its own casino. All 282 spacious guestrooms, including 12 poolside cottages, are air conditioned, with cable TV and telephones; some rooms have balconies with views of the bay. An all-inclusive option covers all meals, beverages, non-motorized water sports, tennis on eight courts (four lighted), use of the fitness center, nightly live entertainment, and taxes and service charges. Facilities include a pool with a swim-up bar, a playground, a shopping arcade, a dive shop, and a water sports center; golf is nearby. There are also three restaurants, including the *Orchid* (see *Eating Out*), and five bars. Deep Bay, 3 miles from St. John's (phone: 462-3733; 800-345-0356; fax: 462-3732).

MODERATE

Admiral's Inn This delightful, 200-year-old brick hostelry is the heart of *Nelson's Dockyard* and dear to history buffs and yachtsmen, who congregate in the bar and restaurant (see *Eating Out*) for sunset cocktails. The 15 well-appointed rooms come in a potpourri of styles and sizes; some are air conditioned, but none has a telephone or TV set. Included in the room rate are snorkel gear, beach chairs, day-sailers, and transportation to nearby beaches. There's also frequent live entertainment. Closed September. English Harbour, 12 miles from St. John's (phone: 460-1027; 800-223-5695;

fax: 460-1534).

Copper & Lumber Store A meticulously restored 1782 warehouse warmed by mellow brass, weathered brick, and hand-hewn beams houses 14 opulent suites named for ships at the Battle of Trafalgar. The suites are contemporary or Georgian-style (with Oriental rugs, antique four-poster beds, and nautical memorabilia) and have fully-equipped kitchens and telephones, but no TV sets. The *Wardroom* restaurant offers fine dining, while the English-style *Mainbrace Pub* does a roaring business during yachting events (see *Eating Out* for both). Or guests may choose to relax on Chesterfield couches in the brick-arcaded courtyard of the *Freelance Bar.* A ferry to the beach is provided, and scuba diving can be arranged; tennis and squash are available nearby. English Harbour, 15 miles from St. John's (phone: 460-1058; 800-275-0877; fax: 460-1529).

Hodges Bay Club Secluded, yet handy to golf, airport, and town, these gleaming Mediterranean-style villas shelter 26 one- and two-bedroom balconied apartments (with cathedral ceilings, Italian tile floors, and kitchens) overlooking a pretty beach with a fine restaurant. All apartments are air conditioned, with telephones and cable TV. There are two championship tennis courts, a pool with a wading pool, and facilities for sailing, windsurfing, and water skiing. Nearby Prickly Pear Island offers first-rate snorkeling and picnicking. Rates include breakfast. Hodges Bay (phone: 462-2300; 800-432-4229; fax: 462-1962).

Inn at English Harbour Within the *National Park* on Antigua's southern coast, this historic small hotel features 22 beachfront rooms, plus six more in hillside cottages; some have telephones, but there are no TV sets. Enjoy excellent fare at the *Terrace* restaurant and bar overlooking Freeman's Bay, or at the beach bar. Water sports are complimentary; also available are racquetball/squash, diving, sailing charters, occasional entertainment, and tennis and riding nearby. A water taxi is available to *Nelson's Dockyard.* English Harbour (phone: 460-1014; 800-223-6510; fax: 460-1603).

Rex Halcyon Cove This haven with 210 newly decorated rooms and one-bedroom suites offers a pool, four lighted tennis courts, and an array of water sports. All rooms (poolside or oceanfront) have air conditioning and telephones, and some have TV sets. There are two restaurants, the *Warri Pier Grill* (see *Eating Out*) and the *Terrace,* as well as an ice cream parlor and nightly live entertainment. On Dickenson Bay, 2 miles from St. John's (phone: 462-0256; 800-255-5859; fax: 462-0271).

Siboney Beach Club Nearly hidden by lush tropical gardens, this intimate hotel features 12 one-bedroom suites in a three-story building with ocean-facing balconies or patios. All have telephones and kitchenettes; some have air conditioning and TV sets. The award-winning *Coconut Grove Beach* restaurant offers Caribbean and continental dishes by the water (see *Eating Out*).

Facilities include a pool, a boutique, water sports, a casino, and golf nearby. On Dickenson Bay, 2 miles from St. John's (phone: 462-0806; 800-533-0234; fax: 462-3356).

INEXPENSIVE

Blue Heron This restful beachfront hotel on Antigua's southwestern tip boasts one of the island's finest reef-protected beaches. Of the 40 guestrooms, 30 are air conditioned, with bath and shower; 10 have ceiling fans and shower only. All have patios and telephones, but there are no TV sets. There's a beach bar, a breezy cocktail lounge, and a restaurant serving local and international dishes. The use of windsurfers, snorkel gear, and Sunfish is complimentary. Johnson's Point Beach, 8 miles from St. John's (phone: 462-8564; fax: 462-8005).

Club Antigua Finally, an all-inclusive Clubs International resort that turns Caribbean fantasy into reality for budget-minded vacationers and families (kids under 16 stay free). Set on 40 landscaped acres on the west coast, it's more a state of mind than a resort, with 470 rooms set in clusters of two-, three- and four-story Spanish-style stucco buildings along the beach. Select from 370 standard rooms, 78 superior, 16 junior suites, and six seaside villas that offer a range of amenities: ceiling fans or air conditioning, shower or bathtub, balcony or patio, and refrigerators. None of the rooms has a telephone or TV set. The rate includes an array of water and land-based sports and equipment: Sunfish sailing, scuba diving with instruction, snorkeling, windsurfing, water skiing, tennis with instruction on eight courts (six lighted), a jogging track, bicycles, a TV/video lounge, squash courts, and a fitness room—even a Kid's Club for children ages four to 12. There are also four restaurants, six bars, a huge pool, an ice cream parlor, boutiques, a disco, and a mini-casino. Golf is nearby at the new 18-hole *Jolly Harbour Golf Club.* Non-guests can enjoy Club Antigua amenities for a daily or half-day rate. Jolly Harbour, 7 miles from St. John's (phone: 462-0061/8; 800-777-1250; fax: 462-1827).

Jolly Harbour Villas This beach resort, marina, and golf club complex with two beaches offers excellent value, with 150 comfortably furnished waterfront villas, each with two bedrooms, two baths, a fully-equipped kitchen, a living/dining area, a private deck, and even mooring for yachts. Facilities include seven restaurants and bars; a pool; one squash court and four lighted tennis courts at the nearby *BBR Sportive Ltd.;* the fabulous 18-hole *Jolly Harbour Golf Club;* and a shopping center. Sailing, diving, and water sports are also available. Children ages two through 12 sharing with two adults stay free. Ask about meal plans and an all-inclusive option that includes dining and use of facilities at the adjacent *Club Antigua.* Jolly Harbour, 7 miles from St. John's (phone: 462-6166; fax: 462-6167).

BARBUDA

VERY EXPENSIVE

K Club Situated on one of the Caribbean's most beautiful beaches, this tranquil, ultra-exclusive property has 33 rooms in 28 bungalows. The airy decor was created by owner Mariuccia Mandelli, head of the Krizia fashion design house. Rooms are spacious and private, with large bathrooms, telephones, and air conditioning, but no TV sets (a main lounge offers satellite TV). There's also a nine-hole golf course. The rate includes all meals at the fine restaurant (alcoholic beverages are extra). No children under 12. Transportation from the airport is provided (phone: 460-0300; 800-235-3505; fax: 460-0305).

MODERATE

Palmetto This beachfront hotel offers 24 guestrooms, nine cottages with kitchens, and three air conditioned villas; none of the accommodations has a telephone or TV set. There's also a variety of water sports, a restaurant, a bar, a tennis court, and a pool. Palmetto Point, 15 minutes from the main town (phone/fax: 460-0440).

EATING OUT

Not including drinks, wine, or tip, expect to pay at least $90 for dinner for two at the restaurants we list as expensive; between $40 and $90 at moderate spots; and less than $40 at places in the inexpensive category. Most restaurants include a 10% service charge, so check before adding any extra gratuity. Unless otherwise noted, all restaurants listed below are open for lunch and dinner, and all are in the 809 area code unless otherwise indicated.

ST. JOHN'S

EXPENSIVE

Chez Pascal Lyons-born owner/chef Pascal Milliat serves fine French cuisine either in a dining room or alfresco in a garden. Specialties include seafood and rack of lamb. Open for dinner only; closed Sundays and the month of September. Reservations advised. Major credit cards accepted. Tanner and Cross Sts. (phone: 462-3232).

MODERATE

Lemon Tree This upbeat eatery offers an international menu and live entertainment (catch the calypso on Saturdays) in a nightclub/casino setting. Closed Saturday lunch and Sundays. Reservations advised. Major credit cards accepted. Long St. (phone: 462-1969/462-0777).

Redcliffe Tavern A restored coffee and sugar warehouse decorated with memorabilia, this family-run bar and restaurant offers a dazzling selection of unusual dishes to suit every budget. Try the pumpkin soup, Bajan beer-battered flying fish, and the tavern's special cheesecake. Open for breakfast, lunch, afternoon tea, and dinner. Closed Sundays. Reservations advised. Major credit cards accepted. In the *Redcliffe Quay* shopping center (phone: 461-4557).

INEXPENSIVE

Commissioner Grill This casual restaurant located in a historic warehouse serves seafood, steaks, ribs, and chicken cafeteria-style. It's a good place to try a typical Antiguan saltfish and avocado breakfast. Open daily. Reservations advised. Major credit cards accepted. Commissioner Alley and Redcliff St. (phone: 462-1883).

Fisherman's Wharf A waterfront view complements this place's extensive seafood and pizza menu. Open daily. Reservations advised. Major credit cards accepted. Lower High St. at Heritage Quay (phone: 462-2248).

ELSEWHERE ON THE ISLAND

EXPENSIVE

Le Bistro One of Antigua's most acclaimed restaurants, with an innovative menu that combines authentic French recipes with Caribbean touches. French chef Roland Boegler's specialties change twice yearly, but there are always a variety of tantalizing soups, hors d'oeuvres, pastas, seafood, and meat dishes. There's also a good selection of French wines. Open for dinner only; closed Mondays. Reservations necessary. Major credit cards accepted. Hodges Bay (phone: 462-3881).

Coconut Grove Beach Nestled beneath palms on a beautiful beach, this award-winning, open-air eatery specializes in seafood (especially lobster) and steaks. There's live entertainment some evenings, when reservations are a must. Open daily for breakfast, lunch, and dinner. Reservations advised. Major credit cards accepted. At the *Siboney Beach Club,* Dickenson Bay (phone: 462-1538 or 462-2162).

Colombo's This place offers a good selection of homemade pastas; the Italian Flag appetizer starts you off with three. There are also lobster, veal, and pork dishes, and fruit ices for dessert. A reggae band plays on Wednesday nights. Open daily. Reservations advised on weekends. Major credit cards accepted. At the *Galleon Beach Club,* English Harbour (phone: 460-1452).

Curtain Bluff Fine international fare, specializing in seafood with an Antiguan touch, served in the handsomely refurbished, flower-filled dining room of the sophisticated resort. Jacket and tie required for dinner. Open daily; closed June to October 10. Reservations advised. American Express accepted. At the *Curtain Bluff Hotel,* Old Rd., Carlisle Bay (phone: 462-8400).

Garden Here diners can enjoy buffet breakfast, lunch alfresco by the sea, and international *table d'hôte* or à la carte dinners with nightly live entertainment. Different days offer different treats, with a lavish Sunday brunch accompanied by steel drum, Tuesday barbecue, and West Indian buffet on Fridays. Open daily. Reservations advised. Major credit cards accepted. *Blue Waters Beach Hotel,* Soldier's Bay, near Boon Point (phone: 462-0290/2).

Orchid This hotel restaurant has an intimate atmosphere and a menu featuring Asian-inspired dishes. Favorites include baked lobster in ginger sauce. Open for dinner only; closed Mondays, Wednesdays, and Fridays. Reservations advised. Major credit cards accepted. At the *Royal Antiguan,* Deep Bay (phone: 462-3733, ext. 5248).

La Perruche West Indian food prepared with a French twist attracts diners to this candlelit garden spot. Try the tenderloin or blackened shrimp in a tomato-mango sauce. Open for dinner only; closed Sundays. Reservations advised. Major credit cards accepted. English Harbour (phone: 460-3013 or 460-3040).

Rainbow Garden Dine on fine continental dishes in this fanciful garden oasis before paying a visit to the disco or casino at this chic resort. There's frequent entertainment. Days open vary, so call ahead. Reservations advised. Major credit cards accepted. *St. James's Club,* Mamora Bay (phone: 460-5000).

MODERATE

Admiral's Inn This historic Georgian inn offers indoor or terrace dining with a view of the harbor. The international and West Indian menu features several good seafood dishes. Open daily for breakfast, lunch, and dinner; closed the month of September. Reservations advised. Major credit cards accepted. *Nelson's Dockyard* (phone: 460-1027 or 460-1153).

Alberto's A choice open-air Italian restaurant with an island ambience. Specialties include conch salad, snapper, linguine with clams, and stuffed clams. Open for dinner only; closed Mondays. Reservations advised. MasterCard and Visa accepted. Near *Nelson's Dockyard* at Willoughby Bay (phone: 460-3007).

French Quarter This place features authentic Cajun and creole dishes with live entertainment nightly. Open daily for dinner only; closed the month of September. Reservations advised. Major credit cards accepted. Runaway Bay (phone: 462-0624).

Jaws Enjoy the view while dining on steaks, seafood, pasta, and local specialties. There's also a dance floor with a DJ. Open daily for dinner only. Reservations advised. Major credit cards accepted. Deep Bay, above the *Royal Antiguan* (phone: 462-2428).

Lobster Pot Breezy seaside dining and brisk service with an extensive international menu. Open daily for breakfast, lunch, and dinner. Reservations advised. Major credit cards accepted. At the *Runaway Beach Club,* Dickenson Bay (phone: 462-2855 or 464-0928).

Pavilion This casual place overlooking a secluded, white-sand beach offers Italian and continental specialties including veal, chicken, and pasta dishes. There's also a varied wine list and frequent live entertainment. Open daily for breakfast, lunch, and dinner. Reservations advised. Major credit cards accepted. At the *Pillar Rock Beach Hotel,* Hope John Bay (phone: 462-2325).

Shirley Heights Lookout Housed in an 18th-century fortification with a view of the harbor, its specialties include lobster, as well as familiar standbys such as burgers and fries. Thursday afternoons, there's a barbecue and steel band concert; Sunday afternoons jump with a not-to-be-missed barbecue featuring non-stop steel drum and reggae. Open daily. Reservations advised. Major credit cards accepted. Shirley Heights, overlooking *Nelson's Dockyard* (phone: 460-1785).

Wardroom Fine international and West Indian fare is served amid foliage and weathered wooden beams in a courtyard setting at the *Copper & Lumber Store* hotel. Open for dinner only; closed Wednesdays. Reservations advised. Major credit cards accepted. English Harbour (phone: 460-1058).

Warri Pier Grill This casual seaside eatery serves seafood, standard grill fare, and international dishes. Open daily. Reservations unnecessary. Major credit cards accepted. At the *Rex Halcyon Cove,* Dickenson Bay (phone: 462-0256, ext. 436).

INEXPENSIVE

Mainbrace Pub A lively eatery offering English pub grub and draft beer in a nautical setting. A DJ and live music are featured on Tuesdays and Fridays. Open daily. Reservations advised. Major credit cards accepted. *Copper & Lumber Store* hotel, English Harbour (phone: 460-1058).

Aruba

Potential visitors once saw Aruba as a less developed and smaller version of Curaçao. There are similarities: Both islands are dry (cacti far outnumber palms) and Dutch; both offer duty-free shopping and casinos; and both have economies that were substantially bolstered by the oil industry.

But Aruba no longer lives in Curaçao's shadow. Tremendous investments in the island's tourism sector during the past several years have turned this 70-square-mile bit of land into one of the Caribbean's fastest-growing destinations. Aruba boasts more than 6,200 hotel rooms, both in the thoroughly modern properties on Palm Beach, a 5-mile stretch of pure white sand that outstrips any strand Curaçao has to offer, and in the first class hotels on smaller Eagle Beach and Druif Bay (both south of Palm, near Oranjestad). Aruba has 10 casinos, with two more under construction and, in season, there are shows most nights in its many hotel nightclubs. In sum, Aruba now caters to vacationers (more than 560,000 annually) in a big way, which is good news for some travelers and not so good for those who crave privacy and quiet.

Aruba was discovered in 1499 by Alonso de Ojeda, who claimed the island for Spain. There is still some question about whether he christened it Oro Hubo—Spanish for "gold was there"—or whether the name came from *ora,* the Carib word for shell, or from *oibubai,* Arawak for "guide." The Spanish did not consider the island worth colonizing, and, therefore, allowed its Arawak Indian population to remain alive. Although some 2,000 Indians were rounded up and shipped off to labor as slaves in the mines of Hispaniola—where the indigenous tribes had been exterminated—Arawak features survive on the faces of many Aruba natives.

In 1636, nearing victory in their 80-year war with Spain, the Dutch turned their attention to the Caribbean. They assessed the area and took over this neglected territory with little opposition from the Spanish. With the exception of a brief period during the early 19th century when the British flag flew over these islands, the Dutch have been in peaceful residence ever since. Of the approximately 79,000 people who live on Aruba today, 75% were born on the island; the rest are Dutch, British, North American, or Venezuelan.

For a time it looked as though Aruba's fortune lay in gold, discovered in 1825 and mined successfully near Balashi. The yield shrank to the point of unprofitability by 1916, but with the opening in 1924 of Esso's Lago Oil Refinery—then the world's largest—the island began to prosper as never before.

When Esso closed the refinery in 1985, Arubans embraced tourism as a way to replace lost jobs and bolster the island's economy. Even with the

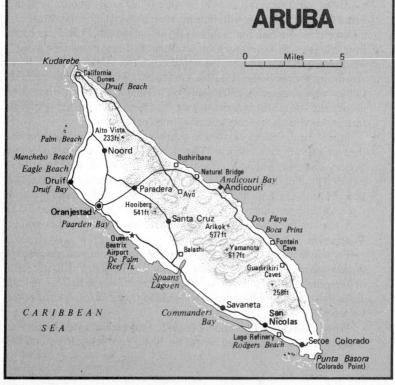

reopening of the oil refinery in 1991 as the Aruba Coastal Refinery, government and citizens alike remain interested in seeing tourism flourish.

It seems to be doing just that—not only because of the sleek hotels and casinos, the extraordinary beaches, and bright, warm sea, but because Arubans make their island an especially pleasant place to visit. They personally bridge the gap between their red-roofed cottages and the tall hotels; they are friendly people, and they want visitors not only to see their island but to understand it. For this reason, taxi touring and small personalized tours here are worth the extra investment. In the course of a half-day tour, you will very likely learn a little Papiamento (derived from Spanish, Portuguese, and Dutch; *bon dia* means "good morning" and *masha danki* means "thank you"), hear about Aruban courtship (before a man may call on a woman seriously, he must build a house), and make at least one Aruban friend—your driver.

You also will learn that Aruban smiles are genuine; they mean *bon bini*—welcome.

Aruba At-a-Glance

FROM THE AIR

Aruba, shaped like a dolphin swimming northwest to southeast toward South America, is the smallest and westernmost of the Dutch "ABC" islands that lie just off the Venezuelan coast (Bonaire and Curaçao are the others). Fifteen miles north of Venezuela and 42 miles west of Curaçao, 72-square-mile Aruba is about 19½ miles long and 6 miles across at its widest point.

The mouth of the dolphin is Rodgers Bay, near the Seroe Colorado residential area at the island's southern point; its right fin is the capital city of Oranjestad, on the west coast; and the end of its tail is a lighthouse on the island's northern tip. *Queen Beatrix Airport* lies a mile southeast of the capital. Jets make the flight from New York in four hours, from Miami in two and a half.

One good way to see Aruba from the air is aboard one of the small commuter planes operated by *Air Aruba* or *ALM* (see *Inter-Island Flights,* below, for both), which make several flights daily between the island and Curaçao and Bonaire. These low-flying craft reveal the dolphin-shaped island in all its diversity, the windswept divi-divi trees along the southern shore, the surf crashing along the east coast, desolate dunes on the northern tip, and all manner of sailing craft at anchor at the southern corner.

SPECIAL PLACES

ORANJESTAD Millions of florins have been spent in recent years spiffing up the capital, which offers quaint Dutch architecture, tempting shopping opportunities, and an agreeably low-key atmosphere. Caya G. F. Betico Croes, its main avenue and most fashionable shopping street, is lined on either side with banks, offices, and stores that offer good duty-free buys from all over the world. Allow at least half a day to explore the city—and travel on foot. Head for the harbor and walk along the wharf where the local fishing boats and island schooners are moored. Fresh fish and produce are sold directly from these boats most mornings. Stroll along L. G. Smith Boulevard (named for an early Lago Oil Refinery general manager) to *Wilhelmina Park,* a triangular patch of tropical gardening on the waterfront. Afterward eat lunch at one of any number of interesting restaurants in the area. Or buy some Dutch cheese and fresh fruit and head north to the picnic grove at Manchebo Beach or a half mile farther to Eagle Beach, which has palm-thatch picnic shelters. Should you choose to tour Oranjestad in the afternoon, remember: Many shops are closed between noon and 2 PM.

ELSEWHERE ON THE ISLAND

The recommended route for touring Aruba heads north out of Oranjestad along Eagle Beach and Palm Beach to the northernmost tip of the island and continues clockwise. Along the way you'll see:

DE OLDE MOLEN This old windmill was brought from Holland, piece by piece, and reconstructed; it's now a restaurant (see *Eating Out*).

CALIFORNIA DUNES At the northernmost tip of the island, the *California Lighthouse* stands on this desolate site (it's not open to the public).

CUNUCU The interior countryside—the flat landscape here—is marked by cactus, huge boulders, aloe and divi-divi trees (the latter, permanently bent by the wind, look as though their branches are blowing away), and pastel houses enclosed by cactus fences.

HOOIBERG (MT. HAYSTACK) This, Aruba's most prominent mountain, is at the center of the island. Several hundred carved steps climb up to its peak, a 541-foot height from which Venezuela is visible on clear days. Mt. Yamanota (617 feet) and Mt. Arikok (577 feet) are less accessible.

CASA BARI AND AYO Here, to the northeast of Hooiberg, are building-size stacks of diorite boulders that look as though they've been dumped on the landscape just to puzzle geologists and impress travelers.

BUSHIRIBANA On the northeast coast are abandoned gold mines (the island's "gold rush" took place between 1824 and 1913) and the ruins of a pirate's castle that legend dates to 1499.

NATURAL BRIDGE Along the east coast, the pounding surf has carved a bridge out of the coral rock. It makes a pretty picture, but it's also a bit touristy; most taxi drivers and tour guides can take you to more remote natural bridges along the shore.

ARIKOK NATIONAL PARK Site of the island's best-preserved Indian drawings, it's near the mountain of the same name. For an insider's view of the park and other ecotourism attractions, contact Ferdi Maduro at *Corvalou Eco-Tours* (see *Sightseeing Tours*).

BOCA PRINS A popular beach area where it's traditional to slide down the sand dunes (wear tough jeans and sneakers).

FONTEIN AND GUADIRIKI CAVES These inland caves are decorated with still-undeciphered ancient Indian drawings.

SAN NICOLAS In the southeast, Aruba's "second city" is a modern community which blossomed during the heyday of Esso's Lago Oil Refinery. Nearby Seroe Colorado was designed and built for North Americans who came to work at the refinery, now the Aruba Coastal Refinery. Visitors are welcome at the *Aruba Golf Club* (phone: 42006), just north of San Nicolas. In town, be sure to stop in at *Charlie's Bar & Restaurant* (see *Eating Out*).

SAVANETA Aruba's oldest town, it's slightly more than midway between San Nicolas and Balashi. This is where the Dutch reestablished control of the island in 1816. There is still a Dutch marine camp at Commander's Bay.

BALASHI Here are the 19th-century ruins of a gold-smelting work and its accompanying settlement. Built during Aruba's "gold rush," it is northwest of Spaans Lagoen, a bit southeast of the island's center.

Sources and Resources

TOURIST INFORMATION

The *Aruba Tourism Authority*'s Oranjestad office (172 L. G. Smith Blvd., phone: 23777; fax: 34702) has a very helpful staff and an excellent collection of maps, guides, and brochures. It's closed weekends. For information on Aruba tourist offices in the US, see GETTING READY TO GO.

LOCAL COVERAGE *Aruba Today* and *The News* are both free English-language newspapers published daily except Sundays and holidays and distributed at the front desk of most hotels. *Aruba Events, Aruba Happy Island, Aruba Nights,* and *The Aruba Experience* are all ad-driven periodicals—distributed free at hotels, the airport, and the tourist office—that provide helpful information and ideas about local activities, shopping, dining, and nightlife. The *Miami Herald* and *The New York Times* normally reach Aruban newsstands on the day of publication.

RADIO AND TELEVISION Aruba has some locally produced television and radio shows in Dutch, English, Papiamento, and Spanish. US TV programs, including CNN, also are available at most hotels. Trans-World Radio broadcasts newscasts in English four times daily.

TELEPHONE When calling from the US, dial 011 (international access code) + 297 (country code) + 8 (city code) + (local number). The access code from other Caribbean islands may vary, so consult the local operator. When calling from a phone on Aruba, use only the local number unless otherwise indicated. Dial 11000 for the police; 115 for an ambulance. *Note:* Changes in local phone numbers began in 1993 and are ongoing. The first digit of phone numbers in many areas, though not Oranjestad, is being changed to make it uniform in a given area. Ask your hotel concierge or the local operator for assistance if you have trouble getting through to a number.

ENTRY REQUIREMENTS For US and Canadian citizens, the only documents required are some proof of citizenship (a passport, or a birth certificate or voter's registration card plus a photo ID; a driver's license alone is *not* acceptable) and an ongoing or return ticket. There is a $12.50 departure tax at the airport.

CLIMATE AND CLOTHES Aruba is one of the few places in the world where newspapers don't publish weather reports. Since only about 20 inches of rain fall annually, the island guarantees one of the most stable year-round climates in all the Caribbean. Temperatures rarely fall below 75F (24C) or rise above 85F (30C), and the trade winds rarely stop blowing. The steady winds keep the humidity down and blow mosquitoes and other insects away from the island (though bites are not unknown). Casual, lightweight resortwear is right for daytime in all seasons. Leave your raincoat at home and use the space for extra swimsuits and scarves. Islanders do not wear shorts or slacks in town, but it's okay for visitors. Bathing suits, however, are strictly for beach or poolside. In the evenings, especially in the casinos in season, women tend to dress up a bit and men occasionally wear jackets.

MONEY Although US dollars are accepted everywhere, the official currency is the Aruba florin (Afl); at press time $1 US equaled approximately 1.77 Afl. Although banks are open from 8 AM to 4 PM on weekdays, there's really no advantage to changing your dollars. Shops give no discount for payment in US dollars and, like most restaurants and hotels, honor major credit cards. All prices in this chapter are quoted in US dollars.

LANGUAGE There probably isn't a more linguistically versatile island in the Caribbean. Arubans speak Dutch (the official language), Spanish, English, Portuguese, and—as if that weren't enough—Papiamento, the local language that's a mixture of all the above and a few words left over from the days of the Arawak. But you'll have no trouble getting along in English.

TIME Aruba is on atlantic standard time all year round. When it's noon in New York it's 1 PM in Aruba; when the eastern US is on daylight saving time, the hour is the same in both places.

CURRENT At 110 volts, 60 cycles, converters and adapters are not necessary.

TIPPING Hotels add an 11% service charge on rooms and a 10% to 15% service charge on food and beverages. Some restaurants add 10% to 15% to cover service; if not, that's the right amount to tip. Airport porters get at least $1 for each bag carried. There is no need to tip taxi drivers except for special services, such as carrying heavy luggage.

GETTING AROUND

BUS The yellow public buses run every 20 to 30 minutes daily (except on Sundays and holidays) between town and the hotels on Eagle Beach and Palm Beach. One-way fare is $1, round trip is $2. However, tourists can buy a round-trip "Yellow Card" from the bus driver (ask for it) for only $1.60. Buses leave from the parking lot on Zoutmanstraat (just behind the mustard-colored government building across from the *Seaport Market Place*). There's also a free shopping-tour bus (you'll know it by its wild colors). It departs every hour starting from the *Holiday Inn* (230 L. G. Smith Blvd.) at 9:15 AM and stops at all the major hotels on its way toward town. The last bus is at 3:15 PM. The bus runs only one way; you'll have to get back on your own.

CAR RENTAL Plenty of cars are available, and renting one is the most pleasant and flexible way to see the island, shop, and dine out. Roads are good and clearly marked, and US or Canadian driver's licenses are valid. Rates vary depending on the type of car. Hotels can make the arrangements for guests who haven't reserved a car ahead of time. All the following international companies have offices at the airport, at hotels, or in Oranjestad, including the following locations: *Avis* (*Queen Beatrix Airport;* phone: 25496), *Budget* (1A Kolibristraat or *Queen Beatrix Airport;* phone: 25423); *Dollar* (9A Camacuri; phone: 22783, 25651, or 35250); *Hertz* (142 L. G. Smith Blvd.; phone: 24400 or 24545); and *National* (170 Tanki Leendert, phone: 21967; or *Queen Beatrix Airport,* phone: 25451). Some excellent local agencies are *Marcos* (27B Noord, phone: 64867; or *Queen Beatrix Airport,* phone: 25295 or 65889); *Topless* (10 Montana; phone: 75236); and *Toyota* (114 L.G. Smith Blvd.; phone: 34832 or 24925).

INTER-ISLAND FLIGHTS *Air Aruba* (phone: 36600), the island's official airline, and *ALM* (phone: 38080) provide connecting service between the island's *Kon Beatrix Luchthaven* (Queen Beatrix Airport) and Bonaire and Curaçao. *General Travel Bureau* (phone: 26609, 26359, or 34717), *Pelican* (phone: 24739, 29134, or 31228) and *De Palm* (phone: 24400 or 24545) offer popular—and interesting—air excursions to both Curaçao and Caracas, Venezuela.

MOTORCYCLES AND MOPEDS Rates vary according to the vehicle. Scooters are cheapest and cost even less for rentals of several days or longer. Contact *Nelson Cycle Rental* (10A Gasperito; phone: 66801); *George's Cycles & Scooters Rental* (136 L. G. Smith Blvd.; phone: 25975 or 31235); *Ron's*

Motorcycle Rental (phone: 17A Bakval; 62090); or *Semver Cycle Rental* (22 Noord; phone: 66851).

SEA EXCURSIONS The *Atlantis Submarine* (at *Seaport Village;* phone: 36090) takes up to 46 passengers 140 feet below the sea to Barcadera Reef. Some hotels distribute discount coupons for this 50-minute plunge in a modern, air conditioned sub. *De Palm* (see *Inter-Island Flights,* above) offers a glass-bottom boat cruise with views of coral reefs, tropical fish, and shipwrecks, and a three-hour sailing and snorkeling cruise on the trimaran *Seaventure,* which includes an open bar, snacks, and snorkeling equipment. The operator also offers sunset and moonlight cruises. *Pelican* (see *Inter-Island Flights*) is the other major tour operator offering day and evening cruises. *Red Sail Sports* (with branches in many hotels; phone: 31603) is known for its friendly staff and its excellent snorkeling and buffet lunch cruises aboard a 53-foot state-of-the-art catamaran, as well as cocktail, sunset, and moonlight sails. Sunset and dinner and dancing cruises on "pirate" ships also are offered aboard the *Tattoo* (at the *De Palm Pier* at the *Aruba Palm Beach* resort, 79 L. G. Smith Blvd.; phone: 28919 or 23513; 65842 after 6 PM), as well as by *Aruba's Pirates* (25 Pindastraat; phone: 24554).

SIGHTSEEING TOURS Aruba cab drivers are genial and informative and usually can serve as superb guides. Hotels can recommend a good driver and make arrangements. *De Palm* (see *Inter-Island Flights,* above), Aruba's largest operator, offers both island excursions and sailing tours. *Pelican* (see *Inter-Island Flights,* above) has excellent tours. Highly recommended is Ferdi Maduro of *Corvalou Eco-Tours* (8 Willemstraat; phone: 35742 or 38383), who offers interesting daytime and sunset tours of the island's hinterland. Eppie Boerstra of *Marlin Booster Tracking* (40 Diamantbergweg; phone: 40457 or 41513) offers wildlife and archaeology tours in five different languages. *Watapana Tours* (phone: 35191) runs several unique tours, including jeep excursions, a four-hour daytime tour that includes a swim and snorkel at Baby Beach, and nightclub outings that include drinks.

TAXI Taxis aren't metered, so agree on the rate with the driver before getting in. Unless your hotel includes ground transfers in your room rate, you will need to take a taxi to your hotel or rent a car. To get a taxi, call *Taxi Dispatch* (phone: 22116 or 21604).

SPECIAL EVENTS

The multi-week celebration of *Carnival* is the year's biggest event. The festivities usually begin the second week in January (with the *Tumba Contest* for musicians) and last until the day before *Ash Wednesday* (February 21 in 1996). For the next few weeks there are children's parades and other festivities; the climax is the *Grand Parade* (the last Sunday in February) and *Jump-up,* an outdoor party with lots of music and dancing (check the exact date of the latter with the tourist office). Banks and stores are closed on the following holidays (although when cruise ships are in port, some stores open for a few hours): *New Year's Day, Betico Croes' Birthday* (January 25), *Carnival Monday* (the day after the *Grand Parade*), *National Anthem and Flag Day* (March 18), *Good Friday* (April 5 in 1996), *Easter Monday* (April 8 in 1996), *Queen's Day* (April 30), *Labor Day* (May 1), *Ascension Day* (May 16 in 1996), *St. John's Day* (June 24), *San Nicolas Day* (December 5), *Christmas,* and *Boxing Day* (December 26). Special annual sporting events include the *Aruba Hi-Winds Pro-Am Windsurfing Tournament* (in June), the *"Caribbean Shootout" International Drag Race* (second week of November), and the annual *Catamaran Regatta* (in early November).

SHOPPING

Technically, Aruba is not a free port, but the duty on most items is so low (3.3%) that Caya G. F. Betico Croes, Oranjestad's shopping hub, is a center for bargains from all over the world; other browsing options abound on the refurbished town square, in the *Seaport Village* mall (connected to the *Aruba Sonesta Resorts* and containing more than 120 stores and eateries), and in the *Seaport Market Place* on the waterfront. But not all the prices are rock-bottom, so be sure to check stateside prices before you leave home. With that in mind, shop for Royal Copenhagen porcelain; Delft pottery; Dutch, Swedish, and Danish silver and pewter; Swiss watches; liquor and liqueurs; Madeira embroidery; Italian woodcarvings; French perfume; British woolens; Indonesian spices; Hummel figurines; and much, much more. For last-minute, no-hassle shopping, most hotels house branches of one or two downtown stores with smaller selections, same prices. Most downtown stores are open daily from 8 AM to 6 PM and are closed Sundays, although some also close for lunch between noon and 2 PM.

Here are some well-known emporiums worthy of a shopper's attention. Stores are in Oranjestad unless otherwise noted.

Artistic Boutique An interesting assortment of Indonesian imports, including ivory pieces and unusual earrings. 25 Caya G. F. Betico Croes (phone: 23142); 82 L.G. Smith Blvd. (phone: 32576); 250 L.G. Smith Blvd. (phone: 70675); and at the *Holiday Inn,* 230 L.G. Smith Blvd., Palm Beach (phone: 63383).

Aruba Trading Company The best place in town for perfume. It also sells cosmetics, jewelry, and both men's and women's clothes. 12 Caya G. F. Betico Croes (phone: 22602) and *Seaport Market Place* (phone: 23950).

De Witt Gift items, toys, and books. 94 Caya G. F. Betico Croes (phone: 21273) and *Seaport Village* (phone: 27358).

Little Switzerland An islands-wide favorite, it offers an array of jewelry, crystal, watches, and gift items. 14 Caya G. F. Betico Croes (phone: 21192).

Palais Oriental A wide selection of crystal. 72 Caya G. F. Betico Croes (phone: 21422).

Spritzer & Fuhrmann A superb selection of fine jewelry, Lalique crystal, and gifts. Two locations: 34A Caya G. F. Betico Croes (phone: 24360) and the *Holiday Inn,* 230 L. G. Smith Blvd., Palm Beach (phone: 64461).

SPORTS

BOATING Most hotels have Sunfish for loan or rent; larger craft can be chartered from boat owners (ask at your hotel or the tourist board). The *Aruba Nautical Club* marina in Balashi, at the mouth of Spanish Lagoon between Oranjestad and San Nicolas, offers reef-protected, all-weather mooring for yachts. Members of other yacht clubs are welcome for a modest fee, charged according to size of craft; for information write to the club (Box 161, Oranjestad; phone: 23022). Farther down the shore, docking facilities also are available at the *Bucuti Yacht Club* (31 Bucutiweg, Oranjestad; phone: 23793).

Pedal boats, sea jeeps, jet skis, and Waverunners also are popular at Aruba resorts. Check at your hotel's water sports facility.

CYCLING Bicycles of all types can be rented at *Donata Cycle Rental* (136D L. G. Smith Blvd.; phone: 22633 or 34343) or *Melchor Cycle Rental* (170A Leendert; phone: 23448).

DUNE SLIDING A sport unique to Aruba at Boca Prins on the north coast; wear sneakers and your strongest pair of jeans.

FITNESS CLUBS *Body Friction* (136A L. G. Smith Blvd.; phone: 24642) is a complete fitness center; guests may use the facility for a daily or weekly rate. It's closed Sundays. The *Holiday Inn Aruba* (230 L. G. Smith Blvd.; phone: 23600) and the *Hyatt Regency Aruba, La Cabaña,* and *Aruba Sonesta* (see *Checking In* for the latter three) allow non-guests to buy day passes to their health spas.

GOLF The 18-hole *Tierra del Sol* (in Arashi, on the northwest coast; phone: 24693) opened in late 1994 to rave reviews. Designed by Robert Trent Jones Jr., these stunningly landscaped championship links managed by Hyatt have already become a big draw for devotees of the game (many hotel golf packages now include this course). The *Aruba Golf Club* near San Nicolas, on the eastern end of the island (phone: 42006), bills itself as an 18-hole course but, in fact, there are 11 Astroturf holes played different ways. The par 72 course is not plush, but it has 25 sand traps, goats, and lots of cacti. There are no caddies, but golf carts are available, as are clubs for rent. Families and miniature-golf fans will enjoy a round at *Joe Mendez Adventure Golf* (Eagle Beach area, across from *La Cabaña* hotel; phone: 76625), where there are two 18-hole mini-golf courses, plus pedal boats, bumper boats, a bar, and a snack stand.

HORSEBACK RIDING Horses are available at *Rancho El Paso* (44 Washington; phone: 23310) and *Rancho del Campo* (22E Sombre; phone: 20290).

LAND SAILING Combine a go-cart with a sailboat and the result is a fast-moving sailcart that just about flies over the huge dirt field at *Aruba Sailkarts* (23 Bushiri; phone: 35133). Helmets, gloves, and instruction—all you need to enjoy this fun and thrilling sport—are provided. Wear clothes that are easy to wash—or that you don't care about very much. Single- and double-seat carts are available.

SNORKELING AND SCUBA DIVING Though not as world renowned as nearby Bonaire, the clear, warm, Aruban waters offer visibility up to 100 feet, and there is a good variety of coral, lacy sea fans, sponges, and multicolored tropical fish for divers to see and photograph. A favorite dive is the 400-foot sunken German freighter *Antilla,* which was scuttled off the northwestern tip of the island during World War II; another popular dive site is the wreck of the *Pedernales,* an oil tanker lying in only 25 feet of water. Arrangements for equipment rental, diving trips, and instruction can be made through your hotel. *Red Sail Sports* (see *Sea Excursions,* above) and *De Palm* and *Pelican* (see *Inter-Island Flights,* above, for both) operate hotel concessions. Beginner's courses are offered, as well as guided trips for the experienced diver with a "C card." Snorkel trips that include equipment can be arranged, or, for snorkeling on your own, equipment can be rented. Some tour operators add a 10% service charge. Other reputable dive operators include: *Charlie's S.E.A Scuba* (phone: 34877), *Aruba Pro Dive* (88 Ponton; phone: 25520), and *Scuba Aruba* (phone: 34142). For those desiring an underwater experience that doesn't include getting wet, there's the *Atlantis Submarine* (see *Sea Excursions*).

SPORT FISHING Aruba's waters are best for sailfish, wahoo, blue and white marlin, tuna, and bonito. Fishing charters can be arranged through your hotel, as well as through *De Palm, Pelican* (see *Inter-Island Flights* for both), or *Red Sail Sports* (see *Sea Excursions*). The cost of a half-day outing includes bait, tackle, soft drinks, and beer. The annual international *White Marlin Tournament,* held at the end of October, lures anglers from the US and South America.

SWIMMING AND SUNNING Gleaming white beaches stretch along the island's western and southwestern shores, which are known as the Turquoise Coast. The best are two strands above Oranjestad: Palm Beach, with a gentle slope that makes it especially good for kids and less adventurous swimmers; and Eagle Beach, closer to town, with thatch-roofed shelters for picnicking. Day-trippers from the Oranjestad area should stop at Baby Beach, a sandfringed shallow lagoon that's perfect for children, located at the eastern tip of the island.

TENNIS A different game here because of the relentless trade winds, but it's popular. The new *Aruba Racquet Club* (21 Rooi Santo; phone: 60215) is a $1.4-million facility with eight championship-quality courts, one stadium court, a clubhouse with a pro shop, a swimming pool, a fitness center, and retail stores. There are also courts at most of the principal hotels on the beach strip: the *Americana Aruba, Aruba Hilton, Aruba Palm Beach, Divi Aruba Beach, Hyatt Regency Aruba, Radisson Aruba Caribbean, Tamarijn Aruba Beach* (see *Checking In* for all), the *Holiday Inn* (see *Fitness,* above), and the *Aruba Beach Club* (51 L. G. Smith Blvd.; phone: 63000; 800-346-7084); the *Hyatt Regency* and *Holiday Inn* seem to have the best wind shields. Several hotels have tennis pros, and a number of the courts are lighted for night play. Tennis is free to hotel guests during the day; some hotels charge for night lighting. Games can be arranged by non-guests when courts are not in use.

WATER SKIING Available at most oceanfront hotels. Lessons are available.

WINDSURFING Aruba is one of the top spots anywhere for this sport, drawing many world class windsurfers for practice and competition. It's also a great place for beginners. *Red Sail Sports* (see *Sea Excursions*) offers equipment and instruction for both novice and advanced windsurfers. "Fanatic" boards (with a special high-tech design) also are available for rent. *Pelican* (see *Inter-Island Flights*) offers boards and lessons.

NIGHTLIFE

Aruba's lively nightlife is centered around its 10 casinos. The plushest and most popular are the *Royal Cabaña Casino* at *La Cabaña All-Suite Beach* resort; the *Hyatt Regency Aruba Casino,* with live entertainment nightly; the *Crystal Casino* at the *Aruba Sonesta;* and the *Aruba Hilton*'s lively *Casablanca* casino (see *Checking In* for all four). Those who feel lucky also may try their hands at blackjack, craps, roulette, or the slot machines at the casinos of the *Americana Aruba, Aruba Palm Beach,* and *Radisson Aruba Caribbean* (see *Checking In* for information on all the preceding), and *Holiday Inn* (see *Fitness,* above); the *Aruba Palm Beach* also has a special room set aside for baccarat. The *Alhambra Casino* (47 L. G. Smith Blvd.; phone: 35000 or 28339) is part of an entertainment complex which also includes the *Aladdin Theater,* more than a dozen shops, several restaurants, and a nightclub. It's near the *Divi Aruba Beach* and *Best Western Manchebo Beach* hotels (see *Checking In* for both). Low betting limits and the absence of high rollers and junket players give Aruba's casinos a pleasantly relaxed atmosphere. Casinos open for action after lunch and keep going until the small hours. For additional details, see *Casino Countdown* in DIVERSIONS. *Note:* No one under 18 is admitted.

Non-gamblers can dance, drink, and watch a show in any of the hotel cocktail lounges or supper clubs. Every night, except Mondays, the *Americana*'s *Jardin Brésilien* lounge features live bands, while its *Las Palmas* nightclub stages cabaret shows. The *Aruba Palm Beach*'s *Oasis Lounge* is a lively venue for drinks, dancing, and occasional entertainment. Cabaret shows and comedy are featured at the *Tropicana* nightclub at the *Royal Cabaña Casino* at *La Cabaña.* The *Holiday Inn* has its *L'Esprit* nightclub for dining, dancing, and occasional shows. Hotel supper clubs require reservations, as they sometimes close for guests-only parties. The *Tamarijn Aruba Beach*'s outdoor bar spotlights local music. Most hotels have theme nights, featuring lavish buffets and entertainment, as regular weekly events; they range from "Carnival Night" on Tuesdays at the *Divi Aruba Beach* to "Fajitas & Ritas Night" on Fridays at the *Hyatt Regency Aruba.* There are also a number of popular dance clubs, although they don't get hopping until after 11 PM. The best ones are *Club Visage* (152A L. G. Smith Blvd.; phone: 33148 or 37451), which caters to a younger crowd; and *Desires* in the *Aruba Sonesta* (see *Checking In*), where the beat is a combination of Latin and top 40. On Tuesday evenings, the *Bon Bini Festival* is held in the outdoor courtyard of the *Fort Zoutman Museum,* located one block north of the *Harbourtown Mall. Bon bini* is Papiamento for "welcome," and this event was designed to introduce visitors to all things Aruban, from folk dancing to crafts, music, and food, for a nominal admission charge. For more information call the tourist office (phone: 23777).

Best on the Island

CHECKING IN

In winter expect to pay $275 or more per day without meals for a double room in a hotel listed below as very expensive; $165 to $275 in those places listed as expensive; from $120 to $165 in moderate places; and from $90 to $120 in an inexpensive hotel. In the off-season (from about May through mid-December) rates are discounted, sometimes as much as 40%. There's a 7% hotel tax, and most hotels add an 11% service charge. Note that all hotels feature air conditioned rooms with color TV sets, telephones, and private baths unless otherwise indicated. When calling from a phone on Aruba, use only the local numbers listed below; for information about calling from elsewhere, see *Telephone* earlier in this chapter.

PALM BEACH

VERY EXPENSIVE

Americana Aruba Here is a lively, rejuvenated place with handsome public areas, 419 rooms and suites (all with balconies and ocean views) in two towers overlooking the pool, two tennis courts, a spectacular swimming pool, a spacious beach, water sports, a fitness center, a beauty salon, a shopping arcade, and a popular children's program. There are also three restaurants (including *Le Petit Café*; see *Eating Out)* and a theater-style nightclub and casino. The all-inclusive option provides a great value. 83 L. G. Smith Blvd. (phone: 64500; 800-203-4475; fax: 63191).

Hyatt Regency Aruba This $57-million property, Aruba's top deluxe resort, has 360 rooms located on 12 beachfront acres on Palm Beach. It boasts a multilevel water display with cascading waterfalls, a slide, gardens, and a lagoon filled with tropical fish. The resort offers all water sports, with instruction available. There are also four restaurants (including *Ruinas del Mar;* see *Eating Out*), a modern health and fitness facility, and a casino with live entertainment. There's also an excellent supervised children's program called "Camp Hyatt." The rooms are decked out in Southwestern decor and boast all the creature comforts. If money is no object, choose one of the concierge-level rooms, which boast two amenity-laden bathrooms and lots of luxurious extras. You won't be disappointed. This is Aruba's top hotel for discriminating travelers who like an informal atmosphere with topnotch service. 85 L. G. Smith Blvd. (phone: 61234; 800-233-1234; fax: 65478).

EXPENSIVE

Aruba Hilton The island's tallest hotel is now one of its top resorts, thanks to a $42 million renovation. All 443 rooms have been redone with new tropical-motif furnishings, stocked mini-bars, cable TV, and balconies overlooking the Caribbean. Highlights include a new free-form pool with lush land-scaping, a fine fitness center, and a well-maintained beach offering a variety of water sports at a quieter end of Palm Beach. There is also a lighted tennis court, a daily breakfast buffet in the *Green House* restaurant, lunch by the beach served at *The Terrace,* and fun theme nights and elegant dining in *Las Antillas Grill Room.* Several bars and lounges stay busy, as do the lively *Casablanca* casino and *Music Hall* nightclub. 77 L. G. Smith Blvd. (phone: 64466; 800-HILTONS; fax: 61941).

Aruba Palm Beach This striking high-rise with 200 oversized rooms, all with private balconies or patios, features Moorish-style lines, a lovely pink color scheme, and beautiful gardens. It boasts a 1,200-foot beach, tennis, a fresh-water pool, water sports, two restaurants, a theater, mini-ballroom, and casino. 79 L. G. Smith Blvd. (phone: 63900; 800-345-2782; fax: 61941).

Mill Condominiums Located adjacent to *De Olde Molen* (The Old Mill) restaurant (see *Eating Out*), a well-known Palm Beach landmark, is a complex of 105 apartment-style suites popular with vacationing families. Junior one- and two-bedroom luxury suites are available, most with full kitchens or kitch-enettes. The beach is a complimentary shuttle ride (or five-minute walk) away, several restaurants are nearby, and breakfast is served poolside. The resort has tennis courts, a fitness center/gym with aerobics classes, a play-ground, pool, children's pool, and mini-market. 330 L. G. Smith Blvd. (phone: 67700; fax: 67271).

Playa Linda Beach A stylish time-share resort with a club-like atmosphere and full hotel services, it has 191 studio, one-, and two-bedroom apartments. Low-rise, with a peaceful atmosphere (no charter groups, no casino), it's within strolling distance of brighter lights. There's a small market, a restaurant, a drugstore, a beach, and water sports; tennis can be arranged. There's a five-night minimum stay year-round. 87 L. G. Smith Blvd. (phone: 61000; 800-346-7084; 201-617-8877 in New Jersey; fax: 63479).

Radisson Aruba Caribbean Set on 1,500 feet of gorgeous beach, this lively resort features 386 spacious rooms and suites with private balconies or patios. It's surrounded by exotic tropical gardens and features three restaurants, a lounge, two bars, a casino, an Olympic-size pool, a health and fitness center, four lighted tennis courts, a shopping arcade, and a complete water sports center. 81 J. E. Irausquin Blvd. (phone: 66555; 800-333-3333; fax: 63260).

EAGLE BEACH

EXPENSIVE

La Cabaña All-Suite Beach This sprawling resort boasts 803 suites, all with pleasant tropical decor, fully-equipped kitchenettes, Jacuzzis, and satellite TV. The *Royal Cabaña Casino* is the island's largest gaming house, and is undergoing an expansion that will make it the largest in the Caribbean. Also on the premises are a complete fitness center, five lighted tennis courts, five restaurants, and water sports facilities. This is an excellent family place, with a supervised children's program and a video arcade to occupy teens. All-inclusive packages are available. 250 L. G. Smith Blvd., Eagle Beach (phone: 79000; 800-223-9815; 212-251-1710 in New York; fax: 75474).

Costa Linda This family-oriented, five-story oceanfront resort has 155 two- and three-bedroom suites. Features include four whirlpools, two pools (one for kids), tennis courts, a fitness center, three restaurants, a nightclub, a shopping arcade, and water sports. 57 L. G. Smith Blvd., Eagle Beach (phone: 38000; fax: 36040).

MANCHEBO AND DRUIF BAY BEACHES

VERY EXPENSIVE

Divi Aruba Beach Formerly known as the *Divi-Divi Beach* resort, this pleasantly rambling low-rise with Spanish architectural accents has 203 lanais and casitas (including three superlative suites); all have either a balcony or patio (some right on the wide, white beach). Features include two freshwater pools, a tennis court, and two bars. For informal, relaxed dining, there's the open-air *Pelican Terrace;* or try *The Red Parrot* for an excellent French dinner. The *Alhambra Casino,* Aruba's most unusual (and only freestanding) casino, with a number of boutiques, is just up the street. 45 J. E. Irausquin Blvd. (phone: 23300; 800-554-2008; fax: 31940).

EXPENSIVE

Best Western Manchebo Beach Considered by many to have one of the best and widest stretches of beach, this friendly, informal resort, especially popular with Europeans, has 71 modern rooms. Guests have exchange privileges at the *Best Western Talk of the Town* (see below). The *French Steak House* is its first-rate restaurant (see *Eating Out*); there's outdoor dancing at night. 55 L. G. Smith Blvd. (phone: 23444; 800-223-1108; fax: 33667).

Dutch Village These sleek townhouses offer all the comforts, inside and out, including satellite TV and Jacuzzis in all 90 studio and one- and two-bedroom apartments, plus a swimming pool, tennis, shops, a restaurant, and a bar. 64 L. G. Smith Blvd. (phone: 31774; 800-367-3484; fax: 20501).

Tamarijn Aruba Beach All of this property's 236 rooms are within a few barefoot steps of its 2,000-foot beach and feature an appealing West Indian decor (the pastel-painted buildings were recently renovated). Other pluses: a pool, two Jacuzzis, a small fitness center, two restaurants, a seaside buffet, two bars (including the intimate *Bunker Bar* directly on the ocean), nightly music by a house band, and weekly theme nights. The all-inclusive package covers all meals and drinks (including alcoholic beverages), a sunset cruise, tennis on two courts, and windsurfing, sailing, and snorkeling equipment and instruction. 41 J. E. Irausquin Blvd. (phone: 24150; 800-554-2008; fax: 31940).

MODERATE

Bushiri Bounty Aruba's first all-inclusive beachfront resort has 153 comfortable, renovated rooms and a staff that's eager to please (it's part of the *Aruba Hospitality Trades Training Center*). Rates include use of the pool and complete water sports and fitness facilities, tennis, all meals and drinks at either of the hotel's two restaurants, daily games and group activities for both children and adults, shuttle service to the casinos, and nightly entertainment. 35 L. G. Smith Blvd. (phone: 25216; 800-GO-BOUNTY in the US; 800-GET-BOUNTY in Canada or Puerto Rico; fax: 26789).

ELSEWHERE ON THE ISLAND

EXPENSIVE

Aruba Sonesta With 300 modern rooms with kitchenettes and 250 one-bedroom suites, this luxury complex located along Oranjestad's scenic harborfront offers pools, three restaurants, and two casinos; guests also have access to Sonesta's 40-acre private island out in the bay, with six beaches, tennis, a health club, a restaurant and bar, and a full water sports program. Two *Seaport Village* marinas and a private yacht offer fishing and sailing charters, and there's an excellent complimentary program of supervised activities for children. The adjoining *Seaport Village* features great shopping, dining, and entertainment. An ideal choice for those who want to be in town, and also enjoy the beach. 82 L. G. Smith Blvd. (phone: 36000; 800-SONESTA; fax: 34389).

Best Western Talk of the Town Known for its excellent restaurant, *Talk of the Town* (see *Eating Out*), this property is popular with budget travelers. There are 63 nicely done rooms overlooking the Caribbean and surrounding an attractive pool/patio. The atmosphere is homey and basic rather than luxurious. Some of the rooms and all the one- and two-bedroom suites have kitchenettes with microwave ovens. It's not on the beach, but there's a pool and an outdoor whirlpool, as well as a bar, a snack bar, and Caribbean entertainment most nights. Guests have full exchange privileges at the *Best Western Manchebo Beach*. A six-minute drive from town, it's a bit out of the way. 2 L. G. Smith Blvd., Oranjestad (phone: 23380; 800-223-1108; fax: 32446).

EATING OUT

Aruba has several notable native dishes. Its tastiest native recipes are *stoba* (a beef, lamb, or goat stew) and *sopito de pisca* (a fish chowder with onions, tomatoes, garlic, peppers, and a bouquet of spices). If you like fish, try it—preferably with *funchi,* a sort of cornmeal pudding. Favorite Aruban snacks include *cala* (a bean fritter), *pastechi* (a meat-stuffed turnover), and *ayacas* (leaf-wrapped meat rolls served mostly at *Christmas*). The most exotic eating around is Indonesian (from another onetime Dutch island), and its most spectacular form is the rijsttafel (rice table), which may be loaded with 25 or more different shrimp, meat, vegetable, and fruit dishes—some spicy hot—to be piled around and eaten with a mountain of rice. A number of Aruban restaurants do a scaled-down version; they also offer other Indonesian specialties like *nasi goreng* (a one-plate rijsttafel of meat, shrimp, chicken, and vegetables crowned with a fried egg), *bami goreng* (the same, with a base of Chinese noodles instead of rice), and *Java honde portie* (literally a Javanese "hound's portion" of rice, beef, vegetables, and fried eggs, all seasoned with curry). Also of Dutch origin (with an island twist): *keshi yena* (Edam cheese stuffed with a savory mixture of beef or chicken cooked with tomatoes, onions, olives, pickles, and raisins) and *capucijners* (mixed beans, meat, marrow, bacon, onions, and pickles). Portions tend to be enormous—or larger.

Most of the big hotels have a terrace restaurant that's casual at lunch and fancier (both dress and menu) at night, plus a more expensive specialty restaurant and/or supper club. In town there are a number of good Aruban and Oriental places. You'll also find Argentinean, Mexican, German, Italian, French, even New York deli–style fare if you look. Major credit cards are generally accepted. In the listings that follow, dinner—without wine, drinks, or 10% to 15% service charge—at a restaurant described as expensive runs $60 or more for two; $30 to $60 at places described as moderate; and less than $30 at spots in the inexpensive category. All restaurants listed below are open for lunch and dinner unless otherwise noted. When calling from a phone on Aruba, use only the local numbers listed below. For information about dialing from elsewhere, see *Telephone* earlier in this chapter.

EXPENSIVE

Ruinas del Mar Romantic fine dining amid the re-created ruins of a gold mine, with stone pillars, candlelit tables, waterfalls, and a lagoon stocked with black swans and goldfish. Reserve a table on the terrace and let the starlit ambience enchant you. The international menu specializes in grilled beef, lamb, chicken, and fish. Open daily for breakfast and dinner. Reservations necessary. Major credit cards accepted. In the *Hyatt Regency Aruba,* 85 L. G. Smith Blvd. (phone: 61234)

MODERATE

Bon Appetit This lovely place has island atmosphere, wood beams, white table-cloths, and a gracious owner/host, Max Croes, who enjoys personally serving his "flaming Max" dessert (vanilla ice cream mixed with caramel, topped with milk chocolate, nuts, and whipped cream and then flambéed with Grand Marnier). House specialties are enormous prime ribs, roast rack of lamb for two, West Indian prawn curry, and shrimp scampi à la Chivas. Open for dinner only; closed Sundays. Reservations advised. Major credit cards accepted. 29 Palm Beach (phone: 65241).

Buccaneer Very popular, it specializes in fish and seafood served in an attractive atmosphere accented by dramatic aquariums. Open for dinner only; closed Sundays. There may be a line, but they won't take reservations. Major credit cards accepted. 11C Gasparito St. (phone: 66172).

Chalet Suisse International fare served in a pleasant Swiss chalet–style building (what else?), overlooking the beach. Open for dinner only; closed Sundays. Reservations advised. Major credit cards accepted. 246 J. E. Irausquin Blvd., Eagle Beach (phone: 75054).

Old Cunucu House International and local dishes are served in a restored country house with live entertainment on Friday and Saturday nights. Service can be slow. Open daily for dinner only. Reservations advised. Major credit cards accepted. 150 Palm Beach, just inland from the resorts (phone: 61666).

De Olde Molen This really is an old windmill, built in Holland in 1804, knocked down, shipped, and reassembled in Aruba in 1960. It's tourist-oriented but nonetheless loaded with cozy atmosphere. The continental menu (steaks, lobster, veal Cordon Bleu) is not surprising, but it's good. Open for dinner only; closed Sundays. Reservations advised. Major credit cards accepted. 330 J. E. Irausquin Blvd., off Palm Beach (phone: 62060).

Papiamento International Cuisine & Grill Delicately lit ficus and palm trees grace the garden patio of this family-run restaurant, located in a restored 130-year-old home decorated with antiques and other charming touches. The menu features creative continental and Caribbean favorites flavored with garden-fresh herbs; specialties include beef and lamb grilled on hot slabs of marble and brought sizzling to the table, as well as fresh seafood. Lovers should request the "Honeymoon Room," a cozy alcove for a tête-à-tête dinner; guests also may be served poolside, by the bar. Open daily for dinner only. Reservations advised. Major credit cards accepted. 61 Washington Noord (phone: 64544).

INEXPENSIVE

Mama & Papa's Aruban specialties—*bakijow stoba seroe patrishi* (stewed cod), *kreeft di cay reef* (broiled lobster), *keshi yena*, and tasty johnnycakes—are served at this popular and truly native-style eatery. There's dancing nightly. Open for dinner only; closed Sundays. Reservations advised. Major credit cards accepted. 41C Noord (phone: 60633 or 67913).

La Paloma Italian restaurants are big on Aruba, and this one offers one of the best overall values. Northern Italian dishes are specialties; try the veal cacciatore or the chicken topped with eggplant and mozzarella cheese. There's pasta and fresh seafood too. Open for dinner only; closed Tuesdays. Reservations advised. Major credit cards accepted. 39 Noord, a five-minute drive from Palm Beach (phone: 62770).

ORANJESTAD

EXPENSIVE

Chez Mathilde Enjoy fine French fare in a 19th-century Aruban house. Small, romantic, and tastefully decorated dining rooms complement the fine food. Jackets required for men. Open daily; no lunch on Sundays. Reservations advised. Major credit cards accepted. 23 Havenstraat (phone: 34968).

MODERATE

Le Petit Café A local favorite, it specializes in steaks cooked on hot stones right at your table. Closed Sundays. Reservations unnecessary. Major credit cards accepted. 7 Schelpstraat, in the *Strada Complex II* (phone: 26577), and in the *Americana Aruba,* 83 L. G. Smith Blvd. (phone: 34368).

Talk of the Town At dinner, this hotel dining room presents a bill of fare that includes escargots *à la bourguignonne,* crabmeat crêpes, veal Cordon Bleu, broiled lobster, and excellent Caribbean frogs' legs, all served by candlelight. Open for dinner only; closed Mondays. Reservations advised. Major credit cards accepted. At the *Best Western Talk of the Town Hotel,* 2 L. G. Smith Blvd. (phone: 23380).

Waterfront Crabhouse Fresh seafood is the specialty here; try the crab or the Maine lobster, and don't miss some of the best fresh-baked cornmeal bread on Aruba. Open daily for breakfast, lunch, and dinner. Reservations advised. Major credit cards accepted. *Seaport Market Place,* L. G. Smith Blvd. (phone: 35858).

Boonoonoonoos This spot specializes in Caribbean fare, with such indigenous dishes as sea terrine, curried goat, Jamaican jerk pork, and roast chicken Barbados (topped with plaintains and coconut). Traditional continental and French items are offered as well. No lunch on Saturdays; closed Sundays. Reservations advised for dinner. Major credit cards accepted. 18A Wilhelminastraat (phone: 31888).

Cocoplum Hearty Aruban dishes such as *keshi yena,* fish soup, or red snapper *crioyo* (prepared in a creole-style sauce) are served at this pleasant, casual indoor/outdoor eatery. Open for breakfast and lunch only (until 6:30 PM); closed Sundays. No reservations. No credit cards accepted. 100 Caya G. F. Betico Croes (phone: 31176).

ELSEWHERE ON THE ISLAND

French Steak House Reopened in 1994 by renowned Aruba hotelier and restaurateur Ike Cohen, this romantic, candlelit spot is well known for its high-quality cuts of North and South American beef. Nightly specials also include fresh-caught fish, and the menu offers several other seafood and poultry dishes. There's an excellent wine list. Open for dinner only; closed Mondays. Reservations advised. Major credit cards accepted. In the *Best Western Manchebo Beach Hotel,* 55 L. G. Smith Blvd. (phone: 23444).

Brisas del Mar Arubans recommend this very casual, friendly place for its fresh fish, seafood, and island dishes; fried plantains and *pan bati* (corn pancake bread) go well with whatever is ordered. Closed Monday lunch. Reservations necessary. Major credit cards accepted. 222A Savaneta, in Savaneta, by the sea just west of San Nicolas (phone: 47718).

Charlie's Bar and Restaurant This legendary place, founded by Dutch expatriates Charlie and Marie Brouns in 1941, has served San Nicolas since its days as an oil boom town. Charlie Jr. now carries on the tradition. The walls and ceiling are packed with a mini-museum of Aruban history, with memorabilia from the island's archaeological, whaling, oil refining, and—most recenty—tourist pasts. Specialties include creole fare, shrimp, and squid. Closed Sundays. No reservations. 56 Zeppenfeldstraat, San Nicolas (phone: 45086).

Mi Cushina This place offers local food served in a homey atmosphere beneath a ceiling cleverly decorated with old coffee sacks. Closed Thursdays. Reservations advised in season. Major credit cards accepted. 24 Noord, Cura Cabai, near San Nicolas (phone: 48335).

Barbados

If you were going to design a pleasure island, chances are it would look a good deal like Barbados: a west coast lined with white beaches and a sea so clear and gentle it looks like polished tourmaline; an east coast pounded by the Atlantic Ocean; southern cane fields that ripple as breezes comb across them; and craggy northern highlands where cool morning mists burn off to reveal sweeps of valley and sea framed by majestic mahogany trees.

Barbados has seaside villages and English country churches that date from the 17th century. Its prettiest hotels, built of pink coral stone, have rambling gardens and lush landscaping, and since the trade winds are steady and the climate kind, their leeward sides are often terraced and open to fresh air and the view. The beach life is superlative; the nightlife, first-rate; golf is great; and there are several superior setups for learning and playing squash and tennis. You also can hike, bike, or ride horseback through the hills of St. Michael or rolling St. Philip Parish. There are plenty of land sites (historic, botanic, and scenic) to explore when you're tired of seeing the sea, and spectator sports (cricket, soccer, horse racing, polo) to watch when you've done enough playing yourself. And it's all pleasantly accessible thanks to the island's compact size.

Although Barbados has been independent since 1966, reminders of the British Empire are everywhere—Nelson's statue on Bridgetown's Trafalgar Square, the middies and wide-brimmed boaters worn by the Harbour Police, and afternoon tea laid out as a matter of course in the lounges of a number of St. James coast hotels. There's also the *Police Band,* resplendent in their white caps and tunics, offering a concert from the gingerbread-frilled Victorian bandstand on the Esplanade; white-wigged magistrates hurrying by on their way to court; and kids in uniforms trooping home from school— all reflective of a system of government, justice, and education built on the British model.

The pervasiveness of British customs on the island is not surprising, considering that Barbados was ruled continuously by Great Britain for over 350 years. Pedro a Campos, the Portuguese sailor said to have discovered the island in 1536, named it Los Barbados—"the bearded ones"—for the banyan trees, with their shaggy, exposed roots, that he sighted on the shore. But presumably because it lay on the Spanish (rather than the Portuguese) side of the line of demarcation established by a papal bull in 1493, he failed to claim the island for Portugal. The British arrived in 1625, found the island uninhabited, and claimed it for King James I. Two years later, 80 British settlers established themselves at Jamestown, later renamed Holetown. The first session of Barbados's Parliament was held in 1639, making it the third oldest in the Commonwealth, after the British House of Commons and the Bermuda House of Assembly.

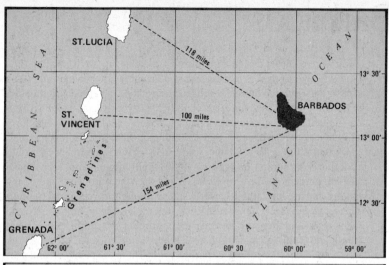

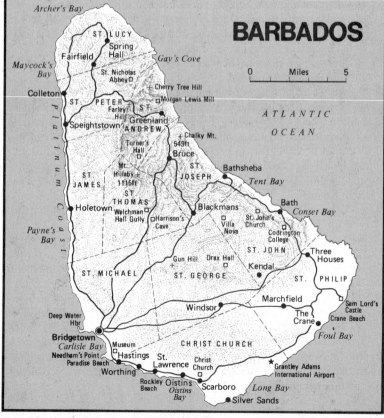

BARBADOS

Archer's Bay

ST. LUCY
Fairfield
Spring Hall
St. Nicholas Abbey
Cherry Tree Hill
Gay's Cove

Maycock's Bay

Colleton
ST. PETER
Farley Hill
Morgan Lewis Mill
Speightstown
Greenland
ST. ANDREW
Turner's Hall
Chalky Mt. 549ft
Bruce

Platinum Coast

Mt. Hillaby 1115ft
ST. JAMES
ST. THOMAS
ST. JOSEPH
Bathsheba
Tent Bay

Holetown
Welchman Hall Gully
Harrison's Cave
Blackmans
Bath
Conset Bay

Payne's Bay

Villa Nova
St. John's Church
Codrington College

Gun Hill
Drax Hall
ST. JOHN
Three Houses

ST. MICHAEL
ST. GEORGE
Kendal
ST. PHILIP

Windsor
Marchfield
Sam Lord's Castle
Crane Beach

Deep Water Hbr
The Crane
Foul Bay

Bridgetown
Carlisle Bay
Museum
Needham's Point
Paradise Beach
Hastings
St. Lawrence
CHRIST CHURCH
Christ Church
Grantley Adams International Airport

Worthing
Rockley Beach
Oistins
Oistins Bay
Scarboro
Long Bay
Silver Sands

ATLANTIC OCEAN

0 Miles 5

Compared to that of its neighbor islands, Barbados's history has been fairly free of strife. Its extreme easterly position, upwind of all the other Lesser Antilles, made it relatively difficult to approach from the west and undoubtedly served as protection from attack by buccaneers. The island's planters, many of whom were either criminals shipped out as indentured servants or dissenters forced to emigrate from England for religious or political reasons, treated the African slaves imported to help cultivate their cane fields in a relatively humane manner, although there were brief slave uprisings in 1672, 1696, and 1702.

Perhaps because of its tranquillity when compared to other islands in the Caribbean, Barbados has been known as a tourist destination for hundreds of years. As early as the 17th century, visitors came to the island for their health. In 1751, George Washington accompanied Lawrence, his tubercular half brother, on a visit to Bridgetown (the only trip abroad Washington ever made). The island was not kind to the future first US president—there he contracted smallpox, the disease that marked him for life. Still, he declared the place "a delight" and was "enraptured with the beautiful prospects."

Today's visitors are delighted, too, which pleases their hosts, whose love of and pride in their island is deep. Bajans are sure—in the nicest possible way—that "Bim" (as they call their homeland) is the best place in the Caribbean, even in the world. As one Bajan put it: "Barbados is where life feels right to me." Bajans want visitors to feel that way too. Their openness and friendliness toward tourists make the island's atmosphere especially appealing.

There has been some trouble in paradise, however. Crime against tourists, mostly in the form of petty theft and robberies, was on the rise in the 1980s and early 1990s; however, a special government task force created to focus on crime against tourists, along with stepped-up police patrols in Bridgetown, have improved the situation in recent years. And although Barbados does face a budget deficit and other economic difficulties, the island's standard of living remains high.

So Barbados is not quite the perfect island. Neither is it the perfect destination for everyone. Downtown Bridgetown is worthwhile for shopping, but it's certainly not sugar-coated pretty. Glitter addicts won't find Vegas shows or gambling, but history buffs will delight in the greathouses, antique churches, and lots more here to explore. To some people, jackets for dinner, still the norm in a few of the posher resorts, are stuffy; to others, they reflect a touch of style. Winter prices will seem astronomical to some; for others the peace and the place will be worth every penny; and still others will wait for summer, when prices drop by at least a third to a half, for the best of both worlds.

Preferences differ, but for many people, Barbados combines all that's necessary for the perfect Caribbean vacation. This island could be where "life feels right" to you, too.

Barbados At-a-Glance

FROM THE AIR

Barbados's bright green sugarcane and cotton fields, neatly framed by hedgerows, look like a tropical translation of rural England, reflecting the country's longtime British ties. The easternmost island of the West Indies, it lies outside the main arc of the Caribbean's Windward Islands chain, about 100 miles due east of St. Vincent and about 340 miles north of Guyana on the north coast of South America. It is small—166 square miles, 21 miles long by 14 miles at its widest point—and relatively densely populated, with about 260,000 inhabitants.

The island is pear shaped, stem end pointing north, with its capital, Bridgetown (pop. 94,000), on the curve of the southwestern coast. Just inland from the southern coast, 11 miles east and slightly south of the city's center, near Seawell, is *Grantley Adams International Airport.* The 2,100-mile flight from New York takes just over four and a half hours (two hours on the new Concorde flights); the flight from Miami (about 1,612 miles) takes about three and a half.

The island is rimmed by beaches. Its eastern edge, above a coast surf-combed by a dark blue Atlantic Ocean, is hilly and rugged, with Mt. Hillaby, at 1115 feet, its highest point; Bathsheba, a small fishing village, sits at the midpoint of the eastern shore. The land along the western coast—on which Bridgetown and the centuries-old settlements of Holetown and Speightstown, as well as most resort hotels, are located—is gentle and rolling, washed by a calmer leeward sea.

SPECIAL PLACES

Except for traffic-tangled Bridgetown, Barbados is the ideal place to explore by car, provided you don't attempt a shortcut from one main route to another without *very explicit* directions or a good map. In Barbados all numbered routes—laid out in a fan-like pattern—lead to or from Bridgetown. Though sometimes narrow, they are reasonably well marked with crossroad signs, and people are pleasant when visitors stop to ask directions. With this in mind, we suggest a two-part itinerary consisting of a sightseeing/shopping morning in Bridgetown, using hotel bus and/or taxi transport, and a day's drive around the island—preferably self-driven, but otherwise in a taxi with a congenial driver—including lunch and sunbathing on the east coast. (In some places, the east coast is great for body-surfing if you're a strong swimmer, but in others, strong currents make the waters unsafe; be sure to check conditions if you plan to swim.) Before setting out, pick up a *Heritage Passport,* which provides reduced admission to 16 sites around the island, from the *Barbados National Trust* (phone: 436-9033 or 426-2421); a mini-pass (entrance to five sites) is also available.

BRIDGETOWN Barbados's capital is an architectural hodgepodge with a network of one-way streets that—during rush hour—seems to epitomize the triumph of car over man. Luckily, the city's few points of interest are within strolling distance of each other and of Broad Street's in-bond (duty-free) shopping. Aim to arrive at Trafalgar Square, the heart of town, at about 10 AM, when the worst of the morning rush hour is over. Like its London namesake, the square (really the area between the edge of the inner harbor and the public buildings across Trafalgar Street) honors Nelson's 1805 naval victory and is endowed with a statue of the great admiral. This Horatio was sculpted and installed in 1813, some three decades before its British counterpart. (Considerably more popular with Bajans is the huge statue of the Freed Slave Bussa, which stands at a crossroads on St. Barnabas Highway just outside Bridgetown.) Other landmarks in and around the square: *Fountain Garden,* with its magnificent three-dolphin fountain, commemorating the advent of piped water in 1861; a memorial cenotaph to the dead of World Wars I and II; and an arch erected in 1987 at the Bay Street entrance to Bridgetown to commemorate the 21st anniversary of independence.

Facing the north side of the square, the great, gray, Victorian-Gothic public buildings (1874) house the Assembly (on the right) and the Senate (in the left-hand towered building). These buildings are open to the public when the Senate and Assembly are not in session. The jarringly modern *Financial Building* dominates the square's east end.

The square's southern boundary is the edge of the old harbor, better known as the Careenage, because from the earliest days, ships were brought in here and careened (tipped on their sides) to have their bottoms scraped, caulked, and painted. Nowadays, island fishing boats berth beside elegant sailing yachts. Keep an eye out for the Bajan harbor police, who wear sailor suits with blue-collared middies and wide-brimmed straw hats.

St. Michael's Cathedral (Anglican) is around the corner and to the right behind the *Financial Building.* Completed in 1665 and rebuilt after hurricanes in 1780 and 1831, it is said to be the place where George Washington worshiped when he visited Barbados with his brother in 1751. Today it offers cool moments on a hot day and a chance to inspect a collection of antique memorial tablets.

The last major site in Bridgetown is the *Barbados Synagogue* on Synagogue Lane, a three-minute walk from *St. Michael's Cathedral* via Magazine Lane. One of the oldest synagogues in the Western Hemisphere, it was originally built in 1654. The structure that now stands on the site, however, was built in 1833, after the first building was destroyed by the hurricane of 1831. The synagogue fell into disuse in the early 1900s, but after extensive restoration by the *Barbados National Trust,* it was reopened in 1992, and it is once again being used as a house of worship. It's closed weekends (phone: 436-8043). The synagogue adjoins the *Jewish Cemetery,* which has tombstones dating back to the 1630s.

That's about it for urban sightseeing (elapsed time: about three-quarters of an hour). Proceed to Broad Street for an hour of intense shopping. If time permits, continue the spree by taking a taxi to nearby *Pelican Village* and the *Handicraft Emporium* (see *Shopping*). Then head for the *Garrison Savannah* (via cab), where the *Barbados Museum,* once the Old Military Prison, built by the Royal Engineers in 1820, features a copy of George Washington's *Barbados Journal,* relics of slavery, geological and archaeological specimens, plantation furniture, china and silver, and West Indian prints dating from the 17th century. A *Children's Gallery* contains lovely dollhouses and historical models. The museum is closed Sundays; there's an admission charge (phone: 427-0201). Nearby lunch choices are the *Brown Sugar* and the *Ocean View* (see *Eating Out*).

Also of interest at the *Garrison Savannah* is the *National Cannon Collection,* an outdoor display of 30 cannons, dating from 1680 to 1770, that were rescued from around the island. The collection is located on a scenic spot that's especially popular with photographers.

On the way out Bay Street, Carlisle Bay and the *Esplanade Pavilion* (where the *Barbados Police Band* holds its concerts) are on the right. A little farther along, across from the entrance to the *Barbados Yacht Club,* Chelsea Road turns off to the left; on its near corner stands the structure apocryphally called "the George Washington House," where—historians agree—it is highly unlikely that either George or his brother ever slept.

ELSEWHERE ON THE ISLAND

Most organized tours travel counterclockwise through Oistins Town, then out to *Sam Lord's,* up the east coast, west across the island, and head back through Speightstown and Holetown. Those touring on their own should do just the opposite: Get an early start, drive north along the island's western edge, and continue clockwise, visiting the following spots.

HOLETOWN This little St. James coast community is the island's oldest British settlement. An obelisk marks the spot where the British ship *Olive Blossom* landed in 1627. *St. James Church,* one of the Caribbean's oldest (dating to 1660), is located here. It looks as though it has been transported—bell tower and all—from England, except for its tropical poinsettia hedge, which blooms bright red at *Christmas.*

GOLD COAST The shore of St. James and St. Peter parishes, it's lined with the island's plushest hotels and winter homes.

SPEIGHTSTOWN Once a major sugar port and still a fishing town, this place features old houses, a picturesque restored church *(St. Peter's)*, and a bustling waterfront. The vendors who sell their piles of produce and crafts on Church Street, the main thoroughfare, remain undaunted by the town's modern shopping mall.

From here turn east on Highway 1 to cross the island.

ST. NICHOLAS ABBEY This Jacobean greathouse, built between 1650 and 1660, is notable for its architecture and antiques, including a stunning 1810 Coalport dinner service and an extensive collection of Wedgwood medallions. The home movie taken by the owner's father of the voyage from Britain and 1930s plantation life is worth the price of admission. Closed weekends. St. Peter (phone: 422-8725).

FARLEY HILL A national park, it features gardens, rich green lawns, and enormous trees surrounding the shell of a once splendid greathouse, partially rebuilt during the filming of *Island in the Sun* in the late 1950s, and later destroyed again by fire. A monument commemorates the dedication of the park by Queen Elizabeth II; there are picnic tables, lookout points, a nature trail, and stunning views. Open daily. Admission charge. Farley Hill, St. Peter (phone: 422-3555).

BARBADOS WILDLIFE RESERVE Across from the entrance to Farley Hill, this four-acre mahogany forest reserve is operated under the auspices of the *Barbados Primate Research Centre,* and is home to rare green monkeys (said to have been brought from West Africa three centuries ago), deer, hares, tortoises, and various birds. Open daily. Admission charge. Farley Hill, St. Peter (phone: 422-8826).

GRENADE HALL FOREST AND SIGNAL STATION Located adjacent to the *Barbados Wildlife Reserve* and *Farley Hill National Park,* this botanic reserve also features a restored 19th-century signal station which was used by the Royal Artillery to communicate with fellow officers in Bridgetown. For additonal details, see *Natural Wonderlands* in DIVERSIONS. Open daily. Admission charge. Farley Hill, St. Peter (phone: 422-8826).

MORGAN LEWIS MILL Turn left (north) below Farley Hill and follow the signs to the only completely intact sugar windmill on Barbados. Open daily. Admission charge.

ANDROMEDA GARDENS Six terraced acres of exotic tropical plants and trees plus a great view of the Bathsheba coast are the highlights here. For additional details, see *Natural Wonderlands* in DIVERSIONS. Open daily. Admission charge. Bathsheba, St. Joseph (phone: 433-9384).

BATHSHEBA This small fishing village, a favorite Sunday beach area for Bajans, gives the coast its name. It's a great place to watch world class surfers do their stuff. Here also, thrusting out of the sea just offshore, are some bizarre, monumental rock formations, their bases eroded so that they look as if, at any moment, they might come crashing down into the surf. Nearby Tent Bay is home port for a fleet of fishing boats.

ST. JOHN'S CHURCH Built during the mid-1600s in the parish of the same name, this church is known for its English look and the tomb of Ferdinand Paleologus, the Emperor Constantine's last descendant. Hwy. 3B, St. John.

CODRINGTON COLLEGE This stately, gray-stone Georgian seminary of the Anglican Community of the Resurrection opened in 1745, making it the oldest seminary in the Western Hemisphere. The campus features an avenue of palms and stunning ocean views. Open daily. Admission charge. On Consett Bay, St. John.

SAM LORD'S CASTLE Once the elegant home of a celebrated 19th-century rogue who, legend has it, made his fortune by the unscrupulous practice of "wrecking." Lord allegedly lured ships onto shoals by hanging lanterns in palms along the shore to simulate port lights, then relieved them of their cargoes. Today, this structure is the centerpiece of the *Marriott* resort hotel complex (see *Checking In*). Open daily. Admission charge. St. Philip.

Other notable sites on the island include:

FRANCIA PLANTATION A stately plantation home in St. George, now open to the public, with mid-19th century furnishings made by Bajan craftsmen and a fabulous map of the West Indies printed in 1522. Still in operation as a vegetable plantation, it boasts exquisite tropical gardens and orchards. Closed weekends. Admission charge. Between Gun Hill and *St. George's Church,* St. George (phone: 429-0474).

TURNER'S HALL WOODS Part of the *Barbados National Trust,* this comprises the last remaining 46 acres of the dense tropical forest that once covered the island. It's inhabited by birds and monkeys and features a boiling spring. Open daily. St. Andrew.

WELCHMAN HALL GULLY This is the site of the *National Trust*'s developing *Botanical Garden* with many marked, tropical specimens set amid natural caves. Occasionally you'll sight wild monkeys. Visiting here is worthwhile—if you're a flower lover. Open daily. Admission charge. Hwy. 2, St. Thomas (phone: 438-6671).

HARRISON'S CAVE The spectacular caverns are endowed with stunning crystal rooms, subterranean streams, waterfalls, and pools where blind crayfish swim. The cave is wonderfully easy to explore thanks to an electric tram that carries visitors down and out again. Open daily. Admission charge. *Welchman Hall Gully,* St. Thomas (phone: 438-6640).

FLOWER FOREST Designed as a living legacy for future generations, this serene 50-acre park and botanical garden features exotic flowers, specimen fruit and spice trees, and a glorious view. Light snacks and fruit are available as refreshments. Open daily. Admission charge. Richmond Rd., St. Joseph (phone: 433-8152).

GUN HILL SIGNAL STATION A lookout point as famous for its 19th-century carved lion and 1818-built lookout tower as for one of the best views of the southern half of the island. Open daily. Admission charge. St. George.

BARBADOS ZOOLOGICAL PARK Located at *Oughterson Plantation,* it contains a collection of Caribbean wildlife, including several endangered species of parrots. The greathouse at the center of the park is full of antiques and interesting curios. Open daily. Admission charge. St. Philip (phone: 423-6203).

SOUTH POINT LIGHTHOUSE Located on the windswept landscape of the south coast and painted in red and white rings, this cast-iron structure is believed to be the only remaining lighthouse of its kind. Though its components were manufactured in England, it was first assembled in Barbados, where it was lit in April 1852. The interior is not open to the public. Christ Church.

SUNBURY PLANTATION HOUSE AND MUSEUM Over 300 years old and still occupied today, the estate house has two-and-a-half-foot-thick walls that shelter an impressive collection of mahogany furniture, 18th- and 19th-century household articles, antiques, and carriages. There's a casual restaurant and, on certain nights, elegant dinners are served in the house's dining room (call for the schedule and to make reservations). Open daily. Admission charge. Near Six Crosses Road, St. Philip (phone: 423-6270).

HARRY BAYLEY OBSERVATORY Built in 1963, this observatory is equipped with a 14-inch reflector telescope. Open Friday evenings only (hours vary, but are usually 8 to 11 PM). Off Hwy. 6, St. Michael (no phone).

MOUNT GAY RUM VISITOR'S CENTRE Take a 45-minute tour of the aging, blending, and bottling facilities used by this famous distillery, the world's oldest. (The distilling part of the process takes place on the northern end of the island in a facility that is only rarely open to the public.) The tour's finale offers an opportunity to sample this fine Barbadian rum. Closed Sundays. Admission charge. Spring Garden Hwy., Bridgetown (phone: 425-9066).

EXTRA SPECIAL

On Wednesday afternoons from mid-January through the first week of April, the *Barbados National Trust* organizes tours to private estates and houses of architectural or historic interest, affording a close look at island antiques as well as the elegant lifestyle of the historic homes' current residents. Tickets benefit the *National Trust.* Watch the Sunday papers, call the *National Trust* (phone: 436-9033), or ask at the tourist office or your hotel activities desk for specifics.

Sources and Resources

TOURIST INFORMATION

The main *Barbados Tourism Authority* office (phone: 427-2623/4) is located at the corner of Redman's Road and the Harbour Road, near the Deep Water Harbour in Bridgetown. There also are tourist information centers at *Grantley Adams International Airport* (phone: 428-0937) and on the cruise ship pier at the Deep Water Harbour (phone: 426-1718). All are closed weekends.

The tourism authority supplies information on attractions and accommodations. It also publishes a season-by-season list of rates and facilities at island hotels, guesthouses, apartments, and cottages, along with details on summer and winter package plans. The tourism authority has two offices in the US (see GETTING READY TO GO).

LOCAL COVERAGE The *Barbados Advocate* and *The Nation* are published daily, but the latter appears as the *Sun* on weekends. Given a two- or three-day time lag, Miami and other US papers (*USA Today* and the *Wall Street Journal*) and the *International Herald Tribune* also are generally available. *Caribbean Week* covers regional news.

The tourism authority's compact *Things You Should Know* brochure covers a good deal of useful information (transport companies and costs, shopping, restaurants, nightspots, and so on), as does the complimentary, pocket-size *Barbados in a Nutshell,* independently published and available at hotels, shops, and restaurants around the island. The *Visitor,* a tourist-oriented tabloid published every Monday by *The Nation,* highlights current nightlife, restaurants, and sightseeing, as does the weekly *Sun Seeker,* published by the *Advocate;* both are distributed free at hotels, the tourism authority office, and other tourist areas.

RADIO AND TELEVISION Barbados Rediffusion Radio; BBS-FM; YESS 104.1 FM; the Voice of Barbados (790 AM); Radio Liberty (98.1 FM); and the Caribbean Broadcasting Corporation (daily radio, morning CNN news from the US, and evening TV) are the island's broadcast media. Channel 8 is the state-owned television station.

TELEPHONE The area code for Barbados is 809. Dial 112 for the police; 115 for 426-1113 for an ambulance.

ENTRY REQUIREMENTS US and Canadian citizens need only proof of citizenship—either a birth certificate or voter's registration card along with a government-approved photo ID (such as a driver's license) or an expired passport (not more than 10 years)—although valid passports ensure easy re-entry home. A ticket for onward or return transportation is also required. There is a departure tax ($12.50 US at press time).

CLIMATE AND CLOTHES Constant sea breezes temper the heat of the sun, which, according to official Barbadian records, shines more than 3,000 hours per (8,760-hour) year. Winter temperatures range from 68F (20C) to 85F (29C); summer temperatures 75F (25C) to 87F (31C). Showers are frequent but brief, and thanks to the trade winds, the air seldom stays muggy for long. Wettest months are September, October, and November; February and March are driest. Rooms at most hotels and guesthouses are at least partially air conditioned.

In terms of attire, only Bermuda is trimmer—a circumstance that, on both islands, can probably be traced to the lingering British influence. The effect is well groomed rather than stuffy: Bajans aren't all that keen on knee socks and walking shorts, but they do appreciate guests neatly turned out. Bare (but not topless) is beautiful on beaches only. Customarily, sun worshipers slip into a shirt or cover-up for lunch on a hotel terrace; a shirt and pants or a skirt or sport dress for daytime sightseeing; something roughly equivalent to what you'd wear on a warm evening at a country club at night. Some hotels and restaurants request jackets, but not necessarily ties, after dark. In summer, dress is less formal.

MONEY The Barbados dollar is pegged to the US dollar; at press time, the official exchange rate was $1.98 Barbados to $1 US. Shops accept both US and Canadian dollars, as well as traveler's checks, but don't offer discounts on purchases paid with them. Some of the larger stores and a number of hotels and restaurants also honor American Express, Diners Club, Visa, and MasterCard, although they may add a 5% surcharge. There usually is little difference between the exchange rate offered by banks and that given in hotels, shops, and restaurants. All prices in this chapter are quoted in US dollars.

Banking hours at *Barclays* are 8 AM to 3 PM Mondays through Thursdays; on Fridays, 8 AM to 5 PM. Most other banks are open 9 AM to 3 PM Mondays through Thursdays, and from 9 AM to 1 PM and 3 to 5 PM on Fridays. Except for the *Caribbean Commercial Bank,* which is also open Saturdays from 9 AM to noon, banks are closed on weekends and holidays. The *Barbados National Bank* operates a currency exchange bureau at the airport from 8 AM until midnight daily.

LANGUAGE Bajans speak English with their own special island lilt.

TIME Barbados time is one hour ahead of eastern standard time (when it's noon in New York, it's 1 PM in Bridgetown), or the same as eastern daylight saving time.

CURRENT 110 volts, 50 cycles; compatible with American and Canadian appliances, though they run a bit more slowly. Some hotels also have 220 volts; many also have adaptors for guests to use, but you may want to bring your own, just in case.

TIPPING The extra 10% added to your bill in most hotels and restaurants covers all but special services. When a service charge is not included, tip waiters 10% to 15%, hotel maids $1 to $2 per room per day, bellboys 50¢ per bag (but not less than $1 per trip for one or two people), and about $1 for a special errand. Airport porters also should be tipped 50¢ per bag; and taxi drivers, 10% of the fare.

GETTING AROUND

BUS Bajans use buses a lot, and more tourists should, since they reach many major interest points and are reliable (if not wildly colorful as buses are on other islands). Bus route No. 1 travels the west coast road from Bridgetown to Speightstown and beyond; Nos. 6 and 7 run between Bridgetown and Bathsheba and Bridgetown and *Codrington College,* respectively. Fare is $1.50 Barbados (US 75¢ at press time) no matter how long the ride, and exact change is required. Ask at the *Barbados Transport Board* (Roebuck St.; phone: 436-6820) for current schedule information. Be sure to put your hand out to flag buses, as they do not automatically stop for passengers, even if you're standing at the bus pole.

Private shuttle vans, owned and operated by a number of hotels, transport guests to and from Bridgetown for sightseeing and shopping several times a day. In some cases, the service is free; in others, there's a small charge.

CAR RENTAL Driving is a great way to get around once you get the hang of keeping left. Rates vary, depending on whether you're renting a no-frills mini-moke or an automatic-shift, air conditioned, four-passenger car, with unlimited mileage and basic insurance. If you don't have a credit card, you'll be asked for a substantial deposit. Rental cars are often in short supply, so early booking is advised. Advance reservations can be made by dialing 800-GO-BAJAN.

Some local firms are *National Car Rental* (not affiliated with the international chain of the same name; Bush Hall, Main Rd., St. Michael; phone: 426-0603); *L. E. Williams* (Hastings, Christ Church; phone: 427-1043 or 427-6006); *Courtesy* (Wildey; St. Michael; phone: 431-4160/1/2); *Rent-A-Moke* (Bridgetown; phone: 429-0364); and *Sunny Isle* (Dayton, Worthing, Christ Church; phone: 435-7979). *Barbados Rent a Car* (Tudor Bridge, St. Michael; phone: 425-1388) also has a booth at the airport (phone: 428-0960). Check the tourism authority for a complete listing. Car rental companies issue visitor's driving permits for a modest fee.

INTER-ISLAND FLIGHTS *American Airlines* and *BWIA* fly between Barbados and San Juan. *Air Martinique, BWIA,* and *LIAT,* and the new *Carib Express* provide air links to other Caribbean islands.

ISLAND-HOPPING TRIPS One-day flying and longer sailing expeditions to nearby Martinique, St. Lucia, St. Vincent, the Grenadines, Grenada, and Tobago include transfers, airfare, lunch, and sightseeing, and are operated by *Chantours Caribbean* (*Sunset Crest Shopping Plaza,* St. James; phone: 432-5591; fax: 432-5540); *Grenadine Tours* (26 Hastings Plaza, Christ Church; phone: 435-8451; fax: 435-6444); and *Palm Tree Tours* (Graeham Hall, Christ Church; phone: 437-1230).

SEA EXCURSIONS Lunch and cocktail cruises are offered by a number of sailing ships. The *Jolly Roger* (phone: 436-6424) provides a snorkeling stop and barbecue, open bar, entertainment by the crew, and transportation from your hotel. The *Bajan Queen* (phone: 436-2149) makes similar trips; the catamaran *Irish Mist* (phone: 436-9201) offers slightly more serene day and evening trips. Lunch and dinner snorkel cruises are offered aboard *Secret Love* (phone: 432-1972). Day cruises are offered by *Tiami Sailing Cruises* (phone: 427-7245) aboard a 60-foot catamaran. For a close-up view of the coral reef, book the submarine *Atlantis* (phone: 436-8929) or the *Jolly Roger*'s semi-submersible, the *Sea World Explorer.*

SIGHTSEEING BUS TOURS *L. E. Williams* (phone: 427-1043; fax: 427-6007) offers an 80-mile tour that takes six hours and circles the island, as well as a four-hour historic and nature tour that covers attractions in the island's interior; both tours include lunch. Other island firms, such as *Chalene Tours* (phone: 428-5645), *West Indian International Tours* (phone: 428-1490), *Dear's Garage* (phone: 427-7853), and *Johnson's* (phone: 426-4205), also organize half- and full-day tours, with special excursions to major island attractions. Be sure to confirm what is included, as some tours require additional fees for certain sites or for lunch.

SIGHTSEEING HELICOPTER EXCURSIONS For a breathtaking (if pricey) view of the island and great photo opportunities, contact *Bajan Helicopters* (*The Wharf,* Bridgetown; phone: 431-0069).

SIGHTSEEING TAXI TOURS A good way to get a close-up of the island for those who prefer not to drive. Bajan drivers are friendly, dignified, and proud of their country. A day's trip with one of them provides visitors with a more personalized feel for the country than a routine bus tour. Optional side trips: a stop for a soda or a rum and Coke at *Barclay's Park* scenic overlook; or lunch and a swim at *Marriott's Sam Lord's Castle* or the *Crane Beach* hotel (see *Checking In* for both).

TAXI Readily available at the airport, at stands in downtown Bridgetown, at the Deep Water Harbour, and outside hotels. They are not metered; but rates are fixed, and drivers carry lists of standard fares to which passengers can refer. Still, it's best to agree on the fare before starting out and to determine whether the quote is in US or Barbadian dollars.

WALKING TOURS The *Barbados National Trust* and *Highland Outdoor Tours* offer a variety of guided walks around Barbados; see *Hiking,* below, for details. *Travel House* (phone: 429-8850) offers guided walking tours of historic Bridgetown Mondays and Thursdays at 10 AM. There's a fee for the tours, which begin at *Queen's Park* restaurant (Queen's Park, Constitution Road).

SPECIAL EVENTS

Barbados's big annual bash is *Crop Over,* a month-long (mid-July through early August) succession of parties, parades, craft displays, plantation fairs, and open-air concerts enjoyed by both Bajans and island visitors. Its climax is the historically rooted *Kadooment*—a day of "jump-up" partying, singing, and dancing with a parade starting from the *National Stadium* and winding up in a central plantation yard.

The official national holidays observed by banks and most businesses include *New Year's Day, Errol Barrow Day* (January 21), *Good Friday, Easter Monday* (April 8 in 1996), *May Day* (May 1), *Whitmonday* (May 27 in 1996), *Kadooment* (first Monday in August), *UN Day* (first Monday in October), *Independence Day* (November 30), *Christmas,* and *Boxing Day* (December 26).

SHOPPING

For best buys (20% to 50% below stateside prices) on classic imports—English bone china, crystal, Japanese cameras and binoculars, perfumes, liquor, watches, jewelry, and clothes (especially British sweaters, tweeds, and sportswear), in-bond (duty-free) sections of major department stores and specialty shops on and around Bridgetown's Broad Street are where it's at. In these designated areas, merchandise is tagged with two prices: in-bond and take-away. The in-bond one is always lowest, but the take-away tag may still represent a saving over what you'd pay back home. For in-bond savings on liquor and tobacco products, visitors must shop at least 24 hours before scheduled departure time and select from display merchandise; purchases are then delivered directly to their plane or ship. All other duty-free items can be taken as they are paid for, provided the purchaser shows proof of being a visitor (airline ticket and passport or ID). At the Deep Water Harbour cruise ship pier there are several duty-free shops set in a West Indian–style arcade. *Mall 34, Norman Centre, Da Costas,* and the *Galleria* are air conditioned malls on Broad Street in Bridgetown. Several smaller malls have sprung up along the south coast, *Hastings Plaza, Sandy Bank,* and *Quayside Centre* among them. These newer shopping havens also have restaurants and bars, and parking is much easier. The selection, however, may not be as extensive as in the central shopping area.

Visitors staying at a west coast hotel can save time and their feet by shopping at the in-bond departments of *Louis L. Bayley, Cave Shepherd, India House,* and others at the *Sunset Crest Shopping Plaza.* The stocks aren't quite as large as those downtown, but neither are the crowds, and the prices are the same. The smaller, double-decked *Skyway Shopping Plaza* at Hastings, handy to South Shore hotels, is stronger on crafts and souvenirs than in-bond buys. There also are coveys of shops (branches and independent boutiques) at the *Hilton* (Needham's Point; phone: 426-0200; fax: 436-8946) and *Marriott's Sam Lord's Castle* (see *Checking In*). If you're in the neighborhood, wander through the *Chattel Village* in St. Lawrence Gap, where the shops are replicas of quaint "Bajan houses," painted in an array of pastel colors and filled with local arts and crafts.

A dozen boutiques—many in hotel gardens or lobby niches—offer sleek sportswear and resort clothes at prices that range from expensive to outrageous. No need to go into town to shop; just start in the Speightstown neighborhood, or at the south edge of the city, and make your way down the coast road. Shopping hours are from 9 AM to 5 PM weekdays; 8:30 AM to 12:30 PM Saturdays.

The following are some of our favorite places to browse or buy:

Articrafts Featuring the work of local artists such as Roslyn of Barbados, this shop offers original wall sculptures, handbags, straw work, and hanging planters, many made from *khus khus* grass, coconut straw, ball thistles, and bamboo. It's associated with the *Pelican Art Gallery* in *Pelican Village. Norman Centre,* Bridgetown (phone: 427-5767).

Barbados Handicraft Center All sorts of local crafts. Bridge St., Bridgetown (phone: 436-6128).

Best of Barbados For top-quality island crafts and prints by local artist Jill Walker. There are several branches, including ones at *Da Costas Mall* (Bridgetown; phone: 431-0013); *Marriott's Sam Lord's Castle* (see *Checking In*); *Mall 34* (Bridgetown; phone: 436-1416); and *Flower Forest* (St. Joseph; phone: 433-8152).

Cave Shepherd With five branches across the island, this department store features locally crafted jewelry, books, leather goods, imported fashions, and perfumes made in Barbados called Camaya and Gina Kaye. Broad St., Bridgetown (431-2121), at the airport (phone: 428-7101), and other locations.

Cotton Days Design Carol Cadogan sells her tropical sportswear at her design studio at *Rose Cottage,* Lower Bay St., Bridgetown (phone: 427-7191).

Flying Fish Inc. This company sells an unusual souvenir—the island's national dish, flash-frozen or vacuum-packed, with a reusable freezer gelpack (approved by major airlines for carry-on). It's also one of the few places that has fresh tropical floral bouquets that have been approved for airline carry-on. (For bouquets including roses, azaleas, camellias, gardenias, or syringa, a certificate from the *US Department of Agriculture* is needed for importation. All other flora can be imported without a certificate, but will be inspected at port of entry into the US.) At the airport departure lounge (phone: 428-1645).

La Galerie Antique China, linen, tapestries, Barbadian furniture. Payne's Bay, St. James (phone: 432-6094).

Handicraft Emporium Stacked to its warehouse rafters with fairly priced woven work, *khus khus* grass wall hangings, and pandanus mats, hats, rugs, and baskets. *Pelican Industrial Park,* Princess Alice Hwy., west of Bridgetown (phone: 426-4391) and at the airport (phone: 428-0932).

Harrison's Duty-free crystal, china, perfume, and cosmetics. 1 Broad St., Bridgetown (phone: 431-5500).

Louis L. Bayley Jewelry specialists. *Da Costas Mall,* Broad St., Bridgetown (phone: 431-0029).

Medford Craft Village These three shops owned by self-taught artist Reggie Medford offer stunning hand-carved mahogany creations and other local crafts. Lower Barbarees Hill, St. Michael (phone: 427-3179).

Royal Shop The place for watch lovers, it sells Piaget, Movado, Raymond Weill, Concord, Citizen, and Casio—to name just a few. Broad St., Bridgetown (phone: 429-7072).

SPORTS

Sun, sand, and sea constitute 90% of what lures visitors to the island, but when the untoward urge for activity strikes, Barbados offers a number of worthwhile alternatives.

BOATING Most hotels have Sunfish, Sailfish, and/or Hobie Cats for loan or rent right on the beach, and most can book sailing yachts for day and party cruising. Individual charters, skippered or bareboat, aren't easy to arrange on the spur of the moment; but ask your hotel travel desk, or call the commodore at the *Barbados Cruising Club* (phone: 426-4434). From January through May, the *Barbados Cruising Club* and the *Barbados Yacht Club* (phone: 427-1125) sponsor frequent regattas. For a truly breathtaking underwater view of the coral reefs, make reservations on the submarine *Atlantis* (see *Sea Excursions*).

CRICKET Inscrutable to most US spectators, it ranks as the number one sport and national passion, with Barbados fielding championship teams at both West Indian and World Test Match levels. The *Advocate* carries match schedules in season (June through January). Though the sport is played on several fields throughout the island, the main one is *Kensington Oval* (Fontabelle, St. Michael; phone: 436-1397).

CYCLING *M. A. Williams Bicycle Rentals* in Hastings (phone: 427-3955) rents bikes, as does *Fun Seekers* (Main Rd., Rockley, Christ Church; phone: 435-6852).

GOLF Barbados boasts what many feel is the finest fairway in the Caribbean.

TOP TEE-OFF SPOTS

Royal Westmoreland Golf & Country Club This new 18-hole course is swiftly transforming Barbados into one of the Caribbean's premier golf destinations. The showpiece of a 480-acre residential country club on Barbados's windswept west coast, the course is already being acclaimed as the finest work of master golf architect Robert Trent Jones Jr., even before the third nine holes open in 1997.

The hilly course was constructed on the site of a former sugar-cane plantation and coral stone quarry. The quarry is in play on five holes, but the crowning achievement here is the sixth hole, where players hit the drive up to a beautiful gully-shaped fairway. Aside from the distraction of the spectacular scenery, other out-of-the-ordinary hazards abound: The steady westerly trade winds were carefully taken into account to create different ways to play the approach shots, and on the third hole wild green monkeys have been known to scamper out of the jungle and quizzically tamper with your ball (if you're lucky, sometimes they'll leave it in a slightly better position). Throughout, the greens have great rhythm, and after a challenging round of play, the last hole plays gracefully downhill to the magnificent clubhouse. Twelve miles from *Grantley Adams International Airport* (phone: 422-4653; 800-283-8666; fax: 422-3021).

There is also an 18-hole, par 72 course at the *Sandy Lane* resort (phone: 432-1405 or 432-1145), as well as three nine-hole courses: at the *Rockley* resort (phone: 435-7873); at *Almond Beach Village* (see *Checking In*); and at *Belair* (phone: 423-4653) in St. Philip Parish, near *Marriott's Sam Lord's Castle* resort. All of the courses are open to the public; some, like the *Royal Westmoreland,* have special golf packages available in cooperation with various hotels.

HIKING The *Duke of Edinburgh Award Scheme* (a program of achievement awards for young people) and the *Heart Foundation of Barbados* in conjunction with the *Barbados National Trust* (phone: 436-9033) sponsor free five-mile guided hikes across Barbados every Sunday. The walks begin at 6 AM and 3:30 PM and take about three hours, with three paces to choose from: fast, medium, and stop-and-stare. *Highland Outdoor Tours* (phone: 438-8069 or 438-8070) offers full-day scenic safari hikes, which include a three-course planter's lunch. If you're keen on walking on your own, you might take the public bus to *Codrington College* and follow the abandoned railway right-of-way along the east coast to the *Atlantis* hotel at Tent Bay (a nice place for an island lunch); bus back from nearby Bathsheba.

HORSEBACK RIDING On hill trails and along beaches in St. Michael Parish and in the countryside around *Marriott's Sam Lord's Castle* in St. Philip, it's as scenic as it is athletic. English saddles predominate, but some western saddles are available. Contact *Brighton Riding Stables* for beach rides (St. Michael; phone: 425-9381). *Caribbean International Riding Centre* (St. Joseph; phone: 433-1453) offers one-hour countryside rides or a selection of other rides, including lunch at *Sunbury Plantation* house. Rates, with a guide, include transportation to and from hotels. *Highland Outdoor Tours* (see *Hiking,* above) offers a guided horseback version of their day-long hikes.

SNORKELING AND SCUBA DIVING The *Eastern Caribbean Diving Association* is having a big impact on the development of diving on the island. In addition to assisting with the operation of a decompression chamber (open 24 hours daily; phone: 427-8819), the association is involved in marine conservation, and was instrumental in establishing minimum standards for safe operating by scuba diving shops. Reefs off the west and south coasts make intriguing day-trip destinations. There's some beach diving on the island, and guided boat excursions seldom take more than 15 to 30 minutes to reach the dive site. Visit the coral reef of the three-zoned (for scientific research; for snorkeling, scuba, and glass-bottom boat trips; for swimming, skiing, sailing, and water sports) *Folkstone National Marine Reserve, Park, and Marine Museum* at Holetown (phone: 422-2314). For experienced divers, the deliberately sunk freighter *Stavronikita* beyond the reef is an added attraction, offering an opportunity for some fabulous underwater photography. The island has a total of five sunken ships that divers may explore. Some hotels have their own diving facilities. Check *Dive Boat Safari* at the *Hilton* (Needham's Point; phone: 427-4350); *Blue Reef Watersports* at *Royal Pavilion/Glitter Bay* (phone: 422-3133); *Shades of Blue* at the *Coral Reef Club* (phone: 422-3215) and *Willie's Water Sports* (Holetown; phone: 432-5980), which also has locations at *Almond Beach Village,* the *Colony Club,* and *Cobblers Cove* (see *Checking In* for all three). Other dive operations include *The Dive Shop* (Aquatic Gap; phone: 426-9947); *Jolly Roger Watersports* at the *Sunset Crest Club* (near Holetown; phone: 432-7090); and two *PADI* five-star training facilities—*Underwater Barbados,* near the *Coconut Court* hotel in Christ Church (phone: 426-0655), and *Exploresub Barbados* in St. Lawrence Gap (phone: 435-6542).

Snorkeling enthusiasts can borrow or rent masks and flippers at most west coast hotels. Also see *Sea Excursions.*

SPECTATOR SPORTS There's soccer from January through June throughout the island; polo July through February at *Holder's* in St. James; and horse racing on alternating Saturdays from January through April and from August through November at the *Garrison Savannah.* The latter features snack booths (fried flying fish is the big seller), steel bands, and all the trappings of a small carnival. Also see *Horse Races* in DIVERSIONS.

SPORT FISHING Not one of Barbados's best sporting attractions, but blue marlin, barracuda, dolphin, wahoo, tuna, and occasional cobia are caught in waters north and south of Barbados. Contact *Blue Jay Charters* (Waterfront Café, Bridgetown; phone: 422-2098) or the *Bill Fisher II* (*The Wharf,* Bridgetown; phone: 431-0741).

SQUASH The *Almond Beach Village* and *Rockley* resorts have two air conditioned squash courts each; the *Almond Beach Club* also has squash facilities (see *Checking In* for all three). Use is free to guests; others pay an hourly rate. Also try the *Barbados Squash Club* (Christ Church; phone: 427-7913).

SURFING Bajans do their surfing at Rockley Beach on the southwest coast between Worthing and St. Lawrence, at Enterprise Beach near Oistins, and at Bathsheba.

SWIMMING AND SUNNING While not very wide (exceptions: the *Hilton*'s broad expanse, shored up by stone jetties—for information, see *Tennis,* below; and Crane Beach, considered by some to be one of the world's best), beaches are pink-tinged coral sand. The majority of hotels command their own stretches of sand (though, technically, all island beaches are public); guests of those that don't are usually just across the road from a beach they can think of as theirs. Most are endowed with chaises, snack and drink bars— all the life-sustaining essentials—so there's not much beach hopping. Barbados has two coasts: the surf-pounded east and the serene west, where most hotels are. Western waters are so clear and buoyant that even real swimming seems to cause unnecessary splashing; you tend to float a lot and/or paddle about on float boards provided by hotels. If you're west-based, you ought to try to make it to the east coast at least once—if only to view the drama of the Atlantic surf. There's swimming on the broad-beached eastern shoreline northwest from Bathsheba, but no regular life-guard service; don't try it alone. *Marriott's Sam Lord's Castle* and the *Crane Beach* hotel (see *Checking In* for both) offer wave-bathing that's safer, with lifeguards on duty.

TENNIS The *Almond Beach Village, Casuarina Beach Club, Crane Beach, Divi Southwinds Beach, Ginger Bay, Marriott's Sam Lord's Castle,* and *Rockley* hotels all have courts, as does the *Hilton* (Needham's Point; phone: 426-0200; fax: 436-8946). *Sandy Lane* not only has courts and pros in attendance, but a setup suitable for exhibition matches. The four courts at the *Sunset Crest Club* near Holetown (phone: 432-1309) are lighted, as are those at *Sam Lord's, Almond Beach Village, Rockley,* and *Divi Southwinds Beach.* Most hotels charge hourly rates for court time. (Unless an address or telephone number is given, see *Checking In* for details about the hotels.) Court time is more expensive at the *Paragon Tennis Club* (Dalkeith's Hill, Brittons Hill, St. Michael; phone: 427-2054). For the best bargain, try the government's grass court at the *Garrison Savannah* (phone: 427-1444).

WATER SKIING Skiing is best on calm western waters. If your hotel doesn't have its own setup, they'll make arrangements with the nearest facility—possibly *Blue Reef Watersports* at *Glitter Bay, Jolly Roger Watersports* at the *Sunset Crest Club,* or *Willie's Water Sports* (see *Snorkeling and Scuba Diving, above,* for all three).

WINDSURFING Many beach hotels offer equipment and instruction. *Club Mistral Barbados* (Benson-on-Sea, Maxwell, Christ Church; phone: 428-7277); *Silver Rock* (Silver Sands Beach, Christ Church; phone: 428-2866); and *Jolly Roger Watersports* (see *Snorkeling and Scuba Diving,* above) also offer rentals and instruction.

NIGHTLIFE

When the sun goes down, even the most laid-back visitor may give in to the temptation to "jump up" (dance) into the beckoning Barbadian night. During the winter season, the larger hotels, particularly *Marriott's Sam Lord's Castle* (see *Checking In*) and the *Hilton* (Needham's Point; phone: 426-0200), feature elaborate entertainment. Steel bands and calypso singers are showcased at various nightspots and hotels around the island. Among the most popular island bands, the *Merrymen, Full Swing, Krosfyah, Spice, Jade, Coalition, Splashband, Square One, Second Avenue,* and *T.L.C.* rank highest; watch the local papers for when and where they'll be performing. The *Plantation Restaurant and Garden Theater* (St. Lawrence Rd., Christ Church; phone: 428-5048) hosts the popular *Barbados by Night* variety show on Wednesdays and Fridays, as well the *Plantation Tropical Spectacular* on Saturday nights.

Those with stout hearts and cast-iron stomachs can dance at sea aboard the *Jolly Roger*'s *Sundowner Calypso Cruise* or the slightly more sedate *Bajan Queen* (see *Sea Excursions*). On land, clubs for the energetic include the *Warehouse* (above the *Waterfront Café;* phone: 436-2897) and *Harbour Lights* (Upper Bay St.; phone: 436-7225), both in Bridgetown. In St. Lawrence Gap, try *After Dark* (phone: 435-6547) or *Captain's Carvery at the Ship Inn* (see *Eating Out*), both on the main road. Clubs in Barbados generally charge admission.

The assortment of British-style pubs on the island includes *Limers* (St. Lawrence Gap; phone: 435-6554); the *Coach House* (Paynes Bay, St. James; phone: 432-1163); the *Boatyard* (Lower Bay St., Carlisle Bay; 436-2622), a nautical hangout; and the *Bamboo Beach Bar* (St. James; phone: 432-0910). Baxter's Road in Bridgetown never seems to close—traditional Saturday night strolls up and down its food stall–lined length provide a real taste of Bajan nightlife; these days, however, fewer tourists venture out here, since shady activities seem to be on the rise.

Best on the Island

CHECKING IN

Barbados hotels are among the pleasantest, prettiest, and most plentiful (140 establishments with over 12,000 beds) in the Caribbean. With their sea views, gardens, beaches, and relaxed atmosphere, staying in one is like being the house guest of rather well-off friends. In summer, a number of establishments offer top-of-the-line elegance and comfort at bargain-basement prices. More moderately priced south coast apartment hotels that ask $80 to $110 European Plan (EP, meaning without meals) daily for two between December 15 and *Easter* tend to be either older places or newer hotels with small rooms designed to handle a continuous stream of charter groups. Suites and apartments with kitchenettes—especially those on the southern shores of Christ Church—often make up in the reasonableness of their cost what they lack in comfort and/or style, but the tasteful-though-barefoot alternative really doesn't exist. Villa suites, apartments (quite a few in hotels), and rental cottages with their own cooking facilities (from $275 a week in summer, about $400 and *way* up in winter) do offer some savings potential. The tourism authority issues seasonal lists of guesthouse, apartment, and cottage rentals and rates.

All-inclusive resorts are becoming more popular in Barbados, offering guests good value at an up-front price, with meals, liquor and soft drinks, sports, some nightly entertainment, airport transfers, and all taxes and tips included in the nightly room rate. Some also offer many more extras in their one-price-covers-all fee. As a rule, these resorts have a three-night minimum stay. The *Elegant Resorts of Barbados,* a group of eight luxurious and very expensive hotels, offers guests a dine-around program among all their hotel restaurants. Reservations for all resorts not listing a toll-free reservations number below can be made through the US central reservations number of the *Barbados Hotel and Tourism Association* (phone: 800-462-2526).

For a double room in winter, the places described below as very expensive cost $360 or more (sometimes *much* more, but meals are generally included); expensive hotels cost $190 to $230 without meals, and between $275 and $360 with breakfast and dinner (Modified American Plan, or MAP); places in the moderate category charge $130 to $180 without meals; and inexpensive places ask $80 to $120 per night. The Modified American Plan can generally be added for about $45 per person per day. A number of hotels offer only MAP rates during the winter season, but several offer dine-around plans that allow guests to eat at the restaurants of other area hotels. All hotel and rental rates are subject to a 5% government tax and a 10% service charge. Unless otherwise noted, hotel rooms have air conditioning, private baths, TV sets, and telephones. All telephone numbers are in the 809 area code unless otherwise indicated.

ST. JAMES

VERY EXPENSIVE

Almond Beach Club Barbados's premier all-inclusive resort (along with *Almond Beach Village,* below) offers a great value, even though it's in our "very expensive" category. There are 151 guestrooms overlooking the beach or one of three freshwater pools, a fitness center, squash and tennis courts, a complete water sports center, two restaurants, and four bars. All meals and drinks (including alcoholic beverages), water sports, live nightly entertainment, island tours, taxes, tips, and airport departure transfers are included in the rate. Guests also have the option, at no extra charge, of dining at several Bajan restaurants. Children under six are not allowed. Vauxhall (phone: 432-7840; 800-4-ALMOND; fax: 432-2115).

Coral Reef Club Family-owned and run with a personal touch, this resort on 12 beautifully landscaped acres offers 81 cottages and suites, all with refrigerators and balconies or patios with sea views (you'll find a selection of paperback books, but don't look for a TV set). The lobby and lounge are open-air and very tropical, and the lovely restaurant overlooks the sea and gardens. There's also a pool and water sports facilities; guests may use the two lighted tennis courts at the *Sandpiper Inn* across the road (see below). In winter, rates include breakfast and dinner; from April through mid-November EP rates (no meals included) are also available. Guests may choose the optional dine-around plan. Closed June and July. St. James Beach, Holetown (phone: 422-2372; 800-223-1108, 800-525-4800, or 800-5-ELEGANT; fax: 422-1776).

Discovery Bay Built in the style of a classic plantation house, this beachfront property, sister to Antigua's *Hawksbill Beach* resort, boasts 84 recently remodeled rooms set among lush, landscaped grounds. Also available are a two-bedroom suite overlooking the gardens and a three-bedroom villa set just 70 yards from the sea. Use of the water sports facilities, two tennis courts, and a pool, plus full breakfast and dinner daily are included in the rate. St. James Beach, Holetown (phone: 432-1301; 800-233-6510; fax: 432-2553).

Glitter Bay This quietly splendid condominium complex, part of the Pemberton chain, exudes luxury and chic in its modern Mediterranean design, flowered landscaping, palms, and half-mile-long sweep of white beach and blue sea. Its focal point is the Great House, built in the style of a Venetian palazzo by shipping magnate Sir Edward Cunard, who lived here in the 1930s. There are 29 rooms and 31 suites, all with a terrace or balcony (TV sets are available for an extra charge, but there's only one channel) and ceiling fans (in addition to air conditioning); suites have full kitchens. Included in the rate is afternoon tea, as well as use of the excellent water sports and boating facilities, a fitness center, and two lighted tennis courts; golf on the nearby *Royal Westmoreland*'s 18-hole championship course and riding can be arranged for an additional charge. There are also two pools (one for children), a shopping arcade, and two restaurants, including the excellent *Piperade* (see *Eating Out*). Guests also may opt to dine at the *Royal Pavilion*'s two restaurants (see below). Hwy. 1, Porters (phone: 422-4111; 800-283-8666; fax: 422-3940).

Royal Pavilion A sister of *Glitter Bay,* this resort set amid 10 acres of tropical gardens and fronted by a half-mile-long beach has taken its place as one of Barbados's top resorts—known for its beautiful grounds, relaxed yet sophisticated atmosphere, and chic clientele. The complex boasts 72 balconied, oceanfront suites and a three-bedroom villa, and amenities include complimentary water sports; tennis on two lighted courts; a pool; elegant duty-free shops; two restaurants and bars, including the refined *Palm Terrace* (see *Eating Out*); and a fitness center. Golf on the *Royal Westmoreland*'s

18-hole course can be arranged at reduced rates, and guests also may dine next door at *Glitter Bay.* Hwy. 1 (phone: 422-4444 or 422-5555; 800-283-8666; fax: 422-3940).

Sandy Lane Managed by the Forte Hotels group, this classic resort is set on a 380-acre former sugar plantation complete with a carefully preserved original façade. Most of its 90 sumptuous rooms, each with a patio or balcony, overlook a half-mile-long crescent-shaped beach protected by sturdy mahogany trees. There are also 30 oversize ocean-view luxury units equipped with every modern comfort, five restaurants and bars, a saltwater pool, five tennis courts, a fitness center, and an 18-hole golf course. Rates include two meals a day, a daily program of activities for children, water sports, and greens fees. Guests are pampered with everything from a Rolls-Royce waiting at the airport to fluffy monogrammed bathrobes. Less costly packages are offered off-season. Hwy. 1 (phone: 432-1311; 800-225-5843 or 800-742-4276; fax: 432-2954).

EXPENSIVE

Colony Club Centered around a rambling, coral stone house, this property offers pleasant service, attractive public rooms with sea views, and 76 villa rooms (none with TV sets) in the garden and near the beach. Breakfast and lunch are served on a lovely waterside terrace, allowing for stay-all-day beach life. There's also a pool. Rates include two meals a day plus a dine-around option. Good summer packages are available. St. James Beach (phone: 422-2335; 800-223-6510; fax: 422-1726).

Sandpiper Inn This pleasant little beachfront resort, sister to the *Coral Reef Club* (above), offers 45 rooms, suites, and one- and two-bedroom apartments. All have balconies or patios and amenities such as refrigerators, hair dryers, safes, even toasters; the apartments also feature full kitchens. None of the accommodations has a TV set, and only the apartments have telephones. There's also a restaurant and bar, a pool, and two lighted tennis courts. Guests may choose a dine-around plan, which offers the opportunity to sample the fare at a number of other participating resorts. Children are welcome, except during February. St. James Beach (phone: 422-2251; 800-223-1108; fax: 422-1776).

MODERATE

Crystal Cove Formerly the *Barbados Beach Village,* this popular beachfront resort has 88 recently renovated rooms (61 double, 27 suites with kitchenettes), two restaurants and bars, three pools, two tennis courts, and entertainment most nights. Guests also may take advantage of the facilities at any of the resort's sister hotels—the *Colony Club, Coconut Creek,* and *Tamarind Cove*—all serviced by complimentary water taxi. Management warns that the layout of units is inconvenient for disabled travelers. Hwy. 1 (phone: 425-1440; 800-223-6510; fax: 424-0996).

ST. PETER

Almond Beach Village Formerly *Heywood's,* this resort has been completely refurbished and is now the most tastefully luxurious all-inclusive resort on the island's scenic northern end. Sister property to the *Almond Beach Club* in St. James, it comprises seven handsome buildings (a total of 288 rooms and suites) set among palms and gardens on an old sugar plantation site. The resort offers a plethora of pools (eight in all), a mile-long white beach with all water sports, five lighted tennis courts, two air conditioned squash courts, a fitness center, planned activities for children, and a nine-hole golf course. There are also two restaurants and bars and an appealing disco; guests may also choose a dine-around option, and are free to use facilities at the *Almond Beach Club.* Speightstown (phone: 422-4900; 800-4-ALMOND; fax: 422-1581).

Cobblers Cove A small, gracious hostelry made special and charming by little touches and attention to detail, this member of the Relais & Châteaux group offers 41 recently renovated luxury suites, each with a balcony or patio, surrounding a pretty, pink main house, which was once a private home. The beach (one of the best coves on Barbados), pool, and bar are within steps of each other. All suites have kitchenettes, but most guests prefer to dine on the terrace, where they can bask in tropical breezes while enjoying excellent continental cooking or Bajan specialties. There are also water sports facilities and a lighted tennis court. Winter rates are MAP. Good summer packages are available. Closed September through October 15. Road View, Speightstown (phone: 422-2291; 800-742-4276; fax: 422-1460).

INEXPENSIVE

Sandridge These 52 balconied hotel rooms, studios, and one-bedroom suites (some are duplexes; some have kitchenettes and TV sets), are all by the sea and surrounded by gardens, with a pool, an appealing beach bar, a restaurant, and a helpful staff. Road View (phone: 422-2361; fax: 422-1965).

ST. PHILIP

EXPENSIVE

Marriott's Sam Lord's Castle The old rascal's elegant mansion—beautifully kept and thoughtfully screened from the 234-room complex—is the centerpiece of this elegant resort. The hotel buildings, three restaurants, three pools, numerous sports, and mile-long beach are located just through the trees beyond. Surf swimming, lighted tennis, and evening entertainment are big features. Horseback riding is available nearby. To our mind, choicest of the resort's rooms are in the "Castle" (furnished with antiques and four-poster beds) and the sleek buildings closest to the sea. Long Bay (phone: 423-7350; 800-228-9290; fax: 423-7350).

MODERATE

Crane Beach What once was an impossibly run-down, old hotel is now one of the island's more appealing properties. Its site, though remote, is spectacular, overlooking the Atlantic, with a stone pool sunk into the cliff edge, a surf beach partially protected by Cobbler's Reef, four tennis courts, and an excellent restaurant specializing in fresh seafood. The 18 rooms and antiques-decorated apartments (all with four-poster beds, kitchenettes, tiled baths, and scenic vistas) may be the island's handsomest. None of the units is air conditioned or has a TV set. Crane Beach (phone: 423-6220; fax: 423-5343).

Ginger Bay This small, intimate place has 16 suites on the Atlantic Ocean, each with a refrigerator, but no air conditioning or TV set. There's also a pool with a Jacuzzi and *Ginger's,* a good outdoor restaurant. Guests get to the beach through a cave on the grounds. Crane Beach (phone: 423-5810; 800-223-9815; fax: 423-6629).

ST. MICHAEL

VERY EXPENSIVE

Sandals Barbados This exclusive, couples-only beachside property has 178 spacious rooms complete with such amenities as hair dryers, safes, and satellite TV. Facilities include two pools, two Jacuzzis, a fitness center, three restaurants, a disco, and a piano bar. The rate includes all land and water sports, meals, drinks (including alcoholic beverages), nightly entertainment, daily activities, plus airport transfers, taxes, and gratuities. About 2½ miles from Bridgetown (phone: 424-0888; 800-SANDALS; fax: 424-0889).

EXPENSIVE

Island Inn Originally part of a garrison where British troops were based, this small, elegant, 23-room, all-inclusive inn has been restored with original stone ballast work. Furnished with antiques and reproductions, it offers elegant surroundings, two bars, a restaurant, a pool, and conference facilities. While not located on the beach, the hotel provides shuttle bus service to one nearby. The rate includes sailing, windsurfing, and snorkeling as well as all meals, some beverages (soft drinks, wine, beer, and rum punch), afternoon tea, and a two-hour cruise. Aquatic Gap (phone: 436-6393; 800-742-4276; fax: 437-8035).

MODERATE

Grand Barbados This high-rise beachfront resort with 133 rooms offers wonderful service and attention to detail. All rooms have satellite TV, hair dryers, and mini-bars; the two executive floors offer additional amenities. The resort also has a pool, complimentary water sports, and two restaurants, one of which features live entertainment nightly. Carlisle Bay, Bridgetown (phone: 426-0890; 800-223-9815; fax: 436-9823).

CHRIST CHURCH

EXPENSIVE

Divi Southwinds Beach Here's a smart, 20-acre hotel-condominium complex with three pools, including a good-looking central pool with an elevated, open-air restaurant; tennis courts; a mini-casino with slot machines; and its own beach club (with bar) on St. Lawrence Beach just across the road. There are 160 units, ranging from pleasantly stylish rooms with king-size beds to one- and two-bedroom duplex suites with living rooms, kitchens, and balconies. St. Lawrence Gap (phone: 428-7181; 800-367-3484; fax: 428-4674).

Rockley A country club atmosphere prevails at this all-inclusive resort, which features 228 smart studios and townhouse apartments scattered in clusters around a nine-hole golf course in the hills. Also on the premises are seven pools, five tennis courts (lighted, with a pro), two squash courts, a boutique, a bar, a restaurant, and a disco. At the beach, a three-minute shuttle ride away, there's a beach club with water sports facilities, a restaurant, and a bar. Use of all the facilities and all meals, drinks, taxes, and tips are included in the room rate. Worthing (phone: 435-7880; 800-223-9815; fax: 435-8015).

MODERATE

Casuarina Beach Club This immensely popular casual resort has 129 rooms (some with kitchenettes), a good-size pool, two tennis courts, and a choice of water sports. Rooms are not furnished with TV sets, although they may be rented for an extra fee. There's also a TV room with satellite reception. St. Lawrence Gap (phone: 428-3600; 800-742-4276; fax: 428-1970).

Seafoam Haciendas These 12 modest but pleasant two-bedroom apartments are especially good for large families, since they can be interconnected. The apartments do not have telephones or TV sets, but they do feature fully equipped kitchens, including microwave ovens and coolers to bring to the beach. Cooking and babysitting services are available. A quiet stretch of Worthing Beach is right outside. Worthing (phone: 435-7380; 800-8-BAR-BADOS; fax: 435-7384).

INEXPENSIVE

Coral Sands This cozy complex of seven two-bedroom apartments and one three-bedroom villa is set right on the beach. The accommodations all have full kitchens (but no TV sets or air conditioning); maid service is included. There's no pool, but the beach, with a wide array of water sports, is only steps away. Monthly rentals are available. Worthing (phone: 428-9828; fax: 428-8119).

Golden Sands A family-oriented hotel with 27 apartments furnished with satellite TV and fully equipped kitchenettes. There's a pool and a restaurant on the property, while the beach is just across the street. Maxwell (phone: 428-8051; 800-742-4276; fax: 428-3897).

EATING OUT

Native Bajan cookery is an interesting blend of Caribbean and continental influences. The tourism authority's emblem, a flying fish, is also the national dish, served broiled, baked, deep-fried, stuffed, and stewed. Delicate and moist, it tastes delicious. Other favorite seafoods: sea eggs (white sea-urchin roe, often mixed with bread crumbs and spices—available only September through December), crab backs, langouste (lobster), dolphin fish, and kingfish. Most meat (except goat and some poultry) is imported. Bajans also fancy pudding (sausage stuffed with mashed sweet potato and spices, with or without blood added); pepper pot (beef and vegetable stew); souse (a mélange of pig parts pickled with onion, cucumber, and pepper); and more generally appealing side dishes like *coo coo* (cornmeal and okra), *conkie* (sweetened pumpkin and coconut), and a *Christmas* specialty called *jug jug* (cornmeal with pigeon peas). Among island-grown fruits: pawpaw (papaya), soursop (luscious in ice cream), avocado, banana, and coconut (super in milk sherbet). Guava is another—stewed, made into preserves, or cooked down and cooled into "cheese."

Mauby, a nonalcoholic liquor brewed from bark, sugar, and spices, is sold down by the Careenage, in neighborhood bars, and is often made and served in Bajan homes; it is spicy and pleasant (if you like liqueurs, you'll probably like it). Falernum, brewed from sugar, is a specialty liqueur. But Barbados rum—the world's smoothest, richest, and best—has no rivals. It turns up in punches, mixed with soda or tonic, and in daiquiris. The "rum snap" and rum cocktail are traditional drinks. Mount Gay brand has fueled generations of yachtsmen, and is sold in a variety of grades from everyday Eclipse to superior, oldest, and darkest Sugar Cane Brandy. Cockspur is another excellent brand. Generally, prices on bottles to take home are half what they cost in the US.

Most of the island's best restaurants fall under one of two headings—continental and expensive, or Bajan and not so—although some combine the two. It's easy to run up a check for $75 or more for two at *La Maison,* while a feast on a pair of flying fish at the *Ocean View* will cost only about $15 per couple. Lunches are even less expensive. Dinner for two (not including wine, drinks, tax, or tip) at those places listed as expensive will cost $65 or more; at a moderate restaurant, dinner will run $30 to $50; and at an inexpensive place, from $15 to $25. Unless otherwise noted all restaurants listed below are open for lunch and dinner. All telephone numbers are in the 809 area code unless otherwise indicated.

ST. MICHAEL

E X P E N S I V E

Brown Sugar In a Bajan home behind the *Island Inn,* its smart setting is an ideal place to sample Bajan specialties like pumpkin soup, pepper pot, and soursop ice cream. There's a very popular noon buffet with traditional Caribbean dishes. Closed weekend lunch. Reservations necessary. Major credit cards accepted. Off Hilton Rd., Aquatic Gap (phone: 426-7684).

M O D E R A T E

Waterfront Café Overlooking the yachts moored in the Careenage, this hot spot attracts an eclectic crowd of sailors, tourists, and well-heeled residents. The menu includes local dishes (flying fish, pepper pot), vegetarian entrées, and innovative appetizer platters, such as "fish melts"—batter-fried flying-fish roe. There's also live entertainment nightly (usually jazz, but also guitar, piano, and Dixieland). Closed Sundays. Reservations necessary Thursday nights, when jazz bands play. Major credit cards accepted. Cavans Lane, Bridgetown (phone: 427-0093).

CHRIST CHURCH

E X P E N S I V E

Da Luciano Italian food is served in this handsomely restored historic mansion. Try the *misto mare* (mixed marinated seafood). Open daily for dinner only. Reservations advised. Major credit cards accepted. Hwy. 7, Staten, Hastings (phone: 427-5518).

Ile de France Excellent French fare served in a garden setting. Open for dinner only; closed Mondays. Reservations advised. Major credit cards accepted. In the *Windsor Arms Hotel,* Hastings (phone: 435-6869).

Josef's Its continental menu rates high marks for unusually good meat dishes (veal Cordon Bleu and Viennoise, filet béarnaise), as well as kingfish Caribe, dolphin meunière, and flying fish creole. Closed for lunch on weekends. Reservations necessary. MasterCard and Visa accepted. Waverly House, St. Lawrence Gap (phone: 435-6541).

Pisces Delicious fish and seafood in a small, pretty house on the shore at St. Lawrence Gap. Recommended: flying fish in wine sauce, snapper Caribe, nutmeg ice cream. Open daily for dinner only. Reservations necessary. Major credit cards accepted. Hwy. 7, St. Lawrence Gap, Christ Church (phone: 435-6564).

M O D E R A T E

Captain's Carvery at the Ship Inn A nautical eatery nestled next to a cozy pub, it features a Bajan buffet at lunch and a variety of fish dishes, including local lobster, at dinner. There's also a salad bar, featuring fresh hot bread. Open daily. Reservations necessary. Major credit cards accepted. St. Lawrence Gap, Christ Church (phone: 435-6961).

Flamboyant This appealing, 80-year-old little Bajan house on the south coast road has a unique menu of European and island dishes. Run by a husband and wife, it has a friendly atmosphere. We especially recommend the rum punches. Open daily for dinner only. Reservations advised. Major credit cards accepted. Hastings Rd. (phone: 427-5588).

Ocean View A pretty green and white seaside dining room, it has a limited—but very good—Bajan and continental menu (savory soup, crisp flying fish). Open daily. Reservations necessary. Major credit cards accepted. In the *Ocean View* hotel, Hastings (phone: 427-7821).

Witch Doctor A casual place featuring jungle decor and tasty island cookery. Favorites are split pea and pumpkin soup, fish fritters, chicken *piri-piri* (marinated in lime, garlic, and chili, then baked), and ice cream with home-made rum-raisin topping. Open daily for dinner only. Reservations advised. MasterCard and Visa accepted. St. Lawrence Gap (phone: 435-6581).

ST. JAMES

EXPENSIVE

La Cage aux Folles In palatial surroundings, this popular dining spot features French, Chinese, and Caribbean fare, with dishes such as sesame prawn pâté, tournedos Rossini, and fresh fruit curries. Open for dinner only; closed Tuesdays. Reservations necessary; reserve *way* ahead. Major credit cards accepted. *Summerland Great House,* Prospect Bay (phone: 424-2424).

Carambola Dine by candlelight on a seaside cliff at this open-air restaurant with a tropical atmosphere. The prize-winning chef presents a menu of French and Thai specialties. There's an extensive wine list, featuring mostly French vintages. Open for dinner only; closed Sundays. Reservations necessary. Major credit cards accepted. Derricks (phone: 432-0832).

The Fathoms Dine outside on the beachfront deck, or in the airy, wood-and-tile rooms at this surfside spot. The menu focuses on seafood prepared with interesting sauces, such as Szechuan-style dorado, and the servings are ample. (But try to save room for the first-rate desserts.) Exotic tropical drinks are also featured. Open daily. Reservations advised for dinner. Major credit cards accepted. Payne's Bay (phone: 432-2568).

Koko's This casual eatery is a real find, offering adventurous "nu-Bajan" cuisine. Try the *koq-ka-doo* (chicken stuffed with banana and rum sauce) or the shrimp kristo (sailing in little *christophine*—a kind of squash—boats). Open daily for dinner only. Reservations advised. Major credit cards accepted. Overlooking the sea at Prospect (phone: 424-4557).

La Maison This restaurant is ensconced in a lovely old Bajan house with tables set right by the water. Try such delectable entrées as marinated red snapper with raspberry sauce, or thin slices of baby veal in a creamy herb sauce. But save room for one of the decadent desserts, such as chocolate cake topped with mousse, ice cream, and chocolate sauce. Closed Mondays. Reservations necessary. Major credit cards accepted. Holetown (phone: 432-1156).

The Mews Continental fare and French wines served in a quaint garden setting. Specialties include tuna carpaccio and kingfish cooked in anchovy butter. Open daily. Reservations advised. Major credit cards accepted. Second St., Holetown (phone: 432-1122).

Palm Terrace The ambience steals the show at this restaurant—a terrace set beneath arches and open to the sea, with piano music played softly in the background (most evenings in season). There are also good continental and Bajan specialties, such as Caribbean shrimp and mango salad, and blackened flying fish. It's a wonderful place to take tea, and Wednesday nights there's a buffet and cabaret show. Open for afternoon tea and dinner only; closed Sundays. Reservations advised. Major credit cards accepted. At the *Royal Pavilion* hotel, Hwy. 1, St. James (phone: 422-4444 or 422-5555; fax: 422-3940).

Piperade Elegant European and island fare served in a romantic island setting. Try the warm artichoke heart and snow crab gratin or the citrus-roasted chicken with basil. Music accompanies your meal. Open daily for breakfast, lunch, and dinner. Reservations advised. Major credit cards accepted. In the garden of the *Glitter Bay* hotel, Hwy. 1, St. James (phone: 422-4111).

Raffles Easily the west coast's coziest, most exotic restaurant, it doesn't stop at creating the best in island atmosphere, but also delivers some of Barbados's best food, including specialties such as Bajan blackened fish and coconut pie. Given such attributes, it's a highly popular place. Open for dinner only; closed Sundays. Reservations necessary. Major credit cards accepted. First St., Holetown (phone: 432-6557).

MODERATE

Coach House An attractive gathering place, popular with locals as well as visitors for its informal English pub atmosphere, simple, excellent food, and a reasonable fixed-price Caribbean/continental menu of prime meat and fresh fish. Dine inside, or order from the more limited bar menu and take a table on the terrace. Live entertainment heats things up at night, and those so inclined can dance. Check the local listings. Closed Saturday lunch. Reservations necessary for dinner. Major credit cards accepted. Payne's Bay near Sandy Lane (phone: 432-1163).

Nico's A cozy restaurant and wine bar located on the second floor of an elegant townhouse. Choose from an excellent selection of wines and champagnes to accompany such dishes as fresh lobster in garlic butter, French cheese and pâté platters, soups, and salads. Open daily. Reservations unnecessary. Major credit cards accepted. Second St., Holetown (phone: 432-6386).

ELSEWHERE ON THE ISLAND

MODERATE

Kingsley Club Once a plantation owners' private club, it's now a charming little inn offering splendid four-course, prix fixe lunches. Specialties include split pea and pumpkin soup, fresh grilled fish, baked yam casserole, and sinfully good coconut meringue pie. Open daily for breakfast, lunch, and early dinner. Reservations advised. Major credit cards accepted. Near Bathsheba, in Cattlewash-on-Sea (phone: 433-9422).

INEXPENSIVE

Atlantis Enid Maxwell sets out one of the island's best Sunday brunches, a buffet laden with Bajan treats such as dolphin, flying fish, turtle steaks, pumpkin fritters, pickled breadfruit, and rum-soaked desserts—all made from scratch in her family-staffed kitchen. Open daily. Reservations necessary for Sunday brunch. American Express accepted. Overlooking Tent Bay near Bathsheba, St. Joseph (phone: 433-9445).

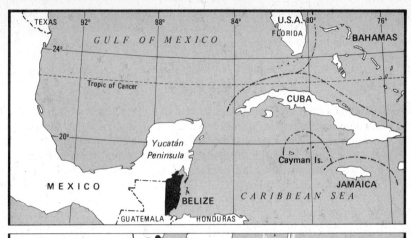

BELIZE

Belize

South of Mexico's Yucatán Peninsula and northeast of Guatemala is the small, wedge-shaped, developing country of Belize, formerly known as British Honduras. It's one of the few places in the Caribbean with literally hundreds of pristine, untouched islands. Even Ambergris Caye, the largest and most developed of these, has mile-long stretches of empty beach, perfect for sunning and swimming. Some of the world's best fishing can be enjoyed in the mangrove swamps and clear flat areas around the cays (pronounced *keys*), and the barrier reef—the longest in the Western Hemisphere and second longest in the world—ensures great diving.

But Belize is far more than the typical fun-in-the-sun, tropical Caribbean getaway. Primarily English-speaking, it offers US visitors the opportunity to explore a Central American country with relative ease, undisturbed by the burgeoning commercialism and crime that plague other Central American tourist destinations. Not far from the beach are dense jungle, majestic karstic mountains, and rain forest. And its history is just as fascinating as its geography. This tiny country has been a melting pot for immigrants from Africa, the Caribbean, Mexico, Central America, Europe, and Asia for 300 years; British pirates, former slaves from East India, and Yucatán refugees from the Caste War all have left their mark here. However, Belize can trace its native culture and ancestry to well before that—to the mysterious ancient Maya, whose immense cities still stand throughout the region. Even while European settlements were being established on Belize's coast, Maya towns existed undetected just a few miles inland, protected by the thick jungle that only the Indians knew how to penetrate with ease. And while many of the early European settlements have been long since washed away, the mammoth religious structures of the Maya—their great temples and pyramids—endure.

Although Spain had claimed this part of the New World for itself, the area's lack of gold, the fierce resistance of the Maya, and the navigational hazards of the barrier reef kept its involvement here to a minimum. In fact, the first white men to colonize Belize were from Great Britain in the early 17th century—and even then only because they were shipwrecked off its coast.

These first British settlers discovered that Belize's swamps and jungles were rich in timber, and almost every type of fish in the Caribbean could be found feeding off the reef. The jungles also were full of game. Trade in logwood, which produces a dye, and then in lumber proved almost as profitable as pirating and, with slaves to supply the labor, were easier and safer.

English soldiers and sailors established logging camps here in the 1690s, and soon afterward Britain challenged Spain's claim to the area. The English government encouraged immigration, providing some limited financial and military support. By 1745, slaves accounted for 71% of the population, and by 1800 the number had risen to 86%. With the shift in economic activity from logwood to mahogany, more slaves, land, and capital were needed, and in 1787 the settlers began to pass a series of laws that soon resulted in a dozen settlers owning four-fifths of all the land.

Slavery was abolished here in 1838, but because most of the land was controlled by "mahogany lords," the freed men were forced to seek employment with their former masters, who passed a system of labor laws designed to keep workers under firm control. In addition, the practice of "advancing" wages bound workers to their employers by keeping them in debt. This system of land and labor control lasted into the middle of the 20th century.

Seeking the protection of the Commonwealth, the colony became British Honduras in 1862; at that time residents feared attacks by Spaniards and mestizos (people of mixed Spanish and Maya ancestry) from Mexico escaping the Caste War (1848–58), a conflict between Mexico's original Indian residents and Spanish colonists. Three years earlier, Great Britain and Guatemala had signed a treaty fixing the borders of Guatemala and Belize. However, boundary problems exist to this day, as Guatemala continues to claim that, as an inheritor of the Spanish lands in the area, it is entitled to Belizean territory. (In late 1991, Guatemala established diplomatic relations with Belize, and for the past several years the two countries have been negotiating a treaty to give Guatemala partial access to Belizean territorial waters in the Caribbean; at press time, a final agreement had not yet been reached. Guatemala has said that if this accord is signed, it will abandon its claim to the rest of the country, but Belizeans remain wary.)

Along with British immigration came the beginnings of a Caribbean influence. The earliest Caribbean immigration was involuntary—slaves brought from Jamaica in the early 1700s to work in the lumber industry. Since then, Belize has become a mosaic of ethnic groups, cultures, and customs. While the country's population was just 6,000 in 1840, it had jumped to over 25,000 by 1861; to 60,000 by 1942; and today stands at about 190,000. The main groups are mestizos; Creoles (people of mixed black and white heritage), who make up the majority of the population; and Garifuna (the progeny of escaped African slaves and Carib Indians). There also are a number of people of Spanish and East Indian descent, some Chinese and Arabs, and a small Mennonite community of European origin. The most recent immigrants are some 5,500 Salvadoran and Guatemalan refugees who have settled in Belize since the late 1980s, fleeing wars in their countries. After a slow process of evolution toward more representative government, a constitution written in 1964 provided total self-government for the first time. As early as 1961, the British government had made it plain that British Honduras (the name "Belize" was officially adopted in 1971) could become independent whenever it wished. However, because of a well-founded fear that without Britain's protection their country would soon be overrun by neighboring Guatemala, Belizeans chose to retain their British ties. After Britain agreed to retain a small protective military presence in the country, Belize declared itself an independent nation on September 21, 1981, and it has managed its own affairs with pride and enthusiasm ever since.

Belize guards its environment as fiercely as it does its freedom. More than 25 wildlife and archaeological reserves have been established in the past 10 years, including the 100,000-acre *Cockscomb Basin Wildlife Sanctuary,* the world's first and only jaguar preserve. One major strategy to reconcile the growing influx of visitors with the country's environmental needs is ecotourism, which encourages people to explore regions without harming the resident wildlife.

Today, it is still possible in Belize to drive along a breathtakingly beautiful mountain road or pause for a dip in a pristine river—and be the only one there. But unless ecotourism is successful, Belize probably will not remain an unspoiled destination much longer. More and more North Americans are discovering its lush, almost virgin coastline and its secluded Maya ruins. While not offering much in the way of creature comforts, Belize does promise adventure and the chance to experience one of the last vestiges of nature in the wild.

Belize At-a-Glance

FROM THE AIR

Belize is a patchwork of subtropical lowlands, marshes, and swamps, with mountains and forests to the west, and beaches, the massive barrier reef, and some 200 offshore cays and islands to the east. It is on the Caribbean coast of the Yucatán Peninsula, separated from Mexico in the north by the Río Hondo and from Guatemala to the southwest by the Sarstoon River. The tiny nation is only 184 miles north to south and 75 miles east to west at its widest point, a total of 9,000 square miles of landmass, one-third of which is used for farming and ranching. The rest is rugged jungle terrain, mountains, and swamps; 266 square miles of offshore cays; and about 300 miles of rivers.

The first view of Belize from the air is of the 185-mile-long barrier reef—second in size only to Australia's Great Barrier Reef. Interspersed are cays and islands of all sizes stretched like a chain set in the blue-green Caribbean Sea. The desolate swamps and deep jungles in the north, dotted with small towns and villages, gradually give rise to the vast Maya Mountains in the southwest. These are topped by Victoria Peak, which, at 3,680 feet, is the highest peak in the entire Cockscomb Mountain range. The country is traversed by a number of rivers: The New River runs parallel to the Río Hondo in the north, and there are several small rivers in the south. The Belize River originates in Guatemala and crosses the country's central region from west to east.

The country sits on a vast continental block of limestone that extends 800 miles north to south, and about 400 miles across. This ledge slopes at a downward angle, so that Belize City on the Caribbean coast is only 18 inches above sea level, and high water easily flows inland, causing bad flooding.

Most visitors will arrive at *Phillip S. W. Goldson International Airport,* 10 miles north of Belize City. Belize has some 190,000 inhabitants, of whom 60,000 live in Belize City. In addition to Belize City, there are seven towns (including Belmopan, the capital), and 160 villages and settlements of varying size. There is more jungle and mountain than rural or urban life, even including the resorts on the coast and the cays.

SPECIAL PLACES

BELIZE CITY Hot, humid, and an interesting mixture of British colonial architecture and small-town ambience, this community is the only real city in the country. It is filled with old, mostly wooden buildings and houses that give the entire place a tumbledown feel, the effect broken only occasionally by Victorian government buildings.

The most colorful things about the city are its street names: The Queen's Square uses animal names such as Antelope, Armadillo, and Seagull Streets; the Mesopotamia area has Middle Eastern names like Euphrates, Cairo, and Tigris; and the Caribbean Shores area relies on church figures for names.

The city's small business and shopping area is located on the few blocks on either side of the Belize Swing Bridge. On the southern side of the bridge are Albert and Queen Streets, which make up the commercial district, and Regent Street, which houses most of the government buildings. On Regent Street is *St. John's Cathedral.* Built between 1812 and 1826, it was the first Anglican church in Central America. A block away, on Southern Foreshore near the Swing Bridge, is the *Baron Bliss Institute,* dedicated to the multimillionaire who left $2 million to Belize in the 1920s; it contains carved stone monuments from the ancient Maya ceremonial center of *Caracol,* in the Maya Mountains. The institute's library is open to the public daily (phone: 2-77267).

Located on the northern side of the Swing Bridge is the Fort George neighborhood, the city's classiest area, with fine old plantation-style homes lining the waterfront. Standing center stage is the *Radisson Fort George* hotel (see *Checking In*), which opened in 1953. At the northeast end of the bridge is the *Paslow Building,* an interesting bit of colonial architecture. It contains the post office (phone: 2-72201), which in turn houses the *Belize Philatelic Bureau.* With drawings of wildlife, shells, historical events, the British royal family, and Belizean patriots, Belizean stamps are unusual and inexpensive mementos. Closed weekends. The nearby *Book Centre* (144 N. Front St.; phone: 2-77457) is a good source for American newspapers and magazines as well as books on Belizean history.

BELMOPAN The capital of Belize was carved out of the jungle in the late 1960s after Hurricane Hattie seriously damaged Belize City in 1961. It was occupied by the government in July 1970. At first, many of the Belizeans who worked in Belmopan commuted from Belize City, but over the years the town's population has grown to about 7,000, and now the capital has developed a personality of its own. Its *Assembly Building,* which dominates the government complex, was designed to represent a Maya temple. On Mondays, Wednesdays, and Fridays from 1:30 to 4 PM, the *Archaeology Commission* conducts guided tours through its vault, which houses a collection of artifacts from the country's archaeological sites. (There is no museum within the country.) Reservations are required at least two days in advance. Admission charge (phone: 8-22106).

GUANACASTE NATIONAL PARK About 2 miles outside Belmopan, at the juncture of the Western and Hummingbird Highways, this park offers 50 acres of forest. The name comes from the colossal guanacaste tree growing on the southwestern edge of the park; it rises to a height of about 400 feet, masked in huge orchids and bromeliads that cling to its branches like giant *Christmas* ornaments. Hundreds of other tree species thrive here, too, including the unusual mammee apple, bookut, and quamwood. Be sure to bring a swimsuit—a dip in the clean, bubbling Belize River is a must. Open daily. Donation suggested (no phone).

BELIZE ZOO In 1982, American biologist Sharon Matola started this zoo with a few primitive pens nestled among the trees. Today, it's an outstanding example of the habitat-style zoo, with more than 100 species of native animals residing in spacious patches of forest veiled in wire mesh. Pebbled paths pass the homes of howler monkeys, crocodiles, jaguars, marguays, king vultures, great black hawks, toucans, pacas, anteaters, and many other beautiful, exotic creatures. Matola, who still runs the zoo, implores visitors to respect the animals with clever, hand-painted wooden signs with messages such as "I'm a great black hawk, but guys who take shots at me are Great Big Turkeys!" Open daily. Admission charge. Take the Western Highway 30 miles west of Belize City, then look for the little wooden sign (no phone).

CAYO DISTRICT This area—Belize's wealthiest—stretches from just west of Belmopan to the Guatemalan border. Savvy adventurers are discovering the region's jungle lodges, guest ranches, Maya ruins, and picturesque byways. A popular day trip is to *Mountain Pine Ridge,* a national forest reserve encompassing hundreds of miles of natural pine, bald hills, orchids, wildlife, and rivulets. Its most famous attractions are the Hidden Valley Falls, which tumble 1,000 feet into the valley below; the inviting pools of the Rio On; and the spectacular Rio Frio Caves. There are 15 miles of roads to cover here, and a picnic should be the order of the day. All necessary facilities are available for travelers, campers, and day-trippers. The reserve is open daily; admission charge (no phone). You also can choose to stay in the area at the *Hidden Valley Inn* (see *Checking In*).

Some of Belize's most compelling scenery lies in Cayo at Spanish Lookout, where Mennonite farmlands cover the landscape. It's reached by a 6-mile trek over a very rocky, rutted road that angles north from the Western Highway west of Belmopan. You can see straw-hatted Mennonite farmers driving horse-drawn buggies laden with watermelon and corn.

San Ignacio, the capital of the district, sits on the bank of the Macal River (a branch of the Belize River) in the misty foothills of the Maya Mountains 72 miles west of Belize City. The town, which is the only source of gasoline and other essentials in the district, can be the jumping-off point for a variety of activities, including exploring Maya ruins, mountain climbing, canoeing in the Macal River, horseback riding, and day trips over the nearby Guatemalan border 9 miles away. High-quality accommodations abound in the area (see *Checking In*). Local hotels and *Mountain Equestrian Trails* (*MET;* see *Horseback Riding*) offer tours into the Maya Mountains and to Tikal in Guatemala. *MET* also can arrange horseback riding trips.

CARACOL ARCHAEOLOGICAL PRESERVE Hidden deep in the tangled jungle at the foothills of the Maya Mountains, a four-hour drive down a bumpy dirt road off the Western Highway, lies the splendid 2,000-year-old Maya city of *Caracol.* The last dirt road to *Caracol* was finished only a few years ago; since then, thousands of visitors have flocked to see this great ancient metropolis, which has been featured numerous times on the public television program "*National Geographic* Explorer." More than 4,000 buildings are sprinkled across 55 square miles, though archaeologists are still concentrating on the city center. Here the magnificent *Caana* (Sky Palace)—Belize's tallest manmade structure—soars 139 feet and is topped with three temples, several pyramids, and a courtyard. More than 55 tombs have been unearthed at *Caracol*—more than at any other Maya site. There is much to see and learn here. All visitors are assigned a guide—either an archaeology student or a local Maya caretaker. Formal tours are offered at 10:30 AM and 1 PM daily. While you can drive to *Caracol* yourself, we recommend hiring a driver; it's a long and rather rough trip. No one is admitted without a visitor's permit (cost: $1), available from the *Forestry Department Station* in the village of Augustine, 30 miles north of *Caracol* (no phone), or from the *Archaeology Department* in Belmopan (phone: 8-22106).

XUNANTUNICH About 80 miles southwest of Belize City, near the Guatemalan border, this archaeological site (whose name is pronounced *Shoo*-nan-*too*-nich) is dominated by its impressive, 130-foot *El Castillo* pyramid. The climb to the top is challenging, but the panoramic view of Belize's mountains and Guatemala provides ample reward. One of the best excavated and most popular of the country's ruins, the site is filled with stone buildings that are more than 1,400 years old and boasts an extensive sampling of artifacts from the ancient Maya civilization. Admission charge. To reach the site, drive southwest on the Western Highway from San Ignacio about 2 miles to the small village of Succotz, then cross the Macal River via the hand-cranked ferry (give the ferry operator a small tip), which operates daily from 9 AM to noon and 1 to 5 PM.

DANGRIGA (STANN CREEK) On a lovely stretch of sand, Dangriga rests along the sea 105 miles south of Belize City. Though accessible by the Southern Highway, the road's rough dirt surface wreaks havoc on cars and passengers alike, and bus service is inconvenient, so the town is best reached by air (*Maya Airways* has daily service). Most of its 8,000 residents are Garifuna, who first settled here in 1823—the event is celebrated here annually (see *Special Events*). The barrier reef is a short boat ride from Dangriga, and fishing, swimming, snorkeling, or diving excursions can be arranged through the *Pelican Beach* resort (see *Checking In*); the *Bonefish* hotel (15 Mahogany St.; phone: 5-22165); the *Rio Mar* (977 Southern Foreshore; phone: 5-22201); and the *Sophie* hotel (970 Chatye St.; phone: 5-22789). For an interesting side trip, stop by the home of painter Benjamin Nicholas across from the *Bonefish* hotel at 25 Howard Street (phone: 5-22785), whose compelling canvases capture Garifuna culture and history. Call ahead for an appointment.

A few miles south of Dangriga, on the beach, is the Garifuna village of Hopkins; the world's first and only jaguar preserve is at the *Cockscomb Basin Wildlife Sanctuary* in Maya Centre, 30 miles south. Although few visitors actually get to see the jaguars here—the animals are nocturnal and afraid of people—they often can see many other exotic creatures. Keel-billed toucans, green parrots, king vultures, coatimundis, anteaters, and boa constrictors are just a few of the animals inhabiting the dense jungle here. Footpaths snake through the forest past rivers and waterfalls. A trail map is available at the visitors' center, but we suggest you hire a guide at Maya Centre or take advantage of the guided tours offered by the *Pelican Beach* hotel and the *Rum Point Inn* (see *Checking In* for both). For additonal details, see *Natural Wonderlands* in DIVERSIONS. For more information, contact these hotels or the *Belize Audubon Society* (12 Fort St., Belize City; phone: 2-35004; fax: 2-34985). Open daily. Admission charge.

PLACENCIA South of Dangriga, this tiny fishing village is strung along the beach of a narrow, 16-mile peninsula. It's reached by boat from either Mango Creek or Big Creek, where there's also an airstrip (stand under the palm tree to wait for your flight). It's also possible to drive here in a four-wheel-drive vehicle, but the access road is not in good condition, especially when it's raining. The beaches here are some of the loveliest in Belize; lately, Americans and Europeans have made this a trendy place for swimming, sunbathing, diving, fishing, and nightlife. There are several good hotels here, particularly the *Rum Point Inn* (see *Checking In*), and nearby Seine Bight, north of Placencia, is an interesting Garifuna village.

PUNTA GORDA Flanked by hills on the west and northwest, Punta Gorda lies at the southern end of Belize. The capital of the Toledo district, its population is primarily a mixture of Garifuna, Creole, Maya, East Indian, and Chinese. The town overlooks the Bay of Honduras, with Guatemala and Honduras only a few miles across the sea. Though Punta Gorda (nicknamed P.G. by Belizeans) is not designed for the tourist trade, it's worth a look, with its funky clapboard homes, roosters wandering the streets, and corner groceries advertising fresh pig snouts and gibnut (a large rodent considered a delicacy). While there are no first-rate hotels here, hard-core adventurers will find plenty to do, as some of Central America's most remote Maya ruins and villages rest in the hills just above town. Also, boats can be hired for river trips to other little-explored areas such as Livingston, Guatemala.

A few miles away from the huge promontory at the southern end of Punta Gorda is the site of the former Toledo settlement, home of US Civil War refugees, and nearby are several picturesque Maya villages. In the tiny village of San Antonio, Maya women and children dry their cacao beans on the hillsides. A mile north of the nearby village of San Pedro Colombia is the path to the ancient Maya ceremonial center of Lubaantun. The mile-long trail to the site is very muddy, except in the dry season. The site itself, however, which is made up of temples built from stone blocks, is well worth the effort. Several miles north of the Punta Gorda–San Antonio turnoff and a few miles south of Big Falls is the trail into *Nim Li Punit,* a Maya ceremonial center noted for its carved stone monuments, or stelae, which show ancient rulers "letting blood" into braziers to appease the gods. Open daily; no admission charge, though it is customary to tip the caretaker (if he's there), who will give you a tour of the ruins.

ALTUN HA Only 30 miles north of Belize City is the ancient Maya ceremonial center of *Altun Ha.* It was here that a carved jade head—six inches long and weighing 10 pounds—of the sun god Kinich Ahau was unearthed during the 1960s by a *Royal Ontario Museum* team. While an important find, it was only one of many artifacts (including bowls and jade objects) discovered in these 3 square miles of ruins. Drive toward Orange Walk on the Northern Highway. Turn right at Maskall Road (also the old highway to Orange Walk) and continue on for about 15 minutes. There is a sign on the left marking the site. Open daily. Admission charge (no phone).

CROOKED TREE WILDLIFE SANCTUARY Located 33 miles northwest of Belize City and 2 miles off the Northern Highway, this wildlife refuge consists of a network of lagoons, swamps, and waterways that provide a variety of habitats for Belize's flora and fauna. There are herons, snowy and great egrets, all five species of kingfisher, crocodiles, black howler monkeys, coatimundi (a tropical mammal related to the raccoon), and many other animals. Further information can be obtained from the *Belize Audubon Society* (see Dangria entry above). Visitors can now stay at the *Maruba* resort (see *Checking In*). Open daily. Admission charge.

LAMANAI Hidden in the jungle of northern Belize, about 50 miles northwest of Belize City, is the fascinating ancient trading and ceremonial center of *Lamanai,* with spectacular temples and masks still intact. The city was probably first inhabited some 3,500 years ago. During the 1970s, a team of archaeologists uncovered more than 700 buildings here. Of those, a 112-foot-high temple is perhaps the most impressive. Because *Lamanai* is spread out along miles of the New River lagoon and can be reached only by a two- to three-hour boat ride, a guide is necessary. The nearby *Maruba* resort (see *Checking In*) offers excellent tours, complete with a tasty picnic lunch.

About 30 miles upriver from Lamanai, and 66 miles north of Belize City, is Orange Walk Town. Though it doesn't offer much of interest to travelers, 3 miles west of here is *Cuello,* the oldest Maya site yet discovered, dating from 2500 BC. It is on Yo Creek Road, behind the Cuello Brothers Rum Distillery, Central America's largest.

COROZAL A Maya stronghold known as Chetumal until the middle of the 19th century, Corozal is the northernmost town in Belize. In addition to its location on Corozal Bay, which is ideal for swimming and fishing, it has *Santa Rita Corozal,* a Maya ruin, and, nearby, *Cerros Maya,* another archaeological site accessible only by boat; make arrangements at *Menzies Travel and Tours* (phone: 4-22725), *Tony's Inn,* or *Adventure Inn* (see *Checking In* for the latter two).

EXTRA SPECIAL

More than 75% of the visitors to Belize spend their vacations on one of the offshore islands such as Cay Caulker, Turneffe Island, Glover's Reef, or St. George's Cay. But Ambergris Caye is the most popular with visitors from the US. The 30-mile-long island sits 36 miles northeast of Belize City, just 15 minutes away by small plane. (Both *Island Air* and *Tropic* Air have daily regularly scheduled flights from Belize City; see *Inter- and Intra-Island Flights,* below.) Arrivals land on the 2,500-foot paved strip that is just a few steps from the heart of the island's only village, San Pedro (pop. 4,000). The streets of San Pedro are pure white sand, and almost everything is just a short, easy stroll away. Most of the places to stay are within a quarter mile of the landing strip. Many resorts are spread out both north and south of the village and can be reached only by boat.

What's most exciting about Ambergris Caye is the magnificent barrier reef just 300 yards offshore. Nearly 185 miles long, it is the longest reef in the Western Hemisphere and a diver's paradise. Underwater visibility is more than 100 feet at Ambergris Caye, and what a spectacle there is: crimson parrot fish and yellowtail damselfish; zebra-striped sergeant majors;

green moray eels (peaceful, unless provoked); and many more sea creatures, gliding and darting amid a staggering variety of coral and sea plants. Off the southern tip of the island, an underwater national park was created to protect the natural beauty of the area. Snorkeling equipment rental, glass-bottom boats, and diving trips can be arranged through most of the hotels in San Pedro. For additional details, see *Sunken and Buried Treasure* in DIVERSIONS.

At night stroll over to the *Navigator Bar*, at the *Barrier Reef* hotel (Main St.; phone: 26-2075). Here you will find a mix of locals, Americans, and visiting British troops who have come for rest and recuperation from their mainland bases. With its white sand floor, bamboo decor, formica tables, and hi-fi tapes, this is *the* nighttime gathering place of Ambergris Caye. Other favorite watering holes are the *Tackle Box* (on the end of a pier at the *Coral Beach* hotel; phone: 26-2013) and the bar at *Ramón's Village* (see *Checking In*).

Sources and Resources

TOURIST INFORMATION

The *Belize Tourist Board* (83 North Front St., Belize City; phone: 2-77213; fax: 2-77490) can provide literature, maps, advice, and help. Newspapers are in English, and there is a tourist guide of sorts, but it's not very helpful. For information about Belize tourist offices in the US, see GETTING READY TO GO.

Note: Due to an increase in robberies and related assaults in Belize (mainly in Belize City), the US State Department cautions visitors to Belize not to walk alone on city streets at night, wear jewelry, carry valuables, or travel alone to remote tourist sites. For up-to-date travel advisory information, check with the US State Department's *Citizens' Emergency Center* (phone: 202-647-5225).

A WORD ABOUT ARTIFACTS

Remember that Maya artifacts are not to be removed from any ruin, and the authorities are very strict about enforcing this rule. This includes items that locals may attempt to sell to you, illegally. Government permits are required for any artifact that is taken from the country.

LOCAL COVERAGE The *Amandala,* the *Reporter,* the *Belize Times, Liberty,* and the *San Pedro Sun* are the major weekly newspapers. The *People's Pulse,* another weekly paper, the *Belize Review,* a monthly, and *Belize Currents,* a bimonthly, also carry information on local events and activities. An American expatriate publishes the indispensable *Emory King's Annual Drivers' Guide to Beautiful Belize* ($8), which features detailed maps and mile-by-mile itineraries. The book is widely available at hotels and tourist destinations.

RADIO AND TELEVISION The Broadcasting Corporation of Belize broadcasts in English and Spanish on television channel 3 (BBC broadcasts in addition to programs from the Caribbean Satellite Network) and on Radio Belize (92.7 FM), with news, talk shows, and light music, and Friends FM (88.9 FM), with Caribbean music and news.

TELEPHONE When calling from the US dial 011 (international access code) + 501 (country code) + (city code) + (local number). To call from anywhere else, the access code may vary, so contact the local operator. When calling from one city in Belize to another, dial 0 + (city code) + (local number). When dialing within a city, use only the four- or five-digit local number. The telephone numbers listed in this chapter include city codes. Dial 911 for the police; 90 for an ambulance.

Many larger hotels have direct AT&T credit card phones for calls to the US. Holders of other companies' long-distance calling cards will be out of luck, since none provide access numbers from Belize.

In the jungle, old-fashioned party-line radio phones are still widely used.

ENTRY REQUIREMENTS To enter Belize, US and Canadian citizens must have a current passport; the immigration office at the point of entry will stamp a visa in your passport. Crossing the border from Mexico or Guatemala to Belize is a fairly simple process, although it can take an hour or more if there are crowds. When you leave Mexico, you must relinquish your Mexican tourist card. If you plan to return to Mexico from Belize, you will be issued a new tourist card upon re-entry. Another option is to stop at the *Mexican Embassy* in Belize City (20 Park St.; phone: 2-30193) to pick up a replacement card.

Note, however, that travel between Mexico and Belize can be difficult unless you're driving your own car. There are no car rental companies in the area on either side of the border, and taxi fares are quite expensive ($15 to $25 just to cross the border). Buses run regularly and are much cheaper, but the trip can be uncomfortable and slow.

CLIMATE AND CLOTHES Belize is a subtropical area with temperatures ranging from the mid-70s F in January to the upper 90s in August. At midday, shade temperatures of 95 to 100F are not uncommon. Rainfall in the northern part of the country averages 50 inches per year, but in the south 200 inches per year is normal. The rainy season generally runs from June through December, and the driest period is from February through May. During the rains, Belize is susceptible to hurricanes, and the humidity hovers around 80%.

Extremely light, informal clothing is the norm, and with good reason. Although some businessmen do wear jackets and ties, it is unnecessary. Women tend to wear summery dresses to dinner, although tropical safari gear will be more appropriate the rest of the time. Shorts are fine on the offshore islands, but not in town. Visitors to the jungle will want to pack long-sleeve shirts and trousers to protect against mosquitoes and other biting insects.

MONEY The official currency is the Belize dollar (BZ), which has been stabilized at $1 US to $2 BZ. Banks generally are open from 8 AM to 1 PM weekdays; on Fridays they're also open from 3 to 6 PM. Hotels usually will exchange currency with little or no commission. If arriving from Mexico, do not exchange Mexican pesos if possible, as the exchange rate is very poor in Belize. All prices in this chapter are quoted in US dollars.

LANGUAGE English is the official language, but it comes with a variety of accents, British, Caribbean, and Spanish among them. Many Belizeans speak Spanish, Chinese, Maya, or Creole, and there are several German-speaking Mennonite settlements.

TIME The country is on central standard time, which means that for most of the year it has the same time as Chicago; when the US switches to daylight saving time, however, Belize does not.

CURRENT Most of Belize uses 110-volt, 60-cycle current, just like the US.

TIPPING Very few restaurants add a service charge, so plan to add 15% if you're satisfied. Many hotels add a 10% service charge, but the staff rarely receives this; leave hotel maids about $1 per day. Taxi drivers should be tipped (about 10% of the fare), and hotel bellhops and airport porters get about 50¢ per bag.

GETTING AROUND

Within the towns, transportation is easy, but once in the countryside, roads are extremely variable. The main highway in northern Belize is very good, and the paved Western Highway also makes for good driving. The washed-out, pothole-riddled Hummingbird Highway south from Belmopan may be the worst road in the country, but it passes through some of the most magnificent scenery. Both the Western and Hummingbird Highways feature mile markers, which are helpful for orientation. The Southern Highway is also treacherous, as it is composed of a hard dirt that can damage a car's suspension and chassis even in good weather; during the rainy season, the road often floods. Beware the "sleeping policemen," speed bumps which can be quite hazardous in villages.

BUS Long-haul buses between towns and villages aren't very comfortable, but they do try to maintain some type of schedule. Fares range from $1 to $4, according to the destination. Local Belize City buses are about 50¢. Bus service to Belize is available from Guatemala City (the fare is about $12), and from Chetumal, Mexico (fare, $3.50), but note that crossing the border by bus can be difficult and time-consuming.

CAR RENTAL Many of the country's roads have been improved, and all major roads in the north are paved. Gas will cost about $1.50 a gallon. Beware of rental companies offering seemingly bargain rates on big, old, American gas-guzzlers. By the time you've paid for gas, you've spent more than if you'd rented a new four-wheel-drive vehicle. Besides, you'll need the four-wheel-drive if you decide to venture off the beaten path—and you should. But before you do any trailblazing, be sure to check with locals for road conditions; after major rainfalls, some jungle and forest roads can become impassable. All the major car rental companies are in Belize City; however, some hotel owners will rent their car (or a friend's) if you decide you need a vehicle in an outlying area. The best rental company in Belize City is *Budget Rent-A-Car* (771 Bella Vista; phone: 2-32435; fax: 2-30237). Other good firms are *Ace* (12 North Front St.; phone: 2-31650 or 2-32637; fax: 2-31586); *World Auto Rentals* (*Phillip S. W. Goldson International Airport;* phone: 25-2586; fax: 2-32940); *National* (126 Freetown Rd.; phone: 25-2294; fax: 2-31586); and *Hertz* (Northern Hwy., 2½ miles from Belize City; phone: 2-32710; fax: 2-32053). A valid US driver's license is all that is needed to drive in Belize.

FERRY The *Andrea I* and *II* run afternoons from Belize City to Ambergris Caye ($10 each way) and Cay Caulker ($7.50 each way). The boats can be boarded at the waterfront at the *Bellevue* hotel on Southern Foreshore Road.

INTER- AND INTRA-ISLAND FLIGHTS *Tropic Air* (San Pedro, Ambergris Caye; phone: 26-2012; fax: 26-2338) has several regularly scheduled flights each day from Belize City to San Pedro on Ambergris Caye and can arrange charters to anywhere in the country. It also flies on an irregular schedule to Tikal, Guatemala. *Maya Airways* (Belize City; phone: 2-72312; 800-522-3419; fax: 2-30585) has daily scheduled flights to towns in southern and northern Belize, and infrequent service to other destinations within the country. *Island Air* (phone: 26-2435 in San Pedro; 2-31140 in Belize City; fax: 26-2192) also has daily scheduled flights to San Pedro.

TAXI There are no meters, but the rates are set by the government. However, if you are leaving from a hotel, check what the fare should be beforehand, as taxi drivers here have been known to overcharge. Also, watch out for drivers who will compute the fare in Belize dollars and try to collect in US dollars.

SPECIAL EVENTS

On March 9, a regatta is held on the Belize River to honor Baron Bliss, an Englishman who, in 1926, left his $2 million fortune to the country to commemorate the kindness Belizeans showed him when he fell ill while sailing near Belize. The *Fiesta de San José* (held in March or April) at San José Succotz climaxes with a reenactment of a battle between the Moors and the Spaniards. In July, the *Fiesta del Virgen del Carmen,* at Benque Viejo del Carmen, features costumes and much dancing in the streets. The *Air and Sea Festival,* celebrated in August on Ambergris Caye, offers booths and carnival rides. *National Day,* the big holiday in Belize, kicks off on September 10 with parades, floats, sports activities, patriotic rallies, and beauty contests. The celebrations culminate on September 21, Belize's

Independence Day. The arrival of the Garifuna from Honduras is celebrated on November 19 in Dangriga and nearby villages with costumed dancers, booths, and displays. Other official holidays when banks, stores, and government offices are closed are: *New Year's Day, Good Friday* (April 5 in 1996), *Easter Monday* (April 8 in 1996; many establishments close for the entire *Holy Week,* but the four days of the long *Easter* weekend are the official holidays), *Labor Day* (May 1), *Commonwealth Day* (May 24), *Columbus Day* (October 12), *Pan American Day* (October 13), *Christmas Eve, Christmas,* and *Boxing Day* (December 26).

SHOPPING

Belize is not exactly a shopper's paradise. The in-bond stores do carry watches, perfume, and other imports at duty-free prices, but it is hardly comparable to other free ports in the Caribbean. There are nice carvings of rosewood and ziricote, the two-tone wood native to the area. Most stores are open Mondays through Saturdays from 8 AM to 5 PM, though some close early on Wednesdays and stay open later on Fridays. The *Belize Chamber of Commerce Handicraft Centre* (Fort St., Belize City; phone: 2-33833) across from the *Four Fort Street* hotel offers a wide variety of locally made items. Good buys include straw goods hand-crafted from jipijapa straw in the Punta Gorda area and slate sculptures by Maya villagers. And though you may be tempted, remember, it's illegal to bring tortoiseshell items into the US.

SPORTS

Fishing in the nation's rivers and off the coast is the main attraction, closely followed by scuba diving and snorkeling in and around the barrier reef.

CLIMBING The Maya Mountains, in the southwest, present a challenge to even experienced climbers. Victoria Peak, at 3,680 feet, crowns the Cockscomb Range. The Chief Forest Officer at the *Ministry of Natural Resources* (Belmopan; phone: 8-22333) will put you in touch with a qualified guide. Also see *Climbing and Hiking* in DIVERSIONS.

HORSEBACK RIDING For guided tours and trail rides, contact *Mountain Equestrian Trails* (*MET;* Mountain Pine Ridge Rd.; phone: 82-3180 or 82-2149; fax: 82-3235).

SNORKELING AND SCUBA DIVING Boasting the second-longest barrier reef in the world and with three of the four authentic coral atolls in the Caribbean, Belize offers every conceivable underwater terrain to divers—from the novice to the most experienced. Experienced divers shouldn't miss Jacques Cousteau's famous Belize Blue Hole cave surrounded by coral reef, considered by some to be one of the Seven Underwater Wonders of the World. Most hotels, especially on Ambergris Caye, Turneffe, Glover's Reef, and Lighthouse Reef, offer year-round open water certification with internationally certified instructors using state-of-the-art equipment. The *Aggressor Fleet* operates the *Belize Aggressor I* and *II,* offering the serious diver Belize's best (phone: 800-348-2628).

The dive shops in San Pedro are very well equipped with state-of-the-art diving equipment. *Reef Divers, Ltd.* (phone: 26-2173; 800-426-0226) and the *Ramón's Village, Sun Breeze, Journey's End Caribbean Club,* and *Victoria House* hotels (see *Checking In* for all) have full-time internationally certified dive masters/guides. Several one- and two-boat operators are also certified. Check before you make reservations. Try snorkeling; it is readily available, and like scuba here, truly spectacular. But be aware that the barrier reef, where the snorkeling is best, is inaccessible from the beach. Your hotel or a local dive shop can arrange for the short boat trip.

SPORT FISHING Any fish in the Caribbean can be caught off the coast of Belize: there's the deep sea for bills and wahoo; reef fishing for barracuda, grouper, and snapper; flat fishing, light tackle, and fly fishing for bone and tarpon; and river fishing for tarpon and snook. The barrier reef paralleling the coast harbors a huge variety of game fish, and there is a number of simple offshore fishing lodges. For more information, contact *Turneffe Island Lodge, Journey's End Caribbean Club, Paradise,* or *El Pescador* (see *Checking In* for all). *Angler Adventures* (PO Box 872, Old Lyme, CT 06371; phone: 203-434-9624) offers fishing safari trips. Most hotels and resorts have facilities available, and private guides can be hired.

SWIMMING AND SUNNING Swimming is good off the sandy beaches of the cays and on the southeast coast. Sunbathing on your very own cay is tops.

TENNIS The two nicest courts are at the *Pickwick Club* in Belize City, but it is open only to members and their guests. The only hotel with tennis courts is *Journey's End* on Ambergris Caye.

NIGHTLIFE

Belize City is not a night town, and what activity there is centers around the hotels (see *Checking In* for details). There's dancing late in the evenings at the *Château Caribbean* hotel and quiet music and conversation at the bar of the *Radisson Fort George*. *Legends* (30 Queen St.; phone: 2-30436) is currently a favorite after-dark gathering place, as is the *Hard Rock Café* (35 Queen St.; phone: 2-32041), although it's not a member of the world-famous chain. Perhaps the best nightclub in Belize is the *Cahal Pech* disco in San Ignacio (phone: 92-2736). Named for nearby ruins and perched on a hill overlooking the Maya Mountains about a quarter mile from the *San Ignacio* hotel, it's a scenic spot that rocks well into the wee hours.

Best in the Country

CHECKING IN

Belize has no luxury hotels, and US travelers may find that none of its accommodations suit sophisticated tastes. But visitors seeking local character, charm, and hospitality will find them in abundance. Jungle lodges and beach villas, many owned and run by American expatriates, offer the chance to get to know this fascinating country on a personal level. Meals are festive events; the owners and guests dine together at one big table, discussing the latest issues in local politics and conservation. In Belize City, several larger chain hotels provide more modern facilities. Offshore, Ambergris Caye offers many comfortable motels and guesthouses, as well as resorts. Lighthouse Reef and Glover's Reef have only one lodge each, and visitors may well feel as if they're living on their own private island.

Many accommodations in Belize have no air conditioning. Generally, air conditioning is unnecessary in the winter, but summer can be suffocatingly hot. Unless otherwise noted, the hotels listed below feature telephones, TV sets, and private baths in the rooms.

In winter, with the exception of some resorts on Ambergris Caye and some fishing resorts, which can be very pricey ($300 or more a night), expect to pay $90 to $150 for a double room, including meals, in hotels we describe as expensive. Places in the moderate range cost between $55 and $90; inexpensive accommodations will cost less than $55 a night. Prices are reduced somewhat in the summer, but the strict Caribbean winter/summer seasonal rate changes don't affect Belize as much as the island nations. All Belize hotels add a 5% room tax, and some will add a 10% service charge. Many hotels also add a 5% surcharge if you pay with a credit card, and a few do not accept credit cards at all. The telephone numbers listed below include city codes. Remember to dial zero before the city code when calling from one city in Belize to another; when calling within a single city use only the local number (the last four or five digits). For information about dialing from elsewhere, see *Telephone* earlier in this chapter.

BELIZE CITY

EXPENSIVE

Biltmore Plaza One of the newer large hotels in Belize. This property has a cozy atmosphere, with 90 air conditioned rooms, a gazebo, and a fish pond and garden inside a central plaza. There's also a pool, restaurant, and bar. On Northern Rd., only 6½ miles from *Phillip S. W. Goldson International Airport* (phone: 2-32302; 800-327-3573; fax: 2-32301).

Radisson Fort George Belize's most upscale property, with 70 air conditioned rooms (30 in a newer, seven-story glass wing). Most popular among businesspeople, older travelers, and families, it makes a good home base for touring the country. There is a gift shop, a fine restaurant with a picture-window view of the harbor (see *Eating Out*), a lounge with music on weekends, and a pool. Marine Parade (phone: 2-77400; 800-333-3333; fax: 2-73820).

Ramada Royal Reef This four-story establishment has 120 air conditioned guestrooms, including a presidential suite. On-premises amenities include a pool, restaurant, gift shop, travel agency, and marina. There are also conference rooms that can accommodate up to 400. Located on the edge of the waterfront on what was originally the Barrach Green, where Charles Lindbergh landed his *Spirit of St. Louis* (phone: 2-32670; 800-228-9898; fax: 2-32660).

MODERATE

Bakadeer Inn This recently opened, 12-room inn run by American expatriates is a very good value, offering comfortable, attractive sleeping quarters with modern amenities at reasonable prices. Air conditioning, cable TV, and mini-refrigerators are included, and inexpensive breakfasts are offered daily to guests in the dining room (no other meals are served). There's also a secured parking lot. 74 Cleghorn St. (phone: 2-31286; fax: 2-31963).

Château Caribbean A converted mansion overlooking the sea, with 25 air conditioned rooms. Off-street parking is also provided, a nice extra. There's also a good restaurant and bar. 6 Marine Parade (phone: 2-30800; fax: 2-30900).

INEXPENSIVE

Colton House One of the best bargains in Belize City, this gem is located a block from the sea in the city's best neighborhood. The 1930s house is inviting, featuring colonial decor and a spacious front porch with swings. The four extra-large rooms (two with private baths) have high ceilings and individual entrances. One of the rooms is air conditioned, but there are no telephones or TV sets (there's a TV set in the main living room). No credit cards are accepted. 9 Cork St. (phone: 2-44666).

Four Fort Street Belize City's first bed and breakfast establishment is in a charming colonial building. There are six rooms (which share two baths), all with ceiling fans but no air conditioning, TV sets, or telephones. (There's a TV in the main living room and a telephone near the guestrooms to share.) There's also *Fort Street,* an elegant restaurant (see *Eating Out*). 4 Fort St. (phone: 2-30116; 800-240-3678; fax: 2-78808).

AMBERGRIS CAYE

VERY EXPENSIVE

Captain Morgan's Retreat This resort features 21 cabañas located directly on the beach, and a lush, tropical ambience. The cabañas have ceiling fans (no air conditioning), and there are no telephones or TV sets. There's a restaurant and bar, but the main attractions here are the beach (there are over-sized hammocks for lolling about), the sea, and the great coral reef. Reef, deep-sea, and fly fishing; scuba diving; snorkeling; and day sailing trips can be arranged. The resort is accessible only by boat (the hotel picks up guests in San Pedro several times a day). On the north side of Ambergris Caye (phone: 26-2527; 800-447-2931).

Journey's End Caribbean Club Featured on "Lifestyles of the Rich & Famous," this resort offers a private coconut-palm-fringed beach, lighted tennis court, oversize swimming pool, Hobie Cats for sailing, a dining room, and a couple of bars. There are 30 villas and 40 double rooms with lagoon frontage (all have air conditioning). Accessible by boat (pickup is in San Pedro) and, thanks to a nearby airstrip, by plane. North of San Pedro (phone: 26-2173; 800-447-0474; fax: 26-2028).

EXPENSIVE

El Pescador With 12 double rooms and one large suite, this remote hostelry is accessible only by boat (the hotel picks up guests in San Pedro). Life here is devoted to fisherfolk. All the rooms have twin beds, ceiling fans, plus verandahs offering striking views of the sea; there's no air conditioning, telephones, or TV sets. There's a seven-night minimum stay; all meals, a daily fishing guide, and round-trip flight from Belize City to Ambergris Caye are included. Three miles north of San Pedro (phone and fax: 26-2398).

Ramón's Village A favorite of young, single Americans and Europeans, this place has an upbeat, often uproarious, atmosphere. The 60 cozy, thatch-roofed bungalows rest on a palmy beach. Some are air conditioned, but there are no TV sets. There's also a swimming pool, a restaurant, and a bar. San Pedro (phone: 26-2071; 800-624-4215; fax: 26-2214).

Victoria House This upscale resort in a beach setting has 29 units (some with air conditioning and telephones, but no TV sets) divided among a Victorian plantation house, Mexican-style casitas, and attractive row houses. There is a restaurant and a bar; complimentary bicycles are also available. Two miles south of San Pedro (phone: 26-2067; 800-247-5159; fax: 26-2429).

MODERATE

Paradise Here is a Tahitian-style resort on Ambergris Caye, offering 18 units (four are air conditioned) in thatch-roofed and bamboo huts. There is a pleasant, family-style dining room, and a bar in a separate building. Fishing and diving facilities are also available. PO Box 888, Belize City (phone: 26-2083).

San Pedro Holiday Caters primarily to deep-sea fishermen, though divers come, too; more than 90% of its business is repeat, a very good sign. Some of the two apartments and 14 rooms are air conditioned, but there are no telephones or TV sets. Cooking is done by the owner, and meals are served in a homey, unpretentious dining room. On the beach at San Pedro (phone: 26-2014; fax: 26-2295).

Sun Breeze This 39-room property features a beachfront setting, air conditioned rooms, a restaurant, a "barefoot" bar and grill, and a dive shop. San Pedro (phone: 26-2191; fax: 26-2346).

INEXPENSIVE

Coral Beach Family-run and catering to divers, it has comfortable accommodations in 19 rooms, all with air conditioning and ceiling fans but no telephones or TV sets. San Pedro (phone: 26-2001; fax: 26-2864).

OTHER CAYS

EXPENSIVE

Lighthouse Reef An island lover's paradise, this resort on the secluded Northern Cay is surrounded by postcard-perfect white sand, coconut palms, and iridescent turquoise sea. It's favored by divers, who can join up to three daily dives to the surrounding atolls. Accommodations are in a two-bedroom villa with clay tile floors; five spacious, modern cabañas; two suites; and two studio apartments. All of the units are air conditioned, but there are no telephones or TV sets (there's a TV with a VCR in the restaurant). The good restaurant and friendly staff complete the inviting picture. Weekly packages only. Northern Cay, in the Lighthouse Reef atoll (phone: 800-423-3114).

Manta Eleven small, simple cabañas and a two-bedroom house strung along the beach of an unnamed island within one of the four atolls in the Western Hemisphere. The house features air conditioning, a kitchen, two baths, a TV set, and VCR but no telephone; the cabañas are very basic and rustic, with fans (no air conditioning), and no TV set or telephone. Popular with scuba divers, it features a huge thatch-roofed cantina perched at the end of a dock over the sea—the nightly gathering spot for guests. Weekly packages are offered, which include meals and boat transport to the island (the resort's launch makes the two-and-a-half hour trip only on Saturdays). Within the Glover's Reef atoll (phone: 2-31895; 800-342-0053; fax: 2-32764, 813-594-5613 in the US).

Turneffe Island Lodge Fishing and diving are the focus of this remote (accessible only by boat) resort 30 miles off the coast. Some of the 12 rooms are air conditioned, but there are no telephones or TV sets. There is a restaurant, bar, and beach. Week-long packages only, including fishing guides or dive masters, boats, and meals. Cay Bokel (phone: 800-338-8149; fax: 3-0236).

ELSEWHERE IN THE COUNTRY

EXPENSIVE

Blancaneaux Lodge Film director Francis Ford Coppola's stunning mountain retreat features seven thatch-roofed cottages decorated in African and Guatemalan motifs and perched in the *Mountain Pine Ridge* forest by the Privassion River. There are also five two-bedroom villas, some of which feature pieces from Coppola's private art collection, and two rooms in the main lodge (with shared bath); none of the accommodations has a telephone or TV set. The restaurant, one of Belize's best, offers superb Italian fare, including pizza from an oven imported from Italy; it also boasts Belize's only espresso machine. The wilds of the jungle are right outside, including lovely waterfalls and dense greenery. This is the perfect place to get away from it all in style. The lodge has its own airstrip, 30 minutes by charter flight from Belize City. Located one-and-a-half hours from the Maya ruins of *Caracol*, the property is on a dirt road off the Western Highway (phone: 92-3878; 800-PINE-RIDGE; fax: 92-3919).

Blue Marlin Lodge Located 35 miles south/southeast of *Phillip S. W. Goldson International Airport*, with 13 rooms (some air conditioned but with no telephones or TV sets) and a restaurant. The barrier reef is 120 feet off the beach. This spot boasts some of the finest, most accessible diving in Belize. South Water Cay, Dangriga (phone: 5-22243; fax: 5-22296).

Chaa Creek Cottages One of Belize's most elegant jungle lodges, in a stunning setting in the jungle-clad hills of the Cayo district. Owned by an Englishman and his American wife, it delivers first-rate service and surroundings. The 19 stucco cabañas, with red stone floors, soaring thatch roofs, and gleaming oak dressers, are sprinkled along a hill overlooking the Macal River. None is air conditioned or has a telephone or TV set. The owners prepare meals, served in a thatch-roofed open-air dining room. Swimming, bird watching, horseback riding, and trips to area ruins and the *Mountain Pine Ridge* reserve are available. Located near the village of Benque Viejo, about 20 minutes southwest of San Ignacio off the Western Highway (phone: 92-2037; fax: 92-2501).

Chan Chich Lodge A truly remarkable place. Built in the center of a Maya ruin in northwestern Belize and surrounded by virgin jungle, this property offers 12 lovely thatch-roofed cabañas with spacious wraparound porches (but no air conditioning, telephones, or TV sets), beautiful landscaping, a bar, and a dining room where the home cooking is first-rate. Toucans, currasows (turkey-like birds), and parrots roam the property freely, and dozens of jungle trails await exploration. Well run and friendly, it is growing very popular—book several months ahead for the *Christmas* holidays and for January and February. Accessible only by chartered plane; the lodge arranges transportation. Located in the old logging town of Gallon Jug (phone: 2-77031; 800-343-8009; fax: 2-77062).

duPlooy's Riverside Cottages Located in western Belize on 20 acres of rolling hills, here are nine units surrounded by lush tropical growth and framed on the eastern and northern sides by the Macal River. The six rooms in the main lodge have shared baths, and there's no air conditioning, telephones, or TV sets. Meals are served in a main dining room. You can swim and canoe in the Macal or hike in the jungle, and the bird watching here is exceptional. Tours can be arranged. Big Eddy, San Ignacio (phone: 92-2188; 800-359-0747; fax: 92-2057).

Hidden Valley Inn Set in a forest of colossal pine trees are 12 stylish stucco cabañas with Mexican tile floors, Guatemalan throw rugs, vaulted ceilings, and wood-burning fireplaces, but no air conditioning, telephones, or TV sets. Cocktails and meals are served in a big, gracious ranch house, which boasts a huge fireplace and an excellent library full of books about Belize. Breakfast is included in the rate. Advance reservations required. Located two hours from the Western Highway in the *Mountain Pine Ridge* reserve (phone: 8-23320; 800-334-7942; fax: 8-23334).

Maruba This remote jungle resort and spa bills itself as being "for the experienced traveler." Located in the heart of the Maya jungle, it features 15 rooms, a pool, a restaurant that serves local fare, a bar, a Japanese hot tub, tropical gardens, and an informal atmosphere. (Note, however, that only some rooms are air conditioned—and minimally at that; there are no telephones or TV sets, but there's a TV set in the main lounge.) Jungle trips on the Northern River and day trips to *Lamanai, Altun Ha,* and other points of interest in the interior are offered. There's also superb fishing and health spa packages. Located 40 miles north of Belize City near the *Crooked Tree Wildlife Sanctuary.* At the 40½-mile mark of the Old Northern Hwy., Maskall Village (phone: 6-23239; 800-552-3419; fax: 218-847-4442).

Rum Point Inn A very special place along some of the prettiest coastline in Belize. The ten futuristic-looking cabañas have gardens and Guatemalan sling chairs, but no air conditioning, telephones, or TV sets. A short stroll away is the picturesque dining room, where innkeepers George and Corol Bevier provide insights on Belize. To get here, guests take a 40-minute flight from Belize City to Placencia. On the beach, 2½ miles north of the village of Placencia (phone: 6-23239; 800-747-1381; fax: 6-23240).

MODERATE

Maya Mountain Lodge Another guest ranch with guestrooms and garden cottages (14 units in all, some with private baths, but no air conditioning, telephones, or TV sets) and delicious food. A number of guided archaeological and natural history tours are offered, as well as hiking, canoeing, and horseback riding. PO Box 46, San Ignacio (phone: 92-2164; fax: 92-2029).

Pelican Beach A very pleasant, family-run place right on the beach with 20 rooms (none with air conditioning, TV set, or telephone) and a restaurant. The owners are hospitable and helpful. Just north of Dangriga (phone: 5-22044; fax: 5-22570).

Turtle Inn Small, but very nice, with six thatch-roofed bungalows and a two-bedroom house on the beach. The rooms have fans (no air conditioning, telephones, or TV sets). A great place to relax, but also popular with active types—the inn is convenient for sport fishing, snorkeling, and scuba diving, and the owners offer a variety of inland tours. Meals are included in the price. Placencia (phone: 62-2069; 303-444-2555).

Warrie Head Lodge This beautiful, 137-acre working farm on the Belize River is a little over an hour's drive from Belize City. It has 500 acres of unspoiled riverside, an adjoining forest, and 10 simple guestrooms (no air conditioning, telephones, or TV sets). The cook, Lydia, is very talented at preparing chicken, steaks, or local vegetables, served family-style in the main house (there is no restaurant). Tours to archaeological sites, reserves, and a zoo can be arranged. Teakettle Village, Cayo (phone: 2-77185, 2-77363, or 2-77364; 800-633-4734).

Windy Hill This complex with 14 cottages with ceiling fans and mini-bars (no air conditioning or telephones) is only a few minutes from the Maya ruins at *Xunantunich* and Tikal, Guatemala. The dining room is for guests only. The staff will provide tours to the *Mountain Pine Ridge* reserve, the Rio Frio Caves, and the swirling waters of the Mopan and Macal rivers. Graceland Ranch, San Ignacio (phone: 92-2017; 800-345-9786; fax: 92-3080 or 504-366-9986).

INEXPENSIVE

Adventure Inn This place features 15 pleasant, thatch-roofed bungalows (with no air conditioning, telephones, or TV sets) overlooking beautiful Corozal Bay, in Consejo Shores, 7 miles north of Corozal. There's also a good restaurant. Corozal Town (phone: 4-22187; 800-552-3419; fax: 4-22243).

San Ignacio Situated on the banks of the Macal River at the threshold of the rain forest, this clean, modern structure is the only full-service hotel in Cayo. There are 23 rooms (none with air conditioning, telephones, or TV sets), a pool, and an excellent restaurant, with a menu that includes beef raised on the owner's own ranch. San Ignacio (phone: 92-2034 or 92-2125; fax: 92-2134).

Tony's Inn A cheery, comfortable motel on a lovely slice of beach in the northern town of Corozal. There are 40 rooms, all with modern decor; some rooms are air conditioned, while others have cable TV and telephones. It also has a congenial staff and the best restaurant in town. Located at the south end of Corozal (phone: 4-22055; 800-633-4734; fax: 4-22829).

Traveller's Inn Despite its location next to the bus stop, this establishment is the only first-rate lodging in Punta Gorda, the southernmost town in Belize. Its eight second-floor rooms feature plush carpets, contemporary dressers and armoires, air conditioning, and cable TV. It also boasts the only fancy restaurant in town. 53 Main St., Punta Gorda (phone: 7-22568; 800-552-3419).

EATING OUT

Fine dining has not yet arrived in Belize, yet this developing country has much to offer in the way of charming eateries. On the cays, it's mainly seafood, with shrimp, Caribbean spiny lobster, conch, and fish (usually snapper or grouper)—ceviche, too—headlining the menus. Order lobster and conch only in season—July 15 to March 15 for lobster; October through June for conch. (If seafood is offered out of season, it's a good bet that the restaurant obtained it illegally from poachers.)

Most hotels prepare meals for their guests, and many will accommodate non-guests if notified in advance. In the jungle lodges, cooks depend on fresh-from-the-garden vegetables and herbs, and tropical fruits culled from the bush country. The official Belizean dish is beans and rice cooked with coconut milk, which can be delicious. Curries, johnnycakes, Tex-Mex fare, and Chinese food are also ubiquitous. For dessert, try a custard apple—it's sweet and creamy, something like pudding. Belikin beer, the only Belizean beer, consumed in great quantities by locals and visitors, is delicious. It costs only $1 a bottle in most places, except on Ambergris Caye, where the price can be double or even triple that. Imported US beer costs $3 and up.

Meal prices are high by Central American standards, but low compared to most Caribbean islands. The cost of a three-course dinner for two, not including drinks or wine, at an expensive place costs $25 or more; expect to pay from $15 to $25 at moderate places; less than $15 at inexpensive places. Reservations are rarely necessary in any restaurant, unless you're dining at the restaurant of a hotel you're not staying at. Unless otherwise noted, all restaurants listed below are open for lunch and dinner. The telephone numbers listed below include city codes. When calling from one place to another in Belize, remember to dial zero before the city code; when calling within a single city use only the local number (the last four or five digits). For information about calling from elsewhere, see *Telephone* earlier in this chapter.

BELIZE CITY

EXPENSIVE

Fort Street In a delightful colonial-style house decorated with flickering oil lamps, eyelet tablecloths, and fresh flowers, this elegant eatery presents fresh seafood, steaks, and chicken. The variable menu, which is printed on a chalkboard, might include such delicacies as Cajun shrimp, kingfish with sour cream and pineapple, or snapper *tic tick* (baked in foil with onions and peppers). Closed Sundays. MasterCard and Visa accepted. 4 Fort St. (phone: 2-30116; fax: 2-78808).

MODERATE

Radisson Fort George This upscale hotel dining room surprises with tasty, imaginative offerings at reasonable prices. Menu items such as shrimp amaretto, lobster thermidor, red snapper creole, juicy burgers, Cobb salad, American-style pizza, and hearty French onion soup are served in a glass-walled dining room with a view of the sea. Open daily for breakfast, lunch, and dinner. Major credit cards accepted. Marine Parade (phone: 2-77400).

Macy's In 1988, the Queen of England ate gibnut (a large rodent whose white meat is considered a delicacy) here and made this funky hole-in-the-wall nationally famous. In addition to the regal gibnut, there's oxtail stew, fried chicken, beans and rice, steamed snapper, and fresh-squeezed papaya and watermelon juices. Open daily. No credit cards accepted. 18 Bishop St. (phone: 2-73419).

Mom's Triangle Café This longtime gathering spot for American expatriates will cure homesickness. BLTs, fried chicken, mashed potatoes, and an irresistible bread pudding are among the offerings. Open daily. MasterCard and Visa accepted. 11 Handyside St. (phone: 2-45523).

AMBERGRIS CAYE

Jade Garden San Pedro's Chinese restaurant is in a beautiful old house right on the beach. The Cantonese fare, which ranges from good to great, includes curries, sweet-and-sour dishes, chow meins, and egg foo yung, as well as fresh seafood. Open daily; closed during October. Major credit cards accepted. Located on the sea, about 1½ miles north of the San Pedro airstrip (phone: 26-2506).

Elvi's Kitchen Extremely popular with locals and tourists alike, this colorful place has a sand floor and a tree growing through the roof. Diners feast on burgers, steaks, rice and beans, and whatever the catch of the day might be. Closed Sundays. Major credit cards accepted. Pescador Dr., San Pedro (phone: 26-2176 or 26-2404).

Mary Ellen's Little Italy The island's best Italian eatery is in a romantic seaside venue. Owned by an attorney from Tennessee, it features lasagna and spaghetti, plus more unusual offerings like shrimp manicotti with white cream sauce. Closed Wednesdays in summer. Major credit cards accepted. Barrier Reef Dr., San Pedro (phone: 26-2866).

Fido's Island Grill Eventually, everyone who comes to San Pedro ends up here (or so the story goes). The restaurant is parked right in the middle of town, and its rambling wood floors and palm thatching make for a comfortable, inviting atmosphere. The quick, filling fare includes Buffalo wings, tuna sandwiches, burritos, fish 'n' chips, and chili dogs. Closed Wednesdays. No credit cards accepted. Barrier Reef Dr., San Pedro (phone: 26-2056).

INEXPENSIVE

Brenda's Soulful Belizean home cooking by a Placencia woman in her backyard. Offerings depend on what's available—and what Brenda's in the mood for—but they're sure to be scrumptious, filling, and a good buy. Her cream pies are legendary. Open daily (except when Brenda doesn't feel like cooking). No credit cards accepted. In Placencia, near the post office, or ask any local to show you the way (phone: 6-23137).

Caladium A choice lunch spot for government employees, this quaint eatery sits in downtown Belmopan. The chalkboard menu outside announces daily specials such as pork chops, fried chicken, gibnut, meatballs, BLTs, cheeseburgers, and heavenly milkshakes. Open daily. No credit cards accepted. Market Sq., Belmopan (phone: 8-22754).

Eva's If ever there was a restaurant that embodied Belize, this is it. The downtown San Ignacio eatery sits at the center of jungle comings-and-goings, catering to every person—farmer, drifter, tourist, or archaeologist—who passes through. The food—typical Belizean fare such as stew chicken, and beans and rice—comes in second to the atmosphere, but it's still good. Open daily. No credit cards accepted. 22 Burns Ave., San Ignacio (phone: 92-2267).

J.B.'s Watering Hole This vast, open-air truck stop attracts locals, American and British expats, backpackers, and anyone else traversing the rain forest. Decorated with memorabilia from the numerous British Army units formerly stationed in the area, the place serves up huge portions of local and Tex-Mex fare at bargain prices. It's truly the atmospheric center of the middle of nowhere. Open daily. No credit cards accepted. Mile 32, Western Highway (phone: 01-49311).

Kingfisher This big, weathered, clapboard building on the sea in Placencia is the place for drinking Belikin, swapping fish tales, and eating fresh seafood. Closed Thursdays and during October. Visa and American Express accepted (phone: 6-23175).

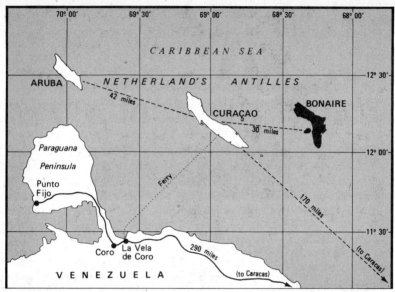

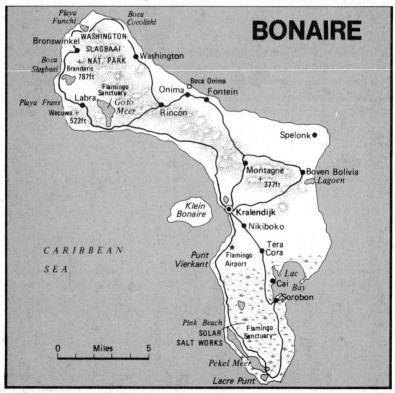

Bonaire

Sleepy little Bonaire has been quietly blooming as a tourist destination for decades. In 1960, a mere 1,555 visitors found their way to its sun-warmed shores. By 1991, that figure had multiplied more than thirtyfold: Some 49,000 people vacationed here, many of them return visitors. And the number of tourists continues to grow. Today, Bonaire rates a place on the savviest list of about-to-be-discovered Caribbean destinations—for good, if not immediately obvious, reasons.

Bonaire is hardly a stereotypical tropical resort. At last count, it boasted fewer than a thousand hotel and condo rooms and a smattering of duty-free shops. But the sudden surge of serious investment interest in Bonaire already is being felt, with the development of several small properties and a few larger projects.

Bonaire's hilly north end is salty, sandy, and dry, but covered with countless species of cactus, century plants, and intriguingly contorted prickly-pear trees. Though a few sections of the island's flat southern end are dotted with mangrove marshes, it is, overall, a desert-like area. Ashore, Bonaire is as intriguing to photographers and naturalists as it is offshore to the hundreds of divers who come to explore its watery depths.

Over the ages, live coral has grafted itself to the island's volcanic limestone base, which slopes steeply into the sea. As a result, Bonaire is surrounded by coral formations and sea gardens, and most of the island's 86 dive sites lie immediately offshore. Moreover, Bonaire offers waters with visibility of 60 to more than 100 feet, nine first-rate diving operations, and a government dedicated to protecting its environment, on land and under the sea. (In 1991, the government appointed a marine park manager, who oversees offshore conservation efforts.)

The discovery of these submarine attractions and tourism's subsequent arrival represent the end of a nearly five-century search by the island's various owners for a viable economic base. Ever since 1499, when the island was discovered by Europeans—led not by Columbus, but by Amerigo Vespucci, who also sailed for the Spanish—governments and private entrepreneurs have tried a variety of ventures on Bonaire. The Spanish, after an unrewarding search for their favorite substance, gold, relied on the island as a source of wood, salt, and meat. They stripped it of its hardwoods and dyewoods, "panned" and dried salt from the sea around it, and hunted its wild goats and sheep.

The Dutch, who arrived in 1623, were no more successful in finding a lucrative use for the island. Nor were the British, who took over Bonaire in the early 19th century. In 1810, they leased the island to a US merchant, Joseph Foulke, who also failed to make good. When the Dutch returned in 1816, they tried harvesting salt, building ships, making brick and tile, raising stock (sheep, horses, and cattle), and weaving hats. Nothing worked. In recent years, Bonaire's men, unable to sustain themselves on the proceeds from the salt lake and the wild goat population, were forced to find work elsewhere, mostly in the oil refineries of Curaçao, Aruba, and Venezuela.

Neighbors on the sister islands and South America, who probably learned about Bonaire from the migrants, began to go there to get away from it all. They fished and lazed and took home tales of the stunning flocks of migratory flamingos at Goto Meer and Pekel Meer. Bird watchers followed; they eventually catalogued 189 species that live on the island in addition to the flamingos—warblers, doves, hummingbirds, sea swallows, gulls, green parrots, white and blue heron, native "lorikeets" or parakeets, and more.

The island's first hotel, the *Zeebad*—originally an internment camp for German prisoners during World War II, now the *Divi Flamingo Beach* resort and casino—opened in 1952. The second, the *Bonaire Beach* hotel (now the *Sunset Beach*), opened in 1962, about the time that the full tourist potential of the island began to be realized. Then the first scuba divers arrived, and with them the awareness that Bonaire's future lay less on its dry land than in the fabulous world below the surface of the sea around it.

Bonaire is a diver's paradise, but it has other attractions, too: its white sand beaches; its natural park; its eerie, sea-carved grottoes; and the petroglyphs left behind by the Caiquetio Indians, its original inhabitants. The sun shines all year, and the capital, Kralendijk (pronounced *Krawl*-in-dike), with its colorful, toy-like houses, is appealing. Residents are courteous and friendly; they seem genuinely happy to see visitors. Their *bon bini*—Papiamento for "welcome"—is genuine. This hospitality and the unspoiled nature attract not only bird watchers and divers, but those who just want to enjoy the serenity—and perhaps snorkel a bit, too.

Bonaire At-a-Glance

FROM THE AIR

The top of a 24-mile-long volcanic ridge poking out of the sea off the South American coast, Bonaire is shaped like a rough crescent, with its back to the trade winds blowing from the northeast. Its windward coast is surf-pounded and wild, but on the leeward side the crescent encloses a natural, protected harbor, with the uninhabited island of Klein Bonaire in the center. In its calm, clear waters a startling variety of marine life flourishes in depths easily managed by snorkelers and novice scuba divers. Beaches stretch to the south and north, but inland, the two halves of the island are quite different. The south is flat and desert-like, and the southern tip is marked by ponds of contrasting colors, where salt is manufactured by solar evaporation. The northern half of the island is hilly with much more greenery, especially within 13,500-acre *Washington-Slagbaai National Park* on the north coast.

The island is 38 miles east of Curaçao, 80 miles east of Aruba, and 50 miles north of the coast of Venezuela. With an area of 112 square miles and only 11,000 inhabitants, Bonaire is one of the most sparsely populated Caribbean islands and consequently one of the most unspoiled. Its capital city, Kralendijk, its major hotels, and its *Flamingo Airport* are on the leeward side near the center of the crescent.

The trip from New York—including flight connecting time—takes about seven hours, or five hours nonstop; from Miami, nonstop flights now make the trip in about 2½ hours.

SPECIAL PLACES

KRALENDIJK A clean, well-kept town, its name means "coral dike" or "reef." Many of the bright buildings are noteworthy examples of Dutch colonial architecture. A half-hour walk can take it all in: the fish market that looks like a Greek temple; the duty-free shops of Kaya Grandi; the waterfront with its promenade and lighthouse; the pier lined with fishing boats and island sloops; and the old fort with three ancient cannon.

BONAIRE MARINE PARK This underwater preserve incorporates the entire coastline surrounding both Bonaire and the offshore island of Klein Bonaire, down to 200 feet. The area is protected by law, and visitors may not take *anything,* alive or dead, from its reefs. Established in 1979, it is one of the few successful efforts in marine conservation in the Caribbean.

ELSEWHERE ON THE ISLAND
An island tour falls naturally into two circuits, northern and southern.

NORTHERN ROUTE Driving northward from Kralendijk, take a paved road that follows the shoreline along low coral cliffs. Every half mile or so there's a place to park and look; it's also possible to leave the car behind to walk along cactus-lined cliffside paths with views of curving beaches. One of these paths, carved from the coral rock, is known as the Thousand Steps (though there aren't really that many). It leads down to one of Bonaire's finest sites for scuba or snorkeling.

The main road continues north along an extraordinary section where a grotto in the hillside forms a natural arch along the roadway. Long ago, the ocean surface, now 30 or 40 feet lower, had been at the level of the roadbed. Over the centuries, waves and tides ate into soft coral rock and created this series of caves that extend deeply inland in some places.

The road turns inland, winds uphill, then dips again to one of Bonaire's most beautiful sites—Goto Meer, a lake that might have been lifted intact from the Scottish moors, except that it's saltwater, with an island in its center. Flocks of flamingos stand along the lake's irregular shoreline.

Follow the road to the right to Rincón, the oldest town on the island, with its distinctive pastel buildings. Stop at *Verona's* bar and restaurant near the center of town (Kaya Para Mira; no phone) for a beer or soft drink, or sample some of the unique, homemade flavors at *Prisca's Ice Cream* shop (phone: 6334) on Kaya Komkomber. The locals will probably stare at you appraisingly; simply say hello and tell them where you're from, and the curtain of aloofness disappears. Bonaireans are friendly and courteous, but they probably won't start a conversation without an invitation.

Those who want to make a day of this excursion should follow the road northwest along Goto Meer, turning left at the crossroad toward *Washington-Slagbaai National Park,* located at the northern tip of the island. This 13,500-acre tract is a preserve interlaced by miles of well-marked, rugged dirt roads. The park is untouched; there's no point in going unless you take the time to explore—set aside at least half a day to do it justice. There are two mapped-out routes to drive through the park, with stops along the way, of course, for exploring on foot: a 15-mile trail marked by green arrows, and a 22-mile one marked by yellow arrows. Pick up an *Excursion Guide,* available at the entrance for about $6; it describes the park's geography, history, geology, and plant and animal life. Watch for goats, donkeys, and iguanas. Though no hunting, fishing, or overnight camping is permitted, Boca Slagbaai (Slaughter Bay) is a favorite with picnickers. Bird watchers will see the most species in the morning. Top birding spots include Salina Mathijs, a salt flat popular with flamingos; the watering hole at Poos di Mangel; and Bronswinkel Well at the foot of Mt. Brandaris.

Along the park's shores are hidden bathing beaches and rocky caves. Swimming, snorkeling, and scuba diving are permitted. Incidentally, the name Washington originated when this area was all one plantation to which the owners had given the name "America." The most important place in "America" was where the workers got their pay, and they called that "Washington." The park is open to the public daily, except holidays, but no one is admitted after 3:30 PM. Admission charge (no phone). Near the entrance is a small museum whose featured exhibit, in addition to cooking utensils and pottery, is an antique hearse.

Afterward, backtrack to Rincón. Or if you've skipped the park and are in Rincón, turn right out of town and head to Onima, on the eastern coast, the site of interesting grottoes. Continue on the paved road for 2 or 3 miles east from Rincón, and then, at the roadside sign, turn left along a dirt road toward Boca Onima. At the end of the road is a parking area along a cliff face, perhaps 50 feet high, honeycombed with odd formations. It's well worth walking a quarter mile or so along the cliff base to look at the patterns carved in the volcanic rock by centuries of wind and water. Once back at the parking area, follow the sign reading "Indian Inscriptions" to the nearby shallow, open caves. The caves' ceilings are inscribed with pink-red petroglyphs designed by Caiquetio Indians at least 500 years ago. These patterns, which have never been deciphered by archaeologists, are repeated in various caves on Bonaire.

When returning to Kralendijk, take a short detour via Seroe Largu (pronounced *Lar*-go) for a special view of the city, the western shoreline, and, just offshore, the island of Klein Bonaire. This observation point is memorable. Drive out again on a brightly moonlit night. It takes only a few minutes, and the reward is splendid: the lights of Kralendijk and the boats in the bay; the lovely coastline; the moon reflected on the water; and a glow on the horizon from the lights of Curaçao, 40 miles away.

SOUTHERN ROUTE The tour south from Kralendijk is totally different. Head down the highway past the airport and the shore homes; about 5 miles away are radio towers belonging to one of the world's most powerful transmitters: the 810,000-watt Trans-World Radio.

After a shoreline drive that features hundreds of sea birds, the road reaches the AKZO Antilles International Salt Company's salt mountains, great pyramids of dazzling white sea salt. They are produced by a distillation process that starts with sea water flowing into a rectangular pond, where the sunshine and trade winds evaporate some of the water; the residue is then pumped to a second pond, where more water is evaporated. This continues in pond after pond, each pond assuming a different hue because of the amount of salt, until the water is completely evaporated. Flocks of pink flamingos feed in these multicolored ponds; they love the briny water and the algae. At two points along the way, the government has restored the tiny, tar-roofed huts where the slaves who worked in the salt ponds slept during the week. On weekends they hiked to their homes in Rincón, 7 miles away. (Slavery was abolished here in 1863.)

The drive now leads past Pink Beach, an incredibly soft stretch of white sand with a pink hue at the water line, followed by *Willemstoren,* the oldest lighthouse on Bonaire (unfortunately closed to the public). Continue past the *Maracultura Foundation,* an aquaculture research center on the south shore that is experimenting with ways to farm fish, shrimp, and conch. It's closed to the public. The road eventually leads to Sorobon, site of the island's only naturalist (clothing optional) resort, and Lac Bay. The road is bordered by mangrove swamps, unique to this part of Bonaire.

If you've brought a bathing suit or picnic lunch, take a 4-mile drive off the main road to Cai, a little settlement on Lac Bay. The swimming and snorkeling here are delightful (bring your own snorkeling gear), and there are shelters to provide shade for a picnic, as well as a snack bar and a small restaurant. The drive back to Kralendijk passes through two villages with the exotic names of Tera Cora and Nikiboko.

Sources and Resources

TOURIST INFORMATION

The *Tourism Corporation of Bonaire* has an office in Kralendijk (12 Kaya Simón Bolívar; phone: 8322 or 8649; fax: 8408). Closed weekends. For information about Bonaire tourist offices in the US, see GETTING READY TO GO.

LOCAL COVERAGE *Bonaire Holiday,* published three times a year, has information on events, shopping, and sightseeing. It's available free at the airport, tourist office, and hotels.

For background reading, pick up the *Guide to Corals and Fishes in the Caribbean* (published by the Island Territory of Curaçao, it's $8; a waterproof version is $13) and the colorful, informative *Guide to the Bonaire Marine Park,* by Tom van't Hof (published by Stinapa, the Netherlands Antilles Park Foundation; $20). Both are available in bookstores on the island.

RADIO AND TELEVISION Trans-World Radio (880 AM) has English newscasts three times a day. Most hotels have cable TV, which carries CNN, ESPN, and other English-language channels.

TELEPHONE When calling from the US, dial 011 (international access code) + 5997 (country code) + (local number). To call from another Caribbean island, the access code may vary, so contact the local operator. Dial 11 for emergency assistance.

ENTRY REQUIREMENTS Proof of citizenship (a passport, or an original or notarized birth certificate or voter's registration card with photo ID) and an ongoing ticket are all that US and Canadian citizens need.

CLIMATE AND CLOTHES Constant cloudless days (yearly rainfall totals only about 22 inches) keep the temperature about 82F (28C), although the thermometer sometimes may reach as high as 90F (33C) in September or as low as 74F (23C) in January. The island's heat and humidity are well tempered by trade winds blowing from the northeast at an average 16 mph. Casual resortwear is the general rule for both men and women. You'll need some type of long-sleeve cover-up to slip on when you've had enough sun. Shorts or slacks are okay for women in town, but bikinis should be confined to the beach or pool. Short-sleeve sport shirts are always permissible. *Note:* The effects of salt water and the constant Antillean breeze make simple hairstyles nearly essential for women; ditto head scarves for the beach and sightseeing drives.

MONEY The Netherlands Antilles florin, or guilder (NAf), is the official monetary unit, with a rate of exchange of approximately 1.80 NAf to $1 US. US dollars and traveler's checks are accepted everywhere; Canadian dollars are somewhat less negotiable, so they should be exchanged for florins. Banking hours are 8 AM to 4 PM weekdays. Stores offer no discounts for payment in US dollars. Major credit cards are honored in most shops, hotels, and restaurants. All prices in this chapter are quoted in US dollars.

LANGUAGE *Bon bini* might be the first words you hear; that's "welcome" in Papiamento, the language unique to the Netherlands Antilles. But don't worry; almost everyone connected with tourism understands and speaks English. Dutch is the official language, but since South America is so close, Spanish also is spoken widely.

TIME Bonaire is on atlantic standard time, which puts its clocks an hour ahead of eastern standard time (when it's noon in New York, it's 1 PM in Bonaire). During daylight saving time, the hour is the same in both places.

CURRENT Outlets are 127 volts, 50 cycles. American appliances work, though a bit slowly; adapters are recommended.

TIPPING A 10% to 15% service charge is added to most hotel bills to take care of chambermaids and other staff, and to restaurant checks. An additional tip is not needed unless some special service has been provided. Taxi drivers appreciate tips (10% of the fare) but it's not mandatory. Give airport porters and other bellhops about 50¢ per bag.

GETTING AROUND

CAR RENTAL The roads are narrow but in good to excellent condition, and with bird watching to do, numerous beaches to visit, and many diving sites just offshore (look for yellow markers beside the road), it's nice to have your own wheels. It's not expensive; daily rates include unlimited mileage, but there's a nominal government tax for each day the car is rented. US and Canadian driver's licenses are valid for driving on the island; the driver must be at least 21. For reservations call *Avis* (phone: 5795), *Budget* (phone: 8300 or 8315), *Dollar* (phone: 5588 or 8888), *A. B. Car Rentals* (phone: 8980), or *Island Car Rentals* (phone: 5111). *Bonaire Bicycle and Motorbike* (phone: 8226) and *S. F. Wave Touch* (phone: 4246) rent scooters, with free pickup and delivery.

INTER-ISLAND FLIGHTS *ALM* and *Air Aruba* (phone: 8300 for both) offer flights from Bonaire to Aruba, Curaçao, and Caracas, Venezuela. Direct charters are available as well.

SEA EXCURSIONS There are four-hour evening sails aboard the 60-foot Siamese junk *Samur* (phone: 5433). The *Samur* also offers snorkel cruises, sunset cruises, and barbecue trips to the uninhabited island of Klein Bonaire, off Kralendijk. Half-day snorkel cruises and sunset cruises also are offered aboard the 42-foot cutter *Oscarina* (phone: 8290) and the 37-foot trimaran *Woodwind* (phone: 8285). Glass-bottom boat tours are available aboard the *Bonaire Dream* at the *Harbour Village* marina (phone: 7500 or 4536).

Dive-Inn at the *Sunset Beach* hotel (phone: 8448, ext. 200) runs seagoing tours (diving, snorkeling, fishing, and sailing). Rates often include transport, beverages, and lunch, and vary according to sport and destination. *Dive-Inn, Captain Don's Habitat,* and *Peter Hughes Dive Bonaire* (at the *Divi Flamingo Beach* resort; see *Checking In* for the latter two) offer water-taxi rides to Klein Bonaire; they'll take passengers over in the morning, leave them for a few hours of snorkeling, beaching, and picnicking, and pick them up in the afternoon.

SIGHTSEEING BUS TOURS *Bonaire Sightseeing* (phone: 8300 or 8778) and *Ayubi's Tours* (phone: 5338) offer a choice of two-hour guided trips: a northern tour (not including *Washington-Slagbaai National Park*) and a southern tour. *Bonaire Sightseeing* also offers a three-hour guided town-and-country tour, a three-hour tour of *Washington-Slagbaai National Park,* and a full-day tour of the park (minimum four people).

TAXI The cabs are unmetered; government-established rates are posted in hotels and the airport, and each driver has a list. Rates increase 25% from 7 PM to midnight, and 50% from midnight to 6 AM. Hotels can get a cab in a matter of minutes, or you can call the central dispatcher at 8100. Drivers are good guides to island attractions and will take a party of up to four on a half-day tour.

SPECIAL EVENTS

Bonaire's biggest wingding is the *October International Sailing Regatta,* four days of racing, steel band music, dancing, and feasting not only for the crews of participating fishing boats, yachts, sloops, Sunfish, and Sailfish, but for the entire island and its visitors. *Carnival* time from late February to early March is observed with costumed parades and more dancing. Occupying a week in June, the *Nikonos Shootout* is an annual event for underwater-camera buffs. There's also lots of folk dancing and singing on *Día de San Juan* (St. John's Day, June 24) and *Día de San Pedro* (St. Peter's Day, June 28). More photography occurs, this time on land, during the *Birdwatching Olympics* (August 17–24). August is also *Bonaire Family Month,* with island-wide programs and special hotel rates geared toward making family travel fun and affordable. Official holidays, when banks and shops are closed (although some shops stay open when a cruise ship is in port), include *New Year's Day, Carnival Monday* (March 2), *Ash Wednesday,* the *Queen's Birthday* and *Rincón Day* (April 30), *Good Friday, Easter, Labor Day* (May 1), *Ascension Day* (May 28), *Whitmonday* (June 5 in 1995), *Bonaire Day* (September 6), *Kingdom Day* (December 15), *Christmas,* and *Boxing Day* (December 26).

SHOPPING

Bonaire shopping—like that in Curaçao and Aruba—though technically not entirely duty-free, offers substantial savings on a long list of imported luxuries: Swiss watches, English china, French perfume, Danish silver, Scandinavian crystal, jewelry, and more. On the whole, Bonaire's inventory doesn't begin to compare with that of its sister islands, though the opening of the *La Terraza* shopping mall in Kralendijk has considerably increased the selection. Store hours are 8 AM to noon and 2 to 6 PM; closed Sundays. The following stores are in Kralendijk unless otherwise noted.

Aries Boutique Good buys in 14K and 18K gold jewelry, watches, Delft china, and semi-precious gems. Dutch specialty foods also are on sale here. 33 Kaya Grandi (phone: 8091).

Caribbean Arts & Crafts A good place for locally crafted black coral, Mexican onyx, painted wooden fish, sterling silver jewelry, Peruvian tapestries, and decorative stone carvings. 38A Kaya Grandi (phone: 5051).

d'Orsy's You'll find a good selection of duty-free perfume and famous-name cosmetics, plus jewelry. *Harborside Mall* (phone: 5488).

Fundashon Arte Industria Bonariano Local crafts and souvenirs at a not-for-profit workshop. Located next to the post office on J. A. Abraham Blvd. (no phone).

Ki Bo Ke Pakus The "do-what-you-want" shop is the island's best boutique, offering a good selection of bikinis, dashikis, caftans, and pareos at nice prices. At the *Divi Flamingo Beach Hotel* (phone: 8239).

Littman Jewelers This is the place to shop for fine jewelry and watches. 33 Kaya Grandi (phone: 8160).

Maharaj Gift House The island's widest selection of fine stainless steel cookware and glassware. *La Terraza* (phone: 4402).

Spritzer & Fuhrmann A local branch of the well-known island chain of very fine jewelry shops. 31 Kaya Grandi (phone: 5488).

Things Bonaire A little bit of everything can be found here, from Indonesian clothing and jewelry, to delftware, to hats and visors. At the *Sunset Beach Hotel* (phone: 8190) and 38C Kaya Grandi (phone: 8423).

SPORTS

BIRD WATCHING Bird watchers flock to Bonaire and for good reason: close to 190 species live here. The roseate flamingos are the most famous, and there are pelicans, parrots, herons, doves, cuckoos, and such exotic birds as the groove-billed ani, the black-whiskered vireo, and the Caribbean eleania. Birding is best on the northern part of the island in valleys, ponds, and Washington-Slagbaai National Park. Flamingo sanctuaries are at Goto Meer on the northern coast and at Pekel Meer on the southwest coast. The largest colony lives at the salt flats at the southern end. For flamingo watching, take binoculars and a telephoto lens for your camera. A listing of most of the species of Bonaire birds is available at the tourist offices in New York and Bonaire.

BOATING If you're on Bonaire at *International Regatta* time in October, you're likely to be recruited by one of the skippers as crew or just ballast. A Sunfish can be rented at your hotel. The *Harbour Village* marina has 60 slips for various types of vessels.

SNORKELING AND SCUBA DIVING Bonaire is ideal for snorkeling, and scuba is the island's varsity sport. Divers come from everywhere to take part or to take advanced certification courses. Novices come to learn the sport and be certified by one of the island's teaching and training facilities. The island is special for diving because it's an underwater mountain fringed by coral reefs. That means you don't have to travel far to find the dive spots; most are right off the beach or a very short boat ride away. Beginning just offshore, the reef slopes gently downward at a 45-degree angle. Visibility in these calm waters is generally 60 to 100 feet, sometimes more. Of special interest is the *Hilma Hooker,* a 238-foot freighter wrecked off the southwest coast, which swarms with fish and other sea creatures. It is only 50 feet from the surface and can be viewed by snorkelers as well as divers. A decompression chamber is available next to the *St. Franciscus Hospital* in Kralendijk (phone: 8187 or 8900). Anyone planning to dive in the *Bonaire Marine Park* must purchase a dive tag, which entitles you to one calendar year of unlimited diving. Tags can be purchased at any dive shop or at the park headquarters in the *Old Fort* in Kralendijk (phone: 8444).

Of special interest is the island's reef preservation program, which offers visiting divers free buoyancy-control workshops (to prevent damage caused by divers' touching the reefs), with special sessions for advanced divers and photo buoyancy control. Check with any of the island dive shops for the schedule. Captain Don Stewart, leader of Bonaire's determined movement to preserve its reefs and marine life, runs *Captain Don's Habitat* (see *Checking In*), a five-star scuba training facility with multilingual instructors; it is rated one of the Caribbean's best. Another *PADI* five-star training facility is *Sand Dollar Dive and Photo* (phone: 5252) at the *Sand Dollar Beach Club.* It offers scuba instruction in four languages (English, Spanish, French, and Dutch/Papiamento), from beginner through advanced courses, including one in underwater photography.

Similar scuba programs are offered by *Peter Hughes Dive Bonaire* (with 11 dive boats and complete underwater-photography facilities) at the *Divi Flamingo Beach; Dive-Inn* at the *Sunset Beach;* Bruce Bowker of the *Carib Inn; Great Adventures Bonaire* at the *Harbour Village Beach;* and *Neal Watson Undersea Adventures* at the *Coral Regency* (see *Checking In* for all five). All local dive centers offer many boat dive and shore dive packages; prices vary. A unique diving opportunity is offered by Dee Scarr (phone: 8529; 215-473-3702), whose Touch the Sea underwater tours emphasize close yet nonintrusive interaction with sea creatures large and small (minimum two people). Or put on a mask and fins and swim out on your own (but never alone). Just don't spearfish or collect any coral or other marine souvenirs while underwater—it's strictly against the law. (It's okay to pick up shells on the beach.)

Dive packages are available through *Bonaire Tours* (phone: 800-526-2370; 908-566-8866 in New Jersey).

SPORT FISHING Local skippers are prepared to take visitors in search of dorado, yellowfin tuna, sea bass, grouper, marlin, sailfish, bonito, and pompano. Bone fishing is also available in the miles of flats and mangroves off the southern part of the island. Make arrangements through your hotel or contact *Captain Rich* (phone: 5111), *Piscatur Charters* (phone: 8774), *Captain Bob* (phone: 7070), or *Good Life Watersports* (phone: 4588).

SWIMMING AND SUNNING Few hotels have beautiful beaches. The best are found at *Sunset Beach* and *Harbour Village Beach* hotels (see *Checking In*). In general, Bonaire's shore is lined by low coral cliffs, with paths and stairways leading down to small coves of sandy beaches. A few of these spots have changing facilities, but most are too secluded to require them. No beach is ever crowded, even those in front of the hotels. In addition to the beaches just above and below Kralendijk, others worth a special visit include Pink Beach on the southwest coast; Sorobon and Cai on Lac Bay on the southeast coast, where you can watch the conch fishermen and help yourself to conch shells for souvenirs; and, on the northern end of the island, the coastline of *Washington-Slagbaai National Park,* including Playa Funchi, black coral Boca Bartol, and Playa Chiquito (Little Beach), walled on three sides by low coral cliffs.

TENNIS Not a major drawing card on Bonaire, but there are two courts at the *Sunset Beach,* two at the *Sand Dollar Beach Club,* and one at the *Divi Flamingo Beach* (see *Checking In* for all). Non-guests can play for free during the day and for an hourly charge in the evenings at the *Divi Flamingo Beach;* free tennis clinics are here Tuesday and Wednesday mornings.

WATER SPORTS Lac Bay, a 3½-mile-long, shallow, protected cove on the east coast, is ideal for windsurfing, especially for novices (there's no way to be blown out to sea). *Windsurfing Bonaire* (phone/fax: 5363) offers courses and board rentals and arranges free hotel pickup and drop-off. *Good Life Watersports* (see *Sport Fishing,* above), with desks at the major hotels, offers parasailing, water skiing, and banana-boat rides, plus boat and fishing charters. *Jibe City* (phone: 7547) offers windsurfing and sea kayaking on Lac Bay or through the nearby mangroves.

NIGHTLIFE

Most is at the hotels, with performances by local folk dancers, steel bands, or a local combo. The *Divi Flamingo Beach*'s informal gaming room—billed as "The World's First Barefoot Casino"—is open nightly except Sundays and occasionally has entertainment (for additional details, see *Casino Countdown* in DIVERSIONS. The island has two downtown nightclub/discos,

E Wowo ("The Eye" in Papiamento) and the new *Fantasy* disco (Kaya L. D. Gerharts; phone: 0434). The *Divi Flamingo Beach* resort and casino and the *Sunset Beach* hotel plan something a little different each evening during the winter season, with music and dancing several nights a week (see *Checking In* for both). Hotel happy hours and special theme nights featuring international buffets also are specialties, all pleasantly casual. For downtown mingling, stop in any evening (except Mondays) at *Karels* bar (Kaya J. N. E. Crane; phone: 8434), located on the waterfront across from the *Zeezicht* restaurant.

Best on the Island

CHECKING IN

The majority of Bonaire's hotel rooms are concentrated on the shore in or near Kralendijk. To keep hotel architecture and commercial growth in harmony with the island's simple beauties and relaxed atmosphere, expansion is being firmly controlled. Hotel prices range from expensive ($160 and more a night for a double room, without meals, in winter), to moderate (between $100 and $160 a night), to inexpensive (less than $100 a night). Off season (from May through about mid-December) rates are discounted anywhere from 20% to 40%. Many hotels offer an optional breakfast and dinner plan (Modified American Plan, or MAP) for about $35 per person per day, less for children under age 12. A government room tax adds to the bill $4.10 per person per night, and most hotels add a 10% to 15% service charge. A list of inexpensive guesthouses and rental apartments is available from the tourist office. All rooms listed below have private baths unless otherwise indicated. When calling from a phone on Bonaire, use only the local numbers listed below. For information about dialing from elsewhere, see *Telephone* earlier in this chapter.

EXPENSIVE

Captain Don's Habitat This property offers 11 two-bedroom cottages, 30 deluxe oceanfront hotel rooms, and 15 oceanfront luxury villas. Rooms and villas are air conditioned and feature terraces; none has a TV set or telephone. The *Kunuku Terrace Bar,* the casual *Rum Runners* restaurant, and a full-fledged scuba training facility (see *Snorkeling and Scuba Diving,* above) round out the amenities. Northern coast (phone: 8290; 800-327-6709; 305-373-3341 in Miami; fax: 8240).

Coral Regency A luxury property with 32 one- and two-bedroom suites, each with a full kitchen, air conditioning, private patio or balcony, TV set, and direct-dial telephone. Dive facilities, a casual restaurant, seaside bar, gift shop, and pool complete the picture. Quiet—ideal for those who want an upscale getaway. Next to *Captain Don's Habitat* (phone: 5580; 800-327-8150; fax: 5680).

Divi Flamingo Beach Hip and pleasantly informal, with 145 mostly tired-looking (but air conditioned) rooms, some with balconies over the water and some with TV sets. There also are 40 deluxe studios with kitchenettes and TV sets in the on-premises *Club Flamingo* complex, which includes a separate dive shop/pier next to the main resort. None of the guestrooms has a telephone. The two open-air dining rooms, *Chibi Chibi* (see *Eating Out*) and *Calabas Terrace,* overlook the beach and sea. There are also two bars, a casino, two freshwater pools, and a Jacuzzi; scuba diving is offered by *Peter Hughes Dive Bonaire.* The all-inclusive package is a good value. J. A. Abraham Blvd., between the airport and town (phone: 8285; 800-367-3484; fax: 8238).

Harbour Village Beach This is the top island choice for couples who want an upscale dive vacation; it is also one of the few resorts here with an excellent beach. All 70 recently renovated rooms and suites have ceiling fans (in addition to air conditioning), as well as direct-dial telephones, cable TV, and balconies or patios overlooking the marina or the beach. There are two restaurants (including *Kasa Coral;* see *Eating Out*), two bars, a pool, four lighted tennis courts, a dive shop, a 60-slip marina, a water sports center, and a new European-style spa and fitness center. At press time, a nine-hole golf course was set to open, and plans called for completion of a new casino sometime this year. Kaya Governador North, on the northwest coast at the marina (phone: 7500; 800-424-0004; 305-567-9509 in Florida; fax: 7507 or 305-567-9659).

Port Bonaire Set to open at press time, this property offers 20 one- and two-bedroom apartments and penthouses, as well as three two-bedroom beach houses. All accommodations are air conditioned, and each has a full kitchen, cable TV, a telephone, and a balcony or terrace. There's also a large pool, a dive center, and a bar/coffee shop. Opposite the airport on the waterfront (phone: 5636; fax: 5639).

Sand Dollar Beach Club These 85 comfortable studio, one-, two-, and three-bedroom condominium units have air conditioning, TV sets, and complete kitchens; a few have telephones. Two tennis courts, a pool, the *Green Parrot* restaurant (see *Eating Out*), and a *PADI* five-star scuba training facility (see *Snorkeling and Scuba Diving*) also are on the premises. There's a grocery store nearby. The place has a fun, upbeat atmosphere, and with the bonus of an activities program for children, it's popular with families. On the northwest coast (phone: 8738; 800-328-2288; fax: 8760).

MODERATE

Sorobon Beach An unusual "naturalist" resort, it has 20 one-bedroom cottages with kitchenettes, but no air conditioning, phones, or TV sets. Facilities include a beach and a restaurant. The big draw: Clothing is optional. Curiosity seekers are turned away at the front door. On Lac Bay (phone: 8080; 800-828-9356; fax: 5363).

Sunset Beach A popular group destination, this two-story property with 120 old-looking but amenity-laden rooms and suites is a link in the Golden Tulip hotel chain. All rooms are air conditioned and have TV sets, telephones, coffee makers, and mini-refrigerators. There is a nice beach, two bars, the *Playa Lechi* restaurant (see *Eating Out*), a coffee shop, and a beach pavilion for lunch; also shops, mini-golf, a pool, tennis courts, and a playground. *Dive-Inn* operates a full water sports program on the premises (see *Sea Excursions*). On the northwest coast (phone: 8448; 800-344-4439; fax: 8118).

INEXPENSIVE

Buddy Dive Resort There are a range of options at this growing resort. The original guestrooms are 10 tiny apartments along the ocean; each has a kitchenette, a shower, and twin beds. Only five are air conditioned; none has a phone or TV set. There is also a newer building, with 15 one-, two-, and three-bedroom apartments, and at press time another complex of 15 units was slated for completion this year. These apartments don't have phones either, but all feature air conditioning, kitchenettes, and TV sets. Just a few dollars more than the original apartments, they are well worth the extra cost. The *Buddy Watersports Center* offers scuba diving and other water sports. There's no restaurant. On the northwest coast (phone: 5080; 800-786-3483; fax: 8647).

Carib Inn This friendly roost is one of the island's best buys. Once a private home, it now is the base for Bruce Bowker's scuba operation; arriving in 1973, Bowker was Bonaire's first "imported" scuba instructor, and his hospitality is much of the inn's appeal. There are seven nicely renovated, unpretentious rooms (five with full kitchens), one sizable seaview suite with kitchen, and one efficiency apartment for rent to divers, plus a pool and patio. All the rooms have air conditioning and TV sets, but no phones. There's no restaurant. About 1½ miles outside of Kralendijk (phone: 8819; fax: 5295).

Sunset Inn Across the street from a small beach, this place offers five rooms and two one-bedroom suites, all air conditioned. The rooms have TV sets, telephones, and refrigerators. There's good snorkeling offshore, and car rentals are available at excellent rates. There's no restaurant. Just outside of town at 29 Kaya C. E. B. Hellmund (phone: 8448; 800-344-4439; fax: 8118).

EATING OUT

Food on Bonaire is generally acceptable, simply cooked, but there's not much variety. The *Sunset Beach* and *Divi Flamingo Beach* hotels try for international standards, and feature good, fresh fish plus an occasional rijsttafel—the traditional Indonesian "rice table" made up of many deliciously spiced dishes. The *Harbour Village Beach* hotel offers a good combination of continental, American, and native Caribbean fare. Hotels also serve native island dishes, but they don't always put them on the menu, so it's a good idea to ask about unlisted specials. Worth sampling: *keshi yena,* a tasty, if hefty, mixture of chicken or beef cooked with onions, tomatoes, olives, pickles, and raisins, then baked in a round of Edam cheese; *stobi,* a casserole of lamb served with rice and banana fritters; goat stew (nicely seasoned, it tastes a lot like veal); and fish chowder. Dinner for two (including tip but not drinks) will cost $50 or more at a restaurant in the expensive category; $25 to $45 at places listed as moderate; and less than $25 at inexpensive eateries. Unless otherwise noted, all restaurants listed below are open for lunch and dinner. Our recommendations are all in or near Kralendijk. When calling from a phone on Bonaire, use only the local numbers listed below. For information about dialing from elsewhere, see *Telephone* earlier in this chapter.

EXPENSIVE

Bistro des Amis Cozily French and one of the island's top restaurants for romantic dining, with Gallic specialties such as escargots, *coquilles St-Jacques,* and carpaccio in mustard-dill sauce. Several entrées combine the best of French and Caribbean flavors. Open for dinner only; closed Sundays. Reservations advised. American Express and Visa accepted. 4 Kaya L. D. Gerharts (phone: 8003 or 4191).

Kasa Coral Start off the day at this open-air restaurant with a breakfast buffet of familiar American dishes. Lunch entrées are mostly native dishes, while dinner is a prix fixe menu offering varied selections such as fresh seafood and rack of lamb. Open daily for breakfast, lunch, and dinner. Reservations advised. Major credit cards accepted. In the *Harbour Village Beach* resort, on the northwest coast (phone: 7500).

Raffles This Kralendijk restaurant in an old Bonairean home features Indonesian and continental cooking. The chef is especially well known for his sweet-and-sour shrimp and mango parfait. Open daily. Reservations advised. Major credit cards accepted. 5 Kaya C. E. B. Hellmund (phone: 8617).

MODERATE

Chibi Chibi Alfresco dining in a two-story wood building overlooking the beach. With an eclectic menu featuring a range of West Indian, American, and continental dishes plus seafood specialties, highlights include an extensive wine list and a weekly Sunday night all-you-can-eat buffet. Open daily for dinner. Reservations advised. Major credit cards accepted. At the *Divi Flamingo Beach* resort, between the airport and town (phone: 8285).

Den Laman This seafood spot has an inviting bar and delightful decor, with an aquarium full of tropical fish lining one wall. House specialties are fresh local fish and homemade cheesecake, and there's a salad bar. There's dancing and live entertainment most Saturday nights. Dinner only; closed

Tuesdays. Reservations advised. Major credit cards accepted. Shoreside between the *Sunset Beach Hotel* and the *Sand Dollar Beach Club* (phone: 8955).

Green Parrot Located on the beach, this is the perfect spot for sunset viewing. Burgers, seafood, steaks, and local specialties are served in a casual atmosphere. There's entertainment Saturday nights. Open daily. Reservations advised for dinner. Major credit cards accepted. At the *Sand Dollar Beach Club,* on the northwest coast (phone: 5454).

Playa Lechi Tropical dining in an attractive beach hut, where offerings include surf and turf. A weekly Bonairean Night on Saturdays features a buffet of island specialties and a floor show with local music. Open daily for dinner. Reservations advised on weekends. Major credit cards accepted. At the *Sunset Beach* hotel, on the northwest coast (phone: 8448).

Richard's A favorite of locals and visitors alike, this casual open-air eatery boasts lots of greenery and a gleaming wood bar. Chef Bonito specializes in seafood; his most popular dish is shrimp *primavera.* Boaters can dock at the pier out front. Open for happy hour and dinner; closed Mondays. Reservations advised. Major credit cards accepted. 60 Abraham Blvd. (phone: 5263).

Zeezicht That's Dutch for "sea view." It's a popular bistro right on the waterfront— good for sampling local specialties, including conch stew, goat curry, or fresh fish platters. Happy hour features live entertainment nightly. Open daily. Reservations advised. Major credit cards accepted. 10 Curaçaostraat (phone: 8434).

INEXPENSIVE

Otello This casual place, set on a corner and open on two sides, serves up traditional Italian fare, featuring homemade pastas with fabulous sauces. Open daily. Reservations unnecessary. No credit cards accepted. Kaya Prinses Marie (phone: 4449).

Rendez Vous This place offers a café atmosphere and seafood dishes, salads, steaks, several vegetarian dishes, and good desserts. Espresso and cappuccino are served in the bar. Dinner only; closed Sundays. Reservations advised. Major credit cards accepted. 3 Kaya L. D. Gerharts (phone: 8454 or 8539).

British Virgin Islands

The British Virgin Islands appear on most maps as a spray of dots not far from Puerto Rico; the general impression is that the cartographer spattered ink over a quarter inch of parchment, which makes for frustrating map reading. Sailors, however, have had no trouble finding the 50 landmasses—rocks, cays, fragments, spits, volcanic atolls, as well as full-fledged islands—that make up the group. For years—indeed, centuries—boats have sailed around and through them, putting in at completely empty cays for a night's rest or to lie in wait for richly laden galleons on their way to Europe, as 17th- and 18th-century pirates were fond of doing. More than 200 ships have run aground here over the centuries and tales of sunken treasure abound, especially off the Anegada Reefs. (Robert Louis Stevenson's *Treasure Island* is popularly believed to be BVI's Norman Island, but some think it's actually a tiny cay called Dead Chest off Peter Island, because of the book's famed ditty "Fifteen men on the Dead Man's Chest—Yo-ho-ho, and a bottle of rum!")

Christopher Columbus discovered the entire Virgin Islands chain in 1493, although it was forgotten almost immediately. In 1595 Sir Francis Drake sailed into the channel south of Tortola that now bears his name. Within 30 years the English had established a legal claim to at least some of the islands, although the claim was disputed—by the Spanish and the Dutch primarily—until 1672, when Tortola was annexed by the English government.

In the meantime, Tortola became a pirates' haven, and there was much coming and going from many of the smaller cays. By the end of the 17th century, Tortola had begun to attract English planters as well; they firmly established the British right to the island. By 1850 or so, a Quaker colony had been established, the planters far outnumbered the pirates, and the Quakers and the planters tried to form their own constitutional government.

Occasional talk of independence through the years notwithstanding, the British Virgin Islands remain linked to the British Commonwealth. The governor is appointed by the queen, but laws are made and administered by a locally elected chief minister and legislative council. You'll find a portrait of the queen in most hotels and shops and British courtesy everywhere. But, oddly enough, you'll also find only US currency in the British Virgin Islands.

Even more than their sisters, the US Virgin Islands, the British Virgins are for tourists who want sun, sea, and nature. Fewer than ten of the islands have accommodations for tourists, although yachtspeople and day sailors in the know often drop anchor off several of the others. The uninhabited coves of Fallen Jerusalem, Great Dog, Ginger, Norman, and little Prickly

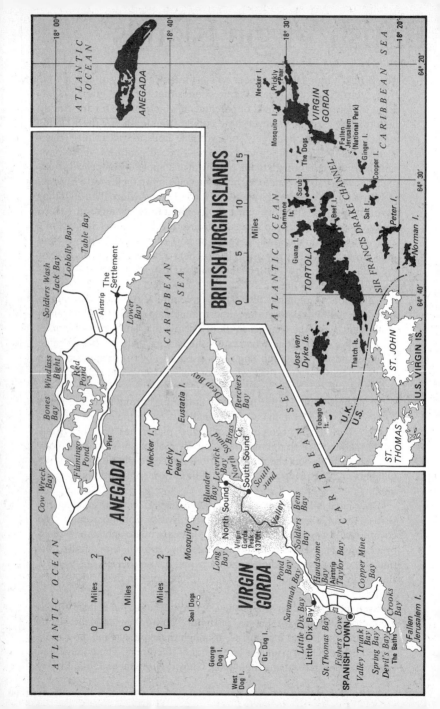

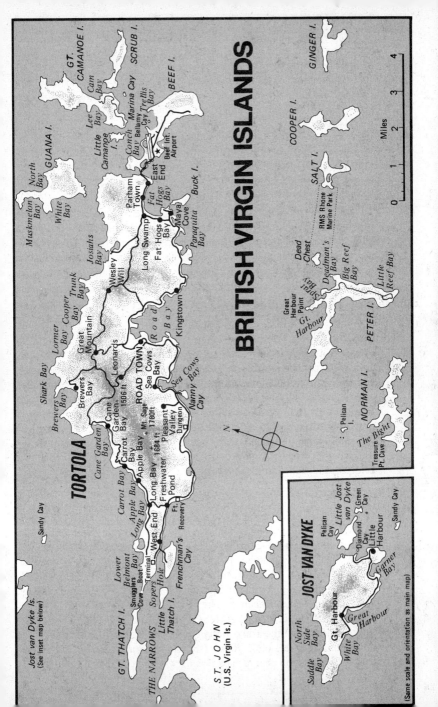

BRITISH VIRGIN ISLANDS

TORTOLA

Jost van Dyke Is.
(See inset map below)

Sandy Cay

GT. THATCH I.

Lower Belmont Bay
Smugglers Cove
Soper's Boat
West End
Little Thatch I.
THE NARROWS
Frenchman's Cay

ST. JOHN
(U.S. Virgin Is.)

Shark Bay
Brewers Bay
Cane Garden Bay
Carrot Bay
Apple Bay
Long Bay
Ft. Recovery

Lormer Bay
Cooper Bay
Trunk Bay
Great Mountain
Leonards
Garden
Carrot Bay
Mt. Sage 1780 ft
Long Bay 1684 ft
Freshwater
Ft. Pond
Pleasant Valley
Dungeon

Muskmelon Bay
North Bay
White Bay
GUANA I.

Josiahs Bay
Wesley Will

ROAD TOWN
Sea Cows Bay
Sea Cows Bay
Nanny Cay

Long Swamp
Fat Hogs Bay
Kingstown
Paraquita Bay

Lee Bay
Little Camanoe I.
Conch Bay
Marina Cay
Bellamy Cay
Trellis Bay
Cam Bay
GT. CAMANOE I.
SCRUB I.

Parham Town
East End
Fat Hogs Bay
Maya Cove
Buck I.
Beef Int. Airport
BEEF I.

N

Great Harbour
Gt. Harbour
Spirit Bay
Deadman's Bay
Dead Chest
Big Reef Bay
Little Reef Bay

RMS Rhone Marine Park

Pelican I.
The Bight
Treasure Pt. Cave
NORMAN I.

PETER I.

SALT I.

COOPER I.

GINGER I.

0   1   2   3   4
Miles

JOST VAN DYKE

North Side Bay
Saddle Bay
White Bay
Gt. Harbour
Great Harbour

Pelican Cay
Little Jost van Dyke
Diamond Cay
Green Cay
Little Harbour
Garner Bay
Sandy Cay

(Same scale and orientation as main map)

Pear are especially beckoning to the carefree bareboat visitor, while the seven relatively "built-up" British Virgin Islands (those with five or more guestrooms) are ready for vacationers who yearn for tranquil cottage resorts at the edge of the sea.

Development for tourism proceeds with great caution because much of the pleasure these cays and islands give tourists is in their isolation and tiny size. The BVI have been much less commercialized than other islands because of transportation difficulties; no major airlines have direct flights from North America, so ferries or small planes must be used. However, a recently opened cruise ship dock in Road Town can berth up to two ships daily (though far fewer than that currently stop here), and the airport will be enlarged over the next year or so to accommodate jets flying direct from the US.

Despite such developments, it is likely that these islands will remain the province of those lucky people who sail around them. The British Virgin Islands offer a quiet retreat, without hotel chains, fancy restaurants, or casinos, but with magnificent scenery, perfect sailing conditions, personalized hotels, secluded beaches, and welcoming, friendly islanders.

British Virgin Islands At-a-Glance

FROM THE AIR

The British Virgin Islands are made up of more than 50 islands, rocks, and cays, many of which are clustered around the Sir Francis Drake Channel, a historic waterway 20 miles long and 5 miles wide. The chain lies 60 miles east of Puerto Rico and directly northeast of St. John, one of the US Virgin Islands. Only 16 of the islands are inhabited; all told, they have a population of approximately 16,300 people and a total area of only 59 square miles. The major inhabited islands in the chain are Tortola, with the islands' capital, Road Town; Virgin Gorda; Beef Island (connected to Tortola by a bridge); Anegada; and Jost Van Dyke.

SPECIAL PLACES

TORTOLA Road Town, the capital of the BVI and home to about half of its residents, is where most activity begins and ends on Tortola. There are about a dozen shops to browse through all along Main Street, a colorful market at the edge of town, and any number of sailing craft to take you away for the day. Several of the colorful old wooden buildings have been preserved, even though a shopping plaza and several modern government buildings have gone up in the city center. The *Virgin Island Historical Society*'s small *Folk Museum* (Main St.; phone: 44811) has a pictorial display of island history, artifacts from the Taíno Indian and plantation eras, and items from the famous shipwreck of the *Rhone* (see *Snorkeling and Scuba* below). Open daily. No admission charge. The *Botanic Garden* (no phone), on the outskirts of town, has a fine collection of tropical flora and fauna—including palm and cactus collections—on four acres. It makes a very pleasant outing. Open daily. No admission charge, but charges for guided tours. To explore the island, head west from Road Town toward Sage Mountain, the island's highest point (1,780 feet) and the focal point of *Sage Mountain National Park* (no phone). On its slopes, what was once a primeval rain forest makes the ideal spot for a picnic overlooking the neighboring islands and cays. The temperature drops as you reach the summit, where three trails lead past huge trees and giant elephant vines, and hummingbirds and mockingbirds flit about. Open daily. No admission charge.

The coast road continues west past *Fort Recovery*, built in 1660 by the Dutch. Just beyond the anchorage at Sopers Hole (if you're thirsty, have a drink at *Pusser's Landing*) is West End town, the takeoff point for St. Thomas–bound ferries. Around the island's western tip lie the north shore's splendidly unspoiled white beaches: Smuggler's Cove, with its garden of snorkeling reefs; sweeping Long Bay; Apple Bay; Carrot Bay; Cane Garden Bay (where *Stanley's Beach Bar* sets up frosty drinks and snacks); beautifully protected Brewer's Bay (which features campgrounds and the remnants of a rum distillery); and Josiah's Bay near Tortola's eastern end. Turn south and cross the Queen Elizabeth Bridge to Beef Island, site of *Beef Island International Airport,* launch departures for Marina and Bellamy Cays, and untrammeled shelling and sunning beaches. Then head back to Road Town.

VIRGIN GORDA The highlight of a visit to this island (third-largest in the chain, with a population of about 2,500) is a trip to the Baths, where gigantic rocks and boulders, shaped by volcanic pressures millions of years ago, have formed strange entrances to water grottoes and shaded pools. Crawl through one formation to find yourself ankle-deep in cool water; through another to find a long stretch of sand and sunlight. Virgin Gorda boasts some 20 beaches; favorites include Spring, Trunk, and Devil's Bays. There is also a 1,370-foot mountain peak in the north, off the main road, that's suitable for hiking. An abandoned 17th-century copper mine on the southeast tip, with its chimney and boiler house still standing, offers fine photo opportunities from your car; the area is currently unsafe to walk around, although plans to reinforce the ground have been discussed for years.

ANEGADA The only coral island of the group (the rest are volcanic), its highest point is just 28 feet above sea level. It's home to a human population of only 150, as well as to a rare species of rock iguana. Dozens of shipwrecks off the reefs tempt divers. One of the sunken ships, the *Paramatta,* has rested 30 feet down for more than a hundred years; another, the 18th-century British frigate HMS *Astrea,* sank in 1808. There is also a Greek freighter, sunk in the middle of this century. Although there is little left of the ships, each wreck still holds the promise of hidden treasure.

JOST VAN DYKE Off this island's East End Harbour, close to Little Jost Van Dyke, lies Diamond Cay, home to terns, pelicans, and boobies; it has been designated a national park. Open daily. No admission charge (phone: 42069 or 43904).

Sources and Resources

TOURIST INFORMATION

The *British Virgin Islands Tourist Board* on Tortola is in the *Joseph Josiah Smith Social Security Building* (Waterfront Dr., Road Town; phone: 43134; fax: 43866). The *National Parks Trust* (Road Town; phone: 43904), which is working to protect 682 acres in the BVI, provides brochures and maps on many sites. For information about BVI tourist offices in the US see GETTING READY TO GO.

LOCAL COVERAGE The *Welcome* is a most informative free bimonthly guide. The *Island Sun* and *BVI Beacon* are the weekly BVI newspapers. Florence Lewisohn's *Tales of Tortola and the British Virgin Islands* (International Graphics; $8) is a readable history of the islands that is available at island shops. *The Cruising Guide to the Virgin Islands,* which is almost as valuable to landlubbers as to sailors, can be ordered directly from its publisher, Cruising Guide Publications (1130-B Pinehurst Rd., Dunedin, FL 34698; phone: 800-330-9542) for $16.95 (plus $3.75 shipping and handling).

RADIO AND TELEVISION ZBVI-AM (780) is the main island station, broadcasting adult contemporary and Caribbean music, as well as local and regional news and BBC World News. The FM station ZROD (103.7) is another option, playing Top 40 rock and pop music, news, sports, and weather. Channel 10 picks up programming from the CBS affiliate in St. Thomas, while cable TV beams 18 channels throughout the area.

TELEPHONE When calling from the US, dial 1 + 809 (area code) + 49 (country code) + (local number). Area codes from other Caribbean islands may vary, so contact the local operator. When calling within the British Virgin Islands, use only the local number unless otherwise indicated. Dial 999 for emergency assistance.

ENTRY REQUIREMENTS A current passport is the preferred entry document, but proof of citizenship (birth certificate or voter's registration card, along with a photo ID) is acceptable. An ongoing or return ticket is also required. There is a departure tax of $8 per person leaving by air; $5 per person leaving by sea.

WARNING

There currently is a law prohibiting members of the Jamaican Rastafarian movement from entering the BVI (purportedly because of concerns about drug smuggling). Rastafarians who must visit for a specific reason, such as business (vacations don't qualify), must have an island official file an application in advance with the immigration authorities. Also, there have been reports of immigration officials turning away tourists wearing clothes or hair styles (such as dreadlocks) that are commonly worn by Rastafarians, even if the tourists are not from Jamaica and not members of the sect. For more information contact the tourist office in New York before you leave (phone: 212-696-0400 or 800-853-8530).

CLIMATE AND CLOTHES The British Virgin Islands enjoy temperatures that range from 77 to 90F (25 to 32C) all year. The air is cooled by trade winds, especially at night, when temperatures drop as much as 10 degrees. Comfortable and casual are the fashion bywords here. Men (except those staying at *Little Dix Bay*) can leave their jackets and ties at home.

MONEY The US dollar is used throughout the islands.

LANGUAGE The queen's English is spoken, often with a West Indian lilt.

TIME Atlantic standard time is in effect all year. In winter, when it's noon in the BVI, it's 11 AM in the US eastern standard time zone; when daylight saving time is in effect, the hour is the same in both places.

CURRENT Outlets are 110 volts, 60 cycles; American appliances need no converter.

TIPPING All hotels add a 10% to 15% service charge to bills; anything additional is up to you. The standard 10% to 15% is expected in restaurants and by cabbies.

GETTING AROUND

CAR RENTAL Only the coolest and surest drivers should take on the roller coaster hills and hairpin turns of the roads in the British Virgin Islands. Vehicles range from Land Rovers, jeeps, and mini-mokes to six- and eight-passenger Suzukis and air conditioned automatic sedans. On Tortola, contact *Alphonso's* (in Fish Bay; phone: 43137 or 44886); *Avis* (opposite police headquarters; phone: 43322 or 42193); *Budget* (Wickhams Cay; phone: 42639; 42531, after hours); *Caribbean Car Rental* (at *Maria's Inn;* phone: 42595); *International Car Rentals* (at *International Motors* in Road Town; phone: 42516 or 44715); *Island Suzuki* (near Nanny Cay; phone: 43666); or *National* at Duffs Bottom (phone: 43197). On Virgin Gorda, try *Andy's Taxi* (Spanish Town; phone: 55511); *Hertz* (The Valley; phone: 55803 or 800-654-3001); *Mahogany* (The Valley; phone: 55469); or *Speedy's Car Rental* (The Valley; phone: 55235 or 55240). A valid US driver's license and a temporary BVI driver's license (good for 30 days; available at police headquarters or the rental agency for $10) are required. Renters must be over 25 years of age, and, remember, driving is on the left.

FERRY SERVICES Travel between Tortola and Virgin Gorda is mainly by local ferry service, which costs about $10 one way. *Smith's Ferry* (phone: 44430, 42355, or 54495) and *Speedy's Fantasy* (phone: 55240 or 55235) both operate from Road Town in Tortola to the Virgin Gorda Yacht Harbour, about a half-hour trip. *Smith's, Inter-Island Boat Services* (phone: 54166), and *Native Son* (phone: 54617) travel between Road Town or West End in Tortola and St. Thomas ($19 one way). *Speedy's* links Virgin Gorda with St. Thomas for $25 one way. The *North Sound Express* (phone: 52271) goes from Beef Island to Virgin Gorda ($18 one way), and *Virgin Gorda Ferry Service* (phone: 55240 or 55542) makes the run from Beef Island to The Valley in Virgin Gorda for $12 one way. *Peter Island Boat* (phone: 42561/2) links that island to Tortola; the trip costs $5 one way. And the *Jost Van Dyke Ferry Service* (phone: 42997) sails for that island from Tortola's West End for about $15 one way. Individual arrangements can be made for separate trips.

INTER-ISLAND FLIGHTS *American Eagle* (phone: 52559; 800-433-7300), *Atlantic Air BVI* (phone: 800-879-0000) and *LIAT* (phone: 43888; 800-253-5011) offer frequent daily flights from San Juan to Tortola and Virgin Gorda. *LIAT* also flies to Tortola from Antigua, St. Kitts, Dominica, and St. Maarten. *Air St. Thomas* (phone: 55935; 800-522-3084; 809-776-2722 on St. Thomas) has daily flights from St. Thomas and San Juan to Virgin Gorda.

SEA EXCURSIONS Day sails (including drinks) to Cooper Island, Anegada, and Peter Island aboard 30- to 50-foot yachts and evening sails to Ginger Island are available through *Misty Isle Charters* (phone: 55643). Similar day- and week-long sails are offered by the amiable crews at *Sunsail* (phone: 54740; 800-327-2276), with a fleet of about 65 sailboats and catamarans.

SIGHTSEEING TOURS On Virgin Gorda, tours are offered by *Andy's Taxi* (phone: 55511) and *Mahogany Taxi Service* (phone: 55469, days; 55322, nights). On Tortola there's *BVI Taxi* (phone: 42322 or 43942), *Style's Taxi* (phone: 42260, days; 43341, nights), *Travel Plan Tours* (phone: 42872), or *Turtle Dove Taxi* (phone: 46274). *Scato's Bus Service,* also on Tortola (phone: 42365), conducts tours on 26-seat minibuses for the budget-minded. *Fly BVI* (Virgin Gorda; phone: 51747) offers 45-minute sightseeing tours by small plane.

TAXI Cabs are readily available only on Tortola, Virgin Gorda, and Anegada; rates are fixed, so ask in advance. "Safaris," attractive open buses painted bright colors, are available through *Mahogany Taxi Service* on Virgin Gorda and *BVI Taxi* on Tortola (see *Sightseeing Tours,* above, for both). You have to call for safaris; they cannot be hailed in the street.

SPECIAL EVENTS

Virgin Gorda holds a three-day festival at *Easter.* The *Spring Regatta* in April on Tortola draws yachts and hordes of spectators from all the Caribbean islands as well as the US. The *BVI Summer Festival* in August is a two-week bonanza of beauty contests, singing, dancing, and parades.

Also in August is the *International Marlin Tournament* held at the *Biras Creek* resort. The *Inter-Airline Regatta,* on Tortola in late September or early October, attracts airline employees from far and wide to compete, uncharacteristically, in a sailing event. Banks and offices close for *New Year's Day, Commonwealth Day* (early March), *Good Friday* and *Easter Monday* (April 5 and 8 in 1996), *Whitmonday* (May 27 in 1996), the *Queen's Official Birthday* (second Saturday in June), *Territory Day* (July 1), *Summer Festival Days* (early August), *St. Ursula's Day* (October 21), the *Prince of Wales's Birthday* (November 14), *Christmas,* and *Boxing Day* (December 26).

SHOPPING

Selections pale beside those in the neighboring USVI, but while Road Town is not a duty-free port, there's no duty on British imports, and some items are bargains. Per-bottle prices on liquor are sometimes lower than those on St. Thomas or St. Croix, but because of the one-liter limit (as opposed to the one-gallon USVI duty-free allowance), most US citizens buy their booze in Charlotte Amalie or Christiansted. Island goods include handmade shell jewelry, cotton resortwear, coral creations, local ceramics, and interesting artwork. Most shops are in colorful old wooden buildings on Road Town's Main Street, with a few more in shopping arcades built into marina developments. General shopping hours are weekdays from 10 AM to 5 PM and Saturdays from 9 AM to 1 PM. Best for buying and browsing on Tortola include the following:

A. H. Riise Smaller version of the St. Thomas store with bargain-basement liquor prices. O'Neal Complex, Port Purcell (phone: 44483 or 46615).

Ample Hamper All sorts of edible and potable temptations from Great Britain and the islands. Wickhams Cay I (phone: 42494) and Sopers Hole, West End (phone: 54684).

Caribbean Handprints Batik fashions for men, women, and children. Main St. (phone: 43717).

Carousel Gift Shop Locally made crafts, including attractive pottery and costume jewelry with island themes. Next to the *Tropic Isles Building,* Waterfront Dr., Road Town (phone: 44542).

Collector's Corner An enormous selection of cut and uncut larimar, a bluish stone mined in the Dominican Republic; also handmade shell jewelry and works of local artists. *Columbus Centre,* Wickhams Cay I (phone: 43550).

Crafts Alive This daily outdoor market, with stalls offering souvenir items and endless T-shirts, is the place to practice your haggling. On Waterfront Dr., near the *BVI Tourist Board* (no phone).

Flamboyance Perfumes and Fendi purses star here. Soper's Hole, West End (phone: 54699).

Kaunda's The spot to pick up calypso and reggae tapes and CDs. Main St. (phone: 46737).

Kids in de Sun Ideal for indulgent grandmas, with fashions including tiny Java Wraps batiks and other hand-painted beauties. Main St. (phone: 43343).

Samarkand Handmade jewelry in an eye-catching pink-and-lilac building. Main St. (phone: 46415).

Sunny Caribbee Spice Company Exotic spices, jams and jellies, mustard, vinegar, herbs, tea, coffee, and hot sauces from all over the Caribbean, plus a fine collection of local art and artifacts. Main St. (phone: 42178).

On Virgin Gorda at Yacht Harbour, *Island Woman* (phone: 55237) has Java Wraps batik clothing and Indonesian crafts; *Kaunda's* (phone: 55636) and the *Virgin Gorda Craft Shop* (phone: 55137) have Caribbean crafts.

SPORTS

BOATING The British Virgins are among the world's best sailing areas, with more than 300 bareboats, almost 100 charter yachts, and the most developed marinas and shore facilities in the Caribbean. More than 70% of the visitors to the BVI are on sailing vacations. Among the dozen yacht charter firms in Road Town, the tops in quality of boats and expertise of personnel is Ginny and Charlie Cary's *Moorings,* the largest yacht operation in the Caribbean (phone: 42331; 800-535-7289 or 800-437-7880; 813-530-9747 in South Florida; or write 19345 US 19N, Suite 402, Clearwater, FL 33546). Also recommended are the *Trimarine Boat Company* (phone: 42490; fax: 45774) and *Tropic Island Yacht Management* (phone: 42450; 800-356-8938). The sailboat *Take Two* is available for charter from the *Prospect Reef* resort (phone: 45208). *Misty Isle Charters* and *Sunsail* (see *Sea Excursions,* above, for both) offer week-long flotilla sailings, where several boats sail together following a lead vessel. Steve Colgate's *Offshore Sailing School* (phone: 800-221-4326) at the *Treasure Isle* hotel offers courses year-round, including a catamaran course. Long-term rentals of bareboats and all-inclusive charters also are available from the *Bitter End Yacht Club* (phone: 42746; 800-872-2392) in Virgin Gorda. *The Cruising Guide to the Virgin Islands* (see *Local Coverage,* above) is an invaluable publication for anyone interested in sailing, diving, or snorkeling.

CAMPING For those who love to rough it, BVI campgrounds offer a variety of options: Rates for two people range from as little as $7 for a bare site to upward of $36 for a tent site outfitted with basic equipment (rates often drop in summer). *Brewer's Bay Campground,* Tortola (phone: 43463), is on a beautiful beach. There's a bar and restaurant; snorkeling gear, tours, and baby-sitters are available. On the coral island of Anegada is the *Anegada Beach Campground* (phone: 59466). Jost Van Dyke's *Tula's N & N*

Campground (phone: 59302; fax: 59296) has a restaurant, a snack bar, a fishing boat, and live entertainment on Mondays.

FISHING Deep-sea fishing is so notable that an International Marlin Tournament is held in August at Biras Creek (phone: 43555 or 43556). The *BVI Yacht Club* (phone: 43286) stages several tournaments annually. Your hotel can arrange hiring boats and equipment.

HIKING *Sage Mountain National Park,* which peaks at 1,780 feet, is an interesting place to hike on Tortola; its three trails lead hikers through a mahogany plantation and past 100-foot-tall trees. Check with the tourist board or with *Shadows Ranch* (phone: 42262), which offers exploration on foot or on horseback. A bonus for bird watchers: A list of birds that live on the islands is available from the *National Parks Trust* (see *Tourist Information,* above).

HORSE RACING There's betting, music, food, and fun at Tortola's makeshift *Little A Race Track* (Zion Hill Road; phone: 44442) one Sunday a month, as well as on holidays and during the *BVI Summer Festival* in August. Check local publications for racing schedules. Also see *Horse Races* in DIVERSIONS.

HORSEBACK RIDING *Shadows Ranch* (see *Hiking,* above) offers several rides, including jaunts to *Sage Mountain National Park* or Cane Garden Bay; rates include a guided tour.

SNORKELING AND SCUBA DIVING There's excellent snorkeling at Virgin Gorda around the Baths, Savannah and Pond Bays, and a dive site called "the Indians" near Peter and Norman Islands. Marina Cay and Cooper Island have good snorkeling from their beaches. Anegada Island, just off the Anegada Reef, has excellent scuba diving and snorkeling sites, although there's not much left of some of the 300-odd ships wrecked here. The most popular dive site in the British Virgin Islands is the wreckage of the RMS *Rhone,* now a British National Monument, close to the western point of Salt Island, a little over 5 miles from Road Town, Tortola. Destroyed by an 1867 hurricane that sank 75 ships and killed at least 500 people, the *Rhone* is one of the Caribbean's most intriguing wrecks. It is broken in half, both parts adorned with colorful fans, corals, sponges, and gorgonians. A huge variety of tame fish cruise through the ship's interior and upright wreckage. It can be reached by commercial dive boat or private charter. Other popular dive sites (there are well over 60) include Blonde Rock, between Dead Chest and Salt Island; Painted Walls (shallow); the wreck of the *Chikuzen* north of Beef Island; and Brenners Bay near Norman. For additional details, see *Sunken and Buried Treasure* in DIVERSIONS.

Among the larger dive outfits in Tortola are *Baskin in the Sun* (phone: 42858 or 54582; 800-233-7938; fax: 45853), with outlets at the *Prospect Reef* and *Long Beach Bay* hotels (see *Checking In* for both), the *Village Cay Resort Marina* in Road Town, and *Sopers Hole Marina; Underwater Safaris,* at the *Moorings* (Road Town; phone: 43235 or 43965; 800-537-7032); and *Blue*

Water Divers (Nanny Cay; phone: 42847). In Virgin Gorda, try *Kilbride's Underwater Tours* (North Sound, Virgin Gorda; phone: 59638) and *Dive BVI* (Virgin Gorda Yacht Harbour, Leverick Bay, and Peter Island; phone: 55513; 800-848-7078). Most of these outfits also offer snorkeling excursions, as do *King Charters* (phone: 45820) and *Caribbean Images* (phone: 52563). The 80-foot traditional schooner *White Squall II,* out of the *Village Cay* marina (phone: 42564), and the catamaran *Patouche II,* at Wickhams Cay I (phone: 46300), offer half- and full-day snorkeling trips to Norman Island; rates include lunch (on day-long trips), drinks, and snorkeling gear.

SURFING Apple Bay is the place. Surfboards are available at *Sebastian's on the Beach* (see *Checking In,* below); *Bomba's Surfside Shack* (Cappoon's Bay; phone: 54148), which looks like a junkyard from the road, is the hangout for the surfing crowd.

SWIMMING AND SUNNING Although almost all of the British Virgin Islands' beaches are lovely, in our opinion, this one is the fairest of them all.

A DREAM BEACH

Cane Garden Bay Acknowledged to be one of the handsomest stretches (1½ miles) of fine, white beach in all the British Virgins, this is the place we choose to spend lazy, sun-filled days. The gentle surf makes it ideal for young children. You have to bring your own snorkel gear, but you can buy a nice island lunch at *Quito's Gazebo* or *Rymer's Beach Bar* (see *Eating Out* for both). For a slightly more formal lunch, walk along the bay to the *Sugar Mill* hotel (see *Checking In*). Except for a tire-and-rope swing, there are no sports facilities. Activities are limited to sunning, splashing, and feeling pleased you came.

Other splendid strands include Smuggler's Cove, with its snorkeling reefs, and the mile-long white sands of Long Bay. But the lazing is lovely and the swimming fine on a dozen lesser-known strands as well. Virgin Gorda is ringed with glorious beaches such as Devil's Bay, Spring Bay, and Trunk Bay. And dozens more on the BVI's small cays and uninhabited isles await discovery.

TENNIS On Virgin Gorda, *Little Dix Bay* has seven courts overseen by *Peter Burwash International* (for guests only); *Biras Creek* has two, also open to guests at the *Bitter End Yacht Club.* On Tortola, *Prospect Reef* has six courts, *Mariner Inn* has two, and *Long Bay Beach* and *Frenchman's Cay* each have one. *Treasure Isle* guests may use the *Mariner Inn* courts across the street. There are also courts at the *Guana Island Club, Necker Island,* and *Peter Island* resorts. (See *Checking In* for all of these hotels.)

For those who have energy left after a day of sun and sea and dinner, there's lots of action after dark. In Road Town on Tortola, the *Paradise Pub* at the *Fort Burt Marina* (phone: 42608) has live entertainment (reggae, jazz, or rock) Thursday through Saturday nights; *Fort Burt* (at the marina; phone: 42587) jumps on Wednesdays; and the *Santa Maria* restaurant (see *Eating Out*) has something going on Tuesdays through Sundays. Look for night action at *Treasure Isle* (see *Checking In*) on Mondays and Fridays.

Elsewhere on Tortola, *Pusser's Landing* in the West End (see *Eating Out*) offers dancing, often to a BVI *fungi* band, a traditional island combo that consists of instruments such as acoustic guitars, squash gourds, ukulele, maracas, banjo, washtub bass, and even an ass pipe (a hollow bamboo reed that makes a sound like a donkey's braying); the festivities here go on till early morning Thursdays through Sundays. The *Long Bay Beach* resort (see *Checking In*) offers entertainment on Tuesdays and Fridays, while *The Apple* (see *Eating Out*) does its number on Wednesdays and Sundays. On the beach, *Bomba's Surfside Shack* (see *Surfing*, above) has local bands Wednesday nights and Sunday afternoons (honeymooners get two drinks on the house), but the party really heats up during each month's full moon. *Sebastian's on the Beach* offers a West Indian *fungi* band Sunday nights, there is reggae at *Rymer's Beach Bar* Friday and Saturday nights, and a steel band plays at *Stanley's* nightly except Sundays. Finally, the delightful Quito Rymer sings folk music at *Quito's Gazebo* five times a week after dinner, with reggae featured Fridays and Saturdays. (See *Eating Out* for details on the four places immediately above.)

On other islands, Virgin Gorda's *Bath & Turtle* (open Wednesdays and Sundays), *Bitter End Clubhouse* (open Mondays, Wednesdays, and Saturdays), and *Pusser's Leverick Bay* (open Thursdays through Sundays) feature live and taped dance music into the wee hours (see *Eating Out* for all). There's night action at the *Virgin Queen* (Virgin Gorda; phone: 42310) on Fridays, live music Mondays and Fridays at the *Olde Yard Inn,* and nightly Caribbean music at the *Pavilion* restaurant at *Little Dix Bay* (see *Eating Out* for the latter two restaurants). On Jost Van Dyke, *Foxy's* (see *Eating Out*), is another popular nightspot right on the sand; Thursday through Saturday nights, guitarist Foxy improvises songs that spoof audience members. *Club Paradise* (see *Eating Out*), just west of the *Customs House,* offers live reggae most weekends. *Tula's N & N Campgrounds* (see *Camping,* above) offers live music Monday nights. A boat takes partyers from Virgin Gorda to Mosquito Island's *Drake's Anchorage* (see *Eating Out*) for live music alternate Tuesdays and Thursdays. For a special treat, arrange to take a dinghy to tiny Bellamy Cay at Beef Island for an evening at the *Last Resort* (see *Eating Out*), where Tony Snell has entertained the boating crowd with risqué one-man shows for more than two decades; dinner is at 7:30 PM, cabaret at 9:30 PM.

Best on the Islands

CHECKING IN

Throughout the British Virgin Islands are some 90 hotels and guesthouses. Although a few of the larger hotels offer special packages that can cut costs considerably, most do not. Expect to pay from about $450 to $690 for a double room (with all meals included) in winter at the hotels we've listed as very expensive. Without meals (European Plan), double rooms in the expensive category will run from about $200 to $425 a night, and our moderate selections will cost $100 to $190 a night. Modified American Plan (including breakfast and dinner) and American Plan (all meals included) rates at places that aren't all-inclusive are higher. Rates drop by as much as 50% in summer. A 7% accommodation tax is added to hotel bills; service charges vary from 10% to 15%. Private homes also are available for rent; check with the tourist board for listings. Many luxurious hotels do not have air conditioning, since the trade winds and ceiling fans are sufficient for most people; however, unless otherwise noted, all hotels listed below have air conditioning, telephones, TV sets, and private baths. Be aware that mosquitoes can plague hotels from time to time; it's a good idea to bring insect repellent from home. The central telephone number for making British Virgin Islands hotel reservations is 800-835-8530 (212-696-0400 in New York; fax: 212-655-5671). When calling from a phone within the British Virgin Islands, use only the local numbers listed below. For information on dialing from elsewhere, see *Telephone* earlier in this chapter.

We begin with our favorite havens, followed by recommended hotels listed by price category.

A REGAL RESORT, A SPECIAL HAVEN, AND ENCHANTED PRIVATE ISLANDS

Little Dix Bay There's sort of a fresh-air exhilaration about life at this 500-acre complex on Virgin Gorda. The guests that gather on its sunny crescent of beach generally love sailing, sunning, swimming, and snorkeling in their own home bay and picnic trips to the island's other blissful beaches; there's also *Peter Burwash International* tennis, horseback riding, and biking. The resort, with 98 beautifully decorated guestrooms and four suites, has undergone a massive renovation which added air conditioning in 44 of the 98 rooms. (There are no TVs, but this is seen as a serene plus here.) The resort's central building is composed of terraces topped with peaked roofs that look like giant beach hats. But during the day you won't find many people under them; everybody's up and about. At night, everyone gathers in the *Pavilion* bar for drinks. Sometimes there's music, dancing, or local entertainment during and after dinner. Outstanding meals are served in the *Pavilion* (see *Eating Out*), and the *Beach Grill* serves grilled Caribbean fare. Full breakfasts are included in the rate, as are water taxi rides to other islands; use of snorkeling and water skiing equipment, Sunfish and kayaks, and daily tennis clinics are also complimentary. The moonrises are spectacular. Our favorite rooms are those in the shingle-topped, hexagonal stilt-houses west of the main buildings, with patios and hammocks underneath; inside, you'll find all the traditional comforts. Its carefree, outdoorsy style makes this a good place for honeymooners, families, and stressed-out corporate types. Little Dix Bay (phone: 55555; 800-928-3000; fax: 55661).

Biras Creek This Virgin Gorda retreat feels far away because it is— a 15-minute taxi ride plus a boat ride (both complimentary) from the Virgin Gorda airstrip. But what a place to soak up sun and unwind. The resort's 140 acres reach from a blue bay on one side, up and over a hill, and then down again to the sea on the other. The 32 beachside suites, including two deluxe suites with sunken tubs, and one two-bedroom villa, are luxurious right down to their plush area rugs—but without such modern intrusions as telephones and TV sets (only one suite is air conditioned). Nothing showy, but lots of traditional Caribbean decor, including touches of wicker and Virgin Gorda stonework. The suites feature airy bedrooms, sitting rooms, patios facing the sea, and discreetly walled outdoor showers that give the feeling of bathing in a waterfall. At the glittering beach there's sunbathing, swimming, snorkeling, sailing, and windsurfing. A permanent dock can accommodate 10 yachts of up to 60 feet long. There's also a small nature sanctuary (the gardener leads tours on Monday mornings) and two tennis courts just a short stroll away. It's a 5-mile hike (or bike trip) to town (bikes are free), but day sailing trips to other beaches are more fun and often include memorable picnics. At cocktail time, everyone sleeks up and gathers in the castle-shaped clubhouse on the heights for drinks, sunset viewing, dinner, and— three nights a week—live music (see *Eating Out*). No children under six. North Sound (phone: 43555/6; 800-223-1108; fax: 43557).

Guana Island Club Green-clad and hilly, this 850-acre island prides itself on "a comfortably casual atmosphere, lots of space, and privacy." A maximum of 30 guests are lodged in 16 whitewashed cottages (with verandahs) that cling to the central ridge among the 18th-century ruins of a Quaker sugar plantation. A recent addition is the totally secluded North Beach Cottage, with a private pool and a kitchen. None of the accommodations has air conditioning (there's great cross-ventilation) or a telephone or TV set—

here the goal is to escape from such reminders of modern life. Guests also can rent the entire island for around $8,500 a day. Seven shining beaches, a salt pond populated by a flock of flamingos, a nature preserve boasting unusual flora and fauna, and intriguing mountain trails provide daytime diversion. Then there's always snorkeling, sailing, fishing, windsurfing, water skiing, tennis, croquet, or simply lazing by the pool; scuba diving can be arranged. All on-premises activities and three meals a day (including wine with lunch and dinner) are included. The island is a 10-minute launch ride from *Beef Island International Airport* on Tortola (phone: 42354; 800-544-8262; 212-696-4566 in New York City; fax: 52900).

Necker Island Advertised simply as "The Island," this 74-acre hideaway, surrounded by its own unspoiled coral reef and flanked by three white sand beaches, may indeed be the ultimate in luxurious retreats. Its owner, Richard Branson, the multimillionaire whiz kid of Virgin Records and Virgin Atlantic Airways, bought this island for his family and friends, but then decided to lease it out when he's not there. Privacy-seeking vacationers have included Oprah Winfrey, Mel Gibson, and Princess Di. The 10-bedroom villa, a remarkable Balinese-style structure, was built from rock that was blasted from the top of Devil's Hill, where it perches, entirely surrounded by terraces with breathtaking views. The sun filters through a lush tropical garden in the center of the spectacular open space, which comprises a living, dining, and bar area decorated with Balinese bamboo furniture and fabrics; above it, a gallery library bulges with books and games for all tastes. First class meals can be enjoyed on the breezy deck, under the retractable roof in the dining room, or at poolside. The villa also features an exercise room, a freshwater pool, and two Jacuzzis. In addition, there are two recently built one-bedroom guesthouses cleverly named "Bali Hi" and "Bali Lo." Each has its own pool, an open-air lounge/dining area, and a kitchen, but no TV set. There's no air conditioning in the villa or the guesthouses, probably because it's really not necessary. Other amenities include tennis, windsurfing, sailing dinghies, water skiing, snorkel equipment, fishing equipment, a full-size snooker table, facilities for small meetings and conferences, and an open bar and wine cellar. The daily rate of up to $15,000 includes all of the above, plus all meals and drinks for 24 people, a staff of 22, and launch or helicopter transfers. Guests are met at *Beef Island International Airport* on Tortola or on Virgin Gorda and are ferried over; the ride takes less than 30 minutes (phone: 42757 or 44492; 800-231-

1445, 800-225-4255, or 800-557-4255; 212-696-4566 in New York City; fax: 212-691-3916).

Peter Island Simple, sleek, and supremely first class, this place acquired its Scandinavian ambience from the source: The eight neat four-unit A-frames that house the resort's 30 original guestrooms were all prefabricated in Norway, shipped out—with all their luxurious garnishes—on the former owner's boats, then reassembled on Sprat Bay around the main clubhouse and marina. The marina and its facilities for sailing, scuba, and fishing are topnotch. There is a meeting room accommodating up to 50 people, a helipad, a fitness center, an up-to-the-minute water sports center, and a freshwater swimming pool. The clubhouse—with its deck, bar, and dining room decorated in shades of coral and sea green—combines eye-pleasing looks and body-cradling comfort. But the adjacent sea and the palm trees that border it are especially appealing, as are the 20 additional luxurious beachfront rooms just over the hill on Deadman's Bay, one of the 2,000-acre island's most beautiful beaches, and four villas, one with its own pool. None of the accommodations has a TV set. Sports include swimming, snorkeling (at a special beach), cruising, water skiing, windsurfing (with lessons available even for kids), Sunfish and Squib sailing, and four Laykold tennis courts with *Peter Burwash International* instructors. The crowd that gathers for dinner each evening in the elegant *Tradewinds* dining room is tanned and glowing. Less formal is the resort's *Deadman's Bay Beach Bar* restaurant. Meal plans are available. Several nights a week a band comes over from Road Town to play dance music (phone: 42561; 800-346-4451; fax: 42313).

TORTOLA

EXPENSIVE

Long Bay Beach This low-rise complex sprawls up a hillside overlooking a truly beautiful mile-long beach, the sea, and nearby islands. The family-friendly resort has 105 units comprised of hillside rooms (some without TV sets) and villas, and beachfront cabañas. There's also a full-service fitness center, conference rooms, a tennis court, a freshwater swimming pool, two bars, and two excellent restaurants—the *Garden* restaurant for more formal dining, and the *Beach* restaurant; meal plans are optional. Be prepared to climb up and down steep hills. Long Bay (phone: 54252; 800-729-9599; fax: 54677).

Sunset House On a hillside above Long Bay with a spectacular view, this place feels like a private, modern home. There are only five rooms in the main house (each with a private balcony, but no telephone or TV set) and another two on the beach. The chef cooks in the common kitchen or at the pool. Other features include ceiling fans (no air conditioning), a pool with bar, and a Jacuzzi. Bring lots of insect repellent—the mosquitoes can be fierce! Long Bay (phone: 42550 or 54220; 800-782-4304; fax: 45866).

MODERATE

Mariner Inn Originally designed for bareboaters, this property with 36 rooms and four suites has attracted other vacationers as well. Some rooms are air conditioned; none has a TV set. Highlights include tennis, a pool, a dive shop, yacht charters, a full-service marina with slips for 140 yachts (many available for charter), a specialty food shop, a good restaurant, and a lively bar overlooking the marina, all within walking distance of Road Town. There's free transportation to *Treasure Isle* (below), which shares facilities. Wickhams Cay II, Road Town (phone: 42332; 800-535-7289; fax: 42226).

Prospect Reef The largest resort (40 acres) in the British Virgin Islands boasts a freshwater junior Olympic-size pool and dive tank, stone-terraced sea pools, two children's pools, two restaurants, and two bars. The 131 comfortable, attractive units include studios (with kitchenettes), suites, and two-bedroom villas; some have air conditioning, and TV sets are available for an extra charge. Other amenities: a large shopping arcade, six tennis courts and a pro shop (lessons are available), a conference center, and a fitness center. Sporting equipment is complimentary, and scuba, snorkeling, sailing, and deep-sea fishing trips can be arranged. Road Town (phone: 43311; 800-356-8937; fax: 45595).

Sebastian's on the Beach Located on a lovely north shore beach, this is one of Tortola's older properties, with lots of island flavor and no pretensions. The 26 rooms—some with air conditioning—have ceiling fans and refrigerators, but no TV sets. Beachfront and back-facing rooms have king- or queen-size beds; the more modest courtyard rooms are a bargain. The restaurant here, called simply *Sebastian's,* serves simple fare and creole specialties (see *Eating Out*), with meal plans available; there's also a friendly beach bar. Closed August and September. Apple Bay (phone: 54212; 800-336-4870; fax: 54466).

Sugar Mill Built on the ruins of an over-350-year-old sugar mill on five acres at Apple Bay, this complex has 21 standard rooms and one- and two-bedroom suites (with kitchenettes), none of which has air conditioning or a TV set. There's also one air conditioned villa with TV set. The estate has a circular freshwater pool, a commendable restaurant (see *Eating Out*), and its own small beach with a shaded bar (where lunch and dinner are also served during high season). The mosquitoes are especially ferocious, so bring lots of bug spray. Apple Bay (phone: 54355; 800-462-8834; fax: 54696).

Treasure Isle One of Tortola's first hotels, this 15-acre complex is a five-minute drive from the center of Road Town. The property, on a hillside overlooking the harbor, features 40 rooms and three suites (with kitchenettes) built around a freshwater swimming pool. Bedrooms have cool terra cotta–tiled floors and rattan furnishings. Rooms on levels three and four offer the most spectacular views, for those who don't mind steep steps. Special features include use of the *Mariner Inn*'s facilities, snorkeling trips, and transport to the island's best beaches. The *Verandah,* an open-air restaurant (see *Eating Out*), is a gathering spot for many yacht charterers. Road Town (phone: 42501; 800-334-2435; fax: 42507).

VIRGIN GORDA

VERY EXPENSIVE

Bitter End Yacht Club This hideaway, at the east end of North Sound, is accessible only by boat. It's a sailor's haven, with more than 100 boats, including sailboats, powered skiffs, rowing sculls, and eight live-aboard yachts. There are some 60 units in marina rooms and in beachfront and hillside villas, with ceiling fans but no air conditioning, telephones, or TV sets. The newer "Commodore Club" offers 39 additional rooms with air conditioning, TV sets, and telephones. There are small beaches and a stunning pool overlooking North Sound; snorkeling, sailing trips, and sailing instruction are available at the *Nick Trotter Sailing School,* including a four-hour introductory class; sailing camp starts with seven-year-olds; and nature packages are available. The *English Carvery* features roasts and grilled meat; the popular *Bitter End Clubhouse* draws boaters (see *Eating Out*). All meals, excursions, and water sports are included in the rate. North Sound (phone: 42746; 800-872-2392; fax: 312-944-2860).

EXPENSIVE

Toad Hall Truly unique, this homey establishment is built into and around the boulders near the Baths. Owners Steve and Marie Green rent the three suites as a unit to one group of family or friends. The design includes some unusual elements: The pool incorporates some of the boulders and boasts its own cave; the rock-walled showers may be curtained by live plants. Rooms boast king-size beds, well-stocked bookshelves, and ceiling fans (no air conditioning) in the raftered, peaked ceilings; the housekeeper can prepare meals in the fully equipped kitchen for an extra fee (the property has no restaurant). There are no telephones or TV sets. A private boardwalk leads over the rocks to the beach, where guests may enter the Baths. The Baths (phone: 55397; fax: 55708).

MODERATE

Olde Yard Inn A breezy gazebo and an extensive library with a piano are among the assets of this personable hideaway. With 14 small, neat, double rooms (four with air conditioning, some with TV sets), it's more retreat than resort. Good food and wines are served at the restaurant (see *Eating Out*). A 20-minute, strenuous walk from Savannah Beach; the Baths are 2 miles away. The Valley (phone: 55544; 800-74-CHARMS; fax: 55986).

JOST VAN DYKE

EXPENSIVE

Sandcastle In this small, secluded colony, four modern octagonal cottages are surrounded by hibiscus and bougainvillea. There's a pleasant outdoor restaurant with a splendid reputation, a bar, and 200 feet of fine sandy beach (complimentary windsurfing and snorkeling are available). This family-run, remote place seems designed for those who *really* want to get away from it all; there are no TV sets, air conditioning, or telephones (though the hotel management does have a cellular phone). All meals are included. The owner picks up guests at Red Hook, St. Thomas, US Virgin Islands. It's also accessible by water taxi from West End, Tortola, and the hotel will pay the fare for guests staying at least six nights (phone: 809-690-1611 or radio VHF Ch. 16; for reservations, call 809-775-5262, on St. Thomas; fax: 809-775-3590, on St. Thomas).

MOSQUITO ISLAND

EXPENSIVE

Drake's Anchorage This secluded resort is named for Sir Francis, who anchored in the harbor while girding to fight the Spanish in 1595. Accommodations are simple (no telephones, TV sets, or air conditioning) and comfortable, with two villas, eight rooms, and two suites that can accommodate up to 38 guests at a time. There are 126 acres of unspoiled island to explore on foot and by bicycle, with four beaches offering excellent snorkeling opportunities. The restaurant here is not to be missed (see *Eating Out*). Mosquito Island, north of Virgin Gorda (phone/fax: 494-2254).

EATING OUT

As in most of the British islands, the best food is simple and straightforward, with seafood a major attraction. Expect to spend $70 and more for a meal for two, not including wine, tip, or drinks, in restaurants listed as expensive; $35 to $70 in those classified as moderate; and less than $35 at places in the inexpensive category. All places listed below are open for lunch and dinner unless otherwise noted. When calling from a phone within the British Virgin Islands, use only the local numbers listed below. For information about dialing from elsewhere, see *Telephone* earlier in this chapter.

TORTOLA

EXPENSIVE

Cloud Room This mountaintop dining spot offers a panoramic view; in good weather, the roof opens to reveal the starry sky. The menu presents a combination of continental and island dishes, including filet mignon, curried shrimp, local fish, and stuffed breast of chicken. Transportation to and from your hotel in a canvas-topped vehicle is included. Dinner only; closed Sundays. Reservations necessary. Major credit cards accepted. Ridge Rd. (phone: 42821).

Sugar Mill California food writers Jinx and Jeff Morgan have found the perfect vehicle for their culinary expertise at this 346-year-old sugar mill. Their menu, considered by many to be the island's best, features garden-fresh ingredients. Each night three entrées are featured: They might include Caribbean-Cajun shrimp and scallops or pork tenderloin marinated in citrus; steaks and fish are always offered. Dessert choices include amaretto soufflé and icebox cheesecake with strawberry sauce. Open daily for breakfast, lunch, and dinner. Reservations necessary. Major credit cards accepted. At the *Sugar Mill Hotel,* Apple Bay (phone: 54355).

Verandah Sailors and local businesspeople like to gather on this gingerbread open-air terrace. Grilled shrimp with aiole (garlic) sauce becomes island-oriented when served with steamed pumpkin flavored with cinnamon; walnut cake is the perfect choice for dessert. On Saturday nights there's a Caribbean barbecue and Wednesday nights feature a cookout with steaks and chicken. Open daily for breakfast, lunch, and dinner. Reservations advised. Major credit cards accepted. *Treasure Isle Resort,* Road Town (phone: 42501).

MODERATE

The Apple Another find on Tortola's northwest coast is tucked into a little West Indian house on pretty Apple Bay. The house drink, "Virgin Souppy," is a must: It consists of soursop juice, Coco Lopez, and local Cruzan rum topped with a sprinkle of nutmeg. Try the pumpkin soup, conch fritters, steamed local fish, or whelks. Open daily. Reservations necessary. Major credit cards accepted. Apple Bay (phone: 54437).

Mrs. Scatliffe's Definitely a family affair, with Mrs. Scatliffe and one daughter in the kitchen, another daughter waiting tables, a son-in-law mixing drinks, and Mr. Scatliffe strumming the guitar. The food is home cooking, West Indian–style, using fresh vegetables from the garden and fish from the sea beneath the terrace restaurant. Favorite dishes include chicken in a coconut shell and curried goat. After dinner, the family jams on the ukulele, merengue box (better known as the marimba), or a handy gourd. Open daily for dinner; occasional lunch (call ahead). Reservations necessary. No credit cards accepted. Carrot Bay (phone: 54556).

Pusser's This chain of three salty dining spots offers English and American-style food, from meat pies to steaks and chicken. There are two branches on Tortola, *Pusser's Landing* and *Pusser's Outpost,* and *Pusser's Leverick Bay* on Virgin Gorda. Open daily; the *Outpost* open for dinner only. Reservations advised for dinner. Major credit cards accepted. Sopers Hole Wharf, West End (phone: 54554); Main St., Road Town (phone: 44199); and Leverick Bay, Virgin Gorda (phone: 57369).

Santa Maria At the *Village Cay* resort, this casual outdoor place lies an arm's length from luxury yachts at anchor at the *Moorings* yacht harbor. Seafood, steaks, a salad bar, and sandwiches are on the menu, and there's an occasional barbecue. A buffet lunch is served Tuesdays and Thursdays. Open daily for breakfast, lunch, and dinner. Reservations necessary in high season. Major credit cards accepted. Wickhams Cay I, Road Town (phone: 42771).

Sebastian's A beachfront dining room that dishes up fare ranging from barbecued chicken to seafood to filet mignon. West Indian entertainment Sunday nights. Open daily for breakfast, lunch, and dinner. Reservations advised. Major credit cards accepted. At *Sebastian's on the Beach,* Apple Bay (phone: 54212, ext. 1313).

Skyworld It's quite a drive up, but this place offers a spectacular view over all the Virgin Islands and fabulous sunsets. Bring a camera (and a sweater if the wind is blowing). Lunches are fairly simple; dinners are either à la carte or six-course affairs featuring local seafood dishes or continental fare such as rack of lamb. The conch fritters are fabulous, as is the "pascha colada," an exotic drink made from passion-fruit juice, cream of coconut, and rum. Open daily; no dinner on Mondays and Tuesdays. Reservations necessary for dinner. Major credit cards accepted. Ridge Rd. (phone: 43567 or radio VHF Ch. 16).

INEXPENSIVE

Quito's Gazebo The personable Quito Rymer serves simple foods, including grilled fish, rotis, and baby back ribs at his beachfront spot, along with entertainment nightly (except Mondays and Wednesdays). Open for breakfast, lunch, and dinner; closed Mondays. Reservations advised. MasterCard and Visa accepted. In the *Ole Works Inn,* Cane Garden Bay (phone: 54837).

Other inexpensive and unpretentious eateries on Tortola include *Stanley's* (phone: 54520) and *Rymer's Beach Bar* (phone: 54639 or 54215) on beautiful Cane Garden Bay; *Peg Leg Landing* (phone: 40028) at Nanny Cay; and *Maria's* (phone: 42595), *Downstairs* at the *Prospect Reef* (phone: 43311, ext. 229), and *Bobby's Fast Food* (phone: 42189) in Road Town. *Marlene's Delicious Design* (Wickhams Cay I; phone: 44634) dishes out homemade pâtés, rotis, sandwiches, cakes, and pastries that can be taken out or eaten in the air conditioned dining room; closed Sundays.

VIRGIN GORDA

EXPENSIVE

Biras Creek The elegant hilltop dining room at this exclusive resort offers one of the most romantic views around. The first-rate food emphasizes light cooking and fresh produce. A five-course set meal is served each night, with a choice of five entrées, including—for an additional charge—lobster. The cold cucumber soup is refreshing, the chicken breast with orange-ginger sauce divine—and the mango mousse is to die for. The wine list here—161 different vintages of US, German, Austrian, French, and Italian origin—is said to rival any in the Caribbean. Open daily for breakfast, lunch, and dinner. Non-guests are welcome for dinner. Reservations advised for dinner. Major credit cards accepted. North Sound (phone: 43555/6).

Olde Yard Inn Small and special, this is the kind of cozy inn one dreams of coming home to after a long day. Exquisite meals are served alfresco on a terra cotta–floored gallery to soft classical music; a guitarist entertains on Monday and Friday evenings. Homemade fettuccine makes a terrific starter; breads and pastries are freshly baked on the premises; fresh local fish or veal served with shrimp and herbs are perfect. There's also a small, well-chosen wine list. Open daily for breakfast, lunch, and dinner. Reservations advised. Major credit cards accepted. The Valley (phone: 55544).

Pavilion Candlelit dinners served in the dining room of the *Little Dix Bay* resort are nothing short of romantic—and are now open to non-guests. The prize-winning French chef, Benoit Pepin (formerly of *La Samanna* in St. Martin), whips up international dishes and Caribbean specialties, including sautéed red snapper infused with ginger and curry, and roast rack of lamb with a garlic breadcrumb crust. Open daily for lunch, tea, and dinner. Reservations necessary. Major credit cards accepted. Little Dix Bay (phone: 55555, ext. 174).

Other Virgin Gorda dining options include the moderately priced *English Carvery* (serving steaks and roasts) and the less formal *Bitter End Clubhouse* (for fresh fish and buffets), both at the *Bitter End Yacht Club* (phone: 42746 or radio VHF Channel 16); *Chez Michelle* (in The Valley; phone: 55510) for continental choices (though a little short on ambience); the pub-type *Bath & Turtle* (at the Virgin Gorda Yacht Harbour; phone: 55239); *Fischer's Cove Beach* (St. Thomas Bay; phone: 55252); the *Crab Hole* (Spanish Town; phone: 55307); and *Teacher Ilma's* (next to the laundromat on Virgin Gorda; phone: 55355).

OTHER ISLANDS

MODERATE

Club Paradise Turn left at Jost Van Dyke's *Customs House* to discover this friendly local spot, which offers excellent island fare prepared by congenial hosts

Dorsey Chinnery and Pat Tonness. There's entertainment most weekends. Open daily. Dinner reservations necessary. MasterCard and Visa accepted. Great Harbour, Jost Van Dyke (phone: 495-9267; fax: 495-9633).

Drake's Anchorage Caressed by sea breezes, this delightful pavilion restaurant in the resort of the same name presents five-course dinners featuring seafood, some West Indian fare, and other choices with a French flair. Dolphin with curry sauce and bananas is the most popular entrée, with grilled rack of lamb a close second. Close to Virgin Gorda; the inn sends a boat over to pick up guests. Open daily for breakfast, lunch, and dinner. Dinner reservations necessary by 3:30 PM. There's a musician on alternate Tuesdays and Thursdays. Major credit cards accepted. Mosquito Island (phone: 42254 or radio VHF Channel 16).

Foxy's An institution since 1968, this hot spot with sand on the floor and patrons' business cards stapled to the ceiling features West Indian food such as roti (curried chicken and potatoes wrapped in dough) and sweet *soca* (spicy steamed shrimp). Live music adds to the fun Thursday, Friday, and Saturday nights (see *Nightlife*). Open daily. Reservations unnecessary. Major credit cards accepted. Great Harbour, Jost Van Dyke (phone: 59258 or radio VHF Channel 16).

Last Resort On its own little islet in the middle of a circular bay, with great anchorage for yachtsmen, this popular port of call features a fairly routine British-style buffet (from 7:30 PM till it's gone), followed by a rather bawdy show by owner/entertainer Tony Snell, an amazing one-man band (see *Nightlife*). Come over by dinghy, or call and they'll send one for you. Closed Sundays. Reservations necessary. Major credit cards accepted. Bellamy Cay, Beef Island (phone: 52520 or radio VHF Channel 16).

Cayman Islands

Once upon a time, if you mentioned the Cayman Islands, the response was likely to be "Cayman who?" followed by "where?" and "why?" Today, however, Grand Cayman is considered the Caribbean's condominium capital and the center of the offshore financial industry, as well as one of the region's fastest-growing beach spots and most popular scuba diving destinations. Its two small sister isles also are being discovered by scuba enthusiasts and anglers who enjoy not only superlative sporting opportunities but also the islands' peaceful isolation.

The Cayman Islands are a trio of tiny coral dots poking out of the western Caribbean. Called Grand Cayman, Little Cayman, and Cayman Brac, they are outcroppings of the Cayman Ridge, a submarine mountain range extending from Cuba's Sierra Maestra to the Misteriosa and Rosario Banks that point their underwater way southwest toward Belize. Grand Cayman, the largest and most developed, and Little Cayman are mostly flat—the highest point on Grand Cayman rises 60 feet above sea level. Mountainous by comparison, Cayman Brac has a bluff running up its spine that starts from sea level on the west end and rises 140 feet to a cliff at its easternmost point (thus the island's name—"brac" means "bluff" in Gaelic, a legacy of the Scots who helped settle the islands). All three islands are formed entirely of calcareous rock so porous that there are no streams. There are, however, freshwater wells throughout the islands and, on Grand Cayman, a large modern desalination plant that provides the bulk of the island's water supply. Many islanders still maintain cisterns that catch and store rainwater.

Columbus found the Cayman Islands by accident when, en route from Panama to Hispaniola in 1503, he was blown off course. The islands' large turtle population led Columbus to call them Las Tortugas. The label did not stick, however; the current name comes from *caymanas* (the Spanish-Carib word—nowadays evolved to *caimanes*—for "alligators"), although the *caymanas* referred to were probably iguanas.

In the 16th and 17th centuries, ships plying the Caribbean called at the islands for supplies of turtle meat and fresh water, but there was no rush to settle them. It was not until 1655 that the first colonists—deserters from Oliver Cromwell's army who, according to legend, sneaked off from Jamaica when England took it from the Spanish—arrived. Fifteen years later the Treaty of Madrid made the Cayman Islands a British possession. This status has been a source of pride to loyal islanders ever since.

For a relatively quiet destination these islands have had a rowdy history. Pirate tales of buried treasure and sunken fortunes abound. But the sea story Caymanians love best is the "Wreck of the Ten Sails." On a dark February night in 1794, a convoy of merchant ships was passing east of

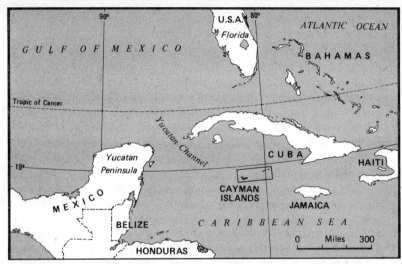

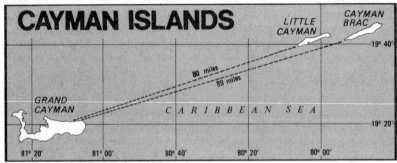

CAYMAN ISLANDS

LITTLE CAYMAN

CAYMAN BRAC

19° 40'

80 miles

89 miles

GRAND CAYMAN

C A R I B B E A N   S E A

19° 20'

81° 20'   81° 00'   80° 40'   80° 20'   80° 00'

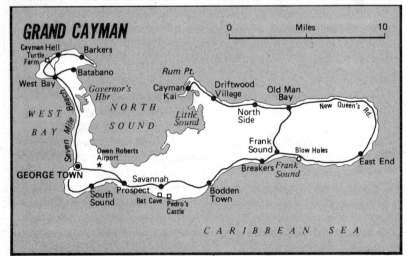

GRAND CAYMAN

0   Miles   10

Cayman Hell
Turtle Farm   Barkers

West Bay   Batabano

Governor's Hbr   Rum Pt.

Cayman Kai   Driftwood Village   Old Man Bay

W E S T   B A Y   N O R T H   S O U N D   Little Sound   New Queen's Rd.

Seven Mile Beach   North Side

Owen Roberts Airport   Frank Sound   Blow Holes

GEORGE TOWN   Savannah   Breakers   Frank Sound   East End

South Sound   Prospect   Bodden Town

Bat Cave   Pedro's Castle

C A R I B B E A N   S E A

Grand Cayman when the lead ship struck the reef. Her warning signal was misunderstood, and nine more vessels piled up with her. Residents of East End risked their lives in heavy seas to rescue many of the ships' passengers, including, according to local lore, the Prince of Wales—the future King William IV (though historians have recently disproved this royal embellishment). Popular belief further has it that after this Caymanian display of bravery, a grateful King George III granted the islands freedom from taxation or, according to other sources, freedom from wartime conscription—benefits that the islanders still enjoy.

Despite the generous spirit shown to the shipwrecked travelers, Caymanians' reaction was less enthusiastic when the first tourists found their way here in the early 1950s. A request for travel information in those days brought a boat-mailed reply, mimeographed slightly off center on a single legal-size sheet. It pointed out the disadvantages of potholed roads, disintegrating cars, a large number of insects, and an uncertain electrical supply. Its tone wasn't "Stay away," but, more candidly, "Don't say we didn't warn you."

But fishermen and beach nuts, undaunted, continued to arrive in increasing numbers. In the early 1960s divers discovered the islands' spectacular underwater sites. In 1966 the Legislative Assembly passed a series of laws creating a variety of tax-haven investment opportunities on Grand Cayman favoring offshore banking, trust-company formation, and the registration of companies. These enticements spurred considerable outside interest, and there are now more than 500 banks on Grand Cayman. The Cayman economy has been improving dramatically ever since, and tourism has come to stay.

Also in 1966 a tourist board was established to encourage and control the industry. It set up a system of hotel inspections that have raised standards—though there is still room for improvement—and it has ridden herd on tour operators and the quality of their offerings. Cayman accommodations may be attractive, clean, and well maintained, but only a few resorts can honestly be labeled "luxurious." Restaurants aren't inexpensive either—although the food is only occasionally first-rate (at *Lantana's* and *The Wharf,* for example). There are a few interesting historic sights and a handful of nightlife and dancing options on Grand Cayman.

But the coral gardens, dramatic sheer walls, and sloping drop-offs of these islands' undersea world are undoubtedly their most famous natural attractions. The variety of marine life, ideal diving conditions (calm seas, mild current, superb visibility), and the largest number of professional dive services in the Caribbean combine to create an underwater nirvana.

Other water sports, from parasailing and sailboarding to glass-bottom boat rides and jet skis, beckon the non-divers. Would-be Jules Vernes can voyage to the bottom of the sea aboard one of the island's three submarines. Last but certainly not least, the islands offer superb sport fishing with year-round action from bonefish (particularly good on Cayman Brac, outstanding on Little Cayman), small tarpon, and, further offshore, blue marlin, wahoo, yellowfin tuna, dolphin, and other game fish. Indeed, when it comes to things aquatic, these islands lack nothing except an underwater hotel.

Topside, there may be no spectacular land vistas, but there are patches of real loveliness—rows of royal palms, tall pines moving in soft breezes, and splashes of floral and faunal color. Cayman beaches, found primarily on Grand Cayman's west and north coasts, rank among the most beautiful in the Caribbean, including Seven Mile Beach (in reality, about 6 miles long) and the quiet and unspoiled area of the Cayman Kai Retreat section of the North Side.

Caymanians contribute their fair share to the islands' appeal: Even the smallest and humblest house in the Cayman Islands is tidy and often brightened with flowers. The islands have one of the highest standards of living in the entire Caribbean, hospitable and courteous residents, and only a rare instance of panhandling. The squadrons of souvenir hawkers who stalk visitors on other shores are absent—a fact that makes Grand Cayman one of the top cruise ship ports in the Caribbean. The Cayman Islands remain a safe, comfortable spot with a very North American atmosphere. Their pleasant people, stable government, and crime-free atmosphere keep many visitors returning each year. For those requiring only sun, sand, and sea—in a non-exotic wrapper—the Cayman Islands might be paradise at any price.

Cayman Islands At-a-Glance

FROM THE AIR

The three Cayman Islands together have a total land area of about 96 square miles. Grand Cayman, looking vaguely like a sperm whale from the air, is 76 square miles, about 22 miles long and 8 miles wide at its broadest point. Some 80 miles east-northeast of Grand Cayman is Little Cayman, resembling a sea slug, with only 10 square miles of land ringed by crystal white beaches. Eel-shaped Cayman Brac, just 5 miles due east of Little Cayman, has a total of 14 square miles.

The hallmark of Grand Cayman is West Bay Beach (that's the official name; everybody calls it Seven Mile Beach), which runs in a gentle curve along the western shore and has the majority of the resort hotels. The western half of the island is sculpted by huge North Sound, whose entrance is entirely protected by a giant coral reef. North Sound digs into the body of the island and deprives it of what would be another 40 square miles of land. Grand Cayman, site of the islands' capital, George Town, has the bulk of the population, just over 28,050 of the 29,700 total. Of the remaining 1,650 practically all live on Cayman Brac. Little Cayman is home to just 50 permanent residents. Grand Cayman is almost precisely due south of Miami, some 480 miles and a little over an hour's plane ride away. Jamaica lies 180 miles east-southeast. Jets land at *Owen Roberts International Airport,* just outside George Town, in the southwest corner of the island, a few miles from Seven Mile Beach.

SPECIAL PLACES

GEORGE TOWN The small, clean, unpretentious capital, where building heights are limited to five stories, keeps the blue sky in sight at all times, and there seem to be sea views from everywhere. Sights include a clock monument to King George V, located at the corner of Fort and Edward Streets; the *Legislative Assembly* on Fort Street; the *Courts Building* opposite; the *Government Administration Building* on Elgin Avenue, called "the Glass House" by locals; the neat little *Cayman Islands Public Library* on Edward Street, which stocks English novels and magazines; and the *General Post Office* (also on Edward St.), near the town center, where you can buy popular stamps at cost in the *Philatelic Bureau.* The *Cayman Islands National Museum,* on the waterfront at Hog Sty Bay, has some 2,000 fascinating exhibits about the islands' history. The collection includes shipbuilding tools, weapons, coins, and books. Closed Sundays. Admission charge (phone: 949-8368).

ELSEWHERE ON GRAND CAYMAN

To see more than George Town on Grand Cayman, it's necessary to hire a cab or rent a car, motorbike, or bicycle. Some of the island's attractions can be seen by driving out along Seven Mile Beach, past the beachside residence of His Excellency the Governor to the vicinity of the settlement of West Bay. Noteworthy sights and stops include:

HELL Supposedly named by a former commissioner who said, after seeing its weird coral and rock formations for the first time, "This is what Hell must look like." To capitalize on the name, there is a post office nearby where the postmistress stamps all cards and letters "Hell, Grand Cayman." There is a ramp leading to a photo vantage point above the limestone fields, and two gift shops where visitors can buy Hell memorabilia and refreshments. The nearby *Club Inferno* bar (phone: 949-3263) is owned by the McDoom family!

BATABANO On North Sound, this small fishing village in the West Bay district is where local fishermen bring their catch and where fresh fish, lobster (in season), conch, and turtle meat are sold. North Sound's reef is an outstanding site for divers and sport fishermen.

CAYMAN TURTLE FARM Established in 1968 by a private enterprise and now owned by the Cayman government, this is the only commercial green sea turtle farm in the world. The reptiles are hatched and raised through young adulthood on the premises. There are educational exhibits and a gift shop selling items with a turtle motif, souvenirs, and tortoiseshell crafts. *Warning:* Because of the US Government's ban on endangered species, "look but don't buy" are the watchwords for Americans where tortoiseshell jewelry and other turtle souvenirs are concerned. Open daily. Admission charge. Northwest Point Rd., near Mount Pleasant (phone: 949-3894).

STINGRAY CITY Just 15 minutes by boat off Grand Cayman's Rum Point, this is one of the few places in the world where you can swim, snorkel, or simply stand waist deep among friendly (or at least non-stinging) sting rays. This not-to-be-missed experience can be arranged through most of the island's dozens of dive shops and water sports concessions.

For the sights in the other direction, head east out of George Town to:

SOUTH SOUND ROAD On this pine-lined street, one of the most attractive on the island, are quaint old wooden Caymanian houses. Look for one on the seaward side painted with colorful abstract designs by the owner, a Caymanian lady who prefers to remain an obscure artist-in-residence and not a tourist attraction. Look, enjoy, and pass on, please.

BODDEN TOWN Currently with a population of a little over 3,400, this was the islands' first capital. Its chief claims to present fame are Gun Square (marked by two cannon, stuck muzzle-first into the ground, that were used to guard the reef channel in the 18th century), and Pirates Cave, where human bones and cannonballs have been found, indicating (perhaps) that it was once a pirates' hideout. The cave, located on the edge of town, is open daily; there's an admission charge (phone: 947-3122).

QUEEN ELIZABETH II BOTANIC PARK One of Grand Cayman's loveliest attractions, with a nearly mile-long woodland trail meandering through wetlands, swamps, and exotic native foliage. Visit endangered blue iguanas and walk among wild Zenaida doves and Cayman parrots. Closed Saturdays. Admission charge. Frank Sound Road, North Side (phone: 947-9462).

CAYMAN'S "BLOW HOLES" These are the sprays of water that shoot into the air when waves hit the rocks on the picturesque stretch of old coral formations called "Ironshore." Off Frank Sound, near East End Channel.

EAST END Here, from the *Queen's View* lookout point, a fluke of an anchor said to be a relic of the "Wreck of the Ten Sails" can sometimes be seen sticking out of the water. It's not wise to wade or swim out for a closer look because the reef in that spot is alive with sea urchins. Around a bend, in the main channel through the reef at East End, is a visible wreck of modern times, the MV *Ridgefield.* East End boasts two hostelries: the scuba buff's small *Cayman Diving Lodge* (phone: 947-7555) and the *Morritt's Tortuga Club* complex (see *Checking In*).

NEW QUEEN'S ROAD Opened by Elizabeth II in 1983, it lines a tranquil stretch of totally undeveloped oceanfront between East End and the small settlement at Old Man Bay. From the settlement you can continue west to the *Cayman Kai* resort and the North Sound landing, or south on the cross-island road to Frank Sound through the lushest part of Grand Cayman. With royal palms and orchids growing wild, green Cayman parrots are sometimes spotted here, especially during spring mango season.

Sources and Resources

TOURIST INFORMATION

The *Cayman Islands Department of Tourism* has an office in George Town at *The Pavilion* on Cricket Square (Elgin Ave.; phone: 949-0623; fax: 949-4053); it's closed weekends. There are also tourist information booths at the airport (phone: 949-2635) and at the pier where cruise passengers land (no phone), both open to meet all arriving planes and ships. For information on government-protected parks and nature areas, call the *National Trust of the Cayman Islands* (phone: 949-0121; fax: 949-7494). For information about Cayman Islands tourist offices in the US, see GETTING READY TO GO.

LOCAL COVERAGE The biannual *Key to Cayman* magazine is in all hotel rooms. The *New Star,* a local lifestyle magazine, comes out monthly. For additional current information, the *Caymanian Compass,* the local newspaper, is published weekdays, and the *New Cayman,* a weekly paper, is published on Thursdays.

RADIO AND TELEVISION Radio Cayman is the government-run AM/FM radio station (91.9 FM; 1205 AM or 1555 AM), broadcasting a range of music programming, from gospel to reggae, and international and local news. ZFZZ (99.9 FM) plays light rock music. Cayman also has its own television station on channel 12.

TELEPHONE To call from the US dial 809 (area code) + (local number). When calling from another Caribbean island, the codes may vary, so contact the local operator for assistance. When calling from a phone on the Cayman Islands, use only the seven-digit local number unless otherwise indicated. Dial 911 for emergency assistance.

ENTRY REQUIREMENTS For stays up to six months, visitors from the US and Canada need only a passport or other proof of citizenship (birth certificate or voter's registration card, plus a photo ID) and a return or ongoing ticket. There's a departure tax of $10 per person (payable at the airport).

CLIMATE AND CLOTHES The average winter temperature is 75F (24C); in summer, it's 5 to 10 degrees warmer. May through October is the rainy season, and showers are intense and brief. The Cayman Islands are informal and casual. Women wear bright blouses, skirts, slacks, and shorts (and, on beaches, the inevitable bikini), and men favor slacks, sport shirts, and swim trunks. Evenings, women sometimes dress up a bit in long cotton dresses (to which they might add a sweater or shawl), but jackets and ties are rarely required for men.

MONEY The Cayman Islands have their own currency, the Cayman dollar, which is valued at a fixed ratio to the US dollar ($1 CI equals $1.25 US). Stores, restaurants, and hotels accept US dollars and credit cards (check to see if prices listed are CI or US dollars). Traveler's checks can be cashed at local banks (open 9 AM to 2:30 PM Mondays through Thursdays, 9 AM to 4:30 PM Fridays). All prices in this chapter are quoted in US dollars unless otherwise indicated.

LANGUAGE Caymanians speak a lovely English, accented with bits of West Indian, Welsh, Irish, and Scottish. They pronounce the name of their largest island "Grahnd Cay-*mahn*."

TIME The Cayman Islands are on eastern standard time all year. When daylight saving time is in effect in the US, there's an hour's difference; when it's noon in New York EDT, it's 11 AM in the Cayman Islands.

CURRENT The same as the US, with standard 110-volt, 60-cycle current. No need for converters or adapters.

TIPPING There is no general rule about service charges. Some hotels add 10%, some 15%. At apartment/condominium complexes, several add 5%; a couple, 10%. To avoid double-tipping, check the service charge policy when you check in. If there is a service charge added, figure that it covers everything except extra special services. If not, give room maids $1 to $2 per room per day; bellboys about 50¢ per bag for carrying luggage, with a $1 minimum. There are airport porters, but your taxi driver will generally pick up your luggage and carry it to the car, and unless you're carrying an unusually large load, it is not necessary to tip him for the luggage lift or the ride since he probably owns his own cab.

GETTING AROUND

BUS Operating roughly once an hour from George Town and West Bay along Seven Mile Beach, buses stop at all hotels; fares depend on destination.

CAR RENTAL Easy to arrange and a good way to get about. All the car rental companies listed here have offices just across from the airport. Cars can be picked up there or delivered to your hotel. The following companies include unlimited mileage in their rates: *Budget* (at the airport, phone: 949-9424; Walkers Rd., George Town, phone: 949-5605; and at the *Treasure Island* resort, phone: 949-6432), *Cico/Avis* (three locations: at the airport, and at the *Holiday Inn* and *Hyatt Regency Grand Cayman;* phone for all three: 949-2468), *Coconut Car Rentals* (800-262-6687; at the airport, phone: 949-7703; in the *Nissan Building,* Crew Rd., phone: 949-4037 or 949-4377; and West Bay Rd., phone: 947-4377), *Hertz* (at the airport, phone: 949-2280; at the *Beach Club,* phone: 947-5621; and at the *Radisson Grand Cayman,* phone: 949-8147), and *Dollar* (at the airport; phone: 949-4790). The newest option (and lots of fun) is to rent a four-wheel-drive vehicle from *Just Jeeps Ltd.*

(North Church St., George Town; phone: 949-7263). On Little Cayman, try *McLaughlin Jeep Rental,* near the airport (phone: 948-1000). Remember, you can request a jeep with automatic transmission. Off-season rates for all vehicles are about 25% less than in winter. At the time of rental, the agency will issue a driving permit for $5 to renters who can prove that they're at least 21 years old and have a valid license from home (some firms set a minimum age of 22). *Important:* This is a British world, and driving is on the left. Gasoline is measured by the imperial gallon, which is 25% larger than the US gallon.

INTER-ISLAND FLIGHTS *Air Jamaica* (phone: 800-523-5585) has service from Kingston, Jamaica, to Grand Cayman. *Cayman Airways* (phone: 949-2311; 800-422-9626 in the US) flies direct from Kingston, Jamaica, and connects Grand Cayman with Little Cayman and Cayman Brac. *Island Air* (phone: 949-5252) flies daily among the Cayman Islands; both firms offer special three-island fares plus a choice of daylong fishing excursions and longer vacation packages for all three islands.

MOTORCYCLE RENTAL *Cayman Cycle Rentals* (*Coconut Place,* West Bay Rd., phone: 947-4021; the *Hyatt Regency Grand Cayman,* phone: 949-1234, ext. 3500; and at the *Treasure Island* resort, phone: 949-8711) and *Soto's Scooters* (*Coconut Place,* West Bay Rd., phone: 947-4652) rent motor scooters.

SEA EXCURSIONS The following operations offer a variety of day sails, snorkeling trips, and sunset and dinner cruises (see *Checking In* for locations of hotels): *Aqua Delights* at the *Holiday Inn* (phone: 947-4786 or 947-4444, ext. 686); *Bob Soto's Diving* (800-262-7686; *Holiday Inn,* phone: 947-4631; *Coconut Place,* West Bay Rd., phone: 947-4003; George Town, phone: 949-6469; or the *Cayman Islander,* phone: 949-7834); *Captain Marvin's Aquatics* (next to the *Holiday Inn,* West Bay Rd.; phone: 947-4590); *Captain Crosby's Water Sports* (*Coconut Place;* phone: 947-4049); *Cayman Diving Lodge* (East End; phone: 947-7555); *Don Foster's Dive Grand Cayman* (*Royal Palms,* West Bay Rd., phone: 949-5679; or the *Radisson;* phone: 949-7181); *Ron Ebanks Charter Boat Headquarters* (*Coconut Place,* West Bay Rd.; phone: 947-4340); *Surfside Watersports* (800-543-6828; Rum Point; phone: 947-9098); *Tortuga Surfside Divers* (*Morritt's Tortuga Club;* phone: 947-2097); and *Treasure Island Divers* at the *Treasure Island* resort (phone: 800-872-7552; 949-4456). *Red Sail Sports* at the *Hyatt Regency* (phone: 949-8745) also offers a number of excursions, including cruises on their 65-foot catamaran *The Spirit of Ppalu.*

Grand Cayman is one of the few places in the world where visitors can take submarine trips to view the marine life of a tropical reef system. The 28-passenger *Atlantis* (phone: 949-7700) reaches depths of up to 150 feet and does both day and night dives. The sub leaves the George Town harbor 12 times a day on the hour. Reservations are required. The affiliated

Research Submersibles Ltd. (phone: 949-8296) has two two-passenger Perry craft that stay submerged for as long as three hours and dive to 800 feet.

SIGHTSEEING BUS TOURS Regularly scheduled bus tours are operated by *Evco Tours* (George Town; phone: 949-2118); *Majestic Tours* (at the airport, second floor; phone: 949-7773); *Reid's Premier Tours* (off Walkers Rd., George Town; phone: 949-6531); *Rudy's Travellers Transport* (Fountain Rd., Boatswain Bay; phone: 949-3208); and *Tropicana Tours* (*Dixie Place,* behind the *Merran Bldg.,* West Bay Rd.; phone: 949-0944). The latter offers hotel pickup, air conditioned buses, and friendly, animated guides who are half the fun.

SIGHTSEEING TAXI TOURS Arrange excursions through the *Cayman Island Taxi Cab Association* (West Bay; phone: 947-4491).

TAXI Taxis meet all arriving flights. Rates are fixed by the *Cayman Island Taxi Cab Association* and are published in the tourist department's *Rate Sheet and Fact Folder.*

SPECIAL EVENTS

The biggest annual event is *Batabano,* a carnival featuring parades, exhibits, and dances held in George Town in April; the *Queen's Birthday* celebration in June (on the Monday following the Saturday appointed as her official birthday) is observed with a uniformed parade and a presentation of awards and honors; and the country's national festival, *Pirates Week,* an elaborate week-long celebration with costumes, parades, and swashbuckling special events, is held in late October. On *Ash Wednesday* (February 21 in 1996) there's an *Annual Agricultural Show,* and June is *Million Dollar Month,* featuring an international saltwater fishing tournament with cash prizes for record catches. Other holidays when banks, stores, and government offices are closed: *New Year's Day; Good Friday; Easter Monday* (April 8 in 1996); *Discovery Day* (third Monday in May); *Constitution Day* (first Monday in July); *Remembrance Day* (November 11 in 1996); *Christmas Day;* and *Boxing Day* (December 26).

SHOPPING

The spectrum of merchandise in George Town is quite diverse. The road along Seven Mile Beach has experienced an explosive growth of mini-malls, with shops selling everything from scuba gear to frozen yogurt. Many famous international brand names are imported here with no sales tax added. But sellers are still free to set prices, so some bargains are better than others. Here, as elsewhere, the best protection is knowing US prices—including those at discount stores—especially on cameras and electronic equipment. *Note:* Processed black coral (such as jewelry) may be brought into the US only in small amounts, and tortoiseshell is prohibited completely. Shopping hours are generally from 9:30 or 10 AM to 5:30 or 6 PM Mondays through Saturdays; some stores close earlier Saturdays.

To stock up on typical island products such as hats, baskets, and straw items, try *Heritage Crafts* (on the waterfront in George Town; phone: 949-7093). Here are some other places worth a stop:

Bonnywear High quality island fashions for women, including sportswear, swimsuits, evening wear, and accessories. *Galleria Plaza* shopping center, West Bay Road, George Town (phone: 949-7065).

The Book Nook An excellent selection of travel, fiction, and children's titles. It also sells cards, toys, T-shirts, and gifts. *Galleria Plaza,* West Bay Road (phone: 947-4686) and George Town (phone: 949-7342).

Caribbean Emporium Sand-covered floors and steel-drum music create a fun atmosphere in which to browse for colorful beach towels, T-shirts, snorkel gear, and Cayman spices. George Town (phone: 949-0466).

Caymandicraft Liberty of London fabrics, Irish linen, men's fine silk ties. Church St., George Town (phone: 949-2405).

Le Classique Fine quality leather luggage, handbags, and wallets, in addition to sport and dress shoes for men and women. George Town (phone: 949-7121) and *Galleria Plaza,* West Bay Rd. (phone: 949-7105).

The Jewelry Centre The place for elegant gold necklaces, rings, and bracelets, all in modern designs. Fort St., George Town (phone: 949-0070).

Kennedy Gallery Here you'll find affordable limited-edition prints of Cayman scenes by local artists. Fort St., George Town (phone: 947-5338) and *West Shore Centre* mall, West Bay Road (phone: 949-8077).

Kirk Freeport Plaza A range of shops with the island's largest selection of famous-name crystal, china, and earthenware. Cardinal Avenue, George Town (phone: 949-7477).

Pure Art Gallery Artist Debbie van der Bol sells paintings, prints, and sculptures by local talent. South Church St., George Town (phone: 949-4433).

Savoy Jewelry This store features treasures ranging from Fabergé eggs and Harry Winston watches to jewelry made from ancient coins. Fort St., George Town (phone: 949-7578).

SPORTS

Since the sea is so warm and gentle, most sports activities take place in, on, or under the water.

BOATING Small boats can be chartered from a number of water sports operators, including *Red Sail Sports, Don Foster's Dive Grand Cayman,* and *Ron Ebanks Charter Boat Headquarters* (see *Sea Excursions* for all three). Sunday sailing races are held off Seven Mile Beach; if you want to join in, contact Gerry Kirkconnell (phone: 949-2651 or 949-7477).

GOLF The most recent venue, and the islands' first genuine 18-hole course, is the *Links at Safehaven* (West Bay Rd., Grand Cayman; phone: 947-4155). The complex includes a clubhouse, a restaurant and bar, and a pro shop. The *Britannia* golf course (phone: 949-8020) at the *Hyatt Regency Grand Cayman* is a prototype course specially designed by Jack Nicklaus to accommodate the "short" ball. Because of its weight (about half that of a normal golf ball) and convex dimples (which create aerodynamic drag), the ball flies about half the distance of a standard ball, requiring a much shorter course and making for a much faster game. It tends to equalize player ability, too. An 18-hole, par 72 course is created by playing the 9 holes twice, each time from different tees (the front nine is 3,157 yards and the back nine is 3,092 yards). This unique course is as challenging as it is fun. Those not staying at the *Hyatt* should set up tee times a day in advance.

SNORKELING AND SCUBA DIVING Aficionados rate the Cayman Islands one of the world's top dive areas, and Grand Cayman boasts at least 20 full-service dive operations. Coral reefs and the famous vertical coral walls teeming with marine life surround each island, so the underwater show is close enough to shore for snorkelers and novice divers to take in easily. Some of the best dive sites can be found off Little Cayman and Cayman Brac; Little Cayman's famous Bloody Bay Wall, for example, plunges from a depth of 20 feet to a mile below the surface. Although experienced divers do not really need boats, guided trips are recommended for convenience and safety's sake. Among the brilliant and friendly fish found here are angelfish, butterfly fish, trumpet fish, grunts, squirrelfish, snapper, and grouper. At Stingray City, off Rum Point, stingrays come in to be hand-fed by divers (see *Special Places*). There are also shipwrecks, some close enough to the surface to be viewed by snorkelers (also see *Sunken and Buried Treasure* in DIVERSIONS). Most hotels rent fins, face masks, and snorkels and can arrange scuba trips for you. Resort courses offer non-divers an introduction to scuba and have participants experiencing the underwater wonders (under close supervision) in one day. Many dive shops offer rental equipment (upon presentation of a national diving association certification card only) and instruction, and arrange guided dive trips. First-rate dive shops on Grand Cayman include: *Eden Rock Diving Center* (S. Church St., just south of George Town; phone: 949-7243); *Fish Eye* (*Cayman Falls* shopping center, West Bay Rd.; phone: 947-4209); *Parrot's Landing* (800-448-0428; S. Church St. at Memorial; phone: 949-7884); *Peter Milburn's Dive Cayman* (Seven Mile Beach; phone: 947-5770); *Quabbin Dives* (*Bush Center*, N. Church St., George Town; phone: 949-5597); *River Sport Divers* (*Coconut Place*, West Bay Rd.; phone: 949-1181); *Sunset Divers* (*Sunset House*; see *Checking In*); and *Surfside Watersports* (see *Sea Excursions*, or try their smaller George Town location: N. Church St.; phone: 949-7330). Also first-rate are *Bob Soto's Diving, Captain Marvin's Aquatics, Cayman Diving Lodge, Don Foster's Dive Grand Cayman, Red Sail Sports, Ron Ebanks Charter Boat Headquarters,*

Tortuga Surfside Divers, and *Treasure Island Divers* (see *Sea Excursions* for information on the last eight outfits). On Cayman Brac are *Brac Aquatics* (phone: 948-1429), *Peter Hughes Dive Tiara* at the *Divi Tiara Beach,* and *Reef Divers* at the *Brac Reef Beach* (see *Checking In* for the latter two hotels). On Little Cayman, there are *Reef Divers* at the *Little Cayman Beach* resort (see *Checking In*) and *Paradise Divers* (phone: 948-4550; 800-450-2084). The experienced diver can book a week-long dive expedition aboard the luxury live-aboard dive yachts *Cayman Aggressor I, Cayman Aggressor II,* or *Sea Hunt;* contact *Sea and See Travel* (phone: 800-DIV-XPRT). *River Sport Divers* and *Sunset Divers* offer guided snorkeling trips; also see *Sea Excursions* for a list of other operators offering snorkeling trips.

SPORT FISHING Game fish abundant in Caymanian waters include bonefish, tarpon and, in deeper waters, marlin, yellowfin tuna, yellowtail, dolphin, and wahoo. Charter boats are available from a number of sources; your hotel can make arrangements. Little Cayman's bone and tarpon fishing are tops. You can arrange fishing charters through *Ron Ebanks Charter Boat Headquarters* and *Captain Marvin's Aquatics* (see *Sea Excursions,* above). Spearfishing is not an option for visitors, since spear guns can be used by licensed residents only.

SWIMMING AND SUNNING The most magnificent site is Seven Mile Beach; it is, incidentally, a public beach, and the majority of the island's hotels and villa and apartment complexes are located along its length. Hotels and condos are small enough and far enough apart so that crowding is seldom a problem. In addition, there are coves, bays, and expanses of coastline all around Grand Cayman (and on the other Cayman Islands) that can be all yours for an hour or a day in the sun and sea.

TENNIS No big layouts, but more than 30 courts in all, mostly at hotels (see *Checking In* for all places listed below). On Grand Cayman: at the *Beach Club* and *Caribbean Club* (where non-guests can play). On Cayman Brac: at *Brac Reef Beach* and *Divi Tiara Beach.* On Little Cayman: at the *Little Cayman Beach* resort. On Seven Mile Beach, the following cottage and condo complexes have courts: *Anchorage, Casa Caribe,* and *Christopher Columbus.*

WATER SKIING AND WINDSURFING Water skiing and windsurfing with instruction are offered by several hotels, as well as by *Red Sail Sports* (see *Sea Excursions,* above).

NIGHTLIFE

Nobody comes to the Cayman Islands for after-dark action, but there is casual nightclubbing at *Mingles* (near the *Cayman Islander* hotel off West Bay Rd.; phone: 949-0528), with disco music nightly (except Sundays) and live bands (and occasionally special international performers) on Saturdays. *Island Rock* is a disco upstairs at the *Cayman Falls* shopping center near the *Holiday Inn* (closed Sundays and Mondays; phone: 947-5366). *Silver's*

Night Club at the *Treasure Island* resort (see *Checking In*) is one of Grand Cayman's liveliest nightspots, featuring a variety of island entertainment; it's closed Sundays. Most nightspots charge admission and are open until 1 AM during the week and until midnight on Saturdays; on Sundays dancing is illegal, so there is no music of any kind, anywhere.

Best on the Islands

CHECKING IN

In the conventional Caribbean sense, there are only a few complete resort hotels with all the dining and entertainment facilities built in: the *Holiday Inn Grand Cayman, Clarion Grand Pavilion, Radisson Grand Cayman, Treasure Island,* and *Hyatt Regency Grand Cayman.* All Grand Cayman hotels, as well as condo, apartment, and villa complexes and guesthouses, charge top dollar. On the whole, apartment and villa rentals seem to be the best deal; fully furnished with kitchenettes, they not only allow you to be pleasantly independent, but also to keep meal costs under control. All places listed below have air conditioning, telephones, TV sets, and private baths unless otherwise indicated.

A word about that word "condo." On Grand Cayman, where no building may rise more than five stories, condominiums are not little congested boxes stuffed into a megastructure. Almost all properties are designed to offer spacious living and privacy. These condos offer what Europeans call a "self-catering holiday"—all the comforts of home without the housework. The condo manager often knows the best places to buy groceries and can arrange for a cook and/or maid to take care of everything from shopping to cleanup (for an extra fee). But be sure to arrange for transportation to and from your condo rental. On Little Cayman, *McLaughlin Properties* (phone: 948-1000) has eight very reasonably priced condominiums and cottages for rent on the water near good snorkeling and sunning beaches.

In the listings below expensive lodgings will cost $220 or more for a double room or condo apartment without meals (EP) between December and April; moderate places, between $150 and $220; and inexpensive lodgings, less than $150. For breakfast and lunch or dinner on the Modified American Plan (MAP), where available, add $35 to $45 per person per day. Off-season rates, normally in effect from mid-April to mid-December, are approximately 30% to 40% less. There's a 6% tax on room rates. In addition, most hotels assess a service charge of up to 10% on all bills in lieu of tipping, and in some places an "energy surcharge" is added for air conditioning. The toll-free central telephone number for hotel reservations on the Cayman Islands is 800-327-8777. All hotels are in the 809 area code unless otherwise indicated.

GRAND CAYMAN

SEVEN MILE BEACH

EXPENSIVE

Anchorage This attractive condominium resort encompasses 15 neatly laid out two-bedroom apartments with full kitchens; tennis, a pool, and Seven Mile Beach are all at the door. There's no restaurant. West Bay Rd. (phone: 947-4088; fax: 947-5001).

Beach Club Style that enhances but never stifles the fun is the hallmark here. Rooms with balconies or terraces have garden or sea views. The restaurant offers a laid-back atmosphere with alfresco dining on its terrace. Also here are water sports (scuba, snorkeling, sailing), a smooth swath of beach, tennis, and a new pool. The resort offers notable summer packages. About 2 miles from George Town on West Bay Rd. (phone: 949-8100; fax: 947-5167).

Caribbean Club At the beach's midpoint, it has 18 one- and two-bedroom villas grouped around a clubhouse with a lounge, and *Lantana's,* a first-rate restaurant (see *Eating Out*). There's also a good tennis court. West Bay Rd. (phone: 947-4099; fax: 947-4433).

Casa Caribe Superb tropical decor in all 13 units and a casually elegant atmosphere attract an upscale clientele. The attentive management and staff, plus amenities such as tennis, a pool, a Jacuzzi, and a fine beach, make this resort among the best on Grand Cayman. Its two- and three-bedroom units can be shared by four to six guests. There's no restaurant. West Bay Rd. (phone: 947-4287).

Clarion Grand Pavilion This is one of the top hotels on Grand Cayman—Queen Elizabeth II chose to stay here during her first visit to the Cayman Islands. The hotel's white-and-teal exterior is complemented by the tropical ambience of the public areas and guestrooms. The 93 rooms are equipped with mini-bars, hair dryers, and trouser presses; there's also a nightly turndown service. Other amenities include a pool, a Jacuzzi underneath a lovely waterfall, swimming and water sports at Seven Mile Beach, a fitness center, and a dive shop. There are two restaurants, including the outstanding *Ottmar's* (see *Eating Out*); a concierge and 24-hour room service are available. Seven Mile Beach Rd., between George Town and Bodden Town (phone: 947-5636; 800-CLARION; fax: 947-5353).

Colonial Club You'd expect to find this pastel pink property in Bermuda. Although situated in the heart of the busy Seven Mile Beach strip, this condominium complex has a charming sense of seclusion and good taste. Twenty-four two- and three-bedroom units are attractively furnished and have fully equipped kitchens. In addition, there's tennis, a pool, a Jacuzzi, and lots of beach. West Bay Rd. (phone: 947-4660; fax: 947-4839).

Holiday Inn Grand Cayman No surprises. On the beach, it offers 215 well-appointed rooms and all sorts of built-in beach action. Sports facilities include a full-service water sports center, a dive shop, and two tennis courts next door. There's poolside lunching, a coffee shop, a dining room, and *The Wreck of the Ten Sails,* an English-style pub and comedy club. West Bay Rd. (phone: 947-4444; 800-421-9999 or 800-HOLIDAY; fax: 947-4213).

Hyatt Regency Grand Cayman At this $80-million resort each of the 235 rooms and 40 villas features a mini-bar, spacious bath, and complimentary toiletries. Regency Club rooms, located in a separate wing, are elegantly decorated and feature extra touches, such as comfy robes, complimentary continental breakfast and, in the evenings, cocktails with hors d'oeuvres. Set on lush landscaped grounds, there are four pools, tennis courts, a beach club, scuba and water sports facilities, and a Jack Nicklaus–designed golf course (see *Golf*). Other features include three restaurants—the *Garden Loggia, Hemingway's* (see *Eating Out*), and the *Britannia Golf Grille;* four lounges with poolside entertainment; and conference facilities for up to 350. About 2½ miles from George Town on West Bay Rd. (phone: 949-1234; 800-233-1234; fax: 949-8528).

Indies Suites Close to West Bay about 4 miles from George Town, it's worth the drive to reach this property, Grand Cayman's only all-suite hotel. The resort offers 38 sumptuous Mediterranean-style suites (the spacious kitchens even have microwave ovens) in a 20-acre tropical setting, with a beautifully landscaped courtyard, pool, Jacuzzi, and small grocery store. A secluded part of Seven Mile Beach is a five-minute walk away. A dive operation (for guests only) offers water sports. There's no restaurant, but continental breakfast is included in the rate, and two nights a week there's a special outdoor barbecue or poolside buffet (phone: 947-5025; 800-654-3130; fax: 947-5024).

London House Here are 20 appealing one- and two-bedroom apartments and one three-bedroom apartment, all elegantly furnished in airy rattan and bright colors. All feature patios or balconies with sea views, ceiling fans (in addition to air conditioning), full kitchens, and daily maid service. Pluses include a pool; helpful, accessible management; and a lovely, peaceful beach. There's no restaurant. At the quiet northern end of Seven Mile Beach (phone: 947-4060; fax: 947-4087).

The Palms This beachfront condominium complex has 15 two- and three-bedroom units, a pool, a hot tub, and a tennis court. There's no restaurant. On Seven Mile Beach (phone: 947-5291; fax: 947-5629).

Radisson Grand Cayman This 315-room beachfront property just a half mile from George Town has a pool, a fitness center, and a full range of water sports and activities, including the *Cayman Mermaid,* one of the largest glass-bottom boats in the world. There is good dining in the *Regency Grille* and a snack bar at the beach. West Bay Rd. (phone: 949-0088; 800-333-3333; fax: 949-0288).

Treasure Island This newly renovated, 281-room resort is conveniently located 2 miles from George Town on Seven Mile Beach. The atmosphere is Caribbean, with an open-air lobby where steel drum bands perform nightly except Sundays. There are two large free-form pools with whirlpools and a swim-up bar, and the reef beach is excellent for snorkeling. Enjoy light snacks outdoors at *Captain Flint's* or Caribbean and continental fare at the *Top of the Falls* restaurant. The hotel dive shop offers snorkeling and dive equipment rentals and certification courses. West Bay Rd., Seven Mile Beach (phone: 949-7777; 800-203-0775; fax: 949-8672).

Villas of the Galleon This complex has 75 one-, two-, and three-bedroom units with spacious rooms, fully equipped kitchens, patios or balconies, and golf at the nearby *Links at Safehaven.* Next to the *Holiday Inn* on West Bay Rd. (phone: 947-4433; 800-232-1034; fax: 947-4705).

MODERATE

Beachcomber Here are 23 two- and three-bedroom condominiums with kitchens and ceiling fans (in addition to air conditioning) in a three-story beachfront structure that's near shopping and restaurants. There's also a pool. West Bay Rd. (phone: 947-4470; fax: 947-5019).

Christopher Columbus With 28 two- and three-bedroom apartments, all with kitchens, this complex at the northern end of Seven Mile Beach includes a freshwater pool and two tournament-quality tennis courts. There's no restaurant. Some good package buys. On the beach (phone: 947-4354; fax: 947-5062).

Seagull Nicely decorated, these 32 one-bedroom apartments, all with kitchens, are set right on the beach. There's no restaurant. No packages are offered, but fishing and scuba excursions are easily arranged (phone: 949-5756; fax: 949-9040).

Victoria House Pleasantly decorated and well managed, this attractive apartment complex at the north end of the beach (you'll need a car) has everything from one-room studios to a penthouse; all 25 units have kitchens. There is a tennis court, shuffleboard, a barbecue area, and snorkeling gear rentals. There's no restaurant. Fishing, scuba, and boat trips can be arranged (phone: 947-4233; fax: 947-5328).

INEXPENSIVE

Cayman Islander Set across the road from the beach rather than right on it, this slightly motel-like, 64-room property is friendly, presentable, and a great budget buy (one of the few). Also on the premises are a restaurant, pool, dive shop, and playground for kids (phone: 949-0990; fax: 949-7896).

Sleep Inn This Quality/Comfort Inn property is the closest establishment on Seven Mile Beach to downtown George Town and is also only a few minutes' drive from the *Britannia* golf course as well as *The Links at Savehaven.* There are 116 rooms and eight suites, a pool, a poolside bar and grill, and an on-site dive facility. West Bay Rd. (phone: 949-9111; 800-4-CHOICE; fax: 949-6699).

ELSEWHERE ON GRAND CAYMAN

EXPENSIVE

Cayman Kai This newly renovated and redecorated 10-room property is on the island's quiet and secluded north side. All one- and two-bedroom units have sea views, full kitchens, and screened-in patios. There's excellent snorkeling from a pristine beach, and Stingray City is fifteen minutes away by boat; the nearest dive shop is a 10-minute drive away. Dine outdoors on the hotel patio or in the air conditioned restaurant and lounge. North Side, near Rum Point (phone: 947-9055; 800-223-5427; fax: 947-9102).

Retreat at Rum Point Old friends of Grand Cayman will remember the *Rum Point Club.* The thatch-roofed, barefoot fun is gone, but the lovely beach and splendid solitude remain, now enhanced by one of the island's top resorts—great for those interested in Cayman's advantages without the Seven Mile Beach setting. The 23 well-decorated one-, two-, and three-bedroom units on 1,300 feet of beach are protected by the north coast barrier reef. There's a pool, tennis, sauna, and a small, complete fitness center. *Surfside Watersports,* across the street, handles the scuba and aquatic fun. On the north shore of the island at Rum Point (phone: 947-9135; fax: 947-9058).

MODERATE

Coconut Harbor Located just south of George Town, this neat, efficient property has 35 rooms with kitchenettes and balconies overlooking the sea and the pool. There's also an open-air bar and restaurant. Excellent shore diving. West Bay Rd. (phone: 949-7468; 800-552-6281; fax: 949-7117).

Morritt's Tortuga Club On the grounds of the old *Tortuga Club,* this property has 72 efficiency condominiums available. *Cayman Windsurfing* is on site, renting snorkeling and windsurfing equipment and sailboats; there's also a pool and a full-service dive operation. The restaurant features different themes—from seafood night to a weekly outdoor barbecue. West Bay Rd. (phone: 947-7449; fax: 947-7669).

INEXPENSIVE

Seaview One of the oldest properties on the island, this hostelry just south of George Town has 15 rooms (with no telephones or TV sets), a pool, dining room, piano bar, and diving facilities. S. Church St., five minutes from George Town (phone: 949-8804; fax: 949-8507).

Sunset House Advertised as a hotel for divers by divers, this small, award-winning resort is even more. South of George Town, on the Ironshore (the craggy limestone shoreline with a steel-gray cast), the informal but well-managed property has 59 simple rooms, two apartments, two pools—one freshwater, one saltwater—and one of the Cayman Islands' best-run dive operations. There's a restaurant, and the thatch-roofed, seaside *My Bar* is a great gathering place, day and night. If you can't stay here, at least stop in and toast the sunset. South Church St. (phone: 949-7111; 800-854-4767; fax: 949-7101).

CAYMAN BRAC

MODERATE

Divi Tiara Beach With more than 200 coconut palms adorning a peaceful strand, this resort offers 59 comfortable, newly decorated rooms (some featuring Jacuzzis, vaulted ceilings, and private balconies). Other amenities include a pool, two tennis courts, and a full-service dive shop. There's a restaurant offering open-air buffet dining and a pleasant seaside bar. On the southwest side of the island, 3 miles from the airport near West End (phone: 948-1553; 800-367-3484; fax: 948-1316).

INEXPENSIVE

Brac Caribbean Beach Village This cheerful-looking blue-and-white three-story building on Cayman Brac's southwest side offers 16 two-bedroom condominiums. All have fully-equipped kitchens, pullout couches in the living rooms, balconies with sea views, TV sets with VCRs, and washer/dryer units. There's no restauurant. Stake Bay (phone: 948-2265 or 948-0403; fax: 948-1111).

Brac Reef Beach Designed and built by Bracker Linton Tibbetts—the Floridian considered the godfather of Cayman Brac tourism—this lovely 40-room resort offers a private beach, a freshwater pool, a Jacuzzi, two tennis courts, a restaurant serving superb native and continental food, and a new full-service dive shop, *Reef Divers*. A great place to relax and really get away without roughing it. All rooms are naturally air conditioned by breezes off the cool south coast. Excellent dive and vacation packages year-round (phone: 948-1323; 800-327-3835; 813-323-8727 in Florida; fax: 948-1207 or 813-323-8827 in the US).

LITTLE CAYMAN

MODERATE

Little Cayman Beach Lush flowers and tropical plants surround 32 simply furnished rooms with sea views, a cabana bar, and a freshwater pool and Jacuzzi. The rooms have ceiling fans (to supplement the air conditioning) and satellite TV. Featuring a first-class dive shop on the premises, the famous Bloody

Bay Wall just minutes away, and warm, personal attention from the hotel and dive staff, this all-inclusive property is a divers' favorite. *PADI* certification and underwater photo instruction are available. Also on the premises is the fine *Birds of Paradise* restaurant (see *Eating Out*), a tennis court, and a conference center for up to 60. Packages for non-divers are available, as well. South side of the island, east of the airport (phone: 948-1033; 800-327-3835; 813-323-8727 in Florida; fax: 948-1040 or 813-323-8827 in the US).

Paradise Villas Here are six seaside duplex cottages (each divided into two one-bedroom units) with fully equipped kitchens, pullout couches in the living rooms, ceiling fans (in addition to air conditioning), and verandahs with sea views. *Paradise Divers,* which offers dive and snorkel equipment rental as well as *PADI* certification, is on the premises. There's also a pool and the *Hungry Iguana* restaurant next door (see *Eating Out*). South side of the island, near the airstrip (phone: 948-0001; 800-450-2084; fax: 948-0002).

Pirates Point Run by Texan-born chef-hostess Gladys Howard, this small, very out-island, 10-room lodge offers scuba packages that include all meals (Howard has won awards for her cooking) and two dives daily. Four of the rooms are air conditioned. It's minutes from Bloody Bay Wall, a famous dive spot. Bonefishing and deep-sea fishing also are available. At the southwest tip of the island (phone: 948-1010; 800-327-8777; fax: 948-1011).

Southern Cross Club A hospitable 10-unit sportsperson's enclave, it's casually comfortable from rooftop to terrace. The rooms are not air conditioned, and none have telephones or TV sets. Complete scuba programs, fishing setups with emphasis on fly fishing, guides, and inclusive packages are available. On South Hole Sound (phone: 948-1099; 317-636-9501 in the US; fax: 317-636-9503 in the US).

EATING OUT

Caymanian meals star fresh fish, turtle soup and steaks, codfish and ackee (a Jamaican dish made with this local fruit), conch stew, and native lobster in season (August through January). In George Town and along the beach, the choice ranges from informal hamburger places to an elegant old plantation house where dinner is served by candlelight on the verandah and the tab, including wine and tip, runs to more than $50 per person. Although the sister islands' dining opportunities are mostly limited to hotel dining rooms, Grand Cayman has an eclectic and ever-changing array of ethnic culinary diversions. In places we call very expensive, for a dinner for two, including drinks and service, expect to pay $100 or more; in an expensive restaurant, $80 to $100; in a moderate place, $50 to $80; and in an inexpensive eatery, $50 or less. All are open for lunch and dinner unless otherwise noted. All restaurants are in the 809 area code unless otherwise indicated.

VERY EXPENSIVE

Chef Tell's Grand Old House Run by TV chef Tell Erhardt, this former plantation house is an extra special eating place. Some dishes are better than others, but it is the ambience of the picturesque old house on the seashore that is most memorable. Start with a drink in the *Clown Bar,* then move to the verandah for your meal. Marinated conch, escargots, Cayman land crab, and crêpes *impériales* serve as appetizers; entrées include fresh fish, Cayman lobster, veal *cordon bleu,* deep-fried grouper *beignets,* and fondue *bourguignonne.* Open daily; no lunch on weekends. Reservations necessary. Major credit cards accepted. S. Church St. (phone: 949-9333).

EXPENSIVE

Bella Capri Romantic ambience and excellent Italian cooking are the lures here. The *scaloppine alla piemontese* is recommended. Open daily for dinner only. Reservations unnecessary. Major credit cards accepted. Off Seven Mile Beach Rd., across from the *Holiday Inn Grand Cayman* (phone: 947-4755).

Golden Pagoda Chinese fare, with West Indian nuances here and there. Takeout available. Open daily for dinner only. Reservations advised. MasterCard and Visa accepted. West Bay Rd. (phone: 949-5475).

Hemingway's This open-air restaurant is set in a delightful white pavilion at the center of the *Hyatt Regency Grand Cayman's* beach club overlooking the Caribbean. Rum drinks are served poolside or even on the beach. Try the macadamia-crusted pork with snow peas, leeks, and sweet potato, or the pumpkin-coated mahi-mahi. Open daily. Reservations advised. Major credit cards accepted. At the *Hyatt Regency Grand Cayman,* West Bay Rd. (phone: 949-1234).

Lantana's The charming decor here features pink conch shells, funky painted wood parrotfish, and miniature white ceramic lamps. The menu changes daily and offers astonishing diversity, including Cuban black bean soup, Chinese pot stickers, blackened reef shark, barbecued wahoo, jerk pork, and roast lamb. Chef Fred Schrock has earned well-deserved accolades for his picture-perfect presentation and innovative cooking. Open daily; no lunch on weekends. Reservations necessary. Major credit cards accepted. West Bay Rd. (phone: 947-5595).

Lobster Pot Overlooking the sea, this is an old favorite with both visitors and locals thanks to consistently fine service and good seafood (lobster, conch chowder, and very fresh local fish). The "Cayman Trio" is a popular special consisting of island-style lobster tail, sautéed shrimp, and broiled dolphin (the fish, not the mammal). It's also a great spot to watch the sunset with one of the restaurant's renowned rum punches in hand. Closed Sundays.

Reservations advised. Major credit cards accepted. N. Church St. (phone: 949-2736).

Ottmar's Owner/chef Ottmar Weber, a veteran of such fine island dining spots as the *Grand Old House* and *L'Escargot,* has opened a showplace for his own brand of classic cooking. Attractive and formal, the restaurant's continental dishes often feature rich sauces, and portions are generous. Try the baked gulf shrimp as an appetizer, then move on to chicken breast Oscar or the pan-fried catch of the day. Open daily for breakfast, lunch, and dinner. Reservations necessary. Major credit cards accepted. In the *Clarion Grand Pavilion,* West Bay Rd. (phone: 947-5879).

Pappagallo One of the island's most unusual dining spots, this thatch-roofed waterfront building has an ambience that is both tropical and elegant—the place has both live parrots and waiters in black tie. (Diners need only wear smart casual attire, though.) It features a northern Italian menu, with seafood, veal, chicken, and pasta specialties. Try the chicken breast marinated in olive oil, garlic, rosemary, and lemon, grilled and served with vegetables. Open daily for dinner only. Reservations advised. Major credit cards accepted. Across from the *Villas Pappagallo* resort, about 15 minutes north of George Town in West Bay (phone: 949-3479).

Wharf Waterfront dining in one of the island's prettiest, most romantic settings. You can choose indoor, deck, or terrace seating, all with a lovely sea view. A menu featuring classic continental and Caribbean fare offers a delectable selection, including blackened yellowfin tuna, lobster and shrimp "Port-au-Prince," and key lime pie topped with golden meringue. There's even a floor show provided by nature—the memorable spectacle of huge tarpon leaping around just off the edge of the wharf as they wait to be fed by the restaurant's staff at 9 PM. Open daily; no lunch on weekends. Reservations advised. Major credit cards accepted. Seven Mile Beach (phone: 949-2231).

MODERATE

Almond Tree Here dinner is served island-style on an outdoor garden patio or inside the big, thatch-roofed restaurant. First-rate tropical punches and piña coladas are served, along with good island food such as baked turtle steaks. Open for dinner only; closed Sundays. Reservations advised. Major credit cards accepted. N. Church St. (phone: 949-2893).

Cracked Conch The conch platter—which includes conch stewed, cracked, and as fritters—is delicious, as are the broiled tuna steak, garlic shrimp, and key lime pie. Owner/chef/artist Suzy Soto's innovative Caribbean cooking and her colorful island murals make this a longtime favorite of locals and tourists alike. Open daily. Reservations advised. Major credit cards accepted. West Bay Rd. (phone: 947-5217).

DJ's Café With its bistro atmosphere, good food, and fast service, this is a regular haunt of an interesting local clientele, from divers to bankers. Check the blackboard for entrées ranging from lobster to lasagna. Open daily for dinner only. Reservations unnecessary. Major credit cards accepted. Behind the *Coconut Place* shopping center, West Bay Rd. (phone: 947-4234).

The Edge This rustic seaside restaurant specializes in fresh local seafood. French chef Philippe Gros serves grilled red snapper, shrimp, yellowfin tuna, and green sea turtle in a variety of light sauces, accompanied by homemade bread and superb desserts. Dine inside or on a breeze-swept outdoor deck. Open daily for breakfast, lunch, and dinner. Reservations necessary for dinner. Major credit cards accepted. A 20-minute drive east of George Town, in Bodden Town (phone: 947-2140).

INEXPENSIVE

Billy's Place In a garden of red hibiscus, this pink-and-blue house is popular with locals for jerk chicken and Cayman-style lobster. The Indian *tikka masala* and curry dishes are also excellent. Finish with rum cake or coconut pie. Open daily. Reservations unnecessary. Major credit cards accepted. N. Church St., George Town (phone: 949-0470).

Corita's Copper Kettle There are just eight red-checkered tables in this charming blue-and-white stucco house in downtown George Town. Try ackee and codfish, turtle burgers, or Corita's Special: fritters made with jelly, cheese, ham, and bacon. Open daily. No reservations. No credit cards accepted. Corner of Edward Street and Doctor Roy's Drive (phone: 949-2696).

Crow's Nest, South Sound This tiny, informal, family-style Caymanian eatery serves great seafood, burgers, and West Indian specialties inside or out, overlooking the sea. One of the best buys on the island. Closed Sunday lunch. Reservations advised. Major credit cards accepted. South of George Town on the coastal road (phone: 949-9366).

Eats Café This colorful, casual café is a popular hangout for locals. The grilled jumbo shrimp Caesar salad is excellent, as are the hamburgers, tuna sandwiches, and chili. Open daily. Reservations unnecessary. MasterCard and Visa accepted. *Cayman Falls* shopping center, West Bay Rd. (phone: 947-5288).

Liberty's, West Bay A great dollar-stretching place for those who really want to try West Indian food at its best; the menu includes such exotica as curried goat, codfish and ackee, oxtail, and seafood Cayman-style. Open daily. No reservations. Major credit cards accepted. Reverend Blackman Rd. (phone: 949-3226).

Lone Star The party never stops at this large, noisy restaurant-bar. The food is Tex-Mex, and there's a lot of it; check out the regular daily specials, which sometimes include Cajun dishes. Overhead TV screens continually show what's going on in the world of US and local sports. Open daily. Reservations unnecessary. Major credit cards accepted. Seven Mile Beach (phone: 947-5175).

West Bay Polo Club There's plenty of camaraderie to be found at this sports bar cum billiard hall, a popular watering hole for residents and tourists alike. The chalkboard menu features good snack fare and nearly two dozen varieties of beer. US (and sometimes local) athletic events are shown on multiple TV screens. Open daily. No reservations. Major credit cards accepted. In the *Seven Mile Shops* complex, West Bay Rd. (phone: 949-9891/2).

LITTLE CAYMAN

MODERATE

Birds of Paradise Enjoy a relaxing buffet dinner in a pink-and-green floral dining room or outdoors under the stars. Specialties here include a salad bar, chicken breast with creamed spinach, and homemade carrot cake. There are also weekly barbecues featuring ribs, fish, and jerk chicken. Reservations advised. Major credit cards accepted. At *Little Cayman Beach* resort (phone: 948-1033).

The Hungry Iguana This beachside house is impossible to miss with its huge iguana mural. Enjoy seafood gumbo, marinated conch salad, jerk chicken sandwiches, grilled shrimp, and peach cobbler à la mode. Open daily for breakfast, lunch, and dinner. Reservations advised. Major credit cards suggested. Next to *Paradise Villas* (phone: 948-0007).

Pirates Point Owner/manager Gladys Howard's training with Julia Child and James Beard is immediately obvious from the virtual gastronomic miracles of fish, pork, chicken, and conch she regularly produces. On "Monday Island Night" local foods are showcased, including steamed triggerfish, stuffed *cho cho* (Caribbean squash stuffed with bread cumbs, onions, and nuts), boiled cassava, *callaloo* (a native green sautéed with onions and bacon), peas and rice, and heavy cake (a pudding-like cake) served with a cherry sauce. Open daily. Reservations necessary. Major credit cards accepted. *Pirates Point* resort (phone: 948-1010).

Colombia's Caribbean Coast

The much-publicized violence in Colombia caused by the drug cartels and other outlaw groups, which make law and order in much of the country a some-time thing, has fostered an undeserved image of general lawlessness along the country's Caribbean coast.

Although the US State Department continues to warn against traveling in many parts of Colombia, it considers travel to the Caribbean port cities of Cartagena, Santa Marta, and Barranquilla relatively safe. Major cruise ships and charter flights once again serve the area. Still, while the falling exchange rate makes Colombia a bargain spot in the high-priced Caribbean, visitors should continue to exercise caution.

Topographically, little of Colombia's 1,000-mile Caribbean coast has changed since European ships first landed on its shores at the beginning of the 16th century to claim its sunbaked beaches and virgin forests for Spain. While the coastal area today is home to a substantial fishing industry and ranks as one of the country's major agricultural and cattle raising regions, its population is still relatively small. Tiny fishing villages are scattered along stretches of beach, and large deep-water bays and hidden coves front the jagged coastline from the desolate plains of the Guajira peninsula in the east to the dense jungles of the Gulf of Darién in the west.

Few travelers see these isolated fishing villages and almost uninhabited jungle. What lures contemporary travelers are the coast's two major resort areas—the walled city of Cartagena and historic Santa Marta—as well as the isolated free-port island of San Andrés, located almost 500 miles to the northwest in the Caribbean Sea. The gateway to Colombia's Caribbean coast is the city of Barranquilla, the nation's largest port (pop. 1.7 million).

The first European to set eyes on Colombia's coast was the Spanish explorer Alonso de Ojeda, in 1500. The next year, Rodrigo de Bastidas, a wealthy notary from Seville, explored the entire coast; he returned almost 24 years later to establish the first permanent European settlement on the South American mainland, in Santa Marta. In 1533, Don Pedro de Heredia landed at what was then the Carib fishing village of Calamari, in a natural harbor formed by a bay and a sand-spit breakwater. He promptly renamed it Cartagena de las Indias, and it soon became one of Spain's most prized New World possessions.

The growing Spanish Empire needed gold and silver to finance further expeditions, as well as to pay the military forces needed to protect these new possessions and their supply lines across the Atlantic and Caribbean.

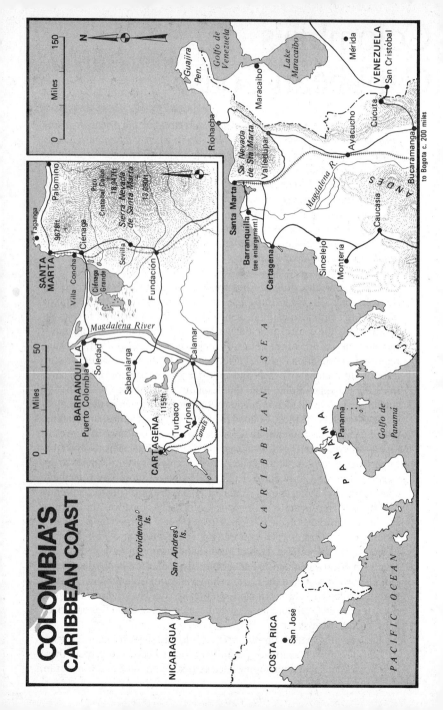

Cartagena became the principal storehouse and the main transit point for the seemingly inexhaustible wealth that flowed to Spain from the New World; it also became a key target for attacks by English, French, and Dutch pirates. It was sacked time and again, only to be reestablished after each attack. Its location made it irreplaceable as a Caribbean port for Spanish galleons loaded with gold, emeralds, pearls, indigo, tobacco, and coffee.

The city was captured and held for ransom by Sir Francis Drake in 1586; consequently, Spanish rulers spent a fortune fortifying it over the next two centuries. Philip II commissioned the top military engineer in Europe to plan the city's defenses, and 23 forts and 7 miles of walls were completed by 1796. Seven of the nine original forts still stand, with their ingenious maze of underground passageways, strategic gun emplacements, cisterns for collecting rainwater, ventilation systems, dungeons, and large storage areas for ammunition and food—most of them 25 feet underground. As part of the defense system, tons of rock were dropped at the wide western entrance to the bay, forming an underwater barrier that prevents ship passage through that point to this day.

A causeway across the strait connects mainland Cartagena with Boca Grande, the newer sand-spit section where the city's major hotels are located. Visitors today can take a cruise that provides a pirate's-eye view of the two forts guarding the passage into the inner harbor, or they can sail the Bay of Cartagena, so large that it once was said to be big enough to hold all the world's fleets. The beaches are so shallow that hostile ships could not come close enough to bombard the city. Although ships were well protected inside the bay, they could fall prey to pirates at those times of the year when the lakes and swamps between the Magdalena River and Cartagena dried up, forcing the ships to put to sea. To transport their riches safely from the interior of the country to the fortress, the Spaniards brought thousands of African slaves to build a 65-mile canal from the Magdalena River to Cartagena that is still in use.

Cartagena (pop. 900,000) remains Colombia's most popular tourist destination, and its appeal seems to be growing. The city combines the colonial antiquity of the Old City, with its crooked narrow streets, impressive fortifications, and well-preserved early churches and palatial homes, with the Boca Grande area's modern, high-rise hotels and smart shops.

The beach resort of Santa Marta and the island of San Andrés also are gaining in popularity, especially among foreign vacationers. Santa Marta is the oldest European-founded city on the continent, and was the favored point of departure of early explorers venturing into the unknown continent in search of gold. Today, tourists bask on the sparkling beaches below the towering snow-covered Sierra Nevada.

San Andrés, set in the Caribbean some 500 miles northwest of the northern coast of Colombia, is a tropical land of lush green hills and coconut groves, with some of the finest weather, clearest waters, and loveliest beaches in the Caribbean. Its inhabitants—descended from the island's English

Pilgrim settlers and their African slaves—still speak English and worship in Protestant churches. In addition, there is a duty-free port and two gambling casinos. Its tiny sister island, Providencia, some 60 miles farther northeast, is becoming increasingly popular with those seeking an off-the-beaten-path, non-touristy Caribbean destination.

Colombia's pride in its colonial heritage, combined with its *mañana* atmosphere, sometimes proves so pervasive that visitors may overlook its current turbulence. However, travelers in Colombia should follow commonsense precautions: Be aware of current conditions in the country; don't carry large sums of money or wear expensive jewelry; and use hotel safes to store valuables—or, better still, leave them at home. Road travel between Colombian cities is dangerous because of robbers and leftist rebels, but the country does have a modern internal air transport system, and it's the best way to travel within the country.

Since the early 1990s, the natural beauty of Colombia's Caribbean coast—and its low prices—have been drawing many new visitors, especially from Canada and Western Europe. Hopefully, conditions in the years ahead will allow even more travelers to discover and enjoy Colombia's wild and beautiful shoreline.

Colombia's Caribbean Coast At-a-Glance

FROM THE AIR

Colombia's Caribbean coast stretches from Panama to Venezuela—1,000 miles of the northernmost edge of South America—in a jagged line of bays, capes, and beaches broken here and there by dense jungle and towering mountains. Only 150 miles across at its widest point, this narrow strip of coastal lowlands occupies a delta-shaped alluvial area between the snow-capped Sierra Nevada and the central and western spurs of the Andes. As travelers look down from the plane approaching Barranquilla, the gateway to Colombia's Caribbean resorts, the sparkling blue sea suddenly gives way to a lush green mat of tropical vegetation that shows scars of civilization. Gray asphalt roads stretch out in long lines toward red-tile rooftops, farmland, large estates, and the helter-skelter of buildings that make up this city.

Just 2½ hours by air from Miami, the busy city of Barranquilla sits at the midpoint of the Colombian coast, on the west bank of the Magdalena River, one of Colombia's principal waterways. A 1,500-meter bridge spans the river and leads to the four-lane Caribbean highway, a direct and sometimes scenic route along the coast that leads east to Santa Marta; to the Sierra Nevada and *Tairona National Park* beyond; and farther still to the little-known beaches, deserts, and Indian country of the Guajira peninsula on the border of Venezuela. West of Barranquilla, in the opposite direction, lies Cartagena.

SPECIAL PLACES

CARTAGENA With some of the best examples of colonial architecture in Americas, the city, once the defender of the New World's riches, is desirable tourist destination. Thanks to a stepped-up police presence in the streets, the tourist areas of the Old City are now reasonably safe for walking. Remember, tourists should not wear expensive jewelry or carry large sums of money, and should avoid deserted streets at night.

Cartagena's once impregnable fortifications are still formidable, blocking the Boca Grande entrance to the harbor (now a causeway to the city) and guarding the Boca Chica mouth of the bay in which the city is nestled. Walls 40 feet high and 50 to 60 feet wide encircle this "heroic city," and seven of its nine original forts—with ingeniously laid out underground passages, barracks, and storage areas—remain standing.

A good way to see the city and get a full appreciation of its strategic importance is to take a boat trip around the harbor. The Old City, with its crooked narrow streets, palm-filled plazas, and stately colonial mansions with wrought-iron gates and balconies, stands out in sharp contrast to the functional high-rise condominiums and hotels, fine restaurants, and fashionable shops in the Boca Grande strip between the bay and the Caribbean.

For a panoramic view of the city and harbor, drive or take a taxi to *El Monasterio del Cerro de la Popa,* a 17th-century monastery at the top of La Popa Hill (open daily; admission charge; no phone). Just below is the city's most important fortification, *Castillo San Felipe de Barajas,* which remains in almost perfect condition. Originally constructed in 1657, it was captured and destroyed in 1697 by a force of 650 French corsairs, pirates, and buccaneers. Between 1762 and 1769 it was transformed into the impressive fort that still guards the harbor. It's open daily; admission charge (no phone). In the plaza in front of the fortress stands a statue of an enormous pair of shoes, honoring one of Cartagena's best-loved poets, Luis Carlos López. López praised the city in one of his poems, saying it inspired as much affection and comfort as an old pair of shoes. The *National Tourist Corporation* can provide more information and recommend guides to both the monastery and the fortress (see *Tourist Information*).

On the western side of Cartagena, along the Caribbean, several early buildings have been restored by public-spirited citizens. The *Iglesia de San Pedro Claver* (Church of San Pedro Claver; Av. San Juan de Dios) is named for the 17th-century Jesuit monk who dedicated his life to helping the African slaves imported by the Spaniards. The remains of this South American saint, canonized in 1888, repose in a chest under the main altar. On the Plaza Bolívar is the former *Palacio de la Inquisición* (Palace of the Inquisition), a splendid example of colonial architecture that now houses the city's tourist office and exhibits documenting the horrors of the Inquisition, as well as memorabilia of the city's past, including the receipt

...ion-peso ransom paid to Sir Francis Drake for not burning
...d weekends; admission charge (no phone).

...dral, which faces the Plaza Bolívar, was begun in a kind of
...e-Andalusian style in 1575 and completed only in this century
...-and-white Moorish tower. Its original hand-carved altar has
...red with gold plating.

...nally across the Plaza Bolívar, a block north and a block west
...the sea), is the oldest church in Cartagena, the *Iglesia de Santo*
...o built at the end of the 16th century. It's easily recognized by its
tow..., part of the original construction, which appears to lean slightly. Of
special interest inside is the statue of the Virgin Mary, wearing a crown of
gold and emeralds.

One block south of the Plaza Bolívar on the Calle de las Damas is a fine
colonial residence where, according to legend, the patron saint of Cartagena
appeared to Fray Alonso de la Cruz and ordered him to build the *Church
of La Popa* on the highest hill in the area. The beautiful patio and elaborately decorated rooms are now the site of *Bodegón de la Candelaria,* a good
seafood restaurant (see *Eating Out*). The house of the Marqués de
Valdehoyos, a man who made a fortune trading in flour and slaves, is nearby
(at Calle Factoria 36-37, Carrera 3), only a block from the cathedral. Its
vaulted Moorish ceilings, double balconies, spiral staircase, and lookout
provide more outstanding examples of colonial architecture. Closed Saturday
afternoons and Sundays; admission charge. The marquis's home also houses
the local offices of *Corporación Nacional de Turismo* (the Colombia National
Tourist Corporation). A few blocks north of here, by the *Parque Madrid,*
is a 17th-century mansion once owned by Don Benito, a gentleman who
ran afoul of the Inquisition for preaching Judaism. It is now a popular handicrafts shop.

The *Parque Morillo,* located opposite the *Clock Tower,* near the center
of the Old City, is a symbol of Cartagena's indomitable spirit and love of
liberty. On November 11, 1811, Cartagena became the first city in what are
now Colombia and Venezuela to declare its independence from Spain.
Freedom fighters expelled the Spanish in 1815 and held the city-state until
Pablo Morillo, leader of the Spanish forces, retook it after a three-month
siege. Upon entering the city, Morillo offered the native freedom fighters
"amnesty in the name of peace," and then proceeded to execute hundreds
of people. Although the park bears the name of the Spanish "peacemaker,"
it commemorates the people he executed.

The *India Catalina* statue (Av. Venezuela and Calle San Pedro Mártir
at Playa San Pedro Mártir), another city landmark, commemorates the
early Carib inhabitants of this area. A beautiful Indian princess, Catalina
was taken prisoner by Spanish conquistadores when she was a child; she
returned as a young maiden with Don Pedro de Heredia to help establish
Cartagena. Today, bronze replicas of her are given out as "Catalinas"—

awards at the annual *International Film Festival* held at the *Baluarte de Santa Catalina,* just off the Plaza Bovedas.

Another of the forts that once protected the city from marauding pirates is the *Castillo de San Fernando,* which has been restored and is well worth a visit. It is on Boca Chica Island, easily reached by boat from the city. Open daily; admission charge (no phone). Several operators offer tours to the *Castillo;* ask at your hotel or contact the *National Tourist Corporation* (see *Tourist Information*).

SANTA MARTA Set between two beaches, Santa Marta is a notable port and commercial fishing center, as well as the capital of a sizable agricultural region where large banana plantations flourish. This 450-year-old city can be reached easily from Barranquilla, Bogotá, and other Colombian cities by plane or car. It is a low-key resort town, with some sightseeing and very little nightlife. What draws people to Santa Marta are the magnificent beaches and the snow-capped Sierra Nevada rising 18,000 feet in the background. Many of the visitors to Santa Marta are Colombians from other parts of the country who come here to sunbathe, scuba dive, and enjoy the scenic mountains just 30 miles from the Caribbean coastline.

Rodadero Beach, east of Santa Marta, between the airport and town, is more modern; it has newer hotels, restaurants, and the only nightlife to speak of in town. Santa Marta Beach, in town, has older (but not necessarily less expensive) accommodations; it is quieter and somewhat isolated.

The area's other attractions are the Sierra Nevada, home of the reclusive Kogi Indians, and the site of the *Ciudad Perdida* (Lost City), accessible only by helicopter (see *Extra Special,* below). Also of interest are the quiet fishing villages of Taganga (about 10 miles north) and Villa Concha (15 miles to the south), and the banana plantations surrounding the area, most accessible from the village of Sevilla (32 miles south of Santa Marta). *Tairona National Park,* located 25 miles northeast of Santa Marta, has what are probably the most beautiful beaches in all of Colombia. Here you can camp or rent grass-roofed huts on a jungle hill overlooking a spectacular beach. For reservations and information, contact *Inderena,* Colombia's environmental agency, in Bogotá (phone: 1-286-8643 or 1-283-0964; fax: 1-283-3458).

La Hacienda de San Pedro Alejandrino, about 3 miles southeast of the city, is another interesting side trip. It was home to the Great Liberator, Simón Bolívar, who was exiled here from his native Venezuela. Totally destitute, he accepted the hospitality of, ironically, a Spanish nobleman whose own fortune had been considerably reduced by Bolívar's Wars of Independence. The final days of Bolívar's life inspired the 1990 novel *The General in His Labyrinth,* by Colombia's Nobel Prize–winning author, Gabriel García Márquez. The Great Liberator died here, disillusioned, on December 17, 1830. Although Bolívar's body was removed to the *National Pantheon* in Caracas, Venezuela, his heart remained (literally) in Santa Marta, kept in the cathedral in a leaden casket, which was lost after a fire in 1872. The stately main house is now a museum, with Bolívar's few possessions on display, and the entire estate is an attractive park with giant shade trees dating from Bolívar's time. Open daily. Admission charge (phone: 54-206589).

SAN ANDRÉS Almost 500 miles northwest of Colombia, San Andrés is actually closer to Nicaragua. This tropical paradise is the largest island of a tiny archipelago that produces coconuts and other fruits. Its main attractions are its luxurious sandy beaches, warm sea, reliable sun, and an almost constant temperature of 80F (27C) 10 months of the year.

Unlike mainland Colombians, most San Andréans speak English. Originally discovered by the Spanish in 1527, the island was settled by English Pilgrims sailing on the *Seaflower,* sister ship to the *Mayflower,* who planted cotton and began importing African slaves to work their plantations. Later the island became a pirate refuge, and buccaneer Henry Morgan set up a base here for his raids on Spanish shipping.

Isolated from the continent, San Andrés has changed little since Morgan's time and has not been tainted by the violence on Colombia's mainland. In fact, Morgan's treasure has never been found and is, according to history and rumor, still hidden in one of the many caves or one of the nearby cays (also see *Sunken and Buried Treasure* in DIVERSIONS).

In 1822, San Andrés became part of the Colombian province of Cartagena and lay quietly in the Caribbean until it was declared a free port in the 1950s. Although regular air service was established at that time, and the free-port status attracts a large number of bargain hunters (from the Colombian mainland as well as the rest of the world), the island has remained fairly primitive and underdeveloped. There are some good hotels and restaurants; however, tap water is undrinkable, hot water often is unavailable, there are occasional blackouts, and restaurant menus depend on ship arrivals.

There are only two towns on the island: San Luis and the self-named San Andrés. The airport is only a short taxi ride from San Andrés, or about a 15-minute walk. Many of the town's 600 or so duty-free shops are clustered around Avenida La Playa, the main street of the resort section of San Andrés; most tourist hotels are nearby. There are several good, paved roads and a scenic route around the island, which meanders through coconut groves and passes what is reputed to be Morgan's Cave. It also skirts the Hoyo Soplador, or Blow Hole, which spouts sea water about 30 feet into the air. San Luis is home to most of the island's residents. A small, primitive fishing village of simple but special beauty, peace, and charm, it is an appealing stop on a San Andrés excursion.

Also be sure to venture beyond the resort and shopping area of San Andrés and into the older section of town, centered around the Baptist church on La Loma Hill, which is the site of many old island mansions surrounded by oleander and banyan trees. From here you can view an incredible seascape of pristine beaches and multihued waters. These beaches and warm waters are perfect for all water sports, and its coral reefs are filled with a variety of colorful fish.

There are several offshore keys; the two that attract most visitors are Johnny Key and Haines Key, accessible by launch from San Andrés. Both have picnic facilities and beautiful waters. Haines Key shelters a natural aquarium within its reefs, and a scuba mask, snorkel, and fins (bring your own) are all that's necessary to explore the colorful world beneath the waves.

PROVIDENCIA This pristine, mountainous island, 60 miles northeast of San Andrés and 900 miles south of Miami, has not yet been developed as a tourist destination. Unlike San Andrés, Providencia is mountainous and volcanic. It features sandy beaches, an extensive coral reef on its east side, a slow pace, and residents who are friendly and who (for the most part) speak English. The island was settled in 1629 by passengers of the *Seaflower,* who began a slave-trading enterprise known as the Providence Company. Today, most of the native residents of Providencia are descendants of the English and Dutch settlers and the many pirates who originally lived here.

Satena airlines (Bogotá; phone: 1-413-8064; fax: 1-413-8178) has daily flights between San Andrés and Providencia. After arriving at Providencia's *El Embrujo Airport,* visitors are transported via taxi-trucks through Santa Isabel, the island's main town, and on to Bahía de Agua Dulce (Sweet Water Bay), where most of the hotels are. All accommodations on the island are modest and small-scale. Stay at the 20-room *Royal Queen* in Santa Isabel (see *Checking In*), or choose from among several properties at Bahía de Agua Dulce.

Things to do on Providencia: Visit the white sand beach at Southwest Bay, eat fresh fish, rent horses, and buy coral handicrafts (forget about tortoiseshell items—you can't bring them into the US). For an interesting inland journey, climb the Peak, at 2,000 feet the highest mountain on the island and, though not a challenge for serious climbers, still a good hike. Ask about hiring a guide at the Bottom House, a village in the southern part of the island, or contact the tourist information office at the airport or on San Andrés (see *Tourist Information*). You also can hire a small boat at Sweet Water Bay and visit isolated Crab Cay, which is one of the best places for snorkeling. Or sail past Morgan's Head, a rock outcropping shaped like a human head, then on to the island of Santa Catalina, site of a fishing village.

EXTRA SPECIAL

The *Ciudad Perdida* (Lost City), containing pre-Columbian ruins of the Tairona Indians, was discovered in 1975 in the Sierra Nevada, just outside of Santa Marta. The Tairona built circular stone platforms, walls, and roads along the crests of the mountains. Their interconnected cities numbered more than 300, and *Ciudad Perdida* was their sacred center. There are no roads leading to the Lost City, but helicopter trips can be arranged in the high season through Flor Rincón at *Aviatur, Inc.* in Bogotá (phone: 1-282-7111; fax: 1-283-0141). Reservations should be booked several weeks in advance; flight schedules are affected by weather conditions and whether there's guerrilla violence in the region.

Sources and Resources

TOURIST INFORMATION

Corporación Nacional de Turismo (the Colombia National Tourist Corporation) has offices in Cartagena at the *Casa de Marqués de Valdehoyos* (Calle Factoria 36-37, Carrera 3; phone: 5-664-7015 or 5-664-7017) and in the old *Palace of the Inquisition* on the Plaza Bolívar (no phone). There also are tourist offices in Santa Marta (3-10 Calle 10, in El Rodadero; phone: 54-229483; fax: 54-227291) and on San Andrés (9-50 Av. Colombia; phone: 811-24230; fax: 811-23832) and Providencia (at the airport; phone: 811-48176). All offices are closed Saturday afternoons and Sundays. The nearest *US Consulate* is in Barranquilla (68-15 Calle 77; phone: 58-459067). For information on tourist offices in the US, see GETTING READY TO GO.

LOCAL COVERAGE *El Caribe Colombia,* a free bilingual magazine published monthly by the *Corporación Nacional de Turismo,* offers the latest information on restaurants, shopping centers, hotels, and tourist sites in Cartagena, Barranquilla, and Santa Marta. It is available in most hotels and many restaurants. On San Andrés, the local newspapers are printed in both English and Spanish.

RADIO AND TELEVISION CNN is broadcast in most of the hotels that have satellite cable access. There are no English-language radio stations on Colombia's Caribbean coast.

TELEPHONE When calling from the US, dial 011 (international access code) + 57 (country code) + (city code) + (local number). The city code for Cartagena is 5; for Santa Marta, 54; and for San Andrés, 811. When calling from Colombia or elsewhere in South America, dial 9 before the city code. To call from anywhere else, the access code may vary, so call the local operator. Note that city codes are included in the telephone numbers listed in this chapter. When calling within a Colombian city, use only the local number. Changes always are being made to the Colombian telephone system; should you have trouble reaching a number, check with your hotel or look at the latest listings in *El Caribe Colombia* (see *Local Coverage,* above), since the number may have changed. Dial 112 for the police; 101 or 103 for an ambulance.

ENTRY REQUIREMENTS US and Canadian citizens need only valid passports and a round-trip ticket or ongoing ticket. Visas are needed for stays of longer than three months, and require presentation of a passport and round-trip or ongoing ticket at the *Colombian Embassy* (see GETTING READY TO GO) or any Colombian consulate (in New York it is located at 10 E. 46th St., New York, NY 10017; phone: 212-949-9898). Smallpox vaccinations and yellow fever or cholera inoculations are required only for travelers coming from an infected area. Those staying more than 24 hours must pay an $18 airport departure tax.

CLIMATE AND CLOTHES Barranquilla is usually very hot and muggy, with the average temperature hovering at 85F (30C). Cartagena is about the same, but the evenings and nights are cooler, as are the beaches, where winds always blow. On San Andrés, the average temperature is 80F (27C) most of the year. The most popular months for a visit are from January through April and from July through September, when it is relatively dry. Spring and fall tend to be rainy and humid.

Daytime dress in the cities and seaside resorts is very casual and informal. Colombians like to dress up in the evenings, especially for dinner at a good restaurant; men will don their fancy *guayaberas,* or sport shirts (but seldom a jacket), and women choose light cocktail dresses. Formal dress is not necessary in the casinos.

MONEY Official currency is the Colombian peso, which has been slowly but steadily losing value against the dollar over the last few years. At press time, the exchange rate was about 820 pesos to $1 US, but the peso's value was likely to continue its slide. Dollars are accepted enthusiastically in most hotels, restaurants, and shops, but changing money at banks ensures a better rate of exchange. *Warning:* Do not be tempted to change money with people offering fantastic rates—even if they are operating within sight of a policeman: When you leave the country, you can exchange a maximum of $100 worth of pesos into US currency at the airport bank, but only with a receipt indicating that the original dollar/peso exchange was effected legally. Banks are open from 9 AM to 3 PM weekdays. All prices in this chapter are quoted in US dollars.

LANGUAGE Spanish is the official language of Colombia, but visitors who don't speak Spanish will have little difficulty in the cities and resort areas of the Caribbean coast, as most hotels, restaurants, and stores cater to English-speaking tourists. On San Andrés, the natives speak English plus an English/Spanish dialect inscrutable to speakers of either of the original languages. Most hotels and restaurants outside the tourist areas are operated by Spanish-speaking Colombians, many of whom speak very little English.

TIME Colombia and the islands of San Andrés and Providencia are on eastern standard time in winter and spring and on eastern daylight saving time in summer and fall, just like the US East Coast.

CURRENT At 110 volts, 60 cycles, it's the same as the US.

TIPPING Some hotels, restaurants, and bars add a 10% to 15% service charge to bills. If they don't, do so yourself. For special service, leave an additional 10%. Taxi drivers do not expect tips, but porters should get about $1 per piece of luggage. If you leave your car under the watchful eye of an attendant, he should get about 50¢, depending on how long it's been in his care.

GETTING AROUND

Note: Colombian street addresses often are written with a compound number before the street name, followed by another number. The first number is that of the street on which the building is located. The second is the building's number on that street. The following street name and number indicate the cross street. For example, the Santa Marta tourist office at 16-44 Carrera 2 is located at 44 Calle 16, at the corner of Carrera 2.

BUS In Cartagena and Barranquilla, buses fall into two categories: large windowless types, which cost only 250 pesos per person (40¢ at press time), and smaller buses with windows, which cost 350 pesos (50¢ at press time). The routes are a little complex, so check with the driver to be sure the bus goes where you want to go. Santa Marta has very little in the way of local bus service, since there are few roads within the town. Carrera 1, which runs along the beach, is the main line; the bus runs from one end of town to the other, making stops throughout the shopping center, and costs 250 pesos (40¢ at press time). There are no buses on San Andrés.

Bus travel between coastal cities is available, but is strongly discouraged. Although it's less likely here than in other parts of Colombia, the possibility still exists of hold-ups or even kidnappings by guerrillas along the route. If you choose to travel on buses, you should avoid carrying valuables. In Cartagena, the two main bus lines operating between Cartagena, Baranquilla, Santa Marta, and other points on the Caribbean coast (as well as Bogotá) are *Copetrán* and *Brasilia.* You can buy tickets at their Cartagena offices (*Copetrán*, 53-89 Av. Buenos Aires at Bosque Diagonal 21st A, phone: 5-662-4363; *Brasilia*, 20D-56 Av. Pedro de Heredia, phone: 5-666-1692 or 5-666-4729; fax: 5-669-0850) or at the main Cartagena bus terminal in the city center at Calle 35 and Avenida Santo Domingo (phone: 5-663-3750). In Baranquilla, the bus terminal is located at 54-35 Calle 72 (phone: 58-455511); or you can contact *Copetrán* (33-120 Calle 45; phone: 58-321151) or *Brasilia* (44-63 Carrera 35; phone: 58-416466). In Santa Marta, both *Copetrán* (phone: 54-212834) and *Brasilia* (phone: 54-234088) have offices in the main terminal at Calle 24 and Avenida Bavaria (phone: 54-231032).

CAR RENTAL If you decide to rent a car, be aware that guerrilla activity in rural areas of the northern coast makes travel outside the major tourist areas of Cartagena, Barranquilla, and Santa Marta unsafe. Car rental is relatively expensive in Colombia; you may get a better rate by making a reservation before leaving the States through a travel agent or the toll-free numbers of the international car rental companies listed. In Cartagena, try *Avis* (6-

94 Av. San Martín, Boca Grande; phone: 5-665-3259) or *Hertz* (at the *Capilla del Mar* hotel, 6-84 Avenida San Martín, Boca Grande; phone: 5-665-3359 or 5-665-2852).

In Santa Marta, there are branches of *Avis* (phone: 54-227807 at the airport; or 54-227046 at the *Irotama* hotel); *Hertz* (7-45 Carrera 4, Suite 9, El Rodadero; phone: 54-227167); and *National* (7-63 Carrera 3, El Rodadero; phone: 54-228078). San Andrés has no public transportation system, so it's either taxis or rental cars. A mini-moke or mini-jeep (Citröen) is a great way to explore the island, and their rental rates are low. Be warned that only a few rental vehicles—dune buggies and motorcycles among them—are available on the island. Check ahead at the tourist office or your hotel desk.

PLANE *Aces* (phone: 1-281-6924), *Avianca/SAM* (phone: 1-410-1011), and *Intercontinental* (phone: 1-287-9777 or 1-288-7266) fly between Bogotá, Barranquilla, Cartagena, San Andrés, and other Colombian cities. *Aces* has the best service; *Avianca/SAM* and *Intercontinental* can be unreliable. There are connecting flights between Santa Marta and Bogotá on *Aces* and *Avianca/SAM*. On *Avianca/SAM,* ask for "R" class tickets, which offer the same service at 50% off the regular price; reserve them in advance, as there is limited availability.

SEA EXCURSIONS *Excursiones Roberto LeMaitre* (4-66 Calle 8, Cartagena; phone: 5-665-5622 or 5-665-2873; fax: 5-665-2872) offers a regularly scheduled trip to El Pirata Island for a fish or lobster lunch and swimming. For a few dollars more, arrange to stay overnight at one of the *LeMaitre* cabañas there, with three meals included. *Caribe Tours* (6-41 Carrera 5, Cartagena; phone: 5-665-5221, 5-665-3352, or 5-665-2542) offers a unique excursion: Given advance notice, they will set would-be Robinson Crusoes adrift on a well-equipped raft headed toward a private beach, where the castaways remain marooned until rescued by motor launch at 4 PM. A one-hour trip to the pristine, white sand beaches of the Islas del Rosario, near Cartagena, can be arranged through your hotel; many boats offer cheap, regular service from the Boca Grande docks.

On San Andrés, excursions are available to Johnny Key and Haines Key. Perhaps the most spectacular way to experience the beauty of the reefs around San Andrés is to take one of the one-hour underwater cruises offered by *Submarinos de Colombia* (*Lord Pierre* hotel, Suite 104; phone: 811-27312; fax: 811-27934). Ticket prices are steep, and reservations should be made well in advance; the tours are not recommended for the claustrophobic. Private sea excursions can be arranged through the *Aquarium Dive Shop* (Av. Colombia, next to the *Aquarium* hotel; phone: 811-23117 or 811-23120). If you go to Providencia, be sure to take a boat trip around the island and to Crab Key. Ask around at Sweet Water Bay or at your hotel.

TAXI Plentiful in all the coastal cities and inexpensive by US standards, taxis cluster at the airports, docksides, hotels, and tourist offices. Taxi fares are based on a mileage rate—but reach an agreement with the driver about the fare before starting the trip. In Cartagena, there is a low minimum fare for short trips to and around the Old City. You can bargain with a taxi driver for an hourly rate, and see the sights of the Old City in comfort. Especially at airports, be wary of illegal taxis, sometimes characterized by two drivers or irregular markings; these can be operated by criminals.

Cartagena also has picturesque horse-drawn carriages, perfect for a romantic nighttime ride through the Old City. Rates are negotiable, and the carriages are available near the large hotels, such as the *Caribe* and the *Cartagena Hilton International* (see *Checking In* for both).

SPECIAL EVENTS

Cartagena hosts the annual *Caribbean Music Festival* in mid-March, but the wildest celebration is for the city's *Independence Day* on November 11. Complete with masks and costumes, dancing in the streets, and fireworks, the party can get a little rough. On the same day, the *Miss Colombia Contest* is celebrated here as if it were a royal coronation. The big party in Santa Marta is the pre-*Lenten Carnaval.* Colombia's *Independence Day* is July 20, and a *Festival of the Sea* is held during late July or early August along the coast. Other holidays when offices, banks, stores, and museums close are *New Year's Day; Epiphany* (January 6); *St. Joseph's Day* (March 19); *Holy Thursday* and *Good Friday* (April 4 and 5 in 1996); *Labor Day* (May 1); *Ascension Day* (May 28); the *Feast of the Sacred Heart* (June 2); the *Feast of Corpus Christi* (May 30 in 1996); the *Feast of Saints Peter & Paul* (June 29); *Battle of Boyacá* (August 7); *Assumption Day* (August 15); *Columbus Day* (October 12); *All Saints' Day* (November 1); the *Feast of the Immaculate Conception* (December 8); and *Christmas.* Banks also close at noon on *Christmas Eve* and *New Year's Eve.* (*Note:* Religious feast days that fall on weekends are officially observed as holidays the following Monday. The same is true of Cartagena's *Independence Day,* Colombia's *Independence Day,* and *Labor Day.*)

SHOPPING

In Cartagena's Old City, keep an eye out for native handicrafts, including *cerámicas,* usually pottery replicas of pre-Columbian art, and *balcones,* replicas of colonial-era decorative woodworking. One of the best places to look is *Las Bóvedas* (Avenida Santander at Centro Murallas), the 23 former dungeons located in the 45-foot-thick city walls. Government shops called *Artesanías de Colombia* also carry a wide array of locally made goods at favorable prices. The stores in the Old City shopping district handle all types of merchandise, from handmade crafts to fine leather goods and Colombian emeralds. The native crafts will probably be the best buy, but if you decide to purchase an emerald, make sure to do so only from a reputable dealer, never from a street peddler. Remember that the deeper the color and greater the sparkle, the more valuable the emerald. *Greenfire Emeralds* (phone: 5-665-0413) has a store in the *Pierino Gallo Centro Comercial* in Boca Grande.

For most other goods, know the prices at home before buying; after paying duty, you may not save much over US discount prices. The exception is coffee, which at about 50¢ a pound is well worth buying in quantity, if there's room in your suitcase. Buy it at a local market, not a tourist shop. Bargains also may be found in the 600-odd duty-free shops on San Andrés. This area, with goods from all over the world, caters primarily to local Colombians and Central and South American travelers. Swiss watches, French perfumes, cameras, and liquor generally are available at prices similar to those in other duty-free areas. Coloma, a local coffee liqueur, is a good buy. Except for a few stores offering inexpensive souvenirs and T-shirts, shopping in Santa Marta is poor. Most shops in Colombian cities are open from 9:30 AM to 7 PM; closed Sundays.

SPORTS

BOATING Most coastal resorts have small boats for rent or charter cruisers. In Cartagena, the *Caribe* hotel (see *Checking In*) rents paddleboats, canoes, and other craft. In Santa Marta, check with Captain Ospina at his beachside stand on Rodadero Beach (see *Sport Fishing,* below). On San Andrés, small boats also can be chartered; check with your hotel or the tourist office. *Excursiones Roberto LeMaitre* (see *Sea Excursions,* above) rents not only boats (with or without crew), but even a private island to escape to. Some of the available islands, which are in the Rosario Archipelago, just 20 miles from Cartagena, are just tiny atolls and reefs, with just enough rock or coral for a small cabin.

SNORKELING AND SCUBA DIVING Wrecks offshore around Cartagena provide excellent diving. Jim Buttgen of *Caribe Tours* (see *Sea Excursions*) runs excursions, rents equipment, and provides supplies. Bill Moore, a treasure hunter, also takes divers out in his boat; ask for him at the *Caribe* hotel (see *Checking In*). On San Andrés, the crystal-clear waters and plentiful marine life make both scuba diving and snorkeling rewarding pastimes; scuba gear rentals and trips on a 40-foot dive boat, the *Karina,* are available through the *Aquarium Dive Shop* (see *Sea Excursions*), and the *Caribe Campo* hotel has a well-equipped dive shop (see *Checking In*).

SPORT FISHING In Cartagena, the *Club de Pesca* (Calle 24, Carrera 17, in the *Fortaleza de San Sebastián;* phone: 5-660-4593/4) can arrange charters. Santa Marta has excellent fishing, from marlin to sea bass, depending on the season, and Captain Ospina will be glad to charter a boat and point out the way. He operates from a stand on Rodadero Beach, and the rates vary, depending on the vessel, the weather, the time of year, and the captain's mood.

SWIMMING AND SUNNING The Boca Grande section of Cartagena has some decent beaches, though much of the shoreline is marred with trash and matted sands. It's worth taking a boat from Cartagena to the Rosario Islands for better beaches (see *Sea Excursions* for information on getting there). Santa Marta has good beaches, as do the islands of San Andrés and Providencia.

TENNIS In Cartagena, the *Cartagena Real, Cartagena Hilton International,* and *Caribe* hotels have courts of their own (see *Checking In*), and three private clubs have playing arrangements with various hotels. Ask your hotel desk to make the reservations; the fees are minimal. The *Irotama* hotel in Santa Marta also has courts (see *Checking In*). On San Andrés, there is a four-court tennis club near the *Isleño* hotel (on Av. de la Playa), with courts available to visitors for a modest fee.

NIGHTLIFE

In general, Colombian nightspots stay open until 3 AM, allowing plenty of time to soak up the atmosphere and a few drinks. Although Colombian nightlife does offer some live shows with local and imported talent, there are few lavish, spectacular floor shows. One exception is the *Cartagena Hilton International,* which regularly features a local dance show (see *Checking In*). Also in Cartagena, the *Casino del Caribe* (*Pierino Gallo Centro Comercial,* Boca Grande; phone: 5-665-0728) has one room devoted to slot machines and another for roulette and blackjack. Minimum table bets are quite low, so the place gets crowded. Also try *Casino Royal* (2-87 Carrera 1; phone: 5-665-0155). Both casinos remain open until 3 AM. For additional details, see *Casino Countdown* in DIVERSIONS. Cartagena bars that are worth a visit include *Club Náutico los Veleros* (Calle Final de las Velas, El Laguito; phone: 5-665-0494) and *Paco's* (at Plaza Santo Domingo; phone: 5-664-4294); both serve food. Three small, bohemian bars in the Old City worth visiting are *El Zorba* (at the *Parque Fernández de Madrid;* no phone); *La Vitrola* (2-01 Calle 33 at Plaza de la Artillería; phone: 5-664-8243); and, best of all, the tower bar in the *Bodegón de la Candelaria* (see *Eating Out*), which features live piano music.

For discotheques, the best bet is the Boca Grande hotel area: Try *La Escollera* (Carrera 1, Calle 5; phone: 5-665-4462 or 5-665-3030; fax: 5-665-3945), which features dancing to US rock or Latin American music. Drinks are inexpensive if you avoid imported brands, including wine, and drink local rums. Tres Esquinas is recommended, and often is mixed with ginger ale.

A disco worth trying on Santa Marta is *La Escollera de la Marina* (1-10 Calle 12, El Rodadero; phone: 54-228186), with an inviting, tropical ambience. On San Andrés, the *Reggae Nest* (Km 6 on Av. Circunvalación) is a popular discotheque, located outside of town, with a laser light show. There also are two casinos in the town of San Andrés—*Casino Internacional* (phone: 811-25931) and *Casino El Dorado–Monte Carlo* (in the *El Dorado* hotel, 1-25 Avenida Colombia; phone: 811-24155); both are at the corner of Avenidas La Playa and Providencia. Minimum bets are low, no jackets are required, and the hours are 9 PM to 3 AM at both.

Best on the Coast

CHECKING IN

The Colombian coastal resort cities have more than 200 hotels and guest-houses, with a total of some 4,000 rooms. Key tourist areas such as Barranquilla, Cartagena, Santa Marta, and the island of San Andrés boast some first class properties. Expect to pay about $85 for a double room without meals in the places listed below as expensive (the *Hilton* is the exception; its rates start at more than twice that during high season); between $55 and $80 a day at hotels in the moderate range; and less than $40 a day in an inexpensive place. Note that nonsmoking rooms are all but unheard of on the Caribbean coast. Unless otherwise noted, all hotels are air conditioned and have telephones, TV sets, and private baths. The telephone numbers listed below include both the city code and the local number. When calling within a city, use only the local number.

CARTAGENA

EXPENSIVE

Las Américas Beach Though it's somewhat off the beaten track in Cartagena, this is the city's newest luxury resort hotel, and also its best. Built in colonial Caribbean style, the hotel has 250 rooms, each with a balcony overlooking the sea, a mini-bar, and a refrigerator. There's also a stretch of virgin beach, three pools connected by a swim-up bar, three restaurants, a fitness center, and a disco. For the active set, the resort offers two tennis courts, a putting green, horseback riding, and water sports. Anillo Vial, Sector Cielo Mar (phone: 5-664-4000 or 5-664-9650; fax: 5-664-9000).

Capilla del Mar On the beach in the Boca Grande section, it has 198 rooms, 47 of which are suites. There are two restaurants, and the top floor has a revolving bar with a spectacular view for great sunset watching. Carrera 1, Calle 8 (phone: 5-665-1666; fax: 5-665-5145).

Caribe With 361 rooms across the street from the beach, this property also has an Olympic-size swimming pool, a tennis court, lush gardens, and shops. The newer section, completed in 1992, has more comfortable, modern rooms, but rooms in the old section (dating from 1939) are still charming and completely refurbished. There's also a restaurant, cafeteria, bar, and casino. 2-87 Carrera 1 (phone: 5-665-0155, 5-663-7811, 5-665-0813, or 5-665-0973; fax: 5-665-3707).

Cartagena Hilton International This deluxe property is in the El Laguito residential neighborhood at the tip of Boca Grande peninsula. It has a beach on three sides, a swimming pool, three lighted tennis courts, water sports, shops, business services, two restaurants, and a bar. All 289 rooms have balconies and lagoon or sea views. El Laguito (phone: 5-665-0666 or 5-665-4657; 800-HILTONS; fax: 5-665-2211).

MODERATE

Cartagena Real An attractive modern resort hotel catering to both vacationers and businesspeople. Across the street from the beach, it has 110 rooms (most are air conditioned), a small pool, a restaurant, and a bar with music nightly. 10-150 Av. Malecón, Carrera 1 (phone: 5-665-3770 or 5-665-5590; fax: 5-665-4163).

Decameron On the Boca Grande hotel strip between the bay and the sea, it has 283 rooms, with no air conditioning or telephones. There's a good restaurant and bar, a pool, and a wide beachfront. 10-80 Carrera 1 (phone: 5-6654400 or 5-665-1472; fax: 5-665-3738).

Las Velas This establishment offers suites and apartments, as well as standard double rooms (105 units in all), and a casual poolside restaurant. On the beach in the Boca Grande section. 1-60 Calle Las Velas (phone: 5-665-0000 or 5-665-6866; fax: 5-665-0530).

INEXPENSIVE

Club Hotel Cartagena Plaza This 319-room hotel in the Boca Grande section has a bar, restaurant, discotheque, and a small swimming pool. 6-154 Carrera 1 (phone: 5-665-4000; fax: 5-665-6315).

El Dorado A high-rise, beachfront property favored by Colombians, it has 336 rooms, with another 250 in a newer, separate annex. There's a restaurant, too. 4-41 Av. San Martín (phone: 5-665-0211, 5-665-0914, or 5-665-0752; fax: 5-665-0479).

Residencias Boca Grande A family hotel with 47 apartments on the beach plus a restaurant. The apartments have fans but no telephones; air conditioning is available for an extra charge. The owners and staff will take very good care of you. 7-187 Carrera 2 (phone: 5-665-4435; fax: 5-665-4437).

SANTA MARTA AND ENVIRONS

EXPENSIVE

Irotama An old-fashioned resort hotel on a fine beach, offering 155 private cottages and two pools; rates include water sports, tennis (there is one court), and meals at the hotel's French restaurant, *La Barra Viva* (see *Eating Out*). Carretera Santa Marta at Km 14, Barranquilla (phone: 54-218121 or 54-218021; fax: 54-218077).

MODERATE

Santamar A resort/convention center complex located on a beautiful beach a mile out of town, it offers 105 rooms, two pools, two restaurants, and 24-hour room service. Km 8 on Via Aeropuerto (phone: 54-228040 or 54-218486; 800-255-3050).

La Sierra This respectable, but no-frills place has 72 rooms, a seafood restaurant, and a bar. El Rodadero Beach (phone: 54-227965; 1-217-6200 in Bogotá; fax: 54-228198).

INEXPENSIVE

TraveLodge Ballena Azul This small hotel is set in a sleepy fishing village. It has 40 rooms overlooking a picturesque bay. Some rooms have air conditioning, but none has a telephone or TV set; there's also a restaurant. While it doesn't offer much in the way of luxury, it's fine for those seeking an authentic, non-touristy Colombian experience. In Taganga, about 15 minutes out of Santa Marta (phone: 54-234328; 1-235-4542 in Bogotá; fax: 1-235-7911 in Bogotá).

SAN ANDRÉS

EXPENSIVE

Aquarium Housed in buildings atop pilings, the 112 guestrooms here not only have a view of the sea, they appear to be floating in it, lending an extra sense of peace and privacy. There's a restaurant and a cafeteria. 1-19 Av. Colombia (phone: 811-23117 or 811-23120; 1-226-9741 or 1-226-9894, Oficina 604 in Bogotá).

Mar Azul Arguably the best hotel on the island, this place has 66 rooms. There are three private beaches, a casino, a restaurant, a bar, and two tennis courts. Water sports also are offered, and the hotel can arrange motorcycle and car rentals. 30-45 Carretera San Luis (phone/fax: 811-23539 or 811-23657).

MODERATE

Caribe Campo This 175-room hotel is perched on a hill overlooking the Caribbean. Amenities include two restaurants, two swimming pools, a small golf course, and water sports. Carretera Harmony Hall (phone: 811-27474/5; fax: 811-23034).

Casa Blanca Small (44 rooms and 14 cabañas, most with air conditioning) and friendly, it caters mostly to young couples and families from the US and Latin America. Just across from the beach, it has a pool, water sports, a restaurant, and a cafeteria. 1-40 Av. Costa Rica (phone: 811-25950).

Decameron The sister property to its namesake in Cartagena, this one is located on San Luis Beach. It offers 27 rooms, a restaurant with the best buffet on the island, and a package that includes meals and water sports, such as water skiing and windsurfing. The rooms are air conditioned and have TV sets but no telephones. Reserve through the main office in Cartagena (phone: 5-665-4400 or 5-665-4401).

Isleño Located on what is considered to be the best beach on San Andrés, within sight of Johnny Key, this place has 47 rooms, a restaurant, and a cafeteria. There's no air conditioning, but the island is always cooled by sea breezes. 5-117 Av. Colombia (phone: 811-23991 or 811-23992; fax: 811-23126).

Lord Pierre This luxurious inn boasts 49 large rooms and ten suites, all with mini-bars and refrigerators. There's also a private dock, two pools (one with a lovely poolside bar), a submarine tour operation (see *Sea Excursions*), and a restaurant. 1B-106 Av. Colombia (phone: 811-27541; fax: 811-25666).

INEXPENSIVE

Cocoplum Beach Located on one of the island's most beautiful beaches and surrounded by coconut palms, this small hotel offers personalized service, spectacular sea views, and modern, albeit simple facilities. Each of its 38 rooms and 14 apartments has a balcony overlooking the sea and a refrigerator. There is also a restaurant, a bar, a private beach where windsurfing is available, and motorcycle and boat rentals. 43-39 Carretera Circunvalar San Luis (phone/fax: 811-24979).

PROVIDENCIA

MODERATE

Cabañas Paraiso These 20 cabañas, all with mini-bars and TV sets and some with sea views, are probably the most comfortable on Providencia. There's no restaurant on the premises. Bahía de Agua Dulce (phone: 811-48038).

Hotel Morgan Despite its unimpressive exterior, this 12-room hotel offers the best accommodations on the island, with friendly, personal service from the owners. All rooms have fans (in addition to air conditioning) and refrigerators. There is also a restaurant that serves simple, but very good food. Bahía de Agua Dulce (phone: 811-48104 or 811-48067).

INEXPENSIVE

Posada del Mar Not on the beach, but the accommodations are the best on the island. The eight rooms are housed in A-frames built around a courtyard restaurant. The rooms have mini-bars but no air conditioning, telephones, or TV sets. Make reservations at your hotel on San Andrés or try calling the restaurant. Bahía de Agua Dulce (phone: 811-48168; fax: 811-48052).

Royal Queen A 17-room hotel with modest facilities. The rooms do not have air conditioning, telephones, or TV sets, but there is a restaurant. Santa Isabel (phone: 811-48138).

EATING OUT

Colombia's coastal resort cities are blessed with some of the finest seafood in the world. However, service on the laid-back Caribbean coast can be maddeningly slow. Choose a place with a pleasant atmosphere, and be prepared to relax, enjoy a drink, and wait.

The most notable culinary choices are the Caribbean lobster (a form of crayfish) and a host of other "fruits of the sea," including squid, crab, oysters, mussels, scallops, jumbo shrimp, red snapper, and even barracuda, which is prepared with local herbs. *Viudo de pescado* (a spicy, baked fish stew) and *escabeche* (pickled seafood) are specialties; soups are super; ditto for the *canasta de coco* (coconut custard in a meringue basket). To avoid contracting dysentery or other GI-tract parasites, steer clear of ceviche (shrimp marinated in lemon juice), especially when you're off the beaten track. Also avoid drinking tap water in Colombia or eating raw vegetables (they may have been washed in it). Stick with bottled water and ice made from distilled water (check with your hotel—most of the larger ones use both). Not including wine, drinks, or tips, dinner for two is about $40 at the most expensive places, between $18 and $30 at moderate establishments, and $15 or less at inexpensive ones. Unless otherwise noted, the restaurants listed below are open for lunch and dinner. The telephone numbers listed below include both the city code and the local number. When calling within a city, use only the local number.

CARTAGENA

EXPENSIVE

Bodegón de la Candelaria Elegantly ensconced in a restored colonial mansion in the Old City, this is one of the country's finest restaurants. Before dinner, stop at the balcony bar to enjoy a drink, cool breezes, and a magnificent ocean view. Seafood and Colombian specialties are served. Open daily in June, July, December, and January; closed Sundays the rest of the year. Reservations advised for large groups. Major credit cards accepted. 3-64 Calle de las Damas (phone: 5-664-7251 or 5-664-4833).

Capilla del Mar A fine seafood restaurant with a French accent, specializing in lobster and shrimp dishes. There's also a fine wine cellar. Open daily in high season; closed Mondays the rest of the year. Reservations advised. Major credit cards accepted. 8-59 Carrera 5, Boca Grande (phone: 5-665-5001).

Classic de Andrei Located in the walled Old City, this spot serves traditional Colombian dishes, though some say the food is not as good as it once was. Open daily; no lunch weekends or holidays. Reservations advised. Major credit cards accepted. Calle de las Damas and Calle Ricuarte (phone: 5-664-2663; fax: 5-664-7321).

La Casa del Pescado All the dishes served here are prepared in authentic Caribbean style, with an emphasis on seafood. Open daily. Reservations necessary for large groups. Major credit cards accepted. *Edificio Trujillo,* Carrera 2, El Pueblito, Boca Grande (phone: 5-665-3686).

Chef Julian Very good seafood, Spanish-style; *triunfo de cocina* is a sampler of lobster done three different ways. Try to save room for the coconut pie. Open daily. Reservations advised. American Express accepted. 8-108 Carrera 3, Boca Grande (phone: 5-664-8220 or 5-665-5220).

Club de Pesca Near the ramparts of an old fort, dine under the stars on seafood specialties (including a fine paella), with a view of the lights of Cartagena shimmering on the bay. Open daily. Reservations advised. Major credit cards accepted. Within the *Fortress del Pastelillo* (phone: 5-660-4601 or 5-660-4594; 5-666-3880 or 5-664-9175).

Doris The place to go for an American and continental menu. Open daily. Reservations advised. American Express and MasterCard accepted. 9-73 Carrera 4 (phone: 5-665-3808).

La Escollera de la Marina Caribbean-style fare in an informal atmosphere, with live music on weekends. No lunch on Fridays and weekends. Reservations advised. Major credit cards accepted. Centro 3-11, Calles San Juan de Dios and Santa Teresa (phone: 5-664-1337, 5-665-3168, or 5-664-2724).

La Fontana di Trevi First-rate Italian fare is served in an elegant (but relaxed) setting. The pasta is highly recommended. Open daily. Reservations unnecessary. Major credit cards accepted. 6-147 Av. San Martín (phone: 5-665-3814).

Nautilus Small, modern seafood eateries, serving only the freshest of fish (when the catch of the day is gone, they close) done in *típico* Cartagena style—broiled, fried, or in an herb casserole. Open daily. Reservations unnecessary. Major credit cards accepted. Two locations: 10-76 Calle San Pedro Martín, Boca Grande (phone: 5-665-3964), and in front of the India Catalina statue (phone: 5-664-4204).

SANTA MARTA AND ENVIRONS

La Barra Viva Probably the best dining spot in town, it serves French and other European dishes as well as steaks from nearby cattle ranches. There's a fine wine cellar. Closed Thursdays. Reservations advised. Major credit cards accepted. In the *Irotama* hotel, Carretera Santa Marta at Km 14, Barranquilla (phone: 54-227643).

Juanillo Excellent Spanish food; the specialty is paella. Open daily. Reservations unnecessary. Major credit cards accepted. 8-59 Carrera 1, El Rodadero (phone: 54-228019).

El Karey One of the many places at which to try fresh seafood prepared in the traditional coastal way, with plenty of spices and coconut milk. Open daily. Reservations unnecessary. Major credit cards accepted. 1-19 Calle 9 (phone: 54-227250).

Pez Caribe This spot offers a varied menu of continental and local dishes. Open daily. Reservations advised. Major credit cards accepted. 11-50 Carrera 4 (phone: 54-227001).

INEXPENSIVE

Pan American A delightful stop if you're downtown, this eatery features light meals and a very informal atmosphere. Open daily. Reservations unnecessary. No credit cards accepted. 1-10 Calle 18 (phone: 54-212901).

SAN ANDRÉS

EXPENSIVE

La Barracuda de los Ojos Verdes A fine selection of contintental and local dishes is served here. Open daily for breakfast, lunch, and dinner. Reservations unnecessary. Major credit cards accepted. 1-19 Av. Colombia (phone: 811-23120, 811-23117, or 811-25953).

MODERATE

La Fonda Antioqueña This is the place to go for Colombian and local specialties like *viudo de pescado* (fish stew with plantains and yucca, in creole sauce), *lechón tolimense* (suckling pig), or *cabrito* (kid) with tamales and yucca. Open daily for breakfast, lunch, and dinner. Reservations unnecessary. No credit cards accepted. 1A-16 Av. Colombia (phone: 811-24185).

INEXPENSIVE

Miss Bess For an authentic Colombian experience, home-cooked meals, native-style. Open daily. Reservations unnecessary. No credit cards accepted. La Loma (phone: 811-25747).

El Oasis Excellent seafood specialties; try *cazuela de mariscos en coco* (seafood casserole cooked in coconut milk). The drinks, primarily rum-based, introduce the meal nicely. Open daily. Reservations advised. Major credit cards accepted. 4-99 Av. Colombia (phone: 811-23819).

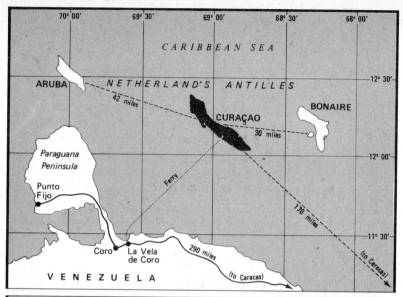

Curaçao

From its very beginning, Curaçao has followed its own unpredictable plan of development. According to geologists, the volcanic isle was reimmersed several times, until its natural, protective coral reef rose permanently above the sea. The present exposed layers of lava and coral (which fringe the island) have been hewn and polished by trade winds to form an intricate filigree of caves and grottoes, interspersed with beaches of coral and volcanic sand, bleached by the Caribbean sun and sea.

When Curaçao was discovered by European explorers in 1499, it was inhabited by the Caiquetio, a tribe closely related to the Arawak. They were natural seafarers who probably landed here during their own voyage of discovery, a journey motivated by a need to escape the fierce Carib Indians who dominated the Lesser Antilles and South America's Caribbean coast. The Caiquetio established the trade link with Venezuela, some 35 miles away, an economic relationship that is still the mainstay of the island's economy. The island's name comes from their language, although several poetic tales claim it is a corruption of the Portuguese word *coração,* which means "heart."

The European colonizers and treasure hunters left the tiny island alone until 1527, when the Spanish returned to occupy it. A century later, Holland began to challenge the Spanish, as the latter's global power began to wane. In 1621 the Dutch West India Company was formed in Holland, both to promote trade and to encourage privateers to further hamper Spanish dominance. In 1634 Van Walbeeck, an officer of the company, claimed the island for the Dutch. They banished the Spanish governor and 400 assorted Spaniards and Indians to Venezuela, and the island became the primary Dutch base for trading with the rest of the Caribbean and South America.

The island flourished under Dutch rule and became one of the most important trading centers along the former Spanish Main (the north and east coasts of South America originally dominated by the Spanish). Jews fleeing persecution in Portugal, Spain, Mexico, and Brazil found a far more tolerant atmosphere in Curaçao and established a sizable community on the island beginning in 1651. Their synagogue, *Mikve Israel-Emanuel,* is the oldest in the Western Hemisphere. Muslims found a welcome here, too, as did English Pilgrims. Simón Bolívar sought asylum here twice during South America's independence struggles. So Curaçao evolved into a peaceful, thriving international community, and as such became an attractive target for greedy pirates and ambitious European nations.

During this initial period, Curaçao's capital city, Willemstad, took on the storybook atmosphere that now characterizes the entire island. The Dutch took great pains to re-create the towns they had left behind, with carefully laid-out streets trimmed with neat, well-constructed homes. The plantation mansions, called *landhuizen,* were patterned after buildings in Holland. One of the colonial governors, however, is said to have complained that the tropical sun reflecting on the white houses gave him severe headaches. According to the story, the obliging citizens painted the houses pink, yellow, purple, and almost every other tropical hue. To this day Willemstad retains an air of unreality, with its small, immaculate streets and 200-year-old pastel houses. Despite its fairy-tale appearance, the city has seen numerous engineering and technological advances, one of the earliest and most significant being the construction of the Queen Emma Pontoon Bridge across the harbor in 1888, connecting both sides of the city.

As wars raged through Europe, Curaçao and its neighboring islands of the West Indies changed hands several times. In 1800, after several attempts, Britain took the island and held it until 1803, when Curaçao-born Pedro Luis Brión, the 21-year-old chief of the island militia, defeated the occupation forces and freed the island. In 1807 the British recaptured Curaçao and retained possession until the island was returned to the Dutch in 1816.

War and the resultant isolation from Europe had taken their toll on the island's economy. Beet sugar had replaced cane sugar on the Continent and, by the mid-19th century, the slave trade had been abolished everywhere. Curaçao retired into a peaceful, isolated existence until 1914, when oil was discovered in Venezuela. Curaçao then emerged as a worldwide trading port.

Venezuelan oil comes to Curaçao for refining and storage, and is thereafter shipped to ports all over the world. The Royal Dutch Shell Company built one of the world's largest refineries on Curaçao, taking advantage of its stable government and the excellent deep-water port, just as the Dutch West India Company had centuries before. Today it's the Curoil Refinery, leased by Venezuela.

A $1.5-million port expansion was completed in 1987, making Curaçao's facilities among the Caribbean's finest. Willemstad is now the seventh-largest harbor in the world (and among the busiest), hosting ships of virtually every international flag. The oil-based prosperity has brought a tremendous influx of refinery and shipping workers, and, in turn, merchants and businesses from around the globe. In addition, Curaçao has developed a reputation as a financial center, and international corporations manage the distribution of their products to the Caribbean and South America from here. Today, some 79 nationalities are represented on Curaçao, including Dutch, English, Spanish, Chinese, Portuguese, East Indian, Venezuelan, and Caiquetio. The island also has a jetport, the *Hato International Airport,* with the longest runway (11,148 feet) in the Caribbean.

Curaçao is part of the kingdom of the Netherlands (and in 1993 a majority of Curaçao's citizens voted in a referendum to remain so); the other Dutch island territories—Bonaire, Saba, St. Eustatius, and St. Maarten—are administered through Willemstad, the capital city for the

Netherlands Antilles. This status explains the city's many fine buildings, offices, and public spaces.

Curaçao, with its quaint towns, beautiful beaches, and its exceptional spots for diving, snorkeling, and other water activities, also is coming into its own as a popular tourism destination. The island currently has 1,800 rooms in large hotels and over 330 rooms in smaller lodgings. In conjunction with major expansion and renovation projects at many hotels in recent years, the island has launched an aggressive tourism promotion campaign. By the turn of the century, tourism officials predict, there will be more than 450,000 visitors to the island each year.

Curaçao At-a-Glance

FROM THE AIR

At 38 miles long, from 2 to 7½ miles wide, and pinched to a narrow "waist" near its middle, Curaçao looks a little like the wings of a bird in flight. Lying diagonally, northwest to southeast, 35 miles north of the Venezuelan coast, it is 42 miles east of Aruba, 30 miles west of Bonaire, and about 1,710 miles south of New York. It is the largest and most populous (170,000 inhabitants) of the five islands that make up the Netherlands Antilles.

The topography of Curaçao is similar to that of the American Southwest—fairly flat, arid, but not quite desolate. Instead of green Caribbean palms, the island's flora are an amalgam of browns and russet. Willemstad, the capital, is just to the southeast of the island's narrow center, occupying the southern shore. Half the residents of Curaçao live in Willemstad; the rest occupy the many small villages scattered along the shores and flatlands. The countryside, or *cunucu,* is flat and dotted with cacti rising as tall as 20 feet and divi-divi trees forever bent before the fierce trade winds. Mt. Christoffel, at the northwestern end of the island, is the highest point—1,239 feet above the sea. The coast is ringed with coves, beaches, caves, and underwater grottoes—reminders of the island's volcanic origin.

SPECIAL PLACES

WILLEMSTAD

With St. Anna Bay facing Venezuela and its long, narrow channel leading into a totally sheltered harbor, this was a natural berthing place for the Spanish and Dutch. By adding a couple of forts on either side of the channel to guard the entranceway, they made the capital of Curaçao a virtually impregnable trading port. The city grew on both sides of the channel, with the eastern side becoming known as the Punda and the west as the Otrobanda, literally "other side."

KONINGIN EMMABRUG (QUEEN EMMA BRIDGE) Originally, there were roads around the harbor and a ferry across the canal. In the late 1800s, however, American consul Leonard Burlington Smith suggested a means of crossing the harbor without interfering with the shipping traffic in the canal: a pontoon bridge. Fixed on one end only, it could swing out of the way when ships passed through the canal. The bridge, completed in 1888, opens over 30 times a day to admit the 8,000 oceangoing ships that use the harbor canal each year. In the bridge's early years only barefoot travelers could cross free of charge, while a toll of 2¢ was charged to anyone wearing shoes (sort of a rich man's tax); today it's free to everyone. Any tour of Willemstad must begin here. Spend half an hour beside the bridge, watching the supertankers pass. The contrast between the ultramodern ships and the 17th-century houses on either side is striking. From the center of the bridge, look north to the "new" Queen Juliana Bridge. Completed in 1974, it spans 1,625 feet; and at almost 200 feet high it is the tallest bridge in the Caribbean.

WATERFORT AND FORT AMSTERDAM The *Waterfort,* which originally guarded the mouth of the canal on the Punda side, is now the site of the *Van der Valk Plaza* hotel; its task of standing guard has been left to *Fort Amsterdam,* just behind it and also overlooking the canal. The plaza between the two forts is dedicated to General Manuel Carlos Piar, a Curaçao native and member of the Great Liberator's (Simón Bolívar's) staff.

The far side of *Fort Amsterdam* is at the foot of the pontoon bridge, and the yellow-and-white section of the fort facing the canal, along Handelskade, is now the *Governor's Palace.* A walk through its archway into the courtyard beyond is a bit like stepping back in time. The entire structure dates to the 18th century. Open for groups by special arrangement only (no phone). The old Dutch church directly opposite still has an English cannonball embedded in its walls (from 1804). Open daily; no admission charge (no phone). The intersection of Handelskade and Breedestraat, by one corner of the fort, is the beginning of Curaçao's main shopping district.

FLOATING MARKET At the north end of Handelskade, just a few minutes' walk from the bridge, is an inlet of St. Anna Bay known as Waaigat, and along this channel runs Shon Sha Capriles Kade, a street named after a well-known local composer and banker, Shon Sha Capriles ("Mr." Sha Capriles in Papiamento). Here Venezuelan schooners and sailboats still tie up, bringing a true floating market to Curaçao. This market continues a trading tradition begun by the Caiquetio well before Spain claimed this land. The South Americans mostly bring tropical fruits and vegetables to Curaçao, but also haul dried meat, fish, spices, and cloth. Cash is now the accepted medium, but in years past this was more a bartering and trading market; even now haggling is the norm. Nearby is an enclosed public market for those who prefer to do business indoors, but it's just not the same.

MIKVE ISRAEL-EMANUEL SYNAGOGUE Located on the corner of Columbusstraat and Kerkstraat, between Shon Sha Capriles Kade and the fort, this is the oldest continuously operating synagogue in the Western Hemisphere. Built in 1732, it is not only a historic house of worship but also an excellent example of colonial Dutch architecture. There is a central courtyard, and the interior of the building is carpeted with the traditional layer of white sand, symbolic of the Jews' journey through the desert to the Promised Land. The Reader's Platform is set in the center, so the congregation surrounds it in much the same way the tribes are presumed to have gathered in the desert. Four 24-candle brass chandeliers, three of which are more than 250 years old, hang from the original mahogany ceiling; they are replicas of the candelabra in the *Portuguese Synagogue* in Amsterdam. Closed weekends, except for services: English and Hebrew services are held Fridays at 6:30 PM and Saturdays at 10 AM.

JEWISH HISTORICAL AND CULTURAL MUSEUM Next door to the synagogue, this building, which dates to 1728, was once a rabbi's house and later a Chinese laundry, until a centuries-old *mikvah* (a communal bath used for ritual purifications) was uncovered in its courtyard. Since then the building has undergone considerable restoration. On display here are utensils for kosher butchering, beautiful silverwork, various religious articles, scales, and a Torah said to date from 1492. Closed weekends and on all Jewish and public holidays. Admission charge. 26-28 Kuiperstraat (phone: 611633).

BRIÓNPLEIN On the Otrobanda, at the foot of the pontoon bridge, this plaza is the site of a statue of Curaçao's favorite son and best-known war hero, Pedro Luis Brión. Born in 1782, this fierce and clever fighter is credited with quashing several British invasions. After they finally took the island in 1800, Brión, then chief of militia of Curaçao, led the island forces in their resistance against the invaders and forced the British withdrawal in 1803. The *Riffort,* once guardian of the canal on this side, now houses a French restaurant, *Bistro Le Clochard* (see *Eating Out*, below).

WEST OF WILLEMSTAD

It's roughly 100 miles around Curaçao, and as the roads vary between good and excellent, the route can be driven easily in a matter of hours. Although Willemstad is the island's principal attraction, the *cunucu* (countryside) should not be ignored. Some of the best examples of Dutch architecture, the *landhuizen* (mansion houses) of the old plantations, are here.

CURAÇAO MUSEUM A short distance from the Queen Emma Bridge, on Van Leeuwenhoekstraat, is the *Curaçao Museum*. Built in 1853 as a seamen's hospital and restored in 1942, it contains relics of the Caiquetio Indians, including a funeral urn, some pottery, beautiful bits of Caribbean coral, and cradles. The cockpit of the Fokker F-XVIII trimotor (the *Snipe,* or *Snip)* that made the first commercial crossing of the southern Atlantic from Holland to Curaçao in 1934 also is on display. In addition, the museum has a replica of a colonial kitchen, painted brick red with white polka dots, either to ward off evil spirits or to conceal kitchen spatter and confuse the flies. The museum gardens contain specimens of all the island's plants and trees. Closed Mondays and the last Sunday of each month. Admission charge (phone: 623873).

LANDHUIS JAN KOCK (JAN KOCK HOUSE) Traveling northwest along the highway that heads toward the tip of the island, you'll come to this yellow-and-white *landhuis.* Built in 1650, it's the oldest continually inhabited building in Curaçao. The plantation here originally produced salt, but it's now a private home owned by Jeannette Leito, who offers one-hour tours through the antiques-filled rooms while regaling visitors with ghost stories. Tours are by appointment only; admission charge (phone: 648087). Sunday mornings, Ms. Leito opens the *Fungi Pot* restaurant behind her home and serves delicious homemade Dutch pancakes; she sometimes stays open for lunch and dinner, too.

LANDHUIS ASCENCION (ASCENCION PLANTATION) Continuing west along the north coast, the road leads to this stately 17th-century *landhuis,* now a rest and recreation center for the Dutch Marines. Open to the public the first Sunday of each month, with live music, folkloric dancing, local handicrafts, and food. No admission charge (phone: 641950).

MT. CHRISTOFFEL Continuing northwest along the coast, this peak, the highest point in the Netherlands Antilles, rises 1,239 feet on the left. It's almost in the center of this end of the island, but on the flat *cunucu,* it can be seen for miles.

CHRISTOFFEL NATIONAL PARK Nature fans may want to detour to visit this 4,450-acre preserve before continuing around the island, or to save a visit here for another day. The park, with its centerpiece, Mt. Christoffel, is dedicated to the conservation of flora (rare palms, cacti, and the bent divi-divi trees) and fauna (iguanas, rabbits, deer, and a number of bird species). The visitors' center, housed in an outbuilding of the privately owned 18th-century *Landhuis Savonet,* serves as park headquarters and sells a guide to the park. An eastern trail leads to four caves embellished with Indian signs and unusual rock formations; another trail winds through nature paths, passes stately ruins, and climbs into the hills. Hikers can follow yet another winding trail 1,239 feet up to the top of the mountain, where they'll be rewarded by stunning views of the island. The park is open daily; no one is admitted after 2 PM, as the circuit takes approximately 3½ hours to complete. No admission charge for children under 6.

Also in the park is the *Savonet Museum of Natural and Cultural History,* a former plantation house with remains and artifacts from Curaçao's pre-Columbian inhabitants, as well as exhibits highlighting some of the island's present-day natural environment. The museum also features a collection of cave drawings made over 500 years ago by the Caiquetio. Open daily.

No admission charge to park visitors (phone: 640363 for both the park and the museum).

BOCA TABLA GROTTO Still heading northwest, a small sign on the right will lead to Boca Tabla on the coast. This is a good place to stop for a short rest. It's also the best known of the hundreds of grottoes that dot the coastline of Curaçao. The coral and limestone-pitted landscape—some of it smooth, other parts sharp—resembles a savage moonscape. Wear sturdy sneakers so that you can climb into this famous cave carved out by the sea and listen to the waves outside. Some parts of these caves are below water, so be careful.

WESTPUNT AND WESTPUNT BAY On the far western tip of the island are some of Curaçao's best and most appealing small beaches, all apt to be crowded with residents on weekends. During the week, however, fishermen can be seen casting their nets and gutting their catch on the beach. It's only an hour's ride from Willemstad. After a swim, stop at one of Westpunt's restaurants for a tasty lunch (see *Eating Out*). There are no changing facilities here, though each secluded sandy spot has its own little cove; if they're not too crowded, most restaurants will allow patrons to use their restrooms for changing. Follow the south shore road back to Willemstad.

NORTH AND EAST OF WILLEMSTAD

ROOSEVELT HOUSE Beyond the business district, on the peninsula formed by the Waaigat and an inlet of the harbor, is the *US Consulate,* known as *Roosevelt House.* On Ararat Hill overlooking the city and the approach to the Queen Juliana Bridge, it was a gift from the Dutch in appreciation for the US's protection during World War II.

FORT NASSAU Located just northeast of the city, on the same peninsula as *Roosevelt House,* this fortress (ca. 1796) has an imposing view from 200 feet above the inner harbor. From here Willemstad resembles a city of dollhouses, and the mammoth ISLA Refinery looks like a toy. Open daily; no admission charge (no phone).

BOLÍVAR MUSEUM On Penstraat, along the coast to the southeast of town near the *Avila Beach* hotel, is this odd little museum, also known as the *Octagon House.* Bolívar (1783–1830) visited his two sisters here during the wars of South American independence. The mansion's rooms have been restored and furnished with period pieces. Open daily. Admission charge. 126-8 Penstraat (phone: 612040).

AUTONOMY MONUMENT From the *Bolívar Museum* swing north, traveling along the east side of the harbor, to the intersection of Fokker Weg and Rijkseenheid Boulevard, where this modern monument stands. Dedicated to the stable, essentially self-governing island of Curaçao, the piece was created by native designer J. Fresco.

AMSTEL BEER BREWERY Turn left at the *Autonomy Monument* and go north on Rijikseenheid Boulevard until the smell of hops signals your arrival at the only brewery in the world to make beer from distilled sea water. (Since 1929, Curaçao has relied upon water produced in its own desalination plants, made by evaporating sea water and then condensing the vapor into virtually pure drinking water.) It takes two weeks to make a good brew at this modern facility, where 40,000 bottles are filled each hour. Tours, followed by complimentary beer tastings, are offered Tuesdays and Thursdays. The brewery is closed from June 15 to August 6. No admission charge. Rijkseenheid Blvd. (phone: 612944).

CHOBOLOBO (CURAÇAO DISTILLERY) Continue east and north around the harbor for a treat—the home of the original Curaçao liqueur. The famed after-dinner drink is produced from a secret family recipe on this 17th-century estate of Senior & Co. Two hundred gallons of the liqueur, uniquely flavored by the sun-dried unripened peel of the Curaçao golden orange (called the *laraha*), are made each week in the one-room distillery. The *laraha* grows only on Curaçao; when planted anywhere else, it simply grows into a regular-size orange. Open weekdays for self-guided tours. Afterward, sample the half-dozen liqueur flavors produced here at the free tastings table. No admission charge (phone: 378459 or 616946).

CUROIL REFINERY The area of the island that extends across the north end of the harbor, along Schottegatweg Noord and Schottegatweg West, is the site of the Venezuelan oil refinery and other Shell-created facilities, including a golf club, yacht club, and country club.

BETH HAIM CEMETERY Northwest of town, on the western fringe of the Curoil Refinery, is the oldest Caucasian burial ground still in use in the Western Hemisphere. Consecrated before 1659, it contains 2,500 graves on three acres of land. Note the intricate stonework on the unusual 17th- and 18th-century tombstones. On Schottegatweg West.

EAST END

SEAQUARIUM To get here, follow the coast road from Willemstad past the zoo and botanical gardens (neither is exceptional) about 2 miles to Jan Thiel Bay. The extraordinary *Seaquarium* occupies six acres next to the *Lions Dive* hotel (see *Checking In*) and the *Underwater Marine Park*. It's the world's only public aquarium that raises and cultivates sea creatures by completely natural methods, with 46 glass tanks that house more than 400 species of marine creatures found in local waters. The best time to come is in the morning, when the fish are fed. Outside, a viewing platform overlooks the wreck of the steamship HMS *Oranje Nassau,* which sank in 1906 and now sits, coral-encrusted, in 10 feet of water. A big draw here is the newly opened, interactive "animal encounters" exhibit, featuring stingrays, giant tortoises, and sharks. The complex also has two restaurants, an open-air bar, and the

Seaworld Explorer, a "semi-submarine" that takes visitors over the underwater park reefs just offshore (operated by *Shore Tours;* phone: 604892). The nearby manmade beach is a perfect spot to relax or to engage in some sailing, fishing, or sailboarding. Changing rooms are available. Open daily. Admission charge (phone: 616666).

FORT BEEKENBERG From the *Seaquarium,* head east along the coast to Caracas Bay, where this fairly well-preserved colonial fort towers above the cruise ship docks. Across the neighboring bay, four yacht clubs line the shore at Spanish Water and fleets of sail and power boats do their Sunday cruising. Open daily; no admission charge (no phone).

SANTA BARBARA PLANTATION South of *Fort Beekenberg* and past Tafelberg, a unique phosphate mountain, is this private plantation, near beautiful Santa Barbara Beach. Visitors can swim in the turquoise waters here, and there are changing rooms, restrooms, a snack bar, Sunfish and windsurfer rentals. The beach is open daily; admission charge (no phone).

ELSEWHERE ON THE ISLAND

HATO CAVES Located near the airport, these caves, opened in 1992 and operated by the *Holland* hotel, are the island's newest tourist attraction. Inside the incredible network of caverns, hidden lights illuminate the white limestone formations while gravel walkways lead through the tunnels. One-hour guided tours are offered daily (except Mondays). Admission charge. F. D. Rooseveltweg (phone: 680379).

Sources and Resources

TOURIST INFORMATION

The *Curaçao Tourist Board* has offices in Willemstad at 19 Pietermaai (phone: 616000; fax: 612305) and at the *Waterfort Arches* (phone: 613397), with another office at the airport (phone: 686789). The Willemstad offices are closed weekends, while the airport office is open daily until after the last flight of the day arrives. Maps, folders, and multilingual staff members are available at all three locations. Radio Paradise (phone: 636105) also has information on activities and events. For information about Curaçao tourist offices in the US, see GETTING READY TO GO.

LOCAL COVERAGE *Curaçao Holiday,* a quarterly island publication in English, carries useful information on special events, shopping hints, restaurants, and nightlife; it's free and distributed at the airport, tourist offices, and hotels.

RADIO AND TELEVISION Curaçao has some locally produced television and radio shows in Dutch, some in English, some in Papiamento, and some in Spanish. Radio Paradise (103.1 FM) broadcasts news in English every hour on the hour daily. Most hotels offer cable television.

TELEPHONE When calling from the US, dial 011 (international access code) + 5999 (country code) + (local number). Access codes from elsewhere in the Caribbean may vary, so contact the local operator. When calling on Curaçao use only the six-digit local number unless otherwise indicated. Dial 114 for the police; 112 for an ambulance.

ENTRY REQUIREMENTS US and Canadian citizens need a passport or other proof of citizenship (a birth certificate or voter's registration card, plus a photo ID), and a return or continuing ticket to a destination beyond the Netherlands Antilles.

CLIMATE AND CLOTHES The average annual rainfall is only 21 inches, and the day-time temperatures remain in the low to mid-80s F (high 20s C) on Curaçao. Because of the trade winds, it does get cool enough at night to make a sweater or light wrap useful. Casual clothes are fine during the day, but beach clothes and shorts are frowned upon in town. In the evening, ties are never required and men seldom wear jackets. If you plan to explore the beaches and grottoes of the island, wear rubber-soled walking shoes or sturdy sneakers, since many of the access trails are rough.

MONEY The coin of the realm is the Netherlands Antilles florin or guilder (the two names are interchangeable), written NAf (at press time $1 US equaled about 1.80 NAf). US dollars and all major credit cards are accepted virtually everywhere, so there is no need to convert any cash unless it benefits you; check prices beforehand. Banks are open weekdays from 8 AM to 3:30 PM. All prices in this chapter are quoted in US dollars unless otherwise noted.

LANGUAGE The official tongue is Dutch, but English and Spanish are spoken widely. The native language is Papiamento, a blend of Spanish, Dutch, French, English, and Portuguese, plus some Caribbean and Indian dialects.

TIME Curaçao is on atlantic standard time all year long. It is one hour later than eastern standard time, but the same as daylight saving time on the US East Coast.

CURRENT Local electricity is 110 to 130 volts AC, 50 cycles, with US-style outlets. This is fine for razors and most hair dryers. If you need a converter your hotel will probably supply one.

TIPPING Most restaurants add a 10% service charge, while hotels add 12%, which covers bartenders, bellhops, chambermaids, and waiters; for special services an additional 5% may be added at your discretion. Taxi drivers should be tipped only for special services such as helping with bags, and porters should be tipped on a per-bag rate (50¢ each).

GETTING AROUND

Most of the sights and shopping in Willemstad are within walking distance of one another, and hotels outside the town usually provide complimentary shuttle bus service. Public buses are available from the downtown area to several island destinations (just check the sign on the front of the bus or ask the driver), with fares ranging from 40¢ to 80¢ NAf (about 23¢ to 45¢ US). Some private vans function as buses as well; they can be boarded at bus stops. They will list destinations on their windshields and show the word "Bus" on their license plates. The minimum fare is about 50¢.

CAR RENTAL Available from *Avis* (phone: 611255 or 614700); *Budget* (phone: 683466 or 683198); *National* (phone: 680373, 636182, or 683489); and *Dollar* (phone: 613144). Local agencies are *Caribe Rentals* (phone: 613089 or 615666) and *Star* (phone: 627444). They all have offices at the airport and also will deliver cars to your hotel. The rates vary by company and vehicle; unlimited mileage rates apply to rentals of three days or more. A valid US or Canadian driver's license is all that is required.

INTER-ISLAND FLIGHTS Both *Air Aruba* and *ALM Antillean Airlines* offer daily flights from Curaçao to Aruba and Bonaire. *ALM* also has frequent flights to Caracas, Venezuela. Charter aircraft can be arranged through either the *Curaçao Aero Club* (phone: 681050) or *Oduber Agencies* (phone: 615011 or 615837). Day and overnight packages are available.

SIGHTSEEING BUS TOURS Choices offered by *Taber Tours* (phone: 376637 or 376713) and *Daltino Tours* (phone: 614888) range from a 2½-hour to a full-day tour. *Casper Tours* (phone: 653010 or 616789) offers custom-tailored tours around the island in an air conditioned van.

TAXI Curaçao's taxis are easily identified by the signs on their roofs and the letters "TX" after the license number. There are taxi stands at the airport (phone: 681220) and all hotels. Cabs are not metered, but there is an official tariff sheet, which drivers must carry. Ask to see the driver's copy, or ask the bell captain in your hotel for a copy. Always come to an agreement on the fare with the driver before starting, and be aware of whether the price stated is in dollars or florins (guilders). For an hourly rate, taxis can be hired for tours of the island. To take a taxi from town to your hotel, get in the cab on the same side of the canal as your hotel. It costs nothing to walk across Queen Emma Bridge, but your fare can double by crossing the Queen Juliana Bridge.

WALKING TOURS *Old City Tours* (53 DeRuyterkade; phone: 613554) offers fascinating walking tours of the old residential neighborhoods of the Otrobanda, sometimes guided by local architect Anko van der Woude. The itineraries include some renowned plantation houses. Tours are on Tuesdays and Saturdays, with pickup at your hotel. Special tours can be arranged for groups of four or more. Prices vary.

SPECIAL EVENTS

Curaçao's *Carnival* begins in January with costume parades, dancing in the streets, and pervasive partying with little restraint. Prime *Carnival* activity occurs the weekend immediately preceding *Ash Wednesday* (February 21 in 1996). Other festivals include the *KLM Jazz Festival* and the *Curaçao Salsa Festival,* both held in June, and October's *Curaçao Caribbean Jazz Festival.* Also celebrated are *New Year's Day* (and *Eve*), the *Queen's Birthday* (April 30), *Good Friday, Easter Monday* (April 8 in 1996), *Labor Day* (May 1), *Ascension Day* (May 16 in 1996), *Flag Day* (July 2), *Christmas,* and *Boxing Day* (December 26). Stores and banks are generally closed on these holidays.

SHOPPING

Willemstad's six square blocks of luxury-stocked shops testify to the fact that shopping has ranked as a leading indoor/outdoor sport in Curaçao since the days of the first cruise ships. Facilities became even more attractive with the addition of the 32-shop *Waterfort Arches* in downtown Willemstad. The local import tax is still so low that prices are virtually duty-free, but be aware of US prices to help you choose the real bargains. There are excellent buys—at 20% to 25% below stateside prices—on many true luxury imports, especially fine English bone china, porcelain, crystal, Swiss watches, and precious jewelry. And "closeout sale" shelves may save you as much as 50% over stateside prices. Since this is a prime cruise port, the best shopping hours are in the morning, before the ship passengers disembark. Generally, stores are closed Sundays and holidays. Although many shops close for lunch from noon till 2 PM, some stay open to accommodate the extra volume on heavy traffic days, and many will open on Sunday if a cruise ship is in port. The small plaza where Breedestraat and Heerenstraat intersect is the place to start.

Among others, these Willemstad shops are tops:

The Black Coral Shop This beachfront boutique specializes in unique black coral jewelry, hand-crafted on the island. Although collecting black coral from the sea is forbidden by law, the proprietor has been granted special permission by the Curaçao government to gather his off the north coast, then bring it ashore to carve into exquisite jewelry, which is sold at reasonable prices. In the *Princess Beach Holiday Inn Crowne Plaza,* 8 Dr. Martin Luther King Blvd. (phone: 652122).

Boolchand's Now that electronics are duty-free on Curaçao, this is a good stop. 50 Breedestraat (phone: 616233).

Gallery 86 The place for original art, including oil paintings, watercolors, sculptures, and ceramics. Tromp St. (phone: 613417).

Gandelman Jewelers Specializing in intricate, uniquely Curaçaoan gold pieces, in a wide array of contemporary designs and settings. 35 Breedestraat (phone: 611854).

J. L. Penha & Sons This shop in the city's oldest building (ca. 1708) stocks French perfume; European clothing; Delft and Hummel collectibles; leather goods from Italy, Spain, and South America; knits and cashmere items from the British Isles. At the corner of Heerenstraat and Breedestraat (phone: 612266).

Little Switzerland Featuring precious jewelry, Swiss watches, Rosenthal china, crystal, and flatware. 44 P. Breedestraat (phone: 612111).

Salas Books, prints, and other reading matter. 50 Fokkerweg (phone: 612303).

Sparky's A first-rate emporium for a wide variety of perfume and cosmetics. 23 Breedestraat (phone: 617462).

Spritzer & Fuhrmann The island staple for fine jewelry and gifts is still alive, well, and offering impressive savings. *Gomez Plaza,* Breedestraat (phone: 612600).

Yellow House For perfume, cosmetics, and accessories. 46 P. Breedestraat (phone: 613222).

SPORTS

BOATING Call *Coral Cliff Diving* (phone: 642822) for 21-foot sailboat rentals. If you're a yacht club member at home, the *Curaçao Yacht Club* may be able to make some arrangement for you. The club is at Spanish Water (toward the southeast end of the island; phone: 674627) and welcomes visitors who give advance notice. The *Top Watersports* facility (phone: 617343) at the *Lions Dive* hotel has Sunfish and catamarans for rent. *Seascape Dive & Watersports* at the *Curaçao Caribbean* hotel (see *Checking In*) runs deep-sea fishing charters, and rents pedal boats and Sunfish. Hour-long morning, afternoon, and evening harbor cruises are available aboard the HMS *Hilda Veronica* (phone: 611257). Sunset cruises and day trips to Klein (Little) Curaçao Island are available aboard the *Miss Ann* (phone: 671579 and 601367).

FITNESS CENTERS Locals and visitors alike head to the *Rif Recreation Area,* locally known as the *Corredor,* the public oceanfront recreational area between the *Curaçao Caribbean* and *Holiday Beach* hotels. It has been upgraded to include a jogging track and a children's playground, plus barbecue and picnic areas. The *Sundance Health & Fitness Center* (J. F. Kennedy Blvd.; phone: 627740) offers saunas, Turkish baths, whirlpool baths, weight and fitness training, massage and beauty treatments, and rejuvenation therapies, all under the supervision of a professional medical and paramedical staff. The *Ooms Sports Institute* (phone: 657969), at the *Lions Dive* hotel (see *Checking In*), features state-of-the-art fitness equipment as well as exercise classes; it's open to non-guests of the hotel for an extra charge.

GOLF The *Curaçao Golf and Squash Club* (Schottegatweg Noord; phone: 373590), near the oil refinery, has a nine-hole course with oiled sand "greens." Open to the public by prior arrangement (call the day before you wish to play).

HORSEBACK RIDING If you wish to ride, have your hotel contact Joe Pinedo (phone: 681181). Fees include transportation. *Ashari's Ranch* (phone: 686254) also offers horseback riding.

SCUBA DIVING AND SNORKELING Curaçao is becoming better known as a scuba destination, and now has several topnotch dive and water sports operations. Snorkels, masks, and fins are available for rent at most hotels. *Seascape Dive & Watersports* at the *Curaçao Caribbean* hotel (see *Checking In*) offers beginning scuba diving courses, dive packages, certification courses, and snorkeling trips. *Underwater Curaçao* (phone: 618131), located at the *Lions Dive* hotel and marina, is a *PADI* five-star training facility, with the largest air station in the Caribbean, a fully equipped dive shop and school, two modern dive boats, and a full range of diving and snorkeling activities, including daily one- and two-tank dives, underwater still and video photography, and certification courses. *Top Watersports* (see *Boating,* above) offers snorkel gear rentals and lessons. *Peter Hughes Divers* (phone: 658991) is a full-service facility at the *Princess Beach Holiday Inn Crowne Plaza* resort (see *Checking In*).

The island's most extensive snorkel and scuba environment, the *Underwater Marine Park,* starts at Jan Thiel Bay and stretches from the *Princess Beach Holiday Inn Crowne Plaza* along 12½ miles of shore to the island's eastern tip. It is fringed by a virtually untouched coral reef that starts 150 feet offshore and slopes gently downward from a depth of 30 feet to 120 feet, where the drop-off occurs. The park boasts several sunken ships plus 22 mooring buoys that mark top dive and snorkel sites. Hook and line fishing is permitted throughout the park, but spearfishing and coral collecting are not. Also off Princess Beach is a unique manmade reef, created in 1968 when the government sank two huge barges and 30 wrecked cars and trucks; it's now a gathering place for fish and coral in all colors of the rainbow. In nearby Caracas Bay wreck enthusiasts also can explore a 15-foot tugboat encrusted with stag, elkhorn, head, and flowering orange tube coral. *Note:* A fully equipped decompression chamber is available 24 hours a day at *Sint Elizabeth Hospital* (Breedestraat, Otrabanda; phone: 624900).

SQUASH The *Curaçao Golf and Squash Club* (see *Golf*) has two non–air conditioned courts (with ceiling fans) available to non-members daily until 6 PM (after 6 PM, you must be with a member to play). There's a charge by the half-hour, and squash rackets can be rented.

SWIMMING AND SUNNING Curaçao's public beaches—at Westpunt, Knip, Klein Knip, Daaibooi, and Santa Barbara—are among its very best. There's also swimming at most of the hotel beaches, where basic water sports equipment can be rented. The island has a number of small cove beaches, many attached to hotels. What nature has not provided, man has, with artificial beaches near the *Curaçao Caribbean* and the *Princess Beach Holiday Inn Crowne Plaza* hotels (see *Checking In* for both).

TENNIS Most of the hotels have courts; if yours doesn't, check with the activities desk to see if they have any arrangements for play elsewhere. If not, call the *Santa Catherina Sports and Country Club* (phone: 677030), where non-members may play for a charge; it's advisable to call ahead for reservations, especially in the evenings. The country club also offers lessons and clinics through the *Salas Tennis Academy;* make arrangements at the club or directly through *Salas Sports Shop* (21 Mahaaiweg; phone: 370282).

WINDSURFING The first *Pro-Am World Cup Windsurfing Championship* was held off Curaçao in 1986; now held here every June, it attracts much local and international talent. *Top Watersports* (see *Boating,* above) and *Seascape Dive & Watersports* at the *Curaçao Caribbean* hotel (see *Checking In*) rent windsurfers and offer instruction, as does *Sail Curaçao* on Spanish Water Bay (phone: 676003).

NIGHTLIFE

Curaçao's 11 casinos—in the *Holland* hotel (phone: 688044), *Las Palmas* hotel (phone: 625200), the *Porto Paseo* complex (de Rouville Weg; phone: 627878), the *San Marco* (phone: 616640), the *Van der Valk Plaza* (Waterfort; phone: 612500), and the *Coral Cliff, Curaçao Caribbean, Holiday Beach, Otrobanda, Princess Beach Holiday Inn Crowne Plaza,* and *Sonesta Beach* hotels (see *Checking In* for information on the last six hotels)—start their action around midday and remain open until 4 AM. For additional details, see *Casino Countdown* in DIVERSIONS. The big hotels feature entertainment and dancing several nights a week. There also are regularly scheduled entertainment nights at some of the hotels, such as the *Curaçao Caribbean*'s folk-loric evenings, Thursday-night "shipwreck" (read: rum) parties, and beach-side barbecues, and the *Avila Beach*'s Saturday nights shows (see *Checking In* for both). Nightclubs include *Infinity* (at *Fort Nassau;* phone: 613450), *L'Aristocrat* (at Salina; phone: 614353), and *Façade* (Lindberghweg; phone: 614640).

Best on the Island

CHECKING IN

Most hotels are in Willemstad or have shuttle bus service to and from town, so wherever you stay, you'll be able to get to town easily. Almost every hotel has a private (albeit small) beach, and there are beautiful public beaches all around the island. Since considerable international trade is conducted continuously on the island, hotels can be crowded anytime. You can make reservations at several island hotels conveniently by calling the *Curaçao Hotel and Tourism Association*'s reservations hotline daily except Sundays (phone: 800-328-7222). At hotels we describe as expensive, rates range from $180 to $250 per night, double occupancy, without meals in winter; suites cost more. Hotels listed as moderate will cost between $130 and $170 a day, and those in the inexpensive category charge between $80 and $120 a day. These prices can drop by 15% to 30% between April 15 and December 15. There is an additional 12% service charge and 7% tax. Most of the hotels are on the European Plan (no meals), but offer an add-on Modified American Plan (breakfast and dinner) for about $20 to $35 per person per day. All hotel rooms listed below have air conditioning, private baths, telephones, and TV sets unless otherwise indicated.

Many hotels and restaurants do not bother with street names, which can complicate things if you choose to rent a car, but directions are easily obtained by calling ahead or asking any cab driver. When calling from a phone on Curaçao use only the six-digit local numbers listed below. For information about dialing from elsewhere, see *Telephone* earlier in this chapter.

EXPENSIVE

Kadushi Cliffs In the beautiful, lush, and hilly far western end of the island, this complex offers 22 two-bedroom, two-bath modern villas filled with eye-pleasing furniture and luxury appointments. It's a true get-away-from-it-all place, with not much to do on premises except relax around the pool or on the tiny beach below the eponymous cliffs. There's a restaurant for alfresco dining. Management will arrange for scuba and fishing excursions. A rental car is a must here. Westpunt (phone: 640200; 800-448-8355 or 800-KADUSHI; fax: 640282).

Princess Beach Holiday Inn Crowne Plaza With 341 rooms and suites, this is the island's largest resort. It has its own beach and diving facilities, two pools, a shopping arcade, fine dining, and a lively nightspot and casino. Value-seekers should note that the garden room rates fall into the moderate price category. 8 Dr. Martin Luther King Blvd. (phone: 367888; 800-HOLIDAY; fax: 614131).

Sonesta Beach This $41-million, 248-room property is Curaçao's finest—and most expensive—resort. Amenities include a wonderful beach, a free-form pool with swim-up bar, a wading pool, a health spa and fitness center with exercise classes, two tennis courts, water sports (including scuba diving), three restaurants, a shopping arcade, and a 5,000-square-foot casino. There also are children's free supervised activities and meeting facilities both on premises and at the *Curaçao International Trade Center* just across the street. While the rooms are not oversize, they feature upscale appointments, stocked mini-bars, and balconies or patios. Piscadera Bay (phone: 368800; 800-SONESTA; fax: 627502).

MODERATE

Avila Beach Right next door to the *Bolívar Museum* stands this stately yellow mansion dating to 1780. A fairly recent expansion nearly doubled its previous capacity; there are now 90 rooms and 18 apartments. The older rooms are modest and pleasant (and fall into our inexpensive price category), but the newer rooms in *La Belle Alliance* section are much more comfortable; all have mini-refrigerators and terraces. The surrounding area is residential, and the well-managed hotel overlooks the ocean and its own beach. There is an outdoor bar, a restaurant, and a tennis court. 130-34 Penstraat (phone: 614377; 800-448-8355; fax: 611493).

Curaçao Caribbean This all-inclusive 200-room resort isn't luxurious, but it has all the basics: a small beach, a pool, a complete water sports and dive center, and tennis. Its location on Piscadera Bay is convenient, and there's a shuttle to downtown shopping. There are three restaurants, and at night, there's dining, dancing, entertainment, and action at the casino. John F. Kennedy Blvd., Piscadera Bay (phone: 625000; 800-328-7222; fax: 625846).

Holiday Beach This property now boasts a remodeled lobby and a beach bar and restaurant. The 200 rooms have been tropically redecorated as well; all have one king- or two queen-size beds, sleek bleached wood and rattan furnishings, and balconies. A big pool is a center of daytime action, while a lovely half-moon, manmade beach protected by a manmade reef offers shallow swimming and water sports. There also are two lighted tennis courts and a dive shop. Beach barbecues and steel bands add to the festive atmosphere. There's considerable evening activity, especially in the casino—the largest on the island. 31 Pater Euwensweg, Piscadera Bay (phone: 625400; 800-223-9815 or 800-328-7222; fax: 624397).

INEXPENSIVE

Coral Cliff A simple, low-rise retreat with 35 apartments (ask for a renovated one), each with its own kitchenette. While the rooms have no TV sets and there's no pool, diversions include its own beach, water sports, tennis, a children's playground, a terrace restaurant, a bar, and a small casino with slot machines, blackjack, and a roulette wheel. Its proximity to prime diving, plus a complete *PADI* dive shop, make this a popular site with underwater enthusiasts. On secluded Santa Marta Bay, 14 miles (23 km) west of Willemstad (phone: 641610; 800-223-9815; fax: 641781).

Lions Dive Adjacent to the *Curaçao Seaquarium,* it caters to the scuba crowd, Dutch business travelers, and an upscale young clientele in search of value. It offers easy access to the island's underwater park and other premier dive sites. *Underwater Curaçao,* the island's largest dive facility, is located here (see *Scuba Diving and Snorkeling*). All 72 rooms have ocean views and private balconies. There are also three restaurants, including *Rumours* (see *Eating Out*), and the state-of-the-art, air conditioned *Ooms* health club and fitness center. About 2 miles east of Willemstad on Jan Thiel Bay (phone: 618100; 800-223-9815; fax: 618200).

Otrobanda The first harborfront property in the Otrobanda, this 45-room hostelry has views of passing cruise ships and of the gabled Dutch architecture of

Punda across the water. A casino, coffee shop, and open-air restaurant and bar with a panoramic view of the harbor entrance complete the offerings here. Popular with business travelers. Breakfast is included in the rate. Breedestraat, Oost (phone: 627400; 800-328-7222 or 800-448-8355; fax: 627299).

EATING OUT

Curaçao dishes have been influenced by the cooking of some 40 countries, although everything is flavored by Dutch overtones. One of the most popular dishes is Indonesian: rijsttafel, a rice-based banquet served with up to 24 side dishes. Other island specialties include *keshi yena* (baked Gouda cheese stuffed with a spicy meat filling) and, for the adventurous, iguana soup, which locals say is an aphrodisiac. Expect to pay $45 or more for dinner for two (not including drinks and service) at restaurants described as expensive; between $25 and $45 at a moderate place; and less than $25 at an inexpensive place. There is an additional 10% service charge. Few restaurants require jackets in the evening. Keep an eye out for Amstel beer, brewed right on the island (see *Special Places*). All restaurants listed below are open for lunch and dinner unless otherwise noted. When calling from a phone on Curaçao, use only the local numbers listed below. For information about dialing from elsewhere, see *Telephone* earlier in this chapter.

WILLEMSTAD AND ENVIRONS

EXPENSIVE

Baffo & Bretella An Italian bar and restaurant known for homemade pasta, fresh fish, and typical Italian fare. Open daily for dinner only. Reservations advised. Major credit cards accepted. At the *Seaquarium,* Jan Thiel Bay (phone: 618700).

Fort Nassau Inside the old fortress, with a commanding view of the inner harbor and the town. Generous portions of Dutch and continental specialties are served in a glass-enclosed, air conditioned dining room; you also can get drinks at the outdoor terrace bar. The food is good, but it's overshadowed by the spectacular view. Open daily; no lunch weekends. Reservations advised. Major credit cards accepted. *Fort Nassau* (phone: 613450 or 613086).

Landhuis Zeelandia Situated in a 150-year-old plantation house in the Salina area, this place offers beef, chicken, lamb, and fish prepared in continental style, as well as an extensive wine list. Open for dinner only; closed Sundays. Reservations advised. Major credit cards accepted. Polarisweg (phone: 614688).

De Taveerne In the wine cellar of a remarkable, octagonal, restored antique *landhuis,* once the residence of a Venezuelan president, the town's handsomest eating place features a cooked-to-order, à la carte menu that changes every five weeks. Sole meunière and steaks are first-rate. Closed Sundays. Reservations necessary. Major credit cards accepted. *Landhuis Groot Davelaar* (phone: 370669).

MODERATE

Bistro Le Clochard The French connection on the other bank—the Otrobanda. One of Curaçao's best bistros, it's housed in a renovated 18th-century harbor fortress. Specialties are fresh fish and steaks. No lunch Saturdays; closed Sundays. Reservations advised. Major credit cards accepted. *Riffort* (phone: 625666).

Bon Appétit This cozy Dutch coffeehouse in the heart of the shopping center serves great breakfasts (try the Dutch pancakes) and filling lunches and dinners, all easy on the wallet. Open for breakfast, lunch, and dinner; closed Sundays. Reservations unnecessary. Major credit cards accepted. 4 Hanchi Snoa (phone: 616916).

Grill King In the heart of town, this casual and popular waterfront eatery serves grilled seafood, steaks, and chicken. Live music weekends. Open daily; no lunch Sundays. Reservations advised. Major credit cards accepted. At the *Waterfort Arches* (phone: 616870).

El Marinero Excellent seafood and Spanish specialties are served at this nautical restaurant. Try the sea bass, Caribbean lobster, or the seafood paella, and come hungry—the portions are large. Open daily. Reservations advised. Major credit cards accepted. 87-B Schottegatweg, east of Willemstad (phone: 379833).

La Pergola This northern Italian eatery with a good wine list offers both indoor and seaside dining. Choose from homemade pasta, veal chops, and dishes prepared with local seafood. Open daily; no lunch Saturdays. Reservations advised. Major credit cards accepted. At the *Waterfort Arches* (phone: 613482).

Rijsttafel Restaurant Indonesia One of Curaçao's not-to-be-missed dining experiences, this place features lavish, authentic Javanese specialties, with the 20-course rijsttafel (the house specialty) served buffet-style. The bar is a popular local gathering place. Open daily; no lunch on Sundays. Reservations advised. Major credit cards accepted. 13 Mercuriusstraat (phone: 612606 or 612999).

Rumours An open-air eatery that features salads, meat dishes, and fresh catch of the day. Open daily. Reservations advised. Major credit cards accepted. At the *Lions Dive Hotel,* about 2 miles east of Willemstad on Jan Thiel Bay (phone: 617555).

Wine Cellar Wooden tables and candles add to the atmosphere at this intimate, award-winning French restaurant. Choose simple or elaborate fare; there's a superb wine list. No lunch weekends; closed Mondays. Only eight tables, so reservations are advised. Major credit cards accepted. Concordiastraat (phone: 612178).

INEXPENSIVE

Fort Waakzaamheid This place with a friendly tavern atmosphere serves Dutch and island specialties, good fish, steaks, and sandwiches at lunch. Open for dinner only; closed Tuesdays. Reservations advised. Major credit cards accepted. On the Otrobanda in Seru di Domi (phone: 623633).

Golden Star Though very basic, this place has a friendly Curaçaoan atmosphere and superior Antillean fare. Open daily. Reservations unnecessary. Major credit cards accepted. 2 Socratesstraat (phone: 654795).

Great Wall The current wok-away winner in the island's Chinese restaurant sweepstakes, it offers savory selections in all columns. No atmosphere and no frills, just good food. Open daily. Reservations unnecessary. Major credit cards accepted. In *Centro Comercial Antilia* (phone: 377799).

WESTPUNT AREA

INEXPENSIVE

Jaanchie's Opened in 1930 by the present owner's father, this delightful alfresco place serves fine local food with the accent on seafood specialties. Call ahead if you want iguana soup. Open daily for lunch only. Reservations unnecessary. No credit cards accepted. 15 Westpunt, near *Christoffel National Park* (phone: 640126).

Playa Forti Offered here at no extra charge is one of the most scenic views on the island, overlooking Westpunt Bay. Specialties at this hilltop eatery include lamb, red snapper, and a native conch stew. Open daily. Reservations unnecessary. American Express and Diner's Club accepted. On Westpunt Bay (phone: 640273).

Dominica

The island of Dominica (pronounced Dom-i-*nee*-ka) is still the primitive garden that Columbus first sighted in 1493—filled with tropical rain forests, flowers of incredible beauty, and animals that exist nowhere else in the world. Also living on Dominica are the last remnants of the fierce Carib Indian tribe whose ancestors prevented European settlements on this island for years.

Not everyone wants to visit an island that has so few white sand beaches, no casinos, no duty-free shops, no glittering nightlife. Still, it appeals to travelers who want to immerse themselves in its mountain jungles—botanists, serious explorers, seekers after its special and uncompromising solitude.

On November 3, 1978, the 485th anniversary of its discovery by Columbus, Dominica became an independent nation within the British Commonwealth. The government pledged both to encourage tourism and to protect the island's enormous natural beauty. To date, this promise has been kept. Having quickly recovered from devastating hurricanes in 1979 and 1989, Dominica today remains an untamed, beautiful land. Its primary allures are its wild mountains; deep rain forests; and the splendor of the Emerald Pool, a grotto fed by a waterfall, lined with giant ferns, and home to darting lizards and tropical birds. The peak of Morne Diablotin, 4,747 feet above sea level, is usually swathed in a cloudy mist. The island's profuse plant life is fed by "liquid sunshine," a native term for mist so fine it can only be seen against a backlight of sunshine. Everything planted on this island grows well and quickly in the rich, volcanic soil; even power and phone lines are interwoven with blossoming vines.

When Columbus discovered Dominica (so named because he first glimpsed its shores on a Sunday), he found it inhabited by the fierce and determined Carib Indians, whose poisoned arrows frustrated his search for fresh water (a pity, because Dominica is filled with beautiful, crystal clear streams). Although the might of the French, Spanish, and British fleets won the Europeans control of most of the Indian lands, the Carib could not be forced to abandon Dominica. Its rain forest interior provided them with protected bases from which to raid the European settlements, as well as the villages of other Indians.

In 1748, the French and English signed the Treaty of Aix-la-Chapelle, agreeing that neither would attempt to settle the island. However, the agreement was a failure, and Dominica was awarded to the British in 1763, taken by the French in 1778, won back by the British in 1783, and finally, raided by the French in 1805, after which the British paid the French $60,000 to be left alone. Through all this, both sides were harassed by the Carib. In 1903, the British forced the Carib to accept fixed boundaries. About a thousand pure-blooded Carib, along with another 1,500 people of mixed ances-

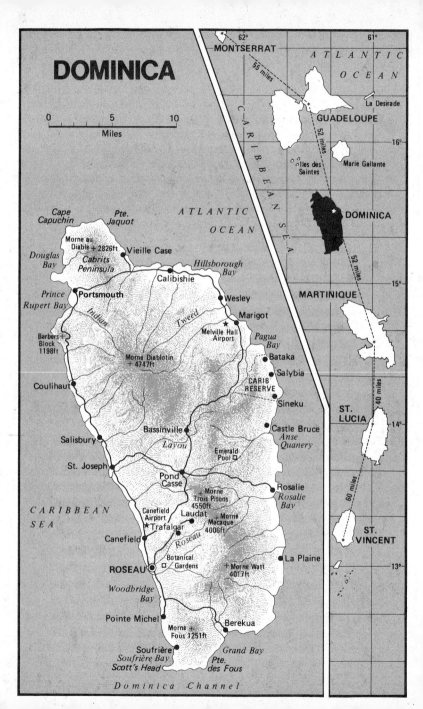

try—Carib and descendants of African slaves—live in what is known today as the *Carib Indian Territory* on the northeast coast of the island. Visitors are welcome to tour this area.

The Carib presence prevented the island from being developed into plantations until just before the abolition of slavery in 1832. As a result, the island's population did not grow during the period of European colonization throughout the rest of the Caribbean. Though it is the largest of the Windward Islands, its population, at 72,000, is the smallest in the group.

This island is the only home of the sisserou, or imperial parrot *(Amazona imperialis)*, a large, purple-breasted parrot facing extinction. The endangered jacquot, or red-necked parrot *(Amazona arausiaca)*, is also a Dominican native. Both are protected. And only on Dominica will you hear the native solitaire, or siffleur, whose call sounds like the opening of Beethoven's *Fifth Symphony.* In the island's forests are gommier and *châtaignier* trees, some reaching 150 feet, not to mention mahogany, cedar, bamboo, giant tree ferns, and palms.

Bananas have replaced lime juice as the island's major export, and the government is looking for light industries to bolster its economy. Careful control over the growth of tourism—especially hotel building—still has top priority. The lack of such "improvements" as a jet airstrip, superhighways, and towering hotels is more than part of the reason that the rush of rivers still drowns out traffic noise on island roads. Dominica remains an ideal island for vacationers looking to escape the "realities" of tourism for just a little while longer.

Dominica At-a-Glance

FROM THE AIR

Dominica lies south of Guadeloupe, just north of Martinique, and is separated from both neighbors by wide channels. It is 29 miles long and 16 miles wide at its widest point, with a total of 298 square miles of very rugged terrain culminating in the peaks of Morne Diablotin. (There are actually three mountain ranges on the island.)

Flying time from New York is a little over four hours to Antigua, followed by a 40-minute connecting flight to Dominica. Flying into Dominica is like arriving nowhere else in the world. Larger airplanes (44-seaters) still land at *Melville Hall Airport,* at the island's northeastern edge. It was carved out of a coconut plantation, and planes make their approach over thick mountain jungles and hill after tree-covered hill. Twenty feet from the airport a broad river rushes by, nearly drowning out the sound of the propellers.

At first glance Dominica is like a terrarium, with giant ferns, feathery foliage, and mists that rise from the valleys and hover over palmy hillsides. It is said that there are 365 rivers on Dominica, one for each day of the year. The one-hour (minimum) taxi drive from *Melville Hall Airport* to Roseau takes the visitor through some of the most spectacular mountain scenery in the tropics.

Smaller aircraft (up to 19 seats) land at *Canefield Airport,* only five minutes from Roseau. Crosswinds here often make for an exciting landing between the mountains and the deep blue sea. Served regularly by *LIAT, Winair, Air Guadeloupe,* and *Cardinal Airlines, Canefield* brings the capital within day-trip range of Antigua, Guadeloupe, and other neighboring islands.

SPECIAL PLACES

ROSEAU At first glance, Dominica's capital city is a curious mixture—a few streets, a jumble of two-story buildings ringed by several blocks of single-story houses. The older buildings are wooden, and the two-story structures have balconies overhanging the sidewalks, with shutters pinned back and wooden railings set in floral designs or starburst patterns. Newer buildings are concrete block or stucco, built in the same style as the earlier ones. Many buildings are painted in bright, contrasting colors. The new market is near the river. The old market, once a slave trading site, has been converted to a crafts market for tourists and houses a tourist information center. Roseau is dotted with local restaurants and "cool out" spots offering refreshing drinks and a break from shopping.

The peak of Morne Bruce stands behind the city and can be reached by car via the winding road past some of the nicer residences, or by the footpath from the nearby *Botanical Gardens.* There is a large cross at the top, several shade trees under which to rest, and an excellent view of Roseau. From here you can see the Roseau River as it meanders through town. The town of Roseau was named after the reeds that grow in profusion along the banks of the river. The Carib used them to make poison-tipped arrows; today they are woven into baskets.

A popular stop is Roseau's *Botanical Gardens,* on the outskirts of town, filled with 500 species of plants from all the surrounding islands, including beautiful flamboyant trees and luscious orchids, as well as Dominica's national flower, the *Bwa Kwaib,* or Carib wood. Open daily; no admission charge (phone: 448-2401, ext. 3414).

The *Fort Young* hotel, located on the waterfront, has been rebuilt within sections of the 18th-century fortress where the French and English battled over the island. Some of the earliest and most persistent visitors to the island were missionaries, and the results of their work are obvious. The Anglican church across the street from *Fort Young* was rebuilt after being destroyed by Hurricane David in 1979. Though Anglicanism is a tangible force in the country, Catholicism dominates Dominica, and the *Cathedral of Our Lady of Fair Haven* on Virgin Lane is suitably impressive.

The historic Roseau Bayfront was renovated during 1993 and 1994. The project included a complete replication of the buildings' original architecture and the creation of a lighted, tree-lined promenade facing the seawall. A new berth for cruise ships also has been completed recently.

SCOTT'S HEAD At the southern tip of the island past Pointe Michel and Soufrière, where there are sulfur springs, the base of Scott's Head may be reached from the west coast by car or private boat. From here, the climb to the top on foot, along a road mostly of stones and dirt, is not difficult. The view at the crest is incredible—the Atlantic on one side, the Caribbean on the other, Martinique in the distance, and Dominica stretching out ahead with its valleys of trees and mountainous peaks capped with lush green vegetation. The Atlantic side of the island is lined with beaches, some covered with gray volcanic sands, others with smooth stones that tumble and make wonderful music as the waves splash against the shores.

MORNE TROIS PITONS NATIONAL PARK Located at the southeast end of the island, this is a primordial rain forest. Some of the trails through the park are marked, and plants are identified, but even with this help, the sheer profusion of green life is staggering. No tree trunk is bare of some kind of vine or symbiotic growth; giant ferns flourish on the shady ground, and anthurium, *z'ailes mouches,* and bromeliads live on the limbs and trunks of trees. An easy 30-minute walk through lush forest leads to beautiful Emerald Pool, a grotto carved into black rock, filled by a waterfall, and surrounded by lovely ferns, a few orchids, and tropical vegetation. Among the park's other natural high points, figuratively and literally (bring a windbreaker up here): Fresh Water Lake, accessible by four-wheel-drive vehicle, affords an expansive view of the island's eastern coast; Boeri Lake, a short hike away, is rimmed with volcanic rock; and Boiling Crater Lake, a rather arduous half-day hike, is the largest of its kind in the world. This lake's water is kept bubbling by the volcanic heat of the crater in which it is cupped. There's also the aptly named Valley of Desolation, where bubbling sulfur springs make the place look like a blighted alien planet. For additional details, see *Natural Wonderlands* in DIVERSIONS. It's best to explore the park with a guide; your hotel, the tourist office, or the *Forestry Division* (see *Sightseeing Tours*) can make arrangements. Open daily. No admission charge.

PORTSMOUTH Dominica's second town faces the Caribbean on the northern end of the island. A cruise ship berth opened at Prince Rupert's Bay in mid-1992; it's the best anchorage on the island, and several hotels and small restaurants now line the palm-fringed, gray sand beach. The town, however, still consists of only three streets parallel to the bay. It's filled with colorful houses, each with its own little garden, hibiscus plants growing in tin cans, and conch shells trimming neat paths. On the green behind the town, there's a cricket pitch where Saturday afternoon matches are played. *Cabrits National Park,* Portsmouth's most historic site, is also one of picturesque natural beauty, a forested peninsula north of town, between Prince Rupert's Bay and Douglas Bay. Once called Prince Rupert's Head, it is dominated by two steep hills covered by one of the Caribbean's few dry woodland areas. Its 18th-century *Fort Shirley* was the scene of a locally famous mutiny in 1802 and abandoned as a military post in 1854; some 50 structures survive. Much of the fort has been restored. There is a small museum, snack bar, and gift shop. The fort is closed weekends; no admission charge (no phone). The marine section of the park, in Douglas Bay, has fascinating rock and coral formations under cliffs, great for snorkeling. The park is open weekdays; contact the *Forestry Division* for weekend hours (see *Sightseeing Tours*). There's no admission charge. To the south, emptying into Prince Rupert's Bay, is the mangrove-lined Indian River, a popular tourist attraction. Boat rides are best arranged through members of the *Portsmouth Indian River Tour Guide Association;* contact the *National Development Corporation* in Roseau (see *Tourist Information,* below) or the *Portsmouth Town Council* (phone: 445-5212) to pre-arrange a tour. Insist on going by rowboat so as not to disrupt the peaceful atmosphere.

TRAFALGAR FALLS In the south-central section of the island, 5 miles from Roseau, the road runs high along the walls of a valley, passing through the tiny village of Trafalgar. The final approach to the falls is by foot, about a 15-minute walk until the cascading water comes into view. There are two major falls (one hot, the other icy cold), which rush and tumble into rocky pools below. The third (often called the "baby" falls) only flows heavily during the rainy season. Visitors can splash in the pools among the rocks.

SULPHUR SPRINGS Near the falls are these two remnants of the island's volcanic origins—hot pools of mud that bubble like a witch's cauldron, belching smelly, sulfurous fumes. They leave little doubt that the island is alive and will likely erupt again. East of Roseau, near the village of Wotton Waven.

OLD MILL CULTURAL CENTER Dominica's agricultural and industrial heritage is reflected at this site, an accurate reproduction of a 1774 sugar mill. Exhibits trace the development of the sugar and agricultural industries on the island. Closed weekends. Admission charge. Located near *Canefield Airport* (phone: 449-1032).

TITOU GORGE A deep, narrow gorge in the village of Laudat where visitors can swim beneath a waterfall (depending on the seasonal rainfall), then warm up in a hot sulfur spring nearby. A guide is a must, however, as the swim can be dangerous when the falls are flowing heavily; ask your tour operator, the tourist board, or the *Forestry Division* (see *Sightseeing Tours*).

SYNDICATE This is a true bird watcher's paradise. About 200 acres of this area on the northwest part of the island have been designated as a home for both endangered species of Dominican parrot. Other birds that make their nests here include the blue-headed hummingbird (found only on Dominica and Martinique), the red-necked pigeon, and the broad-winged hawk. To see the parrots, it's advisable to start your half-hour hike before daybreak. The rugged trail that climbs 3,000 feet to the summit of Morne Diablotin also begins in this area. A guide is recommended for both trails. Check with your tour operator, the tourist board, or the *Forestry Division* (see *Sightseeing Tours*). To get there, follow the Syndicate Road from the village of Dublanc.

EXTRA SPECIAL

The *Carib Indian Territory*, a reserve on the northeastern coast of Dominica created by the British at the turn of the century, consists of six villages: The largest are Salybia, where there's a church with an Indian canoe for an altar; Bataka, with the native school; and Sineku, from where a 15-minute walk leads to *L'Escalier Tête Chien*, an 800-foot cascade of lava that resembles the head of a giant serpent crawling up the shore (even though its name literally translates "Dog's Head Staircase"). There is much discussion about how many pure-blooded Carib are left, since women of other Indian tribes and black women have married into the tribe (the Carib will accept no non-Carib males into their community). Pure-blooded Carib have distinctive Asian features—almond-shaped eyes, high cheekbones, and straight black hair. Their territory is now accessible—whatever the weather—thanks to a paved road that crosses a wide river and passes through a swamp and over a small mountain, offering a spectacular view of the valleys and cliffs.

The Carib formerly used two languages: Carib for the men and Arawak for the women; now they speak English and the patois of the island, a type of French Creole. They still have a tribal chief and remain the independent race of people who once held their island home against the might of two of the 18th century's greatest nations. However, visitors will find them friendly, hospitable, and rather shy. Their simple homes have flower gardens in front and are flanked by fruit and vegetable patches. Several small shops sell the famed Carib baskets and straw mats; fresh fruit, vegetables, and flowers also are available for purchase—just ask. The enterprising and very charming Charles Williams offers rustic overnight accommodations and local food (phone: 445-7256).

Sources and Resources

TOURIST INFORMATION

The *Division of Tourism* of the *National Development Corporation (NDC)* has an office in Roseau at Valley Road. It's closed weekends. Mailing address: PO Box 293, Roseau, Dominica, WI (phone: 448-2045; fax: 448-5840). There's also a tourist information booth in Roseau at Old Market Plaza; closed Saturday afternoons and Sundays (phone: 448-2045, ext. 118).

For information about Dominica tourist offices in the US, see GETTING READY TO GO.

LOCAL COVERAGE The *Dominica Chronicle* and *Tropical Star* are published weekly. *Isle of Adventure* by Dominica authority Lennox Honychurch (privately published; $10) is available at local bookstores. The government's *Cultural Division* in Canefield (phone: 448-2401) publishes two informative booklets, *Dominica's Arts and Artists* and *Dominica's Arts and Culture* for $4 each; both are also available at the *NDC* office in Roseau (see above). The *Forestry Division* (see *Sightseeing Tours*) also sells a selection of good guidebooks.

RADIO AND TELEVISION Dominica has four radio stations that carry programming in English and Creole: DBS Radio (595 AM or 88.1 FM); VOI Radio (860 AM or 96.1 FM); VOL Radio (106 AM; 102.1 and 90.6 FM); and Radio GNBA Mango (93.5 FM). There are two cable TV stations, on Channels 5 and 7, which air CNN and US news.

TELEPHONE When calling from the US, dial 1 + 809 (area code) + (local number). To call from another Caribbean island in the 809 area code, you also must dial 809 first, then the local number. To call from other islands, the access code may vary, so call the local operator. When calling from a phone on Dominica, use only the local number unless otherwise indicated. Dial 448-2222 for the police; 999 for an ambulance.

ENTRY REQUIREMENTS US and Canadian citizens need only a valid passport or other proof of citizenship (birth certificate or voter's registration card, along with a photo ID) and a return or ongoing ticket. Departure and security taxes add up to about $10.

CLIMATE AND CLOTHES Daytime temperatures range from 75 to 85F (24 to 28C). However, it may drop to the mid-50s during the day in the mountains. Rainfall on the coast averages 75 to 80 inches, but the interior rain forest receives some 250 to 400 inches per year. Some days it rains a dozen times, the sun and showers creating magnificent rainbows. January through April is the "dry" season, while July through October is particularly wet. In the mountains it seems to rain most of the year.

The island is very casual. In this climate, light, comfortable cotton clothes are all that are required: shorts, slacks, jeans, swimsuit, walking shoes, maybe a pair of deck shoes if you expect to do any boating. A waterproof windbreaker, a long-sleeve shirt, and good hiking shoes will be very useful for those who plan to go into the mountains. Take along a light sweater for the cooler nights, especially if you plan to stay at a mountain resort. A waterproof bag for your camera also is advisable. Swimsuits are not worn in the streets. Evenings are informal, but conservative.

MONEY The Eastern Caribbean dollar is the official currency, at press time valued at about $2.70 EC to $1 US. American currency is accepted throughout the island, but buying power can be increased a little by exchanging currency in a bank. Most banks are open Mondays through Thursdays from 8 AM to 3 PM and Fridays from 8 AM to 5 PM. Credit cards are accepted at most hotels and restaurants (some add a surcharge of up to 5% on credit card purchases). All prices in this chapter are quoted in US dollars.

LANGUAGE The official language is English, but most of the natives also speak a French Creole patois.

TIME In the winter Dominica is one hour ahead of eastern standard time; when it is 11 AM in Roseau, it is 10 AM in New York; in summer, when the US is on daylight saving time, the time is the same in both places.

CURRENT Electricity is 220–240 volts, 50 cycles, AC, often with British three-square-pin outlets. American appliances must have a converter; it's a good idea to bring your own.

TIPPING A 10% service charge is added by most hotels and some restaurants in lieu of tipping. For special services, an additional gratuity is left to your own discretion. When a service charge is not included (if in doubt, ask) tip waiters 10% to 15%, hotel maids $1 per room per day, and bellhops 50¢ per bag. Airport porters should also be tipped 50¢ per bag. Taxi drivers do not receive tips unless they perform a special service (such as unloading a lot of luggage).

GETTING AROUND

BUS Bus transport can be quite an adventure, as they don't run on any set schedule or at all on Sundays. The trip from Roseau to Portsmouth costs about $8 EC ($3 US at press time).

CAR RENTAL In the Roseau area the following agencies will drop rental cars off at your hotel: *Valley Rent-a-Car* (phone: 448-3233; fax: 448-6009); *Avis Car Rental* (phone: 448-2481; fax: 448-6681); *Budget Car Rental* (phone: 449-2080; fax: 449-2694); *Wide Range Car Rentals* (phone: 448-2198; fax: 448-3600); *STL Car Rental* (phone: 448-2340; fax: 448-6007); *Anselm's Car Rentals* (phone: 448-2730; fax: 448-7559); *Jerry's Car Rentals* (phone: 448-2559; fax: 449-2071); *Pierro Auto Rental and Nature Safari* (phone: 448-2292; fax: 448-5826); *Sag Motors* (phone: 449-1093; fax: 449-1098); and *Tropical Jeep Rentals* (phone: 448-4821). *Valley Rent-a-Car* also has a Portsmouth location (phone: 445-5252). Driving is officially on the left, but some of the roads are so narrow that, in effect, local practice is the horn method: Blow to signal your approach, and/or pull over to the side—just fight your instinct to veer to the right. (A note of warning: Thursdays are banana days. Banana trucks don't—and sometimes can't—stop for anything.) A local driver's permit can be obtained for $12 at the *Traffic Department* on High Street in Roseau (closed weekends) or at either of the airports on arrival. Applicants must show a valid driver's license.

FERRY Making the run from Guadeloupe in the north to Dominica and on to Martinique in the south are *Caribbean Express,* a 200-seat, air conditioned catamaran (phone: 448-2181) and *Madikera,* a 352-seat ferry (phone: 448-6977). The trip, four hours from end to end, can be a bit rough (uneasy sailors, beware). For schedule information contact the ferries directly, or check with the tourist office.

INTER-ISLAND FLIGHTS *LIAT* has several flights daily from Antigua, Barbados, Guadeloupe, Martinique, San Juan, and St. Lucia. *Cardinal Airlines* connects from St. Maarten and Antigua; *Winair* flies out of St. Maarten; and *Air Guadeloupe* flies twice daily from Guadeloupe. *Canefield* accommodates small planes (up to 19 seats), so only passengers on the larger *LIAT* aircraft have to make the hour-long (minimum) taxi ride from *Melville Hall.*

MOTORBIKES *Pierro Auto Rental* and *Nature Safari* (see *Car Rental,* above) rent motorbikes; a driver's permit is required (see *Car Rental* for details).

SEA EXCURSIONS *Dominica Tours* (phone: 448-2638) and *Dive Dominica Tours* at *Castle Comfort Lodge* (see *Checking In*) offer extremely popular whale- and dolphin-watching trips. Species usually sighted include spinner and spotted dolphins, pilot whales, pseudorcas, and pygmy sperm whales; occasionally, bottlenose and Risso dolphins and melon-headed whales are spotted.

SIGHTSEEING TOURS There is a lot to see on Dominica, and many ways to travel; tours can be arranged on land or water. For taxi sightseeing, ask any driver at the airport. A number of tour operators in Roseau organize bus, car, four-wheel-drive, and hiking trips to the island's most famous spots. They include: *Emerald Safari Tours* (phone: 448-4545); *Dive Dominica Tours* at *Castle Comfort Lodge* (see *Checking In*); *Paradise Tours* (phone: 448-5999), *Dominica Tours* (see *Sea Excursions,* above); *Mally's Tours* (phone: 448-3114); *Nature Island Taxi and Tour* (phone: 448-3397); and *Didier's Tours* (phone: 448-3706). They will arrange drivers, guides, rentals, and whatever else is needed. For exploring the more remote regions, as well as any other tour, contact *Ken's Hinterland Adventure Tours,* the only operator with full communications from any point on the island (phone: 448-4850), *Rainbow-Rover* (phone: 448-8650), *Antours* (phone: 448-6460), or *Roxy's Tours* (phone: 448-4845), all also in Roseau. *Whitchurch Travel Agency* (Roseau; phone: 448-2181) arranges tours and also handles charters and air reservations. *Nature Island Dive* in Soufrière (phone: 449-8181; fax: 449-8182) offers mountain-bike trips and hiking tours, as well as unique hourly, half-day, or full-day kayaking tours with optional stops for snorkeling. For wildlife tours, contact the *Forestry Division* at the *Botanical Gardens* near Roseau (phone: 448-2733 or 448-2401, ext. 417; fax: 448-5200). Ask for the forestry director or park superintendent. The tourist office can also be very helpful in arranging special-interest tours for groups and in locating naturalist guides (see *Tourist Information,* above).

TAXI Rates are set by law. The trip from *Melville Hall Airport* to Roseau (37 miles) currently costs $16 per person.

SPECIAL EVENTS

Carnival in Dominica is a big 10-day pre-*Lenten* festival that ends on the Tuesday before *Ash Wednesday.* Festivities include nightly shows, band competitions, a parade of floats, and dancing in the streets. *Domfesta* (the *Dominica Festival of Arts*) is spread out over weeks, usually beginning in July and continuing through August, and features art exhibits, music and dance, literary workshops, readings, lectures, films, and street bazaars. On *Creole Day,* celebrated the last Friday in October, Dominicans all turn up at work or school attired in national dress, and restaurants feature local dishes. *National Day* (November 3) is preceded by a month of events celebrating Dominica's independence and culture with creole songs, dances (both the African-influenced *belaire* and the French quadrille), folk narratives or *contes,* and arts and crafts displays—graced by island women in *wob dwiyet,* the madras-and-foulard, draped national dress; the festivities culminate with evening "jump-ups" (dancing in the streets). *New Year's Day, Merchant's Day* (January 2), *Good Friday, Easter Monday* (April 8 in 1996), *Labor Day* (May 1), *Whitmonday* (May 27 in 1996), *Emancipation Day* (first Monday in August), *Christmas,* and *Boxing Day* (December 26) are all public holidays.

SHOPPING

There is no duty-free shopping on the island; there are, however, some excellent buys on native products. The Bello Company produces delicious jams from pineapple and passion fruit, guava jelly, fruit syrups, hot pepper sauce, gourmet coffee, and bay rum after-shave in gift packs and individual containers. Coconut Products, Ltd. produces soaps (some in the shape of the endangered sisserou parrot), hair care products, body lotions, and sunscreens. Windward Processors makes aloe vera products—including skin lotions and a sports tonic drink—from locally grown plants. Jas. Garraway & Co., the local tobacco company, produces cigarettes, cigars, and pipe tobacco (very strong) packaged in attractive gift boxes. A Carib straw basket, lined with colorful madras material and filled with assorted local products, makes a wonderful gift. Pottery also is made locally and available in a number of shops. Artwork is on display (and for sale) at such restaurants as the *Orchard, Guiyave,* and *Cartwheel Café* (see *Eating Out* for all three). The *National Development Foundation* has opened the *NDF Small Business Complex,* a little mall housing eight crafts shops (9 Great Marlborough St., Roseau; phone: 448-0412); it's a great place to find paintings by local artists, jewelry, batiks, hand-painted T-shirts, and other crafts. In addition to those mentioned, good places to shop are:

Baroon's Jewelry A wide selection of jewelry, both imported and locally made (shell and coral work), and with semi-precious and precious stones. In *Canefield Industrial Estate* (phone: 449-2888).

Blooms Tropical cut flowers, packed to go. They also provide a plant inspection certificate. Hanover St., Roseau (phone: 448-7402).

Blows Tea A good selection of tea, spices, and local herbs. Valley Rd., Roseau (phone: 448-6504).

Brother Matthew Luke An arts and crafts studio and gallery, with T-shirts hand-painted with lovely island designs, hand-carved calabash gourds, and even cassettes of Brother Matthew Luke's music and poetry. If you're driving near Emerald Pool, by all means stop off to see his handiwork. Pont Casse, off the Imperial Hwy. (phone: 449-1836).

Candle Industries A factory that produces a variety of candles; some are decorated with images of the popular Dominican parrot. Items are inexpensive, and also can be found in some shops in town. *Canefield Industrial Estate* (phone: 449-1006).

Carib Territory Crafts Center The big scene-stealer here is a remarkable traditional bag. It's made of two layers of reeds, which create an incredible tricolor effect thanks to a natural processing technique. These two layers sandwich a third layer of a broad, banana-type leaf that makes the whole thing waterproof. A series of six little baskets that fit into one makes a nice, affordable gift (about $10). *Carib Indian Territory* (no phone).

Cee Bee's The best source of books about Dominica, past and present. 20 Cork St., Roseau (phone: 448-2379).

Dominica Export/Import Agency Fresh island-grown grapefruit can be purchased by the box here in season (approximately August through March). The necessary agricultural papers for passing through customs are provided, but be sure to ask. Arrangements need to be made a day or two in advance. On the Bayfront, Roseau (phone: 448-3494).

Floral Gardens This gift shop sells only high-quality local products, including handmade coconut and wooden jewelry, straw items, pottery, food products, and skin care items. In the *Floral Gardens* hotel, Concorde (phone/fax: 445-7636).

Front Line Cooperative An eclectic selection of books on local folklore and culture can be found here, including the complete line of works by famed native writer Jean Rhys. Queen Mary St., Roseau (phone: 448-8664).

Leathercraft Stop off to order handmade leather bags, shoes, and sandals. Elliot Ave., Roseau (phone: 448-3598).

Tropicrafts Locally produced straw mats are woven into intricate designs; place-mats, handbags, and other souvenirs are also available. Queen Mary St., Roseau (phone: 448-2747) and Bay Street, Portsmouth (phone: 445-5659).

SPORTS

BOATING The *Anchorage* and *Castaways* hotels (see *Checking In* for both) offer six-hour motorboat and sailboat trips, which include lunch, and two-hour snorkeling trips; all trips are for a maximum of six people. Also try tour operators (see *Sightseeing Tours*).

HIKING There's a variety of spectacular terrain to be experienced on Dominica. For the very physically fit visitor, the *Morne Trois Pitons Trail* and Boiling Crater Lake (both in *Morne Trois Pitons National Park*; see *Special Places*) and Victoria Falls, near the village of La Plaine on the eastern coast of the island, are a must. For moderately demanding hikes, Boeri Lake (also in *Morne Trois Pitons National Park*), Sari Sari Falls (also near La Plaine), and the *Syndicate* (see *Special Places*) are highly recommended. The hikes to the Emerald Pool (in *Morne Trois Pitons National Park*), Trafalgar Falls (see *Special Places*), and the trails in *Cabrits National Park* (see "Portsmouth" in *Special Places*) are less strenuous still, and definitely worth the effort. For more information on trails and guides, contact the tourist office (see *Tourist Information*) or the *Forestry Division* (see *Sightseeing Tours*). Many local tour operators also offer trips to these sites (see *Sightseeing Tours*). Also see *Climbing and Hiking* in DIVERSIONS.

HUNTING Visitors are prohibited from hunting land crabs, *crapauds* (frogs, locally called "mountain chickens"), river fish, and other wildlife.

SNORKELING AND SCUBA DIVING The island has the fully equipped, *NAUI*-certified *Dive Dominica,* operated by Derek and Ginette Perryman, based at *Castle Comfort Lodge.* The Perryman's expeditions explore virtually virgin southern and western coastal waters; rental equipment, night dives, and snorkel trips are available, too. *Anchorage Dive Centre,* affiliated with the *Anchorage* hotel, is a *PADI* dive center offering scuba diving and water sports. It also has locations at the *Portsmouth Beach* (P.O. Box 34, Picard; phone: 445-5131; fax: 445-5599) and *Picard Beach* resorts, but anyone can arrange dives through their central location at the *Anchorage. East Carib Dive* (at Salisbury Beach; phone: 449-6602; fax: 449-6603) and *Dive Castaways* at the *Castaways* hotel offer a full line of water sports, including water ski-ing, sailing, diving, windsurfing, and snorkeling. Dive packages are available. *Nature Island Dive* (see *Sightseeing Tours,* above) offers small group dive and snorkel trips. See *Checking In* for information on the hotels listed above.

SPORT FISHING Charters for up to six people can be arranged through the *Anchorage, Castaways,* and *Coconut Beach* hotels (see *Checking In* for all three). Paul Wren at *Gamefishing Dominica* (in the *Siserou* hotel, Castle Comfort; phone: 448-7285) arranges full- and half-day trips.

SQUASH The only squash court available to visitors is at the *Anchorage* hotel (see *Checking In*).

TENNIS Both guests and non-guests can play at *Reigate Hall* and the *Castaways* hotel (see *Checking In* for both).

NIGHTLIFE

The best thing to say about activities after dark in Dominica is that it's a beautiful island, and the rum drinks are tasty and inexpensive. Only some of the hotel lounges stay open until 11 PM or so, but the bar at *Reigate Hall* (see *Checking In*) often jumps until later. There is music on weekends during the winter season at several of the hotels. *Fort Young* (see *Checking In*) has a happy hour with live entertainment Fridays. For island barbecue and entertainment, reserve at *Reigate Waterfront* (Castle Comfort; phone: 448-3111) Wednesday nights. The *Good Times Bar-b-que* (see *Eating Out*) is a casual restaurant with a popular bar with music. It's open Wednesday through Sunday nights and stays open as long as there's something going on. On weekends there is music, mostly calypso and reggae, at the *Warehouse* (about 3 miles from Roseau; phone: 449-1303).

Best on the Island

CHECKING IN

Dominica hotels and guesthouses are all quite moderately priced compared to those on other Caribbean islands. The most expensive room on the island is probably a VIP suite at the *Reigate Hall* hotel, which goes for about $190 per night. The expensive hotels here charge $100 to $150 for a double room with breakfast; those in the moderate category run $60 to $100; and places listed as inexpensive charge less than $60. Some places lower their rates slightly (10% to 30%) from April 15 through December 14, but most offer pretty much the same prices year-round. There is a 5% room tax, a 10% service charge, and some places charge an additional fee of up to 5% for payment by credit card. Hotels are divided into three categories: beachfront, country and mountain retreats, and within the city of Roseau. While prices are pretty much the same throughout the island, appeal varies greatly, so look around—you're sure to find one to your liking. Unless otherwise noted, all hotels listed below have private baths, air conditioning, telephones, and TV sets. All hotels are in the 809 area code unless otherwise indicated.

EXPENSIVE

Castaways A longtime favorite, set on a gray beach, with 26 seaside rooms (no air conditioning). There's also a popular alfresco bar and the spacious *Almond Tree* restaurant overlooking the beach (see *Eating Out*). Nicely landscaped, clean, and friendly, the resort also has a dive center, water sports, two tennis courts, and tours. Mero, 11 miles north of Roseau (phone: 449-6244; 800-322-2223; fax: 449-6246).

Fort Young This charming and historic hotel was built into the stone walls of the original 1770 fort. Its 33 bedrooms, some split-level with sitting areas, all have hardwood decks and ceiling fans (in addition to air conditioning). There's also a swimming pool, a restaurant (see *Eating Out*), a bar, and a boutique. Victoria St. (phone: 448-5000; 800-223-6815; fax: 448-5006).

Lauro Club Each of the 10 brightly painted villas at this Swiss-owned development has a panoramic view of the coast. None has air conditioning, telephones, or TV sets. The restaurant offers seafood dishes and continental fare (see *Eating Out*). There's also a pool, access to a small beach, and a water sports and dive center. Salisbury (phone: 449-6602; 800-742-4276; fax: 449-6603).

MODERATE

Anchorage Here are 32 simple but agreeable rooms built around a pool that faces a dock, a small beach, and a curving bay where yachts anchor. There is a steady stream of visiting yachtsmen in the cocktail lounge and restaurant at night. This is a family business, which offers the added benefits of water sports and the *Anchorage Divers* facility on the premises. Castle Comfort, a half mile south of Roseau (phone: 448-2638; 800-223-6815; fax: 448-5680).

Castle Comfort Lodge Only 10 rooms here (none with a TV set), completely renovated and overseen by a genial hostess: Mrs. Perryman runs a "family home," and you're soon a part of it. The restaurant features delicious creole food (see *Eating Out*). Operated in conjunction with *Dive Dominica* (see *Scuba and Snorkeling*), the lodge's guests enjoy complimentary snorkeling gear. Castle Comfort (phone: 448-2188; 800-468-4748; fax: 448-6088).

Coconut Beach Five cottages and 16 apartments at the end of Prince Rupert's Bay near Portsmouth, a stone's throw from Indian River. Only some of the accommodations are air conditioned. Dock facilities, water sports, and a beachside restaurant (see *Eating Out*). This hotel offers a seaside advantage—much less rain than inland—and is a good jumping-off point for touring in the north. Picard Beach, Portsmouth (phone: 445-5393; fax: 445-5693).

Evergreen A friendly, family-style establishment with 16 attractive rooms of stone and brick. The two seaside rooms are somewhat larger, while four on the street in back have porches with mountain views. The dining room serves excellent food, and there is a swimming pool. Guests share diving facilities with *Castle Comfort Lodge* next door. Castle Comfort, 1 mile south of Roseau (phone: 448-3288; fax: 448-6800).

Picard Beach Here are eight cottages with full kitchens, but no air conditioning or TV sets; each sleeps up to four people. There's a pool, a restaurant, a dive shop, and water sports equipment (all shared with the hotel next door). This is another good spot to stay if you're exploring the northern part of the island. Picard Beach, Portsmouth (phone: 445-5131; 800-223-6815; fax: 445-5599).

COUNTRY AND MOUNTAIN RETREATS

EXPENSIVE

Petit Coulibri Guest Cottages These six secluded cottages are perched 1,000 feet above sea level on an old sugar and cocoa plantation at the island's southern tip. The cottages are equipped with full kitchens; there is no air conditioning at this solar-powered resort, but the breezy elevation makes it unnecessary. There are also a pool, a TV lounge, and a bar, but no restaurant. Guests may rustle up their own meals (some groceries are available in nearby Soufrière, and more extensive shopping can be done in Roseau), or cooking services may be arranged. Pointe Def, 10 minutes from Soufrière (phone: 446-3510; fax: 449-8182).

Reigate Hall Nestled on the mountainside a mile above Roseau is one of Dominica's top hotels. Local stonework and wooden finishings and floors handsomely contrast with white-walled interiors. The 16 rooms are tastefully appointed, and there are two VIP suites—each with a four-poster bed and Jacuzzi. Facilities include a pool with a nice view, a meeting room, tennis court, sauna, gym, and gameroom. The bar is a popular gathering spot, and the restaurant features continental and local dishes (see *Eating Out*). Mountain Rd., Reigate, 10 minutes outside Roseau (phone: 448-4031; 800-223-9815; fax: 448-4034).

MODERATE

Floral Gardens This place is an attraction in itself, with 18 rooms (all with ceiling fans, but no air conditioning, telephones, or TV sets) set in a tropical garden with a small wildlife park housing indigenous animals. The hotel's restaurant serves creole dishes. There's no pool, but river bathing is nearby, and the hotel can arrange hiking and safari-van trips into the rain forest. Located in the country on the northeast side of the island near the *Carib Indian Territory* (phone: 445-7636; fax: 445-7636).

Layou River This 36-room, five-suite resort is set right on the riverbank and almost lost in lush green vegetation. Choose a swim in the pool or the river, or take a jaunt to the beach, a five-minute drive away, or to the nearby Emerald

Pool in *Morne Trois Pitons National Park*. The restaurant serves creole dishes and a nice Sunday brunch. Ten miles north of Roseau in Clark Hall, just south of St. Joseph (phone: 449-6281; 800-742-4276; fax: 449-6281).

Papillote Wilderness Retreat This is a very special place for nature lovers, dreamers, and children (who usually are both of the former). Anne and Cuthbert Jean-Baptiste take a personal interest in the well-being of their guests, starting with a good orientation to the island's many offerings. Kids love the hotel's pets, jungle setting, birds, river bathing, hot mineral pools, and the 10-minute nature trail up to Trafalgar Falls. There are seven comfortable rooms, with no telephones, TV sets, or air conditioning (the mountain breezes are sufficient to keep the place cool). The delightful garden restaurant is popular with weekend day-trippers (see *Eating Out*). A masseuse trained in shiatsu, reflexology, and acupressure conducts three-week sessions in the hot mineral water twice yearly. Closed the month of September. Trafalgar Falls Rd., in the foothills of Morne Macaque, a 20-minute drive from Roseau (phone: 448-2287; fax: 448-2285).

Springfield Plantation Picturesque Victorian plantation house and outbuildings with six rooms plus three cottages and three apartments, furnished mostly with antiques. There are stunning views, a river-fed natural pool, and trail maps for hikers. There are no TV sets or air conditioning—nights are often cool enough for a fire in the main lounge. High in the hills, 2 miles from the *National Park* entrance (phone: 449-1401; fax: 449-2160).

ROSEAU

EXPENSIVE

Garraway Heritage Located along the Roseau Bayfront, its 31 attractive guestrooms are furnished with ceiling fans (in addition to air conditioning), direct-dial telephones, and satellite TV. Facilities include an elegant restaurant and bar, and a fully equipped conference room. There is also a lovely terrace and courtyard. Bayfront (phone: 449-8800; fax: 449-8807).

MODERATE

Ambassador's Located in a largely residential area near *Canefield Airport,* this tiny hotel offers 10 guestrooms (all with cable TV); its conference facilities make it popular with businessfolk. On the eastern side of the airport (phone: 449-1501; fax: 449-2304).

INEXPENSIVE

Continental Inn Located in the center of Roseau, it has 10 rooms, half with private baths, and some air conditioned; none has a TV set. The restaurant features tasty local cookery. A good choice for bargain-hunting businesspeople. 37 Queen Mary St. (phone: 448-2215; 800-742-4276; fax: 448-7022).

EATING OUT

Because of a restriction on hunting, some island specialties—land crab, *crapaud* ("mountain chicken" in local jargon, but actually a large land frog), crayfish, and *manicou* (an animal similar to possum)—are unavailable from March through August. There are no restrictions, however, on the abundant seafood, available year-round.

Island cooking styles include creole, continental, and North American, but the native dishes tend toward creole foods like fried *tee-tee-ree* (tiny freshly spawned fish), *lambi* (conch), *callaloo* (a blend of locally grown greens and smoked meat) or pumpkin soup, and crab backs (the backs of red and black land crabs stuffed with crabmeat seasoned creole-style). Bello Hot Pepper Sauce, made on Dominica, is served everywhere, with almost everything. The island fruit juices—pineapple, pawpaw, guava, and lots more—are out of this world, as are the rum punches ("A day without rum punch is no day at all" is a common island saying). Bartenders also blend a terrific coconut rum punch, made fresh from coconut milk, sugar, rum, and bitters. Liquor, and local rum especially, is inexpensive; wine is not. Many brands of beer are also available.

Food prices on Dominica are consistently reasonable. Not including drinks, wine, or tip, expect to spend $50 to $70 for two at places we call expensive (usually in hotel restaurants); $30 to $50 in moderate restaurants; and less than $30 at an inexpensive place. (Note that some restaurants add a surcharge if you pay with a credit card.) All are open for lunch and dinner unless otherwise noted. All restaurants are in the 809 area code unless otherwise indicated.

EXPENSIVE

Almond Tree Pleasant service, fine sea view, and good creole food. A Sunday brunch and evening beach barbecue, as well as special holiday events, are highlights. Open daily for breakfast, lunch, and dinner. Reservations unnecessary. Major credit cards accepted. In the *Castaways* hotel, Mero, 11 miles (a half-hour drive) north of Roseau (phone: 449-6244).

Coconut Beach Featuring large portions of traditional Dominican fare, with daily lunch specials. Its location near Portsmouth makes it the place for lunch on a northern day tour. The candlelit dinners are served alfresco. Open daily for breakfast, lunch, and dinner. Reservations advised. Major credit cards accepted. In the *Coconut Beach Hotel,* Picard Beach, Portsmouth (phone: 445-5393).

Fort Young The open-air setting enhances the atmosphere of this large dining room at the eponymous hotel. The à la carte menu features European and West Indian specialties, including crab backs, "mountain chicken," lobster, and steaks. Open daily. Reservations unnecessary. Major credit cards accepted. At the *Fort Young Hotel,* on the waterfront (phone: 448-5000).

Lauro Club European dishes and fresh conch and lobster are served in an airy, attractive setting. Open daily. Reservations advised. Major credit cards accepted. At the *Lauro Club Hotel,* Salisbury, on the island's leeward coast (phone: 449-6602).

Reigate Hall More continental than creole, its European versions of local dishes—such as "mountain chicken" in champagne sauce—are often interesting. Service is smooth and sweet, and the ambience, with candles and a splashing paddle wheel, is romantic. The bar also is popular. Open daily for breakfast, lunch, and dinner. Reservations advised. Major credit cards accepted. In the *Reigate Hall* hotel, Mountain Rd., 10 minutes outside Roseau (phone: 448-4031).

La Robe Créole Noted for its decor, ambience, and excellent, spicy creole cooking. The menu features creole lobster, freshwater shrimp and crayfish, "mountain chicken," *lambi* (conch), grilled meat and fish, good soups (pumpkin, *callaloo,* crab), fruit punches, salads, and even hamburgers. Air conditioned and popular with both tourists and businessfolk. Closed Sundays. Reservations advised. MasterCard accepted. Victoria St., across from the *Fort Young* hotel, Roseau (phone: 448-2896).

MODERATE

Castle Comfort Lodge Delicious, fresh, local creole food served right by the sea. Added attractions: a tropical garden and nautical decor. Open daily for breakfast and dinner. Reservations necessary. Visa and MasterCard accepted. In the *Castle Comfort Lodge,* Castle Comfort, 1 mile south of Roseau (phone: 448-2188).

Floral Gardens Located just outside the *Carib Indian Territory,* it's a nice lunch stop after a tour. Local fruits and vegetables and freshwater crayfish are the specialties. Open daily. Reservations unnecessary. Visa and MasterCard accepted (phone: 445-7636).

Guiyave Specialties include island dishes such as curried beef, highly seasoned baked *crapaud,* and crayfish when available. Congenial atmosphere, popular for business lunches. Breakfast and lunch only; closed Sundays. Reservations advised. Major credit cards accepted. 15 Cork St., Roseau (phone: 448-2930).

Orchard Filled with tropical plants, it offers a variety of chicken and beef pies and rotis (chicken or beef with vegetables in pastry). Open daily; no dinner on weekends. Reservations unnecessary. MasterCard and Visa accepted. King George V St., Roseau (phone: 448-3051).

Papillote A very popular outdoor hotel restaurant near Trafalgar Falls, a sort of oasis in the rain forest. After lunching on *bookh* (tiny river shrimp) or crayfish with delicate homegrown salads, ask proprietor Anne Jean-Baptiste to take you around her tropical gardens. Then take the short hike to the falls, and have a swim in the cool mountain river and a hot bath in the natural mineral pools. This is a place to spend the day. Open for lunch only (dinners by request); closed Sundays and the month of September. Reservations necessary well in advance. Major credit cards accepted. In the *Papillote Wilderness Retreat* hotel, Trafalgar Rd., in the foothills of Morne Macaque, a 20-minute drive from Roseau (phone: 448-2287).

Wykie's Trends This charming, rustic, bamboo bar and restaurant specializes in local goodies such as court bouillon (boiled fish) and *cochan pafimé* (smoked pork soup). If you're lucky, you might catch a "jing ping" session—performances that take place on occasional Friday nights and feature local instruments such as the boom-boom and the shak-shak. Closed Sundays. Reservations unnecessary. No credit cards accepted. 51 Old St., Roseau (no phone).

INEXPENSIVE

Callaloo As its name implies, a hearty bowl of *callaloo* is the specialty here, along with lobster, crayfish, and "mountain chicken" (in season). Open for breakfast, lunch, and dinner; closed Sundays. Reservations unnecessary. No credit cards accepted. King George V St., Roseau (phone: 48-3386).

Cartwheel Café A cozy corner for sandwiches and hot food, featuring a display of local art that attracts Dominicans and visitors alike. Breakfast and lunch only; closed Sundays. Reservations unnecessary. No credit cards accepted. Corner of Bay St. and John's La., Roseau (phone: 448-5353).

Good Times Bar-b-que Not surprisingly, barbecued chicken, pork, steaks, fish, and lamb—all served with salad and French fries—are the specialties here. Open for dinner only; closed Mondays and Tuesdays. Reservations unnecessary. Major credit cards accepted. Canefield, about 3 miles from Roseau (phone: 449-1660).

World of Food Dominican specialties, including roti and crab backs (in season), are the highlights. Located in the former home and courtyard of famed Dominican novelist Jean Rhys. Open daily. Reservations unnecessary. No credit cards accepted. In *Vena's Guest House,* 48 Cork St., Roseau (phone: 448-3286).

Dominican Republic

The Dominican Republic, sprawled over the eastern two-thirds of the big island of Hispaniola (the western third is Haiti), can claim more "oldests" than anywhere else in the Caribbean—indeed, in the Western Hemisphere: Its capital, Santo Domingo, is the oldest city in the Americas, with the New World's oldest street, oldest house, oldest cathedral, oldest university, and the ruins of its oldest hospital.

These historical distinctions are due in large part to the Columbus clan. Christopher found the island on his first voyage in 1492, and his brother Bartolomeo founded Santo Domingo four years later. In 1509 Christopher's son Diego became the colony's governor, serving as viceroy when the Dominican Republic, then the colony of Santo Domingo, was the provisioning port and launching spot for Spain's greatest expeditions into (and out of) the Americas. From Santo Domingo Velázquez sailed to settle Cuba; Juan Ponce de León to colonize Puerto Rico; and Cortés to conquer Mexico. Britain's Sir Francis Drake ended this golden age when he attacked, sacked, and set fire to the capital in 1586. The city took centuries to regain its lost grandeur.

In the interim, the colony was claimed first by France, then Spain; in 1821 it enjoyed the brief "Ephemeral Independence" proclaimed by José Núñez de Cáceres, but, shortly thereafter, came under Haiti's rule. It was not until February 27, 1844, that the country achieved lasting independence under Juan Pablo Duarte's La Trinitaria movement. The country has been independent ever since, though unrest has led to brief periods of foreign control: In the early 1860s revolts led government leaders to make the island a province of Spain. Civil disorder prompted occupation by the US Marines from 1916–24, and during a 1965 civil war Lyndon Johnson sent in the Marines once more.

Strongman rule has been something of a tradition here, and visitors often are a bit surprised to see armed military and policemen stationed throughout the country (though their presence as preservers of law and order can be seen as curiously reassuring). Much of the Dominican Republic's 20th-century history has been shaped by Generalissimo Rafael Leónidas Trujillo, who took power in 1930 and held fast until his assassination in 1961. Although Trujillo helped establish a degree of economic order in the country, he also siphoned off enormous sums of money for himself and his friends during his increasingly oppressive dictatorship. When the populace objected, he simply tightened his grip. The authoritarian Joaquín Balaguer, the country's current president, was chosen by Trujillo to succeed him in 1960, but was deposed two years later. After the turmoil of the early and mid-1960s died down, Balaguer again took office (this time after winning an election) and, except for a period from 1978 to 1987, has

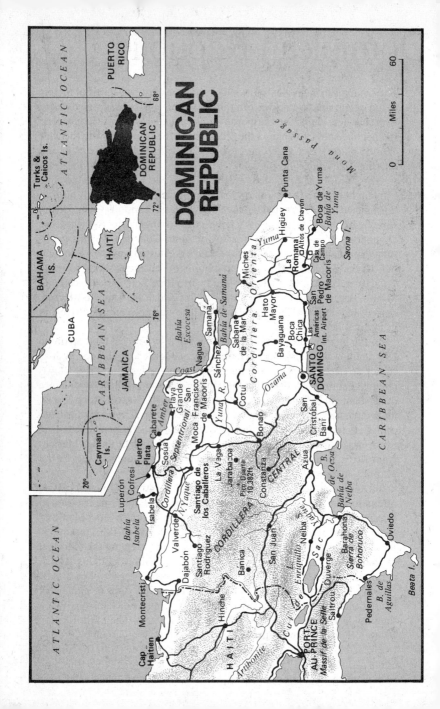

been the freely elected president ever since. These days, however, Balaguer is elderly, feeble, and almost completely blind, and many Dominicans are looking for possible successors.

Due to the baleful influence of Trujillo, the Dominican Republic has only recently become a popular destination for the current generation of American island lovers. In spite of the deluxe hotels and gambling casinos in the capital, which was called Ciudad Trujillo between 1936 and 1961, Trujillo and tourism were incompatible. What once had been a steady stream of business and pleasure traffic slowed to a trickle and, in the late 1950s, almost stopped entirely.

The country did not really get back into the mainstream of the Caribbean travel picture until the early to mid-1970s, when the government invested many millions of dollars in resort infrastructure and hotel development. Tourism also received sizable support from the Gulf + Western conglomerate (now Paramount Communications), which built the super development complex called *Casa de Campo* on the south coast (since sold, and recently given a $3-million overhaul) and two hotels in the capital. In the late 1970s, the first cabinet-level minister of tourism was appointed, and since then the government has steadily promoted tourism. For example, a concerted effort was made to draw visitors to the country in 1992 to commemorate the 500th anniversary of Columbus's arrival in the Americas. Unfortunately, the festivities fizzled due to controversy surrounding the building of the $70-million-plus *Faro a Colón* (Columbus Lighthouse) and the question of whether Columbus's actions were actually worth celebrating.

Nonetheless, the volume of Dominican tourism has climbed from a meager 87,000 visitors in 1967 to an average of more than two million people in 1994. The Dominican Republic offers the same sea, sand, and sun as many other Caribbean destinations, as well as several superb resorts—at substantially lower costs.

The country does have problems—unemployment is high, corruption is rampant, and electricity frequently fails (although most hotels now have back-up generators to guarantee guests' comfort). The number of hotel rooms continues to rise in response to demand, and new properties were under construction at press time at Barahona, Sosúa, Juan Dolio, Punta Cana, Santo Domingo, and in the Playa Grande area. As part of its continued efforts to woo tourists, the nation is now promoting itself with the name "Dominicana," an abbreviated version of *La República Dominicana,* its official Spanish name. No matter what the country is called, you'll find that its people seem genuinely delighted to greet North American travelers.

Dominican Republic At-a-Glance

FROM THE AIR

The island is almost a primer in basic geography, illustrating many kinds of topography. Rugged peaks, rolling hills, rich valleys, lush sugarcane plantations, and fine white beaches are all part of the terrain. The Dominican Republic and Haiti share Hispaniola, the second-largest of the Greater Antilles islands (only Cuba is bigger), which is situated along the upper arch of the Caribbean archipelago. The country is washed by the Caribbean on the south, the Atlantic on the north, and the 75-mile-wide Mona Passage, which separates it from Puerto Rico, on the east. It is also a neighbor of Jamaica (300 miles west) and Cuba (150 miles northwest).

The Dominican Republic is large compared to other Caribbean island countries—19,120 square miles, with a population of 7.6 million. Its principal mountain range—the Cordillera Central—boasts the highest peak in the West Indies, Pico Duarte, rising 10,417 feet above sea level. Three other ranges run almost parallel, west to east, across the country, and four major rivers—of which the longest is the 125-mile Río Yaque del Norte—flow from the mountains to the ocean and the sea.

Santo Domingo, the sprawling capital (pop. 2.4 million), is at the mouth of the Ozama River in the center of the southern coast. A wide, landscaped highway leads to *Las Américas International Airport,* about 20 miles east of the city on the edge of the Caribbean. It's about three and a half jet hours from New York, about two hours from Miami, and about 40 minutes from Puerto Rico.

Almost one-third of the coastline is edged with beaches. For visitors, the most appealing north coast seaside towns are Puerto Plata, around which a resort area has been developed and continues to grow; Sosúa, founded by Jewish refugees from Europe in the 1940s; and Samaná, a fishing village populated by the descendants of escaped American slaves—they still speak English, though they've been loyal Dominicans for generations. The resorts at Punta Cana, on the island's eastern tip, also boast a spectacular 20-mile stretch of sand—the longest beach in the Caribbean. The best southeastern beaches are near Boca Chica and La Romana. The towns of Jarabacoa, Constanza, and Santiago (the Dominican Republic's second city), nestled in the central mountains, are a cool change from the tropical sea scene.

SPECIAL PLACES

While modern beach resorts are popping up all over the island, the country's capital remains its historic and cultural center. Efforts to spruce up the colonial quarter for the 500th anniversary of Columbus's landfall took longer than expected (the work has continued up until the present), but the effort has finally paid off; the colonial district has shed its neglected image and is once again radiant with newly-planted trees and refurbished buildings. In Santo Domingo, a combination of walking and taking taxis is probably the best way to get around. In the colonial area, parking can be a problem, but everything there is within walking distance. Otherwise, driving is comparatively easy (though road signs are few and often confusing), and Dominicans are usually happy to offer directions to those who get lost. Within the colonial district, non-Spanish-speaking visitors are advised to join an organized tour with an English-speaking guide; few locals, aside from staff in the major hotels and restaurants, speak English. Guides for walking tours can be hired at the plaza in front of the *Catedral de Santa María la Menor* (see Parque Colón, below). Keep in mind that some sites may close each day for an hour or more between noon and 3 PM.

COLONIAL SANTO DOMINGO

Seeing the sights—modern and historic—in Santo Domingo can fill several days, especially for those who take the time to trace all of the city's roots. But the major points can be covered in a day if you move fast.

FARO A COLÓN (COLUMBUS LIGHTHOUSE) Set in a park across the Ozama River, this complex was inaugurated in 1992 in honor of the Columbus quincentenary. A longtime dream of President Joaquín Balaguer, it nevertheless caused a firestorm of protest because of its expense (estimates range from $70 million to $250 million), the scarcity of available electricity to light the beacon (at press time it was not lit on Mondays and Tuesdays, but the schedule often changes), and controversy about Columbus himself. The seven-story monument sits on a bluff in the area's southeastern corner. At the center of the cross-shaped building, which is nearly 700 feet long and 132 feet wide at its widest point, is an impressive marble sarcophagus that purports to contain the remains of the explorer. (The true identity of the body is uncertain, however, as the city of Seville in Spain also claims to be Columbus's final resting place.) Emanating from this point are various exhibits relating to the Dominican Republic's *post*-Columbian history. Cloudy nights are best for viewing the lights, which form a cross in the sky. Guided tours available. Closed Mondays. Admission charge. Off Av. España in *Parque Mirador del Este* (phone: 592-5217).

PARQUE COLÓN (COLUMBUS SQUARE) A large bronze statue of the discoverer stands watch here. On the south side of the square is the *Catedral de Santa María la Menor* (on Calle Arzobispo Meriño), a classic example of Spanish Renaissance architecture. Completed in the early sixteenth century, it is the oldest cathedral in the Western Hemisphere, and it was in the 450-year-old nave that what are said to be the mortal remains of Christopher Columbus resided before being moved to the *Faro a Colón*. Be sure to take a tour with one of the expert guides; they speak English and Spanish and will point out details of the cathedral—the gold and silver treasures, delicate carvings, elaborate altars and shrines—that visitors might otherwise overlook. Tip guides about $1 for the half-hour go-round (phone: 682-3848).

Other square landmarks: *Alcaldía de Santo Domingo* (the old City Hall—now empty, though the government is planning to open a museum here) to the west and, on the east, the *Palacio de Borgella,* headquarters of the Haitian governor during the Haitian occupation of 1822–44 and now the home of government offices. Nearby, at the corner of Calles Padre Billini and Arzobispo Meriño, the *Museo de la Familia Dominicana* (Museum of the Dominican Family) in the *Casa de Tostado* (Tostado House) exhibits mementos of a well-to-do Dominican family of the Victorian era. Closed Wednesdays and weekend afternoons. Admission charge (phone: 689-5057).

Upon leaving the museum, go east on Calle Padre Billini, then north on Calle Las Damas, where you'll see the restored walls of the *Fortaleza Ozama* (Ozama Fortress), with its 1503 *Torre del Homenaje* (Tower of Homage), a massive structure where guards stood watch and condemned prisoners awaited their fate. Inside the fort you can also view the powder house, where ammunition was stored, and the old shooting platforms. Open daily. Admission charge (phone: 685-8472).

CALLE LAS DAMAS (LADIES STREET) The oldest and one of the most beautiful streets in the Americas, Calle Las Damas (named for the ladies of the viceregal court who once lived here and promenaded in the evenings) offers a number of excellent examples of 16th-century colonial architecture. One is the *Casa Bastidas* (Bastidas House), now the site of national museum workshops and small exhibits. Open daily. No admission charge (phone: 688-7601). Another is the house of Governor Nicolás de Ovando, who planned and presided over the building of the city in the early 16th century; it is now the *Hostal Palacio Nicolás de Ovando,* a small, charming hotel with a palm-lined bar that's great for a refreshing pause on your tour (see *Checking In*).

The *Panteón Nacional* (National Pantheon), just across the street, is a must for buffs of both history and art. Built as a Jesuit monastery between 1714 and 1745, its austere lines and massive size contrast with the graceful, smaller-scale colonial houses that surround it. Inside, note the commemorative ceiling mural above the altar; the massive bronze and onyx chandelier, a gift of Spain's Generalissimo Francisco Franco; and the ornate grilles bedecked with what look like crosses from one direction and swastikas from another. Many national heroes are buried within these walls. Open daily; no admission charge, although the guides will expect about a $1 tip (no phone). Also along Calle Las Damas are the *Capilla de los Remedios* (Chapel of Our Lady of Remedies), where the first colonists attended mass, and an antique sun clock.

MUSEO DE LAS CASAS REALES (MUSEUM OF THE ROYAL HOUSES) Opened during the state visit of King Juan Carlos I of Spain in 1976, this museum is housed in what was once the "Audiencia Real," a high tribunal which had jurisdiction over all of Spain's holdings in the Americas. Its handsome displays include models of Columbus's original three ships and a map that traces with lights his four voyages of discovery. Also on display are a re-created courtroom, pharmacy, and sugar mill, plus an excellent display of tapestries. Antique artifacts tell the story of local life and government during Santo Domingo's glory days. Upstairs are offices resembling throne rooms, with crystal chandeliers and paintings of 16th- to 18th-century Spanish kings; the offices were once used by the dictator Trujillo. Closed Sunday afternoons and Mondays. Admission charge. Calle las Damas (phone: 682-4202).

ALCÁZAR DE COLÓN (COLUMBUS PALACE) This castle at the foot of Calle Las Damas was built in 1510 for Christopher's son, Diego Colón, who ruled as first Spanish viceroy from 1509 to 1516. It was so painstakingly and authentically restored in 1957 that Don Diego would probably feel completely at home today among the black-and-white terrazzo floors and hand-carved wooden beds. On view are the dining room, several bedrooms, the kitchen, reception rooms, and the private chapel. Closed Tuesdays. Admission charge (phone: 687-5361).

Directly across the street from the *Alcázar* are the gleaming white walls of La Atarazana, once a dock and trading area that housed the city's first customs office. It dates from 1507 and has been restored to house shops, restaurants, and galleries (see *Shopping*, below).

CASA DEL CORDÓN (HOUSE OF THE CORD) Located near the *Alcázar*, at the corner of Calles Emiliano Tejera and Isabel la Católica, this is where Diego Colón and his wife, María de Toledo, lived while they waited for the *Alcázar* to be completed. Somehow it has survived hurricanes, earthquakes, and the ravages of Sir Francis Drake to become the oldest house in the New World. It now houses periodic art exhibits and serves as the executive offices of the Banco Popular Dominicana. Closed weekends. No admission charge (phone: 682-4333).

MONASTERIO DE SAN FRANCISCO (SAN FRANCISCO MONASTERY) Built early in the 16th century, this structure was plagued by earthquakes, pillaged by Sir Francis Drake, and bombarded by French artillery. Amazingly, much of it still stands. On Calle Emiliano Tejera at Calle Hostos; old stone paving leads to the site. Closed Saturday afternoons and Sundays. No admission charge (phone: 698-0510).

HOSPITAL SAN NICOLÁS DE BARI (ST. NICHOLAS OF BARI HOSPITAL) This was the first hospital in the Americas, founded by Governor Nicolás de Ovando in 1503. Visitors may walk among the ruins, located on Calle Hostos (at Luperón). Open daily. No admission charge (no phone).

Santo Domingo has many interesting attractions outside the colonial area, including:

PARQUE INDEPENDENCIA (INDEPENDENCE PARK) At the intersection of Avenida Independencia and Avenida Bolívar, this large city square, where independence was proclaimed in 1844, marks the beginning of modern Santo Domingo. A shrine housing the remains of the country's three fathers (Juan Pablo Duarte y Diez, Francisco del Rosario Sánchez, and Ramón Matías Mella) dominates the square.

PLAZA DE LA CULTURA (CULTURE PLAZA) North of Avenida Bolívar, on Avenida Máximo Gómez, this complex of modern buildings stands on the site of Trujillo's mansion. Here are the impressive *Teatro Nacional* (National Theater; phone: 682-7255) as well as four museums: the anthropological *Museo del Hombre Dominicano* (Museum of the Dominican Man; phone: 687-3623); the *Museo de Arte Moderno* (Museum of Modern Art; phone: 685-2153); the *Museo Nacional de Historia y Geografía* (National Museum of History and Geography; phone: 688-6952); and the *Museo Nacional de Historia Natural* (National Museum of Natural History; phone: 689-0106). All are closed Mondays and charge admission.

PARQUE ZOOLÓGICO NACIONAL (NATIONAL ZOO) This free-space zoological park deserves a visit. The animals roam natural landscapes that are surrounded by a moat. Closed Mondays. Admission charge (phone: 562-3149). The nearby *Jardín Botánico* (Botanical Garden) features carriage rides through several sections—an English garden, a Spanish garden, and so on. Closed Mondays. Admission charge (phone: 565-2860). The zoo and the garden are in the Arroyo Hondo neighborhood, on the Avenida Tiradentes at Avenida de los Arroyos.

LOS TRES OJOS (THE THREE EYES) Ten minutes from Santo Domingo on Las Américas Highway, these three subterranean lagoons of fresh, salt, and sulfur water are fed by an underground river and surrounded by rock formations and lush vegetation. Cool, beautiful, and worth a trip. Open daily. No admission charge, but guides expect a $1 tip (no phone).

ACUARIO NACIONAL (NATIONAL AQUARIUM) A beautifully landscaped park, opened in 1992, features giant turtles living in natural surroundings and sharks circling for prey in glass-enclosed exhibits. Well worth a visit. Closed Mondays. Admission charge. Av. España in Los Mameyes sector (phone: 593-0029).

SOUTHEAST COAST

Outside Santo Domingo, driving is the best way to get around. Most roads are adequate to good, and gas stations are reasonably spaced. Dominicans are more than happy to help with directions, but if you don't speak Spanish, it's a good idea to carry a Spanish phrase book; by all means pick up a road map from the tourist office or a gas station.

LA ROMANA One of the most enjoyable day trips (or, better yet, an excursion of several days) is the *Casa de Campo* complex at La Romana, about 75 miles east of the capital along the southeast coast. This beautifully situated resort offers a broad range of sports facilities, including tennis, golf, skeet shooting, hunting, sailing, and sport fishing (see *Checking In*). On the way, stop and sample the beaches at Boca Chica or the rum at the Pedro Justo Carrión distillery in San Pedro de Macorís. The drive from downtown Santo Domingo takes about two hours.

EXTRA SPECIAL

Altos de Chavón is a re-creation of a 16th-century village, built about a decade ago near *Casa de Campo* by an Italian set designer. Designed to be part living museum, part artisans' colony, part tourist diversion, it now comprises the small, ornate stone *Iglesia San Estanislao* (St. Stanislaus Church), a Grecian-style amphitheater, a museum exhibiting artifacts of the extinct Taíno Indians, and workshops, studios, and galleries where visitors may not only buy but learn to make jewelry, macramé items, art prints, and more. There are also continental, Italian, and Mexican restaurants, and a terrace café. Adding to the appeal is the village's site above the winding green Chavón River. For more information call the *Casa de Campo* resort (see *Checking In*).

NORTH COAST

The country's most ambitious tourist developments are located on the north coast, where the mountains of the Cordillera Central meet long, white sand beaches along the Atlantic Ocean. This area is also known as Costambar (the Amber Coast) because of the large deposits of the substance in the nearby hills.

PUERTO PLATA (PORT OF SILVER) This town set on a crescent-shaped bay is located 130 miles northwest of Santo Domingo (about a three-and-a-half-hour drive). From Santo Domingo, take the main Duarte Highway; at Santiago de los Caballeros, the Puerto Plata road branches off to the north. At the western end of Puerto Plata, near the tourism pier, a funicular runs to the top of Isabela de Torres peak, where there's a spectacular view of the ocean and countryside. The funicular is open daily; admission charge (phone: 586-2122). The local airport has seen an increasing number of international arrivals as the development boom continues on this coast. Outside town, at Playa Dorada, a number of resort hotels are clustered around the Robert Trent Jones Sr. golf course. Another ambitious development, farther east at Playa Grande, currently is under way.

SOSÚA Ten miles east of Puerto Plata, following a strip of beautiful beaches along the coastal highway, Sosúa Beach is a veritable tourist bazaar: Vendors emerge from the shacks lining the beach, hawking imitation Limé ceramic figures, Haitian art, and inexpensive, made-to-order jewelry, while "secretaries" mob tourists, offering their services as gofers. Many small resort hotels, restaurants, and clubs present a striking counterpoint to Puerto Plata. Sosúa has had an interesting history: It served as a haven for Jews fleeing the Nazis at the start of World War II. While some left their Caribbean refuge at the end of the war, many more remained. Sosúa has become a popular spot for Canadian and European package tours. Most Americans, however, have yet to discover this bargain destination.

CABARETE This windsurfing town located another 8 miles east of Sosúa along the coast road resembles Malibu before it was built up. Its lovely beach is under development—hotels are popping up, houses are available for rent, and restaurants are opening here and there. The *Punta Goleta* resort is popular with French Canadians (see *Checking In*).

PLAYA GRANDE This long, nearly deserted stretch is among the Caribbean's best. Day trips (which include a boat ride through the mangroves of the Gú-Gú lagoon) are available from Puerto Plata and Sosúa, and the new *Caribbean Village Playa Grande* (see *Checking In*) can accommodate overnighters. An 18-hole golf course near the hotel was under construction at press time. Ten miles east of Cabarete via the coastal highway.

SAMANÁ This remote fishing village on a peninsula jutting out of the northeast coast is located about 120 miles east of Playa Grande along the coastal highway (count on at least a three-hour drive). During the 1820s, thousands of escaped American slaves settled here, establishing an English-speaking, Protestant community in a Spanish-speaking, Catholic country. Selected by the government as a potential tourism center, today this small, peaceful town combines isolation with development. There are a variety of accommodations available here, from simple guesthouses to luxury resorts such as the *Gran Bahía* and the *El Portillo Beach Club* (see *Checking In*). Day trips are also available to *Los Haitisses,* a national park in nearby Sánchez where ancient Taíno inscriptions still adorn the walls of caves.

Sources and Resources

TOURIST INFORMATION

In Santo Domingo, the *Dominican Tourist Information Center* (at the corner of Avs. México and 30 de Marzo; phone: 221-4660; 800-752-1151; fax: 682-3806) can answer questions, as can centers in Puerto Plata (Av. Hermanas Mirabel; phone: 586-3676) and in Santiago at the *Alcaldía* (City Hall; Av. Duarte; phone: 582-5885). All are closed weekday afternoons after 2:30 PM and on weekends. There is also an information counter at the airport that's open daily (phone: 542-0120). For information about Dominican Republic tourist offices in the US, see GETTING READY TO GO.

LOCAL COVERAGE The weekly *Santo Domingo News,* distributed free at hotels and shops, carries a current entertainment section that is directed more toward English-speaking residents than to tourists. The bilingual *Bohío,* a free quarterly tourist magazine, is obviously ad-oriented, but helpful.

La Cotica: National Tourism Guide to the Dominican Republic, the most complete and available guidebook, is $2 to $3 at hotel newsstands and sundry shops, or can be obtained free from the tourist offices. In addition to a comprehensive view of the country, it offers useful addresses and phone numbers. *Viejo Santo Domingo* is an excellent free guide with a map and a bit of history; it's published by the *Dominican-American Cultural Institute* and can be found at many bookstores and newsstands.

Listín Diario, El Caribe, El Siglo, Nuevo Diario, Hoy, El Nacional, La Noticia, and *Ultima Hora* are the local Spanish-language dailies. The English-language daily *San Juan Star* from Puerto Rico and day-old Miami and New York papers are available in hotels.

RADIO AND TELEVISION Although local radio and TV stations broadcast only in Spanish, many of the larger hotels offer cable TV from the US.

TELEPHONE The area code for the Dominican Republic is 1 + 809. Dial 911 for emergency assistance.

ENTRY REQUIREMENTS A $10 tourist card, valid for up to 90 days, is required, and can be obtained by presenting a valid passport or other proof of citizenship (a birth certificate or voter's registration card, along with an official photo ID such as a driver's license) to a consulate, carrier, or—on arrival—an immigration official. An ongoing or return ticket also is required. The departure tax is $10.

CLIMATE AND CLOTHES The island of Hispaniola lies on the same latitude as Hawaii. Sweeping trade winds and the warm Caribbean help keep temperatures pleasant year-round. Daytime winter temperatures range between 75F (24C) and 80F (27C), with cooler breezes at night. Summer temperatures run from about 80F (27C) to 90F (32C); August is the warmest month. May–June and October–November are the rainiest, but rainfall often comes in short downpours followed by clear skies and fresh, clean air.

In general, daytime dress is casual and comfortable. Lightweight sportswear—slacks and shirts, skirts and dresses in natural fabrics or wash-and-wear blends—are fine for sightseeing; active sports clothes (for beach, tennis, golf, and so on) are right for resorts and the pools and courts of hotels in town. Pack a light sweater or jacket for cooler winter evenings or air conditioned restaurants and clubs. Evenings tend to be a touch dressier, with jackets (but not necessarily ties) for men suggested at better restaurants and hotels. Santo Domingo also has some spots—for example, the *Alcázar* dining room of the *Santo Domingo* hotel, the *Lina* restaurant in the *Gran Hotel Lina,* and *Mesón de la Cava* (see *Eating Out* for all three)—for those who like to get decked out for a night on the town.

MONEY At banks and exchange houses, $1 US buys nearly 13 Dominican pesos; the exchange rate at shops and restaurants may be somewhat less favorable. Try not to have a surplus of pesos at departure time; it's difficult and time-consuming to exchange them.

Shops and hotels happily accept US dollars, but often won't take Canadian currency. Many larger stores accept major US credit cards, as do most hotels and restaurants. Traveler's checks are welcome everywhere, but no discounts are given for payment in either cash dollars or traveler's checks. All prices in this chapter are quoted in US dollars.

LANGUAGE Spanish is the Dominican Republic's official language, but most Dominicans in tourist-related businesses speak some English. Outside of the prime tourist areas, visitors who don't speak Spanish may run into some language problems, but Dominicans are friendly, helpful people who will find a way to communicate.

TIME The Dominican Republic runs on Atlantic standard time. In late fall, winter, and early spring, noon in New York is 1 PM in Santo Domingo; when daylight saving time is in effect in the US, the time is the same in both places.

CURRENT Same as in the US and Canada—110 volts, 60 cycles.

TIPPING Local law requires that hotel bills and restaurant checks include a 10% service charge, which is supposed to cover all tips. For especially good service, however, it's customary to add 5% to 10% more—especially in restaurants not connected with hotels. Tip hotel maids $1 to $2 per day per room, bellboys and airport porters 50¢ per bag (with a $1 minimum). Give taxi drivers 10% to 15% of the fare.

GETTING AROUND

BUS In Santo Domingo they are sometimes crowded, but also inexpensive and efficient, and they cover the entire city. Both buses and minibuses have set routes around the city, and bus assistants often yell out the streets being passed along the route. Prices range from about 2 to 5 pesos (26¢ to 65¢ at press time). Air conditioned bus service from Santo Domingo to other towns—Bonao, Jarabacoa, La Romana, La Vega, Puerto Plata, San Pedro de Macorís, Santiago, and Punta Cana—is comfortable and offers travelers the chance to meet local people and see the country. Check the number of stops, however; some routes offer a bit more local color than you'll want. For schedule and route information, call *Compañía Nacional* (phone: 565-6681), *Metro Tourist Services* (phone: 566-7126), or *Caribe Tours* (phone: 221-4422). Fares vary, but the 3¾-hour ride to Puerto Plata is a bargain any way you look at it.

CAR RENTAL International car rental agencies will make reservations through their US toll-free phone numbers or the following local numbers: *Hertz* (phone:

221-5333), *Budget* (phone: 567-0173), *National* (phone: 562-1444), and *Avis* (phone: 562-6820). They all have desks at the airports in Santo Domingo and Puerto Plata, and at some hotels, as does *Nelly Rent-A-Car,* one of the best local firms (phone: 549-0509 at the Santo Domingo airport; 688-3366 in Santo Domingo; 586-0505 in Puerto Plata; 800-526-6684). *Pueblo* (phone: 689-2000) and other local companies often have representatives in the better hotels. All companies listed above have drop-off centers at the Puerto Plata and Santo Domingo airports. A special license is not necessary to drive in the Dominican Republic; a valid US license is good for 90 days.

Note that Dominican drivers tend to use their horns instead of their brakes. In Old Santo Domingo, the streets are narrow, with blind corners, so be alert. In the countryside, limit your driving to daylight hours; the roads aren't lit, and a meandering mule could wipe out more than your front end.

Also be aware that police often flag down drivers—both tourists and local residents—for dubious alleged infractions. Though you can always test the Dominican system by refusing to submit to this petty extortion, you might prefer to continue your vacation in peace by doing what the locals do: Give the policeman a $5 *"regalo"* (gift) and be on your way.

INTER-ISLAND FLIGHTS *American Eagle* (phone: 542-5151) has daily flights from San Juan, Puerto Rico, to *La Unión International Airport,* near Puerto Plata and the north coast, to the La Romana airport in the *Casa de Campo* complex, and to the *Punta Cana Airport* on the country's east coast. There also are frequent charter arrivals in Puerto Plata and charter flights out of Santo Domingo. *ALM* (*Antilles Airlines*; phone: 687-4569) links Curaçao, Aruba, and Bonaire with Santo Domingo; and *VIASA* (phone: 687-2688) connects Santo Domingo and Caracas, Venezuela.

SIGHTSEEING BUS TOURS Excursions on air conditioned buses, with English-speaking guides, are offered by a number of local companies. *Prieto Tours* (Santo Domingo; phone: 688-5715) is one of the best. *Metro Tours* (phone: 566-7126 in Santo Domingo; 583-9111 in Santiago; 586-6063 in Puerto Plata) also is good. Others to check out are *Omni Tours* (phone: 565-6591) in Santo Domingo, and *Puerto Plata Tours* (phone: 586-8165) or *Apolo Tours* (phone: 586-2751) in Puerto Plata. On the south coast, *Tropical Tours* at *Casa de Campo* is a topnotch operator (phone: 556-3636). Tour options include beach trips, city and country sightseeing, shopping, sports packages, and visits to the mountain towns of Jarabacoa, Constanza, and Santiago.

SIGHTSEEING TAXI TOURS These cost more than bus tours, but are a great way to see the country, provided you can find a driver who speaks your language, knows Dominican history and sights, and has good springs in his car. Consult your hotel travel desk for specific names. Otherwise, you're better off on a bus tour with an English-speaking guide.

TAXI There are plenty of cabs at the airports and in town. But they aren't metered, so make sure the fare (and the number of passengers for which it pays) is understood and agreed upon beforehand. Numerous *conchos*—small taxis following a set route, with passengers getting in and out along the way—serve Santo Domingo and outlying cities. Other transportation alternatives include hopping onto a *motoconcho,* a motorbike taxi that is an increasingly popular mode of transportation, especially in Puerto Plata and other cities on the north coast; vans also shuttle passengers between Puerto Plata and Sosúa on the north coast.

SPECIAL EVENTS

The Dominican Republic's big week-long celebration is the *Festival de Merengue* (Merengue Festival), held in Santo Domingo in late July. Rum flows freely and everyone takes to the dance floor—or the street or nearest tabletop—to do the rhythmic national dance. If your merengue is a little rusty (or nonexistent), don't worry; there'll be more than enough volunteer instructors around to help. *Carnaval,* another traditional celebration, is held on *Día de la Independencia* (Independence Day; February 27).

Legal holidays—when banks, businesses, and most government offices are closed—are *New Year's Day, Epiphany* (January 6), the *Day of Our Lady of Altagracia* (January 21), *Duarte's Day* (January 26), *Independence Day* (February 27), *Good Friday* (April 5 in 1996), *Labor Day* (May 1), *Corpus Christi Day* (May 30 in 1996), *Restoration Day* (August 16), the *Feast of Our Lady of Mercy* (September 24), and *Christmas.*

SHOPPING

Among the best buys in the Dominican Republic are jewelry and decorative pieces made from amber. Some pieces encase insects, leaves, or dew drops, which make them more valuable. Color can range from crystal clear to almost black; gold is most common. But buy amber only in established shops; that nice amber piece that a street vendor offers may actually be plastic.

Larimar, or "Dominican turquoise," is another popular local stone. Milky blue and perhaps even prettier than turquoise, it's often mounted with wild boars' teeth or silver. Polished pink pieces of conch shell also are crafted into striking jewelry.

Other worthwhile take-home items include *mecedoras* (rocking chairs—very popular in the Dominican Republic, sold disassembled and boxed for easy transport), woodcarvings, macramé, baskets, and leather goods. Limé (pronounced "Lee-*may*") figurines, the Dominican Republic's answer to Spain's Lladró, are also very popular; less expensive replicas are sold at roadside and beachside stands. Be sure to haggle with the seller—about half the asking price is usually fair. Many jewelry and gift items sold in the Dominican Republic are made from tortoiseshell. Be aware, however, that because many species of tortoise are on the US endangered species list, any tortoiseshell item you bring home can be confiscated by a US customs officer. La Atarazana (The Shipyard), a winding street across from the *Alcázar* and near the river, is lined with gift shops and galleries. Savvy shoppers browse here, then move on to Calle El Conde in the colonial district, the oldest and most traditional shopping area in the city, now open to pedestrians only.

The *Mercado Modelo,* Santo Domingo's model native marketplace (on Av. Mella), is full of stalls that offer all kinds of craft items. If you don't speak Spanish, you may want to ask your cab driver to come along as interpreter, or give one of the small boys at the gate $1 to lead you through and fend off some of the more eager merchants. With or without escort, you won't be hassled, but you should bargain before you settle on a final buying price. Also look for Dominican coffee, sold unground; it's good, strong, and less expensive than special roasts back home.

In Santo Domingo, duty-free shops at the Centro de los Héroes, La Atarazana, *Las Américas Airport,* and the *Santo Domingo, Sheraton,* and *Embajador* hotels in town (see *Checking In*) carry the usual range of French perfume, liquor, camera equipment, watches, and jewelry. Travelers choose items from the stock on hand; duplicates of the selected merchandise are delivered to their planes or ships. The *Plaza Criolla* (downtown, on Av. 27 de Febrero) is a center for fine jewelry shops and other boutiques. Excellent amber items are sold there, as are silver pieces from some of the oldest wrecks sunk off the island.

Generally, shops are open Mondays through Saturdays from 8:30 or 9 AM to noon, close for siesta, then reopen from 2:30 until about 6:30 PM. Here are some places where the time (and money) might be well spent:

Ambar Maldo Besides the standard amber, *larimar,* and coral items, this store carries pottery, masks, and local artworks. Open during siesta. 1 La Atarazana, Santo Domingo (phone: 688-0639).

Arawak Galería de Arte Native art, including silk-screens, drawings, and paintings, lures collectors here. 104 Av. Pasteur, Santo Domingo (phone: 685-1661) and 22 Calle Bellar, Puerto Plata (phone: 562-8678).

El Conde Gift Shop The place to find rocking chairs, along with other Dominican wares. 153 Calle El Conde, Santo Domingo (phone: 682-5909).

Harrison's Fine jewelry and hand-crafted gift items made from local amber, *larimar,* and coral are this establishment's stocks in trade. Open during siesta. Two locations in Puerto Plata: *Plaza Isabela* near the Playa Dorada complex (phone: 320-2219) and 30 Calle John F. Kennedy (phone: 586-4468). Also in Sosúa at the corner of Calle Pedro Clisante and Calle Dr. Rosen (phone: 571-2022).

La Casa del Cigarro (The Cigar House) For sale here are exquisite Dominican cigars, which many say now outrank Cuban cigars as the best in the world. The owners will also hand-roll cigars for visitors. *Casa de Francia* on Calle Las Damas, Santo Domingo (phone: 685-7083).

Museo del Ambar (Amber Museum) More a shop than a museum, this place may house the best collection of local amber, *larimar,* and coral jewelry for sale on the north coast. It also has ceramics and Limé dolls, as well as second-floor displays tracing the history of amber (admission charge). Open during siesta. 61 Calle Duarte, Puerto Plata (phone: 586-2848).

Noveau Paintings, sculpture, and silk screens are featured at this gallery. 354 Av. Independencia, Santo Domingo (phone: 689-6869).

Rainbow A wonderful treasury of amber, black coral, and *larimar* jewelry, and it's all made in the store's own atelier in the back. 22 Calle Duarte, Puerto Plata (phone: 586-3005).

Sala de Arte Rosa María Good local paintings in a lovely patio setting. 7 La Atarazana, Santo Domingo (phone: 688-2744).

SPORTS

Fine weather year-round, lots of unspoiled land, and beautiful water—as yet not overpublicized—make the Dominican Republic a great place to feel the sun and sea, meet the challenge of a tough par 4 hole, or fight it out with a blue marlin. The country's sporting facilities are top quality now, and—with the further development of resort areas like those at Puerto Plata—they'll be expanding.

BASEBALL *El béisbol* is a national obsession. At any given time, 50 Dominican Republic–born players are in the US majors (current and previous players include former MVP George Bell, All-Star shortstop Tony Fernández, and Pedro Guerrero). Major league coaches frequently arrive to scout potential players. The professional winter season runs from October to the end of January; the summer season is April to September. Check local papers for schedules at five stadiums, or ask any Dominican for the location of the nearest game.

BOATING Small sailboats are available through hotels in Santo Domingo and on the north coast; *Club Mediterranée* and the *Punta Cana Beach* resort at Punta Cana and *Casa de Campo* at La Romana have their own fleets (see *Checking In* for all three). Large-boat charters aren't always easy to arrange; hotels and the tourist offices may have information on boats available in the Santo Domingo area. Try the *Actividades Acuáticas* in Boca Chica (phone: 523-4511) or Puerto Plata (phone: 320-2567); or *Club Náutico de Santo Domingo* in Santo Domingo (phone: 566-4522). Better still, arrange ahead by corresponding through your home yacht club or marina. The *Punta Cana Beach* resort can accommodate yachts of up to 85 feet at its 80-slip marina.

COCKFIGHTING The violence, bloodshed, and smell may turn you off, but there's no denying it's part of the Latino scene. Cockfights are regularly held at the *Coliseo Gallístico,* Av. Luperón, Herrera (phone: 565-3844).

DOG RACES Greyhound races were held year-round at the *Canódromo El Coco,* about 15 minutes north of the capital (phone: 565-8333 or 567-4461), but at press time the track was closed until further notice (for updated information consult your hotel's concierge or the tourist board).

GOLF In addition to several other good layouts, the country boasts two of the world's finest championship courses.

TOP TEE-OFF SPOTS

Casa de Campo The two greats are right here, but if it were necessary to choose just one island course on which to play, it would have to be the one known—for good reason—as "The Teeth of the Dog." Unquestionably Pete Dye's finest island work, this seaside course presents more excitement, interest, and sheer brawny challenge than any golf course we've ever seen. Seven holes play directly along the seaside, and they are unlike any other such water holes you have heretofore experienced. Just standing on one of the championship tees can be an exercise in sheer terror, as the terrain between tee and green occasionally looks as if it might be inhabited by the Loch Ness Monster. In this instance, said monster would be a welcome relief from the rigors that Dye has wrought.

In addition to the superb seaside stretch, the other 11 holes are scarcely less challenging. Dye's unique inclination to enclose terrain within wooden retaining walls and to create traps that look like the Sahara are only part of the picture that greets each golfer. And lest you think the second course at *Casa de Campo* is any real respite, "The Links" is thought by many to be even more difficult. There is a third course, *La Romana Golf Club,* but to play here you must make contact with a member. If you are introduced by a member but play on your own, it's twice as expensive as when a member accompanies you. The real bonus from the third course is that its members—mostly local Dominicans—no longer clog up the fairways at *Casa de Campo*'s two courses (see *Checking In* for details on the resort).

There is also a handsome Robert Trent Jones Sr. course at the Playa Dorada complex, near Puerto Plata (check with any of the Playa Dorada hotels for more information; see *Checking In*), and visitors can play the *Santo Domingo Country Club* course (phone: 530-6606 or 530-6571), but only on a members-first basis—which practically rules out weekend play for visitors. In addition, 18 holes of a Robert Trent Jones Sr.–designed golf course were scheduled for completion at Punta Cana this year (for information, call the *Punta Cana Beach* resort; see *Checking In*), and another 18-hole Robert Trent Jones Sr. course is under development at Playa Grande near the new *Caribbean Village Playa Grande* (see *Checking In*). The *Bávaro Beach* complex has an 18-hole course, and the *Gran Bahía* in Samaná has a nine-hole course (see *Checking In* for both).

HORSE RACES Held year-round every Tuesday, Thursday, and Saturday, and the last Monday of each month at the *Hipódromo Perla Antillana* (Av. San Martín, Santo Domingo; phone: 565-2584). At press time, a new racetrack was under construction on Avenida Las Américas in Santo Domingo; an opening date has not been set, but plans call for it to be the largest track in the Caribbean and Central America (for further information contact the tourist board).

HORSEBACK RIDING Dominicans love riding, and their country offers some of the best in the Caribbean. Rarely do you find a horse that even remotely resembles the stereotypical tired hack. The best place to ride on the south coast is in La Romana, where about 700 homegrown steeds are available at *Casa de Campo's Equestrian Center.* Here you can arrange to ride with a guide (required) for up to three hours on a horse suited to your skill. Or take private or group lessons in riding or polo through the activities office at *Casa de Campo* (see *Checking In*). Horseback riding also is featured at the *Punta Cana Beach* resort (see *Checking In*); three-hour guided trail rides lead to a working cattle ranch, past some Arawak ruins, and along the beach. On the north coast, try *Rancho Montaña* in Cabarete (phone: 571-0836).

PARASAILING *Actividades Acuáticas* (see *Boating,* above) provides the island's only outlet for this sky-high sport.

POLO The polo season runs from November through May, and there are regular games at *Casa de Campo* near La Romana (see *Checking In*). Visitors may join the twice-a-week competition (though first preference goes to registered guests of the resort), as long as they've brought their handicap from a home club. Mallets are appreciated, too, but they can be provided in a pinch. This also is the place to learn to play polo, or to improve your game if you already play, in a glorious setting with patient instructors and usually some 100 polo ponies from which to choose.

SNORKELING AND SCUBA DIVING *Actividades Acuáticas* (see *Boating,* above) offers lessons and tours. *Treasure Divers* (phone: 523-5320) offers night dives, wreck dives, and cave dives at the *Don Juan Beach* resort in Boca Chica. Some of the most spectacular underwater scenery is at La Caleta, near the entrance to *Las Américas International Airport,* where there are miles of coral reefs, caves, and fissures more than 40 feet deep. Snorkel gear is loaned or rented for a small fee by resort hotels. *Casa de Campo* guests can sail to nearby Catalina Island aboard the 52-foot sailboat *Merengue* for a half-day guided snorkeling tour. The *Casa de Campo*'s *Sea Horse* catamaran takes guests on full-day snorkeling excursions, with lunch included (make reservations for either boat one day in advance). Twice-daily snorkeling sails (including equipment) are free to guests of the *Punta Cana Beach* resort. The waters off the shores of *Club Mediterranée* are filled with spiny urchins, snails, and tropical fish, as well as huge quantities of brain coral; snorkeling equipment is free to guests. (See *Checking In* for all hotels listed.) On the north coast, try *Caribbean Marine* in Puerto Plata (see *Sport Fishing,* below); *Northern Coast Aquasports* in Sosúa (phone: 571-1028); or *Tropic Diving Center* in Samaná (phone: 240-6110). For additional details, see *Sunken and Buried Treasure* in DIVERSIONS.

SPORT FISHING Offshore waters are home to marlin, sailfish, dorado, bonito, and other game fish. The best spots are Cumayasa, La Romana, and Boca de Yuma on the east coast; Palmar de Ocoa and Barahona on the south; and Monte Cristi and Samaná on the north. Have your hotel arrange for charter fishing boats, or try the *Club Náutico de Santo Domingo* or *Actividades Acuáticas* (see *Boating,* above, for both); *Haina* (Sánchez Hwy., Santo Domingo; phone: 537-3961); or *Caribbean Marine* (in Puerto Plata; phone: 320-2249). In La Romana, *Casa de Campo* offers deep-sea and river fishing (see *Checking In*). Flatboats, with guides, can be hired for half-day river fishing for snook and tarpon at La Romana, Boca de Yuma, and on the north coast around Samaná. Inquire at your hotel.

SWIMMING AND SUNNING The country's most beautiful strands are those on the north coast, where resort development has grown up around the town of Puerto Plata, about a three-hour drive north of Santo Domingo. Beach addicts drive up, lunch in the hills at Santiago (the Dominican Republic's second city), and stay for two or three days to sample the pleasures of the miles of powdery sand beaches that line the coast of the Atlantic. Here are a couple of the best.

DREAM BEACHES

Playa Grande This nearly deserted sweep of picture-perfect sand on the north shore is a great place to spend a long, lazy day (bring a picnic, playthings, and maybe a beach umbrella).

Sosúa The next beach over from Playa Grande, this semicircle of sand is flanked by the town of the same name, whose cafés, shops, hotels, and friendly atmosphere have made it popular with Canadians, Europeans, and—more recently—Americans.

Also on the north shore, Playa Dorada offers great sunning, swimming, snorkeling, and beachcombing.

The coast is craggy at Santo Domingo, with no sand beaches. The nearest good ones are Boca Chica, just beyond the airport, and Juan Dolio, about 40 to 45 minutes east of town. About two hours out, guests at *Casa de Campo* swim at pretty Las Minitas or Bayahibe; the *Punta Cana Beach* resort and *Club Mediterranée* are situated on a magnificent stretch of beach at Punta Cana on the island's far eastern tip (see *Checking In* for all three).

TENNIS Santo Domingo offers an impressive number of courts for racketeers—from rank beginners to pros.

CHOICE COURTS

Casa de Campo The tennis segment of this 7,000-acre complex is first class; everything works, and everything is in absolutely mint condition. At *La Terraza Tennis Village*—a five-minute jitney ride from the main building—are 13 clay-composition courts (three are stadium courts, ten are lighted). There is a resident pro. Eight to 12 people also can set up their own daily clinic at rates that vary according to the season. There's also a ball machine and a pro shop. Court fees are slightly higher for night play. Tennis packages are offered year-round. A roster of terrific local players makes it possible to guarantee guests games at all levels of skill. Non-guests of the resort may use the facilities, but only if openings remain after all registered guests have been accommodated, which is often unlikely, especially around *Christmas* (see *Checking In* for hotel information).

In Santo Domingo, the *Sheraton Santo Domingo, Santo Domingo,* and *El Embajador* hotels and the *Dominican Fiesta* (Av. Anocaona; phone: 562-8954) have courts (some lighted), pro shops, and teaching pros. In addition to courts, the *Jaragua Renaissance* boasts an 800-seat tennis stadium and usually has a highly ranked tennis pro. The *Gran Hotel Lina* has courts, too. Puerto Plata has good courts at the *Jack Tar Village, Playa Dorada, Club on the Green,* and *Villas Doradas;* those at the *Montemar* in Puerto Plata (Av. Circunvalación del Norte; phone: 586-2800) and the *Cofresí* hotel in Costambar are on the rustic side. At Punta Cana, courts at the *Punta Cana Beach* resort, *Bávaro Beach,* and *Club Mediterranée* are first-rate. (See *Checking In* for hotel information if not listed above.)

TRAP AND SKEET SHOOTING You can perfect your aim at *Casa de Campo* (see *Checking In*). Basic shooting orientation is free for beginners; clinics and lessons are available for experienced marksmen. Non-guests of the resort may take advantage of the facilities, but only if there are still openings after registered guests make reservations.

NIGHTLIFE

Take your pick: A Vegas-style revue, a lounge with a cabaret singer or show tunes played on a piano, New York–style disco dancing, a wild night of merengue, casinos where you can play until dawn, or a quiet drink in a café by the ocean—the Dominican Republic has them all, and until all hours of the morning, since there is no set law on bar closing hours. (Unless otherwise noted, see *Checking In* for more information on the hotels mentioned below.)

Santo Domingo hotels offer traditional, small-scale shows most evenings. A current smart spot is *Las Palmas* in the *Santo Domingo* hotel, with live music Monday through Thursday nights. *L'Azotea,* the lounge atop the *Dominican Fiesta* (see *Tennis*) and *El Yarey* at the *Sheraton Santo Domingo* are catching on with the tourist crowd, while the *Embassy Club* at the *El Embajador* is still a favorite with both Dominicans and visitors. Places for Latin music include *Mesón de la Cava* (see *Eating Out*), with folkloric music; the *Gran Hotel Lina's Salón La Mancha;* the *Maunaloa* (207 Mauricio Báez, Centro de los Héroes; phone: 533-2151); *El Castillo* in the *San Gerónimo* hotel (1067 Av. Independencia; phone: 535-1000); and the *Merengue Lounge* at the *Jaragua Renaissance.* The *Jaragua* also features Vegas-style shows in its 1,600-seat *La Fiesta* showroom about twice monthly. For drinks and 16th-century Dominican ambience, try *Drake's Pub* (25 La Atarazana; phone: 687-8089), a favorite expatriate hangout. The *Golden Café* (14 Calle R. Pastoriza; phone: 565-2616) is also popular for drinks.

You can relieve disco fever at the *Sheraton Santo Domingo's* slick *Omni* (jacket required), and *Alexander's* (23 Av. Pasteur; phone: 685-9728), which draws discoing Dominican preppies. The *Guácara Taína* in *Parque Mirador del Sur* draws Dominicans to an underground cave for dancing and folkloric shows (phone: 530-2662 or 533-1051). Later, if you're still ready to roll, there's *Neon* at the *Hispaniola* hotel. Most places in town with entertainment have an admission charge.

Casino action can be found at the *El Embajador, Hispaniola, Gran Hotel Lina,* and *Sheraton Santo Domingo* hotels, the *Dominican Fiesta* (see *Tennis*), and the *San Gerónimo* and *Maunaloa* (see above). The *Jaragua Renaissance* boasts the Caribbean's largest gambling facility. Casinos throughout the Dominican Republic can set their own hours, but are normally open from 4 PM to 4 AM. For additonal details, see *Casino Countdown* in DIVERSIONS.

Out of town, at *Casa de Campo,* options are limited but pleasant, with nine dining spots at the resort and at the artisans' village of Altos de Chavón; Altos is also the site of the supersound disco called *Genesis.* A special spot for drinks and nightly entertainment is *La Caña,* a thatch-roofed bar perched over a swimming pool (see *Checking In* for information on all of the *Casa's* nightspots).

In the Playa Dorada resort complex near Puerto Plata, the *Playa Dorada* hotel has the hottest nightspot on the beach. Two more popular discos are at *Heavens* (phone: 320-5250) and *Paradise Resort* (phone: 320-3663), also in the Playa Dorada area.

Casinos buzz at *Jack Tar Village* and the *Playa Dorada* at Playa Dorada, and at the *Puerto Plata Beach* resort in Puerto Plata (Av. Malecón; phone: 562-7475). There also are casinos at the *Punta Cana Beach* and *Bávaro Beach* resorts, both in Punta Cana. Other casinos on the island are at the *Matum* hotel in Santiago (Av. La Carrera; phone: 581-3107) and the *Decameron Club* in Juan Dolio.

Merengue music and folkloric shows are often featured poolside at the *Punta Cana Beach* resort. The resort's *La Tortuga Beach Club* (with the largest thatch-roofed building on the island) has disco dancing nightly.

Best on the Island

CHECKING IN

The Dominican Republic has about 32,000 hotel rooms, with choices in all price categories. Santo Domingo hotels cater to a fairly sophisticated crowd of history buffs, shoppers, nightlife lovers, businesspeople, gamblers, and some quickie divorcers. La Romana offers a tops-in-class sports resort, *Casa de Campo*. Puerto Plata, on the north coast, features luxury beach hotels, including, outside of town, the Playa Dorada complex, which includes 14 resort properties. Sosúa is also a rapidly developing area, and hotel plans are on the drawing boards for neighboring north coast areas.

As in most other Caribbean destinations, prices at most hotels here are higher between December 15 and April 15. And winter prices can be steep—La Romana's *Casa de Campo* costs about $240 a day, including government taxes, for a "casita" room for two without meals. Summertime prices drop 40% to 50%, and there are attractively priced packages. Hotels beyond Santo Domingo, La Romana, and Puerto Plata are considerably less expensive, whatever the season.

With the exchange rate favoring the dollar, food and beverage costs at even the finest restaurants can be attractive, so it's a good idea to book your room without meals (European Plan) and sample some of the country's many interesting restaurants. However, the Modified American Plan (MAP, including breakfast and dinner) may be a good option at the largely self-contained *Casa de Campo*.

In the listings below hotels classed as expensive charge $100 and more per night for a double without meals; hotels in the moderate category charge in the $50 to $100 range; at inexpensive places the rate is less than $50. Some places offer a Modified American Plan for an additional $20 to $25 per person per day. Hotels tack on an additional 13% in taxes plus a 10% service charge. Unless otherwise noted, all hotels listed below have air conditioning, telephones, TV sets, and private baths. All telephone numbers are in the 809 area code unless otherwise indicated.

We begin with our favorite haven, which falls in the "expensive" category, followed by recommended hotels listed by price category.

A REGAL RESORT

Casa de Campo The aim was—quite simply—to build the perfect sports resort. The result was this big complex built on 7,000 acres near the old sugar mill town of La Romana. Guests of the resort are met at the airport by a hostess and shown to an air conditioned courtesy suite where they can wait comfortably until all the guests have assembled. The resort recently completed a $3 million renovation of its rooms and grounds. The accommodations, which Dominican-born designer Oscar de la Renta had a hand in decorating, consist of 300 rooms in *casitas* (bungalows), as well as 150 luxury villas with one to four bedrooms and maid and butler service (family villas come with baby-sitters). Indeed, there's just about everything here: two great Pete Dye golf courses, a terrific 13-court tennis layout called *La Terraza*, stables (both English- and Western-style riding), three polo fields (with a coach in attendance), guides and boats for deep-sea and river fishing, trap- and skeet-shooting ranges, and an activities program for children ages five through 12. The sandy beach of Las Minitas is a short golf-cart ride from the main complex; its pleasures include swaying palms, showers, changing facilities, and a snack bar with super hamburgers. The place to be at sunset is *La Caña*, a thatch pavilion with a 360° view. There's dinner in the main dining room (grilled meat and local lobster are specialties). Other appetizing options: the country inn–like *La Piazzetta* (elegant Italian); the *Casa del Río* (with French fare and a spectacular view); and the *Café del Sol* (pizza and ice cream) built into Altos de Chavón, the re-creation of a 16th-century artisans' village atop a nearby hill (see *Eating Out* for information on these three restaurants). *La Caña* offers a variety of entertainment, including folkloric shows and merengue, while *Genesis* in Altos de Chavón is a lively disco (phone: 523-3333; 800-877-3643; fax: 523-8548).

SANTO DOMINGO

EXPENSIVE

Jaragua Renaissance The grande dame of Santo Domingo hotels, now part of the Ramada chain, this 355-room complex occupies 14 acres on the *malecón*, the city's ritzy seaside strip. It boasts four lighted clay tennis courts (plus a tennis pro and an 800-seat tennis stadium), a pool, a European-style spa, and a 20,000-square-foot casino, touted as the largest in the Caribbean. Other drawing cards: four restaurants, including the *Manhattan Grill, Figaro* (see *Eating Out* for both), and a 24-hour deli; Las Vegas–style entertainment in *La Fiesta Showroom;* a lounge for dancing; business services; and a disco. 367 Av. George Washington (phone: 221-2222; 800-228-9898; fax: 686-0528).

Santo Domingo Facing the sea, this luxurious 220-room city hostelry, with interiors by Oscar de la Renta, is a top choice. The decor features elegant latticework, tall potted palms, and locally made furnishings; some rooms face the ocean. The Premier Club, a concierge floor, has beautifully decorated rooms and a most accommodating staff. The hotel offers a large pool and a sun deck with a bar, a sauna, and three tennis courts. Business services are available. There are three restaurants, including the excellent *El Alcázar* dining room (see *Eating Out*). *Las Palmas* is the nightspot, a pianist plays in the lobby bar every afternoon, and there's another most agreeable breeze-conditioned bar. Av. Independencia and Av. Abraham Lincoln (phone: 221-1511; 800-877-3643; fax: 535-4050).

V Centenario Inter-Continental Named in honor of the quincentennial of Columbus's landing on the island, this hotel is right on the *malecón.* It has 201 luxurious rooms with fabulous sea views; amenities include a concierge, a tennis court, a pool, water sports, a gym and spa, two bars, a casino, and the country's first underground parking garage. Guests can enjoy a choice of Spanish and French fare at the hotel's two dining rooms. 218 Av. George Washington (phone: 221-0000; 800-327-0200; fax: 686-3287).

MODERATE

El Embajador On a slight hill in the western part of town, this property has 300 rooms, some overlooking the sea, others on an executive floor, the Club Miguel Angel. There's a nice Olympic-size pool, four tennis courts (one clay), basketball and volleyball courts, three bars, a disco, a coffee shop, a casino, evening entertainment at the *Embassy* nightclub (a smart-set favorite), and two restaurants—*La Terraza* for informal continental dining and *Jardín de Jade* (see *Eating Out*) for Chinese fare. Av. Sarasota (phone: 221-2131; 800-457-0067; fax: 532-4494).

Gran Hotel Lina The reincarnation of a longtime local favorite, it has 220 rooms, a pool, tennis courts, an exercise room, a casino, and *Lina,* one of the capital's best Spanish restaurants (see *Eating Out*). Rooms are simple but attractively furnished. Av. Máximo Gómez and Av. 27 de Febrero (phone: 563-5000; 800-942-2461; fax: 686-5521).

Hispaniola This is the well-liked but less sumptuous sister of the luxurious *Santo Domingo* across the street (see above). Actually, it's a modest yet pleasant and comfortable place, very popular with Dominicans and business travelers; the staff is most hospitable. Some of the 165 rooms on the south side have sea views. Guests may use of all the facilities at its sister hotel (all the play for less pay). Facilities include a pool and sun deck, an outdoor coffee shop, and a pool bar. There's also *La Piazzetta,* an Italian restaurant (see *Eating Out*); the swinging *Neon* disco; and a casino. Av. Independencia and Av. Abraham Lincoln (phone: 221-7111; 800-877-3643; fax: 535-4050).

Palacio Nicolás de Ovando In the heart of Old Santo Domingo, overlooking the Ozama River, it's called "the oldest hotel in the New World." In fact, it's the restored colonial home of Nicolás de Ovando, who supervised the building of the city; the reigning King and Queen of Spain have stayed here. The 45 rooms boast high, beamed ceilings, charming windows, and 16th-century–style furniture. This is the place if you love atmosphere and history and don't care about sports. There's a small pool, a restaurant, and a patio bar with a light menu and piano music weekends. 53 Calle Las Damas (phone: 688-9220; fax: 688-5170).

Sheraton Santo Domingo Most of the 260 rooms (except those on the third floor) have sea views; suites have terraces. Basically a business hotel in a convenient location, it has a good-looking modern design with lush potted plants and management that's skilled and thoughtful. There are three restaurants, including *Antoine,* which serves luncheon buffets only, and the less formal *La Terraza.* Other amenities include a lounge, a nightclub, a pool, a health club with sauna and massage, business services, two lighted tennis courts, a Jacuzzi, a stylish casino, and a top-flight disco. 365 Av. George Washington (phone: 221-6666; 800-325-3535; fax: 687-8150).

INEXPENSIVE

Cervantes This comfortable 172-room hotel is popular with both business travelers and families. It's conveniently located within walking distance of the colonial quarter, Plaza de la Cultura, and the nightlife on Avenida George Washington. There's a 24-hour restaurant, a bar, a pool, and a beauty salon. A good value. 202 Calle Cervantes (phone: 686-8161; fax: 686-5754).

PUERTO PLATA

EXPENSIVE

Club on the Green The 336 rooms and suites here are set in clusters of two-level *casitas,* designed in island-Victorian style. Each unit has a kitchenette and a terrace; many overlook the Robert Trent Jones Sr. golf course. There are three good restaurants, including the elegant *La Condesa* (see *Eating Out*), a pool with a swim-up juice bar, a gym and sauna, seven tennis courts, and constant poolside activity: aerobics, volleyball, Spanish lessons, merengue dancing to local bands, even chicken races. The beach is within walking distance; *La Tortuga Loca* offers beachgoers drinks and snack lunches, and snorkeling and sailing equipment is provided at no charge to guests. The all-inclusive plan features three meals a day and a plethora of activities. Playa Dorada (phone: 320-1111; fax: 320-5386).

Dorado Naco This luxury component in the Playa Dorada complex has 150 one- and two-bedroom and penthouse condominium apartments (each with a full kitchen), rentable when owners are away; interiors have attractive Dominican furnishings, though some are a bit the worse for wear. Features include the *Flamingo* restaurant (see *Eating Out*), a coffee shop, a cocktail lounge, live entertainment, a laundry, and a small supermarket, as well as a swimming pool, a super beach, and horseback riding; golf is on the adjoining Robert Trent Jones Sr. course. Playa Dorada (phone: 320-2019; 800-322-2388; fax: 320-3608).

Flamenco Beach With 310 rooms, this resort offers a wide range of activity: Horseback riding, bicycling, several water sports, tennis on two courts, and a daily activities program are all complimentary. Also on the premises: a golf course, a children's pool, two restaurants, a bar, and live shows nightly. Playa Dorada (phone: 320-5084; 800-545-8089; fax: 320-2775).

Jack Tar Village A club-like, all-inclusive complex, with 240 rooms and suites, catering to all—singles, couples, and families—in a lush setting on the sands at Playa Dorada. There are all kinds of activities—sailing, snorkeling, horseback riding, golf, tennis (two courts, one night-lit), a program for kids, and bicycling. There's also a restaurant and a pool-side grill. The casino is open to the public. Playa Dorada (phone: 320-3800; 800-999-9182; fax: 320-4161).

Playa Dorada Promoted as "a luxury beach resort," this all-inclusive place has 254 deluxe rooms with terraces, balconies, and contemporary furnishings. The public areas have island-Victorian decor. With three restaurants, a pool with swim-up bar, full water sports center, lighted tennis courts, golf on the Robert Trent Jones Sr. course, horseback riding, a piano bar, disco, casino, and nightly entertainment. Request an ocean-view room. 102 Av. 12 de Julio, Playa Dorada (phone: 320-3988; 800-545-8089; fax: 320-1190).

Villas Doradas A first class all-inclusive resort with 207 rooms and suites, it has a pool and kiddie pool, two tennis courts, three restaurants (one features Chinese food), and three bars. There's a beach, water sports (many of which are included in the rate), a jogging track, bicycling, horseback riding, and golf available within the complex. Playa Dorada (phone: 320-3000; 800-545-8089; fax: 320-4790).

MODERATE

Victoria With 190 rooms and suites, this resort within the Playa Dorada complex has a restaurant, piano bar, and pool. Complimentary tennis is available at a nearby hotel. Golf course and private beach are within walking distance.

Rates include water sports, horseback riding, and bicycling. Playa Dorada (phone: 320-1200; fax: 320-4862).

SOSÚA

EXPENSIVE

Sand Castle Perched atop a cliff above the water is this 240-room, pink, Moorish-style, all-inclusive resort. There are two pools, two tennis courts (with five more a short walk away), a fitness center, four restaurants, five bars, plus a disco, a shopping arcade, and meeting facilities. A full program of water sports is available. All rooms have cable TV. Puerto Chiquito Beach (phone: 571-2420; 800-446-5963; fax: 571-2000).

Sosúa By-The-Sea Right on Sosúa Beach, these 81 studios and apartments with rattan furnishings overlook either a swimming pool or the ocean. There also are two restaurants. Sosúa Bay (phone: 571-3222; 800-531-7043; fax: 571-3020).

MODERATE

Casa Marina Directly on the beach, this 202-room hotel is set amid lush vegetation. Guests can enjoy a pool, a Jacuzzi, cable TV, and the on-premises restaurant. *Casa Marina* also operates the 32-room *Club Marina* just around the corner, a small, cozy inn with a bar (but no restaurant), a pool, and a Jacuzzi. Sosúa Bay (phone: 571-3690; fax: 571-3110).

La Esplanada On the outskirts of Sosúa, this all-inclusive resort has 210 rooms, more than half of which are junior suites. Activities include windsurfing, tennis, and volleyball; there's also a pool and a playground. Baby-sitting services are offered. The atmosphere is less crowded and more relaxed than at most of the other resorts. Calle Pedro Clisante (phone: 571-3333; 800-423-6902; fax: 571-3922).

Hotel Coralillo Overlooking Sosúa Bay, this establishment offers great views, a charming Spanish atmosphere, and direct access to the beach. Sixty-five guestrooms, including five cabañas, are set amid gardens. Rooms do not have telephones, and only the cabañas have TV sets. There's also a pool, an outdoor dining terrace, a pizzeria, and a restaurant. 1 Calle Alejo Martínez (phone: 571-2645; fax: 571-2095).

INEXPENSIVE

Tropix Small and casual, this comfy getaway has 10 rooms, each with a refrigerator, clustered around a pool and beautifully maintained gardens. Only some of the rooms are air conditioned (the others have fans), and there are no telephones or TV sets. There's a communal kitchen, and from December through August an inexpensive prix fixe dinner, served alfresco, draws guests and non-guests alike. The beach is a short walk away. Off the main highway between Puerto Plata and Sosúa (phone: 571-2291).

CABARETE

MODERATE

Punta Goleta This distinctive property is a complete resort across from the beach. Its 126 large, attractive rooms have terraces and are decorated with local contemporary art, but there are no telephones. Facilities include horseback riding, a pool, a restaurant, beach and pool bars, and even a lagoon for rowboating. Windsurfing, Cabarete's main attraction, is available, as are two lighted tennis courts, three racquetball courts, and a disco. Playa Cabarete (phone: 571-0700; fax: 571-0707).

PLAYA GRANDE

EXPENSIVE

Caribbean Village Playa Grande This new, 300-room resort overlooks one of the prettiest beaches in the Caribbean. All rooms have cable TV and balconies with a view of either the ocean or the 18-hole Robert Trent Jones Sr. golf course, which was still under construction at press time. There's also a pool, beach club, cafeteria, and restaurant. Playa Grande (phone: 582-1170; fax: 582-6094).

COSTAMBAR–COFRESÍ

EXPENSIVE

Cofresí In a spectacular setting by the sea on the northern "Amber Coast," this all-inclusive resort offers 192 rooms, two pools, two tennis courts, an hour of horseback riding on the beach, all meals and drinks at the restaurant, a bar, a disco, and nightly shows. Rooms are basic: They're not air conditioned, and only some have fans, though there are pleasant ocean breezes; there are no TV sets either. Go for the sports and pools, or visit the property with a daily pass that includes meals, drinks, and use of facilities. This place fills up with Europeans and Canadians in winter, so book early. Playa Cofresí (phone: 586-2898; fax: 586-8064).

Villas Marlena An apartment hotel offering 33 immaculate studios and one-, two-, and three-bedroom units with kitchenettes, but without air conditioning or telephones. There's a pool, a restaurant, and a bar. A five-minute walk from the beach. Playa Costambar (phone: 586-5393; fax: 586-5373).

ELSEWHERE IN THE COUNTRY

EXPENSIVE

Bávaro Beach At the eastern end of the island, this five-hotel complex with 1,952 rooms offers just about everything: five pools, an 18-hole golf course, six tennis courts, 14 restaurants, 18 bars and lounges, and all kinds of water sports. The *Bávaro Beach* and *Bávaro Garden* hotels are on the beach, the

Bávaro Casino is near the casino, and the *Bávaro Golf* and the new *Bávaro Palace* are near the golf course. Rates include breakfast and dinner; the *Bávaro Palace* is all-inclusive. Bávaro Beach, near Punta Cana (phone: 686-5797; 800-879-8687; fax: 686-5680).

Decameron This all-inclusive resort offers 292 air conditioned rooms with kitchenettes set in Victorian-style four-story buildings, a good beach across the street, a variety of beach activities, a pool, a fitness center, and three tennis courts. There's also a casino, a restaurant, a nightclub, and a disco. Juan Dolio, about 45 minutes from Santo Domingo (phone: 526-2009; fax: 526-2310).

Gran Bahía Perched on a bluff on the Samaná Peninsula, this Victorian-style hostelry boasts two sand beaches. There are 96 rooms and suites, two all-weather lighted tennis courts, a nine-hole golf course, a pool, horseback riding, croquet, a fitness center, and a private dock with a boat for fishing. Most water sports are complimentary. An unusual activity is watching whales mate in the bay. Pluses include a dining room serving continental fare, a café for dining alfresco, and a piano lounge. No children under age five permitted. Samaná (phone: 538-3111; fax: 538-2764).

Metro Set in three buildings amid tropical gardens on the beach, the 220 rooms face either the sea or the pool. Facilities include two restaurants, a beach bar, two lighted clay tennis courts, a marina, a pool, and a kiddie pool. Lessons in Spanish and merengue are offered. Juan Dolio (phone: 526-2811; fax: 526-1808).

Punta Cana Beach The beauty of this resort is its location—on 2,200 feet of white sand beach dotted with coconut palms. Each building is designed in an eclectic mix of island-Victorian architecture, thatch roofs, and Greek columns. The 350 studio rooms, suites, and villas have a tropical decor, with Dominican marble tiles and wicker furniture, kitchenettes, and balconies. All-inclusive rates cover breakfast and dinner, plus a roster of activities such as tennis, boat rides, theme parties, and bicycling. Also available are snorkeling trips, deep-sea fishing excursions, and horseback riding nearby. Guests can dine either outdoors (at lobster barbecues and Dominican pig roasts), or more formally at the *Mama Venezia* restaurant. There are evening performances by folkloric groups, a piano bar, and merengue and disco dancing until the wee hours. Other facilities include an 18-hole golf course (which was scheduled for completion at press time), a marina, four tennis courts, a huge pool with a swim-up bar, a shopping center, a health club, and a casino. Punta Cana (phone: 541-2714; fax: 541-2286).

MODERATE

Club Mediterranée A 600-room village of three-story bungalows facing long, white, thickly palm-studded beaches. Rooms have no telephones or TV sets. There's a central entertainment complex, a freshwater pool, three restaurants, and a disco. Included in the rates are tennis (10 courts, including five lighted), water sports, a circus workshop (trapeze, tightrope, clowning), group games (including soccer), nightly entertainment, and all meals (with wine or beer; alcoholic drinks outside of meals are additional). There's also a highly regarded Mini-Club for children, and those under five stay free at certain times of year. Optional local excursions cost extra. Punta Cana (phone: 686-5500; 800-CLUB-MED; fax: 686-2896).

Hamaca Beach At Boca Chica, the closest beach to Santo Domingo, this 256-room resort offers its guests both the cosmopolitan attractions of a major city and the natural pleasures of the beach. The well-appointed rooms, good restaurant, hot, jazzy nightlife, and land and water sports combine to make this a fun place to stay. Boca Chica Beach (phone: 523-4611; 800-472-3985; fax: 523-6767).

El Portillo Beach Club This property is still charmingly rustic, even though it has been converted to an all-inclusive resort. On a beautiful beach called Las Terrenas, there are 171 rooms (none with telephones, TV sets, or air conditioning, though they have fans), sailing, windsurfing, two tennis courts, and volleyball. Liquor and food are available to guests throughout the day. Av. Francia, Samaná (phone: 688-5715 or 688-5749; fax: 685-0457).

Talanquera Located on the sunny south coast, this is a contemporary enclave of 275 rooms and one- and two-bedroom villas. There are two tennis courts, horseback riding, bicycling, a solarium, a pool, water sports on a private beach, a bar, a cafeteria, and a restaurant. Linked in combination packages with *El Embajador* in town. Juan Dolio (phone: 526-1510; fax: 541-8431).

INEXPENSIVE

Punta Garza A cluster of small beachfront cottages with 151 rooms, it's clean and pleasant, with a market and nice beach nearby. Some rooms are air conditioned, while others have fans, but there are no telephones or TV sets. A pool, restaurant, bar, and disco complete the picture. Juan Dolio (phone: 526-3506; fax: 526-3814).

EATING OUT

Native Dominican cooking is appealing rather than wildly tempting. Beef can be expensive (Dominicans raise fine cattle, but export most of the meat). Still, there's lots of very fresh fish and seafood, in addition to island-grown tomatoes, lettuce, papaya, mangoes, passion fruit, and citrus fruits, all of which are delicious. Roast pork and goat are big local favorites, as are *chicharrones* (crisp pork rinds), *chicharrones de pollo* (small pieces of fried chicken), and fried *yuca* (cassava). Dominicans also are fond of *sopa criolla dominicana,* a native soup of meat and vegetables; *pastelón,* a baked vegetable cake; *sancocho,* a stew made with anywhere from seven to 18 ingredients; *mero* (bass) done in half a dozen delicious ways; and such Latin

American standbys as arroz con pollo (chicken with rice) and *pastilitos* (meat pies). Two desserts are stellar: *cocoyuca,* a *yuca* flan with chunks of coconut, and *majarete,* a delicious corn pudding. (*Note:* Dominicans like their coffee strong, and decaffeinated is sometimes hard to find.)

Local beers, including Dominican Presidente, Quisqueya, and Bohemia, are first-rate; so are rum drinks (Brugal and Bermúdez are the local brand names to remember); rum *añejo*—dark and aged—on the rocks makes a good after-dinner drink.

Dress is often informal, although better restaurants discourage shorts. It's best to check ahead to find out if a jacket is required. At places we list as expensive, expect to pay $60 or more for two, including drinks, tax, and tip; at moderate places, $40 to $60; and at inexpensive places, $40 and less. By law, a 10% service charge is added to all bills; reward extra-special service with an additional tip. There's also an 8% food-and-beverage tax. Still, dining out is surprisingly inexpensive. Unless otherwise noted, all restaurants listed below are open for lunch and dinner. All telephone numbers are in the 809 area code unless otherwise indicated.

SANTO DOMINGO

EXPENSIVE

El Alcázar In the *Santo Domingo* hotel, this dining spot is a treat for the eyes and the palate. Designed by Oscar de la Renta in a Moorish motif, it sparkles with tiny mirrors and antique mother-of-pearl; yards and yards of tenting fabric are overhead. A different elaborate international lunch buffet is served each day; elegant continental dinners each evening. Reservations advised. Major credit cards accepted. Av. Independencia and Av. Abraham Lincoln (phone: 221-1511).

La Briciola Formerly *Il Buco,* this is one of the newest restaurants in the capital, serving Italian fare in a Spanish colonial atmosphere just steps away from the *Catedral de Santa María la Menor.* The restaurant's three owners already serve up delicious pasta in three *Briciola* restaurants in Italy; this is their first branch outside Milan. Open for dinner only; closed Mondays. Reservations advised. Major credit cards accepted. 152-A Arzobispo Meriño (phone: 688-5055).

Café St. Michel First class continental and Caribbean food and ambience are found here. The escargots and steak tartare are excellent. Open daily. Reservations advised on weekends. Major credit cards accepted. 24 Calle Lope de Vega (phone: 562-4141).

Figaro Italian food, prepared in an open kitchen, is served at this trattoria-style spot in the *Jaragua Renaissance.* Choices range from eggplant parmigiana to tournedos Rossini. A delicious vegetable lasagna on the regular menu is also prepared, on specified nights, according to the requirements of the resort's spa menu. Try the creamy corn pudding for dessert. Dinner only;

closed Sundays. Reservations advised. Major credit cards accepted. 367 Av. George Washington (phone: 221-2222).

Jai-Alai This eatery features Peruvian and Dominican fare. Delicious seafood (try the Peruvian ceviche) is served in a simple setting with tables outdoors and in. Evenings, there's guitar music, sometimes with a Spanish sing-along. Open daily. Reservations unnecessary. Major credit cards accepted. 411 Av. Independencia (phone: 685-2409).

Lina Lina herself came from Spain, was once Trujillo's personal chef, and left to open her own place in the *Gran Hotel Lina.* International fare with a strong Spanish accent is featured; everyone talks about the paella. The decor is contemporary, the food, great—especially shrimp dishes and *mero* (bass) done several ways, including *à la zarzuela,* in a casserole and faintly flavored with Pernod. Open daily. Reservations advised. Major credit cards accepted. Av. Máximo Gómez and Av. 27 de Febrero (phone: 563-5000).

Manhattan Grill The *Jaragua Renaissance*'s premier eatery, which is a member of the prestigious Chaîne des Rôtisseurs, offers steaks, lamb, and lobster prepared in an open kitchen. The service is attentive. Dinner only; closed Mondays. Reservations advised. Major credit cards accepted. 367 Av. George Washington (phone: 221-2222).

La Piazzetta Italian choices served in a gaily decorated dining room, featuring comfortable wicker chairs and murals of tropical plants. Antipasto is served all day. Try the *penne Cavour*—pasta with ham and mushrooms in a cream sauce. Open daily for dinner. Reservations unnecessary. Major credit cards accepted. At the *Hispaniola Hotel,* Av. Independencia and Av. Abraham Lincoln (phone: 221-7111).

Reina de España A highly praised restaurant featuring international fare, with creole and Spanish specialties. The mixed seafood grill and paella are extremely popular. Open daily. Reservations necessary on Fridays and Saturdays. Major credit cards accepted. 103 Calle Cervantes (phone: 685-2588).

Vesuvio I One of the best Italian restaurants this side of Italy. The irresistible—and always fresh—fare includes seafood, pasta, homemade cheese, meat, a feast of antipasto, and a dessert tray that will dissolve even the firmest willpower. Open daily. Reservations advised on Fridays and Saturdays. Major credit cards accepted. 521 Av. George Washington (phone: 221-3333).

MODERATE

Crucero del Mar In business since the 1920s, this restaurant at the far eastern end of the *malecón* is a true find. The location is ideal—close to the colonial district, but far from the crowds—but it's the food that will bring you back. All the local seafood dishes are delicious, and the grouper stuffed with shrimp or lobster and covered with just enough hot sauce is out of this world. If a waiter recommends something, try it. Open daily. Reservations unnecessary. MasterCard and Visa accepted. 27 Av. George Washington (phone: 682-1368).

Fonda de la Atarazana In a restored colonial building across from the *Alcázar,* this is the ideal lunch spot on a shopping/sightseeing day. It's highly regarded for its native menu (try the pork and lobster dishes). At night, musicians perform on the back terrace. Open daily. No reservations. Major credit cards accepted. 5 La Atarazana (phone: 689-2900).

Jardín de Jade Elegant, spacious, leisurely, authentically Asian—and less expensive than you'd think from the atmosphere. The chef woks his way expertly through five-, seven-, and 10-course meals; specialties include Peking duck and shrimp with Chinese black bean sauce. Open daily. Reservations advised. Major credit cards accepted. In the *El Embajador* hotel, Av. Sarasota (phone: 221-2131).

Mesón de la Cava This have-to-see-it-to-believe-it restaurant is in a natural cave, complete with stalagmites and stalactites. The chef's meat dishes are his pride. It's a popular hangout, with good merengue, folkloric entertainment, and disco music nightly. Open daily. Reservations advised. Major credit cards accepted. 1 Av. Mirador del Sur (phone: 533-2818, 533-4840, or 532-2615).

Vesuvio II Known as *Vesuvito,* the little brother of *Vesuvio I* (see above) serves pasta, pizza, and shrimp that are delectable. Open daily; especially popular at lunch. No reservations. Major credit cards accepted. 17 Av. Tiradentes (phone: 562-6060).

INEXPENSIVE

La Fromagerie A popular spot for French fondue and creole cooking in a modern atmosphere. Open daily. Reservations advised. Major credit cards accepted. In *Plaza Criolla,* Av. 27 de Febrero at the corner of Máximo Gómez in front of *Olympic Park* (phone: 567-8606).

Grand Café Adjacent to and owned by the same people as *Café St. Michel* (see above), this establishment features light café fare with a DJ nightly and live jazz and rock Wednesday nights. Open daily for dinner. Reservations unnecessary. Major credit cards accepted. 26 Calle Lope de Vega (phone: 541-6655).

PUERTO PLATA

EXPENSIVE

De Armando Guests at Armando Rodríguez Pelegrin's award-winning restaurant feel as though they're dining in an elegant home. The service is topnotch, and the food is splendid. The menu features nine soups (try the delicious pumpkin), super ceviche, steaks, and heavenly lobster *atlántica* in a special house sauce. Two of the desserts are themselves worth the visit: *cocoyuca* (a flan with chunks of coconut) and *majarete* (a traditional corn pudding). A guitar trio serenades nightly. Open daily. Reservations advised in high season. Major credit cards accepted. 23 Av. Mota (phone: 586-3418).

La Condesa In the *Club on the Green,* this elegant dining room features the tenderest local beef and the freshest fish and seafood on its continental menu. The wine list, which is quite lengthy, includes some excellent Chilean vintages. Jackets required. Open daily. Reservations advised during holiday seasons. Major credit cards accepted. Playa Dorada (phone: 586-5350).

Flamingo At the *Dorado Naco,* this is one of the best eating spots in Puerto Plata. Try the medallions of beef, veal, and chicken in a medley of three sauces. Open daily for dinner. Reservations advised. Major credit cards accepted. Playa Dorada (phone: 320-2019).

Neptune With the waves crashing against the windows and a statue of the god of the sea in plain view, this is the ideal place to dine on seafood, although the chicken pâté appetizer and the shish kebab also are excellent. Open daily. Reservations advised. Major credit cards accepted. This *Puerto Plata Beach* resort's restaurant is right on the beach, just across the *malecón* from the hotel (Av. Malecón; phone: 586-4243).

Roma II This cozy spot offers excellent service and a huge selection of pizzas—with toppings including olives and garlic or even ham and pineapple. The menu also includes fish soup, paella, lobster, and shrimp. Open daily. No reservations. Major credit cards accepted. Av. Beller at Av. Emilio Prud'homme (phone: 586-3904).

INEXPENSIVE

Porto Fino An Italian eatery with casual indoor/outdoor dining and a fluorescent-green decor. Try the heavenly lasagna or some of the Dominican dishes. Crab creole with French fries is a bargain. Open daily. Reservations unnecessary. Major credit cards accepted. Av. Hermanas Mirabal (phone: 586-2858).

Wienerwald One of several beachside cafés that are great for snacks. This one, with just a few tables facing the ocean, is also the best breakfast place in town. Go for owner Hansi's Austrian omelette, homemade strawberry jam, and the friendly staff. Sandwiches, soups, and Wiener schnitzel are also on the bill of fare. Open daily until 2 AM. No reservations. No credit cards accepted. Long Beach (phone: 586-2551).

SOSÚA

INEXPENSIVE

Tree Tops Lounge An airy, upstairs meeting place for drinks and backgammon. The decor is tropical, with rattan, ceiling fans, and lots of greenery. Order a pizza from the pizzeria downstairs (15 varieties from which to choose) and relax with a piña-banana colada, the house specialty. Open daily from 4 PM to 3 AM. Reservations unnecessary. No credit cards accepted. Calle Pedro Clisante (phone: 571-2141).

ELSEWHERE IN THE COUNTRY

EXPENSIVE

Casa del Río Perched on a cliff, with breathtaking views of river and valley, this *Casa de Campo* eatery provides a rustic setting for nicely done seafood dishes, along with glazed duck, roast lamb in hazelnut sauce, and veal in lemon sauce. Open daily for dinner only (the restaurant may close for some time in October). Reservations necessary. Major credit cards accepted. Altos de Chavón (phone: 523-3333, ext. 2345).

Giacosa Mediterranean food is featured in this cozy spot on the second floor of a stone building. Try the risotto with squid, the roast lamb, or the veal medaillons with wild mushroom sauce. Open daily for dinner only. Reservations advised. Major credit cards accepted. Altos de Chavón (phone: 523-8466).

La Piazzetta Ensconced in *Casa de Campo*'s re-created 16th-century village above the winding green Chavón River, this *ristorante* supplies a romantic change of scene. Mood and food are elegant Italian, with excellent pasta, steaks (try the filet mignon with green peppercorn sauce), seafood, and a good wine list, plus violin music and candlelight. Open daily for dinner. Reservations necessary. Major credit cards accepted. Altos de Chavón (phone: 523-3333).

MODERATE

Atarraya Catch a great sunset and a great meal at this gem of a restaurant overlooking the Chavón River. Specialties at the open-air eatery include steaks, pasta, and seafood. Closed Mondays; no lunch weekdays. Reservations advised. Major credit cards accepted. Boca de Chavón, just outside of Altos de Chavón (phone: 545-1139).

De América Generous portions of fresh and beautifully prepared seafood, creole dishes, and international fare are served in a charming atmosphere (with local art and ceiling fans). Popular with the locals, this place also has great margaritas and good service. Closed Sundays. Reservations necessary. Major credit cards accepted. 52 Calle Castillo Marqués, La Romana (phone: 556-4582).

Shish Kabab What's a nice Middle Eastern restaurant like this doing in a small eastern Caribbean sugar mill town? Well, a Jordanian chef married a Dominican woman, and now they make beautiful lamb and beef kebabs, *kipes* (Middle Eastern meatballs rolled in wheat and fried), and *pasteles en* *hojas* (Dominican spiced ground meat wrapped in plantain dough and cooked in a plantain leaf) together. They also do great shakes (banana, pineapple, papaya, orange) and a luscious concoction of orange juice, milk, sugar, and vanilla called *morir soñando* (literally, "to die dreaming"). Closed Mondays. No reservations. No credit cards accepted. 32 Calle Castillo Marqués, La Romana (phone: 556-2737).

INEXPENSIVE

Café del Sol An open-air place for pizza and ice-cream extravaganzas. Open daily. No reservations. Major credit cards accepted. Altos de Chavón (phone: 523-3333).

WORTH A DETOUR

The picturesque fishing village of Bayahibe, about 20 miles from *Casa de Campo,* has an excellent beach and several open-air restaurants that serve locally caught fish and lobster. Excursions to Bayahibe can be arranged at *Casa de Campo.*

Grenada

Grenada has been called "all the Caribbean islands in miniature" for good reason. Like so many of its neighbors, it is of volcanic origin, it is endowed with lush green mountains and beautiful beaches, it was discovered by Columbus, and it has had a dramatic history, from the seesawing French-English struggles of the 17th and 18th centuries to its own 20th-century quest for identity and independence.

Columbus found Conception Bay—now called Levera Beach—at the island's northern tip in 1498. Though whether he actually came ashore is open to debate, it is certain that he never explored the island in depth. (That failure is ironic in that, of all the islands he was to visit, Grenada came closest to meeting his original goal—a source of spices accessible by sailing west from Europe instead of east.) Spanish sailors dubbed the island Granada because its hills reminded them of home. The French, in their turn, referred to it as Grenade; and the British made the final adjustment to Grenada (pronounced Gren-*ay*-da).

In the century and a half that followed its discovery by Columbus, neither the British nor the French were able to establish settlements on the island. It was not until 1650 that a party of 200 Frenchmen sailed from Martinique and succeeded in purchasing land from the chief of the Carib people living there—literally for some glass beads and a selection of metal knives and hatchets. Soon the Carib, realizing their chief's mistake, began a futile struggle to retake the island from the French. After a series of battles, the 40 remaining Carib men threw the tribe's women and children over the northern precipice (now called Morne des Sauteurs, or Carib's Leap) and followed them to their deaths on the jagged rocks below.

But this bloody event did not give the French undisputed possession of the island. The familiar French-British conflict began anew on Grenada. Amassing troops at opposite ends of the island, the two nations built substantial fortifications and battled stubbornly for decades. The capital city of St. George's is flanked by two impressive historic landmarks: *Fort George,* built by the French in 1705, is on a promontory overlooking the harbor, and overlooking the town on the southern part of the island is *Fort Frederick,* begun by the French and completed by the British after they took control of the island as a result of the 1783 Treaty of Versailles. Grenada became a Crown Colony in 1877. After an abortive attempt to form a federation with nine other UK-associated islands, Grenada was declared a British Associated State in 1967.

During the 1960s Grenada emerged as one of the eastern Caribbean's first tourist destinations. St. George's, with a superb natural harbor, is perhaps the most beautiful Caribbean town. In addition, there are lovely mountains, waterfalls, colorful flowers, fine white and black sand beaches, and

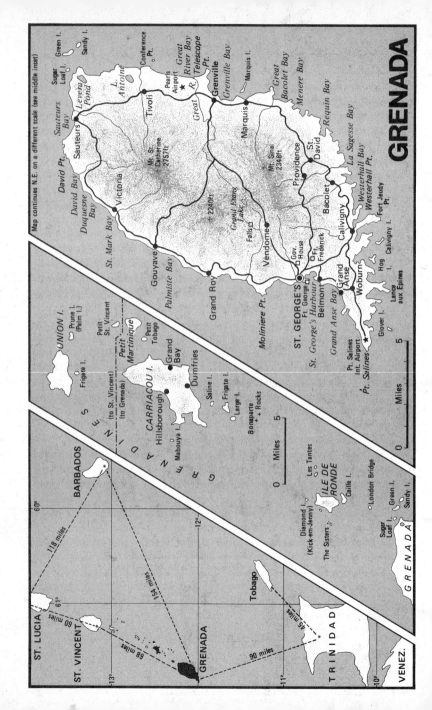

GRENADA

Map continues N.E. on a different scale (see middle inset)

Green I.

Sugar Loaf I.

Sandy I.

Conference Pt.

Great River Bay

Telescope Pt.

Sauteurs Bay

David Pt.

Levera Pond

L. Antoine

Pearls Airport

Great R.

Grenville Bay

Marquis I.

Great Bacolet Bay

Menere Bay

David Bay

Duquesne Bay

Sauteurs

Tivoli

Mt. St. Catherine 2757ft

Grenville

Victoria

Marquis

St. Mark Bay

+2240ft

Grand Etang Lake

Mt. Sinai 2348ft

Providence

St. David

La Sagesse Bay

Gouyave

Falls

Vendome

Bacolet

Westerhall Bay

Westerhall Pt.

Palmiste Bay

Gov. House

Ft. Frederick

Calivigny

Fort Jeudy Pt.

Grand Roy

Grand Anse

Belmont

Woburn

Hog

Calivigny I.

Moliniere Pt.

ST. GEORGE'S Ft. George

Grand Anse Bay

Glover I.

Lance aux Epines

St. George's Harbour

Pt. Salines Int. Airport

Pt. Salines

0   5

Miles

UNION I.

Prune I. (Palm I.)

Petit St. Vincent

Frigate I.

Petit Tobago

Petit Martinique

(to St. Vincent)

(to Grenada)

Grand Bay

Dumfries

Saline I.

Frigate I.

CARRIACOU I.

Hillsborough

Large I.

Mabouya I.

Bonaparte Rocks

G R E N A D I N E S

0   5

Miles

Les Tantes

ILE DE RONDE

Diamond I. (Kick-'em-Jenny)

Caille I.

The Sisters

London Bridge

Sugar Loaf I.

Green I.

Sandy I.

G R E N A D A

60°

BARBADOS

61°

ST. LUCIA

ST. VINCENT

60°

118 miles

154 miles

58 miles

60 miles

12°

13°

GRENADA

Tobago

Trinidad

45 miles

90 miles

11°

10°

VENEZ.

TRINIDAD

the sea. But the early 1970s brought the issue of independence, and with it an identity crisis that split island politics right down the middle. In late 1973 and early 1974 a general strike actually closed the island down, but in February 1974, independence was at last proclaimed, and the island slowly started to recover. Unfortunately, Prime Minister Sir Eric Gairy proved a less than inspiring administrator, seemingly more interested in black magic and UFOs than in island economics. When his dictatorial regime was ousted in March 1979 by Maurice Bishop's New Jewel Movement, hopes rose. But they fell abruptly once Prime Minister Bishop, a protégé of Cuban president Fidel Castro, invited Cuban military advisers to Grenada. Visitors began staying away.

On October 25, 1983, units of the US Marines and Army landed on Grenada to spearhead the rout of a combined Grenadian/Cuban defense force. Along with forces from Barbados, Dominica, Jamaica, St. Lucia, and St. Vincent, the US troops deposed the former colleagues of Maurice Bishop, who had had Bishop assassinated a week earlier for not being radical enough. The lessons of its turmoil have been deeply impressed on the country, especially a keen shock at Grenadians having killed Grenadians (many died with Bishop prior to the intervention). More than one American tourist has been told, "You rescued us."

Grenada's civil authority is now on its own; the US and eastern Caribbean troops—supplemental police, really—have departed. Political stability appears assured. Since March 1990 Nicholas Brathwaite of the National Democratic Congress has been prime minister; his plan is to keep the flow of visitors rising without making major changes to the island.

Bolstered by US aid, substantial improvements in basic services and island infrastructure have been made, and the outlook is for steady, moderate tourism growth. Touch-tone telephones and cable TV are no longer curiosities, and paved roads have halved travel times to most parts of the island. The once controversial Cuban-constructed airport runway at Point Salines now lies next to a full-fledged, comfortable, modern international terminal building, complete with duty-free shopping. It is not surprising that Grenada's tourism numbers have been growing steadily each year; recently, an increasing number of European visitors have contributed to the growth.

For visitors who have come to love the island as it was (and still mostly is), perhaps slow change is best. Grenada retains a lush, unspoiled character that any neighbor nation might covet.

Grenada At-a-Glance

FROM THE AIR

Grenada, the southernmost island of the Windward Antilles, 90 miles north of Trinidad, looks like an oval fish swimming northeast with its mouth open as though to swallow the tiny islands of the Grenadines strung between it and the island of St. Vincent 68 miles northeast. The "mouth" of the fish is Sauteurs Bay; its tail is the beach-bordered peninsula called Point Salines, extending below the capital of St. George's (pop. 11,000) and forming the island's southeastern tip.

The island is only 21 miles long and 12 miles wide at its widest point; its 120 square miles encompass green jungle-covered mountains, racing rivers and streams, waterfalls and lakes, and a ring of beaches of extraordinary beauty. The central mountain range, reaching heights of over 2,000 feet, divides the island diagonally in half, with stretches of desert and cactus to the southwest and cane fields, coconut groves, and banana and spice plantations stretching from the southeast to the northwest.

The highest, wettest, coolest, most densely forested areas of the island are found near the city of Grenville, halfway up the eastern coast. The route from there to the southwest, where most of the hotels are located, passes through the island's driest section. The drive from *Point Salines International Airport* to the hotel district takes 10 minutes.

Fifteen miles off Grenada's northern tip lie the nation's major dependencies, Carriacou and Petit Martinique, which are part of the island group known as the Grenadines.

SPECIAL PLACES

ST. GEORGE'S Grenada's capital is one of the Caribbean's most picturesque ports. Its landlocked inner harbor is actually the crater of a dead volcano. The waterfront, known as the Carenage, is lined with pink, ocher, and brick-red commercial buildings and warehouses, many of which date from the 18th century. Behind them, narrow streets climb green hills dotted with neat red- and green-roofed houses. The Esplanade (or Outer Harbour) area of the city is on St. George's Bay; it's connected to the Carenage area via Sendall Tunnel, a one-way traffic and pedestrian passage cut through St. George's Point, which divides the harbor and the bay.

The French built St. George's in 1732, and French architecture—like the wrought-iron work along the Esplanade and Market Square—survives among the British Georgian–West Indian buildings in a charming blend of European and tropical island styles. Wood has been a forbidden building material since a number of disastrous fires in the island's earliest days, so most buildings are built of brick brought over as ballast on British trading ships.

The most appealing sights in St. George's are vistas of the city and harbor from high points around the town. If you're sightseeing by taxi, let the driver know you'd like to stop wherever the view is especially fine, such as the lookout point built at the *Fort George Cultural Landmark* downtown. Better still, take a good hour to walk and climb around the city (it's not very big), sampling the view whenever you please.

Make your first stop the *Grenada Board of Tourism* on the St. George's Pier (see *Tourist Information,* below), where you can pick up maps and sightseeing information. Walk westward along the edge of the Carenage, where schooners, sailboats, yachts, and dinghies are tied up to concrete posts containing old spiked cannon. Call at the *Grenada National Museum* (Young St.; phone: 440-3725), which offers both historic exhibits and a cool refuge on a too sunny day. The museum is closed Saturday afternoons and Sundays. Admission charge. Above, on the hill, stands the town's dominant structure, *Fort George* (Grand Etang Rd.; no phone), built by the French as *Fort Royal* in 1705; it is now the headquarters of the Grenada police force. On its ramparts, ancient cannon, still used for official salutes, are aimed out across the water. The fort is open daily. No admission charge.

From the fort, go back down the hill, turn right, and follow Young Street to the Carenage, then go right, right again, and left through Sendall Tunnel, built by the French in the 18th century. This is the west side of town, where the principal shops run along the waterfront Esplanade and up Granby Street. Follow Granby one block east to Market Square, where on Saturday mornings Grenadian women in bright cotton dresses, aprons, and wide straw hats pile their produce—mangoes, coconuts, spices, pineapples, and pawpaws (papayas), among others—on rough cloths and flour bags for sale. Also on the square, the *Straw Mart* offers crafts made of straw and coconut. (There are also tortoiseshell items here, but don't buy them; they cannot be imported into the US.)

From Market Square head east on Granby, which turns into Lucas, to *Fort Frederick* on Richmond Hill. Construction of the fort was started by the French in 1779 and completed by the British in 1791; its battlements command a magnificent view of the city and its harbors. Open daily. No admission charge (no phone). Nearby is *Government House,* the residence of the queen's official representative, the governor-general. It was built in the late 18th century; later additions—particularly the 1887 façade—are not all considered architectural triumphs. But the view of the port, the harbor, and the town is indisputably beautiful.

Turn back down Lucas Street. At the Church Street intersection, turn right up the hill to visit the Roman Catholic cathedral, where dark plaster saints oversee both petitioners and their prayers. Also on Church Street, left of Lucas, is the 168-year-old Anglican church. It's pink with heavy stained glass windows, frescoes, and stone memorial tablets carved in England and dedicated to British soldiers who fought against the French. Farther along Church Street, *St. Andrew's Presbyterian Church,* built in 1830, is crowned with the square-spired clock tower that's a trademark of the town skyline. After a visit (or an admiring glance in its direction), head back down the hill to the Carenage for lunch or a rum punch at *Rudolf's* or the *Nutmeg* (try one of their Nutmeg Special drinks), nearby restaurants popular with locals and visitors alike (see *Eating Out* for both).

Two lush spots not far from St. George's are worth visiting for their lavish landscapes. *Bay Gardens,* about a 20-minute drive east of town in the suburb of St. Paul, encompasses six dense acres of tropical flora and mostly feathered fauna (you may not see the island's favorite pripri birds, but you'll certainly hear them). For a small charge, a guided tour will introduce you to an abundance of exotic fruits and spices in their natural state. The feeling is a little like strolling through a primitive island painting. The gardens are open daily from 7 AM to sunset; no admission charge.

Annandale Falls are a 20-minute drive northeast of St. George's, just off Grand Etang Road. Here, young boys eagerly climb the surrounding tall trees to pluck orchids for visiting ladies (don't encourage them to dive off the top of the falls into the placid pool 50 feet below, which they do for tips—it's illegal and dangerous). Visitors can swim here, and the surrounding forest is great for exploring.

NORTH OF ST. GEORGE'S

To explore the spice country, coastal beaches, and villages of the island's northern reaches, head north out of St. George's along the western coastal road. You'll pass curving bays, small seaside settlements, and shores where fishermen with small boats and big nets bring in their catches.

A NOTE OF PERSPECTIVE

Most of Grenada's limited wealth flows to the southwest corner of the island, where tourism is concentrated. Grenadians are among the friendliest, most courteous people in the Caribbean, and a vast majority favored the US–East Caribbean intervention. But in the many small settlements in parishes north and east of St. George's, where most people are poor and have few immediate prospects for significant advancement, they are likely to be less outgoing and to resent being photographed without permission.

CONCORD FALLS Not far off the western coastal road, a turnoff leads to the falls, a wildly beautiful yet accessible picnic destination. Spread out your lunch (most hotels will be happy to pack one; order the night before) in a hideaway setting festooned with liana vines, feathery rock plants, giant elephant ears, and other greenery, while water cascades down a 50-foot fall into a blue-green pool. Afterward, you can swim beneath the waterfall, then hike along the river through the tropical forest to a more remote, second fall.

GOUYAVE Back on the western coastal road, head farther north to the village of Gouyave, which looks like an island painting, with weathered red-roofed houses along the sea wall dwarfed by the Anglican and Catholic churches behind them. Gouyave is a center of the nutmeg and mace industry (both are produced from a single fruit). The *Gouyave Processing Station,* where nutmeg is processed, is open to the public (closed Sundays; admission charge for guided tours; phone: 444-8337 or call the *Grenada Cooperative Nutmeg Association* at 440-2117). Just inland, on the *Dougaldston Estate,* you can see most of the island's spices growing naturally, and being sun-dried and sorted. Closed Sundays. No admission charge (phone: 444-8213).

SAUTEURS From Gouyave proceed along the coast to Sauteurs, at the north end of the island. Behind *St. Patrick's,* a Roman Catholic church, are the cliffs called Carib's Leap, where, in the 17th century, the last of the Carib Indians are said to have jumped to their death rather than submit to slavery under the French. East of Sauteurs is pretty, palm-edged Levera Beach, an ideal spot for a picnic and a swim (if the Atlantic is not in one of its occasionally rough moods). Nearby is the *Levera National Park and Bird Sanctuary,* with bird watching lookouts, and marked nature trails that lead around Levera Pond. Open daily. No admission charge (phone: 442-1018). The sulfurous Chambord Boiling Springs are also in this area. Not far south is the *River Antoine Rum Distillery* (phone: 442-7109), an amazing establishment dating from the 18th century and one of the last agro-industrial enterprises in the hemisphere still powered by a waterwheel. On weekdays the foreman is happy to provide guided tours and to explain the process of turning sugarcane into potent rum. No admission charge.

EXTRA SPECIAL

Lunch at Betty Mascoll's *Morne Fendue* is an ideal stop on any island tour. This plantation house, home to three generations of Betty's family, is worth a visit as much for her stories and pleasant presence as for the food, which is island fare, handsomely served and delicious. The menu might include *callaloo,* ginger chicken, savory pepper pot, vegetables from the garden, and homemade guava ice cream. A meal will cost about $20 per person, including drinks. Open for lunch only; closed Sundays. Reservations necessary. No credit cards accepted. Near Sauteurs, St. Patrick's Parish, a 90-minute drive from St. George's (phone: 442-9330).

GRENVILLE From Sauteurs head south along the east coast to Grenville, Grenada's second city. There are two lively markets here: the waterfront fish market, which does a brisk business every day except Sunday; and Saturday's fruit and vegetable market. Visitors are welcome at the spice factory at the edge of town, where spice baskets and aromatic souvenirs are sold. Closed Sundays. Admission charge (phone: 442-7241).

INLAND ROAD From Grenville turn inland toward the heart of the island along a road that passes small spice farms, young girls sorting nutmegs, and cacao plantations with trays of chocolate-brown pods drying in the sun. Follow the road as it winds up and up into the mountains, with each hairpin curve bringing a surprise view of lush, fern-covered hillsides, nutmeg trees brimming with yellow fruit, cacao and banana groves, and mountain streams tumbling toward the sea. The road reaches its peak at *Grand Etang National Park* (no phone), a national reserve filled with giant ferns, towering trees, and tropical flowers in a profusion of colors. If you are quiet—and lucky—

you may also see luminescent blue butterflies, mona monkeys, mongooses, and the emerald-throated hummingbird. Nature lovers can follow the path through the rain forest to Grand Etang Lake, a shimmering cobalt lake that fills the crater of Grenada's extinct volcano. The park also has a nature-oriented interpretation center, a snack bar, and a souvenir shop. It is closed Sundays; admission charge. The return trip down the same road offers tantalizing glimpses of blue-and-white-coved shoreline all the way to St. George's.

SOUTH OF ST. GEORGE'S

South of St. George's lie the superb beaches and rambling resorts of the Grand Anse and L'Anse aux Epines districts. To tour this end of the island, follow the Royal Drive, so named because it's the route along which Elizabeth II was escorted during her 1966 visit. Leaving St. George's, past *Government House* and the panoramic overlook at Richmond Hill, the drive proceeds down to Westerhall Point, a beautifully landscaped residential development on the southern coast, through the fishing village of Woburn, and the cane fields of Woodlands. At *La Sagesse Nature Center* (phone: 444-6458), there are plenty of trails, wild birds, a banana plantation with guided nature walks, and a lovely beach for relaxing. The center is open daily; no admission charge. Past the nature center, closer to the eastern side of the island, is Marquis Village, renowned for its expert straw weavers. Here artisans weave wild palm leaves into sturdy hats, baskets, handbags, and placemats.

GRENADINES

CARRIACOU One of Grenada's island dependencies, it lies 23 miles northeast of St. George's, a 13-square-mile retreat where Grenadians "get away from it all." It is a special favorite with yachtsmen. In winter the chain of hills extending down its center is fresh and green; in summer the land dries to pale beige, and islanders declare "leggo" season—when goats, cows, and sheep are let go to forage for themselves and gardeners guard their flowers with their lives. Whatever the season, Carriacou's attractions include excellent beaches and natural harbors (Tyrell Bay is especially beautiful), plus the prospect of relaxed living among people who seem genuinely to enjoy having visitors.

Ruins of greathouses in the hills testify to Carriacou's once-thriving sugar industry; now cotton, peanuts, and limes are grown on the island. Its strongest surviving heritages are African (most black islanders can trace their ancestry to a particular tribe) and Scottish. The McLarens, MacLaurences, McQuilkins, MacFarlands, and Comptons of Windward on the east side of the island still hand-build some of the Caribbean's finest sailing workboats. The sprinkling of goat's blood and holy water at launchings recognizes both cultural influences.

Excepting the annual August regatta—when 2,000 people have been known to squeeze themselves onto the island and 300 or 400 manage to dance all night—launchings are Carriacou's biggest parties, sometimes lasting for days. Otherwise, things are pretty quiet here. Visitors laze, swim, sail, snorkel, and dive (nearby Sandy Island has some interesting reef formations), search for seashells, poke about the ruins, and gather at dusk in Hillsborough, the island's only town. From his Hillsborough office, a senior executive officer, supervised by a parliamentary secretary, administers the affairs of both Carriacou and Petit Martinique, the island 3 miles due east.

PETIT MARTINIQUE The residents of this island have a reputation as master sailors (each year they carry off the lion's share of prizes from the regatta) and—some say—smugglers. Whether or not the latter is true, it has inspired some wonderful stories, such as this one, told by Frances Kay in *This—Is Carriacou:* "A very strict customs official from Grenada was sent to Petit Martinique to make a thorough check. When he arrived, he found the entire population standing mournfully around an open grave. 'Who died?' he asked. 'Nobody,' came the matter-of-fact reply. 'We dug it for you.'"

These days, Petit Martinique's approximately 600 French-descended inhabitants are polite, even pleasant, to sailors who drop anchor overnight in their harbor. But there are few accommodations for visitors on this 3-square-mile island. Privacy is still an important commodity.

Grenada's other island dependencies—Ile de Ronde, Kick-em-Jenny (possibly from *caye qui gêne,* or "troublesome shoal"), Green Bird, and Conference among them—are small, picturesque land dots, important only as landmarks for cruising yachtsmen. Other Grenadine islands are administered by St. Vincent, which serves as the administrative center for the entire chain.

EXTRA SPECIAL

Grenada's People-to-People program puts travelers in touch with Grenadians who have similar jobs, hobbies, and interests. Visitors may play a round of golf, go to a church service, have a traditional island meal, or simply see the sights with a local resident. People who have participated in this program have found it to be both enlightening and a lot of fun. There's no charge, though you might want to pick up part of the tab for any excursion. To make arrangements before arriving, contact *New Trends Tours,* PO Box 797, St. George's, Grenada, West Indies (phone: 444-1236; fax: 444-4836).

Sources and Resources

TOURIST INFORMATION

The *Grenada Board of Tourism* on the St. George's Pier in St. George's (phone: 440-2279 or 440-2001; fax: 440-6637) can supply information, maps, literature, and answers to visitors' questions. They also can brief you on excursions to and lodging on Carriacou and Petit Martinique. For information on Grenada tourist offices in the US see GETTING READY TO GO.

LOCAL COVERAGE Consult the *Grenadian Voice, Grenada Today,* or the *Informer,* the island's three weekly newspapers, for sports schedules and special events information. Books about Grenada and the West Indies can be found at *Sea Change Ltd.* on the Carenage, and at *St. George's Bookshop* on Halifax Street (see *Shopping* for both).

RADIO AND TELEVISION There are two television stations: GBC-TV (on channel 7 or 11), which carries CNN news, and Lighthouse TV (channel 5 or 13). There are four radio stations: GBC Radio (535 AM; 105.5 FM), Spice Capital Radio (90 FM), 1400 AM, and YSFM (96.3 FM and 101.7 FM), all of which broadcast local and international news and music.

TELEPHONE When calling from the US dial 1 + 809 (area code) + (local number). To call from another Caribbean island in the 809 area code, you also must dial 809 first, then the local number. From other islands the access code may vary, so contact the local operator. When calling on Grenada, dial only the local number. Dial 911 (throughout the island) for the police; for an ambulance, dial 434 in St. George's, 724 in St. Andrews Parish, 774 on Carriacou.

ENTRY REQUIREMENTS Visitors to Grenada must present a valid passport or proof of citizenship (a birth certificate or voter's registration card *plus* a photo ID), and an ongoing or return ticket. A departure tax of $14 is collected at the airport.

CLIMATE AND CLOTHES At the beach, the daytime temperatures stay close to 80F (27C) year-round, with cooling trade winds. In the mountains (around Grand Etang Lake, for example), it can be as much as 10 degrees cooler; you may even be glad you brought a light sweater along. During the rainy season (June to December), there's a shower for about an hour or so almost every day, and the countryside is at its greenest. Casual, lightweight resort clothes are most comfortable and appropriate for both men and women. Though bathing suits and short shorts are fine on the beach, they are frowned on in St. George's. In the evenings—especially during the winter season— people tend to dress up a bit for dinner in the better hotels and restaurants. But men can leave sports coats at home, and women should skip high heels. If you plan to hike around Grand Etang Lake, bring some sturdy sneakers.

MONEY Grenada's official currency is the Eastern Caribbean dollar (EC); at press time $1 US equaled approximately $2.70 EC. On the islands, prices are usually quoted in EC dollars, but sometimes shopkeepers will quote them in US dollars to US citizens in an effort to be helpful. Know which dollars are being quoted before committing to a purchase or a cab ride. Banking hours are 8 AM to 2 PM Mondays through Thursdays; 8 AM to noon and 2:30 to 5 PM on Fridays. Traveler's checks are accepted by stores, restaurants, and hotels; most honor major credit cards as well. No shops offer discounts for payment in US dollars. All prices in this chapter are quoted in US dollars unless noted otherwise.

LANGUAGE Grenada is a former British Crown Colony, and English is spoken everywhere with a Caribbean lilt. You occasionally may hear islanders speaking among themselves in their own patois—mostly French with some African words and rhythms mixed in.

TIME Grenada is on atlantic standard time, one hour ahead of eastern standard time (when it's noon in New York, it's 1 PM in Grenada); during daylight saving time, Grenada and New York are in sync.

CURRENT It's 230 volts, 50 cycles AC, so an adapter is needed for American appliances. Some hotels supply them, but it wouldn't hurt to bring one along.

TIPPING Hotels add a 10% service charge to your bill, which takes care of bellhops, waiters and waitresses, bartenders, and maids. If you visit a dining room at a hotel you're not staying at, or at non-hotel restaurants, tip 10% to 15% of the check. Taxi drivers do not expect tips unless they help you with your baggage at the airport (give $1 or so unless your load is very heavy).

GETTING AROUND

BUS The older models, painted kindergarten colors, take off from the Market Square in St. George's for all parts of the island, but since seats are boards, springs are hard to come by, and schedules are erratic, they aren't recommended for anything except photographs. Many visitors have taken to the minibuses that travel between island points and charge from $1.25 to $4.50 EC, depending on your destination.

CAR RENTAL A good idea if you enjoy exploring on your own. Reliable agencies include *McIntyre Bros.* (phone: 440-2044 or 444-2901), *Royston's* (phone: 444-4316), and *Spice Isle/Avis Rentals* (phone: 440-3936 or 440-2674). All will deliver cars to the airport and pick them up at the end of your stay. Visitors must obtain a local driving permit, which can be purchased from most car rental companies and at the fire station on the Carenage. Remember: Driving is on the *left,* British-style.

INTER-ISLAND FLIGHTS *BWIA* and *LIAT* (phone: 440-2796) both have flights to Grenada from Trinidad and Barbados; *LIAT* also flies between Antigua and Grenada (with as many as seven stops en route) and has daily flights to Carriacou. Also flying daily to Carriacou is *Airlines of Carriacou* (phone: 444-3549 or 444-2898). *New Trends Tours* (phone: 444-1236) offers flights to Union Island in the Grenadines with a return trip by schooner, and day trips to Margarita Island and Venezuela. *HelenAir* (phone: 444-2266 or 444-4199, ext. 290) provides air taxi service to nearby islands, as well as to St. Lucia, St. Vincent, and Barbados.

SEA EXCURSIONS The glass-bottom boats *Rhum Runner* and *Rhum Runner II* (phone: 440-2198 or 440-3422) sail from St. George's Harbour Saturdays at 7 PM for a 2½-hour sunset cocktail cruise; the fare includes rum punches and steel band music to watch fish by and limbo to. Trips to view the reef may be scheduled on the days when cruise ships are in port; call to check. The same operator offers snorkeling excursions on the 32-foot *Havadu*. *World Wide Watersports* (phone: 444-1339) offers glass-bottom boat tours, sunset cruises, and a popular calypso cruise.

Windward Islands Travel (phone: 444-4732) offers daily charters and tours to Carriacou. Also, freighters sail from Grenada to Carriacou five times a week, leaving anytime between 7 and 10 AM for the three- to four-hour trip. Check with the tourist board for details.

TAXI While taxi rates are fixed, the cabs are unmetered, so be sure to establish the price of the trip with the driver before getting into the cab (there's a surcharge at night). Although not specially trained as such, island taxi drivers are good guides and can tell you lots about the island. Hotels can arrange all-day, around-the-island cab tours; usually, the cabs are shared by two or three people, depending on the size of the car and how cozy you like to be. Water taxis will whisk you from the beach at Grand Anse to town and back—it's cheaper than a land taxi, but your feet might get wet.

TOURS *Henry's Tours, Ltd.* (phone: 444-5313) and *Arnold's Tours* (phone: 440-0531 or 440-2213) arrange custom excursions for adventurous and fit tourists who wish to hike into the interior for a picnic, to swim by a jungle waterfall that even few Grenadians see, or to visit lakes and other natural wonders. Hiking segments range from one hour to a half day. On Carriacou, the *Silver Beach* resort (see *Checking In*) offers 2½-hour tours of the island.

SPECIAL EVENTS

Carnival is Grenada's annual national festival, celebrated for four days and nights during the second week in August with lots of steel band and calypso music, processions, pageants, and beauty contests, and climaxing in a "jump-up" parade of bands, floats, and street dancers. Carriacouans prefer their own smaller but equally festive "old-fashioned" pre-*Lenten Carnival;* they really cut loose at their early August *Regatta.* Other holidays when banks and businesses are closed: *New Year's Day, Independence Day* (February 7), *Good Friday* (April 5 in 1996), *Easter Monday* (April 8 in 1996), *Labour Day* (first Monday in May), *Whitmonday* (May 27 in 1996), *Corpus Christi Day* (June 6 in 1996), *Emancipation Day* (first Monday and Tuesday in August), *Thanksgiving Day* (the fourth Monday of October, commemorating the intervention of US and other military forces against the Communist-backed People's Revolutionary Government), *Christmas,* and *Boxing Day* (December 26).

SHOPPING

The big-tag items are luxury imports (especially British) at prices that aren't literally duty-free, but close. The little-tag buys are uniquely Grenadian, such as the woven "spice baskets" full of fresh island-grown nutmeg, mace, cinnamon, cloves, and more. Roughly a thousand times more aromatic than those fading on the supermarket shelves back home, they make great souvenirs for yourself, or gifts for favorite cooks. *Straw Mart* (on Granby and Young Sts.; no phone) and market ladies have big supplies; *Sea Change Ltd.* (on the Carenage; phone: 440-3402) has individually packed spices; and the *Grand Anse Shopping Centre* has strolling spice vendors every day. As for imported buys, brand names like Liberty, Pringle, Waterford, Wedgwood, Bing & Grøndahl, and Dior—at 40% to 60% below stateside prices—will tempt you.

Of the three main shopping areas, the largest is on the Esplanade side of *Fort George* around Market Square and in the shops facing the harbor along Melville Street; the second is on the Carenage side along the waterfront and on Young Street; and the third, and fastest-growing, is in and near the *Grand Anse Shopping Centre,* handiest to hotels. Most shops are open from 9 AM to 5 PM weekdays, from 9 AM to 1 PM Saturdays, and closed Sundays. Some good places include the following:

Best Little Liquor Store Good selection of local rum, vodka, and gin, as well as imported wines and spirits. Two locations: the Carenage (phone: 440-2198) and *Point Salines International Airport* (phone: 440-3422).

Bon Voyage Duty-free crystal, china, watches, and jewelry. Located both on the Carenage (phone: 440-4217) and at the airport (phone: 444-4165).

Creation Arts and Crafts Craftwork by artisans from Grenada and other Caribbean islands, as well as Africa. Also features leather shoes and handbags, batik items, and jewelry. The Carenage (phone: 440-0570).

Frangipani Tie-dyed batik, patchwork apparel, and watercolors by local artists. The Carenage (no phone).

Gift Shop Well known for its duty-free crystal by Waterford, Orrefors, Lalique, and Daum; it also has Coalport and Wedgwood china, watches, and jewelry. In the *Grand Anse Shopping Centre* (phone: 444-4408).

Gifts Remembered Locally made handicrafts, straw work, and jewelry. Cross St. (phone: 440-2482).

Gitten's Duty Free Name-brand cosmetics and perfumes, including Clinique, Estée Lauder, Calvin Klein, Christian Dior, Oscar de la Renta, and Ralph Lauren. Located in the Carenage (phone: 440-3174) and in the departure lounge at the airport (phone: 444-4101, ext. 272).

Grand Bazaar One-of-a-kind, hand-painted play and party clothes. Considering the designs are originals, the prices are very reasonable. On the Carenage (phone: 440-3712).

Imagine High-quality gift items, crafts, and resortwear from Grenada and other islands. In the *Grand Anse Shopping Centre* (phone: 444-4028).

St. George's Bookshop Wide selection of news magazines and works by Caribbean writers. Halifax St. (phone: 440-2309).

Spice Island Perfumes Makes and sells scents and potpourris concocted from island flowers and spices. A real treat for the nose, and a great place to buy locally made perfumes, colognes, lotions, and even sunscreens. The Carenage (phone: 440-2006).

Tikal Cheerfully stocked with straw bags, hats, baskets, mats, rugs, crafted mobiles, shell jewelry, local pottery, and batik, plus some imported porcelain and glass. Easily the best shop in town for browsing. Young St. (phone: 440-2310).

Yellow Poui Run by Jim Rudin, formerly of New York City's *Museum of Modern Art,* this gallery displays the best artwork—be it paintings, sculpture, prints, or maps—from Grenada and neighboring Caribbean islands, as well as from North America. Above *Gifts Remembered* on Cross St. (phone: 440-3001).

SPORTS

Not surprisingly, considering the splendid white and black sand beaches and calm blue sea that surround it, Grenada's active sports life is centered on the shoreline and in the water.

BOATING Yachtsmen rate the sailing conditions from Grenada north through the Grenadines to St. Vincent as some of the best in the world. There are about 80 miles of coastline and about 65 bays. On a small scale, there are Sunfish, Sailfish, and Hobie Cats to rent for just-offshore fun on hotel beaches. For those venturing farther out, not only does St. George's have first-rate marina facilities, but Grenada is headquarters for a number of charter operations that can arrange skippered or bare-boat charters for a week or longer. Among them: *Grenada Yacht Services* (St. George's; phone: 440-2508 or 440-2883); *The Moorings* (Secret Harbour; phone: 444-4439 or 444-4549); *Go Vacations* (Prickly Bay; phone: 444-4924 or 444-4342); *Spice Island Marine Services* (L'Anse aux Epines; phone: 444-4257); and *Starwind Enterprises* (440-3678). Prices vary enormously according to size and style of boat, provisioning, crew, and so on, but fall by about 20% in summer.

CRICKET This cousin of US baseball is played from January to May on pitches (fields) ranging from exquisitely manicured greens like *Queen's Park* to vacant lots. Cricket is a spectator sport that is also a social event. For a schedule of upcoming matches, check with the tourist board or consult the sports section of the island newspaper.

GOLF The two-way view of the Atlantic and the Caribbean is the most noteworthy thing about the nine holes at the *Grenada Golf Club* in St. George's (phone: 444-4128).

HIKING A favorite islanders' pastime, accessible to visitors thanks to government encouragement and a supportive system of national parks. The tourist board will brief you on location of trails and level of expertise required, provide maps, and—with a day's notice—can put you in touch with expert guides. The *Grand Etang National Park* (see *Special Places*) has maps of marked nature trails (also see *Climbing and Hiking* in DIVERSIONS). Climbing Mt. Qua Qua along a well-marked footpath is a challenging afternoon's hike, and affords stunning views of the surrounding vistas. The Morne LaBaye Trail, which begins behind the national park, is a scenic journey through ferns, palms, and lush flowery vegetation. Several adventures involving hiking are offered by *Henry's Tours, Ltd.*, which also has the best trail maps and information (phone: 444-5313).

SCUBA DIVING AND SNORKELING Along the submerged reef that parallels most of the island's west coast, you can see and photograph a fascinating underwater world of coral formations, submarine "gardens," and friendly schools of exotic fish (blue-headed wrasse, gobies, French angelfish). Experienced divers can also explore the 594-foot-long wreck of the sunken ocean liner *Bianca C*, just offshore. Snorkeling and dive trips can be arranged through *Grand Anse Aquatics* at their *Coyaba* resort location (phone: 444-4219, ext. 144) or the *Dive Grenada* water sports concession (phone: 444-4371). *Grenada Yacht Services* (phone: 440-2883 or 440-2508) offers snorkeling day trips on the 40-foot *Flamingo*.

SPORT FISHING Best in Grenadian waters from November to May, when the catch includes sailfish, blue and white marlin, yellowfin tuna, dorado, kingfish, and wahoo. Fishing charters can be arranged through hotel water sports desks. Jason Fletcher of *Tropix Professional Sport Fishing* (phone: 440-4961 or 444-1422) offers charters on his 28-foot Grady-White fishing boat, while Bob Evans of *Evans Chartering Service* (phone: 444-4422 or 444-4217) runs deep-sea charters on his 35-foot Bertram. *Captain Peters* (phone: 440-1349) offers a four-hour fishing trip for two people, including crew, bait, and tackle. The annual *International Game Fishing Tournament* takes place sometime in January, depending on the moon.

SWIMMING AND SUNNING Grenada has 45 beaches, many with fine white sand, and all free and open to the public. Grand Anse Beach is the long, beautiful, famous one. A number of hotels and guesthouses are on or just across the road from it, so chances are the place you stay will border a piece of it too. (You also can visit strips along hotels you're not staying at, though they are likely to charge a small fee for the use of changing facilities and chaise longues.) The beaches at Calabash and Horseshoe Bays are other southern beauties. At the other end of the island, Levera Beach on the northeastern shore, where the Atlantic and the Caribbean meet, is palm-lined, uncrowded, and a favorite picnic place. Carriacou's most seductive sands line Paradise Beach and small Sandy Island offshore.

TENNIS The *Grenada Renaissance, Secret Harbour, Spice Island Inn, Coyaba, Calabash, Coral Cove, Twelve Degrees North, LaSource, Rex Grenadian* (see *Checking In* for all), and *Holiday Haven Cottages* (L'Anse aux Epines; phone: 440-2606 or 444-4325) have facilities; non-guests can play (if courts are available) for a nominal (and sometimes no) fee. The *Richmond Hill Tennis Club* will arrange one-month memberships (contact Richard Hughes; phone: 440-2751); non-members can play here for a nominal per-person, per-hour charge. The Grand Anse tennis courts are open to the public free of charge on a first-come, first-served basis (no phone).

WINDSURFING Equipment is available for rent at hotels.

NIGHTLIFE

For visitors, it's centered at hotels, each of which holds buffets, barbecues, island shows, and dancing (to a combo one night, a steel band the next) several nights a week in season, less often in summer. (The *Grenada Renaissance* and *LaSource* hotels and the *Spice Island Inn* are the most active in this department; see *Checking In.*) You can hotel-hop, but most people are content to sit, sip, and talk on their own terraces after dinner. On weekends, islanders and visitors alike dance into the wee hours at *Le Sucrier* in the sugar mill on the Grand Anse roundabout (phone: 444-1068) and at *Fantasia 2000* at the *Gem Holiday Beach* resort (Morne Rouge Bay; phone: 444-3737).

Best on the Islands

CHECKING IN

Grenada has a total of about 1,400 rooms. The *Grenada Hotel Association* (phone: 444-1353; 800-322-1753; fax: 444-4847) provides room availability and rate information, and a free reservations service. In the US and Canada, reservations also may be made by calling 800-223-9815.

Grenada's better hotels offer a more casual, understated style of elegance than found elsewhere in the Caribbean. Don't be surprised if a hotel advertised as "deluxe" turns out to be somewhat shy of services—what you're paying for here are some of the most charmingly situated resort hideaways anywhere in the Caribbean, not marble and mirrors. All hotels are low-rise—the rule in Grenada is that no building may be taller than the tallest palm tree.

In-season rates are very reasonable compared to those on a number of neighboring islands, and most establishments deliver comparatively good value in quality of accommodations, food, and pleasantly rendered service; use of water and land sports equipment is generally included. Expect to pay $200 or more for a double room without meals during the winter season in hotels we list below as expensive, from $125 to $200 in moderate places, and $125 or less at inexpensive properties. The cost of adding breakfasts and dinners (Modified American Plan) varies from $30 to $45 extra per person, per day. (Most hotel restaurants fall into the expensive range, so the MAP prices make sense.) Note that rates do not include the 8% government hotel tax or the 10% service charge automatically added to your bill. Hotel rates generally drop 20% to 30% in the off-season. Unless otherwise noted, all hotels listed below feature air conditioning, telephones, TV sets, and private baths. All telephone numbers are in the 809 area code unless otherwise indicated.

GRAND ANSE BEACH

EXPENSIVE

Grenada Renaissance The island's second-largest resort, complete with 19 acres of beachfront property and 186 rooms. Each guestroom features a patio or balcony, a hair dryer, and a direct-dial phone. There are lots of shady palms, a lounge bar, two synthetic-surface tennis courts, a pool, and four shops. Also offered: all water sports, including diving excursions via a concessionaire. Dining is alfresco or indoors with air conditioning in the *Greenery* (open sporadically, and in the winter season only), and there's nightly entertainment (phone: 444-4371; 800-228-9898; fax: 444-4800).

Rex Grenadian The island's newest, biggest (212 rooms) hotel is decorated throughout in breezy, tropical colors. The building, featuring panoramic views across the bay to St. George's, is set in landscaped gardens with a three-acre lake and a giant fountain. The garden rooms have ceiling fans (no air conditioning), while all the ocean-view rooms are air conditioned. In addition to banqueting and conference rooms, four restaurants, three bars, and a courtyard terrace café, there are two beaches, a swimming pool with a waterfall, a children's pool, a full range of water sports, two tennis courts, and a fitness center. There is also live entertainment most evenings. Point Salines (phone: 444-3333; 800-255-5859; fax: 444-1111).

Spice Island Inn Stretching along 1,200 feet of perfect white beach are 56 pleasantly contemporary and spacious suites (all with double whirlpool baths but no TV sets); 17 have private pools and gardens. There's a tennis court with floodlights for night play; a fitness center; a range of water sports, such as snorkeling and windsurfing; and good food and service. "Spice," as it's known locally, has an impressive repeat business clientele. There's usually something interesting going on in the evenings, including a popular Grenadian creole buffet accompanied by a band Wednesday nights, a barbecue Fridays, and a calypso band that plays Saturday nights. Good summer packages (phone: 444-4258; 800-742-4276; fax: 444-4807).

Blue Horizons Spruced up and landscaped, its 32 cottage suites (all with kitchenettes, ceiling fans *and* air conditioning, hair dryers, and clock radios) are
reasonably priced even at the height of the season. There's a pool, whirlpool,
small playground, and an outstanding restaurant, *La Belle Creole* (see *Eating
Out*). For those who prefer to eat in, cooks are available. Grand Anse is
300 yards down the road, and guests can use the beach and water sports
concessions at the nearby *Spice Island Inn* (see above). Children under 12
may stay free in their parents' room (phone: 444-4316; 800-742-4276; fax:
444-2815).

Coyaba This resort occupies a lovely 2½-acre site on Grand Anse Beach. The central pavilion, which houses the reception area, two bars, a lounge, a boutique, and two open-air restaurants, is surrounded by three two-story lodges,
with 40 rooms. All accommodations feature private verandahs with views
of the sea or St. George's Harbour (sometimes both). Facilities include a
pool with swim-up bar, the *Grand Anse Aquatics* dive operation, volleyball,
tennis courts, and a playground (phone: 444-4129; 800-223-9815; fax: 444-
4808).

INEXPENSIVE

Flamboyant On the hillside at the end of Grand Anse Beach, the 41 recently refurbished units (studios, one- and two-bedroom apartments, and two-bedroom cottages) have fabulous views of St. George's and the harbor. The
apartments and cottages have full kitchens. There's also a pool, the *Beachside
Terrace* restaurant, and a bar (phone: 444-4247; fax: 444-1234).

L'ANSE AUX EPINES

EXPENSIVE

Calabash Thirty suites are set in 10 buildings spread over eight landscaped acres
along a pretty beach. All rooms have a verandah just steps from the water's
edge; six have private Jacuzzis, and eight have private swimming pools. A
maid comes in to prepare and serve breakfast each morning. Other pluses
are a large pool, a lighted tennis court, billiard room, one of the island's
best restaurants (see *Eating Out*), and entertainment five nights a week.
The place draws a lot of repeat business, so book early (phone: 444-4334;
800-223-9815; fax: 444-4804).

Secret Harbour A marvelous Spanish-Moorish design, complete with tiled roofs,
terraces, arches, and opulent finishing touches (stained glass, sunken tubs,
and two big four-poster beds per room), sets the ambience here. All of the
20 units have a small fridge wedged into the dressing area; it's a draw, primarily for long-term visitors, but does nothing for the otherwise charming
atmosphere. The rooms don't have TV sets (there's one in the main lobby).
Pluses include a sandy beach, a tile-framed swimming pool, a tennis court,

the antiques-filled *Mariners* restaurant, and an extensive water sports concession, including a 50-slip marina under the aegis of *The Moorings*. Evenings are very quiet (phone: 444-4439; fax: 444-4819).

Horse Shoe Beach This lushly landscaped property has 12 elegant Mediterranean cottages and six suites that recently have been spruced up (including hand-carved four-poster beds) plus six newer and more modern suites. All units have patios. The view from the *Horse Shoe Beach Supper Club* is marvelous, and the food's pretty good, too (see *Eating Out*). There's a small beach, a pool, and a complete water sports center (phone: 444-4410; 800-223-9815; fax: 444-4844).

Twelve Degrees North Tastefully done, these eight one- and two-bedroom cottages are designed for island housekeeping the easy way. Maids, on duty from 8 AM until 3 PM, clean, launder, and cook. Beach amenities include a dock, a Sunfish, a Boston Whaler, windsurfing and kayaking equipment, and a thatch bar and barbecue setup. There's also a pool and a tennis court. If you ask, the day staff will prepare dinner ahead of time for you; otherwise, you're on your own. Apartments are fully stocked with groceries for arriving guests. It's all very relaxing. No children under age 15 (phone: 444-4580; 800-322-1753; fax: 444-4580).

Coral Cove Here are 18 guestrooms with kitchenettes, including one and two-bedroom units overlooking a white sand beach suitable for some water sports (the water is very shallow in this area). The rooms have fans (no air conditioning), and there are no TV sets. There's no restaurant, but a pool and tennis court round out the facilities. Full maid and laundry service; car rentals and charter fishing can be arranged (phone: 444-4422; 800-223-9815; fax: 444-4847).

No Problem Apartment Hotel A 20-suite complex surrounded by tropical gardens and less than a mile from the airport, the rooms here are pleasant, with twin beds, a sofa bed, and a fully equipped kitchen. There's a conference center, a pool, a bar, a casual restaurant, and free bicycle use. A complimentary shuttle provides transport to the airport, town, and Grand Anse Beach (five minutes away). Children under 12 may stay for free in their parents' room (phone: 444-4634/5; 800-223-9815; fax: 444-2803).

ELSEWHERE ON THE ISLAND

LaSource The first all-inclusive resort on Grenada, this sister of *LeSport* on St. Lucia is nestled on 40 acres near the island's southwest tip. The upscale property has 100 rooms and suites decorated with bright fabrics and marble touches and featuring sea-view balconies, direct-dial phones, and radios (but no TV sets). There are two lovely beaches, a free-form pool with a waterfall, two restaurants, and two bars. Meals, snacks, land and water sports (including scuba), first-rate spa services, tips, and airport-to-hotel transfers all are included in the rate. Pink Gin Beach (phone: 444-2556; 800-544-2883; fax: 444-4966).

La Sagesse Nature Center A gracious old manor house has been converted to three apartments (none with air conditioning, TV set, or telephone) on this 77-acre former banana plantation, now home to a nature sanctuary bordered by a pretty beach. There's a bar and a seafood restaurant on the premises. Located in the lush countryside a half-hour drive north of St. George's. St. David's (phone: 444-6458; fax: 444-4847).

CARRIACOU

Caribbee Inn A refuge for writers, poets, and quiet souls, with two rooms, two suites, and a two-bedroom villa gracing a lush hillside with a view of the ocean. The accommodations have ceiling fans (no air conditioning, but there are constant trade winds), louvered windows, and four-poster beds (no telephones or TV sets). The suites and the villa also have refrigerators and private sundecks. Home cooking is supervised by the British owners, and is prepared with a creole touch. There's a small library, several bicycles are available, and water sports are nearby. Swimming is at two secluded beaches. Near Bogles Village (phone: 443-7380; fax: 443-8142).

Silver Beach Located smack on Beausejour Beach, this property has 18 simply furnished units ranging from basic rooms to self-contained apartments with kitchenettes—all with patios (with either a sea or garden view) and ceiling fans, but no air conditioning, telephones, or TV sets. *Dive Paradise,* a water sports and scuba diving operation, is on site. Beausejour Bay (phone: 443-7337; 800-223-9815; fax: 443-7165).

EATING OUT

Grenadian food owes its special flavor to good island cooks and very fresh ingredients: just-caught fish, lobster, crab, and conch (called *lambi*), just-picked garden vegetables, and tropical fruits in great variety. Island dishes to try: pumpkin soup; *callaloo,* with greens and crab, ranging in thickness from soup to stew; conch (in conch and onion pie, or curried); turtle steaks; and soursop ice cream. "Oil down," virtually the national dish, consists of breadfruit and salt pork covered with dasheen leaves and steamed in coconut milk. The national drink is rum punch, *always* with freshly grated Grenadian nutmeg on top; local Carib beer is also quite good.

Food at Grenadian hotels is generally excellent. Most have continental chefs and menus that feature continental specialties, plus a few West Indian choices. Since most hotel dining rooms are small, with only limited space for outside guests, it is essential to call ahead for reservations if you want to sample the food at another hotel. Expect to pay $40 to $50 for a dinner for two at any of the places listed below as expensive (which includes most hotel restaurants); $22 to $35 at spots described as moderate; and less than $22 at an inexpensive place. Prices don't include drinks, wine, the 8% tax, or tips. Unless otherwise noted, all restaurants listed below are open for lunch and dinner. All telephone numbers are in the 809 area code unless otherwise indicated.

ST. GEORGE'S AND ENVIRONS

MODERATE

Mamma's A friendly, home-like atmosphere prevails at this informal eatery. No menu, just a profusion of truly memorable West Indian offerings (up to 25 courses, served family-style, are the rule for large parties) that have made this place a must-stop for authentic island cooking. Always ask if there's any turtle available, and be sure to try the sea moss ice cream. Any cab driver can find it, but make reservations well in advance, as there are only a few tables on the back-to-basics patio and inside. Open daily for dinner; lunch is served depending on the weather and the disposition of the chef, so check ahead. No credit cards accepted. Old Lagoon Rd., Belmont (phone: 440-1459).

Rudolf's A Swiss-owned spot for lunch or dinner in a pub-like setting. The menu is international, including fish and chips, and lobster-as-you-like-it; there are also a few local specialties and potent rum punches. Try the crab back, and finish up with homemade soursop ice cream. Closed Sundays. Reservations necessary for dinner. No credit cards accepted. North corner of the Carenage (phone: 440-2241).

INEXPENSIVE

Nutmeg Overlooking the Carenage, this is the most popular noontime spot in town, and a good place for drinks, snacks, or a full meal almost anytime. Chatty and easygoing, it's popular with visiting yachtspeople. Have a rum punch, *callaloo,* lobster, or *lambi.* Open daily; dinner only on Sundays (unless a cruise ship is in port). Reservations unnecessary. MasterCard and Visa accepted. The Carenage (phone: 440-2539).

Tropicana This casual restaurant, frequented by locals and tourists alike, serves a unique combination of authentic West Indian and Chinese cooking. Open daily. Reservations advised. Major credit cards accepted. Lagoon Rd. (phone: 440-1586).

GRAND ANSE

EXPENSIVE

La Belle Creole For the real island McCoy, this small and cordial balcony dining room is the scene of some highly imaginative West Indian meals in the Hopkins family tradition. One of the island's best. Open daily. Reservations necessary. Major credit cards accepted. In the *Blue Horizons Hotel*, 200 yards down the road from Grand Anse Beach (phone: 444-4316).

Canboulay Definitely in the don't-miss category, it sits on the hillside above Grand Anse Beach and features fantastic views of the entire town. Traditional ingredients are served in such dishes as *moko jumbies* (jumbo shrimp served on skewers), *parang poulet* (chicken in orange-ginger sauce), and red snapper steamed in banana leaves. Good starters are the coconut buns stuffed with salt fish *souse* (salt fish marinated in olive oil, peppers, and onions), and breadfruit with pickled cucumber. Closed Sundays. Reservations necessary for dinner. Major credit cards accepted. Morne Rouge (phone: 444-4401).

L'ANSE AUX EPINES

EXPENSIVE

Calabash This prize-winning restaurant in the hotel of the same name offers the handiwork of chef Cecily Roberts. Fresh seafood and island-grown fruits and vegetables are prepared in Grenadian style and served on a flower-draped terrace. Open daily for breakfast, lunch, and dinner. Reservations necessary for dinner. Major credit cards accepted (phone: 444-4334).

Red Crab Upscale dining in a relaxed atmosphere is the attraction here. Seafood dishes such as shrimp crêpes are specialties. Closed Sundays. Reservations advised. Major credit cards accepted (phone: 444-4424).

MODERATE

Boatyard A convivial eatery featuring fish and chips and burgers for lunch and seafood dishes for dinner. Famous for the crowded happy hours. Closed Mondays. Reservations unnecessary. Major credit cards accepted. In the *Spice Island Marina* compound at Prickly Bay (phone: 444-4662).

Horse Shoe Beach Supper Club West Indian specialties such as pumpkin soup and fish creole are served in this open-air dining room. The sinful homemade desserts include nutmeg mousse and rum raisin ice cream. Open daily for breakfast, lunch, and dinner. Reservations unnecessary. Major credit cards accepted. At the *Horse Shoe Beach Hotel* (phone: 444-4410).

Guadeloupe

Like its sister island Martinique, Guadeloupe has its own dormant (more or less) volcano, tropically forested mountains, an impressive *Parc National,* cane fields, banana plantations and pineapple stands, a surf-pounded Atlantic coast and calmer leeward bathing beaches, creole cooking, and the beguine— a dance resembling the rumba. Each island has *région* status and is governed as if it were physically attached to France. The people are French citizens, vote in French national elections, are entitled to French social benefits, and are bound by France's compulsory educational requirements.

But there are significant differences. Guadeloupe is actually two islands linked by a drawbridge over the Rivière-Salée (the river that connects the Caribbean and the Atlantic). In addition, Guadeloupe has a number of dependencies: the nearby islands of La Désirade, Marie Galante, and Iles des Saintes (also called Les Saintes), plus the French half of the island of St. Martin and tiny St. Barthélemy. It offers not only the stunning scenery of its own two islands to explore, but day or overnight trips to its intriguing, unspoiled, dependent islands as well.

In 1493, nine years before he found Martinique, Christopher Columbus happened upon Guadeloupe, christening it Santa María de Guadalupe de Estremadura to fulfill a promise made to the monks of the Spanish monastery of the same name. The French landed on both islands in 1635. But while Martinique flourished, Guadeloupe foundered—thanks to the ineptitude of its leaders and the lack of farming skill among its volunteer settlers, all of whom were indentured to work three years without pay in exchange for their passage from France.

The French Revolution goaded Guadeloupe into asserting itself: Infuriated by the Declaration of the Rights of Man and the abolition of slavery (which doomed their cane fields), the islanders declared themselves autonomous, inviting the enemy English to invade and stay awhile. In 1794, the Committee of Public Safety in Paris dispatched a force of 1,150 men to discipline the islanders. They ousted the English, set up guillotines in the main squares of Basse-Terre and Pointe-à-Pitre, and beheaded 4,000 Guadeloupeans before being removed to Guiana. Slavery was reestablished under Napoleon. The British reconquered Guadeloupe in 1810, surrendered it to Louis XVIII during the Restoration, reoccupied the island when Napoleon staged his 100-day comeback, and gave it up for good when the Little Emperor was permanently exiled to St. Helena in 1815. Guadeloupe has been French ever since, but it has developed its own character—a unique blend of France and the West Indies.

Guadeloupe's hotels generally follow the large, luxurious, made-in-France pattern, with *tous* sports built in, or the small, French-speaking hostel-on-the-beach design. More than two thirds of the 330,000 tourists who

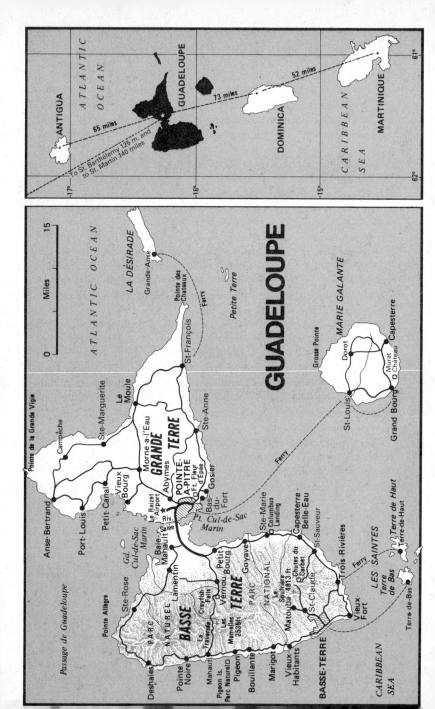

visit Guadeloupe each year come from Europe, particularly France. Guadeloupe's capital is a small port city called Basse-Terre, which could be described as dull in comparison to its working heart, bustling Pointe-à-Pitre. Despite its high-rise housing and burgeoning industry, Pointe-à-Pitre moves to a distinctly Caribbean beat. To feel it, stroll down to the waterfront, lined with chunky island boats, where blue-eyed Iles des Saintes fishermen hawk their morning catch, or pay an early-morning visit to market stalls piled with fruits and spices dear to the soul of Guadeloupe's creole cooks.

This creole fare—vying with traditional French specialties—fires the Guadeloupean spirit. Classic French restaurants like *La Plantation* (see *Eating Out*) are respected and admired, but the real heroines of this island's kitchens are Prudence, Félicité, Trésor, among others, who conjure up their magic *blaffs* (fish soups), *boudins,* and *crabes farcis* in plain places in the hills and along the shores. The whole island celebrates their art with a grand parade, a cathedral blessing, music, dancing, and a five-hour feast at the annual August *Fête des Cuisinières* (Women Chefs' Festival). At any time of year, though, lunch or dinner is an adventure and—when your eye and palate have become acclimated to the spices and surprises—a special delight.

If you're looking for a place with fine beaches that's a bit offbeat, and if you can say *"Vive la différence"* with feeling, Guadeloupe is for you.

Guadeloupe At-a-Glance

FROM THE AIR

Guadeloupe is a butterfly-shaped formation of two islands, Grande-Terre (218 square miles) and Basse-Terre (312 square miles), separated by a narrow strait called the Rivière-Salée and connected by a drawbridge. It has a total area of 582 square miles and a population of 408,000. One of the Leeward Islands, its nearest neighbors are Antigua (65 miles northwest), Dominica (73 miles south), and Martinique (121 miles south and slightly east).

Guadeloupe's two islands are quite different topographically. Basse-Terre has mountainous terrain inland and a rugged coastline with few (but good) beaches suited to daylong basking. Grande-Terre consists of flat cane fields and low, chalky hills rimmed by a number of appealing beaches. The city of Basse-Terre (population 14,000), on the southwest edge of the island of the same name, is the capital of the *région;* but the larger city of Pointe-à-Pitre (population 100,000), on the southwest coast of Grande-Terre, near the point where the Rivière-Salée separates the two islands, is its commercial center.

SPECIAL PLACES

Most island visitors stay on Grande-Terre at the shore hotels of Bas-du-Fort, Gosier, Ste-Anne, and St-François, or at any of the 20-odd members of the Relais Créoles group, an association of modest hotels and country inns that conform to high standards of service and comfort. Visitors typically spend half a day shopping and strolling around Pointe-à-Pitre, and make a day-tour visit to Basse-Terre's *Parc National* (also known as the *Parc Naturel*), one of France's seven national parks, and the city of Basse-Terre. Some travelers rent cars to explore on their own, but since Basse-Terre's roads tend to be mountainous inland and sharply curved along the shore, most visitors sign up for organized bus tours at hotel travel desks. Athletic types can climb to the top of Soufrière, the island's dormant volcano. Day trips via ferry or plane to Iles des Saintes and Marie Galante combine sightseeing with a chance to laze on pleasant, secluded beaches (Petite Anse, a long, golden stretch of sand on Marie Galante, is one of the best).

POINTE-À-PITRE Guadeloupe's port and chief city, on Grande-Terre, likes to call itself the "Paris of the Antilles," but it looks more like a Riviera port than the city on the Seine. Apartments and condominiums form a high-rise backdrop for its 19th-century cathedral, tree-planted squares, and boat-lined harbor. It is busy, but not so bustling or big that you can't see it all and get in your shopping, too, in half a day—preferably morning, when the waterfront and outdoor markets are liveliest.

Start by picking up brochures and a map of Guadeloupe (including a street map of Pointe-à-Pitre) at the tourist office, housed in a white colonial building across from the Place de la Victoire. The park-like area is shaded by flamboyants and palms as well as antique sandbox trees planted by Victor Hugues, whose victory over the British in 1794 gave the square its name. It was here that Hugues, Guadeloupe's first dictator, erected a guillotine to execute enemies of the Revolution.

A short walk from the tourist office along Quai Layrie, which turns into Quai Lardenoy, is the *Centre St-John Perse,* a $20-million waterfront complex. Its several buildings include the headquarters of Guadeloupe's *Port Autonome* (Port Authority), an array of boutiques, including duty-free shops selling local rum and French perfume; many restaurants, most notably *La Canne à Sucre* (see *Eating Out*); and the *St. John Anchorage* hotel (see *Checking In*).

Rue Duplessis, at the Place de la Victoire's southern edge, runs along La Darse, the old port where inter-island ferries leave for Marie Galante and Les Saintes, schooners tie up, and where, farther out, cruise ships drop anchor. West of the harbor, the shopping district's narrow streets are crowded with shops that range from sidewalk stalls to boutiques full of French perfumes and sportswear. Chief shopping streets are Rue de Nozières and Rue Frébault (both of which run north and south) and Rue Achille René-Boisneuf (usually referred to by its hyphenated name alone), running east and west. At 54 Rue René-Boisneuf, a plaque marks the birthplace of St-John Perse, the French poet who won the Nobel Prize for

Literature in 1960, and nearby on the same street is the *Musée St-John Perse.* The museum's first floor is furnished like a 19th-century colonial home, while the second floor contains some personal belongings of Perse along with some fascinating photographs of Pointe-à-Pitre and the Guadeloupe countryside during the 1800s and early 1900s. Closed Saturday afternoons and Sundays. Admission charge (phone: 900192). A block north, bounded by Rues Schoelcher, Peynier, Frébault, and St-John Perse the open-air market hums with the give-and-take of housewives and female vendors—some straw-hatted, some wearing traditional madras turbans—bargaining across stacks of fire-red pimientos, papayas, pineapples, mangoes, and spices. Behind the market is the *Musée Schoelcher* (24 Rue Peynier; phone: 820804), dedicated to Victor Schoelcher, the man credited with abolishing slavery here. Through photographs, newspaper clippings, and graphics, the museum traces the history of slavery on Guadeloupe and the slaves' fight for freedom. Closed Wednesdays, Saturday afternoons, and Sundays. Admission charge (phone: 820804). A short walk north and east brings you to the peaceful Place de l'Eglise, and its yellow-and-white *Cathédrale de St-Pierre et St-Paul* (Cathedral of St. Peter and St. Paul), nicknamed "the Iron Cathedral" because of its skeleton of bolted iron ribs, designed to keep the church standing through hurricanes and earthquakes.

ELSEWHERE ON GRANDE-TERRE

Most points of interest are along the shores east of Pointe-à-Pitre. As you drive east from town, they are:

FORT FLEUR D'EPÉE The well-preserved battlements and dungeons of this 18th-century fortress are located 3 miles east of Pointe-à-Pitre. They command a view of the city, the nearby islands of Marie Galante and the Iles des Saintes, and in the distance the mountains of Basse-Terre and the island of Dominica. Open daily. No admission charge (phone: 901461). On the shore below, Bas-du-Fort is the site of several late-model resort hotels and vacation condominiums. Not far from the marina at Bas-du-Fort is the large *Aquarium de la Guadeloupe,* with over 150 species of fish and tropical plants. Open daily. Admission charge. Pl. Créole, Bas-du-Fort (phone: 909238).

GOSIER Four-and-a-half miles east of Pointe-à-Pitre, this shoreside center has an extensive beach, site of many of the island's major resort hotels. The main thoroughfare, Avenue Général de Gaulle, is dotted with restaurants, boutiques, and busy outdoor cafés.

STE-ANNE This tiny village has become a hot spot for tourism, with windsurfing, kayaking, and snorkeling available at nearby beaches. The town boasts a pastel-yellow *Hôtel de Ville* (Town Hall), a pretty church, and Place Schoelcher, the town's main square, dominated by a statue of emancipationist Victor Schoelcher. It was erected by the island's citizens to commemorate the end of slavery in 1848. The all-inclusive *Caravelle Club*

Méditerranée resort (see *Checking In*), six small Relais Créoles inns, and extensive beaches are nearby.

ST-FRANÇOIS This fishing village has long, white sand beaches, many good creole and French restaurants, and the *Marina de St-François*—a resort that continues to expand, with a marina, casino, and golf course.

POINTE DES CHÂTEAUX The easternmost tip of Grande-Terre, the Atlantic and the Caribbean meet here. There's a towering castle-like rock formation, crowned by a rugged cross that has survived more than a century. Despite the crashing waves, the tranquil, coved beaches make this a fine picnic destination.

LE MOULE There's a long crescent beach at this small coastal fishing village and antique sugar port northeast of Pointe-à-Pitre. The fascinating and attractively designed historical and archaeological *Musée Edgar Clerc* is here. Closed Wednesday afternoons. Admission charge. Parc de la Rosette (phone: 235757). At the Beach of Skulls and Bones, the ocean has uncovered graves and petrified remains, macabre relics of once savage warfare between the Carib and the French and British invaders.

Interesting places along the coastal road north of Pointe-à-Pitre include:

PORT-LOUIS AND ANSE-BERTRAND These fishing villages have good beaches nearby.

POINTE DE LA GRANDE VIGIE At the northernmost tip of the island, it is named for the sweeping Atlantic view from the top of its rocky cliffs.

BASSE-TERRE

To see Basse-Terre, which is west of Pointe-à-Pitre, across the drawbridge over the Rivière-Salée, head west on La Traversée, the highway that crosses Basse-Terre through the lush highlands of the *Parc National,* then go south along the west coast to the capital city of Basse-Terre and return via the island's east coast. Alternatively, you can take the coastal roads first and return on La Traversée, traveling west to east. If you follow the latter route, you'll encounter:

STE-MARIE Columbus landed on this spot during his second voyage in 1493; he left in a hurry, however, when the Carib started peppering his crew with arrows. Today, a statue of Columbus stands in the town square, and the area is largely populated by descendants of the East Indian laborers imported to work plantations after the 1848 emancipation of black slaves. Just south of town is much-photographed Allée Dumanoir, a half-mile stretch of road lined on both sides with tall palms planted in the last century by Pinel Dumanoir, whose major claim to fame was—surprisingly—his French dramatization of *Uncle Tom's Cabin.*

LES CHUTES DU CARBET (CARBET FALLS) This trio of waterfalls impressed Columbus's crew, who—when they sighted them from the sea—thought they were "avalanches of white stones." For a closer look, take the road inland from the coastal town of St-Sauveur past the mountain lake called Grand Etang and up Soufrière Mountain to a viewing point near the three cascades. The lowest is between 60 and 70 feet high; the second and top falls are over 300 feet each. A 25-minute walk brings you to the pool at the foot of the lowest waterfall.

TROIS-RIVIÈRES This seaside settlement has a modern *Hôtel de Ville* (Town Hall), but the older sights here are much more interesting: Near the harbor where ferries depart for Iles des Saintes, rocks in a small park bear pre-Columbian inscriptions, and for a few francs one of the local boys will show you the portrait of a chieftain on the wall of a nearby grotto.

BASSE-TERRE Guadeloupe's capital is a small, neat city of narrow streets and palm-filled parks set between the sea and the green heights of La Soufrière. Chief points of interest: the nicely designed administrative buildings that make up the old Carmel quarter; the 17th-century *Cathédrale de Notre Dame de Guadeloupe* (Cathedral of Our Lady of Guadeloupe) in the St-François section; and *Fort Delgrès,* which has stood guard over the city since its founding in 1643. The fort is open daily. No admission charge (phone: 813748).

LA SOUFRIÈRE This tenuously dormant volcano has given Guadeloupeans some anxious moments, often breathing steam from its fumaroles (steam holes) and burping sulfurous fumes from its pits and mud cauldrons. The foot of the crater can be reached by car; there, at the Savane-à-Mulets parking lot, spectators feel the heat of the subterranean lava and enjoy a magnificent view of Basse-Terre, the sea, Iles des Saintes, and Dominica. Adventurous types can climb one of four marked trails to the edge of the crater to view its five-acre center of bubbling lava and eerie rock formations. Trail maps are available at island bookstores and at the *Club des Montagnards* (see *Hiking,* below). Round-trip treks take from one to three hours, depending on your stamina. Guides are strongly recommended because of sudden mountain mists and shifting paths (due to fast-growing vegetation); the *Club des Montagnards* has a list of guides.

LA TRAVERSÉE The well-maintained Transcoastal Highway provides a convenient way to see the *Parc National* en route from Basse-Terre to Pointe-à-Pitre. You reach its western end by driving north along the coast past black sand beaches; the small town of Vieux-Habitants; Bouillante, boiling with hot springs and geysers; and the spot where dive trips and glass-bottom boat rides leave for Ilet Pigeon (Pigeon Island) and the nearby underwater reserve. La Traversée starts just north of Pigeon at Mahaut and travels 10½ miles east through a pass between mountains graphically referred to as Les Deux Mamelles (The Two Breasts). The road offers a broad view of the hills, valleys, and coasts of Basse-Terre, and the bays called Grand and Petit Cul-de-Sac, plus the park's forests, lakes, and waterfalls. Halfway along the route is *La Maison de la Forêt* (Forest House), an information center with wall maps that indicate various hiking trails off La Traversée; the longest trail takes three hours. Closed Mondays (no phone). Along the route, you also can stroll in the *Parc Zoologique et Botanique* at Bouillante (open daily; admission charge; phone: 988352) or perhaps swim in the pool at the bottom of the Cascade aux Ecrevisses (Crayfish Falls). The eastern end of La Traversée joins the road that crosses the drawbridge back to Pointe-à-Pitre. For additional details, see *Natural Wonderlands* and *Climbing and Hiking* in DIVERSIONS.

EXTRA SPECIAL

Iles des Saintes and Marie Galante are two unspoiled offshore island destinations that are perfect for daylong getaway plane trips or ferry crossings that can be organized by tour operators or arranged on your own. Marie Galante offers a bit of sightseeing—the sunny little town of Grand-Bourg, sugar mills, pastoral landscapes, and fine white beaches, along with the architecturally splendid *Château Murat*, a former plantation house that recently has been restored. The château is closed Wednesdays; there's no admission charge (phone: 974141). Pack a picnic, or lunch on creole fare at *Touloulou* (phone: 973263), or try *lambi* at *Békéké* (phone: 972224); both eateries are on the sand near Capesterre. Visitors who want to skip the sightseeing can take jitneys or buses from the market or bus depot a couple of blocks away to Capesterre Beach (cost is about $1 per person), about 7 miles (11 km) from town. When you've had enough sun, just stand on the highway and hail a bus headed back toward town.

Most Iles des Saintes plane trips land breathtakingly (it's a very short runway with a mountain-pass approach) on Terre-de-Haut Island. There are minibuses, *"taxis de l'île,"* but it's a very short walk past the cemetery, with its white tombs, hand-carved crucifix, and conch shell–framed grave sites, and over the hill to the town, which is one of the Caribbean's prettiest. There's a quaint, tiny town square, rows of miniature, uniquely painted houses, and flowers everywhere. There are a number of good places for lunch: In Pointe Coquelet eat at the terrace café at the *Kanaoa* hotel (see *Checking In*) or *Le Mouillage* (phone: 995057) near the pier, then bask on a beach nearby; or take the launch from the town pier or a taxi out to the *Bois Joli* hotel (see *Checking In*) for lunch and a choice of clothed, topless, or bare beaching. There are a number of good hotels if you'd like to stay overnight (see *Checking In*). Big round salako straw hats (like those worn by Chinese peasants), unique to these islands, make super souvenirs—when you can find them.

Sources and Resources

TOURIST INFORMATION

The *Office Départemental du Tourisme de la Guadeloupe,* near the waterfront in Pointe-à-Pitre (5 Pl. de la Banque; phone: 820930; fax: 838922), supplies maps, information, and advice. The staff also will answer phone queries in English. There are two other tourist offices, one in Basse-Terre at the *Maison du Port* (Rue du Cours Nolivos; phone: 812483), and another in St-François (Av. de l'Europe; phone: 884874). All three offices are closed Saturday afternoons and Sundays. For French West Indies tourist offices in the US, see GETTING READY TO GO.

LOCAL COVERAGE The local French-language newspaper, *France-Antilles,* is published daily except Sundays. The *International Herald Tribune* is available in some bookstores and large hotels; also try *La Gazette* newsstand on Place de la Victoire, Pointe-à-Pitre. *Bonjour Guadeloupe,* the island's official tourist booklet, published periodically in both French and English, is distributed free at the tourist office, at the airport, and in hotels. It is full of useful information, plus up-to-date specifics on excursions, restaurants, and nightlife. A booklet called *Guadeloupe Excursions* details six excellent itineraries for touring the islands by car; it is available from the tourist office in Pointe-à-Pitre.

Guadeloupe, a book of color photographs collected by Hans W. Hannau, can orient you to what the island looks like. *A Woman Named Solitude,* a novel by André Schwarz-Bart (Atheneum, 1973), incorporates much Guadeloupean history and atmosphere, as does *Between Two Worlds* (Harper & Row, 1981) by Schwarz-Bart's wife, Simone. (All three books are out of print, but check your local library.)

RADIO AND TELEVISION Television is in French, but radio, which is locally produced or picked up from neighboring islands, broadcasts in several languages, including English. Most hotels have satellite-dish facilities.

TELEPHONE When calling from the US, dial 011 (international access code) + 590 (country code) + (local number). From another Caribbean island, the access code may vary, so call the local operator. When dialing on Guadeloupe, use only the local number unless otherwise indicated. Dial 17 for the police; 18 for an ambulance.

ENTRY REQUIREMENTS For stays of up to three weeks, a current or expired passport (not more than five years old) or proof of citizenship in the form of a voter's registration card or birth certificate with raised seal accompanied by an official photo ID (such as a driver's license) is necessary. A return or ongoing ticket also is required. For longer stays, a valid passport is necessary. US and Canadian citizens need no vaccination certificates.

CLIMATE AND CLOTHES The weather is tropical, tempered by trade winds and with thermometer readings varying considerably between sea level and the mountains. At beach resorts on the southern coast of Grande-Terre, temperatures range from an average low of 75F (24C) to an average high of 86F (30C). In the higher, cooler inland regions, the averages run from 66 to 81F (19 to 27C). September and October are the wettest months—not immune to hurricanes; November through May, the driest. But even in the residential suburb of St-Claude, where the climate is said to be perfect—sunny, cool, and breezy year-round—it showers almost every day. Most tourist accommodations are air conditioned.

Topless sunning is taken for granted just about everywhere. There are officially designated nude beaches on Guadeloupe proper and on Iles des Saintes. Off the beach, lightweight sportswear is most comfortable. Both men and women should pack some sort of cover-up—long-sleeve shirts or beach caftans—to slip on for lunch or when you've simply had enough sun. Slacks and sport shirts for men and slacks or skirts for women are right for downtown shopping, lunching, or excursions. For the *Parc National,* wear sturdy, crepe-soled shoes or sneakers, and take along a light jacket (preferably waterproof) or sweater in case of a chilly spell or shower. At night, especially in the large hotels, women wear casual dresses or nice slacks; men wear slacks and open-neck shirts. Ties are seldom, if ever, required, but you might pack one just in case.

MONEY Guadeloupe's currency is the French franc, whose value in US dollars is quoted in the business sections of most major daily US metropolitan newspapers; at press time it was 4.8 francs to $1 US. Though most hotels will exchange a limited number of dollars for francs, banks or *bureaux de change* offer the most favorable exchange rates. (French francs can be reconverted to dollars only at banks.) Like most Guadeloupean businesses, banks are closed for lunch between noon and 2:30 PM. You may get more for your shopping money if you can pay for your purchases in dollar-denomination traveler's checks; some tourist-oriented Pointe-à-Pitre merchants discount prices an extra 20% when paid in traveler's checks or with a major credit card. Some shops accept payment in dollars, but don't give the additional discount when they do. All prices in this chapter are quoted in US dollars.

LANGUAGE Guadeloupe's official language is French, with Creole (African words and rhythms grafted onto French stems) a virtual second tongue. You can count on English-speaking tour guides (if you've specified beforehand) and on some personnel in hotels and tourist-frequented shops who understand English. But since the majority of visitors to Guadeloupe come from France, the tourism industry here is geared toward French speakers; if your French is rusty to nonexistent, carry a dictionary or phrase book.

TIME Guadeloupe time is one hour later than eastern standard time (when it's noon in New York, it's 1 PM in Pointe-à-Pitre); it's the same as eastern daylight saving time. Local time is also measured on a 24-hour clock, so that 1 PM is 13 *heures.*

CURRENT Local electricity is 220 volts AC, 50 cycles. Large hotels sometimes have adapters to lend, but if your travel kit includes essential electric gadgets, better bring your own adapter plugs.

TIPPING French law requires that a 15% service charge be automatically added to all restaurant and bar bills. Tip room maids about $1 or $2 a day. Porters should be tipped about 85¢ per bag. Most taxi drivers own their own cars and do not expect tips.

GETTING AROUND

BUS The least expensive and most colorful way to go land roving is by bus—if your French and hang-loose spirit are up to it. Small, late-model jitney vans leave from two stations in downtown Pointe-à-Pitre: the *Gare Routière de Bergevin* for Basse-Terre destinations; the *Gare Routière de la Darse* for Grande-Terre hotels and resorts. They depart every 10 to 30 minutes (generally when they are full), depending on the importance of the route. A one-way trip between Ste-Anne and Pointe-à-Pitre is about $2.

CAR RENTAL Rental car agents are reluctant to rent for just one day, even in off-season. Also, rates are higher at hotel locations than at the airport or in town. Major international agencies—*Avis* (phone: 823347), *Budget* (phone: 829558), *Hertz* (phone: 820014), *EuropRent* (phone: 914216), and *Europcar* (phone: 825051)—have offices in the arrival area of *Le Raizet Airport.* Local firms—also with airport offices—include *Guadeloupe Cars* (phone: 832288), *Jumbo Car* (phone: 836074), and *Azur Auto* (phone: 843056). *Avis, Budget, Hertz, Jumbo, Europcar,* and *Azur Auto* also have desks at the larger hotels.

Cars with automatic transmission are in short supply. A valid driver's license is required; minimum renting age varies from 21 to 25 (depending on the agency), and you must have had at least one year's experience as a licensed driver.

Using government-designed self-drive tours and the tourist board's big, clear map, it's easy to plot your own trip. *One caution:* Driving on Grande-Terre, where roads are good and the land rolls gently, is easy going. Basse-Terre's mountain roads—with their steep ascents, descents, and switchbacks—are different; if you're nervous about driving, it's wiser to go by bus.

FERRY SERVICES Guadeloupe can be reached by ferries operated by *Antilles Trans Express* (phone: 831245; fax: 911105), which make several trips a week to and from Dominica, Martinique, and St. Lucia, as well as daily expeditions to Iles des Saintes and Marie Galante. In winter, an expanded schedule includes the islands of St. Martin, St. Barts, Antigua, St. Kitts, and St. Vincent. Several ferries run among these five destinations: Pointe-à-Pitre, Basse-Terre, Trois-Rivières, Les Saintes, and Marie Galante. There is also ferry service from St-François to Les Saintes, Marie Galante, and La Désirade.

INTER-ISLAND FLIGHTS *American* has regular flights from San Juan, Puerto Rico. *Air Guadeloupe* serves San Juan, St. Barthélemy, St. Martin, and St. Thomas. Several local operators provide the same service for groups of four or more: *Carib Jet* (phone: 822644), *Georges Marie-Gabrielle* (phone: 820538), *Petrelluzzi* (phone: 903777), and *Safari* (phone: 843073), which specializes in sightseeing air excursions. *LIAT* provides air links with several neighboring islands, and *WINAIR* flies directly from Dutch St. Maarten. *Air St. Barthélemy* also has small charter planes. Since the outer islands are popular destinations for Guadeloupeans, book as early as possible.

SEA EXCURSIONS Day sails to nearby islands or to secluded beaches from docks convenient to your hotel can be arranged through hotels or local tour operators. Sailboats up to 50 feet and catamarans can be rented, and the long-established glass-bottom boat *Papyrus* is available for day, twilight, or moonlight sails that leave from the Bas-du-Fort marina (phone: 909298).

SIGHTSEEING BUS TOURS Organized by local operators, these range from a half day of Grande-Terre sightseeing with shopping in Pointe-à-Pitre to a whole day's exploration of Basse-Terre. Among the best and most personalized are the tours put together by *Georges Marie-Gabrielle,* with headquarters at the airport (phone: 820538). It's a very good idea to check tour offerings for special features; when lunch is included, ask where before making reservations. Your concierge or hotel travel desk will have current details and rates on available tours and can make arrangements that include pickup at your hotel.

SIGHTSEEING TAXI TOURS These are reasonable if you can put a group together to share the fare. Ask your concierge or desk clerk to get you a driver-guide and to determine the rates—standardized by the government.

TAXI It will cost about $15 (not inexpensive, but a Mercedes often arrives) for the under-10-minute trip from the airport to your Gosier hotel; at night and on Sundays the rates are at least 40% higher. Since there is no airport limousine service, and buses are provided only for groups, you'll have to take a taxi from the airport unless you rent a car.

There are taxi stands in Pointe-à-Pitre and Basse Terre, and at all the major hotels. Radio cabs are available by calling 207474, 830955, or 836394.

SPECIAL EVENTS

Carnaval on Guadeloupe is more than a few days' revelry—it's a season that stretches from the first Sunday in January through *Ash Wednesday,* the first day of *Lent,* with all sorts of celebrations (masked parades, beguine contests, a beauty pageant, song competitions) scheduled each Sunday and a five-day super-gala that begins the Saturday before *Mardi Gras* and doesn't quit till the King of *Carnaval*—Vaval—goes up in smoke *Ash*

Wednesday evening. On that climactic weekend, everyone heads into town for nonstop partying; no islander thinks about much else for the next week. From a tourist's point of view, the Sunday events can be great fun; they also can be ignored if you're so inclined. Not so, the last bash. So if crowd scenes and slightly distracted service would spoil your fun, schedule your visit for another time. Other special occasions: *Mi-Carême,* a mid-*Lenten* break with processions and the funeral of King Vaval; *La Fête des Cuisinières* (the Women Chefs' Festival) held in early August with a parade and much feasting (your hotel can arrange for tickets to the banquet); the *Tour de la Guadeloupe* (mid-August), a 10-day international cycling race; *Festival of the Sea* (celebrated August 15, along with the *Feast of the Assumption,* on Iles des Saintes); *All Saints' Day* (November 1), observed with candle lighting in cemeteries; *St. Cecilia's Day* (November 22), celebrated with musical fetes in cities and towns; and *Young Saints' Day* (December 28), marked with a special mass and children's parade. *Easter Monday* (April 8 in 1996), *Ascension Day* (May 16 in 1996), *Pentecost Monday* (May 20 in 1996), *Bastille Day* (July 14), *Schoelcher Day* (July 21), *Assumption Day* (August 15), *Armistice Day* (November 11), *Christmas,* and *New Year's Day* are also public holidays.

SHOPPING

Most of the shops in Pointe-à-Pitre are centered around Rue de Nozières, Rue Frébault, and Rue Schoelcher. Stores are open from 9 AM to 1 PM and 3 to 6 PM on weekdays, and 9 AM to 1 PM on Saturdays. If there's a cruise ship in port, shop hours often are extended. Some merchants offer 20% discounts to those paying with US dollar denomination traveler's checks or credit cards. Chanel perfume, Orlane and Dior cosmetics, Hermès scarves, Baccarat and Lalique crystal, and the other standard imports are all here, but stocks are smaller and not so enticingly displayed as in Martinique's Fort-de-France, and the language barrier is harder to surmount. If you've a choice of islands and a long French-import shopping list, you'll probably do better faster on Martinique.

Local products? The best are coffee and rums that range from new and fiery white to 12-year-old and mahogany-colored—a take-home most North Americans sip and savor like a liqueur. Other souvenirs include some nicely made baskets, straw hats (both the wide-brimmed bakoua and flat salako shapes), hammocks, shell items, and creole dolls. Shops to seek out:

Les Artisans Caraïbes Lots of locally crafted items of wood, cloth, and other local materials, including unique chess sets, toy buses painted in colorful island style, wall hangings, and painted woodcarvings. *Little Gallery,* Av. de l'Europe, St-François (phone: 908728).

Centre d'Art Haïtien Paintings, painted metal cutouts, textiles, and wall hangings by Haitian artists. 69 Montauban, Gosier (phone: 840484).

Floral Antilles Experts in packing island flowers for your trip home. 50 Rue Schoelcher, Pointe-à-Pitre (phone: 829765).

Grain d'Or Local branch of a Paris shop offering stylish gold jewelry. 84 Rue de Nozières, Pointe-à-Pitre (phone: 834645).

L'Ile au Trésor Island-made madras sportswear in both adult and children's sizes, dashikis, island souvenirs. Ave. de l'Europe, St-François (phone: 884827).

Phoenicia Brand-name perfume and cosmetics (20% off if paid in US dollars). Three locations: 8 Rue Frébault, Pointe-à-Pitre (phone: 835036); 121 Rue Frébault, Pointe-à-Pitre (phone 822575); and Grande Escale, Gosier (phone: 908556).

A La Recherche du Passé Bibelots, antique books, and nautical items. At the marina, Bas-du-Fort (phone: 908415).

Rosébleu Offers the largest stock and widest choice of French cosmetics, fashion accessories, and crystal. At two locations: 5 Rue Frébault, Pointe-à-Pitre (phone: 20098) and a duty-free shop at *Le Raizet Airport* (phone: 829343).

Seven Sins Fine selection of French wines, but no great bargains on the "duty-free" hard liquor. 6 Rue Frébault, Pointe-à-Pitre (phone: 828839).

Tim Tim A worthwhile antiques shop run by the well-known French author André Schwarz-Bart and his Guadeloupean wife, Simone, also a writer. 15 Rue Henri IV (also known as Rue Jean-Jaurès), Pointe-à-Pitre (phone: 834871).

SPORTS

Guadeloupe's action is largely land-based on Basse-Terre (hiking in the *Parc National* and the climb to the top of 4,813-foot La Soufrière) and sea-linked on Grande-Terre, where the best beaches are, although the beach at Deshaies on Basse-Terre is excellent. If your French isn't fluent, ask your hotel to help you make sports arrangements.

BICYCLING An inexpensive way to get around, but not recommended for long hauls or on Basse-Terre's mountain roads. Rentals are available at *Espace VTT* (phone: 887991) in St-François and *Karucyclo* (phone: 822139) in Pointe-à-Pitre.

BOATING Sailing, on a small scale, is as easy as walking out to the hotel beach and renting a Sail- or Sunfish. Yacht charters can be arranged through *The Moorings* (phone: 908181; 800-535-7289)—bare boat, with a four-day minimum; *ATM Yachts* (phone: 909202; 800-634-8822)—both bare boat and crewed, three-day minimum; or *Massif Marine Antilles* (phone: 908280), which offers a fleet of cruising sailboats—both bare boat and crewed, with no minimum.

Visiting yachts dock at one of three marinas: the fully equipped, 1,000-berth *Port de Plaisance* at Bas-du-Fort (often locally referred to as simply the "Marina du Bas-du-Fort;" phone: 908485); the 250-berth *Marina de St-*

François (phone: 884728); or the 300-berth *Marina de Rivière-Sens* (phone: 817761), at Gourbeyre near Basse-Terre, within touring distance of La Soufrière volcano. (Note that only a few slips are reserved for visiting boats at the *Marina de Rivière-Sens,* so call in advance.) Marie Galante and Iles des Saintes—both within easy cruising distance—offer protected anchorages, too.

GOLF There's only one major course on Guadeloupe, but it's a beauty.

TOP TEE-OFF SPOT

Golf International de St-François For a long time, this course provided a source of comedy for the entire French Caribbean, as its opening took what seemed to be eons. But the long wait turned out to be worthwhile, since the 6,755-yard, par-71 course has been praised as one of the best in the eastern Caribbean. There are water traps on six of the 18 holes, and with the winds on this part of the island, this course offers many challenges. Designed by Robert Trent Jones Sr., its operation is under the aegis of the St-François municipality. The pro is multilingual. Maintenance has improved steadily, and there appears to be a real effort to attract golfers to the southeastern corner of the island (phone: 884187).

There's also a nine-hole course at *Plantation Ste-Marthe* (see *Checking In,* below).

HIKING Basse-Terre's *Parc National* is possibly the best in the Caribbean. Well-marked trails lead through deep green rain forests past waterfalls, mountain pools, and steaming fumaroles to the edge of La Citerne crater. The following organizations can provide information on trails and arrange guided hikes: *Organisation des Guides de Montagne* (Organization of Mountain Guides; *Maison Forestière,* Matouba, St-Claude 97120; phone: 800579); and *Emeraude Guadeloupe* (St-Claude; phone: 801609; fax: 812117).

HORSEBACK RIDING Lessons and trips can be arranged at *Le Criolo* in St-Félix (phone: 843890). Trail rides are available at *La Ferme de Campêche* (phone: 821154), *Poney Club* in Le Moule (phone: 240374), and *La Martingale* in Baie-Mahault (phone: 262839).

SNORKELING AND SCUBA DIVING Especially rewarding in waters off the western and southern coasts of Basse-Terre. Most hotels rent snorkeling equipment and can arrange guided snorkelers' excursions. Jacques Cousteau has spent considerable time under the local waters and described those around Ilet Pigeon as one of the world's ten best areas. US divers should be aware that most instructors and guides are certified under the French *CMAS* rather than *PADI* or *NAUI,* which may make a difference in the type and amount of gear you want to bring along. Complete rental outfits are available, but all components are French. *Chez Guy et Christian* (phone: 988243) and *Les Heures Saines* (phone: 988663; fax: 955090), which face Ilet Pigeon across from the beach at Malendure, specialize in diving excursions to the island. But wherever you stay, lessons for beginners and excursions for experienced divers are easily arranged through the *Aqua-Fari Plongée* at the *Créole Beach* hotel (see *Checking In*). The *Centre Nautique des Saintes* in Terre-de-Haut on Iles des Saintes (phone: 995425) also has good facilities. For any serious diving, a license and certification book, doctor's certificate, and insurance coverage are required. Single-tank dives, multiple dives, and week-long packages are available.

SPECTATOR SPORTS Cockfighting is in season from November through April; if you're interested, check with your hotel. There are periodic horse races at the *St-Jacques Hippodrome* at Anse-Bertrand (phone: 221108). Check with the tourist office for a schedule.

SPORT FISHING For barracuda and kingfish (January–May) and tuna, dolphin, and bonito (December–March), the fishing is best off the leeward coast of Basse-Terre. *Fishing Club Antilles* on Route de Birloton (phone: 907010) has day and weekly charters with bungalows for rent. Your hotel can arrange half- or full-day charters for up to six people. Other operators include *Le Rocher de Malendre* near Ilet Pigeon (phone: 987325) and *Caraïbe Pêche* at the *Bas-du-Fort Marina* (phone: 909751).

SWIMMING AND SUNNING These are major preoccupations, and Guadeloupe rises to the occasion in style.

DREAM BEACHES

Pointe des Châteaux On the east-pointing tip of Guadeloupe's Grande-Terre "wing," there are several sand beaches from which to choose: one of them, Pointe Tarare, is dedicated to au naturel bathing, and another (and more traditional) one is in nearby St-François. The rocky cliffs also shelter several sandy coves, all of which are fine for a picnic and a dip. There's a nature trail that rambles among sign-posted native trees and other vegetation, eventually leading to a spectacular viewpoint atop a promontory.

Petite Anse, Marie Galante, near Guadeloupe On the cookie-shaped island, which is a 10-minute flight from Guadeloupe's *Le Raizet Airport,* this beach is where the Guadeloupeans—who consider it their secret—go for their weekend picnics. It's long and golden, with no improvements or facilities except for a few simple creole restaurants. No excitement, but true beach buffs will find it worth the trip.

Beaches on the island vary in texture and color. On rugged Basse-Terre, west coast beaches are surf-combed, usually gray or black sand in the south and orange sand in the north. Grande-Terre has long stretches of white sand along its shores—narrow artificial beaches on the southern coast between Bas-du-Fort and Gosier; beautifully natural stretches from Ste-Anne to the tip of Pointe des Châteaux; and sandy strands along the northeastern coast at Le Moule and northwest at Anse-Bertrand and Port-Louis.

Chances are you'll spend most of your sand-and-sea time on your own hotel's beach, but if you want to visit others, most hotels will welcome you (there's usually a small fee for changing facilities, chaises, and towels). On Guadeloupe's public beaches, there's no charge or only a small fee for parking. They're fine for picnicking, but most also have small seafood restaurants where you can pick up an inexpensive creole lunch. Public beach names to know: Ste-Anne, Raisins Clairs at St-François, Anse Laborde and Anse-Bertrand on the northeast coast, Anse du Souffleur near Port-Louis, and La Grande Anse near Deshaies. In addition to Pointe Tarare, other nudist beaches include: those on Ilet Gosier, a tiny offshore land dot to which several Gosier hotels provide boat transportation (it's clothed on Sundays); at *Caravelle Club Méditerranée;* and behind the *Bois Joli* hotel, on Terre-de-Haut in the Iles des Saintes.

TENNIS There are floodlit courts at many island hotels; daytime play is free all around, but some hotels charge for night games. Hotels with courts include *Arawak, Auberge de la Vieille Tour, Canella Beach, Caravelle Club Méditerranée, La Cocoteraie, Créole Beach, Fleur d'Epée, Golf Marine Club, Golf Village, Hamak, Marissol, Méridien, Plantation Ste-Marthe, Relais du Moulin, Holiday Inn SunSpree Resort Salako,* and *La Toubana* (see *Checking In* for all). Visitors may also be able to arrange to play at the private *Marina Club* at Pointe-à-Pitre (phone: 908408) and *Centre Lamby Lambert* in Gosier (phone: 909097).

WATER SKIING AND WINDSURFING Water skiing is offered by most seaside hotels, as is windsurfing (which is so good that major international events are held here). The *Union des Centres de Plein Air* (*UCPA;* phone: 886479) in St-François offers week-long packages with daily lessons.

NIGHTLIFE

No matter where the beguine began (Guadeloupeans swear it was here), they dance it with gusto throughout the island, as they do the *zouk,* a newer dance craze. Guadeloupeans love to dance; hang a bit loose and they'll have you swinging right along in no time. Folkloric companies perform the old-fashioned dances at some of the larger hotels (don't miss them). Dinner dancing clubs and hotel discos (all very intimate, oozing trendiness, and favored by as many islanders as tourists) update the movements, and play into the small hours. Current favorites in Gosier include the *New Land* (Rte. de la Riveria; phone: 843791); the very popular *Mandingo* in the

Domaine Caribéen (Plage du Gosier; phone: 843559), which also has a restaurant; and *Le Caraïbe* at *Holiday Inn Sunspree Resort Salako* (see *Checking In*). *La Victoria* (Rte. du Bas-du-Fort; phone: 909776), *Marissol*'s *Fou Fou* (see *Checking In*), and *Elysées Matignon* (Rte. des Hôtels; phone: 908905) are hot at Bas-du-Fort. More casual clubs include the *Jardin Brésilien* (phone: 909931) in Pointe-à-Pitre and *La Chaîne* (no phone) at the marina in Bas-du-Fort. Elsewhere, *Caravelle Club Méditerranée* (see *Checking In*) prides itself on new shows nightly (lots of staff participation). At St-François there's a small discotheque called *Acapulco* (phone: 884490) and the *Blue Sea* (no phone), a music bar where things always seem to be stirred up.

There are also two casinos: one at St-François called *Casino de la Marina* (Av. de l'Europe; phone: 884131) and one at Gosier on the grounds of the *Arawak* (see *Checking In*) called *Casino Caraïbe Club* (43 Pte. de la Verdure; phone: 841833). Both offer roulette, blackjack, and baccarat from 9 PM to 3 AM (the Gosier casino may stay open until dawn, depending on the crowd); slot machines are available starting at 3 PM in St-François, from noon in Gosier. The casino in St-François is closed Mondays; the one in Gosier is closed Sundays. There is an admission charge. Minimum age is 21. Proofs of age and identity—with photo—are required. For details, see *Casino Countdown* in DIVERSIONS.

None of the island's late-night entertainment is inexpensive. Count on $10 and up for admission at clubs and discos (usually with one free drink), about $6 a drink for gin or whiskey, a bit less for rum or local beer.

Best on the Island

CHECKING IN

Guadeloupe offers a wide range of hotels in terms of size, location, ambience, and price. The smaller ones are more intimate and service-oriented; the larger resorts attract an active, sports-minded clientele. The approach is much more continental than Caribbean, since so many of Guadeloupe's visitors are Europeans. Hotels have relatively high standards of service, and offer a broad range of on-site activities and food that's good even in coffee shops. Unless otherwise indicated, all hotels listed below have air conditioning and private baths.

Where to stay? If you like hotel hopping, the answer is the Gosier strip of three- and four-star resort hotels along the beach, or Bas-du-Fort, just down the shoreline, with more three-star establishments. Farther out at Ste-Anne and St-François on Grande-Terre, there's a choice of self-contained, multi-activity resorts. Other choice places include more modest resort hotels and country inns, many of which now belong to an association called Relais Créoles (phone: 820930). In the list that follows, very expensive is defined as $250 or more per night for two including continental breakfast in winter; expensive is $200 to $250; moderate, $125 to $200; and inexpensive, less than $125. Summer rates are from 25% to 35% less. As a rule, hotel room rates quoted in dollars are guaranteed for the whole season—winter or summer—whatever the franc's fluctuations. Virtually all hotels, large and small, accept US credit cards. When calling from a phone on Guadeloupe, use only the local numbers listed below. For information about dialing from elsewhere, see *Telephone* earlier in this chapter.

GOSIER

VERY EXPENSIVE

Auberge de la Vieille Tour The sugar mill tower in front, dating from 1835, was the inspiration for the French colonial architecture here. The 160 guestrooms have ocean-view balconies, and there is a bar, a good dining room (see *Eating Out*), and a poolside restaurant. The steep, stone steps everywhere will ensure you get enough exercise even if you don't use the lighted tennis court, volleyball court, or pool. The property is operated by Pullman, the French hotel chain. On its own small beach, Montauban (phone: 842323; 800-221-4542; fax: 843343).

EXPENSIVE

Arawak With 150 trim rooms and six penthouse suites, this eight-story property offers a big pool, a beach, all sorts of sports, and plenty of services. There's also a restaurant serving French and creole fare, a popular terrace bar, and the *Caraïbe Club* casino. Pointe de la Verdure (phone: 842424; 800-223-6510; fax: 843845).

Créole Beach Part of the Leader Hôtels group, this bustling and cheerful place has 156 rooms, eight duplex apartments, a pool, a large beach, top water sports, and tennis. The restaurant has French and creole chefs. Pointe de la Verdure (phone: 904646; 800-322-2223; fax: 904666).

Holiday Inn SunSpree Resort Salako Despite its name, this 120-room property is French-speaking and modern, with stylish guestrooms, two restaurants, a disco (see *Nightlife*), two tennis courts, all water sports, and planned activities for children. The *Caraïbe Club* casino is right next door. Pointe de la Verdure (phone: 826464; 800-HOLIDAY; fax: 826400).

Canella Beach There are 146 studios (some of them duplexes), junior suites, and duplex suites here, set in three-story, Caribbean-style buildings. All units have a kitchenette, a TV set, a safe, and a balcony or terrace. A pool, four tennis courts, all water sports, and *La Véranda,* a fine restaurant (see *Eating Out*), are on the premises. Pointe de la Verdure (phone: 904400; 800-322-2223; fax 904444).

MODERATE

Callinago Beach Right on Gosier Beach, this hostelry has 40 recently refurbished rooms with mini-bars, a restaurant serving French and creole fare, and a poolside eatery. The water sports are among the best on the island. A buffet breakfast is included. Pointe de la Verdure (phone: 842525; 800-223-6510; fax: 842490).

Callinago Village A simple, attractive complex of apartments (93 studios, 22 duplexes), it's adjacent to the affiliated *Callinago Beach* (see above) and has use of its facilities. A good buy for families, all units have complete kitchenettes and balconies; there's a small supermarket on the premises. Pointe de la Verdure (phone: 842525; 800-223-6510; fax: 842490).

Cap Sud Caraïbes A very charming Relais Créoles property in a tranquil setting, it offers 12 rooms with sea-view balconies. Chemin de la Plage, near Petit-Havre Beach (phone: 859602; fax: 858039).

INEXPENSIVE

Carmelita's Village Caraïbe Just outside Gosier, this 18-bungalow enclave with a restaurant overlooks the beach and mountains. The units have kitchenettes and balconies. There's horseback riding at *Le Criolo* nearby. St-Félix (phone: 842828; fax: 845812).

BAS-DU-FORT

EXPENSIVE

Fleur d'Epée Here are 190 rooms (most with balconies) in a waterfront hotel with a Y-angled trio of three-story wings. Together with its sister hotel, the *Marissol* (see below), there are four restaurants serving a variety of creole and international fare, and lots of sports options. The landscaped gardens next to the beach add to the charm. Beachfront (phone: 908149; 800-221-4542; fax: 909907).

Marissol Two rambling two- and three-story buildings house 200 cheerful rooms. There's a marina nearby, all water sports, two tennis courts, a disco (see *Nightlife*), and weekly folkloric shows. The informal staff makes guests feel welcome. Beachfront (phone: 908444; 800-221-4542; fax: 908332).

MODERATE

Relais Bleus du Gosier An attractive condominium/hotel on the lagoon, it has 20 studios and 10 apartments grouped around a pool and garden. All have kitchenettes and balconies or patios. Rates include weekly maid service. There's a car rental agent on site. Guests may use the nearby *Marissol*'s beach and sports facilities. Rte. de l'Aéroport (phone: 908146; fax: 820026).

Sprimhotel This complex of 17 studios and three apartments features kitchenettes and daily maid service. A beach (at the *Marissol*, see above), sports facilities, shopping, and restaurants are nearby. Porte des Caraïbes (phone: 908290; fax: 828763).

Village Soleil These 81 hilltop units include studios with kitchenettes and one-bedroom suites designed for self-catering stays. Among the facilities are a pool, a snack bar, a restaurant, and a small market. It's a short drive to the beach; *Port de Plaisance* restaurants and entertainment are within walking distance. *Port de Plaisance* marina (phone: 908576; fax: 909365).

STE-ANNE

EXPENSIVE

La Toubana These 32 bungalows—each with garden, terrace, kitchenette, and telephone—offer a super view from atop a high cliff. There's a tennis court, a pool, and a small beach. The staff is happy to assist with car rentals and excursions. The dining room serves French and creole specialties. Overlooking Caravelle Beach (phone: 882578; 800-322-2223; fax: 883890).

MODERATE

Caravelle Club Méditerranée One of the many *Club Med* resorts in the Caribbean, this 300-room, all-inclusive establishment feels vast, with a beach to match (nude bathing area included). Lots is always happening, from every kind of water sport imaginable to a staff-produced show several nights a week. Facilities include two restaurants, six lighted tennis courts, and a fitness center. The clientele includes many singles over 30, as well as quite a few couples. On the beach (phone: 882100; 800-CLUB-MED; fax: 880606).

Relais du Moulin This country retreat consists of 40 cottages around an antique sugar mill. The emphasis is on peaceful, casual relaxation, with water sports available on a nearby beach. Pool, tennis, car rental, and riding stables on premises; "adventure" activities organized for more active guests. There's also a very good restaurant serving casual creole lunches and more formal French fare at night. Châteaubrun, between Ste-Anne and St-François (phone: 882396; 800-223-9815; fax: 880392).

Le Rotabas Right on the water, this relaxed and cordial place has 44 rooms, and a good French-creole restaurant. Water sports and beach are nearby. Management is very helpful with excursion arrangements. Beachfront (phone: 882560; fax: 882687).

ST-FRANÇOIS AND ENVIRONS

VERY EXPENSIVE

La Cocoteraie One of the loveliest and newest hostelries on the island, this place is ideal for those who want to be isolated but be near sports activities. Pastel colors and colonial architecture provide an intimate ambience. Both an octagonal bathtub and a balcony in the 52 deluxe suites overlook the lagoon; the guestrooms are also equipped with minibars, safes, television sets, and direct-dial telephones. There is a private beach, swimming pool, tennis courts, and a variety of water sports. It's also close to the island's best tee-off spot, the *Golf International de St-François* (see *Golf*). The restaurant and bar are right next to the swimming pool. Av. de l'Europe, St-François (phone: 887981; fax: 887833).

Hamak Recently reopened after a $1-million renovation, this elegant, peaceful, and very private retreat offers 56 stylish bungalows in a tropical garden setting, each with a patio and terrace. There's no swimming pool; all water sports take place on a private artificial beach. A good restaurant serving a buffet breakfast overlooks the sea, and other restaurants and nightlife are within walking distance. There's also a private airstrip, and the excellent, 18-hole *Golf International de St-François* (see *Golf*) is next door. Av. de l'Europe, St-François (phone: 885999; 800-633-7411; fax: 884192).

Méridien One of the French chain's Caribbean outposts, this hotel's 265 rooms are undistinguished, though comfortable. But this property is well equipped for sports—especially tennis (4 courts) and water sports on a fine beach. It's adjacent to the *Golf International de St-François* (see *Golf*); a marina is nearby. Activities include rentals of ULMs, low-power seaplanes you can operate yourself. There are three restaurants, and the nightlife is fairly active. Near the casino, St-François (phone: 885100; 800-543-4300; fax: 884071).

EXPENSIVE

Golf Marine Club Located opposite the *Golf International de St-François* course (see *Golf*), this modern complex has 58 rooms and suites, a restaurant, a bar, and a lovely pool; the club will arrange transport to the nearby beach. Av. de l'Europe, St-François (phone: 886060; 800-223-6510; fax: 887467).

Golf Village Here are 16 pretty bungalows and 20 studios on 10 garden-filled acres. Each unit has a kitchenette, living room, terrace, outside shower, and direct-dial telephone. There are also tennis courts, a pool, putting green, and gameroom. The property looks over the sea and the island's golf course; the beach is about 900 yards away. The restaurant serves creole fare. Breakfast is included in the rate, and MAP rates are also available. Ste-Marthe, above St-François (phone: 887373; fax: 886170).

MODERATE

Les Marines de St-François This 10-acre enclave of 230 sleek, contemporary studios, apartments, and duplexes borders the marina. Each unit has a fully equipped kitchenette; weekly maid service is available. Many of the units are occupied by long-term residents. There are two swimming pools, with water sports at the nearby *Méridien* and sailing from the adjacent marina. Golf, restaurants, and a casino are at its doorstep. Minimum one-week stay. *La Marina de St-François,* St-François (phone: 885955; fax: 884401).

Plantation Ste-Marthe This retreat exudes tropical elegance. Built on the site of a former sugar plantation, the 15-acre property is set in the hills above the St-François resort area, near the golf course and some of the island's best beaches. The 120 rooms are decorated in traditional style, with mahogany furniture, French fabrics, and a wrought-iron balcony offering a lovely countryside view; each has such modern amenities as cable TV and hair dryers. Facilities include the largest pool on the island, four lighted tennis courts, a health club, horseback riding, a nine-hole golf course, and water sports. There's also the excellent *Vallée d'Or* restaurant (see *Eating Out*). Ste-Marthe (phone: 884358; 800-223-9815; fax: 887247).

ELSEWHERE ON THE ISLAND

MODERATE

Auberge de la Distillerie Surrounded by fields of pineapple, this tranquil, tile-roofed country inn has 12 comfortably rustic rooms and six bungalows (all with TV sets); there are no room numbers—all are adorned with the name and painting of different flowers. Dining options include a restaurant serving creole and international fare, an informal eatery, and a bar; continental breakfast is included. There is tennis and a small garden pool. Rte. de Versailles at Tabanon, Petit-Bourg on Basse-Terre (phone: 942591; 800-322-2223; fax: 941191).

Relais Bleus du Raizet Guadeloupe's only good hotel near the airport, it's a modern motel-style building with 60 well-equipped, comfortable units and a pool. Le Raizet on Grande-Terre (phone: 900303; fax: 820026).

Relais de la Grande Soufrière The mountain views are wonderful at this former hillside manse with 22 rooms and a restaurant that serves French and creole fare. St-Claude on Basse-Terre (phone: 800127; fax: 801840).

La Sucrerie Guadeloupe's newest hotel sits by the sea on the grounds of a former rum distillery. The 52 guestrooms feature terraces and creole decor. Amenities include a pool, tennis, a restaurant, and a bar set into natural volcanic rock. Comté de Lohéac, Ste-Rose on Basse-Terre (phone: 286017; fax: 286563).

Tropical Club Nestled in a coconut grove just off the beach on the northeastern coast, this property has 72 guestrooms with terraces and ocean views, kitchenettes, TV sets, and ceiling fans. Amenities include a restaurant, a snack bar, two bars, a pool, tennis, windsurfing, scuba diving, and golf at the *Golf International de St-François* just 6 miles away. Each unit can accommodate up to four people, which makes the hotel an economical choice. Just outside Le Moule at Plage de l'Autre Bord on Grande-Terre (phone: 939797; 800-322-2223; fax: 939700).

St. John Anchorage On the waterfront at Pointe-à-Pitre, this hostelry has 44 rooms decorated with locally crafted mahogany furniture. Some rooms have private terraces; all have spectacular views of the harbor and bay. Conveniently located in the *Centre St-John Perse,* with its many shops and restaurants. Pointe-à-Pitre (phone: 825157; fax: 825261).

OFFSHORE—TERRE-DE-HAUT, ILES DES SAINTES

MODERATE

Auberge les Petits Saints aux Anacardiers With its charming village atmosphere and 11 comfortable, hillside rooms, this place is a good value. The units, distributed between the main house and a newer bungalow, are furnished with antiques but have such modern amenities as mini-bars. There's a pool, a sauna, and a boat to take guests on excursions. Its excellent restaurant (*Les Petits Saints aux Anacardiers*; see *Eating Out*) features French and creole dishes and has a view of Baie des Saintes. La Savane (phone: 995099; 800-322-2223; fax: 995451).

Bois Joli In a tranquil hilltop setting, with a great view of the bay, are eight beach bungalows and 21 small, neat rooms (13 air conditioned); most rooms have telephones and showers (no TV sets), but for those who don't mind roughing it, some less expensive rooms have a washbasin only. Features include two pretty beaches (one is the nearby Crawen Beach, where bathing is au naturel) and a pool; water sports and boat trips are available. Good creole food is served in the restaurant, with the emphasis on seafood. There's a bus and boat shuttle to town. Anse à Cointe (phone: 995038; 800-322-2223; fax: 995505).

Village Créole The best-appointed of Les Saintes' accommodations, its 22 bayfront two-bedroom apartments have kitchenettes. Take a moped ride to the good beach and other attractions (scuba diving, boating, museums, forts) nearby, or rent the yacht for excursions to other islands. No restaurant. Pointe Coquelet (phone: 995383; 800-322-2223; fax: 995555).

INEXPENSIVE

Kanaoa On the water at Pointe Coquelet, with 19 rooms and two bungalows (request an Anse Mire cove view), its amenities include all water sports, a snack bar, and an inviting restaurant. Anse Mire (phone: 995136; 800-755-9313; fax: 995504).

EATING OUT

Guadeloupe's favorite food is creole—probably because its cooks are great at it. Specialties: *crabes farcis* (stuffed crabs), *accras* (hot, puffed, cod fritters), and *boudin* (blood sausage) for appetizers; lots of fresh fish and seafood—especially *vivaneau* (red snapper), *lambi* (conch), and langouste (lobster); spicy fish stews and curries zinged with turmeric, mustard, and seven kinds of hot peppers; plus native vegetables like *christophine,* breadfruit, and fried plantain. For dessert, sample some tropical-flavored ice cream: guava, pineapple, papaya, coconut, or mango. But there are classic French restaurants, too. A three-course meal with wine for two will cost $150 or more at a restaurant we describe as very expensive, $90 to $140 at expensive places, $60 to $90 at places in the moderate category, and less than $60 at eateries listed as inexpensive. A 15% service charge is added to the bill.

Meals, whether French or creole, are usually accompanied by French wine, which is plentiful and reasonably priced. But before and after, Guadeloupeans most often order a punch in one of several dynamite variations: 'ti-punch, a fiery rum in a small glass that packs a large wallop; plain punch, white rum with lemon; and, after the meal, a *vieux* punch of dark rum, cane syrup, and lime. Restaurants tend to be small; some close on Sundays. Unless otherwise noted, restaurants are open for lunch and dinner, and reservations are advised for dinner, particularly during high season and on weekends. When making a call from a phone on Guadeloupe, use only the local numbers listed below. For information about dialing from elsewhere, see *Telephone* earlier in this chapter.

GOSIER

EXPENSIVE

Auberge de la Vieille Tour In the hotel of the same name, this place is as charming as ever. Local seafood and spices are used to produce delicious nouvelle cuisine, such as lobster salad, and duck breast with sweet-and-sour pineapple sauce. Extensive wine list. Open daily. Major credit cards accepted. On the beach, Montauban (phone: 842323).

La Véranda Among the best restaurants on the island, this dining room at the *Canella Beach* hotel features a creole and French menu. All the dishes, including smoked marlin, a lobster-and-shrimp soup, grouper flavored with ginger *en papillote,* and filet of red snapper with cucumbers, are beautifully prepared and presented. An unusual highlight is the wine list with offerings not only from France, but from California, Chile, and Italy. A live band plays nightly—everything from beguine to waltzes. Open daily. Major credit cards accepted. Pointe de la Verdure (phone: 904400).

MODERATE

Le Bananier Cornélia, formerly head of the *Auberge de la Vieille Tour* dining room, runs this place, which serves excellent creole fare cooked in nouvelle cuisine style. The wine list is extensive. Closed Mondays. Major credit cards accepted. Rte. de Gosier (phone: 843485).

La Chaubette A small, friendly spot offering baby clam soup, langouste, and coconut ice cream. Closed Sundays. Major credit cards accepted. Rte. de Ste-Anne (phone: 841429).

Au P'ti Paris This friendly place serves up thin-crust pizzas (one of which makes a meal in itself) and pasta dishes in a colonial white building with seating indoors or on a wide verandah. Open for dinner only; closed Mondays. No reservations. No credit cards accepted. Rte. de Ste-Anne (phone: 845665).

BAS-DU-FORT

La Plantation Set in a typical tropical house with a verandah, this chic, popular spot—run by the former chef of the *Carlton* hotel in Cannes—is one of the finest classic French restaurants in the Caribbean. The menu features Bordeaux specialties, as well as dishes with a creole touch, such as saffron ragout of shark, and game hen cooked with cocount and fresh ginger. Closed Saturday lunch and Sundays. Major credit cards accepted. *Galerie Marina* (phone: 908483).

Rosini The Rosini family goes to great lengths to serve classic, authentic Italian dishes in a warm, welcoming setting. Try the mixed homemade pasta (in Italian-flag colors—red, white, and green), local river shrimp *fra diavolo,* and homemade desserts. Open daily. Major credit cards accepted. Rte. du Bas-du-Fort (phone: 908781).

Tropicabana This place serves up an eclectic menu that suits its funky decor of old art posters and record covers. The steaks are superb, and the banana flambé is a great way to finish the meal. Open for dinner only; closed Wednesdays and September. Major credit cards accepted. Rte. du Bas-du-Fort (phone: 907311).

POINTE-À-PITRE

La Canne à Sucre Arguably the best kitchen in the Caribbean, it's on the waterfront, with a brasserie on the street level and a quieter, 60-seat dining room upstairs. Chef Gérard Viginius turns out the nouvelle creole specialties that have gained him fame throughout the islands. His creations include *beignets* (fritters) of pumpkin and malanga, savory *crabes farcis,* parrot fish prepared with anise seeds, and *coupe Canne à Sucre* (crème Chantilly and coconut sherbet with banana caramel, aged rum, and a bit of cinnamon). Fine wines, too. Closed Saturday afternoons and Sundays. Major credit cards accepted. *Centre St-John Perse* (phone: 821019).

MODERATE

Le Big Steak House Serving lunch only and geared toward the business crowd, this air conditioned eatery emphasizes steaks—entrecôtes, tournedos, rib steaks, you name it—all with a choice of five sauces: shallot, chive butter, green peppercorn, roquefort, or mustard. Closed Sundays. Major credit cards accepted. 2 Rue Delgrès at the Quai Lardenoy (phone: 821244).

Normandie A pleasant spot on the main square, with either out- or indoor seating. The menu features salads, pasta, pizza, grilled meat, and fish; there's a daily three-course special for less than $20. Most of the youthful, energetic staff speak at least some English—as well as Italian, Spanish, and Dutch. Open daily. Major credit cards accepted. 14 Pl. de la Victoire (phone: 823715).

ST-FRANÇOIS

EXPENSIVE

La Louisiane A charming, colonial house where traditional French fare with creole influences is served. Closed Mondays. Major credit cards accepted. Quartier Ste-Marthe, just outside St-François (phone: 884434).

Vallée d'Or The fare at the elegant *Plantation Ste-Marthe* dining room consists of light, contemporary versions of French dishes. French cheeses and wines round out the meal. Open daily. Major credit cards accepted. Ste-Marthe, near St-François (phone: 884358).

MODERATE

Café Gourmand The ambience is typically French and the food is very good at this tiny sidewalk bistro, the best in town for salads, pizza, or ice-cream sundaes. Closed Mondays. Major credit cards accepted. In the *Gulf Marine Club* hotel (phone: 886939).

Chez Honoré This homey, unpretentious place serves very good fresh fish and seafood dishes (caught by the owner). Open daily. Major credit cards accepted. 5 Pl. du Marché (phone: 884061).

La Langouste A casual beach spot; not surprisingly, grilled lobster is its specialty. The quality is consistent with the owner's other restaurant, *Chez Honoré* (see above). Open daily for lunch. Reservations unnecessary. Major credit cards accepted. Anse à la Gourde (phone: 885219).

Zig Zag André Rojchouze, the owner, offers an excellent varied menu, with choices ranging from creole (fricassee of octopus and curried goat) to continental (veal scaloppine Milanese, entrecôte in green peppercorn sauce). Open for breakfast, lunch, and dinner; closed Mondays. Major credit cards accepted. Port de Pêche (phone: 884273).

Le Mareyeur The fixed price lunch at this open-air creole dining spot—Antillean salad, grilled fish, and *glace* for dessert—is a rare and tasty bargain at about $12 per person. Closed Tuesdays and September. Major credit cards accepted. Rue de la République, overlooking the waterfront (phone: 884424).

ELSEWHERE ON GRANDE-TERRE

EXPENSIVE

Les Oiseaux In a pastoral setting, with stone walls and open windows, this friendly eatery delivers first-rate creole cooking, with a welcome touch of country French. Highlights include fish fondue, gratinéed lobster steaks, marinated conch. Closed Mondays, Tuesday lunch, and September. Major credit cards accepted. Anse des Rochers (phone: 885692).

MODERATE

Château de Feuilles A delightful terrace on an old country estate, it offers such unusual specialties as Tahitian fish soup, seafood sauerkraut with green papaya, and tropical fruit charlotte. Closed Mondays and September. Reservations necessary for dinner. Major credit cards accepted. Near Anse-Bertrand, Campêche (phone: 223030).

BASSE-TERRE

EXPENSIVE

Karacoli, Grande Anse One of the best places for such creole specialties as *colombos* (island curries) and *coquilles Karacoli* (coquilles St. Jacques with creole spices), served indoors or on a tree-shaded terrace by the beach. English-speaking staff. Open daily for lunch. Major credit cards accepted. Plage Grande, Anse Deshaies (phone: 284117).

MODERATE

Chez Paul Located in an East Indian Basse-Terre neighborhood, the specialties here are curries and creole dishes. The menu changes daily; when you call for reservations, check what's on. Open daily for breakfast and lunch. Major credit cards accepted. Matouba (phone: 802920).

INEXPENSIVE

Chez LouLouse Cheerful and rustic, it's a favorite spot for divers returning from Ilet Pigeon. The menu *touristique* features salad, fresh grilled fish, curried chicken, rice, wine, and fruit. No extra charge for spontaneous song accompaniment. Open daily. Reservations unnecessary. No credit cards accepted. On the beach, Malendure Beach (phone: 987034).

La Touna There's always a warm welcome at this open-air spot, which is also the *Fishing Club Antilles.* The menu depends on what the boat brings in. Closed

Sunday dinner, Mondays, and September. Reservations advised for dinner and Sunday lunch. Visa accepted. Pigeon Galet in Bouillante (phone: 987010).

OFFSHORE—TERRE-DE-HAUT, ILES DES SAINTES

MODERATE

Les Petits Saints aux Anacardiers The terraced hotel dining room is well known for its fine seafood, especially the smoked local kingfish, as well as stuffed squid and sea urchin *blaff* (stew). It's poolside, so take a dip before dining. Open daily. Major credit cards accepted. In *Auberge les Petits Saints aux Anacardiers,* La Savane, Terre-de-Haut (phone: 995099).

Pizzeria le Genois Cozy waterfront spot with all kinds of—you guessed it—pizza. Try the Santoise, topped with cheese and minced conch. There's also a Buccaneer's Platter of smoked marlin, tuna, and marinated local fish. Open daily. Reservations unnecessary. Major credit cards accepted. Terre-de-Haut (phone: 995301).

Le Relais des Iles A 10-table dining room in the home of chef Bernard Mathieu and his gracious wife. There's a fresh lobster tank on the terrace. Seafood specialties on the menu include pâté of fish and creamy scallops Florentine; try the lemon sherbet with vodka for dessert. Closed Tuesdays. Reservations advised for dinner. Major credit cards accepted. Rte. de Pompière, Terre-de-Haut (phone: 995304).

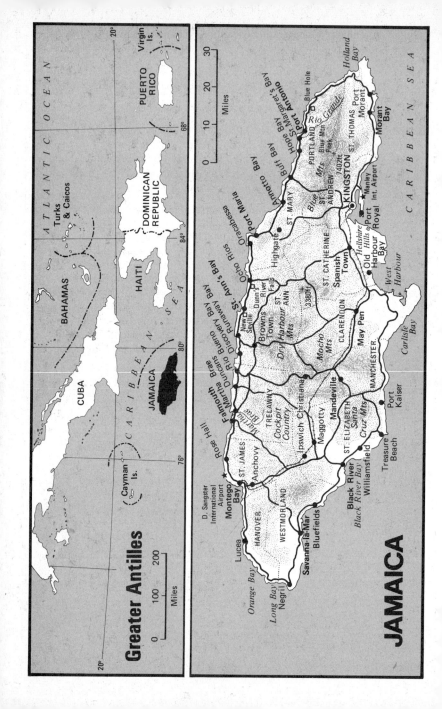

Greater Antilles

ATLANTIC OCEAN

BAHAMAS

Turks & Caicos

CUBA

Cayman Is.

C A R I B B E A N   S E A

JAMAICA

HAITI

DOMINICAN REPUBLIC

PUERTO RICO

Virgin Is.

Miles
0   100   200

JAMAICA

D. Sangster International Airport
Montego Bay
Rose Hall
Anchovy
ST. JAMES
Lucea
HANOVER
Orange Bay
Long Bay
Negril
WESTMORLAND
Savanna-la-Mar
Bluefields
Falmouth
Martha Brae
Rio Bueno
Duncans
Discovery Bay
Runaway Bay
St. Ann's Bay
Ocho Rios
Oracabessa
Port Maria
Martha Brae
TRELAWNY
Cockpit Country
Ipswich Christiana
Maggotty
Mandeville
MANCHESTER
Santa Cruz Mts
ST. ELIZABETH
Black River
Black River Bay
Williamsfield
Treasure Beach
Port Kaiser
New Seville
Browns Town
Dry Harbour Mts
ST. ANN
St. Faith's
3380 ft.
Mocho Mts
CLARENDON
May Pen
Highgate
ST. MARY
Blue
Mts
ST. CATHERINE
Spanish Town
Old Harbour Bay
West Harbour
Hellshire Hills
Port Royal
Manley Royal Int. Airport
KINGSTON
ANDREW
7402 ft.
Blue Mtn Peak
PORTLAND
Buff Bay
Annotto Bay
Hope Bay
St. Margaret's Bay
Port Antonio
Blue Hole
Rio Grande
Holland Bay
ST. THOMAS
Port Morant
Morant Bay
Carlisle Bay

C A R I B B E A N   S E A

Miles
0   10   20   30

Jamaica

Jamaica is one of the most provocative Caribbean islands, tempting visitors with a diversity of dramatic landscapes and seascapes, a greater variety of flora and fauna than any of its Greater Antillean neighbors, and a rich culture that has seduced even the most seasoned traveler. The real Jamaica is found in the Jamaicans themselves, 2.5 million people whose features may be African, European, Arabic, Chinese, or East Indian, and who embody the country's motto, so similar to our own: "Out of many, one people."

The third-largest Caribbean island, Jamaica has an area of 4,411 square miles (slightly smaller than Connecticut). On the southeastern coast is the busy capital of Kingston, one of the commercial hubs of the West Indies. On the north coast are the fine powdery beaches of Montego Bay and Ocho Rios. Negril's 7-mile expanse of white sand beaches at the island's northwestern tip—a fast-growing resort area—adds yet another dimension. And the broad selection of hotels, luxury villas, evocative guesthouses, and charming small inns sprinkled throughout the island makes Jamaica one of the Caribbean's most interesting destinations.

Rugged highlands and mountains dominate the landscape: More than half of Jamaica rises 1,000 feet above the sea. The highest point, Blue Mountain Peak, provides the stunning backdrop for Kingston, towering over the capital at 7,402 feet. From the plunging waterfalls and languorous Rio Grande of Port Antonio to the surrealist moonscape of Cockpit Country in the northwest, Jamaica is a study in dramatic contrasts.

With the hypnotic, haunting rhythms of reggae and the breeze-cooled, hidden beaches of elegant resorts, Jamaica offers both stimulation and relaxation. Water sports aplenty can be pursued under and upon the turquoise waves, and Jamaica also has 12 championship golf courses, hundreds of tennis courts, and a first-rate equestrian center near Ocho Rios.

The Jamaican people create memories as vivid as the varied landscape of their country. Proud, resourceful, and extremely creative in fields from literature and music to arts and crafts, their unrelenting good humor, ingenuity, and natural hospitality make them among the most accessible of all Caribbean peoples. While some visitors are taken aback by their gregariousness, most find it engaging.

Many have described Jamaica as seductive, and it has cast its spell over adventurers and rogues, as well as some of the most civilized bon vivants of this century. Ian Fleming wrote his "007" series at his house in Oracabessa, while Noël Coward produced some of his finest works at *Firefly,* his hilltop retreat at Port Maria (see *Special Places*).

Christopher Columbus sighted the island's north coast in May 1494. His first visit was relatively uneventful; after sighting land in the neighborhood of Rio Bueno, he sailed to Montego Bay before returning to Cuba. His second call, in 1503, was stormier; foul weather and two crippled ships forced him to put in at St. Ann's Bay, where he and his crew were marooned until the jealous governor of Hispaniola saw fit to send a ship to rescue them a year later.

In 1510, after his father's death, Christopher's son Diego, then based in Santo Domingo as governor of all the West Indies, sent Juan de Esquivel to found a permanent Spanish settlement in Jamaica. Twenty-four years later, the town called New Seville (near the site of present-day Ocho Rios) was abandoned in favor of a new capital at Villa de la Vega (Town on the Plain), now called Spanish Town.

In 1655 Britain's Oliver Cromwell dispatched 6,000 men to counter Spain's claim to Jamaica. They drove out the 500 Spaniards then residing on the island and almost immediately set up privateering headquarters at Port Royal, across the harbor from what is now Kingston. The settlement soon earned a reputation as "the wickedest city on earth." Henry Morgan, the notorious buccaneer, took charge and carried out a series of raids that climaxed with his sacking of the Spanish colony at Panama and Spain's ultimate recognition of England's claim to Jamaica. The end of Port Royal's era of outrageous fun and profit came in 1692 with the literal fall of the city—during a severe earthquake, more than half the town slid into the harbor.

Agriculture then became the colony's chief concern. After unprofitable attempts at the commercial growing of indigo, tobacco, and cotton, the planters settled on sugarcane as their main crop. And sugar meant slaves. By the end of the 18th century, Jamaica's population consisted of roughly 300,000 African slaves and 20,000 whites. Adding to the mix were "free coloureds," the offspring of white men and slave women, and Maroons (from the Spanish *cimarrón,* meaning "untamed"), descendants of freed slaves. (Descendants of the Maroons still live in the hilly Cockpit Country to the west and at Moore Town in the hills of Portland to the east.) Plantation owners were constantly harassed by the Maroons' guerrilla-style raids—so much so that the government signed a formal treaty with them, guaranteeing them freedom within specified tax-free boundaries in return for their help against "enemies of the government" and the return of runaway slaves. Though this last provision was rarely honored, the Maroon threat was lessened.

Revolts by the slaves themselves began during the mid-1700s. The most serious of these broke out in 1760 and continued on and off until December 1831, when a bloody clash took place in Montego Bay. Sparked by now-hero "Daddy" Sam Sharpe, a Baptist deacon and slave (who was hanged in the square that bears his name today), the confrontation hastened the end of slavery in Jamaica. Seven years later the institution was abolished throughout the British Empire.

For a number of reasons—including abolition and increased competition from Cuba—sugarcane became less and less profitable. In 1865 drought struck and, pushed beyond endurance, the impoverished and desperate black population of Morant Bay rioted, killing a government official. The uprising was summarily put down, but in the process the Jamaican Assembly, which had previously exercised considerable control over island affairs, surrendered much of its power to the governor. As a result, in 1866 Jamaica was designated a British Crown Colony, which it remained until 1944, when full adult suffrage was granted.

The emergence of bananas as a major crop, the very profitable discovery of bauxite, and the rise of year-round tourism shored up the economy. Eighteen years later, Jamaica became fully independent within the British Commonwealth. But autonomy does not ensure stability, and since its independence ceremony on August 6, 1962, Jamaica has had its share of traumatic ups and downs.

The basic problems were both economic and political. During the mid-1970s unemployment and the cost of living were up, incomes down. Further, the left-leaning statements of Prime Minister Michael Manley—and his government's apparent coziness with Cuba—gave rise to the worldwide belief that the island was about to go Communist. Stories of violence—many true—were dramatically reported. Visitors began staying away in droves. To try to set the economy right, the government declared a massive austerity program and devalued the Jamaican dollar several times.

Devaluation boosted the tourist trade by keeping hotel and package prices low, and the island's natural beauty made it one of the most appealing tropical destinations. Tourism began a slow recovery, which got a boost with the election of Manley's more conservative Jamaica Labour Party opponent, Edward P. G. Seaga. Seaga's victory inspired hope for Jamaica's economic recovery and reassured its neighbors—including the US. It also gave tourism an immediate and enormous lift that led, ultimately, to an all-time high of 1.6 million visitors in 1993. At the same time, resort projects built largely by foreign investors added nearly 19,000 guestrooms and introduced significant vitality and vivacity.

In the 1989 elections a more moderate Manley regained power. In contrast to his fiery rhetoric of a decade before, Manley vowed to pay Jamaica's debt and to encourage tourism, by then Jamaica's largest industry. Manley retired in 1992 at the age of 67; his successor, Percival J. Patterson, chairman of the People's National Party and a former Deputy Prime Minister, also supports tourism. And Patterson's 1993 re-election (though marred by violence during the campaign and at the polls) is good news for those who wish to visit the country.

Should you grab your bathing suit and sunblock and take off for Jamaica? The answer is an equivocal "yes," as long as you exercise the same common sense that you would at home: Don't leave your wallet unattended at the beach, or your camera on the front seat of your rental car, and don't go strolling down dark, deserted streets alone (especially in Kingston). There are police foot patrols in all major tourist areas, and both major political parties have made a commitment to "encourage decorum and law and order."

One thing to watch out for, however, is the overexuberance of some islanders. In Jamaica it doesn't matter that you just told four taxi drivers that you don't need a cab; the fifth will solicit you anyway. Ditto the craft vendor trying to sell you wares. Do beware of the young men who want to guide you around town; they expect a tip for their service. Your "no" needs to be polite but very firm. More recently, a government-sponsored education campaign has had some success in toning down aggressive sales pitches from street vendors and others.

In terms of cost and comfort, the overall picture in Jamaica has been steadily brightening. No longer must villa renters tote in staples and foodstuffs, although savvy sportspersons still bring their own equipment. The rising cost of imported food and oil has sent restaurant, taxi, and car rental prices up, but no more so than on other Caribbean islands. On the other hand, hotel prices remain reasonable. Winter occupancies have climbed back to the 80% to 90% range, due in no small part to Jamaica's pioneering of all-inclusive resorts. From Negril to Port Antonio, more and more vacationers are lolling on Jamaica's beaches, splashing in its sea, seeking its pleasures—and finding them.

Jamaica At-a-Glance

FROM THE AIR

Jamaica is shaped something like a swimming sea turtle, and measures 146 miles from east to west and 51 miles from north to south at its broadest point, with a total land area of 4,411 square miles and a population of 2.5 million. Dark green mountains rise from foothills in the west, stretch the length of the island, and reach their highest point at Blue Mountain Peak (7,402 feet) in the east. The island's best-known resort areas—Montego Bay (or "MoBay"), Negril, Runaway Bay, Ocho Rios, and Port Antonio—lie along the gently curved north coast. In contrast, the long southern shoreline forms a deeper curve irregularly notched by coves, bays, and harbors, the most important of which is the eastern harbor on which Kingston (pop. 750,000), Jamaica's capital and chief port, is located.

The island is about 90 miles due south of Cuba and approximately the same distance from its two other near neighbors, Haiti to the northeast and the Cayman Islands to the northwest. Its gateway airports are *Norman Manley International*, about 20 minutes from downtown Kingston, and *Sir Donald Sangster International* (where most vacationers deplane), about a 10-minute drive from Montego Bay. International flights stop at both airports. Flight time from Miami (about 590 air miles) is about an hour and a half; from New York (about 1,450 air miles), less than four hours; from Atlanta (1,120 air miles), 2½ hours.

SPECIAL PLACES

Jamaican sightseeing isn't an obligation; it's a delightful diversion. Each of the island's vacation areas, as well as its capital, has sights worth seeing, and there also are old Georgian towns and plantation greathouses to explore.

NEGRIL In the northwesternmost corner of Jamaica, this area was one of the island's last secret places. But sleepy, bohemian Negril has developed rapidly over the last 20 years, and today has many hotels, villas, and cottages—including several luxurious all-inclusive resorts. There also are campsites at *Roots Bamboo* and the *Negril Lighthouse Park* (both off West End Rd.; no phones).

Negril is famous for its laid-back village atmosphere, its 7 miles of beaches dotted with sea grape and coconut palm, its tranquil turquoise seas, superb scuba diving, golf, and tennis, and its unforgettable sunsets that set the clouds afire with color. (*Rick's Café*—see *Eating Out*—is one of the best spots to view the latter; while sipping a cocktail and waiting for the sun to sink to the horizon, you can watch divers jump off the cliffs into a deep pool below.) According to law, none of Negril's buildings may be taller than the tallest palm tree, so no ultramodern high-rises mar the skyline.

Excursions from Negril include visits to Booby Cay, a small island across from Rutland Point that is popular with nude sunbathers; Bluefields, a small fishing village with an attractive swimming beach; Bloody Bay, an intimate beach so named because whalers used to butcher their catch there; and the Roaring River Caves, located in Savanna-la-Mar. Or opt for a leisurely sunset cruise on the *Sunsplash,* a 55-foot catamaran (book through *Sandals Negril;* see *Checking In*), or a stroll through the outdoor *Craft Market* and the indoor *Vendors' Arcade* (both open daily).

At one time Negril's free-wheeling ways weren't ideal for family vacationing, but things have changed: *Anancy* (phone: 957-4100), a children's amusement park, petting zoo, and cultural center, has opened across from *Poinciana Beach,* a family resort (see *Checking In*). Still, Negril also remains great for singles, couples, and sports enthusiasts. The beach resorts along Norman Manley Boulevard are where most people stay, but there's also a thriving nightlife, several good eateries, and a number of popular watering holes along West End Road.

About halfway between Negril and Montego Bay is the village of Lucea, where the *Hanover Museum* (Watson Taylor Dr., next door to the church; no phone) has displays on local history, as well as an art gallery and a gift shop. The museum is closed Sundays; there's an admission charge. Other sites here are the 18th-century *Fort Charlotte* battlements, an interesting clock tower shaped like a German World War I helmet, and the 1725 *Hanover Parish Church.* The nearby thousand-acre *Belvedere Estate* (Hanover, 15 miles west of Montego Bay; phone: 952-6001 or 957-4170) is set amid lush tropical forest and features a historical village and living museum where visitors can watch coffee beans, sugarcane, and cacao being processed the old-fashioned way and view the greathouse ruins, a reconstructed cookhouse, and an old sugar mill. The estate is closed Sundays; there is an admission charge.

MONTEGO BAY This second-largest city in Jamaica (and the capital of Jamaican tourism) offers enough attractions, excellent beaches, restaurants, and nightlife to make it a desirable spot, especially for those who like to sightsee (though it's rather short on picturesque views).

The city's center is the Parade (also known as Sam Sharpe Square), with its 1804 *Old Courthouse* (closed weekends; no admission charge). *St. James Parish Church* (open for Sunday 11 AM service only; St. Claver and Church Sts.; phone: 952-2775) is a faithful restoration (after severe damage by a 1957 earthquake) of the Georgian original (1775–82). Regarded as one of the finest churches on Jamaica, it is surrounded by tropical gardens and is full of fascinating monuments. Church Street itself boasts some handsomely restored Georgian homes. The *Town House,* a Georgian red brick structure (16 Church St.), was built in 1765 as the town residence of a wealthy sugar planter. Today it houses a restaurant (see *Eating Out*). Also worth visiting on Sam Sharpe Square is the *Cage,* an 1806 jail that was used for slaves and runaway seamen (closed weekends; no admission charge; no phone), and *Fort Montego* (no phone), which still has two old cannon turned toward the sea.

An excellent excursion is the bus ride up to the *Appleton Sugar Estate and Rum Distillery* (Moggotty; phone: 963-2210/6) where rum and sugar have been produced since 1749. Buses to the estate run daily; book the tour through your hotel. Another is the the *Mountain Valley Rafting Tour* (see *Getting Around*). Birders flock to *Rocklands Feeding Station* in Anchovy (turn left onto Rte. B8 south of town). Established by artist-writer-naturalist Lisa Salmon, the sanctuary is home to some 100 species, a number of which arrive to be fed promptly at 4 PM. Many birds, including the Doctor Bird hummingbird, will eat right out of your hand. Bring a camera and arrive at 3 PM. No children under 5 allowed. Open daily; admission charge (phone: 956-4019).

In the early 17th century, some Maroons hid on the Cockpit Mountains and warded off all attempts by the British to return them to slavery. The *Maroon Tourist Attraction Co.* (phone: 952-4546) offers guided historical tours from Montego Bay to Accompong Town, a Maroon village high up in the mountains.

Water sports enthusiasts will enjoy the *Montego Bay Marine Park,* a national underwater preserve. The 6,000-acre park stretches from the airport to the Great Rivers. Closed weekends; no admission charge (phone: 952-9709).

Montego Bay was once a major port for sugar and bananas. Today the main remnants of this industry are the magnificent houses of the sugar barons, such as *Greenwood Great House* and *Rose Hall.* The *Greenwood Great House,* which belonged to members of Elizabeth Barrett Browning's family, exhibits original books, letters, musical instruments, furniture, and other household items dating back over 200 years. It is very close to the Trelawny–St. James Parish line, outside of Montego Bay on the way to Falmouth (open daily; admission charge; phone: 953-1077). While *Greenwood* gives a truer picture of plantation life, *Rose Hall,* about 10 miles east of Montego Bay on Rose Hall Rd., is Jamaica's best-known greathouse, partly due to the legend of its second mistress, Anne Palmer, the infamous voodoo-practicing White Witch, who disposed of husbands and lovers by murdering them. The tour guide's tale of love, lust, and unbridled passion is itself worth the price of admission. Afterward, you can sit in *Annie's Pub* (where the dungeons were located) and sip a drink called "the Witch's Brew." *Rose Hall* is open daily; there's an admission charge (phone: 953-2323). At *Belfield Great House and Barnett Estates Plantation* (phone: 952-1709 for the greathouse; 952-2382 for the plantation) overlooking Montego Bay, two tours are available, one of the working sugarcane plantation and the other of the greathouse, where 11 generations of the Kerr-Jarrett family lived and hosted distinguished guests including US presidents and British royalty. The plantation is open daily; there's an admission charge.

Closer to Falmouth (follow the signs) is *Jamaica Safari Village.* Kids will love this bird sanctuary, petting zoo, and crocodile exhibit and farm. It's located on the film set of the James Bond movie *Live and Let Die.* Closed Sundays; admission charge (phone: 954-3065).

FALMOUTH This small 18th-century port town on the north coast, about 23 miles east of Montego Bay, is an interesting destination for a drive. The historic district has been declared a national monument due to its splendid array of Georgian architecture, with some of the finest examples in the Caribbean. Park on or near Water Square and take half an hour to explore on foot. Among the noteworthy sites in the town center are the courthouse, a reconstruction of the 1817 building; the customs office; the 1796 parish church; and *William Knibb Memorial Church,* at George and King Streets (the present church building is new, but ask about its predecessors).

Leaving town, turn south (away from the water); at the town of Martha Brae the road forks. If greathouses intrigue you, take the right, then—almost immediately, when the road divides again—take the left fork to visit *Good Hope,* the 18th-century home of one of the wealthiest planters in Jamaican history, John Thorpe. The main house and outbuildings have been impeccably restored and recently opened as a hotel; there are stables, and horseback riding is offered daily on trails through the estate's 2,000 acres. Call ahead to make reservations for the tour, which includes a welcome drink. Admission charge (see *Checking In*). Bearing left at Martha

Brae town (following the signs) leads to *Rafters' Village,* where visitors can take a raft ride on the Martha Brae River (see *River Rafting,* below), enjoy a dip in the pool, then have lunch in the thatch restaurant (Jamaican food at reasonable prices).

Before returning to Montego Bay, drive 2 miles east of Falmouth on the main road to the *Caribatik* factory (see *Shopping*). Owner Muriel Chandler has an open-air studio with batik items for sale, and a gallery displaying many of her paintings. Just east of *Caribatik,* stop at *Glistening Waters Marina* (see *Eating Out*) for a cool drink or some seafood and a look at beautiful Oyster Bay, which glows with bioluminescence caused by microorganisms in the water. Boat rides depart from the main dock every evening except Sundays; reserve at the marina in advance.

NORTH SHORE DRIVE The trip from Montego Bay to Ocho Rios (a 67-mile drive) can be a day's excursion (to Dunn's River Falls for lunch and back) or a link between stays in Montego Bay and Ocho Rios or Port Antonio. The sea is on the left as you drive east; to the right is Jamaican plantation country. Some of the land is devoted to sugarcane, some to pimiento, and some is now pastureland. Detours along any one of a dozen narrow roads will reveal antique greathouses and little old settlements. Going from west to east on the main road (A1), beyond Falmouth, you'll come to:

RIO BUENO A tiny fishing village with old stone houses, a photogenic church, a fort, and Joe James's art gallery (no phone); sample pepper pot soup and seafood in his adjoining restaurant. The historian Samuel Eliot Morison believed that Columbus did not find Discovery Bay until his fourth and final voyage, and that he actually landed in Rio Bueno first, in 1494.

DISCOVERY BAY The spot where Columbus landed is marked by *Columbus Park,* with a small outdoor exhibit of artifacts of old Jamaica. Open daily. No admission charge (no phone).

RUNAWAY BAY Once a tourist satellite of Ocho Rios, it is now a resort in its own right, with several hotels. The area is named for escaped slaves, who hid in nearby caverns. Not far beyond, off the main road, is *Chukka Cove Farm* (see *Horseback Riding,* below), an equestrian center where polo matches often are held.

ST. ANN'S BAY A few miles farther east along A1, past the ruined church at Priory, is the *Columbus Monument* at the entrance of the *Seville National Park.* The monument commemorates the explorer's year-long stay here as well as the site of Jamaica's first Spanish settlement, nearby Sevilla la Nueva (New Seville), founded in 1510 by Christopher's son Diego. The park, operated by the *Jamaica National Heritage Trust,* features a recently restored 18th-century greathouse overlooking the site of New Seville, as well as the ruins of a 19th-century English factory complex. The greathouse museum (phone: 972-2191) contains locally discovered artifacts dating back to 900 AD. The museum is closed Mondays. Admission charge.

DUNN'S RIVER FALLS Located in Ocho Rios, these famous, stair-stepped cascading falls splash wonderfully down the mountainside on the right, rush under the road, and join the sea by the white sand beach on the left. This is a must-see attraction, even if you decide not to participate in the popular get-wet tour up the falls. (It's quite safe, but a little scary!) There are steps and an overlook beside the falls for those who don't want to get wet. Wear sneakers and bring your camera for some unforgettable pictures. There are changing facilities, lockers, and a snack bar. Admission charge (the local guides who lead groups up the falls also expect a tip). Ocho Rios (phone: 974-2857).

OCHO RIOS On the northern coastline, midway between Montego Bay and Port Antonio, this spot is ideal for tourists who want upscale resort pampering plus some of the island's best scenery. The town has maintained its charm in spite of extensive building and the cruise ships calling at its port.

In addition to Dunn's River Falls, another local attraction is Fern Gully, on Route A3, the main road to Kingston, a 3-mile-long dry riverbed surrounded by giant ferns, which grow along the steep hillside and intertwine in spots to form a natural roof over sections of the gully. Naturalists also can head over to the 34-acre *Shaw Park Botanical Gardens.* Located on a hill above town, the gardens offer a spectacular view. Open daily. Admission charge (Milford Rd.; phone: 974-2723). Also in *Shaw Park* is a new island attraction, the *Coyaba River Garden and Museum.* The exhibits here focus on Jamaica's heritage—from pre-Columbian Arawak relics to tributes to Bob Marley—while the gardens are lush with native flora. Open daily; admission charge (phone: 974-6235).

Several working plantations in the vicinity offer jitney or horseback tours of their grounds. The most interesting of these (and the one closest to town, off Rte. A1) is *Prospect Plantation;* a jitney tour of the plantation is included in the admission charge. Also offered (at additional cost) are 1½-hour horseback tours along trails through groves of citrus and coffee trees, past impressive stands of mahogany, and along the banks of the White River. Open daily (phone: 974-2058).

Harmony Hall, built toward the end of the 19th century as the greathouse of a small pimiento estate, is a few miles east of Ocho Rios on the main road. Now an art gallery, it has an excellent selection of Jamaican artwork and handicrafts for sale (see *Shopping*), plus an excellent restaurant. Open daily (phone: 975-4222 for the gallery; 975-4785 for the restaurant).

From Ocho Rios the North Shore Road wends east through Oracabessa, a small banana port. Four miles farther on, at *Sun Valley Plantation,* a tour recounts the story of plantation life from colonial times to the present. Open daily; admission charge (phone: 995-3075).

PORT MARIA Three miles east of Oracabessa is Port Maria, site of *Firefly,* the tiny home high on the hill where British playwright Noël Coward lived and wrote from 1950 until his death in 1973. After a $250,000 restoration, *Firefly* has been opened to the public. The simplicity of the house and its mementos (Coward's paintings and clothes are just where he left them) is immensely touching; the view of the curved harbor below is breathtaking; and there's a small restaurant and bar. Once a month, on the weekend night closest to the full moon, the museum hosts a party where guests can enjoy a moonlight picnic while being serenaded by a jazz band. Open daily; admission charge (phone: 997-7201). The road briefly takes to the hills in the coconut and banana country beyond, before being joined by the railroad right-of-way at Albany. Continue on to Annotto Bay. Watch closely for signs to *Crystal Springs,* a 350-acre natural garden with rivers, waterfalls, birds, hundreds of orchids, and a restaurant (open daily; admission charge; phone: 929-6280). The main road then goes through Buff Bay, Hope Bay, and St. Margaret's Bay, crosses the Rio Grande, Jamaica's original rafting river, and leads into Port Antonio.

PORT ANTONIO A miniature island port built around two picture-book harbors, it is 67 miles east of Ocho Rios and 134 miles east of Montego Bay. Its quaint buildings extend onto the peninsula between the two harbors and up into the hills behind. It is famous for quiet beauty, deep-sea fishing, and river rafting, which Hollywood legend Errol Flynn invented as a tourist attraction when he saw the skinny bamboo craft islanders used to ferry bananas to the port for shipping. Another Flynn landmark is Navy Island, in Port Antonio Harbor. Once his private hideaway, this 64-acre retreat now comprises the *Navy Island Marina* resort (see *Checking In*). It can be reached by ferry from the Navy Island land base in Port Antonio.

Port Antonio itself boasts two intriguing architectural sites. The first is the *Folly,* the crumbled ruins of a splendid concrete mansion built on a headland at the eastern end of town by millionaire Connecticut Yankee Alfred Mitchell in 1906. Open daily; no admission charge. The second building, a turreted fantasy castle designed by architect Earl Levy, commands the rockbound shoreline east of the *Trident* hotel (see *Checking In*). Check with your hotel to see if the house is currently open to the public; no admission charge. History buffs also may want to take a short detour to Fort George Street, where the remains of *Fort George,* built in 1865 by the British, can be seen on the grounds of *Titchfield High School* (open daily; no admission charge). Neighboring natural wonders include the Blue Hole, a 282-foot-deep lagoon (off Rte. A4); Somerset Falls, in the gorge of the Daniel River above Hope Bay, where visitors can take a gondola ride to hidden cataracts; and the Caves of Nonsuch, unique for their fossilized sea life (open daily; no admission charge). Fabulous vistas also can be seen from the Blue Mountains—a tropical version of the soaring peaks of Switzerland. Hiking and bicycling excursions are available (see *Cycling* and *Hiking,* below).

(Bring a sweater, as the temperature drops about 20 degrees at higher elevations.) Reach Falls, at Machioneal, offers a lovely view of what many consider Jamaica's finest waterfalls, but it's a steep climb even for hardy souls.

KINGSTON

Jamaica's capital is a two-hour drive from either Ocho Rios or Port Antonio. Like Port Antonio, it is a good base for daylong explorations of the Blue Mountains. While far from being a resort area, Kingston is undergoing something of a cultural and architectural renaissance, particularly close to the harbor, where the *Convention Centre, National Gallery, Bank of Jamaica* (which houses the *Museum of Coins and Notes*), and other modern buildings are located, and in the New Kingston business district farther north. Kingston is the seat of government and a major port. It's also Jamaica's business, political, commercial, and industrial center. Businesspeople and West Indies scholars and enthusiasts will enjoy its schools, its museums, and Port Royal. Briefly, here's what's where.

DOWNTOWN

INSTITUTE OF JAMAICA Founded in 1870, it has one of the most extensive and scholarly collections of West Indian and Jamaican books, prints, and historical documents in the world. It contains both a *Natural History Museum* and a *Historical Gallery,* and its *West Indian Research Library* is the best of its kind outside Great Britain. Closed Fridays and Saturdays; no admission charge. 12 East St. (phone: 922-0620).

KINGSTON CRAFTS MARKET The stalls are laden with Jamaica's largest assortment of handmade items. Open daily. On the waterfront, at the end of Harbour St.

NATIONAL GALLERY OF JAMAICA In its own building near the waterfront in Kingston, it features Jamaican art. Although it contains 17th-century portraits of planters and their families, the gallery concentrates largely on the period from the 1920s to the present. Impressionist paintings, colorful portrayals of all aspects of Jamaican life, and abstracts are included in the impressive collection. Closed Sundays. Admission charge. *Roy West Building,* Orange St. and Ocean Blvd. (phone: 922-1561).

NATIONAL HEROES PARK Formerly *George VI Memorial Park* and a racecourse (not at the same time), there are now 74 acres of playing fields, gardens, and memorials to Jamaica's national heroes. Government buildings line the eastern edge. At the north end of East St.

THE PARADE Where King and Queen Streets meet. There is a public park, the historic *Ward Theatre,* and the *Kingston Parish Church.*

DEVON HOUSE This is the handsomely restored 19th-century home of George Stiebel, one of the Caribbean's first black millionaires. It boasts several elegant rooms with period furnishings, china, and other decorative items. In addition to the restored rooms are three pleasant restaurants for patio or verandah dining (see *Eating Out*), and the handsome *Things Jamaican* shops, which offer the nation's best collection of island-crafted furniture and gifts (see *Shopping*). The museum is closed Sundays and Mondays. Admission charge. Hope and Waterloo Rds. (phone: 929-7029).

BOB MARLEY MUSEUM Opened in 1986 to mark the fifth anniversary of the death of the reggae music legend, this stately 19th-century home is where Marley lived with his wife, Rita, and their five children. It features the most comprehensive collection of Marley memorabilia anywhere. Closed Sundays, holidays, and Wednesday and Saturday mornings. Admission charge includes tour. 56 Hope Rd. (phone: 927-9152).

JAMAICA HOUSE AND KINGS HOUSE In a large park where East Kings House Road meets Hope Road, these are the official residences of the prime minister and the governor general (the queen's representative), respectively. *Kings House* is closed Sundays; no admission charge (phone: 927-6424). *Jamaica House* open by appointment only (phone: 927-9941).

HOPE BOTANICAL GARDENS AND ZOO A small zoo, but the lawns and ornamental gardens are big and beautiful. Open daily. Admission charge to the zoo. Old Hope Rd (phone: 927-1085).

SANGSTER'S LIQUORS In the hills of the Blue Mountains is World's End, a community named by Dr. Ian Sangster, a Scottish chemistry teacher turned master liqueur maker. Guided tours are followed by tastings of 15 liqueurs. The rum creams are ambrosial. Stock up, as the prices are less expensive than at the airport. Open by appointment only; no admission charge. Garden Town Rd., World's End (phone: 926-8888 or 926-8211).

THE GAP Ecotourists and hikers will enjoy a day at this Blue Mountain retreat 4,200 feet above sea level. There are several marked nature trails in the nearby *Hollywell Recreation Park* (within the *Blue and John Crow National Park*), as well as a restaurant swathed in clouds that serves memorable soups and lunches, and a gift shop. Closed Mondays. No admission charge (phone: 923-5617 or 923-7078).

ACROSS THE HARBOR

PORT ROYAL These are the remains of what was once Jamaica's number one city and the wealthiest stronghold of 17th-century buccaneers. It was the headquarters of Henry Morgan (sometimes called pirate, sometimes—more respectably—privateer) and his Brethren of the Coast. A large chunk of the city, which is located at the tip of the long, skinny, natural breakwater called the Palisadoes, was toppled into the harbor by an earthquake and subsequent tidal wave in 1692. Surviving are *St. Peter's Church; Fort Charles* (no phone), where British naval hero Admiral Horatio Nelson once served; the *Giddy House* (no phone), an old artillery store, permanently tilted by a 1907 earthquake; and the old *Naval Hospital* (phone: 924-8782, 924-8871, or call the *Jamaica National Heritage Trust,* below), now an archaeological museum. All are open daily and have an admission charge. The *Committee of Friends of Port Royal* at the *Port Royal Brotherhood* (phone: 924-8420) and the *Jamaica National Heritage Trust* (phone: 972-2191) are planning new tours, further reconstruction, and expanded attractions. There's also a small pub-style restaurant, as well as a full-service bar, restaurant, and small hotel at *Morgan's Harbour Marina* (see *Checking In*). For additional details, see *Testaments in Stone: Historic Sites* in DIVERSIONS.

WEST OF KINGSTON

SPANISH TOWN Jamaica's old capital (1534–1872), 13 miles due west of Kingston on Routes A1 (confusingly, two A1s lead out of the city, then they converge into a single highway, also called A1). Its chief architectural monument is much-photographed Antique Square, which might have been designed by a Georgian wedding-cake baker. The cupolaed monument celebrates Admiral Rodney and his 1782 victory over the French navy near Iles des Saintes. Though no Spanish buildings remain, several historical sites still stand around Antique Square: the old British *House of Assembly,* the façade of the *Old King's House* (the governor's residence, now an archaeological museum; phone: 927-6424), the *Old King's House* stables (now the *Jamaican People's Museum of Crafts and Technology*, housing crafts rooted in Africa, Europe, Asia, and Central America; no phone), the *Cathedral Church of St. James,* and a number of other 18th-century buildings. Museums are closed weekends and have an admission charge.

At White Marl, on the way to Spanish Town, is an *Arawak Museum* with displays from Jamaica's pre-Columbian past. Open daily; admission charge (phone: 922-0620).

MANDEVILLE AND THE SOUTH COAST Here visitors will find a quieter, simpler Jamaica. On Friday and Saturday mornings, stop in at the market on Manchester Road in the center of Mandeville to dicker over crafts, clothes, fruits, and vegetables. Bird lovers will want to tour *Marshall's Pen,* an 18th-century greathouse set on a 300-acre wildlife sanctuary west of Mandeville. The Sutton family, which owns the house, has been in Jamaica for more than nine generations. It was built some 200 years ago by Lord Belcarres, then Governor of Jamaica. Open by appointment only; no admission charge (phone: 962-2260). Other highlights include Lover's Leap, a cliff that plunges 1,700 feet to the sea and a spot where the sunsets are truly breathtaking, located in Yardley, Chase, South St. Elizabeth; Bamboo Avenue, a scenic stretch of highway in St. Elizabeth shaded by a natural arch of tall, intertwining bamboo, reached by passing through *Holland Estate,* a former sugar factory; and a boat tour on the Black River—one of Jamaica's largest and longest rivers. *South Coast Safaris* (on the Black River, Mandeville; phone: 965-2513; 962-0220 after 7 PM) offers a 1½-hour excursion covering 10 miles round-trip; participants can see and photograph a wide variety of birds, as well as the American crocodile, indigenous to Jamaica (despite its name). Special tours can be arranged for botanists, and for wildlife and fishing enthusiasts.

South Coast Safaris also offers whole-day tours, including lunch and a boat trip, to the uncommercialized YS Falls (the name is pronounced one letter at a time). Located 40 miles south of Montego Bay and about 25 miles west of Mandeville, these wonderfully scenic tiered cascades have far fewer tourists than the falls at Dunn's River. Nature lovers also will want to visit *Apple Valley Farms,* located in St. Elizabeth. This 418-acre property is built around a former greathouse that now accommodates overnight guests (phone: 997-6000).

Sources and Resources

TOURIST INFORMATION

The *Jamaica Tourist Board*'s main office on the island is at the *Tourism Centre* in Kingston (2 St. Lucia Ave.; phone: 929-9200 or 929-9213; fax: 929-9375). There are regional offices in Montego Bay (Kent Ave., Cornwall Beach; phone: 952-4425/8); Ocho Rios (in the *Ocean Village Shopping Centre;* phone: 974-2570 or 974-2583); Port Antonio (at *City Centre;* phone: 993-3051 or 993-2589); Black River (1 High St.; phone: 965-2076); and Negril (Adrija Plaza; phone: 957-4243). All the offices are closed weekends. They will supply maps and brochures and answer questions about facilities, events, and sightseeing; interested visitors may want to participate in the tourist board's "Meet the People" program, which offers a chance to meet Jamaicans who have similar jobs, hobbies, and interests for a shared excursion or meal. Jamaica also has set up several security/information kiosks to complement the tourist board's offices. These kiosks can be found in Ocho Rios, Montego Bay, and Negril (closed Sundays). For information on Jamaica tourist offices in the US, see GETTING READY TO GO.

LOCAL COVERAGE The *Visitor,* published twice weekly, tells tourists what's going on where. It's free at hotels, airports, and tourist offices. Also free, the *Daily Gleaner*'s widely distributed tourist guide updates shopping, dining, and nightlife every other week. Another useful tourism newspaper is the *Vacationer,* which is published in Montego Bay and updated biannually. The free *Destination Jamaica* magazine, put out by the *Jamaica Hotel & Tourist Association* and updated annually, is available at the tourist board and at hotels. Also look for the biannual *Vacation Jamaica* guide in your hotel room. The local daily newspapers include the *Daily Gleaner,* the *Jamaica Herald,* and the *Star,* and there are the biweekly *Observer* and

Western Mirror. The New York Times is available at hotel newsstands on the afternoon of the day it is published.

RADIO AND TELEVISION Jamaica Broadcasting Corporation (JBC) produces radio and television programs; Radio Jamaica (RJR; 92.9 FM in Montego Bay; 720 AM in Kingston) broadcasts music, news, and features. Other stations are FAME (95.7 FM in Kingston), JBC Radio 2 (560 AM or 91.1 FM), IRIE (107.7 FM), KLAS (89.3 FM), Radio Waves (102.9 FM), LOVE (101.7 FM), and Power 106.5 FM. Most hotels have satellite TV with CNN and several U.S. channels.

TELEPHONE The area code for Jamaica is 809. Dial 911 for emergency assistance.

ENTRY REQUIREMENTS Proof of citizenship (either a passport, or a birth certificate plus an official photo ID) and a return or ongoing ticket are the only documents required of US and Canadian citizens for stays of up to six months. There is a departure tax of $400 JDS (about $12).

CLIMATE AND CLOTHES In winter, daytime temperatures range from the high 70s to the mid-80s F (25 to 30C) (in Kingston, to about 90F, 33C), but these temperatures are moderated by the prevailing trade winds from the northeast. During October and early November and again in May and early June, there are usually brief showers every day, but the sun returns quickly. Lightweight resortwear is right for daytime, plus a jacket or sweater if you're going into the cooler mountains. Short shorts and swimsuits are for beaches, not city streets. Be cautious about sunning, and keep protection (long-sleeve shirt, pants, hat, sunscreen) handy if you're going to be exposed to the sun for a long time—sailing or rafting, for example.

Evening dress varies from barefoot-casual in Negril to quite formal in season in other resort areas, where a few hotels and restaurants still require men to wear jackets and ties at dinner. A rule of thumb: If the restaurant is labeled "expensive" in our *Eating Out* listings, women should wear a dress and men a sport coat (and possibly a tie) in the winter season. Summer is less dressed up everywhere, although a few places still require a jacket (no tie required in summer, except perhaps in Kingston). On the whole, the dress for most restaurants is Caribbean casual, which means a skirt or slacks and a cotton shirt, worn with casual shoes or sandals. In Negril, where the term "casual" is taken more literally, a clean pair of shorts and a T-shirt will suffice at most any restaurant.

MONEY Jamaica's currency, the Jamaican dollar (JDS), is subject to frequent revaluation. At press time the exchange rate was $32 JDS to $1 US. Visitors can use almost any currency here, but be aware that most prices in tourist areas are quoted in US dollars (as are all the prices quoted in this chapter). Some shops and restaurants offer better exchange rates than others, so it's smart to check the official rate at a bank. There's also an exchange bureau at every airport. Traveler's checks are generally accepted, and most hotels and many restaurants and shops honor major credit cards. Banking hours generally are 9 AM to 2 PM Mondays through Thursdays; 9 AM to noon and 2:30 to 5 PM Fridays. Some banks are open Saturday mornings.

LANGUAGE The official language is English. There is also a Jamaican patois, an intriguing British-accented mixture of English, African, and island words and rhythms—plus, some say, a bit of Welsh.

TIME Jamaica is on eastern standard time year-round. During US daylight saving time, when it's noon in New York, it's 11 AM in Jamaica.

CURRENT Electricity varies from hotel to hotel; 110 volts in some, 220 in others. Where necessary, most hotels will supply converters or adapters for electric shavers or hair dryers; check with your travel agent to be sure.

TIPPING Most Jamaican hotels and restaurants add a service charge of 10%; check to see if it's included in your bill. If not, tip waiters 10% to 15%; leave $1 to $2 per person per day for hotel maids. Airport porters and hotel bellhops should be tipped 50¢ per bag (but not less than $1). It's not necessary to tip taxi drivers, although 10% of the fare is appreciated.

GETTING AROUND

AIRPORT TRANSFERS If transfers are included in your package, you'll be given a voucher with the name of the operator, and a company representative will meet you at the airport. Otherwise, have your agent reserve transfer space in advance. Fares in *JUTA* (*Jamaica Union of Travellers Association*) taxis that hold up to five people can run $80 from the nearest airports to hotels in Negril, Ocho Rios, or Port Antonio; fares to more convenient Montego Bay and Kingston are relatively inexpensive. If you're heading outside of Montego Bay (and if you're not in a rush), your best bet is to purchase a seat on one of *Tourwise*'s air conditioned minibuses at their desk just outside the luggage area of *Sangster Airport* (phone: 974-2323). They run to Ocho Rios and Negril and charge a per-person fare. The only drawback is that they usually don't make the trip until the bus is at least half full.

BUS An inexpensive way to get around the Kingston and Montego Bay areas, but they run infrequently and often are crowded and uncomfortable. Fares in Kingston and in Montego Bay change frequently, but are usually the equivalent of 50¢ US or less, depending on the distance traveled. Buses service the rest of the island as well, but again, they often are crowded—not only with people, but also with chickens and produce going to market. Unscheduled, but quite frequent, minibus jitneys serving the same routes are more comfortable. Still, most visitors rent a car or call a cab.

CAR RENTAL Most Jamaican attractions are accessible to visiting motorists, so renting a car is a good idea if you like driving and sightseeing at your own pace, and can handle driving "British-style"—on the left side of the road, as well as roads that are often narrow, winding, and in poor condition. There are 128 agencies on the island, many of which have desks at the Montego Bay and Kingston airports as well as branches in hotels and other sites throughout the island. The major operators are *Avis* (3 Oxford St., Kingston, phone: 926-1560; 924-8013 at the Kingston airport; 952-4543 at the Montego Bay airport); *Budget* (phone: 999-4888 at the Montego Bay airport); and *National* (phone: 924-8344 at the Kingston airport; 952-2769 at the Montego Bay airport). *United Car Rentals,* based in Montego Bay, offers very reasonable rates on good-quality cars (49 Gloucester Ave.; phone: 952-3077). In Ocho Rios there's *Sunshine Car Rental* (154 Main St.; phone: 974-2980) and *Caribbean Car Rental* (19 Gloucester St.; phone: 974-2123). In Port Antonio there's *Eastern Car Rental* (23 Harbour; phone: 993-3624). Major international chains accept bookings through stateside toll-free (800) numbers; be sure to request written confirmation, and bring it along.

Although there are some 2,800 rental cars on the island, it's usually necessary to reserve well before arriving, because they sometimes are in short supply. The renter pays for gas. There's also a 10% government tax. Valid US and Canadian driver's licenses are good on Jamaica, but many agencies require drivers to be over 25. *A word of warning:* Many Jamaican drivers have their "cowboy" moments. The best way to deal with the occasional challenge—at a one-lane bridge, for example—is to yield.

A reasonably priced alternative to regular car rental is the seven-day "Fly-Drive Jamaica/The Great Escape" package, which combines a rental car with air transportation and overnight accommodations. Offered by *Vacation Network* (1501 W. Fullerton, Chicago, IL 60614; phone: 800-423-4095; 312-883-3485 in Chicago), the package includes prepaid accommodations vouchers that are redeemable at any of 45 participating small Jamaican hotels and inns, a guidebook specifically geared for drivers, and road maps.

INTER- AND INTRA-ISLAND FLIGHTS Flights to the island land in either Montego Bay or Kingston. *Air Jamaica* (phone: 800-523-5585) is the island's major carrier. Air taxis save time and aggravation on long transfer runs—between Kingston or Montego Bay and Ocho Rios or Port Antonio, for example. The surest and least expensive way to use them is to book in advance through your travel agent. Local intra-island service is provided by *Trans Jamaican Airlines* (phone: 952-5401 or 952-5403), connecting the various resort centers and providing some nice island views between points. A good local charter service, *TIM-AIR* (phone: 952-2516), based at Montego Bay's airport, offers three tours, all for a minimum of two people, as well as local transportation.

Although now quite modern, Montego Bay's airport has been a frequent scene of frustration for both arriving and departing passengers. We recommend having your hotel reconfirm your return flight three days in advance. Then arrive at the airport for your flight home *at least* two hours before scheduled departure—and after calling the airline to find out when the flight is actually departing.

RIVER RAFTING It's best on Jamaica's original rafting river, the Rio Grande, starting at Rafter's Rest in St. Margaret's Bay, 15 minutes west of Port Antonio; there also are shorter trips available on the Great River west of Montego Bay, on the Martha Brae River in Falmouth, and on the White River in Ocho Rios. A bamboo raft for two, poled by a skilled guide, takes you through jungles of vines and guango trees (where the blue heron live) down to the sea. Wear a bathing suit and swim from the raft (though some rivers, the murky Martha Brae, for example, are less inviting than others). The leisurely Rio Grande trip takes two and a half hours (phone: 993-2778). The one-hour Mountain Valley rafting tour (phone: 952-0527), an expedition on the Great River, begins at the historic village of Lethe, south of Montego Bay, and wends its way through Jamaica's beautiful mountainous interior, ending at a recreational area where there are complimentary donkey rides for kids, an optional hayride, and hammocks to laze in. There's also a one-hour Martha Brae trip (phone: 952-0889) at *Rafters' Village*. The trips operate daily. Arrangements also can be made at hotel tour desks.

SEA EXCURSIONS In Montego Bay, snorkel and sail cruises are offered on the *Calico* (phone: 952-5860) and the *Rhapsody* (phone: 979-0104). One-hour glass-bottom boat rides are offered by most Ocho Rios and north coast hotels. Yacht excursions to Dunn's River Falls, with drinks and dancing on the beach, are offered by *Water Sports Enterprises* of Ocho Rios (phone: 974-2244). Out of Port Antonio, the catamaran *Lady Jamaica* (phone: 993-3318) makes hour-long harbor cruises; 2½-hour cocktail sails include snacks and drinks. *Morgan's Harbour* hotel outside Kingston offers a boat ride to Lime Cay for swimming and/or a picnic (see *Checking In*). In Kingston a 30-minute ferry ride to Port Royal leaves every two hours from the *Craft Centre*, on the harbor. A number of day sailers and motor yachts offer day-long snorkel and party cruises with lunch, drinks, entertainment, and use of snorkeling equipment included in the price. Many also offer sunset and evening cruises. In Ocho Rios contact the *Red Stripe* (phone: 974-2446) or the *Dreamweaver* (*Heave-Ho Charters;* phone: 974-5367). In Montego Bay there's the *Mary-Ann* (phone: 953-2231; ask for the tour desk) or the *Montrose II* (phone: 952-1760 or 952-5484). In Negril try the *Lollypop* (phone: 952-4121 or 952-5133) or the *Eclipse* (*Aqua Nova Water Sports;* phone: 957-4323).

SIGHTSEEING TOURS Local operators include *Jamaica Tours* (686 Half Moon St., Coral Gardens, Rose Hall, Montego Bay, phone: 952-2887; and 152 Main St., Ocho Rios, phone: 974-1673); *Blue Danube Tours* (phone: 952-0886 in Montego Bay; 974-2031 in Ocho Rios); *Greenlight Tours* (phone: 952-2200 in Montego Bay; 974-2266 in Ocho Rios; 929-9190 in Kingston); *Holiday Service* (phone: 974-2948 in Ocho Rios); and *Sun Holiday Tours* (phone:

952-5629 or 952-4585). In Port Antonio contact *JUTA* (phone: 993-2684) or your hotel desk. The most worthwhile excursions from Montego Bay include the greathouse tour (three hours), the coast tour to Ocho Rios and Dunn's River Falls (seven hours), and the Negril Beach circle tour (all day). Excursions available from Ocho Rios include the plantation tour of *Brimmer Hall* (three and a half hours), hour-long helicopter tours offered by *Helitours Jamaica* (phone: 974-2265 in Ocho Rios; 929-8150 in Kingston), and an inland tour to Kingston and Spanish Town (seven hours). *South Coast Safaris* offers nature tours on the Black River in Mandeville, and along the south coast (see *Special Places*). There also are several excellent local airplane tours (see *Inter- and Intra-Island Flights,* above). For tours focusing on Jamaican folk art, birds, gardens, or greathouses, contact the *Touring Society of Jamaica* (phone: 975-7158).

TAXI Recommended for short trips between island points. *JUTA* taxis and coaches are readily available at airports and at most resorts, but if you're going to an out-of-the-way spot, like a restaurant in the hills, arrange with the driver to return to pick you up. Most taxis are unmetered, so be sure to agree on the rate with the driver before you get in the cab, or ask the doorman at your hotel to make the arrangements. If in doubt, ask to see the rate sheet, which all cabs should have. After midnight, there is a 25% surcharge (frequently negotiable). Note that only cabs with red license plates are properly licensed and insured.

Many Jamaican cab drivers also make good guides, but only use those recommended by your hotel or *JUTA.* Hotel travel desks can make the arrangements.

SPECIAL EVENTS

Twice a year, the *Jamaica Tourist Board* publishes a detailed calendar of events, available from their offices in the US and Jamaica. "Junkanoo" is a *Christmastime* celebration throughout the island. Fantastically costumed and masked dancers parade and perform in village and city streets, and there is much feasting and rum punch partying. The *LTM (Little Theatre Movement) Pantomime,* is an annual production with original songs, dances, and stories performed from December 26 through April in Kingston (phone: 922-5988 or 926-6129). *Jamaica Carnival,* which takes place on *Easter Sunday,* is an island-wide celebration with *soca* parties, fetes, calypso and reggae bands, street dancing, and spectacular costumed parades. *Reggae Sunsplash,* a week-long music fest held in August at *Jam World* in Kingston, draws top reggae and rock artists (and huge crowds). *Jamaican Independence Day* (first Monday in August) celebrates the establishment (on August 6, 1962) of Jamaica as a sovereign country; it's an occasion for parades, music, dancing, and an arts festival. August is also when Port Antonio celebrates its 10-day *Portland Jamboree* with colorful parades, beach parties, cultural shows, and sporting events, and when Montego Bay hosts its reggae festival, *Sumfest.* Other holidays, when banks and most stores are closed, are

New Year's Day, Ash Wednesday (February 21 in 1996), *Good Friday* (April 5 in 1996), *Easter Monday* (April 8 in 1996), *Labour Day* (May 23), *National Heroes Day* (third Monday in October), *Christmas,* and *Boxing Day* (December 26). With the exception of *Good Friday,* all public holidays feature numerous island-wide celebrations, including reggae festivals, balls, sporting events, and the like.

SHOPPING

Things to bring home from Jamaica fall into two categories—art and crafts produced on the island, and imports at duty-free prices that often are a good deal lower than what you'd pay in the US. (Note, however, that a 10% General Consumption Tax is added to the prices of all goods and services.) Duty-free shops tend to cluster in shopping centers and larger hotels in each major tourist area. They offer all the classic luxury items: cameras and electronic equipment, Swiss watches, gold jewelry, French perfume, British woolens, liquor, cigarettes, fine European crystal, bone china, and porcelain. Stores specialize in different kinds of merchandise, and each has its exclusive brands and patterns, but prices are roughly standard. Visitors (with proof of identity) pay in Jamaican dollars, traveler's checks, or a wide range of credit cards, and may carry away all duty-free purchases except consumables. Liquor (including Jamaican rums, coffee-flavored Tia Maria, and Rumona, the unique rum liqueur), cigarettes, and those good Jamaican cigars (Royal Jamaica is the top brand) may be picked up at the pier or the airport. With a firm grasp of US prices to help sort out the bargains and a well-planned shopping list, a morning or an afternoon should be enough to cover all the tempting duty-free buying.

Shopping for island-made items is more serendipitous. For unique goods, seek out original work by Jamaican artists, Jamaican fashions, and island-mined gemstone jewelry. Look for carvings—statues, bookends, and other crafts—of lignum vitae, a rosy native hardwood, in the crafts markets and in the concentration of roadside stands along the north shore between Montego Bay and Falmouth. And be sure to try some of Jamaica's (some say the world's) finest brew: its rich, aromatic Blue Mountain coffee (try the *Coffee Mill* shop in the *Montego Bay Airport* for a good selection).

Locally produced straw work, baskets, clothing, and wood items have improved tremendously in the past several years; colorful, attractive, *and* reasonably priced goods are available. The best show up in boutiques at nonnegotiable prices, but a bit of market-stall research in the government-sponsored crafts markets can unearth similar merchandise for less. Try the *Kingston Crafts Market* at the end of Harbour Street or the capital's Saturday *Musgrave Market* on Trafalgar Road; the *Montego Bay Crafts Market* in downtown Montego Bay; the *Port Antonio Craft Market* at the intersection of Harbour and West Streets; and the *Negril Crafts Market* across from the tourist office at Adrija Plaza, as well as the nearby indoor *Vendors' Arcade.* Ocho Rios has several craft markets: the *Ocho Rios Craft Market* (off Main

St. in the center of town); the *Olde Market Craft Shoppes* (next to the *Seow Supermarket*); the *Pineapple Craft Centre* (adjacent to *Pineapple Place* on the main road about a mile east of town); the *Coconut Grove Craft Market* (adjacent to the *Coconut Grove Shopping Centre* on the main road about 2 miles east of town); the *Dunn's River Crafts Market* (at the famous waterfalls); and the *Fern Gully Craft Centre* (at Fern Gully). At all these outdoor sources, asking prices vary and bargaining (or haggling) is okay, even expected.

Art is a source of considerable and justifiable Jamaican pride. Individuality and quality are high; so are prices. The most revered names are those of the painters John Dunkley and Henry Daley, both of whom worked during the 1930s and 1940s, and the late Edna Manley, a major sculptor (and the wife of one prime minister and mother of another). More contemporary artists are Karl Parboosingh, Carl Abrahams, Eugene Hyde, Albert Huie, Barrington Watson, Ralph Campbell, Rhoda Jackson, and Gloria Escoffery. The works of renowned primitive painter and sculptor Kapo (given name: Mallica Reynolds) are in Kingston's *National Gallery* and other island museums. Besides the shops and galleries listed below, places to browse and buy in Kingston include the *Edna Manley School of Art* (at the *Cultural Training Centre,* 1A Arthur Wint Dr.; phone: 926-2800); the *Bolivar Gallery* (Grove Rd. off Half Way Tree Rd.; phone: 926-8799); the *Contemporary Arts Centre* (1 Liguanea Ave.; phone: 927-9958); and the *Frame Centre Gallery* (10 Tangerine Pl.; phone: 926-4644). The latter two have some fine old Jamaican prints and maps at more modest prices.

Island fashion designers are turning out clothes that are clever, stylish, and often made up in colorful fabrics silk-screened on the island. Look for the resort fashions at shopping centers and arcades, both in downtown Kingston and in the hotels of the four major tourist areas. In Negril there's the *Sunshine Village Shopping Centre.* In Montego Bay there's the *Montego Freeport* at the *Seawind Beach* resort near the the harbor; the *City Centre Arcade,* not far from the Parade; and the *Holiday Village Shopping Centre,* on Route A1, Rose Hall. In Ocho Rios, *Pineapple Place,* on the main road about a mile east of town, is an interesting collection of duty-free shops and boutiques, with an adjacent crafts market. A little farther east are *Coconut Grove Shopping Centre,* opposite *Plantation Inn,* also with a neighboring crafts market; *Ocean Village Shopping Centre* on Ocho Rios Bay, next to *Turtle Beach Towers;* the *Little Pub Yard,* with a few small shops adjoining the *Little Pub* restaurant, west of the Ocho Rios roundabout; *Soni's Shopping Plaza* on Main Street; and the *Taj Mahal Shopping Centre,* a duty-free complex on Main Street close to the *Ruins* restaurant. In Port Antonio, there's the *City Centre Shopping Plaza* and *Goebal Shopping Complex,* both on Harbour Street. Kingston has the most shopping plazas. Some of the best are the *New Kingston Shopping Centre,* an enclosed mall on Dominica Drive; the *Sovereign Centre* mall (in Liguanea at the corner of Liguanea Ave. and Hope Rd.); and Mall Row in the Half Way Tree area, which features the *Pavillion, Premier, The Mall, Village,* and *The Springs* shopping centers one after the other. The activities desk at most hotels can arrange shopping tours of the capital, including a few hours at the downtown crafts market. Most shops keep regular hours: 8:30 or 9 AM to 5 PM weekdays, to 6 PM Saturdays. Stores also are open on Sundays when ships are in port.

Here are a few island stores worth checking:

Blue Mountain Gems Unusual gemstone jewelry—coral agate from Jamaican riverbeds, black coral, and other semi-precious finds in original handwrought settings. You can watch the polishing and casting. *Holiday Village Shopping Centre,* Montego Bay (phone: 953-2338).

Caribatik Fine batik resortwear for men and women, paintings, and wall hangings in rainbow-colored hand-dyed silks and cottons—all made on site. Open 10 AM to 3 PM, Tuesdays through Saturdays; closed September 16 to November 15. On the main road, 2 miles east of Falmouth (phone: 954-3314).

Casa de Oro A duty-free shop specializing in perfume, watches, and fine jewelry. *Holiday Village Shopping Centre,* Montego Bay (phone: 953-2600), and at *Pineapple Place,* Ocho Rios (phone: 974-2577).

Gallery of West Indian Art Whimsically painted, hand-carved wooden fish, parrots, chickens, pigs, and alligators from top Jamaican artisans vie for floor and shelf space at this incredible shop. Jamaican and Haitian paintings line the walls. 1 Orange La., at the corner of Church St., Montego Bay (phone: 952-4547).

Harmony Hall Gallery An excellent place to view the works of some of Jamaica's best known as well as some of its undiscovered artists, it has a good selection of artwork and superior-quality crafts. The coveted, locally made Annabella boxes are for sale here, too. There's also an excellent restaurant on the premises. Open daily. About 4 miles east of Ocho Rios (phone: 975-4222).

Institute of Jamaica A good source for color facsimiles of antique Jamaican scenic prints and books about Jamaica. Closed Fridays and weekends. 12 East St., Kingston (phone: 922-0620).

Motta's Carries brand-name electronics, duty-free. At three Kingston addresses: 27 King St. (phone: 922-8640); *Jamaica Pegasus Hotel,* 81 Knutsford Blvd. (phone: 929-8147); and *Norman Manley International Airport* (phone: 924-8023).

Native Shop Woodcarvings, with special emphasis on the works of Lester Clarke; also hand-turned salad bowls, plates, cups and saucers, masks, and pineapple lamps. *Ocean Village Shopping Centre,* Ocho Rios (phone: 974-2348).

Pineapple Shop Island clothes in island prints, ready-to-wear or custom-made at quite attractive prices, and fabrics by the yard. Three locations in Montego Bay: the *Montego Freeport* shopping center; *Fantasy Resort,* on Gloucester Ave.; and *Holiday Inn,* 480 Rose Hall Rd. (phone for all: 952-2750).

Presita Fine electronics and camera equipment. *City Centre Arcade,* Montego Bay (phone: 952-3261).

Ruth Clarage Womenswear in original prints and designs, with accessories and costume jewelry, too. Branches in Montego Bay in the *Montego Freeport* shopping center (phone: 952-3278) and the *Half Moon Golf, Tennis & Beach Club* (Rose Hall; phone: 953-2211); in Ocho Rios at the *Ocean Village Shopping Centre* (phone: 974-2874); and in Kingston at the *Wyndham Kingston Hotel* (77 Knutsford Blvd.; phone: 926-5430).

Swiss Stores Not only famous Swiss watches (Patek Philippe, Piaget, Rolex, Omega, Tissot, Juvenia, and more), but exquisitely hand-crafted jewelry, all duty-free. Branches at the *Half Moon Golf, Tennis & Beach Club* (Rose Hall, Montego Bay; phone: 953-2520); *Ocean Village Shopping Centre* (Ocho Rios; phone: 974-2519); *Jamaica Pegasus Hotel* (81 Knutsford Blvd., Kingston; phone: 929-8147); and the corner of Harbour and Church Sts., Kingston (phone: 922-8050).

Things Jamaican The cream of the hand-crafted crop—from four-poster beds to figurines, appliquéd quilts to antique spoons. *Devon House,* 26 Hope Rd., Kingston (phone: 929-6602); 44 Fort St., Montego Bay (phone: 952-5605); *Norman Manley International Airport* (phone: 924-8556) and *Sangster Airport* (phone: 952-1936).

SPORTS

BOATING Most beach hotels have Sunfish, Sailfish, and/or windsurfers for rent. To charter larger boats, contact the *Royal Jamaica Yacht Club* in Port Royal (phone: 924-8685/8686), the *Montego Bay Yacht Club* (phone: 979-8038), or *Morgan's Harbour Marina* (Port Royal; see *Checking In*), which also has facilities for visiting yachts. Every February, March, or April, the *Montego Bay Pineapple Cup Yacht Race* draws some of the sport's top teams from the US, Canada, and Great Britain to compete in a grueling contest, which ends at the *Montego Bay Yacht Club.* Call the *Jamaica Tourist Board* for details (see *Tourist Information*).

CYCLING Although Jamaican distances and the terrain are daunting except to seasoned bikers, the very active *Cycling Association* organizes races and tours throughout the year. Check with the local *Jamaica Tourist Board* office (see *Tourist Information*) for details of activities during your stay. *Blue Mountain Tours, Ltd.* (West Palm Ave., Port Antonio; phone: 974-7493) takes cyclists by van to the Blue Mountains, where experienced guides lead the group downhill. *Sense Adventures* also arranges cycling tours (see *Hiking*).

GOLF Over the years, Jamaica—an official *PGA* golf destination—has developed some of the Caribbean's most beautiful and challenging courses, and it now offers 12 championship links. Montego Bay is the place for dedicated golfers to stay; there are four courses in the area, and it's not necessary to be a guest at a hotel to play its course. Of all the layouts, however, one is a stand-out.

TOP TEE-OFF SPOT

Tryall About 12 miles due west of Montego Bay, the *Tryall* resort course, site of the annual *Johnnie Walker World Championship,* is without question the finest on Jamaica. Where some courses on this island seem restricted by their flat terrain and rather repetitious hole configuration, *Tryall* (par 71) exults in its 6,680 yards of hills and dales, and no cost seems to have been spared to create the most interesting course possible. These grounds were once one of the island's most productive sugar plantations. All that remains of those days is a rusty old waterwheel and some ruins along the course boundaries, but they do provide a nice context in which to survey the surrounding landscape.

Don't take too much time to reflect on history, however, for the course itself is sufficient challenge for any player. The constantly changing direction of the wind off the nearby sea restructures each hole virtually every day, so there are fresh problems every time you set your ball on a *Tryall* tee (also see *Checking In*).

Other MoBay courses include the 18-hole layouts at the *Half Moon Golf, Tennis & Beach Club* (7,115 yards, par 72; phone: 953-2560), *Wyndham Rose Hall* (6,598 yards, par 72; see *Checking In*), and *Ironshore Golf and Country Club* (6,663 yards, par 72; phone: 953-2800). In the Kingston vicinity there are 18-hole courses at the *Constant Spring Golf Club* (6,196 yards, par 70; phone: 924-1610) and the *Caymanas Golf Club* (6,844 yards, par 72; phone: 997-8026). Near Ocho Rios, there are the *SuperClubs' Runaway Bay Golf Club* (6,884 yards, par 72; phone: 973-2561), and the newly spruced-up *Sandals Golf and Country Club* (6,600 yards, par 71; phone: 975-0119). *Negril Hills Golf Club* (phone: 957-4638 or 955-4165) is the new 18-hole course on the island, located 2 miles east of Negril's town center. Mandeville has a nine-hole course, *Manchester Club* (2,865 yards, par 35; phone: 962-2403), but its 18 tees allow each green to serve as two different holes. There are also miniature golf courses at *Prospect Plantation* in Ocho Rios and at *Anancy Amusement Park* in Negril (see *Special Places* for both).

HIKING The hills above the resort areas of the north coast are a scenic site for walking tours. An especially popular journey on foot in Ocho Rios is the climb (600 feet) to the top of Dunn's River Falls—do it in your swimsuit;

it's a wonderfully damp trip. Serious mountain climbers scale the Blue Mountains in the southeastern part of the island, where the *Forest Department* manages mountain retreats: *Chinchona, Clydesdale Forest Camp, Clydesdale Rest House,* and *Hollywell Recreation Centre;* for information contact the tourist board in Kingston (see *Tourist Information*). Also see *Climbing and Hiking* in DIVERSIONS. The nature-oriented *Sense Adventures* (PO Box 216, Kingston 7; phone: 927-2097) arranges hiking, climbing, and backpacking tours as well as river canoeing and cycling, and low-cost camping and guesthouse accommodations. Special arrangements for the strenuous climb up 7,402-foot Blue Mountain Peak can also be made with John Allgrove (8 Armon Jones Crescent, Kingston 6; phone: 927-0986 after 5 PM) or *Sense Adventures* (phone: 927-2097) for sunrise hikes.

HORSE RACING Races are run at *Caymanas Race Track* on Wednesdays, Saturdays, and some public holidays. It's in Kingston, 7 miles west of the New Kingston area and south of Kemp's Hill (phone: 988-7281). Consult your hotel desk and the newspapers for specific times.

HORSEBACK RIDING A beautiful way to explore Jamaica's backcountry of plantation lands and hills, pine forests, shaded streams, and waterfalls. Some stables are open all year; others take summer vacations on a varying schedule; it's best to ask your hotel to set things up. The top outfit is *Chukka Cove Farm* (Box 160, Ocho Rios, St. Ann, Jamaica; phone: 972-2506) on the old *Llandovery* estate west of Ocho Rios. A complete equestrian operation, it offers trail, picnic, and moonlight rides; it also arranges three- and five-day Horseman's Holiday packages that include trail and picnic rides, lessons, and bus trips to thoroughbred stud farms. It also has complete polo facilities; Captain Mark Phillips, first husband of Britain's Princess Anne and an *Olympic* equestrian, even conducts an annual clinic here. *Wilderness Resorts* (phone: 974-4379) in Ocho Rios also offers riding. In the Montego Bay area *Rocky Point Stables* (just east of the *Half Moon Golf, Tennis, & Beach Club;* phone: 953-2286) offers excellent instruction, as well as beach and trail rides; the *Double "A" Ranch* (phone: 952-3427), opposite the *Holiday Inn* in Montego Bay, offers both plantation and sunset rides. In the Ocho Rios area try *Prospect Plantation* (see *Special Places*) or the *Polo Club* (47 Main St.; phone: 974-5371). In Negril (the only place on the island where riding on the beach is permitted) there's *Negril Rhodes Hall Plantation* (Norman Manley Blvd.; phone: 957-4258), *Western Horseback Riding* (phone: 957-4439), and *Babo's Riding Stable* (phone: 957-3322). In Port Antonio contact the *Bonnie View* hotel (see *Checking In*).

SNORKELING AND SCUBA DIVING Reefs, formed of 50 varieties of coral and populated by brightly colored fish, anemones, lavender fans, and other marine flora and fauna, are accessible within 100 yards of the beach at a number of places along the north coast. Farther out—at about 200 yards—are dropoffs to depths where more seasoned divers can venture down in the clear waters to see and photograph larger fish and explore giant sponge forests, caves, and shipwrecks. Most of the all-inclusive resorts and large hotels have certified on-premises dive shops, fully equipped dive boats, and licensed instructors who run daily dives and teach get-in-the-water-in-one-day resort courses. The best diving on the island is found at Montego Bay, famous for its wall diving, coral caves, tunnels, and canyons, and at Negril, where the reefs are unspoiled. Also see *Sunken and Buried Treasure* in DIVERSIONS. There are 14 *Jamaican Tourist Board*-licensed dive operators (three in Montego Bay, five in Negril, and six in Ocho Rios), and we strongly recommend you use one of them; check with your concierge. Such dive shops, offering rentals, guided snorkel and scuba trips, and usually instruction, include *Poseidon Nemrod Divers Ltd.* at the *Chalet Caribe* hotel in Montego Bay (Rte. A1; phone: 952-3624 or 952-6088) and *Sun Divers* at *Ambiance Jamaica* in Runaway Bay (phone: 973-2346).

SPAS Throughout the island there are several mineral springs—thought to have therapeutic qualities—that have spawned modest spas. The *Bath of St. Thomas the Apostle* (phone: 982-2132), built around thermal springs discovered in 1695, is situated near Morant Bay halfway along the main Port Antonio–Kingston road (A4). It's open daily; there's a small hotel with a restaurant on the premises. At the *Rockfort Mineral Bath,* on Route A4, 5 miles east of Kingston, the turn-of-the-century spa (built on the site of a 1694 fort) has been overhauled and offers a health bar and massage therapy (phone: 938-5055). *Milk River Bath* (phone: 924-9544), with its own 20-room hotel and restaurant, is near Clarendon at the foot of Carpenter's Mountain, 1½ hours west of Kingston off Route A2; here, massage therapy is offered in addition to dips in the warm mineral springs. Since it's a bit tricky to get to on your own, it's best to arrange a tour with an agency such as *JUTA* (see *Sightseeing Tours*). The cool waters at Ocho Rios's plush *Sans Souci Lido* resort (see *Checking In*) were discovered in the 18th century; today, the resort offers additional pampering in the form of massage therapy, whirlpools, sauna, and other spa treatments.

SPECTATOR SPORTS Jamaica's British colonial past is evident today in its spectator sports. Cricket is the national pastime, and matches are played from January through August in *Sabina Park,* Kingston, and at other locations throughout the island. The second most popular sport is football (soccer, that is), played in the fall and winter at Kingston's *National Stadium* (phone: 929-4970) or at the indoor *National Arena* (phone: 968-0061). Polo has more than a century of tradition in Jamaica, and matches are played in Kingston on Thursdays and Sundays year-round at *Caymanas Park,* 7 miles west of the New Kingston area, south of Kemp's Hill; and in Ocho Rios on Saturdays at *Drax Hall* (phone: 972-2438), 5 miles west of town, and at *Chukka Cove Farm* (see *Horseback Riding,* above). Check local newspapers, or consult the tourist board or your hotel's concierge for current schedules.

SPORT FISHING Both fresh- and saltwater fishing are very popular. Jamaica's rivers yield such freshwater game as mountain mullet, hognose mullet, drummer, and small snook. There's also snook and tarpon fishing in the Black River and its tributaries. Deep-sea fishing charters can be arranged through hotels in Port Antonio (one of the outstanding deep-sea fishing centers in the Caribbean), Montego Bay, Ocho Rios, and Kingston. The captain keeps half the catch; the rest you can arrange to have prepared by the chef at your hotel. Billfish run through Jamaica's north coast waters year-round, although local anglers say September to April is the hottest time for blue marlin. The proximity (and proliferation) of billfish in this area has sparked international attention. Other game fish include Allison tuna (March–June), wahoo (October–April), kingfish (October–April), dolphin (April–October), bonito and barracuda (September–April). In the fall Jamaica hosts three international blue marlin and game fish tournaments, in Montego Bay, Ocho Rios, and Port Antonio. Contact the tourist board for exact dates and details.

SURFING The finest is on the north coast east of Port Antonio, where the longest and best breakers roll into Boston Bay. Since no lifeguards are present, surfing by novices is not recommended. Also, there is no place here to rent boards.

SWIMMING AND SUNNING Most of Jamaica's best beaches are on the northern coast, from secluded coves to broad stretches of white sand. Your hotel will have its own—or privileges at one nearby—and there are a number of public beaches you can visit, too. Most famous is Doctor's Cave Beach on Montego Bay, the five-acre strand that helped lure the first tourists to this part of the world; it has changing rooms and snack bars. Doctor's Cave has attracted so many people that the tourist board decided to develop the 300-yard Cornwall Beach, adjacent and to the east; both charge admission. For beachcombers who want more sand to themselves, Negril, at the western tip of the island, 50 miles from Montego Bay, has 7 shining white miles of it. New resorts are being developed in this area, but the beach's northern segment is still far from crowded and worth a special trip. *Hedonism II,* a young, high-energy resort, has nudist beaches (see *Checking In*). Nudist areas also are found on sections of Long Bay Beach and on Booby Island, just offshore. The *Navy Island Marina* resort on Navy Island, Port Antonio, has a good beach and a small nudist cove (see *Checking In*). Jamaica's southern coast has a few good beaches, notably at Hellshire near Kingston and Treasure Beach in St. Elizabeth. Other good beaches for sunning and swimming: Puerto Seco Beach in Discovery Bay; Rio Bueno and Turtle Beach in Ocho Rios; San San, Boston Beach, and Long Beach in Port Antonio; and Lime Cay near Kingston.

TENNIS Plenty of places to play—and many courts are lighted for cooler nighttime play.

Half Moon Golf, Tennis & Beach Club Jamaica's most extensive complex, located in Montego Bay, it has 13 tennis courts (nine lighted) plus four international squash courts occasionally co-opted by the racquetball crowd (Byron Bernard is the pro). Year-round, ex–*Davis Cup*/*Wimbledon* player Richard Russell, the head pro, sets up clinics according to guest interest, with video playback. No charge to hotel guests for play; court reservations necessary only in peak season (see *Checking In*).

Many resort hotels have resident pros, and a number offer tennis packages. The *Jamaica, Jamaica* resort in Runaway Bay offers an ongoing intensive instruction program at its *Tennis Academy*. The *Swept Away* resort in Negril features different US pros each week (see *Checking In* for both of these resorts). In addition, most hotels without courts have access to those of nearby properties; court use usually is complimentary for guests.

WATER SKIING Doctor's Cave Beach in Montego Bay is an ideal location. Water skiing also is part of the water sports program at most beach hotels. Jet skiing is available at Cornwall Beach in Montego Bay, on Turtle Bay in Ocho Rios, and at the *Negril Tree House Club* in Negril (see *Checking In*).

NIGHTLIFE

At the larger resort hotels, after-dark entertainment usually features small combos and occasional guitar-carrying calypso singers, plus (at least once a week) a torchlit Jamaican folkloric show complete with steel band, amazing contortionists, limbo dancers, and masochistic types who eat fire and stomp barefoot on broken bottles for a living. First-timers shouldn't miss it; old island hands, who've seen it a dozen times, can make for the nearest sound-shielded bar and wait for the honky-tonk to go away.

But Jamaica does offer something different. "Boonoonoonoos"—which means something special, a delight, in local patois—is the name of and theme for a series of year-round events and gala parties uniquely Jamaican in setting, food, and—in the case of the river nights—even transport (by dugout canoe). The drinks are rum-based and free-flowing; the entertainment, less stereotyped and with more folk feeling than most hotel productions. Each island area has its own events, which are included in the price of week-long "Boonoonoonoos" tour packages or available to guests on an individual basis. In Negril there's a weekly "Jamaica Night" with island food, music, and dancing at *Hedonism II* (see *Checking In*). In Montego Bay every Monday evening is *MoBay Nite Out,* a festive street fair, sponsored by the tourist board. Gloucester Avenue is turned into a pedestrian mall from *Jack Tar Village* to the *Pelican Grill* restaurant and the street comes alive with mento and steel bands, dancing, mingling, and curbside food and drink vendors. An "Evening on the Great River" is another entertaining option. It begins with a torchlit canoe ride, and ends with drinks, dinner, a show, and dancing in a re-created Arawak village (phone: 952-5097 or 952-5047). Also in Montego Bay is a weekly beach party at Cornwall Beach with buffet, open bar, a show, and beach games; check with your hotel for details. There's a popular Friday-night bash held on Walter Fletcher Beach which also includes dinner and entertainment (phone: 974-2619 for information; ask for Carl Young). *Rock Cliff* hotel in Negril (West End Rd.; phone: 957-4331) is known for its Sunday-night lobster barbecue and roasted suckling pig. The feast is topped off with fire eaters, limbo dancers, and a rocking reggae band. The *Fern Hill Club* (see *Checking In*) has a Monday-night beach party, fashion show, and buffet barbecue; on Friday nights there's a Jamaican buffet. Both events feature live entertainment.

In Negril *Rick's Café* (see *Eating Out*) is literally and figuratively the way-out place to be for sunset and after. Live reggae concerts can be found most evenings at *Kaiser's Café* (on the cliffs at Negril; phone: 957-4070) and in the west end of town at *Sam Sara* (phone: 957-4395), *MX III* (phone: 957-4818), or the *Compulsion Disco* (phone: 957-4416). The *Negril Tree House Club* (see *Checking In*), on the beach, is also popular. MoBay's currently popular watering holes are *Hemingway's Pub* (phone: 952-8606) and *Walter's* (phone: 952-9391), next door to each other on Gloucester Avenue. MoBay's liveliest discos are *Pier 1* (Howard Cooke Blvd. opposite the crafts market; phone: 952-2452), which is open on Friday nights; the *Cave* (at the *Sea Wind Beach;* phone: 979-8070); *Disco Inferno* (at *Holiday Village Shopping Centre* on Rose Hall Rd.; phone: 953-2113); and *Thriller* (at the *Holiday Inn;* see *Checking In*). *Sir Winston's Reggae Club* (on Gloucester Ave., downtown Montego Bay; phone: 952-2084) features live music several times a week and attracts a good local crowd. Ocho Rios's favorite night places are the *Little Pub* (see *Eating Out*); *Silks* (at the *Shaw Park Beach* hotel; see *Checking In*); *Jamaica Me Crazy* discotheque (at the *Jamaica Grande;* phone: 974-2207); and more disco action at the *Acropolis* (70 Main St.; phone: 974-2633). Port Antonio comes alive at the popular *Roof Club* (11 West St.; no phone) and at *Shadows* (40 West St.; phone: 993-3823). Aimless late-night roving in Kingston is not recommended, so hop a cab over to the *Godfather* disco (Knutsford Blvd.; phone: 929-5459) or to *Epiphany* (St. Lucia Ave., off Trafalgar Rd.; phone: 929-1130) on Thursday nights to hear the newest reggae bands. For oldies music, stop in at *The Rock* (Redhill Rd.; phone: 969-8659) on Wednesdays. Wednesday is also the night for jazz in the basement of the *Mutual Life Centre* (on Oxford and Hope Rds.; no phone). There's also the *Wyndham Kingston's Junkanoo* disco (77 Knutsford Blvd.; phone: 926-5430), *Mingles* at the *Courtleigh* hotel (see *Checking In*), and *Illusions* (Lane Plaza on South Ave.; phone: 968-8195).

Best on the Island

CHECKING IN

It's no secret that Jamaica's accommodations are now among the best buys in the Caribbean. Even the country's four Elegant Resorts, an association of the local crème de la crème, are surprisingly reasonable for the value and ambience they offer. They are Montego Bay's *Round Hill* hotel and *Half Moon Golf, Tennis & Beach Club,* the *Plantation Inn* in Ocho Rios, and Port Antonio's *Trident* hotel. The group's all-inclusive Platinum Plan is noteworthy; it includes accommodations, welcoming champagne, three meals daily, all bar drinks, afternoon tea, nightly entertainment, airport transfers, taxes and service charge, plus all land and water sports, including scuba and golf. Guests on the plan can take advantage of the Dine Around/Sleep Around option, which allows them to experience more than one resort during the same week.

In addition, a fair number of Jamaica's hotels are all-inclusive resorts. While most all-inclusive resorts here are for couples only, more and more are welcoming singles and families. (The Sandals chain, which has six all-inclusive resorts for couples on Jamaica, is planning to create an all-inclusive resort for families called *Beaches,* but little progress had been made at press time; call 800-SANDALS for information.) These club-style holidays represent some of the best value-for-the-money vacations in the entire Caribbean. The price covers all expenses—accommodations, meals, snacks, alcoholic and soft drinks, nightly entertainment, all water and land sports plus instruction and equipment, airport transfers, taxes, and tips. In fact, airfare, sightseeing excursions, telephone calls, and souvenirs are the only extras likely to be incurred by most people, although a close reading of the literature may reveal slight variations from resort to resort. (For instance, some rates may not include drinks, or may include only non-motorized water sports.)

Friends and families planning to travel together can benefit from Jamaica's vacation villa and apartment rental system. Several hundred properties—some one-bedroom models but most with two to six bedrooms, with private pools or near the beach—are available for about $550 and more a week in summer, about $650 and more in winter. The price includes staff to take care of you and the place; rental cars and minibuses also can be reserved. Even counting the cost of food, it's a scheme that cuts costs way down. The *Jamaica Association of Villas and Apartments* (*JAVA,* 1501 W. Fullerton, Chicago, IL 60614; phone: 800-221-8830 or 800-VILLAS6; 312-883-3485 in Chicago; fax: 312-883-5140) represents more than 300 properties of all sizes and degrees of luxury in all resort areas. *Villas and Apartments Abroad* (420 Madison Ave., New York, NY 10017; phone: 800-433-3020; 212-759-1025 in New York) lists about 200 select Jamaican properties. Another unique outfit, *Sense Adventures* (PO Box 216, Kingston 7;

phone: 927-2097), arranges low-cost camping and informal guesthouse accommodations, as well as nature- and outdoor-oriented tours of the island.

In addition to the properties mentioned here, the island offers hundreds of other accommodations possibilities, from tiny guesthouses to mega-resorts. For more information on small inns, contact the *Jamaica Tourist Board* for the brochure "Inns of Jamaica," or, for guesthouses and bed and breakfasts, the brochure "Welcome to the Secret Side of Jamaica." Or call one of several reservations services: *Vacation Hotline* for Negril properties (800-325-2485), *Charms* (800-74-CHARMS), *Jamaica Reservation Service* (800-JAMAICA), and *International Travel and Resorts* (800-223-9815; 212-545-8467 in New York).

In the listings that follow, hotels classed as expensive run about $250 and more a day for a double room, including breakfast and dinner (MAP) in season; about $160 and more without meals (EP). Rates at moderate places run about $160 to $250 for two MAP; about $100 to $150 EP. Places in the inexpensive category charge as little as $50 to $100 for two without meals. Between April 15 and December 15, prices all over the island—including those for villa rentals—drop 25% to 40%. Check with your hotel to see if its rates include the GCT (General Consumption Tax), which can vary from 6.5% to 12.5%. Unless otherwise noted, all hotels listed below feature air conditioning, telephones, TV sets, and private baths. All telephone numbers are in the 809 area code unless otherwise indicated.

We begin with our favorite havens, all of which are in the "expensive" category, followed by recommended hotels listed by price category.

REGAL RESORTS AND SPECIAL HAVENS

Ciboney Ocho Rios Nestled in the hills overlooking the sea, this Radisson-run all-inclusive resort boasts 289 luxurious one-, two-, and three-bedroom units in villas or in the resort's greathouse. Privacy and pampering are the key words here. Each tropically decorated villa has an attendant who does everything from unpacking and light ironing to preparing a scrumptious breakfast. The villas feature spacious bathrooms, stocked refrigerators and bars, living rooms with remote-control TV sets and VCRs (movies may be borrowed at the concierge desk), private balconies or patios for dining, and private swimming pools. Open-air jitneys shuttle guests between their villas and the rest of the resort, which spreads over 45 acres. The Grecian-looking but ultramodern spa is a big draw here. All guests receive a complimentary Swedish massage, foot, back and neck rubs, manicure, and pedicure. There also are air conditioned squash and racquetball courts, six lighted tennis courts (plus free clinics), a fitness/weight room, an aerobics room, a steam-room, a sauna, hot tubs, cold plunges, plus a beach and a private beach club. Greens fees and transportation to a nearby golf course are included in the rate. A low-key daily activities program, croquet, scuba and other water sports, four restaurants, two pools (both with swim-up bars), a jogging track, and nightly entertainment in an intimate club round out the amenities. Congenial and plush, it's geared toward luxury-loving singles, couples, and families traveling with children over the age of 16. Ocho Rios (phone: 974-1027 or 974-5600; 800-333-3333; fax: 974-5838).

Round Hill Set in a quiet cove several miles west of the clamor of Montego Bay, this is the sort of traditional resort that hearkens back to the days of colonial Jamaica. It was once so exclusive that the popular impression was that guest privileges were restricted to members of the peerage; today, with recent renovations that have kept it among Jamaica's top resorts, it remains the place celebrities and "society" head for in Jamaica. The protected atmosphere is accentuated by the fact that many "guests" actually own the villas in which they are staying. The facilities include 36 extremely stylish rooms in the very comfortable *Pineapple House,* plus 65 suites in the surrounding 27 villas, which are available when their owners are not in residence. TV sets are available at an extra charge. The hotel operation (including two restaurants) is open year-round and the *Back-in-Shape Spa* has become a major draw. There's a beach, a pool, five lighted tennis courts, a wide array of water sports (snorkeling gear is complimentary), and golf nearby at *Tryall.* You can even arrange yacht and sport-fishing charters. This is by far the toniest address on Jamaica, with prices to match, and if you like to keep your upper lip stiff while sunning and swimming, this is the place for you. Hopewell, Hanover (phone: 952-5150; 800-972-2159 or 800-237-3237; fax: 952-2505).

Trident It's impossibly romantic even in the morning, when the sun finds rainbows in the spray of the waves crashing on the rocks below your terrace and a peacock trails across the lawn to join you for breakfast. The current hotel re-creates the country house charm of its predecessor (destroyed twice by hurricanes). Each villa and tower suite (there are 26 units in all) is individually decorated, full of pastels, pleasing prints, and comforting touches (a cushioned window seat, an antique desk); none has a TV set. Service is individual, too—from breakfast (brought one course at a time to your terrace or balcony) right through the day. There's a small beach, a pool, and two tennis courts; the pleasures of Port Antonio and green-hilled Portland (surf beaches, river rafting, plantation visits, picnics by waterfalls and blue lagoons) are nearby. Afternoon tea is a tradition; dinner is superb—a formal six-course, prix fixe event complete with white-gloved, silver-domed service in the stately dining room (see *Eating Out*). Like all the rest, it's done with great style and personal attention, but utterly (and this is the special delight) without pretension. East of Port Antonio on Rte. A4 (phone: 993-2602 or 993-2705; 800-237-3237; fax: 993-2590).

NEGRIL

EXPENSIVE

Grand Lido Quieter, more elegant, and more luxurious than its Negril neighbors, this all-inclusive sanctuary caters to adults (no guests under the age of 16). The 200 suites are comfortable, with entertainment centers (including satellite TV), patios or balconies, and 24-hour room service. The crowd is international, a section of the beach is reserved for nude sunbathing, and all guests receive complimentary manicures and pedicures. Organized activities and sports, four restaurants, a fabulous midnight buffet, a fitness center, and sunset cocktail cruises on a 147-foot yacht previously owned by Prince Rainier of Monaco (he and Princess Grace honeymooned on board) complete the picture at this architecturally dramatic resort. Bring nice resortwear. Make reservations early at the fine dining room, *Piacere,* then dance the calories off at the modern discotheque. Bloody Bay (phone: 957-4013; 800-859-7873; fax: 957-4317).

Hedonism II The name says it all. This all-inclusive resort attracts pleasure-seeking singles and couples of all ages (no children under 18). There's plenty of action and activity—everything from scuba diving to toga parties. On 22 acres, with 280 large rooms (none with TV sets or telephones), six lighted tennis courts, lots of land and water sports, a famous clothing-optional beach, a fitness center, and a continuous fun-and-games atmosphere. Rutland Point (phone: 957-4200; 800-858-8009 or 800-869-SUPER; fax: 957-4289).

Sandals Negril Set amidst lush foliage on 1,800 feet of Negril's famous 7-mile stretch of beach, this all-inclusive, couples-only resort is perfect for those seeking an active, yet luxurious, getaway. The 199 rooms here are a favorite of scuba divers and snorkelers: Negril has some of the best underwater scenery on the island, and all water sports are included in the package. Accommodations range from garden or beachfront rooms to one-bedroom loft suites to 12 new deluxe honeymoon suites. Features include two freshwater pools, two whirlpools, four tennis courts, squash and racquetball courts, a fitness center, three restaurants (among them the *4 C's* beach restaurant, with light, low-calorie fare), and four bars (including a swim-up pool bar and a disco). There's even an offshore island for sunbathing au naturel. Rutland Point (phone: 957-4216; 800-SANDALS; fax: 957-4338).

Swept Away Although this all-inclusive, couples-only oasis caters largely to fitness-loving duos, you don't have to be a jock to enjoy staying here. The 10-acre sports complex features 10 lighted tennis courts (plus clinics, tournaments, and classes), two air conditioned squash courts, two racquetball courts, a lap pool, an open-air gymnasium with daily exercise programs, and a spa. Just across the road, overlooking the beach and sea, are 26 two-story villas housing 134 Caribbean-style suites (none with TV sets). There's a poolside juice and veggie bar and *Feathers,* a restaurant featuring alfresco dining on Jamaican-style health-conscious fare. Water enthusiasts can scuba dive, snorkel, sail, and windsurf. Norman Manley Blvd. (phone: 957-4040; 800-545-7937; 305-666-2021 in Miami; fax: 957-4060).

MODERATE

Beachcomber Club This small-scale resort offers 45 rooms, including one- and two-bedroom suites with large living rooms, full kitchens, sleeper sofas, and large verandahs (some also have washer/dryers). There are two restaurants, the *Ocean Beach Grill* and the Italian-style *Gambino's,* along with a bar, a duty-free shop, a tennis court, and a children's activities program. Water sports are available at an additional cost. Norman Manley Blvd. (phone: 957-4174 or 957-4170; fax: 957-4097).

Negril Cabins Set on lushly landscaped grounds with its own private beach are twenty-four cabins perched on stilts, each housing two double rooms. Half the rooms currently have air conditioning, telephones, and TV sets; all have ceiling fans and balconies. Refrigerators are available for an extra charge. The resort offers three restaurants, a pool with a swim-up bar, a piano bar with nightly entertainment, a fitness center, an outdoor Jacuzzi, a tennis court, a gameroom, a gift shop, and a children's activities program. Norman Manley Blvd. (phone: 957-4350; 800-382-3444; fax: 957-4381).

Negril Gardens Popular with Europeans, about half of this hotel's 65 rooms are on the beach; the rest are nestled around the pool across the street. None of the rooms has a telephone. Features include a pleasant, open-air restaurant and bar, and a gift shop. A water sports facility is nearby. Norman Manley Blvd. (phone: 957-4408; fax: 957-4374).

Poinciana Beach A relatively intimate all-inclusive resort on Negril's famous beach. The 130 units include two blocks of 22 villas, 12 one-bedroom suites, and six studio apartments, most with sea views and all with satellite TV (only suites and apartments have kitchenettes). This low-key, family-oriented property features programs for toddlers and children. Facilities include two swimming pools, a Jacuzzi, a lighted tennis court, two restaurants, beach and pool bars, water sports, and gift shops. Children under 12 stay for free. Norman Manley Blvd. (phone: 957-4256; 800-468-6728; fax: 957-4229).

MONTEGO BAY AREA

EXPENSIVE

Half Moon Golf, Tennis & Beach Club Here is a luxurious country club–like layout
with 208 beachfront rooms on 400 acres. It offers three restaurants; 13 tennis courts (nine of which are lighted) with a resident pro; an 18-hole championship golf course and clubhouse; full beach facilities for sailing, swimming, and water sports (including scuba); two big freshwater pools; a fitness
center; a new shopping plaza with upscale boutiques; and four squash courts.
The elegant suites in the main house are choice; ditto the Royal Suites, 23
spacious, stylishly private beachfront accommodations, though they're a
long hike from main house doings. Some opulent villa suites have private
pools. The week-long Platinum Plan package is an affordable option. Rose
Hall, on the shore 7 miles east of Montego Bay (phone: 953-2211 or 953-
2615; 800-237-3237; fax: 953-2731).

Royal Sandals Another all-inclusive, couples-only resort, it has 190 rooms in British
colonial–style buildings that, in a previous incarnation, hosted Queen
Elizabeth II. Peacocks stroll along the property's 17 acres of well-tended
gardens and lawns, contributing to the genteel, low-key atmosphere that
attracts couples of all ages. The beach is not huge (about 600 feet), but it
includes a nice wide-open stretch and several small coves, so romantics can
find a quiet spot far away from the volleyball crowd. There are four restaurants, four bars, three pools (one with a swim-up bar), four whirlpools, three
lighted tennis courts, a fitness center, and a walking/fitness trail. Guests
may choose from myriad sports options, including scuba diving, water skiing, and golf at the nearby 18-hole, par 72 *Ironshore Golf and Country Club*
(transportation and greens fees are included in the rate). Special touches
include breakfast in bed, afternoon tea, a private island for sunbathing during the day, and the *Bali Hai* restaurant—offering Indonesian fare served
with a theatrical flair—at night. There is regular shuttle bus service to
Sandals Montego Bay and *Sandals Inn,* where guests also may use the facilities. Mahoe Bay (phone: 953-2231; 800-SANDALS; fax: 953-2788 or 956-
5673).

Sandals Inn The least expensive and most modest of the six all-inclusive *Sandals*
resorts on Jamaica, this property is popular with Europeans and budget-minded travelers who like the intimacy of a small hotel and don't mind the
lack of a private beach on-site. (There's a small beach across the road,
Doctor's Cave Beach is a short walk away, and true beach lovers can take
the complimentary shuttle over to nearby *Sandals Montego Bay* or *Royal
Sandals,* where use of the facilities is included.) The motel-like main building has been nicely renovated to give it a comfortable, tropical atmosphere;
it features 52 guestrooms (some with terraces), two restaurants (plus room
service), two bars, and a small fitness center. The grounds are compact, but
there is a pool, a tennis court, a volleyball court, and water sports and

THE ISLANDS JAMAICA

instruction (including scuba diving, windsurfing, and water skiing). It's a short walk to the shops and nightlife of Montego Bay. Kent Ave. (phone: 952-4140; 800-SANDALS; fax: 952-6913).

Sandals Montego Bay One of the island's most popular and spirited couples-only, all-inclusive resorts, this is the Sandals flagship property. Known for its party atmosphere, it appeals to an active, predominantly young, crowd. The 1,700-foot beach is the largest private stretch of sand in Montego Bay, and the rest of the 19 acres are adorned with orchids and other lush tropical plants. The 243 rooms all have private balconies or patios and a full range of amenities. (Those along the central section of the beach, where the weekly beach party is held, can get a bit noisy at night.) There are two large pools (one with a swim-up bar), a well-equipped fitness club, and four tennis courts. Equipment for and instruction in a complete range of water sports (including scuba diving, water skiing, and windsurfing) and land sports are also part of the deal. Meals are served in three restaurants; there also are five bars, including a popular piano bar and a spacious disco. Other pluses include glass-bottom boat rides, a miniature golf course, and a special lounge that serves all of the *Sandals* resorts' departing guests. (The proximity to the airport is convenient, but it also means a fairly steady stream of planes overhead—those with sensitive ears, beware.) Guests may use the facilities at the other five *Sandals* resorts as well; there is regular shuttle bus service to *Royal Sandals* and *Sandals Inn.* Reserve early—this is a popular place. Kent Ave. (phone: 952-5510; 800-SANDALS; fax: 952-0816).

Tryall This exclusive 2,200-acre resort includes a refurbished 156-year-old greathouse with 52 guestrooms, and 42 luxury villas with two, three, four, or five bedrooms. None of the accommodations has a TV set or telephone. On a hill overlooking a fine curve of beach, it offers quietly elegant country-estate atmosphere, a beach club, pool, and a perfect terrace and bar for sea and sunset watching. It also has the best golfing on the island (see *Golf*). There are nine tennis courts with a resident pro, and free court time in the off-season. The food is good; nights are peaceful. The all-inclusive Platinum Plan is an attractive option. Twelve miles west of town. Sandy Bay, Hanover (phone: 956-5660 or 956-5667; 800-336-4571; fax: 956-5673).

Wyndham Rose Hall Beach With an 18-hole championship golf course, six lighted tennis courts (resident pro, too), all kinds of beach and water sports, and three interconnecting swimming pools, this beachfront property is popular with all types of folk, including golfers, families, honeymooners young and old, and large groups. It has 489 good-looking rooms and 36 suites. There's a choice of five restaurants, including *Ambrosia,* which features excellent northern Italian cooking, and there's refined entertainment in the *Gazebo Bar* and late-night dancing at the *Junkanoo* disco. An all-inclusive package is available. Nine miles (15 minutes) east of the airport. Rose Hall Rd. (phone: 953-2650; 800-822-4200; fax: 953-2617).

MODERATE

Coyaba Beach Resort and Club This resort, whose name is the Arawak Indian word meaning "place of ease and rest," is a wonderful new 50-room beachfront property near Montego Bay. The rooms are light, airy, and exquisitely furnished. On the premises is a pool, as well as a lounge and the popular *Vineyard* restaurant (see *Eating Out*). Rates include airport transfers, snorkeling gear, tennis, continental breakfast, and afternoon tea. Little River, St. James (phone: 953-9150; 800-223-9815; fax: 953-2244).

Gloucestershire Located in downtown Montego Bay, the 88 rooms are just steps away from the public Doctor's Cave Beach. Amenities include a restaurant, tour desk, room service, pool, and Jacuzzi. A meal plan is available. Gloucester Ave. (phone: 952-4420 or 952-4422; 800-742-4276; fax: 952-8088).

Holiday Inn The on-premises beach, a shopping complex just across the street, a lively disco, and reasonable rates make this 516-room resort popular with singles, families, and groups. Facilities include three restaurants, a huge pool, water sports, and four tennis courts. 480 Rose Hall Rd. (phone: 953-2485/6; 800-HOLIDAY; fax: 953-2840).

Sea Wind Beach A high-rise with excellent views, set on a private white sand beach, with 468 standard rooms, suites, and apartments—some with kitchens, none with TV sets. Its amenities include two swimming pools, four tennis courts, three restaurants, five bars, a water sports center, and the popular *Cave* discotheque. An all-around good value with lots of activities; the beautiful beach is the main draw. Across from the *Montego Bay Yacht Club.* Montego Bay, Freeport (phone: 979-8177; 800-223-6510; fax: 979-8039).

INEXPENSIVE

Richmond Hill Although it's not on the beach, this former greathouse, best known for its restaurant (see *Eating Out*), has considerable style and grace. The 20 guestrooms are small but impeccably decorated, and there's a big pool, an extraordinary view of Montego Bay and the Caribbean, and a sociable bar. Union St., on Richmond Hill above town (phone: 952-3859; fax: 952-6106).

FALMOUTH

EXPENSIVE

Good Hope Set on a 2,000-acre working plantation in the mountains, this superb hideaway offers nine guestrooms in a beautifully restored 18th-century greathouse and its coach house. There's also the quaint little Accountant's Cottage, which serves as a honeymoon suite. All the rooms are furnished with antiques or tasteful reproductions (there are no telephones or TV sets to disturb the serene atmosphere); only the five rooms in the coach house are air conditioned, but the greathouse's tall windows admit pleasant breezes. On the premises are gardens, walking trails, horseback riding and tennis facilities, a pool, and a dining room; there's also rafting on the nearby Martha Brae River. Rates include breakfast. Groups may arrange to rent either of the main buildings or even the plantation as a whole. Falmouth (phone/fax: 954-3289; 800-OUTPOST).

Trelawny Beach Though somewhat isolated, this property offers all-inclusive rates and 350 rooms, including cottage rooms (with patios) near the pool, beach, and garden, superior rooms with sea views, or standard rooms with a garden or mountain view. Tennis clinics and four lighted Laykold courts, water sports (including a daily one-tank scuba dive), a shuttle to Montego Bay, nightly live entertainment, and a daily supervised children's activities program are included. There's also a disco and a nude beach area. The *Jamaican Room* offers buffet or four-course dinners every evening; on Tuesdays there's "Jamaican Night" with a poolside buffet. Two meal plans are available. Children 14 and under stay for free in their parents' room during the summer. Ten minutes from Falmouth and Martha Brae rafting (phone: 954-2450; 800-JAMAICA or 800-336-1435; fax: 954-2173).

RUNAWAY BAY

EXPENSIVE

Braco Village Opened last year on what once was the *Braco* plantation near Duncans Bay, this all-inclusive beachfront property is patterned after a traditional Jamaican village. There are 180 airy rooms decorated in pink and yellow with private balconies, and the complex features four restaurants and three bars, plus a sidewalk café, pastry shop, and beach grill. Sports facilities include an Olympic-size pool, tennis courts, a range of water sports, a fitness center, a nine-hole golf course, and cricket and soccer fields where visitors may watch matches played by visiting teams or get involved in the action themselves. Rio Bueno (phone: 973-4882; 800-654-1337; fax: 973-4839; 516-223-4815 in the US).

MODERATE

Club Caribbean All 135 rooms are in cottages in a tropical garden setting; only 30 are air conditioned, and there are no TV sets or telephones. This all-inclusive resort offers a special daily activities program for children, as well as tennis on two courts, snorkeling, windsurfing, water skiing, and sailing. An on-premises *PADI* five-star scuba diving training facility offers a range of dive packages. There's a private beach, a pool, a disco, a bar, and a restaurant. Special rates for children under 12. On the beach (phone: 973-3507; 800-223-9815; 212-251-1800 in New York City; fax: 973-3509).

FDR This upscale all-inclusive property is outstanding for families. The 78 one-, two-, and three-bedroom apartment suites are spacious, and each has a pullout sleep sofa in the living room. In addition, every suite comes with a "Gal Friday" who acts as a nanny, cook, housekeeper, and kitchen stocker. For a small extra charge, she'll even baby-sit in the evening. Rates include all meals, transfers, a shopping trip to nearby Ocho Rios, a glass-bottom boat tour, scuba diving, land and water sports, and nightly entertainment. Golf is nearby. For children and teens there are extensive supervised activities; there's also a petting zoo and a playground. Other features include a pool, a fitness center, an open-air restaurant and beach grill, a piano bar, and—for adults only—a casino room. Across from the beach (phone: 973-4591; 800-654-1FDR; fax: 973-3071).

Jamaica, Jamaica An exuberant all-inclusive member of the SuperClubs group, this 238-room place is notable for its Jamaican decor and dining. Its chefs have won gold medals from the *Jamaican Cultural Commission* for their innovative cooking. Meals and all the usual expenses are covered in the all-inclusive rates, as are such pluses as a pool, horse-and-buggy rides, music, parties, all sports (including excellent scuba facilities), a shopping shuttle, and a cruise. Special complimentary sports clinics include the Tennis Academy (morning and afternoon lectures, video, and sessions with visiting pros) and the Golf Academy (driving range, putting green, and intensive instruction at the nearby championship *Runaway Bay Golf Club*). There's a separate nude beach. No children under 16. On the beach (phone: 973-2436/7/8; 800-859-7873 in the U.S.; 800-553-4320 in Canada; fax: 973-2352).

INEXPENSIVE

Silver Spray Small, serviceable, quiet and basic, this property has 13 rooms on a cliff overlooking the sea. There are no TV sets or telephones. There's a saltwater pool, and a nearby water sports facility offering diving, fishing, and Waverunners (basically waterborne mopeds). The food is good, and a meal plan is optional. St. Ann's (phone: 973-3413; 800-526-2422).

OCHO RIOS AREA

EXPENSIVE

Boscobel Beach This family-oriented SuperClubs member is a lively 207-room, all-inclusive beachfront resort. Fourteen two-bedroom suites are in a building next to the main building. There are three restaurants, two pools, golf, aerobics classes, scuba, a fitness center, four tennis courts, and a fine beach. While the adults play, the kids are kept happy in supervised activity programs. There's even a separate program for teenagers, with a computer classroom, movie theater, mini-farm, video games, donkey rides, picnics, arts and crafts classes, disco, and activities room. Coastal Rd., about 10 miles east of Ocho Rios (phone: 975-7330; 800-859-7873; fax: 975-7370).

Couples The emphasis on romance and relaxed fun at this all-inclusive couples-only resort on the beach draws lots of repeat visitors, and lots of weddings. There are 172 rooms; only the mountain-view ones have TV sets. Weekly rates include everything—room, airport transport, tips, taxes, all meals, water skiing, scuba, kayaking, tennis (five courts), squash (one court), horseback riding, entertainment, wine, bar drinks, even cigarettes. There's a pool, a gym overlooking the ocean, four restaurants, golf nearby, and a nude beach on a small, private island. Tower Isle, St. Mary, about 5 miles east of Ocho Rios (phone: 975-4271/2/3/4/5; 800-859-7873; fax: 975-4439).

Enchanted Garden This resort is surrounded by 20 acres of tropical flowers, cascading waterfalls, and exotic birds. The 112 deluxe one-, two-, and three-bedroom villas all have private patios with magnificent views of Ocho Rios Bay, while 40 feature a private indoor plunge pool. Nightly entertainment, tennis, horseback riding, plus a facial, massage, manicure, and pedicure are included, and there are five restaurants to choose from for all your meals and drinks, also included. Free shuttles are provided to the beach, golf courses, and in-town shopping areas. Eden Bower Rd., in the hills above Ocho Rios (phone: 974-1400; 800-223-6725; fax: 974-5823).

Jamaica Grande This all-inclusive, family-oriented property, a member of the Ramada Renaissance group of hotels, is Jamaica's largest resort, with 731 rooms in high-rise buildings. The island's most extensive convention and meeting facilities are here, so expect large groups of business types. Other amenities include four lighted tennis courts; a pool complex with waterfalls, swim-through grottoes, a swim-up bar, and a children's wading pool; a beach; water sports; fitness center with daily exercise classes; a video room; a disco; five restaurants; seven bars; and a tour desk. There is also a supervised children's activity and day-care program; 24-hour room service; and an impressive open-air reception area. Main St., Ocho Rios (phone: 974-2201; 800-228-9898; fax: 974-2289 or 974-5378).

Jamaica Inn A small, classic island inn offering gentle luxuries—comfortable rooms, thoughtful service, good food (with an orchestra every evening in winter), and relaxed life on a beautiful private beach. There are 45 rooms decorated with antiques, with sea-view terraces and no TV sets; all have been recently renovated. Tennis facilities are around the corner at the *Shaw Park Beach* hotel; riding and golf can be found at *Sandals Golf and Country Club,* a short drive away. The place draws lots of repeat visitors, so book early. About 2 miles east of Ocho Rios (phone: 974-2514; 800-243-9420; fax: 974-2449).

Plantation Inn One of the island's most inviting properties, it features genteel service and a lush garden setting overlooking twin crescent beaches. Here are 76 lovely rooms with private sea-view balconies where breakfast is served each morning. A pool, water sports facilities, two tennis courts, and a health club with sauna are on the premises; riding and golf are nearby; and there's elegant dining and nightly entertainment. About 2 miles east of Ocho Rios (phone: 974-5601; 800-742-4276, 800-752-6824, or 800-237-3237; fax: 974-5912).

Sandals Dunn's River The newest and ritziest of Sandals' all-inclusive, couples-only resorts on the island, it draws a diverse clientele—from young newlyweds (75% of guests are on their honeymoons) to mature couples celebrating their silver anniversaries. The interior features an elegant Italianate Renaissance decor, with marble columns and wrought-iron details, and outdoor life revolves around a huge Mediterranean-style brick-paved plaza. There are 256 rooms in a six-story main building, a five-story west wing, and two lanai buildings; four restaurants; and seven bars and lounges. The good-size beach (800 feet) is complemented by two freshwater pools, one of which—the largest in Jamaica—is complete with a swim-up bar and waterfall. Among the sports facilities are an open-air fitness center, four tennis courts, a jogging course, a pitch-and-putt golf course, three Jacuzzis, and two whirlpool baths. The package includes all land sports (including golf at the nearby 18-hole *Sandals Golf and Country Club*) and water sports (including scuba diving—there's a reef right off the beach). A Dunn's River Falls tour and a 20-minute massage are special complimentary extras. There's a regular shuttle to nearby *Sandals Ocho Rios,* where guests are free to use the facilities. Located a few miles west of Ocho Rios (phone: 972-0563; 800-SANDALS; fax: 972-1611).

Sandals Ocho Rios The majority of guests at this all-inclusive, couples-only haven are in their 20s and 30s, but the atmosphere is lively, not raucous, so vacationers of any age would be comfortable here. The resort occupies 15 acres of beachfront, offering 237 rooms in the balconied, multistory main building (sea or mountain view) or in garden cottages. (The rooms overlooking the beach terrace can be a bit noisy.) The grounds are not vast, but are filled with beautiful tropical greenery. Three freshwater pools complement the modest-size beach (600 feet); there also is a fitness center, two whirlpool baths, two tennis courts, and facilities and instruction for a full roster of water sports (including scuba diving, but not water skiing) and land sports (including golf at the nearby *Sandals* 18-hole course). There's dining in three restaurants, and the four bars (among them a swim-up pool bar, a piano lounge, and a discotheque) provide entertainment. Other nice touches (also included): a 20-minute massage and an excursion to Dunn's River Falls. About 1½ miles east of Ocho Rios center (phone: 974-5691; 800-SANDALS; fax: 974-5700 or 974-2544).

Sans Souci Lido This charming and truly classy all-inclusive enclave, now under SuperClubs ownership, has 111 freshly and stylishly decorated rooms and suites terraced down a lush, gardened hillside above a small private bay. Most accommodations have balcony views; all are sumptuous and spacious. In addition, there are 36 beachfront one-bedroom suites. The resort's three bars and two restaurants include the outstanding *Casanova.* There are two pools (one freshwater, one fed by a mineral spring) and four tennis courts. Complete water sports facilities are on the beach. Guests have privileges at a nearby golf course; riding and polo can be arranged. There's also a spa which features a natural mineral spring (see *Extra Special,* above); fitness holiday packages that include spa dishes are available. Guests can spend part of their day at the *Grande Lido* in Negril, with air transportation included. About 4 miles east of Ocho Rios center (phone: 974-2353/4; 800-859-SUPER; fax: 974-2544).

MODERATE

Shaw Park Beach An appealing place with 118 rooms on a lovely stretch of pure white sand, its atmosphere is active but not frantic. Once so-so, it's been renovated and is now an affordable, yet upscale, beach resort. Features include water sports (including scuba), a pool, two tennis courts, and a helpful tour desk. After dark there's fine dining, entertainment, and *Silks* disco for night owls. About 2½ miles east of Ocho Rios center (phone: 974-2552 or 974-2554; 800-243-9420; fax: 974-5042).

INEXPENSIVE

Hibiscus Lodge This neat little hotel (26 well-kept rooms, nine of which are air conditioned, though there are no TV sets) is very personally—and personably—run. Activities are limited (a pool, sunning and swimming at the adjacent hotel's beach, snorkeling, tennis nearby, and golf privileges at the *Sandals Golf and Country Club*), but it's near the center of town, within walking distance of restaurants and shopping. Outstanding home-style Jamaican food is served at the *Almond Tree* (see *Eating Out*). Main St., Ocho Rios (phone: 974-2676; 800-JAMAICA; fax: 974-1874).

Hummingbird Haven In a garden setting with a sea view, this campground is where backpackers and those on an austere budget can literally pitch their tents. Several spartan cabins also can be rented. It goes without saying that no air conditioning, telephones, or TV sets are to be found hereabouts, but there is a restaurant serving West Indian meals and snacks. Located 2 miles east of the Ocho Rios clock tower, on Main Hwy. (phone: 974-5188; fax: 974-2559).

PORT ANTONIO

EXPENSIVE

Jamaica Palace An international luxury resort richly deserving of its name. This romantic, beautifully appointed hotel offers 65 rooms filled with antiques, crystal chandeliers, and Oriental rugs (no TV sets). There's a shuttle to the beach; guests also can take a swim "around the island" in the 114-foot-long Jamaica-shaped pool. There are two bars, a restaurant serving island and continental fare (see *Eating Out*), gamerooms, and numerous sun decks (phone: 993-2020; 800-472-1149 or 800-423-4095; fax: 993-3459).

MODERATE

Fern Hill Club Port Antonio's only all-inclusive property, it has 40 rooms and suites (none has a telephone). While rates include meals and most sports and nightly entertainment, scuba diving and horseback riding are offered nearby for an extra charge. Located on 40 acres in the hills above San San Beach (phone: 993-3222; fax: 993-2257).

Goblin Hill Villas To the delight of its many longtime guests, this legendary property has reclaimed its original name, after an assortment of monikers. One of the island's most gracious and cherished refuges, it offers the quintessential villa vacation, with 28 fresh, airy, one- and two-bedroom apartments in townhouse-like villas with sea views; none of the apartments has a telephone or TV set. The 700-acre hilltop estate also features two tennis courts, a pool, and snorkeling and swimming at San San Bay; water skiing, scuba, and horseback riding are nearby. There's no dining room, but each apartment has a butler and a maid who shops and cooks. The *Tree Bar* wraps around a gigantic banyan tree. A children's activities program is available. East of Port Antonio at San San Beach (phone: 993-3286; 800-472-1148; fax: 993-9616).

Jamaica Crest Perched on a hill east of Port Antonio near San San Beach, this new property with friendly management offers 14 rooms in studios and one- to three-bedroom villas, some with Jacuzzis and TV sets and all with kitchenettes. At press time a separate building with 60 additional guestrooms was in the planning phase. There's also a pool with a poolside bar and grill, two restaurants, a disco and gameroom, a fitness center, tennis courts, and conference facilities. Shuttle service to the beach is provided. Off Route A4 (phone: 993-8400; fax: 993-8432).

Navy Island Marina This lovely, unspoiled spot was once Errol Flynn's private hideaway. Formerly the *Admiralty Club,* it is reached by a short ferry ride from the Port Antonio marina. It has an eight-slip marina, seven studio cottages, two guestrooms, and three one- and two-bedroom villas (cook/housekeeper optional), all cooled by ceiling fans and tropical breezes (no air conditioning). The accommodations are basic: no TV sets and no telephones. The main building boasts an attractive nautical decor with native wood embellishments plus a waterfront dining room, *Bounty* (see *Eating Out*), with magnificent views of Port Antonio and the Blue Mountains. There's also a pool, a fine swimming beach, the secluded Trembly Knees Cove for nude sunbathing, and a tennis court. Some water sports are on the premises; others can be arranged. There's an Errol Flynn Room with posters and memorabilia. Every Saturday night, there's a reggae party at Crusoe's Beach. Navy Island, Port Antonio Harbour (phone: 993-2667; fax: 993-2041).

KINGSTON

EXPENSIVE

Jamaica Pegasus Consistently topnotch service is found at this well-run city hotel with the feel of an upscale resort. A 17-story high-rise in the New Kingston business district, it's favored by business and pleasure travelers. All its 350 rooms (which include deluxe suites, and rooms on the amenity-laden, extra-service Knutsford Club executive floor) are large and comfortable, but with no TV sets. The pool and bar are popular after-hours meeting places, and a pianist entertains weekdays at the afternoon tea in the lobby. There is a Sunday night poolside barbecue with live entertainment, the elegant *Le Pavillon* restaurant (see *Eating Out*), and the less formal *Country Kitchen* restaurant. There's also a children's pool, a small fitness center, a jogging trail, and tennis court, plus a tennis club across the road. Other amenities include 24-hour room service, duty-free shops, a hair salon, pharmacy, car rental desk, and tour desk. 81 Knutsford Blvd. (phone: 926-3690; 800-225-5843; fax: 929-5855).

Wyndham Kingston Hotel Already a popular executive retreat in Kingston's financial and diplomatic district, this hotel with 303 rooms and suites recently underwent a $15-million renovation. In addition to three restaurants, there are a bar, a disco, a business center, and boutiques. Sports facilities include an Olympic-size pool, a fitness center, and tennis courts. 77 Knutsford Blvd. (phone: 926-5430; 800-WYNDHAM; fax: 929-7439).

MODERATE

Morgan's Harbour This yacht club–like lodging alternative to downtown Kingston is across the harbor at the end of the Palisadoes Peninsula. Life centers on the harborside pool complex; recreational possibilities include swimming, snorkeling, boat trips to the cays, deep-sea fishing trips, a *PADI* diving program, or working out in the small gym. The breezy open-air bar and restaurant have a handsome view of Kingston across the bay. The 66 recently renovated rooms are neat but smallish. Service is friendly. Ten minutes from *Norman Manley Airport,* near Port Royal (phone: 924-8464; 800-526-2422; fax: 924-8562).

Terra Nova What was once a graceful private home is now an elegant inn with 33 rooms, well-tended gardens, and a pool. The restaurant is a favorite of government officials and Kingston's high society. 17 Waterloo Rd. (phone: 926-9334; 800-742-4276; fax: 929-4933).

INEXPENSIVE

Courtleigh Located across the street from the *Japanese Embassy,* this 40-room, elegant hotel is especially popular with Japanese businessmen. The *Courtleigh House,* an adjacent medium-rise building, offers 42 additional one-, two-, and three-bedroom suites. There also are two restaurants, a pool with bar, and the *Mingles* cocktail lounge, one of New Kingston's more popular nightspots on Wednesday and Friday nights. Shops and recreational facilities are nearby. 31 Trafalgar Rd. (phone: 926-8174; 800-JAMAICA; fax: 926-7566).

Four Seasons A beautifully converted Edwardian greathouse, with 39 rooms, all individually decorated (none with telephones). Run by two German sisters, the property is set in a walled tropical garden with a pool, its restaurant is well regarded, and it's close to all New Kingston business, sports, and entertainment. 18 Ruthven Rd. (phone: 929-7655; 800-742-4276; fax: 929-5964).

OUTSIDE KINGSTON

EXPENSIVE

Strawberry Hill This intimate luxury hideaway set in the Blue Mountains 3,100 feet above sea level rewards the tortuous drive to the summit (helicopter service is also available) with spectacular vistas of Kingston. Recently opened by Island Records mogul Chris Blackwell, it features 18 studio and one- to three-bedroom apartments set in white gingerbread villas built in classic 19th-century Jamaican style. The accommodations have a gorgeous, neo-colonial austerity, with four-poster beds draped in mosquito netting, ceiling fans (which, along with the mountain breezes, make air conditioning unnecessary), a sitting room, and wrap-around porches; some have kitchens, and telephones, TV sets, VCRs, CD players, and fax machines are available upon request. Other amenities include a dining room serving creative Jamaican specialties (see *Eating Out*), spa services such as massage and aromatherapy, and a small conference center. Rates include breakfast and pickup from the Kingston airport. Irishtown, a 30-minute drive from Kingston (phone: 944-8400; 800-OUTPOST; 305-531-8800 in Florida; fax: 994-8203; 305-531-5543 in the US).

MANDEVILLE

INEXPENSIVE

Astra Country Inn Cool off at this inn in the Mandeville hills, 2,000 feet above sea level in the island interior. The restaurant and bar serve excellent Jamaican dishes in a Caribbean country inn setting. There's a pool and sauna; tennis is nearby; and golf is available, as are horseback tours of nearby plantations. Its 22 rooms are popular with Jamaicans who want to go rural for a weekend, ecotourists, and bird watchers. 62 Ward Ave. (phone: 962-3265; 800-JAMAICA; fax: 962-1461).

Mandeville A small, informal, and friendly 62-room resort set in tropical gardens, with hints of the Victorian era in its decor. There is a restaurant and bar, and the Wednesday night poolside barbecue is popular with guests. Another cool, country refuge much different from north coast resorts. None of the rooms has air conditioning, and only the more expensive rooms have TV sets. Guests have golf privileges at the nearby *Manchester Club*. 4 Hotel St. (phone: 962-2460 or 962-2138; 800-742-4276; fax: 962-0700).

ST. ELIZABETH

INEXPENSIVE

Invercauld Great House and Hotel This small, pleasant property offers 48 rooms, in addition to a pool, tennis courts, a restaurant, and gift shops. Black River (phone: 965-2750; fax: 965-2751).

Treasure Beach This oasis on Jamaica's sunny, palm-shaded south coast beach features 16 rooms set in several cottages. Among the amenities are a freshwater swimming pool, poolside bar, and two restaurants. Located about 65 miles south of Montego Bay, southeast of Black River, at Treasure Beach (phone: 965-2305; 800-742-4276; fax: 965-2544).

EATING OUT

The trend toward all-inclusive hotel rates means you don't have to eat out. But you will probably want to sample at least a few of the local restaurants, most offering some island dishes as well as continental choices. Jamaican soups are superior—including meaty pepper pot, spicy *callaloo* (a spinach-like green), red pea, and pumpkin. The island's most famous concoction is salt fish and ackee, a mixture of cod and a bland local fruit, which tastes something like flavorful scrambled eggs. Another traditional dish is jerk pork or jerk chicken—the meat is highly seasoned and grilled or smoked for hours over pimiento (allspice) wood and leaves (especially good at the *Pork Pit* in Montego Bay—see below). Most visitors enjoy the spicy Jamaican patties, which are pastry shells filled with beef or vegetables; stamp & go (codfish fritters) or *akkra* (vegetable fritters); cassava bread; and rice and peas (really beans) served as a main or side dish, along with *christophine* (a squash-like vegetable) and yams. Roast suckling pig and curried goat are also favorite main dishes; Jamaican mango chutney is fine with the latter and to take home. Native fruits—mango, sweetsop, soursop, paw paw (papaya), bananas, and the rest—are delicious fresh or made into tarts or ice cream. And Jamaicans are almost as proud of their rich Blue Mountain coffee, first-rate Red Stripe beer, and liqueurs (coffee-flavored Tia Maria, rummy Rumona, and a pimiento liqueur made from ripe, red allspice berries) as they are of their famous rums.

Expect to pay $100 or more for dinner for two (including tax, but without drinks and tip) at the place described below as very expensive; $40 to $100 at places described below as expensive; from $22 to $40 at restaurants in the moderate category; and less than $22 at places listed as inexpensive. The 10% General Consumption Tax may not be included in the listed menu prices; be sure to ask. In the Montego Bay and Negril areas, many restaurants offer complimentary pick-up and drop-off car service to and from hotels. Just request this service when you call to make reservations. Unless otherwise noted, all restaurants are open for lunch and dinner. All telephone numbers are in the 809 area code unless otherwise indicated.

NEGRIL

EXPENSIVE

Rick's Café Negril's most famous eatery, its terrace is set on cliffs that afford matchless views not only of the sunset but also of intrepid divers who plunge into the sea far below. Young folks staying nearby head here as soon as they unpack. Fresh fish and lobster are dinner specialties, while the Sunday brunch features such offerings as eggs Benedict Caribe (with filet of lobster instead of Canadian bacon). Open daily. Reservations advised. Major credit cards accepted. Lighthouse Rd. (phone: 957-4335).

MODERATE

Charela Inn Features à la carte and five-course French and West Indian fare, a good wine list, a nice atmosphere, and good service. Open daily for breakfast, lunch, and dinner. Reservations necessary. Major credit cards accepted. Norman Manley Blvd. (phone: 957-4277).

Cosmo's A casual waterside location just east of town, serving soup, fish, lobster, Jamaican dishes, and good cracked conch. Open daily. Reservations unnecessary. MasterCard and Visa accepted. Norman Manley Blvd. (phone: 957-4330).

Negril Tree House Club Good island fare, especially lobster, is featured, along with a lovely view and live reggae music at sunset. Serves all three meals daily, plus an all-you-can-eat barbecue with live entertainment Monday nights. Reservations unnecessary. Major credit cards accepted. Norman Manley Blvd. (phone: 957-4287).

INEXPENSIVE

Hungry Lion This very casual alfresco eatery on the cliffs features a juice bar and excellent vegetarian and seafood dishes. Open daily for dinner only. Reservations advised. MasterCard and Visa accepted. West End Rd. (phone: 957-4486).

Negril Jerk Centre Serving up jerk chicken, pork, and fish, by the quarter-, half-, or whole pound. Beware the hot sauce—its nickname is Jamaican Hellfire. Wash it all down with coconut water, homemade ginger beer, or a Red Stripe. Open daily for breakfast, lunch, and dinner. Reservations unnecessary. No credit cards accepted. West End Rd., just past the *Sunshine Village Shopping Centre* (phone: 957-4847).

Sweet Spice Located on the road to Savanna-la-Mar, this cheerful restaurant serves Jamaican specialties and does a large take-out business. Open daily. No reservations. No credit cards accepted. White Hall Rd., a half mile east of the Negril roundabout (phone: 957-4621).

MONTEGO BAY AREA

EXPENSIVE

Day O Plantation Operated by well-known local musician Paul Hurlock and his wife Jennifer, this elegant restaurant overlooking the harbor serves up Jamaican and continental specialties with an emphasis on seafood. Open for dinner only; closed Mondays. Reservations advised. Major credit cards accepted. Granville (phone: 952-1825).

Georgian House This beautifully restored 18th-century house, a historic landmark, offers lots of romantic charm. The downstairs dining room has the atmosphere of an old English pub and opens onto a restored courtyard. There is also an elegant dining room upstairs. The seafood is great—try the lobster Newburg, prepared with secret seasonings—or sample the Jamaican specialties. Open daily. Reservations advised. Major credit cards accepted. 2 Orange St. (phone: 952-0632).

Julia's A covered outdoor dining area with a spectacular view of the surrounding town and bay. The excellent Italian menu offers a prix fixe dinner of soup, pasta, main course, and dessert. Open daily. Reservations necessary for dinner. Major credit cards accepted. Bogue Hill (phone: 952-1772).

Norma's at the Wharf House Part of a small inn, this restaurant is set in an 18th-century sugar warehouse with tables on a waterfront deck. Portions are large, the sauces light, and the presentation mouth-watering. The ever-changing menu features chef Norma Shirley's creative local cooking, such as smoked marlin, grilled deviled crab back, pumpkin soup, and curried lobster nuggets. Closed Sundays and Mondays, as well as for lunch Tuesdays and Wednesdays. Live entertainment daily. Transportation from local hotels is complimentary. Reservations necessary for dinner. MasterCard and Visa accepted. Reading, just west of Montego Bay (phone: 979-2745).

Richmond Hill This romantic hilltop restaurant, with a splendid view, is set on the terrace and around the pool of an elegant mansion–turned–small hotel. Lobster is the specialty here. Free transportation provided from hotels. Open daily for dinner. Reservations advised. Major credit cards accepted. Union St., on Richmond Hill (phone: 952-3859).

Vineyard The attractive, airy house restaurant at the *Coyaba Beach Resort and Club* is low-key but elegant, with tiled floors, beamed ceilings, wrought-iron furniture, and lots of greenery. It serves an eclectic mix of Caribbean and continental fare that has made it as popular with locals as it is with visitors. Open daily for breakfast, lunch, and dinner. Reservations advised on weekends. Major credit cards accepted. Little River, St. James (phone: 953-9150).

MODERATE

Marguerite's by the Sea A romantic seaside setting, attentive service, and reliable food make this small, appealing place a favorite with islanders as well as visitors. Lobster dishes, fresh local shrimp, and the catch of the day are recommended; there's a good wine list and a beer garden, too. Open daily. Reservations advised. Major credit cards accepted. Gloucester Ave. (phone: 952-4777 or 952-3290).

Pelican For breakfast, lunch, and dinner, this casual place—one of MoBay's most popular eateries for more than 25 years—serves local soups and Jamaican dishes. The adjacent *Cascade Room,* open for dinner only, is more formal, with lobster and seafood, pricier but still reasonable. Open daily for breakfast, lunch, and dinner. Free transportation provided from hotels. Reservations advised for the *Cascade Room.* Major credit cards accepted. Gloucester Ave. (phone: 952-3171).

Pier 1 On the waterfront, this gathering place for the yachting set and business-people has a casual deck and a more formal dining room. Great seafood soups and tropical drinks, with a nice view of the marina. Free transportation provided from hotels. Open daily; Fridays it becomes one of MoBay's most popular late-night spots, and it serves Sunday brunch. Reservations unnecessary. Major credit cards accepted. Howard Cooke Blvd. (phone: 952-2452).

Town House A colonial atmosphere prevails in the brick-lined basement of a handsomely restored 18th-century home. It's a cool lunch retreat, and quietly stylish at night. There's an outdoor dining room, too. There are very good soups (pepper pot, pumpkin) and a variety of tempting seafood creations. Open daily. Reservations advised. Major credit cards accepted. Church St. (phone: 952-2660).

INEXPENSIVE

Pork Pit A local institution, this small, open-air gazebo in a garden setting serves the best jerk pork, chicken, and ribs we've found. Well worth a stop, if you thrive on spicy local fare. Open daily. No reservations. No credit cards accepted. Off Gloucester Ave. (no phone).

The Grill Good local dishes and continental fare are presented in a clean, simple setting. It's popular with the local crowd and businesspeople at lunch. Open daily for breakfast, lunch, and dinner; Tuesdays feature a special cocktail brunch. Reservations advised. Major credit cards accepted. In the *Wexford Court Hotel,* Gloucester Ave. (phone: 952-2854).

FALMOUTH

Glistening Waters Marina A friendly, informal spot for fresh fish and seafood on the edge of Oyster Bay—brilliantly "phosphorescent" on moonless nights. Run by angler and raconteur Pat Hastings and his wife, Patty, who is the kitchen wizard, it serves great soups, fresh fish, lobster, conch, and Jamaican dishes. Worth the trip from MoBay for a lazy day by the water. Open daily; no dinner on Sundays. Reservations unnecessary. Major credit cards accepted. Located a couple of miles east of Falmouth (phone: 954-3229 or 954-3138).

OCHO RIOS

EXPENSIVE

Almond Tree Attractively set on the *Hibiscus Lodge*'s gingerbread-trimmed back porch, this spot is popular for Jamaican lunch dishes—pepper pot, pumpkin soup, and fish sautéed with lime, onion, herbs, and butter—as well as delectable seafood and continental dinners with an island flavor (try Caribbean bouillabaisse or Jamaican beef tenderloin). The setting is intimate, and the service is good. Open daily. Reservations advised. Major credit cards accepted. Main St. (phone: 974-2813).

MODERATE

Carib Inn With imaginative local and seafood dishes, good service, and an almost elegant atmosphere in a garden setting, this place deserves several visits. Open daily. Reservations advised. American Express and Visa accepted. Main St. (phone: 974-2445).

Evita's A top-flight Italian dining spot, set in an 1860 gingerbread house with an incredible view of Ocho Rios Bay. Specialties include pasta dishes and seafood. Open daily. Reservations advised. Major credit cards accepted. Located next to the *Enchanted Garden Hotel.* Eden Bower Rd. (phone: 974-2333).

Parkway Good, simple soups, seafood, and Jamaican dishes in a coffee shop setting with fast service. Open daily for breakfast, lunch, and dinner. Reservations unnecessary. Major credit cards accepted. Off Main St. (phone: 974-2667).

INEXPENSIVE

Double V Jerk Pork Centre A friendly hangout with some of the best jerk chicken and pork in town. Open 24 hours daily. Reservations unnecessary. Major credit cards accepted. 109 Main St. (phone: 974-2084).

Little Pub This thatch-topped, casual spot is a good choice for lunch (hamburgers or other snacks) and dinner (lobster and Jamaican dishes). It's a popular gathering place, with music and dancing most nights. Open daily.

Reservations unnecessary. Major credit cards accepted. West of the Ocho Rios roundabout (phone: 974-2324).

PORT ANTONIO

VERY EXPENSIVE

Trident A very formal dining room (polished wood, gleaming silver, crystal, five-course place settings), serving fine continental dishes and attended by tuxedoed, white-gloved waiters who take their time to serve you. At the *Trident* hotel, one of Jamaica's four Elegant Resorts, it deserves its top rating. From the excellent wine list to the exquisite pastries, this is a memorable dining experience, whether for a casual garden luncheon or a prix fixe formal dinner. The menu changes daily. Jackets and ties required for dinner. Open daily. Dinner reservations necessary. Major credit cards accepted. East of Port Antonio on Rte. A4 (phone: 993-2602).

EXPENSIVE

Bounty This casual and relaxing place is on a private island that once belonged to Errol Flynn. It offers good seafood, authentic Jamaican dishes, daily specials, and great atmosphere. Sip a cocktail and drink in the scenery of Port Antonio from the bar. There's a prix fixe five-course dinner. Ferry service is provided. Open daily. Reservations advised for dinner. Major credit cards accepted. *Navy Island Marina Resort,* Port Antonio Harbour (phone: 993-2667).

Jamaica Palace Fine Caribbean and continental fare is served in this resort's elegant dining room, appointed with plush upholstery and crystal chandeliers. Jackets are required. Open daily for dinner only. Reservations necessary. Major credit cards accepted (phone: 993-2020).

MODERATE

DeMontevin Lodge A gingerbread-trimmed family hotel that serves delicious Jamaican dinners by appointment. Call a day ahead. American Express accepted. Musgrave and George Sts. (phone: 993-2604).

INEXPENSIVE

Bonnie View This small, hilltop hostelry with the most spectacular view anywhere of Port Antonio (even when it's hot down there, there's a cool breeze up here) serves a traditional afternoon tea and informal Jamaican dinners. Open daily. Reservations unnecessary. Major credit cards accepted. Bonnie View Rd. (phone: 993-2752).

KINGSTON

EXPENSIVE

Le Pavillon Hushed tones prevail within this soft cocoon of pink, mauve, and white. Guests sit upon silk-upholstered chairs and scallop-backed couches, the lighting is low, the service unobtrusive, and the presentation of the creative continental fare *très* elegant. There are excellent seafood, steak, and veal dishes. Come for a splurge, a romantic evening, or for the all-you-can-eat Sunday brunch. Open daily; no lunch Saturdays. Reservations necessary for dinner. Major credit cards accepted. 81 Knutsford Blvd., in the *Jamaica Pegasus Hotel* (phone: 926-3690).

Raphael's This casually elegant northern Italian eatery specializes in homemade pasta and wonderful veal, fish, and chicken dishes. Try the ravioli stuffed with beef, the fettuccine in lime sauce, or the red snapper with lemon and capers. Dining is alfresco, either on the patio beneath the leaves of a huge lignum vitae tree or on the terrace, with romantic music playing in the background. Leave room for dessert—the gelato bar offers homemade Italian ice cream in such flavors as mango, coconut, banana, and tamarind. No lunch Saturdays; closed Sundays. Reservations advised. Major credit cards accepted. 7 Hillcrest Ave. (phone: 978-2983).

MODERATE

Devon House Kingston's government-owned showplace mansion offers two dining options. The elegant *Devonshire,* on the verandah, is a fine restaurant in an intimate garden setting, serving continental fare (closed Sundays; dinner reservations advised). The *Coffee Terrace,* another verandah-style eatery, serves light lunches, teas, and a Sunday Jamaican brunch (open daily; reservations advised). Major credit cards accepted. Hope and Waterloo Rds. (phone: 929-7046 for the *Devonshire;* 929-6867 for the *Coffee Terrace*).

Terra Nova A fashionable favorite with Jamaicans as well as visitors, this elegant eatery features a classic continental menu. There's a popular Friday seafood lunch buffet. Open daily for breakfast, lunch, and dinner. Reservations advised for dinner. Major credit cards accepted. 17 Waterloo Rd. (phone: 926-2211 or 926-9334).

INEXPENSIVE

Chelsea Jerk Centre One of Kingston's most popular casual eateries for jerk pork and chicken, and roasted fish. Closed Sundays. Reservations unnecessary. No credit cards accepted. 7 Chelsea Ave. (phone: 926-6322).

OUTSIDE KINGSTON

EXPENSIVE

Blue Mountain Inn This dining spot, located on the grounds of a former coffee plantation set alongside the Hope River, offers an exceptionally attractive setting. The late-19th-century, wood-shingled building is delightfully decorated with English colonial antiques, mahogany tables, and a working fireplace. Guests begin with drinks on the terrace, then dine indoors in cozy intimacy. The service is attentive, the mood romantic, the wine cellar well stocked, and the fare a blend of continental and seafood specialties topped, perhaps, by baked Alaska. It is well worth the trip out of Kingston. Jackets are required for men. Dinner only; closed Sundays. Reservations necessary. Major credit cards accepted. Gordon Town Rd., 20 minutes from New Kingston (phone: 927-1700 or 927-2606).

Strawberry Hill Set high in the scenic Blue Mountains, this intimate retreat offers exquisitely prepared, inventive Jamaican fare, afternoon tea on weekends, and a panoramic view of Kingston. Signature dishes include pumpkin-crusted snapper, *agnolotti* filled with curried minced goat, and jerk-roasted lamb. Afternoon tea is served on Fridays and Saturdays, and Sunday brunch is accompanied by live music. The wine list is extensive. Open daily for breakfast, lunch, and dinner. Reservations required. Major credit cards accepted. Irishtown (phone: 944-8400; fax: 994-8203).

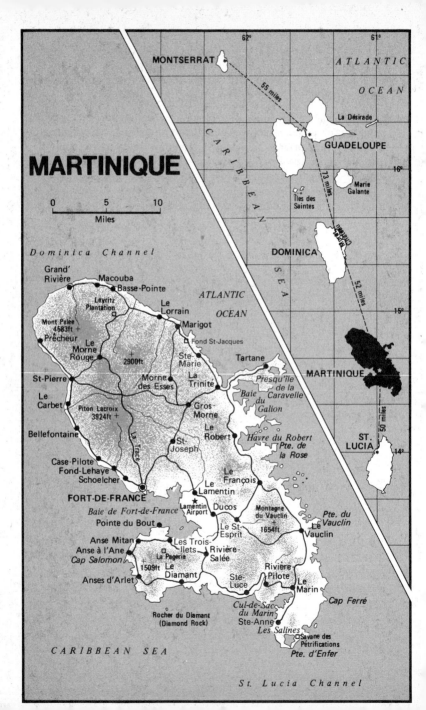

Martinique

"A bit of France in the Caribbean." As clichés often are, this one is largely true. Not that wild, tropical Martinique looks like *la mère patrie.* Unlike France's snow-topped Alps, Martinique's mountains are blanketed with green jungle; thick stands of bamboo and giant breadfruit trees thrive in the island's rain forests, and there's even a patch of desert in the south.

Despite all appearances, though, Martinique is indeed France. It is a *région,* whose citizens exercise the same rights and privileges accorded citizens of France. They are eligible for French social security benefits, health programs, and free compulsory education. (The literacy rate in the French West Indies is over 95%.) In addition to having a local government, island residents vote in French national elections. Few people in Martinique speak of island independence; the majority can't imagine what they would have to gain.

Martinique has a distinctly French *air.* Boutiques are full of Baccarat crystal, Chanel perfume, and Hermès scarves; pâtisseries sell fresh-baked croissants and display cheeses just off the boat from Marseilles; the streets are filled with honking Peugeots and buzzing *bicyclettes;* and French is heard everywhere.

But Martinique has its own personality, too, born of its sensuous climate, its lush landscapes, and its proud people. The island has its own distinctive musical heritage, including mazurkas and waltzes from plantation days, the hot sounds of *zouk* (danceable music with an African/beguine/West Indian sound), and the timeless, sexy beguine. Martinique's food also is distinctive—creole cooking combining native seafood, tropical fruit, and feisty spices.

Martinique's recorded history dates to 1493, when Columbus discovered the island but didn't land here. More than a century later—in 1635—a party of Frenchmen arrived to claim the island for France and begin permanent settlement. The British conquered the island in 1762, only to give it up again a year later under the 1763 Treaty of Paris, in exchange for France's relinquishing her claim to Canada. Martinique has been French ever since.

The island's story is sprinkled with the names of interesting people, such as Victor Schoelcher, a Parisian-born deputy from Alsace who was instrumental in helping to free the island's slaves in 1848. A statue of Schoelcher with a slave child stands in front of the island's *Palais de Justice,* and a Fort-de-France street, a suburb, and the capital's library bear his name. Painter Paul Gauguin lived and worked in Carbet for about five months in 1887. And then there's Marie-Josèphe Rose Tascher de la Pagerie, who became Napoleon's Empress Josephine. Her birthplace in Les Trois-Ilets is now a national museum, and her name is on the tongue of every tour guide. (Her memory is not exactly revered by local people, however. The reason: In the late 1700s, slavery was outlawed in France and all its island properties, but Josephine asked Napoleon to reinstate it in Martinique because her family's sugar plantation had many slaves. As a result, slavery continued on the island for another 75 years.)

In Josephine's day and until the late 19th century, Martinique lived well on its production of sugar and rum. Elegant plantations with large houses, cane processing factories, and round-towered windmills dotted the country. Except for the steepest mountainsides, the island was quilted with green fields of cane. Sugar—and the rum made from it—is still an important crop on Martinique. But growing it requires hard labor. For this reason and because of the gradual decline in sugar prices, crops have been diversified in recent years. More and more banana plantations and bristly fields of pineapple are appearing.

And then there's tourism. Any Francophile will find the combination of Gallic culture, gentle climate, and natural beauty irresistible. The sports facilities are good and varied—visitors can enjoy cycling, fishing, golf, tennis, hiking, boating, windsurfing, water skiing, and scuba diving—and there's also a choice of interesting historic sites.

But can you enjoy Martinique's charms if you don't speak French? That depends on you. In small, out-of-the-way hotels and restaurants, you'll probably have difficulty making yourself understood. One day you might find yourself in front of a shop counter miming a waterproof watch for a puzzled salesgirl who doesn't speak English. If such things bother you, forget about Martinique.

On the other hand, staff members of most tourist hotels, popular shops, and restaurants speak fair-to-excellent English; tours in English are available; and islanders usually are much more willing to bridge the language gap than are their Parisian counterparts. With a good phrase book, a little patience, and a sense of humor, you'll find your room, order a meal, shop, see the sights, and even lose your limit at the casino. If you don't mind occasionally communicating by gestures, and if intriguing foreign places appeal to you, you'll love this "little bit of France in the Caribbean."

Martinique At-a-Glance

FROM THE AIR

The island of Martinique is 50 miles long and 22 miles wide, with a land area of 425 square miles and a population of 360,000. It is the northernmost of the Windward (eastern) Islands in the Lesser Antilles. Its nearest neighbors are Dominica (52 miles north), Guadeloupe (125 miles north), and St. Lucia (50 miles south).

Martinique is shaped somewhat like an elongated right-hand mitten with the space between its west coast thumb-and-forefinger edge forming an admirable deep-water harbor. On the tip of the thumb sits Pointe du Bout, the island's principal resort area, with its highest concentration of medium-rise hotels and condominium apartments surrounding a handsome marina. Directly north of the point—a 20-minute ferry ride across the harbor—is Martinique's only real city, its capital and chief commercial port, Fort-de-France (pop. 105,000).

Lamentin International Airport is just inland of the harbor's eastern edge, about 20 minutes from Fort-de-France and about 30 minutes from Pointe du Bout. The distance from New York is 1,965 miles (about a 5½-hour flight), from Miami about 1,470 miles (about five hours' flying time), and from San Juan, 425 miles (about a two-hour flight).

Martinique's east coast, pounded by Atlantic surf, combines rugged shoreline, occasional wave-combed beaches, and a few small fishing towns: Vauclin, François, Le Robert, Tartane (on the peninsula called Presqu'île de la Caravelle, which is mostly nature preserve), Ste-Marie, and Grand' Rivière. The western and southern coasts are washed by the gentler Caribbean. Lining the shore south of Pointe du Bout are some of the island's best bathing beaches: Anses d'Arlet, Le Diamant, Plage des Salines, and Ste-Anne.

Much of the northern half of the island is covered with rain forests and tall, green mountains. Most famous of these is Mt. Pelée, a now-dormant (but still alive) volcano whose 1902 eruption destroyed the city of St-Pierre. St-Pierre never recovered; the ghost town is a chief sightseeing destination here.

SPECIAL PLACES

FORT-DE-FRANCE Martinique's capital is a small-scale combination of New Orleans and Nice—with narrow streets and iron grille balconies, blue-capped *flics* (cops) marshaling traffic, and a fleet of trim-hulled yachts riding at anchor in its Baie des Flamands. It's where the banks, the shops, and some of the best restaurants are, the place everyone visits at least once.

The heart of the city is *La Savane,* the big green park handsomely restored and landscaped with benches, walks, and playing fields. Located here is the once-beautiful statue of Josephine, dedicated in 1859 and mysteriously beheaded in 1991. The beheading, some Martiniquais say, was long overdue because Josephine championed the slavery that cursed their forefathers. On the park's edge, near the harbor, a roofed market shades craftswomen and their stacks of baskets, straw hats, woodcarvings, beads, bangles, and shells for sale. Just across the street is the ferry dock, and on the strategic hilltop to the east looms *Fort St-Louis.*

Walk west along Boulevard Alfassa following the harbor's edge, and you'll find the tourist information center. Along the park's western edge runs the main street, Rue de la Liberté. It's lined with "les quick-snack" vans on the park side and, on the other, the town's chief hotels, the frenetic post office, and the city's library and architectural chef d'oeuvre, *La*

Bibliothèque Schoelcher, imported lock, stock, and trompe l'oeil from Paris after the *Exposition of 1889.* Also here is the *Musée Départemental,* installed in a gracefully restored and air conditioned townhouse. Its collections include relics of prehistoric Arawak and Carib civilizations as well as some pretty pieces of antique furniture. Closed Saturday afternoons and Sundays; admission charge (phone: 715705). Streets leading off Rue de la Liberté to the left (west) shelter Fort-de-France's best-stocked shops, full of perfume, crystal, porcelain, handbags, scarves, and other elegant imports—mostly from France, but from Switzerland, Germany, Japan, and the rest of the world as well. One block west on Rue Schoelcher and opposite its own small square stands the *cathédrale.*

NORTH OF FORT-DE-FRANCE

ST-PIERRE Once the Paris of the West Indies and now its Pompeii, the remains of this city are Martinique's top day-trip destination. Only the ruins of the theater, the cathedral, and the broken gray walls remain of what were once homes, gardens, and stately villas before the May 1902 eruption of Mt. Pelée, which killed 30,000 people. A small volcanological museum named for its American founder, Dr. Franck A. Perret, displays pictures and relics—fused coins, a charred sewing machine, petrified spaghetti, a melted bottle with perfume still inside. It's a featured stop on a number of half-day and daylong bus tours departing from Fort-de-France and major tourist hotels. About an hour north of Fort-de-France, it's an easy drive-yourself destination, too. Open daily; admission charge (phone: 781516).

Visitors also can descend 87 yards beneath the waves in the 48-seat *Mobilis* submarine to view the graveyard of sailing ships and giant steamboats sent to the bottom during the Mt. Pelée eruption. The sub also provides a dazzling glimpse of Martinique's colorful marine life. It's operated by *La Compagnie de la Baie de St-Pierre* (phone: 781818), which also runs 100-seat quadrimarans that whisk visitors from Fort-de-France to St-Pierre in just 25 minutes. There's a hefty admission to the submarine ($70 for adults, $35 for children); the quadrimaran costs $14, about the same as a taxi.

SACRÉ COEUR DE BALATA (SACRED HEART OF BALATA) Perched in the hills above Fort-de-France, this church, which resembles Paris's *Sacré-Coeur,* is visible from a distance. Day tours headed for St-Pierre and *Leyritz Plantation* give a closer look. Or drive up and see for yourself—especially on Sundays, when families promenade in their brightest and best. Route de Balata.

JARDIN DE BALATA (BALATA BOTANICAL PARK) On Route de Balata, about a 10-minute drive from *Sacré Coeur de Balata,* this idyllic spot is a veritable feast for the senses. Waves of brilliant hibiscus, orchids, anthuriums (the island's official flower), flaming red torch lilies, and thousands of other tropical beauties bloom across the hillside. Open daily. Admission charge (phone: 644873).

CARBET Columbus landed here in 1502; Gauguin lived here for five months in 1887. Today it's a small fishing village with a photogenic shoreline and Martinique's only Olympic-size swimming pool built into the hills. The pool, at the town's center, is open daily; admission charge (phone: 780770). Also visit the *Jardin Zoologique Amazona* (Amazona Zoological Garden), home to 60 animal species, mostly from the Amazon Basin and Africa. It's at Le Coin and open daily; admission charge (phone: 780064). The local botanical garden boasts the *Vallée des Papillons* (Valley of the Butterflies). Set in a steep ravine, over 1,500 species flutter through both a large tropical conservatory and gardens growing among the ruins of a large plantation destroyed by the eruption of Mt. Pelée. Open daily. Admission charge (*Habitation Anse Latouche;* phone: 781919). There's also a little Gauguin museum (Turin Cove; phone: 782266), with several reproductions but, unfortunately, no originals. Open daily; admission charge.

FOND ST-JACQUES Dominican fathers established a community here in the hills above the Atlantic in 1658. The most famous of them, Père Labat, lived here from 1693 to 1705. His *Voyages to the American Islands* could be considered the first Caribbean guidebook. The chapel, rebuilt in 1769, still stands, as do the partially restored buildings of a sugar estate. Most impressive: the vast purgery—the room where sugar was dried—with its great, arched, beamed ceiling. This is a stop on the all-day tour to *Leyritz* (see below). Open daily. No admission charge (no phone).

LA TRACE A serpentine road through Martinique's rain forest, it scales the heights from the north side of Fort-de-France to towering Morne Rouge and offers great views. From Fort-de-France, follow the signs for Balata to get to La Trace.

LEYRITZ The best-restored plantation on the island, it's now an inn (see *Checking In*), a restaurant, a working banana concern, and a doll museum housing miniatures of celebrated women, each doll made of plant materials. This is the final destination of some day tours; a swim-and-lunch stop on others. Open daily. Admission charge to the gardens and the main house (phone: 785392).

CERON PLANTATION This magnificent old estate, located near Le Prêcheur on the northwest Caribbean coast of the island, makes for an out-of-the-ordinary daylong excursion. Lovingly restored, the estate, which dates from 1670, includes a main house (now the owners' residence), a sugar refinery (now a restaurant), an immense garden, and a number of well-preserved ruins of other structures. Visitors may stroll about the grounds and the nearby forest, or swim in the estate's river. Trips to the beach and boating also may be included in the excursion. Open daily. Admission charge (phone: 529453 for tour information).

LA PAGERIE Located near Les Trois-Ilets, this ruin evokes another era. Its crumbled stones outline the plantation house, the sugar factory with its tall chimney, and the grounds that Marie-Josèphe Rose Tascher de la Pagerie (later Napoleon's Empress Josephine) called home. The cottage that was the plantation kitchen is a government-operated museum whose displays include paintings, a white net stocking (monogrammed and mended) and other bits of clothing, Josephine's childhood bed, and a smoldering love letter from Napoleon (with an English translation) that is worth the trip in itself. Some southbound tours combine this with a beach outing and lunch at Le Diamant. From Pointe du Bout, it's a reasonable destination for a moped ride, or stop on the way to the golf course at Les Trois-Ilets. There's a refreshment stand. Closed Mondays. Admission charge (phone: 683455).

DIAMOND ROCK Looming out of the Caribbean off the south-coast beach at Le Diamant, it is the only rock ever commissioned as a ship in the British Navy. For 18 months between 1804 and 1805, it was—officially—the HMS *Diamond Rock,* manned by the British and bombarded by the French, who were in firm possession of the rest of Martinique. The siege failed miserably until (legend says) the French smuggled some rum within striking distance of the British, then re-took the rock while the British crew was under the influence.

PRESQU'ÎLE DE LA CARAVELLE Jutting dramatically into the Atlantic, this peninsula is part of the big *Parc Naturel,* which also encompasses the tropical mountains in the north and the highlands as far south as Les Salines. A nature preserve with good campsites, it's embellished with the ruins of the 18th-century *Château Duboc,* ancestral home of the Sultana Validé, another Martiniquan woman who was destined, like her cousin Josephine, to rule in another country. In the case of the Sultana, born Aimée Duboc de Rivery, it was not by choice. Kidnapped by pirates on the journey home from her school in France, she was sold into slavery and later presented as a gift to the Sultan of Constantinople, becoming his wife and the mother of Sultan Mahmoud II. Just inside the entrance of the château are copper pots the size of wading pools, once used to boil sugarcane. A path leads from the ruins of the stone buildings down to a cove that was a favorite launching spot of pirates. Open daily. Admission charge (no phone). For information on trails and campsites in the preserve, call the *Syndicat d'Initiative* (see *Hiking*).

EXTRA SPECIAL

Much of Martinique's sugarcane ends up at one of the 14 *rhumeries* sprinkled across the island, where the juice is squeezed from the cane, boiled into syrup, and distilled into a knock-your-socks-off potion. Free rum tasting and distillery tours are offered at each *rhumerie;* arrive during rum season (August through December) and you can watch the machines in action. The *St. James Distillery* (Ste-Marie; phone: 693002) has a small but interesting museum, set in a lovely creole house, with 200 years of rum-making artifacts and a museum store. Closed weekend afternoons; no admission charge. For a list of additional distilleries, contact the *Martinique Tourist Office* (see *Tourist Information*).

Sources and Resources

TOURIST INFORMATION

The tourist information center along the waterfront in Fort-de-France (Blvd. Alfassa; phone: 637960; fax: 736693) is closed Saturday afternoons and Sundays. The tourist office's airport information desk (phone: 512855) is open daily until after the last flight arrives.

For details on Martinique tourist offices in the US, see GETTING READY TO GO. In addition, information about the island is now available via computer; the Martinique menu on the World Wide Web is accessible at http://www.nyo.com/martinique.

LOCAL COVERAGE *Une Histoire d'Amour Entre Ciel and Mer,* published seasonally by the tourist office in French and English, is available free at the airport, hotels, and the Fort-de-France tourist information center, and gives up-to-date information on hotel facilities, sightseeing, restaurants, shopping, and entertainment. It includes a map of Fort-de-France, as well as briefings on culture and history. The tourist office also publishes a helpful monthly bilingual newspaper called *Bienvenue en Martinique.* The privately published (every two weeks) English-language *Choubouloute*—also free—covers much of the same material and includes a clear color map of the island. *Ti Gourmet* is a handy guide to Martinique restaurants, updated annually, with color photographs and sample menus as well as a section on nightlife. It's available free from many hotels and shops.

The daily French-language newspaper, *France-Antilles,* carries easily understood (even for those who don't speak French) entertainment ads. Parisian papers and the English-language *International Herald Tribune* normally arrive on the island the day after publication.

The deluxe picture book—one of a number for sale locally—called *Martinique* (Editions Exbrayat; about $30) is worth having for its short, readable essays by local experts on island history and culture, as well as for its dramatic photographs.

RADIO AND TELEVISION Television is in French, but radio (which is produced locally or picked up from neighboring islands) broadcasts in several languages, including a nightly English news program on Martinique-Inter (1350 AM). Most hotels have satellite-dish facilities.

TELEPHONE When calling from the US, dial 011 (international access code) + 596 (country code) + (local number). To call from another Caribbean island, the access code may vary, so call the local operator. When calling from a phone on Martinique, use only the local number unless otherwise indicated. Dial 17 for the police; 18 for an ambulance.

ENTRY REQUIREMENTS In addition to an ongoing or return ticket, a current passport, a passport expired not more than five years, or other proof of citizenship (voter's registration card, or birth certificate with raised seal, plus official photo ID, such as a driver's license) is required for stays of up to three months. A visa is needed for longer visits.

CLIMATE AND CLOTHES The average year-round temperature is 79F (26C). The weather is tropical and tends to be humid at sea level during the day, but can be 5 to 10F cooler—and breezy—in the hills. Even summer days are tempered by trade winds; expect high 60s or low 70s (20 to 23C) at night. November through April are the driest months; July through September, the wettest; but it doesn't rain every day even in the wet season, and more than a few dry-season days have a shower or two—especially in the rain forest areas around Morne-Rouge and La Trace.

For daytime, wear lightweight sports clothes, bikinis or monokinis (female) and bikini trunks (male) on the beach. Caftans and djellabas make popular beach robes for both men and women. For touring and shopping, slacks and tops, cool cotton dresses or separates are suggested for women; slacks and knit or cotton-blend sport shirts for men. Shorts are less well received. Nights are dressier—especially in season. For women, that could mean a cocktail dress or fancy pants and top; for men, a long-sleeve, open-neck shirt and slacks. Jacket and tie are seldom, if ever, required. Women might want a light sweater or shawl for breezy nights and air conditioned restaurants and discos.

MONEY Martinique's official currency is the French franc, whose day-to-day dollar value is quoted in the business sections of major metropolitan US newspapers; at press time it was about 4.8 francs to $1 US. Banks pay a little more for US currency than for traveler's checks. However, several tourist-oriented shops offer an additional 20% discount when shoppers use traveler's checks or credit cards (but not cash dollars) to pay for purchases. Francs are best for restaurant meals, taxi fares, and other day-to-day expenses.

Banks (at the airport and in Fort-de-France) offer the best rate of exchange. Hours are approximately 7:30 AM to 4 PM, but they close for lunch between about noon and 2:30 PM, and in the afternoon preceding a public holiday. Hotels usually cash traveler's checks at a slightly lower francs-per-dollar rate. French francs can be reconverted to dollars only at banks (including the one at the airport), not at hotels. Your home bank will charge an unconscionable amount for the reconversion service (and only exchange paper bills), so allow enough time to reconvert leftover francs at the airport before you leave. All prices in this chapter are quoted in US dollars.

LANGUAGE Most native-born Martiniquais speak both French and Creole—a mélange of French with African words and rhythms. Some employees at major tourist hotels and popular shops speak English, but country people are less likely to. If you're not fluent in French, carry a dictionary or phrase book.

TIME Martinique is on atlantic standard time, one hour later than eastern standard time. When it's 7 PM EST in New York, it's 8 PM on Martinique. When New York is on daylight saving time, the Martinique hour is the same. As in France, a 24-hour clock is used, so 1 PM becomes 1300 hours; 2 PM, 1400 hours; and so on.

CURRENT Local electricity is 220 volts AC, 50 cycles, so North American visitors need a converter and an adapter. Several large hotels lend them; to be sure, bring your own.

TIPPING French law requires the automatic addition of a 15% service charge to all restaurant and bar bills. If you decide to tip extra in a restaurant or nightclub, be sure to leave cash. Credit card gratuities go directly to the establishment, not to the individual server. Give bellboys and porters about $1 per bag. Most cab drivers own their cars and do not expect tips.

GETTING AROUND

BUS There are a few point-to-point buses on the island. The system is pretty informal; hail them on the street. For more information, contact the tourist office (see *Tourist Information*). Taxis Collectifs, or TCs, are eight-seat limos or vans that provide most of Martinique's public transport for rates that run from 8 francs (about $1.50 at press time) to 45 francs (about $8.65 at press time), depending on distance. The Fort-de-France departure point for most TCs is Pointe Simon on the waterfront. They operate from early morning until early evening. To travel on them confidently, you should be able to speak a little French or know exactly where you want to go. Again, check with the tourist office (close by Pointe Simon) for schedules and fares.

CAR RENTAL Easy to arrange, and rates aren't exorbitant. Many companies offer a choice of day rate plus mileage or unlimited-mileage rate—whichever computes more favorably for the renter at turn-in time. Weekly rentals offer a 10% discount. The renter pays for gas, insurance, and 14% local tax; renters with no credit card will have to put down a cash deposit of about $300 to $350. A driver's license from home is good in Martinique for up to 20 days; for longer stays, obtain an international driver's permit (about $10) from a local *American Automobile Association* chapter before leaving home (you don't have to be a member). Renters must be at least 21 to 25 years old, depending on the rental company, with at least one year's experience as a licensed driver. Make advance reservations with the following international companies via their toll-free numbers, or at their airport branches or through your hotel after arrival: *Avis* (phone: 512686 or 511770), *Budget* (phone: 512288, 513656, or 636900), *Europcar* (phone: 513333 or 510196), *Hertz* (phone: 512822 or 606464), and *Thrifty* (phone: 510373 or 507550). Local firms (whose rates occasionally are lower than the international companies') include *Citer–LAM* (17 Rue de Redoute de Marouba, Fort-de-France; phone: 726648 or 724013; and at the airport; phone: 516575), *Pop's Car* (Rue Ernest DeProge, Fort-de-France; phone: 700070; and at the airport; phone: 510272), and *Europcar* (28 Rue Ernest DeProge, Fort-de-France; phone: 733313). The major rental agencies and many of the local companies accept one or more credit cards, although some smaller ones may operate on a cash-only basis.

Martinique has more than 175 miles of well-paved but sometimes zigzagging main roads. Driving is on the right. The tourist office has outlined seven self-guided driving tours that take a half to a full day to cover (see *Tourist Information*). But if strange, sometimes steep, and curving roads make you nervous, opt for the bus.

FERRY SERVICE Runs from early morning until after midnight between Fort-de-France, at Desnambuc Quay opposite *La Savane,* and Pointe du Bout, where a number of the best-known tourist hotels are. *Somatour* (phone: 730553) operates a ferry on the 15-minute route. *Madinina Vedette* (phone: 630646) links Fort-de-France with Anse Mitan and Anse à l'Ane from morning until late afternoon.

INTER-ISLAND FLIGHTS *American* (phone: 511229) flies from San Juan, Puerto Rico, daily, but arrival time is close to midnight; return flights depart in the early morning. *Air Martinique* (phone: 516868) flies to and from most of its Antillean neighbors. There are frequent daily flights to and from Guadeloupe on *Air Guadeloupe* (phone: 590-822835 or 590-901225 on Guadeloupe) and *Air France* (phone: 553333). *LIAT* (phone: 511000 or 512111) also flies to and from neighboring islands. *Antilles Aero Service* (phone: 516688) at *Lamentin Airport* rents small planes, with or without pilot, by the day or the hour.

MOPEDS AND MOTORCYCLES Mopeds may just be the best way to take a jaunt to *La Pagerie* or to get to the golf course at Les Trois-Ilets. Vespas, on which two can ride comfortably, also are available for rent. Reserve a day ahead; you'll need a credit card or a cash deposit of about $225. In Fort-de-France, *Funny* (80 Rue Ernest DeProge; phone: 633305) rents Vespas, mopeds, and motorcycles.

SEA EXCURSIONS Several excursion boats operate out of the *Pointe du Bout Marina,* the *Méridien* and *La Batelière* hotels (see *Checking In* for both), and other docks for daylong trips to St-Pierre in the north and Diamond Rock in the south. These include the schooner *Toumelin* (at the *Méridien* marina; phone: 493501). The catamaran *Emeraude Express* (at the Basin de Redoub, Fort-de-France; phone: 631211; fax: 633447) makes several trips a week to and from Guadeloupe and Dominica. Geologist Jacques Meneau offers informative daytime tours on the glass-bottom *Seaquarium* (*Pointe du Bout Marina;* phone: 660550), as well as evening cruises on the bay with a bar, a buffet, steel band entertainment, and an impressive, illuminated underwater show. Hour-long undersea excursions in Aquascopes—odd, bug-shaped metal pods that poke around the ocean floor and allow passengers to view the scenery through big glass windows—are offered several times a day in Ste-Anne (phone: 748741) and at the *Pointe du Bout Marina* in Les Trois-Ilets (phone: 683609).

SIGHTSEEING BUS TOURS Local operators offer day and half-day tours along five key routes; each combines historical sites, scenery, and—often—a sample of good creole cooking. The standard itineraries (with departures from *La Savane* in Fort-de-France and some tourist hotels): north to St-Pierre or *Leyritz Plantation* or both; east to the Atlantic coast; south to the village of Ste-Anne and the beach at Les Salines, or to *La Pagerie* and Le Diamant with its white sand beach and landmark rock. Among the best operators: *Caribtours* (Pointe du Bout; phone: 660256), *Madinina Tours* (89 Rue Blénac, Fort-de-France; phone: 706525), *CaribJet* (*Lamentin Airport;* phone: 519000), and *S.T.T. Voyage* (23 Rue Blénac, Fort-de-France; phone: 716812 or 733200). Guides are pleasant and speak English well. Buses are air conditioned. Book tours directly, or through your travel agent, your hotel, or the tourist office (see *Tourist Information*).

SIGHTSEEING TAXI TOURS These are a good choice when several passengers share the ride and split the cost. Typical itineraries: a half-day trip from Fort-de-France to Les Trois-Ilets and Le Diamant Beach; or to St-Pierre via the Caribbean coast, then on to Morne Rouge and La Trace. Be sure to agree upon the cost of the ride before starting. Drivers speak some English, but it's a good idea to take along a map and a sightseeing guide. One excellent tour guide is Bernadette Ducteil (phone: 513187). A lover of Martinique history, folklore, and flora, she speaks fluent English and often works for the tourist office.

TAXI Travel by taxi is expensive. The fare for two people from *Lamentin Airport,* where all international flights land, to Pointe du Bout hotels is about $28 during the day, about $45 at night. From Fort-de-France to Pointe du Bout, the day fare is about $35; after 8 PM there's a 40% surcharge. Since drivers own their vehicles, tips are not expected.

SPECIAL EVENTS

The most festive time of the year is *Carnaval.* Just before *Lent,* it involves days of parading, masquerading, and celebrating. But before that come weeks of dancing and gala goings-on to get everyone in condition for the main event. It builds to a wild climax on *Ash Wednesday* (February 21 in 1996) when Vaval, the spirit of *Carnaval,* is burned in effigy on a giant bonfire off *La Savane.* Martinique calls a halt to fasting with *Mi-Carême* (mid-*Lent*); May 1 is *La Fête du Travail* (Labor Day) with workers' parades. Fort-de-France stages its *Festival de Fort-de-France,* a celebration of local arts and culture, every July. The *Tour de la Martinique,* a thrilling week-long bicycle race, takes place in mid-July; and the *Tour des Yoles Rondes,* a week-long yawling contest, is in late July. During the first two weeks in December the biennial *Martinique Carrefour Mondial de la Guitare* (Martinique World Guitar Festival; to be held this year) and the *Jazz à la Martinique* festival alternate. *New Year's Day, Easter Monday* (April 8 in 1996), *Pentecost Monday* (May 27 in 1996), *Ascension Day* (May 16 in 1996), *Slavery Abolition Day* (May 22), *Bastille Day* (July 14), *Assumption Day* (August 15), *All Saints' Day* (November 1), *Armistice Day* (November 11), and *Christmas* also are public holidays.

SHOPPING

The brightest bargains around are French imports—Lalique crystal, Limoges dinnerware, fashions and fragrances from the best-known Paris houses—all at prices 25% to 40% below US, with an additional 20% discount if you pay in traveler's checks (some shops extend the extra discount to purchases made with major credit cards). The prices not only beat those in many of the world's so-called free ports, but those in Paris boutiques as well. Finds include cosmetics made in France, French food (truffled pâté, quail eggs, mustard), kitchen gadgets (graters, food mills, crêpe pans), and liqueurs and brandies. Martinique's own favorite rum comes in shades from Vieux Acajou (dark, mellow "Old Mahogany") to Jeune Acajou (newer, paler "Young Mahogany") to clear white (fiery, 100 proof). The connoisseur's buy: deep brown, liqueur-like, 12-year-old rums bottled by St. James, Bally, and Clément.

On the whole, Martinique's crafts are not remarkable. By far the most fun are big, bright, appliquéd hangings depicting island folks and folkways. The ubiquitous Martiniquais doll, in her *madras et foulard* national dress, is available in every size. There also are some nicely woven straw hats (the pointed *bakoua* is the island's official topper), baskets, and placemats. The open-air market at *La Savane* is best for browsing.

A Caribbean shopping survival tip: Try to avoid cruise ship crowds. Check with your hotel desk or the tourist office downtown (see *Tourist Information*) and plan to shop when the fleet's not in. Shopping hours are from 9 AM to 12:30 PM and 2:30 to 6 PM; closed Saturday afternoons, Sundays, and holidays. Some shops, like *Roger Albert,* stay open during lunchtime as well.

Some notable shops in Fort-de-France:

Albert Venutolo Moderately priced gold and silver jewelry, tea services, and crystal; 20% off for payment with US dollar traveler's checks or a credit card.

Four locations: 17 Rue Victor Hugo (phone: 725744); 17 Rue Antoine Siger (phone: 714334); *Centre Commercial* in Cluny (phone: 735013); and Rue Ernest André in Lamentin (phone: 511158).

Boutique Michel Montignac A must for lovers of fine foods and preserves, with jellies, fresh pasta, foie gras, pastries, chocolates, breads, vinegars, teas, fruit juices, sparkling wines, and health products. 77 Rue Blénac (phone: 702169).

Boutique Mounia High-style Parisian fashions. 26 Rue Perrinon (phone: 737727).

Cadet-Daniel The place to look for gold and silver chains and other real jewelry at prices well below those back home. 72 Rue Antoine Siger (phone: 714148).

Carambole A cut above typical tourist souvenirs, with arts and crafts by local, Haitian, and other Antillean artisans, jewelry, books on Martinique, swimwear. Two locations: 17 Rue Victor Hugo (phone: 734651) and 20 Rue Ernest DeProge (phone: 639363).

Forum Africain Superb selection of colorful imported African batik clothing and fabrics, fine leather, woodwork, jewelry, paintings, and original accessories. 100 Rue Victor Hugo (phone: 602012).

Galeries Lafayette This three-story branch of the French department store has an excellent selection of clothing, cosmetics, perfumes, lingerie, leather handbags and belts, and more, all with typical Parisian panache. The store offers 20% off purchases made with US dollar traveler's checks or a credit card. Corner of Rues Schoelcher and Siger (phone: 718950).

Hit Parade Featuring the latest island discs, as well as recorded folk songs, beguines, *zouk*, and mazurkas. 55 Rue Lamartine (phone: 700151).

Merlande Smaller and not as crowded as *Roger Albert*, but still offering 20% off purchases made with US dollar traveler's checks or a credit card. Good selection of fragrances and cosmetics; also sunglasses, hats, and pocketbooks. Corner of Rues Schoelcher and Siger (phone: 718950).

Othello A real men's haberdashery, with suits, jackets, slacks, shirts, and ties. Two locations: 43 Rue Blénac (phone: 635659) and 37 Rue St-Germain (phone: 713838).

Roger Albert Fort-de-France's best-known and biggest specialty shop stocks just about everything from chic watches to Limoges place-card holders. The shop offers an extra discount on purchases made with major credit cards. Just off *La Savane*, at 7 Rue Victor Hugo (phone: 714444), and at the *Méridien Trois-Ilets Hotel* (see *Checking In*).

Salines Shop Delightful interior with small catwalks over a miniature lagoon, with a good range of classy women's swimwear, exotic batik clothing and fabrics, embroidered dresses, and fun childrenswear. 66 Rue Victor Hugo (phone: 702828).

Thomas de Rogatis For gold and silver chains, watches, crystal, and other fine jewelry at discount prices. 24 Rue Antoine Siger (phone: 702911).

L'Univers Youthful Parisian-style fashions for men and women, with brand names such as Chevignon, and a varied selection of tropical shirts, fine shoes, and accessories. 90 Rue Perrinon (phone: 638884).

The following shops, located outside of the capital, also are recommended:

Ella Purveying an intriguing assortment of homemade tropical jams, purées, preserves, and liqueurs, as well as island-grown spices, this *boutique gourmande* is in the village of Bézaudin near Ste-Marie (no phone).

La Paille Caraïbe Outside the little town of Morne des Esses is this market, island-famous for its basketry (*vannerie*), with small shops and stands selling all styles and sizes. In the village of Bézaudin near Ste-Marie (no phone).

SPORTS

The Martiniquais attitude is that sports are to play, not to work at. So you won't find super pro golf clinics, tennis camps, or any of the popular American sweat-and-learn setups. But there are plenty of opportunities for activity and better-than-adequate equipment.

BOATING One- or two-seater Sunfish, Sailfish, Hobie Cats, or other small craft are rented by the hour from kiosks on most hotel beaches. Yacht charters, both bareboat and skippered, are available from numerous sources. Fort-de-France boasts two yacht clubs: *Club de la Voile de Fort-de-France* (phone: 616949) and *Yacht Club de la Martinique* (Blvd. Chevalier Ste-Marthe; phone: 632676). Among the firms offering yacht charters or boat rentals at the *Pointe du Bout Marina* in Les Trois-Ilets are *Tropic Yachting* (phone: 660385); *Star Voyages* (phone: 660072); and *Cat Club* (phone: 660301). *ATM* (at Port de Plaisance du Marin in Le Marin; phone: 749817) has the largest fleet on the island. Also in Le Marin with an all-catamaran fleet is *Bambou Yachting* (phone: 747805), and specializing in motor boats is *Ecole Nautisme Accastillage* (Cité Mansarde in Le Robert; phone: 651818). The *Affaires Maritimes* (Blvd. Chevalier Ste-Marthe; phone: 719005) is a good source of nautical information. In addition, the 140-page, French and English *Guide Trois Rivières: A Cruising Guide to Martinique* is a highly regarded boating manual, available for about $25 in island bookstores or from the publisher (Editions Trois Rivières, BP 566, Fort-de-France 97242; phone: 750707).

CYCLING Rent all-terrain bikes at *VT Tilt* in Anse Mitan (phone: 660101) and *Basalt* in Bellefontaine (phone: 550184). The *Comité de Randonnées Pédestres* (Quartier Bouillé, 9 Blvd. Général de Gaulle, Fort-de-France; phone: 731930) has developed some unusual itineraries for cyclists.

GOLF The *Golf de l'Impératrice Joséphine* (in Les Trois-Ilets; phone: 683281) is a good, sporty Robert Trent Jones Sr. course (6,640 yards, par 71). It has a well-stocked pro shop, English-speaking pro, rental clubs, carts, caddies, and *Le Country* bar/restaurant. Its greens adjoin *La Pagerie*'s premises. Lessons also are available. Ask your hotel to arrange a tee-off time.

HIKING It's best in the nature preserve on Presqu'île de la Caravelle, where, in addition to trails that explore the ruins of the *Château Duboc* and exotic, tropical landscapes (some stamina but no special skills required), you'll find safe surf beaches (this is the Atlantic side of the island) and a fishing village called Tartane. For more information, contact the *Syndicat d'Initiative* in La Trinité (phone: 582681). For more serious trekking, contact the *Parc Régional de la Martinique* (see *Cycling,* above) to arrange a guide for the two-hour Mt. Pelée climb (as trails are often overgrown with dense foliage, a guide is essential; because of cloud cover, the view from the top can't be guaranteed), or a trek through the Gorges de la Falaise (moderate length, not too difficult) or the rain forest between Grand' Rivière and Le Prêcheur (choice of trails, several degrees of difficulty). *Cariballad* (phone: 545198) offers some off-the-beaten-track treks, which include bus departure, lunch, and guides. Also see *Climbing and Hiking* in DIVERSIONS.

HORSEBACK RIDING Rides along scenic hillside and banana country trails are offered at *Ranch-Jack* (phone: 683769) in Morne Habitué, 10 minutes from Pointe du Bout; the ranch also runs half-day group rides through nearby mountains, cane fields, and around sea coves. The ranch is a part of the *Commune des Trois-Ilets* organization, and arrangements can be made through local member hotels. Also offering riding excursions are *Black Horse* in Les Trois-Ilets (near *La Pagerie* hotel; phone: 683780) and *La Cavale* in Le Diamant (near the *Diamant-Novotel;* phone: 762294).

SNORKELING AND SCUBA DIVING The best diving spots are off Ste-Anne, Anses d'Arlet, Ilet Ramier, Cap Saloman, and the shipwrecks at St-Pierre. The following operations offer a variety of packages: the *Union Centre de Plein Air* (*UCPA;* in Anse Coré, just north of St-Pierre; phone: 782103); the *Club Subaquatique* (in Case-Pilote, halfway between Carbet and Fort-de-France; phone: 787375); *Tropicasub* (on the beach in St-Pierre; phone: 783803; and at *La Batelière;* see *Checking In*); *Bathys Club* (at the *Méridien Trois-Ilets,* Pointe du Bout; see *Checking In*); and the dive boat *Planète Bleue* (at the marina; phone: 660879). *Diamant-Novotel*'s *Sub Diamond Rock Club* has daily excursions around Diamond Rock and offers packages at sea (see *Checking In*). Also in the area are *Bleue Marine* (at the *Marine* hotel; see *Checking In*) and the *Okeonos Club* (in Le Diamant; phone: 762176).

Snorkeling fins and masks are available at many hotels, including *Le Bakoua, Bambou, La Batelière, Buccaneer's Creek/Club Med, Diamant-Novotel, Frantour, Marine, Méridien,* and *Novotel Carayou* (see *Checking In* for all). A variety of snorkeling excursions sail from the Pointe du Bout hotels as well as *La Batelière* and the *Diamant-Novotel;* ask at your hotel activities desk.

SPECTATOR SPORTS Cockfighting is the big spectator sport for Martiniquais. Mainlanders may call it cruel or revolting, but it is far and away the Sunday favorite from December through July. The place and time of the action shifts from week to week, though there's usually something going on Saturday afternoons at *Le Pitt de Balata* (Km 8, Rte. de Balata, north of Fort-de-France). If you'd like to see what it's all about, ask at the tourist office or at the travel desk of your hotel; they may be getting a group together. Try to find a taxi driver or guide who'll stick with you and explain the action and the betting. Note: For the blood-sport enthusiast, snake and mongoose matches also are staged, but on irregular schedules.

There's also a good deal of island soccer playing, and it draws sizable crowds; local papers and hotel desks will have schedules. If there's a yawling regatta in town, don't miss it. It's a great thrill to see skilled seamen hanging from the rigging of a yawl (a fishing boat) with its huge, colorful sails, while racing at daredevil speeds.

SPORT FISHING Captain Joseph Alaric and his 36-foot *Eureka I* (at the *Auberge du Varé* at Case Pilote; phone: 788056) offer full-day excursions for up to six people, including lunch, drinks, tackle, and everything else the serious angler needs. *Bathys Club* (at the *Méridien;* see *Checking In*) offers half-day trips aboard *La Mauny.*

SWIMMING AND SUNNING Fine, if not fantastic. Martinique doesn't possess endless miles of beach. However, with 6½ miles of bright sand facing the landmark HMS *Diamond Rock,* Le Diamant is a favorite swim-and-picnic destination. Bring snorkel equipment (rented from your hotel), beach towels, and a picnic. Also, most hotels have their own beaches—natural, or helped along with imported sand and groin-jetties to keep it in place. As a result of such assistance, Pointe du Bout beaches have never been better. The natural beach at Anse Mitan just down the shore serves small, mostly French-speaking hotels such as *Bambou* (see *Checking In*) and *Auberge de l'Anse Mitan* (phone: 660112). Beaches north of Fort-de-France tend to be soft, volcanic gray; those to the south are whiter, and all are public, though hotels charge non-guests a small fee for lockers and changing cabañas. Many hotels that are not on or near the beach have swimming pools. To escape the hotel scene, plan a day's picnic trip to the pretty, palm-treed shores at Ste-Anne, Les Salines, Le Diamant (see above), or Anses d'Arlet. (Topless sunbathing is okay on beaches and at poolside, but tops are de rigueur at beach bars and restaurants.)

TENNIS Courts are part of the big-hotel scene. Most are complimentary for guests during the day, with a small fee after dark; for non-guests, there is an hourly rate. Court time should be reserved in advance. *Le Bakoua, La Batelière, Buccaneer's Creek/Club Med, Diamant-Novotel, Habitation LaGrange, Leyritz*

Plantation, Marine, Méridien, and the Novotel Carayou hotels (see Checking In) have tennis courts on their grounds; all except the Plantation's have lights. Buccaneer's Creek/Club Med and La Batelière have teaching pros, as does the Golf de l'Impératrice Joséphine (see Golf, above) with its three lighted courts. Serious players also can arrange temporary memberships at private clubs in Fort-de-France like the Tennis Club de Fort-de-France (Anse Madame, Schoelcher; phone: 612001) and Tennis Club du Vieux Moulin (Rue de Didier and Rte. des Rochers; phone: 644818)—and games with local players—via hotels, the tourist office, or La Ligue Régionale de Tennis (Rue Petit Manoir, Fort-de-France; phone: 510800).

WATER SKIING AND WINDSURFING Available at Le Diamant, Ste-Anne, La Batelière, Buccaneer's Creek/Club Med, and Bathys Club at the Méridien (see Checking In), within easy reach of Pointe du Bout and Anse Mitan hotels. The best windsurfing site away from hotels is Cap Michel, near Cap Chevalier in the south. There is no rental equipment here, however. Passeport pour la Mer (Bois Lézards, Gros Morne; phone: 640448) offers classes in scuba, parasailing, jet skiing, and other water sports from its catamaran D'Lo.

NIGHTLIFE

Most nightspots on Martinique close around midnight, though hotel bars and nightclubs often stay open later. (Unless otherwise noted, see Checking In for more information on the hotels mentioned below.)

Wherever you stay, don't miss Les Grands Ballets de Martinique, performances by a bouncy young troupe of teenage singers, dancers, and musicians playing weekly at larger hotels (Le Bakoua, La Batelière, Diamant-Novotel, Méridien, and Novotel Carayou) as well as on visiting cruise ships. By combining stories of plantation days with choreographed waltzes, beguines, and mazurkas, they give you a special feeling for island history and seem to have a terrific time doing it.

Small hotels have dance music one or two nights a week, sometimes more often during high season; the larger places tune up most evenings— more or less sedately during dinner, fairly frenetically in their discos later on. The Méridien's Cocot-Raie is small, dark, and loud; La Paillote at the Novotel Carayou has live entertainment, including steel band dinner-dances on Sundays and Mondays, and fabulous views across the bay to Fort-de-France. Le Bakoua has dinner dancing, limbo shows, ballet performances, steel bands—something different every night; La Queens at La Batelière is perched on the water's edge and offers dance music that mixes some hustle, updated beguine, a few Latin beats, and zouk, the most popular style on the island.

For something a bit more native, try the clubs in downtown Fort-de-France. There's dancing and song at Le New Hippo (24 Blvd. Allègre; phone: 602022); entertainment at the open-air and tropical Cocoloco (Rue Ernest DeProge and Blvd. Alfassa; phone: 636377); and jazz at La Carafe (Rue Lamartine; no phone). A short cab ride from downtown are the Palace Club (at Palmiste near *Lamentin Airport;* phone: 505638) and *Le Manoir* (Rte. des Religieuses; phone: 702823), a popular weekend spot for dancing to local rhythms. In La Trinité, *Le Top 50* (Quartier Bac; phone: 584336) is a sizzling discotheque. Nightclubs and discos exist in the smaller towns and resort areas as well, but finding them after dark is sometimes difficult, so ask for directions from your hotel desk.

Caution: Disco drinks, especially scotch and whiskey, are expensive—starting at about $8 each with the taxes and service charge. Rum drinks and local Lorraine beer (quite good) cost less.

The island's only casino is at the *Méridien Trois-Ilets.* Games are American and French roulette and blackjack. Jackets and ties are not required. Croupiers are European-trained islanders. Hours are 9 PM to 3 AM nightly; there is an admission charge. *Note:* The legal gambling age is 18; casinos require photo ID. Also see *Casino Countdown* in DIVERSIONS.

Best on the Island

CHECKING IN

Martinique hotels range from charming Relais Créole country inns and seaside cottages to sprawling 300-room high-rise resorts. Food, even in very small places, tends to be quite good.

Martinique hotel choices hinge on location. Choose Pointe du Bout if you want to be where the other tourists are, make the most of sports, dine around, and take in all the nightlife. For a quieter time, pick a self-contained resort or a country inn farther out (*Leyritz Plantation* or *St-Aubin,* for example). By far, the best beaches are found in the southeastern part of the island. All hotels listed here are air conditioned and have private baths unless otherwise noted. In this listing, including breakfast, very expensive is defined as $225 and up for two; expensive is $175 to $225; and moderate, from $100 to $175. Inexpensive accommodations cost less than $100 for two without meals. Prices run about 25% to 35% less in summer. As a rule, hotel room rates quoted in dollars are guaranteed for the whole season—winter or summer—whatever the franc's fluctuations. When calling from a phone on Martinique, use only the local numbers listed below. For information about dialing from elsewhere, see *Telephone* earlier in this chapter.

POINTE DU BOUT

VERY EXPENSIVE

Le Bakoua A Sofitel resort affiliated with the prestigious Accor Loisir group, this 139-room facility is one of the island's best. Public areas are decorated in Caribbean colors and native woods, and there's a squash court, workout room, small library, and gameroom. All guestrooms have patios or balconies, and feature such amenities as telephones, TV sets, and hair dryers. There also are two good restaurants, two bars (including one that floats in the lagoon), a big pool, water sports, and two tennis courts. On the beach (phone: 660202; 800-221-4542; fax: 660041).

Méridien Trois-Ilets This property has 300 small, but bright rooms with balconies and wonderful views, all equipped with telephones and TV sets. There's still a strong chain-hotel feeling, but it's hardly a major deterrent with the pleasant indoor-outdoor lobby with restaurant, attractive and busy cocktail bar, casino, and *Roger Albert* boutique. There are facilities for most water sports, a spacious pool, and two tennis courts. The well-run activities center offers scuba and deep-sea fishing excursions. Evening entertainment, a disco, and good food—especially beachside dinners at *La Case Créole*—complete the picture. Convenient location on the beach near the ferry dock and marina (phone: 660000; 800-543-4300; fax: 660074).

EXPENSIVE

Novotel Carayou The informal atmosphere makes this a good choice for families. The 197 rooms have summer cottage decor (rattan chairs and tables, striped fabrics), telephones, TV sets, and mini-bars. There are three restaurants and *La Paillote* bar. Located on a nice, but small beach; there's also a pool, tennis courts, archery, golf practice areas, and water sports equipment. Scuba, fishing, and boat trips can be arranged; water skiing, golf, and horseback riding are nearby. On the beach (phone: 660404; 800-221-4542; fax: 660057).

MODERATE

PLM Azur La Pagerie A good spot for do-it-yourselfers, this place features balconied studios—64 with kitchenettes, 28 with refrigerators—all with telephones and TV sets. A nice choice of restaurants and beaches are within walking distance, and a small supermarket and the ferry are nearby. There's a swimming pool, and guests may use the facilities at the nearby *Novotel Carayou*. The lobby bar is a congenial gathering place. Near the marina (phone: 660530; 800-221-4542; fax: 660099).

INEXPENSIVE

La Karacoli Hidden along a hill overlooking the bay, this charming family-owned inn has 18 modern rooms and 8 one-bedroom apartments. Each has a terrace, kitchenette or full kitchen, and telephone. Some rooms do not have private baths, and some are not air conditioned, but trade winds create a nice breeze, even in the heat of the day. There's a TV set only in the main salon. A little beach rims the water out back, though bigger beaches are within walking distance. Other features are a swimming pool and solarium. Breakfast is included for an extra charge. In the hotel area near the *PLM Azur La Pagerie* (phone: 660267).

ANSE MITAN

Bambou A casual beach hotel, it has 118 rooms in 60 rustic, tile-roofed chalets. The decor is simple but functional. The rooms have telephones, but no TV sets or private baths. There's a pool and a busy terrace restaurant with a panoramic view of the bay. On the beach (phone: 660139; fax: 660505).

Rivage A stone's throw from the beach, this cheerful little property has 17 garden studios with kitchenettes and telephones. TV sets are available for an extra charge. There's a pool, barbecue pit, snack bar, and English-speaking staff. A good buy. On the beach (phone: 660053; fax: 660656).

ANSE À L'ANE

MODERATE

Frantour With peach buildings sitting right on the beach, this pretty place has 74 renovated units, all with telephones, TV sets, and mini-bars. The grounds are studded with palm trees, and there's a lovely pool and a restaurant. The staff is extra friendly, and a delicious daily breakfast is included. On the beach (phone: 683167; fax: 683765).

Le Panoramic Located on the hillside above the *Frantour,* here are 36 large, balconied rooms that can accommodate up to four people. Each unit has a kitchenette, telephone, and TV set, and there's a swimming pool on the premises. There's no restaurant, but your first breakfast is complimentary; after that you're own your own. Short walk to the beach (phone: 683434; fax: 500195).

FORT-DE-FRANCE AND ENVIRONS

EXPENSIVE

La Batelière About a 10-minute drive north of Fort-de-France on the sea, this place has 215 large rooms, each with a telephone, TV set, and balcony with fine sea views. There also are six lighted tennis courts, water sports, a nice small beach, a sun deck, a sauna, a pier, three dining rooms (including a seaside restaurant and bar), and a disco. In Schoelcher on the beach (phone: 614949; 800-888-4747; fax: 617057).

MODERATE

Squash Three squash courts are the main attraction of this hostelry with 108 rooms, all with telephones and TV sets. It also boasts a fitness center, a Jacuzzi, and a small outdoor pool, but no restaurant. 3 Blvd. de la Marne, overlooking the harbor just outside Fort-de-France (phone: 630001; fax: 630074).

INEXPENSIVE

Impératrice A dependable old standby, it's attractively set on Place de la Savane, with an Art Deco façade and 24 rooms with creole decor and telephones (no TV sets). There's a busy sidewalk café and a dining room serving creole fare. 15 Rue de la Liberté, Fort-de-France (phone: 630682).

Martinique Cottages Handsomely landscaped, well-managed, and 15 minutes from town, this property has eight modern bungalows set in a flowery hillside; each unit has a kitchenette, private verandah, TV set, telephone, and fan, but no air conditioning. Facilities include a pool, Jacuzzi, and *La Plantation* restaurant (see *Eating Out*). Pays Mélé Jeanne d'Arc (phone: 501608; fax: 502683).

LE DIAMANT

VERY EXPENSIVE

Diamant-Novotel Set on a jutting peninsula, offering a postcard-perfect panorama of Diamond Rock, this five-acre resort is dotted with well-manicured tropical gardens and boasts a freshwater pool with a dramatic footbridge. There are 181 rooms (all with telephones and TV sets), three small white sand beaches, two tennis courts, and *beaucoup de* water sports among the many amenities. A riding stable is nearby. The restaurant offers superb wining and dining, and there's a bit of nightlife and a few English-speaking staff members. Honeymooners love this spot. Just outside Le Diamant, about 20 minutes south of the airport via the highway (phone: 764242; 800-221-4542; fax: 762287).

MODERATE

Diamant-les-Bains A very homey atmosphere. There are 24 units, including a few bungalows on the beach, all with TV sets and telephones. Amenities include a flower-rimmed swimming pool, a bar, and a terrace restaurant serving fine creole fare. The dining room is closed Wednesdays; the whole inn closes for September. In the village, with a great view of Diamond Rock offshore (phone: 764014; 800-322-2223; fax: 762700).

Marine This establishment offers 150 rooms with balconies, kitchenettes, TV sets, telephones, and fabulous views. There's a restaurant, a bar, a large pool, a water slide, two lighted tennis courts, and a boat pier. On a hillside overlooking the sea and Diamond Rock (phone: 764600; 800-221-4542; fax: 762599).

Plein Sud Another residential hotel run by the Groupe Archipel. Like the *Hameau de Beauregard* (see below), this 53-unit property features apartment-style accommodations for up to three people, equipped with complete kitchenettes, telephones, and TV sets. Concierge service is provided by a local couple. There's also a large pool and a shopping arcade, but no restaurant.

Located across the road from Le Diamant Beach and a short stroll to the center of town (phone: 762606; fax: 762607).

Relais Caraïbes Just down the street from the *Diamant-Novotel,* these 16 bungalows are neat, clean, and comfortable. The hillside location offers great sea views, and a lush garden provides plenty of privacy. All rooms have TV sets and direct-dial phones. There's a restaurant, and guests may use the *Novotel*'s beach. Just outside Le Diamant (phone: 764465; 800-223-9815; fax: 762120).

STE-ANNE

Note: All hotels in this small village are located along the main road.

EXPENSIVE

Anse Caritan Very casual and relaxed, this is an ideal place for families. It has 96 rooms with TV sets, telephones, and kitchenettes, a tiny beach, a pool, water sports, and a restaurant (phone: 767412; 800-322-2223; fax: 767259).

MODERATE

Buccaneer's Creek/Club Med A sprawling property with 300 small, spartan rooms in a beach and garden setting; none of the rooms has a TV set or telephone. Activities offered include water sports, tennis (seven courts, six of which are lighted), aerobics, basketball, and more. There's a lovely dining room, along with a theater, bar, marina café, late-night restaurant, and disco. As with every Club Med village, the draw here is that all activities and meals are included in a weekly package price. However, when it comes to island congeniality and plushness, the facilities can't compare with Martinique's premier resorts. On the beach (phone: 767452; 800-CLUB-MED; fax: 767202).

La Dunette Here are 18 rooms, with telephones, but no TV sets; most have sea views and terraces. There's also a good seafood restaurant (phone: 767390; fax: 767605).

Hameau de Beauregard This residential hotel, run by the Groupe Archipel, features 90 apartment-style units with fully equipped kitchenettes, TV sets, and telephones; each unit can accommodate three guests. There's also a restaurant, a large pool and lovely aquatic gardens. Concierges assist with excursions and offer recommendations. Located very near the beach (phone: 767575; fax: 732075).

THE NORTH

VERY EXPENSIVE

Habitation LaGrange This luxurious establishment is set on the 7½-acre grounds of a former sugar plantation and rum distillery. Seventeen rooms are located in an 18th-century creole mansion and in three newer cottages built around a pool. A nostalgic ambience prevails—a horse-drawn carriage transports guests from the entrance to the manor house, staff members wear period costumes, and the rooms are furnished with antiques and four-poster beds (as well as such modern amenities as telephones, TV sets, VCRs, and mini-bars). There's a restaurant and bar, and a lighted tennis court. Guided hikes, sailboat excursions, and other activities can be arranged. The best beach for swimming is about 20 minutes away. Marigot (phone: 536060; 800-633-7411; fax: 535058).

MODERATE

La Baie du Galion This hotel's hilltop location provides panoramic views of the bay from every balconied room. All 146 rooms have TV sets and telephones; 55 also have kitchenettes. In addition, the hotel offers a fitness center overlooking the pool, a bar, a restaurant that features a Martiniquan theme night once a week (with French and creole specialties at other times), and shuttle service to a private, crescent-shaped beach less than a mile away. Tartane, on the Presqu'île de la Caravelle (phone: 586530; 800-528-1234; fax: 582576).

Bel Air Village Located in the Morne Vert hills, just a short drive to the beach, this place features four studios and 12 one-bedroom apartments, decorated in creole style and equipped with kitchenettes, TV sets, and telephones, but no air conditioning. Guests have the choice of hiking in the nearby mountains and rain forests, or relaxing on the beach at Carbet, just 1½ miles away. There's also a swimming pool, but no restaurant. Quartier Bout Barrière, Morne Vert (phone: 555294; fax: 555297).

Leyritz Plantation In the idyllic landscape of Martinique's lush north, this 70-room inn is set among lawns and tropical gardens. Surrounding the beautiful property is a 25-acre banana and pineapple plantation. The focal point is a restored antiques-filled 18th-century manor. Traditional island furnishings decorate the remaining accommodations, all in rebuilt dwellings and equipped with modern plumbing. All rooms have TV sets and telephones. There is a restaurant, and a tennis court and swimming pool. The nearest beaches are about 30 minutes away; transportation is provided. Near Basse-Pointe (phone: 785392; fax: 789244).

Primerêve With 111 units, it's one of the largest properties on the island's northeastern coast. Perfect for families, there are 25 single and double rooms and 86 suites that accommodate up to four people, all in sea-view bungalows with TV sets and telephones. There's a secluded beach, a large pool, two lighted tennis courts, a variety of water sports facilities, a restaurant, a bar, and a beachside snack bar. Anse Azerot (phone: 694040; fax: 690937).

St-Aubin This impressive French colonial *maison de campagne* is set in sugarcane country, above the Atlantic coast. The 15 guestrooms are surprisingly spartan, with telephones, but no TV sets (there's one in the main salon); the gardens and pool are lovely. The beaches and water sports of the Caravelle

Peninsula are just 15 minutes by car from this very quiet retreat. Dining (for guests only) is a big draw. In Trinité, near the Presqu'île de la Caravelle (phone: 693477).

INEXPENSIVE

L'Auberge de la Montagne Pelée These eight modest bungalows, all with telephones and TV sets (there's no air conditioning), provide the ultimate retreat. Located in a remote jungle setting that's often masked in mist and clouds, the sunsets here are spectacular. Dining in the inn's creole restaurant is an exceptional experience. Located near Morne Rouge, about an hour's drive from Fort-de-France (phone: 523209; fax: 732075).

OFFSHORE ISLANDS

VERY EXPENSIVE

Les Ilets de l'Impératrice These two private islands under the same ownership as *Habitation LaGrange* (above) offer a luxurious, secluded getaway. Each island has a rustic creole-style guesthouse staffed with a maid, cook, and boatman and equipped with a beach and boat dock. The house on Ilet Oscar has five guestrooms with private baths. The house on Ilet Thierry has six rooms, all with toilets and sinks, but shared showers. There is no air conditioning, telephones, or TV sets—this really is a place to "get away from it all." Rates include airport transportation, all meals, drinks, water sports, and use of a motorboat. Off the windward coast of the island (reserve through *Habitation LaGrange;* phone: 536060; 800-633-7411; fax: 535058).

EATING OUT

Two things are true of the French West Indies that aren't true anyplace else in the Caribbean: Local people eat much the same food as visitors, and the local food is exceptionally good. Restaurants range from casual to elegant; the only big restaurants on the island are in hotels, but all care a great deal about their food.

The fare falls into two categories—French haute and island creole—with most restaurants serving a combination of the two. Steaks are available, but delicious fish and seafood (sometimes exotic) are staples. Most common fowl are pigeon and peacock, as well as chicken and duck *à l'orange.* Roast suckling pig often appears on buffets.

Favorite appetizers include *accra* (delicately flavored cod cakes), *crabes farcis* (deviled crab with bread crumbs and seasoning, served in its own shell), *soudons* (small, sweet clams), and *coquille de lambi* (minced conch in a creamy sauce served in a shell). Entrée specialties are red snapper, *cribiches* (large river shrimp), langouste (clawless rock lobster), *lambi* (conch), *oursins* (sea urchins), and *chatrou* (octopus). *Colombo* is the creole version of curry (usually chicken, mutton, or goat); *pâté en pot* is a thick creole mutton soup. *Blaff* is an aromatic, spicy creole stew whose name—they say—comes from the sound the poor fish makes when it's plopped into the kettle. For dessert: tropical fruit served fresh with imported French cheeses, or, more elaborately, transformed into coconut cake or rum-fired banana flambé.

With dinner, the Martiniquais serve French wines that are good to great, and priced accordingly. Before and after, the drink of choice is local rum—in several different forms. Tourists tend to opt for *les planteurs*—the familiar planter's punch with a sweet fruit juice base. Islanders prefer a *décollage*—a blast-off of aged, herbed rum with a fruit juice chaser—or a white *ti punch* (*ti* means small) of rum, sugar syrup, and lime. For an after-dinner *digestif*, try 12-year-old Bally or Clément rum.

Dinner for two, including wine and service charge, will cost more than $100 at restaurants described below as expensive; from $50 to $100 at moderate places; and less than $50 at inexpensive places. Unless otherwise noted, all restaurants listed below are open for lunch and dinner. If you're having language difficulties, ask the hotel desk to make reservations for you. When calling from Martinique, use only the local numbers listed below.

FORT-DE-FRANCE AND ENVIRONS

VERY EXPENSIVE

La Plantation The award-winning dining room of *Martinique Cottages.* The seafood ratatouille alone is worth the drive. Fish, fowl, beef, and lamb are prepared in delicious, inventive ways, and the owners love discussing their culinary art. Closed Saturdays at lunch and Sundays. Reservations necessary. Major credit cards accepted. Pays Mélé Jeanne d'Arc, Lamentin (phone: 501608).

EXPENSIVE

La Belle Epoque With a well-deserved reputation for fine food, this spot serves haute cuisine in a turn-of-the-century setting befitting its name. Closed Saturday lunch, Sunday dinner, and Mondays. Reservations advised. Major credit cards accepted. 97 Rte. de Didier, in the suburb of Didier (phone: 646724).

Le Dôme This restaurant atop the new *Hôtel Valmenière* affords diners panoramic views of the mountains and the bay. The service is excellent, and the menu features a creative blend of classic French and local cooking; try the fish soup, a meal in itself, or order the three-course prix fixe dinner. Open daily. Reservations advised. Major credit cards accepted. Av. des Arawaks (phone: 757575).

La Fontane This private home decorated with period antiques has a very elegant, tranquil ambience and a most imaginative menu featuring French and creole fare. Sample delectable specialties such as pumpkin cream soup and noisettes of lamb in mango sauce. Closed Sundays. Reservations necessary—the restaurant frequently closes for private parties and large groups.

Major credit cards accepted. Km 4, Rte. de Balata, north of Fort-de-France (phone: 642870).

La Grand' Voile Seafood and classic French provincial specialties are served at this spot on the second floor of the town's yacht club. There's a fine wine cellar. Closed Sundays. Reservations necessary. Major credit cards accepted. Rue Schoelcher, Pointe Simon, Fort-de-France (phone: 702929).

Le Mareyeur Seafood specialties include all the creole favorites—*lambis, soudons, palourdes,* and *oursins*—carefully prepared and beautifully presented. Try *blaff de poisson* (steamed fish in local spices), shark in coconut milk, or, better yet, order the *assiette* for a smorgasbord-like taste of all the house specialties. No lunch on Saturdays; closed Sundays. Reservations advised. Major credit cards accepted. 183 Blvd. Pointe des Nègres, Fort-de-France (phone: 617470).

La Mouina A delightful old colonial villa above the town. Impeccably prepared creole and French dishes (bonito *en papillote,* avocado sherbet) are served on the villa's terrace. Presidents George Bush and François Mitterrand dined here in 1991. Closed weekends. Reservations necessary. Visa accepted. 127 Rte. de la Redoute, Fort-de-France (phone: 793457).

Le Verger Enjoy lunch or dinner on the terrace of a big country house set in a fruit orchard. This is gracious dining, with many specialties from Périgord (foie gras, *confit* of duck, cassoulet, pheasant, and more). There's also a variety of local creole dishes. Closed Sundays. Reservations advised. Major credit cards accepted. Place d'Armes, Lamentin (phone: 514302).

Le Second Soufflé Haute cuisine for vegetarians in an airy first-floor room overlooking the cathedral square, with deliciously blended fruit juices, salad combos, homemade tofu, breads, yogurts, hot dishes cooked in coconut milk or curried creole-style, and tangy homemade fruit desserts. Closed weekends. Reservations unnecessary. No credit cards accepted. 27 Rue Blénac, Fort-de-France (phone: 634411).

Le Vieux Milan Bright and bustling, this Italian eatery serves up generous portions of pasta, including gnocchi with gorgonzola and tagliatelle with salmon. Other specialties include thin-crusted pizza, carpaccio, and *tiramisù.* Closed Saturday afternoons and Sundays. Reservations advised. Visa accepted. Located along *La Savane,* 60 Av. du Caraïbes, Fort-de-France (phone: 603531).

POINTE DU BOUT

La Marine This spacious dockside patio restaurant is popular with local boaters and tourists. The atmosphere is upbeat, the food good to very good. Brick-oven pizza, chicken, and creole dishes are the bill of fare. The adjoining bar is a good place to have a beer or a *planteur* punch. Open daily. Reservations advised. Major credit cards accepted. At the marina (phone: 660232).

ANSE MITAN

MODERATE

L'Amphore Guy Dawson's second spot in Anse Mitan (see *La Villa Créole,* below), with lobster as the prime drawing card, prepared in any number of delicious ways. Fish, curries, and entrecôte (steak) also are on the menu. A pretty seaside location and a good guitarist enhance the atmosphere. No lunch on Tuesdays; closed Mondays. Reservations advised. Major credit cards accepted (phone: 660309).

La Petite Louisiane Formerly *Le Matadore* and now under new ownership, this spot still features creative creole cooking, with seafood, fish curries, soups, langouste, flambés, and sorbets. Open daily. Reservations advised. Major credit cards accepted (phone: 660536).

La Villa Créole Guy Dawson's perfect combination of soft lights, music, and excellent food served in a romantic garden has made this a most popular spot in Anse Mitan. The predominantly creole menu includes *blaff* of sea urchins, court bouillon (a local soup), conch tart, terrine of local redfish, curried chicken, pork, and lamb. Live entertainment nightly. No lunch on Mondays; closed Sundays. Reservations advised. Major credit cards accepted (phone: 660553).

GRAND' ANSE

EXPENSIVE

Le Flamboyant des Isles Named for the gorgeous flamboyant trees that speckle the property, this romantic place features candlelit dining on a deck that extends over the sea. The view of the ragged crescent coastline is stunning. The fare is creole *et gastronomique,* with specialties such as octopus salad, shrimp fritters, conch fricassee, fish *colombo* (curry), and flambéed bananas. Buffet dinner Sundays; closed Tuesdays. Reservations advised. MasterCard and Visa accepted. Anses d'Arlet (phone: 686775).

MODERATE

Ti' Sable Set in a typical creole-style house, with verandahs and an adjoining canopied terrace, this laid-back place offers traditional island dishes—rich seafood, grilled meat, curries, and a salad bar. The beach site is accessible by car or boat. Open daily in high season; in low season open weekends only for dinner. Reservations advised. Major credit cards accepted. Anses d'Arlet (phone: 686244).

LE DIAMANT

MODERATE

Chez Lucie Two distinct menus are available here: One offers Vietnamese and Chinese specialties such as stir fry, *satays,* and curries; the other features creole preparations including *blaff* of seafood or sea urchins, turtle steaks, and shrimp. Almost every seat faces the sea; service is slow. Open daily. Reservations advised for lunch. Major credit cards accepted. On the waterfront (phone: 764010).

Le Coin Tranquille Creole cooking is featured at this country inn. A family operation—mom and dad greet guests and daughter serves. No lunch Wednesdays and Thursdays. Reservations advised. No credit cards accepted. Bitaille (phone: 764112 or 762282).

STE-ANNE

MODERATE

Poï et Virginie A waterfront spot with lots of tropical character: bamboo walls, ceiling fans, and drinks garnished with big flowers. Seafood platters, curries, and steaks are quite good, but the menu highlight is the luscious lobster and crab salad. A fine choice for both lunch and dinner. No lunch Tuesdays; closed Mondays. Reservations advised. Major credit cards accepted. On the waterfront (phone: 767222).

INEXPENSIVE

Athanor Favored by locals, it's set in a little brick courtyard beneath an *arbre à pain,* a breadfruit tree. Choose from creole creations such as sea urchin tart and avocado stuffed with crab, or opt for the brick oven–baked pizza. Open daily. Reservations advised for dinner. Major credit cards accepted. On the main road away from the beach (phone: 767293).

Le Touloulou Among the many shacks on Ste-Anne Beach offering tasty fare, this one stands out. The breezy dining room is decorated with island posters and sits right on the sand. The *colombo* (curry-style) preparations are delicious, as are the grilled *lambi* (conch) and *poulet* (chicken). There's a steel band on Wednesday and Friday nights. Open daily in high season; in low season, call ahead to confirm hours. Reservations advised for Sunday dinner. Major credit cards accepted. Ste-Anne Beach (phone: 767327).

THE NORTH

EXPENSIVE

Le Brin d'Amour Set in a gracious manor house on gorgeous grounds, serving local seafood, French, Italian, and Indian fare, and creole dishes. No dinner

Sundays. Reservations advised. Major credit cards accepted. Brin d'Amour, near Trinité (phone: 585345; fax: 584782).

Le Colibri Diners have a wonderful hillside view and are given royal treatment at the home of Mme Palladino, whose sea urchin *tarte,* roast suckling pig, stuffed pigeon, and crab *callaloo* are scrumptious. Open daily. Reservations necessary. Major credit cards accepted. Morne des Esses (phone: 699195).

Le Madras A lively place, especially on weekend nights during the summer months, when islanders come to hear local bands play rousing music. A more subdued band plays Sunday afternoons. Specialties include medallions of beef with goat cheese, and the catch of the day. Open daily. Reservations unnecessary. Major credit cards accepted. Overlooking the beach in the tiny town of Tartane (phone: 583395; fax: 583363).

MODERATE

La Belle Capresse A worthwhile place to stop for lunch while on a northern tour. Original creole creations such as shark pâté, fried sea urchins, crab soufflé, pork flambéed in aged rum, and chicken in coconut milk are specialties. Open daily. Reservations advised for dinner. Major credit cards accepted. Le Prêcheur (phone: 529623).

Chez Mally Edjam A 73-year-old virtuosa cook serves seafood and creole meals in her modest home at the island's northernmost tip. Open daily; closed mid-July through mid-August. Reservations necessary for dinner. Visa accepted. Rte. de la Côte Atlantique, Basse-Pointe (phone: 785118).

Le Fromager Perched on the side of Mt. Pelée with a panoramic view of St-Pierre and the bay, this place features creole specials and seafood. Open daily for lunch. Reservations advised; necessary Sundays. Major credit cards accepted. Rte. de Fonds St-Denis, St-Pierre (phone: 781907).

Le Vieux Galion Beyond a lush garden entrance is this beachfront seafood restaurant, which specializes in shrimp dishes and creole fare. Enjoy the sunset from the restaurant's broad patio, while sampling one (or more) of the fifty varieties of local, homemade rums. Closed Sundays. Reservations unnecessary. American Express accepted. Rte. de Tartane, Anse Bellune, Trinité (phone 582058).

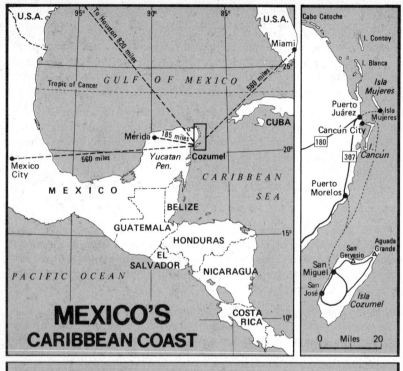

MEXICO'S
CARIBBEAN COAST

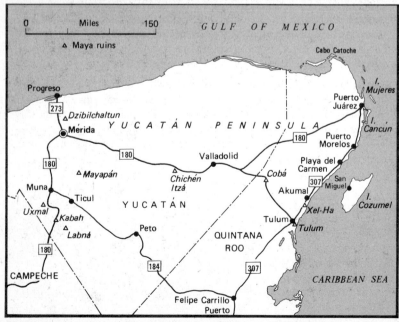

Mexico's Caribbean Coast

CANCÚN, COZUMEL, AND ISLA MUJERES

For many years, small groups of divers and determined sun worshipers had the lagoons, beaches, and islands of Mexico's Caribbean coast along the Yucatán Peninsula almost to themselves. People planning a trip to the Yucatán had to choose among the Maya ruins at *Chichén Itzá, Cobá, Uxmal,* and *Tulum;* sun and sea sports along the coast of Quintana Roo, including *Xel-Ha* (pronounced Shell-*Hah*) and Akumal; or the islands of Isla Mujeres, Cancún, and Cozumel. Transportation was too difficult to make all sides of the vacation coin easily accessible. In those days, Mexico's largest island, Cozumel, was the preferred Caribbean destination of less well-heeled travelers, and Cancún was an undeveloped spit of land off the coast to the north.

All that changed when *FONATUR,* the government agency charged with improving Mexico's tourist facilities, chose Cancún as its first multimillion-dollar experiment in resort development. Cancún had all the natural attributes of a resort area—beautiful sea and some of the best diving in the world, adequate space and facilities, and proximity to the ruins. So new it wasn't even marked on road maps 25 years ago, Cancún has blossomed into one of the world's most bustling resorts—to the point, some feel, of overdevelopment. It has become Mexico's leading tourist destination, attracting 19% of the country's visitors.

One of the major dividends of Cancún's development is that travelers no longer have to choose between culture and carousal. Part of the original 15-year Cancún master plan was a system of transportation and communications that connects the resort area to important indigenous ruins and to Mérida, the closest major city. Both Cancún and Cozumel benefit from a direct road from the sea to *Chichén Itzá,* along which tour buses roll daily. And both are helped by the improvement of the shoreline road to *Xel-Ha,* the small seacoast ruins at *Tulum,* and the huge site of ancient *Cobá,* overgrown by jungle.

But the sea is still the major attraction. The crystalline Caribbean offers visibility to a hundred feet, and the stretch of sea along the peninsula and into Belize is world-famous as an area rich in fish, coral, and wrecks. Unruffled Laguna Nichupté, which separates Cancún from the mainland, has been cleaned up over the past few years. Protected from the open sea, it offers a tranquil place for sailing or water skiing.

Since Cancún's inception, the Mexican government has poured some $100 million into the area to assure a complete resort infrastructure, including the development of recreational facilities such as an 18-hole Robert Trent Jones Jr. golf course, ships for touring, boats for sailing, and a panoply of hotels. Paseo Kukulcán (Kukulcán Boulevard), the boulevard running from one end of Cancún to the other, also has been expanded from two lanes to four, and the 12,000-seat *Centro de Convenciones* (Convention Center) was renovated extensively in 1994 and now includes facilities for musical and theatrical performances. There are now about 100 hotels in Cancún and Cancún City, plus condominium buildings, shopping centers, restaurants, and marinas, scattered along Paseo Kukulcán. In short, Cancún's weather and manmade attractions are an authentic lure, although this is not the place for those who prize peace and privacy.

Although Cozumel was the first island in the area to be developed, it has grown at a much slower pace than Cancún, and tends to attract visitors who are more interested in fabulous skin diving and fishing than in glitz and glamour. Plans for several new hotels were dropped for fear of damaging the island's ecological system—not to mention its tranquillity.

Isla Mujeres, with a few charming but fairly simple hotels and wide expanses of beaches, has a small but loyal following. Guests here must be willing to give up certain luxuries (such as air conditioning) in exchange for lower prices and access to *El Garrafón,* an underwater national park famous for its coral reef and tropical fish.

The Quintana Roo area on the mainland known as the "Cancún-Tulum Corridor" is peppered with delightful hotels and restaurants set at the edge of the sea. It's hard to tell how many more years of peace and tranquillity remain for this area, however, as two large resort development projects, Puerto Aventuras and Playacar, are well under way.

Mexico's Coast At-a-Glance

FROM THE AIR

Mexico's Caribbean islands are grouped around the northeastern corner of the Yucatán, the chunky peninsula that divides the Gulf of Mexico from the Caribbean Sea. They are flat, sunbaked, and sea-washed bits of land. Their centers are dense green brush and coconut palms rimmed by white limestone sand beaches. Cancún is flanked to the southeast by Cozumel and to the northeast by Isla Mujeres.

The islands are about 560 miles southwest of Miami (about an hour and 45 minutes by jet), about 640 miles (two hours) east of Mexico City, and about 185 miles (35 minutes) east of Mérida, capital of the Mexican state of Yucatán.

Cancún (pronounced Kahn-*koon*), 14 miles long and a quarter mile wide, is shaped like a sea horse, connected by a causeway at its nose to Cancún City—the support city on the mainland where most of the area's over 300,000 residents live. (Cancún's jetport is 12 miles/19 km southwest of the city.) For most of the rest of its length, Cancún is separated from the mainland by Laguna Nichupté. Most of the island's resort hotels are set along the skinny east-west sand spit that forms the sea horse's head. Along its back, the Caribbean surf rolls in over 12 miles of intermittent beaches and hotel sea walls.

Already prosperous, Cancún City has an even brighter future. One project currently in the works is the $600-million, 330-acre Malecón Cancún, which will include homes, shops, restaurants, offices, and a park overlooking the lagoon and Cancún's Hotel Zone. Environmental regulations, however, are slowing the development's progress.

Cozumel (pronounced Ko-soo-*mehl*), 33 miles long and 9 miles wide, lies about 50 miles south of Cancún and about 2 miles off the Yucatán coast. Its almost straight eastern shoreline is pounded by rough, windward seas; on its leeward (western) side, the waters off its resort beaches are calm, the shore notched with sandy coves. The coral reefs that surround it—especially the sunken mountains of the Palancar reef chain—make it a prime skin divers' destination. Most of the island's resort hotels are just north of its only town, San Miguel, on the northwest coast, where most of the island's 60,000 inhabitants live. The jet airport is between the hotels and town.

Isla Mujeres (pronounced *Ees*-lah Moo-*hair*-ehs), 5 miles long and a half mile wide, is 6 miles north of Cancún and 6 miles off Puerto Juárez at the tip of the Yucatán Peninsula. It has a tiny town, beautiful beaches, lagoons, reefs, and transparent waters that make it a super retreat for snorkelers, skin divers, and loafers. There's a lovely lookout point and a Maya "lighthouse" at the southern end of the island. It's no longer a sleepy little island; most places have phones; the few roads are paved; and there are even several discos.

SPECIAL PLACES

There's little sightseeing on Mexico's Caribbean islands. Each has a town with restaurants and at least a few shops. There are, however, a number of interesting excursions from the resort areas, including some of the Yucatán mainland's most intriguing archaeological sites. Fascinating *Chichén Itzá* and the ruins of the coast city of *Tulum* are both easy to reach. You really should see at least one of the two, preferably *Chichén Itzá,* although *Tulum*'s cliffside setting is spectacular.

CANCÚN

CENTRO DE CONVENCIONES (CONVENTION CENTER) Completely rebuilt in 1994 at a cost of $90 million, it accommodates up to 12,000 people and has facilities for theater performances, concerts, expositions, and conferences. The center also has a large shopping center, and future plans include the addition of an observation deck, a disco, and a revolving restaurant atop a 50-story "needle" tower. Km 9 of Paseo Kukulcán (phone: 98-830199).

CANCÚN CITY On the mainland, Cancún City, like the resort itself, did not evolve but was built from scratch as part of a *FONATUR* master plan. It didn't exist at all in 1970; now it's home to about 322,000 people—many of them native Yucatecans—almost all of whom work on the resort island. There are a number of restaurants and shops, most located along the main thoroughfare, Avenida Tulum, and Avenida Yaxchilán, which is two blocks west and parallel to Avenida Tulum.

EL REY These modest Maya ruins on the lagoon at the southern end of the island are hardly impressive compared with those at *Tulum* or *Cobá,* let alone *Chichén Itzá,* but they are worth a visit. All of the structures that can be seen here today date from the 12th and 13th centuries. When the ruins first were excavated in the l950s, the skeleton of a human male was discovered, as well as scattered remains of other bodies, apparently human sacrifices. Some anthropologists suggest that the main skeleton was that of a chieftain (hence the name "rey," king in Spanish). Unfortunately, the site had been sacked by looters before archaeologists found it, so there is little evidence of just what purpose this ancient temple served in Maya times.

SOUTH OF CANCÚN

JARDÍN BOTÁNICO DR. ALFREDO BARRERA MARÍN (DR. ALFREDO BARRERA MARÍN BOTANICAL GARDENS) Located about 24 miles (38 km) south of Cancún, just off the coast highway, this nature preserve covers 150 acres. Trails wind through the semi-evergreen tropical forests that border a mangrove swamp. Closed Mondays. Admission charge (no phone).

PUERTO AVENTURAS About 49 miles (78 km) south of Cancún, this resort area features the largest marina in Mexico, an 18-hole golf course built around several pre-Columbian structures and a couple of ancient cenotes (sinkholes), and a tennis club (see *Sports* for descriptions of all three). Puerto Aventuras is nestled in the natural beauty of the region and enhanced with Asian palms and orchids brought in from the Brazilian Amazon. A glimpse of the area's maritime history can be seen at the *Pablo Bush Romero Centro de Exploración de Arqueología Marina (CEDAM;* Km 98 of Route 307; no phone, but information is available from the *CEDAM* dive center at 987-35129), whose collection includes 18th-century silver goblets, gold coins, and other relics salvaged from the *Matanceros,* a Spanish merchant ship that sank off the coast of Akumal in 1741. The collection is closed Tuesdays; there's no admission charge. The area has several hotels (see *Checking In*), and many villas and condominiums are currently under construction.

AKUMAL About 10 miles (16 km) south of Puerto Aventuras, this town gained international status in 1958, when a diving exploration headed by Pablo Bush, a Mexican philanthropist, stumbled across the sunken remains of the *Matanceros,* a Spanish galleon that had been lost at sea about two centuries earlier. Since the discovery, the place has become the unofficial scuba and snorkeling headquarters for the *Mexican Underwater Explorers' Club.* Akumal also has one of the loveliest beaches in the area, with excellent snorkeling. There are dive shops on virtually every corner. The *Club Akumal* hotel (Km 104, Carr. Cancún-Tulum; phone 987-22532) is a great spot for lunch.

CHEMUYIL About 6 miles (10 km) south of Akumal, a sign welcomes visitors to "the most beautiful beach in the world." Accommodations here include a charming, albeit nameless, hotel and bar run by the Román family (see *Checking In*).

XEL-HA Another 4 miles (6 km) farther south, this is the site of a national park where a lagoon forms a natural aquarium for snorkeling (though the water is somewhat murky at times due to the large number of visitors the park receives). Snorkeling equipment, as well as scuba gear and kayaks, can be rented here; there are also a few scattered ruins and several small restaurants. *Xel-Ha* is open daily, and there's an admission charge (no phone).

TULUM Once a thriving Maya city-fort built on a cliff above the sea about 81 miles (129 km) south of Cancún, *Tulum* lacks the magnitude of earlier cities such as *Chichén Itzá* and *Uxmal,* but its beautiful setting makes it a compelling destination nonetheless. It was the largest city of a postclassic Maya civilization that established a trade empire along the Caribbean coast, from the northwestern Yucatán to Honduras. There are 25 major structures, including the city wall, a large temple overlooking the sea, a number of other temples with brightly colored frescoes and relief carvings, and several platforms that were used for dances and ceremonies. *Tulum* commands a magnificent view of the Caribbean, and the small beach below the main pyramid is the perfect place to cool off after a hot day among the ruins. The ruins are open daily; no admission charge on Sundays (no phone).

   Tulum is connected to Cancún by daily bus service (plan on a one-and-one-half-hour ride each way). A number of tour companies offer excursions to *Tulum,* with stops at Akumal and at *Xel-Ha* for snorkeling. Half- or full-day trips are offered, but we recommend the latter, with its more leisurely pace and the beach lunch at Akumal. Ask at your hotel's activities desk for details.

COBÁ Archaeology buffs won't want to miss this, one of the most recently excavated and potentially most intriguing of Maya ruins. A half hour away from *Tulum,* and about two hours from Cancún, this jungle-bound site was discovered in 1897 by Teobert Maler, but exploration and excavation did not begin until 1974 and are still far from complete. The city is believed to have been a major trade center, connected by a network of highways with other major Maya cities such as *Chichén Itzá* and *Uxmal.* The painstaking process of reclaiming the ancient ruins from the jungle (archaeologists believe some 6,500 structures once stood here) has only just begun; *Cobá* presents travelers with the rare chance to see an archaeological site before it is completely uncovered and understood. A tour of the main sites involves a 2-

mile walk along jungle paths (bring insect repellent). The ruins are not labeled, but informational booklets in English are sold at the small gift shop at the entrance to the site, and guides are available for a small fee. Among the ruins are several large pyramids, including the tallest Maya pyramid in the Yucatán (130 feet); visitors may climb its 120 steps for a sweeping view of the jungle. The site is open daily; no admission charge on Sundays. *Cobá* is easily reached by car: Turn inland at the marked road just south of *Tulum;* it's 26 miles (42 km) straight ahead. *Club Med's Villa Arqueológica* (phone: 5-203-3833 or 5-203-3086 in Mexico City; 800-CLUB-MED) is nearby for lunch and/or overnight lodging.

SIAN KA'AN Stretching south of *Tulum* to Punta Allen is a 1.3-million-acre nature reserve containing tropical forests, mangrove swamps, salt marshes, palm-rimmed beaches, archaeological ruins, and coral reefs. Pronounced *See-ahn Cahn,* it's a paradise for bird watchers and crocodile and butterfly lovers. If you venture far enough into the jungle (not recommended as a solo journey), you're likely to come across a jaguar or some other large cat. There are two hotels on the reserve geared especially toward sportspeople who come here for the bonefishing: the pricey *Club de Pesca Boca Paila,* represented by *Frontiers* (PO Box 959, Wexford, PA 15090-0959; phone: 987-21176 on Cozumel; 800-245-1950), and *Pez Maya* (no local phone; 305-664-4615 in Florida; 800-327-2880 elsewhere in the US). Considerably more rustic accommodations are available at *El Retiro* at Punta Xamach (clean cabins, but no private baths; no phone) or at *Posada Cuzan* at Punta Allen (thatch tepees; no phone, but there's a public fax nearby: 983-40383). At *Posada Cuzan,* Sonia López will provide a good meal if you ask nicely, or try *Restaurant Candy* (no phone), which serves delicious local lobster and fish. For guided visits, contact the *Amigos de Sian Ka'an, A. C.* (Association of Friends of Sian Ka'an; Plaza Américas, Suite 50, Cancún 77500, QR, México; phone: 98-849583; fax: 98-873080).

COZUMEL

PLAZA The heart of Cozumel (and of San Miguel) is a wide plaza near where the ferry docks; most of the shops and restaurants are here. There's an esplanade on the sea side, and the *malecón,* the road that follows the shore north and south, is lined with relaxed cafés and tourist shops. If you're traveling to the plaza by motor scooter, find somewhere else to park: parking is forbidden here.

MUSEO DEL CARIBE (MUSEUM OF THE CARIBBEAN) Formerly the *Museo Cozumel,* this museum exhibits impressive three-dimensional models of tropical fish, of human-eating sharks, and of the underwater caves in the offshore reefs, plus historical and ethnographical exhibits. Other features are temporary exhibits, a library, a crafts shop, and a restaurant. Closed Saturdays. Admission charge. Av. Rafael E. Melgar between Calles 4 and 6, in San Miguel (phone: 987-21545).

LAGUNA CHANKANAB AND JARDÍN BOTÁNICO (CHANKANAB LAGOON AND BOTANICAL GARDENS) About 5 miles (8 km) south of town is a natural aquarium filled with multicolored tropical fish. Because suntan lotion collects in the water and harms the fish, swimming and snorkeling in the lagoon are sometimes prohibited, but they're always permitted at the nearby beach. The gardens boast more than 400 species of tropical plants. Open daily. Admission charge (no phone).

PLAYA SAN FRANCISCO On the southern tip of Cozumel, the island's most popular beach is accessible via a paved road, but it's also fun getting there aboard one of the vessels making the *El Zorro* cruise (see *Cruises*). If you're not on a cruise that provides lunch, try the *San Francisco* restaurant (see *Eating Out*).

PUNTA MORENA At this beach on the open Caribbean side of the island, the surf is rough, and swimming can be dangerous. Since the undertow can be tricky, check the currents before you take the plunge (plan to enter the water at one point, exit at another), and never swim alone. There's a sheltered lagoon nearby. If you get hungry, *Mezcalito's* is a good place to stop for some grilled fish and a beer (see *Eating Out*).

A NOTE ON COZUMEL RUINS

There are archaeological ruins in the island's interior, but they're mostly overgrown and not worth the buggy, sweaty, dusty trip unless you're a serious archaeological enthusiast. On a day's drive around the southern end of the island, a sandy detour off the main paved road leads to "The Tomb of the Snail," but if you're planning an excursion to *Tulum, Cobá,* or *Chichén Itzá,* don't bother. Day trips to *Tulum* and *Xel-Ha* (by boat and bus, including lunch) are available from Cozumel (see *Tours*).

ELSEWHERE ON THE COAST

ISLA MUJERES The name means "Isle of Women"; the Spanish so dubbed it because they found many sculptures of females here. A dot 5 miles long and a half mile wide, it is 6 miles north of Cancún and 6 miles off Puerto Juárez on the Yucatán Peninsula. The island's tiny town, beautiful beaches, lagoons, reefs, and transparent waters make it a pleasant retreat for snorkelers and skin divers. Hotels and restaurants are moderate to inexpensive. Ferries run regularly from Puerto Juárez and Punta Sam on Cancún (see *Ferry, below*). Several outfits operate excursions to Isla Mujeres, some of which include snorkeling (see *Cruises, below*). The island's most famous attraction is *El Garrafón* ("The Jug"), an underwater national park located at the southern end and renowned for its crystal-clear waters, coral reef, tropical fish, and great snorkeling. There's a sea museum at *El Garrafón* with an aquarium and pieces of wrecked historic galleons. The park and museum are open daily and charge separate admissions (no phone).

ISLA CONTOY (CONTOY ISLAND) Declared a National Wildlife Reserve in 1961, this tiny, uninhabited coral island is 25 miles (40 km) north of Cancún. A favorite destination for bird watchers, it is home to over a hundred species, although their numbers are, unfortunately, diminishing. It's also an important migratory point for other birds, and an egg-laying spot for sea turtles. *Warning:* If you should happen upon a sea turtle, look, but don't touch! Disturbing these creatures is considered a very serious crime in Mexico, punishable by a long jail sentence (and the government recently stepped up its enforcement of environmental regulations here). Daily boat excursions to the island, which include lunch, are offered by several companies (see *Cruises,* below). The trip is not for landlubbers—it's a two-and-one-half-hour sail each way, and the actual time spent on shore is short (about three-and-one-half hours), but very sweet. The island is beautiful and completely undeveloped except for a small museum and research center. The afternoon can be pleasantly spent lying on the narrow and nearly deserted beach on the island's leeward shore; swimming and snorkeling (though the visibility is not great here) in the warm water; taking a boat ride into the island's interior lagoons, where bird nesting areas are visible; or doing a bit of exploring. Isla Contoy is not for thrill seekers, but it is perfect for those who seek a soothing cruise, a pristine beach, an untouched landscape— and a respite from the crowds of Cancún.

EXTRA SPECIAL

A trip to the ruins at *Chichén Itzá* (which date to the early 11th century) is the best way to experience the buildings of the Maya civilization. The most famous and complete of the ancient Maya cities, this site is a testament to their engineering genius. Here are temples, sacrificial wells, sacred ball courts, reclining idols, and the great *El Castillo* pyramid. The ruins are located in the interior of the Yucatán Peninsula, about a two-and-one-half-hour drive from Cancún. All hotel travel desks book the daylong, air conditioned bus trip, or it may be included in your travel package. Prices include the admission charge, guided tours of the site, and lunch. The ruins are open daily. For additional details, see *Testaments in Stone: Historic Sites* in DIVERSIONS.

Sources and Resources

TOURIST INFORMATION

The *Mexican Ministry of Tourism* is the best source of brochures and background material on all of Mexico. Information can be obtained by contacting any of their US offices (see GETTING READY TO GO).

The information available through the local tourist offices, however, is very limited. In Cancún, there's a modern information center (Avs. Tulum and Tulipanes, near the *Mercado Ki-Huic;* phone: 98-848073) and a tourist office (Avs. Cobá and Nader; phone: 98-843238; fax: 98-843438); both are open daily. On Cozumel, the tourist office is upstairs in the *Plaza del Sol Building* (closed weekends; Av. Rafael E. Melgar and Calle 8; phone: 987-20972). There are also information booths at the tourist dock and at the airport; their hours coincide with plane and boat schedules. The *Delegación Estatal de Turismo de Isla Mujeres* (Isla Mujeres Tourist Office; 6 Hidalgo; phone: 988-70316) is closed weekends. Hotel personnel and travel desks are other good sources of information; there's also a toll-free, 24-hour tourist-information hotline (phone: 91-800-90392).

LOCAL COVERAGE In Cancún, two English-language periodicals—the comprehensive biannual *Cancún Tips* and the quarterly *Cancún Tips Magazine*—contain good background information, ads, and some handy listings of happenings, hotels, restaurants, shops, nightspots, and tour operators. Two similar publications, the quarterlies *Cozumel in One Day* and *Blue Guide to Cozumel,* are distributed on Cozumel. On Isla Mujeres, *The Islander,* published weekly, lists current events.

Newspapers from Mexico City (including the *News,* a national English-language daily) arrive on Cozumel and Cancún the day they're published, as do the *Miami Herald,* the *Houston Chronicle,* and *USA Today.* Local daily newspapers (in Spanish) include *Quintana Roo, Novedades de Quintana Roo, El Tiempo de Cozumel,* and *Diario de Quintana Roo.* They're available on all three islands. In addition, we immodestly suggest that you pick up a copy of *Birnbaum's Cancún, Cozumel, & Isla Mujeres 96* (HarperCollins; $12).

RADIO AND TELEVISION There are no local English-language radio or television stations. Most hotels have satellite access to CNN and other English-language stations.

TELEPHONE The city code for Cancún is 98; the city code for Cozumel and Isla Mujeres is 987. When calling from the US, dial 011 + 52 (country code) + (city code) + (local number); when calling from other parts of the Caribbean, dial 52 (country code) + (city code) + (local number). When calling from anywhere on Cancún, Cozumel, or Isla Mujeres to any other location on Cancún, Cozumel, or Isla Mujeres, simply dial the number without the city code. Note that all telephone numbers in this chapter include city codes.

ENTRY REQUIREMENTS A US citizen must have proof of citizenship (either a current passport or a birth certificate, naturalization certificate, or Armed Forces ID card, along with a photo ID); a Canadian citizen needs a current passport or birth certificate. Each must have a tourist card, obtainable free at Mexican embassies and consulates, airlines and travel agencies booking trips to Mexico, *Mexican Ministry of Tourism* offices, *Greyhound Bus Line* offices, or *American Automobile Association* offices. Carry the card with you at all times.

CLIMATE AND CLOTHES Year-round temperatures average in the low 80s F (about 27C). From October through April, sunny days prevail; in July, August, and September there are brief showers, usually in the afternoons. At the resorts, most days call for beach clothes, with cover-ups or caftans for protection from too much sun. Tennis clothes (though not necessarily all white) and tennis shoes are requested on the courts. For sightseeing trips, light dresses, skirts, or pants are most comfortable for women; slacks and shirts for men. Mexicans generally do not wear shorts outside of beach areas, so you shouldn't either. Nights also are casual but neat (for the most part, discos bar T-shirts and sneakers). Neither coats nor ties are required for men, but many women tend to dress up a bit—dresses or dressy pants and tops—at Cancún's posher hotels. The same, on a slightly more casual level, goes for Cancún's smaller hotels and Cozumel. On Isla Mujeres, a fresh shirt and a pair of slacks are as dressy as evening attire ever gets.

MONEY The official currency in Mexico is the *nuevo* (new) *peso,* which was instituted about three years ago. Be aware, however, that old pesos (distinguished by having three zeros) may still be in circulation, so check when exchanging money or making a purchase. The exchange rate was N$7.5 to $1 US at press time; however, there was continuing instability in the value of the peso due to deregulation, so the rate could change significantly by the time of your trip. It's a good idea to check the current rate in the *International Herald Tribune* or *Wall Street Journal* before making your travel plans. In Cancún, US currency is accepted almost everywhere, as are most credit cards and traveler's checks. Banks generally are open from 9 AM to 12 PM and from 2 PM to 6 PM weekdays. Most major hotels also have currency exchange desks, typically open daily from 8 AM to 8 PM.

LANGUAGE Spanish is the official language, but some English usually is understood and spoken in tourist areas of Cancún, Cozumel, and *Chichén Itzá.* Its use is somewhat rarer on Isla Mujeres, but with a little patience and a phrase book, non-Spanish speakers usually manage fine.

TIME Mexico's Caribbean islands lie in the central standard time zone. When it's noon on Cozumel, Cancún, and Isla Mujeres, it's noon in Chicago and 1 PM in New York. Since Mexico does not observe daylight saving time, from spring through fall, when it's noon on these islands, it's 1 PM in Chicago and 2 PM in New York.

CURRENT Electricity on Cancún, Cozumel, and Isla Mujeres is 110 volts, 60 cycles. However, the safety feature on most US plugs—a fatter prong—makes it impossible to use most of the outlets without an adapter.

TIPPING No service charge is added to hotel bills, so give the room maid $1 to $2 per person per day; the bellhops get $1 to $2 for two to three bags and $1 for calls that require a trip to your room. Give the doorman 50¢ when he calls a cab for you; taxi drivers get 10% of the tab, if they seem to charge a fair price. Airport porters get the same amount as bellhops. In Cancún, you don't have to leave any additional sum when a 15% service charge is added to your food or drink bill; on Cozumel and on Isla Mujeres, where there is seldom a service charge, tip 10% to 15%. Also, tip gas station attendants about 35¢ for service.

GETTING AROUND

BUS Inexpensive vans that depart promptly and handle all luggage travel between the airport and hotels. From 6 AM to midnight, a flock of buses runs between Cancún City and the island's hotels and shopping area; the fare is 2.5 new pesos (about 35¢ at press time). *FONATUR* buses—with reclining seats and air conditioning—travel a similar route; the cost is 3 new pesos (about 40¢ at press time).

CAR RENTAL Several agencies in Cancún City offer rental cars and jeeps: *Avis* (phone: 98-830803 or 98-860002); *Dollar* (phone: 98-844101 or 98-860165); *Econo-Rent* (phone: 98-841826); *Kokai Rent a Car* (phone: 98-843643); and *Monterrey Rent* (phone: 98-847843 or 98-860239). On Cozumel, *Rentadora Cozumel* (phone: 987-21120) rents jeeps—the best bet for local roads.

CRUISES Numerous voyages depart from Cancún and nearby points. The *Columbus* (phone: 98-831488 or 98-833268), a motorized replica of a 15th-century sailing vessel, sails around Laguna Chankanab nightly at sunset; dinner is included. The trimaran *Aqua Quin* (phone: 98-831883) sails daily to Isla Mujeres from Cancún, with snacks included. If you think getting there is half the fun, you might opt for a leisurely crossing to Isla Mujeres on the *Tropical Cruiser* (phone: 98-831488), which includes a full-day tour complete with a buffet lunch, soft drinks, a musical show, and a snorkeling trip to *El Garrafón*. It sails Mondays through Saturdays at 10 AM. Also available in Cancún is the *Nautibus Yellow Submarine* (phone: 98-833552), a catamaran with seats and windows in the keel to provide a panoramic view of sea life. If you're on Cozumel and want to go to Playa San Francisco—the best beach on the island, at the southern tip–try the *El Zorro* cruise (phone: 987-20831).

Cruises leave from Cancún and Isla Mujeres for the approximately two-and-a-half-hour journey to Isla Contoy (see *Special Places*). The *Contoy II* (phone: 98-871862 or 98-871909 on Cancún) runs all-day trips to the island from the *Playa Linda Pier* in Cancún. The cruises, which include lunch, soft drinks, and alcohol, depart Mondays through Saturdays at 9 AM. The *Cooperativa Transporte Turística* (phone: 987-70274 on Isla Mujeres) offers prearranged package tours of Isla Contoy that leave daily at 9 AM from the waterfront docks on Isla Mujeres; the cost includes a light breakfast, lunch, and snorkeling equipment.

FERRY There's ferry service from Playa del Carmen on the mainland 40 miles (66 km) south of Cancún to Cozumel; the trip takes about 35 minutes. The ferry to Isla Mujeres from Punta Sam on the mainland carries both vehicles and people. Most visitors, however, take the passenger boat from Puerto Juárez (on the mainland north of Cancún City); the trip takes an hour.

INTER-ISLAND FLIGHTS *Cancún Avioturismo* (phone: 98-830315), across the street from *Casa Maya* in Cancún, has a Cessna 206 that can transport up to five passengers to Cozumel, *Tulum, Chichén Itzá,* Mérida, Chetumal, and other destinations. (Flights to *Tulum* and *Chichén Itzá* have a two-hour stopover to see the ruins before returning to Cancún.) The company also has a one-passenger ultra-light seaplane that makes a 15-minute tour of the Hotel Zone. In Cozumel, *Aviomar* (phone: 98-848831 or 98-848841; fax: 98-845385) has plane tours to *Chichén Itzá. Aero Cozumel* (Av. Tulum and Av. Uxmal, Cancún, phone: 98-842000) makes connections between Cancún and Cozumel, as well as several other cities on the Mexican mainland.

MOPED Small motorbikes are an easy way to get around and are available at many Cancún hotels, including the *Casa Maya* and the *Krystal Cancún* (see *Checking In*). On Cozumel, rent mopeds at *Rentadora Cozumel* (172 Av. 10 Sur; phone: 987-21120 or 987-21503) or at the southern end of San Miguel at the *Plaza las Glorias* hotel (see *Checking In*), where bicycles also are available. On Isla Mujeres, motorbikes are the only way to go; they're available from *Rent Me* (Av. Juárez at Calle Morelos, about 50 paces from the ferry dock; no phone).

TAXI Small green-and-white cabs are available at reasonable fares, according to zone, in the Cancún area. On Cozumel, meterless island taxis operate by arrangement; i.e., you and the driver agree on a price for the proposed trip before you get into the cab. When you talk pesos, make sure you and your driver are speaking the same language (see *Money*).

TOURS There are dozens of tour operators on Cancún, all of them with hotel offices on the island. Arrange excursions directly or through hotel travel desks. Boat, bus, taxi, and automobile tours are available.

SPECIAL EVENTS

Isla Mujeres hosts regattas from St. Petersburg, Florida, and Galveston, Texas, between April and June. A unique attraction on the first day of spring or fall is the *Chichén Itzá* phenomenon, when light and shadow strike *El Castillo* pyramid in such a manner that the snake god Kukulcán appears to be slithering along the side of the monument. The annual *Feria de Cancún* (Cancún Fair) takes place in November, with cockfights, dances, and shows.

Mexicans enjoy celebrating so much that they often take off the day before and the day after a holiday, as well as the big day itself. Most banks, businesses, and government offices are closed on the following days: *New Year's Day, Constitution Day* (February 5), *Juárez's Birthday* (March 21), *Easter* (and often much of the preceding week), *Labor Day* (May 1), *Anniversary of the Battle of Puebla* (May 5), *Independence Day* (September

15–16), *Columbus Day* (October 12), *President's State of the Nation Address* (November 1), *All Saints' Day* and the *Day of the Dead* (November 1–2), *Anniversary of the Mexican Revolution* (November 20), *Feast of the Virgin of Guadalupe* (December 12), and *Christmas.*

SHOPPING

In addition to traditional Mexican crafts (silver, ceramics, papier-mâché, alabaster, leather, and straw goods), there are boutiques stocked with imported perfumes, fashions (especially accessories), crystal, china, and more. Mexican resortwear (embroidered and lace-trimmed caftans, beach cover-ups, and shirts) is brightly colored, fun, and remarkably reasonable in price, considering the amount of handwork involved. But before you buy, be sure to try on those classic Yucatecan take-homes—*huipiles* (loose white dresses embroidered at neck and hem) and *guayabera* shirts (dressy-casual with tucked fronts, sometimes embroidery)—they can look either terrific or very tacky. Sisal mats, hats, rugs, and bags are other local specialties.

Shops on all three islands generally are open daily from 10 AM to 2 PM and from 4 to 7 PM; most major stores on Cancún stay open until 9 PM. Hotel shops are generally open daily from 10 AM to 8 PM, with no downtime for siesta. Downtown Cancún's tourist shops are along Avenida Tulum, between Avenidas Uxmal and Cobá, and range from superior to so-so. On Cozumel, the work of some 200 first-rate Mexican artists is displayed and sold at *Bazar Cozumel* (Av. Juárez). There isn't much good shopping on Isla Mujeres, with the exception of *Rachat & Romé* (see below), so head for the beach instead.

The booklet *GSP & the Traveler,* available free from the US Customs Service (PO Box 7118, Washington, DC 20044), has information about duty-free items.

DOWNTOWN CANCÚN

La Casita Arts, crafts, decorative items, leather, jewelry, and Mexican-inspired clothing. 115 Av. Tulum, Cancún City (phone: 98-841468).

Sybele High-quality imports from around the world, ranging from men's suits and women's lingerie to leather briefcases and fine perfume. 109 Av. Tulum, Cancún City (phone: 98-841181), and *Plaza Caracol* (phone: 98-831738).

HOTEL ZONE

The most elegant shops in the *zona turística* generally are located in the many shopping centers, all along Paseo Kukulcán: *Flamingo Plaza, La Hacienda, Kukulcán Plaza, La Mansión–Costa Blanca, Mayfair, El Parián, Plaza Caracol, Plaza Lagunas, Plaza Náutilus,* and *Plaza Terramar.*

Anakena Maya temple rubbings, pre-Columbian reproductions, and unique jewelry. *El Parián* (phone: 98-830539).

Artland Rubbings, batik items, paintings, and jewelry, all inspired by Maya designs. *Plaza Terramar* (phone: 98-831562).

Los Castillos and Joyas Caroli Jewelry and art objects crafted from sterling silver and semi-precious stones by two of Taxco's best jewelers. *Flamingo Plaza* (phone: 98-850882).

Chantal Select pieces of hand-crafted silver jewelry. The shop has a stunning African motif. *Plaza Caracol* shopping center (phone: 98-830450).

Galerías Colonial Tableware with beautifully painted patterns, carved marble knick-knacks, and chess sets. *Plaza Caracol* (phone: 98-830914).

Onyx and Handicrafts Good quality and prices for onyx pieces and other handi-crafts. *Plaza Náutilus* (phone: 98-830699).

Ronay One of Mexico's most prestigious jewelers, specializing in gold designs. *Plaza Caracol* (phone: 98-831261).

Sebastián The very finest in designer silver jewelry. *Plaza Caracol* (phone: 98-831815) and *Plaza Náutilus* (phone: 98-831949).

Xcaret An unusual and varied selection of some of the very best of Mexico's hand-icrafts—ceramics, textiles, papier-mâché—at reasonable prices. *Flamingo Plaza* (phone: 98-833256).

COZUMEL

All shops listed below are in San Miguel.

La Casita The parent of the Cancún store and the source of more smashing Mexican resort clothes, as well as Sergio Bustamante's imaginative animal and bird sculptures. Av. Rafael E. Melgar (phone: 987-20198).

Pama High-quality, duty-free imports, from jewelry and perfume to silk ties and women's fashions. 9 Av. Rafael E. Melgar (phone: 987-20090).

Plaza del Sol A nest of nearly a dozen art, crafts, jewelry, and import boutiques including *Los Cinco Soles,* which has a good selection of handicrafts from throughout Mexico. Av. Rafael E. Melgar at Calle 8 (no phone).

ISLA MUJERES

Rachat & Romé Outstanding jewelry designed and crafted by the friendly Cuban shop owner. In the flamingo-colored building steps from the ferry dock, at Av. Rueda Medina and Calle Morelos (phone: 987-70250).

BEACH (AND STREET) VENDORS

Although "legally" outlawed in this part of Mexico, these ambulant sales-people materialize on almost every beach. They can be persistent, but unless you are interested in their wares, make your feelings understood with a firm "no."

SPORTS

As on most islands, water activities come first, and they're most of what it's all about on Cozumel and Isla Mujeres. But on all the islands, especially Cancún, the possibilities don't end there.

BICYCLING A serpentine 6-mile path of pink brick bordered by garden plants and the seashore winds through Cancún, with *palapa*-topped rest stops along the way. In Cancún, rent bikes at the *Cancún Bicycle Club* (two locations: *Plaza las Glorias,* at Km 3.5 of Paseo Kukulcán, and the *Radisson Sierra Plaza;* see *Checking In;* phone for both: 98-843299). On Cozumel, try *Rentadora Cozumel;* on Isla Mujeres, *Rent Me.* (See *Mopeds,* above, for both.)

BOATING Craft large and small, power and sail, crewed and uncrewed, are available on Cancún. Make arrangements at any hotel travel desk; at the *Royal Yacht Club* (Km 16.5 of Paseo Kukulcán; phone: 98-852360 or 98-852930); at *Marina Aqua Ray* (Km 10.5 of Paseo Kukulcán; phone: 98-833007 or 98-831763); or at the marinas of the *Camino Real, Club Lagoon,* or *Presidente* hotels (see *Checking In*).

BULLFIGHTS Cancún's small bullring, the *Plaza de Toros* (Av. Bonampak and Calle Sayil, in the south of Cancún City; phone: 98-845465), occasionally attracts major matadors. Corridas are held Wednesdays at 3:30 PM. The modern, three-tiered arena has a seating capacity of 6,000 and provides ample parking.

FISHING Strong men and women do battle on the deep sea with sailfish, bonito, and mahimahi (in season from March through July), white marlin (April through May), bluefin tuna (May), wahoo and kingfish (May through September), and barracuda, red snapper, grouper, and mackerel (year-round). Closer to shore, light tackle anglers attempt to hook the elusive permit (tour operators can help you get one). Boats, both large and small, are available at *Marina Aqua Ray* and *Royal Yacht Club* (see *Boating,* above, for both), *Marina del Rey* (Km 15.5 of Paseo Kukulcán; phone: 98-831748), and *Aqua Tours* (Km 6.5 of Paseo Kukulcán; phone: 98-830227 or 98-830400). Here again, hotels can make all the arrangements. On Isla Mujeres, *Cooperativa Transporte Turística* (see *Cruises,* above) can arrange trips.

GOLF *Club de Golf Cancún* (formerly *Pok-Ta-Pok;* phone: 98-831230), the famous Robert Trent Jones Jr. golf course (par 72), offers gently rolling fairways bordered by palms. There's an 18-hole championship course at the *Caesar Park Beach and Golf Resort,* and the *Meliá Cancún* hotel has an 18-hole golf course (see *Checking In* for both hotels). The *Puerto Aventuras Golf Club* (Km 269.5 of Carretera Chetumal; phone: 987-22211 or 987-22233), about 61 miles (98 km) south of Cancún, has an excellent 18-hole course that was built around several pre-Columbian structures and incorporates ancient cenotes (sinkholes).

HORSEBACK RIDING *Rancho Loma Bonita* (Km 49 of Rte. 307; phone: 98-840907 from Cancún or 987-42113 from Cozumel or Isla Mujeres) escorts riders through the jungle daily at 8 and 10:30 AM and 1:30 PM.

JET SKIING Laguna Nichupté is great for this water sport, which requires a minimum of learning time. Jet skis are available at *Marina Aqua Ray* and the *Royal Yacht Club* (see *Boating,* above, for both).

SNORKELING AND SCUBA DIVING The variety of the reefs and the clarity of the water (average undersea visibility, year-round, is 100 feet, but you can often see much farther) make Mexico's Caribbean a top area for underwater exploring. Cozumel takes the diving honors. (But beware: Currents are strong on Cozumel, so don't dive without a guide.) Its prime attractions are the reefs 500 yards off the island's leeward shore along El Cantil (the Drop-Off), the edge of the shelf that borders the Yucatán Channel to the south. Famous 6-mile-long Palancar Reef has—in addition to forests of black, staghorn, and other species of live coral and friendly swarms of Day-Glo–colored fish—a number of antique wrecks in which to poke around. You can dive to look and take pictures, but removing flora or fauna is strictly forbidden. There are several dive shops along the waterfront in San Miguel on Cozumel, including *Aqua Safari* (phone: 987-20101) and *Big Blue* (phone: 987-20396). In addition, several shops based at local hotels—including *Casa del Mar* (located next to the hotel of the same name; phone: 987-21900); *Del Mar Aquatics* (at *La Ceiba* hotel); *Viajes y Deportes de Cozumel* (in the *Presidente Cozumel*); and the dive shop at the *Plaza las Glorias* hostelry (see *Checking In* for details on hotels)—offer rental equipment, instruction, and dive trips to Palancar. Most hotels also have diving facilities at somewhat higher rates, but you may feel that the convenience is worth the added cost. Scuba classes range from pool instruction (about three hours) to four- or five-day seminars with a certified instructor that include theory, shallow shore dives, a boat dive to a shallow reef, and a full boat dive to Palancar Reef. Rent underwater cameras at *Cozumel Images* at the *Casa del Mar* hotel (on the waterfront; phone: 987-21944).

Though great for scuba diving, Cozumel seems short on good snorkeling spots; best are the shallow reefs to the south, where depths range from 5 to 35 feet. Laguna Chankanab, midway down the leeward coast, with its underwater grottoes and fairly large fish population, is a good place for beginners to get their fins wet. (However, since suntan lotion collects in the water and harms the fish, swimming and snorkeling are not always permitted.)

Cancún's best scuba diving and snorkeling are found at Punta Nizuc, off the island's southern point. Dive trips and equipment rental can be arranged through your hotel. Guided scuba trips, including equipment, are available here, too; some offer two hours of morning scuba instruction in the lagoon and an afternoon dive. You also can rent snorkel or scuba gear from *Scuba Cancún* (Km 5.5 of Paseo Kukulcán, across from the *Casa Maya* hotel; phone: 98-831011) or *Marina Aqua Ray* (see *Boating,* above).

Isla Mujeres is surrounded by reefs, so snorkeling is fairly good along its shores. Snorkelers and scuba divers can rent equipment from *La Bahía,* which also organizes dives, across from the ferry dock (phone: 988-70340), and *Cooperativa Transporte Turística Isla Mujeres* (see *Cruises,* above). These operations also arrange dive trips, including equipment and two dives.

SWIMMING AND SUNNING The texture and whiteness of Cancún's sand are so distinctive they inspired special studies by geologists, who found that many of the sand's individual grains contain microscopic, star-shaped fossils of an organism called discoaster, extinct for 70 million years. Through the ages, the sea has ground and polished these grains till they've become brilliant and powder soft. What's more, their limestone composition has a cooling effect that makes the island's sand—even under the noonday sun—feel comfortable to bare feet. Unless you stay right in Cancún City, chances are your hotel will have its own beach as well as a pool, but there also are several public strands—Playa Tortuga and Playa Chac-Mool are just two examples.

Cozumel's beaches—shaped into distinctive coves—are mostly on the island's leeward side, north and south of San Miguel. The majority of hotels are there, too, and visitors will probably spend most of their sun and sea time beside their own hotel or on nearby sands. Other beaches to visit include the lengthy one about 10 miles (16 km) south of San Miguel at Playa San Francisco (a bit crowded these days, particularly on weekends); and Punta Morena, on the rough side with a sheltered lagoon nearby. Because the undertow can be tricky, it's a good idea to observe the currents before you take the plunge (plan to enter the water at one point, exit at another), and never swim alone.

On Isla Mujeres, *El Garrafón* (see *Special Places*), the southern beach and underwater national park with intriguing undersea formations, is the target of many day trips from Cancún. Sand seekers tend to congregate on the manmade beaches that have been built on platforms against the hill that leads up to the shops and restaurants. Playa Tortuga and Playa María, on the western shore of the island along the road (Av. Gustavo Rueda Medina) that leads to *El Garrafón,* are less crowded.

TENNIS Cancún and Cozumel are ideal tennis destinations, as many major hotels offer tennis facilities. (See *Checking In* for all hotels mentioned in this section.) On Cancún, there are courts at the *Aristos, Caesar Park Beach and Golf Resort, Calinda Beach Cancún, Camino Real, Casa Maya, Continental Villas Plaza, Fiesta Americana Condesa, Fiesta Americana Coral Beach, Hyatt Cancún Caribe, Krystal Cancún, Marriott Casa Magna, Meliá Cancún, Oasis, Presidente, Sheraton Cancún,* the *Villas Tacul* hotels, and the *Club de Golf Cancún* (see *Golf,* above; phone: 98-830871). On Cozumel, courts are available at *La Ceiba, Club Cozumel Caribe,* the *Fiesta Americana Sol Caribe,* the *Fiesta Inn,* the *Holiday Inn Cozumel Reef,* the *Meliá Mayan Cozumel,* the *Presidente Cozumel,* and the *Villablanca* hotels. No courts are available on Isla Mujeres.

WATER SKIING Laguna Nichupté—behind the island of Cancún—is the ideal place to learn or perfect this exhilarating sport. Make arrangements at any island hotel; *Marina Aqua Ray* (see *Boating,* above); or at *Marina del Rey* (see *Fishing,* above).

WINDSURFING Lessons are available at several Cancún hotels, including the *Club Lagoon* (see *Checking In*). Boards are available for rent; several places offer weekly rates that include lessons. There are regattas Sundays at *Club Cancún* (Km 4.5 of Paseo Kukulcán; phone: 98-830855), a condominium complex with a private marina.

NIGHTLIFE

Reigning Cancún dance clubs are easily discernible by the crowds gathering outside before opening time (around 10 PM). Unless otherwise noted, see *Checking In* for more information on hotels mentioned below. Current hot spots are *La Boom* (Km 3.5 of Paseo Kukulcán; phone: 98-831372); *Dady'O* (near the *Centro de Convenciones,* Km 9.5 of Paseo Kukulcán; phone: 98-833333); *Christine* at the *Krystal Cancún;* and the *Hard Rock Café* (at the *Plaza Lagunas* shopping center; phone: 98-832024). *Carlos 'n' Charlie's* (on the marina; phone: 98-830846) is a good place for food, drink, dancing, and meeting people; it's open until midnight. *Daphny's* at the *Sheraton Cancún* is a popular video bar with live and taped music for dancing. *Sixties,* in the *Marriott Casa Magna,* plays dance music from the 1950s, 1960s, and 1970s. The *Camino Real* offers a nightly cabaret of Cuban music and dance. *Batachá Tropical* in the *Miramar Misión* hotel (Km 10 of Paseo Kukulcán; phone: 98-831755) is a swinging disco that features live salsa music.

Unusual options for nightlife include *Jai Alai Cancún* (Km 4.5 of Paseo Kukulcán; phone: 98-833910 or 98-833916), which offers pari-mutuel betting on this fast-paced team sport, with live action nightly. There also is a restaurant, bar, and sports betting parlor on the premises. *Mexico Magico* (Km 12 of Paseo Kukulcán; phone: 98-834980), a big, garish theme park, presents six buffet dinner-theaters, in both English and Spanish, and an equal number of non-dinner shows. Each focuses on a different culture (Mexican fiesta, Italian opera, and so on), and features costumed dancers lip-synching to popular American and Mexican tunes.

For more silly fun, there's the "Pirate's Night Adventure" cruise (phone: 98-831488), which includes dinner and a musical show, available on both Cancún and Cozumel. Not to be missed is the *Ballet Folklórico,* which is presented nightly at the *Continental Villas Plaza* hotel; the show includes dinner and drinks. There is a flamenco dinner show at *Gypsy's* (see *Eating Out*) with after-dinner dancing by the pier. A torchlit beach, a delicious buffet, and exotic drinks make for a romantic evening at the *Hyatt Cancún Caribe*'s "Mexican Night," which takes place Mondays, Wednesdays, Fridays, and Saturdays at 7 PM. The *Sheraton Cancún* hosts a similar event Wednesdays at 7:30 PM; *Plaza las Glorias* offers one Tuesdays.

On Cozumel, *Scaramouche* (downtown, on Av. Rafael E. Melgar near Av. Dr. A. Rosario Salas; no phone) is a lively disco that attempts sophistication. The other possibility is *Neptuno* (Av. Rafael E. Melgar; phone: 987-21537), next to the *Acuario* restaurant. No matter where you go, it's mostly a young crowd.

On Isla Mujeres, there's *Jimbo's* (Av. Rueda Medina at Playa Norte; no phone), for salsa and reggae; and romantic *La Peña* (5 Calle Guerrero; no phone), which features live music and candlelight. Beach parties and night cruises complete the after-dark scene here.

Best on the Coast

CHECKING IN

Cancún's hotels are relatively new, aspire to be lavish, and boast some of the highest prices in Mexico. Many of the hotels on the island fall within an area along Paseo Kukulcán known as the Hotel Zone. Travelers on a budget can find less costly accommodations in Cancún City, away from the major beaches. During high season (December through early May), expect to pay $180 to $270 per day for a double room in a very expensive hotel (the highest price would be for a two-bedroom villa); $110 to $175 in an expensive one; $75 to $100 in a moderate place; and $60 or less in an inexpensive one. Prices drop as much as 50% during the summer months. Although it has more than 24,000 hotel rooms, Cancún really does not have enough accommodations to meet the demand during the winter months, so it is best to go only with a confirmed, prepaid reservation.

Cozumel's more luxurious hotels are in either the North Zone or the South Zone, above and below the town of San Miguel. The in-town hostelries (most have neither beach nor pool) appeal most to budget travelers. Hotel prices on Cozumel are comparable to those on Cancún, and, as on Cancún, we recommend that you arrive with a confirmed reservation. Most hotel rates on Isla Mujeres fall into our moderate and inexpensive categories. All hotels listed have air conditioning and private baths unless otherwise indicated; virtually all hotels have satellite TV with remote control. *Note:* Parking can be a problem at some hotels. Telephone numbers here include both the city code and the local number. When calling from anywhere on Cancún, Cozumel, or Isla Mujeres to any other location on Cancún, Cozumel, or Isla Mujeres, use only the local number. For information about dialing from elsewhere, see *Telephone* earlier in this chapter.

BE FOREWARNED

Visitors should be aware that the word *motel* has a very different connotation in Mexico than in the US. While a Mexican hotel provides accommodations similar to the US version, a *motel* often serves one purpose and rents rooms by the hour. These *auto-hoteles,* as they are also advertised, have curtained garages to insure the privacy of any "guests" who might not like their license plates seen. Many an unsuspecting tourist has pulled into a *motel* hoping to enjoy a relaxing evening, only to discover that there is no furniture (other than one very conspicuous bed), no closet, and no phone in the room.

CANCÚN AND THE MAINLAND

HOTEL ZONE

VERY EXPENSIVE

Caesar Park Beach and Golf Resort Run by the Westin group, this immense new luxury property is sited on 240 well-landscaped acres. The main building is a modern, somewhat pyramidal structure containing 448 rooms and suites, an atrium lounge with a waterfall, a restaurant serving Mexican, Italian, and Argentine fare, a health club, and even a shopping mall. Several additional buildings house the deluxe *Royal Beach Club,* which offers 80 rooms and two suites. All guestrooms are decorated simply but comfortably, with marble baths, private balconies with panoramic views of the Caribbean, mini-bars, and in-room safes; members of the *Royal Beach Club* receive complimentary continental breakfast and evening cocktails. A narrow strip of white-sand beach (though the surf is rough for swimming), seven pools, an open-air eatery featuring seafood dishes and Japanese specialties, two lighted tennis courts, and an 18-hole championship golf course all combine to make this a true resort. Km 17 of Paseo Kukulcán (phone: 98-818000; 800-228-3000; fax: 98-818080).

Camino Real A ritzy pleasure palace, it has a total of 381 rooms situated in two beautiful buildings, both affording magnificent views of the Caribbean. The older, main structure (designed by Ricardo Legoretta) reflects Maya architecture. The newer *Camino Real Beach Club Room* building offers 67 deluxe guestrooms and 18 suites, all with such amenities as concierge service, complimentary continental breakfast, and afternoon tea. All rooms have balconies and are decorated in a colorful Mexican design. A freshwater pool with a swim-up bar, a saltwater lagoon, three restaurants (including *Calypso;* see *Eating Out*), tennis courts, and plenty of water sports make this hotel one of the best around. On the northeast tip of the island (phone: 98-830100; 800-722-6466; fax: 98-831730).

Continental Villas Plaza Splendid is the only way to describe this 626-suite coral-toned complex that sprawls over seven blocks of oceanfront. Among the amenities are seven restaurants, three swimming pools, two tennis courts, and private Jacuzzis in most rooms. Km 11 of Paseo Kukulcán (phone: 98-831022 or 98-851444; 800-88-CONTI; fax: 98-832270).

Fiesta Americana Condesa Each of its three towers has its own atrium lounge covered by a glass, *palapa*-shaped roof. The decor is mostly rattan complemented by fresh, vivid colors. There are 502 rooms—including 27 suites with Jacuzzis on private terraces—plus a split-level pool with a 66-foot waterfall, three indoor tennis courts (all air conditioned), a jogging track, a spa, a small beach, five restaurants, and a lobby bar where live music is played in the evenings. Km 15.5 of Paseo Kukulcán (phone: 98-851000; 800-FIESTA-1; fax: 98-851800).

Fiesta Americana Coral Beach Designed in Mediterranean style with a definite calypso accent, this super-luxurious, massive, flamingo-pink complex is considered by many to be a true Mexican masterpiece. There are several restaurants and bars, a nightclub, a huge pool, tennis courts, and a gym. Km 8.5 of Paseo Kukulcán (phone: 98-832900; 800-FIESTA-1; fax: 98-833084).

Hyatt Cancún Caribe A graceful white arc a short walk from the *Centro de Convenciones,* this 198-room resort has 39 villas, several restaurants, including the superb *Blue Bayou* (see *Eating Out*), tennis courts, three pools, a Jacuzzi, water sports, and an art gallery in the lobby. There are also gardens spread out over 10 acres. Km 8.5 of Paseo Kukulcán (phone: 98-830044; 800-233-1234; fax: 98-831514).

Hyatt Regency Beautifully housed under a glass atrium, this hotel has 300 rooms, all with ocean views. There's also a pool, three bars, and three restaurants (the best is *Scampi;* see *Eating Out*). Paseo Kukulcán, on the northern tip of the island (phone: 98-831234; 800-233-1234; fax: 98-831349).

Krystal Cancún With lush, thick greenery outside and in, it offers 316 rooms and suites, tennis, and five fine restaurants (our favorites are *Bogart's* and *Hacienda el Mortero;* see *Eating Out* for both). Km 9 of Paseo Kukulcán, on the northern tip of the island (phone: 98-831133; 800-231-9860; fax: 98-831790).

Marriott Casa Magna This six-story hostelry of contemporary design is stunningly decorated with Mexican textures and colors. All 450 rooms have balconies affording a view of either the Caribbean or the lagoon. On the premises are four restaurants, including a Japanese steakhouse; a nightclub; a pool; a Jacuzzi; and two lighted tennis courts. Km 14.5 of Paseo Kukulcán (phone: 98-852000; 800-228-9290; fax: 98-851731).

Meliá Cancún With a waterfall cascading over part of its entrance, this 450-unit marble-and-glass complex has a huge central atrium that looks and, unfortunately, *feels* like a tropical jungle. The hotel's newest feature is a full-service spa with exercise classes, massage, facials, and other beauty treatments. Other facilities include four restaurants, five bars, two pools, three tennis courts, and a small, par 54, 18-hole golf course. Km 15 of Paseo Kukulcán (phone: 98-851114; 800-336-3542; fax: 98-851260).

Meliá Turquesa A giant white pyramid sloping down to the beach, it offers 446 rooms decorated in soft colors and equipped with mini-bars and safe-deposit boxes. There also are two restaurants, three bars, a coffee shop, and two lighted tennis courts. Km 12 of Paseo Kukulcán (phone: 98-832544; 800-336-3542; fax: 98-851241).

Oasis Built in the tradition of an ancient Maya city, this 1,000-room complex of angled structures offers seven restaurants, nine bars, four tennis courts, a nine-hole golf course, and the longest swimming pool (nearly a third of a mile) in Cancún. The downside: Its location, way north of town. Km 47 of Paseo Kukulcán (phone: 98-850867; 800-44-OASIS; fax: 98-833486).

Omni All 334 rooms here have large terraces; there also are 35 suites and 27 villas. Facilities include eight restaurants, bars, a gameroom, two lighted tennis courts, and a health center. There's not much of a beach, but guests seems to enjoy lounging and sipping tropical drinks on hammocks strung up by the sea. Km 16.5 of Paseo Kukulcán (phone: 98-850714; 800-THE-OMNI; fax: 98-850184).

Presidente On the edge of the *Club de Golf Cancún* golf links (see *Golf,* above) and a peaceful lagoon, this stately, 298-room hostelry offers a tennis court, fishing, and water skiing—thus its popularity with sports enthusiasts. Its beach—one of the calmest in the area, and perfect for children—and location are among the best on Cancún. Four restaurants and a pool complete the picture. Km 7 of Paseo Kukulcán (phone: 98-830200, 98-830202, or 98-830414; 800-447-6147; fax: 98-832515).

Radisson Sierra Plaza The 261 rooms are elegantly decorated in a Southwestern style, with bright colors and tile floors. The oceanfront property features two restaurants, three lounges, two snack bars, an outdoor pool, a fitness center, two tennis courts, and plenty of water sports. Km 10.5 of Paseo Kukulcán (phone: 98-832444; 800-333-3333; fax: 98-833486).

Ritz-Carlton Cancún This super-luxury resort features 370 guestrooms (including 54 suites). All rooms offer private balconies with sea views, mini-bars, refrigerators, and two bathrooms. On premises: a health club, two pools, tennis courts, and three dining rooms. 36 Retorno del Rey, off Paseo Kukulcán (phone: 98-850808; 305-446-0776 in Florida; 800-241-3333 elsewhere in the US; fax: 98-851015).

Villas Tacul Each of the 23 Spanish-style villas in this colony has a garden, a patio, a kitchen, and two to five bedrooms. On a narrow but pleasant beach, it also offers a restaurant and two tennis courts. It's perfect for families or congenial two- or three-couple groups. Km 5.5 of Paseo Kukulcán (phone: 98-830000; 800-842-0193; fax: 98-830349).

Westin Regina In this complex are 385 rooms, each with an ocean or lagoon view; the 94 tower rooms have private balconies (as do some in the low-rise building). Facilities include five outdoor pools, two lighted tennis courts, a health club and recreation center, a water sports center, and a boat dock for access to evening cruises and water sports. There also are two restaurants and two lounges. Punta Nizuc, at the south end of the island (phone: 98-850086; 800-228-3000; fax: 98-850074).

EXPENSIVE

Calinda Beach Cancún Situated on the best beach on the island, between Laguna Nichupté and Bahía de Mujeres, this hostelry isn't as lavish as many of its neighbors, but it's nonetheless a favorite, as attested to by its loyal following. A restaurant, bars, tennis courts, and a gym also contribute to its popularity. All 460 rooms have ocean views. Km 4 of Paseo Kukulcán (phone: 98-831600; 800-228-5151; fax: 98-831857).

Casa Maya Originally built as condominiums, the 356 rooms and suites here are large, with immense walk-in closets, sinks the size of bathtubs, and tubs the size of swimming pools. Among the amenities are a pool, two lighted tennis courts, mopeds for rent, a restaurant, and cordial service. The place seems to be especially popular with families. Km 5 of Paseo Kukulcán (phone: 98-830555; 800-44-UTELL; fax: 98-831188).

Club Med Boasting one of the island's widest beaches, this is one of the prime places to stay on Cancún. The 410 rooms, each with two wide single beds and traditional Mexican decor, are set in three-story bungalows facing either the ocean or the lagoon. Windsurfing, sailing, snorkeling, and scuba diving (including scuba instruction) are included in the basic rate, as are all meals. There's entertainment nightly. Punta Nizuc, at the south end of the island (phone: 98-852929; 800-CLUB-MED; fax: 98-830904).

Fiesta Americana Each of the 280 rooms has rattan furnishings and a balcony overlooking the water. The pool area is nicely laid out, with a *palapa* restaurant and two bars, beyond which lies the aqua-blue bay. Snorkeling gear is available poolside. The fountain-filled lobby is a pretty place for before-dinner cocktails. Km 8 of Paseo Kukulcán (phone: 98-831400; 800-FIESTA-1; fax: 98-832502).

Playa Blanca A pioneer among Cancún's hotels (it opened in 1974), this link in the Best Western chain has 161 rooms, a pool, a small beachfront, and every water sport imaginable. Since it's next door to the marina, the boating facilities are excellent. There's also a restaurant. Km 3 of Paseo Kukulcán (phone: 98-830071; 800-528-1234; fax: 98-830904).

Royal Solaris Caribe A Maya pyramid–like structure, it has 280 rooms (including 13 junior suites), three restaurants, an Olympic-size pool, a pleasant beach, a health club, and social programs. Km 23 of Paseo Kukulcán (phone: 98-850600; 800-368-9779; fax: 98-850354).

Sheraton Cancún This self-contained, 748-room gem is set apart on its own beach, which it shares with a small Maya temple. Other draws: six tennis courts, six pools, five dining rooms, *Daphny's* video bar (with live and taped music), aerobics classes, and scuba lessons. Km 12.5 of Paseo Kukulcán (phone: 98-831988; 800-325-3535; fax: 98-850083).

MODERATE

Aristos A friendly scale and typical Mexican hospitality make for easy comfort here. There are 222 smallish but pleasant rooms, an inviting pool area, a beach, two lighted tennis courts, and a restaurant. Km 9.5 of Paseo Kukulcán (phone: 98-830011; 800-5-ARISTOS; fax: 98-830078).

Club Lagoon On a quiet lagoon, this secluded collection of 89 adobe-type dwellings (the best face the lagoon), including rooms and two-level suites, is a real find. One picturesque courtyard opens onto another, with flowers playing colorfully against the white cottages. It also has two restaurants, two bars, and a nautical center. Laguna Nichupté (phone: 98-831111; fax: 98-831808).

Holiday Inn Express Club de Golf Cancún This no-frills, 120-room establishment adjoins the famous *Club de Golf Cancún* course (see *Golf,* above). Though the hotel has neither a restaurant nor a beach, it does boast a pool with two waterfalls, as well as complimentary transportation to a nearby beach club. It's one of the best values in the Hotel Zone. 21 Paseo Pok-Ta-Pok (phone: 98-832200; 800-HOLIDAY; fax: 98-832532).

CANCÚN CITY

MODERATE

América At this pleasant place are 177 large rooms, each with its own terrace. Though it's not right on the beach, it does provide complimentary shuttle service to its own beach club. There's a pool, restaurant, bar, and coffee shop. Av. Tulum, Cancún City (phone: 98-847500; fax: 98-841953).

INEXPENSIVE

Plaza Caribe Downtown, across from the bus station, the 140 rooms here fill up fast. Public buses will take you to the beach, 2 miles (3 km) away. Other facilities include a restaurant and a coffee shop. 36 Av. Tulum, Cancún City (phone: 98-841377; 800-528-1234; fax: 98-846352).

Plaza del Sol Shaped like a half-moon with two stylized canoes over its portals, it has 87 rooms, a pool, a restaurant, a bar, and complimentary transportation to and from the beach. 31 Av. Yaxchilán, Cancún City (phone: 98-843888; fax: 98-844393).

ELSEWHERE ON THE MAINLAND

EXPENSIVE

Diamond Playacar This gem of a resort has 300 luxury rooms and suites in jungle lodge–style four-plexes with thatch roofs and ceiling fans. Facilities include two pools, two restaurants, three bars, four tennis courts, water sports equipment rentals, and miles of uncrowded beach. Rates include all meals and the use of all facilities. Playa del Carmen (phone: 987-30341/2; 212-251-1816 in New York State; 800-642-1600 elsewhere in the US; fax: 987-30348).

Oasis Club de Playa Part of the beautiful Puerto Aventuras resort area (see *Special Places*), this beachfront property has 36 rooms, a restaurant, and a pool. Puerto Aventuras (phone: 987-35101; 800-44-OASIS; fax: 987-35051).

Oasis Marina Mar Another Puerto Aventuras resort, this establishment has 309 rooms, all with fully equipped kitchens. Located next to the marina, it has a pool and a restaurant. Km 269 of Carretera Chetumal, Puerto Aventuras (phone: 987-23287 or 987-23376; 800-44-OASIS; fax: 987-23332).

La Posada del Capitán Lafitte Located in Punta Beté, about 21 miles (38 km) south of *Cancún Airport,* this beachfront complex has 39 bungalows (no fans or air conditioning), a dining room, a billiards hall, a pool, a dive shop, and reefs just 100 yards offshore (phone: 99-230485 or 99-239082 in Mérida; 303-674-9615 in Colorado; 800-538-6802 elsewhere in the US).

On quiet Chemuyil Beach, the Román family runs a 10-cabaña, moderately priced hotel (with no formal name, air conditioning, or private baths) that also has 12 tents for campers and additional camping space, plus a lively bar that offers drinks, snacks, and local-catch seafood. Relax on a hammock and sip a cocktail out of a fresh coconut. For further information on the beach, the bar, the hotel, and camping, write to *Don Lalo Román Chemoir Fideicomiso* (*Xel-Ha,* Tulum, QR 77500, México), the trust that maintains the beach. Km 123 of Carretera Tulum (no phone).

COZUMEL

VERY EXPENSIVE

Club Cozumel Caribe A twisting, palm-canopied drive leads to this expansive 260-room beachfront property with attractive grounds. It offers tennis, a restaurant, and a bar. Unfortunately, it's so far removed from everything else on the island that you may have trouble getting a taxi to Palancar Reef or San Miguel. Playa San Juan (phone: 987-20100; 800-327-2254).

EXPENSIVE

Coral Princess Club A posh resort, it offers 70 units, each with kitchenette and private terrace. There's also a restaurant and video bar. On the north end of the island (phone: 987-23200 or 987-23323; 800-272-3243; fax: 987-22800).

El Cozumeleño This property has 80 large rooms, three restaurants, a bar, a tennis court, and a free-form pool. Playa Santa Pilar, on the north end of the island (phone: 987-20050; 800-437-3923; fax: 987-20381).

Fiesta Americana Sol Caribe A beautiful 322-room resort 'twixt beach and jungle, it has three tennis courts, good diving facilities, and a fine dining room.

South Zone (phone: 987-20466 or 987-20700; 800-FIESTA-1; fax: 987-21301).

Holiday Inn Cozumel Reef In this inn are 165 guestrooms, three restaurants, two bars, two lighted tennis courts, a health spa, and a private boat dock. South Zone (phone: 987-22622; 800-HOLIDAY; fax: 987-22666).

Meliá Mayan Cozumel Set on the isolated north end of the coast, this 12-story high-rise on the beach has 200 rooms and suites, two restaurants, an abundance of terraces, two tennis courts, a Mexican fiesta on Thursdays, and a Caribbean fiesta on Fridays. Playa Santa Pilar (phone: 987-20411 or 987-22109; 800-336-3542; fax: 987-21599).

Plaza las Glorias It's the only luxury hotel in town that is on the beach. A 170-room complex, each room has a private balcony and an ocean view. There are also a private marina, two restaurants, a lobby bar with live music, a scuba diving school, and a pool. South Zone (phone: 987-22000; 800-342-AMIGO; fax: 987-21937).

Presidente Cozumel Cozumel's original luxury establishment (and still one of its best) offers 253 rooms, an excellent dining room, a nice pool, a pleasant beach, tennis, and a variety of water sports, including scuba diving, snorkeling, and game fishing. On the northern end of the island (phone: 987-20322; 800-447-6147; fax: 987-21360).

MODERATE

La Ceiba Well equipped and conveniently located for scuba divers, this 115-room hostelry has a spa, tennis, a restaurant, and a cocktail lounge. Punta Paraíso, south of town (phone: 987-20844; 800-777-5873; fax: 987-20064).

Fiesta Inn The three-story, colonial-style link in the Fiesta chain has 178 rooms and two suites. Surrounded by beautiful gardens, it's connected to the beach by a tunnel. Other pluses: a large pool, a tennis court, motorcycles for rent, a dive shop, a restaurant, a bar, and a coffee shop. Km 1.7 of the Costera Sur (phone: 987-22899; 800-FIESTA-1; fax: 987-22154).

Fontán Most of these 48 rooms face the lovely beach. There's also a pool, a restaurant, and a dive shop. North Zone (phone: 987-20300; 800-221-6509; fax: 987-20105).

La Perla Right on the beach, this four-story, 22-room hotel has its own swimming cove and a pier for private yachts. A pool, dive packages, a deli-bar, and a quiet, comfortable, and unpretentious atmosphere round out the amenities. Km 2 of Av. Rafael E. Melgar (phone: 987-20188; 800-852-6404; fax: 987-22611).

Playa Azul A family favorite, this member of the Best Western group offers 60 rooms and suites, a restaurant, a bar, and water sports. North of San Miguel, at Km 4 of the Carretera San Juan (phone: 987-20033; 800-528-1234; fax: 987-20066).

Sol Cabañas del Caribe Informal and friendly, this semitropical hideaway on one of the island's best beaches has 50 rooms, a small pool, and nine individual cabañas. There is a restaurant. Playa Santa Pilar (phone: 987-20072; 800-336-3542; fax: 987-21599).

INEXPENSIVE

Villablanca Though its draws—a tennis court, a pool, a dive shop, a boat for up to 60 divers, and classes in all water sports—compare with those usually found only at a resort hotel, this property has only 50 rooms and suites, some with Jacuzzis. Across the street, on the water's edge, is *Amadeus,* its restaurant/bar/beach club. Across from Playa Paraíso, south of town (phone: 987-20730; 800-DIVE-MEX; fax: 987-20865).

ISLA MUJERES

EXPENSIVE

Cristalmar Tucked away on the inward coast, this 38-suite property has deluxe one-, two-, and three-bedroom units. The hotel also boasts its own secluded beach, a good restaurant, an excellent dive shop, and the nicest pool in town. Fraccionamiento Paraíso Laguna (phone: 987-70007; 800-441-0472; fax: 987-70509).

MODERATE

Cabañas María del Mar It has 48 units (including 10 cabañas), a restaurant, and a full-service, 20-slip marina. The proprietors, the Limas, make everyone feel at home. At the north end of the island, on Av. Carlos Lazo (phone: 987-70213).

Perla del Caribe This three-story hotel offers 90 rooms, all with balconies. There also are a restaurant and a pool. 2 Av. Madero (phone: 987-70444; 800-258-6454; fax: 987-70011).

INEXPENSIVE

Berny In this hostelry are 40 rooms, a restaurant, and a spacious lobby. Downtown, on Av. Juárez (phone: 987-70025; fax: 987-70026).

Perla del Caribe II Under the same management as its relative on Avenida Madero (see above), this less expensive version contains 34 basic but pleasant rooms, all with a view. There's also a restaurant. Avs. Nicolás Bravo and Vicente Guerrero (phone: 987-70586/7).

Posada del Mar This pleasant 42-room hostelry is one of the best on the island, with palm-shaded grounds, a fine restaurant (*Los Pájaros;* see *Eating Out*), a bar, and laundry facilities. Across from the beach, at 15 Av. Rueda Medina (phone: 987-70212 or 987-70300; fax: 987-70266).

EATING OUT

Hotel food in Cancún is better than average because the hoteliers want to keep the money spent on food in the house; this means that the non-hotel restaurants must work extra hard to lure customers. Be sure to try Yucatecan specialties, which are quite different from standard Mexican fare. Start the day with eggs *moltuleños*—fried eggs on a tortilla—black beans, and a spicy sauce. Don't miss delicious and filling Yucatecan lime soup, which also contains chicken, vegetables, and tortillas. All restaurants listed below accept MasterCard and Visa, and a few also accept American Express and Diners Club; it's a good idea to call ahead and check. Expect to pay $40 to $60 for dinner for two at restaurants we describe as expensive, about $30 at places in the moderate category, and less than $25 at spots listed as inexpensive. Prices do not include tax, tips, wine, or drinks. Note that there is a 15% tax on restaurant meals; calculate the tip on the bill before tax.

Almost all the restaurants on Cozumel are in town, although a few, open only for lunch, are out on the beaches. Restaurant prices here, as well as on Isla Mujeres, are more moderate than those on Cancún. *Note:* On Isla Mujeres, it is best to avoid drinking tap water and eating unpeeled, raw vegetables that may have been washed in tap water. In Cancún or in any major resort hotels, there's generally nothing to worry about. Unless otherwise noted, all restaurants listed below are open for lunch and dinner. The telephone numbers listed include both the city code and the local number. When calling from anywhere on Cancún, Cozumel, or Isla Mujeres to any other location on Cancún, Cozumel, or Isla Mujeres, use only the local number. For information on dialing from elsewhere, see *Telephone* earlier in this chapter.

CANCÚN AND THE MAINLAND

HOTEL ZONE

EXPENSIVE

Augustus Caesar Seafood and traditional Italian dishes are served with panache in pretty surroundings. Live music is featured nightly from 8:30 PM to midnight. No shorts or T-shirts allowed. Reservations advised. *La Mansión–Costa Blanca* shopping center (phone: 98-833384).

Blue Bayou Customers nosh on Cajun and creole fare and sip specialty drinks in a multilevel dining area suspended among waterfalls and lush tropical greenery. There's live jazz nightly. Closed for lunch. Reservations necessary. *Hyatt Cancún Caribe,* Km 8.5 of Paseo Kukulcán (phone: 98-830044, ext. 54).

Bogart's International dishes are served with quiet elegance in exotic Moroccan surroundings. No shorts or T-shirts allowed. Closed for lunch; dinner seatings are at 7 and 9:30 PM. Reservations advised. At the *Krystal Cancún,* Km 9 of Paseo Kukulcán (phone: 98-831133).

Calypso The decor at this dining spot combines elegance and a tropical exuberance, with fountains, pools, and live reggae music enhancing the romantic seaside ambience. The menu features first-rate Caribbean fare, with an emphasis on seafood—try the braised fish with lobster medallions and scallion sauce. Closed for lunch. Reservations advised. At the *Camino Real,* on the northeast tip of the island (phone: 98-830100, ext. 8060).

Grimond's The mayor's former home has been gussied up with European furniture, Oriental rugs, English china, and French crystal. Diners choose from four sitting rooms, a dining room, and an upstairs piano bar, all duly elegant. The French chef recommends shrimp sautéed in a cherry wine sauce. No shorts or beach sandals allowed. Closed for lunch. Reservations advised. 8 Pez Volador, next to the *Casa Maya* hotel (phone: 98-830438).

Gypsy's A touch of Spain in the Mexican Caribbean, this rustic-looking eatery specializes in Iberian cooking (the paella is exceptional). Flamenco dancers entertain nightly. Closed for lunch. No reservations. Laguna Nichupté, across from the *Continental Villas Plaza* (phone: 98-832015 or 98-832120).

Hacienda el Mortero A convincing copy of a hacienda in Súchil, Durango (complete with an impressive stone fountain and lots of plants), it specializes in steaks and Mexican haute cuisine. The service is attentive and friendly, and the atmosphere is enhanced by live mariachi music in the evenings. Reservations advised. In the *Krystal Cancún,* Km 9 of Paseo Kukulcán (phone: 98-831133).

Iguana Wana This trendy spot—which bills itself as "a contemporary Mexican café and bar"—offers live jazz and a varied menu, including Tex-Mex chili and buckets of peel-your-own shrimp. No reservations. *Plaza Caracol* shopping center (phone: 98-830829).

Jaguari's Here's the place to sink your teeth into a thick, juicy steak. Run by a Brazilian, it offers premium beef cuts served with a South American–style *churrasquería* (barbecue) sauce. Reservations advised. Playa Gaviota Azul (phone: 98-832880).

Lorenzillo's Set under a giant *palapa* extending over Laguna Nichupté, this restaurant specializes in soft-shell shrimp and rock lobster. Casual dress is acceptable, but shorts and T-shirts are not allowed. Open daily for breakfast, lunch, and dinner. Reservations unnecessary. Km 10.5 of Paseo Kukulcán (phone: 98-833073).

Scampi Superb northern Italian fare—delicious pasta, meat, and seafood—is served in a beautiful setting. The service is impeccable. At the *Hyatt Regency,* Paseo Kukulcán, on the northern tip of the island (phone: 98-831234).

Seryna This pretty place offers Japanese specialties such as sushi, *teppanyaki,* sukiyaki, *shabu-shabu,* and tempura. Reservations advised. *Flamingo Plaza* shopping center (phone: 98-851155 or 98-832995).

Bombay Bicycle Club Casual and comfortable, the menu is strictly US-style fare—good hamburgers, barbecued ribs, and calorie-filled desserts. The service is excellent and friendly. Open 7 AM to 11 PM. No reservations. Paseo Kukulcán, across from Playa Tortuga (98-831281).

INEXPENSIVE

100% Natural The menu consists of fresh fruit drinks, salads, sandwiches, and fruit and vegetable platters; there's live jazz music nightly. No reservations. Three locations: 6 Calle Sunyaxchen, downtown (phone: 98-843617); *Plaza Terramar* shopping center, Paseo Kukulcán (phone: 98-831180); and *Plaza Kukulcán* shopping center, Paseo Kukulcán (phone: 98-852904).

CANCÚN CITY

EXPENSIVE

La Dolce Vita Modern decor supplies the backdrop for intimate dining at this place, where the sweet life is manifested in tasty pasta and seafood dishes. Closed for lunch. Reservations advised. 87 Av. Cobá (phone: 98-841384).

La Habichuela The place locals go for a night out and for *mar y tierra* (surf and turf) in a Maya garden replete with miniature ruins. Reservations advised. 25 Margaritas (phone: 98-843158).

El Pescador Perhaps the best seafood eatery in Cancún dishes up fresh lobster, shrimp, and red snapper on Mexican pottery. Don't miss the Yucatecan lime soup and the hot rolls, and try for a table outside on the fan-cooled terrace. Closed Mondays. Reservations unnecessary. 28 Av. Tulipanes (phone: 98-842673).

MODERATE

Johnny Rockets Rock 'n' roll and a 1950s theme attract visitors to this hamburger eatery–video bar. The music is hot, the food even hotter. Definitely not a place for easy listening. No reservations. *Plaza Terramar* shopping center (phone: 98-833092).

Pizza Rolandi All kinds of Italian dishes are offered in an informal, outdoor setting. Reservations unnecessary. 12 Av. Cobá (phone: 98-844047).

Torremolinos Paella, crayfish, and crab prepared the Spanish way. No reservations. Av. Tulum and Calle Xcaret (phone: 98-843639).

INEXPENSIVE

Los Almendros Under the same management as its famous Mérida namesake, this eatery draws repeat customers for its authentic Yucatecan food. Reservations unnecessary. 60 Av. Bonampak (phone: 98-840807).

Amsterdam Bistro European dishes are served in this intimate bistro. The delicious bread is baked on the premises, and there is a huge salad and fresh fruit bar. Open for breakfast, lunch, and dinner; closed Mondays. Reservations unnecessary. 70 Av. Yaxchilán (phone: 98-844098).

COZUMEL

EXPENSIVE

Acuario Once a real aquarium, it's now an elegant seafood restaurant, with entertainment provided by an immense tankful of exotic tropical fish in the middle of the room. Reservations advised. Av. Rafael E. Melgar at Av. 11 Sur, San Miguel (phone: 987-21097).

Donatello A premier Italian dining place with a New Orleans French Quarter ambience, it serves superb fresh pasta and offers a beautiful ocean view. Closed for lunch. Reservations advised. 131 Av. Rafael E. Melgar Sur, San Miguel (phone: 987-20090 or 987-22586).

Morgan's Lobster thermidor and special coffees are favorites at this comfortable, popular wood cabin. Good steaks and seafood also are served. Reservations advised. On the main plaza, in San Miguel (phone: 987-20584).

Pepe's Grill This romantic spot by the waterfront has excellent seafood and steaks. A variety of live music is featured nightly. Reservations advised. Av. Rafael E. Melgar, San Miguel (phone: 987-20213).

MODERATE

Casa Denis The menu varies at this cozy eatery, where Yucatecan dishes are served outdoors under a tropical fruit tree. Reservations advised. Off the south side of the main square, in San Miguel (phone: 987-20067).

Mezcalito's Set on the surf-pounded Caribbean side of the island, this large open-air *palapa* serves up some of the tastiest grilled shrimp and fish on the island. The atmosphere—white sand, ocean breezes, and friendly chatter—is unbeatable. A good spot, too, just to stop for a cold beer or a piña colada. No reservations. Punta Morena (no phone).

Las Palmeras Opposite the ferry dock, it's a great meeting place offering a varied menu for every meal, including breakfast. The homemade biscuits and French toast are a real treat. Reservations unnecessary. On the *malecón,* San Miguel (phone: 987-20532).

Pancho's Backyard The food is just what you would expect—good and plenty—served on hand-crafted ceramic pottery. Strolling mariachis give this place a certain *sabor mexicano.* No reservations. On the waterfront at Calle 8, San Miguel (no phone).

Plaza Leza A sidewalk café, it prepares good Mexican snacks, charcoal-broiled steaks, and seafood. Reservations advised. 58 Calle 1 Sur, San Miguel (phone: 987-21041).

INEXPENSIVE

San Francisco The fare is—what else?—seafood (try the snail ceviche), and a band plays in the afternoons. Closed for dinner. Reservations unnecessary. A quarter mile from Playa San Francisco (no phone).

Sports Page If you can't survive without the *Super Bowl* or the *World Series,* stop in and watch the games on TV while munching on a burger and fries. No reservations. Av. 5, San Miguel (phone: 987-21199).

ISLA MUJERES

EXPENSIVE

Ciro's Lobster House A wide selection of Mexican wines accompanies the lobster and red snapper served here. Reservations advised. 11 Matamoros, in town (phone: 987-70102).

MODERATE

Gomar Lobster and fresh fish are best enjoyed on the romantic terrace, where tables sport bright, striped Mexican cloths during the day, elegant white tablecloths at night. You also can dine indoors. Reservations unnecessary. Avs. Hidalgo and Madero (phone: 987-70142).

Hacienda Gomar Exotic drinks and a good seafood buffet are what attract patrons to this eatery. Reservations unnecessary. On the west side of the island on the road to *El Garrafón* (no phone).

Los Pájaros Facing the beach on the north end of town, this *palapa*-style eatery serves good Mexican fare. Reservations unnecessary. *Posada del Mar* hotel (phone: 987-70044).

INEXPENSIVE

Buho's Paradise Remaining open until the wee hours, this nightclub/restaurant is great for late snacks. Reservations unnecessary. Next to *Cabañas María del Mar,* at the island's northern tip (phone: 987-70179).

Pizza Rolandi Pizza cooked in a wood-burning oven and other Italian dishes are the attractions here. Reservations unnecessary. Av. Hidalgo, between Avs. Madero and Abasolo (phone: 987-70430).

Montserrat

There may not be leprechauns on this verdant, idyllic island, but there is a feeling of Irish magic. The Irish who settled on Montserrat in the early 1600s nicknamed it the Emerald Isle because of the greenery that grew beyond its gray and black volcanic beaches.

The tiny island (population 12,000), which sits between Antigua and Guadeloupe in the Leeward Islands, was initially sighted by Columbus during his second visit to the Caribbean. It was later settled by the British, held on two occasions by the French (after bitter fighting), used as a deportation colony by the British, and finally became a British Crown Colony. Named by Columbus for the quiet hills surrounding the Abbey of Montserrat in Spain, this serene haven—the epitome of peace today—knew little tranquillity for almost 250 years.

The British decision to settle Montserrat was based primarily on their occupation of neighboring St. Kitts and Nevis. About 20 years after the initial English settlement, a large contingent of Irish was sent to the island; whether these people had been deported directly from Ireland because of their involvement in the rebellions suppressed by Oliver Cromwell or whether they left (or were forced to leave) St. Kitts is an unresolved historical question. The island's Irish heritage is reflected today in the number of red-haired islanders (who even have a hint of a brogue), in the Irish names for many locations (Carr's Bay, *Galway's Plantation*, Fergus Mountain), and in the Irish shamrock that graces the immigration stamp. At the same time, this is one of the most West Indian of all the Caribbean islands, intensely uncommercial, and very proud of its culture and customs.

Shortly after the Irish settled Montserrat, the French became interested in the island. In 1664 the British governor ordered a new fort to be built. It was considered impregnable because of its position on a steep hill, yet was taken a year later by a French and Carib force. After four years, the island again came under British control. Then, in 1783, the French retook Montserrat. It was returned to Britain by treaty shortly after the American Revolution, and it has remained British ever since.

Both the British and the Irish worked to make Montserrat into a farm and plantation island. Slaves were imported to develop sugar and lime plantations, and crops of potatoes, tomatoes, and other vegetables were planted. But however perfect for semitropical wild growth, the terrain was simply too rugged for the kind of agriculture planned by the colonists. The plantations never did turn the island into the boomtown and trading port the British had envisioned. With the abolition of slavery in the mid-1800s, large-scale agriculture on the island was finished for good.

Since that time, Montserrat has been more or less dependent on Britain for its economic livelihood. Though it produces enough fruit and vegeta-

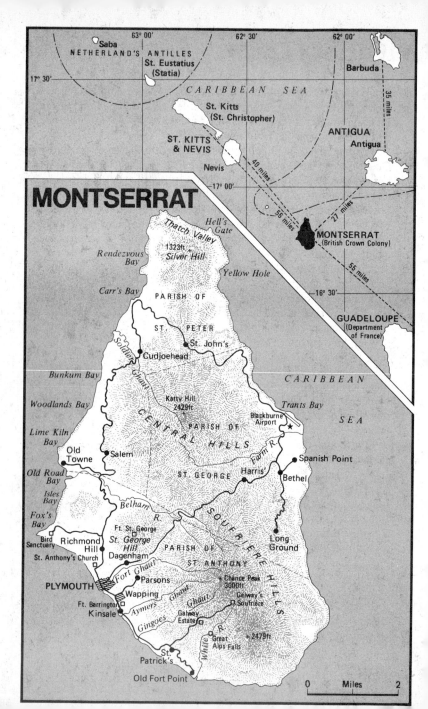

bles for its own needs—and even exports bumper crops like tomatoes—the island essentially remains undeveloped. Offered associate statehood by the British in 1966, Montserrat chose to remain a Crown Colony.

In more recent years, tourists began to discover this tiny isle. Montserrat's mystique was enhanced by Air Studios, a state-of-the-art recording studio built in the lush northern hills. It brought the likes of Stevie Wonder, Paul McCartney, Sting, and Elton John to Montserrat to cut albums and to relax in the tranquil beauty. As word spread, the hills became alive with music. Unfortunately, Hurricane Hugo pulled the plug in 1989. Air Studios suffered major damage and is still up for sale.

Today, Montserrat offers visitors luxury villas, several first class hotels and restaurants, and a welcoming atmosphere. A $30-million seaport was completed in mid-1993 in the town of Plymouth so that cruise ships may once again dock here. Phase two of the development will include bayside shops and dining facilities. Montserrat is unhurried, uncommercialized, and for the most part, undiscovered. But then, peace and privacy are a large part of this island hideaway's appeal.

Montserrat At-a-Glance

FROM THE AIR

Montserrat is a pear-shaped island about 27 miles southwest of Antigua and 275 miles southeast of Puerto Rico. Only about 11 miles long and 7 miles across at its widest point, almost a third of its 39 square miles is either virgin forest or unsuitable for any agricultural purpose. Half of what is left is devoted to tree crops or is otherwise cultivated. The remainder is developed or urban land. The island is volcanic, and active sulfur vents may be found in the mountain region. It is renowned for its black sand beaches and thick tropical vegetation. The majestic Chances Peak, the tallest point on the island, rises 3,002 feet above sea level. Flying time is three-and-a-half hours from New York to Antigua, followed by a 15-minute connecting flight.

SPECIAL PLACES

PLYMOUTH This colorful, charming port is marvelously West Indian in flavor, although a touch of the British influence remains. It's an easy town to explore on foot, but dress properly; residents here don't appreciate bathing suits or other ultra-informal dress. A small town of 3,500 people, Plymouth stretches along the Caribbean. A dock was constructed for small cruise ships and visiting yachtsmen in 1993. The streets are quiet and clean; the entire town is very proper, neat, and serene. A walking tour of Plymouth takes about an hour and a half, and it's best to start with *Government House* (Pebbles St.; phone: 491-2409). This delightful Victorian structure, surrounded by well-maintained lawns and gardens of flowering poincianas, is decorated with a shamrock, in honor of the Irish who settled and cultivated the island. The house is closed to the public, but visitors may stroll through the gardens; they're closed weekday afternoons and on weekends. There's no admission charge.

Fridays and Saturdays are market days; early on those mornings rural islanders bring their produce into Plymouth, and city merchants prepare for a big day of shopping. Vegetables, fruit, fresh fish, and tidbits of gossip are rapidly exchanged, and villagers and farmers discuss island politics, the weather, and prices in an age-old island ritual.

While in town, check out the *Philatelic Bureau* (phone: 491-2996), one block from *Government House,* where there are displays of current and past stamp issues, prized by collectors and souvenir seekers alike.

Also of interest is *St. Anthony's Church,* on Church Road on the northern outskirts of town. Originally constructed in 1636, the church has been destroyed—by earthquake, hurricanes, invasion, and fire—and rebuilt five times. Displayed inside the church are two silver chalices, gifts from emancipated slaves. On Richmond Hill, the tiny *Montserrat Museum,* ensconced in an antique sugar mill, displays a collection of artifacts, some of which date back to Carib and Arawak times. It's open Sundays and Wednesdays from 2:30 to 5 PM and at other times by arrangement for groups. There's no admission charge (phone: 491-5443).

Fort Barrington, between Kinsale and Wapping on the cliff above the banana pier, was built in the 18th century but saw little action. It's closed weekends; no admission charge (no phone). *Fort St. George,* on St. George's Hill overlooking Plymouth, about a 10-minute drive from town, was thrown together in 1782 as a defense against an oncoming force of French and Carib invaders. It's open daily; no admission charge (no phone). These forts did not prevent the French from taking the island a second time.

ELSEWHERE ON THE ISLAND

CHANCES PEAK The tallest point on Montserrat offers an incredible panorama when clear of clouds. Local folklore tells of a beautiful mermaid who lives in a pond at the summit. The lucky person who is able to capture her comb will be blessed with riches. There are two routes to the top. The easiest is to climb the 2,003 steps built into the side of the mountain (bring a canteen and wear sneakers or sturdy shoes). The other option is to hike up the mountain itself, which can be difficult and hazardous without a guide, so arrange for one at any hotel or the tourist office (see *Tourist Information,* below) before setting out. The round trip takes about two hours. The mountain is at the southern end of the island in St. Anthony's Parish. Also see *Climbing and Hiking* in DIVERSIONS.

FOX'S BAY BIRD SANCTUARY Fifteen acres of mangrove swamp at Bransby Point on the northwest side of the island have been turned into a preserve for nesting colonies of Caribbean coots, green herons, the rare little blue herons, ringed kingfishers, and numerous other avian species. There are no organized tours, but marked trails lead to the circular pond. Open daily. No admission charge. To get there, turn left off Grove Rd. just beyond the *Montserrat Museum* to Bransby Point (phone: 491-3086).

GALWAY'S PLANTATION On the way south to Galway's Soufrière (see below), this historic sugar plantation is the site of picturesque ruins, which include a greathouse, a boiling house, a windmill, two reservoirs, a large barn and warehouse, what appears to have been a rum still, and a slave village. Open daily. No admission charge (no phone).

GALWAY'S SOUFRIÈRE In the south-central region of Montserrat, this small (about four feet across), open crater bubbling with grayish-yellow molten sulfur is a vivid reminder that the volcano beneath the island's surface still lives. In addition to giving off sulfur fumes (*soufrière* is French for sulfur), the crater allows experts to monitor volcanic activity under the island. Visitors can drive the steep, paved road, which passes *Galway's Plantation,* to the path to the crater's rim, then hike 15 minutes to the crater itself.

BAMBOO FOREST Near Galway's Soufrière, this two-hour walk climbs to a ridge from which there are excellent views down the White River valley to the south coast of the island. Massive bamboo stands line the path. The national bird of Montserrat, the black-and-yellow Montserrat oriole, can be seen in this area of the island. A guide is recommended and can be obtained through the tourist office (see *Tourist Information,* below).

GREAT ALPS WATERFALL At the end of a healthy 1-mile hike (which takes about 45 minutes) through dense rain forest, this small waterfall drops 70 feet into a pool of clear water, making a perfect stop for a quick cool shower. At noon, the overhead sun turns the mist over the pool into rainbows. It's best to hike in the cool morning air; be sure to wear sturdy shoes. The roadway from which to start is about a 15-minute drive south of Plymouth on the White River.

RENDEZVOUS BEACH On the far northwest coast is the island's only white sand strand, a popular swimming, sunning, and picnic destination. The easiest way to get there is by boat; otherwise it's a half-hour hike over the hills from Little Bay. Boat transportation can be arranged through the *Vue Pointe* hotel in Old Towne; many local fishermen in nearby Carr's Bay also will ferry visitors over to the beach. (Also see *Sailing Cruises,* below.)

Sources and Resources

TOURIST INFORMATION

There's a small tourist office in Plymouth (closed weekends; Church Rd.; phone: 491-2230; fax: 491-7430). Since it's a friendly town, don't hesitate to ask questions of passersby. For information about Montserrat tourist offices in the US, see GETTING READY TO GO.

LOCAL COVERAGE Maps and guides are periodically available through the tourist office in Plymouth. The *Montserrat Reporter* and *Montserrat News* are the island's weekly newspapers.

RADIO AND TELEVISION Radio stations broadcasting on Montserrat are Radio Antilles (930 AM), which features regional music and news, plus British and American programming; Radio Montserrat (885 AM; 92.5 FM), playing reggae, calypso, soul, and R & B music plus regional news; and the GEM Radio Network (94.5 FM), which features adult contemporary music, with both American and regional programs. The only local TV station is the Local Access Foundation, which broadcasts on cable channel 5; otherwise, cable television on Montserrat features 27 stations in all.

TELEPHONE When calling from the US, dial 1 + 809 (area code) + (local number). When calling on Montserrat, dial the local number unless otherwise indicated. Dial 491999 for the police; 911 for an ambulance.

ENTRY REQUIREMENTS British, US, and Canadian citizens need only proof of citizenship (a current passport, or an original or certified birth certificate plus an official photo ID such as a driver's license) and a return or ongoing ticket.

CLIMATE AND CLOTHES Temperatures in Montserrat vary between the mid-70s F (20s C) and about 90F (35C), and the humidity is quite low. Rainfall averages about 60 inches per year, with the wettest months being July through September. Dress tends to be more formal here than on other islands, so don't wear short shorts or swimsuit cover-ups in town. Evenings call for something slightly dressy, such as casual resortwear. A sweater or jacket is recommended for evenings in December and January. Bring deck shoes or sneakers for boating and sturdy, comfortable shoes for walking.

MONEY Montserrat currency is the Eastern Caribbean dollar (EC), called the "Bee Wee" by local people. The current exchange rate is about $2.70 EC to $1 US. US dollars are accepted at most places in Montserrat, as are traveler's checks and major credit cards; Canadian dollars are not. Banking hours are from 8 AM to 3 PM Mondays through Thursdays; 8 AM to 5 PM Fridays. The *Bank of Montserrat* (Parliament and Chapel Sts., Plymouth; phone: 491-3843; fax: 491-3163) also is open 8:30 AM to 12:30 PM on Saturdays. All prices in this chapter are quoted in US dollars.

LANGUAGE English is spoken with the usual West Indian lilt and an occasional hint of Irish brogue.

TIME Montserrat is on atlantic standard time. When it is noon in New York, it is 1 PM in Plymouth. During daylight saving time, island and US East Coast times are the same.

CURRENT Some hotel outlets are 220 volts, 60 cycles, AC. A converter is needed for all US appliances here; some hotels will provide one. The newer or renovated hotels have installed 110 volts, 60 cycles. Be sure to check.

TIPPING Hotels add a 10% service charge to bills, which takes care of room maids and other staff. Restaurants frequently add a 10% service charge; check to be certain. Airport porters should get about $1 per bag. Taxi drivers and providers of other services should be tipped 10%.

GETTING AROUND

CAR RENTAL There are 119 miles of well-paved (though winding and twisting) roads on Montserrat. Your hotel desk or the tourist board can arrange for a rental car, or in Plymouth contact *Pauline's Car Rentals* (phone: 491-3846; fax: 491-2434), *Neville Bradshaw* (phone: 491-5270; fax: 491-5069), or *Jefferson's Car Rental* (phone: 491-2126). Mini-moke rentals are available at *Reliable Car Rental* (Marine Dr.; phone: 491-6990; fax: 491-8070). A temporary island driver's license is required. They cost about $12 and are available at *Blackburne Airport* or at the *Traffic Department* (open weekdays from 8:30 AM to 2:30 PM) on Strand Street in Plymouth. Driving is on the left, British-style.

INTER-ISLAND FLIGHTS *LIAT,* through *Montserrat Aviation Services* (*MAS;* phone: 491-2533 or 491-2362) offers regular service between Antigua and *Blackburne Airport* on Montserrat. The flight takes 15 minutes. *Winair* (phone: 491-8022 or 491-2713) offers daily 40-minute flights between St. Maarten and Montserrat. *Montserrat Airways Charter Service* (phone: 491-5342, 491-6494, or 491-2713) runs nine-seater charters and sometimes sells individual tickets. There is a $10 departure tax (save your ticket receipt and boarding pass, as in-transit passengers do not need to pay Antigua's departure tax).

TAXI Rates are standardized by law—and rather expensive. Taxis also may be hired at an hourly rate for tours of the island. It's best to agree on the fare ahead of time and determine whether the quote is in $US or $EC. If you need a taxi and one's not around, call the *Taxi Stand* (phone: 491-2261) in Plymouth.

SPECIAL EVENTS

Montserrat is the only Caribbean island that observes *St. Patrick's Day* (March 17) as a public holiday; this Irish–West Indian celebration actually lasts for several days with events centered in the village of St. Patrick at the southern end of the island. In August, Montserrat natives living abroad return home to visit during the month-long festivities of the *Montserrat Annual Pilgrimage. Christmastime* is celebrated throughout the island from December 16 through *New Year's Day* with parades, masquerades, parties, dinners, and dances, all accompanied by singing and steel and string bands. Other public holidays are *Good Friday* (April 5 in 1996), *Easter Monday* (April 8 in 1996), *Labor Day* (first Monday in May), the *Queen's Birthday* (early June), *Whitmonday* (May 27 in 1996), *August Monday* (first Monday in August; commemorates the 1834 abolition of slavery), *Christmas Day, Boxing Day* (December 26), and *Festival Day* (December 31).

SHOPPING

Not a major preoccupation, since there are few duty-free imports to consider, but local crafts grow more interesting by the season. The best buys are pottery and ceramic jewelry (especially from *Dutcher's Studio;* see below), china, hand-screened prints and T-shirts, anything made from Sea Island cotton, leather sandals, local jams and jellies, and Perk's Rum Punch. In general, shops are open from 8 AM to noon and 1 to 4 PM; Wednesdays and Saturdays, hours are 8 AM to 12:30 PM. The following shops are worth looking into.

Arrow's Man Shop Owned by Alphonse "Arrow" Cassell, king of *soca* music and famous for the song "Hot! Hot! Hot!" This boutique specializes in clothing, shoes, bags, and luggage for men. 6 Marine Dr., Plymouth (phone: 491-2993).

Dutcher's Studio Intriguing decorative pieces made from salvaged bottles, tile, glass, and other materials. Ceramic jewelry made at the studio is an especially good buy. Olveston (phone: 491-5823).

Island House This art gallery specializes in Haitian paintings, as well as crafts, pottery, and prints by local artists. John St., Plymouth (phone: 491-3938).

Jus' Looking A wide selection of island-made items—straw bags from Barbados, the Sunny Caribbee herb and spice line from the British Virgin Islands, works by West Indian artists such as Jill Walker of Barbados, and handmade batik from St. Kitts. Great for shopping—or "jus' looking." George St., Plymouth (phone: 491-4076), and at the airport (phone: 491-4040).

LeatherCraft Center Hand-tooled leather items—shoes, sandals, belts, bags, key rings, bookmarks—are sold here. Groves (phone: 491-4934).

Montserrat Sea Island Cotton Company Features useful and wearable items, including blouses, sundresses, and piles of table linen, much of it handwoven from locally grown fiber. George St., on the bayfront, Plymouth (phone: 491-7009).

Montserrat T-Shirts Locally made and imported all-cotton T-shirts, polo shirts, and "shirtjacs" (loose-fitting men's cotton shirts commonly worn in the tropics) printed with island scenes and tropical flora and fauna. Also handmade African jewelry and accessories. Parliament St., Plymouth (phone 491-4661).

Tapestries of Montserrat Don't miss the island-made rugs, wall hangings, totes, and mats displayed here; they also will create custom designs. Duty-free crystal, watches, and jewelry are in stock, too. In the *John Bull Shop,* Parliament St., Plymouth (phone: 491-2520).

SPORTS

BOATING The *Vue Pointe* hotel can arrange day cruises around the island for up to 12 people (see *Checking In*). Several other yachts and some small craft also may be available for rent from individual owners. There are no formal rental facilities, but check the bulletin board at the tourist office (see *Tourist Information,* above) or ask at your hotel. Visiting yachtsmen can check out the *Montserrat Yacht Club* (Wapping; phone: 491-6963).

CYCLING *Island Bikes* (Plymouth; phone: 491-4696) rents mountain bikes by the day, week, or month. Pedal on your own, with a guide, or on an organized tour along back roads and goat trails. Two spin-off trips feature a bike/van journey for the less energetic and a bike/hike adventure to the Great Alps Waterfall for the physically fit.

GOLF The *Montserrat Golf Club* (Belham Valley; phone: 491-5220) maintains a challenging year-round 11-hole course that can be played as a complete 18-hole course by playing some holes twice. Non-members are free to play the course on payment of the greens fee. Clubs and pullcarts also can be rented. Local members can arrange permission for guests to use the clubhouse, and visitors are welcome to enter the island's major tournament, the *Montserrat Open,* in March. Other, less formal, tournaments are held as well.

HIKING AND MOUNTAIN CLIMBING The 3,002-foot Chances Peak affords spectacular views of nearly the entire island. Among Montserrat's other fine spots for hiking are *Fox's Bay Bird Sanctuary,* the Bamboo Forest, and the Great Alps Waterfall (see *Special Places* for information on all of the above). To arrange a guide for any hiking or mountain climbing expedition or for more information on hiking sites, contact the tourist office in Plymouth (see *Tourist Information*); or call Gerard Gray, the Chief Forestry Officer, or Claude Gerald, the Director of Agriculture, at the *Department of the Environment* (the Groves, Plymouth; 491-2075/76).

SAILING CRUISES Day cruises around Montserrat on Captain Martin Haxby's 46-foot trimaran, the *John Willie,* provide access to Rendezvous Bay (and on request, the offshore island of Redonda which is owned by Antigua and Barbuda), along with an open bar and snorkeling gear. Arrangements can be made through Captain Haxby (phone: 491-5738) or the *Vue Pointe* hotel (see *Checking In*).

SCUBA DIVING AND SNORKELING Montserrat's unspoiled reefs boast a variety of corals and sponges. *Sea Wolf Diving School* (George St., Plymouth; phone: 491-7807) offers one-and two-tank dives as well as certification courses. The *Vue Pointe* hotel (see *Checking In*) offers its guests complimentary use of snorkeling equipment (none is available for non-guests). *Aquatic Discoveries* (Old Road Bay next to the *Vue Pointe* hotel; phone: 491-FISH) offers all levels of *PADI* certification, whale watching, evening sea-turtle watching, and underwater videotaping. *Danny's Watersports* (Old Road Bay; phone: 491-5645) rents equipment and offers lessons in snorkeling, wind-surfing, sailing, and water skiing. Otherwise, you'll need to bring your own equipment or take one of the sailing cruises offered (see above). Woodlands and Lime Kiln are the most popular beach choices for snorkeling and diving.

SPORT FISHING The fish are out there, but special arrangements must be made to get at them. The tourist board (see *Tourist Information*) or your hotel can set up something with a local fisherman. Bringing your own tackle will facilitate matters. *Danny's Watersports* (see *Scuba Diving and Snorkeling*, above) also offers half- and full-day charters.

SWIMMING AND SUNNING The most popular and crowded beach for sunning is Old Road Bay Beach. There are volcanic sand beaches on both coasts, which are easily reached by car or are within walking distance of most hotels. The island's only stretch of white sand, Rendezvous Beach, can be reached either by boat (see *Sailing Cruises,* above) or by a 30-minute hike from Little Bay. Most of the hotels and villas have pools and lounging areas.

TENNIS The *Vue Pointe* hotel has two lighted, hard-surface courts on which non-guests can arrange to play for a small fee. The *Montserrat Springs* hotel also has two lighted courts (one hard surface and one grass court). The hourly rates increase for night use. See *Checking In* for details on both hotels.

NIGHTLIFE

Nights, which tend toward the quiet, cognac-and-conversation side here, are occasionally enlivened by island entertainment (dance bands, singers) at local clubs or at the main hotels. The island has a disco—*La Cave* (Evergreen Dr., Plymouth; no phone)—where the locals dress to the teeth and dance until dawn. Other favorite "liming," or watering, holes are the *Green Flash* (Wapping, Plymouth; phone: 491-7557); the *Village Place* (see *Eating Out*); the *Hilltop* (see *Eating Out*); and the *Las' Call Beach Bar* (near the *Montserrat Springs* hotel on Richmond Hill; phone: 491-6738). Hotel parties—such as the Wednesday-evening barbecues and the Friday-night dinner dances at the *Vue Pointe* (see *Checking In*)—feature steel band music, occasional crab races, and relaxed fun.

Best on the Island

CHECKING IN

Montserrat offers a remarkable variety of accommodations to suit all preferences and pocketbooks. These range from luxury hotels to modest guesthouses, from studio apartments to six-bedroom villas. Most accommodations are located on the island's western coast, north of Plymouth. In the winter season, expect to pay from $210 to $250 per night for a double room with breakfast and dinner at hotels we've listed as expensive. A double room without meals will cost $85 to $100 at moderate places and less than $85 at inexpensive lodgings. Rates drop by about a third during the off-season. Hotels tack on an additional 10% service charge and 10% government tax (7% for villas).

Private villa rentals are an established part of tourism on Montserrat, and the primary choice of residence among island visitors. Be aware that most villas are set on breezy hilltops and not on beaches; however, most have private pools. Winter weekly rates run from about $900 to $3,000 and in the summer from $600 to $2,000. There is usually a one-week minimum stay, but occasionally bookings for five nights are accepted. Prices generally include maid service, gardeners, round-trip transfers to the airport, an orientation tour of the island, and refrigerators stocked with groceries; cooks and baby-sitters are available on request. Cribs, rollaway beds, and rental cars are also available at daily rates. Villa rentals can be booked through *Caribbean Connection Plus* (PO Box 261, Trumbull, CT 06611; phone: 203-261-8603), or on the island through the *Neville Bradshaw Agencies* (PO Box 270, Plymouth, Montserrat, BWI; phone: 491-5270; fax: 491-5069); *Montserrat Enterprises, Ltd.* (PO Box 58, Plymouth, Montserrat, BWI; phone: 491-2431; fax: 491-4660); *Montserrat Villas Unlimited* (PO Box 421, Plymouth, Montserrat, BWI; phone: 491-5513; fax: 491-7850); or *Tradewinds Real Estate* (PO Box 365, Plymouth, Montserrat, BWI; phone: 491-2004), among others. A complete list of agencies is available from the tourist offices in Montserrat and in the US (see *Tourist Information* and GETTING READY TO GO). *Caribbean Connection Plus* will also handle hotel reservations. Unless otherwise noted, all hotels listed below have air conditioning, telephones, TV sets, and private baths. All hotels are in the 809 area code unless otherwise indicated.

EXPENSIVE

Montserrat Springs This property, with its sweeping views of the mountainside, is within walking distance of town. There are 34 garden rooms plus six one- and two-bedroom suites equipped with kitchenettes. Amenities include two floodlit tennis courts, a beach bar, a 70-foot pool, a restaurant, and room service. There are also two hot tubs, one filled with fresh water and the other brimming with therapeutic mineral spring water that the hotel taps from a rivulet flowing from Galway's Soufrière. The Friday-night barbecues held in the winter are quite popular. Meals are not included in the rate. On Richmond Hill, overlooking Jumby Beach, to the north of the city (phone: 491-2481; 800-742-4276; fax: 491-4070).

Vue Pointe Overlooking the Caribbean and adjacent to the *Montserrat Golf Club*, this charming, truly first class hotel has 28 individual cottages and 12 double rooms in connected units (none of the accommodations is air conditioned). There's also a pool, two lighted tennis courts, a beach bar, and the island's most complete water sports setup. The dining room is one of the best on the island, with a very popular Wednesday-night West Indian buffet/barbecue (see *Eating Out*). The *Michael Symons Osborne Complex* is a multipurpose conference center and venue for theater productions. Old Towne, north of Plymouth (phone: 491-5210; 800-742-4276; fax: 491-4813).

MODERATE

Belham Valley Inn Small and intimate with only three units (a studio, a freestanding studio cottage, and a two-bedroom suite—none with air conditioning), these comfortable accommodations overlook the *Montserrat Golf Club* and are a five-minute walk from the beach. The cottage and the two-bedroom suite have kitchenettes, but don't miss the fine dining on the premises (see *Eating Out*). Old Towne, near Isles Bay (phone: 491-5553; 800-692-4105; fax: 203-261-8295 in the US).

Providence Estate House Set in a lovely, restored turn-of-the-century plantation house on a hill overlooking the northwest coast, this is a Caribbean-style bed and breakfast establishment surrounded by extensive gardens. Two guestrooms with timbered ceilings and stone walls open onto a poolside patio, where they share an outdoor kitchenette; there's no air conditioning, but the hilltop location makes it unnecessary. The rooms also share a living area with a telephone. Breakfast, which features fruit right off the 10-acre estate, is included, and dinners are available on request. Several beaches are a short drive away. St. Peter's, about a 20-minute drive north of Plymouth (phone: 491-6476; fax: 491-8476).

INEXPENSIVE

Shamrock Villas These 50 fully furnished one- and two-bedroom apartment-villas are a good value, with kitchens, white tile floors, pastel color schemes, and ceiling fans (no air conditioning). Some have TV sets, some views of the sea, and the complex is 400 yards from the beach. There's no restaurant on the premises. Pluses include a freshwater pool and twice-weekly maid service for a small additional charge. Richmond Hill (phone: 491-2431; fax: 491-4660).

EATING OUT

"Goat water," a rich, meaty stew laden with fresh vegetables (derived from Irish stew), is the island's unofficial national dish. Try a bowl of it at *Mrs. Morgan's* (see below). Another local delicacy is "mountain chicken," actually legs of the large frog native only to this island and nearby Dominica. Rum punches are the island's real specialties—each hotel and bar seems to have its own recipe. The most powerful belongs to J. W. R. Perkins, who bottles Perk's Punch, a rum-based brew with the kick of an island mule (it makes a great gift for the folks back home). Not including drinks, wine, or tips, expect to pay $50 and more for dinner for two at restaurants we've listed as expensive; from $20 to $50 at places described as moderate; and less than $20 at any of the restaurants listed as inexpensive. Restaurants generally add a 10% service charge to the check. Unless otherwise noted, all restaurants listed below are open for lunch and dinner. All restaurants are in the 809 area code unless otherwise noted.

EXPENSIVE

Belham Valley A stylish establishment with a romantic setting and a view of Old Road Bay, this was once a private home. Island drinks, fine French wines, and continental and West Indian dishes are served with piano accompaniment. Thursday's menu features Chinese food. Open daily; closed for lunch on weekends and Mondays. Reservations necessary for dinner. Major credit cards accepted. Located at the *Belham Valley Inn,* Old Towne, near Isles Bay (phone: 491-5553).

Vue Pointe A five-course *table d'hôte* as well as an à la carte dinner menu are offered at this dining room overlooking the sea. Especially good are the West Indian curried chicken, Bessie's beautiful lime pie, and the guava cheesecake. Don't miss the Wednesday-night barbecue; it's a real feast, with steel band music. Open daily for breakfast, lunch, and dinner. Reservations necessary. Major credit cards accepted. At the *Vue Pointe* hotel, Old Towne, north of Plymouth (phone: 491-5210).

MODERATE

Blue Dolphin With an eye-catching view of the town and the harbor, this eatery is plain, but it has the best local food on the island; the house specialty is mountain chicken. Open daily. Reservations unnecessary. Major credit cards accepted. Parsons Rd., on the outskirts of Plymouth (phone: 491-3263).

Emerald Café Set beneath a canopy of blooming hibiscus, this garden restaurant features seafood and sandwiches. Try a slice of fresh coconut meringue pie for dessert. Open daily. Reservations unnecessary. Major credit cards accepted. Wapping, Plymouth (phone: 491-3821).

Hilltop The weekend party place, featuring live music, a stocked bar, and an excellent restaurant serving a blend of continental and West Indian fare. Open Fridays and Saturdays from 6 PM to midnight; Sunday champagne brunch served from 10 AM to 2 PM. Reservations unnecessary. Major credit cards accepted. St. Peter's (phone: 491-8707).

Village Place The closest thing to a soul food restaurant on Montserrat, it was once the favorite local haunt of superstar musicians Elton John, Sting, Mick

Jagger, and others who used to record their albums at the now-defunct Air Studios. "Goat water" and fried chicken are the most popular dishes. Dinner only; closed Tuesdays. Reservations unnecessary. No credit cards accepted. Salem (phone: 491-5202).

INEXPENSIVE

Mrs. Morgan's This is the place to try the local stew called "goat water," a big favorite among the islanders. Open Fridays and Saturdays only. Reservations unnecessary for lunch; open for dinner by advance request only. No credit cards accepted. St. John's (phone: 491-5419).

Puerto Rico

Puerto Rico is finally overcoming its image problem. In the past, if you asked most mainland Americans, "Quick, name three things you expect to find on Puerto Rico," without hesitation they'd usually list glitzy hotels, Vegas-style gambling and nightlife, and poverty. All of these still exist, but they are just part of the picture. To a certain extent, they describe the city of San Juan, which is too often mistaken for the whole 3,435-square-mile commonwealth (more than a third of Puerto Rico's 3.6 million people live in the metropolitan area).

In fact, Puerto Rico offers extraordinary vacation variety, but in the past travelers in search of great sports, escapist resorts, and lush tropical atmosphere have looked to other islands—even though all of that can be found within an hour's drive of *Luis Muñoz Marín International Airport.* Today, however, more and more travelers are finding that Puerto Rico is—as it's described on local license plates—an "Island of Enchantment." Puerto Rico offers a fascinating blend of historical sites and natural beauty (from its 258 miles of beaches to its lush forests); sporting pursuits and museums; fine dining and exciting urban nightlife; and quiet fishing towns. Tourism is now booming, with visitor arrivals totaling more than four million in 1994.

Evidence of the tourism turnaround has appeared all over the island—more than $100 million has been spent to spruce up San Juan's old buildings and construct new plazas, with much of the work unveiled in 1992 during the island's commemoration of Columbus's discovery of the Americas. Marina Street, parallel to the cruise ship piers, is undergoing a complete $100-million renovation; it is also the site of a new hotel, the 242-room *Wyndham Old San Juan,* which is slated to open late this year. In the southern coast city of Ponce, $450 million has been invested in refurbishing historical sites, and another $70 million has been spent on renovation projects in 79 smaller towns and cities across the island.

Ecotourism continues to grow as well; in the spirit of renewed interest in nature and the environment, many travelers are taking day trips from San Juan to visit *Las Cabezas de San Juan Nature Reserve* near Fajardo, the *Río Camuy Cave Park* south of Arecibo (one of the largest underground river systems in the world), and Mona Island, home of rare, three-foot-long iguanas, among other exotic creatures. For astronomy fans, the *Arecibo Observatory* houses the world's largest radar/radio telescope; a new visitor's center is scheduled to open early this year.

Puerto Rico also offers accommodations throughout the island in a wide range of styles and price categories. San Juan does have some luxury properties as tall and determined to dazzle as those along the Atlantic City boardwalk, but it also provides alternatives ranging from smaller hotels and condominiums to well-run guesthouses. There are even more choices *en la*

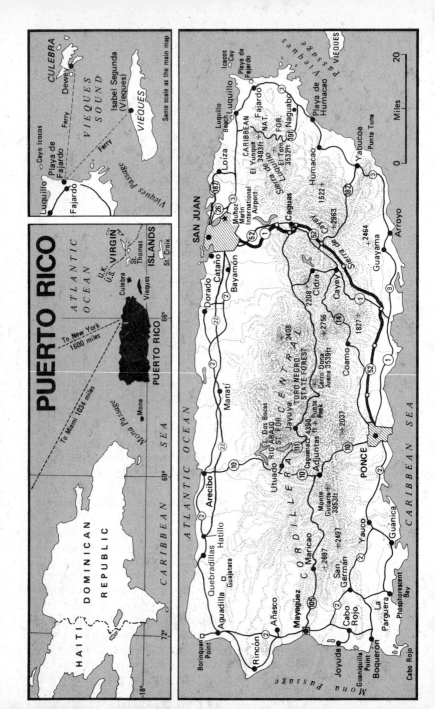

isla ("out on the island," meaning beyond San Juan), from fine resorts and sports-oriented villages (such as the *Hyatt Dorado Beach–Cerromar* complex and *Palmas del Mar;* see *Checking In*) to casual seaside towns like Rincón, Guánica, and La Parguera (a favored spot for fishing). Finally, there is Puerto Rico's network of paradors, inns that have been awarded government sponsorship because of their unique atmosphere, interesting sites, fine food, and high standards of service and cleanliness.

San Juan's nightlife, while not so lavish in scale, often outstrips that of Las Vegas in variety and local color. The big hotels split their year's billings between imported stars and the best Puerto Rican performers, and they downplay their casinos, which are basically low-key and carefully regulated. There are also San Juan's flamenco shows and cafés—plus a number of late-playing discos. Dining out options include some outstanding hotel dining rooms, as well as good Chinese, French, German, Mexican, Italian, Argentine, Spanish, US-style, and Puerto Rican restaurants.

As for poverty, Puerto Rico—like every other island in the Caribbean—has its share, although Puerto Rico boasts one of the region's highest per capita incomes. But the progress that started with 1949's "Operation Bootstrap"—a program offering tax exemptions and other incentives to lure industry and new jobs to the island—has continued.

Operation Bootstrap was the first in a series of self-help programs that have changed the face and future of Puerto Rico. In the program's early days, the seven-block-square area within the Old City walls of San Juan was declared a historic zone, and 10 years' tax exemption was offered to anyone who would buy and restore one of its buildings. The result was the salvation of what is now known as Viejo (Old) San Juan, the city founded by Juan Ponce de León, who arrived on the island with Columbus in 1493. Ponce christened the island for his patron saint, San Juan (although the name the native Taíno Indians had for the island—Borinquen—is still used with affection and pride by Puerto Ricans).

After he became governor of the island, the first settlement Ponce de León established, in 1509, was at Caparra, south of San Juan Bay. By 1520 the Spaniards' hopes for finding gold here had dwindled, but the island's strategic importance had increased, so the following year the settlement moved to the more defensible peninsula on which it now stands. Since the name San Juan already belonged to the island, Ponce had to pick another for the city. Optimistically, he called it Puerto Rico, "rich port." Later, the city and island swapped names.

Building began on the massive fortifications still standing today; later a cathedral, a convent, and homes were erected. One of the prettiest of the latter, the *Casa Blanca,* was built in 1521 as Ponce's residence. But Ponce de León took off on his fatal search for the fountain of youth and never lived there. Today the building houses two museums (see *Special Places,* below). Its restoration, along with that of numerous other irreplaceable Old San Juan landmarks, has been accomplished under the caring eye of the *Institute of Puerto Rican Culture,* created in 1955 to foster the arts and an appreciation of Puerto Rico's heritage and folklore.

After a prolonged struggle, the island achieved autonomy under Spanish rule in 1897. It had barely begun to enjoy it when, in the course of the Spanish-American War, American troops landed at Guánica on July 25, 1898. With the signing of the Treaty of Paris in April of 1899, Puerto Ricans took a giant step backward and again became subjects ruled by a foreign power—this time, the US. It was not until 1917 that Congress granted them American citizenship, and not till 1952 that the island, as a one-of-a-kind commonwealth (*estado libre asociado,* or "free associated state") under the US flag, was given its own constitution and government. While support for statehood has gained momentum in the past two decades, Puerto Ricans nevertheless opted to remain a US commonwealth in 1993, a decision that should keep the island's unique relationship with the US intact for the foreseeable future.

One battle the government and residents are still fighting is a high incidence of crime, especially in San Juan. Visitors should take the same commonsense precautions here that they would in any large city: Keep a close watch on personal belongings, avoid wearing jewelry in the streets and on the beaches, and be sure not to walk around deserted areas after dark. Another continuing problem has been the occurrence of occasional cases of dengue fever. This disease is carried by local mosquitoes, so remember to bring a good supply of bug repellent with you.

Nevertheless, it is easy to see why Puerto Rico is the Caribbean's most popular tourist destination, far ahead of any other island in the region. In addition to its varied attractions, it offers mainlanders especially an appealing blend of the familiar and the foreign. Puerto Ricans buy (and sell) American products (the island is the tenth-largest overseas market for goods manufactured on the mainland), crack American jokes, and watch American cable television; at the same time, they maintain a strong sense of pride and heritage, and relish being able to impress it on visitors. "I know this is a great place to live," said the owner of a Humacao Exxon station, chatting as he pumped gas into a rental car. "So . . . I guess it's a great place to visit, right?" No arguments here.

Puerto Rico At-a-Glance

FROM THE AIR

Puerto Rico is the smallest and the easternmost of the group of islands known as the Greater Antilles, which also includes Cuba, Jamaica, and Hispaniola (the island shared by Haiti and the Dominican Republic). With a landmass of more than 3,500 square miles (measuring 110 miles from east to west and 35 miles from north to south), it is roughly three-fourths the size of Jamaica, and about as rectangular as an island can get. The commonwealth's nearest neighbors are the Dominican Republic, about 54 miles west, and the US Virgin Island of St. Thomas, 40 miles east.

Its capital, San Juan (pop. 1.5 million), is on the north coast; Ponce, its second city, overlooks a bay in the center of the southern coast; and Mayagüez, the third-largest metropolis, is at the middle of the western shoreline.

Puerto Rico's 272-mile coastline is rimmed with beaches, but its mid-island spine of mountains—the Cordillera Central, plus the northeastern Luquillo and southeastern Cayey Ranges—creates a lush interior, a green northern sector, and a drier southern coastal strip, with a desert-like west end complete with cactus and arid soil. The commonwealth also has several offshore islands. Vieques and Culebra (to the east) are basically dry with some hills and uncrowded beaches; with 8,708 and 1,515 inhabitants respectively, both serve as getaway vacation places for islanders as well as for a few peace-seeking visitors. Icacos, a sandy spit a few miles northeast of Las Croabas at Puerto Rico's northeastern corner which is easily visited from *El Conquistador* resort, is uninhabited, but a favorite snorkel-trip destination; and little, round Mona Island, plunked down in the western sea passage of the same name, is barren plateau and cliffs.

From flight height it's not difficult to spot several of the island's most distinctive geographical features: El Yunque, the rain forest in the northeast; La Parguera's Bahía Fosforescénte (Phosphorescent Bay) in the southwest; the central island's mountain lakes, waterfalls, and teak forests; and the dramatic karst area, limestone earth pocked with deep, conical sinkholes and dotted with small haystack hills, north of the Cordillera Central. You also will see evidence of farming: sugarcane in the northern coastal plains; tobacco and plantains in the foothills; and pineapple in the center of the northern plain.

Luis Muñoz Marín International Airport on the eastern outskirts of San Juan, a modern, cosmopolitan, air conditioned facility, is 1,000 miles (2½ hours' flying time) southeast of Miami; 1,500 miles (3½ hours) south of New York City. Flying times from Chicago and Los Angeles are 4½ and six hours, respectively. Service also has expanded at the *Rafael Hernández Airport* in Aguadilla and the *Mercedita Airport* in Ponce.

SPECIAL PLACES

As they are in most old cities, the capital's streets are narrow and teeming with traffic. But exploring the seven-block-square Viejo San Juan Historic Zone on foot is pleasant and rewarding; pick up a map at the tourist office by the docks or use the one in *Qué Pasa,* the official visitors' guide. You'll spot more than 400 restored buildings, some almost 500 years old, with charming Spanish architecture of iron or carved wood balconies clinging to pastel-painted buildings.

Depending on your interests, you could easily spend two days exploring the nooks and crannies of Old San Juan, or spend a half day visiting the historic highlights and a half day browsing in the stores. The next most popular site after the historic district is undoubtedly El Yunque, the island's exotic rain forest. Tour companies offer dozens of guided half-day and all-day trips to El Yunque, and you can easily book one through your hotel travel desk. If you aren't all that interested in flora, you may want to substitute a day's snorkeling trip (see *Snorkeling and Scuba Diving,* below). Better still, rent a car, and combine an El Yunque visit with a drive across the island. There's much that's surprising and pleasing—including genuine charm and beautiful countryside—about the vast area beyond San Juan.

With first-rate roads circling the island and a superhighway from San Juan to Ponce, driving here isn't the bumpy adventure it once was. However, if you're visiting out-of-the-way places, factor in some getting-lost time, as many side roads aren't marked clearly. Also, modern roads haven't eliminated traffic jams—especially during traditional commuting hours and on weekends. To bypass the traffic, try to avoid—especially during rush hour—Route 26 to the airport, which joins Route 3 to El Yunque, and use the recently constructed Route 22 through Bayamón and westward onto Dorado and Arecibo whenever possible. Also, plan to do as much of your touring as you can on weekdays because residents take advantage of their free time on weekends to explore the island by car, causing increased traffic congestion. Or make the most of your time by flying to a point out on the island (like Ponce, Mayagüez, or Aguadilla), picking up a car there, and taking a slow, meandering route back to San Juan. Wherever you stay on the island, you should see something of the following:

VIEJO SAN JUAN

The seven-block-square area on the tip of the peninsula that forms the westernmost part of the city, Old San Juan was once completely encircled by the city wall—part of which still stands—and guarded by *Fuerte San Cristóbal* and *Fuerte San Felipe del Morro. Administered by the US National Park Service,* which provides tours of each, the forts are massively impressive and well preserved.

Two parking garages can be found on Calle Recinto Sur. If they are full, try the parking lot at La Puntilla, the waterfront district, which is located past the pink colonial customs house. Buses from the Isla Verde and Condado sections of San Juan leave passengers at the Covadonga parking facility or Plaza Colón. Free open-air buses and trolleys run through some parts of the area, including a route between Plaza Las Armas and Covadonga, but you will still have to walk to catch all of the sites. Walking along Old San Juan's hilly streets can be tiring, especially in the midday sun; bring a hat and wear comfortable walking shoes. Also see *Testaments in Stone: Historic Sites* in DIVERSIONS.

Note: Many attractions are closed or have shorter hours on some public holidays (the schedules are variable from year to year, so it's a good idea to call ahead or check with the tourist office).

Start your tour at Paseo de la Princesa (Princess Promenade), a tree-lined walkway that skirts the city wall. About halfway down the promenade, stop in at *La Princesa,* built as a prison in 1837. Now headquarters for the *Puerto Rico Tourism Company,* the building has been renovated as part of a major Old San Juan waterfront renewal project. Three cells have been reconstructed, and there's a restored courtyard, with fountains and royal palms. The 15-foot-high brick ceilings, massive mahogany doors, and brass accents provide a showcase for works by Puerto Rican artists. Closed weekends. No admission charge (phone: 721-2400). Continue along the promenade, which curves behind the seawalls and leads to the *Puerta de San Juan* (San Juan Gate) built in 1639 and formerly the principal entry into the walled city. Turn left onto Recinto de Oeste and left again at Caleta de Las Monjas. A shady path here leads to *El Morro.*

FUERTE SAN FELIPE DEL MORRO (EL MORRO FORT) Though smaller than *Fuerte San Cristóbal,* this fort (also known as simply *El Morro*) is more dramatic. Housed within its gray, 16-foot-thick walls is a museum with artifacts from early colonial times. The main battlements were built in 1591 on a foundation of earlier defense works that dated back to 1539. In 1595, *El Morro* was credited with preventing Sir Francis Drake from entering San Juan Harbor. It was attacked many times—mostly unsuccessfully. Since 1783 the fort has been a single compact unit with six levels looming 140 feet above the sea and its large land area laced with many tunnels. (If you arrive by taxi, have the driver take you all the way into the fort; you'll get all the exercise you need on the long walk out.) Open daily. Guided tours are at 10 and 11 AM and 2, 3, and 4 PM. No admission charge. Calle Norzagaray (phone: 729-6960).

MUSEO DE LAS AMÉRICAS (MUSEUM OF THE AMERICAS) Housed in the *Cuartel de Ballajá,* where Spanish troops once were quartered, this museum contains anthropological exhibits and folk art such as ceremonial masks from Puerto Rico and several countries in Latin America. It also hosts periodic exhibits of well-known Latin American artists. Closed Mondays. No admission charge. On the west side of the Plaza del Quinto (phone: 724-5052).

FUERTE SAN CRISTÓBAL (FORT ST. CHRISTOPHER) From *El Morro,* follow Calle Norzagaray along the ocean until you reach this fort. Rising 150 feet above the sea on 27 acres of land and consisting of five independent units connected by tunnels and dry moats, it walls the north side of Avenida Muñoz Rivera, the route that brings you from the Condado hotel strip to the old sector. The fort was built from 1766 to 1772 to supplement *El Morro* and defend the land side of the city. Open daily. Tours are at 10 and 11 AM and 2, 3, and 4 PM. No admission charge. Calle Norzagaray (phone: 729-6960).

MUSEO DE ARTE E HISTORIA (ART AND HISTORY MUSEUM) Across the street and a short stroll westward from *Fuerte San Cristóbal* is this museum set in a former marketplace. This institution houses a small number of artifacts from Puerto Rico's colonial period. (Unfortunately, many of its treasures were destroyed during the storm or stolen in the looting that followed, but the government plans to replenish the collection over time.) Several galleries display changing exhibits as well. Closed weekends. No admission charge. Calle Norzagaray (phone: 724-1875).

PLAZA DEL QUINTO CENTENARIO (QUINCENTENNIAL PLAZA) West of the *Museo de Arte e Historia* and facing Calle Norzagaray is one of the newest plazas in Old San Juan. Opened in 1992 during the island's festivities to commemorate Columbus's arrival in the Americas, this controversial square created from a parking lot has been criticized by local residents because its modern touches clash with the surrounding architecture. The most intriguing sight here is a 40-foot-high sculpture covered with black granite and ceramic fragments, which its creator, Jaime Suárez, used to symbolize the earth and clay of America. The plaza also has a fountain with 100 streams that symbolize the first 100 years after Columbus's discovery, and three flights of stairs to represent the next 300 years. Two needle-shaped columns point to the North Star, the explorers' guiding light.

IGLESIA DE SAN JOSÉ (CHURCH OF ST. JOSEPH) On the east side of Plaza del Quinto facing Plaza de San José, this is the church of Juan Ponce de León's descendants and the second-oldest church in the Western Hemisphere. The statue on the square is that of Juan Ponce himself. The famous conquistador's body was buried in this church from 1559 until 1908, when it was moved to the cathedral. His coat of arms still hangs above the *San José* altar. The vaulted Gothic ceilings are reminiscent of 16th-century Spain. Calle Cristo (phone: 725-7501).

MUSEO DE PABLO CASALS (PABLO CASALS MUSEUM) At the corner of Plaza de San José, adjacent to the church, this museum houses memorabilia Casals (1876–1973) left to the people of Puerto Rico—including manuscripts and the cello of the Catalan maestro. Closed Sundays and Mondays. Admission charge (phone: 723-9185).

CASA DE LOS CONTRAFUERTES (HOUSE OF BUTTRESSES) Also on Plaza de San José, this is thought to be the oldest private residence on the island. Built in the early 18th century, it now houses the tiny *Museo del Grabado Latinamericano* (Museum of Latin American Graphics) on the second floor, where periodic exhibitions are held, and the one-room *Museo de Farmacia* (Pharmacy Museum), with a collection of porcelain and glass jars displayed in a replica of an old apothecary's shop. Both museums are closed Mondays and Tuesdays. No admission charge (phone: 724-5477).

EL ASILO DE BENEFICIENCIA (WELFARE HOUSE) Just across the street from *Museo de las Américas* is this handsomely restored 19th-century building, which was once used as a mental hospital. Today it is the headquarters of the *Institute of Puerto Rican Culture* and displays rotating exhibits of Puerto

Rican and Latin American art. Exhibition rooms closed Mondays and Tuesdays. No admission charge (phone: 724-5949).

CASA BLANCA (WHITE HOUSE) On Calle San Sebastián next to *El Asilo de Beneficiencia* is a serene white house that was built for Ponce de León (he never lived in it, however). After his death, his son-in-law, Juan García Troche, had the original frame house replaced with the present masonry one, where his descendants lived for 250 years; it was later a residence for both Spanish and US military commanders. The house is now the site of two museums: the *Museo Juan Ponce de León* (Juan Ponce de León Museum), whose exhibits illustrate 16th- and 17th-century Puerto Rican life, and the *Museo Etnohistórico del Indio de América* (Taíno Indian Ethno-Historic Museum), whose exhibits focus on the lives and history of the Taíno Indians. The gardens are open daily; the museums are closed Mondays and Tuesdays. Admission charge for the museums (phone: 724-4102).

Exit the *Casa Blanca* on Calle del Sol past "step streets" on either side, and turn right—downhill again—on Calle Cristo. A block's walk brings you to a shaded square. Facing it, on the east side of Cristo, is the city's main cathedral.

CATEDRAL DE SAN JUAN (SAN JUAN CATHEDRAL) First built in 1540, and extensively restored in 1977, the circular staircase and four nearby rooms with vaulted Gothic ceilings are all that remain of the original structure; the rest is predominantly early 19th century. The body of Ponce de León now rests in a marble tomb near the transept; a supposed relic of the Roman martyr San Pío (St. Pius) is enshrined near it. Guided tours weekdays by appointment. 153 Calle Cristo (phone: 722-0861).

EL CONVENTO (THE CONVENT) The imposing building with great wooden doors facing the square (on your right as you leave the cathedral) was built as a Carmelite convent in the 17th century. Nowadays it's a hotel (see *Checking In*) with a patio that's convenient for lunch or a refreshing drink.

At this point, those who've had enough sightseeing can continue down Calle Cristo, where they'll find some of the city's most enticing boutiques; to explore a bit more history, follow the Caleta de las Monjas (Little Street of the Nuns) from *El Convento* downhill to the Plazuela de la Rogativa at the city wall. Turn left on Calle Recinto Oeste and walk downhill to the *Puerta de San Juan.*

LA FORTALEZA (THE FORTRESS) Just past the *Puerta de San Juan,* this is the Western Hemisphere's oldest governor's mansion in continuous use. Its original single tower and patio were built in 1540, while its more palatial elements were 19th-century additions. Note especially the polished reception rooms, stately mahogany staircase, the mosaic-lined chapel, and the gardens. Free guided tours are given. Closed weekends and holidays. No admission charge. Calle Fortaleza (phone: 721-7000).

Leaving *La Fortaleza,* walk east (toward the city's center) on Calle Fortaleza and turn right on Cristo. At the end of the street on your right is a small park.

PARQUE DE LAS PALOMAS (PIGEON PARK) Named for its resident birds, this is a good place to rest and admire the surrounding cluster of antique buildings. Notice the tiny *Capilla de Cristo* (Christ Chapel), with its silver altar visible through glass doors. It's open Tuesdays from 10 AM to 3:30 PM. Also nearby is the *Casa del Libro* (House of Books), a scholarly book and bookmaking museum set in an 18th-century house. The collection of 5,000 volumes includes two original decrees signed by King Ferdinand and Queen Isabella; special exhibitions are held on the first floor. Closed Sundays, Mondays, and holidays. No admission charge. 255 Calle Cristo (phone: 723-0354).

BASTIÓN DE LAS PALMAS (PALM BASTION) Follow the wall east one block to reach this defense emplacement–turned–park for a great view of the bay and the mountains beyond.

From the park, turn north on Calle San José and walk two short blocks.

PLAZA DE ARMAS (PARADE GROUND) The former heart of the city, this plaza is faced on the west by the neo-classical *Intendencia* (Administration Building), which houses some Justice Department offices, and on the north by the *Alcaldía* (City Hall), where you can get tourist information at the center near the main entrance. Closed weekends. No admission charge (phone: 724-7171).

PLAZA COLÓN (COLUMBUS PLAZA) Located five traffic-filled blocks east of the Plaza de Armas whichever *calle* you take (San Francisco and Fortaleza are both major tourist shopping streets), this plaza is the site of the graceful *Teatro Tapia* (Av. Ponce de León; phone: 722-0407), a theater now restored to its 19th-century elegance and presenting ballet, concerts, and dramatic performances. If you're feeling hungry at this point, try *La Bombonera* (259 Calle San Francisco; phone: 722-0658), open daily with an inexpensive menu of tasty sandwiches and pastries; *Bistro Gámbero* (320 Calle Fortaleza; phone: 724-4592), serving pasta dishes on a patio decorated with plants and flowers; or the *Hard Rock Café* (253 Calle Recinto Sur; phone: 724-7625), another incarnation of the popular worldwide chain.

EAST OF SAN JUAN

LOÍZA As you follow Route 187 out of Isla Verde, the scenery quickly changes from a developed tourist zone into tranquil, rural countryside. About 15 miles east of San Juan, the palm-lined road reaches Loíza, one of the most colorful towns in Puerto Rico. With one of the highest percentages of African descendants in all of Puerto Rico, this town is known for its festive *Carnaval* (in July) and its shops; in particular, look for *vejigante* masks (brightly colored faces carved from coconuts). *Herencia Africana* (201 Calle

5; phone: 876-7006) is one of the best crafts stores. In late July the town holds an eight-day observance in honor of St. James the Apostle (see *Special Events*).

EL YUNQUE Continue on Route 187 to Río Grande, then pick up Route 3 and head east about 6 miles to Route 191, which climbs up into the forest surrounding El Yunque's 3,493-foot peak and that of its taller brother, El Toro (3,523 feet). The trip will take about 45 minutes from downtown San Juan. Officially called the *Caribbean National Forest,* this area was set aside by the Spanish Crown in 1876; later designated a forest reserve by Theodore Roosevelt, its 28,000 acres make up the only tropical rain forest in the US national system. El Yunque boasts 240 different species of trees, only six of which are indigenous to the continental US; it is also a bird sanctuary, and one of the few places where you can hear the call of Puerto Rico's national mascot—the tiny tree frog called *coquí*—in the daytime. There's also a waterfall-fed swimming hole (picturesque, but cold) and a rustic restaurant. It is almost certain to shower while you're there (100 billion gallons fall here each year), but don't worry: Rains are brief, and there are lots of shelters. For additional details, see *Natural Wonderlands* in DIVERSIONS. The *Sierra Palm Visitors Center* on Route 191 gives nature talks and slide shows. Open daily. No admission charge (phone: 887-2875 or 766-5335).

LUQUILLO BEACH Returning to Route 3, travel 5 miles farther east to this popular strip of sand. About 30 miles east of the capital, it is certainly the most famous of the 13 government-built *balnearios* (beaches with lockers, showers, and parking facilities available for a small charge). It's gorgeous, too—long, white, and lined with palms, but apt to be crowded on weekends. Bring your own towels; lunch or snacks ranging from lobster rolls to coconut milk, *pionoños* (spicy ground beef enclosed in strips of ripe plantains), and *pasteles* (meat pies, usually pork, wrapped in plantain leaves) are available at stands near the entrance. Tent sites also are available. Facilities are closed Mondays during winter months, *Good Friday,* and *Election Day.*

LAS CABEZAS DE SAN JUAN NATURE RESERVE Continue along Route 3 and follow the signs to this 316-acre nature reserve, which features forest land, mangroves, lagoons, cliffs, beaches, coral reefs, offshore cays, and a 19th-century lighthouse. The reserve is better known as *El Faro* (The Lighthouse) and is surrounded on three sides by the Atlantic Ocean. Open Fridays through Sundays by reservation only; guided tours are given at 9:30 and 10:30 AM, and 1:30 PM (be sure to call well in advance since tours fill up quickly). Admission charge. Off Rte. 987, Fajardo (phone: 722-5882; 860-2560 on weekends).

FAJARDO About 5 miles south of *Las Cabezas* on Route 3, this small east coast seaport is bustling but relaxed. Ferries leave from here every morning and afternoon for Vieques and Culebra (see *Ferry Service,* below). At the small harbor at Las Croabas, you can hire a native sloop (capacity: six passengers) to take you out to Icacos for a swim; bring equipment if you want to snorkel. An ocean of water-based activities is available at the *Puerto del Rey Marina* (see *Boating*), including deep-sea fishing and day sails.

HUMACAO From Fajardo, continue along Route 3 another 20 miles or so until you reach this small town. Though not oriented toward tourists, it has a splendid *balneario*-equipped beach (facilities closed Mondays during winter months, *Good Friday,* and *Election Day*) and snack stands, too. Detour south to the beautiful 2,750-acre sports resort called *Palmas del Mar* (see *Checking In*). Have a swim and a rum punch (at the beach, not the pool—which tends to get overcrowded), and stay over in comfort. Or travel along Route 3 to Arroyo (another public beach—Punta Guilarte—is just east of town) and Guayama, where you turn right (north) on Route 15, which wends through the foothills of the Cayey Mountains. This road meets Highway 52 (the Luis A. Ferré Expressway, formerly known as Las Américas Expressway), which leads back to San Juan.

SOUTH OF SAN JUAN

PONCE From San Juan take Route 18 to Highway 52. About 70 miles south and west of the capital, Ponce is the island's second-largest city. Incorporated in 1692 and named after Juan Ponce de León, it runs the architectural gamut: Some buildings are handsomely historic, such as the dignified *Catedral de Nuestra Señora de Guadalupe* (Cathedral of Our Lady of Guadalupe), which dominates the central plaza; and some are notably modern, such as the small *Museo de Arte de Ponce* (Ponce Museum of Art), designed by Edward Durell Stone, architect of the Museum of Modern Art in New York City; and others are just plain kooky, like the red-and-black-striped *Parque de Bombas* (Firehouse) with green and yellow fanlights.

The *Museo de Arte de Ponce* (Las Américas Ave.; phone: 848-0511) is the best in the Caribbean, with a 2,000-piece collection. Its exhibitions feature the works of contemporary Latin American artists and European greats such as Rubens and Rodin, though it is best known for its pre-Raphaelite paintings and its baroque paintings and sculpture from Italy, Spain, and France. Included in the museum's permanent collection are several works by Puerto Rican artists Miguel Pou and Francisco Oller. The museum is open daily; admission charge.

A 40-by-80-block area of the city has been designated a National Historic Site and Treasure; walk around and see some of the 1,000 colonial buildings and lovely Victorian houses and banks (almost half of these were restored with funding from Spain and the Puerto Rican government for the 1992 celebration of the Columbus quincentennial and the city's 300th anniversary). Streets are again edged with pink marble and illuminated by replicas of 19th-century gas lamps. If you're in the mood for a cool drink or a bite to eat, stop at the *Meliá* hotel (see *Checking In*) off the main plaza, Plaza de las Delicias.

Then follow narrow Bertoly Street until you see a huge pink palace perched on a hill overlooking the city. This is *Castillo Serrallés,* a mansion built in the 1930s by the Serrallés family (makers of Don Q rum). The 15-room Spanish Revival house has been refurbished to look as it did during the 1930s. Most impressive are the huge windows that make the landscape— the Caribbean Sea to the south and the Cordillera Central to the north— seem like part of the building itself. Tours in English and Spanish are offered. There's also a display on rum production and a café. The house is closed Mondays; admission charge (phone: 259-1774).

Next to *Castillo Serrallés* is the 100-foot-tall, cross-shaped *El Vigía* (The Lookout) observation tower, which offers the best view of the surrounding area. The tower has been closed recently, but at press time was set to reopen. Call ahead for hours; admission charge (phone: 840-4141).

Just north of town on Route 503, the *Tibes Indian Ceremonial Center* is well worth a visit. Its exhibits include pre-Taíno ruins from AD 700 that have been restored to comprise a re-created village, a museum, and seven intact ceremonial ball courts. The center is closed Mondays; admission charge (phone: 840-2255).

On Route 10, *Hacienda Buena Vista* is a restored coffee plantation featuring re-creations of mechanical mills, slave quarters, a coffee husker, and photographs from the plantation as it was in 1870. Open Fridays through Sundays; reservations necessary. Admission charge (phone: 722-5882 or 848-7020).

COAMO Though nothing fancy, this mineral springs resort in the hills about 20 miles northeast of Ponce on Route 14 is a popular getaway for local residents. The on-site spa parador, *Baños de Coamo* (see *Checking In*), makes a pleasant detour or overnight spot.

TORO NEGRO (BLACK BULL) STATE FOREST In the central mountains on Route 143, 10 miles north of Ponce, the 7,000-acre preserve has the island's tallest peak—the 4,390-foot Cerro Punta—plus waterfalls, picnic tables, barbecue pits, a spring-fed pool (open during the summer), and an observation tower. With an early start it could be a day trip from San Juan, but it's easier from Ponce. There's a ranger's office on Route 143, where you can ask for maps and trail information. Open daily. No admission charge (phone: 724-3724).

WEST OF SAN JUAN

DORADO This town is about 20 miles from San Juan off Route 693, which turns north off Route 22 a few miles west of Bayamón. There are a few interesting gift and crafts shops on the main drag and a shopping center as you exit town to the north. It's the nearest town to the sister resorts of *Hyatt Regency Cerromar Beach* and *Hyatt Dorado Beach* (see *Checking In*), two good places to have lunch or a drink.

ARECIBO Return to Route 22 and continue another 30 miles west to this commercial town (pop. 93,000) by the sea known for its lighthouse, its beaches, its rum distillery (Ron Rico), and its goat cheese. This is also a tour turning point, with interesting attractions in several directions. To the south, Route 10 leads to a mixed bag of sites:

RÍO ABAJO STATE FOREST The entrance to this forest (10 miles south of Arecibo) is off Route 621, which intersects with Route 10. A 5,800-acre woodland (predominantly teak); it has a camping ground and recreation area (very pretty for picnicking), and a big, blue, artificial lake called Dos Bocas, on which there are launch trips. Also, two pools were under construction at press time. Park information is available at the ranger's office on Route 621. Open daily. No admission charge (phone: 724-3724).

CAGUANA INDIAN CEREMONIAL PARK Several miles farther south on Route 111 off Route 10 near the coffee town of Utuado, this is a 13-acre landscaped park with paved walks and plazas, and monoliths put here by the Taíno Indians 800 years ago. Open daily. No admission charge. Route 111, Km 12.3 (phone: 894-7325).

ARECIBO OBSERVATORY A special place with special visiting hours: between 1 and 4:30 PM on Sundays, and between 2 and 3 PM Tuesdays through Fridays. It has the world's largest radio telescope, with a 20-acre curved reflector installed over a natural karst sinkhole 1,300 feet wide by 300 feet deep. A new $2.5-million educational and visitors' center is scheduled to open early this year. If astronomy fascinates you, it may be worth the 35-minute drive from Arecibo, via Routes 129, 134, 635, and 625. No admission charge (phone: 878-2612).

RÍO CAMUY CAVE PARK The highlight of this 250-acre park just southwest of *Arecibo Observatory* is a series of limestone caves with stalactites and stalagmites, accessible by trolley cars. Guides lead visitors (45-minute tours are offered in English and Spanish) through the very cool caves 200 feet underground. There are also sinkholes (depressions in the earth made from the river eroding the land) that are open to visitors. The caves are two hours from San Juan. No reservations are necessary, but it's wise to call ahead to see if space is available. Closed Mondays and Tuesdays. Admission charge. Rte. 129, south of Camuy (phone: 898-3100.)

JAYUYA (PRONOUNCED HAH-*YOO*-YAH) East and a little south of Utuado on Route 144 (about 30 miles from Arecibo), this is Puerto Rico's highest town, and the site of a former coffee plantation house, *Parador Hacienda Gripiñas* (see *Checking In*), which is now a most appealing inn. There's nothing to do but enjoy the view, the peace, the good food, the pool, the mountain air, and the evening cacophony of the *coquíes* (Puerto Rico's tiny tree frogs).

You may, however, want to skip this detour and head west from Arecibo along Route 22, picking up Route 2 near Hatillo; about 15 miles from

Arecibo is Quebradillas, site of the island's first parador, the *Parador Guajataca* (stop for turtle steaks, smashing views of the sea, and/or an overnight stay—see *Checking In*). A bit farther west is Aguadilla, site of a moderately-priced parador called *Faro* (phone: 882-8000).

RINCÓN Another 25 miles southwest of Aguadilla via Route 2 and Route 115 (there's a turn-off at Aguada, about 10 miles north of Rincón, or a bit farther on, just before Rincón—both take about the same time), this laid-back fishing town is famous for its great surfing beaches, such as Steps Beach, Dogman's Beach, and the Point (surfing's *World Championships* were held at Rincón in 1968 and 1988). It's also a good place for whale watching, as humpback whales can be seen off the west shore between December and March. For overnight stays there are several small, casual hotels, plus one of the island's finest, the *Horned Dorset Primavera* (see *Checking In*).

MAYAGÜEZ About 10 miles from Rincón on Route 2, this is Puerto Rico's third-largest city. A friendly, busy port that is known for its Victorian and Baroque architecture, it shines as a headquarters for exploring the western and southwestern sections of the island. Mayagüez once was considered the needlework capital of Puerto Rico, and intrepid shoppers may still be able to unearth fine embroidery and drawn-thread work in the older shops downtown. Adjacent to the western campus of the *University of Puerto Rico,* the *Tropical Agricultural Experimental Station* (Rte. 2, take the Ave. Post exit; phone: 831-3435) has grounds worth seeing, along with the Western Hemisphere's largest collection of tropical plants. It's closed weekends; no admission charge. There is also *Zoorico* (Rte. 108, behind the *University of Puerto Rico* campus; phone: 834-8110), the island's only zoo. It's closed Mondays; admission charge.

MONA ISLAND About 50 miles west of Mayagüez, this rugged island is inhabited by colonies of sea birds and yard-long iguanas. Its breathtaking, 200-foot cliffs have caves said to have been hiding places for pirate booty, and beautiful white sand beaches line the shore. The island is protected by the *National Park Service* and the *Puerto Rico Natural Resources Department.* Overnight camping is allowed (permits required) and there are also some cabins available for lodging. Several tour companies have begun arranging trips to Mona; for example, *Eco-Logic* in Mayagüez offers a six-day camping trip (phone: 832-7933). For more information or to apply for a camping permit, contact the *Puerto Rico Natural Resources Department,* located next to *Club Náutico de San Juan* in Miramar (phone: 724-3724; fax: 721-5984); or write to the department at PO Box 5887, Puerta de Tierra, PR 00906.

BOQUERÓN BEACH The government has installed several small cottages at this mile-long west coast gem of a beach located 20 miles south of Mayagüez on Route 101. There are *balneario* facilities, and the prices for overnight accommodations are very low (about $20 a night), provided an application is mailed four months in advance to the *Recreation and Sports Department* (Box 2923, San Juan, PR 00903; phone: 722-1551, ext. 225). *Note:* Weekends attract lots of local families and teens with boom boxes. *Balneario* facilities are closed Mondays during winter months, *Good Friday,* and *Election Day.* A little to the north of here are Guaniquilla Point, with a lagoon filled with spikey limestone boulders; tiny Buyé Beach; and a proliferation of seafood restaurants at Joyuda Beach.

EL FARO (CABO ROJO LIGHTHOUSE) At the island's southwesternmost corner at the end of narrow, bumpy Route 301, this century-old Spanish lighthouse (not to be confused with the town of the same name farther north) is worth seeing. The bright blue structure overlooks red cliffs and the ocean; locals claim that this is the best place on the island to view the sunset. The lighthouse itself is closed to the public (no phone).

SAN GERMÁN On Route 102 about 25 miles beyond *Cabo Rojo Lighthouse,* the island's second-oldest city (pronounced Sahn Her-*mahn*) offers tourists a couple of pretty plazas, a colonial atmosphere, interesting architecture (shops and homes with turrets and gingerbread trim), and the island's oldest church (1606), the winsome *Porta Coeli* (Heaven's Gate), now a museum of religious art with some pieces dating from the late 16th century. The museum was closed for restorations at press time, but is scheduled to reopen late this summer (phone: 892-5845). A charmingly restored hotel, the *Parador Oasis* (see *Checking In*), is also here.

LA PARGUERA On Route 304, this tiny fishing village on the south coast 12 miles south of San Germán is a popular tourist spot among Puerto Ricans: there's a friendly inn, the *Villa Parguera* (see *Checking In*), several casual, open-air seafood restaurants, and the famous Phosphorescent Bay, where micro-organisms cause the water to glow eerily in the dark. There are nightly glass-bottom boat tours of the bay (which also is reachable by car via Route 324); sport fishing is popular here as well.

GUÁNICA A small beach resort about 15 miles from La Parguera on Route 116, also on the south coast, this is where US troops first landed on the island during the Spanish-American War of 1898. It's got lots of sand, space, and an informal (and moderately priced) hotel, the *Copamarina Beach* (phone: 821-0505; 800-981-4676; fax: 821-0070). Also here is the dry Bosque de Guánica (Guánica Forest) on Route 333, with 40 species of birds and 12 hiking trails. It's open daily; no admission charge (phone: 724-3724).

EXTRA SPECIAL

The Ruta Panorámica (Panoramic Route) meanders across the Cordillera Central and the Cayey Range from Mayagüez on the west coast to Yabucoa and *Punta Tuna Lighthouse* at the southeast corner of the island. Built for scenery, not speed, it comprises 40 roads over 165 miles that offer stunning vistas all the way, often with rain forest on both sides. It intersects with principal north-south routes so even if you can't spare the three days recommended to drive the route, you can enjoy random samples. Several inns and paradors lie a few miles north or south for comfortable overnight accommodations. The *Puerto Rico Tourism Company's* publication *Qué Pasa* contains a map highlighting points of interest on the route (see *Local Coverage*). Manual transmission and good reflexes are advised for the often twisting, turning route, and those susceptible to motion sickness should be forewarned.

Sources and Resources

TOURIST INFORMATION

The *Puerto Rico Tourism Company* operates several US offices (for information, see GETTING READY TO GO). They also maintain information centers at two key tourist points in San Juan: at the *Luis Muñoz Marín International Airport* (phone: 791-1014 or 791-2551) and *La Casita Information Center* in Old San Juan (Plaza Darsenas, near Pier One; phone: 722-1709; fax: 722-5208). Both are open daily. In Ponce, there's a small tourism office on the second floor of the *Citibank* building (Dedetao St., Plaza de las Delicias; phone: 841-8044). Elsewhere on the island, tourist information is available in the city halls of Adjuntas, Añasco, Bayamón, Cabo Rojo, Camuy, Culebra, Dorado, Fajardo, Guánica, Jayuya, Luquillo, Mayagüez, Naguabo, and Vieques. All are closed weekends.

LOCAL COVERAGE The *San Juan Star,* Puerto Rico's English-language newspaper, is published every morning. *El Vocero* and *El Nuevo Día* are Spanish-language dailies. New York City and Miami newspapers usually are available on the day of publication in hotels and at the *Bookstore* (255 Calle San José, Viejo San Juan; phone: 724-1815).

Qué Pasa, the free official visitors' guide published quarterly by the tourist office, is the best of its kind in the Caribbean, with information on special events, sports, sights, lodging, restaurants, transportation, and shopping in San Juan and out on the island. Get one at your hotel desk or at any information center. Ask at the tourist office for maps of historic sites and material on galleries and craft studios. A magazine/guide available only in Puerto Rico, *Walking Tours of Old San Juan* (Publishing Resources, Inc.; $2), packs in lots of visitors' information. *Puerto Rico: A Political and Cultural History,* by Arturo Morales Carrión (W. W. Norton; $13.95), is good reading for history buffs, as is *A Short History of Puerto Rico,* by Morton J. Golding, which is out of print (but you may be able to find a copy at the library).

RADIO AND TELEVISION WOSO-AM (1030 AM) broadcasts in English local and international news, talk shows, music, and sometimes major stateside sports events; NewsTalk (1560 AM) is a new English-language station offering news and talk shows. Several cable stations offer TV programs from the mainland.

TELEPHONE The area code for Puerto Rico is 809. Dial 343-2020 for the police; 754-2222 for an ambulance in San Juan; 754-2250 for an ambulance elsewhere on the island.

ENTRY REQUIREMENTS Neither passports nor visas are required of US or Canadian citizens, but Canadians must carry some form of identification (such as a birth certificate).

CLIMATE AND CLOTHES It's warm and sunny year-round on the island's resort coasts, always 5 to 10F cooler in the mountains. Winter temperatures in San Juan range from the low 70s F (about 22C) to the low 80s F (27 to 29C). In summer, the spread edges up about 5F. The wettest months are May to December; you're least likely to need an umbrella in March and April. As a general rule, however, there's more rain on the north coast than in the south.

In San Juan, clothing needs range from daytime beachwear to nighttime casino attire. But keep in mind that, beyond the hotel strip, San Juan is both a city and Spanish in its heritage. That means no short shorts downtown, in churches, or in public buildings. And it means nights are dressier—especially in casinos, nightclubs, and the tonier restaurants. Women should carry sweaters or light wraps to foil air conditioning drafts.

At the larger sports resorts out on the island (*Hyatt Dorado Beach, Hyatt Regency Cerromar Beach,* and to a somewhat lesser extent, *Palmas del Mar*), days call for classic sports clothes (tennis togs are required on the courts); nights go tieless but call for a certain sense of style, with blazers or jackets preferred for men, casual resort eveningwear for women.

Both in cities and out on the island, dress is generally more casual at smaller hotels and guesthouses.

MONEY The US dollar is official in Puerto Rico, though some places will—reluctantly—accept Canadian currency. Major credit cards are widely accepted in Puerto Rican hotels, restaurants, and shops. Banking hours are from 9 AM to 2:30 PM on weekdays, except holidays. The big US banks all have branches on the island.

LANGUAGE In cities and major tourist resorts, English is always understood, usually spoken. With islanders, however, the homegrown variety of Spanish is still *número uno*.

TIME Clocks keep atlantic standard time—that's one hour ahead of eastern standard time, the same as eastern daylight saving time. So in winter, when it's noon in New York it's 1 PM in San Juan. From April until late October, noon in the eastern US is noon in Puerto Rico.

CURRENT It's 110 volts, 60 cycles—the same as in the continental US and Canada.

TIPPING The commonwealth's system is like that in the continental US. Airport porters expect $1 per bag; taxi drivers, 15% of the fare. Leave $1 to $2 per room per day for the hotel chambermaid; give the doorman 50¢ to $1 for calling a cab. The standard tip in hotel dining rooms and supper clubs is 15%; and, unless the package tour you bought specifically states otherwise, remember that the included meal coupons usually do not cover tips, so leave 15% of your estimated cost of the meal.

GETTING AROUND

BUS Neat, handy, and inexpensive, they run day and night for a fare of 25¢ or 50¢, depending on the route. City terminals are at the Plaza Colón and the Covadonga parking garage; elsewhere, bus stops are marked by yellow posts or metal standards reading "Parada" or "Parada de Guaguas." Routes to note: No. 1, marked "Río Piedras," which goes through the banking district in Hato Rey to the *University of Puerto Rico;* and No. A7, which runs from Old San Juan to Condado, Isla Verde, and the airport. Bus lanes run against traffic on main thoroughfares. For additional information call 250-6064 or 763-4141.

CAR RENTAL Rental cars are easy to come by. *Avis* (phone: 721-4499), *Budget* (phone: 791-3600), *Hertz* (phone: 791-0844), *National* (phone: 791-1805 or 791-1851), and *Thrifty* (phone: 253-2525) are all represented in downtown San Juan, some Condado and Isla Verde hotels, *Isla Verde Airport,* and in Ponce and Mayagüez as well. Local firms like *Afro* (phone: 724-3720 or 723-8287), *L&M* (phone: 725-8416 or 725-8307; 800-666-0807), and *Target* (phone: 783-6592 or 728-1447) offer special low cash deals; they do take credit cards, but don't have reassuring offices out on the island. For a day trip out of San Juan, they're okay. For longer tours, the internationals are probably a wiser choice. Always opt for air conditioning.

Puerto Rican speed limits are given in miles per hour, but road signs show distances in kilometers. (A kilometer equals roughly 0.6 of a mile.) Also, the car horn remains a basic Puerto Rican driving tool. On twisting roads out on the island, it's imperative that you honk when approaching blind curves to warn oncoming cars to keep right.

FERRY SERVICE Boats sail every half hour from the small pier next to Pier One for the little town of Cataño across the bay; it's a neat $1 (round-trip) way to cool off any day, but in July, when the population stages a fiesta in honor of its patron saint, it's a ticket to a party with parades, booths, rides, dancing, and all sorts of fun in the streets. From Fajardo, at the eastern end of the island, a *Port Authority* launch makes daily morning and afternoon trips carrying passengers only to the islands of Vieques and Culebra. One-way fare: about $2 per person. Weekdays, a ferry carrying cars also makes trips. If you want to take a car (a good idea for visiting all the hidden beaches on these islands), call the *Port Authority* (phone: 863-0705; 800-981-2005 in

Puerto Rico) weekdays for reservations and a current schedule; the round-trip fare is $25.

INTRA- AND INTER-ISLAND FLIGHTS In Puerto Rico, *American Airlines' American Eagle* (phone: 749-1747) flies from San Juan to Ponce and Mayagüez. *Vieques Air-Link* (phone: 722-3736) offers frequent daily flights (in small eight-seaters) from San Juan's *Isla Grande Airport* to Vieques. The airline also flies from Vieques to St. Croix. *Flamenco* (phone: 723-8110) flies to Culebra from *Isla Grande Airport,* next to the downtown area and handy to Old San Juan and close-in Condado hotels. Numerous flights (95 daily) connect Puerto Rico and other Caribbean islands. St. Thomas is a short 30 minutes away, and St. Croix, 45 minutes. *American Eagle* has daily service to St. Thomas and to La Romana in the Dominican Republic. Charters are available to other parts of the Caribbean through *Pravco* (phone: 253-3000) at *Luis Muñoz Marín International Airport.*

PÚBLICOS Cars or minibuses whose license plate numbers are followed by the letters "PD" or "P" provide point-to-point transport all over the island for reasonable rates. Basic routes run from Town A plaza to Town B plaza, with drivers stopping to pick up or drop passengers anywhere along the route. They are insured, and the *Public Service Commission* sets the prices. If your Spanish is in working order and your schedule is flexible, you might give them a whirl.

SEA EXCURSIONS A 2½-hour sunset cruise around San Juan Harbor is offered by *Caribe Aquatic Adventures* (phone: 724-1882); the cost includes beer and refreshments. The *Condado Plaza* (see *Checking In*) has dinner cruises for groups of 10 or more.

The *Palmas del Mar* marina, near Humacao, arranges skippered charters for a day or longer (phone: 852-6000). And from La Parguera (the *Villa Parguera* pier), boats depart from 7:30 PM through 12:30 AM (depending on demand) on moonless nights for a firsthand look at the luminous wonders of Phosphorescent Bay. Even on evenings when the moon is out, you can witness the sparkling phenomenon on early trips; best are the glass-bottom boats.

SIGHTSEEING BUS TOURS A number of firms offer daily rain forest tours and assorted trips to the Bacardi rum distillery, *El Comandante* racetrack, and Ponce. Principal companies are *Gray Line* (phone: 727-8080), *United Tour Guides* (phone: 725-7605 or 723-5578), *Angelo Tours* (phone: 784-4375), and *Rico Suntours* (phone: 722-2080 or 722-6090). Offerings change, so consult *Qué Pasa* or your hotel travel desk about current best values.

TAXI Cabs are found at the airport, near the cruise piers, and in lines outside major San Juan hotels. All cabs authorized by the *Public Service Commission* are metered (although the meter is not used on trips outside normal taxi zones;

for these, you and the driver should agree on a price in advance). San Juan drivers don't offer much taxi touring.

SPECIAL EVENTS

Puerto Rico has more festive occasions than any other Caribbean island. Numerous *Carnaval* celebrations take place in February; the city of Ponce holds one of the most exciting, with masqueraders, live music, and lots of street parties. The *Casals Festival,* begun in 1957 by the Spanish-born cellist-conductor-composer Pablo Casals, takes place in San Juan and at other spots throughout Puerto Rico, usually during the first two weeks in June. The festival features performances by the *Puerto Rico Symphony Orchestra* with internationally known guest musicians. Tickets are very hard to come by; for details, write as far in advance as possible to *Corporación de las Artes Escénico-Musicales* (Apt. 41224, Minillas Station, Santurce, PR 00940-1227). Every town has its patron saint, and holds a one- to three-day fiesta marking his or her feast day each year. On June 24 (though celebrations often start the day before), San Juan celebrates the *Fiesta de San Juan Bautista* (Feast of St. John the Baptist), when resort hotels often sponsor beachside barbecues that culminate at midnight in a traditional mass dunking—for good luck—in the surf. The eight-day *Loíza Festival* in honor of *Santiago Apóstol* (St. James the Apostle), one of the island's most festive celebrations, starts on July 25 in Loíza; there are 75 to 80 other such events. More than 130 Puerto Rican craftspeople participate in the 33-year-old *Barranquitas Artisans Fair* in mid-July in Barranquitas. Colorful masks and folk music characterize the *Festival de las Máscaras de Hatillo* (Hatillo Festival of the Masks) in late December in Hatillo. The *Bacardi Arts Festival* is a major annual arts and crafts festival held in December on the grounds of the *Bacardi Rum Plant* in Cataño.

Puerto Rico also seems to have more than its share of public holidays. Official national holidays include *New Year's Day, Three Kings Day* (January 6), *Martin Luther King Day* (January 15 in 1996), *Washington's Birthday, Palm Sunday* (March 31 in 1996), *Good Friday* (April 5 in 1996), *Easter* (April 7 in 1996), *Memorial Day, Fourth of July, Columbus Day, Veterans' Day, Thanksgiving* (November 28 in 1996), *Christmas,* and *New Year's Eve.* The island also celebrates its own *Día de la Constitución* (Constitution Day; July 25); *Cumpleaños de José Celso Barbosa* (José Celso Barbosa's Birthday; July 26); and *Día del Descubrimiento* (Discovery Day; November 19). On these days, banks, businesses, government offices, schools, and many museums are closed; when holidays fall on a Sunday (*Easter,* for example) the holiday usually carries over to Monday. But there are also half holidays, when banks and businesses remain open but government offices, schools, and some museums close. These include the *Cumpleaños de Eugenio María Hostos* (the birthday of educator and patriot Eugenio María de Hostos; January 11); *Día de Emancipación* (Emancipation Day; March 22); and the

Cumpleaños de Luis Muñoz Rivera (the birthday of the early-20th-century journalist and statesman; July 19).

LeLoLai, a musical expression borrowed from the song of the Puerto Rican *jíbaro* (freely translated as "hillbilly"), is the name of a year-round festival of weekly events sponsored by the *Puerto Rico Tourism Company,* which features native dance, music, and foods, as well as discounts on guided tours, restaurants, and car rentals. The events are included free in many tour packages. You can also buy tickets for individual events from information centers and hotel travel desks. For details, contact the company's New York office (575 Fifth Ave., 23rd Floor, New York, NY 10017; phone: 800-223-6530; 212-599-6262 in New York).

SHOPPING

The good news is that there's no duty on anything you take home to the continental United States from Puerto Rico. That's because US import taxes have already been paid. Which brings us to the bad news: Since the island is not a duty-free port, you'll find no ultra-low-price imported bargains. What you will find is a number of specialized stores and boutiques staffed with helpful people and stocked with island crafts that aren't for sale at home.

Island crafts take many forms: predictable (straw work, ceramics); useful (hammocks, men's *guayabera* shirts, *mundillo* or handmade bobbin lace fashioned into collars and tablecloths); surprising (weird *vejigante* masks, cheery papier-mâché fruit); and unique (guitar-like *cuatros,* hand-carved wooden *santos* figures).

Crafts centers include *Galería Epoca en Tourismo* (an open-air collection of artisans' stands clustered around *La Casita Information Center;* no phone); *Iquitos* (103 Calle Cristo; phone: 722-4212); and the *Centro Nacional de Artes Populares y Artesanías* (National Center of Popular Arts and Crafts; 253 Calle Cristo; phone: 722-0621), all in Old San Juan. In addition, two artisans' markets are open on weekends: *Mercado de Artesanía Carabalí* (phone: 722-0369) and *Mercado de Artesanía Puertorriqueña–Hermandad de Artesanos* (Puerto Rican Artisans' Market–Artisans' Brotherhood; no phone). Both are in Puerta de Tierra, between Old San Juan and the Condado strip.

To visit artisans' shops "out on the island"—*santeros* (*santos* makers) and mask makers in Ponce, basket weavers in Jayuya, or hammock makers in San Sebastián—visitors can contact the government-sponsored crafts program (phone: 758-4747, ext. 2291) or the *Tourism Artisan* office (phone: 721-2400, ext. 2201) to find out which artisans welcome visitors. Other excellent sources for authentic handicrafts are the craft festivals held annually throughout the island. They include the *Puerto Rico Weave Festival,* held in the northwestern coastal town of Isabela (May); the *Artisans Fair* in Barranquitas (mid-July); and the *Bacardi Arts Festival* at the *Bacardi Rum Plant* in Cataño (December).

The art scene on the island is alive and exciting, with contemporary Puerto Ricans working in every medium. Jan d'Esopo is a well-known local painter (and part-owner of the *Galería San Juan*—see *Checking In*) whose images of island life are sold in the *Galería San Jerónimo* in the *Condado Plaza* (phone: 722-1808). Luis Hernández Cruz, Myrna Báez, Francisco Rodón, Rafael Tufino, and Julio Rosado del Valle are among the island's best-known artists.

Rum, another source of Puerto Rican pride, sells for about half its stateside price, and there's no limit to the tax-free bottles you can bring home. Ask at your hotel for a nearby shop that sells stamped bottles (the average Puerto Rican liquor store does not), where you'll have a bigger selection than at the airport shop. Most Puerto Rican rums are fine and light, but the connoisseurs' choice is aged *añejo*, which has the smoothness and power of a good brandy. An excellent one, Ron del Barrilito, sells for under $10 on the island, just a little more than half its typical stateside price.

For a tasty education in the history and art of making rum, visit the *Bacardi Rum Distillery* in Cataño (take the ferry from Old San Juan and then a *público* or taxi to the distillery). The distillery is closed Sundays; no admission charge. Rte. 22 (phone: 788-1500).

Puerto Rican coffee, which is grown in the central mountain range and is noted for its rich and aromatic flavor, can be purchased in all grocery stores. Look for such brands as Café Crema, Café Rico, Rioja, and Yaucono, which all sell for about $3.60 per pound.

In Old San Juan, the good jewelery shops are clustered along Calle Fortaleza, including *N. Barquet* (phone: 721-3366) and *Letran* (phone: 721-5825), both at No. 201, as well as *Yas Mar* (No. 205; phone: 724-1377). Travelers looking for wearable souvenirs can browse along Calle Cristo between Calle Fortaleza and Calle San Francisco, the main shopping street for apparel in Old San Juan. For couture of an haute-er order, stroll along Ashford Avenue in Condado, where boutiques feature the originals of such locally known designers as Nono Maldonado, Fernando Peña, Annie Lago, and Milli Arango.

Most major hotels have shops that are branches of downtown establishments. In these, as well as in downtown stores and at most places on the island, price tags mean what they say. There's no haggling. Stores are generally open from 9 AM to 6 PM, Mondays through Saturdays; in Old San Juan, shops may extend their hours during high season if several cruise ships are in port; the 250 stores at *Plaza Las Américas* in the Hato Rey section of town are open until 9 PM on Fridays and from noon to 5 PM on Sundays. Major credit cards are accepted, except where noted. Among the many places where you might want to part with your money (all are in San Juan unless otherwise noted):

Bared and Sons Fine imported china and crystal, which the staff claims are 30% to 35% below US mainland prices. There are four stores in Old San Juan, all along Calle Fortaleza at: Calle San Justo (phone: 724-4811), Calle Tanca (phone: 725-7005), Calle Cristo (phone: 724-3215), and Calle San José (phone: 725-1731).

Galería Botello Among the best galleries on the island, it showcases the work of Botello and other Latin American artists, and has a fine *santos* collection. 208 Calle Cristo (phone: 723-9987) and at *Plaza Las Américas* (phone: 754-7430).

Gillies & Woodward Cigars made of island-grown tobacco. 253 Calle San Justo (phone: 725-5280).

Leather & Pearls Majólica pearls and Gucci, Fendi, and Mark Cross products at a slight discount. 202 Calle Cristo (phone: 724-8185).

London Fog Factory Outlet More than just rain gear, here are men's, women's, and children's fashions—all at substantial discounts. 156 Calle Cristo (phone: 722-4334).

Lord Jim Leather Imports Fine leather goods—from purses to wallets to suitcases— line the shelves here. 250 Calle San Francisco (phone: 722-3589).

M. Rivera Miniature Spanish-style houses (*casitas*), starting at $15, make unique gifts. 107 Calle Cristo (phone: 724-1004).

Nono Maldonado Trendy men's fashions for the *GQ* set. Two locations: 1051 Ashford Ave., Condado (phone: 721-0456) and at *El San Juan* hotel (phone: 791-7550).

Olé *The* place for crafts, including hand-painted watercolors and prints by island artists, leather sandals, and gourd masks. Antiques are sold at the back of the shop; the most interesting items are the *santos* from Puerto Rico and Latin America. 105 Calle Fortaleza (phone: 724-2445).

Polo/Ralph Lauren Men's, women's, and children's clothing, including jeans, at discounts of 30% to 50%. 201 Calle Cristo (phone: 722-2136).

Puerto Rican Art & Crafts The finest in artisanry from all over the island, including choice ceramics, sculpture, leather goods, and costume jewelry. 204 Calle Fortaleza (phone: 725-5596).

Riviera A must-see for anyone in the market for jewelry set with fine stones. 205 Calle Cruz (phone: 725-4000).

Spicy Caribbee An offbeat shop offering Caribbean spices, top-quality Puerto Rican coffee beans (selling for around $10 per pound), and cookbooks featuring local recipes. 154 Calle Cristo (phone: 725-4690).

SPORTS

The hotels along the San Juan–Condado–Isla Verde coastline naturally concentrate on beach and water sports, plus some tennis and spectator sports. San Juan's marina is a major departure point for deep-sea fishing boats. If you're really serious about your sporting life, head for one of the four extraordinary playing places out on the island: Dorado with its *Hyatt Dorado Beach* and *Hyatt Regency Cerromar Beach* hotels, the *El Conquistador* at the island's northeast end, and *Palmas del Mar* near Humacao (see *Checking In* for all). *El béisbol* (baseball) is big here, and soccer (called *fútbol*) is quite popular, too. Occasionally San Juan is the scene of title boxing bouts.

BASEBALL As beloved on the island as on the mainland. Games are played in stadiums in San Juan, Mayagüez, Ponce, Arecibo, Caguas, and Santurce from October to mid-April. Nascent North American stars often play with Puerto Rico's six teams during the winter season.

BOATING From San Juan, up to six people may sail on the 35-foot sloop *Airborne*, with drinks included, through the *Caribbean School of Aquatics* (1 Calle Taft; phone: 728-6606) in Condado. At *Palmas del Mar's Marina de Palmas* near Humacao, you can sign up for a full-day or half-day sail on a captained yacht to offshore Monkey Island through *Riviera Yacht Charters* (phone: 852-6000), or take sailing instruction (see *Checking In*). *Villa Marina Yacht Harbor* (phone: 863-5131 or 728-2450) in Fajardo also rents and charters boats. There is a massive marine complex at the upscale *Marina Puerto del Rey* (phone: 860-1000) in Fajardo, where the hurricane-proof harbor has 740 wet slips to handle boats up to 200 feet long and haul-out and repair facilities for vessels up to 90 feet long. The 600-acre *Marina Puerto del Rey* project is also home to *Club Náutico International Powerboat Rentals* (phone: 860-2400) and *Sea Ventures*, a dive shop that also has boats for rent (phone: 863-3483). Hotels offering rentals on a very-small-boat scale (Sunfish, Sailfish) include the *Condado Plaza, Palmas del Mar* in Humacao, and the *Hyatt Dorado Beach* (kayaks) near Dorado (see *Checking In* for all). Rowboats can be rented at the Condado Lagoon pier, and boating equipment is also available at *San Juan Bay Marina* (phone: 721-8062), *Isleta Marina* (phone: 863-0370), and *Puerto Chico* (phone: 863-0834) in Fajardo, and *Marina de Salinas* (phone: 752-8484) in Salinas.

COCKFIGHTING In Puerto Rico this gruesome "sport" is as civilized as it ever gets (which is not very) in the *Coliseo Gallístico* (air conditioned, with comfortable seating, a restaurant, a bar, and a fake-grass-carpeted pit) in Isla Verde. The feathers fly Saturdays from 2 to 9 PM (phone: 791-1557 to confirm).

CYCLING The *Hyatt Dorado Beach* (see *Checking In*) rents bicycles. Morning group bike rides are led by the activities coordinator assistant, who points out trees and tells tales of the plantation house.

GOLF Out on the island, more than 10 championship courses await the golf aficionado.

El Conquistador The 18-hole, 6,700-yard, par 72 championship course created by Robert Von Hagge that opened here in 1967 has been redesigned by Arthur Hills & Associates. The original course has been greatly altered, with 16 holes in completely different configurations. While the course features undulating fairways and greens, the severe rolling hills of the old course—never popular with amateur duffers—have been trimmed away. Nonetheless, the elevation and the winds combine to make this a real challenge. The location is as stunning as ever—atop a cliff at the northeast corner of the island, where the Atlantic and Caribbean converge, with spectacular views of the water and the El Yunque rain forest in the distance. The course is restricted to guests of the *El Conquistador* hotel. Las Croabas (see *Checking In*).

Hyatt Dorado Beach The two topflight Robert Trent Jones Sr.–designed courses that wind their way through this former grapefruit and coconut plantation are sufficiently difficult to make players regularly wish the land had been left in citrus cultivation. But that is only for those for whom the final score is everything. In fact, these are as good a pair of golfing tests that exist side by side on any island, and among the liveliest arguments heard around the 19th hole here are the discussions about which course is best (we vote for the East).

And if even these two fine layouts are not enough to satisfy your desire for assorted golfing venues, there is the added attraction of the two sister courses (also designed by Jones) just down the road at the *Hyatt Regency Cerromar Beach* hotel. Having all four of these to choose from permits the playing of your own private "Dorado Open," and that has got to be bliss for any golfer. Rte. 693, Dorado (see *Checking In*).

Palmas del Mar This resort near Humacao has what are considered by many the toughest 18 holes on Puerto Rico. Designed by Gary Player, its 6,600-yard, par 72 layout is a magnet for top tee-ers. Resident pro Seth Bull is the guy to go to for advice on the course's most challenging holes—11 through 15. He might also warn you about the 18th hole (par 5), which is as tricky as they come hereabouts. Golf packages are available at either of *Palmas del Mar*'s hotels—the *Palmas Inn* or the *Candelero*. Rte. 3, Km 86.4, Buena Vista, Humacao (see *Checking In*).

Other island greens: There's an 18-hole course under construction at the *Ponce Hilton* (see *Checking In*). *Punta Borinquen* at the old *Ramey Air Force Base* in Aguadilla (phone: 890-2987) has an 18-hole course. Other

18-hole courses are the new *Bahía Beach* course (Rte. 187, Km 4.2; phone: 256-5600) and *Club Riomar* (Rte. 968, Km 1.2; phone: 887-3964 or 887-3064), both in Río Grande, about 16 miles east of San Juan. The highly regarded *Berwind Country Club* (phone: 876-3056), just across the street from the *Bahía Beach* course, is the only private 18-hole layout on the island, but it does allow non-members to play, except on Wednesdays and weekends. The *Mayagüez Hilton* (see *Checking In*) arranges for guests to play at the private *Club Deportivo del Oeste*'s nine-hole course (Cabo Rojo; phone: 851-8880). At press time the nine-hole course at *Dorado del Mar Country Club* in Dorado was closed, with the reopening date uncertain (phone: 796-2030). Golf carts are necessary, as there are no caddies; clubs and shoes are available for rent at some courses.

Major tournaments include the *New York Life Champions Senior PGA Tournament* at the *Hyatt Dorado Beach* in December or January, and the *Rums of Puerto Rico National Pro Am* at the *Hyatt Regency Cerromar Beach* in November (see *Checking In* for both hotels).

HIKING The *Caribbean National Forest* has three verdant and well-maintained trails: El Yunque (from an easy 15 minutes to a more difficult two hours), Mt. Britton (1¼ hours), and El Toro (most ambitious, at eight hours). The *Sierra Palm Visitors Center* is near the park entrance (see *Special Places* for details).

HORSE RACING *El Comandante* racetrack in Canóvanas, east of San Juan (Rte. 3, km 15.3), is cheerful, colorful, and fun. Post time is 2:30 PM on Wednesdays, Fridays, Sundays, and holidays; admission charge. For additional details, see *Horse Races* in DIVERSIONS. The 900-seat, air conditioned restaurant opens at 12:30 PM on race days (for reservations, call 724-6060). Check with your hotel about packages including transport and entrance fee. Also ask at tourism information centers about *paso fino* meets (races between horses with a tiny, high-stepping gait) and rodeos.

HORSEBACK RIDING *Palmas del Mar* (see *Checking In*) has its own equestrian center and scenic paths that wind through a pine-laden nature preserve; trail rides, as well as jumping and riding instruction, are available. *Le Petit Chalet Mountain Inn* (see *Checking In*) offers rides on the beach at Luquillo or in El Yunque rain forest. You also can arrange to ride at the *Hacienda Carabalí* at Mameyes near Luquillo Beach (by reservation only; phone: 889-5820 or 887-4954) or the *Caribbean School of Aquatics* (see *Boating,* above).

RUNNING The annual *San Blas Half Marathon* draws international competitors each February in Coamo.

SNORKELING AND SCUBA DIVING Available through water sports desks at several major San Juan hotels. The *Caribe Hilton,* the *Condado Plaza Watersports Center,* and the *Hyatt Dorado Beach* (see *Checking In* for all) offer instruction and equipment rental. Coral reefs, cays, and mangrove clumps along the coast make for interesting snorkeling. From Fajardo, several tour operators go to the numerous cays and islands off the coast for a day of snorkeling and swimming (including lunch). Try *Sea Ventures* (see *Boating*, above) or *Spread Eagle* (phone: 863-1905). The best dive sites are off the *Caribe Hilton*'s beach (outside the reef there's a 33-foot drop with underwater caves) and a considerable distance out to sea. The *Caribbean School of Aquatics* (see *Boating*, above) offers daily scuba and snorkeling trips, as well as a five-day scuba instruction package. Or try *Caribe Aquatic Adventures* at San Juan Bay Marina (see *Sea Excursions*, above). Elsewhere on the island, *Coral Head Divers* (phone: 850-7208 or 800-635-4529), at the *Palmas del Mar* resort near Humacao, operates Puerto Rico's largest diving fleet. You also can rent equipment in La Parguera, Vieques, and Culebra.

SPORT FISHING More than 30 world-record fish have been taken in these waters. The catch: blue marlin (April through November); white marlin (April through June, October, November); sailfish (October through June); also wahoo, Allison tuna, dolphin, mackerel, tarpon, and snook, plus fighting bonefish in the shallows. José Castillo operates half- and full-day trips aboard his 38- and 48-foot yachts at the *ESJ Towers* in Isla Verde (phone: 791-6195 days; 726-5752 evenings). *Marina de Palmas* at *Palmas del Mar* offers half-day and overnight trips from *Karolett Fishing Charters* (phone: 850-7442) and *Maragata Charters* (phone: 850-7548). Rates usually include bait, tackle, beer, and soft drinks. The priciest trips available are aboard Captain Mike Benítez's island-famous yachts, the 45-foot *Sea Born* and 61-foot *Sea Born II,* which are berthed at the private *Club Náutico de San Juan* (phone: 723-2292); the day rate is about $625 to $1,200 for up to six people. *Club Náutico* is also the site of the *International Billfish Tournament,* a week-long event held every year in late August or early September.

SURFING A north and west coast pursuit. Pine Grove Beach in Isla Verde (north) and Punta Higüero, near Rincón (west), are the most popular surfing beaches. Rincón, site of the *World Surfing Championships* in 1968 and 1988, has been called the "Hawaii of the Caribbean." Within 10 miles, favorite surf spots include Tres Palmas, Steps, Indicators, Dogman's, and Dome's, possibly the most crowded. The best time to hit the waves is from October through February, at 6 AM. Punta Borinquen, near Aguadilla (west), is a good area for body-surfing, especially at Wilderness, Surfers, and Crashboat Beaches. Other popular places include Los Turbos in Vega Baja and La Pared in Luquillo. Mainland travel agencies that can arrange specific surfing tours include *Surf Express* (phone: 407-783-7184) for custom arrangements and *Par Avion Travel* (phone: 800-927-3327) for professional surfing groups.

SWIMMING AND SUNNING On the beach or by the pool, both are only an amble away from your room at the big strip hotels. But all San Juan hotel beaches are not created equal—check the hotel's setup before you make reservations. The *Caribe Hilton* and the *Condado Plaza* are among the best in the

Condado section (the *Hilton*'s beach is actually right on the border of Puerta de Tierra). In San Juan, the Isla Verde section has the best beaches by far. One caution: Rough sea conditions can sometimes create local rip currents or undertow off the Condado–Isla Verde hotel beaches, some of which do not provide full-time lifeguards. Puerto Rico's nicest beaches are away from the city. Out on the island, the *Hyatt Dorado Beach* and *Hyatt Regency Cerromar Beach* resorts have especially fine sandy shores. By law, all Puerto Rican beaches are open to the public. But the government has installed special *balneario* facilities (lockers, showers, changing rooms, and parking, available for a small charge) at 13 of the island's most beautiful strips, including one on Vieques (now referred to as "public" beaches). The facilities are closed Mondays during the winter, *Good Friday,* and *Election Day.* Luquillo, on the north coast about 30 miles east of San Juan, is most famous (although not as clean as it was pre–Hurricane Hugo) and most popular (too much so on weekends) with islanders as well as tourists. In San Juan, there's Escambrón in Puerta de Tierra and Carolina in Isla Verde. On the east coast, there's Humacao. Along the south coast are two beaches: Punta Guilarte, near Arroyo, and Caña Gorda, near Guánica. On the western shore there's Boquerón and Añasco (the latter not highly recommended). Along the north coast west of San Juan: Cerro Gordo, about 25 miles from the city; La Sardinera, near Dorado; and Punta Salinas, between Dorado and Cataño. Sombé Beach (called "Sun Bay" by locals) is on the offshore island of Vieques; with all the *balneario* accoutrements, but with a special sense of faraway privacy, it is very beautiful. Although it has no *balneario* facilities, Flamenco Beach on Culebra ranks among the best in the Caribbean.

TENNIS It's big stuff throughout Puerto Rico with about 100 courts in and beyond the San Juan city limits.

CHOICE COURTS

El Conquistador This sprawling resort offers seven Har-Tru courts (four are night-lighted). There's also a pro, a complete instruction program, and a clubhouse. If you don't have a partner, the hotel will find one for you. Only guests can play here, however (see *Checking In*).

Hyatt Regency Cerromar Beach/Hyatt Dorado Beach Courts are scattered all around this two-resort complex; if tennis is your consuming interest, be sure your room is near one of them. Both resorts host tennis weeks and offer special packages. At *Cerromar* there are 14 Laykold courts—one is a stadium court; two are lighted. At *Dorado* there are five Laykold courts by the pro shop, two courts at the west end of the property; two are lighted. *Peter Burwash International* handles instruction at both hotels. Given notice, they'll arrange videotaping and tournaments for groups (see *Checking In*).

Palmas del Mar A complex of condominiums at Humacao, where you should be sure to stay in the tennis village. Facilities are excellent; 20 courts, of which five are Har-Tru (more like clay), 15 Tenneflex (a harder surface), and seven lighted. Private lessons and instruction packages with the pro are available (see *Checking In*).

Another major complex is located at *Club Riomar* in Río Grande (phone: 887-3964 or 887-3064), with 13 courts (four lighted), lessons, and a pro shop.

In the San Juan area, the *Carib-Inn* hotel (phone: 791-3535) has four clay and four Laykold (and lighted) courts; instruction may be arranged. The *Caribe Hilton* has a topnotch setup—six lighted courts, a pro shop, instruction, and a program that matches guests with local players of equal talent; the *Condado Plaza* and *San Juan Marriott* also offer tennis (see *Checking In* for all three). You can also play daily on 17 lighted public courts in *San Juan Central Park* (phone: 722-1646). Out on the island, there are courts at *Punta Borinquen* in Aguadilla (phone: 890-2987); the *Mayagüez Hilton, Parador Guajataca, Ponce Hilton* (see *Checking In* for information on these three) and *Parador Vistamar* (phone: 895-2065) in Quebradillas; *Parador Villa Antonio* in Rincón (phone: 823-2645); *Hacienda Juanita* in Maricao (838-2550); and the *Baños de Coamo* in Coamo (see *Checking In*).

WINDSURFING Best setups are at *Palmas del Mar,* the *Condado Plaza,* and the *Hyatt Dorado Beach,* where rentals and instruction are available (see *Checking In* for all). *Ocean Park* in San Juan and Boquerón Bay are popular windsurfing spots.

NIGHTLIFE

Dining, going to the theater, dancing, gaming, and *LeLoLai* happenings are the options for a night out on Puerto Rico. The *Centro de Bellas Artes* (Fine Arts Center, Stop 22, Ponce de León Ave., Santurce; phone: 725-7334) presents a full range of concerts, theater, opera, and dance performances. More than a dozen casinos—where games range from baccarat to blackjack—are among the island's big draws. By law, all are in hotels with 100 or more rooms. In the San Juan area, they include the *Caribe Hilton, Condado Plaza, El San Juan, Sands,* and the new *San Juan Marriott* hotel; elsewhere on the island, there are casinos at *El Conquistador, Hyatt Regency Cerromar Beach, Hyatt Dorado Beach, Mayagüez Hilton, Palmas del Mar,* and the *Ponce Hilton.* (See *Checking In* for details on all of the above.) The atmosphere at the casinos is a bit formal and somewhat subdued. No drinking is permitted at the tables (you may order free coffee or soft drinks and sandwiches). Dressy (but not formal) attire for women and jackets and ties for men are firmly suggested after dark (especially at the *Caribe Hilton,*

Condado Plaza, and *Sands*). Casinos are open from noon until 4 AM; you must be at least 18 to enter. Also see *Casino Countdown* in DIVERSIONS.

The *Chart House* (see *Eating Out*) remains the best spot to kick off the evening with drinks in a congenial atmosphere. All the big hotels have nightclubs; in season, the *Caribe Hilton*'s classy *Caribar* (phone: 721-0303, ext. 1587) spotlights the best Latin talent; the *Condado Plaza*'s *Fiesta Lobby Lounge* (see *Checking In*) features a Latin revue, and its piano bar draws a crowd.

Other, less expensive alternatives are hotel lounges with combos for dancing and a minimum but no cover charge. *The Patio* at *El Convento* hotel provides piano serenades (see *Checking In*); the piano bar at the *Regency* hotel (phone: 721-0505) in Condado is popular with the business set; and the *Player's Lounge* at the *Sands* in Isla Verde features live music from noon to 4 AM (see *Checking In*). All of the flamenco shows are mild compared to the authentic, wailing Andalusian version. *El San Juan*'s *Club Tropicaro* and the *Palacio de Congresos* (Convention Center, phone: 722-8433) next to *La Concha* are some places to watch dancers click their heels; of the current crop of discos, one of the most popular is *Amadeus* at *El San Juan* (see *Checking In*). *Peggy Sue* (1 Robert H. Todd Ave.; phone: 722-4750) features 1950s and 1960s rock 'n' roll. For live jazz, try *Café San Juan Bistro* (152 Calle Cruz, Viejo San Juan; phone: 724-1198). *Shannon's Irish Pub* (1503 Loíza St., Santurce; phone: 728-6103) features rock 'n' roll bands, while the *Hard Rock Café* (253 Calle Recinto Sur, Plaza Colón; phone: 724-7625) sometimes brings in live rock and blues bands. If you want to belly up to a bar, try *El Batey* (101 Calle Cristo, Viejo San Juan; no phone) where graffiti-covered walls provide a colorful atmosphere for late-night conversations. *Café Violeta* (56 Calle Fortaleza; phone: 723-6804) offers a serene open-air setting for after-dinner drinks and occasional guitar serenades. After dancing, snack on burgers and omelettes at the *Green House* on Condado (see *Eating Out*) till 4:30 AM.

Out on the island, all's relatively quiet outside the hotels. The *Hyatt Regency Cerromar Beach* features music videos at *El Coquí;* the *Bacchus Music Club* at the *Mayagüez Hilton* also does its share of swinging; and there's live music at the *Vista Terrace Lounge. El Conquistador* lures latenighters with live entertainment and its *Amigos* nightclub. (See *Checking In* for details on hotels listed above.)

Best on the Island

CHECKING IN

In San Juan, accommodations range from very expensive, full-service resort hotels to small, cheerful guesthouses. Their counterparts out on the island are low-slung luxury hotel and villa complexes and the island's unique network of country inns called paradors (double rooms from $55 to $90), which can be booked in the mainland US by calling 800-443-0266 or the *Puerto Rico Tourism Company* (phone: 800-223-6530). (Note that paradors require a minimum two-night stay on weekends, and three nights on a weekend followed by a Monday holiday.) For information on individually run hotels, small to large, contact the *Puerto Rico Home and Tourism Association* (phone: 725-2901). The newest addition to the hotel scene is the *Wyndham Old San Juan;* scheduled to open late this year, this 242-room property on Old San Juan's waterfront will feature two restaurants, two lounges, a pool, a health club, conference facilities, and a 10,000-square-foot casino. For more information, call 800-822-4200. Other major new hotels in the works on the island include a beachfront resort at the *Marina Puerto del Rey* in Fajardo, and a Westin resort at Río Grande near Luquillo Beach.

Whatever the season—but especially in summer—check out package deals offered by airlines, tour operators, or travel agents. At the very least, they can mean free *LeLoLai* parties, special perks (waived greens fees for a round of golf, a San Juan bay cruise), and souvenirs.

For families, Puerto Rico's hundreds of rental and/or resort condominiums and hotel suites equipped with kitchens not only mean substantial savings on food costs, but added scheduling flexibility. Be aware, however, that the word *motel* in Puerto Rico usually means a place that caters to illicit lovers.

Hotels listed here as very expensive ask more than $300 (EP—no meals) per night for a double room in season; expensive, $200 to $300; moderate, $100 to $200; inexpensive, $75 to $100. Modified American Plan (MAP) arrangements—including breakfast and dinner—are often available for an extra charge of about $50 per person per day. Expect to pay 25% to 50% less during the off-season. There is a 7% room tax at hotels without casinos, 9% at hotels with casinos. Unless otherwise noted, all hotels listed below have air conditioning, telephones, TV sets, and private baths. Unlike on most other Caribbean islands, many of Puerto Rico's hotels have complete facilities for the business traveler. Properties listed as having business services usually include such conveniences as a concierge, meeting rooms, photocopiers, computers, and express checkout, among others. Call the hotel for additional information. All phone numbers are in the 809 area code unless otherwise indicated.

We begin with our favorite havens, both of which fall in the "very expensive" category, followed by recommended hotels listed by price category.

A REGAL RESORT AND A SPECIAL HAVEN

El Conquistador A massive $250-million development with 918 rooms in five "environments," this ultra-posh (and ultra-pricey) resort overlooks the Atlantic and the Caribbean from a 300-foot cliff. The property incorporates some structures from the original hotel on this site, built in 1962, while introducing such innovations as glass funiculars that transport beach-loving guests to the sand below. Sports-minded visitors have their choice of activities—there are 18 great holes of golf (see *Golf*), seven tennis courts (see *Tennis*), six pools, a health club and spa, a private marina with fishing and sailboats available for charter, and a private 100-acre island set aside for water sports. There are 16 restaurants and lounges, including fine dining at *Isabela's* (Caribbean), *Blossom's* (Oriental), and *Otello's* (Italian). A casino, evening entertainment, a children's camp, and business services complete the enormous picture. This resort is like a self-contained country whose raison d'être is your enjoyment. Guests are greeted by hotel personnel at the airport and transported in air conditioned luxury to the resort. 1000 El Conquistador Ave. (Rte. 987), Las Croabas, near Fajardo (phone: 863-1000; 800-468-5228 or 800-468-8365; fax: 863-8377).

Horned Dorset Primavera This hostelry with the unusual name is often described as Puerto Rico's most exclusive resort (and the island's only Relais & Châteaux member as well). It certainly is one of the island's most expensive properties, but in this case it's definitely worth it. Located on the west coast near Rincón's great surfing beaches, the inn, built of white stucco with a red-tile roof, has 30 small, elegant suites, some with balconies overhanging the sea. Each room has a four-poster bed and painted tiles on the floors, and flowers can be seen just about everywhere. There's also a swimming pool and a spectacular beach. The hotel is run by a twosome who have an inn in upstate New York—also called *Horned Dorset*—and the pervasive mood is one of tranquillity and serenity. Visitors feel as if they're staying in a luxurious private hacienda (with stunning appointments) rather than a public hotel. The food is also first class (see *Eating Out*); there are six-course dinners with fine wines and excellent service. Breakfast and lunch are served on a lovely outdoor patio. No children under 12. Bo Barrero, Rte. 429, Km 3, Rincón (phone: 823-4030 or 823-4050; fax: 823-5580).

SAN JUAN–CONDADO–ISLA VERDE AREA

VERY EXPENSIVE

Caribe Hilton Among the best hotels in town, this place has 668 well-tended rooms and suites, including a deluxe executive floor, plus landscaped grounds complete with an antique fort. The service is smooth more than 90% of the time—good by any island standard. Other features include a casino, beach, excellent tennis facilities, air conditioned racquetball and squash courts, two pools, children's summer and holiday day camp, a health club, three restaurants, business services, and the *Caribar* outdoor café. The poolside bar is yacht-size. Modified American Plan available in winter. Old San Juan is a short cab ride away. Calle San Jerónimo, Puerta de Tierra (phone: 721-0303; 800-HILTONS; fax: 724-6992).

El San Juan The centerpiece of this landmark is its Palm Court lobby—with a massive chandelier, rose marble floor, and hand-carved mahogany ceiling—where guests can enjoy afternoon tea and chamber music. Near the airport, it has 392 rooms, including guesthouses with private patios, one of San Juan's largest casinos, a nightclub, 24-hour café, lounge, the *Amadeus* disco (see *Nightlife*), the island's only *cruvinet* wine bar, and five restaurants, including *Back Street Hong Kong* (see *Eating Out*). There also are two pools, water sports facilities, a fitness center, and three lighted tennis courts. Isla Verde Rd., Isla Verde (phone: 791-1000; 800-468-2818; fax: 791-0390).

EXPENSIVE

La Concha Part of the so-called "Condado Beach Trio" which includes the *Condado Beach* hotel (see below) and a convention center, this property features a pleasant, large (but heavily populated) pool surrounded by fountains. There's a lovely beachfront with lanais, two tennis courts, water sports (including scuba), business services, a restaurant, a lobby lounge with flamenco shows, a poolside bar, and 235 rooms, all of which have terraces and ocean views. 1071 Ashford Ave., Condado (phone: 721-6888; 800-468-2775; fax: 724-7222).

Condado Beach Pretty though not plush, this Art Deco–style hostelry was built in 1919. It has fine service, 245 rooms (half with ocean view), the international *Vivas* restaurant, a pool, business services, and use of the tennis courts at *La Concha* next door. A dine-around plan for MAP guests is offered. VIP guests have a club floor, honor bar, and other privileges. 1071 Ashford Ave., Condado (phone: 721-6888; 800-468-2775; fax: 724-7222).

Condado Plaza A best seller for good reason: good looks, good service, 566 rooms outfitted with plenty of luxury amenities, three pools, tennis, fitness and conference centers, lots of daytime action, and varied nightlife, with several winning restaurants (notably the darkly elegant *L. K. Sweeney & Son Ltd.;* see *Eating Out*), and a big casino. The Plaza Club floor offers on-floor concierge service, key-only elevator access, a private lounge, and complimentary breakfast and snacks. The two-hotel complex includes the original beachfront property, plus the Laguna section, linked by a walkway across Ashford Avenue. 999 Ave. Ashford, Condado (phone: 721-1000; 800-468-8588; fax: 721-4613).

Radisson Normandie Built in 1939 to resemble the celebrated French ocean liner, it lay in ruins for years—little more than an Art Deco hulk opposite the

Caribe Hilton. Now beautifully restored, and a National Historic Landmark, this gem boasts 177 rooms (more than half are suites), and all the amenities for upscale leisure and business travelers (including two corporate floors), small groups, and conventions. Features include the handsome *Atrium Café,* a beachfront pool, and a jogging track. Calle Muñoz Rivera, corner of Rosales St., Puerta de Tierra (phone: 729-2929; 800-333-3333; fax: 729-3083).

San Juan Marriott The former *Dupont Plaza* was devastated by fire in 1986, but has reopened at last. The Marriott hotel group has spent about $130 million on rebuilding and refurbishing this luxury getaway, which features 525 rooms (including 13 suites), most with views of the ocean, and all with balconies and mini-bars. Five executive-level floors offer extra amenities and services. There are also three restaurants, two pools, two lighted tennis courts, a lounge with nightly entertainment, an 11,000-square-foot casino, a health club, and business services. 1309 Ashford Ave., Condado (phone: 722-7000; 800-228-9290; fax: 289-6060).

Sands Next to *El San Juan* in Isla Verde, this property offers 418 rooms (including 51 suites), all with private balconies. Situated on five acres along a stunning crescent beach, it features a huge casino, an enormous pool with waterfalls and a swim-up sandwich bar, four restaurants, a nightclub/disco, gift shops and boutiques, 24-hour room service, business services, baby-sitting, and a sophisticated sports and recreation program. The property offers an all-inclusive option; 90 rooms of the hotel comprise the "Diamond Club," where guests pay one all-inclusive rate for accommodations, all meals and liquor, shows, casino game lessons, non-motorized water sports, and more. Isla Verde Rd., Isla Verde (phone: 791-6100; 800-443-2009; fax: 791-8525).

MODERATE

Casa San José This charming inn, fashioned from a four-story 17th-century mansion, has 10 rooms and suites with old marble floors and antique furnishings (none with TV sets), an interior patio, and a large and comfortable upstairs salon, where afternoon tea and cocktails are served, though there's no restaurant as such. Rates include continental breakfast and evening drinks. No children under age 12 allowed. 159 Calle San José, Viejo San Juan (phone: 723-1212; fax: 723-7620).

El Convento Once a 17th-century Dominican convent in Old San Juan, this hotel now has all the modern conveniences. The 100 rooms and suites are smallish and the hotel in general could stand a major sprucing up, but antique touches add style. An ideal base for seeing the city or for pre- and post-cruise stays. Except for a small pool and sun decks, there are no sports facilities on the premises, but the desk will arrange tennis, golf, or fishing. *El Patio* is a favorite in-town lunch spot. 100 Calle Cristo, Viejo San Juan (phone: 723-9020; 800-468-2779; fax: 721-2877).

Galería San Juan The quarters for the Spanish artillery in the 18th century is now a charming bed and breakfast establishment, with the ambience of a private home and art studio. The building has been restored, and its public areas are filled with paintings, drawings, and sculptures by owners Jan D'Esopo and Héctor Gandia, as well as other artists. The eight rooms and suites (seven air conditioned, the other fan-cooled) are individually decorated and feature lovely views of the harbor, the ocean, or the area's historic forts. Some rooms have TV sets and telephones. A simple breakfast buffet is included in the rate, and several restaurants are nearby. It's a special place. 204 Calle Norzagaray, Viejo San Juan (phone: 722-1808 or 725-3829; fax: 724-7360).

INEXPENSIVE

El Canario Inn Located in the heart of the Condado hotel strip, this delightful 25-room guesthouse is San Juan's most famous and attractive small hotel. It is near, but not on, the beach. Rooms have cable TV. There's no restaurant, but continental breakfast is included. 1317 Ashford Ave., Condado (phone: 722-3861; 800-533-2649; fax: 722-0391).

DORADO

VERY EXPENSIVE

Hyatt Dorado Beach Lushly landscaped, this two-level, 298-room resort boasts a casino, super golf and tennis (see *Sports*), two pools, a Jacuzzi, long sweeps of beach, snorkeling, miles of bike paths, and weekly nature walks. The intimate *Su Casa* restaurant, in a separate colonial mansion, provides fine dining (see *Eating Out*). The main building houses the glass-walled *Surf Room,* serving continental food with a spotlighted view of the ocean, as well as an inviting lobby. There's also an open-air (breakfast and lunch) dining area, where netting has stymied the invasion of annoying blackbirds. If you can, book one of the attractive and comfortable waterfront casitas. Ground-floor units have patios. A convention center and ballroom, in a separate building, continue the resort's tradition of erecting buildings no higher than the palm trees. The *Caribbean Sports Academy* offers golf, tennis, or windsurfing instruction for adults and children. There also are excellent summer sport packages, a free summer and holiday camp for kids, and activity programs for teenagers. Rte. 693, Dorado (phone: 796-1234; 800-233-1234; fax: 796-6560).

Hyatt Regency Cerromar Beach Far less lush and more commercial than the *Hyatt Dorado Beach,* it's a renovated high-rise with 504 rooms, two Robert Trent Jones Sr. golf courses and 14 tennis courts (see *Sports*), a health club with sauna and exercise classes, a pool, a small beach, and a gigantic lawn. Eateries include *Medici's,* serving northern Italian fare, *Sushi Wong's* for Far Eastern food, and the trilevel outdoor *Swan Café.* What some claim is the world's largest swimming pool (*Guinness* doesn't agree) is actually an artificial river, a third of a mile long, with currents, a waterfall, peripheral hydromassages, and other diversions. *El Coquí* sports bar, a nightclub, and a casino enliven nights. *Camp Hyatt* is a weekend, summer, and holiday day camp for kids ages 3 to 12; *Rock Hyatt* is designed for 13- to 15-year-olds. The *Caribbean Sports Academy* offers instruction in a wide variety of sports. Summer sport packages are excellent buys. Rte. 693, Dorado (phone: 796-1234; 800-233-1234; fax: 796-6560).

PONCE

EXPENSIVE

Ponce Hilton Set on 80 acres overlooking the Caribbean, there are 156 rooms and suites, a beach, a pool with cascading waterfall, a jogging trail, a bicycle path, two night-lighted tennis courts, a casino, two restaurants, a disco, and a lounge. An 18-hole golf course was being built at press time, and a practice range has recently opened. A convention center that accommodates 1,000 and an executive business center are aimed at attracting the brief-case crowd. On the outskirts of Ponce in the La Guancha area (phone: 259-7676; 800-HILTONS; fax: 259-7674).

MODERATE

Meliá Popular with business travelers, it's a good choice for a night or two in town because of its setting (facing the Plaza de las Delicias across from the funky, striped firehouse) and Spanish-accented atmosphere, but beware: The 1908 architecture is interesting, but the 80 rooms are disappointing and sometimes shabby. There's a good restaurant, but no pool. Continental breakfast included. 2 Calle Cristina, Ponce (phone: 842-0260; fax: 841-3602).

ELSEWHERE ON THE ISLAND

EXPENSIVE

Mayagüez Hilton This place features 145 big rooms, personal service, an Olympic-size pool, a bar, two restaurants, a disco, three tennis courts (two lighted), a casino, a fitness circuit, a walking trail, a mini-gym, and landscaped grounds with a pond and outdoor Jacuzzi. Golf is nearby. Rte. 104, Km 0.3, Mayagüez (phone: 831-7575; 800-HILTONS; fax: 834-3475).

Palmas del Mar A 2,700-acre Mediterranean-style resort composed of the luxury 23-room *Palmas Inn,* the 102-room *Candelero* hotel (group- and family-oriented, slightly less pricey), and 400 stylish villas (about 150 available for rent) grouped around a marina, a championship golf course, and a 20-court tennis complex with a pro. Other features include children's programs and teen activities, a miniature golf course, nature and bike trails, an equestrian center, a palm-lined beach, deep-sea fishing, water sports, a fitness center, a casino, and seven restaurants. Hotel and villa accommodations have been gradually renovated and updated over the past few years. Dine-around plan for MAP guests includes theme-night parties and choice of nearby island restaurants. Rte. 3, Km 86.4, Buena Vista, Humacao (phone: 852-6000; 800-468-3331; fax: 852-6320).

Baños de Coamo A modest government parador with 48 clean and simply furnished rooms. The grounds in the mountain foothills—with thermal and fresh-water pools where water-therapy programs are offered—are pleasant. There's also a swimming pool and tennis court. The charming, old-fashioned dining room serves generous portions of simple Puerto Rican fare. Not by any means a lavish spa, it's still a favorite weekend retreat for locals, and FDR and Frank Lloyd Wright once "took the waters" here. Rte. 546, Coamo (phone: 825-2186 or 825-2239; 800-443-0266; fax: 825-4739).

Parador Casa Grande Another government parador, this 75-year-old restored hacienda offers 20 suites with balconies and fans (no air conditioning, TV sets, or telephones), a swimming pool, and a restaurant with a lounge. It's located in the central mountains close to the *Arecibo Observatory* and *Río Camuy Cave Park.* Rte. 612, Utuado (phone: 894-3939; 800-443-0266).

Parador Guajataca Set on a dramatic sweep of beach, this parador has 38 basic rooms with balconies, two pools, tennis, golf nearby, a restaurant (buffets on Sundays and Wednesdays), and an informal ambience. During your stay, visit the roadside *La Granja de Guajataca* and sample *queso do hoya* (white layered cheese) and *tembleque* (a gelatinous sweet). Rte. 2, Km 103.8, Quebradillas (phone: 895-3070; 800-443-0266; fax: 895-3589).

Parador Hacienda Gripiñas Edgardo and Milagros Dedos's genuine pleasure in pleasing guests makes this place special. On the grounds of a former coffee plantation, it's a 150-year-old house set in lush foliage; the 19 rustic rooms vary in size (some are rather small) but are pin-neat and cheery. Rooms are cooled by fans; there are no telephones or TV sets. There's a chilly mountain pool and excellent, reasonably priced Puerto Rican food. But the chance to relax in a rocker or loll in a hammock on the verandah sipping a piña colada is what it's really about. In Jayuya; no matter what the map says, heading south on the Ponce Speedway, then north at Juana Díaz, is the fastest route from San Juan. Route 527, Km 2.5, Jayuya (phone: 828-1717; 800-443-0266).

Parador Martorell For beach nuts only, it offers nine super-neat rooms in a former private house. Only some rooms are air conditioned (others have fans); none has a telephone. There is a patio, but no surrounding grounds, pool, or dining room. The famous beach is only half a block away. Buffet breakfasts on the patio are included in the room rate. 6A Ocean Dr., Luquillo (phone: 889-2710; 800-443-0266; fax: 889-4520).

Parador Oasis A 200-year-old family mansion and winery, now a hospitable inn, it has 52 rooms and a pretty courtyard dining area, a pool and gym. It's within walking distance of the town's historic sites. 72 Calle Luna, San Germán (phone: 892-1175; 800-443-0266; fax: 892-1175).

Le Petit Chalet Mountain Inn This guesthouse in the rain forest has long been a secret favorite of bird watchers and scientists visiting El Yunque. There are 10 rooms with fans, but no air conditioning. A TV set may be requested, and, though the rooms have no phones, you're free to take the house's portable phone to your room. Breakfast is included in the rate, although some cottages have kitchens. A highly regarded restaurant is also on the premises (see *Eating Out*). Activities include hiking in the rain forest, horseback riding on the beach and in the rain forest, and trips to *Arecibo Observatory*. A children's sleepaway camp is also located here. Advance reservations are required. Near El Yunque (phone: 887-5802 or 887-5807; fax: 887-7926).

Posada Guayama Jag Mehta, who also owns *Casa San José,* has created a 20-room inn in Guayama, a small, historic town on the island's south side. Rooms have verandahs. There's a restaurant and bar, a pool, and night-lighted tennis and basketball courts, which can keep you amused after you've seen the town, with its steepled churches and *Casa Cautiño,* a museum featuring turn-of-the-century furnishings. Rte. 3, Km 138.5, Guayama (phone: 866-1515; fax: 866-1570).

Villa Parguera Another government parador, this inn catering to fishing enthusiasts is rustic but comfortable; the dining room specializes in fresh seafood, and Saturday nights there's plenty of music and dancing. With 61 rooms and a pool, the parador is adjacent to Phosphorescent Bay. Rte. 304, La Parguera (phone: 899-3975; 800-443-0266; fax: 899-6040).

ON THE OFFSHORE ISLANDS

MODERATE

Club Seabourne This laid-back property has four rooms, eight villas, two cottages, and one room in a crow's nest (the only room with a TV set—there's a big-screen TV in the main lounge). None of the units has a telephone. It boasts the only pool on the island and also has a bar and restaurant. Continental breakfast is included in the rate. Located just outside of Dewey on Culebra (phone: 742-3169; fax: 742-3176).

INEXPENSIVE

Casa del Francés This turn-of-the-century sugarcane plantation house on Isla de Vieques (it resembles Tara in *Gone With the Wind*) is a delightful, 18-room guesthouse run by an informal, convivial owner/manager team. Rooms are fan-cooled (there's no air conditioning). It's only a 15-minute walk to spectacular Sombé Beach, or a 10-minute stroll to the lively, funky fishing village of Esperanza, with its harborside restaurants and bars. Delicious, imaginative meals are served at *La Casa* on the attractive back patio, and the poolside bar is a local favorite. A perfect refuge from television, telephone (none are to be found here), and tension. Carr. 996, Esperanza, Isla de Vieques (phone: 741-3751; fax: 741-2330).

Trade Winds Even less expensive than *Casa del Francés,* this guesthouse offers 10 no-frills rooms (no TV sets or telephones, and only some rooms have air conditioning) and a restaurant and bar overlooking the ocean. It's close to *Bananas,* the popular nighttime bar, and within walking distance of Sombé Beach. Esperanza, Vieques (phone: 741-8666).

EATING OUT

San Juan is a city with a predictably citified selection of continental restaurants and steakhouses, with many European-trained chefs. In addition, there are several restaurants dedicated to the Puerto Rican way of cooking (in some ways similar to, but not as olive oil–based, as Spanish fare, nor as fiery as Mexican food). Lately, there has been a trend toward including island dishes on more hotel menus. Worth sampling: black bean soup (very rich), often served with chopped raw onion; *bacalaitos* (codfish fritters); *morcillas* (spicy blood sausages); *pionoños* (spicy ground beef enclosed in strips of ripe plantains); *tostones* (deep-fried plantain slices, often served as a side dish); *pescado* (any fresh fish, especially good in seaside restaurants out on the island); *asopao* (a soupy but generally delicious concoction of chicken or seafood with rice); *arroz con pollo* (chicken and rice); *jueyes* (land crabs, often deviled and served in the shell); *lechón asado* (roast suckling pig); and, for dessert, Puerto Rican pineapple or guava (preserved halves or squares of "paste") served with white cheese. To drink: Puerto Rican coffee (which is the dark, strong stuff you get when you order a "small" cup), light Puerto Rican rum, and island-brewed Medalla and India beer.

Lunch is generally served from noon to 2:30 PM; 8 to 10 PM is the most popular dinnertime for vacationers, though Puerto Ricans usually eat earlier, between 5:30 and 7:30 PM. Outstanding independent restaurants are often found in hotels. A three-course dinner for two including tip, but no drinks, will cost more than $70 at a restaurant we describe as expensive; from $40 to $65 at a place in the moderate category; and less than $30 at spots listed as inexpensive. Lunches run a couple of dollars less. Unless otherwise noted, all restaurants listed below are open for lunch and dinner. All phone numbers are in the 809 area code unless otherwise indicated.

EXPENSIVE

Augusto's This impressive place specializes in continental dishes combined with local ingredients, such as venison medallions with polenta and fresh foie gras. Closed Saturday lunch, Sundays, and Mondays. Reservations necessary. Major credit cards accepted. *Hotel Excelsior,* 801 Av. Ponce de León, Miramar (phone: 725-7700 or 721-7400).

Back Street Hong Kong The Chinese food is authentic, priced higher than its New York equivalent, and the decor is mysterious and unique—it's the set from the Hong Kong pavilion at the *1964 World's Fair* in New York. Open daily for dinner and Sunday lunch. Reservations advised. Major credit cards accepted. In *El San Juan Hotel,* Isla Verde Rd., Isla Verde (phone: 791-1224).

Horned Dorset Primavera Overlooking the beach, the elegant dining room of this inn of the same name has high ceilings and black-and-white tiled floors. It offers a semiformal, six-course, $45 prix fixe dinner (although special dietary requests are honored). Excellent French fare with a tropical accent (try the smoked dorado and the chocolate mousse cake) is matched by the wine list and service. Open daily; dinner only. Reservations advised. Major credit cards accepted. Bo Barrero, Rte. 429, Km 3, Rincón (phone: 823-4030).

Il Perugino Recently reopened in a new, larger location, this highly regarded Italian restaurant is as good as ever. In a lovely, restored colonial building, owner/chef Franco Seccarelli serves up specialties that include lettuce soup, beef medallions, and salmon carpaccio. Closed Mondays, Tuesday and Wednesday lunch, and the month of July. Reservations advised. Major credit cards accepted. 105 Calle Cristo, Viejo San Juan (phone: 722-5481).

L. K. Sweeney & Son Ltd. Richly decorated with green leather, dark wood, and crystal chandeliers, this dining spot specializes in the freshest of seafood. The almond pudding with Fra Angelica sauce is a heavenly experience, and the oyster bar is the largest in the Caribbean, and has been expanded recently to include Spanish-style *tapas.* Open daily; dinner only. Reservations advised. Major credit cards accepted. In the *Condado Plaza,* Ashford Ave., Condado (phone: 723-5551).

Ramiro's This highly regarded restaurant serves creole and Spanish food in a graceful old Condado townhouse. Open daily; no lunch on Saturdays. Reservations advised. Major credit cards accepted. 1106 Av. Magdalena, just off Ashford, Condado (phone: 721-9049).

Su Casa International delicacies served in one of the most romantic settings possible, in a 1928 oceanfront plantation mansion complete with iron grillwork, tinkling fountains, and strolling musicians. Try the grilled rack of lamb with roasted garlic, with a side order of *tostones* (fried plantains). Diet-conscious fare also is available. Open daily for dinner only. Reservations necessary. Major credit cards accepted. *Hyatt Dorado Beach,* Rte. 693, Dorado (phone: 796-1234).

La Zaragozana Longtime favorite for its Spanish-Cuban–Puerto Rican menu and the dim, romantic atmosphere. Black bean soup and the chicken *à la andaluza* are top choices. Strolling musicians on weekends; nightly in season. Open daily. Reservations necessary in season. Major credit cards accepted. 356 Calle San Francisco, Viejo San Juan (phone: 723-5103 or 725-3262).

MODERATE

Chart House This graceful, verandah-enclosed townhouse surrounded by well-kept gardens is the pride of the Condado strip. Extremely handsome, with dark polished woodwork and excellent artwork (both traditional and modern), it serves flawless steaks, lobsters, rack of lamb, and the freshest salads in a variety of settings: a bar room, up- and downstairs parlors—even a treehouse. The piña coladas are the best in town. Open daily; dinner only. Reservations advised. Major credit cards accepted. 1214 Ashford Ave., Condado (phone: 728-0110).

Che's Popular with locals, this restaurant specializes in Argentine fare. The steaks are hard to resist, but make sure you're hungry when you come—the portions are *big.* Open daily. Reservations unnecessary. Major credit cards accepted. 35 Caoba St., Punta Las Marías, Santurce (phone: 726-7202).

La Mallorquina In the heart of Old San Juan, this popular and venerable spot (established in 1848) is perfect for lunch or dinner following a shopping tour. Puerto Rican and Spanish specialties (black bean soup, *asopao,* beans, and rice) are served. Closed Sundays. Reservations advised for dinner. Major credit cards accepted. 207 Calle San Justo, Viejo San Juan (phone: 722-3261).

La Monserrate Sea Port Diners are served inside or on the terrace overlooking the water. Seafood with a Spanish flavor is the specialty here; the *empanadillas* and corn sticks are wonderful. Open daily. Reservations necessary for large groups. Major credit cards accepted. Rte. 2, Ponce (phone: 841-2740).

Los Naborias One of the *mesones gastronómicos* (gastronomic inns recognized by the government for serving excellent Puerto Rican food at moderate prices), here is a fine place to try traditional dishes such as black bean soup and coconut flan. Open daily; dinner only. Reservations advised for large groups. Major credit cards accepted. Rte. 690, Vega Alta, about 20 miles west of San Juan via Rte. 2 (phone: 883-4885).

El Patio de Sam A casual, congenial oasis in Old San Juan, it has an imaginative menu (savory black bean soup, seafood crêpes Mornay, daily specials, plus great burgers). It's also known for its fruit drinks, served both with and without rum, and its Sunday brunch. Open daily. Reservations unnecessary. Major credit cards accepted. 102 Calle San Sebastián, Viejo San Juan (phone: 723-1149).

Le Petit Chalet Rarely found by tourists, this little gem is in a private home, where the dining room seats no more than 40 people. Specialties include leg of lamb and grilled red snapper. Closed Mondays (except for group functions). Reservations necessary one or two nights in advance. Major credit cards accepted. Near El Yunque (phone: 887-5802 or 887-5807).

La Tasca del Callejón Traditional Spanish dishes are served in this charming, restored colonial home. Best are its hot and cold *tapas,* which are served, along with sandwiches, during the day; a full menu is available for dinner. The waiters also sing and entertain. Closed Sundays. Reservations advised. Major credit cards accepted. 317 Calle Fortaleza, Viejo San Juan (phone: 721-1689).

INEXPENSIVE

Amanda's Café A delightful hideaway facing the sea, this tiny French-Mexican café specializes in drinks that are close cousins to desserts (Amanda Robles inherited her know-how from her dad, who was bar manager at the old Lindy's in New York and invented the Black Russian). Black bean soup, gazpacho, guacamole, enchiladas, French-Mexican fish soup, and frappés are among the offerings. This is a late-night spot, open until 2 AM during the week and until 4 AM Fridays through Sundays. Reservations advised for groups. Major credit cards accepted. To get here, follow the road uphill by *Fuerte San Cristóbal.* 424 Calle Norzagaray, Viejo San Juan (phone: 722-1682).

Butterfly People Both an unusual gallery (with exotic butterflies mounted in plastic cases) and an extremely pleasant lunch stop in Old San Juan. Soups, salads, local grilled specialties, and sandwiches are served on the upstairs balcony surrounding the atrium. Open for breakfast, lunch, and dinner; closed Sundays. Reservations necessary for large parties. Major credit cards accepted. 152 Calle Fortaleza, Viejo San Juan (phone: 723-2432).

Criollíssimo Puerto Rican dishes are served at this hot spot in a San Juan suburb, including stuffed *mofongo* (fried, mashed plantains shaped into a bowl and filled with beef, chicken, pork, or seafood) and homemade soups for lunch and dinner. Open daily. Reservations unnecessary. Major credit cards accepted. 300 F. D. Roosevelt Ave., Hato Rey (phone: 767-3344).

Green House What it lacks in atmosphere, it more than makes up in good food, cordial service, and reasonable prices. Stop in for burgers, omelettes, daily specials, and divine desserts. Popular with residents. Open daily until 4:30 AM. Reservations advised on weekends. Major credit cards accepted. 1200 Ashford Ave., Condado (phone: 725-4036).

Metropol This chain of eateries serves perhaps the best Cuban food on the island. The menu is basically the same at each location: stuffed Cornish hen, red snapper, steaks, and even liver—all prepared Cuban-style. All locations are open daily. Reservations unnecessary. Major credit cards accepted. 105 De Diego, Condado (phone: 268-3075); 124 F. D. Roosevelt Ave., Hato Rey (phone: 751-4022); Isla Verde Rd., Isla Verde (phone: 791-4046).

Saba

For years there was a shakily handwritten sign just outside the two-room airport at the edge of the tiny airstrip: "Welcome to Saba, the Storybook Island." The sign is gone, but the fairy-tale appeal remains.

Saba (pronounced *Say*-bah) is mite-size, beachless, and mountainous. Most of the island's five square miles seem to go either straight up or straight down, and "The Road"—Saba's only major thoroughfare—switches back and forth like a dragon's tail, and never stops ascending or descending. Everything looks doll-size: the gingerbread-trimmed houses of Hell's Gate clinging to the mountain; English Quarter, with its picture-book church; and Windwardside, where the island's only museum is an antique home just a bit larger than a child's playhouse. Seen from The Road above, even The Bottom, Saba's capital, looks like a miniature town in a toy train set.

Grouped with St. Maarten and St. Eustatius in the Windward Islands of the Netherlands Antilles, Saba has been Dutch since 1812. Its prime spoken language, however, is English—the legacy of the Shetland Islanders who were its first residents.

For centuries the steep hillsides kept Saba isolated from the rest of the Caribbean. Its people became expert seamen, fishermen, and longshoremen. They learned to unload vital cargo offshore, wrestle the stuff through the surf, and haul it up the cliff—no matter what the object's size or shape.

Perhaps because of its isolation, what would be minor events anywhere else are major historical landmarks for Saba—including the opening of Windwardside's first supermarket (1963), the arrival of Saba's first cruise ship (the *Argonaut,* in 1966), and the arrival of a jeep in 1947. Lashed to two rowboats, the island's first car narrowly missed being swamped as 50 men lifted it ashore. Decades later, there are still fewer than 300 automobiles on Saba.

Saba is an island scaled to individuals (there are only 1,200 residents) and, if you're lucky, you'll meet its memorable ones. They include Will Johnson, a former chairman of the *Saba Tourist Board,* who edits and publishes the monthly mimeographed *Saba Herald* (which he began in 1968) and serves as Senator of Saba; and Pauline Paul, who gives piano lessons to young and old.

Of all citizens of the Kingdom of the Netherlands, only Sabans—because of the extreme ups and downs of their island's topography—are permitted to bury their dead in their own yards. Although the burial custom is fading with rising property values, almost every old house has its flower-garden grave site, and the effect is more cheerfully practical than gloomy. Sabans are self-reliant and kind, to each other and to visitors. It's an unwritten rule of The Road that anyone with wheels who's going your way will stop and offer a ride.

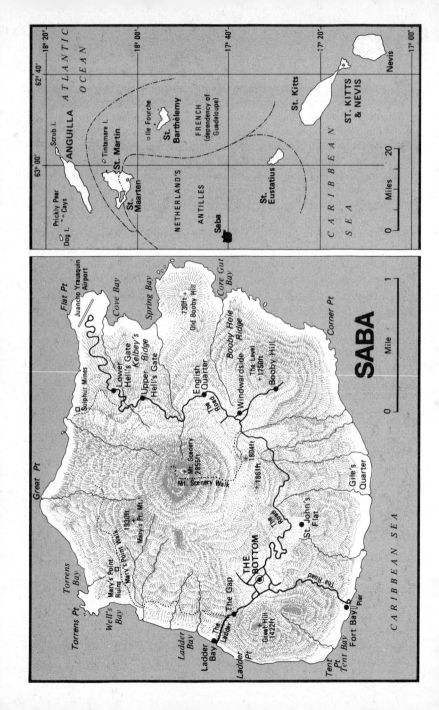

There is some development in progress on Saba, but on a very modest scale. In 1989 the island added a fiber-optic phone system for clearer reception and better intra-island access. The following year it acquired a decompression chamber from the Royal Dutch Navy, making it the only eastern Caribbean island with this diving equipment. Dutch investors recently built the *Queens Gardens* resort (see *Checking In*), but at press time the opening was mired in legal delays. Two Dutch investment firms also are building *Saba Villas,* which will consist of several luxury villas, each with a price tag of $1 million; at press time, only one villa had been completed. Another new hotel, the *Cottage Club,* features 10 gingerbread-style cottages built on a ridge overlooking the tiny village of English Quarter (see *Checking In*).

Friday and Saturday night dances are as exciting as Saba ever gets. There are no casinos, no beaches, no golf courses, no marinas, and no big glitzy resorts. If you are not a mountain climber, botanist, or scuba diver, there's a limited amount to see and do. After you've taken the two-hour all-island tour, there are still two "step roads" (steep, narrow paths traveled via hand-hewn stone stairs) to explore: One leads to the top of Mt. Scenery, the other down to Ladder Bay. There also are seven marked hiking trails, mostly footpaths trod by farmers for centuries.

Otherwise there are several small hotel pools, three small dive operations, and a quasi-tennis court at The Bottom. You can read or snooze in the sun, walk around a bit, meet a few people, and take pictures. You can hike, bird watch, take naturalist tours or marine ecology seminars, or join the Wednesday-morning social breakfast at *Scout's Place,* where "the purpose is just to come together and have interesting talks" (see *Eating Out*). After the day's inactivity, you can return to *Scout's* for more conversation. The slow pace would drive some people crazy. For others, it's addictive— the perfect escape.

Saba At-a-Glance

FROM THE AIR

Saba is green, round, and tiny—about 5 square miles. At 2,855 feet above sea level, about 28 miles (15 minutes' flying time) south of the Dutch/French island of St. Maarten/St. Martin and 150 miles east of Puerto Rico, it looks like a mountain up to its shoulders in sea—which is exactly what it is. Eons ago its highest peak—2,855-foot Mt. Scenery—was an active volcano. Now its crater is dead, and a rain forest grows on its sides. Mt. Scenery and surrounding high points (variously and whimsically christened The Level, St. John's Flat, Bunker, Booby, and Old Booby Hills, and ranging from just over 1,000 to just under 1,700 feet) produce Saba's extreme vertical topography. So suddenly does the island rise out of the Caribbean that for years not a road, but a series of steps called The Ladder, climbing up its western cliffs, provided the only access to its capital town, The Bottom. Landing at

Juancho Yrausquin Airport on northeastern Flat Point is akin to putting down on an aircraft carrier: The 1,312-foot airstrip, one of the world's shortest, is 130 feet above sea level, with cliffs at either end. Visitors are then taxied through Lower Hell's Gate and Upper Hell's Gate, southwest across the island to English Quarter and Windwardside, then down again via St. John's to The Bottom. The impossible Road, which divides the island diagonally, ends at Fort Bay on the southwestern edge at a pier.

Saba has no real beaches. In 1989 Hurricane Hugo washed a tiny sand patch ashore at Fort Bay, but it disappeared later that year, never to return. There also is the "Wandering Beach" at Well's Bay. True to its name, the narrow spit of sand wanders off for about five months of every year.

SPECIAL PLACES

The Road, which climbs, hairpin-curving, from the airport up the steep side of the island to reach Saba's interior, is the island's first special sight. After every expert pooh-poohed the idea, Josephus Lambert Hassell took a correspondence course in engineering and in the 1930s began work on The Road, which he and his fellow Sabans built by hand over the next 20 years—thus demonstrating the Saban will and spirit. Reconstruction of The Road has been completed from The Bottom to the airport.

HELL'S GATE, UPPER HELL'S GATE, AND ENGLISH QUARTER These neighborhoods, which consist of clusters of houses, neatly painted in white with contrasting shutters, bright red roofs, and jigsaw-cut gingerbread trim, line the way to the island's top settlement.

WINDWARDSIDE At the top of The Road, slightly east of the island's midpoint, at 1,804 feet, is Saba's second-largest settlement, site of a number of tourist shops and the greater part of the island's guestrooms. Windwardside also is the site of the *Harry L. Johnson Memorial Museum.* The former home of a Dutch sea captain, the museum is filled with a growing collection of antique Saban furnishings, a lovely rock oven, crisp curtains of Spanish lace, a few pre-Columbian stone tools, and touching mementos of the severe hurricane of 1772 (don't miss the letter Sabans sent to the Dutch government soliciting its help). Also be sure to check out the guestbook—the sixth signature is that of Jacqueline Kennedy Onassis, from her visit of March 28, 1978. Closed weekends. Admission charge (phone: 62359). In the grassy meadow just above the museum is a bust of Simón Bolívar, commemorating his 1816 visit to recruit help for his struggle to free South America from its colonizers. A little beyond Windwardside, a set of 1,064 hand-hewn steps scales the side of Mt. Scenery through a rain forest where some wild orchids still bloom (look, don't pick) and ferns grow taller than children.

THE BOTTOM Saba's capital town lies in a round valley 820 feet above sea level. It takes its name from the fact that the valley is bowl-shaped (*botte* is Dutch for bowl). Actually, its official name is not "The Bottom" at all. In the late 19th century the local council voted to change it to Leverock Town in honor of Moses Leverock, a Saban who had done much for the island. His memory is still revered, though the name never took hold. Among The Bottom's top sites: the governor's official residence, painted sunny peach and white, and the small garden park adjoining it; *Heleen's Art Gallery,* with lovely watercolors and an old fireplace (open weekdays or by appointment; phone: 63348); and *Cranston's Antique Inn* (see *Checking In*), once the government's guesthouse, now a private hotel and late-afternoon watering spot. Northwest of town, a set of concrete and stone steps called The Ladder lead to a rocky beach and the sea.

FORT BAY At the end of the 9-mile cross-island Road is the island's power plant, its only gas station, the *Saba Deep Dive Shop, Wilson's Dive Shop,* and the *Saba Marine Park* (see *Snorkeling and Scuba Diving*), and the 250-foot pier where imports and some visitors are landed. Sabans and visitors often swim here, making their way to the water via the remaining steps from the old pier.

Sources and Resources

TOURIST INFORMATION

The *Saba Tourist Bureau Office* is in Windwardside, in the renovated *Lambert Hassell Building* (closed weekends; phone: 62231; 800-SABA-DWI in the US; fax: 62350). For information on Saba tourist offices in the US, see GETTING READY TO GO.

LOCAL COVERAGE For a little island, Saba is covered with newsprint. The *Saba Herald* is a lively, mimeographed roundup of island news and political opinion that comes out on the 24th of every month. The *Chronicle,* a daily paper, and the *Caribbean Herald,* a weekly—both printed on St. Maarten—are delivered to Saba subscribers the day they are published.

Two delightful books worth investigating are *Saban Lore—Tales from My Grandmother's Pipe,* by Will Johnson ($10), and *Saba—The First Guidebook,* by Natalie and Paul Pfanstiehl ($10). In St. Maarten you might be able to find historian Dr. J. Hartog's *St. Maarten, Saba, St. Eustatius* ($4) and his *History of Saba* in the paperback English translation ($7). Divers will want the *Guide to the Saba Marine Park* by Tom van't Hof ($14), published by Stinapa (the Netherlands Antilles Park Foundation) and available at the park office and most island bookstores. Heleen Cornet's *Saban Cottages* features reproductions of her watercolor paintings and information on local architecture.

RADIO AND TELEVISION There are several English-language radio and television programs. The island's two radio stations are PGF-1 (93.9 FM) and PGD-2 (1410 AM), with music and local and international news. All of the hotels have cable access and receive CNN.

TELEPHONE When calling from the US, dial 011 (international access code) + 5994 (country code) + (local number). To call from another Caribbean island the access code may vary, so check with the local operator. When calling from a phone on Saba, use only the local number listed unless otherwise indicated. Dial 63237 for the police; 63288/9 for an ambulance.

ENTRY REQUIREMENTS All that is required of US or Canadian citizens is a current passport, or one that expired less than five years earlier, or other proof of citizenship (an original or certified birth certificate or voter's registration card plus a photo ID) and a return or ongoing ticket.

CLIMATE AND CLOTHES Temperatures range from a high of about 85F (about 30C) on a sunny day in Hell's Gate to about 65F (around 19C) on a cool night in Windwardside. Take cottons and polyester blends that can easily be laundered; there are no dry cleaners. Dress is informal. You'll probably need rubber-soled hiking shoes and a sweater for cool evenings.

MONEY Official currency is the Netherlands Antilles florin, also known as a guilder, and abbreviated NAf. The current exchange rate is about 1.80 NAf to the US dollar, but US dollars are accepted throughout the island; Canadians should change their money for florins before departing from St. Maarten, or in Windwardside at either the *Banco Barclays Antilliano* (open 8 AM to 4 PM weekdays) or the *Commercial Bank* (open from 8:30 AM to noon weekdays). Credit cards are accepted at some island restaurants and shops. All prices in this chapter are quoted in US dollars.

LANGUAGE Though all of the public signs are written in Dutch, the island's official language, everybody on the island speaks English, the native tongue of Saba's original Scottish-English-Irish settlers. The national greeting exchanged by Sabans passing on steps or road is "Howzzit? Howzzit?" delivered with a very slight raised-hand salute.

TIME Saba operates on atlantic standard time, one hour ahead of eastern standard and the same as eastern daylight saving time. In winter, when it's noon in New York, it's 1 PM on Saba; during daylight saving time, the time is the same in both places.

CURRENT Electricity is 110 volts, 60 cycles—no problem for North American travel appliances.

TIPPING A 10% to 15% service charge is usually added to restaurant, bar, or hotel bills. If not, that's the right amount to leave. Give cab drivers $1 or $2. Don't worry about tipping airport porters—there are none, so travel light to Saba.

GETTING AROUND

CAR RENTAL The island's fleet of 16 rental cars is distributed among *Scout's Place* (see *Checking In*), *Johnson's Rent-A-Car* (phone: 62269), *Mike's Car Rental* (phone: 63259), and *Doc's Car Rental* (phone: 62271). The rates include a tank of gas and unlimited mileage. Your hotel can make arrangements, but considering the precipitous Road and difficult parking, hitchhiking is both friendlier and easier.

HITCHHIKING An approved way of getting around. Just start walking, and in minutes a Saban will stop and give you a lift as far as he's going in your direction. Wherever he drops you, someone else is sure to pick you up. It's a great way to get to know the people and the island.

INTER-ISLAND FLIGHTS *Windward Island Airways* (*WINAIR;* in St. Maarten; phone: 5995-54237 or 5995-54210) flies STOL (short takeoff and landing) craft on the 15-minute route from St. Maarten's *Juliana Airport* to Saba five times daily. In the past such flights were thought to be impossible—like The Road—until aviation pioneer Rémy de Haenen (former mayor of St. Barts) built the amazing 1,312-foot airstrip, little more than half as long as the much-maligned strip on St. Barts. Flight schedules permit visitors to spend most of the day sightseeing and lunching on the island before catching the afternoon flight out, or to plan longer stays. Organized full-day tours leave St. Maarten almost daily and include air transport, sightseeing, and lunch at *Captain's Quarters* (see *Eating Out*). For more information try *Irish Tours* on St. Maarten (phone: 5995-53663).

TAXI Several taxis meet every arriving flight and ship; they serve both as point-to-point transport and tour vehicles. Taxi drivers are not only proficient in negotiating the zigs, zags, ups, and downs of The Road, but they will be glad to fill you in on island lore. After an island tour you can be dropped off at *Scout's Place* or *Captain's Quarters* for lunch (see *Eating Out* for both). The driver also will pick you up afterward in time to make an afternoon flight. If you're traveling alone, look for a minibus, as they usually will load up with a group of people for a 1½-hour tour of the island for much less than the cost of hiring a taxi on your own.

WALKING Can be a challenge—even within a limited area such as the lanes of Windwardside. Inclines are steep, and the concrete slippery. Sturdy, ground-gripping shoes are a must.

SPECIAL EVENTS

The Queen's Birthday (April 30) honors Beatrix of the Netherlands with sports events, parades, and fireworks. Ten days in late July are dedicated to the *Saba Summer Festival,* with shows, games, contests, steel bands, and dancing. During *Saba Days,* held the first weekend in December, there are greased-pole and spearfishing contests, swimming, games of all sorts, maypole dances, and lots of partying. Legal holidays include *New Year's Day, Good Friday, Easter Monday* (April 8 in 1996), *Labor Day* (May 1), *Ascension Day* (May 16 in 1996), *Christmas,* and *Boxing Day* (December 26).

SHOPPING

It's more like stepping into someone's parlor. The shops to see are in Windwardside and easy to handle in an after-lunch stroll; store hours are from approximately 9 AM to noon and 2 to 6 PM. Local art and crafts are the most interesting items for sale here.

For 125 years Saban women have been famous for their drawn-thread work called Saba lace. Introduced on the island in 1870 by Mary Gertrude Johnson, who learned it from nuns in her convent school in Caracas, Venezuela, it's a form of needlecraft that involves drawing and tying selected threads in a piece of linen to produce an ornamental pattern. Though the number of women skilled in it has dwindled, the *Community Center* (in Hell's Gate; phone: 62300) still offers lace-worked blouses, sheets, pillowcases, tablecloths and napkins, and handkerchiefs. The remarkably delicate tatting can be beautiful, but it does require careful laundering and can be expensive. Marguerite Hassell, one of the island's expert needleworkers, sells her own Saba lace from her Windwardside home (phone: 62261).

Today's most visible island craft is silk-screen printing on cotton, handsomely practiced by the *Saba Artisans Foundation* (phone: 63260) in a wide array of imaginative designs. At their main shop and workroom in The Bottom you'll find everything from head scarves, T-shirts, and placemats to full-length dresses. Also for sale here are leatherwork and dolls from Curaçao.

Another local specialty is "Saba Spice"—an aromatic blend of 151-proof cask rum, brown sugar, anise seed, cinnamon, nutmeg, and secret ingredients—home-brewed by many locals, including Patsy Hassell of Hell's Gate (she has a small stand—ask any local to point you in the right direction). While no two bottles are exactly alike (each brewer uses his or her own recipe), the drink is sweet, spicy, and packs quite a wallop.

Other spots, all in Windwardside: *Breadfruit Gallery* (in the *Lambert Hassell Building;* phone: 62509) for a large selection of original paintings, prints, and other fine art by local artists; *Saba Tropical Arts* (in the same building; phone: 62373), for a little bit of everything the island produces; and the *Little Shop* (phone: 62231) for clothing and local pottery.

SPORTS

HIKING Allow three to four hours for the trek up the 2,855-foot extinct volcano Mt. Scenery, but if a cloud hovers at the peak, wait until the morning mist burns off or go another day. Try to start out as early as possible. Wear good walking shoes and sunscreen; bring a camera and a canteen. Begin the climb either from Windwardside at the road sign "Mt. Scenery" or from midway up at the end of Mountain Road, where a 1,064-step concrete stairway leads to the top. (This can be slippery, but is well worth any scrambling.) A tropical paradise of giant elephant ears and ferns, palms, banana and mango trees, heliconias, and 17 species of wild orchid prepares you for the spectacular view from the summit. If you're uneasy going it alone, Glenn Holm at the tourist bureau (see *Tourist Information,* above) may be able to provide a guide, or to accompany you himself. He has catalogued a list of over 16 island trails, of which seven are mapped out, complete with instructions, trail hazards, and a description of the sights en route. James Johnson (phone: 63307) offers a four-hour hike from the sulfur mine to Well's Bay (the price drops if there are more than three people) and fills the hours with historical information, island trivia, and ecological insights.

SNORKELING AND SCUBA DIVING Saba has become one of the premier diving locations in the Caribbean, and it has 38 officially designated dive sites around the island. You can dive very close to shore, and underwater visibility, normally in excess of 100 feet, can reach up to 200 feet. There are both shallow and very deep dives; some of the reef structures include lava flows, towering vertical walls, underwater caverns and caves, and even underwater mountains. The black sand bottom accents the striking colors of large purple sponges, breathtakingly huge stands of black coral, and abundant fish. Even the most seasoned diver will be stunned by the site called Outer Limits, which features a huge mountaintop under 90 feet of water.

Another highlight is the *Saba Marine Park (SMP),* which Saba established in 1987 to protect its still virgin marine life. The park encircles the island and includes the waters and seabed from the high-water mark down to 200 feet. The *SMP*'s Edward S. Arnold Snorkel Trail at Torrens Point is well thought out, informative, and fun. Rent a laminated trail map that can be read underwater; it's useful as you follow the arrows leading to the 11 sites. Arrangements can be made with any of the three island dive shops (see below). The *SMP* also maintains a system of 38 permanent mooring buoys (including four overnight yacht moorings) to facilitate diving and to prevent anchor damage to coral. An information office is located at Fort Bay (phone: 63295), and complimentary slide shows are offered to all visiting dive groups. A diving decompression chamber is housed at the *Saba Marine Park Hyperbaric Facility* (phone: 63295) in Fort Bay.

The three diving operations on Saba are *Saba Deep Dive Shop* (Fort Bay; phone: 63347; or contact its US representative, *Surfside,* in Scranton, PA; phone: 717-346-6382); *Sea Saba,* owned by Louis and Joan Bourque, both PADI instructors (Windwardside; phone: 62246); and *Wilson's Dive Shop* (Fort Bay; phone: 63410). All offer single-tank, two-tank, and night dives, as well as longer-term packages. Special arrangements can be made for marine ecology seminars, slide presentations, underwater photography instruction, and fishing excursions to Saba Bank. *Sea Saba* and *Saba Deep* also offer five-day Open Water certification courses. Snorkeling trips and equipment rental can be arranged through *Wilson's.*

A live-aboard dive boat that offers week-long dive trips, mooring around the island, is the *Caribbean Explorer* (phone: 800-322-3577). *Go Diving* (phone: 800-328-5285) arranges dive packages from the US. Several St. Maarten–based firms also offer dive excursions on Saba. *Rising Sun Tours* (phone: 5995-42855 or 5995-52055) or *Irish Tours* (see *Inter-Island Flights*) have one-day packages from St. Maarten, including two dives, all equipment, transport, lunch, and sightseeing. Arrangements for other packages can be made through *Maho Watersports* on St. Maarten (phone: 5995-52801, ext. 1871, or 5995-54387).

SPORT FISHING Contact Michel Peterson (phone: 62359), who will motor you in his 22-foot vessel to Saba Bank, 3 miles offshore and known for its excellent catches. *Wilson's Dive Shop* (see *Snorkeling and Scuba Diving,* above) will arrange fishing trips. And if you can twist his arm, Arrindell Hassell (phone: 62261) will occasionally take deep-sea fishing charters. Saba Bank is 32 miles long and 20 miles wide, mostly six to 20 fathoms deep, and in some areas the bottom can be seen clearly.

SWIMMING Seasonal swimming is possible at Well's Bay. Otherwise, there is a lovely pool clinging to the top of the mountain at *Captain's Quarters,* as well as pools at *Scout's Place, Juliana's, Willard's of Saba, Queens Gardens,* and *Cranston's Antique Inn* (see *Checking In* for all). You don't need to be a hotel guest to use the pools.

TENNIS Few people take advantage of the cement tennis court at The Bottom (free and open to all). If the net isn't up, ask around (there's no phone). There also is a court at *Willard's of Saba* hotel, and a court was being built at press time at *Queens Gardens* (see *Checking In* for both).

NIGHTLIFE

The weekly Friday and Saturday night dances—to which everyone is invited and just about everyone goes—are held at *Guido's* (Windwardside; phone: 62230). Other action can be found at *Inner Circle* (The Bottom; phone: 63218). If there is a party, most everyone on the island will know. Ask at your hotel. That's it—although people have been known to sit up late and swap yarns and philosophical observations around the bar at—guess where—*Scout's Place* or the *Captain's Quarters* (see *Eating Out* for both).

Best on the Island

CHECKING IN

Saba has several hotels, plus a fine selection of less expensive vacation apartments and guesthouses, including some traditional Saban wood cottages that rent on a daily, weekly, or monthly basis. Apartment prices stay fairly stable year-round, although some landlords discount their rates by 10% to 15% in the summertime. Most are completely equipped. Contact the *Saba Tourist Bureau* in the US or on Saba for a full listing, and then contact the landlord directly. Several large, fully furnished villas with private pools—such as *Saba Villas* (phone: 62236)—also are available for rent. Again, ask at the tourist bureau.

At the hotel listed here as very expensive expect to pay $240 or more for a double in peak season; at expensive places $125 to $240; moderate $75 to $110; inexpensive $65 or less. A 5% room tax and a 10% to 15% service charge are additional. Unless otherwise noted, credit cards are accepted, and all rooms listed below have private baths. Since nights tend to be cool, most Saban hotels are not air conditioned; also, most do not have TV sets or telephones in the rooms (unless otherwise noted). When calling from a phone on Saba, use only the local numbers listed below. For information about dialing from elsewhere, see *Telephone* earlier in this chapter.

VERY EXPENSIVE

Queens Gardens Saba's first luxury resort was built by a group of Dutch investors. Unfortunately, the opening has been delayed, and at press time, the property was mired in legal problems. However, it's worth checking to see if the problems have cleared up and the place has opened. Located on eight acres of tropical gardens on the slopes of Troy Hill, the hotel has 12 studios and suites, all with living rooms and kitchens. Other amenities include a swimming pool and a small fitness center. Troy Hill (phone: 63339; fax: 62450).

EXPENSIVE

Cottage Club A cluster of 10 beautiful, new gingerbread cottages overlooking the tiny village of English Quarter. The sparkling-clean, spacious cottages have balconies and fully equipped kitchens. The lobby of the main building is decorated with antiques, including Italian Renaissance chairs. There's no restaurant, but a swimming pool and Jacuzzi were planned at press time. Special scuba packages are available. Windwardside (phone: 62486).

Willard's of Saba Situated 1,700 feet above sea level is this small, intimate resort with an outdoor Jacuzzi overlooking the sea. The seven guestrooms (cooled by ceiling fans and tropical breezes) are in bungalows, most with balconies or patios, and all with spectacular views. Telephones and TV sets are available upon request. There's a fine dining room, a heated swimming pool, and a tennis court on the premises. Booby Hill (phone: 62498; 800-883-SABA; fax: 62482).

MODERATE

Captain's Quarters Recently renovated, but still long on old-fashioned charm, its two houses are 100 and 175 years old, with much furniture to match. The 10 rooms are big, airy, and island-stylish (fresh colors, four-poster beds, sisal rugs, antique touches). The view, the terrace, dining room, bar, and swimming pool are all mighty attractive, and the fare has improved greatly in recent years (see *Eating Out*). Rates include continental breakfast. Windwardside (phone: 62201; 800-223-9815; 212-251-1800 in New York City; fax: 62377).

The Gate House This small hostelry offers a warm and friendly atmosphere in a quiet village, with six bright and arty rooms decorated by a former graphic artist from New York. Two of the rooms include kitchens, and there's a restaurant. Rates include continental breakfast. Dive packages are available. Hell's Gate (phone: 62416; 708-354-9641 in the US; fax: 62529).

Juliana's Here are 10 no-frills, functional units—eight double rooms, a one-bedroom apartment, and a two-bedroom cottage. The double rooms have ceiling fans and private balconies, and the apartment and cottage have full kitchens and patios. There's a pool, cable TV in a recreation room, and the *Tropics Café* restaurant which serves breakfast and lunch. Windwardside (phone: 62269; 800-223-9815 or 800-328-5285; fax: 22289).

Scout's Place It describes itself as "Bed 'n' Board, Cheap 'n' Cheerful." In addition to the older four doubles, there are 10 double rooms in a newer section—all with four-poster beds and balconies—and an apartment with a full kitchen. There is a small pool, and the view is great. Visitors and locals alike stop by late in the day to drink a cold beer, enjoy the island cooking, and discuss life (see *Eating Out*). Windwardside (phone: 62205; fax: 62388).

INEXPENSIVE

Cranston's Antique Inn At press time, much-needed renovations at this small guesthouse were slated for completion this year. The six rooms have four-poster beds and patios, but not all have private baths. There's a pool, and the restaurant serves West Indian dishes. No credit cards accepted. The Bottom (phone: 63203).

EATING OUT

Most visitors to Saba eat at their guesthouse restaurant, but there are a few other options. Not including wine, drinks, or tip, expect to pay $30 to $40 at places in the moderate category, less than $25 at inexpensive places. Unless otherwise noted, all restaurants listed below are open for lunch and dinner. When calling from Saba use only the local numbers listed below. For information about dialing from elsewhere, see *Telephone* earlier in this chapter.

WINDWARDSIDE

MODERATE

Brigadoon Saban-born chef Greg Johnson serves up the best food on the island, an enticing menu of Caribbean and continental dishes ranging from fresh fish to succulent steaks. Leave room for his homemade desserts. Open daily for dinner. Reservations unnecessary. Major credit cards accepted (phone: 62380).

Captain's Quarters This popular dining room serves a variety of West Indian and American dishes in an enchanting alfresco setting. Open daily for breakfast, lunch, and dinner. Reservations necessary for groups of eight or more. MasterCard and Visa accepted. In the *Captain's Quarters* hotel (phone: 62201).

Scout's Place A popular eatery connected with the guesthouse of the same name (see *Checking In),* it serves Caribbean dishes and other favorites, from stewed goat and mutton to well-prepared fish dishes. The open-air dining room has a sweeping view of the sea. After dinner, stick around for some conversation or join in a card game. Open daily for breakfast, lunch, and dinner. Reservations advised. MasterCard and Visa accepted (phone: 62205).

INEXPENSIVE

Corner Deli Pick up the makings for a deluxe picnic at this deli run by a New York expatriate (who else?). It offers excellent sandwiches, plus an assortment of homemade sausages and smoked fish and meat. It's also the only place on the island to get a cappuccino. Open 7:30 AM to 6 PM; closed Sundays. No reservations. No credit cards accepted (phone: 62517).

Guido's The island's combination rec room and pizza place, it offers decent pizza, subs, and standard rib-sticking Italian favorites. Part of the draw here is the large-screen TV set, the dart boards, pool tables, and the loud stereo, which sometimes prompts dancing at night. Open daily for dinner. Reservations unnecessary. No credit cards accepted (phone: 62230).

Saba Chinese The menu features more than 100 Chinese choices and a few Indonesian dishes. With good food and a funky decor, it's one of Saba's weekend hot spots. Open daily. Reservations unnecessary. No credit cards accepted (phone: 62268).

THE BOTTOM

INEXPENSIVE

Lollypops This unassuming place offers home cooking Saba-style, with good local fish, goat, and chicken dishes. Saturday nights there's a chicken-and-ribs barbecue. Free transportation is available to and from Windwardside hotels. Open daily. Reservations unnecessary. Visa and MasterCard accepted (phone: 63330).

Queenie's Serving Spoon Authentic and plentiful family-style West Indian food, served in an eight-table appendage to Queenie's home. Chicken with peanut sauce, pumpkin fritters, and homemade soursop ice cream are all specialties. Open daily. Reservations necessary by about noon. No credit cards accepted (phone: 63225).

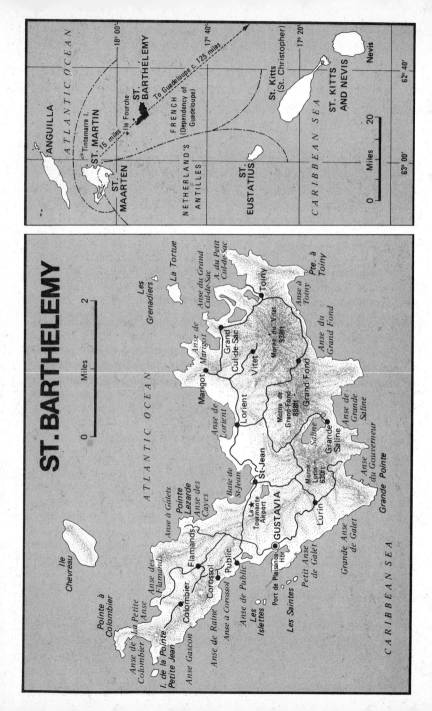

St. Barthélemy

People tend to be protective about St. Barts—both for the island's sake and their own. It is tiny—only 8 square miles—and beautiful, endowed with mellow green mountains, coral sand coves, a dollhouse-size capital port, and a free-and-easy pace. Its vacation life is unprogrammed, its sands uncrowded, and its denizens—including wealthy Americans and European aristocrats—want it to stay that way. Over the past 10 years or so, St. Barts has been discovered, but, with fewer than 700 hotel rooms, an airstrip accommodating nothing larger than a 20-seat short takeoff and landing (STOL) plane, and (for the most part) astronomic prices, most visitors still come from among the privileged. The masses are limited to day-trippers from cruise ships or from nearby St. Martin/St. Maarten.

Discovered by Columbus in 1493 and named for his brother Bartolomeo, the island received its first French settlers in 1648. Except for a takeover by the British in 1758 (when French-speaking inhabitants temporarily fled to neighboring islands), it remained firmly Gallic until 1784, when islanders awoke to the astounding news that one of Louis XVI's ministers had traded the island—lock, stock, and citizens—to Sweden for trading rights in Göteborg.

While the island's inhabitants continued to eke out a living from the stone-walled fields and sea, the Swedes took over, rechristened the island's capital Gustavia in honor of their king, declared it a free port, and began trading—and prospering. In 1878, when St. Barts became French again, the free-port status remained—along with such Viking legacies as neat-lined buildings and Swedish names on tombstones, streets, and, of course, Gustavia.

St. Barts' residents look like few other Caribbean islanders. About 90% of the population of just over 5,000 are descendants of the island's first settlers—from the Normandy, Brittany, and Poitou regions of France—and are white-skinned and blue-eyed. They're a sober-looking group, whose *anciennes dames* pad barefoot about the village of Corossol and weave exquisite handicrafts of undyed *latania* (straw).

But St. Barts is also St. Tropez French—a playground of monokinis and beach café lunches brimming with wine and laughter. Evenings are reserved for intimate restaurants, where cuisine is spelled with a capital "C" and wine cellars are well stocked. Late-night activity might include a leisurely stroll along the yacht-filled waterfront, where the occasional strains of jazz can be heard, or lingering over a cognac at the *Castelets* hotel, basking in the moonlight and picking out lights on the boats anchored in the bay below. There's no big-city hustle and bustle here—just a laid-back atmosphere and gem-like perfection. You'll either be bored to tears, or you'll love it.

If the latter is the case, you'll soon find yourself feeling protective about St. Barts, too.

St. Barts At-a-Glance

FROM THE AIR

The V-shaped island of St. Barts lies 125 miles northwest of Guadeloupe, of which it is a dependency, but only 15 miles (a 10-minute flight) southeast of St. Martin/St. Maarten. Its topography boasts lush hillsides born of ancient volcanoes, deep valleys, and white-gold beaches with bays scooped into the shoreline. Its capital, Gustavia, is built around a harbor 13 to 16 feet deep, which cuts into the island's southwest coast. The town is home to less than 15% of St. Barts' population. *Gustav III Airport* at La Tourmente—which well describes the emotion first-timers feel when they contemplate its short runway—lies north of town on the road to St-Jean. The beach at Baie de St-Jean is the most famous strand on the island, with a number of small hotels, restaurants, bistros, and water sports. It is washed with gentle waves, as are most leeward shores. By contrast, the surf is sometimes quite strong along Anse du Grand Fond (part of which is aptly nicknamed the "Washing Machine") and Anse de Toiny on the windward (southeastern) coast. Roads are, for the most part, well paved and easy to cope with in the lowlands and valleys, but they sometimes scale hills at an angle only a chamois could love.

SPECIAL PLACES

GUSTAVIA St. Barts' capital lines the three protective sides of the harbor, or *port de plaisance.* Too small for most cruise ships, it's a favorite layover for sailing yachts. When a liner or large windjammer anchors offshore, tenders ferry passengers to the principal quay on the east edge of the port. The focal point of town activity, the quay is surrounded by boutiques offering duty-free French imports. The town, with its cafés and restaurants in old houses and its architectural mix of Swedish colonial (the *Town Hall,* the former yacht club, the old *Clock Tower* at the foot of Morne Lurin) and French creole (almost everything else), is quaint, pretty, and pin-neat. There are only a few historic monuments, and although pirates prowled here in the 18th century, they left no souvenirs.

A stroll around the whole town takes only an hour or two, depending on your café-resistance threshold. Park at the quay, then browse down the Rue de la République and the Rue Général-de-Gaulle; turn right and follow Rue du Centenaire along the harborside, past the old 10-ton English anchor (marked "Liverpool Wood–London," the type used by 18th-century warships) perched over the harbor opposite the Anglican church; then, if you still feel like walking, turn right and take Rue Jeanne d'Arc along the harbor's third side. Here you may want to stop at the terrace of the popular *L'Escale* restaurant (see *Eating Out*) for a glass of Beaujolais on the waterfront. Continue a couple of blocks down Rue Jeanne d'Arc to La Pointe, where you'll find the *Musée Municipal de Saint-Barthélemy* (near *Le Wall House;* phone: 278907), with a modest collection of historical photos and mementos. Most displays are in French. Closed Friday mornings, Saturday afternoons, and Sundays. Admission charge. From here, stroll back to town for refreshment at the snack bar *Chez Joe* (Rue du Roi Oscar II; phone: 276146), *Le Sélect,* or the *Bar de l'Oubli* (see *Nightlife* for the latter two). At sunset, take a two-minute drive to the edge of town (near Anse de Public) and climb atop the ruins of the 18th-century *Fort Gustav.* Here you can end your tour with spectacular views across St. Bart's high-peaked mountains and the surrounding sea. (A display map identifies the islands in the distance.)

ELSEWHERE ON THE ISLAND

GRAND FOND ROUTE Drive east past the Baie de St-Jean and a succession of stunning beaches (Anse de Lorient, Anse de Marigot, Anse du Grand Cul-de-Sac, and Petit Cul-de-Sac). Picnic or stop for a seafront lunch at *Chez Francine, Le Pélican,* or at the peaceful *Marigot Bay Club,* where the snorkeling is fine (see *Eating Out* for all three). Then turn south and swing along the surf-pounded shore of the pastoral Grand Fond district, a miniature otherworld of stone-fenced farms and tile-roofed houses with hills for backdrop and waves breaking at their feet. Return through the mountains to rejoin the north shore road. The circuit takes less than an hour, not including lunch and swim time.

COROSSOL ROUTE This second, somewhat shorter drive explores the northwest end of the island. Take a sharp left at the crossroads between town and the airport and look for the sign for *Les Grands Vins de France.* In a room adjacent to his home, wine importer Jean Patrick Gay and his assistant Stéphane Dantec offer more than 400 vintages at below-retail prices. The amiable Monsieur Gay will gladly let you taste his wares. Closed afternoons during summer and Sundays year-round (phone/fax: 277744). From the winery, the Route de Corossol parallels the Anse de Public past the cemetery to the "straw village" of Corossol. Here live the descendants of the earliest French settlers. Old, barefoot women, a few wearing starched white Breton poke bonnets, sell fine straw hats, placemats, and similar items made in small home-parlor shops. (They are shy about being photographed, so ask before you snap.) Tucked among the straw stands is the tiny gallery of Marion Vinot (phone: 277897), whose vivid canvases portray stylish Frenchwomen à Paris; it's usually closed Sundays, but hours are variable, so call before going. Before leaving Corossol, visit Ingénu Magras's *Inter-Océans Museum,* which houses a remarkable collection of seashells. Open daily. Admission charge (phone: 276297). Returning to the main road, turn left toward Quartier du Colombier for a drink or a meal at the gracious

François Plantation (see *Eating Out*). Just past the plantation, where the road ends, is a windy promontory that affords a spectacular vista out over the cobalt sea. Back toward Colombier, detour to the gleaming sands of Anse des Flamands, or the Petite Anse beyond, for a swim or a snorkel, then head back over the hills for "home."

Sources and Resources

TOURIST INFORMATION

The *Office du Tourisme* in Gustavia is located on the Quai Général-de-Gaulle, across from the *Capitainerie* (the port authority). It's closed Saturday afternoons and Sundays (phone: 278727; fax: 277447). The information booth at the airport is open during arrival and departure hours. For French West Indies tourist offices in the US, see GETTING READY TO GO.

LOCAL COVERAGE Both *Bonjour St-Barth!* (Editions du Pélican; $18)—a good French-English guide with whimsical illustrations, maps, practical information, and charming tales about the island's history and traditions—and Georges Bourdin's more scholarly *History of St. Barthélemy* (Porter Henry; $30) are usually available at *Le Colibri* (Rue de la République; phone: 278708) in Gustavia. The *Saint Barthélemy Vendôme Guide,* published by the West Indies Management Company (WIMCO), covers restaurants, hotels, and villa rentals. It is available for $11 from *SIBARTH Rental and Real Estate/WIMCO* (Rue Général-de-Gaulle, Gustavia; phone: 276238; 800-932-3222; 401-849-8012 in Rhode Island; fax: 276052). *St. Barth Magazine,* published regularly from November through May, is free and distributed widely. The *Ti Gourmet* guide is published annually and distributed free on the island (or for $5.50 subscription, phone: 279389; fax: 279848). Other annual publications include the *Guide St. Barth,* published by the hotel association, and *Tropical St. Barth.*

RADIO AND TELEVISION Radio St. Barths (98 FM) broadcasts "This Week," featuring English news and variety programs, at noon on Mondays and Thursdays; in addition, the island receives several English-language stations broadcast from St. Maarten. Most large hotels have satellite access to US television programming.

TELEPHONE When calling from the US, dial 011 (international access code) + 590 (country code) + (local number). When dialing a number on St. Barts, use only the six-digit local number unless otherwise indicated. To call St. Barts from Dutch St. Maarten, dial 6 plus the local six-digit number; from French St. Martin, as well as other French West Indies islands, dial only the local number. Codes may vary from other islands in the Caribbean, so seek operator assistance. To call the US from St. Barts, dial 19, wait for a second tone, then dial 1, plus the area code and number. Collect calls cannot be made from the island. There are few coin-operated public pay phones; it's best to purchase a *Télécarte* (a debit card good for local or international calls) at a post office or gas station. Visitors with phones restricted to local calls may access international service via *Liaisons Mondiales* by dialing 277991. Dial 17 for the police; 18 for an ambulance.

ENTRY REQUIREMENTS For stays up to three weeks, US or Canadian citizens must present proof of citizenship (a current passport or one that has expired within the past five years, or a birth certificate with raised seal or voter's registration card accompanied by a government-authorized photo ID such as a driver's license) in addition to a return or ongoing ticket. For longer periods, a valid passport is required.

CLIMATE AND CLOTHES With low annual rainfall and average daytime temperatures of 72 to 84F (about 22 to 29C), St. Barts's climate is right for light cotton and cotton-blend sports clothes—especially with a French casual chic. That means T-shirts, jeans, casual mini-skirts, shorts, pareos, or loose cotton shirts; on the beach, bikinis or monokinis are de rigueur. Nighttime dress is slightly spruced up, but still casual, except possibly at *Castelets*, *François Plantation,* the *Carl Gustaf,* the *Manapany Cottages,* the *Guanahani,* or *La Toque Lyonnaise* at *El Sereno Beach,* which call for something a shade dressier (though still no jacket and tie).

MONEY Currency is the French franc (FF). Stores and restaurants freely accept US dollars and traveler's checks (but offer no discount for them) and quote prices in US dollars; Canadian currency is accepted a bit less frequently. At press time, the exchange rate was about 4.8 FF to $1 US. Banking hours in Gustavia are 8 AM to noon and 2 to 3:30 or 4 PM weekdays; closed weekends, holidays, and afternoons preceding holidays. Credit cards are not universally honored, so ask ahead of time at hotels or restaurants. All prices in this chapter are quoted in US dollars.

LANGUAGE Pervasively French—you'll feel at home if you can *parlez* a little, but language won't be a barrier. In most shops, hotels, and restaurants, there's someone who speaks some English; and with a phrase book and patience, you'll be okay. St. Barts' second language—one you probably won't hear much—is the Norman dialect spoken by the old-timers of Corossol.

TIME St. Barts runs on atlantic standard time year-round—the same as eastern North America's daylight saving time and an hour ahead of eastern standard time (e.g., when it's noon in New York, it's 1 PM in Gustavia). Times are referred to the French way (that is, midnight is 24:00).

CURRENT Electricity is 220 volts, 60 cycles; adapters and a converter kit are needed to use American appliances.

TIPPING A 10% to 15% service charge is usually added to both hotel bills and restaurant checks and is adequate except in the case of extra special service. If no service charge has been added, give the waiter 15% of the total bill. For an errand above and beyond the call of duty, tip 5 francs or a $1 bill (American coins are hard for islanders to exchange). Taxi drivers, most of whom own their own cars, don't expect a tip.

GETTING AROUND

CAR RENTAL Offering more fun and freedom than taxis, car rentals are easy to arrange (during peak season, advance reservations are strongly advised), providing you're of legal driving age and have at least one year's licensed driving experience. In the off-season (May through November), a canopied mini-moke or a Suzuki Samurai can be picked up at the airport with a minimum of red tape. Considering the hilly terrain, these "mechanical mountain goats" make the most sense, but you must be able to operate a stick shift comfortably. Hotels with rental fleets may request you book through them.

Agencies at the airport include *Avis,* represented by *Robert Lédée* (phone: 277143); *Budget,* through *Jean-Marc Gréaux* (phone: 276743); *Guy Turbé* (phone: 277142 or 276070); *Hertz,* represented by *Francine Gréaux* (phone: 277114 or 276021); *Maurice Questel* (phone: 277322 or 276405); *Soleil Caraïbe* (phone: 276718 or 276506); and *USA,* through *Jean-Claude Gréaux* (phone: 277001 or 276643). In Colombier, there's *Edmond Gumbs* (phone: 276193 or 277532); *Europcar,* through *Alain Jeanney* (phone: 277333); in Terre Neuve, *Odette Brin* (phone: 276399); and in Gustavia, *Charles Gréaux* (phone: 276190) and *Ernest Lédée* (phone: 276163). At *Mathieu Aubin Car Rental* in Vitet (phone: 277303 or 277198), M. Aubin is particularly knowledgeable about island happenings.

Check the brakes carefully before charging off into the countryside. When maps advise the use of first gear to climb hills, PAY ATTENTION!

There are two gas stations. The one near the airport is open Mondays through Saturdays from 7:30 AM to noon and 2 to 5 PM, and sells debit cards for self-service on Sunday and after hours. Visa cards are accepted. The one in Lorient opens from 7:30 AM to 5 PM; it's closed Thursday and Saturday afternoons and all day Sunday. Gas currently costs about $3.25 per gallon.

FERRY SERVICES For a smooth, fast ride, the new catamaran *The Edge* (phone: 5995-42640 on St. Maarten) makes the run from Dutch St. Maarten's Simpson Bay to Gustavia and back (a 40-minute trip each way) on Monday, Tuesday, Thursday, and Saturday mornings (during winter) for $50 for a single day's round trip or $70 if you travel each leg on different days (plus the $5 St. Maarten departure tax). This is an excellent way to arrive in St. Barts for those who tremble at the thought of landing on the airstrip's short runway. Call ahead for reservations. Another power cat, the *White Octopus,* charges $25 one-way (plus the $5 tax) and can be reserved through *Bobby's Marina* (Philipsburg, St. Maarten; phone: 5995-23170). Making a round trip Mondays through Saturdays, the *St. Barth Express III* (phone: 277724 or 276238; fax: 277723) is an inter-island ferry that departs daily from Gustavia in the early morning and returns late afternoon from *Port la Royale Marina* in Marigot on St. Martin and from *Bobby's Marina* in Philipsburg on Dutch St. Maarten. One-way fare is $35; round-trip $50. The new *Dauphin II* ferry links Gustavia and Marigot, St. Martin (phone: 278438 or 276287). *Bateau Dakar* (phone: 277005) services both St. Martin and Guadeloupe. For help with travel plans, *Saint-Barth Voyages* (Rue Duquesne, Gustavia; phone: 277979; fax: 278045) and *Agence Charles Gréaux* (Rue Victor-Hugo, Gustavia; phone: 276663 or 276444; fax: 278502) are full-service agencies that also offer excursions. Ticket agencies include *Mast'Air* (Galeries du Commerce, St-Jean; phone: 277037 or 277743; fax: 277033).

INTER-ISLAND FLIGHTS From St. Maarten's *Juliana Airport* (the principal US gateway to the area), reserve *Windward Islands Airways* (*WINAIR;* phone: 276101 on St. Barts; 5995-44230 or 5995-44237 on St. Maarten) or *Air St. Barthélemy* (phone: 277190) for the 10-minute hop to St. Barts; the latter also has daily flights from Puerto Rico and *Espérance Airport* on French St. Martin. Both airlines offer charters, as does *Air Caraïbes* (phone: 279941; fax: 279942). There is a $5 departure tax from Dutch St. Maarten. *Air Guadeloupe* (phone: 276190 or 276444) makes the short flight from French St. Martin's *Espérance Airport* and also schedules daily flights to and from Guadeloupe (about one hour flying time) and flights from St. Thomas several days a week. *Air St. Thomas* (phone: 277176) also serves St. Barts with 45-minute flights from St. Thomas. Helicopter charters are offered by *Héli-Inter* (phone: 277114; fax: 278711). There is an airport departure tax of $2 to French St. Martin or Guadeloupe and $3 to other destinations. It is imperative to confirm return flights on all airlines, or you may inadvertently extend your visit.

MOPEDS AND MOTORCYCLES Motorbikes, mopeds, and scooters are plentiful and fun, but may not climb some steep hills. French law requires that you wear a helmet and have a motorbike or driver's license. In Gustavia, check with Denis Dufau's *Rent Some Fun* (phone: 277059), which also carries 18-speed mountain bikes; *Ernest Lédée* (see *Car Rental,* above); *Frédéric Supligeau* (phone: 276789); *Chez Beranger* (phone: 278900); or *Ouanalao Motors* (phone/fax: 278874).

SEA EXCURSIONS Opportunities to cruise the waves abound in St. Barts: day and sunset sails around St. Barts or to neighboring islands, snorkeling trips, and even underwater outings to view sunken shipwrecks aboard the semi-submersible *L'Aquascope.* To arrange any of these, contact the multi-faceted *Marine Service* (Quai du Yacht Club, Gustavia; phone: 277034; fax: 277036), or try *Océan Must Marina* (La Pointe, Gustavia; phone/fax: 276225). *Kachina* offers day sails aboard a 53-foot catamaran (phone: 276698). *Stardust Marine* (Rue Victor Hugo, Gustavia, phone: 277981; fax: 277982) and *St. Barth Ship Service* (Quai de la République, Gustavia, phone: 277738; fax: 276795) also offer day sails.

SIGHTSEEING BUS TOURS The *Office du Tourisme* (see *Tourist Information,* above) offers three minibus tours of the island that depart from Quai Général-de-Gaulle in Gustavia. The moderately priced trips last from 45 minutes to one-and-a-half hours and are designed for small groups. Independent tour operators include *Céline Gréaux* (phone: 276598), *Bruno Béal* (phone: 276005), *Emile Gréaux* (phone: 276601), *Florian Laplace* (phone: 276358), *Hugo Cagan* (phone: 276128), *Jean Brin* (phone: 276390), *Marie-Claude Lédée* (phone: 276054), *Raymond Gréaux* (phone: 276632), *Rémy Gréaux* (276360), *René Bernier* (phone: 276375), and *Robert Magras* (phone: 276312).

SIGHTSEEING HELICOPTER TOURS *Trans-Hélico-Caraïbes* offers aerial tours for about $65 (*Espérance Airport,* St. Martin; phone: 274068 or 290541; fax: 290541); also try *Héli-Inter* (phone: 277114; fax: 278711).

TAXI Taxi stands are located at the airport (phone: 277581) and on Rue de la République in Gustavia (phone: 276631). Dozens of drivers meet morning arrivals, but only a few are on call in the evenings; try *Raymond Gréaux* or *Robert Magras* (see *Sightseeing Bus Tours,* above, for both), *Jean-Paul Janin* (phone: 276186), *Mathilde Laplace* (phone: 276059), or *Lina Bernier* (phone: 276054). Flat rates apply for taxi runs up to five minutes, increasing thereafter every three minutes. There is a surcharge for nights, Sundays, and holidays.

SPECIAL EVENTS

In January or February, St. Barts stages its annual *Festival de Musique,* featuring classical and jazz artists and ballet. In February, the island has a small *Carnaval,* climaxing with *Mardi Gras* costume parades and *Ash Wednesday*'s burning of Vaval, King Carnival. August kicks off with the *Fête de Gustavia* (Gustavia Festival), followed by the August 24 *Fête de St-Barthélemy,* when pealing church bells, flying flags, festive balls, regattas, and fireworks celebrate the island's patron saint. The *Fête de St-Louis,* on August 25 in Corossol, features *pétanque* (a French bowling game similar to *bocce*), traditional *belote* dances, and a ritual blessing of the sea; Lorient's *Fête du Vent* (Festival of the Wind) celebrates with similar activities during the last weekend in August. In December, the annual *La Route du Rosé Regatta* reaches St. Barts from St. Tropez, some 4,000 miles away, bearing its cargo of rosé wines, in keeping with the tradition first established by tall ships trading between free ports. Legal holidays include *New Year's Day, Easter Sunday/Monday* (April 7 and 8), *Labor Day* (May 1), *V-E Day* (May 8), *Ascension Day* (May 16 in 1996), *Pentecost Monday* (May 27 in 1996), *Jour de l'Abolition de l'Esclavage* (Slavery Abolition Day; June 27), *Bastille Day* (July 14), *Assumption Day* and *St. Barths/Pitea Day*—Pitea is the island's Swedish sister town—(both on August 15), *All Saints' Day* (November 1), *All Souls' Day* (November 2), *Armistice Day/WWI* (November 11), *Christmas Eve, Christmas,* and *New Year's Eve.*

SHOPPING

Duty-free prices are good on island-brewed liquor and imported watches, crystal, porcelain, and other luxuries—especially French perfume, cosmetics, and name-brand sportswear. Among island crafts, traditional straw work, block-printed cotton, hand-painted silk, shellwork, and island artwork are most likely to please. Should you feel an irrational craving for one of those white sunbonnets (called *calèche* or *quichenotte*) the ladies of Corossol wear, they will make one to order in three to five days for about $35. Works by local artists Arden Rose and Jean-Paul Sorel are available in several shops. Among St. Barts' most beautiful buys are the brilliantly colored, hand-blocked cotton and silk fabrics created by Jean-Yves Froment, either sold by the meter or transformed into everything from skirts to bikinis. Beauty lotions and oils from local plants, such as those created for the *Produits M* line by Hervé Brin in Lorient (phone: 278263), make unusual gifts and are sold in shops around the island. Massage therapists Hélène Muntal and Franck Garcia in Marigot (phone: 278545) market a line of fragrant oils and bottled rum punches known as *Belou's "P"* (for *"parfums et punchs"*). Their products can be found at *Le Ti Marché* in Gustavia (see below); the punches are also served or sold to take away at *Bar de l'Oubli* (see *Nightlife*).

Most shops are open Mondays through Saturdays from 9 AM to 7 PM, with a two-hour break for lunch. In St-Jean, the best shopping is at *Centre Commercial de St-Jean* and *Centre Commercial de la Villa Créole* right next to it on Rue St-Jean. Though a tad pricier than town, these shops stay open until 8 PM. The attractive *La Savane Centre Commercial,* opposite the airport, offers more chic shops. Some of our favorite places:

Les Artisans Choice selection of local arts and crafts: hand-painted silk scarves, custom silver and gold jewelry, Elsie Questel's delicate straw work, pottery by Stanislas Carrelet, *quichenottes,* and batik clothing. Open during lunch. Level Two, Carré d'Or, Gustavia (phone/fax: 275040).

Carat I & II Twin treasure troves of fine jewelry, gems, china, porcelain, and watches. Rue de la République, Gustavia (phone: 276722 or 279919).

La Cave An amazing collection of France's top vintages, stored in climate-controlled cellars. Rue Marigot, Marigot (phone: 276321). A branch in Gustavia, called *La Cave du Port Franc,* Quai de la République (phone: 276527), also carries artwork and antique objets d'art.

Le Comptoir du Cigare A new shop with a superb collection of tobacco products (including Cuban cigars) stored in a temperature- and humidity-controlled cigar cellar, along with humidors and other accessories. Open during lunch. Rue Général-de-Gaulle, Gustavia (phone: 275062).

Hermès Synonymous with the ultimate in luxury: handbags, linen, scarves, jewelry. *Not* for the budget-minded. Quai de la République, Gustavia (phone/fax: 276615).

Kornérupine Resident gemologist-jewelry designer, Dominique Elie, sells his own creations and those of other top jewelers. *Villa Créole,* St-Jean (phone: 276811). Elie also deals in gems, gold, and watches at a branch in Gustavia called *Diamond Genesis,* Rue du Roi Oscar II (phone: 276694).

Loulou's Marine An institution for yachtsmen, featuring nautical sportswear, deck shoes, courtesy flags, and custom canvas totes. Rue de la France, Gustavia (phone: 276274).

La Maison de Free Mousse Down-to-earth collection of cotton and linen robes, table linen, natural fragrances, essential oils, quilts, pottery, pillows, and bath accessories. Carré d'Or, Gustavia (phone: 277504).

Manuel Canovas An array of designer home furnishings, fabric, bath and table linen, coordinated china and linen breakfast services, beach towels, luggage, and some bathing suits. Quai de la République, Gustavia (phone: 278278).

Pati's Tee Shirt Factory Pati Guyot—creator of the island's official logo—offers a complete line of sportswear and accessories, including her own newest creations and children's wear. Rue Schoelcher, La Pointe, Gustavia (phone: 278261) or at a boutique specializing in crafts, *Pati de St-Barth,* Rue Jeanne d'Arc (across the street from the post office), Gustavia (phone: 279880).

Privilège Emporium for duty-free perfume, cosmetics, and jewelry. Rue Général-de-Gaulle, Gustavia (phone: 276743) and *Centre Commercial de St-Jean,* St-Jean (phone: 277208).

La Rôtisserie A long-established deli that provides hors d'oeuvres, pâtés, French sausages, roast chicken, salads, and fine wines for an elegant picnic. Rue Lafayette and Rue du Roi Oscar II, Gustavia (phone: 276313) and Rue St-Jean, St-Jean (phone: 277346).

Sophie Laurent Men's and women's fashionable sportswear. They will, if you wish, imprint their tasteful logo on your purchase. Rue du Roi Oscar II, Gustavia (phone: 276757).

Stéphane & Bernard Smart boutique carrying women's international designer collections. Rue de la République, Gustavia (phone: 276569) and *La Savane Centre Commercial* at the airport (phone: 276913).

Le Ti Marché Gustavia's outdoor crafts market, where artisans sell everything from murals and straw weavings to lace-trimmed table and bed linen and coconut sculptures. Its most famous vendor is the *Belou's "P"* booth, offering home-brewed body oils and shampoos, luxurious perfumes, and herb-spiked rum and *digestifs.* On Rue du Roi Oscar II. Mornings only; closed Sundays.

SPORTS

The *St. Barth Sports Agency* (phone: 277725 or 276806) will arrange everything from windsurfing and water skiing to hiking, horseback riding, and tennis.

BOATING Sunfish and small boats can be rented at most beaches near hotels for an hourly fee. Private charters can be arranged through *La Calèche Yacht Charter* at *SIBARTH/WIMCO* (phone: 276238; fax: 276052), *St. Barth Ship*

Service (see *Sea Excursions*), or *Yacht Charter Agency* in Gustavia (phone: 277034). St. Barts can accommodate 500 yachts, mostly at anchor. Gustavia Harbor has mooring and limited docking facilities for yachts.

FITNESS CENTERS The *St. Barth's Gym* at the *St. Barth's Beach* hotel (see *Checking In*) features licensed sports trainer Dr. Harvey Maron, who'll custom-design a fitness program. *A.S.S.C.O.* (Sports Center of Colombier; phone: 276107) offers body-building. Many hotels, such as the *Christopher* and the *Carl Gustaf* (see *Checking In* for both), offer health and fitness programs.

HORSEBACK RIDING *Ranch des Flamands* is located at Anse des Flamands (phone: 278072).

SNORKELING AND SCUBA DIVING Several of the beachside hotels provide or rent gear. For scuba diving, contact *Marine Service* or *Océan Must Marina* (see *Sea Excursions*); *Dive With Dan* at the *Emeraude Plage* hotel (see *Checking In*); *Rainbow Dive* (phone: 273129 or 279170) in Gustavia; or *Scuba Club La Bulle* (St-Jean; phone: 276893). *St-Barth Plongée* (Quai de la République, Gustavia; phone: 274333 or 273110) offers snorkel and dive trips, some to nearby Saba.

SPORT FISHING Tuna, marlin, bonito, wahoo, dorado, and barracuda are found in the waters north of Lorient, Flamands, and Corossol. *Marine Service* and *Océan Must Marina* (see *Sea Excursions* for both) offer half- and full-day fishing trips. Trips with private fishermen can be arranged by your hotel, given a day's notice. Bring your own tackle. *Warning:* Some tropical fish species can be toxic. Get an expert opinion before consuming your catch.

SURFING Surfers should contact Eric Chaumant of the *Reefer Surf Club* (Lorient; phone: 276763) for hot spots.

SWIMMING AND SUNNING The island's combination of gleaming stretches of sand and unique isolation makes it irresistible to unwinders.

DREAM BEACHES

Grande Saline and Gouverneur These two glorious crescents of beach, cushioned between jagged mountains marbled with cacti, slope into blue-green sea. Named for nearby salt pans, Grande Saline is noted for its wild beauty and pounding surf. Gouverneur is smaller and calmer, a secluded stretch of porcelain sand edged with sea grape that requires a bit of a walk to reach it. Be sure to explore the cave in the cliffs of Grande Pointe, on the western end of Gouverneur, where the 17th-century pirate Monbars the Exterminator is said to have stashed his treasure. The newly-paved road and landscaped parking area at Saline has increased its popularity, and these days it's sometimes crowded. Bring your own provisions. Even though nude sunbathing is illegal, the rule isn't strictly enforced at Grande

Saline, and visitors have been known to bask au naturel here; in general, however, it's a practice reserved for tots only.

Other super strands: Baie de St-Jean, a popular beach for people watching; secluded Marigot, favored by locals for picnics; Lorient, ideal for children with its gentle surf and shady spots; Colombier, a 20-minute walk from Petite Anse, but worth the effort; Grand Cul-de-Sac, a calm lagoon with great windsurfing and beachfront restaurants; and Anse des Flamands, a classic Caribbean beach dotted with small hotels and homes. Watch the undertow, especially on windward beaches like Anse de Toiny and Anse du Grand Fond. No hotel really owns a beach, but some collect a small fee for the use of their facilities.

TENNIS Reservations are necessary at all society clubs and hotel courts (where guests have priority). There are two lighted courts at *A.S.S.C.O.* (see *Fitness Centers,* above), and one lighted court at *Centre Association des Jeunes Ouvriers & Etudiants* (*A.J.O.E.;* Youth Association of Lorient; off the main road; phone: 276763). Private courts include *Guanahani,* with two lighted, artificial grass courts; *Le Flamboyant Tennis Club* in Grand Cul-de-Sac, with two lighted courts (phone: 277565 or 276982); and *Isle de France, Manapany Cottages, St. Barth's Beach, Les Islets de la Plage* (St-Jean; phone: 276238), and *Taïwana* (Anse des Flamands; phone: 276501), all with one court each. Pro Yves Lacoste gives lessons in Toiny through *SB Sports Agency* (phone: 276806). Unless otherwise noted, see *Checking In* for the hotels listed above.

WATER SKIING For equipment and instruction, contact Stéphan Jouany at *Marine Service,* or call *Océan Must* (see *Sea Excursions* for both).

WINDSURFING Pascal Vallon's *Wind Wave Power,* at the *St. Barth's Beach* hotel (Grand Cul-de-Sac; phone: 278257) and at *Guanahani* (see *Checking In*), offers instruction and equipment rental. Jean-Michel Marot's *Windsurfing Paradise* (phone: 277122), also offering lessons and equipment, operates off the beach at St-Jean. Rentals are available at the *Filao Beach* hotel in St-Jean (see *Checking In*); at *Ouanalao* in Gustavia (phone: 278127); and on the beach at Marigot Bay. Windsurfing is also popular at Anse des Flamands and Lorient.

NIGHTLIFE

Anyone who cares about food and ambience should savor a whole evening—from aperitifs through *digestifs*—at one of these outstanding restaurants: *Carl Gustaf,* with its spectacular view of Gustavia's harbor, nightly live music, and piano bar; *La Table des Castelets,* with its breathtaking vistas from atop Morne Lurin; *La Toque Lyonnaise* at suave *El Sereno Beach; Manapany Cottages,* where softly sung traditional ballads complement the cuisine; and the peaceful, mountaintop *François Plantation* in Colombier (see *Eating Out* for all). In Gustavia, *L'Ananas* (see *Eating Out*) and *L'Hibiscus* (Rue Thiers; phone: 279696) have pleasant piano bars. Visitors can dine while taking in magician Dominique Webb's mesmerizing nightly show at the *Magic House* (6 Rue Jeanne d'Arc; phone: 279991). *Eddy's Ghetto* (see *Eating Out*) is a good choice for a vibrant scene, casual dining, and frequent live music. *Rock and Roll Marine* (Rue du Bord de Mer; phone: 276999) offers a *tapas* menu until midnight. No visit to the island is complete without a "Cheeseburger in Paradise" at *Le Sélect* (Rue Général-de-Gaulle; phone: 278687), where Jimmy Buffet himself is a frequent visitor, or a cocktail and some prime people watching across the street at the slightly more St. Tropez–like *Bar de l'Oubli* (phone: 276940 or 277006). For late-night disco in Gustavia, check out *Le Petit Club,* next to the *Côté Jardin* on Rue du Centenaire (phone: 276633). Outside Gustavia, at Anse de Public, *Maya's* (see *Eating Out*) attracts a lively crowd for cocktails and dinner. In St-Jean, *Le Pélican* has a piano bar and features live jazz and dancing (phone: 276464; closed Sundays), while *Topolino* (see *Eating Out*) is a good bet for jazz. At Lorient, *La Licorne* is a popular dance club that attracts a young late-night crowd, especially on Saturdays (phone: 278394 or 276074); *La Banane* offers a dinner cabaret revue (see *Eating Out*). In Lurin try *Le Why Not?* nightclub and bar for dancing (phone: 278867; closed Sundays through Tuesdays in summer). At Grand Cul-de-Sac, *Guanahani*'s *L'Indigo* (see *Eating Out*) puts on a fabulous poolside dinner show on Wednesdays.

Best on the Island

CHECKING IN

The largest hotel on St. Barts might be considered mid-size elsewhere, but the special charm of the island lies in its intimacy—with tiny, often luxurious hotels, many of which are actually a string of cottages clinging to a hillside or bungalows scattered among sea grapes along a beach. The island has become so fashionable that prices have skyrocketed. For a double room without meals (EP) in winter (December 15 to April 15), our expensive category starts at $250 a day (*Le Toiny, Carl Gustaf,* and *Manapany Cottages* are very expensive, with rates as high as $800 a day in season). The moderate range is $130 to $250; anything less than $130 is considered inexpensive (and you won't find a room much under $75 in high season). Continental breakfasts often are included. Some hotels include tax and service charge in their quoted rates, while others tack on from 5% to 15% for taxes and/or a 10% to 15% service charge. Many hotels have steep paths or are set on sprawling properties that may pose a problem for some; if this is a concern, ask if your room is easily accessible. Unless otherwise indicated, the accommodations below feature private baths, air conditioning, telephones, and TV sets.

A number of furnished hillside and beach villas are rented by the week or month through *Ici & La* (Quai de la République, BP 219, Gustavia 97096, St. Barthélemy; phone: 277878; fax: 277828). *SIBARTH Rental and Real Estate/WIMCO* (Rue Général-de-Gaulle, Gustavia; phone: 276238; 800-

932-3222; 401-849-8012 in Rhode Island; fax: 276052) can arrange a stay in one of over 200 different villas and bungalows, ranging from one-bedroom beach cottages to lavish six-bedroom estates perched atop cliffs. Rates vary considerably, with weekly winter rents starting at about $1,200 for a one-bedroom, one-bath bungalow. Summer rates are 25% to 40% less. When calling from St. Barts, use only the local number. For information about dialing from elsewhere, see *Telephone* earlier in this chapter.

We begin with our favorite havens, all of which fall in the "expensive" category, followed by recommended hotels listed by price category.

SPECIAL HAVENS

Carl Gustaf Named for the King of Sweden, this is arguably *le dernier cri* (the last word) in luxury, with 14 exquisite one- and two-bedroom suites perched on a hillside overlooking Gustavia's harbor. The suites, each with a Jacuzzi plunge pool, marble-floored living room, and kitchenette, are surrounded by exotic gardens of bougainvillea and birds of paradise. All rooms feature stereos, fax machines, and mini-bars. Continental breakfast is served on your private terrace, while dinner is a deluxe affair at the hotel's restaurant (see *Eating Out*). There's also a fitness center and a pool with a piano bar, and the beach is a short stroll away. Rue des Normands, Gustavia (phone: 278283; 800-322-2223; fax: 278237).

Les Castelets This place has the feel of a small, very elegant part of France transported to an island mountaintop. Now under the expert management of seasoned Parisian hoteliers M. and Mme. Laugeois, this *très* chic resort has eight luxury guestrooms and two suites, which feature either cream-colored carpets or marble floors, high French provincial beds, gleaming bathrooms, handsome fabrics, and balconies with exquisite views; all rooms have mini-bars and refrigerators (no TV sets). Outside, sloping stone trails wend their way between poinciana trees. Meals in the refined dining room are superb (see *Eating Out*). There's a *petite* pool with a compelling view; Gouverneur and Grande Saline Beaches are a short stroll away. Continental breakfast is included in the rate. Closed May through October. Morne Lurin (phone: 276173 or 277880; 800-322-2223; fax: 278527).

François Plantation The serene mountain retreat of François and Françoise Beret, this elegant resort comprises 12 pastel colonial-style bungalows with terraces set on a lush, flower-filled hillside. The bungalows are decorated with antique reproductions, such as four-poster beds, and Provençal print fabrics, while the spacious bathrooms are fashioned from striking keystone coral and marble and furnished with oversize towels. All rooms have ceiling fans, refrigerator/mini-bars, and safes. Full American breakfast is served in the garden-side dining room or, for a small charge, on your private terrace; dinner is French and fabulous (see *Eating Out*). The pool at the top of the property provides an eagle's-nest view of the sea and surrounding countryside. Colombier (phone: 277882; 800-932-3222; fax: 276126).

Guanahani St. Barts' largest hotel, with two beaches and 91 rooms scattered among colorful West Indian–style cottages with peaked roofs and laced in gingerbread trim. There are 61 rooms and 19 one-bedroom suites, each with either a small private pool or an outdoor Jacuzzi. All accommodations feature ceiling fans, mini-bars, and covered verandahs with ocean views. Rooms differ in size and layout; some may be combined to form larger units to accommodate groups. Amenities include two pools, exemplary 24-hour room service, two lighted tennis courts, complete water sports facilities, and two restaurants—*Bartolomeo,* serving French haute cuisine, and the informal pool/beach café *L'Indigo* (see *Eating Out* for both). Grand Cul-de-Sac (phone: 276660; 800-223-6800; fax: 277070).

Le Toiny This sumptuous retreat rests on a rolling hillside suspended above a splendid sea tableau. Each of the 12 cottage suites—with its own garden, picket fence, and swimming pool—gives the feeling of a luxurious home. Gleaming hardwood floors, mahogany four-poster beds with canopies, designer draperies, plush fabrics, and Italian tile baths provide a sense of plantation-era elegance. Each villa also features a kitchenette, fax machine, VCR, safe, and fitness equipment. Continental breakfast is served on your terrace, and *Le Gaïac* restaurant offers excellent French cuisine (see *Eating Out*). To top it all off, the service is world class. Closed September through October. Anse de Toiny (phone: 278888; 800-932-3222; fax: 278930).

GRAND CUL-DE-SAC–MARIGOT–VITET

EXPENSIVE

St. Barth's Beach Set on a peninsula between a calm beach and a lagoon, Guy Turbe's older but pleasant property is favored by families for its water sports, tennis, and saltwater pool. The 36 comfortable rooms feature Mexican tile floors, vaulted ceilings, and balconies; there are also eight newer deluxe two-bedroom villas with spacious living rooms, VCRs, and ocean-view terraces. There's also a bar and restaurant, *Le Rivage* (see *Eating Out*). The hotel shares facilities with Turbe's adjacent *Grand Cul-de-Sac Beach* hotel (where there are 16 additional bungalows). Grand Cul-de-Sac (phone: 276070; 800-223-9815; fax: 277557).

El Sereno Beach A *petit bijou* (jewel) with 20 bungalow-style rooms boasting Mexican tile floors, vaulted ceilings, hammocks, and private gardens and terraces; all rooms have refrigerators and safes. There are also nine one-bedroom villas on a nearby hillside, each with a living room, kitchen, and large terrace. There's a big pool, a fitness center, and plenty of water sports. The hotel boasts one of St. Barts' most acclaimed restaurants, *La Toque Lyonnaise,* plus the beachside bistro *La Lagon Bleu* (see *Eating Out* for both) and two bars. Closed September through mid-October. Grand Cul-de-Sac (phone: 276480; 800-322-2223; fax: 277547).

MODERATE

Hostellerie des Trois Forces This "New Age" country inn is a remote mountainside cluster of 12 bungalows, each designed after a different sign of the zodiac and all with terraces and handmade furnishings; a two-bedroom villa is also available. Some of the accommodations are air conditioned and have tubs and showers, while others have ceiling fans and showers only; none has a telephone or TV set. French astrologer-owner-chef Hubert de la Motte conducts yoga classes by the pool (with swim-up bar) and holiday cooking classes. The poolside restaurant features French and creole dishes (see *Eating Out*). Closed the months of June and October. Vitet (phone: 276125; 800-932-3222; fax: 278138).

Marigot Bay Club This charming, bungalow-style hotel across from the beach has six one-bedroom studio apartments that are always in demand. All units have kitchens, terraces, and living rooms, but no telephones. Guests need travel no farther than the restaurant here for a memorable meal (see *Eating Out*). Marigot (phone: 277545; fax: 279004).

Sea Horse Nestled on a hillside with views of the bay below, this intimate hotel offers 10 airy one-bedroom suites with high ceilings, kitchenettes, living rooms, and ocean-view terraces; there's also a two-bedroom villa. The recently redecorated rooms have tile floors, ceiling fans, and handmade-tile showers (no TV sets). There's also a pool and an outdoor grill area. A restaurant and the beach are a five-minute walk away. Airport transportation is included in the rate. There's no charge for children under 12. Marigot (phone: 277536; fax: 278533).

LORIENT

EXPENSIVE

La Banane This unforgettable gem, in a lush tropical setting near the beach, offers nine cottages (five are air conditioned) with interesting interiors: One has a tub and shower near the four-poster bed, as well as live plants and trees throughout. Bungalow Nos. 2 and 3 can be rented together, and No. 4 has a very private terrace. All have VCRs and mini-bars. There's a bar and a poolside restaurant that features a French cabaret show (see *Eating Out*), as well as two freshwater pools. Continental breakfast is included in the rate. Near Lorient Beach (phone: 276825; 800-932-3222; fax: 276844).

Christopher This Sofitel property is set on a dramatic promontory above the ocean. The 40 spacious rooms open onto terraces surrounded by lush tropical gardens; all are furnished with polished mahogany pieces and Mexican tile floors. The large baths feature oversize tubs and separate showers. There's a fitness center, large pool, good French and creole dining at the increasingly popular *L'Orchidée,* and casual lunches and tropical cocktails at *Le Mango.* The beaches at Lorient and Marigot are a five-minute drive away. Full American breakfast is included in the rate. Pointe Milou (phone: 276363; 800-763-4835 or 800-221-4542; fax: 279292).

MODERATE

Les Islets Fleuris A relaxed mountaintop inn with a panoramic view of offshore islands, this tranquil spot has six large studios and one suite in a tropical garden setting with a pool. All units are attractively furnished and have kitchenettes, showers, balconies, and ceiling fans (no air conditioning); several have ocean views, and two have TV sets. There's no restaurant, but breakfast is available on request (at an extra charge). MasterCard accepted (phone: 276422; 800-223-9815; fax: 276972).

INEXPENSIVE

Le Manoir de Saint-Barthélemy Jeanne Audy Rowland—architect, designer, museum curator, and author—presides over this most unusual bed and breakfast, long a favorite of French artists. The lobby and public areas are in a 17th-century country house and barn from Normandy, which is surrounded by five one-to three-bedroom villas with kitchenettes and ceiling fans (none with air conditioning, telephones, or TV sets). The grounds are studded with mango, lime, and papaya trees, and a small waterfall flows into a fish pond. It's all very relaxed (hammocks, huge cushions, and macramé sculptures everywhere) and very, very romantic. There's no restaurant, but breakfast is available at an additional charge. A short walk from the beach (phone: 277927; fax: 276575).

La Normandie This hospitable guesthouse has eight modest, but immaculate rooms, decorated in pretty floral fabrics; there are no telephones or TV sets. There's a small pool, garden, and bar/restaurant. Just a few minutes' walk from the beach and the village. No credit cards accepted (phone: 276166).

ST-JEAN

EXPENSIVE

Eden Rock St. Barts' first inn, built on a magnificent quartzite promontory flanked by two perfect beaches, boasts a cluster of red-roofed cottages. The six rooms are individually decorated in elegant tropical style, with clay tile floors, mini-bars, and beds draped in either mosquito netting or canopies; most have terraces with compelling views of the ocean and mountains. Room No. 1 boasts antique furnishings, a four-poster bed, and a beautiful view. There are no TV sets. Continental breakfast is included in the rate, and there's an informal restaurant—see *Eating Out* (phone: 277294; fax: 278837).

Emeraude Plage Grouped around a secluded tropical garden right on the beach are 24 comfortably furnished, two-bedroom bungalows, three suites, and one villa, all with kitchens and terraces. There's no restaurant, but there's a bar, and several dining spots are nearby; there's also an on-site dive shop (phone: 276478; fax: 278308).

Filao Beach At the island's only member of the prestigious Relais & Châteaux group of hotels, 30 rooms in bungalows named for French châteaux form a crescent around the beach and pool; most rooms have ocean-view terraces, and all have sitting areas, ceiling fans, refrigerators, and safes. Water sports and boat charters are available. There's also a popular, casual poolside restaurant and bar (see *Eating Out*). Continental breakfast is served on your private terrace or poolside. Closed August 29 through October 15 (phone: 276484; 800-372-1323; fax: 276224).

MODERATE

Tropical Gingerbread trim adds to the attraction of 20 twin-bedded rooms clustered around a fountain garden, each with a verandah or ocean-view balcony, as well as shower, fan, and refrigerator (none has a TV set, but there's a main music/reading room with a TV set and VCR). There is a small pool, a bar, a breakfast terrace, and a snack bar. The beach and restaurants are nearby (phone: 276487; 800-223-6510; fax: 278174).

Village St. Jean This 25-room property perched on a hill above Baie de St-Jean has a variety of accommodations: guestrooms, one- and two-bedroom suites, deluxe one-bedroom cottages with full kitchens, and a deluxe one-bedroom suite with a Jacuzzi. All have ceiling fans, kitchenettes, and terraces. A stone path leads to an attractive pool with a waterfall and Jacuzzi that command a breathtaking view of the bay below. There's a commissary, a library/listening room, and *Le Patio* restaurant (see *Eating Out*). The beach is a five-minute walk away. Closed September and October (phone: 276139; 800-322-2223; fax: 277796).

INEXPENSIVE

Tom Beach Right on the beach, this basic but charming hotel offers easy access to Gustavia shops and restaurants. All 10 rooms have balconies and kitchenettes, and there's an open-air bamboo bistro for casual lunches (phone: 277096; fax: 277277).

GUSTAVIA

INEXPENSIVE

Sunset The upper floors of a lovely old building have been turned into an eight-room hotel; all rooms are simple but comfortable, with mini-bars. Best views are from rooms facing the harbor, though the inner rooms are quieter. Continental breakfast is included in the rate. Rue de la République, Gustavia (phone: 277721; fax: 278340 or 278159).

ANSE DES CAYES–COLOMBIER–ANSE DES FLAMANDS

VERY EXPENSIVE

Manapany Cottages A posh colony of 52 luxury units in red-roofed gingerbread cottages sprawled along a private beach or tiered on the flowered hillside above. Best are the extravagant beachfront Club Suites—each with a large marble bath, full kitchen, and open-air living room/dining area. The other accommodations consist of smaller double rooms and adjoining suites with kitchenettes, and large living room/dining terraces; some can be rented as a combined unit. All accommodations have views of the ocean. Amenities include a large oval pool, lighted tennis court, Jacuzzi, fitness center, and a variety of water sports. There's also a bar, a billiards room, and two restaurants, *Le Ballahou* and *Ouanalao* (see *Eating Out* for both). Anse des Cayes (phone: 276655 or 277526; 800-847-4249; fax: 277528).

EXPENSIVE

Isle de France Considered one of the island's finest addresses, this stylish 30-unit beachfront hotel is an informal but elegant refuge. Its bungalows, suites, and studios are richly adorned with marble floors, rattan furniture, showers and sunken tubs, and wide terraces with unbeatable views of the beach and sea. There are two pools, a fitness center, restaurant, tennis court, and the island's only air conditioned squash court. Closed September through mid-October. Anse des Flamands (phone: 276181; 800-322-2223; fax: 278683).

MODERATE

Auberge de la Petite Anse Mother Nature designed the decor for this serene, get-away-from-it-all collection of bungalows linked to the beach by paths. Set on a hillock above the sea, its 16 rooms (two per balconied house) are immaculate but spartan, with kitchenettes but no telephones or TV sets. There's no restaurant, but a grocery store is nearby. No credit cards accepted. Petite Anse des Flamands (phone: 276460; 800-223-6510; fax: 277230).

Baie des Anges A beachside bungalow complex that's great for families; there are nine units, each with a kitchenette and a terrace facing the ocean. Best are the two units right on the beach with full kitchens. All rooms are simply but comfortably furnished (no TV sets or telephones). There is a restaurant. Anse des Flamands (phone: 276361 or 277825; 800-932-3222; fax: 278344).

Baie des Flamands A two-story beachfront inn popular with families, it's one of St. Barts' older properties. The 24 rooms are good-size, all with balconies or terraces. Lower-level rooms have kitchenettes, while upper-level ones have refrigerators only; there are no telephones or TV sets, and all rooms have showers only (no tubs). There is a large saltwater pool, a terrace bar, and *La Frégate* restaurant. Airport transfers are included in the rate, and car rental is available. Anse des Flamands (phone: 276485 or 276476; 800-44-PRIMA; fax: 278398).

Le P'tit Morne In a stunning setting, this breezy, friendly mountaintop retreat has 14 spacious and pleasantly decorated studio apartments, each with a full kitchen. There's a pool with a snack bar serving breakfast and lunch. One of the island's best values. Closed June. Colombier (phone: 266264; fax: 278463).

White Sand Beach Cottages Great for families, these four pretty pink bungalows all have kitchenettes, terrace/living rooms, sun decks, and gardens, but no telephones or TV sets. A restaurant and grocery store are nearby. Anse des Flamands (phone: 278208; fax: 277069).

INEXPENSIVE

Auberge Terre-Neuve Ten simple bungalows with kitchenettes (but no air conditioning, TV sets, or telephones) on the island's western tip, far from the crowds. A good value, with rental car included in the rate. There's no restaurant. Petite Anse des Flamands (phone: 277532; fax: 277899).

EATING OUT

St. Barts offers some 65 options for eating out—snack places and town bistros, informal beachside cafés featuring charcoal-grilled steaks and fresh lobster, several spots for island cooking, and restaurants serving haute cuisine. Only a select few can really be considered inexpensive. St. Barts has several native dishes, such as *funghi* (cornmeal and okra dumplings), *boudin* (spicy blood sausage), *colombo de poulet* (curried chicken), and creole-spiced fresh fish and lobster. The cost of a three-course dinner for two, not including wine, ranges from "inexpensive" (less than $75), to moderate ($75 to $150), to expensive ($150 and up, up, up!). Unless stated otherwise, all restaurants listed below are open for lunch and dinner, and dinner reservations are necessary—especially in season and on weekends. When calling from St. Barts, use only the local numbers listed below. For information about dialing from elsewhere, see *Telephone* earlier in this chapter.

GUSTAVIA

EXPENSIVE

Carl Gustaf This elegant hillside dining room offers a premier gastronomic experience in a captivating setting, with candlelight, romantic piano music, and harbor panoramas. Chef Patrick Gateau prepares a stellar three-course prix fixe lunch; the à la carte dinner menu features such delicacies as Maine lobster in golden puff pastry, lobster ravioli with *pistou* and shellfish cream sauce, and prime rib of lamb with garlic cream sauce. The chocolate cake flavored with passion fruit is to die for. The piano bar is a choice spot to view *un magnifique coucher de soleil* (sunset) while sampling the excellent wine cellar. Open daily. Closed September through mid-October. Major credit cards accepted. At the *Carl Gustaf Hotel*, Rue des Normands (phone: 278283; fax: 278237).

Au Port One of St. Barts's oldest and most hospitable restaurants sports a new decor and serves a French and Antillean menu featuring a prix fixe creole dinner, as well as à la carte house foie gras, steamed snapper with passion fruit, lobster cassoulet, and tangy fresh-fruit soup. Open for dinner only; closed Sundays in the off-season. Reservations advised. Major credit cards accepted. Rue du Centenaire (phone: 276236).

Le Sapotillier Across from the quay, this cozy place accommodates guests indoors or under its namesake sapotilla tree. The new menu features duck foie gras with juniper berry sauce, snail lasagna in garlic sauce, veal stew with Roquefort, and traditional French fish dishes. Outstanding desserts include rich "white-and-black" chocolate mousse. Open for dinner only; closed Sundays. Reservations advised. MasterCard and Visa accepted. Rue du Centenaire (phone: 276028).

MODERATE

L'Ananas Set on a verandah dripping with bougainvillea in an elegant historic home overlooking the harbor, this intimate spot is set apart by its ambience and creative West Indian menu, which features such specialties as pan-fried prawns and creole lobster. Arrive in time to watch the sunset from the piano bar with a homemade-rum cocktail. Open for dinner only; closed Tuesdays. Major credit cards accepted. Rue Thiers (phone: 276377).

Eddy's Ghetto Recently relocated to a new site across from *Le Sapotillier* (above), this is the current "in" spot for nighttime fun, especially when Eddy Stakelborough's musician buddies drop by. (Eddy's father, Marius, founded *Le Sélect* just two blocks away.) The changing French and creole menu also offers occasional Brazilian specialties; Chef Filou Burlot's pumpkin soup, crab salad, conch *colombo,* beef ragout, and chocolate mousse are crowd pleasers, so it's best to arrive early if you don't want to wait. Open for dinner only; closed Sundays, and the months of June, September, and October. No reservations. No credit cards accepted. Rue du Centenaire (no phone).

L'Escale A popular spot to view the yachting scene, this casual waterfront alfresco eatery furnished in white wicker features an array of Italian pasta, pizza, appetizers, and salads, as well as seafood grilled over a wood fire. Open daily. MasterCard and Visa accepted. Rue Jeanne d'Arc, on the far side of the harbor (phone: 277033 or 278106).

Maya's Specials change nightly, but fresh seafood, grilled lobster, and tasty creole dishes are staples at this open-air waterfront terrace run by Martinique-born Maya Gurley. The sherbets and pastries are homemade (try the dense chocolate cake). This is a nice spot for sundowner cocktails. Open for dinner only; closed Sundays. Closed mid-June through mid-July and September through October. Reservations advised. Major credit cards accepted. Anse de Public, just outside Gustavia (phone: 277361 or 277573).

Le Repaire Gustavia's biggest harborfront café features a stylish alfresco setting with ceiling fans, a fish pond, and upbeat recorded music. Daily French and creole specials supplement a menu that includes imported, fresh mussels (on Fridays), lobster, beef, fish—even *les burgers avec frites.* Save room for some ice cream or sorbet. Open daily for breakfast, lunch, and dinner. Reservations unnecessary. MasterCard and Visa accepted. Quai de la République (phone: 277248).

Le Saïgon Thai, Vietnamese, Chinese, and Indian food is served at this popular family eatery. Some dishes are familiar—sweet-and-sour pork, Peking duck, fried wontons—while others are more exotic—Vietnamese egg rolls (*nem*) and *crevettes au curry Indien et au lait de coco* (curried shrimp with coconut milk). Closed Tuesdays off-season. MasterCard accepted. Rue du Roi Oscar II (phone: 278137).

Le Wall House Gérard Pagan's chic terrace eatery on the harbor offers a traditional French menu; try the roast lamb, shrimp stew, the *menu dégustation* (sampling of several dishes), or the special prix fixe lobster menu. Open daily. MasterCard and Visa accepted. La Pointe, on the far side of the harbor (phone: 277183).

INEXPENSIVE

Le Bistrot des Arts A favorite with celebrities and artists (it has its own contemporary art exhibit). Traditional French bistro fare, plus barbecue and pizza, is served on a terrace overlooking the harbor. Open daily. MasterCard and American Express accepted. Rue Jeanne d'Arc, La Pointe (phone: 277000; fax: 277407).

Côté Jardin This inviting garden terrace, next to *L'Ananas* (above), features French and Italian specialties (including pizza), and grilled meat, chicken, and fish;

there's also a children's menu. Open daily for dinner only. MasterCard accepted. Rue du Centenaire (phone: 177047).

La Marine If you like mussels, reserve a week in advance for the Thursday special at Pierre Gallic's pretty waterside terrace restaurant. There's also an affordable prix fixe dinner and an à la carte menu featuring more mouthwatering seafood dishes—try the fresh sautéed Dover sole, lightly seasoned with *herbes de Provence*. Closed Sundays. Major credit cards accepted. Rue Jeanne D'Arc, on the far side of the harbor (phone: 277013 or 276891).

ST-JEAN

EXPENSIVE

Adam This hillside terrace restaurant is small and charming, with a menu that offers classic French cuisine with a twist—lobster tabbouleh or salmon *tartare* with oysters and caviar—as well as a fine, affordable prix fixe menu. For dessert, sample the excellent *crème brûlée*. Open for dinner only; closed Tuesdays. Reservations advised. Major credit cards accepted. St-Jean Carénage (phone: 279322).

Filao Beach Tempting, light lunches—lobster salad with trout caviar, warm goat cheese salad with walnuts, snapper with sea urchin purée—are served in the café bar or around the pool of this beachfront hotel. Lobster, tuna, and duck often appear on the menu, with coconut soufflé a featured dessert. Open daily for lunch only; closed August 29 through October 15. Visa and American Express accepted. Baie de St-Jean (phone: 276484; fax: 276224).

Le Patio Bouillabaisse and Italian specialties are the draw at this casual Caribbean-style eatery on a terrace overlooking the bay. The changing menu features homemade pasta and pizza with more than a dozen toppings (even lobster). Also featured are veal, fish, and chicken dishes, as well as classic desserts such as chocolate *gâteau*. Live jazz is featured on Friday and Saturday nights in season. Open for dinner only; closed Wednesdays and mid-September through mid-October. Reservations advised. Major credit cards accepted. At the *Village St. Jean* (phone: 276139; fax: 277796).

Topolino This attractive poolside spot serves homemade foie gras, charcoal-grilled fish, lobster, and steaks, as well as French, creole, and Italian dishes. It's a good place for family dining—kids love the adjacent ice-cream parlor. There's nightly live music in season. Open daily; closed for lunch in the off-season. No reservations. MasterCard and Visa accepted. Across the street from the *Filao Beach Hotel* (phone: 277092; fax: 278033).

MODERATE

Brasserie La Créole This open-air spot serves breakfast and lunch, but really turns on the authentic creole cuisine for dinner, with dishes like *soukai* (mango marinated with herbs and lime) and *bélélé* (a pork stew from Martinique).

Open daily. No reservations. American Express accepted. In the *Centre Commercial de la Villa Créole* (phone: 276809).

Chez Francine The attractions of this beach café are many: the view of a turquoise lagoon, carefree clientele, and the delicious French and creole food. Highly recommended are the fresh langouste (possibly the island's best), *boudin créole* (blood sausage), and chicken, fish, or steak platters; for dessert, try the fresh-baked *tartes maison.* Open daily; closed Monday dinner (except holidays). Reservations advised. Major credit cards accepted. Baie de St-Jean (phone: 276049; fax: 279306).

Eden Rock Enjoying the hilltop view of the bay at St. Barts's original hostelry, this recently reopened bar and restaurant's rustic flavor makes it a popular spot for spicy barbecue and creole dishes or just for evening cocktails. Open daily. Visa accepted. At *Eden Rock Hotel,* Baie de St-Jean (phone: 277294; fax: 278837).

Le Pélican An island institution noted for its jazzy nightlife, this large beachside terrace restaurant is equally famous for its grilled lobsters (pick your own from the tank), shrimp brochettes, and fresh mussels flown in from France (on Thursday and Friday nights). Open daily. Reservations advised for dinner. Major credit cards accepted. Baie de St-Jean (phone: 276464; fax: 276001).

ANSE DES CAYES–COLOMBIER

EXPENSIVE

Le Ballahou Overflowing with greenery and overlooking the ocean, this elegant poolside dining room at the *Manapany Cottages* is the perfect romantic setting, complete with flowers, candlelight, and soft piano music. Chef Gilles Berthaud creates classic and nouvelle French dishes, ranging from an *assiette norvégienne* (smoked salmon with dilled whipped cream) to escargot turnovers. Homemade pastries, sherbet, and tropical fruit are among dessert choices; there are also exotic cocktails garnished with fresh flowers, and an elaborate wine list. Reservations advised. Open daily for dinner only; closed mid-April through mid-November. Major credit cards accepted. Anse des Cayes (phone: 276655; fax: 278714 or 277528).

François Plantation The bloom-covered arbor, mahogany furnishings, and tropical garden provide the first hint of the haute cuisine experience to come in this elegant dining room that ranks among the island's finest. Chef Christophe Picard, trained in Paris's famed *Taillevent,* combines imagination and unusual spices to create the subtly-flavored house specialty, Coutancie rib steak with *gratin dauphinois* potatoes, and equally delightful dishes such as tournedos of ostrich, balsamic-baked salmon, and lamb tournedos sautéed with bacon and juniper. The innovative touches carry over to dessert, with pears poached in cardamom and white pepper, served with *glace à la Livèche* (celery-flavored ice cream), or a *marquise* of bitter chocolate with pistachio sauce. The extensive wine cellar boasts several rare vintages. Open daily for dinner only. Major credit cards accepted. Colombier (phone: 277882; fax: 276126).

Taïwana This informal, beachside bistro with excellent soups, salads, and grilled meat dishes is where the rich and famous retreat for *le déjeuner*. Open daily for lunch only. No credit cards accepted. At the *Hôtel Taïwana,* Anse des Flamands (phone: 726501; fax: 276382).

MODERATE

Le Ouanalao This bright and breezy spot, sheltered beneath a poolside pavilion, serves Italian and creole specialties with a French touch, such as veal scaloppine with ham and cheese, and lobster in Mornay sauce au gratin. Sunday Brunch is popular, as are Wednesday creole and Friday barbecued lobster nights. Open daily. Reservations advised. Major credit cards accepted. At the *Hôtel Manapany Cottages,* Anse des Cayes (phone: 276655; fax: 277528).

INEXPENSIVE

New Born This popular eatery has possibly the best creole seafood on the island—managers Frankie and David Gréaux even catch their own lobsters and stock the restaurant's aquarium themselves. The decor is nothing fancy, but the setting—in a spacious home just a stone's throw from the beach—is pleasant. Menu staples include *accras* (fritters), *boudin* (sausage) and *callaloo* (dasheen soup), as well as homemade *tartes,* coconut flan, and *bananes flambées.* Specialties may include turtle steaks, curried shrimp, and salt cod salad. Open for dinner only; closed Sundays. Major credit cards accepted. On the road to the *Manapany* hotel, marked by a sign with a nursing baby. Anse des Cayes (phone: 276707 or 276511).

GRAND CUL-DE-SAC–MARIGOT–VITET

EXPENSIVE

Le Gaïac The *ne plus ultra* of wining and dining, this idyllic spot in the greathouse of *Le Toiny* hotel offers exemplary French cuisine in a romantic hillside setting. There's indoor or outdoor dining for 30 with a sea view across a shimmering pool that seems to spill over the mountainside. Chef Maxime des Champs blends traditional French with island cuisines to create appetizing mushroom and conch ravioli with garlic sauce, steamed red mullet with fennel and tomato marinade, and roast saddle of lamb with plantain and sweet potato pie. Devastating desserts include frozen chocolate mousse cake with orange flavored sauce. There's a special Sunday brunch buffet. Open daily; closed Tuesdays in the off-season and September through October. Reservations advised. Major credit cards accepted. Anse de Toiny (phone: 278888; fax: 278930).

Lafayette Club This *très chic* spot packs in an attractive crowd (including the occasional celebrity) whose noonday ritual includes swimming (in the ocean or the pool), drying off under a palm tree while sipping a tall rum *planteur,* then feasting on lobster salad, crispy duck, or fish with hot pepper sauce, topping it all off with a delectable chocolate *marquise.* Fashion shows from the restaurant's own boutiques (on the premises and at *Villa Créole* shopping center) are part of the fun. Open daily for lunch only; closed May through October. Reservations advised in season. Major credit cards accepted. Grand Cul-de-Sac (phone: 276251; fax: 278631).

MODERATE TO EXPENSIVE

Le Bartolomeo An elegant dinner retreat in a tropical garden, where Chef Patrick Guerry creates an ever-changing menu of French fare with an emphasis on seafood and innovative preparations of lamb, local wildfowl, beef tenderloin, rabbit, and veal. The wicker and mahogany furnishings, along with the bar-salon and piano entertainment, lend to the sophisticated ambience. Open daily for dinner only; closed September through October. Reservations advised. Major credit cards accepted. At the *Guanahani Hotel,* Grand Cul-de-Sac (phone: 276660; fax: 277070).

Le Flamboyant Set in Albert Balayn's hillside stucco house with an ocean view, this eatery's French fare centers on its creole *plat du jour* and prix fixe menu. The house specialty is *cassoulet de langouste.* There's a good wine list. Open for dinner only; closed Mondays. Reservations advised. Major credit cards accepted. Grand Cul-de-Sac (phone: 277565).

Hostellerie des Trois Forces If astrologer/chef/proprietor Hubert de la Motte is keyed into the cosmic truth that "food is love," then this rustic inn offers some of the most romantic cuisine around. His wood-burning grill turns out shrimp, lobster with basil, and fish with fennel, while potatoes slow-roast among the ashes. Other specialties include fish soufflés and, for dessert, lovely swan-shaped profiteroles. Open daily; closed Sunday lunch. Reservations advised. Major credit cards accepted. At the inn of the same name, Vitet (phone: 276125; fax: 278138).

La Toque Lyonnaise This dining room *par excellence* has earned the right to its name (Lyons being the gastronomic capital of France), combining the creative talents of its chef with the freshest produce, finest French cheeses, and choicest cuts of meat to present delightful dishes such as marinated salmon in ginger cream, grilled lobster flavored with vanilla bean, and crayfish with *pistou* sauce. Many make the pilgrimage here for the three-course *menu dégustation* (tasting menu), which may comprise a terrine of Roquefort with poached pears in Sauternes, chicken breast in an oregano-flavored pastry shell, and a cracknel of "ebony-and-ivory" for dessert. The wine list is superb. Open daily for dinner only; closed June through August.

Reservations advised. Major credit cards accepted. At *El Sereno Beach Hotel,* Grand Cul-de-Sac (phone: 276480; fax: 277547).

MODERATE

L'Indigo This poolside café and bar is a wonderful place for a casual luncheon overlooking the lagoon. Typical French lunches—light, but with three courses—as well as some sandwiches are served. Among the specialties are rack of lamb with java beans, duck *confit,* and fish tart with leeks and tomatoes. There's a good wine list. Open daily for breakfast and lunch only, except Wednesday nights for barbecue and cabaret; closed September through October. Reservations advised. Major credit cards accepted. At the *Guanahani Hotel,* Grand Cul-de-Sac (phone: 276660; fax: 277070).

La Lagon Bleu This beachside spot serves terrific tuna (*tarte de thon*) with candied tomatoes and basil, warm goat cheese salad with smoked bacon and walnuts, and grilled lobster or fish. Open daily for lunch; also open for dinner June through August. No reservations. Major credit cards accepted. *El Sereno Beach Resort,* Grand Cul-de-Sac (phone: 276480).

Marigot Bay Club At this intimate, 16-table hideaway swathed in greenery and palm trees, patrons can watch the surf between courses of lobster bisque, secret-recipe conch fritters and conch sausage, or *christophines* (squash) stuffed with lobster, then concentrate on the French or creole-inspired duck, veal, chicken, filet mignon, or seafood cooked to perfection and served with a smile. Treat yourself to some mango sorbet and a visit to the bar for a cappuccino and perhaps a chat with the amiable (and English-speaking) owner, Jean-Michel Lédée. Closed Monday lunch and September through October. Reservations advised. Major credit cards accepted. At the *Marigot Bay Club,* Marigot (phone: 277545; fax: 279004).

Le Rivage Nestled on the sandy beach, this friendly creole and French eatery offers midday selections of grilled lobster, beef or lamb kebab, and sandwiches. The dinner menu is more extensive, with homemade duck liver pâté, melon marinated in wine, crayfish with creole sauce, and tasty desserts (try the passion-fruit mousse). Closed Thursdays and the month of September. Major credit cards accepted. At the *St. Barth's Beach Hôtel,* Grand Cul-de-Sac (phone: 278242).

INEXPENSIVE

Chez Pompi Good local fare and plenty of it. A highlight is the gallery of owner-artist Louis "Pompi" Ledec's paintings of local landscapes and people. Closed Sundays. Reservations advised. Major credit cards accepted. Grand Cul-de-Sac (phone: 277567).

La Petite Bouffe This tiny café and bakery is set high on a hill, with its windows thrown open to the sea breezes. The menu varies, but generally includes omelettes and French toast for breakfast, burgers and sandwiches for lunch, and grilled beef, lobster, and fish for dinner. It's one of the best dinner values on the island. Open daily. Reservations unnecessary. No credit cards accepted. Pointe Milou (phone: 276583).

LORIENT

EXPENSIVE

La Banane This small and charming tropical paradise offers a refined French *table d'hôte* dinner to be savored at a leisurely pace while watching owner/entertainer Jean-Marie Rivière's Paris cabaret show. Specialties include frogs' legs Provençal and, for dessert, Antillean bananas flambé. Open for dinner only; closed Wednesdays and the months of May, June, September, and October. Reservations advised. Major credit cards accepted. At *La Banane* hotel, Lorient (phone: 276825; fax: 276844).

ELSEWHERE ON THE ISLAND

EXPENSIVE

La Table des Castelets Serving fine cuisine in the grand French culinary tradition, this chic little restaurant is committed to the rediscovery of simple and genuine tastes. Chef Patrick Lavergne has introduced a new, lighter touch with dishes such as roasted scallops with julienne endives and banana tartlet with caramel. The dining room is tastefully furnished with antiques and offers breathtaking views. Closed for lunch January through March, and on Tuesdays the rest of the year. Reservations advised. Major credit cards accepted. In the *Hôtel Castelets,* Morne Lurin (phone: 276173 or 277880; fax: 278527).

MODERATE

Le Tamarin This hip eatery is named for the ancient tamarind tree that shelters guests swaying blissfully in a hammock while sipping cocktails to classical music. Tables are arranged on a porch and surrounding lawn (ruled over by Cooky, a mischievous parrot). Owner Cat Cent and crew stay busy taking orders from the blackboard menu for grilled chops, chicken with honey and prunes, carpaccios of meat, tuna, and salmon, and fanciful desserts. Open daily for lunch; dinner served only Thursdays through Saturdays in season. Closed mid-June through mid-July and September through October. Reservations advised. Major credit cards accepted. Anse de Grande Saline (phone: 277212).

St. Eustatius

St. Eustatius, the small Dutch island everybody calls Statia, is very quiet these days. But around 1650 Oranjestad's harbor was a pivotal point in international trade, with the Lower Town buzzing with activity from merchant ships. Not only Dutch but French and Spanish merchants sold everything from sailors' pants and iron pots to silver plates, painted silks, and Portuguese wines. Unlike its neighboring islands, whose fortunes were tied to agriculture, Statia's prosperity was due to its importance as a transshipment location for sugar, cotton, and other commodities smuggled out of their nearby home islands by the British and French in protest against monopolies and taxes imposed by their governments. It also specialized in selling arms—at a goodly profit—to the North American rebels for use in their revolt against the British. During the 1770s the island was known throughout the Caribbean as the "Golden Rock."

In subsequent centuries, however, a series of incidents changed Statia from a bustling commercial center to a sleepy vacation spot. The first, on December 20, 1780, was Britain's declaration of war on the Dutch. The second came less than two months later, when Admiral George Bridges Rodney led an army onto St. Eustatius, confiscated everything on the island, and began selling off goods at considerable profit. Not satisfied with found riches, he kept the Dutch flag flying from *Fort Oranje* for a month, entrapping a total of 150 ships. Six months later, in August 1781, he left an island that was considerably poorer, but virtually undamaged. That November, the French, under the Marquis de Bouillé, governor of Martinique, drove the British out. Three years later, the French also left, returning Statia to the Dutch.

By 1786 the island seemed as bustling and prosperous as ever, but appearances were deceiving. Island life was elegant, but wealth had made Statia's merchants corrupt and lazy. So eager were they to make money for themselves that there was little left for the Dutch West Indies Company, which had bankrolled the island's original settlement and had headquarters there. It foundered and, in 1791, left the island. From that point the island experienced a steady decline.

Statia's fortifications, which had never amounted to much anyway, had deteriorated to the point of uselessness. In 1780 a Dutch ship's officer reported that *Fort de Windt*'s four cannon were manned by a constable, a small boy, and a maid. *Fort Oranje*'s big guns could not be used because chunks of the supporting cliff dropped away every time the cannon fired. But people were too busy making money to pay attention, and the French easily reconquered the island in 1795. When the British took over in April 1801, all trade stopped.

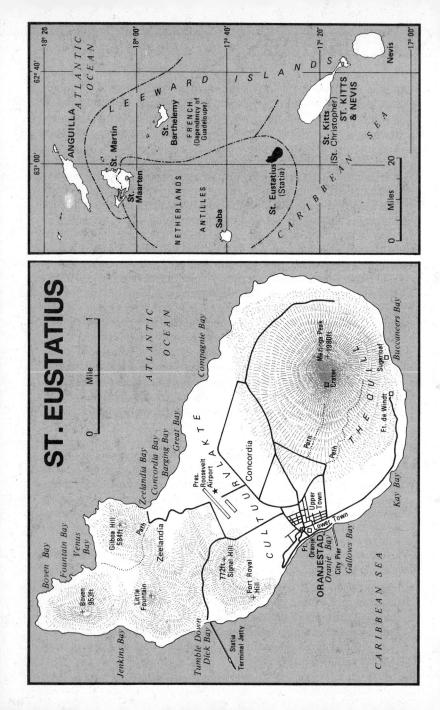

Statia finally was returned to Dutch hands in 1816, but the island never recovered its former economic strength. Plantations had long since been allowed to go to seed in favor of the island's more profitable, less troublesome trade, and now empty warehouses also were left to crumble into ruins, or to be pushed over by hurricanes. When storms ruptured the seawall, built—in Dutch fashion—to reclaim land from the sea, no one bothered to repair it. Eventually the water returned, swallowing the foundations beneath it. On land, the old *Customs House* (now the headquarters of *Dive Statia*—see below), two brick warehouses, and a network of ruined walls survive. A number of old buildings and substantial ruins are clustered near *Fort Oranje* in the Upper Town, and the *St. Eustatius Historical Foundation* is doing its best to shore them up and save them.

The island's population—officially counted at 7,830 in 1790—has dwindled to some 2,080. About 25 of these residents are retired North Americans who've built villas in the hills overlooking the sea. Two Americans provided Statia with its first real spark of tourist life. About 20 years ago they built a small inn called the *Old Gin House* (that's "gin" as in "cotton") on the foundations of an old building in the Lower Town. These days, its patio is a gathering place for islanders and visitors alike.

Today, tourists trickle through Statia at the rate of about 23,000 a year. Many are attracted by the unique diving possibilities opened up by *Dive Statia,* a full-service dive operation located next to the *Old Gin House.* Perhaps they also are attracted by Statia's safety, tidiness, and lack of hassles. Others do the standard sightseeing tour—which holds few thrills—and wonder why they bothered. But a few become so addicted to the island's relaxed, unstructured life and easy friendliness that they return again and again, join the historical foundation, and become a part of the place.

Statia is still very quiet—perhaps too quiet for most people, with its largest hotels offering just 20 rooms. But it may be just the retreat you've been looking for.

St. Eustatius At-a-Glance

FROM THE AIR

Little 11.8-square-mile St. Eustatius looks like a lozenge-shaped table, slightly above sea level, with a sawed-off volcano at its southern end and a pile of lower hills pointing northwest at its other tip. Lying diagonally southeast to northwest, Statia forms a 2½-by-five-mile barrier between the Atlantic Ocean and the Caribbean. It is about 35 miles south of St. Maarten, about 17 miles southeast of its sister island of Saba, and about 11 miles northwest of the British Leeward Island of St. Kitts. The volcano, known as the Quill (a corruption of the Dutch word *kuil,* meaning pit, presumably referring to its crater), is almost symmetrical. You can climb up the mountain and look down into the dense green rain forest cupped in its burnt-out top.

But what strikes most visitors first is the utter flatness of Statia's central plain, De Cultuurvlakte, with *Franklin D. Roosevelt Airport*'s 1,900-foot airstrip at the center. About a mile south of the airport, the island's capital, Oranjestad, occupies land on top of and beneath the pink-gray coastal cliffs. Soft gray volcanic beaches dot the leeward (Caribbean) side of the island from just south of Gallows Bay below Oranjestad to the base of Fort Royal Hill in the northwest. (Unfortunately, hurricanes have claimed some of them.) Beaches also line the shore of Tumble Down Dick Bay a bit farther north (where an oil storage facility has been installed with the hope of boosting the island economy). On the northeast-facing windward side, surf from the deep blue Atlantic rolls in along the island's most picturesque gold sand beaches at Zeelandia, Concordia, Barging, and Great Bays—good spots for experienced surfers, but not advisable for swimming because of the fierce undertow.

SPECIAL PLACES

A list of Statia's monuments has a way of sounding more impressive than the collection actually looks. Before booking an extended stay, remember that when Statians talk about *ruins,* they mean just that. But the remains are nevertheless arresting, and history buffs will feel right in their element.

ORANJESTAD St. Eustatius's capital is, in a sense, a ghost town, only now coming out of the coma into which it lapsed in the early 19th century. Your first stop should be *Fort Oranje,* where, at the tourist office, you can pick up the booklet *Get to Know St. Eustatius* (about $1.75 per copy) or the historical foundation's *Walking Tour Guide* ($2 per copy; also available at the *St. Eustatius Historical Foundation Museum*—see below). This spot also offers a fine view of the Lower Town. It is difficult to believe that the skeletal stone walls below are the vestiges of what was once the immensely rich port known as the Golden Rock.

Fort Oranje, with its three bastions, is in the best shape of any Statian landmark, having been extensively restored in honor of the US bicentennial celebration of 1976. Now its ramparts bristle with shiny black cannon, and it houses the post office and several other government offices, as well as the *St. Eustatius Historical Foundation Museum.* Here are exhibits on the island's history, including re-created 18th-century rooms with period furniture, blue glass beads (used to measure a slave's value), a few Amerindian skeletons, slave lists, and shipping logs. The aforementioned booklets, a few souvenirs, and postcards are sold here. Open daily. Admission charge (phone: 82288). Restoration of the fort is still in progress. A plaque commemorates the return of the salute fired by the US brig *Andrew Doria* on November 16, 1776, by which "sovereignty of the United States of America was first formally acknowledged" by a foreign government (though *Fort Frederik* on St. Croix, then owned by the Dutch, claims to have made a similar acknowledgment a few weeks earlier). Since *Fort Oranje*'s act helped to bring on war with the British, it is one that islanders may have regretted later.

Leaving the fort, turn right on Fort Oranjestraat and, following the *Walking Tour Guide* map, visit the Upper Town's other sights, many of which are part of a $20-million restoration project: the *Public Library* on Fort Oranjestraat; the renovated barracks-like *Government Building* just across the street (formerly the *Government Guesthouse,* it now houses government offices, the tourist office, a handicraft center, and a snack bar), near which the remains of four old buildings were found; the gingerbread-frilled house at 4 Fort Oranjestraat, a 20th-century building constructed in keeping with the surrounding 18th-century architecture; and, behind it, the remains of the 18th-century house called *Three Widows Corner* with its restored cookhouse, patio, and herb garden.

The beautifully restored *Simon Doncker House* (on Wilhelminaweg in the center of Oranjestad; phone: 82288), once the home of a wealthy merchant, became Admiral Rodney's headquarters after he captured the island in 1781. The house is open daily; admission charge. The *Town House* on the corner of the continuation of Fort Oranjestraat and Bredeweg is on the verge of tumbling down, but it still provides a glimpse of classic Statian stone-and-wood construction. Just behind it, on Synagogpad, stand the ruins of the *Honen Dalim* (Charity to the Poor), the second-oldest synagogue in the Western Hemisphere (begun around 1740). Its yellow brick outer walls are intact. On the outskirts of town on Princessweg, there is a tiny, lovingly tended Jewish cemetery with some 20 legible tombstones dating from 1742. Next to it is a ruin of what some believe was a *mikvah* (Jewish ritual bath); other folks speculate that it was part of an old rum factory.

ELSEWHERE ON THE ISLAND

If you're touring by car or taxi, be sure to stop at the stately ruins of the *Dutch Reformed Church* (c. 1755) on Kerkweg as you head out of town toward *Fort de Windt.* The church's stone tower and choir loft have been restored by the historical foundation and the churchyard is full of fascinating stones dating from 1775—a find if stone rubbing is your hobby. Other places to explore are the ruins of the old sisal factory and sugar mill just beyond the church, *Fort Nassau,* and tiny *Fort de Windt,* part of a 16-emplacement chain of defenses dotted around the island's periphery. Out of town, on the *Lynch Plantation* (on Kortelsweg; no phone), the tiny, charming *Domestic Museum of the Berkel Family* chronicles one family's life through the 19th and 20th centuries, with farm tools, family photos, and exhibits labled "Ma's Bible" and "Pa's Parting Words." Open daily. No admission charge.

The strong of lung and limb can climb the slopes of the Quill. Since this mountain gave up smoking some centuries back, a lush rain forest has grown in its tip; the views from the trail and the flora within the crater make the effort worthwhile. It's a half-day trip that takes more energy than skill, and there are rest spots along the way. Guides are available, but usually they're not essential—even for the novice. In all, the tourist office has 12 mapped nature trails, from the Crater Track down into the Quill, to the easy White Bird Track along Oranjestad Beach beneath Powder Hill, where "white birds" or tropic birds rest and nest. A guide is a good idea, however, for hiking into the Quill's crater, since this can be tricky due to paths not well marked or maintained. Contact the tourist office (see *Tourist Information,* below) or the *Old Gin House* (see *Checking In*) to arrange for a guide.

At this point, unless you've brought a picnic, head back for the terrace of the *Old Gin House* and lunch. Then—to get the real feel of the island—change into a bathing suit and a pair of expendable sneakers and go exploring among the ruins and along the shore in either direction. Shards of pottery and glass, coins, buttons, bones, and other remnants of Statia's rich past are still found all over the island, above *and* below the water. Another option is just to sit in the sun and absorb the peace.

Sources and Resources

TOURIST INFORMATION

If you're flying in from St. Maarten (you probably will be) and have a chance to visit Philipsburg before taking off for Statia, stop in at the tourist office at the head of the Little Pier for brochures about Statia. Also look in a St. Maarten bookstore for Dr. J. Hartog's *St. Maarten, Saba, St. Eustatius.* The *St. Eustatius Tourist Office* (phone/fax: 82433), located in Oranjestad's 201-year-old *Government Guesthouse,* and the historical museum at *Fort Oranje* also distribute printed information (although they occasionally run out). In addition, the friendly people at the *Gertrude Judson Library* and at the historical foundation's headquarters on Prinsestraat will do all they can to help you. For information on tourist offices in the US see GETTING READY TO GO.

MAIL NOTE

When sending mail to St. Eustatius's capital, leave the name of the city out of postal addresses to avoid having your letter detoured to the other Oranjestad, capital of the better-known island of Aruba, hundreds of miles to the south.

LOCAL COVERAGE The *Guardian,* the *Herald,* and the *Chronicle,* English dailies published on St. Maarten, arrive late each morning. An invaluable resource is *St. Eustatius, A Short History,* by Ypie Attema (De Walburg; $11.50), which can be obtained at the tourist office, the historical foundation, the museum, and the *Mazinga Gift Shop* (see *Shopping,* below).

RADIO AND TELEVISION Radio broadcasts and television programs in English are available throughout the island. Most hotels have cable TV access.

TELEPHONE When calling from the US dial 011 (international access code) + 599 (country code) + 3 (city code) + (five-digit local number). To call from another Caribbean island, the access code may vary, so contact the local operator. When calling from a phone on St. Eustatius, use only the local number unless otherwise indicated. Dial 82333 for the police; 82211 or 82371 for an ambulance.

ENTRY REQUIREMENTS US and Canadian citizens need only proof of citizenship (a current passport or one that expired less than five years ago, or a voter's registration card or birth certificate with raised seal *and* a photo ID), plus a return ticket. There's a departure tax of $10 if you're going to the US; $4 if you're heading for any other Dutch Caribbean island.

CLIMATE AND CLOTHES The climate is comparatively dry (only 45 inches of rain a year) with daytime temperatures in the mid-80s F (29 to 30C) and nights in the 70s F (23C) all year. The word "casual" is a shade overstated to describe the island's mode of dress. People are neat, but style couldn't matter less. Bring some old sneakers for walking through the ruins along the shoreline. There are no real dress-up occasions on Statia.

MONEY Official currency is the Netherlands Antilles florin (abbreviated NAf), also called the guilder, valued at about 1.80 NAf to $1 US. US dollars are acceptable for all tourist purposes, but Canadians should change their money for florins before departing from St. Maarten or on Statia at Barclays Bank (Wilhelminaweg; phone: 2392), open from 8:30 AM to 2 PM weekdays and also from 4 PM to 5 PM Friday afternoons, or at Windward Islands Bank (Mazinga Arcade; phone: 2846/7/8), open from 8:30 AM to 12 PM and from 1PM to 3:30 PM Mondays through Thursdays and from 8:30 AM to 12 PM and 2 PM to 4:30 PM Fridays. Credit cards generally are not accepted except in hotels and some restaurants. All prices in this chapter are in US dollars.

LANGUAGE Most public signs are written in Dutch, the island's official language, but everybody speaks English. The common greeting is, "Awright, ok-a-a-y."

TIME Statia is on atlantic standard time—which is one hour ahead of eastern standard time—year-round. In winter, when it's noon in New York it's 1 PM on Statia; in summer, when daylight saving time is in effect in the US, the time's the same in both places.

CURRENT Electricity is 110 volts, 60 cycles AC—which means no trouble for American travel appliances.

TIPPING A 15% service charge is added to restaurant, bar, and hotel bills, and that takes care of waiters, maids, bartenders, et al. Don't worry about bellhops and porters; there aren't any. Tip taxi drivers $1 to $2.

GETTING AROUND

CAR RENTAL Rental cars are available from several sources, a list of which is available at the tourist office. *Avis* now has offices in town and at the airport (phone: 82303 or 82421). You'll be asked to show your license; other formalities are minimal.

INTER-ISLAND FLIGHTS *Windward Island Airways (WINAIR)* flies STOL (short takeoff and landing) planes from St. Maarten's *Juliana Airport* to Statia five times daily; the trip takes about 16 minutes. *WINAIR* also flies between Statia, St. Kitts, and Nevis. Private charters can be arranged from St. Croix or St. Thomas. There are also day tours from St. Maarten (daily except Sundays); the cost includes airfare and lunch (St. Maarten; phone: 5995-322700, ext. 82).

TAXI Cabs meet all incoming flights and cruise ships. A two-hour taxi tour, which includes a cassette-taped commentary in English, French, Dutch, Spanish, or German, is available; ask for the amiable Josser Daniel (phone: 82358). Local historian Ellis Lopes also conducts tours (phone: 82288). A couple of hours' touring will cover the Upper and Lower Towns, plus a ride out the southwestern coast road to *Fort de Windt,* below the side of the Quill they call White Wall, where there's a spectacular view of St. Kitts. When you get back to the Upper Town, ask to be dropped at the tourist office or the museum, where you can pick up a guidebook with a map and continue on your own. If you're not staying overnight, set a time with the driver to be taken back to the airport.

SPECIAL EVENTS

The *Queen's Coronation Day* (April 30) is celebrated with fireworks, sports events, music, and dancing. *Statia Carnival* (concluding with *Carnival Monday*) in July and *Statia-America Day* (November 16), commemorating the first salute to the American flag by a foreign government, in 1776, are the year's big celebrations, with sunup to way-past-sunset parading, partying, and the like. Other legal holidays include *New Year's Day, Good Friday* (April 5 in 1996), *Easter* and *Easter Monday* (April 7 and 8 in 1996), *Labor Day* (May 1), *Ascension Day* (May 16 in 1996), *Christmas,* and *Boxing Day* (December 26).

SHOPPING

There's not much. Visitors can find a few imported Dutch items, jewelry, toiletries, liquors, cigarettes, magazines, and books among the general stock at the *Mazinga Gift Shop* in Upper Town (Fort Oranjestraat; phone: 2245), which is open weekdays from 8 AM to 6 PM and to 8:30 PM on Saturdays. T-shirts, island wear, and the local exportable elixir, Mazinga Mist (soursop schnapps), are available at *Dive Statia's* boutique next to the *Old Gin House* (open daily from 8 AM to 4:30 PM; Fishermen's Beach, Lower Town; phone:

2435). There's a limited selection of postcards and books at the museum at *Fort Oranje*.

SPORTS

The scale is small, but the hiking and water sports potential is considerable and unique.

HIKING Trekking up the side of the Quill, a former volcano now endowed with rain forest and spectacular scenery, is a rewarding hike (see *Special Places*).

SNORKELING AND SCUBA DIVING Most fun is found among the underwater ruins in Oranje Bay; contrary to off-island legend, you won't find a whole city buried intact, but there are enough submerged masonry, cannon, old coins, wine bottles, and coral to make it interesting. Historians believe there are more than 250 old ships sunk in this untouched bay; the government hopes divers won't pocket their finds, but that they'll be recorded and placed in the museum for all to enjoy. For additional details, see *Sunken and Buried Treasure* in DIVERSIONS. Visibility isn't the greatest, but it is worth an underwater visit. Snorkelers have to swim over depths of only eight to 10 feet to see the ruins, and about five square miles of reef harbor virtually every Caribbean fish. *Dive Statia* (Fishermen's Beach, Lower Town; phone: 2435; 405-843-3040 in the US), a dive shop next to the *Old Gin House,* offers a full range of instructional programs, and occasionally a shared one-week plan (half the week on one island, half on the other) with Saba, Statia's equally unspoiled neighbor. It also rents snorkel equipment. A 31-foot dive boat, underwater camera rentals, and computer diving capability have been added; *PADI* and *SSI* instruction are also available.

SWIMMING AND SUNNING Pleasant areas for quick dips or leisurely swims are on all the small volcanic beaches on the southwest shore. The northeast, or windward, beaches—such as Zeelandia and Lynch—are beautiful for walking or sunning, but very dangerous for swimming due to the strong undertow.

TENNIS The single concrete court at the *Community Center* (on Rosemary La.; phone: 2249) is rudimentary, but it's open daily and lighted for night play; players must bring their own equipment.

NIGHTLIFE

The biggest show is an occasional weekend concert by the *Statia Steel Band,* the *Killy-Killy String Band,* the *Re-creation Roots* combo, or local reggae/calypso groups such as the *In-Laws* and *Roots-2.* For live music check out *The Golden Era* (Sundays only; Lower Town, Oranjestad; phone: 2345), *Talk of the Town* (Fridays only; on the Airport Rd.; phone: 2236), or the local disco, *Lago Heights* (no phone). Otherwise, evenings consist of sipping brandy, talking, and early to bed.

Best on the Island

CHECKING IN

Statia's 93 hotel rooms are a mixed bag. Roughly half are in three proper hotels overlooking either Oranje Bay or the Atlantic. Unless otherwise noted, those listed here have air conditioning, telephones, TV sets, and private baths. Their in-season rates range from about $110 (expensive) to $80 (moderate) to $65 (inexpensive) for two without meals; breakfast and dinner will add another $30 to $40 per person a day. Additional hotel charges usually total another 20% or so for service, utilities, and a 7% government tax.

Guesthouses offer basic, inexpensive accommodations costing the bargain-hunter anywhere from a rock-bottom $7 to about $35 per day for a double room. A list of guesthouses is available at the tourist office (also see those noted at the end of the hotel entries). When calling from a phone on St. Eustatius, use only the local numbers listed below. For information about dialing from elsewhere see *Telephone* earlier in this chapter.

EXPENSIVE

Old Gin House Set on the main street of what was once the richest port in the Caribbean, this restored 18th-century cotton warehouse is fitted out with 20 antiques-filled guestrooms with ceiling fans, though no air conditioning, telephones, or TV sets (the larger rooms are oceanside); a pool; the *Mooshay Bay Publick House,* a snug pub walled with brick from the original cotton gin; and the cool, high-ceilinged *Mooshay Bay Dining Room* (see *Eating Out*). The ambience is nostalgic; the decor is casual (if somewhat run down). Dive packages also are available (the operator *Dive Statia*—see *Snorkeling and Scuba*—is right next door). The seaside *Terrace* restaurant serves breakfast, lunch, and Saturday barbecue. If you wonder what else there is to do, you probably shouldn't be here. But if you have too much to do everyplace else in your world, this could be your spot to unwind. Children under 10 are not permitted. Bay Road, Lower Town (phone: 82319; fax: 82555).

MODERATE

Golden Era Simple but comfortable, this establishment overlooking Oranje Bay offers 20 harborfront rooms (although some of the balconies face concrete walls). The beach is a tenth of a mile away, and there's a pool on the property. The restaurant/bar's decor won't win any awards, but the food is good, reasonably priced island fare. Lower Town, Oranjestad (phone: 82345; 800-562-9807; fax: 82445).

Kings Well A small, new hotel on a cliff overlooking the sea, a short walk from the beach below. At press time four of the 20 rooms projected were completed, and a pool and Jacuzzi also are planned. Rooms are spacious and comfortable (one has a water bed) and have terraces, VCRs, and refrigerators.

There's also a restaurant, with the health-conscious owner of the hotel as chef. Lower Town, Oranjestad (phone/fax: 82538).

La Maison sur la Plage "The House on the Beach" with 10 bungalows overlooks an isolated, lovely two-mile stretch of sand on the dramatic ocean side of the island. The rooms are clean, fresh, and simple; there's no air conditioning, telephones, or TV sets. There's a pool, and continental breakfast is included. The restaurant is known for its fine French fare (see *Eating Out*). Zeelandia Beach (phone: 82256; fax: 82831).

Talk of the Town This place, above one of Statia's finest restaurants (see *Eating Out*), is considered one of the island's best lodging choices. Near many historical sites, the 18 modern rooms (one with kitchenette) have cable TV. Furniture is locally hand-crafted. Amenities include a pool and a boutique. Buffet breakfast is included. L. E. Saddlerweg (phone/fax: 82236).

INEXPENSIVE

Airport View Apartments Formerly the *Henríquez Apartments,* here are 18 comfortable units next to (you guessed it) the airport, each with a refrigerator, coffee maker, and cable TV, but no telephone. There's a bar/restaurant and an outdoor patio with barbecue. Carine Henríquez sometimes comes over from *L'Etoile* restaurant (see *Eating Out*) to cook, depending on where the demand is. Oranjestad (phone: 82474; fax: 82517).

GUESTHOUSES

Recommended guesthouses include *Country Inn* (phone: 82484) and *Daniel's Guest House* (phone: 82358).

EATING OUT

For a meal for two, expect to pay about $65 in a restaurant listed as expensive, between $35 and $60 in places in the moderate category, and less than $35 in inexpensive spots. Prices do not include drinks or service charge. Unless otherwise noted, all restaurants listed below are open for lunch and dinner. When calling from a phone on St. Eustatius, use only the local numbers listed below. For information about dialing from anywhere else, see *Telephone* earlier in this chapter.

EXPENSIVE

Mooshay Bay Dining Room A la carte or prix fixe dinners ($22 per person, including two wines) might begin with grapefruit soup, followed by chateaubriand in *dijonnaise* sauce or lobster sautéed with garlic, butter, and chives; homemade snow orange or key lime pie rounds out the meal. This rustic dining room draws guests back year after year. Open daily for dinner. Reservations advised. MasterCard and Visa accepted. At the *Old Gin House,* Lower Town (phone: 82319).

La Maison sur la Plage Excellent French food is served at this trellis-adorned restaurant—the island's best—with Atlantic views. Popular dishes include escargots, steak with roquefort or green peppercorn sauce, and crêpes *à l'orange* or profiteroles for dessert. Open daily; breakfast served only to guests staying at the hotel of the same name. Reservations advised for parties of more than four people. MasterCard and Visa accepted. Zeelandia Beach (phone: 82256).

INEXPENSIVE

L'Etoile A simple upstairs snack bar–restaurant where Carine Henríquez prepares West Indian dishes such as salt fish and spareribs (when she's not cooking for guests at the *Airport View Apartments;* see *Checking In*). The menu also includes hamburgers, hot dogs, and drinks. A great place to stop for lunch. Open daily for breakfast, lunch, and dinner. Reservations advised. No credit cards accepted. 6 Van Rheeweg, Upper Town, Oranjestad (phone: 82299).

Talk of the Town Definitely the best choice for local fare. Ask for a table on the sea-view sun terrace. The menu beams with the best available ingredients; choices include chicken, seafood, steaks prepared Statian-style, and sandwiches. Open daily for breakfast, lunch, and dinner. Reservations unnecessary. Major credit cards accepted. L. E. Saddlerweg (phone: 82236).

ISLAND EATS

Other Oranjestad eateries include the *Chinese Bar and Restaurant* (in Upper Town; phone: 2389), and, for lighter meals, the *Old Gin House Terrace* (see *Checking In*), *Sunny's Place* (in Upper Town; phone: 2609), *Kool Corner* (in Upper Town; no phone), the *Blue Bead* (phone: 82873), and *B's Garden* (phone: 82733).

St. Kitts and Nevis

They call themselves "the secret Caribbean" in tourism promotions and, to most of the world, they are. The intimate islands of St. Kitts and Nevis are gorgeous, green, and volcanic; they offer some of the Caribbean's most dramatic panoramas—as well as one of its warmest welcomes. But their strongest attraction is their "Old West Indies" charm and their small, gracious hotels and inns, in which visitors can savor a vanishing way of life.

Despite very British roots and lingering traditions (as in most of the West Indies, cricket is a national passion, driving is on the left, and English is spelled, honourably, the Queen's way), the islands are now determined, in a peaceful and stable way, to establish their own identity as the Caribbean's newest independent country. The Federation of St. Kitts–Nevis was established as a nation within the British Commonwealth in September 1983.

For the past several decades, the whimsical politics of these islands has seemed to be the only thing of interest to the press. Few people heard about the lush cane fields, the volcanic vistas, the rain forests, and the black and blonde sand beaches that make St. Kitts a visual jewel; the superb, palm-cloaked, beige sand beaches of Pinney's Bay and the secluded coves on Nevis; or the charming, centuries-old inns and rare serenity awaiting visitors to either island. They did hear bizarre tales of sibling rivalry and petty political diatribes exchanged with the distant triplet, Anguilla (a coral isle 60 miles north, with little in common with St. Kitts and Nevis other than British rule). The skirmishes were part of an ongoing familial flap that got its start back in 1825, when the British made a single Crown Colony of the three. It was a union that just didn't work.

When Anguilla declared itself independent of the St. Kitts–Nevis association in 1967, the press portrayed the event as a West Indian version of *The Mouse That Roared*. There even was talk of invasion by the hostile twins to the south to bring the recalcitrant island back into line. To forestall any such local moves, a British "peacekeeping force" landed on Anguilla's beaches in 1969, and in 1971, the Mother Country reassumed full responsibility for the island—much to its citizens' delight. Without further ado, the islands returned to relative obscurity, except for an occasional rumor that the two remaining siblings, St. Kitts and Nevis, had a violent rivalry and planned to ask for separate independence decrees.

There is a small grain of truth in that gossip, although the *real* rivalry is more a matter of pride than prejudice. Kittitians are more business-minded, tense, and anxious for development—or so the Nevisians claim. Kittitians, on the other hand, refer to their neighbors as "lazy and sometimes snooty, taking too much advantage of the special, easygoing atmosphere of Nevis." They are merely jealous, Nevisians insist, pointing out that every weekend and public holiday, their pristine beaches are a magnet for weary Kittitians,

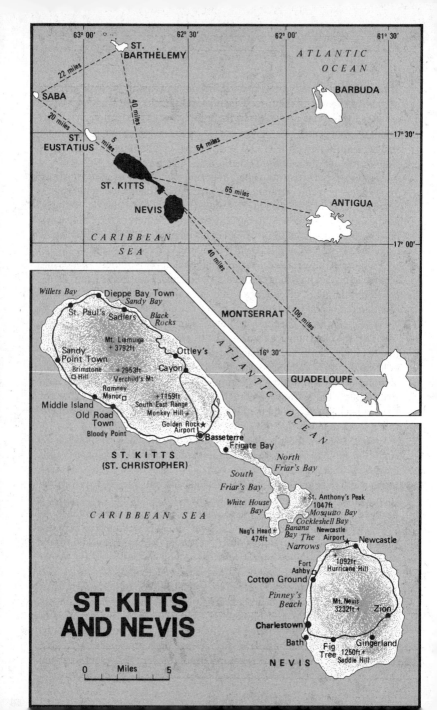

ST. KITTS AND NEVIS

0 — Miles — 5

who make the swift 2-mile crossing as quickly as they can to unwind from life in "the big city." It's a very amusing story—especially to anyone who has visited both islands and knows how beautiful and slow-moving each actually is.

Sugar and cotton, once sources of tremendous wealth for both islands, are no longer cash crops for Nevis, which makes tourism its primary industry. St. Kitts continues to raise cane commercially, but here, too, tourism is first. The southeast peninsula road, opened in 1989, is spurring development that eventually will result in over 300 additional hotel rooms at the island's southernmost tip.

The country is a model of stability in the Caribbean. Peaceful, quiet surroundings and congenial, caring people are the trademarks of St. Kitts and Nevis, and the islands are so far from being a tropical trouble spot that it's difficult to imagine their turbulent history. Columbus sighted them during his second voyage in 1493, and it was he who named them: St. Christopher—for either himself or the patron saint of travelers (the British gave the island its nickname, St. Kitts); and Nevis—originally Las Nieves, Spanish for "the snows"—because of the snow-white clouds clinging to its peak. Then Columbus sailed on, leaving the islands and their resident Carib Indians undisturbed.

More than a century passed before the British settled at Old Road Town on St. Kitts in 1623. In 1625, they were joined by the crew of a French ship seeking refuge after a skirmish with a Spanish warship. The two groups wiped out the Carib and then divided the island strangely, but peaceably—the French took both ends and the English, the midsection. In 1629, the two groups again joined forces to resist a Spanish attack, then turned their attention to the many islands around them. During the next decades, the British, from their St. Kitts base, fanned out to colonize Antigua, Barbuda, Tortuga (Ile de la Tortue), and Montserrat. The French sent landing parties to claim Martinique and Guadeloupe. St. Kitts earned its credentials as "Cradle of the Caribbean" in two languages. Then intra-island friction sparked a seesaw struggle: By 1664, the French managed to squeeze the British off the island. The British retook it in 1689. The French returned in 1782 to lay siege to the British *Brimstone Hill Fortress.* It eventually fell, despite a brave defense. In 1783, the Treaty of Versailles restored both fort and island to Britain once and for all, leaving the islanders free to concentrate on sugarcane crops and business.

At one time, Nevis's sugar trade made the island even more prosperous than St. Kitts; it was nicknamed "the Queen of the Caribbees." By the late 18th century, the elegant *Bath* hotel just outside Charlestown, the capital of Nevis, was attracting 4,000 tourists each year (a remarkable number for those times, although small compared to the more than 95,000 per annum who visit St. Kitts and Nevis today).

In 1834, the abolition of slavery meant the beginning of the end of the sugar culture, and with it the eventual decline of Nevis's fortunes. St. Kitts, still deeply involved in cane production today, fell into a partial slumber as the world demand for its sugar decreased.

Since then—apart from the flurry surrounding Anguilla's declaration of independence—St. Kitts and Nevis have been relatively quiet in terms of politics, but much busier as far as tourism is concerned. St. Kitts now has an 18-hole and a nine-hole golf course, many hotels, a casino, a deep-water port, and an airport with both nonstop and direct jet service from the US and Canada. For its part, Nevis offers one of the choicest resorts, the *Four Seasons,* with 196 rooms and an 18-hole golf course (see *Checking In*).

Today only the impressive *Brimstone Hill Fortress,* overlooking the south coast of St. Kitts from an imposing perch at 800 feet, lingers as a reminder of these islands' uneasy history. Little disturbs the order and tranquillity of these tiny islands. But they are attracting more and more visitors each year; if you want to beat the crowds, you'd better hurry.

At press time, plans were underway to build a new cruise facility in Basseterre, St. Kitts. The project will include a new marina, cruise ship berth, and boardwalk for crafts vendors, boutiques, and restaurants.

St. Kitts and Nevis At-a-Glance

FROM THE AIR

St. Kitts is a 68-square-mile island shaped (as Kittitians insist) like a cricket bat, with the wide end pointing northwest toward the Dutch island of St. Eustatius, about 5 miles away, and the handle pointing toward Nevis, the 40-square-mile "ball" that lies to the southeast across a 2-mile channel called The Narrows. St. Kitts is only 5 miles across at its widest and 23 miles long from tip to handle. St. Kitts has a population of only 40,000; Nevis, about 9,500.

Basseterre, the capital of St. Kitts, is tucked into a harbor on the southern shore. *Golden Rock Airport* is a mile from town, 75 minutes by air from San Juan, and 30 minutes from Antigua or St. Maarten. The route to most of the island's resorts leads through Basseterre. Bay Road, the capital's main street, connects with the principal Circle Road that follows the shoreline all the way around the island. All of St. Kitts' principal settlements lie along it.

At the island's northwest end, Mt. Liamuiga (3,792 feet), its highest peak, is surrounded by sugarcane fields. Pronounced Lee-*a*-mwee-ga, the dormant volcano's name means "the fertile land" in the Carib language. On the coast south of the peak, on top of 800-foot cliffs, sits *Brimstone Hill Fortress,* an impressive landmark that made St. Kitts "the Gibraltar of the Caribbean." Among other scenic assets are a crater lake—Dos d'Anse Pond—caught in the top of Verchild's Mountain (2,953 feet), virgin tropical forests, tall palms, and innumerable poincianas, the flame-bloomed tree now found throughout the Caribbean but nurtured and developed here.

Nevis, lush, green, and ringed with beaches, lies south of the Dutch islands of Saba and St. Eustatius and due west of Antigua. From the air it looks like a cone, with cloud-capped Nevis Peak its 3,232-foot central apex; it is bracketed by Saddle Hill (1,250 feet) to the south and Round Hill (1,014 feet) to the north.

Like several other British islands, Nevis is divided into parishes: St. Thomas Lowland, St. James Windward, St. Paul Charlestown, St. George Gingerland, and St. John Fig Tree. On the island's west side, massed rows of palm trees form a coconut forest, while single palms bend in the breeze along the windward eastern coast. The black (actually dark gray) sand beaches at Jones and Mosquito Bays in the northwest rank high as sight-seeing attractions, but the white sand beaches to the north and west are more appealing for swimming.

SPECIAL PLACES: ST. KITTS

This island is ideal for leisurely touring, discovering bays and beaches, exploring small fishing villages, and meeting people. The action, such as it is, centers around Basseterre, a quaint, friendly, and very photogenic West Indian port with a colorful harbor. Small craft and, about twice a week, a large cruise liner, lie at anchor in the waters offshore; ferryboats chug off to Nevis across the way.

BASSETERRE The town has looked as it does (West Indian with British overtones) for centuries, but it is punctuated with modern accents. An easy and safe place for a walking tour early in the morning or later in the afternoon (to avoid the heat), it boasts what have been called some of the most perfect examples of West Indian architecture in the islands. The black and white *Treasury Building* on the waterfront is a fine specimen; others are the two-story buildings surrounding the Circus, which forms the hub of the city.

The Circus won't remind you much of Piccadilly, but its centerpiece is the island's *"Big Ben,"* the *Berkeley Memorial Clock,* an ornate, cast-iron, Victorian clock tower with four faces, columns, coats of arms, and a fountain in its base. A few blocks away is Independence Square (formerly Pall Mall), where a park has taken the place of the old slave market. Nearby *Government House* is properly Georgian, as are several antique townhouses surrounding the Circus; they have small, fenced gardens in front, first stories of cut volcanic stone, second stories of shingled cedar wood bordered by arched galleries, wide terraces trimmed with gingerbread, and steep roofs. Other town landmarks include the Anglican *Church of St. George* (Cayon St.), plagued by disasters, including an earthquake, since its first incarnation in 1670; its churchyard, where graves date back to the early 18th century; and the post office and its *Philatelic Bureau* (Bay Rd.; phone: 465-2521), where you can buy St. Kitts and Nevis stamps, outranked in popularity only by those of the British Virgin Islands in the world of Caribbean philately.

THE CIRCLE ROAD

Taxi drivers on both islands are some of the most entertaining guides in the eastern Caribbean, well known for their running commentary of island life and lore. While it's safe and easy to drive yourself, it's much more fun to sit back and listen to the amazing history and island gossip a reliable taxi driver can provide. Whether you travel by taxi or in your own rental car, take the Circle Road tour. You can make it all the way around the island in a little over three-and-a-half hours, but do it more slowly. Pack a picnic, or call ahead to make lunch reservations at *Rawlins Plantation* or at the *Golden Lemon,* near Dieppe Bay (see *Eating Out* for both). Starting north from Basseterre and traveling clockwise, you'll see:

ST. KITTS SUGAR FACTORY The factory, located at the edge of Basseterre, provides a look into the island's history. The best months to visit are February through July, when cane is ground and you can see the entire sugar-making process, from raw cane to bulk sugar. Tours are available at no charge, but you must call ahead to make an appointment (phone: 465-8157).

CARIB BEER BREWERY Near the *Sugar Factory,* the brewery offers a tour and a complimentary tasting by appointment only. No admission charge. (phone: 465-2309).

FOUNTAIN ESTATE High on a hill north of town, it was the home of Philippe de Longvilliers de Poincy, who was for 20 years governor of the French Antilles and for whom the royal poinciana (or flamboyant) tree was named. Though a landmark, the estate is private property; no tours are offered.

BLOODY POINT Here the British and French massacred the Carib Indians in 1626. Stone Ft. River, 7 miles northwest of Basseterre.

ROMNEY MANOR After a scenic drive through a tropical rain forest, visitors will reach a 17th-century house surrounded by five acres of well-tended gardens, with a huge saman tree ("rain tree") said to be over 350 years old. Today it is home to the *Caribelle Batik* factory and shop (see *Shopping*); visitors are invited inside to watch craftsmen make the colorful cloth. There is a fine selection for sale here, but shoppers also may custom-order clothing and wall hangings. Closed weekends. No admission charge (phone: 465-6609 or 465-6253).

OLD ROAD TOWN This was the first permanent British settlement in the West Indies and the early capital of the island. There are Carib petroglyphs—carvings on a small cluster of boulders—on *Wingfield Estate* nearby. Ask your driver to point them out, or ask directions at *Romney Manor.*

MIDDLE ISLAND VILLAGE Here Sir Thomas Warner, leader of the original British landing party, is entombed under a cracked marble slab—with a weighty epitaph written in Old English—in the yard of *St. Thomas Church.*

HALF-WAY TREE VILLAGE A giant tamarind tree here marks the midpoint of Britain's holdings when the island was shared with France.

SANDY POINT The first British settlers landed at this spot in 1623, in the shadow of Mt. Liamuiga.

DIEPPE BAY This is a pleasant spot for swimming and picnicking. *Gibbons Pasture* estate, which overlooks it, was once a combined sugar mill and fort; two cannon have been found on the reef below, but that's just about all that's left of the place. The sands of Dieppe Bay are volcanic gray to black. In fact, from here around the northeast coast of St. Kitts to Black Rocks, the beaches are of black sand. While not every beach lover's ideal (you'll find it hard to remove from your skin when dry), black sand has its own startling beauty, especially under bright sunlight.

BLACK ROCKS On the island's windward (Atlantic) side, these are eerie lava formations deposited over the years by the now dormant Mt. Liamuiga.

MONKEY HILL A green, 1,319-foot knoll west of Basseterre, named for the local population of green vervet monkeys, originally imported by the French as pets and left behind when their masters moved on. Lucky shutterbugs will sight a few in their camera viewfinders. In any case, the view from the top is worth the trip. You drive part of the way up the hill, and then walk the rest. On the way up, you'll pass the ruins of a picturesque two-story greathouse called the *Glen,* now tangled in green overgrowth. Call the tourist board (see *Tourist Information*) for more information.

FRIGATE BAY Near the beginning of the skinny handle of land that extends east from Basseterre, this area boasts two beaches—a surf-pounded one on North Frigate Bay on the Atlantic (or windward) side, and a calmer strand on South Frigate Bay on the Caribbean (or leeward) side. Designated a tourist zone by the government in order to preserve the rest of the island in a more pristine state, Frigate Bay is the site of a number of hotel and condominium projects, including the *Jack Tar Village* resort (see *Checking In*) and the island's 18-hole golf course. North Friar's Bay and South Friar's Bay are farther to the southeast.

ELSEWHERE ON ST. KITTS

SOUTHEAST PENINSULA Before the opening in 1989 of Dr. Kennedy Simmonds Highway—a 6-mile road that starts from the Frigate Bay area and stretches across the island—a boat was necessary to get here. The roadside has some of the island's most beautiful scenery, including nine unspoiled beaches, lagoon-like coves, pastures of tall guinea grass, and the Salt Pond (which looks pink because of the millions of tiny red krill shrimp inhabiting it).

The peninsula is largely uninhabited except by black-faced vervet monkeys, white-tailed deer, and tropical birds. Camping is permitted, though you must bring everything you need with you. The *Turtle Beach Bar & Grill* (phone: 469-9086) is a good choice for lunch; their Sunday buffet, accompanied by a steel band, is popular and well attended. A free shuttle offers transportation from the *Ocean Terrace Inn* hotel (see *Checking In*), or just follow the paved road out to the peninsula, bearing left when it splits—it leads right down to the beach and the restaurant.

BRIMSTONE HILL FORTRESS No trip to St. Kitts is complete without a day spent at *Brimstone Hill.* Named for the faint fume of sulfur that lingers around it, the fort (800 feet above the Caribbean) commands a spectacular view of six islands (Nevis, Montserrat, Saba, Statia, St. Martin, and St. Barts). Because of its site and size, it took 105 years to build. Its massive volcanic stone walls, seven to 12 feet thick, link a number of bastions and enclose the remnants of extensive life-sustaining installations (hospital, storerooms, cookhouses, asylum, cemetery, and freshwater cistern system) as well as the predictable parade, barracks, officers' quarters, and mess. There has been meticulous restoration of the *Prince of Wales Bastion;* it includes a visitors' center and souvenir shop. The fortress was attacked only twice. In 1782, before it was completed, 8,000 French troops under the Marquis de Bouillé mounted a siege that finally exhausted the British. They surrendered and were permitted—as a tribute to their bravery—to march out in uniform with drums beating and colors flying. A year later, the British retook the fort under the terms of the Treaty of Versailles and accorded the French the same honor. An information sheet is available for a nominal fee from the guard at the bottom of the steps. Pack a picnic to spread on a grassy hilltop after or midway through your explorations. (A small bar and restaurant offers supplementary drinks and snacks.) Open daily; admission charge (phone: 465-6771).

SPECIAL PLACES: NEVIS

The island's capital, Charlestown (pop. 1,200), is a miniature West Indian port whose life revolves around the arrival of the ferries from St. Kitts. Since almost everything Nevisians want or need has to be imported, a small crowd gathers when a ferry docks to wait for wares to be unloaded and transferred to the open market on the waterfront.

CHARLESTOWN A walking tour of the town needn't take more than an hour, but it often does. You can go on your own or take the historical society's walking tour, given weekly in winter. The schedule varies for the one-hour trek, so call ahead to make a reservation (phone: 469-5786). Leave the pier, turn right at the old *Cotton House and Ginnery,* and stroll through the marketplace. At the dead end, turn left on Prince William Street and follow it along to Memorial Square, dedicated to the dead of World Wars I and II. The coral stone building with the box-shaped clock tower overlooking the square is the courthouse (downstairs) and public library (upstairs). Visitors who plan to drive on the island and haven't yet gotten their local driver's license should detour right on Main Street to call at the police station. Otherwise, turn left for the heart of town, which is roughly three blocks long. Turn into Happy Hill Alley and follow your nose to the *Nevis Bakery* for bread, coconut tarts, and cookies warm from the oven. Nearby is the modern *Administration Building.* Directly behind it sits an old, one-story stone building, which until 1993 was used as a government storage shed. That year, the curator of the *Nevis Historical and Conservation Society,* David Robinson, discovered that the building is the remains of either Nevis's lost Jewish synagogue or its *mikvah* (a ceremonial bathhouse). Robinson's findings have been confirmed by an archaeological team from the US. The building may date back to the early 1650s, which would make it one of the oldest synagogues in the Western Hemisphere. Visitors can arrange to see the magnificent stone columns and stone barrel-vaulted ceiling by contacting Joan Robinson (phone: 469-5786; no admission charge). Behind this building is a stone-walled path, known as "Jews' Walk." The approximately 200-foot-long path leads to the old Jewish cemetery at the corner of Jews' Street and Government Road, where 19 worn gravestones date from 1658 to 1758.

Head back toward Main Street and cross to the tourist office (handsome wall maps are for sale here) and the *Nevis Philatelic Bureau,* whose stamps are one of the island's popular souvenir buys (see *Shopping*). Farther along on Main Street, note the customs house and the post office (stamps are for sale here, too, but not first covers). Past Chapel Street, on Low Street, is the site of Alexander Hamilton's birthplace, the town's most interesting stop for most Americans. The original is gone, but a replica on the spot houses the *Museum of Nevis History* downstairs and meeting quarters of the *Nevisian House of Assembly* upstairs. The museum has exhibits on Hamilton and island history and culture, and the gift shop sells various guides to the island. Closed Sundays; admission charge (phone: 469-5786). Farther down Main Street stands *St. Paul's Church,* first built in the 17th century and rebuilt several times since.

About 1½ miles north of town lies *St. Thomas Church* (ca. 1640), the oldest on the island, which has been reincarnated several times after natural disasters, including earthquakes and hurricanes.

ELSEWHERE ON NEVIS

The tricky, rutted roads climbing inland up the sides of Mt. Nevis are best left to intrepid island drivers. The best route is the (relatively) good main road that circles the island. Virtually all of Nevis's remaining landmarks lie along it; more important, so do vistas and ruins that offer a sense of the days when Nevis was the Queen of the Caribbees. Plan to stop for lunch or a picnic and a swim at Pinney's Beach or *Nisbet Plantation* (see below for both). If you do drive, be alert. Even on the main drag you're likely to round a curve and suddenly find yourself tailgating a flock of goats, a sauntering donkey, or a slow-rolling cart.

Heading north from Charlestown and proceeding clockwise, you'll come to:

PINNEY'S BEACH One of the island's best beaches. The reef-protected waters here are clear and fine for swimming and snorkeling, and there are several miles of sand near the *Four Seasons* resort (see *Checking In*). Don't leave without discovering the sleepy lagoon (very *South Pacific*) that lies through the palms at the beach's windward edge.

COTTON GROUND A village whose chief claim to fame is Nelson's Spring and its lagoon, where Horatio Nelson is said to have replenished the freshwater supply of his flagship *Boreas*.

FORT ASHBY This overlooks what is thought to be the site of Jamestown, a settlement that slid into the sea—the victim of an earthquake and tidal wave—around 1680. There's nothing much left of the fort itself, either.

ROUND HILL The view from the top of this hill takes in St. Kitts and Booby Island, named after the brown pelican, Nevis's national bird.

NEWCASTLE A tumbled old village near the airport, it's known for its fishing fleet and as one of the best places to buy (in the morning) fresh lobster, conch, and fish.

NISBET PLANTATION A restored greathouse-hotel that serves good island lunches, it overlooks a gorgeous beach and an elegant, formal sea vista lined with grass lawns and tall palms. As at all Nevis beaches and restored greathouses, you're welcome to stop, sup, and swim (see *Checking In*).

EDEN BROWN ESTATE Now a gaunt, gray ruin that is said to be haunted, this estate was built and elegantly furnished by a wealthy planter for his daughter, then abandoned after her fiancé and his best man killed each other in a drunken duel on the eve of the wedding.

NEW RIVER ESTATE Nevis's last operating sugar mill ceased operation in 1956, but you still can wander through the stone ruins at your leisure.

MONTPELIER ESTATE Now the site of the *Montpelier Plantation Inn* (the original gateposts stand), this was the scene of the marriage of "Horatio Nelson, Esquire, Captain of his Majesty's Ship, the *Boreas*, to Frances Herbert Nisbet, Widow," on March 11, 1787. So reads the entry on a tattered page of the register displayed in *St. John's Church,* Fig Tree. The scrawled signature below is that of the Duke of Clarence—later William IV of England—who witnessed the ceremony. The church sexton can be coaxed to say a few words about the Nelson-Nisbet nuptials, but he'd rather talk about Sunday's hymns, or the church itself, or the mossy old graveyard where stones date back to 1682. The estate is closed from mid-August through September (see *Checking In* for more information).

LORD NELSON MUSEUM An astonishingly complete collection of mementos of the great admiral, as well as 18th-century period clothing are displayed here. Closed weekends (but open Saturdays in winter). Admission charge. Located next to the *Government House* (phone: 469-0408).

BATH HOTEL The remains of an 18th-century watering place that put Nevis on the map as "the West Indian spa" for more than a hundred years. Its social life was the talk of the islands, and its guest list included not only British gentry from all over the Caribbean, but European nobility as well. Although they are very basic, five mineral-steeped spa baths have been restored and are now open for visitors' use; there is speculation that the massive hotel, which is still standing, may be restored as well. Closed Sundays. Admission charge (phone: 469-5521, ext. 2117).

Sources and Resources

TOURIST INFORMATION

The local *St. Kitts Tourist Board* (*Pelican Shopping Mall,* Bay Rd., Basseterre; phone: 465-4040 or 465-2620; fax: 465-8794) is close to the center of things. The staff is pleasant and helpful, although sometimes short on printed information. There's also a desk at *Golden Rock Airport* (phone: 465-8970). The *Nevis Tourist Office* (Main St., Charlestown; phone: 469-1042; fax: 469-1066) has brochures and current rate sheets on the island's hotels. Both the islands' tourist offices are closed weekends. For information on tourist offices in the US, see GETTING READY TO GO.

LOCAL COVERAGE Two newspapers are published on St. Kitts: the weekly *Democrat,* which is published every Saturday; and the *Labor Spokesman,* published Wednesdays and Saturdays. A daily paper, *The Chronicle,* comes from St. Martin. Stateside papers generally aren't available, and nobody minds much.

Useful guides include the locally published *A Motoring Guide to St. Kitts* (about $4) and *Discover St. Kitts,* by Amalia Stone and Frank Sharman (about $9). Both are available at *Wall's Deluxe Record and Book Shop* in Basseterre (see *Shopping*); your hotel also may have copies for sale. A tourist map, indicating hotels and points of interest on both St. Kitts and Nevis, is available free at the tourist office and sells for about $1 at local shops. The tourist board also makes available, at no charge, the *Traveller Tourist Guide,* with information on sightseeing, dining, shopping, and entertainment. For background reading, pick up *Fire and Brimstone,* by military historian Victor Smith (published by Creole Graphics; about $10); it's available at the *Brimstone Hill Fortress* gift shop and at *Wall's Book Shop.*

No newspapers or tourist periodicals are published on Nevis. Island papers occasionally are ferried over from St. Kitts, but on no regular schedule. If you're going to do any exploring, be sure to get a good map from the tourist office or your rental car agency. Also invaluable is the *Walking and*

Riding Guide of Nevis, available free from the tourist board or for $1 at the *Museum of Nevis History* (see *Special Places*). For background reading, try *Swords, Ships, and Sugar,* by Vincent K. Hubbard (published by the *Nevis Historical and Cultural Society;* about $10), or *Nevis, Queen of the Caribees,* by Joyce Gordon (Macmillan; about $12.50), which can be found at the gift shop at the *Four Seasons* resort (see *Checking In*).

RADIO AND TELEVISION There are three radio stations: ZIZ Radio (555 AM and 96 FM), Voice of Nevis (VON; 895 AM), and Radio Paradise (825 AM); there's also a local television station, ZIZ-TV (channel 5). All carry local programs plus US and BBC pickups. The Trinity Broadcasting Network (TBN) transmits religious television programs via satellite and also airs some local programs. Satellite TV is available at most hotels.

TELEPHONE The area code for St. Kitts and Nevis is 809. Dial 911 for emergency assistance.

ENTRY REQUIREMENTS A passport or other proof of citizenship (a voter's registration card or birth certificate *and* an official photo ID such as a valid driver's license) and a return or ongoing ticket are all that's required of US and Canadian citizens for short visits to either island. There's a $10 departure tax, payable at the airport when you check in to leave (*not* when going from one island to visit the other).

CLIMATE AND CLOTHES The temperature on St. Kitts ranges from about 78 to 85F (25 to 30C) during the day all year long; at night, it sometimes drops to 68F (20C). Nevis maintains about the same temperatures. Both islands can be uncomfortably humid during the summer, even though they are cooled by trade winds. During the rainy season (mid-June through mid-November), it can shower heavily, but the downpour lasts only an hour or two.

On St. Kitts, dress is for casual comfort, not for fashion; cotton and cotton-blend sports clothes are fine for daytime and touring whatever the season. Be sure to pack sturdy walking shoes or sneakers, plus several swimming changes. Even for the June to November showers, you probably won't need a raincoat. Evenings, wear what you please, but the northeast trade winds keep it cool enough for a light wrap on winter evenings.

Daytime dress is similar on Nevis, but swim clothes are worn only at the beach or pool; you'll want a shirt or a cover-up at lunchtime or when you've had enough sun. At night, jackets and ties are never required for men, but something about the greathouse atmosphere makes many women enjoy dressing up a bit in long (but casual) skirts or summer evening dresses.

MONEY Currency on both islands is the Eastern Caribbean dollar (EC), valued at about $2.70 EC to $1 US. Except at hotels, most prices on the islands are quoted in $EC. US and Canadian bills generally are accepted, but foreign coins are not welcome because they're difficult for islanders to exchange. It's a good idea to have some EC currency handy for small purchases. Most banks are open from 8 AM to 3 PM Mondays through Thursdays and from 8 AM to 5 PM Fridays. The *St. Kitts–Nevis National Bank* (Independence Sq., Basseterre; phone: 465-2204) also is open Saturdays from 8:30 to 11 AM, while the *Bank of Nevis* (Main St., Charlestown; phone: 469-5564) and the *St. Kitts–Nevis-Anguilla National Bank* (West St., Charlestown; phone: 469-5123) also are open Saturdays from 8 to 11 AM. In general, the exchange rate at hotels and shops is the same as the bank rate. All prices in this chapter are quoted in US dollars.

LANGUAGE English, spoken with an island lilt, has been the official language on St. Kitts and Nevis for more than 350 years, although there's also a local patois.

TIME St. Kitts and Nevis clocks are set to atlantic standard time throughout the year, one hour ahead of eastern standard time in winter (when it's noon in New York, it's 1 PM in Basseterre and Charlestown), the same as eastern daylight saving time in summer.

CURRENT Here 220 volts predominate, though a number of hotels are now wired for 110 volts (standard in the US and Canada). Check beforehand, or bring a converter just in case.

TIPPING Hotels add a 10% service charge, which really covers everybody. If you're eating out and no service charge is included, tip 10% to 15%; the same goes for taxi rides. On St. Kitts, give an airport porter 50¢ per bag, with a $1 minimum (there are no porters on Nevis).

GETTING AROUND: ST. KITTS

BUS These run between island villages, but tourists seldom use them because taxis are always handy and provide round-trip transportation (not always easy to plot using bus schedules) to exactly the place you want to go. The fare depends on how far you're going, but it's likely to be around $1.50 EC (about 56¢ US at press time), and you must use local currency. There are no airport buses.

CAR RENTAL Easy to arrange, car rental costs include unlimited mileage; gas is on you. A local driver's license is required; it's available at the fire station in Basseterre, where you'll need to present your driver's license from home. *Avis* (S. Independence Sq. St.; phone: 465-6507); *Caine's* (Princes St.; phone: 465-2366); *Delisle Walwyn & Co.* (Liverpool Row; phone: 465-8449); *Island Car Rental* (12 W. Independence Sq. St.; phone: 465-3000); *Sunshine* (11 Cayon St.; phone: 465-2193); and *TDC* (W. Independence Sq. St.; phone: 465-2991) are good firms in Basseterre. Shop around; some companies offer free pickup and drop-off. For moped rentals, call *Easy Ride Rentals* (phone: 465-3429). Don't forget to drive on the left!

FERRY SERVICES The government-operated ferry makes one or two trips between St. Kitts and Nevis daily except Thursdays and Sundays. The 45-minute crossing is generally calm and pleasant, and costs about $8 per person round trip. Contact the *St. Kitts Tourist Board* (see *Tourist Information*) for exact departure times. The *Spirit of Mt. Nevis,* a private ferry run by the *Mt. Nevis* hotel, makes one or two runs per day on Thursdays and Sundays between Basseterre and Charlestown; the fare is $12 per person round trip (phone: 469-9373).

INTER-ISLAND FLIGHTS *LIAT* has flights to St. Kitts from Nevis; Antigua; San Juan, Puerto Rico; St. Thomas; St. Croix; and St. Martin/St. Maarten. *American Eagle* flies from San Juan and St. Thomas to St. Kitts; the regional flight from St. Kitts to Nevis can be booked through on the same ticket. *Winair* (phone: 465-2186) and *Nevis Express* (phone: 469-3346) offer frequent flights between St. Kitts and Nevis; they also fly to other nearby islands. *Carib Aviation* (phone: 465-3055) and *Air St. Kitts–Nevis* (phone: 465-8571) offer charters.

SEA EXCURSIONS Trips to neighboring islands, sunset cruises, and deep-sea fishing and scuba trips are arranged through hotels or directly with *Kantours* (phone: 465-2098, 465-2040, or 465-3128), *Tropical Tours* (phone: 465-4039 or 465-4167), and *Kenneth's Dive Centre* (phone: 465-7043 or 465-2670). *Tropical Dreamer* (phone: 465-8224), a glass-bottom sailing catamaran, offers full-day sails to Nevis with snorkeling and beach barbecues, plus sunset cruises. Half-day snorkeling and sailing excursions and sunset cruises also are offered aboard the catamaran the *Spirit of St. Kitts* (phone: 465-7474). A day trip to Nevis is a must if time permits; take the ferry (see *Ferry Services,* above).

SIGHTSEEING TOURS *Kantours* and *Tropical Tours* (see *Sea Excursions,* above) both offer three-and-one-half-hour historic and sightseeing tours. Taxi tours also are popular because hotels try to team visitors with a driver who'll make the trip pleasant (although if exact dates and statistics matter to you, take your guidebook along). If you'd like extra stops or time, negotiate—or ask your hotel to—before you take off. *Greg's Safari Tours* (phone: 465-4121/2) specializes in ecotourism, offering tours full of information on the island's history, ecology, and folklore.

TAXI The transportation mainstay here, taxis are found waiting at the airport and at the Circus in Basseterre, and each hotel has a coterie of loyal drivers waiting outside in the shade or at the other end of a phone call. You also can call for a taxi (phone: 465-2050). Cabs are not metered, but the *Taxi Association* (phone: 465-4253) publishes a list of point-to-point rates (look for it in local tourist guides, or ask for a copy). Even so, the price should be settled before you start off (establish whether the rate quoted is in EC or US dollars). Remember that fares increase by 50% between 11 PM and 6 AM.

GETTING AROUND: NEVIS

BUS There's bus service between villages, but no set schedule; taxis are much easier. Here again, the fare depends on how far you're going, but is usually around $1.50 EC (about 56¢ US at press time) and must be paid in local currency.

CAR RENTAL Japanese and American cars and a few open-air mini-mokes are available. Rentals are easily arranged—ask your hotel to do it. The rates include unlimited mileage and a full tank of gas to start you off (generally, you won't need a refill). You'll need a Nevis driver's license, available at the police station in Charlestown (bring your driver's license from home). Reputable car rental agencies include *Avis* (phone: 469-1240), *Strikers* (phone: 469-2654), and *TDC* (phone: 469-5690). Remember—keep left!

FERRY SERVICES See listings for St. Kitts, above.

INTER-ISLAND FLIGHTS See listings for St. Kitts, above.

SEA EXCURSIONS Mostly plan-it-yourself, using the local ferry services or tour operators (see listings for St. Kitts). The other option: *Newcastle Bay Marina Watersports Centre* (next to the *Newcastle Airport;* phone: 469-9395) offers half-day snorkel tours and sunset cruises aboard their 55-foot motor yacht.

SIGHTSEEING TAXI TOURS Simple to negotiate. Your hotel will find you a driver. Minivan and minibus tours also are available through *All Season Streamline Tours* (phone: 469-1138).

TAXI Unlike the yellow metropolitan cabs on St. Kitts, the system here is individual car-and-driver. Rates are fixed and published in the tourist guides available at the airport and at the tourist office. Before taking any trip, confirm whether the fare is quoted in EC or US dollars. Also remember that fares increase 50% between 10 PM and 6 AM. Taxis are available at the airport, or any hotel can call one for you.

SPECIAL EVENTS

Carnival—December 20 through January 2—is the big party on St. Kitts, complete with parades, music, and dancing. Summer's *Culturama* (late July, early August) brings calypso shows, dances, parties, and festive events to Nevis. *Tourism Week,* held in late October or early November in St. Kitts and February 6 through 12 in Nevis, is another big celebration, with cultural programs, water sports, competitions, and fishing tournaments. Legal holidays on both islands include *New Year's Day, Good Friday* (April 5 in 1996), *Easter Monday* (April 8 in 1996), *Labour Day* (first Monday in May), *Whitmonday* (May 27 in 1996), the *Queen's Birthday* (early June), *August Monday* (first Monday in August), *Independence Day* (September 19), *Christmas,* and *Boxing Day* (December 26).

SHOPPING

Duty-free shopping is relatively new to St. Kitts, but liberalized licensing legislation has resulted in an increasing number of shops that feature imported merchandise—perfume, jewelry, watches, china, and crystal. There is some rather good local crafts work, interesting local jewelry, and island casualwear. Be sure to sample (and take home) a bottle of CSR (Cane Spirits Rothschild), a St. Kitts–made cane spirit delicious in mixed drinks. Two shopping plazas in the center of town, *Palms Arcade* and *TDC Mall*, are worth a visit, as is the *Pelican Shopping Mall* on Bay Road, near the pier in Basseterre; it has 26 shops, a covered bandstand, two lounges, and a restaurant in an Old World setting. The selection of goods on Nevis has increased, with many new shops offering island fashions in addition to the predictable souvenirs, T-shirts, and some fairly routine island crafts (shell and straw, mostly). Almost all the shops are in Charlestown, along Main Street and one or two side streets.

ST. KITTS

Ashburry's Duty-free fine watches, jewelry, fragrances, cosmetics, sunglasses, and skin-care products. On Liverpool Row, Basseterre (phone: 465-8175).

Caribelle Batik Dresses, skirts, blouses, shirts, pareos (sarongs), and wall hangings in batik, tie-dyed, and hand-painted Sea Island cotton fabrics are made and sold here. All are brightly colored, in island-inspired designs, and guaranteed colorfast and washable. *Romney Manor* near Old Road Town (phone: 465-6253).

Little Switzerland The only authorized agent of Rolex watches on the island. Figurines, crystal, and a good selection of fine jewelry—all available duty-free. *Pelican Shopping Mall,* Basseterre (phone: 465-9859).

The Palms Resortwear designed by Canadian John Warden and made in St. Kitts; also Sunny Caribbee brand spices and teas, tropical costume jewelry, and scarves. *Palms Arcade,* Basseterre (phone: 465-2599).

Plantation Picture House Portraits, still lifes, and landscapes in watercolors and oils by local artist Kate Spencer. At *Rawlins Plantation* (see *Checking In*) and Fort St., Basseterre (phone: 465-7740).

A Slice of the Lemon French perfume, imported jewelry, watches, china, crystal—the largest selection and the best brands and buys, all duty-free. Fort St., Basseterre (phone: 465-2889).

Spencer Cameron Art Gallery Locally produced silk-screened fabrics, watercolors, and other paintings. N. Independence Sq., Basseterre (phone: 465-1617).

Splash T-shirts, jazzy island clothing, batik cotton sportswear, bathing suits, and woodwork. *Pelican Shopping Mall,* Basseterre (phone: 465-9640 or 465-9279).

Wall's Deluxe Record and Book Shop Good selection of books about the area, works by West Indian authors, and records of calypso, reggae, and steel band music. Fort St., Basseterre (phone: 465-2159).

NEVIS

Batik by Carvelle Formerly the *Nevis Craft Studio* (in fact, its sign still says so), this is a good source for batik fashions. Main St., Charlestown (no phone).

Caribbean Confections Baskets of jams, jellies, and candies to take home, plus fresh tropical-fruit ice cream for immediate consumption. Main St., Charlestown (phone: 469-5685).

Gallery of Nevis Art Local artwork is featured. Main St., Charlestown (phone: 469-1381).

The Island Hopper A selection of the batik, tie-dyed, and hand-painted clothing and wall hangings made at *Caribelle Batik* (see St. Kitts listing). Main St., Charlestown (phone: 469-5430).

Knick Knacks Local art and handmade dolls, as well as men's and women's cotton sportswear and batik clothing. Main St., Charlestown (phone: 469-5784).

Nevis Handicraft Co-operative A wide selection of crafts and locally made preserves, such as guava and soursop jellies, mango chutney, and hot sauce. Next to the tourist office, Main St., Charlestown (phone: 469-1746).

Nevis Philatelic Bureau Magnificent, colorful island stamps. The postcards already come with the prettiest stamps available. Just off Main St., Charlestown (phone: 469-5535).

Newcastle Pottery Gift items and cooking pots; visitors may watch the merchandise being made and fired over burning coconut shells. Just east of the airport, Newcastle (phone: 469-9746).

Sandbox Tree Gifts, souvenirs, and clothing for men, women, and children, including embroidered placemats, hand-carved wooden fish, and an entire room full of toys and books. *Evelyn's Villa,* Cedar Trees, Charlestown (phone: 469-5662).

Williams Eulalie Main Street Grocery Nevis hot pepper sauce, among the Caribbean's best, is a good souvenir or gift. CSR, the St. Kitts–made cane spirit, also is available here. Main St., Charlestown (phone: 469-5226).

SPORTS: ST. KITTS

BOATING Day sails to Nevis, moonlight cruises, and coastal cruises are offered by a number of outfits in Basseterre, including *Tropical Tours, Kenneth's Dive Centre* (see *Sea Excursions* for both), *Leeward Island Charters* (phone: 465-

7474), and *Fisherman's Wharf*, the restaurant/boating facility of the *Ocean Terrace Inn* (see *Checking In*).

GOLF *Jack Tar Village* has the *Royal St. Kitts* golf course, an 18-hole championship layout at Frigate Bay (phone: 465-8339). The par 72, 160-acre course incorporates seven lakes and is bounded by the Caribbean and the Atlantic. Use of the greens (but not the carts) is complimentary for *Jack Tar Village* guests; non-guests pay greens and cart rental fees. Caddies are not available, but lessons are. There is also a nine-hole course at the *Golden Rock Estate* (phone: 465-8103).

HIKING AND MOUNTAIN CLIMBING No fully marked trails exist on St. Kitts, so either hire a local guide through your hotel or take a tour. Monkey Hill is rated an easy climb, but the trail is hard to find. The two-and-one-half-hour hike to the crater rim of dormant volcano Mt. Liamuiga is moderately strenuous, but rewarded by a spectacular vista of steaming sulfur and lush greenery. The full-day hike up Verchild's Mountain and back is more difficult; make sure you're in good physical shape before you go. Another possibility is a rain forest hike up hidden mountain trails and past waterfalls and dense vegetation where monkeys, mongooses, and hummingbirds often are seen. *Greg's Safari Tours* (see *Sightseeing Tours*) and *Kris Tours* (phone: 465-4042) offer half-day rain forest tours, as well as full-day tours to Mt. Liamuiga that include lunch and drinks.

HORSEBACK RIDING *Trinity Stables* (phone: 465-3226 or 465-9603) offers one-hour beach rides, and *Royal Stables* (phone: 465-2222) runs half-day riding trips to the rain forest.

SNORKELING AND SCUBA DIVING The reefs are mostly pristine, and popular dive sites include underwater caves, coral grottoes, and several wrecks. Instruction, equipment, dive and snorkeling trips are offered by *Pro Diver* (two locations: at the *Ocean Terrace Inn*'s *Fisherman's Wharf*—see *Checking In*—and at Turtle Beach; phone: 465-3223) and *Kenneth's Dive Centre* (see *Sea Excursions*).

SPORT FISHING St. Kitts's waters abound with fish, including dorado, kingfish, wahoo, and tuna. Charter boats for deep-sea fishing are available from the *Ocean Terrace Inn*'s *Fisherman's Wharf* (see *Checking In*), *Kenneth's Dive Centre* and *Tropical Tours* (see *Sea Excursions* for both), *Jeffers M. C. Enterprises* (phone: 465-1900), and *Sam Lake* (phone: 465-8225). The cost includes tackle, bait, and drinks on board. If you land anything, *Fisherman's Wharf* will prepare it for dinner that night with their compliments (though they might charge you if you made the catch on another outfit's boat).

SWIMMING AND SUNNING The widest and whitest sands are at the southern end of the island, and the best of these is at Sand Bank Bay. Frigate Bay and Friar's Bay have beaches on both the Atlantic and Caribbean (there's surf on the windward side of Frigate Bay). White House Bay is just south of

Friar's Bay; Banana Bay and Cockleshell Bay, on the island's southernmost shore, beyond Great Salt Pond, are other good names to know. Unusual black sand beaches rim the northeast coast of St. Kitts from Dieppe Bay to Black Rocks. Few hotels are directly on the beach, though most aren't far away and will arrange transportation; most have swimming pools.

TENNIS If you're addicted, stay at the *Jack Tar Village,* which has four courts (two lighted) and a pro; non-guests can use the courts by purchasing a day pass that entitles them to use all the resort's facilities. There is also a court at the *St. Kitts Bridge and Tennis Club* (at Fortlands in Basseterre; phone: 465-2938); the *St. Kitts Lawn Tennis Club* (Victoria Rd., Basseterre; phone: 465-2051) has two courts and will grant temporary membership to visitors. The following hotels have tennis for guests only: *Bird Rock Beach* (two courts), the *Golden Lemon* (one court), *Rawlins Plantation* (a grass court), and *Sun 'n' Sand* (two courts). (See *Checking In* for all hotels mentioned.)

WATER SKIING Go to *Roy Gumbs Watersports* (phone: 465-8050), on the Caribbean beach at Frigate Bay. Jet skis are available for rent through *Kenneth's Dive Centre* (see *Sea Excursions*).

WINDSURFING For lessons and board rental, try *Roy Gumbs Watersports* (see *Water Skiing*) or *Tropical Surf* (Turtle Beach; phone: 465-2380 or 469-9086).

SPORTS: NEVIS

CYCLING Both mountain and speed bicycles are available for rent at *Meadville* (Craddock Rd., Charlestown; phone: 469-5235).

GOLF There's only one, but it's tops.

TOP TEE-OFF SPOT

Four Seasons Nevis's first course is a real gem. With 18 holes designed by Robert Trent Jones Jr., the course begins at sea level, slopes toward 3,232-foot Mt. Nevis, and ends up on the beach. The 15th hole, which features a ravine and a 600-yard drop to the green, is the most challenging. With its beautiful layout, uncrowded fairways, stunning views, and crew of staff members who patrol the course with refreshments, a round here is bound to be memorable, regardless of your score (see *Checking In*).

HIKING AND MOUNTAIN CLIMBING Climbing to the top of Nevis Peak, the dormant volcano, is not difficult, though the dirt path can be muddy from April through November. Wear sturdy climbing shoes or sneakers and hardy, easily washed clothes. The climb takes about six hours round trip, and most hotels will pack a lunch. A guide is recommended; your hotel can make arrangements. Try *Eco-Tours Nevis* (phone: 469-2091) for historical and ecological walks; or *Top-to-Bottom* (phone: 469-5371), which offers more strenuous hikes to the peak.

HORSE RACING There are races six times a year at the *Indian Castle Race Track* on the beach in Gingerland (no phone): *New Year's Day, Easter Monday, Labour Day* (the first Monday in May), *August Monday* (the first Monday in August), *Independence Day* (September 19), and *Boxing Day* (December 26).

HORSEBACK RIDING Riding can be arranged through Ira Dore at *Garner's Estate* (phone: 469-5528). The charge includes a guide and a one-and-a-half-hour ride. The *Hermitage Plantation* (see *Checking In*) offers one-hour horseback rides and either 15-minute or one-hour horse-drawn carriage rides. Hotels will often make riding arrangements for you.

SPORT FISHING Barracuda, shark, kingfish, wahoo, and snapper can all be caught in local waters. Contact *Sea Nevis* (phone: 469-9239) or your hotel desk to arrange for an outing with a reputable guide. Or call Captain Ken at *Newcastle Bay Marina Watersports Centre* (see *Sea Excursions,* or try him at 469-9373).

SWIMMING AND SUNNING All beaches are public. Pinney's Beach on the Caribbean side is the longest and the best. Of the island's hostelries, only the *Four Seasons, Nisbet Plantation, Oualie Beach,* and *Pinney's Beach* are on beaches (see *Checking In* for all). Other hotels have large swimming pools, usually well placed for views, and offer complimentary transportation to private cabañas on Pinney's Beach.

TENNIS Nevis offers excellent racket sports for both novices and more experienced players. Hotel courts are open to non-guests for an extra charge.

CHOICE COURTS

Four Seasons This resort offers six courts with all-weather surfaces and four of red clay (a rare treat in the Caribbean). Three of the courts are lighted for nighttime play. There also are round-robin tournaments and topflight instruction (see *Checking In*).

Other tennis options: There is one court each at the *Golden Rock, Montpelier Plantation, Nisbet Plantation,* and *Pinney's Beach* hotels (see *Checking In* for all), and at the *Rest Haven* hotel (Charlestown; phone: 469-5208).

WATER SPORTS The *Oualie Beach* hotel (see *Checking In*) rents Sunfish; *Scuba Safaris* (also at the *Oualie Beach* hotel; phone: 469-9518) offers a full range of snorkeling, scuba diving, and *NAUI* instruction. Glass-bottom boat trips also are available. *Newcastle Bay Marina Watersports Centre* (see *Sea Excursions*) offers sailboat and kayak rentals, half-day snorkel tours, water skiing, and windsurfing—lessons and board rentals.

NIGHTLIFE

Low voltage. Most hotels have string or steel band performances on regular schedules in season. On St. Kitts, the *Ocean Terrace Inn* hosts a steel band and a fashion show Wednesdays, and a West Indian buffet or barbecue accompanied by a steel band Fridays; call ahead for reservations (see *Checking In*). A night pass, available with or without dinner, will get you into *Jack Tar Village* for the evening's show (see *Checking In*). The *Royal St. Kitts Casino*—the only one on the island—also is there. The casino is open daily from 7 PM to 2 AM and offers slot machines, roulette, craps, blackjack tables, and a disco. There's no admission charge, and a complimentary casino bus shuttles to and from several island hotels. For additional details, see *Casino Countdown* in DIVERSIONS. Late-late nightspots include *Reflexions* at *Flexes Fitness Centre* (Frigate Bay Rd.; phone: 465-7616) and the *Cotton Club* disco at *Canada Estate* (phone: 465-5855).

On Nevis, a happening Friday night spot is *Prinderella's* (phone: 469-1291), popular for its sunset "Happy Night," which includes excellent munchies; on Saturday nights there's local music and dancing at *Dick's Bar* (at Brick Kiln, in the northeast; phone: 469-9182); the bar at the *Oualie Beach* hotel (see *Checking In*) is a popular place for just hanging out. What action there is usually winds down by midnight.

Best on the Islands

CHECKING IN

Hotels on St. Kitts tend to be small, low-profile, charming resorts, with lots of personality (island law decrees that no building can be higher than the tallest palm tree). But few qualify as luxurious. Construction in the Frigate Bay area, including several large-scale projects, has added to the island's supply of 840 guestrooms.

Accommodations on Nevis consist mainly of inns and condo complexes that range from small to tiny—except for the luxurious *Four Seasons,* with its 196 rooms. Much of the appeal of these inns lies in their origins as sugar plantations. Most innkeepers describe their places as "more of a house party, really." Guests who meet for the first time over after-dinner drinks often end up planning an outing together for the next day, and by the end of the week they may plan to vacation together the following year. All hotel rooms listed below have air conditioning, telephones, TV sets, and private baths unless otherwise indicated.

Many of the hotels operate on a Modified American Plan (MAP), which means that breakfast and dinner are included in the room rate. Most of the others offer an MAP at an additional $30 to $60 per person per day. Those operating on the European Plan (EP) do not include meals in the room rate. Properties described below as expensive charge $275 and more for a double room with meals, $210 and more without meals. Those listed as moderate charge between $125 and $210 for a double room without meals, and inexpensive places charge less than $125 for a double without meals. Prices drop by about 35% in summer. A 7% tax and 10% service charge is added to hotel bills. A few hotels may require a deposit to hold a reservation.

Rental cottages, a less expensive option, go for about $175 and more a week. Arrange cottage, house, and villa rentals through *Seashell* (Main St., Charlestown, Nevis; phone: 469-1675; 800-457-0444), or obtain a list of addresses from the islands' tourist offices (see *Tourist Information*, above). All telephone numbers are in the 809 area code unless otherwise indicated.

We begin with our favorite haven, followed by recommended hotels listed by price category.

A SPECIAL HAVEN

Four Seasons, Nevis Nestled within a former coconut palm tree grove is this island's largest and most luxurious (and most expensive) resort. Its 196 rooms situated in 12 two-story buildings overlook either the pristine sands of Pinney's Beach or the scenic rolling hills of the first-rate 18-hole Robert Trent Jones Jr. golf course. The quiet center of this complex is the plantation-style greathouse, which contains two excellent restaurants (see *Eating Out*), a library, a main bar, and a nightclub. A marble staircase leads to two pools on a pavilion, a poolside restaurant, a beach, and a dock. Flowering yellow bells, hibiscus, and bougainvillea line the walkways. Each guestroom is a tropical oasis, with either one king-size or two full-size beds, a stocked mini-bar, large closets, a mahogany armoire with TV set and VCR, a huge tile-and-marble bathroom, and a private patio or screened-in balcony. For children, there's a supervised daily activities program. Other pluses include a complete health club and fitness center, a spa, water sports facilities, 10 tennis courts, and an attentive, pleasant staff. This well-run resort is easy on the mind and the body—a topnotch getaway for those who want pampering and relaxation. Pinney's Beach (phone: 469-1111; 800-332-3442; fax: 469-1112).

ST. KITTS

BASSETERRE

MODERATE

Ocean Terrace Inn One of St. Kitts's best, on a hilltop at the far west hook of Basseterre Harbor, this place has many appealing qualities. The 54 rooms (including eight attractive one- and two-bedroom apartments) have tiled floors, tropical decor, and breezy terraces from which to watch the harbor life. The grounds are charming, and the restaurants and two bars have a lively, congenial atmosphere. Various meal plans are available, and guests may choose either the hotel's dining room (indoors or out, with an ocean view) or its *Fisherman's Wharf* restaurant and bar, a five-minute walk away (see *Eating Out* for more on both). Other pluses: a boating and scuba facility at *Fisherman's Wharf,* two pools, and a complimentary shuttle to Frigate Bay's Caribbean beach and to *Turtle Beach Bar & Grill* on the Southeast Peninsula. Fortlands (phone: 465-2754 or 465-2380; 800-524-0512; fax: 465-1057).

INEXPENSIVE

Fort Thomas This extensively refurbished, modern hotel offers 64 guestrooms overlooking the harbor. Each features pink and green appointments and a balcony or patio. The place boasts the largest pool on the island, plus an open-air lobby, a restaurant, a terrace bar, complimentary shuttles to the beach (about five miles away) and golf, and a gift shop. Tennis is nearby. One of the island's best values. Just outside of Basseterre (phone: 465-2695; 800-851-7818; fax: 465-7518).

FRIGATE BAY

EXPENSIVE

Island Paradise Beach Village The first condominium development in Frigate Bay, with 35 one-bedroom, 19 two-bedroom, and four three-bedroom apartments, all with fully equipped kitchens. None of the apartments has a telephone, and only some have air conditioning and TV sets, so if these are important to you, be sure to request them. There's a pool and the Atlantic beach, plus a pizza and snack restaurant, a food market, a liquor store, and a small souvenir shop. No credit cards accepted. Across from the golf course (phone: 465-8035; 800-828-2956; fax: 465-8236).

Jack Tar Village Royal St. Kitts Rates at this all-inclusive resort cover everything from accommodations in its 242 rooms to meals, cocktails, water sports, tennis, nightly entertainment, and tips. All this, plus an adjoining 18-hole golf course and a casino, make it the place for those seeking an active vacation at a typically modern resort. Closer to the Atlantic than the Caribbean beach, with complimentary shuttle service to the latter. Those not staying here can buy a day pass permitting use of all facilities. While expensive, this is not a luxury hotel; however, with so much to offer, it is a good value. On Frigate Bay (phone: 465-8651; 800-999-9182; 214-987-4909 in Dallas; fax: 465-1031).

MODERATE

Colony Timothy Beach Now managed by the Colony hotel group, this property, with a total of 61 rooms and suites, is at the foot of Sir Timothy Hill on a golden sand beach. Rooms feature patios or balconies; studios and suites also have full kitchens. TV sets are available for an extra charge. There's a pool on the premises; water sports and complimentary tennis are nearby. The beachside restaurant specializes in seafood cooked over an open grill. Golf packages in connection with the *Jack Tar Village* course (see above) are available. About 3 miles from Basseterre (phone: 465-8597; 800-777-1700; fax: 465-7723).

InterGrande Frigate Bay Located on the Caribbean side of the bay, a five-minute stroll from the beach, this place has 64 spacious units in low-rise, Mediterranean-style buildings clustered around a big, handsome pool. All accommodations have ceiling fans (to supplement the air conditioning) and patios, and junior, one-, and two-bedroom suites also have kitchenettes or full kitchens. There's also a restaurant and bar. A meal plan is available at extra charge (phone: 465-8935; 800-226-2185; fax: 465-7050).

Sun 'n' Sand Beach Village Just off the wild Atlantic and behind a hedge of sea grape bushes are 18 cottages (each with two bedrooms, two baths) and 32 studio apartments. The cottages are simple, but pleasant, with high ceilings, fully equipped kitchens, and air conditioned bedrooms. The studios have kitchenettes and ceiling fans (to supplement the air conditioning). There's a small grocery and drugstore, as well as a casual beachside pub, two tennis courts, and a pool. Continental breakfast is included; attractive weekly rates make it a good choice for families traveling on a budget, especially off-season, when the rates drop by as much as 50% (phone: 465-8037; 800-223-6510; fax: 465-6745).

INEXPENSIVE

Leeward Cove A small condominium hotel opposite the *Jack Tar Village* golf course, with 38 spacious and comfortably furnished one- and two-bedroom units with kitchenettes (but without telephones). TV sets are available for an extra charge. The complex offers access to the Atlantic beach, a tennis court, and complimentary use of the golf course. There's a three-night minimum stay in winter; if you stay a week, your apartment comes with a car at no extra charge. On five acres; within walking distance of restaurants (phone: 465-8030; 800-223-5695; fax: 465-3476).

ELSEWHERE ON ST. KITTS

EXPENSIVE

Golden Lemon "For the discriminating few who like to do nothing, in grand style" is how the brochure puts it. A beautifully refurbished 17th-century greathouse, this is one of the few inns where as much attention has been lavished on guestrooms as public areas. Eleven rooms are in the greathouse itself and there are eight individually decorated, stylish villas with small private pools at the water's edge. The rooms are cooled by sea breezes and ceiling fans; there are no air conditioners or TV sets, and only the villas have telephones. The inn has lovely gardens and courtyards, a tennis court, a pool, a small black sand beach, superb food (see *Eating Out*), and *Lemon-aid,* an exclusive boutique. Rates include breakfast, afternoon tea, and dinner. No children under age 16 allowed. At Dieppe Bay, on the island's northwest coast (phone: 465-7260; 800-633-7411; fax: 465-4019).

Ottley's Plantation Inn A hostelry on an old sugar plantation near the foot of Mt. Liamuiga, it is high enough to offer scenic views from its 35 acres. The 15 rooms are either in the restored, verandah-girded greathouse, where an English country look prevails, or in stone cottages within walking distance of the rain forest. None of the rooms has a TV set, but a TV room in the greathouse provides cable TV, a VCR, and an extensive film library. There's a spring-fed swimming pool, as well as shuttle service to beach, golf, tennis, and shopping. The restaurant borders the rain forest. MAP is available at an additional charge. *Ottley's Estate,* north of Basseterre (phone: 465-7234; 800-772-3039; fax: 465-4760).

Rawlins Plantation This owner-operated country estate, a 12-acre, onetime sugar plantation, lies on a hilltop with beautiful gardens and arresting views of the ocean. The main building, constructed on the foundations of the 17th-century greathouse, houses the dining room (see *Eating Out*); the 12 guestrooms are in the renovated outbuildings scattered around the breezy hillside site. The rooms do not have telephones, TV sets, or air conditioning, but they do have ceiling fans and verandahs or patios. There's a pretty pool and a grass tennis court; a beach is a short drive away. Rates include breakfast, afternoon tea, dinner, and laundry service. Closed mid-August through mid-October. At Mt. Pleasant, near Dieppe Bay on the north coast (phone: 465-6221; 800-621-1270 or 800-346-5358; fax: 469-4954).

White House A restored 18th-century greathouse, decorated with antiques and mahogany, this establishment has only 10 guestrooms—one in the converted stable, four in the old carriage house, and five in new, but traditionally designed, stone cottages. All are cooled by ceiling fans (no air conditioning); none has a telephone or TV set. The main house has two dining rooms (see *Eating Out*). There's also a pool and a tennis court. Rates include breakfast, afternoon tea, and dinner. In St. Peter's, at the foot of Monkey Hill, about 3 miles north of Basseterre (phone: 465-8162; 800-223-1108; fax: 465-8275).

INEXPENSIVE

Bird Rock Beach The 38 rooms here are set in two-story cottages perched on a cliff overlooking the water. The rooms have tile floors, and each has an oceanfront patio or balcony. One restaurant is on the premises and another, run by the same owner, is five minutes away. There also are two tennis courts, a pool with swim-up bar, and scuba gear rentals. Centrally located; the capital is nearby (phone: 465-8914; 800-621-1270; fax: 465-1675).

NEVIS

EXPENSIVE

Hermitage A heavenly island-farm property with the oldest wooden greathouse in the Caribbean. There are 14 rooms in gingerbread cottages painted in pleasant periwinkle, melon, and lemon tones, sprinkled among lush hills dotted with tropical flowers. The friendly owners grow their own fruit trees and herbs and raise their own chickens and pigs, ensuring that the freshest meat and produce go into their excellent meals. Facilities include a pool, a tennis court, and horseback riding. Rates include a full breakfast and a four-course dinner. St. John Fig Tree (phone: 469-3477 or 469-2201; 800-682-4025 or 800-742-4276; fax: 469-2481).

Montpelier Plantation Inn The prettiest of the old estate inns, it has 17 rooms in private cottages set on the grounds of an elegant old greathouse. The spacious rooms feature porches, marble-tiled baths, four-poster beds, hair dryers, coffee and tea makers, and ceiling fans (there's no air conditioning—none needed with the island's sea breezes—or TV sets). Flowers bloom everywhere: a large, flaming-orange, flamboyant tree canopies a walkway, and a blooming jasmine shrub sweetens the breeze at the large lap pool. The inn's dinners are bountiful and superb, and the owners are delightful hosts. There's also a tennis court, and transportation is provided to a private cabaña on Pinney's Beach. Rates include a full breakfast (with fresh fruit from the property's trees), and MAP rates are available. In the hills east of Charlestown (phone: 469-3462; 212-599-8280; fax: 469-2932).

Nisbet Plantation Inn Built on the site of an 18th-century plantation, this is a perfect place for those who want to be steps away from the beach. A long alley of towering coconut palms runs from the manor house to the inn's silky white sand beach. The 38 ultramodern private cottages are spread over immaculately trimmed lawns and have tile baths, patios, mini-refrigerators, coffee and tea makers, hair dryers, and ceiling fans (no air conditioners or TV sets). The antiques-filled manor house is where everyone congregates for dinners that rank among the best on the island (see *Eating Out*). There's a large beachside pool and a casual restaurant for breakfast and lunch. Rates include breakfast and dinner. Newcastle (phone: 469-9325; 800-724-6008; 410-628-1718 in Maryland; fax: 469-9864).

MODERATE

Croney's Old Manor Estate Set in the island's most extensively restored cut-stone plantation house and outbuildings are 15 spacious rooms and suites with four-poster beds, ceiling fans (there's no air conditioning), and antique fixtures in some of the baths. None of the rooms has a telephone or a TV set.

The dining room serves wonderful meals, and the pool is one of the most unusual around—it was the plantation's former cistern. Both MAP and EP rates are available. In the hills of St. George Gingerland (phone: 469-3445; 800-892-7093; fax: 469-3388).

Golden Rock Estate An 1815 stone plantation house forms the core of this 100-acre estate criss-crossed by delightful nature trails where monkeys are a common sight. The 16 pleasant guestrooms are in cottages around the estate, and there is also a lovely two-bedroom cottage inside an old stone windmill. All rooms have island-made canopy beds and ceiling fans (no air conditioners, TV sets, or telephones). There's also a dining room, a beach restaurant, a tennis court, a pool, and a complimentary shuttle to two private beaches. The staff is friendly, and the knowledgeable innkeeper is happy to chat about island history and lore. Both MAP and EP rates are available. In the hills of St. George Gingerland (phone: 469-3346; fax: 469-2113).

Mt. Nevis Hotel and Beach Club A spanking modern condominium hotel with 16 deluxe rooms and another 16 suites (sleeping up to four people), all with TV sets with VCRs, plus private balconies from which to view the southern shore of St. Kitts. Some units have kitchens, and there's a freshwater pool. The beach—where the hotel maintains a restaurant and water sports facilities—is a quarter mile away; complimentary shuttle service is provided. Other features include a 110-passenger launch that ferries between Nevis and St. Kitts and is used for luncheon and sunset cruises when off duty. Newcastle (phone: 469-9373; 800-75-NEVIS; fax: 469-9375).

Oualie Beach This resort offers 24 rooms in pretty pastel gingerbread cottages on a lovely beach. An excellent choice for scuba divers, it is home to *Scuba Safaris,* at press time the only dive operator on Nevis; ask about special dive packages. The rooms are immaculate and have screened-in porches, mini-bars, and ceiling fans; most have air conditioning, and some have full kitchens. There's also a restaurant and a popular beach bar. Rates include full breakfast. Oualie Bay (phone: 469-9735; 800-682-5431; fax: 469-9176).

INEXPENSIVE

Pinney's Beach A comfortable establishment in a convenient location (a seven-minute walk to Charlestown) on one of the island's nicest beaches. The 36 spacious rooms all have patios with beach or ocean views and are equipped with coffee makers. There's a dining room, pool, and tennis court; fishing, sailing, and horseback riding can be arranged. Pinney's Beach (phone: 469-5207; 800-742-4276; fax: 469-1088).

EATING OUT

All kinds of dishes—including roast suckling pig, crab backs, mutton stew, turtle steaks, and creole fried fish—appear on the menus of island restaurants, which cater to all tastes. Expect to pay $60 and more for dinner for two, excluding wine, drinks, and tips, in the restaurants we list as expensive; between $30 and $50 at places in the moderate category; and less than $30 at inexpensive spots. Unless otherwise noted, all restaurants are open for lunch and dinner. All telephone numbers are in the 809 area code unless otherwise indicated.

ST. KITTS

EXPENSIVE

Golden Lemon With an eclectic international menu, charming atmosphere, and grand service, this spot is a must for all island visitors. Open daily for breakfast, lunch, and dinner. Reservations necessary for dinner. Major credit cards accepted. At the *Golden Lemon Inn,* on Dieppe Bay (phone: 465-7260).

Ocean Terrace Inn Centrally located, with a sweeping view of the harbor, the dining room here serves continental and island dishes in a tropical setting, indoors or outdoors. On alternate Fridays, the menu features either a West Indian buffet or a barbecue with steaks, lobsters, and Cornish game hens. There's steel band entertainment Wednesdays and Fridays. Open daily for breakfast, lunch, and dinner. Dinner reservations necessary for those not staying at the hotel. Major credit cards accepted. Fortlands, Basseterre (phone: 465-2754; fax: 465-1057).

Rawlins Plantation Arguably the best dining on the island, with its panoramic view and cool country setting, this lovely spot is where savvy Kittitian professionals entertain luncheon guests. It's located in the main house of a country estate that was built on the foundations of an old sugar works. Lunch is a West Indian buffet, dinner a four-course prix fixe meal with a classic French menu that changes daily. Open daily; closed mid-August through mid-October. Reservations necessary by noon. Major credit cards accepted. Mt. Pleasant (phone: 465-6221).

White House Dine outdoors or in the exquisite original dining room of this 18th-century greathouse. The atmosphere is sophisticated. Lunch and a multi-course, prix fixe dinner, with West Indian and continental dishes, are served daily, as is afternoon tea. Jackets are suggested for men, but not required. Reservations necessary. Major credit cards accepted. St. Peter's, about 3 miles north of Basseterre (phone: 465-8162).

MODERATE

J's Place In the foothills of the *Brimstone Hill Fortress,* it's a good spot for lunching on local fare. Open daily. Reservations unnecessary. No credit cards accepted. Main Rd., Sandy Point (phone: 465-6264).

Lighthouse Good food, fine service, and a sophisticated atmosphere prevail at this place serving West Indian and continental fare. There are panoramic views over Basseterre from the east side of town. Dinner only; closed Sundays and Mondays. Reservations advised. American Express and Visa accepted. Centrally located at Bird Rock, Basseterre (phone: 465-8914).

INEXPENSIVE

Ballahoo In the heart of Basseterre, this is a charming, cozy, upstairs eatery serving tasty West Indian dishes, sandwiches, and steaks, with tables on a balcony overlooking the hustle and bustle below. Open for breakfast, lunch, and dinner; closed Sundays. Reservations unnecessary. Major credit cards accepted. On the Circus, Basseterre (phone: 465-4197).

Chef's Place West Indian dishes are served in a casual atmosphere. Open for breakfast, lunch, and dinner; closed Sundays. Reservations unnecessary. No credit cards accepted. Church St. (phone: 465-6176).

Fisherman's Wharf Seafood, chicken, and ribs are served at the picnic tables here, plus conch chowder, a house specialty. A very casual place at the water's edge, it belongs to the *Ocean Terrace Inn,* a short walk away. Open daily for dinner. Reservations advised Friday nights, when a steel band plays. Major credit cards accepted. Fortlands, Basseterre (phone: 465-2754).

NEVIS

While Nevis has virtually no restaurants other than inn dining rooms, it still is a place to unbuckle your belt and enjoy things culinary. Nevis grows much of its own food; consequently, the fruits and vegetables are plentiful and very fresh. The papaya you have for breakfast is likely to have come from a tree outside your door. Likewise, the fish is of the just-caught variety. Good ingredients inspire good cooking—whether at an inn or a casual beachside pub, the quality of the food here is unusually high.

Most of the inns operate on the Modified American Plan, which means breakfast and dinner are included in the daily rate. There are no dine-around plans, and most visitors will do just fine if they stay put, but those who want to sample fare at other inns may patronize them for lunch or for special dinners, such as *Nisbet*'s Thursday night buffet barbecue feast of fresh fish, lobster, and steaks. Most of the inns also host cookouts or West Indian buffets. Call to find out when and where, and, in general, call ahead for reservations if you plan to dine at another hotel. All plantation estates create superb meals, but *Montpelier* in particular offers an extraordinary dining experience (reservations advised). The *Four Seasons* resort offers good fare; reservations and appropriate dress are advised for the excellent main dining room. (See *Checking In* for all hotels listed above.)

In Charlestown, *Muriel's Cuisine* (Upper Happy Hill Dr.; phone: 469-5920) and *Unella's* (on the waterfront; phone: 469-5574) are local favorites, serving West Indian cooking. *Caribbean Confections* is good for a light snack (see *Shopping*). For an authentic local scene and West Indian food, try *CLA-CHA-DEL* (Shaws Rd., Newcastle; phone: 469-9640).

St. Lucia

St. Lucia's location hints at its tempestuous past. Midway between French Martinique and British St. Vincent, the island has spent a good part of the last 300 years bouncing between Britain and France as those two countries fought over control of the West Indies.

Focusing only on St. Lucia's location, however, is to ignore the island's intoxicating beauty. St. Lucia has some of the most magnificent shoreline in the entire island chain; remote Anse Chastanet and Marigot Bay, as beautiful a sea cove as exists in the world; and inland jungles with two lushly forested mountains, the Pitons. St. Lucia is endowed with stands of towering bamboo trees and tropical rain forests filled with giant ferns, colorful parrots, and hummingbirds. It even has a quiescent (but still bubbling) volcano, Mt. Soufrière, where tourists can amble among smoking sulfur pits and gurgling mudholes.

The peaceful Arawak Indians apparently arrived on the island hundreds of years ago to escape the fierce Carib Indians. Remains of their villages have been found on Pigeon Island, just off St. Lucia's northern tip (today joined to St. Lucia by a causeway). Soon enough the Carib arrived on St. Lucia, however, and it was that tribe—not the Arawak—whom the Spanish found when they discovered the island. (Just when that was is open to debate. The island celebrates December 13, 1502, as its discovery day; but the French have a counterclaim based on a colony of shipwrecked French sailors who found their way to the island at about the same time.)

Over the next 200 years the island changed hands between the French and the English more than 10 times. During the French Revolution the British took possession of the small island but, finding that French republican terrorists made it too difficult to control, abandoned it. In May 1706 a force of 12,000 British troops retook St. Lucia. The Treaty of Amiens, in March 1802, awarded St. Lucia to the French, but a year later the two countries were at war again, and an invading English force stormed the fortifications on Morne Fortune with fixed bayonets and recaptured the island.

The island remained under British control until 1967, when St. Lucia became a self-governing state in association with Great Britain; on February 22, 1979, it was granted full sovereignty and became a full-fledged member of the British Commonwealth.

St. Lucia, whose current population is 153,000, is now undergoing the development it missed during its turbulent earlier years. The growth of tourist facilities and immigration are proceeding at a controlled rate, and there has been some industrial expansion to support the new economy. And the island received international attention in late 1992, when native poet and playwright Derek Walcott was awarded the Nobel Prize for Literature. Yet, in spite of "progress," St. Lucia retains a unique sense of

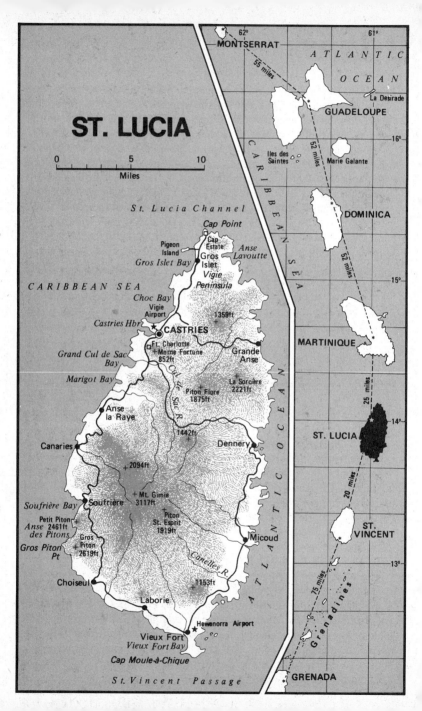

ST. LUCIA

0   5   10
Miles

MONTSERRAT   62°   61°

ATLANTIC
OCEAN

55 miles

La Desirade

GUADELOUPE   16°

C
A
R
I
B
B
E
A
N
S
E
A

Iles des
Saintes   Marie Galante

52 miles

DOMINICA

52 miles

St. Lucia Channel

Cap Point

Pigeon
Island   Anse
Lavoutte

Cap
Estate

Gros Islet Bay   Gros
Islet

Vigie
Peninsula   15°

Choc Bay   1359ft

Vigie
Airport

Castries Hbr.   CASTRIES   MARTINIQUE

Ft. Charlotte   Grande
Morne Fortune   Anse

Grand Cul de Sac
Bay   852ft

La Sorcière
2221ft   25 miles

Marigot Bay   Piton Flore
1875ft

Anse
la Raye   14°

1442ft

Canaries   Dennery   ST. LUCIA

2094ft

Soufrière Bay   Soufrière
Mt. Gimie
3117ft   Micoud   ST.
VINCENT

Petit Piton
2461ft   Piton
St. Esprit
1919ft   13°

Anse
des Pitons

Gros
Piton
2619ft

Gros Piton
Pt.   Canelles R.

Choiseul   1153ft   75 miles

Laborie   Grenadines

Vieux Fort   Hewanorra Airport

Vieux Fort Bay

Cap Moule-à-Chique   GRENADA

St. Vincent Passage

simplicity and pride that have earned it its deserved reputation as one of the still unspoiled islands in the Caribbean today.

St. Lucia At-a-Glance

FROM THE AIR

St. Lucia is shaped almost like a leaf, the stem at its base being the peninsula of Moule-à-Chique. Its Barre de l'Isle ridge of mountains divides the island horizontally, with a network of rivers carrying water down the slopes, like the veins of the leaf. The island's mountainous terrain is softened in appearance by a gentle covering of tropical trees and flowering plants. The highest peak is Mt. Gimie, 3,145 feet, but more prominent are the twin half-mile-tall volcanic cones called the Pitons. To the west, Petit Piton stands straight up from the Caribbean to a height of 2,460 feet; just to the east, Gros Piton rises to 2,619 feet. In between is Jalousie Bay and the stretch of land known as Anse des Pitons.

St. Lucia is 25 miles south of Martinique and 20 miles north of St. Vincent. From New York it is about 2,020 miles (a three-and-a-half- to four-hour flight) to St. Lucia.

SPECIAL PLACES

CASTRIES This is the island's capital (pop. 55,000) and, with a natural harbor, its major port. Its architecture is basically bland and modern, the result of severe fires in 1948 and 1951 that swept through the older buildings. Still, it's a lively West Indian town. The morning market is very active, especially on Saturdays, when it fills up with small farmers and craftspeople, everybody buying, selling, and bartering. Fresh fish, plantain, mango, and pawpaw (papaya) are among the foodstuffs traded and sold here.

Just behind the city rises Morne Fortune, from whose heights the French and the British alternately defended the island and its port and whose slopes they in turn charged in hopes of final victory. At the crest of the hill stands *Fort Charlotte,* an 18th-century fortress that changed hands about a dozen times during the years of English-French colonial warfare. The stone buildings of the French occupation forces contrast with those of the British, who built their structures of brick. Constant change of ownership resulted in a hodgepodge of materials and styles, and many buildings started by one side were completed or repaired by the other. The fortress is open daily; no admission charge (no phone). But even more attractive to visitors than Morne Fortune's history is the view from its peak—north to Pigeon Island, south to the Pitons, and a panorama of the harbor at Castries and of the Vigie Peninsula. Vigie itself was the site of two major battles—both of them victories for the British.

PIGEON POINT North of Castries, off the west coast, this was formerly a separate island, but now is linked by a causeway to the town of Gros Islet. The ruins of 275-year-old *Rodney Fort* are here, and it was from this island that the fleet commanded by British admiral George Rodney sailed to intercept the French in the Dominica Passage, resulting in the Battle of the Saints. The fort has been designated a historic site. (The island, by the way, gets its name from Rodney's hobby of breeding pigeons.) A small museum, the *Pigeon Island Interpretation Centre,* displays exhibits on the island's history; under the museum, in the cellar of the old officers' quarters, there's a pub. Closed Sundays; admission charge (no phone). Guided tours of the island are available from any tour operator, or you may explore on your own; more information is available from the *National Trust for Pigeon Island* (phone: 452-5005). Also on the island is *Jambe de Bois,* a casual restaurant serving good food (no phone). A short distance north of Pigeon Point, at the very tip of St. Lucia, is *Cap Estate,* the site of a land development. On a clear day, it is possible to see Martinique from the gentle hills of the Cap area.

MARIGOT BAY On the west coast, south of Castries, is a yachtsman's haven. Most of the palm-lined shore remains primitive, but some sections are being developed with shops. It is still one of the most beautiful coves in the entire Caribbean. Just a few miles south along the coast is the little fishing village of Anse La Raye, where fishermen repair their nets and gut their catch on the beach, and workmen still build canoes in much the same manner Carib warriors did 400 years ago. A little farther south, just below the midpoint of the island, the village of Canaries lies where one of the island's many rivers meets the sea. Here native women can be seen washing their clothing in the river.

Just inland from Marigot Bay itself are two large banana plantations. *Cul-de-Sac* (phone: 451-5505) is slightly north of the bay, the *Roseau Estate* (phone: 451-4242) just to the south. Visitors are welcome daily at both plantations; no appointment is needed, and there's no admission charge. Two other working plantations that offer tours are *Marquis Plantation,* a banana plantation in the northeast, and, in the south, *Errard Plantation,* known for nutmeg, sugarcane, coffee, and citrus fruits. Tours of *Marquis Plantation* are available on Tuesdays and Thursdays; admission charge. For tour information, contact *Sunlink Tours/St. Lucia Representative Services* (see *Sightseeing Tours,* below). Tours of *Errard Plantation* are offered on Fridays through *Barnard's Travel* (see *Sightseeing Tours*); admission charge. Your hotel's travel desk may also be able to arrange tours of both plantations.

SOUFRIÈRE On the west coast of the island, about a third of the way from the southern tip, is the village of Soufrière, St. Lucia's second-largest community. From here, too, fishermen still put out to sea in the same kind of narrow dugout canoe used in this area for centuries, and cast with homemade nets. Beyond the town, past the hill of green vines and trees that helped to hide the town from attackers, the Pitons stand over half a mile high, stretching from the shore of the Caribbean. The remains of the island's once-active volcanoes, they are formed from lava and coated with fertile volcanic topsoil and tropical forest.

MT. SOUFRIÈRE The dormant volcano near Soufrière is a rocky moonscape of pits and open craters of boiling sulfur, which looks like bubbling grayish-yellow mud. A walk through the area, with its clouds of sulfur-reeking mist and intense earth-born heat, is like a visit to Dante's *Inferno*. Here also are some natural spring-fed pools of heated waters containing traces of sulfur and other minerals. A sample sent to King Louis XVI was found to have a mineral content similar to the baths of Aix-la-Chapelle. A guide is required for exploring Mt. Soufrière; they're available at the entrance to the park area. Open daily; admission charge. The natural baths at neighboring Diamond Falls are cooler and sweeter smelling than those at Mt. Soufrière. The privately owned *Diamond Mineral Baths* are located on the *Soufrière Estate,* where visitors can bathe in the waters from natural springs. Open daily; admission charge (phone: 459-7250).

MOULE-À-CHIQUE Near the southern tip of the island, this mountain peak affords views of the Caribbean's distinctly blue-green waters as they mix with the Atlantic's very different blue, and of the nearby island of St. Vincent to the south and slightly west. You can drive up and walk around, but there are no formal trails.

FRIGATE ISLAND A rocky spur off the east coast of St. Lucia, it is home to the rare frigate bird (called *ciseaux* or "scissors" by islanders). The area, inaccessible from the mainland, is one of the few remaining places the bird can be observed nesting and roosting. The *St. Lucia National Trust* now manages the island and arranges tours (ask for Barbara Jacobs; see *Hiking,* below).

Sources and Resources

TOURIST INFORMATION

On St. Lucia, the main tourist office is at Pointe Seraphine in Castries (closed weekends; phone: 453-0053 or 452-4094; fax: 453-1121), with a branch at Jeremie Street (closed Saturday afternoons and Sundays; phone: 452-5968). There also are visitor information centers at *Vigie* (phone: 452-2596) and *Hewanorra* (phone: 454-6644) airports (always staffed at flight arrival times), on Bay Street in Soufrière (phone: 459-7419), and at Pointe Seraphine (phone: 452-7577); the last two are closed weekends except when cruise ships pull in. All the offices can provide brochures and maps (most are free). Hotels also provide information for tourists. For information about St. Lucia tourist offices in the US, see GETTING READY TO GO.

LOCAL COVERAGE There are three local weekly papers—the *Crusader,* the *Weekly Mirror,* and the *Star;* there's also the *Voice of St. Lucia,* published three days a week. *Caribbean Week* is a weekly published on Barbados. *The New York Times* is also available, usually two days late.

RADIO AND TELEVISION Radio St. Lucia (99.9 FM) and Radio Caribbean International (101.1 FM) broadcast local and regional programming, and TV stations HTS (Channel 4) and DBS (Channel 2) carry local as well as some US programs. Most hotels have cable TV.

TELEPHONE When calling from the US, dial 1 + 809 (area code) + (local number). From other Caribbean islands the code may vary, so contact the local operator. When dialing on St. Lucia, use only the seven-digit local number unless otherwise indicated. Dial 999 for emergency assistance.

ENTRY REQUIREMENTS US and Canadian citizens need only a passport or other proof of citizenship (a birth certificate or voter's registration card plus an official photo ID) and a return or ongoing ticket. There is an airport departure tax of about $10.

CLIMATE AND CLOTHES Winter temperatures range between 65 and 85F (19 to 30C); in summer, between 75 and 95F (24 to 35C). Summers tend to be a little rainy, but winters are dry. Summer clothing is worn year-round; cottons are prevalent. Casual resortwear is fine for both men and women during the day, although shorts and bathing suits should not be worn into town. In the evening women wear dresses, or dressy pants or skirts and tops; for men, jackets and occasionally ties are required only at the larger hotels and a few restaurants during the winter season.

MONEY St. Lucia uses the Eastern Caribbean dollar, which at press time was valued at the rate of $1 US to about $2.70 EC ($2.50 EC in hotels and stores). In general, banking hours are from 8 AM to 3 PM Mondays through Thursdays, 8 AM to 5 PM Fridays. US and Canadian dollars are accepted by stores, restaurants, and hotels, as are traveler's checks and most major credit cards (check when making reservations for meals or accommodations). All prices in this chapter are quoted in US dollars.

LANGUAGE English is the official tongue of St. Lucia, and it is spoken by almost all the inhabitants. A French-Creole patois, similar to that of Guadeloupe and Martinique, also is spoken.

TIME St. Lucia is on atlantic standard time, an hour ahead of eastern standard time. In winter, when it's noon in New York, it's 1 PM in St. Lucia. During US daylight saving time the hour is the same in both places.

CURRENT Electricity is 220–230 volts, 50 cycles, AC. Most hotels have provisions for electric shavers and can supply the converters needed for hair dryers and other small appliances.

TIPPING A 10% service charge is included on hotel bills; it covers room maids and other hotel staff. Extra tipping is called for only if some special service is rendered. Restaurants add a 10% service charge to the check, which covers the waiter's tip. Cab drivers should be tipped about 10% of the fare. Airport porters depend on tips for a substantial portion of their income; tip 50¢ per bag, with a $1 minimum.

GETTING AROUND

CAR RENTAL Major firms with desks at both airports for pickup and drop-off are *Avis* (*Vigie Airport,* phone: 452-2046; *Hewanorra Airport,* phone: 452-6325; and John Compton Highway, Castries, phone: 452-2700 or 452-2202), *National* (*Vigie Airport,* phone: 452-3050; *Hewanorra Airport,* phone: 454-6699; Gros Islet, phone: 450-8500; and at *LeSport,* phone: 450-9406), and *Hertz/Sun Fun Car Rentals* (*Vigie Airport,* phone: 451-7351; *Hewanorra Airport,* phone: 454-9636; Rodney Bay, phone: 452-0680 or 452-8857; and the *Royal St. Lucian* hotel—see *Checking In*). *Budget* (phone: 452-0233) has a location at *Hewanorra Airport.* Elsewhere, agencies include *St. Lucia Yacht Service Car Rentals* (Vigie Cove; phone: 452-5057), *Dollar* (Reduit; phone: 452-0994; fax: 452-0102), and *CTL Rent-A-Car* (Rodney Bay Marina; phone: 452-0732). Most agencies offer free drop-off and pickup, and several also have desks at resorts. All take at least one major credit card. Rates drop slightly during the off-season (April 15 through December 15). An international or St. Lucia driver's license is required. Those with international licenses must have them endorsed; most car rental agencies will do it (there's no charge). If you don't have an international license, a St. Lucia license can be obtained through most rental agencies on the island for about $14; you must present a valid US, Canadian, or UK license.

INTRA- AND INTER-ISLAND FLIGHTS *Eastern Caribbean Helicopter, Ltd.* (phone: 453-6952; fax: 453-6956), a Canadian-owned company, offers shuttle service from both *Vigie* and *Hewanorra Airports* to many of the island's major hotels. If you're less than eager to spend 1½ hours driving from *Hewanorra* to one of the northern resort areas, this may be a good option. *St. Lucia Helicopters, Ltd.* (phone: 453-6950) also charters helicopters. *American Eagle* (phone: 452-1840) flies between St. Lucia and San Juan, Puerto Rico. For connections to other islands, small plane charters can be arranged with *Air Martinique* (phone: 452-2463), *Eagle Air* (phone: 452-1900), and *Helenair* (phone: 452-7196; fax: 452-7112).

SEA EXCURSIONS Most popular is the daylong sail from Castries to the Pitons, with a shore trip to Soufrière's Sulphur Springs. Lunch, drinks, a swim and snorkeling stop, plus steel band music en route are included. The square-rigged brig *Unicorn* (phone: 452-6811) sails twice a week. *Motor Vessel Vigie* (phone: 452-3762), *Endless Summer I and II* (phone: 452-8651), and *Surf Queen* (phone: 452-8351) also offer day sails from Castries. Tour operators also book sea excursions.

SIGHTSEEING TOURS There are tours to suit almost any desire: all-inclusive day trips to other islands (Martinique and the Grenadines), half- or full-day island tours, rain forest walks, and shopping tours. For details contact *Barnard's Travel* (Castries; phone: 452-2214; fax: 453-1394), *Sunlink Tours/St. Lucia Representative Services* (Reduit Beach Ave., Rodney Bay; phone: 452-8232; fax: 452-0459). *Eastern Caribbean Helicopter, Ltd.* offers two chopper tours—a northern and a southern one (see *Intra- and Inter-Island Flights,* above). A complete list of tour operators is available from the tourist office (see *Tourist Information*). The travel desk at any hotel also can help with arrangements for excursions.

TAXI Unmetered rates are fixed by the government and the *Taxi Association*. A list of point-to-point fares is available from the tourist office (see *Tourist Information*). However, drivers do not always stick to the official rates, so confirm them in advance and also establish whether the fare quoted is in US or EC dollars. The fare from *Hewanorra Airport,* the island's international airport, to the hotels in the Castries area (an hour's drive) runs a good $60 for up to four people.

SPECIAL EVENTS

On *New Year's Day* and January 2, a festival in Vigie Field is part of the traditional French celebration of *Le Jour de l'An,* a holdover from the island's days as a French colony; there are dances, picnics, and partying throughout the island as well. *Carnival,* usually in late February, is the year's big festival, with the crowning of a Carnival Queen, dancing, costumed parades, steel band music, and calypso singing. The *St. Lucia Jazz Festival,* with performances by such internationally acclaimed musicians as Wynton Marsalis, Vanessa Rubin, McCoy Tyner, and the *Kenny Barron Trio,* is held in mid-May. Other holidays when most stores and businesses close are *Independence Day* (February 22), *Good Friday* (April 5 in 1996), *Easter* and *Easter Monday* (April 7 and 8 in 1996), *Labor Day* (May 1), *Whitsuntide* (the long weekend of May 25-27 in 1996), *Corpus Christi* (June 6 in 1996), *Emancipation Day* (first Monday in August), *Thanksgiving Day* (first Monday in October), *National Day* (December 13), *Christmas,* and *Boxing Day* (December 26).

SHOPPING

Castries's big department store is *J. Q. Charles, Ltd.* (on Bridge St.), worth browsing through. The outdoor market on Jeremie Street sells fresh produce and also has a wide array of handmade goods such as pottery and small straw baskets filled with local spices and herbs (nutmeg, cinnamon, and bay leaves). A new market that sells local arts and crafts opened recently on John Compton Highway. The entire area has recently undergone a major face-lift, and improved facilities have been added. Pointe Seraphine, just outside of Castries toward *Vigie Airport,* offers duty-free and late-evening shopping for the convenience of cruise ship passengers.

The following shops offer some of the best buys and most intriguing merchandise:

Artsibits Gallery Features paintings, pottery, and woodcarvings, all by the finest local artists. On the corner of Brazil and Mongiraud Sts., Castries (phone: 452-7865).

Bagshaws Studios A must-stop for unique hand-screened fabrics and fashions. Three locations: La Toc Rd., Castries (phone: 452-2139), Pointe Seraphine (phone: 452-7570), and Marigot Bay (phone: 451-4378).

Caribelle Batik A fine fabric emporium with a selection of island prints. Old Victoria Rd., Castries (phone: 452-3785).

Choiseul Arts and Crafts Locally crafted baskets, woodwork, and straw articles such as hats and placemats. In the LaFargue area of Choiseul (phone: 459-3226).

Gablewoods Shopping Mall This modern strip mall offers 20 stores and extended shopping hours. Wares include everything from jewelry to home accessories and tropical artwork. Choc Highway, Castries.

Noah's Arkade The place to shop for high-quality West Indian gift items. Four locations: Jeremie St., Castries (phone: 452-2523); Bridge St., Soufrière (phone: 459-7514); Pointe Seraphine (phone: 452-7488); and *Hewanorra Airport* (phone: 454-5288).

SPORTS

BOATING St. Lucia, with excellent anchorages at Marigot and Rodney Bays and in Castries Harbour, is rapidly growing in popularity with yachtsmen. The island is the finishing point for the *Atlantic Rally for Cruisers (ARC),* the world's largest annual transoceanic sailing rally, with more than 150 yachts arriving between November and the end of December. For information contact the *St. Lucia Tourist Board* in Castries (see *Tourist Information*). Yachts can be chartered through *Sunsail* (Rodney Bay; phone: 452-8648; fax: 452-0839; US address: 3347 NW 55th St., Ft. Lauderdale, FL 33309; phone: 800-327-2276; 305-484-5246 in Florida; fax: 305-485-5072); the *Moorings* (Marigot Bay; phone: 451-4357; fax: 451-4353; US address: 1305 US 19S, Suite 402, Clearwater, FL 33346; phone: 800-334-2435; fax: 813-530-9747); and *Trade Wind Yacht Charters* (Rodney Bay; phone: 452-8424; fax: 452-8442; US address: 1186 Cot Circle, Gloucester, VA 23061; phone: 800-825-7245; 804-694-0881 in Virginia; fax: 804-693-7245). Rates depend on the craft, the season, and whether the rental is crewed or bareboat. Most hotels also have Sunfish for loan or rent.

GOLF *Cap Estate* (phone: 450-8523), at the northern tip of the island, has a nine-hole course, though it is not very challenging. The course also rents clubs and pull carts; caddies are available only on weekends. *Sandals St. Lucia* also has a golf course, available to guests at no extra charge and open to visitors for a nominal greens fee; reservations are necessary (see *Checking In*).

HIKING Organized hiking is limited, but there are trails all over the island, and the Pitons are a time-honored climbers' challenge. Petit Piton (Little Piton) has been officially closed until further notice due to a fire caused by climbers that greatly damaged the area, but Gros Piton (Big Piton) is still open to hikers. The *St. Lucia National Trust* (phone: 452-1654 or 452-5005) and the *Forestry Division* (phone: 450-2086) have developed several nature walks, as well as more advanced climbs, and can provide details and arrange guides for a small fee. None of the island's peaks should be attempted without a guide, because of frequent—and sudden—mists and rains, which make visibility a problem. For additional details, see *Climbing and Hiking* in DIVERSIONS.

HORSEBACK RIDING *Trim Stables* (Cas-en-Bas; phone: 450-8273) offers all levels of riding. The charge for a 1¼-hour ride includes transportation from your hotel. Horse-and-buggy rides also are available.

SNORKELING AND SCUBA DIVING St. Lucia's reefs are beautiful to explore, and the Anse Chastanet area—where there's good diving right off the beach—is the most popular. For snorkeling and scuba equipment, reef and wreck trips, and instruction, contact *Scuba St. Lucia* (at the *Anse Chastanet Beach* hotel, phone: 459-7355; and at the *Rex St. Lucian*, phone: 452-8009); the *Moorings Scuba Centre* (Marigot Bay; phone: 451-4357); *Dolphin Divers* (Rodney Bay; phone: 452-9922; fax: 452-8524); or *Buddies Scuba* (at *Vigie Marina;* phone/fax: 452-5288; and at *Windjammer Landing;* see *Checking In*). A number of all-inclusive resorts offer complimentary dive courses to guests, including *Club Med, Club St. Lucia, Rendezvous, Sandals St. Lucia, Sandals Halcyon,* and *Wyndham Morgan Bay* (see *Checking In* for information on all). Most hotels will provide snorkeling gear gratis.

SPECTATOR SPORTS The cricket season runs from January through June. Football—we call it soccer—is played from July through January. Both sports are played at sites throughout the island. Check local newspapers or ask at your hotel desk for schedules. Tennis tournaments, some of international standing, are held periodically at the *St. Lucia Racquet Club* at *Club St. Lucia* (see *Checking In*).

SPORT FISHING Game fish in these waters include barracuda, mackerel, kingfish, tuna, wahoo, swordfish, sailfish, and cavalla. If your hotel doesn't have boats of its own, it can make arrangements for one. Or contact *Barnard's Travel* (phone: 452-1615), *Captain Mike* (phone: 452-7044), or *Mako Watersports* (phone 452-0412).

SQUASH Courts are available at *Club St. Lucia* (see *Checking In*), the *St. Lucia Yacht Club* (Rodney Bay; phone: 452-8350), and *Cap Estate* (see *Golf*).

SWIMMING AND SUNNING Beautiful white beaches edge the calm leeward side of the island. These are the best swimming beaches; the eastern, windward side is rugged and often has rough surf that makes swimming unsafe and sometimes simply impossible. Outstanding strands include Vigie Beach, just north of Castries Harbour; Choc Bay, in the same area; Reduit Bay, well north along the coast from Castries; and Pigeon Island off the northern shore. To the south of the island are La Toc Bay, the black volcanic sand beach at Soufrière, and the reef-protected beaches of the Vieux Fort area. Most St. Lucia hotels are on a beach.

TENNIS *Club St. Lucia* has seven lighted courts and offers temporary memberships at its tennis club, the *St. Lucia Racquet Club. Windjammer Landing* has two lighted courts; the *Rex St. Lucian,* with two courts, also has a pro (see *Checking In* for information on all three hotels). Most hotels have at least one court or will arrange for guests to play at a nearby resort.

WATER SKIING Most hotels have the equipment available or will make arrangements for guests.

WINDSURFING The *Rex St. Lucian* hotel, the local affiliate of *Windsurfing International,* offers a certification course of three one-hour lessons (see *Checking In*). Most beach hotels will rent windsurfers to non-guests.

NIGHTLIFE

Most of the island's nightlife is confined to the hotels; they have entertainment on a regular basis in season and sometimes during the off-season. Friday night is "jump-up" (party) night, and everyone at the north end of the island heads for Gros Islet for a big street party. A steel band usually performs, while residents and visitors dance together in the street. At Marigot Bay they head for the *Hurricane Hole* hotel's bar (phone: 451-4357). *Rain,* a fun and atmospheric restaurant and bar, stays open late some evenings; the *"A" Pub* features karaoke on Saturday nights; and there are shows and live entertainment several times a week at the *Green Parrot* (see *Eating Out* for more on all three). Other popular nightspots include *The Lime* (and the upstairs *Late Lime;* see *Eating Out*); *Fisherman's Wharf Disco* (at the *Sandals Halcyon;* see *Checking In*), with live music and disco on a covered jetty over the water; and *Splash,* the disco at the *Rex St. Lucian* (see *Checking In*).

Best on the Island

CHECKING IN

St. Lucia offers three types of accommodations: relatively expensive luxury hotels, a number of all-inclusive resorts (at which rates typically cover all meals, drinks, activities, airport transfers, and more), and less costly "self-catering" setups in apartment or villa complexes. Most places offer optional Modified American Plan (MAP) arrangements (including break-fast and dinner), which add between $50 and $60 per person to the daily room rate.

At all-inclusive resorts, two people should expect to pay winter rates from $375 to $715 per night at places listed as expensive, $200 to $375 per night at those listed as moderate, and less than $200 a night at those we call inexpensive. At "traditional" hotels expect to pay from $275 to $700 a day for a double room, excluding meals, at the places we list as very expensive; $225 to $275 at establishments in the expensive category; $125 to $225 at places we call moderate; and less than $100 at places listed as inexpensive. Rates drop 30% to 50% during the summer season. Many hotels will add a 10% service charge, and there is an 8% government tax. All hotels listed below have air conditioning, telephones, TV sets, and private baths unless otherwise noted. All hotels are in the 809 are code unless otherwise indicated.

We begin with our favorite havens, followed by recommended hotels listed by price category.

SPECIAL HAVENS

Anse Chastanet Beach One of the great small island retreats (and moderately priced to boot), it's not really a hotel in the usual sense, but a cluster of octagonal cottages perched on cool green hillsides above the Caribbean. Most of the 36 hillside rooms (none is air conditioned) have wraparound views of St. Lucia's twin trademark mountains—the jolly green Pitons—their lush valley, and the sun-glinted sea beyond; there also are 12 beachside units. The view is beautiful and so is the privacy—ideal for reading, writing, loving, sleeping, or just watching the bougainvillea ruffle in the breeze. TV sets and telephones, of which there are none, would be intrusions here. When you're ready, the beach is down 125 steps, a trip you aren't likely to make more than once a day. Happily, the fine gray sands below are equipped with a life-sustaining snack bar, chaises, Sunfish, and snorkel and dive gear. At the end of the day, to reward your upward climb the main building offers a congenial bar, good company, and food to match. Soufrière, a truly unspoiled West Indian town, is only a short drive away. Soufrière (phone: 459-7000; 800-223-1108; fax: 459-7700; 914-763-5362 in the US).

Ladera This special 19-unit hideaway won the St. Lucia National Hospitality Award in 1993 as the most outstanding small resort on the island. Since then, like fine wine, it has only improved with age (and, also like fine wine, its charms command high prices). Decorated in charming, casual West Indian style, the suites and villas are like luxurious tree houses, with a wall that folds back completely to expose the grandeur of the nearly 3,000-foot-high Pitons framed by the Caribbean Sea. Mosquito netting draped over your four-poster bed is all that separates you from this glorious outside world. The six one-bedroom suites each have a private bath and a living room, while the 13 three-bedroom villas have two baths, full kitchens, and spacious living rooms. Most have private swimming pools with Jacuzzis. The units have no telephones or TV sets—believe us, you won't miss them—and with all the balmy mountain air and open vistas, air conditioning isn't an issue. There is a free-form pool for all guests, as well as a library, TV room, and botanical garden. The restaurant, *Dasheene,* has garnered high acclaim. There's a shuttle to the beach, located at *Anse Chastanet.* Between Gros and Petit Piton (phone: 459-7323 or 800-841-4145; fax 459-5156).

CASTRIES AND NORTH

VERY EXPENSIVE

Royal St. Lucian A luxury resort with 98 modern one-bedroom suites overlooking the beach (one with its own pool), complete water sports facilities, a pool, a restaurant, and nightly entertainment. Reduit Beach (phone: 452-9999; 800-225-5859; fax: 452-9639).

Windjammer Landing This hillside resort features 59 one- to four-bedroom villas with full kitchens (some even have small private pools) and 56 studio condominiums with kitchenettes; all the accommodations have terraces. There are four restaurants, including *Jammer's Bar and Grille* and *Papa Don's,* which serves pasta and pizza. Also on the premises are four pools, two tennis courts, and extensive water sports facilities. Labrelotte Bay, Castries (phone: 452-0913; 800-743-9609; fax: 452-9454).

EXPENSIVE

LeSport Facing the sea at the northernmost tip of the island, is this 102-room all-inclusive resort and spa. None of the rooms has a TV set (but you'll never miss it). An active beach vacation, with three pools, tennis, water sports, and golf nearby, can be combined with thalassotherapy (seawater massages, jet baths, toning) and a healthful diet, *"cuisine légère."* Guests also can rent *Manderley,* a plantation house with three bedrooms, its own pool, and 13 acres of gardens and panoramic vistas set on a hilltop a five-minute drive from the resort. Anse de Cap Beach (phone: 450-8551; 800-544-2883; fax: 450-0368).

Sandals Halcyon On Choc Bay, this all-inclusive place, recently acquired by the Sandals chain, has 180 cabaña-style rooms with patios, most with sea or garden views. There are two pools, two tennis courts, and full water sports facilities. Dining is at a popular, casual wharfside eatery and a more formal restaurant, and there are three bars. The disco (also at wharfside) has shows Mondays, Wednesdays, and Fridays. Four miles from Castries (phone: 452-5331; 800-SANDALS; fax: 452-5434).

Wyndham Morgan Bay Located on a four-acre nature preserve, this property features 240 rooms decorated with floral pastels and wicker, two restaurants, a lounge, a pool, and a small beach. The all-inclusive package provides a choice of 25 sports activities, including tennis, a wide array of water sports, and golf nearby, plus two island sightseeing trips. Five miles from Castries (phone: 450-2511; fax: 453-6214).

MODERATE

Club St. Lucia This 372-bungalow all-inclusive property has a panoramic view of the curved stretch of Smuggler's Cove, plus three free-form pools and a casual bar. Some of the bungalows are air conditioned; most have telephones and TV sets. There are two restaurants, seven lighted tennis courts, one squash court, a gym, and a children's program; all water sports, except scuba diving, are included in the rate. *Cap Estate* (phone: 450-0551; fax: 450-0281).

Rendezvous Formerly *Couples St. Lucia,* this couples-only (and adults-only) all-inclusive resort set on Malabar Beach, among lushly landscaped grounds, is now under the same management as *LeSport* (above). All sports (including scuba diving), two day excursions, and nightly entertainment are included in the package. The 100 rooms are in beachside cottages or in the hotel section, none with TV sets, but all with plenty of gorgeous water to gaze at. Recent additions and renovations include a pool with a swim-up bar and two dining rooms. Malabar Beach (phone: 452-4211; 800-544-2883; fax: 452-7419).

Rex St. Lucian Set along the beach in pastel-colored buildings are 260 rooms, some air conditioned but with no TV sets. Facilities include a pool, two tennis courts, and all water sports (which, except for scuba diving, are included in the rate). There's also *Flamingo,* a fine restaurant (see *Eating Out*), and evening entertainment at *Splash,* the hotel's popular disco. Reduit Beach (phone: 452-8351; fax: 452-8331).

INEXPENSIVE

Harmony Marina Suites A family-run, family-welcoming cluster of 21 two-bedroom apartments, each with living/dining room, one or two baths, kitchen, and a sizable balcony; air conditioning is optional. There's a freshwater pool and a restaurant. On Rodney Bay Lagoon (phone: 452-0336; fax: 452-8677).

Orange Grove This small colony of eight one-bedroom and three two-bedroom cottages with living rooms and kitchenettes—all immaculately kept—overlooks the island's northern tip and Reduit Bay. The view is spectacular. There's a pool, and once-a-day transport to Reduit Beach, a 10-minute drive away. The restaurant features local dishes. Castries (phone: 452-8213; fax: 452-4115).

SOUTH OF CASTRIES

EXPENSIVE

Jalousie Plantation One of St. Lucia's newer all-inclusive resorts, this 114-room property (including suites and one-bedroom cottages) is located near Soufrière on a beach between the Pitons. Amenities include four good restaurants and a fully equipped spa. There are also complete sports facilities, including four tennis courts (three lighted), horseback riding, an Olympic-size pool, and a wide range of water sports, including scuba, with lessons available. Newly added is a three-hole golf facility that offers the possibility of playing a nine-hole round by playing each hole three different ways. Near Soufrière (phone: 459-7666; 800-392-2007; fax: 459-7667).

Sandals St. Lucia Formerly the *Cunard La Toc* and *La Toc Suites,* it's now part of the Sandals chain of couples-only all-inclusive resorts. Before its reopening in 1993 the resort underwent major renovations, including refurbishing the 273 rooms and suites, enlarging the main pool (there are two) and fitness center, and adding a swim-up bar (for a total of five bars and three dining rooms). The resort is on the beach, and there are a nine-hole golf course and five lighted tennis courts. All suites feature four-poster beds and satellite TV; some have private pools. La Toc (phone: 452-3081; 800-SANDALS; fax: 453-7089).

MODERATE

Club Med Set on 95 acres on the southern tip of the island, this all-inclusive property has 256 rooms and a well-equipped sports facility with eight lighted tennis courts, volleyball, soccer, archery, basketball, softball, windsurfing, and a workout center—all part of the package (diving and horseback riding are available for an extra charge). There's a pool (with a mini-pool for children) and a beach with lounge chairs and umbrellas. The resort has a main dining room and two other restaurants. There's also a circus school and "Mini-Club" for children. All rooms have balconies (some with sea views) but no telephones or TV sets. On Savannes Bay, just five minutes from *Hewanorra Airport* (phone: 454-6546; 800-CLUB-MED; fax: 454-6017).

The Moorings Marigot Bay Situated along one of the Caribbean's most beautiful anchorages, this complex has two places to stay—*Dolittle's,* a small inn with 16 one-bedroom cottages, and the *Hurricane Hole* hotel, with 14 studios and nine one- and two-bedroom villas. There are also boutiques, two restaurants (including *Dolittle's;* see *Eating Out*), two bars, a full water sports center, and yacht berths. The villas and cottages have full kitchens. *Hurricane Hole* has a pool, open to all guests at the complex. None of the resort's units is air conditioned or has a TV set. On Marigot Bay, 9 miles from Castries (phone: 451-4357; 800-334-2435; fax: 451-4353).

EATING OUT

American, Chinese, and European dishes are all available on St. Lucia, but island specialties are really excellent. Be sure to try the fresh produce and distinctive island dishes: *callaloo* soup, stuffed breadfruit, banana bread, fried plantain, pumpkin soup, fried flying fish, crab backs stuffed with spiced crab and lobster meat, and baked lobster. Expect to pay $85 and more for dinner for two, with tip and drinks, at places listed below as expensive; $60 to $85 at those listed as moderate; and less than $60 at spots described as inexpensive. Unless otherwise noted, all restaurants listed below are open for lunch and dinner. All numbers are in the 809 area code unless otherwise indicated.

CASTRIES

EXPENSIVE

Bon Appétit This tiny, charming eatery is perched on top of Morne Fortune, offering diners a spectacular view of Castries and the harbor, Pigeon Island, and Martinique beyond. Specialties include rib steaks, lamb shanks, and shrimp creole. Open daily. Reservations advised. Major credit cards accepted. Red Tape La., Morne Fortune (phone: 452-2757).

Chez Paul This restaurant's sultry decor is in true South Seas style, from its tin roof on down. The rum drinks are powerful, and the menu features an eclectic range of French and exotic Pacific Rim dishes such as crispy duck breast in a ginger and honey liqueur sauce, and stir fried flying fish, prawns, and squid in a black bean and sherry sauce. Best "meet me at" place in town. Open daily. Reservations advised. Major credit cards accepted. Derek Walcott Sq. (phone: 452-3022).

Great House Built upon the foundations of an estate owned by one of the island's 18th-century French military commanders, this elegant restaurant features terrace dining, European-style service, and an imaginative French and creole menu. Attire is casually elegant—no shorts. A 25-seat private dining room is available. Open daily for dinner only. Reservations advised. Major credit cards accepted. *Cap Estate,* Gros Islet (phone: 450-0450).

Green Parrot The St. Lucia–born owner-chef, trained at *Claridge's* in London, is an inventive interpreter of French and creole dishes, with a distinctly English bent. Try soup *oh-la-la,* a spicy pumpkin mixture that earned its sobriquet from a French patron's instant appreciation; the mixed grill; or the steaks. On Morne Fortune with fabulous views of Castries, this is a fun spot, popular with visitors and locals. Live shows Mondays and Wednesdays, jazz on Friday nights. Monday is also Ladies' Night: If a woman wears a flower in her hair and is accompanied by a man wearing a jacket and tie, her meal is on the house. Open daily. Reservations advised. Major credit cards accepted. Red Tape La., Morne Fortune (phone: 452-3167).

San Antoine Overlooking Castries harbor, one of St. Lucia's most elegant dining spots serves fine continental fare in a century-old building rebuilt after a fire in 1970. Specialties include filet mignon stuffed with crayfish, and breast of chicken in puff pastry with spinach. Closed Saturday lunch and Sundays in season; call ahead to check closing times off-season. Reservations advised. Major credit cards accepted. Old Morne Rd., Morne Fortune (phone: 452-4660).

MODERATE

Jimmie's At *Vigie Cove Marina,* it has a superb view of the harbor. Local fare is served; fish, octopus, and *lambi* (conch) dishes usually are available. Closed Sunday lunch and mid-July through August. Reservations advised. Major credit cards accepted. *Vigie Cove Marina* (phone: 452-5142).

SOUFRIÈRE

EXPENSIVE

Hummingbird A lovely place on the waterfront for a lingering lunch featuring a glorious Piton view, a pool to cool off in, and a creole menu with lobster, shrimp, and fish prepared lots of ways. But the real treat is freshwater crayfish in lime or garlic butter (when available). Open daily. Reservations advised. MasterCard and Visa accepted. Soufrière (phone: 459-7232).

MODERATE

The Still An old rum distillery, now an excellent eatery. Much of what is served is grown or produced on the owners' plantation. The creole buffet at lunch is a real treat. Dinner is a relaxed affair, with lots of island favorites on the bill of fare. Open daily. Reservations advised. Major credit cards accepted. On the south end of the island, between the Pitons (phone: 459-7224).

NORTH

EXPENSIVE

Capone's Southern Italian dishes are featured here; there's also pizza, and a complete ice-cream parlor for dessert choices. The interior decor combines a Jazz Age 1920s motif with Art Deco touches from the 1930s. Closed Mondays. Reservations advised. Major credit cards accepted. Rodney Bay (phone: 452-0284).

Charthouse Wood paneled, full of plants, and open to the breezes from the yacht harbor it overlooks, this is a handsome steak and lobster house. Open for happy hour and dinner only; closed Sundays. Reservations necessary. Major credit cards accepted. Rodney Bay (phone: 452-8115).

Flamingo The menu in this hotel dining room changes frequently, offering a variety of continental and Caribbean dishes with the emphasis on fresh local seafood. Open daily for breakfast, lunch, and dinner. Reservations advised. Major credit cards accepted. At the *Rex St. Lucian* hotel, Reduit Beach (phone: 452-8351, ext. 403).

Mortar & Pestle On the waterfront, with a wonderful variety of Caribbean specialties: *ackee* (a fruit) and salt fish from Jamaica, flying fish from Barbados, Guyana pepper pot, and stuffed jack fish from Grenada. Open daily. Reservations necessary well in advance. Major credit cards accepted. Rodney Bay (phone: 452-8756).

MODERATE

"A" Pub Another dining spot facing the waterfront on Rodney Bay, it has a friendly pub atmosphere, with a local following and happy hour every evening. Selections include local roti (pastry stuffed with curried chicken, vegetables, or beef) and Mexican dishes. Saturdays are *karaoke* nights. Open daily for dinner only. Reservations unnecessary. American Express and Visa accepted. Rodney Bay (phone: 452-8725).

Banana Split Sitting right on the beach in the town of Gros Islet, it's open-air and casual, the kind of place to linger over a long lunch. The menu offers creole dishes, West Indian curries, conch, boiled lobster, grilled steaks, and—what else?—banana splits. Go on Friday night, when the whole town is something like a carnival and the restaurant stays open until the band packs up. Closed Sundays. Reservations advised. No credit cards accepted. Gros Islet (phone: 450-8125).

Lime A nice little spot for a quick lunch, with eight tables inside, five alfresco. Lunch here is very inexpensive; you'll have a tough time spending $7 per person for *rôti*, sandwiches, or dishes like fish lasagna and steak-and-kidney pie. Dinner runs the gamut from seafood and chicken to chops and steaks. Closed Tuesday and the first three weeks of September. Reservations unnecessary. MasterCard and Visa accepted. Rodney Bay (phone: 452-0761).

INEXPENSIVE

Bread Basket Fresh-baked bread and pastries; also light snacks. Open daily for breakfast, lunch, and tea. Reservations unnecessary. No credit cards accepted. Rodney Bay (phone: 452-0647).

MODERATE

Chak Chak This spot features West Indian creole cooking as well as some continental dishes. There are two bars and a large courtyard with frequent entertainment. Open daily for breakfast, lunch, and dinner. Reservations unnecessary. Major credit cards accepted. Near Vieux Fort, close to the airport (phone: 454-6260).

Dolittle's Simple island foods pleasantly presented in a special bayside setting. Open daily for breakfast, lunch, and dinner. Reservations unnecessary. Major credit cards accepted. At the *Marigot Bay* resort on Marigot Bay (phone: 451-4246).

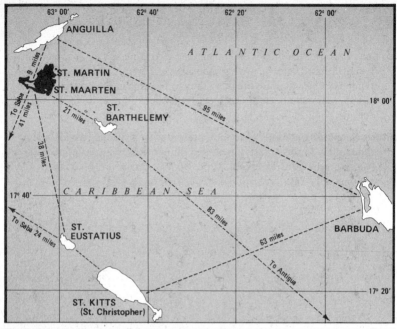

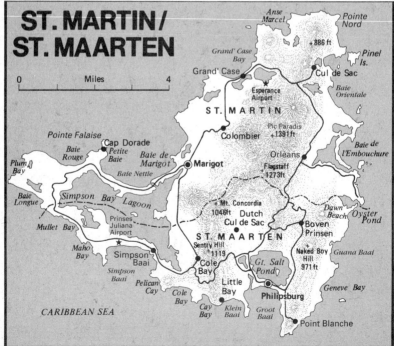

ST. MARTIN/ ST. MAARTEN

St. Maarten/St. Martin

People have all kinds of ways of picking a particular vacation spot in the Caribbean. Some go for super sports facilities or health spas. Others look for culture, historic sights, social cachet, or nightlife. Still others seek that rare 20th-century commodity—total relaxation on memorable beaches.

St. Martin/St. Maarten (the island is divided into French and Dutch territories) offers only modest quantities of the above features, with the exception of its abundant beaches. Its sports facilities are good, but not spectacular; culturally, it can't compete with Puerto Rico or Jamaica; and there aren't many distinguished reminders of the island's history. Socialites and celebrities who visit the island tend to keep to themselves; they own or lease villas, or else they take a secluded suite at *La Samanna* or *La Belle Créole.* Nightlife here is equally subdued, although there are casinos on the Dutch side, one or two "shows," and a handful of discos.

Nevertheless, St. Martin has boomed enormously in the past few years. Annually, between cruise ship passengers and overnight vacationers, the island hosts more than a million visitors. The secret of the island's considerable success with tourists is simple. People can relax here. Its sun is dependable, and its sea and beaches are beautiful. There are plenty of activities to amuse you (though sightseeing isn't one of them). Favorite diversions include golf, tennis, and sea excursions to Saba, St. Barts, Anguilla, or uninhabited Ilet Pinel. You can scuba under the sea, water-ski across it, or catch the end of a spinnaker and fly over it. Visitors feel at home very quickly, because St. Martin remains "the Friendly Island," in spite of its ever-increasing popularity and large-scale development. (With development, however, has come an increase in crime, particularly theft. Although you may feel as if you're in paradise, you should take the same precautions you would in any urban location: Check the security arrangements provided at your hotel, be careful with your possessions, and avoid walking in deserted areas at night.)

The arrival of Christopher Columbus in 1493 signaled the beginning of the end of the island's Carib Indian civilization. Over the next 150 years, the island languished unnoticed by Europeans, until, with the boom in West Indies trade in the 17th century, the Dutch arrived in 1631 to challenge Spain's claim to St. Maarten/St. Martin. The Spanish finally pushed out the Dutch in the 1640s, but they surrendered the island to them peacefully a few years later. However, by the time the Dutch returned to take possession of the island, the French had beat them to it. After a few skirmishes, St. Martin/St. Maarten was divided in 1648, when (according to local legend) a Frenchman and a Dutchman (the former fueled by wine, the latter by gin) started out back to back and walked in opposite directions around the periphery of the island until they met on the other side, each claiming the land they had paced off for their country. A border marker by the side of the Philipsburg-Marigot road commemorates the first Dutch-French treaty of friendship, signed that same year. Actually, island land changed hands at least 16 times after that, but a final settlement was reached in 1816, and relations between the two countries have been serene ever since.

If it weren't for the monument and the sign that reads *"Bienvenue Partie Française,"* you probably wouldn't know that you were crossing the border. There are no guards, no customs officials. Differences between Dutch and French portions of the island are a matter of style. The island's biggest hotels traditionally have been on the Dutch side, which, on the whole, has been more developed than the French. But building activity has been on the upswing on the French side, too. In fact, although the Dutch side has more total rooms, the French side now has more properties. In addition, the harbor area has been expanded, and with the *Port la Royale* complex, Marigot now boasts well over 250 chic shops.

Philipsburg, the Dutch capital, is a charming, but bustling, town three streets wide. In midday or late afternoon traffic, it can take almost as long to drive from one end of Front Street to the other as to cross Manhattan. Shops full of duty-free luxuries from all over the world prosper here, especially on a busy cruise ship day (there can be as many as eight ships in port at once), when Front Street is literally crammed with shoppers and (mercifully) closed to traffic. The primary language is English (Dutch is seen mainly on street signs), but the mobs can be heard comparing prices in every language from Japanese to Papiamento, the Dutch Caribbean patois.

The French side is basically bucolic; even on cruise ship days, there's a slightly calmer (though still busy) air about Marigot, the French capital. Boutique windows display the finest crystal, porcelain, and perfume, along with the latest styles in jewelry, bikinis, and clothing of French and Italian design. Shops are busy, but not overcrowded, with vacationers staying at the low-key French-side resorts, yachtspeople, and a smattering of cruise ship passengers. French—some pure, some patois—is most often heard in shops, hotels, and restaurants, although English is widely spoken and understood.

The border is so invisible that visitors forget it and move about as mood and mission dictate: to the French side in search of a secluded beach; to the Dutch to catch the boat or plane for Saba or to play a round of golf; to either side to shop, depending on the kind of bargain they're after. At night, Dutch-side guests cross over for a drink and dinner at one of the pleasant outdoor cafés. French-side guests reciprocate with a visit to one of the casinos on the Dutch side, finishing with a disco stop on the way home. The unique combination makes a trip to St. Martin/St. Maarten a bit like having two vacations in one.

St. Martin/St. Maarten At-a-Glance

FROM THE AIR

With a coastline of beaches notched by large and small bays, St. Martin/St. Maarten looks like an island jigsawed by a Victorian gingerbread addict. This is especially true of its southwestern section, where a curlicued framework of land surrounds a large body of blue water known as Simpson Bay Lagoon (sometimes spelled Simson). *Prinses Juliana Airport,* now the second busiest in the Caribbean (after San Juan's), occupies a slender strip of land on the south side of the lagoon. To the north is the town of Marigot, the capital of French St. Martin. Southeast, where the horseshoe of Groot Baai (Great Bay) curves into the coast, is Philipsburg, the capital of Dutch St. Maarten, occupying a narrow isthmus between the sea and Great Salt Pond.

St. Martin/St. Maarten, approximately 6 miles long and 6 miles wide for a total area of 37 square miles, is the world's smallest island divided between two sovereignties. The island has a population of about 60,000 (28,000 on the French side; 32,000 on the Dutch). St. Maarten in the south (16 square miles) is part of the Netherlands Antilles, along with the neighbor islands of Saba and St. Eustatius and the larger Aruba, Curaçao, and Bonaire off the coast of South America. Like St. Barthélemy, the St. Martin half (21 square miles), is a dependency of Guadeloupe, 140 miles to the southeast, and is part of the French West Indies. The island's nearest unrelated neighbors are Anguilla, 9 miles north, and St. Kitts, some 50 miles south. Puerto Rico is a 30-minute, 144-mile flight west. Miami lies 1,223 miles (roughly 2½ hours flying time) northwest, and the 1,460-mile flight from New York takes about 3½ hours. Its position in the midst of so many small islands and the frequency of landings at *Juliana Airport* make it one of the Caribbean's crossroads.

SPECIAL PLACES

If you love poking around in little out-of-the-way places, this is the island for you. St. Martin's pleasures lie in the unexpected discoveries you make on your own: an empty beach, a seascape, old houses, and sugar mill towers moldering away in nameless valleys. Rent a car and take off *ex tempore.* The best overview of the entire island—not to mention the views of Anguilla and St. Barts—is to be had by driving up Pic Paradis (Paradise Peak), at 1,400 feet the island's highest point. Heading north from Marigot, take the road that turns right at Rambaud. For visitors who hate to drive, there are guided tours by small bus or taxi. Roads are simply laid out and in good repair. Watch out for animals in the road, especially at night.

PHILIPSBURG Take an hour or two to stroll through the Dutch capital. Its central square (renamed Cyrus W. Wathey Square, but still De Ruyterplein to most), a long, narrow rectangle located a few blocks east of the midpoint of Front Street, is usually so jammed with islanders, taxis, and visitors toting shopping bags that at first you're likely to mistake it for an impossibly clogged intersection. At the southern edge of the square, the Little Pier, from which several excursion boats depart and where cruise passengers land, juts into the harbor. Across Front Street, opposite Little Pier, stands one of the town's two notable buildings: the 1793 courthouse (now the post office and *Town Hall*), restored to its 1826 post-hurricane incarnation. At the other end of Front Street is the *St. Maarten Museum* (119 Front St.; no phone), a restored 19th-century West Indian house operated by the *St. Maarten Museum Foundation;* it displays exhibits on St. Maarten's history and archaeological finds on the island. Closed afternoons and weekends. Admission charge.

Once there were only Front and Back Streets; now a third street—built on land reclaimed from the Old Salt Pond and generally called Pond Fill Road—has been added to relieve congestion. But Front Street still is clogged with traffic struggling east, except on major cruise ship days, when people rather than vehicles cause the congestion. Turning east from the square and creeping along with the traffic, you'll pass a jumble of shops, restaurants, and business places—a few in modern buildings, some in old Dutch West Indian–style arcades and courtyards, still others in old, pastel-painted houses with porches in front. One such building on the beach, once the official government guesthouse, forms the central section—lobby, bar, and dining terrace—of the *Pasanggrahan Royal Inn* (see *Checking In*). A bit farther, behind an old house on the north side of the street, are brick ruins reputed to be the remains of a 17th- or 18th-century synagogue. Facing the head of Front Street is the *Buncamper House,* a handsomely proportioned structure with a front staircase and wraparound verandah. Built by an old island family, it is one of the island's purest examples of upper class West Indian architecture.

MARIGOT More picturesque than Philipsburg, the French capital is a good distance from most cruise ships and is somewhat less crowded and easier to explore, with expanded parking at the waterfront. The bustling harbor, busy with Anguilla-bound traffic, is alive with tropical sounds and colors, and fragrant with West Indian spices and French croissants, especially on Saturday mornings, when the waterfront market is liveliest; here a wide selection of souvenirs also attracts visitors. Old West Indian buildings line the quay, many now gracious restaurants and elegant shops. On the main corner, opposite *La Vie en Rose* restaurant (see *Eating Out*), is the tiny tourist office with a few brochures (and public washrooms). Near it stands a small museum, *On the Trail of the Arawaks,* which traces local prehistory and history beginning in 1,500 BC through artifacts and photographs. Open daily; no admission charge (no phone). The two main shopping streets are Rue de la République and Rue de la Liberté, while the *Port la Royale* complex at the southern end of town has an impressive marina and an array of chic boutiques, cafés, and bistros, which come alive at sunset with live music and beautiful people.

ELSEWHERE ON THE ISLAND

A circle tour of the island might start at Philipsburg and travel clockwise past the old cemetery at the foot of Front Street, then toward the 17th-century reconstructed *Fort Amsterdam* and past Cay Bay, where Peter Stuyvesant—later governor of New Amsterdam—lost his leg in a skirmish with the Spanish. Backtrack, and go just over Cole Bay Hill, then turn right and take the most direct route to Marigot, passing the obelisk *Border Monument* and Mt. Concordia, where the original Dutch-French treaty of peaceful coexistence was signed. For a longer, more scenic route, turn left and follow the road that loops around Simpson Bay Lagoon, where you may want to stop at the *St. Maarten Zoological and Botanical Garden,* located on three acres at *Madame Estates.* The two walk-through aviaries are filled with exotic birds from the Caribbean and South America. The petting area provides children with opportunities to feed and touch such creatures as golden lion tamarind monkeys. Open daily; admission charge (phone: 22748). From here the route passes the airport; the green, sprawling *Mullet Bay* resort complex and nearby *Maho Beach* resort; gleaming white *La Samanna;* and Pointe des Pierres à Chaux, on which stands the brainchild of the late Claude Philippe of the *Waldorf-Astoria: La Belle Créole* luxury resort (see *Checking In* for details on all four resorts). Drive on to Marigot, with its satellite, the St. Tropez–style complex *Port la Royale Marina,* and to the small, picturesque French settlements of Grand Case and Orléans. Newly opened on Le Galion Beach Road near Baie Orientale (commonly known by its English name, Orient Bay), the *Butterfly Farm* is a tropical garden with waterfalls, pools, fountains, and hundreds of butterflies. It's open daily; admission charge (no phone). Make a stop at landlocked Oyster Pond Harbor, then continue around Naked Boy Hill and along the road that skirts the Great Salt Pond and returns to Philipsburg. Don't hesitate to stray from the route any time a beach or a picnic spot beckons or when lunch—especially at Marigot or Grand Case—seems like a good idea.

Sources and Resources

TOURIST INFORMATION

The *St. Maarten Tourist Bureau,* with maps of the island and literature, is on Cyrus W. Wathey Square, formerly called De Ruyterplein, Philipsburg's small, crowded main square at the head of the Little Pier. Closed Saturday afternoons and Sundays (phone: 22337 or 22868; fax: 24734). There also is a tourist office on the French side, in its own building near the taxi stand at the corner of the harbor in Marigot. Closed weekends (phone: 875721;

fax: 875643). For information on St. Maarten/St. Martin tourist offices in North America, see GETTING READY TO GO.

LOCAL COVERAGE *St. Maarten Holiday,* a Dutch-side monthly guide in English, is available free at the airport, the tourist bureau, and hotels, and contains much useful, up-to-date information on shopping, restaurants (including a few on the French side), hotels, nightlife, special events, and religious services; maps of Philipsburg and the island are included. Other free publications include the annually updated *St. Maarten/St. Martin Visitors' Guide and Map, St. Maarten Events,* and *Discover St. Maarten/St. Martin;* the biannual *Focus St. Maarten/St. Martin, Living in St. Maarten/St. Martin,* and *St. Maarten Nights;* and the weekly *St. Martin's Week, Today,* and *Day Breaks.*

The New York Times, New York Daily News, New York Post, USA Today, and *San Juan Star* arrive on St. Maarten newsstands the day they are published. Many hotels provide a free *New York Times Fax Sheet,* a daily fax compilation of the front page, the business page, and other important pages from the newspaper. The *International Herald Tribune* also is available.

RADIO AND TELEVISION Radio and television broadcasts in English are available in most hotels on the island. Some hotels have satellite or cable TV with stateside programming.

TELEPHONE When calling the Dutch side of the island from the US, dial 011 (international access code) + 5995 (country code) + (five-digit local number). When calling the French side dial 011 (international access code) + 590 (country code) + (six-digit local number). To call from another Caribbean island, the access code may vary, so call the local operator. When calling the Dutch side from the French, dial 195995 + (local number); when calling the French side from the Dutch, dial 06 + (local number). When dialing within one side of St. Martin/St. Maarten, use only the local number unless otherwise indicated. On the Dutch side, dial 22222 for the police; 22111 (from a rotary phone) or 130 (from a touch-tone phone) for an ambulance. On the French side, dial 875004 for the police; 878625 for an ambulance. From a cellular phone, dial 911 for all emergency services on either side of the island.

ENTRY REQUIREMENTS A current passport, an expired one less than five years old, or other proof of citizenship (either a birth certificate with raised seal or photocopy with notary seal or a voter's registration card, *plus* a driver's license or other government-approved photo ID) and an ongoing or return ticket are the only documents required of US and Canadian citizens for indefinite stays on the Dutch side. On the French side, the same documentation (without the ongoing or return ticket) is needed for stays of up to three months; for longer periods a visa, plus an ongoing or return ticket, is required. There is a $10 departure tax at *Juliana Airport;* from *Espérance Airport,* the French side's small airport used for inter-island flights, the 15 franc departure tax is included in the airfare.

CLIMATE AND CLOTHES The island is sunny and warm year-round, and constant trade winds take the edge off the heat. Average daytime temperature during winter is about 80F (27C); summer's a few degrees warmer and more humid. Average annual rainfall is about 45 inches, which means more air cooling thanks to occasional showers, especially in late summer and early fall. Daytime dress for both men and women is neat but comfortably casual. Proper tennis attire—not necessarily all white—is requested on most courts. Take two swimsuits, minimum, plus some sort of cover-up to wear for lunch or when you've had enough sun but don't want to leave the beach; you'll also want a beach hat. Both the French and the Dutch are easygoing about beachwear (although nudity is not allowed on Dutch beaches), but swimsuits are for beaches only—not hotel lobbies or downtown streets. Evenings are informal, although men may want to have a jacket and women a shawl or sweater to wear in the air conditioned casinos and some of the restaurants and hotels.

MONEY Currency on the Dutch side is the Netherlands Antilles florin or guilder (NAf), valued at 1.80 NAf to $1 US at press time, but most transactions are made in US dollars. Currency in French St. Martin is the French franc, at press time valued at 4.8 francs to the dollar (the unofficial rate is lower, about 5.5 francs to the dollar). Since US currency is accepted everywhere, there is no reason to exchange US dollars for local money, but Canadian dollars are not as readily accepted and should be exchanged for florins or francs. In some shops and restaurants, prices are given in both local currency and US dollars, sometimes only in US dollars. A few shops offer discounts for payment in US cash, but not in traveler's checks. Banking hours on the Dutch side are normally 8:30 AM to 3:30 PM Mondays through Thursdays and 8:30 AM to 4:30 PM Fridays. Some banks may open Saturdays 8:30 AM until noon. On the French side, banks are open 8:30 AM to 1:30 PM weekdays. The American Express representative is on the Dutch side: *S. E. L. Maduro & Sons* (Emmaplein, Building 1, Philipsburg; phone: 22678). All prices in this chapter are quoted in US dollars.

LANGUAGE Dutch is the official language of St. Maarten, and French is the official language of St. Martin, but English is spoken nearly everywhere. Some of the natives on the Dutch side speak Papiamento, the patois unique to the Netherlands Antilles.

TIME The island is on atlantic standard time; in fall and winter when it's noon in New York, it's 1 PM in Philipsburg and Marigot. When the US East Coast is on daylight saving time, the hour is the same there as it is on the island.

CURRENT Most hotels on the Dutch side are wired for 110 volts, as are the US and Canada; on the French side, all run on 220-volt, 60-cycle current. If you depend on travel appliances, bring a converter and adapter plugs.

TIPPING Hotels add a 10% to 15% service charge to bills, which is supposed to take care of room maids and other staff members. In some establishments, however, personnel see little, if any, of this sum, so a small gratuity for good service always is appreciated. Most restaurants on the French side include at least a 10% service charge on the check; on the Dutch side some do, some don't. Always make sure, so you won't double-tip (or zero-tip). The customary tip to taxi drivers is 50¢ or $1; the expected tip for tours is bigger. For airport porters, $1 per bag is about right.

GETTING AROUND

BUS There is regularly scheduled bus service to main points throughout the island, in addition to the Philipsburg–Marigot–Grand Case round trip. Buses run from 6 AM to midnight daily. Flag buses down anywhere on the road; fares, which may be paid in $US, are $1 to $2, depending upon destination.

CAR RENTAL Enthusiastically recommended for those who want to sample several of the island's beaches, restaurants, and shops, rather than just stay put at a hotel (at some resorts, such as the 172-acre *Mullet Bay*—your own wheels are handy for getting from cottage to beach, golf course, or restaurant). Gas usually is not included in rental rates, and tanks aren't likely to be full. If you don't use a credit card, a deposit of $350 to $1,500 normally is required. There is an extra daily charge for the optional Collision Damage Waiver, which may be advisable here because you may be liable for damages even if an accident is not your fault. A US or Canadian driver's license is valid for island driving. *Note:* The number of car thefts and burglaries (stealing batteries is common) has been on the rise. *Never* leave anything in your car (especially the trunk) that you would mind losing, and always be sure to lock it.

On the Dutch side, car rental agencies have booths inside the *Juliana Airport* as well as sharing a building not far from the terminal, and many have offices in Philipsburg or at major hotels: *Avis* (at the airport, contact through any of the other locations: Cole Bay, Philipsburg, phone: 42322; *Great Bay Marina,* phone: 42316; or *Little Bay Marina,* phone: 44265), *Budget* (at the airport, phone: 54030), *Caribbean* (phone: 45211), *Hertz* (phone: 54542), *Lucky Car Rental/National* (phone: 42268), *Risdon Car Rentals* (phone: 54239), *Sandyg* (at the airport; phone: 53335), and *Sun 'n Fun* (phone: 52706). On the French side, car rentals are available at *Avis* (Bellevue, Marigot; phone: 875060), *Budget/Dan's* (French Cul-de-Sac; phone: 54030 or 873822), *Dan's* (Baie Nettle; phone: 872191), *Hertz* (10 locations, including *Le Grand St. Martin* hotel, Rue de Gallisbay, Marigot; phone: 877301), *Sandyg* (Sandy Ground, phone: 878825; fax: 879838), and *Espérance* (Rue de la République, Marigot; phone: 875109). By local law, car rental agencies may not garage cars at the airport, so rental cars must be delivered to your hotel (agencies will deliver to both sides of the island) or picked up outside the airport. The car rental building near *Juliana Airport* is only a short distance from the terminal, and some agencies offer shuttle service there, or you can take a taxi. On departure day you can drop off the car at the airport or at one of the agency's other locations.

INTER-ISLAND FLIGHTS *American Airlines* (phone: 52404; 800-433-7300) connects the island to San Juan, Puerto Rico. *LIAT* (phone: 54203; 800-468-0482) schedules regular flights between St. Maarten and several other Caribbean destinations. *ALM Antillean Airlines* (phone: 54240) offers flights to Aruba, Curaçao, and Bonaire, among other islands. *WINAIR* (phone: 54230) has daily flights from St. Maarten to Dominica, Montserrat, Nevis, Saba, St. Eustatius, St. Kitts, and St. Thomas and schedules flights several times weekly to Tortola; *WINAIR* also offers flightseeing excursions. *Air Guadeloupe* (phone: 875374, French side; phone: 54212, Dutch side) makes the 15-minute flight to St. Barts several times a day from *Espérance Airport* on the French side. *Air St. Barthélemy* (phone: 53150, Dutch side; phone: 871343 or 871307, French side) runs a regular shuttle between *Juliana Airport* and St. Barts until dusk and also schedules flights out of *Espérance Airport.*

MOPEDS AND MOTORCYCLES These can be rented from several firms: On the Dutch side, try *Honda Super Bikes* (Union Road, Cole Bay; phone: 42775). On the French side, there's *Bike Power Cycle* at *Le Pirate* hotel (Marigot; phone: 871374) and *Moto Caraïbes* (St. James, Marigot; phone: 872591). However, we strongly discourage this mode of transport here; the roads are often crowded and dangerous.

SEA EXCURSIONS Several day sails are available, all requiring reservations, from *Bobby's Marina* (phone: 22366), *Great Bay Marina* (phone: 22167), and Little Pier, all in Philipsburg. A number of catamarans offer trips to St. Barts, including the *White Octopus* (phone: 23170), which sails from *Bobby's; Quicksilver* (phone: 22167), which leaves from *Great Bay Marina;* and *The Edge* (phone: 42640), which leaves from Simpson Baai (Simpson Bay). The crossing takes about 90 minutes. *El Tigre* (phone: 44309 or 42503) sails from the *Pelican Marina,* at the *Pelican Beach* resort in Simpson Bay, to St. Barts or Anguilla, with lunch included. Several boats at the Philipsburg marinas offer excursions to the Dutch island of Saba. *Dockside Management* (phone: 24096), based at *Bobby's Marina,* offers full-day sails aboard the *Inspiration* and half-day, full-day, and sunset sails on the *Gabrielle.* Both *Watersports* at *Mullet Bay* (phone: 52801, ext. 337; or 54363) and *Watersports Westport* at Kimsha Beach (phone: 42557) offer a number of sailing or cruising options, including excursions to Saba, Anguilla, St. Barts, and the deserted Prickly Pear Island.

On the French side, *Marine Time,* with locations in Marigot (Chemin du Port; phone: 872028) and Oyster Pond (phone: 873831, ext. 453) can arrange a wide array of excursions, including catamaran trips to Anguilla, St. Barts, Prickly Pear Island, and Tintamarre, with lunch and drinks included; power boat excursions to Saba; and dinner cruises. Check with *Port la Royale Marina* (phone: 872043) and the marina at Anse Marcel (Port Lonvilliers; phone: 873194) for other day trips, as well as sunset sails and dinner cruises. Ferries headed for Anguilla operate on regular schedules from the waterfront in Marigot for about $9 (plus a $2 departure tax) at press time each way. On both sides of the island, be sure to ask if the boat you choose is a member of the *Charter Boat Association* to ensure reliability and safety.

The *Star Flyer,* the first clipper ship to be launched in 125 years, has cruises out of Philipsburg. The world's tallest sailing ship, with four masts that tower 220 feet above the deck, the 360-foot vessel can accommodate 180 passengers in 90 staterooms. The ship makes seven-day cruises, alternating between the Leeward Islands and the British and US Virgin Islands. For information, contact *Star Clippers* (4101 Salzedo Ave., Coral Gables, FL 33146; phone: 800-442-0551; 305-442-0550 in Florida).

For a different sort of marine experience, try the *Seaworld Explorer* (Grand Case Pier; phone: 24078, Dutch side) a semi-submarine that allows passengers to view sea life below the waterline; *Marine Time* (above), on the French side, also books semi-submarine tours.

SIGHTSEEING BUS TOURS Principally designed for cruise passengers, eight- to 40-passenger buses are operated by *St. Maarten Sightseeing Tours* (Philipsburg; phone: 22753) and *Calypso Tours* (Cole Bay; phone: 42858), with representatives at eight of the larger hotels. Other outfits, including *St. Maarten Taxi Association* (Cole Bay; phone: 55329), *Rising Sun Tours* (Marigot; phone: 871422; and at *Simpson Bay Yacht Club*; phone: 42799 or 43356), and *S. E. L. Maduro & Sons* (Philipsburg; phone: 22678), will arrange similar excursions.

SIGHTSEEING HELICOPTER TOURS Pricey but dramatic views are available from *Héli-Inter Caraïbes* (at the *Le Privilège* complex at Anse Marcel; phone: 873588), for a maximum of five passengers. For a special treat, hop one of their helicopters for lunch at Anguilla's *Gorgeous Scilly Cay* (see *Eating Out* in *Anguilla,* THE ISLANDS). Also on the French side are *Marine Time* (see *Sea Excursions,* above) and *Trans-Hélico-Caraïbes* at *Espérance Airport* (phone: 274068 or 290541; fax: 290541).

SIGHTSEEING TAXI TOURS This is the way to see the island if you don't want to drive. A private taxi tour of the entire island takes about two-and-a-half hours. Your hotel activities or travel desk will arrange for a car with a driver-guide. Or arrange it yourself with *R & J Tours* (Marigot; phone: 875620).

TAXI They are ready and waiting at *Juliana Airport* and hotels. Since there are no limos, and rental car companies aren't allowed to garage cars on airport property, cabs often provide the best transport to your hotel when you land. (Although you can also take a cab to the car rental building near the *Juliana Airport* terminal to pick up your car; see *Car Rental.*)

Cabs are unmetered, but drivers are required to carry booklets listing rates for destinations throughout the island. Rates go up 25% after 10 PM and 50% after midnight. For late-night service on the Dutch side, call the taxi stand in town (phone: 22359) or at *Juliana Airport* (phone: 54317); on the French side, call 875654 or 877579. *Ste. Transport Touristique de St. Martin* (see *Sightseeing Taxi Tours*) offers bus transfers from *Juliana Airport*. *Mullet Bay Marina* (see *Sea Excursions,* above) provides water taxis to Marigot; passengers need not be registered hotel guests.

WALKING TOURS A guided walking tour of Marigot is offered twice daily, at 9 AM and 3 PM. It departs from *La Petite Auberge Café* at *Port la Royale Marina* (phone: 875631).

SPECIAL EVENTS

The annual *St. Maarten/St. Martin Heineken Regatta,* one of the largest in the Caribbean, is held the first weekend in March. A Dutch national holiday, the *Queen's Birthday* (April 30), and a French one, *Bastille Day* (July 14), are celebrated on both sides of the island with fireworks, dancing, and sports events. At the end of May, the annual *St. Martin Food Festival* is held on the French side. On *Schoelcher Day* (July 21), French St. Martin celebrates the end of slavery in the French West Indies with music, African dances, and feasting. On *St. Martin's* or *Concordia Day* (November 11), Dutch-French friendship is celebrated with parades and ceremonies at the border. Other holidays when banks and many stores close include *New Year's Day, Carnival* (pre-*Lent* on the French side, in mid- to late April on the Dutch), *Good Friday* (April 5 in 1996), *Easter Monday* (April 8 in 1996), *Labor Day* (May 1), *Ascension Day* (May 16 in 1996), *All Saints' Day* (French side, November 1), *Christmas,* and—on the Dutch side—*Boxing Day* (December 26).

SHOPPING

St. Martin/St. Maarten is that rarity—a truly duty-free island. No tax is paid on imports arriving on either side of the border. But that fact alone does not guarantee that all that glitters in either Dutch- or French-side shop windows is a bargain worth bringing home; individual merchants are free to set their own prices. In addition, certain manufacturers—especially of world-marketed items like calculators, cameras, and electronic equipment—work hard to fix prices across the international board; you often can do as well or better at your local discount store. Check prices before leaving home and, if possible, shop twice—first to research, and second, after a cooling-off period, to buy.

On the Dutch side, shopping hours are normally 8 AM to noon and 2 or 2:30 to 6 PM. Some shops remain open at lunchtime; many also open for a few hours on Sundays or holidays when cruise ships are in port. Most take credit cards. Philipsburg's Front Street is lined with shops offering everything from delftware, Swiss watches, French perfume, and British cashmeres to Chinese embroidery, Japanese cameras and electronics, Indonesian batiks, Italian leather goods, fine jewelry, crystal, linen, porcelain, liquor, and more. About a block behind *Town Hall* on the right is a permanent market offering the works of local craftspeople. In addition, several street vendors are usually set up just off the pier. Try to avoid shopping on Front Street on cruise ship days, particularly Tuesdays, when you are better off taking a taxi to the *Maho Plaza Shopping Center,* near the *Maho Beach* and *Mullet Bay* resorts; to the *New Amsterdam Mall,* not far from Philipsburg; or to the French side.

On the French side, there are few cruise crowds, but also fewer bargains. Small, elegant boutiques—a number with island exclusives on French and Italian fashion names—are featured here. Though priced below US levels, many are still very expensive—but the same clothing may not be available back home. You can save on French perfume, cosmetics, fashion accessories, porcelains, and crystal at Marigot's duty-free shops along Rues de la Liberté and de la République. The city's other top shopping centers are *Galerie Périgourdine, Palais Caraïbe,* and *Port la Royale Marina,* a most attractive area for strolling and watching yachts or people from the many cafés and bistros along the wharf. Major US credit cards are accepted almost everywhere, but sometimes paying cash with US dollars can make for a better bargain. Some shops are open from 9 AM to noon or 12:30 PM and 2 to 6 PM, but many now keep the later hours set by the chic *Port la Royale* arcades (10 AM to 1 PM and 3 to 7 PM).

In addition, there are a number of galleries to visit in Marigot. Outside of town, off the main road to Rambaud on the left side, the French painter Alexandre Minguet has a studio (phone: 879514). In Orléans, visit artist Roland Richardson at his lovely home. His watercolors, etchings, and charcoal and oil paintings of island life and architecture have been exhibited internationally and make beautiful gifts. He receives visitors on Tuesdays, Thursdays, or by appointment (phone: 873224).

ON BOTH SIDES OF THE ISLAND

Colombian Emeralds Designer jewelry, all of which comes with guarantees honored by their Miami service office. At two locations in Philipsburg: Front St. (phone: 22438) and *Old Street Shopping Center* (phone: 23933); and Rue de la République, Marigot (phone: 878605).

Dalila Exotic batik at an exotic boutique. Old St., Philipsburg (phone: 24623); *Port la Royale,* Marigot (phone: 872206); and Baie Nettle (phone: 871778).

Goldfinger For 14k and 18k finery and Swiss watches. 109 *Old Street Shopping Center,* Philipsburg (phone: 24661), *Marina Royale* in Marigot (phone: 877051), and Rue de la République, Marigot (phone: 875950).

Gucci The one and only. Designer creations, still expensive, but duty-free. 83 Front St., Philipsburg (phone: 23537), and Rue de Général de Gaulle, Marigot (phone: 878424).

Little Switzerland Luxury merchandise: English bone china, French crystal, and, of course, Swiss clocks and watches. *Hint:* Resist seemingly sensational buys in waterproof, shockproof, what-have-you-proof watches with unfamiliar names, no matter how glowing the guarantees that come with them, unless the salesperson can give you the name of a stateside organization that will make good on the claims. 42 Front St., Philipsburg (phone: 22523), and Rue Gourbeyre, Marigot (phone: 875003).

La Romana Up to 40% discounts on Fendi and other fine leather labels at four locations: 82 Front St., Philipsburg (phone: 22181), *Mullet Bay* resort (phone: 54310), *Juliana Airport* (phone: 52181), and Rue de la République, Marigot (phone: 878816).

Sparky's International scents, cosmetics, and other grooming aids. At two locations along Front St., Philipsburg (phone: 24912 and 23017), at *Juliana Airport* (phone: 54217), and at *Port la Royale,* Marigot (phone: 875962).

Spritzer & Fuhrmann An island staple for fine jewelry and gifts, it continues to offer golden (literally) opportunities. *Juliana Airport* (phone: 54217) and Rue de la République, Marigot (phone: 875962).

THE DUTCH SIDE

Artistic Fine gold jewelry, Mikimoto cultured pearls. 55 Front St., Philipsburg (phone: 23456).

Butani Jewelers Unusual jewelry created in its own workshops. 86 Front St., Philipsburg (phone: 32118).

Greenwith Galleries Features the work of more than 40 local artists. 25 Front St., Philipsburg (phone: 23842).

H. Stern The reputable firm, whose elegant jewelry comes with ironclad (or should we say, platinum-clad) guarantees. 56 Front St., Philipsburg (phone: 23328; 800-524-2024).

Java Wraps Exotic batiks to slip around head, shoulders, or waist, for men, women, and children. *Old Street Shopping Center,* Philipsburg (phone: 24605).

Lil' Shoppe Everything from swimwear to eel-skin wallets and handbags to pearls. Just off the Little Pier, Philipsburg (phone: 22177).

Little Europe Movado, Piaget, Corum watches; precious stones and jewelry; 18K and 24K jewelry. 74 Front St., Philipsburg (phone: 24371).

Mille Fleurs Fairly sparkles with exquisite crystal; china; jewelry; and unset, cut, and polished stones. 36 Front St., Philipsburg (phone: 22473).

New Amsterdam For anyone on the lookout for jewelry, linen, and good buys on Swatch watches. 54 Front St., Philipsburg (phone: 22787 or 22788).

THE FRENCH SIDE

Animale Elegant French designer fashions and accessories for the woman who wants to buy the very best—and spend a lot for it. *Port la Royale,* Marigot (phone: 879987).

Bastringue Prêt-à-porter by Gaultier, Hamnett, and other top designers. *Port la Royale,* Marigot (phone: 878342).

Beauty and Scents Cosmetics and fragrances from international perfume houses. Rue de Général de Gaulle, Marigot (phone: 875877).

Boutique Jet Set Menswear for the island hopper—and shopper. Rue de Général de Gaulle, Marigot (phone: 878706).

Carat Mainly 14- and 18-, gold, that is. Rue de la République, Marigot (phone: 877340).

Gingerbread Gallery Haitian art and handicrafts. *Port la Royale,* Marigot (phone: 877321).

Lipstick Offering massages and all sorts of salon treatments, plus French cosmetics and other *attendrissements.* Two Marigot locations: *Port la Royale* (phone: 875392) and Rue du Président-Kennedy (phone: 871914).

Marithé and François Girbaud Same owners as *Bastringue.* Designer clothing for men and women that can be found only in Paris, Tokyo, and, at 10% less, here. Rue de la Liberté, Marigot (phone: 879458).

Oro de Sol Offering Ebel watches; Pratesi linen; fine china and crystal by Villeroy & Boch, Lalique, and Baccarat; and exquisite jewelry, among other luxury goods. Three Marigot locations: Rue de la République (phone: 875651), Harborfront (phone: 878098), and *Cosmetic Oro de Sol* (specializing in cosmetics), Rue de la République (phone: 871666).

Paris 7 Art Gallery Mini-conglomerate of fine art run by Christine Pelletier. 10 La Fregate, *Port la Royale,* Marigot (phone: 878503).

SPORTS

BICYCLING On the Dutch side, *Trisport* rents mountain bikes by the day or week. Delivery and pickup are available (8 Airport Blvd., Simpson Bay; phone: 54384).

BOATING Most hotels have Sunfish or Sailfish for loan or rent, and there are larger boats available for charter, particularly on the French side. Ask your hotel travel desk, or try *The Moorings* at Oyster Bay (phone: 873255); *ATM Yachts* at Port Lonvilliers (phone: 874030); *Dynasty Yachts* at *Port la Royale Marina* (phone: 878521); or *Marine Time* (see *Sea Excursions*). Sailing instruction and sailboat rental are available from *Mullet Bay Marina* (phone: 52801, ext. 337; or 54363). *America's Cup Yacht Racing* (*Bobby's Marina;* phone: 43354) offers visitors the opportunity to experience the excitement of world class sailboat racing aboard the multimillion-dollar *Canada II* and *True North;* on the French side, try *Marine Time,* which organizes weekly regattas (naturally, with drinks included). For the real thing, check out the big annual race, the *St. Maarten Trade Winds Regatta,* which takes place every year in early March.

FITNESS CENTERS AND SPAS *L'Aqualigne* (phone: 42426), the health spa–beauty clinic at the Dutch side's *Pelican Beach* resort, isn't flashy, but it does offer a full range of treatments and equipment for men and women, including exercise machines; sauna, steamrooms, and whirlpool baths; dance, aerobics, and yoga classes; a health bar; Swedish and shiatsu massages; cellulite treatments, waxings, and facials; and cosmetics and health foods. Weight-loss programs and even cosmetic surgery are available, with weekly, monthly, and daily programs. *Mullet Bay*'s fitness center includes state-of-the-art exercise equipment, plus health programs and aerobics classes; non-guests of the resort may use the facilities for an extra charge. *La Samanna* provides exercise equipment and daily aerobics classes; the *Sheraton Port de Plaisance*'s *Spa and Tennis Center* offers exercise equipment and a complete range of spa services, including Sea Mud Envelopment (seaweed and other ingredients are used as a body mask) and anti-stress massage: Facilities at both are for use by registered guests only. (See *Checking In* for information on all hotels mentioned above.) Sports facilities at *Le Privilège* (phone: 873737), the French side's chic complex at Anse Marcel, include a pool, six tennis courts, two squash courts, jogging, weightlifting, yoga, archery, shooting, and *pétanque,* a version of bowling played in France; there's also a full range of spa services.

GOLF The windy, Joseph Lee–designed layout at *Mullet Bay* (see *Checking In*) is a bit too gimmicky to please purists, but has good views of the water at 14 of its 18 holes. It extends along the palm-lined shores of the bay on one side and the lagoon on the other. The island's only 18-hole course, it is primarily for the use of hotel guests, island residents, and cruise ship passengers who purchase a golf package; however, when tee times are available, other visitors may play by pre-arranging and prepaying for a round.

HIKING *Action Nature* (36 Spring Hills, Marigot; phone: 879787) offers guided hiking tours on Tuesdays and Saturdays. Tours cover a variety of terrain, from difficult climbs up Pic Paradis (Paradise Peak) to easier rambles around archaeological sites on the island.

HORSEBACK RIDING On the Dutch side, *Crazy Acres Riding Center,* on the *Wathey Estate* in Cole Bay (phone: 42793), offers daily two-hour beach rides; book two days in advance. Private beach picnics can also be arranged, and riding instruction is available. On the French side, the *Coralita Beach* resort at Baie Lucas has a small stable (phone: 873035); *Bayside Riding Club* at *Le Galion* in Orient Bay offers moonlight rides (phone: 873614); *Caïd & Isa* at *Le Méridien L'Habitation* in Anse Marcel offers beach rides (phone: 874570); and *Marine Time* (see *Sea Excursions*) offers a choice of three different two- to two-and-a-half-hour rides.

JOGGING Several hotels have jogging on the beach, as does *Le Privilège* spa at Anse Marcel (see *Fitness Centers and Spas,* above). The *Road Runners* club meets Wednesday evenings at the *Raoul Illidge Sports Complex* on Welgelegen Road in Cay Hill and Sunday mornings in the main parking lot of the *Pelican Beach* resort for 5- or 10-kilometer runs. Races usually are held once a month. Visitors are welcome. For information, contact Dr. Fritz Bus of the *Back Street Clinic* (phone: 22467) or Ron van Sittert (phone: 22842).

PARASAILING Rides are offered at *Watersports* at *Mullet Bay Marina* (see *Sea Excursions*).

SNORKELING AND SCUBA DIVING Diving off the island is excellent, with underwater visibility running from 75 to 125 feet. Dutch-side water sports centers that offer equipment rental, instruction, and dive and snorkel trips include *Maho Watersports*—which also offers dive packages to Saba (based at Mullet Bay; phone: 54387, ext. 379); *Ocean Explorers* (Simpson Bay; phone: 45252); *Little Bay Watersports* (at the *Divi Little Bay Beach* hotel, near Philipsburg; phone: 22333/4); *Watersports* (at *Great Bay* hotel; see *Checking In*); and *Pelican Watersports and Excursions* (*Pelican Marina,* Simpson Bay; phone: 42640 or 42503, ext. 1553). On the French side, operators include *Lou Scuba Club* (Laguna Beach; phone: 871661); *Blue Ocean* (at *Le Pirate,* Marigot; phone: 878973); *Marine Time* (see *Sea Excursions*); and *Diving* (at *Le Méridien L'Habitation* resort; see *Checking In*). The waters around the island are clear (75- to 125-foot visibility), with a fair amount of reef life to explore. Pinel Island, just offshore, also offers good snorkeling and shallow diving, and a mile off the coast of St. Maarten, near Great Bay, is a sunken 1801 British man-of-war, the *Proselyte,* replete with cannon and anchors, as well as a variety of coral and fish. Another way to see the aquatic world is offered by *Ocean Explorers*—their "sea walk" permits visitors to walk underwater wearing a specially constructed bronze diving helmet; on the French side, *Marine Time* also offers "sea walks." A cruise on the *Maho Beach* resort's glass-bottom boat (phone: 52115, ext. 4240) is another option. Also see *Sunken and Buried Treasure* in DIVERSIONS.

SPORT FISHING Marlin, barracuda, tuna, kingfish, and dolphin fish are the best catches in the nearby fishing grounds. Tuna is fished year-round; dolphin, kingfish, and barracuda from December through March. Plenty of boats are available for hire on the Dutch side at *Bobby's Marina* and the *Great Bay Marina* in Philipsburg (see *Sea Excursions*), as well as at Simpson Bay; arrangements can be made through your hotel. *Mullet Bay Marina* (see *Sea Excursions*) also runs fishing trips. On the French side, check *Sailfish Caraïbes,* based at Port Lonvilliers (phone: 873194), or *Marine Time* (see *Sea Excursions*). Charters usually include tackle, bait, food, and drink.

SQUASH There are two courts at *Le Privilège* (see *Fitness Centers and Spas,* above) and a squash and raquetball court at the *Tennis and Fitness Center* in the Dutch Cul-de-Sac (phone: 23685).

SWIMMING AND SUNNING The 37 beaches around the island are top attractions. Your hotel will likely have its own stretch of sand, but visit some of the others, for there is a great variety of wide, white expanses and secluded, shady coves to enjoy. Non-guests can use changing facilities at most hotels for a small fee; at many beaches, you won't need any facilities because nobody else will be there. You'll find very few people on the hideaway sands of Long Bay, on the French side north of *La Samanna,* and at Plum and Rouge Bays, north of Long Bay. It's not a good idea to leave belongings unattended at these secluded spots. There is one designated nudist beach, on— *naturellement*—the French side, at Orient Bay, where there's also a simple nudist resort. But even at other French-side beaches, the general attitude toward bikinis, monokinis, and *sans 'kinis* is pretty relaxed.

TENNIS Very popular. At last count there were more than 70 courts on the island, 14 of them at the *Mullet Bay* resort (two lighted). Most of the larger hotels have at least one court: *Captain Oliver's, Great Bay, Summit,* and *La Flamboyant* have one each; the *Divi Little Bay Beach* and *Marine, Simson Beach* have one each, lighted; *Grand Case Beach Club* has one lighted "omnisport" court; *Oyster Bay* (Oyster Pond; 875472) and *Oyster Pond* have two; *Club Orient, Esmeralda, Dawn Beach,* and *Mont Vernon* have two each, lighted; *Belair Beach* (Little Bay Beach; phone: 23366), *Laguna Beach, Nettle Bay Beach Club,* and *La Samanna* have three each; *Pelican Beach* resort (Pelican Keys, Simpson Bay; phone: 42503) and *Maho Beach* each have four, as does *La Belle Créole* (all lighted); *Le Privilège* has six courts (four lighted) and a practice wall (see *Fitness Centers and Spas*); and *Le Méridien L'Habitation* has six lighted courts as well. *Sheraton Port de Plaisance* offers seven lighted courts and a 500-seat stadium, with tennis programs under the direction of *Peter Burwash International.* (See *Checking In* for more information on all of the above hotels, unless otherwise noted.) Some hotels have instructional programs and pro shops. In the Dutch Cul-de-Sac, the *Tennis and Fitness Center* (see *Squash,* above), with two lighted courts and a pro shop, is operated by tennis pro Michael Sprott. Lessons and clinics are available at the center, or Sprott will visit your hotel; the first lesson is a complimentary introduction.

WATER SKIING Available at most beachside hotels and on calm Simpson Bay Lagoon or try *Watersports* at *Mullet Bay Marina* (see *Sea Excursions*).

WINDSURFING Available at many Dutch-side beachfront hotels, including *Mullet Bay* resort (see *Checking In*), *Little Bay Watersports* at the *Divi Little Bay*

Beach hotel (see *Snorkeling and Scuba Diving,* above), *Dawn Beach* (serving Oyster Pond; see *Checking In*), and on Simpson Bay Lagoon. Most French-side beach hotels also are equipped or will make arrangements. On Orient Bay, *Sport Away* provides instruction and holds races (phone: 879324), and *Nathalie Simon Windsurfing Club* (*Résidence Plantation;* phone: 874034) offers lessons, rentals, and races.

NIGHTLIFE

With some 300 restaurants on the island, dining out is the most popular pastime. On the Dutch side, nautical types usually begin their evenings at *Berrymore's* (Front St.; no phone). Later, many hotels on both sides have "West Indian nights" (such as the Saturday-night Caribbean party with a steel band at *Great Bay*), dancing under the stars, or discos. A popular dance club on the Dutch side is *Mullet Bay*'s *Studio 7,* while *Great Bay*'s *Chrysalis* features international entertainers. The *Dawn Beach* hotel features steel bands on Thursday nights in season. (*Note:* Unless otherwise noted, see *Checking In* for more information on hotels mentioned in this section.) *Coconuts Comedy Club,* upstairs at the *Maho Beach* hotel's *Casino Royale* (phone: 52602), hosts local and international comedians; it's closed Mondays. Also at *Maho Beach,* the *Regards Theatre* offers an entertaining send-up of island life in a nightly musical comedy revue. *Cheri's Café* (next to the *Casino Royale;* phone: 53361) draws crowds with live reggae and Latin music nightly. *Lynnette's* (near *Juliana Airport;* see *Eating Out*) features reggae on Tuesday and Friday nights, and *Turtle Pier Bar* (on Simpson Bay Lagoon; phone: 52230) offers live music, including a sing-along, on Sunday nights. *L'Escargot* (see *Eating Out*) features a cabaret with dinner on Sundays. There's crowded late-night activity in Philipsburg at the *Greenhouse* at *Bobby's Marina* (phone: 22941).

All of the island's casinos are on the Dutch side. Hotel casinos include the *Belair Beach* (Little Bay Beach; phone: 23366), *Pelican Beach, Maho Beach, Mullet Bay* resort, *Great Bay Beach,* and *Sheraton Port de Plaisance* (phone: 44334). At Cupecoy Beach, there's the *Atlantis* (phone: 54600/1). In Philipsburg, visitors may try their luck at the *Seaview* (67 Front St., Great Bay Beach; phone: 22323), the *Coliseum* (Front St.; phone: 32101), and *Rouge et Noir* (Front St.; phone: 43326). Near the airport, *Lightning Casino* offers betting on televised sports events shown on 15 large-screen TVs (Airport Blvd.; phone: 43290). Most casinos offer craps, roulette, blackjack, and slot machines. Before playing, check the house rules, for they vary slightly from one casino to another; minimum playing age is 18. Some casinos have nightclubs that feature live entertainment; all serve complimentary drinks, and most open at lunchtime and stay open until 2 AM. Several French-side hotels provide free transport to casinos for their guests. For additional details, see *Casino Countdown* in DIVERSIONS.

On the French side, dining begins with an aperitif at one of the lively café-bars or bistros of the chic *Port la Royale Marina,* where live music often fills the air as the temperature cools down. French-side nocturnal types also are found at *Port la Royale Marina,* at *L'Atmosphère* (phone: 875024), the marina's *très chic* disco, or at *Café de Paris* (Rue du Président-Kennedy; phone: 879936 or 290579), which offers cabaret on Friday nights. At *Le Privilège* (see *Fitness Centers and Spas*) there's a nightclub and restaurants that serve food into the wee hours. The *Sheraton Port de Plaisance* offers nightly live entertainment. A more local flavor can be savored at *Night Fever* near Colombier (take the road from Marigot toward Grand Case, and turn right where marked; no phone). You can party till the wee hours at *La Bar de la Mer* on the beach in Marigot (phone: 878179).

Best on the Island

CHECKING IN

The Dutch side has more than 4,000 rooms and efficiency apartments with kitchenettes. Accommodations range from modest guesthouse rooms to big hotels by the sea. But, unlike the French side, the Dutch side offers no truly luxurious resorts. In fact, many of the bigger Dutch-side resorts have become more interested in selling time-share slots than in providing good service to hotel guests. Other hotels rely heavily on back-to-back charter bookings, and their beaches and facilities are always crowded.

Rooms on the French side number over 3,500, ranging from small efficiency apartments to lavish (and astronomically priced) resorts. For information on small inns on the French side, contact *Les Hôtels de Charme* (phone: 800-GO-TO-SXM).

A number of fully staffed private homes are rented by the week or month on each side of the border. Prices start at about $800 a week in winter and range *way* up from there. Best contacts: Ms. Judy Shepherd at *St. Maarten Rentals* (Pelican House, Beacon Hill, St. Maarten, NA; phone: 54330 or 55443) or *Carimo* (23 Rue de Général de Gaulle, PO Box 220, Marigot 97150, St. Martin, FWI; phone: 875758).

Best reservations advice: Shop carefully to make sure what you want is what you get (especially in the atmosphere department), and book early because there are many winter weeks when the island is almost sold out. Among our recommendations below, expensive translates to $225 and more (much more) for a double without meals in winter; moderate, from $150 to $225; inexpensive, $150 and less. In summer, rates drop as much as 60% on the Dutch side; by about a third on the French side. On the Dutch side, there's a 5% tax on hotel rooms and usually a 15% service (or 10% service and 5% "energy") charge. French hotels add a 15% service charge, and a 2- to 7-franc government tax per person per night, which is sometimes incorporated into the room rate. All hotels listed below have air conditioning, TV sets, telephones, and private baths unless otherwise noted. When calling from a phone within one side of St. Martin/St. Maarten, use only the local numbers listed below. When calling the Dutch side from the French, dial 195995 + (local number); when calling the French side from the Dutch, dial 06 + (local number). For information about dialing from anywhere else, see *Telephone* earlier in this chapter.

We begin with our favorite havens, all of which fall in the "expensive" category, followed by recommended hotels listed by price category.

REGAL RESORTS AND SPECIAL HAVENS

La Belle Créole Conceived by the late Claude Philippe (of New York's *Waldorf-Astoria*), this 156-room luxury resort is modeled after a typical fishing village on the French Riviera. Its 27 one- to three-story villas are linked by cobblestone streets, sidewalks, and courtyards, all surrounding a village square. All units are decorated in a Provençal motif and have mini-bars, and cable TV. Some have beamed ceilings, and most have private terraces overlooking Baie de Marigot or the lagoon. Amenities include three beaches, a freshwater pool, four tennis courts with pro shop, a fitness center, and a full range of water sports. Boutiques, secretarial services, a drugstore, car rental agency, and concierge also are on the premises. The resort's excellent *La Provence* restaurant (see *Eating Out*) features international and creole cuisine; a poolside café-bar serves light meals and snacks; a beach bar and a main bar offer regular entertainment. Children under 12 stay with their parents free of charge. Pte. des Pierres à Chaux (phone: 876600; 800-445-8667; fax: 590-875666).

Le Méridien L'Habitation and Le Domaine Tucked under Pigeon Pea Hill on one of St. Martin's most beautiful beaches, this place sprawls over 150 of the island's choicest acres. A member of the French Méridien group and St. Martin's largest hotel, the property has a large freshwater pool, four restaurants, nightly entertainment, water sports, a 100-slip marina, and *Le Privilège* sports complex nearby. *Le Domaine,* a $45-million luxury wing, has 125 rooms and 20 suites in five two- and three-level buildings, as well as a pool, a bar, and an open-air restaurant. Each room has a round bathtub with an ocean view, a terrace or patio, as well as a direct-dial telephone, mini-bar, and safe. *Le Domaine* buildings feature traditional creole architecture and are set in tropical gardens. The original *L'Habitation* complex, designed in pure West Indian style, comprises five two-story buildings (overlooking a lagoon) and three three-story structures that make up the main building, which houses the deluxe rooms and suites, three restaurants, including the elegant *La Belle France* (see *Eating Out*), and entertainment facilities. *L'Habitation* offers 189 rooms and 73 one- and two-bedroom suites, each containing spacious, well-appointed baths. All rooms have private balconies or terraces, direct-dial phones, and mini-fridges; some have kitchenettes. Each of the one-bedroom marina suites also includes a private patio (with a hammock, table, and chairs) and a fully equipped kitchen. A $1-million landscaping project has enhanced the gardens and grounds. The *Pirate's Club* provides activities for kids two to 14. Although large and rambling (for St. Martin), this property has a lot of charm and a professional, efficient management. Anse Marcel (phone: 876700; 800-543-4300; fax: 873038).

Oyster Pond In spite of its rustic name, it's actually a small Moorish structure on the far side of the Dutch portion of the island. Beautifully secluded on a remote point of land, it's cut off from the rest of the world by sudden hills on one side and a blue lagoon and the sea on the other. The ride down to the hotel can be slightly hair-raising, but this retreat is still the choice of many high-powered financial types, including at least one former head of the New York Stock Exchange. Beyond the breezy lobby, furnished in white wicker with Pierre Deux fabrics, and lush with tropical plants and flowers, lies a sun-dappled patio and stairs that lead up to some of the best-looking rooms in the Caribbean. All 40, including the tower suites, are pastel-coordinated, with ceiling fans (plus air conditioning) and their own terraces. Most have smashing views of the sea, but garden-view rooms are available for considerably lower rates—worth checking into if you're on a budget, but still want the benefits of a luxury hotel. The beach (called Dawn) is perfect for swimming and picnicking, and for a quick dip there's a choice: the wood-decked swimming pool or the coral-protected lagoon beside the hotel. Scuba is available by arrangement, and other water sports are nearby; so is deep-sea fishing, and a charter boat is at the ready to cruise to offshore islands. Two tennis courts are also on the premises. French cuisine is served in the candelit dining room (see *Eating Out*). There's never a crowd: perhaps 60 guests at most, plus a few drop-in yachtsmen. Regrettably, the *Dawn Beach* condo and hotel crowd next door has meaningfully increased the area's population. No children under 10. Near the French-Dutch border (phone: 22206 or 23206; 800-839-3030; fax: 25695).

La Samanna This spot, owned by the prestigious Rosewood hotels, is where celebrities come to soak up some rays as anonymously as possible. The quarter-mile crescent of white sand beach is merely perfect, and the Mediterranean-Moorish design enhances the Arabian nights mystique. The resort is sleek, chic, more than slightly sexy, and *très* expensive. All 80 villas (with one, two, or three bedrooms) are designed with tropical elegance, featuring bamboo furnishings and shades of coral, blue, and green. All have spectacular sea views, full kitchens, living rooms, terraces (though no TV sets), and many open onto the silky sand. The most popular is the Terrace Suite, which (befitting its name) has myriad balconies, including one with a thatch roof. Elaborate, complimentary (at these rates, they should be) breakfasts are delivered to your terrace each morning; and *The Restaurant,* candlelit and cooled by sea breezes, offers some of the *haute*-est French cuisine on the island (see *Eating Out*). Also complimentary are use of the pool, fitness pavilion, and three tennis courts, plus water sports and daily aerobics classes. Closed September and October. Long Bay (phone: 876400; 800-854-2252; fax: 878786).

THE DUTCH SIDE

NEAR THE AIRPORT

EXPENSIVE

Atrium The newest hotel on the island, it's under the same management as the *Pelican Beach* and *Royal Palm Beach Club* (see below). This sleek, sophisticated property on the beach offers 90 one- and two-bedroom apartments, all with kitchens, ceiling fans (in addition to air conditioning), and balconies or terraces. There's a pool, with a pool bar that serves light snacks, and the popular *Old Rock Café* is directly across the street. Guests have full use of the facilities at the nearby *Pelican Beach,* a short walk or complimentary ferry ride away. Pelican Rd., Pelican Keys, Simpson Bay (phone: 42126; 800-626-9637; fax: 42503).

Cupecoy Beach Club Situated on a cliff overlooking a generous stretch of Cupecoy Bay Beach, this property features 52 beautifully furnished, Mediterranean-style one- to three-bedroom apartments, all with fully-equipped kitchens and such amenities as cable TV, VCRs, and safes. The property features a large pool with swim-up bar and a beach bar (but no restaurant). The *Atlantis* casino is across the street, and nearby are restaurants, shops, and evening entertainment at the *Maho Plaza Shopping Center* and *Mullet Bay* resort (phone/fax: 52243).

Maho Beach The largest property in St. Maarten, this beachfront property has 624 rooms, some with kitchenettes, and many amenities, including a beach, two pools, four tennis courts, and full water sports facilities. There also are several restaurants, a casino, a disco, the *Coconuts Comedy Club,* and even a medical clinic. Shopping and more night spots are nearby at the *Maho Plaza Shopping Center.* Mullet Bay (phone: 52115 or 52119; 800-223-0757; fax: 53180).

Mullet Bay This sprawling 172-acre condominium-cum-resort hotel, with 611 spacious rooms and suites, has just about everything in the way of facilities: a water sports center, 18 holes of golf, 14 tennis courts, one freshwater and one saltwater pool, a casino, a disco, seven restaurants (including the *Frigate*—see *Eating Out*), a grocery store, a clinic, a shopping plaza, a branch of Chase Manhattan Bank, and regular shuttle service to Philipsburg and *Juliana Airport* (although a car helps a lot). It's all remarkably self-sufficient. On Mullet Bay, about 4½ miles from *Juliana Airport* (phone: 52801; 800-4-MULLET or 800-325-0446; fax: 54281).

Ocean Club Set right on a small, crescent-shaped beach down a secluded road, this property offers 20 luxury suites and one- and two-bedroom villas with full kitchens, decks, and cable TV; some units boast large Jacuzzis and laundry rooms. There's a pool, and a variety of water sports is available. There's no restaurant on the premises, but restaurants, casinos, evening entertainment, and shopping are a five-minute drive away. Cupecoy Bay (phone: 54632; 800-223-9815; fax: 54434).

Pelican Beach This resort has 424 guest accommodations ranging from studios to two-bedroom apartments. All feature full kitchen facilities, ceiling fans (in addition to air conditioning), balconies or terraces, satellite TV, and even a stereo system. The resort offers a choice of two beaches, and there are three restaurants with a variety of menus. Other facilities include a marina, a European-style spa, a casino, five swimming pools, four tennis courts, Jacuzzis, a shopping arcade, a mini-market and deli, and a medical clinic. A complimentary ferry transports guests to and from the resort's sister properties, the nearby *Atrium* (above) and *Royal Palm Beach Club* (below); guests at any of the three properties have full privileges at the others. Pelican Rd., Pelican Keys, Simpson Bay (phone: 42503 or 44308; 800-626-9637; fax: 42133).

Royal Palm Beach Club Set on Simpson Bay Beach, this property has 140 beachfront accommodations ranging from studios to two-bedroom apartments, all with kitchens, ceiling fans (to supplement the air conditioning), and balconies or terraces. There's a restaurant, a pool with a swim-up bar, a fitness center, a mini-market, and a deli. All the facilities of the sister *Pelican Beach* and *Atrium* resorts are available to guests; a complimentary ferry transports guests among the three resorts. Airport Blvd., Simpson Bay (phone: 42503; 800-626-9637; fax: 42133).

Sapphire Beach Club Privately located near the end of the road leading to Cupecoy Bay, this resort overlooks the beach, with 102 studio- to two-bedroom apartments (including 14 luxurious two-bedroom beachfront villas that are privately owned, but sometimes available for rent)—all with fully-equipped kitchens and most with either a small private pool or a Jacuzzi on the balcony. There's a pool with a pool bar offering a light menu. 147 Lowlands (phone: 52179; 800-435-8122; fax: 52178).

Sheraton Port de Plaisance Located on 200 acres on Simpson Bay Lagoon, this oasis of red-roofed and trellised buildings offers unique pampering. The 88 rooms and suites are decorated in a breezy island style of light colors and rattan; each has a full kitchen. The resort boasts a stunning casino, four restaurants, a shuttle to the beach, two pools—a lap pool and another featuring a waterfall—and two Jacuzzis. The *Spa and Tennis Center* has state-of-the-art equipment and a complete range of spa services. The seven lighted tennis courts include a 500-seat stadium court and clinics under the direction of *Peter Burwash International.* Union Rd. (phone: 45222; 800-325-3535; fax: 42315).

Towers at Mullet Bay This mid-rise condominium property under the same management as the *Mullet Bay* resort (above) overlooks a lagoon. Eighty-four elegant guest accommodations, ranging from studios to three-bedroom suites, feature fully-equipped kitchens, cable TVs with VCRs, and stereo systems. There's a pool on the premises with a poolside bar. Guests enjoy full privileges at *Mullet Bay.* Mullet Bay, 4½ miles from *Juliana Airport* (phone: 53069; 800-235-5889; fax: 52147).

MODERATE

Mary's Boon The service is excellent at this hotel, which has 12 rooms, each with a kitchenette and seaside patio. Decorated with a blend of antiques and tropical wicker, sisal, and bamboo, the rooms are breezy, but not air conditioned, and there are no telephones or TV sets. Highlights include a great beach, an honor bar, and an unregimented atmosphere. Pets are welcome; children under 16 aren't. Delicious French cuisine with an American accent is served in the dining room. No one seems bothered by its location next to the *Juliana Airport* runway. No credit cards are accepted. Airport Rd., Simpson Bay (phone: 54235; 800-223-9815; fax: 53403).

Summit One of St. Maarten's older properties, this informal place set on a bluff overlooking Simpson Bay Lagoon has a faithful following and an Italian restaurant (under a French chef). The 32 pleasant one- and two-story chalets have porches (often looking onto the neighboring chalet); some have kitchenettes, but they're not air conditioned, and there are no telephones or TV sets. There's also a large pool and a tennis court. A free shuttle bus transports guests to beaches (a quarter of a mile away) and casinos (phone: 52150; 800-622-7836; fax: 52150).

PHILIPSBURG

EXPENSIVE

Great Bay One of Philipsburg's oldest hotels, it has 285 spacious rooms, each with a king-size bed or two double beds and direct-dial telephone. Amenities include three restaurants and bars, a disco, a casino, a beach, two pools, a lighted tennis court, water sports, and seemingly endless activities. Popular with package tours. All-inclusive rates are available. There's a Saturday-night Caribbean party with a steel band. At the western end of Great Bay Beach, just outside town (phone: 22446; 800-223-6510; 212-969-9220 in New York City; fax: 23859).

MODERATE

Divi Little Bay Beach Occupying its own beach-surrounded peninsula, this resort, one of the island's older properties, is one of the few on the Dutch side that offer standard hotel rooms. Its 157 recently renovated beachfront and casita (garden) rooms feature ceiling fans (in addition to air conditioning) and satellite TV; some suites with kitchens are available. The resort has two restaurants, two pools (one with a whirlpool section), water sports, a lighted tennis court, a casino, and a gameroom. Klein Baai (phone: 22333/4; 800-367-3484; fax: 23911).

Holland House Beach Set on Great Bay Beach in the heart of Philipsburg, this intimate hotel is built on the site of what once was the governor's headquarters. All of the 54 rooms feature satellite TV and hardwood or tile floors, and all but eight have kitchenettes. Some boast balconies with picturesque views of the bay. There's also an open-air restaurant and bar. The hotel is within easy walking distance of shopping, restaurants, nightspots, and casinos (phone: 22572; 800-223-9815; fax: 24673).

Horizon View Beach Conveniently located in the heart of Philipsburg, this pleasant beachfront hostelry has 30 units—studios, one-bedroom suites with living rooms and beach views, and two-bedroom penthouse suites with patios and Jacuzzis. All units have kitchenettes, cable TV, and direct-dial phones. There's a restaurant and a gift shop on the premises. 39 Front St. (phone: 32120 or 32121; fax: 32123).

Town House Villas Each of these 11 attractive beachfront townhouses in the middle of Philipsburg has two bedrooms, 1½ baths, two patios, a complete kitchen and living/dining area, but no telephone or TV set. Located on the edge of town. On busy Front St., Great Bay Beach (phone: 22898; 800-223-9815; fax: 22418).

INEXPENSIVE

Pasanggrahan Royal Inn Formerly a governor's home, this historic West Indian building on the beach is St. Maarten's oldest inn and a favorite of many repeat visitors, from statesmen to salesmen. In an annex there are 30 charming, if small, rooms (no telephones or TV sets). The main house offers a pleasant seaside bar and restaurant, where guests can take afternoon tea and hobnob at a social cocktail hour. Front St., at the beach (phone: 23588; 800-223-9815; fax: 22885).

ELSEWHERE ON THE DUTCH SIDE

EXPENSIVE

Dawn Beach Here are 155 spacious rooms, each with a kitchenette and a terrace, but no telephone, on one of the island's most beautiful reef-protected beaches (the surf can be choppy on windy days). The units on the beach are by far the most desirable. The attractive open-air dining room and bar are raised to catch the view and sea breezes. Other highlights: a freshwater pool with waterfall, two lighted tennis courts, water sports, and a popular Sunday brunch. All-inclusive packages are available. On Dawn Beach, near the border (phone: 22929; 800-351-5656; fax: 24421).

THE FRENCH SIDE

MARIGOT

INEXPENSIVE

Le Pirate A gleaming white property within walking distance of Marigot, it has 55 large studios (with kitchenettes and terraces) and 11 duplexes. Units are not air conditioned, and have no telephones or TV sets. Amenities include a small pool, a beach within strolling distance, an informal waterfront snack bar, and a restaurant. Near Sandy Ground (phone: 877837; 800-666-5756; fax: 879667).

GRAND CASE

EXPENSIVE

Grand Case Beach Club On one of St. Martin's most splendid beaches, this property features 72 airy, attractive studios and one- and two-bedroom apartments; all units have kitchens and private terraces. Swimming, sailing, water sports, tennis, *pétanque* (the Provençal equivalent of *bocci*), a bar, a panoramic restaurant called—not surprisingly—*Café Panoramique* (see *Eating Out*), and friendly and gracious management. On Grand Case Bay (phone: 875187; 800-223-1588; 212-223-2848 in New York City; fax: 875993).

MODERATE

L'Esplanade Perched on a hillside above Grand Case Bay, this property's three buildings give the place the feel of three very small hotels in one. Each building houses 24 studios and one-bedroom suites with kitchen facilities and balconies or terraces (views from the latter have earned the place the title "Best Porch and Garden View in the Caribbean" from *Caribbean Travel and Life* magazine). There is a pool with a swim-up bar nestled among the lushly landscaped grounds, and the beach is just down the hill. There's no restaurant (phone: 870655; fax: 872915).

BAIE NETTLE

MODERATE

Anse Margot In a lush tropical garden, these 95 rooms in trilevel buildings are set on a lagoon. There are two moderate-size swimming pools, two Jacuzzis, a bar, and a first class restaurant. Just west of Marigot (phone: 879201; 800-742-4276; fax: 879213).

La Flamboyant Among the pluses at this 271-room establishment are two fresh-water pools, a Jacuzzi, a tennis court, a restaurant with panoramic views, and a brasserie on the beach level. Some rooms have kitchenettes. In the off-season, packages are available that include all meals, drinks, entertainment, water sports, an island tour, and more. At the marina on Simpson Bay Lagoon, next to the *Nettle Bay Beach Club* resort, Rte. des Terres Basses (phone: 876000; 800-221-5333; fax: 879957).

Laguna Beach A somewhat smaller and less posh sister of the *Anse Margot,* this 62-room hostelry has two beachside two-level buildings overlooking a swimming pool. The rooms are spacious and have terraces. Amenities include a restaurant, two bars, shops, and three tennis courts. Just west of Marigot (phone: 879175; 800-223-9815; fax: 878165).

Marine, Simson Beach Featuring creole architecture, with wooden, balconied loggia and stylish wicker furniture in the lounges, this place offers 128 studios and 48 duplex apartments (with no air conditioning, telephones, or TV sets), a pool, a lighted tennis court, a bar, and a restaurant. In the Baie Nettle area (phone: 875454; 800-221-4542; fax: 879211).

Nettle Bay Beach Club This beachfront resort offers 201 modern, comfortable accommodations in a variety of settings: the inn, the gardens, and the villas. There's also a pool, three tennis courts, and a casual French restaurant, *Lafayette* (phone: 876868 or 879704; 800-223-9815; fax: 872151).

ATLANTIC COAST

EXPENSIVE

Esmeralda This delightful property on 100 secluded acres near Orient Bay has 14 villa-like structures with a total of 51 rooms designed in a mix of Antillean creole and Spanish Mission architecture. Most villas have three guestrooms plus a large luxury suite. All units have private entrances, sitting areas, kitchenettes, and terraces, but no telephones or TV sets. There's a pool for each building, two lighted tennis courts, complete water sports facilities, and a main pool area with an extensive deck overlooking the ocean. The restaurant offers French, creole, and continental dishes, and there is also a beachfront grill and bar. Orient Bay (phone: 873636; 800-622-7836; fax: 873518).

Mont Vernon These 394 units in junior and two-room suites have terraces with ocean views; none has air conditioning, telephone, or TV set. There is a large swimming pool, two lighted tennis courts, a water sports center, three restaurants, and a lounge with nightly entertainment. Bilingual staff. Orient Bay (phone: 876200; 800-223-0888; fax: 873727).

MODERATE

Belvédère Here are 132 studio apartments (all with kitchenettes, but no TV sets) facing an excellent crescent beach on the Atlantic. There are two restaurants and a pool. Cul-de-Sac (phone: 873789; fax: 873052).

Captain Oliver's Straddling the Dutch/French border is this French luxury complex. Each of the 50 bungalows offers a kitchenette, a terrace, a direct-dial phone, a radio (but no TV set), and room service from the eponymous waterfront restaurant (see *Eating Out*). Many rooms have ocean views. A pool and a tennis court complete the picture. Oyster Pond (phone: 874026; 800-223-1588; fax: 874084).

Club Orient A "clothing optional" naturist resort on a lovely, windswept, 1½-mile-long beach. Accommodations are in 91 prefabricated red pine chalets imported from Finland; all have kitchens and living rooms, but no air conditioning, telephones, or TV sets. Some accommodate up to four people. A beach bar/restaurant, water sports facilities, two lighted tennis courts, a boutique, and a basic grocery store are on the premises. No frills—but getting back to nature is what this place is all about. Orient Bay (phone: 873385; 800-452-9016; fax: 873376).

St. Tropez Set right on Orient Bay Beach, this resort has 84 junior suites, all with refrigerators. There's also a pool and a tennis court, but no restaurant (phone: 874201; 800-622-7836; fax: 874169).

INEXPENSIVE

Jardins de Chevrise This property has 29 studios and duplexes in West Indian–style bungalows around a pool. Each room has a kitchenette and patio or terrace, but no telephone or TV set. There's a casual restaurant, and the beach is a five-minute walk away. On the hillside at Mont Vernon overlooking a lagoon (phone: 873779; fax: 873803).

EATING OUT

St. Martin/St. Maarten offers a wealth of dining options. French cuisine, in both its classic version (escargots, frogs' legs, langouste flambé) and its creole variations (the savory fish stew called *blaff, crabes farcis,* curried conch, and chicken *colombos*), is prepared very well on both sides of the island. But if you're smitten with a sudden craving for bagels and lox, prime ribs, or a chocolate soda, these are available here, too. For lobster lovers, this island comes close to heaven (although most of the restaurant supply is now shipped over from nearby Anguilla). The meat is sweet and tender, and the price—compared to stateside levels—also is palatable. There's lots of good fish, but beware—sometimes it is "fresh frozen," that is, caught on the island but frozen instead of being served immediately. Several restaurants, including *Le Mini Club, Chez Martine,* and *La Belle France,* offer prix fixe dinners. There's also plenty of good French wine (served by the carafe or bottle), and lots of tasty Dutch beer.

At lunch, nobody bothers about reservations; for dinner, they're usually a good idea. Most restaurants add a 10% to 15% service charge in lieu of tip, but neither government taxes meals. Not including tip, wine, or drinks, expect to pay over $160 for dinner for two at restaurants described below as very expensive; from $100 to $160 at expensive places; from $60 to $100 at places in the moderate category; and less than $60 at eateries listed as inexpensive. Unless otherwise noted, all places below serve lunch and dinner. When calling from a phone within one side of the island, use only the local numbers listed below. When calling the Dutch side from the French, dial 5995 + (local number); when calling the French side from the Dutch, dial 6 + (local number).

THE DUTCH SIDE

PHILIPSBURG

EXPENSIVE

Antoine The best lobster thermidor on the island, plus duck Montmorency (with a cherry brandy sauce), conch fricassee, and soufflés grace the menu at this romantic restaurant set on the waterfront, next to the pier. Closed Sundays. Reservations advised. MasterCard and American Express accepted. Front St. (phone: 22964).

Le Bec Fin This long-established gastronomic address proffers elegant dining in a lovely 18th-century courtyard. The French chef offers a fairly traditional menu, albeit with some tempting deviations, such as lobster salad with mango sauce, smoked duck salad, and marinated salmon. Definitely worth checking out. Open daily. Reservations advised. Major credit cards accepted. 119 Front St. (phone: 22976).

Dario's Piccola Trieste On the water across from the *Caribbean* hotel, it features outstanding northern Italian fare, just like its sister restaurant of the same name on New York's Long Island. The grilled red snapper with garlic and olive oil, and the veal chop Dario (lightly breaded, sautéed in white wine, and smothered in fontina cheese) are specialties. All meat is imported from the United States. Open daily. Reservations advised. Major credit cards accepted. 103 Front St. (phone: 23834).

L'Escargot In an old townhouse, this is one of the island's oldest restaurants (celebrating its 24th anniversary this year). True to its name, the restaurant's snails are memorable; try them in puff pastry, *à la provençale, de bourgogne,* or in fresh mushroom caps. Other items include crisp duck in guavaberry sauce, lobster thermidor, and the famous white chocolate mousse for dessert. Every Sunday there's a cabaret with dinner. Open daily. Reservations advised. Major credit cards accepted. 84 Front St. (phone: 22483).

Da Livio The island's best Italian restaurant enjoys a seafront setting that's perfect for alfresco lunches on the terrace or casually elegant candlelit dinners. The menu features a myriad of pasta, veal, chicken, and seafood dishes. A few that are extra special: manicotti with spinach and ricotta cheese, scampi in garlic butter, lobster *fra diavolo,* and ricotta cheesecake with pine nuts. The owner, Livio, could not be more gracious. Closed Sundays. Reservations advised. Major credit cards accepted. 159 Front St. (phone: 22690).

MODERATE

Seafood Galley and Raw Bar Fresh oysters, mussels, clams, and other seafood landed locally or imported from New England (when unavailable, guests are advised of "fresh frozen" backups) and served au naturel at the raw bar or, if you prefer, sautéed or grilled. Chicken and steaks are available for landlubbers. Right on the dock, it's a pleasant, breezy place, perfect for boat watching. Open daily, with a happy hour. Reservations advised. Major credit cards accepted. At *Bobby's Marina* (phone: 23253).

Shivsagar Serving the only authentic Indian cuisine on St. Maarten, this eatery features a variety of savory kebabs, nans, and rotis prepared before guests in a traditional tandoori oven. Open daily. Reservations advised. Major credit cards accepted. Front St. (phone: 22299).

Wajang Doll Popular spot for authentic Indonesian feasting on rijsttafel, with a sampling of 14 or 19 different exotic dishes. Highly acclaimed by Dutch expatriates who know their rijsttafel well. Dinner only; closed Sundays. Reservations advised. Major credit cards accepted. 137 Front St. (phone: 22687).

INEXPENSIVE

Café Rembrandt For those who feel adventurous or who want to experience the Caribbean version of a typical Amsterdam pub. There's a long lineup of such Dutch-Indonesian delights as *kroket* (crusty egg-batter roll with ragout of mildly spiced meat), *bami* (spicy fried rice or noodles with chopped vegetables in an egg-batter crust), and *satay* (grilled chunks of pork or chicken on a skewer with hot peanut sauce). Reproductions of the Old Master's works hang on the walls. Open daily. Reservations unnecessary. Major credit cards accepted. 15 Rembrandtsplein (phone: 24715).

EXPENSIVE

Frigate Diners flock here for steaks and seafood, a casual atmosphere, and a lovely view of the shimmering lagoon. Open daily for dinner only. Reservations advised in high season. Major credit cards accepted. At the *Mullet Bay* resort, about 4½ miles from the airport (phone: 52801, ext. 331).

Oyster Pond All meals at this retreat in the *Oyster Pond* hotel are special. Whether dining in the elegant, breezy, candlelit dining room with fine linen, Rosenthal china, and fresh flowers, or lunching informally under the umbrellas of the quiet courtyard, the ambience alone rates five stars. To that, add the superb cuisine: Before overdosing on minted cold cucumber soup, fresh asparagus in puff pastry with chervil butter, or medallions of lobster with truffles, tomato, and basil, remember to save room for the banana, chocolate, or raspberry dessert soufflé. Open daily for breakfast, lunch, and dinner. Reservations advised. Major credit cards accepted. Oyster Pond (phone: 22206).

Le Perroquet Named after Chicago's bastion of French cuisine, this tropical version overlooking the quiet waters of Simpson Bay Lagoon, not far from the airport, is another Dutch-side favorite. The West Indian–style house offers breezy dining on a lush garden porch. The menu features such unusual fare as breast of ostrich, alligator, and black bear, as well as more familiar foods, such as fresh salmon lightly smoked in herbs at your table (a truly memorable dish). Also good are mussels with leeks in muscadet sauce. Charming ambience, smiling service, and a good wine list add to the experience. Dinner only; closed Mondays and during June and September. Reservations advised. Major credit cards accepted. Airport Rd. (phone: 54339).

Spartaco Since its smashing debut 10 years ago, this excellent northern Italian restaurant just seems to get better and better. It's in an early-19th-century West Indian plantation house, where the late afternoon sun shines through a louvered verandah onto black Alessi china and sparkling crystal, and mock Roman statuary lines the long stairs leading through the gardens to a flowered pool area with a view of the lagoon. Service is superb, the ambience quietly romantic, and the food excellent. Rich in snob appeal, yet friendly. Dinner only; closed Mondays in low season. Reservations advised. Major credit cards accepted. Almond Grove, Cole Bay (phone: 45379).

MODERATE

Lynnette's This is the place everyone's talking about. It features local fare such as fried fish creole, curried goat, and stuffed crab backs, as well as fancier dishes like rack of lamb *bouquettière* (baked in mustard) and tomatoes stuffed with snails and mushrooms in a creamy Pernod sauce. Both indoor and outdoor dining is available. Open daily; no lunch Mondays. Reservations advised for dinner. Major credit cards accepted. Simpson Bay Blvd., near *Juliana Airport* (phone: 52865).

Old Rock Café and Grill One of the newest dining additions to the island, this casual spot is a creation of the owners of the successful *Lynnette's* (above). Set in a historic, West Indian–style home, the restaurant features gingerbread woodwork, ceiling fans, and "Lover's Row"—tables set by the windows that have old-fashioned porch swings instead of chairs. Breakfast and lunch are casual affairs; the atmosphere at dinner, which features seafood, steaks, and local specialties, is more elegant. The ample Sunday brunch is a popular event, and there's live entertainment some evenings. Open daily. Reservations advised for dinner and Sunday brunch. MasterCard and American Express accepted. Onyx Road, Simpson Bay (phone: 42369).

La Rosa, Too The traditional Italian menu features several of Giuseppe La Rosa's own Sicilian recipes, such as *ziti alla Norma* (named after the opera, it's made with fried eggplant and plenty of parmesan), as well as classic pasta, meat, and seafood dishes. A favorite dish is veal chop Regine (made with mushrooms and a light cream-and-wine sauce). Open daily for dinner. Reservations advised. Major credit cards accepted. In the *Maho Plaza Shopping Center,* a half mile west of *Juliana Airport* (phone: 53470).

Rumboat Café Easygoing island pleasures and international haute cuisine await at this casual bistro restaurant. Naturally, a wide selection of rums and rum liqueurs from around the Caribbean are offered. Open daily for dinner only. No reservations. Major credit cards accepted. *Maho Plaza Shopping Center,* Maho Bay (phone: 71006).

INEXPENSIVE

Paradise Café If you get a hankering for Mexican or Tex-Mex, this is the place for such traditional fare as burritos, tacos, and nachos, along with beef, chicken, and seafood specialties grilled over mesquite coals at the outdoor barbecue. Informal alfresco dining at tables overlooking a swimming pool, which guests are encouraged to use. Open daily, including weekend brunch; no lunch Mondays. Reservations unnecessary. Major credit cards accepted. Across from *Maho Beach* resort, Mullet Bay (phone: 52842).

Turtle Pier Bar There's a sun deck with lounge chairs for lazing around this relaxed, comfortable watering hole, which also has its own boat dock and a menagerie of monkeys and parrots. The day begins with full breakfast, and a menu of barbecued chicken and ribs, burgers, and fish and chips is offered throughout the day and evening; there's also a children's menu. Showers are available for boaters. Open daily. Reservations unnecessary. MasterCard and Visa accepted. Simpson Bay Lagoon (phone: 52230).

THE FRENCH SIDE

MARIGOT AND ENVIRONS

VERY EXPENSIVE

Le Poisson d'Or Small and select, this dining spot on the seaside terrace of a restored stone warehouse is one of Marigot's best. Start with the house aperitif—passion fruit, Armagnac, and champagne—before choosing from an exciting menu, which might include fresh lobster bisque, cassoulet of snails, or home-smoked spiny lobster in champagne butter. Try the chocolate cake; it's just this side of paradise. There is a charming art gallery in the historic building. Open daily. Reservations advised. Major credit cards accepted. Off Rue d'Anguille, a short walk from the port (phone: 877245).

Le Santal Housed in a splendid seaside villa just outside Marigot, this is one of the island's most refined dining rooms. The blue-and-white decor of the scalloped terrace matches the spectacular sea scenery reflected in cleverly placed mirrors. The enticing menu, in French and English, is pricey, but neither the food nor the service will disappoint. Very special are the fried rack of lamb with thyme and caramelized tomatoes, and the broiled red snapper with fennel, which is flambéed with Pernod. Open daily, but check ahead—the hours change frequently. Reservations advised. Major credit cards accepted. Seaside, west of Marigot Bridge (phone: 875348).

La Vie en Rose Overlooking Marigot's picturesque waterfront, this popular restaurant is as gastronomically appealing as it is astronomical in price. If you would like a table on the small seaside balcony, say so when you reserve. There are young geniuses in the kitchen, preparing a rather modified nouvelle cuisine, with menus that change daily with the availability of ingredients. A specialty is baked lobster with truffle sauce. Generally, the seafood is fresh and local and most meat imported, as are many vegetables and fruits. Certain seafood much loved by the French (scallops, shrimp, and fish such as monkfish or salmon) also are imported—at great expense. There's a pleasant tearoom downstairs. Open daily for dinner. Reservations necessary. Major credit cards accepted. Marigot Harbor (phone: 875442).

EXPENSIVE

La Calanque Marigot's landmark harborside restaurant for more than 25 years. In keeping with the French tradition, the menu changes frequently, but poultry and lobster always are featured in one or more variations, as are such French classics as chateaubriand and rack of lamb. Upstairs is an open terrace with a pretty view of the bay. Open daily; no lunch Sundays. Reservations advised. Major credit cards accepted. Blvd. de France (phone: 879967).

Davids The spinnaker hung in the rafters gives away the fact that it was two yachts-men, both Englishmen named David, who created this plain and very pleas-ant place. They serve conch fritters and beef Wellington as well as good, hearty steaks, poultry, and fish. A patio at the back puts you under the stars. The two bars are popular with jolly expats. Open daily; no lunch weekends. Reservations advised. Major credit cards accepted. Rue de la Liberté (phone: 875158).

Le Mini Club One of Marigot's oldest terrace restaurants, still under its original ownership, it is known especially for its big French/creole buffet (more than 35 dishes and endless carafes of French wine), usually offered Wednesday and Saturday evenings. The court bouillon (fish soup, creole-style), stuffed land crab, and dessert soufflés are all excellent. Open daily; no lunch Sundays. Reservations advised. Major credit cards accepted. Rue de la Liberté (phone: 875069).

GRAND CASE

EXPENSIVE

L'Auberge Gourmande This homey-chic country inn (lanterns, crystal, louvered windows, beams) serves such fine French fare as frogs' legs and beef ten-derloins with morel mushrooms. Because the chef hails from Burgundy, the menu emphasizes that region, including classic snails *bourguignon*. There's also a delicious cream of shrimp and scallop soup. Dinner only; closed Wednesdays and the months of June and July. Reservations neces-sary. MasterCard and Visa accepted (phone: 877337).

L'Escapade This eatery is in a pretty house with a softly lit, appealing dining room. The seafood is first-rate, with red snapper and lobster among the more popular main dishes, or duck breast with raspberry sauce for poultry fanciers. The escargots are as good as you will find on the island, while dessert favorites include creole pie (made with bananas and rum) and a creamy chocolate mousse cake. Open daily, with seatings at 7 and 9 PM; closed Mondays from April through December. Reservations advised. Major credit cards accepted. Seaside (phone: 877504).

Hévéa French cuisine with Niçoise accents is served in a tiny (10 tables) dining room decorated with china and island antiques. Specialties include duck liver pâté, red snapper *en papillote, noisettes d'agneau* (those little lamb riblets the French adore) in thyme and garlic sauce, and seafood and fish steamed in morel sauce. Open daily for dinner; closed the month of September. Reservations necessary. MasterCard and Visa accepted. At the *Hévéa* guesthouse, Grand Case (phone: 875685).

Rainbow A very pretty, very exclusive terraced dining room overlooking the begin-ning of Grand Case Beach serves "New American, freestyle" fare, meaning "a melting-pot menu of all nationalities." The menu changes frequently but might include smoked salmon sushi, or fricassee of shrimp and scallops with Caribbean chutney; fresh fish always is available. One of the more exquisite desserts is a strawberry, chocolate, and vanilla soup in a puff pastry. No pets, cigars, pipes, or children under 16. Seatings at 7 and 9:30 PM; closed Sundays. Reservations advised. Major credit cards accepted. 176 Blvd. de Grand Case (phone: 875580).

MODERATE

Café Panoramique This place is strikingly situated on a promontory between two beaches. The menu includes shrimp, broiled stuffed lobster tail, veal Milanese or Marsala, steaks, pasta, and more. Open daily. Reservations advised. Major credit cards accepted. In the *Grand Case Beach Club* (phone: 875187).

Chez Martine This intimate guesthouse dining room is warm pink, with a gingerbread terrace overlooking the beach. The menu includes winners like raw salmon and scallops marinated in lime juice, olive oil, and basil; snails in pastry with garlic and parsley sauce; quail and goose liver *en gelée de porc;* red snapper soufflé in two sauces; chicken breast stuffed with mushrooms and cranberries; and wonderful tournedos in roquefort sauce. Open daily. Reservations advised in season and on weekends. Major credit cards accepted. On the beach (phone: 875159).

ELSEWHERE ON THE FRENCH SIDE

VERY EXPENSIVE

The Restaurant Justifiably well-regarded, it's elegant and formal, with an airy arched terrace overlooking Long Bay, and the air fragrant with tropical flowers and West Indian spices. Ask for a table at the outer edge, under the thatch roof. The food is prepared by chef Marc Ehrler, a native of southern France, and the menu changes regularly according to the availability of fresh ingredients. Specials might include roasted rack of lamb or rock lobster *millefeuille,* layered with mashed potatoes and shredded black truffles. There's caviar—beluga, sevruga, and oscetra—for those who care to indulge. The ambience is romantic, and there's also a very respectable selection of French wines. Open daily for breakfast, lunch, and dinner; closed September and October. Reservations necessary. Major credit cards accepted. At *La Samanna,* Long Bay (phone: 875122).

EXPENSIVE

La Belle France Breezy West Indian–style restaurant at *Le Méridien L'Habitation* resort, where the house cocktail combines blue curaçao, amaretto, lemon juice, and champagne in a drink that promises to make your tastebuds sit up and take notice. Presentation is everything, whether it's the lobster salad with walnut oil or a whole local lobster that looks almost too good to eat. The filet mignon of veal with morel cream sauce is another aesthetic adventure, and desserts, with specials every day, are nothing short of sinful, including *blancmange* with pears and pear liqueur, mango melba, and *crème caramel*. Open daily for dinner. Reservations advised. Major credit cards accepted. Anse Marcel (phone: 876700).

Captain Oliver's Right on the border of the French and Dutch sides, across from the luxury complex of the same name, the seaside terrace here faces St. Barthélemy. The menu includes creamed crayfish soup, tuna tartare, grilled lobster flambéed in cognac, chicken *colombo,* and steak *frites.* Open daily. Reservations advised. Major credit cards accepted. Oyster Pond (phone: 873000).

Le Privilège *Le Privilège* complex (with its marina/shopping plaza behind *L'Habitation* and sports complex/disco on the cliff above) boasts two restaurants: *Le Privilège Grill,* featuring vichyssoise, *grillades* of fish, and salads; and the main dining room, which offers a conventional menu (fresh salmon stew with truffle juice; chicken breast with shrimp and ginger) as well as a low-calorie haute cuisine menu. Open daily. Reservations advised. Major credit cards accepted. Anse Marcel (phone: 873737).

La Provence This is the main restaurant of the deluxe *La Belle Créole* hotel, featuring fine French and creole specialties. Elegant dishes include salmon steaks with oysters in champagne sauce; earthier choices are available at the Monday-night barbecues. With an expansive view of the lagoon and ocean, the posh atmosphere extends from a formal indoor dining room to seating out on the terrace. Open daily for breakfast, lunch, and dinner. Reservations advised. Major credit cards accepted. At Pointe des Pierres à Chaux (phone: 875600).

La Rhumerie If it's authentic creole cooking you're after, this restaurant in a private house won't disappoint. Specialties include *poulet boucanne créole* (home-smoked chicken with baked green papayas and steamed, buttered cabbage hearts), herbed conch, curried goat, salad of *poisson coffre* (a local fish), and flavorfully spiced vegetables. There's also French fare, such as escargots, frogs' legs, and duck *à l'orange.* Open daily; no dinner Thursdays. Reservations advised. MasterCard and Visa accepted. Off the Marigot–Grand Case road near Colombier (phone: 875698).

MODERATE

Mark's Place Rather out of the way (unless you're staying at *L'Habitation* or planning to hit the *Privilège* disco at Anse Marcel) in a country setting, this extremely popular informal restaurant (it was recently chosen by the readers of *Caribbean Travel and Life* as among the best restaurants in the Caribbean) specializes in very fresh lobster and seafood, plus good creole dishes. Daily specials are listed on a blackboard and might include octopus or goat *colombo* (curried), while the *assiette créole* (*accra, boudin,* crab and *christophine farci*) is an interesting menu staple. Huge portions of very good food at very reasonable prices and the rustic atmosphere, overlooking the surrounding countryside and bay, have contributed to the restaurant's overwhelming success. Closed Mondays. Major credit cards accepted. French Cul-de-Sac (phone: 873450).

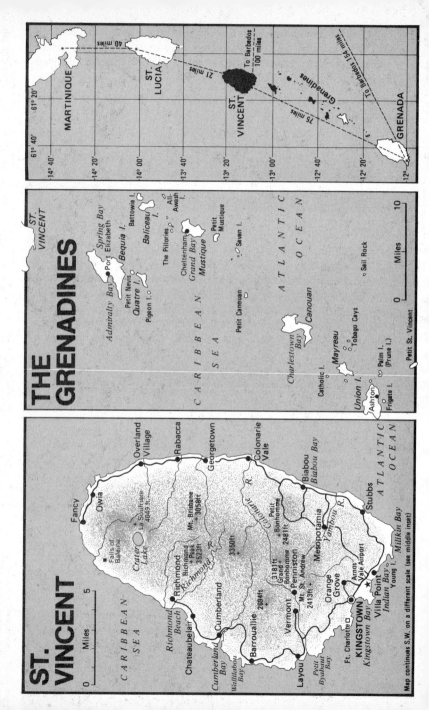

ST. VINCENT

CARIBBEAN SEA

0   Miles   5

Fancy

Owia

Overland Village

Rabacca

La Soufrière 4049 ft.

Crater Lake

Falls of Baleine

Richmond Beach

Chateaubelair

Richmond

Richmond Peak 3523 ft.

Mt. Brisbane 3058 ft.

Georgetown

Colonarie Vale

3350 ft.

Petit Bonhomme 2481 ft.

Biabou

Biabou Bay

Cumberland

Cumberland Bay

Barrouallie

2684 ft.

Vermont

Grand Bonhomme 3181 ft.

Mt. St. Andrew 2413 ft.

Penniston

Mesopotamia

Stubbs

Layou

Petit Byahaut Bay

Orange Grove

Arnos Vale Airport

Villa Point

Indian Bay

Young I.

Milikin Bay

KINGSTOWN

Ft. Charlotte

Kingstown Bay

ATLANTIC OCEAN

Map continues S.W. on a different scale (see middle inset)

THE GRENADINES

ST. VINCENT

Spring Bay

Port Elizabeth

Bequia I.

Admiralty Bay

Petit Nevis

Quatre I.

Pigeon I.

Battowia I.

Baliceau I.

Ali-Awash I.

The Pillories

Cheltenham Grand Bay

Mustique

Petit Mustique

Savan I.

CARIBBEAN SEA

Petit Canouan

Charlestown Bay

Canouan

Mayreau

Tobago Cays

Catholic I.

Sail Rock

Union I.

Ashton

Palm I. (Prune I.)

Frigate I.

ATLANTIC OCEAN

0   Miles   10

Petit St. Vincent

MARTINIQUE

ST. LUCIA

ST. VINCENT

To Barbados 100 miles

Grenadines

To Barbados 154 miles

GRENADA

40 miles

21 miles

75 miles

61° 20'

61° 40'

14° 40'

14° 20'

14° 00'

13° 40'

13° 20'

13° 00'

12° 40'

12° 20'

12°

St. Vincent and the Grenadines

A chain of more than 32 islands and cays anchored in the southeast Caribbean between St. Lucia and Grenada, St. Vincent and the Grenadines have long been known to sailors and yachtsmen for their many quiet bays, beautiful beaches, pristine water, and coral reefs. The island of St. Vincent, known locally as "the mainland," has a largely unexplored interior of staggeringly verdant mountains, alive with rushing rivers and waterfalls. The tiny Grenadines offer both the luxury and charm of the Caribbean, with none of the commercial clamor of its so-called glamor destinations.

Lively Kingstown, the major port and capital of St. Vincent, is not postcard pretty—this is still a Third World country—but it's a bustling center of inter-island sea traffic and trade. The island's uncluttered black sand volcanic beaches and tropically forested, mountainous landscapes make it a joy to explore: Hundreds of yachtsmen make it a regular stop on their annual voyages around the Caribbean, and land-based visitors fly in from the US, Canada, Europe, and surrounding small islands to relax here. A steady breeze provided by the northeast trade winds creates pleasant year-round temperatures of 78 to 80F. The moderate climate, plus St. Vincent's healthy supply of rain and fertile terrain, have made it one of the most cultivated isles of the West Indies, producing an abundance of fruits, vegetables, and arrowroot (once more popular as a medicinal herb, and now a coating for computer paper).

St. Vincent was one of the last strongholds of the Carib Indians; they managed to retard European colonization for almost two centuries after Columbus discovered the island and claimed it for Spain. However, by the 18th century, the French and the English were engaged in a bitter struggle for control of the Caribbean, and St. Vincent and the Grenadines were as much embroiled in the ongoing hostilities as any of the other islands. St. Vincent was passed between Britain and France three times during the 18th century, but in 1789 it became a British Crown Colony. It remained so until 1969, when it became a British Associated State. On October 27, 1979, St. Vincent and the Grenadines proclaimed complete independence from Great Britain. Still, emotional and economic ties remain strong, though unofficial.

Today, the islands reflect traces of many cultures—not just the English and the French. During the 18th century, while the Carib Indians were fighting off shiploads of Europeans, they were welcoming stranded black slaves from a ship wrecked off the coast. As a result of their hospitality, a new race of black Carib developed, which soon outnumbered the original tribe. During the mid-18th century, an influx of East Indian laborers and Portuguese settlers added new elements to the multiracial population (which currently numbers just over 106,000). But the lasting influence of the French and the English still can be observed in both language and local architecture.

The Grenadines have served as safe harbors and prime ports-of-call for yachts for years. The islands and cays are beautiful—with exquisitely clear water and white powder beaches—but economically poor. To sustain themselves, most Grenadinians turn to boat building, to seasonal labor on other islands, and, according to legend and local lore, to smuggling.

Life on St. Vincent and in the Grenadines is slow, simple, and relaxing. Tourists are welcomed with warmth and hospitality, but Tourism—with a capital T—has yet to hit these islands (though, judging from plans for building a cruise ship port in Kingstown, it's on its way). While Vincentians tend to be formal and reserved at first, their friendliness soon becomes apparent. Note that no one comes to these islands to shop or eat—these are not duty-free ports, and truly fine dining is found only at pricey resorts. Several of these have made some islands (like Mustique and Petit St. Vincent) the exclusive retreats of extremely well-off travelers; however, many spots on the islands are still inexpensive or moderately priced and very comfortable. If you don't mind unannounced changes in inter-island boat schedules, planes that may not arrive on time, and the occasional lack of hot water—and if you really want to do nothing but relax and enjoy the sea and some very nice people—St. Vincent and the Grenadines may well be the perfect group of hideaway islands for you.

St. Vincent and the Grenadines At-a-Glance

FROM THE AIR

St. Vincent looks like an imperfectly shaped oval kite with the Grenadines trailing below as its tail. Although only 18 miles long and 11 miles wide, St. Vincent has a richly varied terrain: many black sand beaches washed by calm waters on the west (Caribbean) coast, breakers rushing against steep cliffs and rocks on the east (Atlantic) coast, plantations, fertile valleys, rolling hills, winding rivers, forests, and, inland, a 4,049-foot volcanic mountain, La Soufrière. The island's capital, Kingstown, is a harbor city on the southwest corner of the island. Two miles from Kingstown is *E. T. Joshua Airport,* where flights land from Barbados and St. Lucia (the connecting point for flights from North America to St. Vincent and the Grenadines). St. Vincent lies 100 miles due west of Barbados, 24 miles south of St. Lucia, and 75 miles north of Grenada; it's about 1,600 miles from Miami and 2,100 miles from New York.

Although there are over 100 bodies of land in the Grenadines chain, the major islands running southward from St. Vincent are Bequia, Mustique, Canouan, Mayreau, Union, Palm, and Petit St. Vincent. Nearby Carriacou and Petit Martinique are part of the multi-island country of Grenada.

SPECIAL PLACES: ST. VINCENT

KINGSTOWN St. Vincent's capital and commercial center, with a population of roughly 15,500 is a lively, busy port. The waterfront, with island schooners unloading their cargoes and transatlantic freighters loading bananas and other island produce, is fascinating to watch. On Saturday mornings, the marketplace at the south end of town bursts with color and buzzes with activity when small farmers, fishermen, and merchants from all over the island come to town to sell yams, breadfruit, mangoes, papayas, soursop, colorful fish, and butchered meat. On Grenville Street is the 19th-century *St. Mary's Catholic Church,* a photogenic mishmash of architectural styles redesigned in the 1930s by a Flemish monk whose grasp of Romanesque, Gothic, and Moorish architecture was fanciful but flawed. Two more charming churches are on adjacent corners. On the north side of town, *Fort Charlotte* sits at the end of a winding road, on a promontory rising 636 feet above sea level. Named after the wife of King George III, the fort was built by the English to defend the island against the French. Three of the original cannon remain in place, and the living quarters of the military personnel have been turned into a museum containing a series of murals that depict black Carib history. The biggest attraction of *Fort Charlotte,* however, is the magnificent view of St. Vincent and the Grenadine Islands beyond. The fort is open daily. No admission charge (phone: 456-1165). East of the fort, on the north side of Kingstown, are the *Botanical Gardens,* the oldest of their kind in the Western Hemisphere (founded in 1765). The gardens cover 20 acres and encompass a formidable display of tropical plants, including a breadfruit tree grown from the original plant brought to St. Vincent from Tahiti by Captain Bligh in 1793. Open daily. No admission charge (phone: 457-1003). The gardens also are the site of the small, artifact-filled *National Museum,* which is open Wednesday mornings, Saturday afternoons, and when a cruise ship docks. Admission charge (phone: 457-1003).

LEEWARD HIGHWAY North from Kingstown, the road climbs a series of steep hills with magnificent views all along the way before descending close to the sea and leading to the village of Layou. Ask any of the villagers to show you the picture rock, which is one of several petroglyphs carved by Carib Indians over 13 centuries ago. Farther north is the whaling village of Barrouallie, where fishermen set out with harpoons in small, brightly painted boats to hunt pilot whales, just as they did in the 18th century. Barrouallie and the nearby Grenadine island of Bequia are two of the few places in the world where this type of whaling is still done. To finish your excursion with a swim, and perhaps lunch or a drink, continue on the Leeward Highway to Wallilabou Beach near Richmond before returning to Kingstown.

WINDWARD SIDE HIGHWAY A drive along St. Vincent's eastern Atlantic coast from Kingstown features the coastal surf pounding against rocky shores, banana and coconut plantations, arrowroot fields, and gently sloping hills set in a peaceful landscape. However, things here aren't always so peaceful; tropical storms can seriously damage St. Vincent's banana and coconut crops. You may need a four-wheel-drive vehicle to venture past Rabacca Dry River (actually an old lava flow path) to the northern tip of the island. Check with the tourist board before setting out (see *Tourist Information, below*). A popular excursion is the hike up La Soufrière, which starts at Bamboo Range. Hikers pass from a lowland forest into a tropical rain forest and finally into cloud cover as they climb to the lip of the volcanic crater. A guide for this hike is advisable (see *Mountain Climbing, below*).

MARRIAQUA VALLEY (ALSO CALLED THE MESOPOTAMIA VALLEY) Another area worth visiting on St. Vincent. The journey begins at the Vigie Highway, just east of the *E. T. Joshua Airport* runway, and continues northeast, then north, to the town of Mesopotamia. The route passes freshwater streams, boys on donkeys, terraced farms, winding rivers, and deep forests before heading north to *Montreal Gardens* (about 12 miles from Kingstown), where there are natural mineral springs, as well as tropical flowers and plants. Open daily. No admission charge (phone: 458-5452).

QUEEN'S DRIVE This trip loops into the high hills and steep ridges east of Kingstown. Begin at Sion Hill, just southeast of Kingstown, halfway to the *E. T. Joshua Airport*. After turning northeast and driving a very short distance (about a city block), veer sharply right and climb Dorsetshire Hill to Millers Ridge, where the road will turn south and then head back toward the airport, with breathtaking views of the Grenadines and Kingstown along the way.

SPECIAL PLACES: THE GRENADINES

Most of the 100 or more islands and islets that make up the Grenadines appear as mere dots on yachtsmen's charts. Stretching southward from St. Vincent, the major islands administered by St. Vincent are described below.

BEQUIA Northernmost of the Grenadines and 9 miles south of St. Vincent, Bequia (pronounced *Beck*-wee), a picturesque island, is home to boat builders and sailors, and is one of the last whaling stations in the world where humpback whales still are captured by hand-hurled harpoons. The *International Whaling Federation (IWF)* has granted the country permission to take two whales per year for food, but the whalers will probably become extinct long before the whales do; only one harpooner is still alive, and just one whale has been captured in the last seven years. Bequia's largest town, Port Elizabeth, sits at the edge of sheltered Admiralty Bay. The *Bequia Tourist Bureau* (see *Tourist Information, below*) dispenses information, sells postcards and stamps, and will recommend a driver to take visitors around the island (settle on the price in advance). Be sure to see several sites: the fort, which offers a sweeping view of the harbor; Industry Bay and Spring, where you can stop for a swim and a curry lunch; lovely Lower Bay, with its popular *De Reef* restaurant (see *Eating Out*); the beaches of Princess Margaret and Friendship Bay; Paget Farm, the last whalers' village, opposite Petit Nevis; the steep vista point, which offers a 360-degree view of St. Vincent and the islands south; and Moonhole, a remarkable American community built into the cliffs at the southern end of the island—the cave-like stone homes are private, but daily tours are offered (phone: 458-3277). In town, stop by *Mauvin's* or the *Sargeant Brothers* shop, where artisans craft beautifully accurate sailboat and ship models (see *Shopping*). Be sure to stroll the narrow walkway between the *Porthole* café and the *Plantation House* (see *Checking In*), formerly called and still often referred to as the *Sunny Caribee*. Here is a browse-worthy string of souvenir and craft shops (*Crab Hole,* with its silk-screening studio, is a standout; see *Shopping*), small restaurants, and snack bars. The adventurous can climb the path over the headland to Princess Margaret Beach, with a stone arch and grotto at the far end, then over the next bluff to Lower Bay Beach.

MUSTIQUE Princess Margaret, David Bowie, and Raquel Welch are only the most famous of the wealthy people who own homes on this carefully manicured private island, about 15 miles south of St. Vincent. About half of the mansions can be rented when the owners are not in residence; high-season prices, which include staff and car, range from about $2,500 a week for a two-bedroom villa to $15,000 for a six-bedroom house (Princess Margaret's place goes for a mere $6,500 in high season). Rentals are handled by the *Mustique Co. Ltd.* (see *Checking In*). Among the other lodging possibilities here are *Cotton House,* an exquisitely restored cotton estate, and *Firefly House* (see *Checking In* for more information on both places). Besides the magnificent mansions, don't miss Macaroni Beach, a lovely stretch of powder-white sand flanked by clear turquoise water, or the calmer waters of Gelliceaux Bay. *Basil's Bar* (see *Eating Out*), one of the many enterprises run by successful entrepreneur Basil Charles, is where the yachting crowd gathers to drink and socialize, albeit at exorbitant prices.

CANOUAN Progress has at last hit sleepy little Canouan with the early 1995 opening of the huge (by local standards) 45-room *Tamarind Beach,* a hotel, yacht, and beach club on Charleston Bay (see *Checking In*). Before its arrival, the island had changed little since the 18th century, and most of it will probably remain unspoiled—despite plans for a second, much larger hotel complex in the future. Frequented mostly by yachtsmen, Canouan's many exquisite white sand beaches remain pristine, and there is easy, pleasant hiking to the ruins of an old cathedral in the hills.

TOBAGO CAYS These four tiny islets and their waters are protected as a national park; though uninhabited, they have camping and picnic sites, handsomely protected anchorages for overnighting yachts, and incredibly beautiful snorkeling reefs. A must stop on any cruise.

MAYREAU Long a favorite yacht anchorage and now occasionally visited by cruise ships, this 1½-square-mile island boasts a tropical-gardened, South Seas–style hotel, the *Salt Whistle Bay Club,* with villas, outdoor dining, and some yacht-charter and cruising facilities (see *Checking In*). Its stone villas and dining terrace are set back among sea grape, palm, and casuarina trees, on one of the world's most beautiful beaches. A tiny village (population 190; farm animals, 200+) with three simple, open-air restaurants is a 20-minute walk along a pleasant trail over a cactus-studded hill (wear shoes, not sandals). From the village, the view of Union Island is stunning.

UNION ISLAND The southernmost of the Grenadines, mountainous Union Island is a well-known port of call for yachts. It has a small but busy airstrip, a few small inns, and a very French boaters' hangout, the *Anchorage Yacht Club* (see *Checking In*). It's also a connecting point for launch access to nearby Petit St. Vincent and Palm Island, as well as the secluded islands of Mayreau and the national "water park" that surrounds the uninhabited Tobago Cays. The *Union Island Tourist Board* is open daily (see *Tourist Information, below*).

YOUNG, PETIT ST. VINCENT, AND PALM ISLANDS These three private islands in the Grenadines are essentially resorts whose guests constitute the majority of the population. Young Island, 200 yards south of St. Vincent, is known for its South Seas atmosphere. The other two, about 40 miles south of Kingstown, are reached by flying to Union Island (see *Inter-Island Flights, below*), where the resort's launches pick up guests.

Sources and Resources

TOURIST INFORMATION

The *St. Vincent Department of Tourism* (*Administrative Centre,* Bay St., Kingstown; phone: 457-1502) has information on accommodations and sightseeing and also carries *Escape,* the St. Vincent and the Grenadines tourist guide, which provides helpful facts, background information, and travel advice. The office is closed weekends. A satellite desk is open daily at *E. T. Joshua Airport* in Arnos Vale. There's also a St. Vincent and the Grenadines information desk in Barbados, in the arrivals area at *Grantley Adams International Airport* (open daily until the last flight to St. Vincent has left). Bequia has its own tourist information office (closed Saturday afternoons; on the waterfront in Port Elizabeth; phone: 458-3286), as does Union Island (open daily; at Clifton; phone: 458-8350). For information about St. Vincent and the Grenadines tourist offices in the US, see GETTING READY TO GO.

LOCAL COVERAGE Two weekly newspapers are published on St. Vincent: the *Vincentian* and the *News;* both come out on Fridays. In addition, *Discover St. Vincent,* a free information booklet, is available in most shops and hotels. For an overview, a lovely coffee-table book is available in shops and some hotels: *St. Vincent and the Grenadines—A Plural Country,* by Dana Jinkins and Jill Bobrow (Concepts Publishing; $35).

RADIO AND TELEVISION In addition to the local government-owned AM radio (705) and TV stations, there is cable TV and other television programming beamed in from Barbados by BTS.

TELEPHONE The area code for St. Vincent and the Grenadines is 809. When calling within an island or from one island to another, you need dial only the seven-digit local number. Dial 999 for the police; 61185 for an ambulance.

ENTRY REQUIREMENTS Proof of citizenship (a passport is preferred, but a birth certificate or voter's registration card, accompanied by a photo ID, will do) and a return or ongoing ticket are the only documents required of US or Canadian citizens. St. Vincent charges an airport departure tax of about $7.50 ($20 EC).

CLIMATE AND CLOTHES The thermometer hovers around 78 to 80F (25 to 26C) all year in St. Vincent and the Grenadines, and the northeast trade winds bring gentle breezes that temper the tropical heat. The mountains of St. Vincent attract more rain than the flatter atolls of the Grenadines. Summers are stiller and more humid, while August through December is the rainy season. Dress on the islands is very casual: Women wear bright blouses, skirts, slacks, jeans, and modest shorts; bikinis on the beach, but not in town. (Topless and nude sunbathing are illegal.) Men wear slacks, shorts, and sport shirts; neither jacket nor tie is needed, although St. Vincent is a little more formal than the Grenadines. Few resorts and even fewer restaurants are air conditioned in the Grenadines, so pack accordingly. Insect repellent always is a good idea, especially in the evenings. If you find mosquito netting and "incense coils" in your hotel room, take the hint and use them.

MONEY The Eastern Caribbean dollar is the official currency of the islands. The rate of exchange is currently about $2.70 EC ($2.50 to $2.68 EC in stores) to $1 US. When shopping, always be certain which dollars—EC or US—are being quoted. US and Canadian dollars are accepted in most restaurants, hotels, and stores, as are traveler's checks. Most hotels and many restaurants honor major US credit cards. Banking hours on St. Vincent are weekdays from 8 AM to noon or 1 PM and also Fridays from 3 to 5 PM; *Barclays Bank* is open Fridays from 8 AM to 5 PM. Some Kingstown banks are open Saturday mornings. All prices in this chapter are quoted in US dollars.

LANGUAGE English is spoken, sometimes in a West Indian patois.

TIME St. Vincent and the Grenadines are in the atlantic standard time zone, one hour ahead of eastern standard time (when it's noon in New York, it's 1 PM in St. Vincent). During daylight saving time, the hour is the same in both places.

CURRENT Except for Petit St. Vincent, where the current is 110 volts, 60 cycles, electricity generally operates at 220 volts, 60 cycles. American appliances must have converters. Some hotels can supply them, but it's more prudent to bring one along. Young Island and Mustique's *Cotton House* use British-style three-prong plugs.

TIPPING Most hotels add a 10% to 15% service charge to the bill, and that takes care of room maids and other staff. If a service charge is not added, tip bell-hops 50¢ to $1 per bag (with a $1 minimum), room maids $1 to $2 per person per day; ask the manager what is customary for waiters. Tip taxi drivers 10% of the fare. Restaurants usually include a 10% service charge in the tab; if not, give the waiter a 10% tip, 15% if you're especially pleased with the service.

GETTING AROUND

BUS Small, colorfully painted vans set out from Market Square in Kingstown and run along all the main roads. They are inexpensive, efficient, and fun. Just stick your hand out anywhere along the road and they'll stop for you. You pay when you disembark; rates run from about $1 to $6 EC (40¢ to $2 US at press time). Van owners love music, so be prepared to listen to some mega-decibel reggae.

CAR RENTAL Car rental firms in Kingstown include *David's Auto Clinic* (Sion Hill; phone: 457-1116), *Hertz* (Grenville St.; phone: 456-1743), *Kim's Rentals* (Grenville St.; phone: 456-1884), and *Sunshine* in Arnos Vale (phone: 456-5380). On Bequia, there's *Phil's Rental* (phone: 458-8304). Car rental is more expensive on Mustique; try the *Cotton House* and *Mustique Co. Ltd.* (see *Checking In* for both). A temporary driver's license is required and may be obtained at the airport, or in Kingstown at the police station on Bay Street or the *Licensing Authority* on Halifax Street. A valid US, Canadian, or international driver's license must be presented; there's a $40 EC fee (about $15). Remember that driving is on the *left.* And be very careful; there are lots of curves and sharp turns in the roads—sound your horn beforehand and be certain you're still on the left after the turn.

FERRY SERVICES For information about ferry schedules and services, check the free *Discover St. Vincent* booklet available in most shops and hotels, or just ask at your hotel. Currently, there is service to Bequia daily on the MV

Admiral I and *Admiral II* (phone: 458-3348), plus trips to Union Island via Bequia, to Canouan, and to Mayreau every other day. The island schooner *Sand Island* (phone: 458-3472) is *very* basic, and unpleasant in rough weather; it sails to Bequia every day except Sunday. The MV *Snapper* (no phone), also known as "the mail boat," travels south, making the circuit from St. Vincent to Bequia, Canouan, Mayreau, and Union Island Mondays, Thursdays, and Saturdays; and back north from Union Island to Mayreau, Canouan, Bequia, and St. Vincent on Tuesdays and Fridays; and finally from Union Island nonstop to St. Vincent Saturdays. All vessels take one to one-and-a-half hours to travel between St. Vincent and Bequia and charge the same fare of a few dollars. The trip from St. Vincent to Union Island is about six hours. The *Petit St. Vincent* and *Palm Island Beach Club* resorts arrange launch pickups at Union Island for arriving guests (see "Enchanted Private Islands" in *Checking In*).

INTER-ISLAND FLIGHTS Note that delays are common, but usually not outrageous. Your hotel can book your connecting flight from Barbados when you reserve a room; remember to confirm it and your return flight 72 hours before departure. Many planes have just six or eight seats; bring earplugs if you're sensitive to noise. *LIAT* (phone: 457-2641 or 457-1821) has daily scheduled flights from Barbados to Mustique and Union Island via St. Vincent, and between St. Vincent and St. Lucia and all the way down the chain to Caracas, Venezuela. *Air Martinique* (phone: 458-4528 on St. Vincent; 458-8328 on Union Island; 458-8888 on Canouan) operates twice daily to St. Vincent and Union Island from Martinique, via St. Lucia and Barbados. *SVG Air* (phone: 456-5610; fax: 458-4697) handles local charters, including direct Barbados-Mustique, Barbados-Bequia, and Barbados–Union Island flights. If your destination is one of the other Grenadines, you must take another short flight from St. Vincent or board a boat in Kingstown. The Grenada-based *Airlines of Carriacou* (phone: 444-3549 or 444-2898; reservations also can be booked through *LIAT*) flies daily from Bequia to St. Vincent, then on to Union Island, Carriacou, and Grenada; it also flies nonstop daily from Bequia to Union Island. *Mustique Airways* (phone: 458-4380 in St. Vincent; 458-3183 in Bequia; 800-526-4789, ext. 301; or 201-891-1111 in New Jersey) has frequent and efficient "shared charter" service from Barbados to St. Vincent, Mustique, and Bequia; flights meet and wait for your major carrier's arrival even if it's delayed. *Mustique Airways* also runs a shuttle between St. Vincent and Bequia. *Grenadines Reservations* (phone: 456-5645) can help with schedules and booking.

MOTORBIKES Motorbikes are available on Mustique from *Mustique Co. Ltd.* (see *Checking In*) and on St. Vincent at *Sailor's Cycle & Fitness Centre* (Kingstown; phone: 457-1712).

SIGHTSEEING TOURS Minibus or taxi tours may be arranged through the tourist office, which has a trained Tour Guide Unit; your hotel; or the *Taxi Drivers*

Association (phone: 457-1807). Tour operators in Kingstown include *Barefoot Holidays* (phone: 456-9334), *Global Travel* (phone: 456-1601), *Grenadine Travel Company* (phone: 458-4818), and *Paradise Tours* (phone: 458-5417). On Bequia, try *Sam's Taxi Tours* (phone: 458-3686) or *Lighthouse Tours* (phone: 457-3187). Recommended taxi drivers include Curtis "Challenger" (phone: 458-3811 or 458-3342), Gideon (phone: 458-3760), and Noel (phone: 458-3064). Your hotel also can reach them by marine radio.

TAXI Plentiful and unmetered, with rates set by the government; consult the free *Discover St. Vincent* booklet for information on fares. Agree on the rate with the driver—or ask someone at your hotel to do so—before getting into any cab. On Bequia, water taxis zip to the beaches from the *Frangipani* and *Plantation House* hotels (see *Checking In* for both). Many of the taxi drivers provide good, well-informed, guided tours (see *Sightseeing Tours,* above).

SPECIAL EVENTS

The St. Vincent *Carnival* (also known as *Vincy Mas*), held in late June through mid-July, is a week-long celebration with traditional parades, dancing, music, steel band and calypso competitions, and feasting. Other holidays, when stores and businesses close, are *New Year's Day, St. Vincent and the Grenadines* (or *National Heroes*) *Day* (January 22), *Good Friday* (April 5 in 1996), *Easter Monday* (April 8 in 1996), *Labour Day* (first Monday in May), *Whitmonday* (May 27 in 1996), *Caricom Day* (second Monday in July), *Carnival Day* (second Tuesday in July), *Emancipation Day* (first Monday in August), *Independence Day* (October 27), *Christmas,* and *Boxing Day* (December 26). In December, Mustique entrepreneur Basil Charles and local homeowner Lady Thouche cohost a barbecue on the beach to benefit the tiny *Island School.* But you don't have to pull any strings to get in; just pull out your wallet and pay the hefty admission charge, and you're more than welcome. Details are available at *Basil's Bar* (see *Eating Out*).

SHOPPING

Although St. Vincent and the Grenadines aren't shoppers' paradises, a number of stores offer batik and tie-dyed fabrics, and various handicrafts. The Saturday marketplace in Kingstown has the liveliest shopping, although the bill of fare is fresh produce and staples—there's not much you can carry home, except, perhaps, a bottle of locally made hot sauce (pure fire if taken in heavy doses, but delicious when used sparingly). In general, stores are open weekdays from 8 AM to noon and 1 to 4 PM, Saturdays from 8 AM to noon. Among the stores worth including in your shopping itinerary are the following:

Basil's Boutique Owned by local businessman Basil Charles, this shop offers unusual Balinese batik items, including resortwear, as well as hand-painted T-shirts and curiosities. Mustique (phone: 458-4621).

Crab Hole Nestled on the beach by the *Plantation House,* it features unique clothing and accessories for men, women, and kids. The sports clothes, hats, totes, bikinis, and pareos are all hand-sewn in original silk-screened cottons that you can watch being printed in the workshop out back. Closed July through October. Port Elizabeth, Belmont, Bequia (phone: 458-3290).

Garden Boutique Exquisite hand-dyed blouses, locally made batik dresses, and jewelry. Port Elizabeth, Bequia (phone: 458-3892).

Giggles Fine designer clothes for women. *Cobblestone Arcade,* Kingstown, St. Vincent (phone: 457-1174).

Local Color One of Bequia's best shops, it offers a wide selection of T-shirts, hand-painted bathing suits, jewelry, and tropical clothing. Port Elizabeth, Bequia (phone: 458-3202).

Made in de Shade Imported women's fashions plus the work of local artists. In the *Heron* hotel, Bay St., Kingstown, St. Vincent (phone: 457-2364), and at the *Gingerbread* complex, Port Elizabeth, Bequia (phone: 458-3001).

Mauvin's Model Boat Shop Beautifully hand-crafted model boats; you can even order a copy of your own yacht. Port Elizabeth, Bequia (phone: 458-3669).

Melinda's One-of-a-kind hand-painted T-shirts. Port Elizabeth, Bequia (phone: 458-3895).

Noah's Arkade A must-see for crafts—local and imported—this place also specializes in locally made tropical clothing, herbal teas, spices, and a wealth of books: cookbooks, guidebooks, and children's books, as well as volumes on Caribbean literature, politics, marine life, and nature. Two locations: on St. Vincent at Bay St., Kingstown (phone: 457-1513), and on Bequia at the *Frangipani* hotel, Port Elizabeth (phone: 458-3424).

St. Vincent Craftsmen Center Noted specialists in local and imported crafts, including straw hats, wood bowls, and carvings. Frenches St., Kingstown, St. Vincent (phone: 457-2516).

Sam McDowell Scrimshaw by an expatriate American artist. Paget Farm, Bequia (phone: 458-3865).

Sargeant Brothers Hand-crafted model boats. Port Elizabeth, Bequia (phone: 458-3344).

Solana's A crafts shop featuring the work of Caribbean artisans. Port Elizabeth, Bequia (phone: 458-3554).

Sprotties Original hand-painted and silk-screened clothing. Port Elizabeth, Bequia (phone: 458-3904 or 458-4749), and Bay St., Kingstown, St. Vincent (phone: 456-1647).

Treasure A fine selection of gifts, including local crafts and upscale beachwear in the pink and purple cottages across from *Basil's Bar*. Mustique (phone: 456-3521).

Y. de Lima High-quality jewelry, china, and crystal. Corner of Bay and Egmont Sts., St. Vincent (phone: 477-1681).

SPORTS

Basically it's the sea—swimming, snorkeling, scuba diving, fishing, yachting, and sailing—that brings people here.

BOATING It's a way of life in these islands—the most outstanding sailing grounds of the entire Caribbean. Various types of craft are available: Sunfish or Sailfish can be borrowed or rented from some hotels, such as *Young Island* resort or *Sunset Shores* on St. Vincent (see *Checking In* for both). Also check the *Sunsports* facilities on Bequia (phone: 458-3577), as well as the hotels at Friendship Bay. Day sails are extremely popular in the Grenadines and easily arranged; check with your hotel or call Captain Ivan Oliver on the sailboat *Bella Vita* (phone: 458-4304). The *Young Island, Palm Island,* and *Petit St. Vincent* hotels offer regular day sails, as do the *Canouan Beach* and *Tamarind Beach* hotels on Canouan, and the *Cotton House* on Mustique. On Bequia, day charters on the S/Y *Pelangi* (phone: 458-3255) and the 50-foot catamaran *Passion* (phone: 458-3884) can be arranged to Mustique, the St. Vincent coast, and the Tobago Cays for snorkeling or fishing. Any hotel can recommend other yachts. On Union Island, you can sail on the gaff-rigged schooner *Scaramouche* (phone: 458-8418), with a fine lunch and open bar. *Wind & Sea Ltd.* (phone: 458-8647 or 458-8878; fax: 458-8569) at the *Anchorage Yacht Club* on Union Island also offers group day sails.

Bareboat and skippered yacht charters are also available through *Barefoot Yacht Charters* on St. Vincent (phone: 456-9526), *Nicholson Yacht Charters* (phone: 460-1530 or 617-255-0555), and the *Lagoon Marina* and the *Young Island* resort. On Union Island, Captain Yannis at the *Anchorage Yacht Club* usually knows which yachts are currently offering charters in the Grenadines. On Bequia, check with the *Frangipani* resort or *Bequia Marina* (phone: 458-3272). *Baleine Tours* (phone: 457-4089) offers powerboat rentals. *Dive St. Vincent* (phone: 457-4714), on Villa Beach, a stretch of land opposite Young Island, offers speedboat trips along the west coast to the Falls of Baleine, a 60-foot waterfall, and Wallilabou. For a slower, quieter experience, the *Sea Breeze* guesthouse (Arnos Vale, St. Vincent; phone: 458-4969) sponsors a sailing trip to the Falls of Baleine on a 36-foot sloop that leaves from Indian Bay. (See *Checking In* for hotel information not otherwise given above.)

HORSEBACK RIDING Arrange through Mustique's *Cotton House* (see *Checking In*).

MOUNTAIN CLIMBING St. Vincent is one of the few sites on earth where you can climb an active volcano, the 4,049-foot La Soufrière, which last erupted on

Friday the 13th, 1979 (and is closely monitored by seismologists). A guide is not essential for the four-hour (each way) climb, as the path has been much improved recently. However, it's advisable to hire a guide with a four-wheel-drive vehicle to get you to the starting point. Robert and Andrew have been highly recommended, and your hotel or the tourist board (see *Tourist Information*) can put you in touch with them. (If you go alone, first phone the tourist board for reports of any rumblings that you should know about.) If the summit is obscured by clouds, be patient: The clouds eventually will part, rewarding you with a stunning view of the deep crater itself. From this height on a clear day, you can see Grenada to the south and St. Lucia to the north.

An equally strenuous trek leads through thick bush to Trinity Falls, three waterfalls mid-island that definitely require a guide to reach. Contact Charles Meistrell of the *Petit Byahaut* resort to arrange for a guide (see *Checking In*). A much easier, scenic hike is the *Vermont Nature Trail*, with two circular routes through the forest and spectacular views at the rest stops. It's located 20 minutes from Kingstown on the western side of the island near the village of Vermont. Any taxi driver can take you there; arrange to be picked up about three hours later. For additional details on both treks, see *Climbing and Hiking* in DIVERSIONS.

SNORKELING AND SCUBA DIVING St. Vincent and Bequia are unquestionably among the top dive sites in the Caribbean; the quality, if not the quantity, of reefs easily matches that in the more well-known Caymans and Bonaire. Noted for healthy, colorful, hard and soft coral and abundant fish life, these crystal-clear waters are an underwater photographer's paradise. Remains of a centuries-old galleon were recently discovered in Kingstown harbor at about 80 feet, though the most colorful dives are along the leeward coast. On Bequia, Devil's Table, the Wall, and the Bullet are excellent sites. Sunken freighters, sailboats, and gunboats lie off Bequia, Mayreau, and Mustique. The Tobago Cays are truly world class reefs, and so shallow (15 to 30 feet) that snorkeling will reveal the rich aquatic life just as well as scuba diving.

Snorkel equipment is available at virtually every hotel and beachside restaurant. Most dive shops offer full gear rental and tank fills, plus three-hour, "dive today" resort courses, five-day certification courses, and night dives. (Many shops work together to allow you to complete the course and do your open-water dives as you sail the many islands of the Grenadines; inquire before you fly down.)

Dive St. Vincent (phone: 457-4714) on Villa Beach across from Young Island also does snorkel-dive motorboat trips to the remote and fabulous Falls of Baleine; or try *St. Vincent Dive Experience* (phone: 456-9741). On Bequia, there's *Dive Bequia* (phone: 458-3504); *Sunsports* (phone: 458-3577), next to the *Frangipani* hotel; the *Bequia Beach Club* (phone: 458-3563); and *Dive Paradise* (phone: 458-3563) at the *Friendship Bay* hotel.

Other dive shops include *Mustique Watersports* (phone: 456-3522) on Mustique, *Grenadines Dive* (phone: 458-8138) or *Dive Anchorage* (phone: 458-8221) on Union Island, and *Dive Canouan* (phone: 458-8648) on Canouan.

SPORT FISHING Most hotels and dive shops can arrange a fishing boat. Bring your own rod and reel. Some charter yachts, like the 50-foot catamaran *Passion* on Bequia (see *Boating*), are equipped with deep-sea fishing gear. The catch includes sailfish, marlin, snapper, dolphin, kingfish, tuna, bonito, blue runner, mackerel, jack, grouper, and pompano. Note that spearfishing is not allowed here.

SQUASH The *Prospect Racquet Club* (Prospect, 4 miles outside Kingstown; phone: 458-4866) has two courts, and the *Grand View Racquet Club* at the *Grand View Beach* hotel (see *Checking In*) has one.

SWIMMING AND SUNNING Villa Beach, across from Young Island, is the only white (actually tan) sand beach on St. Vincent; many small hotels are located along it. The rest of St. Vincent's beaches are volcanic black sand, with facilities only at Wallilabou. Use extreme caution on the windward side: The waves are rough and the undertow strong.

All Grenadines beaches are white sand, and some, like Salt Whistle Bay on Mayreau, rank among the world's best (its Saline Bay isn't bad either). On Bequia, try Princess Margaret, Lower Bay, and Friendship Bay; for seclusion and an end-of-the-earth feel, go to the inaptly named Industry Bay and Spring. Other wonderful strands include Charleston and Glossy Bays on Canouan, Macaroni Beach on Mustique, and Richmond and Chatham Bays on Union Island. Private isles Palm and Petit St. Vincent are ringed with white sand.

TENNIS On St. Vincent, courts are at the *Prospect Racquet Club* (see *Squash*, above), the *Emerald Valley* hotel, *Young Island* resort, and the *Grand View Beach* hotel; on Bequia at the *Plantation House, Spring on Bequia, Friendship Bay,* and *Frangipani;* they're also at the *Petit St. Vincent* and *Palm Island* resorts; and on Mustique at the *Cotton House* (see *Checking In* for all hotels).

WINDSURFING Available on St. Vincent at the *Young Island* resort, where lessons also are offered, and on Mustique at the *Cotton House* hotel, which has equipment, but no instruction. Windsurfing boards also are available on Bequia at the *Frangipani, Friendship Bay,* and *Plantation House* hotels, at the *Bequia Beach Club* (see *Snorkeling and Scuba Diving*), and at *De Reef* restaurant (see *Eating Out*). See *Checking In* for hotel information.

NIGHTLIFE

Choices on and around St. Vincent include the tiny *Emerald Valley* hotel casino (see *Checking In*), with blackjack, roulette, and slot machines worlds away from Las Vegas; closed Tuesdays (for additional details, see *Casino Countdown* in DIVERSIONS). In Kingstown, jazz lovers flock to *The Attic* (phone: 457-2558) for dining and music. *Aquatic Club* (Villa Beach; phone: 458-4205), next to the Young Island landing pier, is a popular disco. It has a live band two or three nights a week, followed by disco music until the last guest leaves; Saturday night sees big action here. Otherwise, most after-dark diversion is provided by the hotels. The *Young Island* resort has music four nights a week, but most of the action is over well before midnight; once a week the hotel's guests are shuttled a short distance by boat for a memorable cocktail party on tiny Rock Fort Island, where flaming torches light the hundred stone steps spiraling up to 18th-century *Fort Duvernette* (locally called Rock Fort). Non-guests must reserve, as space on the rock is limited. See *Checking In* for details on hotels listed above.

In the Grenadines, most resort hotels have weekly beach barbecues or jump-ups (so called because the lively island music makes one want to jump up and dance). On Bequia, don't miss the *Frangipani* jump-up on Thursday nights; the *Friendship Bay* hotel also has occasional jump-ups (see *Checking In* for both hotels). On Mustique, there's a jump-up every Wednesday night at *Basil's Bar,* a nightspot that's extremely popular with yachtspeople, jet set execs, and even with some of the island's celebrity homeowners (see *Eating Out*).

Best on the Islands

CHECKING IN

The best hotels on these islands are worlds unto themselves, offering casual, pampered luxury and seclusion. They can be very expensive, but in most cases they are worth it, if you can afford from about $300 to almost $700 for two per day in winter (with all meals). Resorts listed below as expensive run between $170 to $300 a day for two in winter, without meals. Some accommodations offer island ambience and amenities at more moderate prices: $100 to $170 for two per day in winter, and some of these even include breakfast and dinner in the rate. It's also possible to get a basic room without meals for between $50 and $100—such places are listed here as inexpensive. Prices drop by about 30% in summer. A tax of 5% is added to all hotel bills, and most hotels also add a 10% to 15% service charge in lieu of tipping. All hotels listed below accept Visa and MasterCard unless otherwise indicated.

About half of the mansions on Mustique can be rented when their owners aren't around; prices range from about $2,500 a week for a two-bedroom villa to $15,000 for a six-bedroom house in high season, including staff and car. Contact *Mustique Co. Ltd.* (phone: 458-4621 on Mustique; 457-1531 on St. Vincent; 800-557-4255; 212-696-4566 in New York City).

Many hotels, including a number of luxury resorts, do not have air conditioning; the constant tropical breezes and ceiling fans do keep things comfortable, and most accommodations are fully screened. However, the tropics always are somewhat humid, so if air conditioning is important to you, inquire before booking your reservation. Unless otherwise noted, all hotels listed below feature air conditioning, telephones, TV sets, and private baths. All telephone numbers are in the 809 area code unless otherwise indicated.

We begin with our favorite havens (all but *Salt Whistle Bay Club*, in the "expensive" category, considered "very expensive"), followed by recommended hotels listed by price category.

ENCHANTED PRIVATE ISLANDS

Cotton House, Mustique Once part of a working sugar plantation, this gem of a hotel was refurbished and decorated by the late set designer Oliver Messel. Intriguing English and Caribbean antiques—sea chests, silver, brasses, and a marvelous secretary's desk covered with cockle shells—decorate the main building's public room, which is ringed with wide, breezy verandahs. Guest accommodations are in pretty, comfortable cottages spaced widely around the lovely grounds. The 20 rooms (including seven suites) have private patios and stocked mini-fridges (but no TV sets). Daytime is casual, with sunning, lolling, and complimentary water sports as favored activities, though there's also tennis (on two courts), horseback riding, and an elegant hilltop swimming pool. Nights are somewhat dressier, but a jacket is never required. The British-American management is especially warm and welcoming, with one caveat: A British wag once wrote, "Mustique is best described as a house party, to which, if you have not been invited, it might be better not to come." Translation: Rich and famous Mustique homeowners tend to use *Cotton House* as extra guest bedrooms. However, if you seek true seclusion and plenty of rest and relaxation (Mustique has no town, little shopping, and one bar), you'll love it here. Free transportation by van, with un-island-like punctuality. All meals are included in the rate. Mustique (phone and fax: 456-4777; 800-223-1108; 914-763-5526 in New York).

Palm Island Beach Club After sailing around the world solo—and risking death several times to do it—John Caldwell came with his wife, Mary, to the Caribbean. They discovered a bald, 110-acre islet, planted hundreds of palm trees, and opened a small hotel in 1967. They, now with the help of their sons, have been expanding and improving it ever since. Lining stunning Casuarina Beach are 12 homey cottages, each housing two suites with solar-powered hot water. All units feature screened, louvered windows and walls, as well as ceiling fans (but no air conditioning, TV sets, or telephones). This is a classic Caribbean getaway, with a truly exquisite beach, stunning views of craggy Union Island, and no technology to distract you from the glories of nature. A narrow stone path winds among the lush palms, sea grapes, casuarinas, and almond trees to a quiet alfresco bar at the main beach (there are five beaches in all) and a separate sunset bar for the yachting crowd. Enjoy complimentary windsurfing, snorkeling, and Sunfish sailboats; scuba diving is also available, along with a 52-foot sloop and a 52-foot catamaran for fishing trips and catered day sails. A tennis court is nearby, and a jogging and walking trail winds throughout the property. The island is reached via a 45-minute flight from Barbados to nearby Union Island and a 15-minute launch ride from there. Palm Island (phone: 458-8824; 800-776-7256; 301-990-0277 in Maryland; fax: 458-8804; 301-990-0290 in the US).

Petit St. Vincent If you've ever dreamed of leaving the world behind for secluded tropical splendor on your own private island (with elegant service and superb food, of course), this is the place for you. It's entirely possible to spend your whole vacation here at one of the 22 spacious, ceiling fan- and breeze-cooled stone-and-wood houses, complete with private beach and thatch-roofed hammock, without ever having to see another human being (there are no telephones or TV sets to serve as reminders, either). Raising a yellow flag outside your villa means you want room service; after a member of the staff arrives by mini-moke to take your order, don't confuse him or her by hoisting the red "leave-us-alone" flag until your order has been delivered. Manager Haze Richardson is another of those intrepid souls who turned a mosquito-infested swamp of an island into what seasoned travelers now deem one of the top five resorts in the Caribbean. (It's also one of the most expensive—and worth it.) The meat is flown in daily from Julia Child's butcher, and meals attain five-star standards. All non-motorized water sports are included, with charter yachts and scuba diving available at an extra charge; tennis, volleyball, and a Parcours fitness trail (hidden from the beach by skillful landscaping) are complimentary. So are trips to nearby Mopion (also known as Petit St. Richardson), a cinematic little sandbar surrounded by brilliant aqua water. Rates drop from mid-April until just before *Christmas.* Closed September and October. Visa and American Express accepted; personal checks preferred. Petit St. Vincent (phone: 458-8801; 800-654-9326; 513-242-1333 in Ohio; fax: 458-8428).

Salt Whistle Bay Club, Mayreau Not technically a private island, but it might as well be: This uniquely beautiful, low-key resort sits on one of the world's most secluded, magnificent beaches, on a calm horseshoe bay with the rolling Atlantic surf just a stroll away. A stay here is a total getaway; there are no roads, no cars (just two vans), no phones, no TV sets, and no reason to bring more than a few swimsuits and sarongs. (A band used to entertain, but guests complained it made too much noise.) Five two-unit stone bungalows (with ceiling fans, but no air conditioning—and none needed) are hidden among the papaya and palm trees. Most water sports are free to guests; table tennis, darts, volleyball, backgammon, chess, and fishing poles also are available. Diving and boat excursions can be arranged. An alfresco beach bar/restaurant serves tasty West Indian and continental food. If you must, you can walk over the cactus-studded hill to see the tiny village and wide Saline Bay Beach. Mayreau (phone: 458-8444; fax: 458-8944; or radio VHF Ch. 16).

Young Island If Gauguin had lingered in the Caribbean, he might have found barefoot happiness on this 35-acre tropical paradise. Its central indoor-outdoor buildings and 29 individual Tahitian cottages are surrounded by lush gardens. The cottages—king-size retreats in local stone and South American hardwood—feature bamboo and *khus khus* (vetiver grass) decor. They're naturally air conditioned by screened, adjustable jalousies and louvers, plus ceiling fans (there are no telephones or TV sets). Tiled baths lead to sexy outdoor showers secluded by ferns and luxuriant flowers. Several units even have small private pools. There's a pretty beach, a free-form saltwater pool nestled in greenery, water sports (including full diving facilities with instruction and windsurfers), two yachts that make regular day trips to Bequia and Mustique, tennis courts, and lots of relaxing (with lots of hammocks to do it in). The thatch-roofed *Coconut Bar* floats in waist-high water just off-shore, and another bar operates on the beach. Meals are savored under beach gazebos or in a Polynesian pavilion terraced into the rocks above. Several times a week local island bands ferry over to make music in the evening; once a week they play on the nearby, romantically torch-lit Rock Fort Island (see *Nightlife,* above). Otherwise, it's sociable talk over brandy, and a short stroll down the garden path to bed. Yacht cruise packages available. Reached by ferry from the Villa Beach dock on St. Vincent (phone: 458-4826; 800-223-1108; fax: 457-4567).

ST. VINCENT AND JUST OFFSHORE

EXPENSIVE

Grand View Beach Caring family management, smiling, efficient service, beautifully landscaped grounds, and several truly grand views await guests at this elegant, converted turn-of-the-century cotton plantation. There are 19 simple but homey double rooms (including eight built in 1992). All are spacious and breezy; some also have air conditioning (but no TV sets). The photogenic swimming pool sits out on the point, and trails lead down to the small beach. Other pluses: a fitness center, a tennis court, a squash court, summer packages, and West Indian fare in a simple dining room with an excellent view. Rates include breakfast. Villa Point (phone: 458-4811; 800-223-6510; fax: 457-4174).

Browne's on Villa Beach At press time, this hotel, the project of former *Young Island* resort manager Vidal Browne, was set to open, catering to the business traveler, with fax machines, a business center, and valet service. The 25 rooms will have West Indian flair; there also will be a restaurant serving West Indian and international fare. Villa Beach (phone: 457-4000; 800-223-1108; fax: 457-4001).

Lagoon Marina This bright, modern hotel has 19 rooms overlooking a full-service marina with a tennis court. The rooms have ceiling fans, but no air conditioning, telephones, or TV sets. Guests have access to the beach, and there are two freshwater pools atop a hill, surrounded by palms and flowering bushes. Day sails and longer yacht charters are easily arranged. There's also a fun restaurant and bar featuring good seafood and the same great view of the marina. American Express and Visa accepted. Blue Lagoon (phone: 458-4308; 800-74-CHARM; fax: 457-4716).

Petit Byahaut Ecotourists take note: This unusual retreat sits on a horseshoe-shaped bay in a 50-acre private valley accessible only by boat; guests are picked up at docks throughout St. Vincent. The accommodations are very basic—seven open, wooden decks overlooking the sea and secluded from each other by lush foliage. Each has a roof over a large, eight-by-ten-foot tent containing a queen-size bed and solar-powered lights, and on the spacious deck are a table and chairs, a propane lamp, and a hammock. (Needless to say, there's no air conditioning, telephones, or TV sets.) Each "tent-cabin" has its own outdoor flush toilet and an enclosed hot-water shower. Near the 500-foot black sand beach is an open-air patio, where simple, wholesome meals are served. There's equipment for all water sports and superb snorkeling and scuba diving right off the beach. Inter-island excursions can be arranged, as can daylong treks to La Soufrière and Trinity Falls. The rate includes everything but drinks, scuba diving, and tours. For nature lovers who don't mind roughing it a bit to enjoy St. Vincent's staggering natural beauty, this is close to paradise. Located 4½ miles north of Kingstown on the leeward coast (phone: 457-7008; 800-285-2377; 203-838-6864 in Connecticut; fax: 457-7008).

Villa Lodge Here are 10 spacious rooms (with extra beds available for children), each with a mini-refrigerator and a terrace and some with lovely sea views, a five-minute walk from the beach. Guests share a pool with the next-door *Breezeville Apartments* (eight units). Another pleasant amenity is the open-air bar with a view of the harbor. The restaurant specializes in seafood and barbecued steaks. MAP rates (breakfast and dinner included) are available. Villa Point (phone: 458-4641; 800-74-CHARM; fax: 457-4468).

Beachcombers Formerly a stucco and wood family home, this lovely new inn sits amid lawns and tropical gardens on a hill that slopes gently down to an open-air restaurant and Indian Bay Beach. Each room has a covered patio and is simply but appealingly decorated. Six of the ten rooms have air conditioning, telephones, and TV sets; three are beachfront. Full dinners are served, as well as pizza, kebabs, and quiche; continental breakfast is included in the rate. The eighth night of your stay is complimentary. Villa Beach (phone: 458-4283; fax: 458-4385).

Cobblestone Inn A converted 200-year-old sugar warehouse in the middle of town, it has 19 rooms (with TV sets on request), many with views overlooking the harbor; *Basil's,* a popular restaurant and bar (see *Eating Out*); and a pleasant rooftop snack bar. Rates include continental breakfast. A favorite stopover for Vincentian business travelers and boaters. Bay St., Kingstown (phone: 456-1937; fax: 456-1938).

Coconut Beach Inn Right on the beach, this friendly, small place offers eight rooms in bright island style (with no telephones, TV sets, or air conditioning). Wide piers with white wooden benches make it easy to enjoy the view, and there's a charming, welcoming bar. Restaurant dining includes steaks, Cornish hens, and pasta. Indian Bay (phone: 457-4900).

Emerald Valley If you'd prefer to be in the verdant hills rather than at the beach, drive 7 miles from Kingstown to this pretty property that lives up to its name. Twelve rooms in two-unit chalets have kitchenettes and balconies, but no telephones or TV sets. Guests enjoy two freshwater pools, two tennis courts, horseback riding, and horseshoes. The hotel also houses St. Vincent's only casino—a small gaming room with craps, roulette, blackjack, and slot machines. There are excellent nature trails in the surrounding hills; and a courtesy van makes trips to town. Penniston Valley (phone: 456-7140; fax: 456-7145).

Sunset Shores Simple but very comfortable, the 31 airy, balconied rooms, all with satellite TV, surround a swimming pool with a spacious deck; a lawn fronts the white sand beach. Complimentary sailing, snorkeling, and windsurfing equipment are available. Scuba diving, yacht charters, and tennis courts are nearby, and sightseeing and hiking tours can be arranged. The restaurant serves good local and continental fare, and other beach eateries are nearby. Villa Beach (phone: 458-4411; 800-223-6510; fax: 458-4800).

Umbrella Beach Nine simple, budget-priced, efficiency apartments, owned by the next-door *French* restaurant (see *Eating Out*). It's perfect for vacationers and businessfolks who'd rather spend money on good food and wine than on posh accommodations. The apartments have no air conditioning or TV sets. Front rooms have patios on the beach directly opposite Young Island and overlooking a flower-filled garden; several lively cafés are just steps away. Villa Beach (phone: 458-4651; fax: 457-4930).

THE GRENADINES

VERY EXPENSIVE

Canouan Beach New French management has transformed this beachside resort into a charming, friendly, international place (most guests are French or German). Set amid lawns and gardens lining beautiful Glossy Bay Beach are 32 pastel-trimmed bungalows; all have spacious verandahs, but no telephones or TV sets. Eleven rooms in the main building are simpler, but comfortable. Activities include day sails to the Cays and Mayreau, a golf driving range, and *bocci*. West Indian food is served in a spacious open-air restaurant/bar with friendly service; a steel band plays once a week. American Express and Visa accepted. Canouan, near the airstrip (phone: 458-8888; fax: 458-8875).

Plantation House Bequia's prettiest, most upscale waterside property offers 17 simple one- and two-bedroom cottages spaced among postcard-perfect lawns and palm trees; all rooms have ceiling fans (to supplement the air conditioning). Five rooms with marble floors and baths are in the peach-colored main house, which is circled by a wide, terra cotta–tiled verandah where excellent meals are served (see *Eating Out*). The beach is tiny, yet pristine. A small stone pool, a lighted tennis court, a lively seaside drink and snack bar, and most water sports (including full diving facilities) are on the premises. Hospitable new management is adding about 20 cottages on the surrounding hillside, which should be open by press time. Admiralty Bay, Belmont, Bequia (phone: 458-3425; fax: 458-3612).

EXPENSIVE

Anchorage Yacht Club This French-owned inn is popular with yachtspeople and mostly French passersby on their way to the other Grenadines—Union Island offers very little to the land-based traveler. There are 10 motel-modern rooms—some with TV sets—a bar, and a restaurant with a French chef. Great for boating trips and local gossip. Breakfast is included in the rate. Clifton, Union Island (phone: 458-8244; fax: 458-8365).

Spring on Bequia Rustling leaves and singing birds (along with the occasional moo from a Holstein cow grazing among towering palms) provide the music at this exquisitely rustic getaway, part of a 250-year-old working plantation perched on a hillside above Spring Bay. The view from here is of verdant valleys and aqua seas. The 10 cottages are simple, of stone and wood, with verandahs and comfortable chairs for reading and relaxing (no air conditioning, telephones, or TV sets). In the main house is an inviting dining room and bar (try the popular Sunday lunch curry buffet). Tennis courts, a pool, and a beach (good for snorkeling) are a stroll away. Quiet, contemplative, utterly peaceful. Spring, Bequia (phone: 458-3414; 612-823-1202 in Minnesota; fax: 458-3612).

Tamarind Beach Opened early last year to attract a primarily European clientele, this hotel and yacht club on Charleston Bay has three gingerbread-trimmed, motel-like buildings housing 48 small rooms and one suite, all with minibars and balconies overlooking the sea. Dark natural-wood walls and ceilings are brightened with white wicker furniture; there's no air conditioning or telephones, and TV sets are available upon request. Three large, thatch-roofed structures shelter the two restaurants and bars. The big draw here in the main restaurant is the Italian food prepared by the Milanese chef, including superb pizza, pasta, salads, and soups. A 50-foot catamaran makes day sails to neighboring islands. Rates include all meals (but not drinks) and water sports. Canouan (phone: 458-8044; fax: 458-8851).

MODERATE

Firefly House Billy Mitchell sailed the world for 19 years before building one of Mustique's first houses. She now rents four delightful rooms with terraces overlooking Britannia Bay. There are no telephones or TV sets, but air conditioning is available at a small extra charge. Breakfast is included, and there's an honor bar; a restaurant and the beach are both a short walk away. Mustique (phone: 456-3414).

Friendship Bay Owners Lars and Marget Abrahamsson offer 27 very basic—no air conditioning, telephones, or TV sets—bright and cheery rooms (but note that, during rainy weather, the ceiling fans don't banish the humidity). There's also a lovely beach with a Polynesian bar featuring swings for seats, a restaurant serving excellent local seafood, water sports (including parasailing, windsurfing, and full diving facilities and instruction), a yacht for charters and day cruising to Mustique, and tennis courts. Friendship Bay, Bequia, 10 minutes from Port Elizabeth (phone: 458-3222; fax: 458-3840).

Julie's This 19-room guesthouse is right in town and furnished humbly, but it is clean and friendly, with excellent West Indian food. The rooms have no air conditioning, telephones, or TV sets. Breakfast and dinner are included in the rate. MasterCard accepted. Port Elizabeth, Bequia (phone: 458-3304; fax: 458-3812).

Old Fort Bequia's most charming hideaway is the dream-come-true of Otmar Schaedle, a well-traveled history and music professor from Germany who found the ruins of a French fort and rebuilt it in local stone and hardwood for himself and his family. Guests share this special retreat in six breezy, rustic apartments, each with panoramic views from fragrant gardens; they have no air conditioning, telephones, or TV sets. Perched on the lofty heights of Mt. Pleasant, this place is a world away from the bustle of the boating crowds below—on a clear day, you can see beyond the glittering lights of Mustique to distant Grenada. There's a highly praised, open-air restaurant, and MAP rates are available. A gem. Bequia (phone: 458-3440; fax: 458-3824).

INEXPENSIVE

Frangipani Friendly and fun, this is a favorite gathering place for visiting yachts-people, tourists, and locals. There's a popular open-air bar and a Thursday night jump-up, with steel band and great barbecue (but avoid the beef). In the 100-year-old main house are five simple rooms with shared baths and cold water only; the eight garden units have private baths and hot and cold water, but no air conditioning, telephones, or TV sets. There's a tennis court, a dive shop, and a water sports center nearby, plus a phone and fax center for yachters. Port Elizabeth, Bequia (phone: 458-3255; fax: 458-3824).

Kingsville Apartments A two-minute stroll from popular (but never crowded) Lower Bay Beach and several good local cafés, these six modern pink-and-white apartments (with full kitchens and one or two bedrooms; no air conditioning, telephones, or TV sets) are separated by small lawns and gardens; lush green hills rise behind. An excellent value. Lower Bay, Bequia (phone: 458-3404; fax: 458-3000).

EATING OUT

With very few exceptions, dining is limited to hotel restaurants. Most offer hearty, tasty West Indian food—pumpkin and *callaloo* (similar to spinach) soup, local fish or lobster prepared creole style—and what they believe tourists like to eat—usually overcooked steaks, imported frozen shrimp, French fries, and so on. Bartenders pride themselves on variations of rum punch—which are always stronger than they seem. Compared to most Caribbean holiday islands, St. Vincent's prices—outside the luxury hotels—are not bad. Dinner for two (excluding wine, which can be pricey, and tip) at restaurants we list as expensive will run $60 to $80; at places in the moderate category, $30 to $60; at inexpensive places, $30 or less. Normally, a 10% service charge (in lieu of a tip) and 5% government tax are added to the bill. For boaters, most restaurants take reservations via VHF channel 68. The following are a few recommended dining spots and outstanding hotel dining rooms. Unless otherwise noted, all restaurants listed below are open for lunch and dinner. All telephone numbers are in the 809 area code unless otherwise indicated.

ST. VINCENT

EXPENSIVE

Basil's Basil Charles, of Mustique fame, took over the popular ground-floor restaurant of the *Cobblestone Inn*. The lunchtime buffet, served weekdays, has proved a grand success. Other offerings include lobster salad, grilled snapper, omelettes, burgers, sandwiches, escargots, and grilled lobster, with several reasonably priced French wines. Closed Sundays. Reservations advised. Major credit cards accepted. Bay St., Kingstown (phone: 457-2713).

French The chef is from Orléans, and the cuisine an admirable marriage of Gallic savoir-faire with island ingredients and the few available imports. Starters include a luscious lobster crêpe, delicate quenelles, frogs' legs, and escargots. A live lobster pool guarantees freshness, and snapper is nicely prepared in a gratinéed basil sauce. With its delightful alfresco setting opposite Young Island, next to the dock, this is unquestionably the island's best choice for lunch or dinner out. Open daily for breakfast, lunch, and dinner; closed the month of September. Reservations advised. Major credit cards accepted. At the *Umbrella Beach* hotel, Villa Beach (phone: 458-4972).

MODERATE

Aggie's A clean, brightly painted, upstairs café with banners of English football (our soccer) teams hanging over the bar. The menu features such authentic West Indian fare as codfish and breadfruit, as well as dishes like shrimp creole. Open for breakfast, lunch, and dinner; no lunch Sundays. Reservations unnecessary. No credit cards accepted. Grenville St., Kingstown (phone: 456-2110).

Jana's Dolphin This open-air restaurant and bar owned and run by Jana Forde, a friendly young German woman, has a nightly barbecue featuring seafood and beef, and a menu of continental treats such as Hungarian goulash, shrimp cocktail, and sesame chicken wings. Open daily for dinner. Reservations unnecessary. No credit cards accepted. Villa Beach (phone: 457-4301).

Lime 'n' Pub A bright, sometimes noisy tropical pub across from Young Island, serving local specialties. To get here, you have to walk the rocky ledge over the beach. Open daily. Reservations unnecessary. Major credit cards accepted. Villa Beach (phone: 458-4227).

THE GRENADINES

EXPENSIVE

Basil's Bar A Caribbean institution that's been feeding sailors, rock stars, and royalty (British and Hollywood) for decades. This appealing alfresco wicker-and-wood complex opens early and closes late. The menu ranges from full breakfasts to sandwiches, salads, seafood, and homemade ice cream. The Wednesday night jump-up is a must. Open daily. Reservations advised. Major credit cards accepted. Britannia Bay, Mustique (phone: 458-4621 or radio VHF Ch. 68).

Le Petit Jardin An extensive wine list complements the fine food and elegant surroundings at this chalet-style restaurant in town. Owner/chef Owen Belmar trained at the *Culinary Institute of America,* and his food is sophisticated

West Indian. Seafood is a specialty. Open daily. Reservations advised. Major credit cards accepted. Bequia (phone: 458-3318).

Plantation House Bequia's best dining spot features fine presentations of standard island dishes with fresh local seafood. Dine on the breezy, candlelit verandah of the main house or in the open-air *Green Flash* beach bar, with piano music (played nightly on a white baby grand, no less). Saturday barbecue buffets feature a calypso band, and a new wooden floor for dancing. Open daily for breakfast, lunch, afternoon tea, and dinner. Reservations advised for dinner. Major credit cards accepted. Bequia (phone: 458-3425).

MODERATE

Daphne Cooks It There's no set menu here; Daphne simply cooks whatever ingredients were acquired that day, using old Bequian family recipes. Open daily. Reservations advised for dinner. No credit cards accepted. Port Elizabeth, Bequia, across from the vegetable market (phone: 458-3271).

Mac's Pizzeria and Bakeshop On a lovely terrace overlooking the beach on Admiralty Bay, it's renowned for its lobster pizza (when lobster is available, that is), pita-bread sandwiches, quiche, banana bread, and chocolate-chip cookies—all homemade and available to eat there or take out. Open daily for breakfast, lunch, and dinner. Reservations advised; necessary for dinner during high season. MasterCard and Visa accepted. Near Port Elizabeth, Bequia (phone: 458-3474).

Old Fig Tree The young American chef has expanded the menu with excellent, unusual dishes: chicken, beef, pasta, and vegetarian, some with a Thai or Chinese flair. This is *the* place to enjoy drinks and the sunset with bareboaters, full-time sailors, and locals in a Caribbean-as-it-used-to-be seaside café. Open for breakfast, lunch, dinner, and Sunday brunch; closed Thursdays. Reservations advised. MasterCard and Visa accepted. Port Elizabeth, Bequia (phone: 458-3201).

De Reef A popular beach bar and day spot, with a restaurant serving good local food—great conch, whelk, and shrimp dishes, plus sandwiches and *rôtis* (similar to burritos, but stuffed with a spicy, curried chicken, vegetable, or beef filling)—on island time (order, then have a swim; they'll come find you). Showers and lockers are available, as well as windsurfing and snorkeling equipment. Some Saturday nights feature a seafood buffet and live entertainment. Open daily. Reservations advised for dinner. No credit cards accepted. Lower Bay, Bequia (phone: 458-3484 or radio VHF Ch. 68).

Theresa's Located at the far end of wonderful Lower Bay Beach, this dining spot features a rotating selection of huge, tasty, Greek, Indian, Mexican, and Italian buffets on Mondays. The rest of the week, owners Theresa and John Bennett serve West Indian fare. Reservations advised for the buffet. No credit cards accepted. Lower Bay, Bequia (phone: 458-3802; 458-3075).

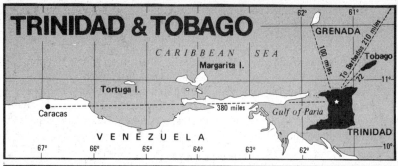

TRINIDAD & TOBAGO

CARIBBEAN SEA

GRENADA

To Barbados 210 miles

Tobago

Margarita I.

Tortuga I.

100 miles

380 miles

Gulf of Paria

Caracas

TRINIDAD

V E N E Z U E L A

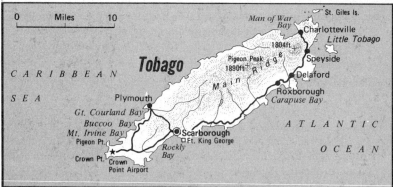

0   Miles   10

St. Giles Is.

Man of War Bay

Charlotteville

Little Tobago

1804ft

C A R I B B E A N

Tobago

Pigeon Peak 1890ft

Speyside

Delaford

Main Ridge

S E A

Plymouth

Roxborough

Carapuse Bay

Gt. Courland Bay

Buccoo Bay

Mt. Irvine Bay

A T L A N T I C

Pigeon Pt.

Scarborough

Rockly Bay

O C E A N

Crown Pt. Crown Point Airport

Ft. King George

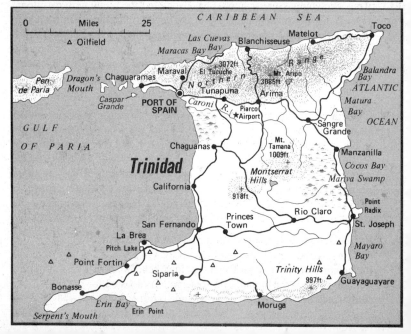

0   Miles   25

△ Oilfield

C A R I B B E A N   S E A

Toco

Matelot

Las Cuevas Bay

Blanchisseuse

Maracas Bay

Range

Balandra Bay

Maraval

El Tucuche +3072ft

+ Mt. Aripo 3085ft

ATLANTIC

Pen. de Paria

Dragon's Mouth

Chaguaramas

Northern

Arima

Matura Bay

Caspar Grande

Tunapuna

Caroni R.

OCEAN

PORT OF SPAIN

Piarco ★ Airport

Sangre Grande

G U L F

O F   P A R I A

Chaguanas

Mt. Tamana 1009ft

Manzanilla

Cocos Bay

Trinidad

Montserrat Hills

Mariva Swamp

California

+918ft

Point Radix

Princes Town

Rio Claro

St. Joseph

San Fernando

Mayaro Bay

La Brea

Pitch Lake □

Trinity Hills

Point Fortin

Siparia

997ft

Guayaguayare

Bonasse

Moruga

Erin Bay

Erin Point

Serpent's Mouth

Trinidad and Tobago

The twin-island nation of Trinidad and Tobago is a study in contrasts—the Caribbean's "yin and yang"—that together make a harmonious whole. Trinidad is large and densely populated with several major towns; Tobago is small and sparsely populated with scattered settlements. Trinidad (named by Columbus for the way its three major peaks recalled the Holy Trinity) is South American; Tobago (a variation on "tobacco") is Caribbean. Trinidad and its capital, Port of Spain, are vibrant, industrial, and cosmopolitan; Tobago and its capital, Scarborough, are unhurried and tranquil, reminiscent of an earlier West Indian era.

Originally inhabited by Amerindians, then settled by the Spanish as a transshipment point for South America's riches, Trinidad became a British colony when it was captured in 1797. Tobago's more turbulent past is peppered with bitter battles and occupations by the Dutch, the Spanish, the British, the French—even Kurlanders from present-day Latvia (for whom Great Courland Bay was named); all told, the island changed hands no fewer than 31 times in the course of three centuries. Not until 1803, when the British won a bloodless victory over the French and occupied Scarborough, was Tobago left to tend its flowing fields of sugarcane in peace.

During most of the 19th century, Tobago's sugar industry prospered, but it began a steady decline when slavery was abolished in 1834. The 1884 bankruptcy of Gillespie & Company, the London firm that monopolized the colony's financial dealings, brought about the final collapse of the industry and, as a result, of the island's economy. Suddenly a poor relation, but still clinging to its distinctive culture—more than 90% of Tobagonians are of African descent—Tobago reluctantly became a ward of the more economically secure Trinidad.

On August 31, 1962, the twin-island nation of Trinidad & Tobago ("TT" in local jargon) became an independent member of the British Commonwealth and, in 1976, a republic within the Commonwealth, with a freely-elected president as head of state. Executive power is vested with the Prime Minister and the Cabinet, while the legislature consists of an elected House of Representatives and an appointed Senate. Tobago has a separate House of Assembly controlling domestic affairs.

The People's National Movement (PNM) was an early force in the drive for independence, and its founder, Dr. Eric Williams, served first as chief minister, then as prime minister of the new nation for 25 years, until his death in 1981. Demonstrating its commitment to democracy, the government changed hands smoothly in 1986 from the People's National Movement, which had been in power since independence, to the National Alliance for Reconstruction (NAR), led by A. N. R. Robinson. In 1990,

Libyan-inspired black Muslims attempted a coup, holding Robinson and other government officials hostage for several days before the rebels surrendered. A little more than a year later, the nation held peaceful elections and a democratic form of government continued under a new prime minister, Patrick Manning, and the People's National Movement.

Major industries in Trinidad and Tobago include steel, natural gas, methanol, agriculture, and tourism. It is oil, however, to which this country owes much of its prosperity and, more recently, its economic malaise (due to erratic world prices which have led the government into increasing foreign debt). Still, Trinidad and Tobago remains the third-largest oil exporter in the Western Hemisphere, and it ranks among the richest and most industrialized nations in the West Indies. Natural gas discovered off Trinidad's coast offers potential for economic expansion, as do sugar, cocoa, coffee, citrus fruits, and coconuts.

For tourists, however, Trinidad's mineral wealth represents a mixed blessing: While the profusion of birds (over 400 species), butterflies (600-plus species), orchids (700 species), reptiles, and other flora and fauna delight and dazzle, visitors may find themselves traveling through an oil refinery to reach a bird sanctuary or rain forest. On the other hand, TT's petrochemical prosperity has, in the past, caused it to pay scant attention to tourism, and it has avoided the overbuilding and damage to wildlife habitats endemic to many other tourist destinations. Now, however, a new era is dawning as the Ministry of Tourism begins implementing a strategy focused on eco-tourism and cultural attractions, backed by extensive hotel construction and infrastructure upgrading on both islands.

Today, Trinidad and Tobago boasts one of the world's most diverse multiracial societies, whose rich fusion of cultures is reflected in its spirited music, dance, art, and cuisine. Building on the heritage of the Amerindians, who are believed to have settled here in about 5000 BC, the culture boasts strong African and East Indian influences flavored with Créole and Portuguese. Add British, Spanish, French, German, Chinese, Lebanese, Syrian, and North American peoples, and you can begin to understand TT's unique personality—one that is reflected in its eclectic architecture and cuisine. In fact, the number of languages heard throughout this "Rainbow Country" (as Bishop Desmond Tutu has called it)—including Hindi, Urdu, Spanish, Chinese, English, and a local patois—is surpassed only by the spectrum of cooking styles. Over half the population is East Indian, both Hindu and Muslim, as is the "national dish"—roti (folded flat bread filled with a chickpea paste called *channa* and curried meat, seafood, or vegetables). During the Indian religious festivals, TT is as close as you'll get to the subcontinent without flying to Calcutta.

The hustle and bustle of life on Trinidad in no way disturbs the calm of nearby Tobago. In fact, Trinidad's nightlife, exotic eateries, and exuberant *Carnival* (the oldest and largest in the Caribbean) are perfectly complemented by Tobago's idyllic beaches and spectacular wildlife. It would be almost impossible to find a better combination for a Caribbean visit than these southernmost islands: Tobago soothes where Trinidad titillates. To visit one without the other is possible, but not wise; the two islands are halves of an ideal vacation whole.

Trinidad and Tobago At-a-Glance

FROM THE AIR

Most of TT's 1.3 million inhabitants live on Trinidad, a rectangular-shaped island, 37 miles by 50 miles, that looks like a jigsaw-puzzle piece ready to be moved into place next to Venezuela, just 7 miles away. Geologists theorize that Trinidad, now separated from the mainland by the Gulf of Paria, was part of South America until about 10,000 BC.

The flora and fauna of Trinidad closely resemble Venezuela's, and the Northern Range mountains, which stretch from east to west, are a continuation of the South American Cordillera. The two highest peaks on Trinidad are El Cerro del Aripo (3,085 feet) and El Tucuche (3,072 feet). The central Montserrat Hills and the Trinity Hills to the southeast are interspersed with valleys and separated by broad plains.

Fish-shaped Tobago, 26 miles long by 7 miles wide, is one-sixteenth the size of its neighbor and has a population of just under 50,000. With its mountainous terrain, Tobago resembles the Windward Islands to the north more than it does Trinidad or Venezuela. Tobago's 1,860-foot hills rolling to white, sandy beaches and aqua seas provided the photogenic island setting for the movie classic *The Swiss Family Robinson,* filmed near Hope Beach.

SPECIAL PLACES: TRINIDAD

PORT OF SPAIN Start your walking tour in the city's pride and joy, the 200-acre playground oasis called *Queen's Park Savannah,* which hosts cricket, rugby, and football (soccer) players, joggers, and vendors hawking everything from coconut water to roasted corn. The 3-mile perimeter of the *Savannah* is perhaps the world's biggest roundabout. On the Maraval Road side are seven imposing, turn-of-the-century mansions christened the *Magnificent Seven,* which serve as architectural evidence of Trinidad's tangled heritage and its plantation owners' individualism. *Queen's Royal College,* the stately structure with lighted tower and chiming clock, was built in German Renaissance style in 1904; its most famous graduate is author V. S. Naipaul (*A Bend in the River*). *Hayes Court* is home to the Anglican bishop. *Roodal's Palace,* known as the "Gingerbread House," sports the extravagant Baroque domes and cupolas typical of the French Second Empire. *Stollmeyer's Castle* is a 1904 replica of a German castle, though its stone turrets and archways more closely resemble those of a Scottish baronial mansion. *Whitehall,* the office of the prime minister, looks like a cross between a wedding cake and a Moorish palace.

Walking southwest from the *Magnificent Seven,* you'll reach the *Queen's Park* hotel and, nearby, on Upper Frederick Street facing *Memorial Park,* the *National Museum and Art Gallery.* In addition to housing the national art collection, including works by Trinidad's notable 19th-century painter Jean Michel Cazabon, this renovated, must-see museum also features an ornate Spanish cannon, Amerindian relics, an exhibit of snakebite cures, and a dazzling display of *Carnival* costumes. Closed Sundays and Mondays. Admission charge (phone: 623-5941).

Turn down Frederick Street, the heart of Port of Spain's shopping district, which presents a cramped jumble of merchandise, a barrage of the latest calypso beats, and olfactory confusion—as coconut oil, roasting corn on the cob, peppers, and sausage compete for your attention. Halfway down Frederick Street lies *Woodford Square,* where Trinidadians speak out on issues of the day. Across the square on St. Vincent Street stands the *Red House,* a neo-Renaissance building that is the seat of government. Perpendicular to *Red House* on Hart Street is the Gothic *Holy Trinity Cathedral* (consecrated 1823), with distinctive altar carvings, choir stalls, and marble monuments to prominent citizens. Set apart from the activity of Frederick Street, a short distance from the *Savannah,* are the *Royal Botanic Gardens.* Covering some 70 acres of a former sugar plantation, the gardens are brimming with such exotic flora as orchids, frangipani, sausage trees, and lipstick plants. Keep an eye out for the raw beef tree, whose cut bark resembles rare roast beef. There are also lotus nymph lilies—sacred to the Egyptians—and the type of holy *peepul* (fig) tree under which the Buddha is purported to have attained nirvana. Open daily. No admission charge (no phone). A fun spot for families, the nearby eight-acre *Emperor Valley Zoo* houses 200 species and habitats that so closely resemble those in nature that some species have achieved rare, in-captivity births. Open daily. Admission charge (phone: 622-3530).

ELSEWHERE ON TRINIDAD

ASA WRIGHT NATURE CENTRE AND LODGE North of Arima on Blanchisseuse Road, about a 90-minute drive from Port of Spain, this 200-acre center is devoted to naturalists and bird watchers. The breeding colony of the nocturnal oilbird *(guacharo)* in Dunston Cave is the world's most accessible, though the trek to the Guacharo Gorge still demands determination and comfortable gear. There are seven additional trails, where overnight guests (see *Checking In*) can enjoy sunset and sunrise bird watching, but even day-trippers will enjoy high tea on a porch surrounded by nature. Make arrangements two days in advance for field trips. Open daily. Admission charge (phone/fax: 667-4655).

POINTE-À-PIERRE WILDFOWL TRUST This 60-acre conservation center on the grounds of the Petrotrin oil refinery has trails and protected breeding areas for reintroducing endangered species of birds. The *Environmental Learning Center* has displays of Amerindian artifacts. Dress appropriately for hikes through the Fairy Woods. Visitors must reserve in advance to view the preserve. Open daily. Admission charge includes guide. Pointe-à-Pierre (phone: 637-5145 or 662-4040).

LOPINOT HISTORICAL COMPLEX This restored cocoa-estate greathouse, once the home of the French Count de Lopinot, is now a plantation museum with displays of period furniture, pottery, and other artifacts; there's also a cocoa drying house and a park. Small groups of musicians playing *parang* (traditional *Christmas* music with Spanish roots) often rove through the complex and the nearby villages, and frequent *parang* competitions are held around *Christmastime* at the complex. Open daily, except holidays. No admission charge. To arrange a guided tour, contact the *Forestry Division* (phone: 622-3153) or *National Parks Department* (phone: 622-4521). Five miles off Eastern Main Rd. up the Lopinot Valley, one hour's drive east of Port of Spain.

CLEAVER WOODS PARK This 31-acre nature preserve showcases Trinidad's flora and fauna. It also has an Amerindian museum, a pine plantation, and picnic sites. Open daily, except holidays. No admission charge. To arrange a guided tour, contact the *National Parks Department* (see *Lopinot Historical Complex*, above). Near the Eastern Main Road, 1 mile west of Arima and an hour's drive east of Port of Spain.

FORT GEORGE Built in 1804 on a 1,500-foot peak, the fort is only 10 miles from Port of Spain along Western Main Road. The drive up affords imposing views of the capital city. Open daily, except holidays. No admission charge. For more information, contact the *National Parks Department* (see *Lopinot Historical Complex*, above).

KNOLLY'S TUNNEL Near Tabaquit, this quarter-mile-long railroad tunnel, the longest in the Caribbean, was used from 1898 to 1965 to transport sugar, cocoa, and passengers to Port of Spain. The tunnel was reopened in 1991 as part of a project to develop the 62-acre reserve that surrounds it. These days, visitors can take horse-drawn carriage rides through the tunnel. *Note:* Stay inside the carriage, since the sleeping bats in the tunnel are disturbed by daytime visitors. There are also three thatch-roofed cabins for overnight stays, a picnic area, and hiking trails. Open daily. Admission charge (phone: 622-5146 or 628-6087).

NORTH COAST BEACHES The 34-mile drive from "the Saddle"—a pass dividing the Santa Cruz and Maraval valleys—across the Northern Range and down to Maracas Bay is exhilarating. The view from 1,500 feet up—a 100-mile sweep from Tobago to Venezuela—is itself worth the trip, as is the *shark-*

and-bake (fried dough stuffed with shark) sold by roadside vendors. Enclosed by lush mountains and swaying palms, Maracas Beach, Trinidad's most popular strand, has changing facilities, snack bars, and good surfing. Take a worthwhile detour inland through the cool Maracas Valley and stop for a 1-mile hike to refresh yourself in TT's highest falls, the Maracas Waterfall, north of St. Joseph. A 10-minute drive from Maracas Bay, Las Cuevas Beach boasts an inviting seascape with waves ranging from the "surf's up" variety to those worthy of a placid tropical lagoon; there are also restrooms, changing rooms, lifeguards, and a snack bar. Watch for warning flags that indicate an undertow. Farther down the coast, scenic Blanchisseuse Beach is seldom crowded (there are no showers or changing rooms, however).

GASPAREE CAVES These grottoes, located on Caspar Grande Island just off the northern peninsula of Chaguaramas, are favorite spelunker haunts, with extraordinary stalactite and stalagmite formations visible from lighted paths. Visitors also can explore the ruins of colonial fortifications. There are picnic facilities adjacent to the caves. Regular ferries run to the island from Chaguaramas, and boats may be booked in advance through Papa Willie (phone: 632-8761) or Elton Pouchet (phone: 622-8974). Open daily until 2:30 PM weekdays, 3PM on weekends. Admission charge includes guide (phone: 625-1503 or 634-4364).

CARONI BIRD SANCTUARY Established in 1965 to preserve Trinidad's national bird, the scarlet ibis, this 450-acre, mangrove-strewn sanctuary lies 7 miles south of Port of Spain. A boat ride through the waterways of the Caroni Swamp is a soothing way to spend an afternoon. At sunset, thousands of ibis swooping in to roost seem to set the mangroves aflame. For additional details, see *Natural Wonderlands* in DIVERSIONS. Winston Nanan of *Caroni Tours* (phone: 645-1305) offers excursions. Boats for the four-hour journey leave the roadside dock daily at 4:30 AM and 4 PM. Needless to say, the afternoon departure has more takers. Reservations are necessary.

PITCH LAKE Near the southern coast town of La Brea (Spanish for "pitch") lies the world's largest asphalt deposit, which continues to yield Ice Age and Amerindian artifacts, as well as enough asphalt to pave the world's highways (though it's being depleted at the alarming rate of 300 tons a day). First discovered by Sir Walter Raleigh, who used the pitch as ship's caulking, the lake is a 114-acre expanse of slowly swirling crude oil and bitumen, which bubble up from a fault 250 feet below the surface. There's a museum here, and guided tours of both the lake and museum are available by arrangement. Open daily. Admission charge (phone: 648-7697).

SPECIAL PLACES: TOBAGO

SCARBOROUGH Tobago's historic capital (pop. 20,000), which has fended off innumerable assaults by quarreling nations, now welcomes visitors arriving by sea with its new *Cruise Ship Complex* in the modern, deep-water harbor.

For a panoramic view of Scarborough and a peek at Tobago's past, visit the prison, officer's mess, and bell tower at *Fort King George*, built by the British in 1777 some 430 feet above Rockly Bay; most of the ramparts have been restored. The fort is open daily. No admission charge (phone: 639-3421). Within the fort is the *Tobago Historical Museum*, housed in the former barracks. Exhibits showcase pre-Columbian artifacts and historical documents. Closed weekends. Admission charge. The fort also houses the *Tobago Centre of Fine Arts*, with a collection of works by local artists. Closed weekends. No admission charge (phone for both museum and *Centre:* 639-3970). African tulip trees and flamboyants add splashes of color to the 17-acre *Botanical Gardens* beneath the fort. Open daily. No admission charge (phone: 639-3421, ext. 273).

PIGEON POINT BEACH RESORT Protected by Buccoo Reef, this palm-fringed, privately-owned beach is Tobago's safest and most popular stretch of powdery sand, with thatch shelters, picnic tables, changing areas, restrooms, and a restaurant/bar. It's a lively spot on weekends and holidays. Open daily. Admission charge. At the northwestern tip of the island near Store Bay (no phone).

BUCCOO REEF For a breathtaking kaleidoscope of tropical fish and corals, don't miss this marine park a mile offshore at Pigeon Point. Here you'll find the transparent Nylon Pool, a tranquil lagoon so dubbed by Princess Margaret during her Tobago honeymoon, and the beautiful Coral Gardens. Glass-bottom boat and snorkel trips to the reef may be booked from Buccoo Point or Pigeon Point/Store Bay. Trips usually include snorkel gear and reef shoes (phone: 639-8582 or 639-8519).

FAIRYHAUS Luise Kimme's workshop and private gallery displays her whimsical sculptures carved from enormous tree trunks. Open Sunday or by appointment, in the hills above Mount Irvine (phone: 639-0257).

CHARLOTTEVILLE For a close-up view of the "real" Tobago, seek out this idyllic fishing village on the island's northeastern tip, where 1,890-foot Pigeon Peak rises majestically above tin-roofed houses with gingerbread trim. One of the Caribbean's finest natural harbors, Man of War Bay's waters nudge against a perfect crescent of white sand; on the beach there's a covered pavilion with picnic tables. Once a haven for buccaneers, nearby Pirate's Bay now offers a secluded beach, with a fine reef and wild parrots for company.

BIRD OF PARADISE WILDLIFE SANCTUARY A tiny cay one mile off the coast near the Atlantic fishing village of Speyside, Little Tobago (known as "Bird of Paradise Island") attracts ornithologists and amateur bird watchers alike, all eager to catch a glimpse of the area's golden-feathered namesake, specimens of which were introduced here from New Guinea in 1909. None has been spotted since 1981, but there are still more than fifty species of South American and Antillean birds breeding on the island, all best sighted during the early morning or late afternoon. For more information, call the *Conservator of Forests* (phone: 660-2079) or the *Botanic Station* in Scarborough (phone: 639-2234). Boat trips to the island are available at the *Blue Waters Inn* (see *Checking In*) or *Speyside Inn* (Windward Road, Speyside; phone: 660-4852) with a day's advance notice. Open daily until 3 PM. Admission charge.

MAIN RIDGE FOREST RESERVE The oldest reserve of its kind in the Western Hemisphere, this mountainous rain forest forms the spine of Tobago, running two thirds of its length. Protected in perpetuity since 1764 (its hardwood trees were used as masts for the Royal Navy), this 14,000-acre jungle of evergreens, flowering plants, palms, and giant ferns serves as a unique habitat for birds and wildlife. Facilities include lookout huts, nature trails, campsites with fireplaces, and restrooms. For more information, call 639-4468, or contact the *Botanic Station* in Scarborough (phone: 639-2234).

Sources and Resources

TOURIST INFORMATION

The new *Tourism and Industrial Development Company (TIDCO)* headquarters are in Port of Spain (10-14 Phillips St., Third Floor; phone: 623-INFO or 623-1932/4; fax: 623-3848). There is also an information office at *Piarco International Airport* (phone: 664-5196). On Tobago, there are information offices in the *NIB Mall* in Scarborough (phone: 639-2125 or 639-3566) and at *Crown Point Airport* (phone: 639-0509). Offices are open weekdays and sometimes staffed on weekends. For tourist offices in the US, see GETTING READY TO GO.

LOCAL COVERAGE Trinidad's English-language daily newspapers include the *Trinidad Guardian,* the *Trinidad Express,* and *Newsday;* there are also the *Mirror* (a bi-weekly) and several local-interest weeklies: the *Catholic News,* the *Tobago News,* and the rather incendiary-sounding *Bomb, Blast, Heat,* and *Punch.* The *Discover Trinidad & Tobago Travel Guide,* updated annually by the Trinidad and Tobago Hotel and Tourism Association, is recommended; it's available free of charge from the tourist office and at other locations around the islands.

RADIO AND TELEVISION Many hotels have cable TV; some have satellite TV. Trinidad and Tobago Television (TTTV, Channels 2, 4, and 6) broadcasts local shows, as well as a broader range of programming in English. The National Broadcasting Company (NBC, 95.3 FM) and Trinidad Broadcasting Company (TBC, 105.1 FM) are the local radio stations.

TELEPHONE The area code for Trinidad and Tobago is 809. Debit cards are convenient for local and international calls from public phones; they're inexpensive and widely available. Dial 999 for emergency assistance.

ENTRY REQUIREMENTS Visitors must show a valid passport. There's a departure tax of TT $75 (about $13 at press time), payable in local currency.

CLIMATE AND CLOTHES Trade winds temper the tropical warmth of these islands, which lie only 10 to 11 degrees north of the equator, receiving nearly 12 hours of sunshine a day. The rainy season lasts from June through December. Average year-round temperatures are 74F (23C) at night, 84F (29C) during the day, so lightweight clothing is in order. A light jacket may be useful in winter months, particularly at higher elevations. Dressy resortwear (including jacket and tie) is often appropriate for evenings on Trinidad, while daytime Trinidad and anytime Tobago are casual (though, away from the water, wear cover-ups over beachwear).

MONEY The TT dollar is based on a floating exchange rate of about US $1 to TT $5.65 at press time. US currency is universally accepted, as are traveler's checks and major credit cards, but purchases made in local currency will occasionally prove less expensive. Most banks are open from 9 AM to 2 PM Mondays through Thursdays and 8 AM to 12 PM and 3 to 5 PM Fridays. Automatic banking machines are available in Trinidad. All prices in this chapter are quoted in US dollars, unless otherwise indicated.

LANGUAGE English is the official language on both islands (though many others are spoken).

TIME The islands are on atlantic standard time, one hour ahead of eastern standard time (when it's noon in New York, its 1 PM in Port of Spain) and the same as eastern daylight saving time.

CURRENT Electricity is 110 or 220 volts, 60 cycles AC. Check with your hotel before plugging in appliances to make sure they're compatible; many provide adapters.

TIPPING A 10% tip is standard, unless a service charge is included in your hotel or restaurant bill (be sure to check to avoid double- or non-tipping); a larger tip is appropriate for better-than-average service.

GETTING AROUND

BUS Trinidad's buses run regularly from Port of Spain to various outlying cities. On Tobago buses are modern, inexpensive, and afford a good view of island life. Fares on both islands start at about $1 and depend on the distance traveled. For information on fares and schedules on both islands, call 623-7872.

CAR RENTAL Rentals are a good choice—that is, if you don't have a problem driving on the left-hand side of the road with a right-hand mounted wheel and can adapt to the flamboyant driving habits of locals. Gas usually costs less than back home. A US, Canadian, or UK driver's license is valid on TT for up to 90 days.

Most rental agencies have desks at *Piarco International Airport,* in addition to other locations. On Trinidad (all the town locations are in Port of Spain) there's *Amar* (Barataria; phone: 674-1783, fax: 675-6227; and other locations on the island), *Autocenter Car* (33-35 Richmond St.; phone: 625-4041), *Auto Rentals* (at the airport, phone/fax: 669-2277; at *Uptown Mall,* Edward St., phone: 623-7368, fax: 675-2258; at the *Cruise Ship Complex,* phone: 624-8687; and other locations on the island), *Econo-Car Rentals Ltd.* (at the airport, phone: 669-2342, fax: 622-8074; and 191-193 Western Main Rd., Cocorite, phone/fax: 622-8074), *Singh's* (at the airport, phone: 664-5417, fax: 664-3860; and 7-9 Wrightson Rd., phone: 623-0150, fax: 627-8476), *Southern Sales and Service* (at the airport, phone: 669-2424; 22 Kew Pl., phone: 625-2461, fax: 623-1546; El Socorro Rd. Extension, phone/fax: 675-2424; and other locations on the island), and *Thrifty* (at the airport; phone: 669-0602). In San Fernando there's *Quality Motors* (23 Scott St.; phone: 652-2795; fax: 657-5755).

On Tobago, there's *Auto Rentals* (at the *Cruise Ship Complex,* Scarborough; phone: 639-5330), *Carlton James* (Crown Point; phone/fax: 639-8084), *Hill Crest Car Rental Service Ltd.* (Mt. Pelier Trace, Northside Rd.; phone: 639-5208), *Peter Gremli Car Rental and Transport Service* (Crown Point; phone: 639-8400), *Quashie's Taxi and Car Rental Service* (*Crown Point Airport;* phone: 639-0350 or 639-8427), *Rattan's Car Rentals Ltd.* (Crown Point; phone/fax: 639-8271), *Singh's* (at the *Grafton Beach* hotel; phone: 639-0624 or 639-0191; fax: 639-0030), *Thrifty* (at the *Turtle Beach* hotel, 201 Courland Bay; phone: 639-8507; fax: 639-0357), and *Tobago Travel* (Store Bay Rd., Crown Point; phone: 639-8778 or 639-8105; fax: 639-8786).

FERRY SERVICES The 450-passenger, high-speed *Sun Island Jet Express* makes the two-and-a-half-hour run daily between the *Cruise Ship Complex* at Port of Spain (phone: 623-0302) and Scarborough (phone: 639-1136) for about $18 one way. For more leisurely travel, there is a ferry that makes the trip in five hours from one or the other *Cruise Ship Complex,* daily except Saturday. For all ferry schedules, call the *Port Authority* (phone: 625-3055 or 639-2417).

INTER-ISLAND FLIGHTS *American Airlines* flies nonstop from Puerto Rico to Trinidad. *LIAT* (on Trinidad, phone: 623-1837; on Tobago, phone: 639-0484) and *Air Caribbean* (phone: 623-2500) schedule daily 20-minute flights between Trinidad and Tobago. *LIAT* also links Trinidad and Tobago with 25 other Caribbean destinations. *Diamond Air* (172 Frederick St., Port of Spain; phone: 624-4555; fax: 623-3300) has daily flights from Trinidad to the Grenadines and other Caribbean islands.

TAXIS Taxis are a good choice for short-term visits. They have plates starting with "H" and can't usually be flagged on the street. Taxis are unmetered, but most routes to downtown areas or hotels have fixed fares (there are surcharges for luggage and late-night trips). Other fares are negotiable, but it's best to agree on a price—and in what currency—before starting. Six-person "mini-taxis" travel certain designated routes (color-coded to the stripes marking the taxis) within cities, while 12-person "maxi-taxis" service set routes to Port of Spain's suburbs.

SIGHTSEEING TOURS Especially for groups, tour operators offer knowledgeable guides and good value; many specialize in wildlife, historical, diving, or fishing tours, so it's a good idea to ask around or consult the tourist office (see *Tourist Information,* above) to locate an outfit that caters to your interests. Some of the best on Trinidad include *AJM Tours/Aerotuy* (90 Queen St.; phone:625-3732; fax: 625-4472), *Classic Tours and Travel Ltd.* (102B Woodford St., Port of Spain, phone: 628-5714, fax: 628-7053; and *Samaroo Building,* 49 Sutton St., San Fernando; phone: 652-3680 or 652-3676), *CTC TNT Explorers* (Royal Palm Plaza, Saddle Rd., Maraval; phone/fax: 628-7487), *Hummingbird Tours* (172 Frederick St., Port of Spain; phone: 624-4555; fax: 627-6110), *Legacy Tours* (7-9 Wrightson Rd., Port of Spain; phone: 623-0150; fax: 627-8476), *Tony's Professional Tour Guiding Service* (Caparita Rd., La Pastora, Upper Santa Cruz; phone: 676-7802), *Travel Centre* (44-58 Edward St., Port of Spain; phone: 623-5096; fax: 623-5101), and *T & T Sightseeing* (*Galleria Shopping Plaza,* 12 Western Main Rd., St. James; phone: 628-1051; fax: 627-0856).

On Tobago, contact *AJM Tours/Aerotuy* (*Crown Point Airport;* phone: 639-0610), *Anjo's Holiday Services* (*Anjo's Villa,* Crown Point; phone/fax: 639-7963), *Ansyle Tours* (Wilson Rd., Scarborough; phone: 639-3865; fax: 639-2829), *Classic Tours and Travel Ltd.* (Friendship Estate; phone: 639-0618), *Good Time Tours* (7 *Cruise Ship Complex,* Scarborough; phone/fax: 639-6816), *Pioneer Journeys* (*Man O' War Bay Cottages,* Charlotteville; phone: 660-4327; fax: 660-4328), or *Tobago Travel* (Store Bay Rd., Crown Point; phone: 639-8778; fax: 639-8786).

SPECIAL EVENTS

A major cultural event is staged somewhere on Trinidad and Tobago every month of the year.

FABULOUS FETES

Carnival The cultural highlight of the year (more properly a state-of-mind than an event) is *Carnival*—where "kalypso" (spelled with a "K" only in TT), *soca,* steel drum, and "playing mas" (masquerade) make time stand still. This late-February bacchanal centers around Port of Spain, though San Fernando, Arima, Scarborough on Tobago, and other outlying areas "jump-up" too. *Carnival* season begins after *Christmas* and officially lasts from *J'Ouvert,* before daybreak on *Carnival Monday,* through midnight on *Carnival Tuesday,* the eve of *Ash Wednesday.* But from the previous *Carnival Saturday* on, the seductively-costumed islanders "tramp" through the streets to the rhythms of large steel-pan orchestras and the satirical lyrics of calypsonians. Music lovers revel in the unique mélange of sounds—from *gospelypso* (gospel and calypso), *rapso* (rap and soul), and *binghi* (hip-hop and calypso), to *chutney* (East Indian and calpyso). If you plan to visit during *Carnival,* make reservations up to a year in advance and expect to pay top dollar for accommodations. For more information on *Carnival,* contact the *National Carnival Commission* (phone:623-8867/9).

The main cultural event on Tobago is the *Tobago Heritage Festival,* which focuses on distinctive traditions in different villages; it's held the last two weeks in July and is highlighted by storytelling, hilarious goat and crab races, folk dancing, and a reenactment of an old-fashioned Tobagonian courtship and wedding. For more information, contact the *Tobago Heritage Office* (phone: 639-4441). Late in July, the world's oldest powerboat race, the *Du Maurier Great Race,* crosses the 86 miles from Port of Spain to Tobago's Store Bay (phone for information: 634-4424 or 634-4449). More goat and crab races are held on *Easter Tuesday* at Buccoo Village.

Around the full moon in March, the *Phagwah Festival of Color* celebrates the Hindu *New Year* (phone for information: 625-3240). In early June Trinidad's St. James, Tunapuna, and southern villages are the place to be for the three-day Muslim festival of *Hosay,* which commemorates the martyrs of the Holy War at Kerbala. Today, the festival features colorful parades of symbolic battle flags, elaborate miniature replicas of the martyrs' tombs *(tadjahs),* and *tassa* drummers.

The *Natural History Festival,* held the first two weeks of October, spotlights TT's natural resources, with the *Orchid Society's Show* a highlight (phone for information: 675-8512). The increasingly popular *Tobago Jazz Carnival* (phone for information: 212-677-3055 in New York City) takes place in late October.

Late October or early November is the time for the *Hindu Festival of Lights,* or *Divali,* best experienced in villages like Chaguanas, where celebrants light thousands of clay lamps *(deyas)* in honor of the goddess Lakshmi (phone for information: 645-3240). Around the same time, a ceremony of purification, *Katik-Nannan,* is performed at Manzanilla to which hundreds of Hindus travel to bathe in the sea. In mid-November, the annual *Pan Jazz Festival* unites international jazz artists with top steel drum masters in a vibrant explosion of new sounds (phone: 628-5476).

Official public holidays, when banks and businesses on both islands are closed, include *New Year's Day, Good Friday* (April 5 in 1996), *Easter Monday* (April 8 in 1996), *Whitmonday* (May 27 in 1996), *Corpus Christi* (May 30 in 1996), *Labor Day* (June 19), *Emancipation Day* (August 1), *Independence Day* (August 31), *Republic Day* (September 24), *Christmas,* and *Boxing Day* (December 26). Moveable festival holidays also include the Muslim *Eid* (in

March) and the Hindu *Divali* (in late October or early November). *Carnival Monday* and *Tuesday* (February 19 and 20 in 1996), though not legal holidays, are in practice observed nationwide.

SHOPPING

Though not a full duty-free port and, as such, not ranked among the Caribbean's shopping meccas, TT has its share of bargains on fine merchandise and exotic gifts. Best buys include clothing, textiles, jewelry, accessories, local music, craftwork (leather, brass, copper, and ceramic), rum, and local artwork. A 15% Value-Added Tax (VAT) is levied on most products, but may be included in the price, so be sure to ask.

Certain "in-bond" stores offer discounted brand-name liquor, perfume, electronics, watches, jewelry, crystal, and more, that can be purchased (and collected upon departure) with the presentation of an air or cruise ticket and passport. Many duty-free shops have outlets at the airports and cruise ship piers on both islands.

Major shopping malls and plazas in Port of Spain and the suburbs (where hours are extended) include the *Long Circular Mall* in St. James, *West Mall* in Westmoorings, the *Cruise Ship Complex* (Wrightson Rd.; phone: 62-SHIPS), *Plaza Aranjuez* (Aranjuez Main Rd., San Juan; phone: 675-1825), *Starlite Shopping Plaza* (Diego Martin Main Rd.; phone: 637-5435), *The Market* at the *Normandie* hotel (10 Nook Ave., St. Ann's; phone: 624-1181), *Valpark Shopping Plaza* (Valsayn; phone: 663-2386), and the *Trinidad Hilton* (Lady Young Rd., Port of Spain; phone: 624-3211). In Maraval, just outside the city, are *Ellerslie Plaza,* the *Kapok Hotel Shopping Arcade* (16 Cotton Hill; phone: 622-6441), and *Royal Palm Plaza* (Saddle Rd.); the *Trincity Mall* is near the airport.

The *Frederick Street* district is the traditional shopping area in Port of Spain, where sidewalk vendors and pushcarts compete with conventional shops. Good buys include porcelain, doeskin gloves, Asian and Indian imports, straw goods, hand-crafted filigree jewelry, music, leather goods, and artwork. Don't miss Port of Spain's *Central Market* on Saturday mornings, when vendors bring their goods—fruit, vegetables, baskets, and vetiver (for sachets)—in from the countryside.

Downtown shopping hours are 8 AM to 4 or 5 PM weekdays, 8 AM to noon Saturdays. In general, malls outside town keep longer hours, usually from 10 AM to 7 PM, Monday through Saturday.

The best shopping is on Trinidad, but shoppers who find themselves going into withdrawal on Tobago can check out the following mini-malls: *IDC Mall* at Sangers Hill, and, in Scarborough, *NIB Mall* near the market, *Cruise Ship Mall* by the ferry terminal, or *Breeze Hall Mall* on Milford Road. Most resort hotels have a boutique or two. Caribbean-colored kiosks on Burnett Street in Scarborough hawk crafts, clothes, and footwear, as do vendors near Pigeon Point. Shopping hours on Tobago tend to be shorter and more erratic than on Trinidad.

For some distinctive gift items, visit any of the following:

TRINIDAD

El Alligator Specializing in leather handbags, briefcases, and accessories. Level Two, *Long Circular Mall,* St. James (phone: 622-7817).

Art Creators & Suppliers Ltd. Trinidad's oldest gallery, representing Geoffrey and Boscoe Holder as well as other fine Trinidadian artists. The gallery also carries books by local authors. In *Aldegonda Park,* 7 St. Ann's Rd., Port of Spain (phone: 624-4369).

The Batique A boutique filled with original batik garments and gift items. 43 Sydenham Ave., St. Ann's (phone: 624-3274).

Begum's Boutique A favorite with an international clientele for custom hand-blocked, appliquéd, and hand-painted collectible clothing by designer Begum Sultana Kazim. At the *Trinidad Hilton,* Lady Young Rd., Port of Spain (phone: 624-3211, ext. 6087).

The Collection Jewelry, china, and collectibles of all sorts. *Town Centre Mall,* Frederick St., Port of Spain (phone: 623-1357).

Fabi Cosmetique et Parfum French and local fragrances and cosmetics. *West Mall,* Westmoorings, Port of Spain (phone: 633-4364).

Lakhan's Bazaar The place for Indian goods, including saris, embroidered purses, and rugs. Bombay St. and Western Main Rd., Port of Spain (no phone).

Meiling One-of-a-kind women's fashion designs, with a distinctive line of island-influenced European styles in linen and batik prints. Two locations: studio at *Satchel's House,* 6 Carlos St., Woodbrook (phone: 627-6975) and boutique at the *Kapok Hotel Shopping Arcade,* 16 Cotton Hill, Maraval, St. Clair (phone: 628-6205).

Patrick's Imported and locally designed fabrics are sold by the yard. Queen and Henry Sts., Port of Spain (phone: 627-9097).

People's Mall Tiny stalls and shops line footpaths with such monikers as Zimbabwe Lane, Freedom Street, and Mandela Way. Many of the items featured have African motifs; most shops accept only cash. Entrances on Frederick St. and Henry St. near Queen St., Port of Spain (no phone).

Rhyner's Record Shop The latest sounds in "kalypso," *soca,* reggae, and *parang.* Two locations: 54 Prince St., Port of Spain (phone: 62-KAISO or 623-5673) and *Rhyner's Music Connection* (duty-free) at *Piarco International Airport* (phone: 669-3064).

Stechers Trinidad's most distinctive retailer, with a stunning array of duty-free crystal, china, watches, jewelry, and other imported luxuries. Main location at 27 Frederick St., Port of Spain, Trinidad (phone: 623-5912 or 623-2586) and six other Trinidad locations; and 45 Carrington St., Scarborough, Tobago (phone: 639-2377).

Trinidad and Tobago Blind Welfare Association Your best bet for rattan and grass weavings—everything from furniture to fruit baskets. Duke and Edward Sts., Port of Spain (phone: 624-3356).

Y de Lima High-quality gold and silver jewelry, duty-free cameras, watches, and a wide selection of crystal and china. There are 15 locations around town and the island, with the main store at 83 Queen St., Port of Spain (phone: 623-1364).

TOBAGO

Gallery Reflections A boutique and art gallery featuring natural-fiber fabric and clothing by the trendiest local designers, plus handwoven African cloth, jewelry, and cosmetics. Buccoo Point. (phone: 639-8463).

Karibik Cotton Batik and tie-dyed clothing and accessories. At *Sandy Point Beach Club,* Crown Point (phone: 639-8391).

Lagniappe Duty-Free Specializing in liquor and tobacco products. At the *Cruise Ship Complex,* Scarborough (phone/fax: 639-7984).

Shore Things Caribbean batik and tie-dyed clothing, plus original watercolors, wood crafts, pottery, hand-crafted jewelry, and beach accessories. At *Conrado Beach Resort,* Pigeon Point (phone: 639-0145).

SPORTS

BICYCLING Biking is a popular pastime on Tobago; contact *Modern Bike Rental* (Scarborough; phone: 639-3275) for bikes or scooters or *Glorious Ride* (Milford Rd., Crown Point; phone: 639-7124 or 639-0617) for bicycles.

BIRD WATCHING Naturalist/ornithologist David Rooks of *Nature Tours* conducts trips to Little Tobago and area rain forests (phone/fax: 639-4276). Also try wildlife photographer Roger Neckles of *Avifauna Tours* (Diego Martin, Trinidad; phone: 633-5614), Pat Turpin of *Pioneer Journeys* (see *Sightseeing Tours*), and Rosemary Hernandez of the *Trinidad and Tobago Field Naturalists Club* (phone: 645-2132). The tourist office also can arrange a number of specialized tours.

CRICKET Played passionately on grounds ranging from manicured ovals to vacant lots, this national spectator sport is also a social event (phone for current schedules: 657-6013).

GOLF Tobago currently has only one golf course, but it's tops. (A second is under construction, but is not expected to open until next year, at the earliest.)

Mount Irvine Golf Club, Tobago It may seem unusual for such a small island to have a championship course, but this one is the quintessence of palm-shaded tropical links (it has been featured on "Wonderful World of Golf"). The 18 holes are set on a taxing 6,793-yard course along the Caribbean coastline, where the vistas are breathtaking. The famed ninth hole is noted for its minuscule green, set at a devilish angle. At the *Mount Irvine Bay Hotel* (see *Checking In*).

The best course on Trinidad is the private 18-hole championship course at *St. Andrews Golf Club* (phone: 629-2314) in Maraval, 3 miles from Port of Spain; temporary memberships are available to visitors. There are also two public, nine-hole courses—the *Chaguaramas Golf Course* on the northwestern coast just outside Port of Spain (phone: 634-4349, ext. 129/145) and the *Brighton Golf Course* at La Brea (no phone).

HIKING On Trinidad, the 1½-mile hike to the Maracas Waterfall north of St. Joseph rewards beginning hikers with a refreshing dip beneath TT's highest falls (300 feet) and views from the Northern Range. The more difficult trek along the Jean-Baptiste Trace from the northern village of Blanchisseuse culminates at a secluded beach. Experienced hikers may attempt a foray (with a guide) into the virgin forest between Blanchisseuse and the village of Matelot, said to be the most beautiful terrain on the island. The *Chaguaramas Development Authority* (Chaguaramas; phone: 634-4227, ext. 104/5) books groups a week in advance for hikes in *Chaguaramas National Park. Hikers 20 Club* (Port of Spain; phone: 622-7731) can schedule groups for a variety of expeditions on Trinidad and Tobago. Hikers also can contact the *Forestry Division* in Port of Spain (phone: 622-4521) for general information.

Favorite haunts of hikers on Tobago are the many old plantation estates, where dirt roads offer easy trekking for beginners. Near Speyside, check out the Merchiston and Belmont Roads. Reached via the Windward Road between Scarborough and Speyside, the area around Hillsborough Dam offers exhilarating views of the coast and excellent bird watching for more accomplished hikers.

HORSE RACING A popular year-round sport with plenty of betting (and breeding programs that are gaining international recognition). The big races are on holidays and during *Carnival* at *Union Park* in San Fernando and *Santa Rosa Park* in Arima. For information, contact the *Trinidad Turf Club* (phone: 625-4122) or the *Trinidad Race Club* at Santa Rosa (phone: 646-0952).

SAILING Racing yachtsmen can check with the *T&T Yachting Association* (phone/fax: 634-4376) for a year-round schedule of races, including dates for the *Angostura Yachting World Regatta* held off Tobago in May. For dockage, contact the *TT Yacht Club* (Chaguaramas, Trinidad; phone/fax: 637-4260). On Tobago, *Sail with Chloe* (phone: 639-9039) and *Loafer* (phone: 639-8555) offer day charters.

SNORKELING AND SCUBA DIVING A largely undiscovered and untouched world class dive destination, Tobago is surrounded by waters with visibility exceeding 100 feet and spectacular coral reefs. The best diving, complete with giant manta rays, is off Speyside, but stunning sites also are found off Charlotteville, Crown Point, and on the West Coast. Buccoo Reef is popular for snorkeling. (*Note:* Learn to identify fire coral, which can deliver a searing burn to snorkelers and divers exploring area reefs.) Certified operators offer a full range of instruction, from resort courses through certification, as well as equipment rental and repair, and boat and beach dives—even drift dives such as the African Express. Several hotels also have facilities for diving. Sean Robinson's *Tobago Dive Experience* at the *Manta Lodge* (see *Checking In*) also has locations at the *Grafton Beach* resort (phone: 639-0191, ext. 39) and at the *Ocean Point Holiday* resort (Milford Rd., Lowlands, Tobago; phone/fax: 639-0973). *Dive Tobago Ltd.*, the oldest dive operation on the island, is at Pigeon Point (phone: 639-0202 or 639-2150; fax: 639-2727). Winston Nanan of *Caroni Tours* (Uriah Butler Hwy., Port of Spain; phone: 645-1305) can arrange diving tours. Also try *Man Friday Diving* (Man of War Bay, Charlotteville; phone/fax: 660-4676), Ellis John's *Tobago Dive Masters* in Scarborough (phone/fax: 639-4697) or at *Palm Tree Village* (see *Checking In*), *Aquamarine Dive Ltd.* at the *Blue Waters Inn* (see *Checking In*), John K. Darwent's *Tobago Marine Sports Ltd.* at the *Crown Reef Hotel* (Scarborough; phone: 639-0291; fax: 639-4416), *Ron's Watersports* (Main Rd., Charlotteville; phone: 622-0459), or *Viking Dive & Yacht Consulting* (Scarborough; phone/fax: 639-9209 or 639-0414).

SOCCER Two major leagues battle it out year-round at the *National Stadium*. The *Trinidad & Tobago Football Association* can provide current schedules (phone: 627-7661).

SPORT FISHING Offshore, coastal, and night fishing charters are available year-round for blue marlin, sailfish, tuna, dolphin, wahoo, kingfish, African pompano, and more. Naturalist David Rooks of *Nature Tours* schedules custom trips (see *Bird Watching,* above). On Tobago, sport fishing charters are also offered by Gerard De Silva on the *Hard Play* (Friendship Estate; phone: 639-7108), Captain Carlos of *RUI Tours* (at *Gomes Sunrise* restaurant, Lower Scarborough; phone: 639-3477), and *Island Yacht Charters* (phone: 637-7389; fax: 628-0437) and *Stanley Dillon* (phone: 639-8765), both at Crown Point. The *Carib International Game Fishing Tournament* is held off Tobago each April; for information, contact the *TT Game Fishing Association* (phone: 624-5304; fax: 627-0391).

SWIMMING, SUNNING, AND SURFING On Trinidad, visitors can choose from the beaches at Maracas and Las Cuevas in the north, Balandra and Toco to the northeast, and Manzanilla and Mayaro in the east. Tobago has a profusion of good beaches. All beaches are accessible by car or bus. Surfing is possible, particularly during winter months, off Tobago's Mt. Irvine Beach, among other areas. Contact the *Surfing Association of Trinidad and Tobago* (phone: 637-4533) for information on current hot spots. Be careful of undertow and strong waves at some beaches, especially on the Atlantic coasts.

TENNIS Most larger hotels have courts; a good one to try is the *Trinidad Hilton* (see *Checking In*), with a new pavilion where non-guests pay an hourly rate. There are public courts in Port of Spain on the grounds of the *Princess Building* off Upper Frederick Street (phone: 623-1121) and in *Skinner Park* in San Fernando (phone: 657-7168). On Tobago, ask about court time at the *Mount Irvine Bay* hotel (see *Checking In*), or *Turtle Beach* hotel (201 Courland Bay; phone: 639-2851).

TURTLE WATCHING From March through August, late-night watching for leatherbacks requires patience, but the reward—the sight of a nesting turtle the size of a Volkswagen—is unforgettable. The leeward side of Tobago and the east coast of Trinidad are favored nesting grounds for this endangered species. Contact the *Wildlife Section* of the *Forestry Division* (phone: 622-4521, ext. 104) for locations and information on permits (which may require a small fee and take a few days to process).

WINDSURFING Contact the *Windsurfing Association of Trinidad and Tobago* (phone: 659-2457) for information on the best current conditions and on places that offer equipment and instruction.

NIGHTLIFE

Port of Spain offers a variety of cultural events—from dance to experimental theater to opera—in venues that include *Queen's Hall* on the grounds of the *President's House* (1-3 St. Ann's Rd.; phone: 624-1284), the *Little Carib Theatre* (White & Roberts Sts., Woodbrook; phone: 622-4644), and the *Space Theatre* (*Bretton Hall,* 16 Victoria Ave.; phone: 623-0732).

Trinidad comes alive after sunset, when the after-work crowd heads to fashionable pubs or bars, but nightclubs don't fill until close to midnight. Most large hotels offer floor shows, music, and dancing. The recently renovated *Carnival Bar* at the *Trinidad Hilton* (see *Checking In*), with an intriguing decor that features Carnival masks and tables that resemble steel drums, is an upscale "in" spot for live music on Friday and Saturday nights. Tuesday evenings, the *Hilton's* Poolside Fiesta draws a crowd for steel drum, calypso, and a Trinidadian buffet. Other nightspots include the English-style *Pelican Inn Pub* (2-4 Coblentz Ave., Cascade; phone: 624-7486) and *Rafters,* which livens up at happy hour (see *Eating Out*). Jazz and calypso clubs in Port of Spain include *Philip & Fraser's,* offering live jazz on Friday nights (16 Phillips St.; phone: 623-7632); *Cricket Wicket* (opposite the *Oval* at 149 Tragarete Rd.; phone: 622-1808); and *Moon Over Bourbon St.* (at *West Mall;* phone: 637-3448). If you can't make it for *Carnival,* the next best thing is to "lime" (what Trinidadians do when they relax and shoot the breeze) at the *Mas Camp Pub* (French St. at Ariapita Ave., Port of Spain; phone: 623-3745), where the locals talk about little else.

Tobago's nightlife is more subdued, except in Scarborough and the Crown Point area, where several discos and bars hop until the wee hours. Gus Goddard's *Cabin Pub* (Carrington St., Scarborough; phone: 639-3196) is a hospitable dockside tavern that's popular with yachtsmen. Locals gather on Fridays and Saturdays at *The Starting Gate* (off Shirvan Rd.; phone: 639-0225), noted for its pub grub, grafitti-covered chalkboard ceiling, and namesake lawn ornament. Larger hotels and resorts regularly offer floor shows, steel drum bands, and limbo exhibitions and contests. The bamboo-and-thatch *Village* resaurant, at the *Kariwak Village* resort near the airport, offers live, *soca*-inflected jazz on Friday and Saturday nights. In addition, watch for posters announcing moonlit beach barbecues and church fund-raisers, which usually feature plenty of music, food, and refreshments. Buccoo Point is the late-night party spot, where Tobagonians attend the weekly "Sunday School," a not-too-pious beach bacchanal that starts late and often extends until dawn on Monday.

Best on the Islands

CHECKING IN

Accommodations on Trinidad run the gamut from deluxe high-rise convention centers in the city to small luxury hotels and condo/villa complexes in suburban areas. For a truer island flavor, there are several rental cottages and guesthouses; those who want to enjoy affordable Trinidadian hospitality should contact the *Trinidad & Tobago Bed and Breakfast Cooperative Society Ltd.* (phone/fax: 627-BEDS) or the *Tobago Bed & Breakfast Association* (phone: 639-3926 or 639-8836; fax: 639-3566).

Many of the larger hotels are near Port of Spain, an advantage for those with sightseeing, shopping, or business on their agendas, but less convenient for the avid beachcomber.

Expect to pay $100 to $200 (or more) a night for a double room, without meals, during the winter season at hotels we place in the expensive category; between $75 and $100 at places in the moderate range; and less than $75 a night for inexpensive accommodations. Rates are subject to a 10% room tax, and some places also tack on a 10% to 15% service charge. Many hotels offer Modified American Plan (MAP) rates, which include breakfast and dinner, at an additional $20 to $40 per person per day. Summer rates on Trinidad are somewhat lower—about 10% to 20% less. Special rates (sometimes twice the regular rates) and multiple-night-stay requirements are often in effect during *Carnival,* when rooms are in short supply. Unless otherwise noted, all hotels listed below accept major credit cards and feature air conditioning, telephones, TV sets, and private baths. All telephone numbers are in the 809 area code unless otherwise indicated.

TRINIDAD

PORT OF SPAIN AND ENVIRONS

EXPENSIVE

Trinidad Hilton Located on a hilltop just 17 miles from *Piarco International Airport,* this 12-story, upside-down hotel (with its lobby on top and guestrooms below) is *the* premier address for both business and leisure travelers. In addition to 394 recently refurbished rooms, all with private balconies offering spectacular views of *Queen's Park Savannah,* the Northern Range, and the Gulf of Paria, it boasts the largest convention facility in the southern Caribbean; the final phase of a multimillion-dollar expansion was set for completion at press time with the opening of a high-tech Executive Business Center and the last of 20 function rooms. Two refurbished restaurants, *La Boucan* (see *Eating Out*) and the *Pool Terrace Garden,* are supplemented by theme buffets held by the two pools (shaped like Trinidad and Tobago). There are also two lighted tennis courts in a new, covered pavilion, a health club with sauna, and a shopping arcade. Lady Young Rd., Port of Spain (phone: 624-3211; 800-HILTONS; fax: 624-4485).

MODERATE

Chaconia Inn This low-rise hotel 10 miles from Maracas Beach is popular with Trinidadians as well as visitors. There are 33 rooms and two-bedroom apartments, 21 of which have kitchenettes. A pool, a sun deck, two restaurants, a popular pub, and proximity to shopping and an 18-hole golf course are among its attractions. 106 Saddle Rd., Maraval (phone: 628-8603/5; 800-223-6510; fax: 628-3214).

Kapok An unpretentious, intimate hotel near the *Savannah* that offers 71 rooms and suites, some with kitchens, just minutes from downtown sightseeing and shopping. Features include a pool, easy access to beach transportation, two restaurants and bars, and boutiques. One child under 12 stays at no charge (two children may occupy an adjoining room at a single-occupancy rate). 16-18 Cotton Hill, St. Clair (phone: 622-6441; 800-74-CHARMS; fax: 622-9677).

Normandie Hotel This historic hotel's 53 units preserve the charm of the original 1930s structure on the site of *La Fantasie* plantation. There are 41 standard and deluxe rooms, plus 12 units with sleeping lofts, some overlooking a pool in a garden setting and all within walking distance of the *Savannah.* Also featured are a conference facility, nightlife at the *Cascade Club,* an aerobics room, and a shopping arcade. Children under 12 stay at no charge.

Be sure to dine at *La Fantasie* (see *Eating Out*) or "take tea" at *Café Trinidad.* 10 Nook Ave., St. Ann's (phone/fax: 624-1181/4).

Valley Vue Just 10 minutes from Port of Spain in lush St. Ann's Valley, this popular hotel has 68 rooms, including 12 suites, and plenty to do. In addition to three 400-foot water slides and a pool, there are squash and tennis courts, a fitness center with sauna, shops, a disco, a restaurant, and a bar. Children under 12 stay at no charge. 67 Ariapita Rd., St. Ann's Valley (phone: 623-3511; fax: 627-8046).

INEXPENSIVE

Monique's Guest House This engagingly informal establishment is the place to experience true island hospitality. There are 20 charming and spacious rooms with carpeted or teakwood floors, some with kitchenettes and TV sets. The *St. Andrew's Golf Club* is nearby. There's no restaurant. Children under 12 stay at no charge. 114 Saddle Rd., Maraval (phone: 628-3334 or 628-2351; fax: 622-3232).

ELSEWHERE ON TRINIDAD

MODERATE

Asa Wright Nature Centre & Lodge Even if you're not a bird watcher, you'll enjoy this Victorian plantation greathouse set in a 200-acre wildlife sanctuary laced with lush rain forest trails (see *Special Places*). Its 20 twin-bedded and three single rooms are comfortable, but none has air conditioning, telephone, or a TV set; guestrooms Nos. 5 or 6 in the main building are large, charming, and high-ceilinged. There's a lovely pool with a waterfall. Rates include three hearty meals. Mile Marker 7½, Blanchisseuse Rd., Arima, 20 miles from Port of Spain (phone: 667-4655; 800-426-7781; fax: 667-0493).

Timberline Nature Resorts The 10 units here are in intriguing converted cocoa houses in an idyllic beachfront setting on Trinidad's north coast. The rooms are simple—there's no air conditioning, telephones, or TV sets. Nature lovers can enjoy the island's most popular beach or bird watching trails. Rates include breakfast and dinner. Maracas Bay Rd., Maracas (phone: 638-2263, evenings).

INEXPENSIVE

Pax Guesthouse These 19 rooms (including one two-room cottage) are part of a monastery at Mount St. Benedict in the breezy hills of Tunapuna, about 20 minutes from Port of Spain. The rooms are spartan, but pleasantly simple and furnished with a few antiques. Some rooms offer cooking facilities, but none has air conditioning, a telephone, or a TV set; five have private baths. Highlights include spectacular views, bird watching, nature trails, three tennis courts, and a dining room that serves a celebrated high tea. Rates include breakfast and dinner (phone/fax: 662-4084).

TOBAGO

Tobago's accommodations range from luxury resorts and villas to small hotels and quaint bed and breakfast establishments. The current island-wide room count (about 800) is expected to triple in the next few years, in conjunction with controlled development designed to protect the environment. The *Tobago Villas Agency* (phone/fax: 639-8737) lists several attractive villas throughout *Mt. Irvine Estate.* Winter rates at expensive hotels run about $175 and more per night for a double room; a moderate place will charge $100 to $175; an inexpensive establishment will cost from $50 to $100. Tobago's rates are considerably lower (40% or so) in summer. Most hotels offer a Modified American Plan at additional cost, and all-inclusive stays are becoming popular. Unless otherwise noted, all hotels listed below accept major credit cards and feature air conditioning, telephones, TV sets, and private baths. Telephone numbers are in the 809 area code unless otherwise indicated.

CROWN POINT–STORE BAY–AIRPORT AREA

MODERATE

Sandy Point Beach Club and Village This resort complex includes condominium, time-share, and hotel units. The 35 units in the *Village* have kitchenettes; upper-level rooms have sleeping lofts. Features include two pools (one with a swim-up bar), the *Man Friday's* (see *Eating Out*) and *Steak Hut* restaurants, and a free shuttle to the beach. Crown Point (phone: 639-8391; 800-223-6510; fax: 639-8495).

INEXPENSIVE

Golden Thistle Hotel A 15-minute walk from Store Bay Beach, this relaxing, small hotel has 36 rooms, all with fully-equipped kitchens (none with telephones). There's a pool and a restaurant. One child under 12 stays at no charge. Store Bay Local Rd., Crown Point (phone/fax: 639-8521).

NORTH SHORE

EXPENSIVE

Arnos Vale All 30 rooms and three suites face the Caribbean at this lush, secluded 40-acre property set on a hillside overlooking the beach. Rooms are large and handsomely furnished (no TV sets, though there's one in the lobby). Features include beach bars, a tennis court, a boutique, a disco, and a pool. The food is first-rate at the two restaurants. Arnos Vale Rd., Plymouth (phone: 639-2881/2 or 639-3247; fax: 639-4629 or 639-3251).

Grafton Beach This award-winning, low-rise resort sits on five beautifully-landscaped acres with a crescent beach shared by the affiliated *Le Grand Courlan* (see below) next door and an adjacent bird sanctuary. There are 112 rooms and two suites with Jacuzzis; all rooms have ceiling fans, mini-bars, satellite TV, and a balcony or patio with ocean views. Facilities include complimentary water sports, a pool with swim-up bar, two air conditioned squash/racquetball courts, a Jacuzzi, a dive shop, a gameroom, a fitness center, and tennis at *Le Grand Courlan*. There are two bars and restaurants, both featuring nightly live entertainment—the excellent *Oceanview* and *Neptune's Seafood* (see *Eating Out* for both). The *Mount Irvine Golf Club* is nearby. Children ages one through four stay at no charge. Black Rock (phone: 639-0191; 800-223-6510; fax: 639-0030).

Le Grand Courlan Unveiled just last year and even more upscale than its sister property next door (see above), this elegant new hotel features 68 luxuriously-furnished rooms (eight with outdoor hot tubs) and 10 suites (with Jacuzzis), each with a balcony commanding a panoramic view. All rooms are equipped with such amenities as mini-bars, safes, cable TV, and two telephones. There's a massive pool with a swim-up bar, tennis and squash courts, a cocktail lounge, spa facilities, and three restaurants. The resort shares a water sports facility featuring scuba diving and complimentary windsurfers, sailboats, and canoes with the *Grafton Beach* hotel. The *Mount Irvine Golf Club* is nearby. Black Rock (phone: 639-0191; 800-223-6510; fax: 639-0030).

Mount Irvine Bay Hotel & Golf Club Set amid 16 tropical acres overlooking the Caribbean Sea, this plush resort features the island's only 18-hole championship golf course (at which guests are entitled to reduced greens fees). There are 114 rooms, including 46 two-room garden cottages, each with a refrigerator and a patio view of the fairways or the sea, and a main building with 52 comfortable rooms that wrap around a pool with a swim-up bar and six one- and two-bedroom suites. There are two lighted tennis courts, a sauna, as well as three choices for fine dining—the *Jacaranda, Le Beau Rivage,* and the *Sugar Mill* (see *Eating Out*). A variety of water sports, including sailing and water skiing, are available. Five miles from *Crown Point Airport* (phone: 639-8871/2/3; 800-44-UTELL; fax: 639-8800).

INEXPENSIVE

Cocrico Inn This charming, island-style inn has a pool, a boutique, and a popular restaurant and bar (see *Eating Out*) that displays works by local artists. Thirteen of the 16 rooms are air conditioned; some have kitchenettes and TV sets (none has a telephone). The beach is a five-minute walk away, and golf and tennis are nearby. Children under 12 stay at no charge. Plymouth (phone: 639-2961; 800-223-9815; fax: 639-6565).

SOUTH SHORE–SCARBOROUGH

MODERATE

Palm Tree Village Popular with families and activity-oriented travelers, this seaside getaway is set on 2 miles of pristine beach great for windsurfing and diving. The resort offers 20 standard rooms with Caribbean-inspired decor, featuring hardwood floors and teak furniture; there are also 20 two-bedroom suites and 18 self-contained villas with full kitchens, large living rooms, and patios. Amenities include a restaurant, a pool, tennis courts, a children's playground, a fitness center, and a conference facility. There's a riding stable nearby. Little Rockly Bay, Milford (phone: 639-4347/9; 800-223-6510; fax: 639-4180).

INEXPENSIVE

Della Mira Guest House Proximity to Scarborough and the beach makes this a popular choice. Its 12 rooms (some with air conditioning and TV sets, none with telephones) are among the best values on the island. There's a restaurant, a beauty salon, a pool, and a nightclub next door. Bacolet St., Scarborough (phone/fax: 639-2531).

EAST END

MODERATE

Richmond Great House With a six-acre hilltop setting, this elegantly restored 1766 sugar plantation greathouse is popular with history buffs and solitude seekers. It offers six generous rooms (none with air conditioning, some with ceiling fans) open to ocean vistas and cooling breezes; a telephone and a TV set are in the common area. Features include a large dining room, a library, a sitting room, a pool, and an interesting, private collection of African art and textiles. Belle Gardens (phone: 660-4467; fax: 623-2213).

INEXPENSIVE

Blue Waters Inn This secluded naturalist's and diver's haven on the northeastern coast is set on 46 lush acres beside a horseshoe-shape bay overlooking Little Tobago and Goat Island. The inn has recently refurbished most of its 38 rooms, which include 31 standard rooms, three pricier one- and two-bedroom bungalows with kitchens, and four efficiencies. All rooms have ceiling fans (air conditioning by request only) and balconies with ocean views, but no telephones or TV sets (there's a main TV lounge). Features include an extensive dive facility, a new 180-foot jetty with facilities for visiting yachtspeople, a tennis court, a restaurant, and a bar that's a popular divers' hangout. There are also a variety of water sports, including kayaking, snorkeling, and windsurfing, and the inn's grounds are great for bird watching. Batteaux Bay, Speyside (phone: 660-4341 or 660-4077; 800-742-4276; fax: 660-5195).

Manta Lodge Newly opened by Sean Robinson to cater to serious divers and bird watchers, this 22-room lodge overlooking the beach was named for the monster manta rays (fondly known as "Tobago taxis") that frequent nearby dive sites. All rooms have ceiling fans; 12 are air conditioned, and some have kitchenettes (no telephones or TV sets). Several two-bedroom tree-top cottages perched on stilts are scheduled for completion this year. Also here are an informal restaurant with an honor bar, nature trails, bird feeding stations, and a full-service dive shop and repair facility that offers daily boat and beach dives. Speyside (phone/fax: 660-5268).

EATING OUT

A wide variety of dishes reflecting these islands' fusion of cultures is available in Trinidad and, to a lesser extent, in Tobago, where traditional delicacies such as *manicou* (opossum) and *tatou* (armadillo) stews seldom appear on menus outside the legal hunting season (the unadventurous can heave a sigh of relief). More commonly served island specialties are crab backs (stuffed crabs), *chip-chip* (tiny clam-like shellfish), and "doubles" (fried *bara* bread filled with curried chickpeas), as well as the national dish—Indian-spiced roti, a folded-up flat-bread sandwich stuffed with curried chickpea paste (*channa*) and meat, fish, or vegetables. Chase a fiery-hot meal with a rum punch made with Angostura bitters (produced exclusively on Trinidad), or a Carib or Stag beer. The deluxe Royal Oak, Vat 19, and White Oak rums are also made at the House of Angostura, as is a coffee liqueur, Mokatia.

In the listing below, dinner for two will cost $60 or more, not including drinks or tip, at restaurants described as expensive; from about $30 to $60 at moderate places; and $30 or less at inexpensive places. Unless otherwise noted, all restaurants listed below are open for lunch and dinner. All telephone numbers are in the 809 area code unless otherwise indicated.

TRINIDAD

PORT OF SPAIN AND ENVIRONS

EXPENSIVE

La Boucan Named for the smoking process used by buccaneers to preserve meat, the *Trinidad Hilton*'s elegant restaurant sports a replica of this cooking apparatus and incorporates its subtle, smoky flavor into some of its international and Caribbean specialties. There's a buffet lunch on weekdays and live entertainment during afternoon tea (Wednesdays through Fridays) and dinner. Closed Sundays. Reservations advised. Major credit cards accepted. Lady Young Rd., Port of Spain (phone: 624-3211).

MODERATE

Café Savanna This romantic spot features Caribbean and creole specialties including *callaloo* (a soup made with a spinach-like green), fish baked in banana leaves, and flying fish. Closed Saturday lunch and Sundays. Reservations advised. Major credit cards accepted. In the *Kapok Hotel,* 16-18 Cotton Hill, St. Clair (phone: 622-6441).

La Fantasie This hotel restaurant features innovative nouvelle cuisine creole, a creative updating of Trinidad's traditional cooking. Menu favorites include crab backs stuffed with herb-seasoned crabmeat, and lobster thermidor with lime-garlic butter, and there's a popular six-course Chinese dinner on Saturdays. Open daily for breakfast, lunch, and dinner; closed Saturday lunch. Reservations advised. Major credit cards accepted. In the *Normandie Hotel,* 10 Nook Ave., St. Ann's (phone/fax: 624-1181).

Rafters A rustic yet private lunch spot that specializes in local seafood and carved meat buffets. A great value, the Wednesday seafood buffet includes everything from lobster to local *chip-chip.* Thursdays through Saturdays, the buffet features roast beef or lamb. It's also known for its popular happy hour (5 to 7 PM). Closed Sundays. Reservations advised. Major credit cards accepted. 6A Warner St., Woodbrook (phone/fax: 628-9258).

INEXPENSIVE

China Palace Trinidadian Chinese restaurants like this one don't include vegetables in meat and fish dishes, and rice must be ordered separately. A tangy starter here is shrimp souse, a variation on traditional Trinidadian souse (pork in a spicy marinade). The Wednesday night buffet offers a sampling of house specialties. Open daily, except holidays. Reservations advised. Major credit cards accepted. In *Ellerslie Plaza,* St. Clair (phone: 622-5866).

Monsoon Busy at lunch, but less hectic in the evening, this authentic Trinidadian-Indian eatery has a modern, stylish decor with attentive service. Closed Sundays. Reservations advised for groups of six or more. Major credit cards accepted. 72 Tragarete Rd., Port of Spain (phone: 628-7684).

Veni Mangé A not-to-be-missed lunch spot in a typical creole home renowned for its gallery of local art and authentic creole cuisine with a French flair. The menu changes frequently, but the flying fish, kingfish, and *callaloo* are popular items, as are the tropical cocktails. Open for lunch Mondays through Thursdays; open Wednesday nights for prix fixe dinner, and Fridays at happy hour for drinks and snacks only. Closed weekends and during *Christmas* holidays. Reservations advised for groups of six or more. Major credit cards accepted. 13 Lucknow St., St. James (phone: 622-7533).

TOBAGO

EXPENSIVE

Neptune's Seafood Enjoy a pampered evening in a splendid bayview setting with an extensive seafood menu presided over by the *Grafton Beach* resort's award-winning chef, Cyril Sammy. There's live entertainment nightly. Open daily. Reservations necessary for dinner. Major credit cards accepted. Black Rock (phone: 639-0191; fax: 639-0030).

Oceanview The *Grafton Beach* resort's open-air verandah offers a panoramic view of Stone Haven Bay for breakfast, lunch, or dinner. It's an informally elegant setting for à la carte Caribbean and international cuisine or theme buffets such as Caribbean Night, Indian Night, and Pirate's Night. There's live entertainment nightly. Open daily. Reservations necessary for dinner. Major credit cards accepted. Black Rock (phone: 639-0191; fax: 639-0030).

Sugar Mill Here, guests dine in a relaxed atmosphere in a 17th-century sugar mill built of coral block. Choose from an à la carte menu or buffet, both featuring local seafood, creole, and international cuisine; there's a special Caribbean/creole dinner on Mondays and a barbecue on Fridays. Open daily. Reservations necessary. Major credit cards accepted. At the *Mount Irvine Bay Hotel & Golf Club* (phone: 639-8871).

MODERATE

Blue Crab On a verandah overlooking Rockly Bay, this lunch spot features seafood and local dishes, including crab backs, conch chowder, and homemade ice cream. Closed weekends. Reservations (by noon) necessary for dinner. Major credit cards accepted. At Main and Robinson Sts., Scarborough (phone: 639-2737).

Cocrico Inn Tobagonian fare and seafood dishes are the specialty here, served in a charming dining room. Open daily. Reservations advised. Major credit cards accepted. Plymouth (phone: 639-2961; fax: 639-6565).

Dillon's Owned by sport fisherman Captain Stanley Dillon, this popular seafood restaurant can get hectic, but the lobster is memorable. Open for dinner only; closed Mondays. Reservations advised. Major credit cards accepted. Milford Rd., Crown Point (phone: 639-8765).

Man Friday's The perfect place to relax beside a sparkling waterfall with a sundowner cocktail, Wendell Newallo's new hot spot at the *Sandy Point Beach Club* features alfresco seaside dining with local and international flair, either à la carte or as a prix fixe buffet. Lobster platters and Thai dishes are specialties. There's also a Sunday brunch and a Thursday night barbecue with steel band (for which reservations are a must). Open daily for breakfast, lunch, and dinner. Reservations advised. Major credit cards accepted. Crown Point (phone 639-9547).

Old Donkey Cart House In an old Edwardian home offering dining in a palm garden or on verandahs, this unique spot owned by Tobagonian Gloria Jones Knapp boasts fine international and local cuisine and a select cellar of European wines. Closed Wednesdays during summer. Reservations advised on weekends. Major credit cards accepted. Bacolet St., Scarborough (phone: 639-3551; fax: 639-6124).

Papillon Managed by Jakob Straessle, this restaurant in the *Old Grange Inn* has long been popular for an extensive menu of international dishes and local seafood specialties, such as mountain stream langoustines. Guests may be seated in the air conditioned dining room or in the adjacent *Grotto Ticino,* a garden patio. There's also a bar and lounge, the *Bijou.* Closed Sundays. Reservations advised. Major credit cards accepted. Buccoo and Auchenskoech Rds. (phone: 639-0275; fax: 639-9395).

La Tartaruga A small dining room featuring Italian and seafood dishes in a homey atmosphere overlooking Buccoo Bay. Open for dinner only; closed Sundays and Mondays. Reservations necessary. Major credit cards accepted. Buccoo Bay (phone: 639-0940).

Village Sample some of the most enticing preparations of Caribbean and international dishes on the island in a rustic bamboo setting at the *Kariwak Village* resort. Open daily. Reservations advised. Major credit cards accepted. Crown Point (phone: 639-8545; Fax: 639-8441).

INEXPENSIVE

Jemma's Seafood Kitchen Serving Tobagonian fare at its best, this charming treehouse restaurant with a bamboo ceiling and antique chairs overlooks a tranquil beach where fishing boats bob at anchor. Open for breakfast, lunch, and dinner Mondays through Thursdays, lunch only on Fridays and Sundays; closed Saturdays. No reservations. No credit cards accepted. Speyside (phone: 660-4066).

The US Virgin Islands

Among the most beautiful islands in the entire Caribbean are the three siblings that make up the US Virgin Islands—St. Croix, St. John, and St. Thomas. Products of a common history, set in the same sea, they are at once the same and very different—St. Thomas with steep, green mountains and lengths of shining sands; St. John with a cover of jungle and its share of beaches, most within the boundaries of the extraordinary *Virgin Islands National Park;* and St. Croix, the most underrated of the three, with nostalgic towns, ruins of plantation houses, and rolling, breeze-combed grass hills and valleys.

Despite their insistent greenery and profuse flowers, the USVI are counted among the dry islands of the Caribbean; just why is most evident on St. Croix, where the landscape gradually browns as the dry season wears on. Prickly fingered cacti are the chief botanical feature of its Atlantic tip—the easternmost tip of US territory. This dry weather, however, means lots of sunshine. Breezes temper the humidity so that even late summer days, with midday temperatures in the low 90s, are fairly comfortable.

The blue and green waters around the islands are clean and clear thanks to the national park, which protects 5,650 acres offshore and 9,000 acres of land on St. John. *Virgin Islands National Park* was established in 1956 after extensive donations of land by Laurance Rockefeller's Rockresort Foundation. It has set the pace for similar preserves on a number of other Caribbean islands.

Since Columbus discovered the islands in 1493, St. Croix, St. John, and St. Thomas have attracted the attention of more outside powers than any other Caribbean isles. The flags of Spain, the Knights of Malta, France, England, Holland, Denmark, and the United States have flown over them. Columbus and his men came ashore near St. Croix's Salt River in search of water, but were repulsed by Carib Indians. Columbus hastily named the island for the Holy Cross (Santa Cruz) and shoved off to discover St. Thomas and St. John. He then named the whole group—which at that time included the British Virgin Islands—for the legendary 11,000 virgin followers of St. Ursula, and moved on to Puerto Rico.

A century later, in 1593, Sir Francis Drake put in at St. Thomas and St. John on his way to attack the Spanish at San Juan. In 1625—although the islands were still technically Spanish—British, Dutch, and French colonists established farms on St. Croix. By 1650, the French and Dutch were gone, and Spain returned to expel the British as well. In 1653, St. Croix was given to the crusaders' Order of St. John, better known as the Knights of Malta. A few years later, France took it over, and for the next half century or so, possession of this largest of the Virgin Islands alternated between the French and the Spanish.

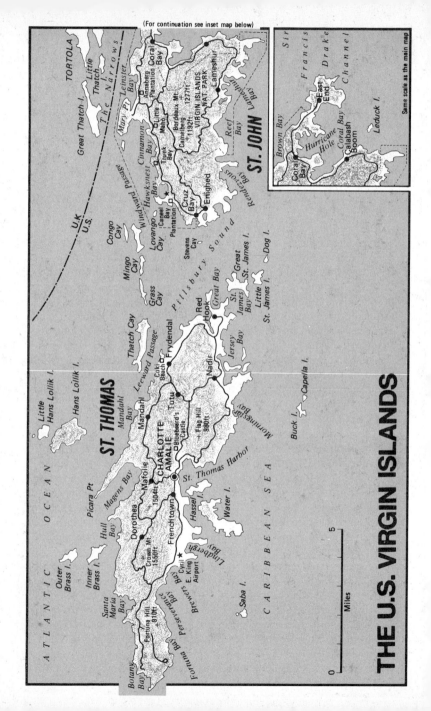

THE U.S. VIRGIN ISLANDS

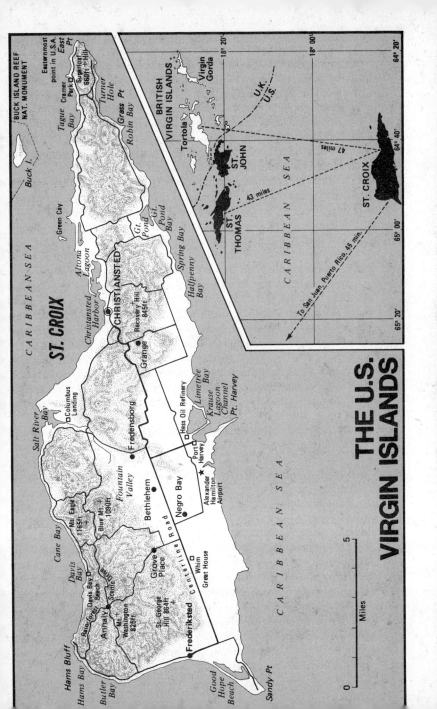

The other two islands, meanwhile, had become the property of the Danish West India and Guinea Company. The company name indicates the three cardinal points of the triangular trade in which it was involved: Denmark, where its investors lived; the West Indies, where they grew and processed sugarcane; and Africa (then called Guinea), where they captured the slaves whose labor made operations profitable. On St. Thomas, the Danes founded the town of Charlotte Amalie (pronounced Ah-*mahl*-yah). At the height of its sugar-producing days in the 17th century, St. Thomas had 170 plantations, but the number dwindled quickly. The terrain proved too rugged for agriculture, and St. Thomas's economic focus shifted to trade. In 1724 it became a free port where goods were exempt from customs duties and regulation. The laissez-faire atmosphere made it a favorite among pirates, especially the infamous Blackbeard and Captain Kidd.

While commerce—legitimate and otherwise—outstripped sugarcane on St. Thomas, agriculture thrived on St. John. When the Danish West India Company first took title, the island was shared by some British squatters and a few established Danes. A quarter of a century later, in 1717, the company set up a permanent colony and port at Coral Bay. It was expected that the town and sturdy *Fort Frederiksvaern,* with its fine harbor, would someday surpass Charlotte Amalie as the principal city of the Danish West Indies. Cane flourished, along with tobacco and cotton. By 1733, there were 208 whites and 1,087 slaves on the island. All seemed prosperous and serene until November 23, 1733, when the slaves revolted, maddened by their masters' cruelty and made distraught by drought, plague, and a crop-leveling hurricane. A number of settlers and the entire white garrison at Coral Bay's *Fort Berg* were killed. On the other side of the island, 40 planters holed up near Caneel Bay; many escaped to St. Thomas.

By the following May, the Danes, backed by two French warships and an army from Martinique, retook the island and subdued the rebel slaves. The island was devastated, but the Danes (and capitalism) prevailed. Homes and sugar factories were rebuilt, cane was replanted, and prosperity returned—for a while.

St. John's story might have unfolded differently had Denmark not fought with France in the Napoleonic Wars. This was just the excuse for aggression for which the British on nearby Tortola had been waiting. They occupied St. John briefly in 1801 and again for seven years beginning in 1807. By the time the Danes regained possession of St. John, the island's economic base had been dealt a mortal blow—not so much by the British as by progress itself. European-grown sugar beets were gradually taking over the sugar market, and in 1848 slavery was abolished on St. John. Even though the steam engine was already replacing manpower in some island sugar mill operations, the plantation lifestyle couldn't adapt to the loss of slave labor. Soon after abolition, the Danish planters who hadn't already left because of failing cane markets sailed for home.

If it had not been for World War I, St. Croix, St. John, and St. Thomas might still be Danish. But when the sugar industry began to crumble, Denmark started looking for buyers. In 1917, the United States, worried about possible unfriendly bases in the Caribbean that might threaten the Panama Canal or the US mainland, bought the three islands for $25 million. Today, although some fine old Danish buildings remain and streets have Danish *gade* (street) signs, the atmosphere of the US Virgin Islands is distinctly American. St. Croix became better known when the *Westin Carambola Beach Resort* opened in 1986, and the condominium developers moved in. Future plans include building a conference center elsewhere on the island. In addition, shallow-draft cruise ships are now docking at Christiansted, and Frederiksted boasts a new, state-of-the-art dock that accommodates most ships. In spite of the increase in development, St. Croix is a surprisingly livable island. Neither as developed as St. Thomas nor as rural and raw as St. John, it boasts a number of historical sites, plenty of water sports facilities, and enough restaurants, hotels, and nightspots to keep most visitors happy.

St. John, which pulled a blanket of jungle over its head when the Danish planters left in 1848, is reawakening. This process first started in 1956, when the national park was established and Laurance Rockefeller built his *Caneel Bay* resort, allowing visitors to enjoy the park in ultra-comfort. A second stage of development was launched in 1976 with the camp-in-comfort *Maho Bay* resort. This attracted a new wave of more adventuresome travelers, intrigued by the park and the island's history. The third stage began in the late 1980s with the opening of the *Hyatt Regency* and the inevitable appearance of condominiums.

St. Thomas, liveliest of the island trio, takes its quickened pace from active visitors who swim, sail, windsurf, dive, and water-ski off its spectacular beaches and explore its up-hill-and-down-dale roads in cars and jeeps. They gather in seafront watering spots and choose from an array of restaurants and nightclubs in the evenings. The press of local hawkers and the onslaught of cruise passengers (often thousands a day) make Charlotte Amalie a good place to avoid on days when several ships are in port (Wednesdays and Fridays are generally busiest). But St. Thomas's boosters believe that the island's beauty and fun more than make up for the inconvenience of crowds.

Residents of all three islands are somewhat ambivalent about the changes wrought by new development. There is controversy concerning the effects of tourism on the environment, and nowhere is that more evident than on St. John, which fears for the future of the national park and is fighting to keep the cruise ships away. As elsewhere in the Caribbean, modern life has intruded to the degree that lonely nighttime walks down dark streets in Virgin Island towns are not recommended; unfortunately, such warnings, sensibly applied, have become a "given" of contemporary travel.

But understanding that few places are exempt from today's tensions or nature's wrath, savvy travelers continue to return to the US Virgins, because they also recognize that few, if any, islands anywhere in the world offer so much in the way of natural beauty and potential pleasure.

US Virgin Islands At-a-Glance

FROM THE AIR

In addition to the three major US Virgin Islands—St. Croix, St. John, and St. Thomas—there are approximately 50 smaller islets and cays, most of them uninhabited. Spread over some 14,000 square miles of Caribbean and Atlantic waters, the US Virgin Islands are part of the Leeward Islands in the Lesser Antilles and have a total population of over 150,000. The center of the island group is about 60 miles east of Puerto Rico and just west of the smaller British Virgin Islands. St. Croix (pronounced *Croy*) is the largest of the group (23 miles long and 6 miles across at its widest point), 40 miles south of the other two main islands and entirely surrounded by the Caribbean Sea. Long, narrow St. Thomas (12 miles long and 3 miles wide) and little St. John (9 by 3 miles) are next-door neighbors, only 3 miles apart, both with northern coasts washed by the Atlantic and southern sides bathed by the Caribbean Sea.

St. Croix looks like a caveman's club floating northeast (handle end) to southwest (round end) in the Caribbean. Its rolling land is still laid out in fields where cane used to grow. About 150 chunky stone towers—former plantation windmills—dot the hills of St. Croix. Most island areas are still identified by names of the original plantations. St. Croix has two towns: Christiansted, tucked into a reef-protected harbor a little east of center on its north coast, and Frederiksted, its deep-water port, in the middle of its western coast. *Alexander Hamilton Airport* is about a 10-minute drive due east of Frederiksted. Farther east along the south shore is St. Croix's major industrial development: the Hess Oil Refinery. The northern road out of Frederiksted leads toward the island's small rain forest and the Scenic Drive, which follows along the crest of these hills, overlooking Fountain Valley to the south and, to the north, Cane Bay and Davis Bay, two of St. Croix's many handsome beaches.

St. John, amoeba-shaped and indented with beach-lined bays, rises to inland heights covered with tropical forest. In the early 1800s, it boasted more than a hundred sugar plantations; now ruins of the old greathouses and sugar mills lie hidden in the undergrowth of the *Virgin Islands National Park,* which covers nearly 60% of the island's 20 square miles. One of the island's most beautiful beaches is Francis Bay, at the end of the road past Little Maho. While Cruz Bay still lacks the sophistication of a modern mainland city, its pace is more frenetic now than it has been.

St. Thomas has an elongated hourglass shape, its waist cinched by a deep-water harbor on the south and horseshoe-shaped Magens Bay on the north. A ridge of mountains forms its spinal column. Surrounding the harbor and climbing the green hills beyond are the red-roofed houses of Charlotte Amalie, St. Thomas's only city and the capital of the US Virgin Islands, with a population of about 25,000. Since it has a major cruise port and an excellent shopping center, Charlotte Amalie's population swells by thousands of visitors whenever ships come into port, which is usually every day. Beyond the town, St. Thomas is a scenic collection of hills rising up to 1,500 feet and sloping steeply down to beaches cupped in curved bays on the jagged southern coast, or down to longer sweeps of white sand on the northern shore. *Cyril E. King Airport* (with its air conditioned terminal and spiffy shops) is on the south shore, about a 10-minute drive west of town. About 20 minutes to the east, at the end of the island, Red Hook Harbor has marina facilities for pleasure and deep-sea fishing boats and docks for ferries and launches that make the trip across Pillsbury Sound to St. John, Tortola, Jost Van Dyke, and other islands.

SPECIAL PLACES: ST. CROIX

CHRISTIANSTED St. Croix's largest town, Christiansted is a cozy and culturally active community. Begin your sightseeing tour in the heart of town, where handsome 18th-century buildings stand near the harbor. Built by the Danish West India and Guinea Company, they're now a US National Historic Site. The *Old Scalehouse,* where Danish customs officers once weighed imports and exports, faces the waterfront; it now houses the *Visitors' Information Bureau,* where a free *Walking Tour Guide,* a map of the four-square-block historic area, and a number of brochures on the island are available. Also see *Testaments in Stone: Historic Sites* in DIVERSIONS.

Just east of the *Scalehouse,* across a small park, stands *Fort Christiansvaern,* painted yellow and built on the foundations of a 1645 French fortress. Inside there are fine harbor views from battlements lined with cannon (never fired at an invader). A free pamphlet provides information about the dungeons, powder magazine, barracks, officers' kitchen, and battery. Five rooms have been designed to look as they did in the 1840s. The fort's single non-military exhibit tells all about Buck Island Reef. Tours are available on request. Open daily; no admission charge for those under 16 or over 62 (phone: 773-1460). A block from the fort, on Company Street, stands the *Steeple Building.* Originally a Lutheran church, it has served as a military bakery, a hospital, and a school; today it's a historical museum with a small collection of Carib and Arawak artifacts, old uniforms, a diorama showing Christiansted as it was around 1800, an exhibit on black urban history during the Danish period, a display of drawings and photos of Christiansted's historic Danish architecture, and a visitors' orientation center. Closed weekends; admission charge (phone: 773-1460). Diagonally across the street, the post office does business in what was once the Danish West India and Guinea Company warehouse, built in 1749.

From the post office, head back toward the *Scalehouse,* turn left, and walk one block up King Street to *Government House,* the impressive cream-and-white former residence of the Danish governor-general. A small red Danish guardhouse still stands at the foot of the formal staircase, which leads from the courtyard to a grand ballroom with chandeliers, chimneyed sconces, and a dining table—copies of the originals—presented by the King and Queen of Denmark when the building was restored several decades ago. Official receptions are still held here, and visitors can look in daily.

At the outdoor market at "Shan" Hendricks Square, a short stroll away on Company Street, stalls are full of island-grown vegetables and fruit, including the pulpy green genips that are island favorites. Be sure to try one. Saturday morning is the best time to check out the market. Between Company Street and the harbor, old buildings, arcades, patios, and walkways are full of shops; a number of them are branches of St. Thomas stores. The harbor itself, with its bustling small boat traffic, is a fascinating sight.

FREDERIKSTED Seventeen miles from Christiansted at the west end of the island, this town comes to life when a cruise ship ties up at its deep-water pier. At other times, the town snoozes, especially during the summer, when a number of its restaurants and shops hang out "Closed for the season" signs. Still, it's worth some browsing time because it is so different from Christiansted.

First of all, it looks different—more Victorian gingerbread than colonial Danish—though a few of its landmarks do date from the 1700s. Most buildings of that era were destroyed in a devastating fire in 1878, however, and Frederikstedders rebuilt the city, elaborate curlicued fretwork replacing the straightforward lines and arches of earlier Danish architecture. Try to go on a day when no cruise ship is in port so that you'll be able to park at the north end of town near the pier. The visitors' bureau at the end of the Frederiksted pier can provide a free *Walking Tour Guide* and a map. *Fort Frederik,* on the other side of Lagoon Street, is the logical place to begin a walking tour. Built in 1752 and now restored and repainted (Danish-fort red and white, naturally), it was the site of the 1848 proclamation freeing the slaves. It also claims to have been the first foreign fort to have fired a salute to the American flag—flown by a US merchant ship—on October 25, 1776. The Dutch island of St. Eustatius files a counterclaim by virtue of its salute to the Stars and Stripes aboard the US man-of-war *Andrew Doria* on November 16, 1776. The issue seems to hinge on the ownership (private or federal) of the vessel involved. At the fort, you can inspect the courtyard, the stable, the canteen, and the art exhibit in the old garrison. Closed weekends and holidays; no admission charge (phone: 772-2021).

Two blocks south and one block east of the fort, at the corner of Prince and Queen Streets, is Market Place. Islanders have sold locally grown produce and herbs here since the town's founding in 1751. A block farther down Prince Street, at the corner of Market, is an interesting, though unrestored, antique masonry and frame residence, beyond which is *St. Patrick's Church,* erected in 1843. On Hospital Street (parallel to Prince Street, one block east) stands an 18th-century building that was originally a residence, then a school. On Strand Street, which runs along the waterfront, the *Old Customs House* (late 18th century), now the headquarters of the Energy Commission, and *Victoria House,* with its elaborate gingerbread trim, are prime examples of Frederiksted's two favorite building styles. Children especially will enjoy the *St. Croix Aquarium* (Strand St.; phone: 772-1345). It's open Wednesdays through Sundays; admission charge.

ELSEWHERE ON ST. CROIX

NORTH OF FREDERIKSTED The shore road north passes *Sprat Hall,* an old plantation home that's now a guesthouse with cottages and a restaurant (see *Eating Out*), to the rain forest, the Scenic Drive (see *From the Air,* above), and 150-foot-high Creque Dam (pronounced *Cree*-ky), surrounded by yellow cedar, mahogany trees, and lilies.

SUGAR COUNTRY The Centerline Road heads northeast from Frederiksted across what was once St. Croix's sugar country. The land is green and rolling, still neatly divided into fields, though it has been a number of years since sugarcane has been cultivated here. (Local distilleries now make their rum from imported molasses.) Old stone mill towers (at Bodkin, Jolly Hill, and Mount Eagle) seem to watch through window eyes as you drive past. The map of this area is scribbled with antique plantation names like Upper and Lower Love, Jealousy, Sally's Fancy, Anna's Hope, and John's Rest. The last is the site of *Estate Whim Plantation Museum,* off Centerline Road a few minutes from Frederiksted. Distinctive in shape, it is a long, graceful oval with rounded ends. There are just three rooms in the main part of the house: a large dining room and a large bedroom, divided by a central reception or living room. It's small—only one story high—but the 16½-foot ceiling and many tall windows give it an airy feeling. The *Landmarks Society* has furnished it with 17th- and 18th-century pieces. Outside there's a watchhouse, the ruins of the sugar boiling factory, a mule mill, a steam chimney, and a windmill with grinding machinery. The slave quarters have been restored, and fields of sugarcane planted. On an island of now-vaneless towers, it is satisfying to see all four of the mill's big sail arms restored. This place provides visitors with a good explanation of how a sugar plantation operated; the demonstrations of johnnycake making are especially interesting. There's also a small museum, including an apothecary from 1832, and a shop (see *Shopping*). Closed Sundays; admission charge (phone: 772-0598).

CRUZAN RUM FACTORY Not far from Christiansted (W. Airport Rd., Estate Diamond; phone: 772-0280/3), the factory offers guided tours weekdays. The admission charge includes rum drink samples.

JUDITH'S FANCY Located off Route 751, northwest of Christiansted, there are impressively proportioned ruins of the onetime home of the Governor of the Knights of Malta. From the hill beyond the structure there's a view of the mouth of the Salt River, where Columbus was driven off by resident Carib Indians in 1493 (he later called the place the Cape of Arrows) and still the only spot in US territory where Columbus is known to have actually landed. Declared a national park in 1992, Salt River was cleaned up of sunken boats and debris left by 1989's Hurricane Hugo, and a commemorative plaque was installed. A popular place for windsurfing and water skiing, there's also a "submarine canyon" here, where the water's depth suddenly drops off to 2,000 feet, making it a fascinating dive site as well.

ST. GEORGE VILLAGE BOTANICAL GARDEN Off Centerline Road, Frederiksted, this is a historically interesting combination of trees, blooms, and village ruins, including slave quarters. The latest addition is a walk-through tropical rain forest. The fine, airy central building is the site of frequent concerts and special events and also houses a gift shop with a selection of Cruzan crafts and edibles. The garden is open Tuesdays through Fridays and on days cruise ships are in port; closed holidays. Admission charge (phone: 772-3874).

SPECIAL PLACES: ST. JOHN

A tour of this island can take no time or forever—it all depends on how interested you are in nature.

CRUZ BAY The island's town is tiny and informal, with a harbor, St. John's Square, a communications center, and a bank. It also has a scattering of boutiques, and the *Mongoose Junction* marketplace, which houses *Paradiso,* one of the island's best restaurants (see *Eating Out*). First check the bulletin board at the ferry dock for news of local happenings, then have a cup of coffee at the *Back Yard* (phone: 776-8553), *Joe's Diner* (phone: 776-6888), or the *Lime Inn* (see *Eating Out*) to pick up some local color.

VIRGIN ISLANDS NATIONAL PARK This is the real place of interest on St. John. Start explorations at the park headquarters on the *National Park Service* dock (along the waterfront to the left as you leave the ferry dock). Regular briefings and slide talks about the park and its flora, fauna, and history take place here. Rangers know all about the area's native birds (from pelicans to sandpipers), trees (including stands of mahogany and bay—from which the "bay" of bay rum comes), and flowers (tamarind, flamboyant, shower of gold). They'll also tell you about the mongooses, imported here to hunt rats. Park guides lead nature walks and set up evening programs on a flexible schedule at *Maho Bay Camps, Cinnamon Bay, Caneel Bay,* and other locations. Open daily. No admission charge. Call 776-6201 for a complete rundown of park activities.

You can rent a car or take a safari bus tour into the park, but you'll have more fun and come home with a better sense of the island if you make your first tour with one of the native drivers who gather near the ferry dock around mid-morning. The classic route takes in Trunk Bay; *Annaberg Plantation,* the ruins of a greathouse that have been marked for self-guided tours; and assorted lookout points. An alternate tour follows the old Danish Centerline Road to the almost forgotten settlement of Coral Bay, with its 18th-century Moravian church and Fort Berg Hill ruins. The park is also crisscrossed with clearly mapped hiking trails, some of which were old Danish roads and all of which—except the steep climb to see the plantation ruins and the petroglyphs above Reef Bay—are reasonably easy going. For additional details, see *Natural Wonderlands* in DIVERSIONS.

If you sail, you can take the sea route to Hurricane Hole, a postcard-perfect harbor surrounded by park wilderness, as well as to Coral Bay, Lameshur Bay, Reef Bay, and Chocolate Hole. Ask at the visitors' bureau in Cruz Bay (see *Tourist Information,* below) for information about local skippered or bareboat rentals. Don't forget that almost a third of the park is under water. There is a spectacular underwater trail at Trunk Bay, which the park service administers and which allows you to snorkel along coral reefs amid schools of tropical fish. In the past, the sheer number of tourists had largely destroyed its appeal; to remedy this situation, the *National Park Service* has set a maximum number of visitors to Trunk Bay to 500 at one time; the limit for smaller beaches is 75.

SPECIAL PLACES: ST. THOMAS

CHARLOTTE AMALIE Charlotte Amalie's harbor has been a haven for ships—merchantmen, naval vessels, and buccaneer galleons—since the 1600s. The town's white and pastel buildings cover the waterfront and three steep hills called (from west to east) Denmark Hill, Synagogue Hill, and Government Hill. Along the harbor, warehouses that in another age held pirates' loot are now chock-full of duty-free shops stocked with imported luxuries that lure shiploads of shoppers docked at the deep-water pier out toward the harbor's east end.

Start your walking tour in the narrow streets near the Charlotte Amalie waterfront at the *Grand* hotel. Built in 1839, it no longer takes guests, but still dispenses hospitality in the Project St. Thomas's ground-floor visitors' center. Next door is *Emancipation Park,* a tiny plot that commemorates the 1848 proclamation that freed the slaves. Across the street to the west of the park is the post office, embellished inside with murals by the illustrator Stephen Dohanos. Beyond the post office lies Main Street and the alleys and passages of the principal shopping district.

Southeast of the park stands *Fort Christian,* a venerable monument painted rust red and topped with a clock tower. Built by the Danes in 1671, it has served as a jail, courthouse, church, rectory, governor's residence, and a police station. Now a national landmark, its dungeons house a small museum with a modest collection of Arawak and Carib relics; there are also displays depicting the life of the early Danish settlement, including a re-creation of a Danish plantation and merchants' furniture made from local mahogany. At press time, the fort was closed for restorations; call ahead to check (phone: 776-4566). The *Legislative Building* is on the harbor side of the fort; visitors can observe when the Senate is in session.

High on Government Hill, overlooking the town and the waterfront, the white brick and wood *Government House,* built in 1867 as a meeting place for the Danish Colonial Council, is now the official residence of the Governor of the US Virgin Islands. The first two floors, where murals portray significant moments in the islands' history, are open to the public daily; no admission charge (phone: 774-0001). There's also a collection of oil paintings by St. Thomian artists, including French Impressionist Camille Pissarro, who lived in the building that now houses a branch of *Tropicana Perfume Shoppes* (see *Shopping*) before moving to Paris. His relatives are buried in the Jewish cemetery in the Savan district, on the low peninsula to the west of town. Its epitaphs date from 1792.

On the same street as *Government House* (Kongens Gade, Danish for King's Street), overlooking *Emancipation Park,* stands *Hotel 1829* (see *Checking In*), originally a mansion built in that year by a French sea captain named Lavalette. (His initials appear entwined in the hotel's wrought-iron balcony.) Between the hotel and *Government House,* the staircase known as the Street of 99 Steps (actually, there are 103) climbs to the summit of Government Hill.

Not far from the stairs are remnants of 17th-century fortifications originally known as *Fort Skytsborg,* now a 24-room hotel called *Blackbeard's Castle* (see *Checking In*). Historically, the name Blackbeard refers to the pirate Edward Teach, who frequented St. Thomas in the 1700s. (Confusingly, there's also a *Bluebeard's Tower* atop another 300-foot hill at the eastern edge of town. This one—its historic origins are vague—has a honeymoon suite on its top floor and is a part of *Bluebeard's Castle* hotel; see *Checking In*.) At the foot of Government Hill on Norre Gade stands the yellow-brick *Frederick Lutheran Church,* built in 1820. Its serene interior is decorated with white pews, a mahogany altar, and impressive antique chandeliers; the church still uses 18th-century ecclesiastical silver brought from Denmark.

The synagogue of St. Thomas's Jewish congregation—*Beracha Veshalom U'Gemilut Hasidim* (Blessing and Peace and Loving Deeds)—overlooks the town from neighboring Synagogue Hill. It is reached by a steep climb from Main Street up to Krystal Gade. Built by Sephardic Jews in 1833, it is one of the Western Hemisphere's oldest synagogues (the oldest is on Curaçao). In the traditional arrangement, benches face inward along three sides and the floor is covered with sand.

Farther west, where Main Street intersects Strand Gade, is Market Square. A slave market before emancipation, it is now a roofed-over, open-air block of stalls where island farmers and gardeners sell their produce. Closed Sundays. (Saturday is the biggest market day.) Action is liveliest and the light for picture taking best in the early morning. After your market rounds, follow Strand Gade to the waterfront, where you can buy a fresh coconut; ask the seller to lop off its top so you can drink the sweet milk from the hull.

ELSEWHERE ON ST. THOMAS

Having seen Charlotte Amalie on foot, get wheels (rental or taxi) to tour the rest of St. Thomas. Head west out of town on Main Street, connecting with Harwood Highway. You also may want to follow Veterans Drive along the waterfront and turn off to the left at the Villa Olga sign to visit Frenchtown (also called Cha Cha Town for the peaked straw hats called "cha chas" that are made and worn there). It is an enclave of descendants of refugees from the Swedish invasion of St. Barthélemy in the late 18th century; residents still speak a Norman French dialect.

Farther west off Harwood Highway, turn right at Contant Hill, and climb Crown Mountain Road for super views of green hills, white beaches, and blue seas. For a stunning view of Drake's Passage, which separates the British and US Virgin Islands, stop at the perch called *Drake's Seat,* where Sir Francis himself allegedly watched the galleons go by. From this point, there's a splendid view of the passage Drake first navigated in 1580, plus an entire panorama of almost a hundred Virgin Islands—both US and British. Another option is to drive higher, to *Mountain Top,* a shopping complex with spectacular views (see *Shopping*).

Continue east along northern roads with fine views of Magens Bay, Mandahl Bay, and others. At the T-shaped intersection near the *Green Parrot* restaurant in the *Magens Point* hotel, continue east, following the signs to the intriguing attraction called *Coral World* (at Coki Beach), a completely remodeled marine park with an underwater observatory tower planted on the sea floor. You climb down 14 feet for a wide-windowed view of reef life. The best time to visit is at 10 and 11 AM, when the fish are being fed. Geodesic domes housing an aquarium, a restaurant, shops, a tropical bird show, and a museum are also part of the complex. It's open daily; admission charge (phone: 775-1555).

On your way to or from *Coral World,* stop at the *Tillett Gardens* silk-screening complex, built around an old sugar mill (see *Shopping*). Watch the silk screeners work and browse through the gallery and boutique here. Arts festivals are also held here three times a year: *Thanksgiving* weekend, in March, and in August.

In a clockwise direction, the road leads past Pineapple, Pelican, and Sapphire Beaches, and Red Hook (where ferries leave for St. John and other ports). Before finishing the circle—back to home base in Charlotte Amalie—stop at the *Havensight Mall* for a brief but panoramic ride up Flag Hill on the *Paradise Point Gondola.* At the top, there are shops and an open-air restaurant where you can relax and take in the scenic view. Open daily. Admission charge (phone: 774-9809). Across the way from the mall on Flag Hill is the site of the *Cultural Center of the Caribbean,* scheduled to open later this year. The focal point of this complex will be an IMAX theater with a six-story-high, 86-foot-wide screen that shows a breathtaking 45-minute film on the Caribbean. Also planned are shops selling local crafts, eateries serving Caribbean food, and—to add to the carnival atmosphere—steel drum players and "moko jumbis"—costumed men on stilts (open daily; no local phone at press time).

Sources and Resources

TOURIST INFORMATION

The *US Virgin Islands Division of Tourism* maintains a number of visitors information bureaus to provide on-the-spot information.

On St. Croix: Tourist bureaus are located at the airport, in the *Scalehouse* at Christiansted's harbor (phone: 773-0495), and at the end of Frederiksted's cruise ship pier (phone: 772-0357). All are open daily.

On St. John: The tourist office is around the corner from the Cruz Bay ferry dock by the post office. Open daily (phone: 776-6450).

On St. Thomas: Offices are at the airport (phone: 774-8784), on the waterfront in Charlotte Amalie (phone: 774-8784, ext. 147), and in *Havensight Mall* near the cruise ship pier (phone: 774-8784, ext. 150). All are open daily. As part of their Project St. Thomas, merchants maintain a hospitality lounge in the *Old Customs House* next to *Little Switzerland,* where visitors can pick up information, rest, even check shopping bags for a small fee; closed Sundays (phone: 774-8784).

The *Division of Tourism* also has branch offices in numerous US cities (see GETTING READY TO GO).

LOCAL COVERAGE There are several sources of up-to-the-minute information: *WHERE, St. Thomas This Week* (which includes St. John information), *St. Croix This Week,* and *Today in St. Thomas* cover special events, shopping, restaurants, and nightlife. *Best Buys* is another source of shopping information, while *What to Do in St. Thomas and St. John* (published biannually) highlights activities. All are available free in airports, hotels, and shops.

St. Thomas's *Daily News,* St. Croix's *Avis,* and St. John's *Tradewinds* cover local, national, and international news. The *San Juan Star* (Virgin Islands edition), *The New York Times, New York Daily News, Wall Street Journal,* and *Miami Herald* are available on newsstands daily. The annual *Virgin Islands Playground* is a tourist-oriented magazine.

Island Insight, a 24-hour cable TV station featuring information on hotels, shopping, and car rentals for all three islands, runs on channel 4.

For history buffs, Florence Lewisohn's lively *The Romantic History of St. Croix* (St. Croix Landmarks Society; $6.95) is required reading, and *The Undiscovered Gifts of the Caribbean,* a historical guide to the entire region, is available for $2 (plus a $2.50 shipping fee) from *Partners for Livable Places* (1429 21st St. NW, Washington, DC 20036; phone: 202-887-5990).

RADIO AND TELEVISION In addition to CBS television programming on channel 10, an ABC News-feed on St. Croix's WSVI (channel 8), and PBS on WTJX (channel 12), many hotels on St. Thomas and St. Croix have satellite reception, which brings in movies and wider TV programming. St. Croix has three FM radio stations: WAVI (93.5 FM), playing urban contemporary music; WJKC, Isle 95 (95.5 FM), playing adult contemporary music; and WVIQ, 99Q (99 FM), with easy listening music. There's also an AM station, WRRA (1290 AM), programming Caribbean music and talk shows. On St. Thomas there are two AM stations: WSTA, Lucky 13 (1340 AM), playing soul, R&B, and Caribbean music, and the local CBS affiliate, WVWI, Radio One (1000 AM), with CBS news and sports, *Wall Street Journal* reports, and weather, as well as adult contemporary and Caribbean music. St. Thomas has five FM stations: WGOD (98 FM), with gospel music and Christian programming; WIYC (104 FM), the sister station to St. Croix's Isle 95, playing adult contemporary hits; WIVI (96.1 FM), playing rock and alternative music; WTBN (102.1 FM), playing jazz, R&B, and reggae; and WVGN (105.3 FM), sister station to St. Croix's WAVI, playing urban contemporary music.

TELEPHONE The area code for the USVI is 809. Dial 911 for emergency assistance.

ENTRY REQUIREMENTS No passports or visas are required of US citizens. If you're contemplating a side trip to the neighboring British Virgin Islands, however, bring proof of citizenship (passport or birth certificate and photo ID). Canadians must have a current passport.

CLIMATE AND CLOTHES The average winter temperature is 77F (25C), with lows around 69F (21C) and highs of up to 84F (29C). The average summer temperature, dehumidified by the trade winds from the east, is 82F (28C), sometimes dropping to 75F (24C). Summer can bring some extremely hot days, but there's usually a brief shower to cool off the evenings. Average annual rainfall is 40 inches, but even in the rainiest months (September through January), days with no sunshine are rare.

"Casual chic" is the tourist office's description of the islands' dress code. In practice, attire is more casual than chic—even the toniest hotels and restaurants rarely hold fast to the tie and jacket rule, even in season. However, wearing shorts indoors after dark in public places is *verboten* at *Caneel Bay.* For men and women, sports clothes are the daytime rule. Cutoffs, jeans, and T-shirts are okay if you're camping or sporting, but not for resort hotels or sit-down restaurants. Wearing an uncovered bathing suit away from the beach is against the law. Evenings call for something a little dressier, and women may want a shawl or sweater on winter nights.

MONEY US dollars are the local currency.

LANGUAGE English is the official language, but you'll still hear Norman French spoken in French Town, and islanders also speak a local patois—English

Creole—that's a puzzling but musical mix of English, African, and Spanish. As there is a large Puerto Rican population—particularly on St. Croix—Spanish can be considered the islands' second language.

TIME The US Virgin Islands are on atlantic standard time, one hour ahead of eastern standard time. When it's noon in Charlotte Amalie, it's 11 AM in New York. When the mainland is on daylight saving time, Virgin Island and East Coast times are the same.

CURRENT Current is 110 AC, the same as on the mainland US, so US-made appliances don't need adapters.

TIPPING When the hotel adds an automatic 10% to 15% service charge, you need not leave tips for the room maid, dining room waiter or waitress, or other hotel personnel. Tips are customary, however, for service above and beyond the expected: give $1 to the bellboy who runs a special errand; $2 to the wine steward who brings and serves your wine. When no service charge is added, give the maid $1 to $2 for each day of your stay, your dining waiter 15% of the check—or $2.50 to $3 per person a day, depending on the class of hotel and number of meals included. Bartenders and bar waiters should be tipped 10% to 15% whenever they serve you. Bellboys and porters get at least 50¢ per bag, and never less than $1 on arrival or departure. Tip taxi drivers 15% of the fare.

GETTING AROUND: ST. CROIX

BUS Modern, air conditioned public buses, called "Vitrans," service the entire island. Fares start at 75¢ at press time; the exact fare depends on how far you're going. Buses run on an irregular schedule from 6 AM to 9 PM daily. Look for bus stops along the island's main thoroughfares.

CAR RENTAL Ideal for exploring on your own. *Avis* (phone: 778-9365; 800-331-1084), *Budget* (phone: 778-9636; 800-472-3325), *Hertz* (phone: 778-1402; 800-654-3131), and local agencies have offices in Christiansted; some firms also have branches in Frederiksted. *Olympic* (phone: 773-2208, 772-1617, or 773-9588; 800-344-5776) is a good local agency with somewhat lower rates. Most car rental agencies will deliver a car to your hotel within two hours of your call. But since demand sometimes exceeds supply, especially in high season, reserve well ahead through your travel agent or the larger rental companies' toll-free reservation services. Driving in the US Virgin Islands is on the left side of the road.

INTER-ISLAND FLIGHTS *American Eagle* (phone: 776-6450; 800-433-7300) provides local service, flying approximately every hour to San Juan, Puerto Rico, and frequently each way from St. Thomas to St. Croix and Tortola. *LIAT* (phone: 778-9930; 800-774-2313) carries passengers from and to St. Maarten, Antigua, Barbados, and other islands to the south. *Air St. Thomas* (phone: 776-2992; 800-619-0013) handles small-plane charters. There are several helicopter operators, among them *Air Center Helicopters* (phone: 775-7335) and *Hill Aviation* (phone: 776-7880; 809-723-3385, in Puerto Rico).

SEA EXCURSIONS *Mile Mark Charters* (at the *King Christian* hotel, Christiansted; phone: 773-2285, 773-2628, or 773-2482; 800-524-2012) runs full- and half-day charters on its sleek trimaran *Trine*. Another option is *Dive St. Croix* (Christiansted; phone: 773-3434; 800-523-DIVE). The *Junie Bomba* (phone: 772-2482) out of Frederiksted offers sunset cruises (limited to six passengers). Your hotel travel desk will have up-to-date information on twilight sails, cocktail cruises, and special excursions.

An all-day sail to Buck Island Reef—the country's only underwater national monument—is a must. The *US Park Service* has laid down an underwater trail marked with surface floats and blue sea-floor signs that identify coral formations and plants for passing snorkelers. The fish are fantastic—90 species swim alongside hawksbill sea turtles. The coral reef, with some of the world's largest specimens of elkhorn coral, rises 30 feet from the sea floor. Guides aboard day-trip boats help beginners get used to the gear and lead snorkelers along the reef (it's easy). Non-swimmers can ride in a glass-bottom dinghy or catch a life preserver tow. Make reservations through your hotel or wander down to the harbor and make your own arrangements on the spot. Beer and soft drinks are provided (sometimes at additional charge), but bring your own picnic (unless a barbecue is included), towel, and an extra T-shirt for sunburn protection while you're swimming along the trails.

Among the charterers offering Buck Island excursions: the *Windancer* (phone: 773-0754), the *Teroro II* (*Green Cay Marina,* Christiansted; phone: 773-3161 or 773-4041), *Big Beard's Adventure Tours* (*Pan Am Pavilion,* Christiansted; phone: 773-4482), and *Mile Mark Charters* (see above). All operate out of Christiansted Harbor.

SIGHTSEEING BUS TOURS Mostly timed and organized with cruise ship passengers in mind. *Travellers' Tours* (at the *Alexander Hamilton Airport;* phone: 778-1636) runs a three-hour island tour; *St. Croix Safari Tours* (2157 King Cross St., Christiansted; phone: 773-6700) offers an especially well guided four-hour bus tour and can arrange minibus tours; and *Smitty's* (King St., Christiansted; phone: 773-9188) gives 4½-hour tours.

SIGHTSEEING TAXI TOURS A good way to see the island. Drivers are usually good guides. Ask your hotel travel desk to recommend one and negotiate a price for the length of tour you'd like.

TAXI Cabs are easy to find in towns and at the airport. No matter how far out your hotel may be, the desk usually can get a taxi within half an hour. As cabs are unmetered, it's best to settle on a price before you get in. At the airport, a list of rates is posted by the baggage counter.

GETTING AROUND: ST. JOHN

BUS Open-air safari buses run from Cruz Bay to points around the island; fares vary, but generally start at around $3.

CAR RENTAL Agencies, all located in Cruz Bay, include *St. John Car Rental* (phone: 776-6103), *Hertz* (phone: 776-6695; 800-654-3001), *St. John Development Corporation* (phone: 776-6343), *Avis* (phone: 776-6374; 800-331-1084), *Delbert Hill Taxi & Jeep Rental* (phone: 776-6637; 800-537-6238), *Spencer's Jeeps & Cars* (phone: 776-6628), and *Denzil Clyne Jeeps & Cars* (phone: 776-6715). Four-wheel-drive is not essential for exploring.

FERRY SERVICES Ferries frequently cross Pillsbury Sound to Red Hook on St. Thomas. The trip takes 20 minutes; one-way fare is $3 per adult, $1.25 per senior citizen, $1 per child under 12. For a current schedule, check with the visitors' bureau, the dockside bulletin board, or the ticket office at the dock in Cruz Bay (phone: 776-6282). Ferry boats also leave from Cruz Bay for Charlotte Amalie on St. Thomas (near the Coast Guard dock) and Tortola, British Virgin Islands. The trip to Charlotte Amalie takes about 45 minutes; one-way fare is $7 per adult, $3 per child. There's also launch service from the *Caneel Bay* resort (see *Checking In,* below) to the *National Park* dock at Red Hook. One-way fare is $9 per person, and the trip takes about 20 minutes. *Sundance* runs frequently between Cruz Bay and West End on Tortola; the 30-minute trip costs $18 one way (phone: 776-6597). The *Mona Queen* (phone: 776-6597) links Cruz Bay with Jost Van Dyke, British Virgin Islands; the 45-minute trip costs $18 one way.

INTER-ISLAND FLIGHTS See listings for St. Croix, above.

SEA EXCURSIONS Several outfits offer *PADI* scuba instruction and certification, equipment rentals, and reef and wreck dives: *Cruz Bay Watersports Co.* (in Cruz Bay; phone: 776-6234); *Low Key Watersports* (in Wharfside Village; phone: 693-8999; 800-835-7718), which also arranges sport fishing and day sailing excursions; and *St. John Water Sports/Hinkley Charters* (in *Mongoose Junction;* phone: 776-6256).

TAXI Available, but not always where and when you want them. If you find a driver you like, take his card so you can get in touch by phone. Tours are also available by cab. License plates on official taxis read "JP."

GETTING AROUND: ST. THOMAS

BUS The air conditioned *Manassah Bus,* or "Vitran" (phone: 774-5678), offers two routes: The Country Bus makes one trip about every hour between town and Red Hook (fare: $1); the City Bus travels between the hospital area west of town into Charlotte Amalie three or four times an hour (75¢). A safari bus also shuttles between downtown Charlotte Amalie's Market Place and Red Hook hourly during the day for about $3 each way. Check your hotel or the tourist office for schedules; ask, too, about shuttle service to *Tillett Gardens* and *Coral World.*

CAR RENTAL Easily arranged, but relatively expensive; weekly rates may provide a better per-day price. Reserve well in advance for *Christmas* and *Carnival* weeks. Honda scooters can be rented by the hour or day. *Avis* (phone: 774-1468; 800-331-1084), *Budget* (phone: 776-5774; 800-626-4516), *Hertz* (phone: 774-1879; 800-654-3001), *National* (phone: 776-3616), *Dollar* (phone: 776-0850), *Thrifty* (phone: 775-7282; 800-367-2277), and *Discount* (phone: 776-4858) have offices at or near the airport. *Avis, Budget, Hertz,* and a number of local operators, such as *Paradise Car Rental* (phone: 775-7282), have downtown offices, too. *ABC* (phone: 776-1222), *Dependable* (phone: 774-2253; 800-522-3076), *Cowpet Auto Rental* (phone: 775-7376; 800-524-2072), *Sea Breeze Car Rental* (phone: 774-7200), and *V.I. Auto Rental* (phone: 776-3616; 800-843-3571) are good local firms that offer bargain rates. Your driver's license is good for up to 90 days on the islands. Just remember to keep left.

FERRY SERVICES There is regular service between Red Hook and St. John (see listings for St. John, above), as well as launch service from Red Hook to Charlotte Amalie (near the Coast Guard dock). The *Reefer* (phone: 776-8500, ext. 625 or 445) connects Charlotte Amalie and *Marriott's Frenchman's Reef* for $3.50 one way. It leaves on the hour from the waterfront and on the half hour from the hotel Mondays through Saturdays.

Native Son (phone: 774-8685 or 775-3111) and *Smith's Ferry* (phone: 775-7292) operate from Charlotte Amalie's waterfront to Tortola's West End (45 minutes each way) and Road Town (1½ hours each way); the round trip costs $35. *Smith's Ferry* also makes the trip to Virgin Gorda (two hours each way) for $50 (reservations necessary), and *Native Son* also links Red Hook and Tortola (30 minutes each way); the round trip costs $31. The *Mona Queen* (phone: 776-6597 or 776-6282) sails to Jost Van Dyke; the round trip costs $31.

INTER-ISLAND FLIGHTS See listings for St. Croix, above.

SEA EXCURSIONS The *Kontiki* (phone: 775-5055), a glass-bottom boat, leaves from the downtown dock several times a day. In addition, the *Atlantis* submarine (*Havensight Mall;* phone: 776-5650; 776-0288, for 24-hour information; 800-253-0493) offers a comfortable two-hour cruise at a depth of 90 feet with good views. The 46-passenger sub with large portholes reveals a world of coral shapes and brilliantly colored fish. It's the next best thing to scuba diving. Children under four are not allowed. Reservations are required.

The motor ship *Bomba Charger* (phone: 775-7292) makes the scenic run to another small world—the British Virgin Island of Tortola. The trip takes 45 minutes each way. Schedules leave time for a look around, lunch, a pint at the *Sir Francis Drake Pub,* and a chance to meet some nice people. For a day trip to St. John, a number of boats sail from Charlotte Amalie every morning. A park tour and a chance to explore the Trunk Bay underwater trail are built into most itineraries. Prices include lunch and drinks. Smaller yachts handle parties of six. For information, ask at the visitors' bureau or at *Sea Tours Transfers* (phone: 774-2990) at *Marriott's Frenchman's Reef*. Or try a trip on one of the picturesque tall ships, such as the *Schooner Alexander Hamilton* (phone: 775-6500).

SIGHTSEEING BUS TOURS These are not a big deal on St. Thomas. Cruise passengers are their principal customers. *Tropic Tours* (phone: 774-1855; 800-524-4334) with its main office in *Havensight Mall* and branches in major hotels, runs 2½-hour safari bus tours, including hotel pickup and drop-off. They also run a full-day tour of St. John, including ferry and lunch at *Cinnamon Bay*.

SIGHTSEEING TAXI TOURS A pleasantly effortless way to see island sights. Many St. Thomas drivers are good guides and can suggest half- and full-day itineraries, including likely lunch spots if you have nothing specific in mind. But don't rely on the luck of the taxi-stand draw. As soon as you know when you want to go, ask your hotel tour desk to make arrangements with a driver they know. Officially licensed taxis have "TP" on their license plates.

TAXI Plentiful, unmetered, and inexpensive. Rates are based on destination rather than mileage. (It's considered okay for the driver to pick up additional people en route if they're going your way.) There's also an after-midnight surcharge. The ubiquitous *Virgin Islands Taxi Association* may be reached at 774-7457. Many hotels operate shuttle services from *Emancipation Park*. *Hint:* If you're shopping downtown and want to taxi back to your hotel, head for the waterfront drive. No cab driver in his right mind would voluntarily tangle with Main Street or Back Street traffic—especially on a cruise ship day.

SPECIAL EVENTS

St. Thomians celebrate *Carnival* (the last two weeks of April) with stilt-walking "moko jumbis" and steel bands that reverberate all day and night; on St. John, *Independence Day* (July 4) is the Big Time, celebrated with music, parades, "moko jumbis," a *Miss St. John* contest, and the traditional fireworks. A smaller carnival is celebrated on St. John during the last week of June. On St. Croix, the *Mumm's Cup Regatta* and the *St. Croix Jazz Festival* liven things up in October. In addition to all the US national holidays (*New Year's Day, Martin Luther King's Birthday, President's Day, Easter, Memorial Day, Independence Day, Labor Day, Columbus Day, Veterans' Day, Thanksgiving,* and *Christmas*), the Virgin Islands celebrate *Three Kings' Day* (January 6); *Transfer Day* (March 31, the day the US flag first flew in the islands); *Holy Thursday; Good Friday; Organic Act Day* (June 16, the day in 1936 when the US Congress granted home rule and suffrage to the Virgin Islands); *Emancipation Day* (July 3, the day in 1848 when slaves were freed in the Danish West Indies); *Supplication Day* (third Monday in July, a day of prayer for protection from hurricanes); *Puerto Rico Friendship Day* (October 12); *Hurricane Thanksgiving Day* for the end of hurricane season (third Monday in October); and *Liberty Day* (November 1, honoring Judge David Hamilton Jackson, who secured freedom of the press and assembly from King Christian X of Denmark). For more information about events on the three islands, call 800-USVI-INFO.

SHOPPING

Three things have made US Virgin Islands shopping famous: low prices (on a list of 20 or so categories of most-wanted merchandise); wide selections; and the fact that US citizens are allowed to carry home, untaxed, $1,200 worth of goods (instead of the usual $400 per person) and five fifths of liquor (six, if one fifth is locally produced) instead of the usual one liter. In addition, stateside residents may ship home from the US Virgin Islands, each day, up to $100 worth of gifts (instead of the usual $50), over and above the $1,200 individual exemption. Products manufactured in the US Virgin Islands are completely tax exempt and do not count in the duty-free allowance.

The low prices are a legacy from the Danes, who stipulated as part of their 1917 treaty of sale that island retailers be forced to pay no more than 6% *ad valorem* duty (property tax) on incoming goods. This is so much less than the tax paid elsewhere that Virgin Islands merchants can afford to sell their luxury imports for 5% to 60% less than most mainland US stores. Selections are large because volume is enormous, swelled by hundreds of thousands of cruise ship passengers' purchases.

A little planning will help you through the maze of shops so that you end up with the goodies you want without spending your entire vacation shopping. Check prices in your hometown stores before you leave so you know whether the Virgin Islands prices are worth the time and effort of long-distance hauling. For example, current savings are minimal on photographic and electronic equipment, more substantial on fine china and crystal (savings from 30% to 50%). Perfume, watches, gold jewelry, and imported beauty products (makeup, bath gels) can sometimes be real bargains. Liquor is a buy at 50% to 65% less than New York prices, and cigarettes by the carton are 40% or so below New York levels.

ST. CROIX

Shopping is better than ever on this island, spurred by increased tourism. More cruise ships are adding St. Croix to their itineraries; most call at Frederiksted (which still has only a few stores), but some shallow-drafted ships dock at Christiansted's Gallows Bay. Bear in mind that Christiansted's shopping area, although colorful, may pose a problem for those who have difficulty walking: Sidewalks are made of brick or stone, and there are numerous short flights of steps to maneuver. Navigation is easier at some of the newer complexes close to the water, such as the *Pan Am Pavilion* or *Caravelle Arcade.*

Most shops in St. Croix are open Mondays through Saturdays from 9 AM to 5 PM. The following shops are in Christiansted, unless otherwise noted.

American West India Company All products here are made or grown in the Caribbean, including spices and coffee, gourmet food, batik clothing, Sea Island cotton fabric, and artwork. Strand St. (phone: 773-7325).

Anything Goes The place to pick up fancy fixings for a picnic. Near the docks at Gallows Bay (phone: 773-2777).

Caribbean Clothing Co. Designer duds, featuring men's and women's sportswear (including Bally men's shoes). 41 Queen Cross St. (phone: 773-5012).

Colombian Emeralds The gorgeous green gems in varied settings. At two locations: 43 Queen Cross St. (phone: 773-1928 or 773-9189) and 2A Strand St., Frederiksted (phone: 772-1927).

Crucian Gold Original fine gold jewelry made on the spot. 57A Company St. (phone: 773-5241).

1870 Townhouse Shoppes Attractive, reasonably priced beachwear and sportswear, and Chinese and African giftware. 52 King St. (phone: 773-2967).

Folk Art Traders A gallery of fine Caribbean art and antiques, featuring an impressive collection of jewelry, books, West Indian artifacts, and art including iron sculpture, woodcarvings, and *Carnival* masks. Strand St., across from the *Pan Am Pavilion* (phone: 773-1900).

From the Gecko A boutique featuring creations by Virgin Islands artists, including beautiful clothing made from hand-dyed silks and hand-painted cottons, jewelry, and leather goods. Queen Cross St. (phone: 778-9433).

Grog & Spirits Portable potables—wine, liquor, beer, and mixers to go, plus picnic fixings. Chandlers Wharf at Gallows Bay (phone: 773-8485).

Java Wraps Dozens of hand-blocked pareos (sarongs), no two alike, in terrific colors; also shirts, sundresses, jumpsuits, and all sorts of resortwear in the same great Indonesian batik prints. The annual October clearance sale yields savings of 50% and more. *Pan Am Pavilion* (phone: 773-3770).

Jeltrup's Books Specializing in Caribbean lore—histories, cookbooks, and gardening; paperbacks, too. 2132 Company St. (phone: 773-1018).

Land of Oz Children's and adult games, including backgammon and wari (an ancient African game that's an island favorite), plus jigsaw puzzles, kites, and lots more. 52A Company St. (phone: 773-4610).

Little Switzerland For fine imported china, perfume, watches, crystal, and porcelain figures. 1108 King St. (phone: 773-1976).

Many Hands Imaginative graphics and crafts at wonderfully non-shock prices; cards, shells, jams and spices, enchanting *Christmas* ornaments, too. 21 *Pan Am Pavilion* (phone: 773-1990).

Pegasus Original jewelry made with gemstones. 58 Company St. (phone: 773-6926).

Royal Poinciana A potpourri of coffees, teas, spices, Caribbean condiments, herbal bath gels and soaps, and tropical perfume. 38 Strand St. (phone: 773-9892).

S & B Liquor The place to stock up on alcohol in Frederiksted. 9A King St., Frederiksted (phone: 772-3934).

St. Croix Shoppes All of Estée Lauder's products, plus Clinique, Aramis, and Prescriptives, in two sparkling side-by-side stores. Other fragrances and makeup are available as well. 53B Company St. (phone: 773-2727).

Simply Cotton Colorful cotton knit clothing for women and kids. 36C Strand St. (phone: 773-6860).

Small Wonder Fine children's clothing (such as Florence Eiseman and Oshkosh togs) and high-quality toys. 4 Company St. (phone: 773-5551).

Violette's Boutique Downstairs is an enormous perfume and cosmetics selection, featuring popular imports; upstairs are Cartier, Fendi, and Gottex boutiques—all at 30% off stateside prices. *Caravelle Arcade,* 38 Strand St. (phone: 773-2148).

Wayne James Boutique Native son Wayne James, who has designed clothing for the likes of the Queen of Denmark (and even the pope), has opened a shop to sell his fashions. 42 Queen Cross St. (phone: 773-8585).

Whim Museum Shop Antique reproductions (door knockers, hurricane globes) and some period pieces (silver, paperweights, Cantonware). All profits go to the St. Croix Landmarks Restoration fund. At *Estate Whim Plantation Museum,* Rte. 70, east of Frederiksted (phone: 772-0598).

Writer's Block Excellent bookstore, with a good travel section and antique maps. 36 S. Strand St. (phone: 773-5101).

ST. JOHN

Shops on St. John, primarily clustered around Cruz Bay, are generally open Mondays through Saturdays from 9 AM to 5 PM.

Lazy Lizard Moderately priced casual island clothing for men and women. *Meadas Plaza,* Cruz Bay (phone: 693-7152).

Mongoose Junction A complex of smart brick and wood studio shops (many open daily; hours vary) in Cruz Bay sheltering such crafts emporia as *Canvas Factory* (seaworthy totes, bags, clothing, as well as sail repair; phone: 776-6196), *The Clothing Studio* (hand-painted garments; phone: 776-6585), *Colombian Emeralds* (a branch of the one on St. Thomas; phone: 776-6007),

Donald Schnell Studio (original pottery, ceramics, and hand-blown glass; phone: 776-6420), *Fabric Mill* (batiks, silk-screen prints; phone: 776-6194), *Mongoose Trading Co.* (hand-painted dinnerware; phone: 776-6993), *R. and I. Patton* (contemporary gold and silver jewelry; phone: 776-6548), *Seasons Boutique* (beachwear for men, women, and children; phone: 776-6130), and *Wicker, Wood & Shells* (gifts, decor items; phone: 776-6909).

Pink Papaya A lovely selection of arts and crafts such as silkscreen prints, ceramics, glassware, placemats, and jewelry. *Lemon Tree Mall,* Cruz Bay (phone: 693-8535).

Sparky's This branch is smaller than its St. Thomas cousin, but it's handy for cigarette and liquor purchases, which they'll deliver to the airport or your ship. 6B Cruz Bay (phone: 776-6284).

Wharfside Village A cluster of pastel-painted stores at the water's edge (many open daily; hours vary) includes *Barracuda Bistro* (freshly baked bread, plus take-out sandwiches and dinners; phone: 779-4944), *Blue Carib Gems* (phone: 693-8299), *Cruz Bay Clothing Co.* (casualwear; phone: 776-7611), *Freebird Creations* (jewelry; phone: 693-8625), *Island Hoppers* (gourmet island foods and collectibles; phone: 693-7200), *Let's Go Bananas* (women's clothing; phone: 776-7055), and *Third World Electronics* (CDs and tapes; phone: 776-6600).

ST. THOMAS

If shopping is your favorite sport, you can spend days searching glassy-eyed through the offerings in Charlotte Amalie's restored warehouse shops—though true bargains are relatively scarce. Of the three US Virgin Islands, St. Thomas has the biggest stores (most in Charlotte Amalie) and the largest stocks (and crowds). Before heading downtown, check *This Week* or *Best Buys* to find out which store sells the most of the brands or kinds of merchandise you want. In general, prices for similar items are the same throughout the islands, so there's no need to comparison shop. (Included in the listing below are toll-free numbers that allow visitors to check prices before leaving home.)

Avoid shopping on crowded cruise ship days whenever possible, and go early in the day—while you and the salespeople are still fresh—or during mealtimes, when many cruisers head back to their ships to eat. Most stores are open from 9 AM to 5 PM, but numerous shops on St. Thomas remain open until 10 or 11 PM for cruise ship passengers. Many close on Sundays, unless ships are in port.

Main Street, also called Dronningens Gade, is the main shopping street. Also check out the shops in *Bakery Square,* Charlotte Amalie's restored shopping complex on Back Street, and the 50 stores at *Havensight Mall* near the West Indian Company dock, just steps from the ships' gangways (thus avoiding the long, traffic-congested ride into town). There's also the *International Plaza* complex at The Waterfront and the *Mountain Top* shopping and cultural complex. The *Vendors Plaza,* an outdoor flea market, is held at *Emancipation Park* Mondays through Saturdays from 6 AM to 6 PM and Sundays from 7 AM to 3 PM when cruise ships are in port. You'll find plenty of T-shirts and designer knockoffs; try your hand at bargaining here. A number of St. Thomas shops have St. Croix branches where the choices may be somewhat smaller, but so are the crowds. If you're planning to island hop, you may want to plan your shopping accordingly.

A discordant note on the St. Thomas shopping scene: The crowds and frequent discourtesy of Charlotte Amalie shopkeepers have been joined by street hawkers and vendors who seem bent on making a sale—regardless of how many times prospective purchasers decline their entreaties. St. Thomas is fast becoming the Mexico City of the Caribbean for shoppers—and that's no compliment.

Here are some of the best-stocked Charlotte Amalie stores.

A. H. Riise Stacks of top-quality china (Wedgwood), crystal (Waterford), watches, jewelry, objets d'art, antiques, and decorator accessories, as well as a large stock of liquor. Nice, helpful people. Two locations: an enormous complex at 37 Main St. (phone: 776-2303) and *Havensight Mall* (phone: 776-2303, ext. 192; 800-524-2037).

Al Cohen's Huge liquor warehouse at *Havensight,* with prices 30% to 60% below US prices, and a few cents below other town shops. Across from the West India Company dock, Long Bay Rd. (phone: 774-3690).

Amsterdam Sauer Internationally known South American jewelry firm shows wares to buyers by appointment only. 14 Main St. (phone: 774-2222) and *Havensight Mall* (phone: 776-3828; 800-345-3564).

Aperiton For fine furs, leather clothing for men and women, and jewelry of Greek and Italian design. 3A Main St. (phone: 776-0780).

Blue Carib Gems Tour this gemstone workshop, where jewelry is created on the spot by in-house artisans. Sometimes, the shop will allow customers to design their own pieces. *Bakery Square,* Back St. at Nye Gade (phone: 774-8525).

Bolero Daum and Danish crystal, English bone china, Omega and Tissot watches, French perfume, men's and women's fashions, and liquor. 34 Main St. (phone: 776-0551).

Cardow Long established, it claims the Caribbean's biggest precious and semi-precious gem collection. Nine locations, including 25-26 Main St., on the waterfront, and *Havensight Mall* (phone for all: 776-1140).

Cartier Stunning jewelry at 15% below mainland prices. Main St. at Trumpeter Gade (phone: 774-1590).

China Embroidery Arts Large selection of embroidered linen. Two locations: 17 Main St. (phone: 776-2521) and the large, air conditioned warehouse at 6-C Wimmelskaft Gade (phone: 776-0726).

Colombian Emeralds Large selection of both set and unset gemstones and famous-name watches. At four locations: Main St. (phone: 774-0581), The Waterfront (phone: 774-1033), *Mountain Top* (phone: 774-3400), and *Havensight Mall* (phone: 774-2442).

Cosmopolitan Bally shoes, a large selection of Gottex bathing suits for men and women, and Fila sportswear at discount prices. At Drake's Passage on the waterfront (phone: 776-2040).

Dockside Book Shop A reliable source of reading matter, with a good travel section. *Havensight Mall* (phone: 774-4937).

Down Island Traders Homemade Virgin Island goods that are tax-exempt—mango chutney and preserves, passion-fruit jelly, papaya and lime marmalades, as well as spices, fancy teas, and Caribbean cookbooks. On the waterfront (phone: 776-4641).

English Shop China, porcelain, and crystal with brands such as Wedgwood, Boehm, and Royal Bierley. On the waterfront above *Cardow* (phone: 776-5399) and at *Havensight Mall* (phone: 776-3776; 800-524-2013).

Gucci The one and only at substantial savings; the October end-of-season clearance sale is worth a trip in itself. Two locations: On the waterfront (phone: 774-7841) and *Havensight Mall* (phone: 774-4090).

H. Stern The prestigious South American jewelry outfit has six locations here: 12 Main St. (phone: 776-1939), two branches across from each other on Main St. at Raadets Gade (phone: 776-3550 and 776-1146), *Havensight Mall* (phone: 776-1223), at *Marriott's Frenchman's Reef* (phone: 774-7658), and *Bluebeard's Castle* (phone: 774-3158). The toll-free number for all stores is 800-524-2024.

Java Wraps Wonderful hand-screened batik clothing printed in Indonesia. An annual sale the first two weeks in October offers 50% to 75% off regular prices. 5141 Palm Passage (phone: 774-3700).

Jonna White Art Gallery Unique etchings on handmade paper. Palm Passage, above *Bared Jewelers* (phone: 774-3098).

Leather Shop Fendi, Bottega Veneta, Desmo, and Furla items at 40% below mainland prices. Check the sale table for some real bargains. 2 Main St. (phone: 776-3995) and *Havensight Mall* (phone: 776-0040).

Linen House Tablecloths and blouses imported from China. Three locations: Main St. (phone: 774-1668), *Royal Dane Mall* (phone: 774-8117), and *Havensight Mall* (phone: 774-0868).

Lion in the Sun Eclectic selection of American and European designer labels, including Donna Karan, Yves Saint Laurent, Sonia Rykiel—some items priced low—for men and women. Riis Alley (phone: 776-4203).

Little Switzerland As might be expected, a high concentration of watches (including Omega and Rolex), music boxes, cuckoo clocks; also elegant china (Rosenthal and Royal Worcester), crystal, jewelry, binoculars. At four locations: 5 Main St., 38 Main St., 48A-B Norre Gade, and the *Havensight Mall* (phone: 776-2010 for all).

Local Color Silk-screened knits and artwork in vibrant colors and designs seen all around the island, but the largest selection is here. 2A Garden St. (phone: 774-3727).

Louis Vuitton Leather products made in Europe, complete with the famous initials, discounted 20% below stateside prices. 24 Dronningens (phone: 774-3644).

Mr. Tablecloth Discount prices on table and bed linen, plus aprons and crocheted scarves. 6 Main St. (phone: 774-4343).

Modamare Izod/Lacoste clothing at 20% discounts. *Havensight Mall* (phone: 776-5067).

Mountain Top An air conditioned shopping and cultural center atop a mountain in the center of the island. Its 18 colorful shops include some branches of in-town stores plus independents such as the *West Indian Museum Shop,* with prints and antique map reproductions, and a jam and spice shop. Scratch bands and weavers of palm hats demonstrate local arts and crafts. There's also an aquarium, a terrarium, an aviary, an outdoor observation deck, and a snack bar. Rte. 33 (phone: 774-2400).

Paradise Point Up Flag Hill above *Havensight,* the first part of a four-building complex has opened with several shops and the *Bar at Paradise Point,* offering a spectacular view. A Swiss-built gondola transports guests from the foot of the hill to the complex. The first stores feature locally made items; eventually a broader selection will be available. Flag Hill (phone: 777-4548).

Polo/Ralph Lauren Factory Store Men's and women's clothing by the famous designer, some items at 30% to 70% off. 2 Garden St., above *Local Color* (phone: 774-3806).

Scandinavian Center Collection of fine wares from top names in Sweden, Finland, Denmark, and Norway, including Royal Copenhagen china, Kosta Boda crystal, and jewelry by Georg Jensen. At two locations: 4 Main St. (phone: 776-0656) and *Havensight Mall* (phone: 776-5030; 800-524-2063).

Signatures An elegant boutique featuring a daily fashion show. 5141 Palm Passage (phone: 776-5900).

Sparky's One of the chain of gleaming shops stocked with best-selling merchandise such as perfume and jewelry, including Gucci and Ebel watches. Best known for liquor and cigarettes. 29-31 Main St. (phone: 776-7510).

Tillett Gardens Jim Tillett's silk-screened fabrics, wall hangings, and paintings are fresh and fun. On the road to *Coral World,* his compound at Estate Tutu—where they also do the screen printing—is a sightseeing must even if you don't buy. 126 Estate Anna's Retreat, Rte. 38 (phone: 775-1405 or 775-1929).

Tropicana Perfume Shoppes The world's largest scents store, it has cosmetics, bath oils, and men's and women's toiletries as well. At two locations: 2 Main St. and 14 Main St. (phone: 774-0010 for both; 800-233-7948).

Zora of St. Thomas Custom-made leather sandals and belts, and canvas bags. 34 Norre Gade (phone: 774-2559).

SPORTS: ST. CROIX

BOATING *Caribbean Sea Adventures* (phone: 778-7004) handles small boat rentals and arranges charters for larger boats, bareboat and crewed. Sunfish and Hobie Cats can be rented at the water sports activity centers of most beach hotels.

For those captains of their own ships, there are repair, service, and docking facilities at *St. Croix Marina* at Gallows Bay (phone: 773-0289; fax: 778-8974), *Salt River Marina* at Salt River (phone: 778-9650; fax: 778-0706), and *Green Cay Marina* on the northeast coast (phone: 773-1453; fax: 773-9651).

GOLF While the number of courses on the island is limited, one stands out from the rest.

TOP TEE-OFF SPOT

Westin Carambola Beach For more than 20 years, this course was known as *Fountain Valley,* one of the most challenging golf courses in the Caribbean, and today this Robert Trent Jones Sr. course is in better shape than ever. It is mostly notable for its route through a deep valley, full of abundant water hazards and an inordinate number of ravines. From its championship tees, it plays to a length of more than 6,900 yards, which should be sufficient to exhaust even the most inveterate ball pounder. With the expanded clubhouse, a practice putting green, and a driving range, a good challenge has been made into a great one. The pro shop has rental clubs and lockers, and there's a restaurant whose steak sandwiches and view make it a recommended lunch stop even if you don't play golf. Davis Bay (phone: 778-5638).

The public also is welcome to play the far shorter course at the *Buccaneer* hotel (see *Checking In*). There is a nine-hole course at the *Reef* (Teague Bay; phone: 773-8844).

HORSE RACING Thoroughbred horses race about twice a month at *Flamboyant Race Track* on Airport Road; check newspapers for race schedules. There's informal betting, food, drink, live music, and a party atmosphere. For additional details, see *Horse Races* in DIVERSIONS.

HORSEBACK RIDING At *Sprat Hall* (Creque Dam Rd., north of Frederiksted; phone: 772-2880 or 772-2627), a plantation homestead–turned–hotel, *Paul and Jill's Equestrian Stable* offers a two-hour trail ride through the rain forest and over the hills beyond. After you've made a daylight excursion, you may qualify for one of their memorable moonlight expeditions; reserve at least a day in advance. *Sprat Hall* has riding packages.

PARASAILING Rides are offered by *Mile Mark Charters* (see *Sea Excursions,* above) and *Paradise Parasailing* (phone: 773-7060). The latter operates from several hotels as well as the Christiansted boardwalk.

SNORKELING AND SCUBA DIVING Waters are so clear and warm, with so many dive sites to see, that you could spend a whole vacation under water and still cover only a fraction of what's there. St. Croix has become known as a top diving destination, offering all types of diving—beach dives, wall dives, reef dives, wreck dives, and nighttime dives. In addition to the underwater trails off Buck Island, the island's most intriguing sites include its coral canyons and the drop-offs at Salt River, Cane Bay, and Davis Bay (site of the 12,000-foot-deep Puerto Rico Trench, the fifth-deepest body of water in the world). For scuba instruction, day and night dives, and equipment rental, contact *Mile Mark Charters* (see *Sea Excursions,* above). Outfits offering *PADI* certification include *Dive Experience* (1 Strand St., Christiansted; phone: 773-3307; 800-235-9047); *Anchor Dive Center* (Salt River, Sunny Isle; phone: 778-1522; 800-532-DIVE); *Cruzan Divers* (12 Strand St., Frederiksted; phone: 772-3701; 800-352-0107); *V.I. Divers* (*Pan Am Pavilion,* Christiansted; phone: 773-6045; 800-544-5911); and *Cane Bay Dive Shop* (phone: 773-9913 or 778-1805).

Snorkeling doesn't require any formal arrangements. There are plenty of good snorkeling spots right off the coast, and even the smallest hotels are likely to have equipment on hand, which they will lend gratis or rent for a small fee. However, most visitors to St. Croix—snorkelers and non-snorkelers alike—make at least one trip to see the Buck Island reef. A number of boats make half- or full-day excursions to Buck Island that include snorkeling in the underwater park and provide the equipment and, frequently, a guide (see *Sea Excursions,* above).

SPORT FISHING Cruzan fisherman go deep for mahimahi, wahoo, snapper, grouper, and blue dolphin (the fish, not the mammal), using light tackle for sporty jack or bonefish closer to shore. Islanders claim to hold the world billfishing record. *Mile Mark Charters* (see *Sea Excursions,* above) arranges deep-sea trips. Since fleet members are limited, advance reservations are always a good idea; most places require a 50% deposit.

SWIMMING AND SUNNING Beach names to know are Cane, Sugar, Pelican, Davis, and Grapetree Bays, as well as La Grange—all pleasant, none spectacular. People staying in Christiansted tend to use the small, pretty beach on Protestant Cay or take a short shuttle out to one of the three beaches at the *Buccaneer* hotel (see *Checking In*). Cramer Park, near the island's eastern tip, has a beach, picnic tables, and changing rooms—but on weekends, it's crowded with locals.

TENNIS The island has courts galore, making it a great locale for both novices and experienced players.

CHOICE COURTS

Buccaneer Unarguably the best tennis in the Virgin Islands. Good for watching (with several annual tournaments) as well as playing. Facilities: eight all-weather Laykold courts (two lighted); ball machine; pro shop. The *Virgin Islands Tennis Championships* usually take place in July; several other tournaments are held during the year (phone: 773-2100; 800-223-1108 for reservations; non-guests of the hotel may use the facilities for a charge).

The *Reef* golf course (see *Golf,* above) has two courts, and the *Westin Carambola Beach* resort has four grass courts at the hotel and five at the golf club (see *Checking In*). Other setups include *St. Croix by the Sea* (four), the *Club St. Croix* (three), *Colony Cove* (two), and *Villa Madeleine* (one); see *Checking In* for information on all of the above. *Chenay Bay* (Rte. 75, Christiansted; phone: 773-2918) has two courts. There also are three public courts at *Canegata Ball Park* (no phone), a half-mile east of Christiansted.

WATER SKIING Boats, skis, and lessons are available through most hotels or *Trade Windsurfing* (phone: 773-7060).

WINDSURFING A very popular sport in these parts, it is available at many hotels, with lessons and rentals at the *Chenay Bay Beach* resort (phone: 773-8195), *Mile Mark Charters* (see *Sea Excursions,* above), and *Paradise Parasailing* (see *Parasailing,* above).

SPORTS: ST. JOHN

BOATING *Cinnamon Bay Watersports* (phone: 776-6330), *Low Key Watersports,* and *Cruz Bay Watersports* (see *Sea Excursions,* above, for the latter two) will arrange daily sails, as will the water sports centers at *Caneel Bay* and *Maho*

Bay (see *Checking In*). *St. John Water Sports/Hinkley Charters* (see *Sea Excursions*) handles both day sails and longer crewed charters.

HIKING An extensive network of trails covers the national park. Take a four-wheeled tour first to get oriented. Then set out on your own with the free trail map and literature from the park service headquarters, located on the *National Park Service* dock to the left as you leave the ferry dock. Two or three times a week—at different locations and on a flexible schedule—a park service guide leads nature walks. Call 776-6201 for more information.

KAYAKING The latest way to cruise these waters is on short kayaking trips arranged through *Cinnamon Bay Campgrounds* (see *Checking In*) or via five- or seven-day excursions with *Arawak Expeditions* (phone: 693-8312; 800-238-8687).

SNORKELING AND SCUBA DIVING There is a fine marked underwater trail at Trunk Bay, with guided snorkel tours Wednesday mornings. Other top spots are Hawksnest Bay, Waterlemon Cay, and Salt Pond. For snorkeling and scuba trips, equipment rental, and instruction, try *St. John Water Sports/Hinckley Charters* in Cruz Bay, *Low Key Watersports,* or *Cruz Bay Watersports* (see *Sea Excursions,* above, for all three). *Caneel Bay* (see *Checking In*) has its own facilities.

SPORT FISHING Book through *Caneel Bay* (see *Checking In*) or check with *Cruz Bay Watersports* or *Low Key Watersports* (see *Sea Excursions,* above). Mary's Creek, near Maho Bay, has excellent bonefishing.

SWIMMING AND SUNNING For such a small island, St. John has more than its share of super, sandy stretches.

DREAM BEACH

Trunk Bay Success hasn't spoiled it one iota, thanks to the diligence of the *National Park Service* rangers who keep watch. Its most famous asset is the underwater trail, with markers to guide you along the reef just off the beach. It's been named one of the world's ten best time and again. A favorite escape destination for *Caneel Bay* guests, it has picnic tables, changing facilities, restrooms, beverage and snack service. Part of the *Virgin Islands National Park,* and open during the daytime only.

In addition, *Cinnamon Bay* and *Maho Bay* campgrounds have their own beaches, and seven more stunning beaches scallop the waters around *Caneel Bay* (see *Checking In* for all). Elsewhere, swim and sun at Hawks Reef and Lameshur Bays.

TENNIS *Caneel Bay* has 11 courts, a pro shop, and a *Peter Burwash International* pro staff. *Cinnamon Bay* and *Maho Bay* campers can arrange to play there. There are also two public courts in downtown Cruz Bay.

BOATING Virgin Islanders do the biggest charter business in the Caribbean. St. Thomas, with its sizable yacht harbors at the *Ramada Yacht Haven Marina* and Red Hook marina, is the heart of the business. Moving out of the Sunfish/Hobie Cat class (both of which can be rented at bathing beach centers), you can rent just about anything that floats—from a 13-foot power boat to an 80-foot schooner, and houseboats, cabin cruisers, and trimarans in between. (*Note:* A proficiency check is a standard pre-takeover requirement.)

For information on day or night sails and boat charters, ask at your hotel's travel desk, or contact *Club Nautico* (Red Hook; phone: 779-2555), *V.I. Charteryacht League* (Flagship; phone: 774-3944; 800-524-2061), or *American Yacht Harbor* (Red Hook; phone: 775-6454); all can put you in touch with any one of the many charter operators in the area. Day sails, which generally include snorkeling and a picnic lunch while anchored in an out-of-the-way cove, are very popular. *Sea Tours Transfers* at the *Marriott's Frenchman's Reef* hotel (phone: 776-8500, ext. 145, or 774-2990) and the activities desk at the *Sapphire Beach* hotel (see *Checking In*) will charter half- or full-day sails. You also can book directly on a variety of craft, including the schooner *True Love* (the very yacht on which Bing Crosby sang to Grace Kelly in the film *High Society*), which has a champagne buffet that sets the standard for day-sail elegance (phone: 775-6547 or 775-6374); and *Nightwind,* a 55-foot yawl (phone: 775-6666 or 775-4110). Dozens of other craft are advertised in local publications; also check with your hotel.

GOLF There's only one course on St. Thomas, but it is a beauty.

TOP TEE-OFF SPOT

Mahogany Run Designed by George and Tom Fazio, it runs along some of the most picturesque parts of the island, through scenery that makes it well worth enduring the few dull stretches. Especially picturesque is the "Devil's Triangle" (holes 13 through 15). Relatively tight and hilly, with small greens, this is not a course for the lover of classic hole configuration, but it provides 18 good reasons for making a Virgin Islands visit. 1 Mahogany Run Rd., near Magens Bay (phone: 775-5000).

HORSE RACING The *Estate Nadir Race Track* (Bovari Rd.; no phone) hosts meets roughly once a month—usually on a holiday or a Sunday. Check the papers for the schedule.

KAYAKING *West Indies Windsurfing* (phone: 775-6530) organizes trips.

PARASAILING *Fat Boys Water Toys* (phone: 775-3055) offers parasailing at the *Point Pleasant, Sapphire Beach, Grand Palazzo,* and *Stouffer Renaissance Grand Beach* resorts. Also ask at *Marriott's Frenchman's Reef* (see *Checking In* for the hotels' phone numbers).

SNORKELING AND SCUBA DIVING You can rent masks and fins for a small fee at all major hotels and on tourist beaches. Snorkel gear is standard equipment on sailing and yacht excursions as well. Off St. Thomas are good beginners' dive spots (Cow and Calf, St. James Island, Stevens Cay, Coki Bay) plus any number of fascinating underwaterscapes (Congo Cay's lava archways, Thatch Cay's tunnels, Eagle Shoal's submerged mountain) for more advanced divers. From St. Thomas (or St. John) you can make the all-day dive trip to the wreck of the Royal Mail packet boat *Rhone* (now a British national park) off the British Virgin Islands. Night dives are available for intermediate and advanced divers only.

   Some firms that offer diving trips, instruction, and equipment on St. Thomas are *Aqua Action* at Secret Harbour (phone: 775-6235 or 775-6550), *Caribbean Divers* at Red Hook (phone: 775-6384), the *Coki Beach Dive Club* at Coki Beach (phone: 775-4220), the *Watersports Center* at the *Sapphire Beach* resort (see *Checking In*), *Virgin Island Diving Schools and Divers' Supplies* (phone: 774-8687), and *Joe Vogel Diving Company* (phone: 775-7610) at the *Galleon House* in Frenchtown. The *St. Thomas Diving Club* (phone: 776-2381) sponsors daily dives from a choice of three island take-off points—the two docks at *Bolongo Club Everything* or a dock at *Bolongo Elysian Beach*—and offers instruction and certification aboard two dive boats.

SPORT FISHING There's year-round fishing for wahoo, Allison tuna, bonito, sailfish, and marlin. Blue marlin angling is best between June and August, white marlin in spring and fall, tarpon and bonefish in spring, wahoo from September to May, and sailfish and blackfin tuna in January and February.

   American Yacht Harbor at Red Hook (phone: 775-6454) is prime deep-sea headquarters with boats in fine fighting trim. They can arrange on- or offshore fishing for half days, full days, or longer. Captain Al Petrosky skippers angling trips on the *Fish Hawk,* out of East End Lagoon (phone: 775-9058). The *Sapphire Beach* resort (see *Checking In*) and *Sea Tours Transfers* (see *Boating,* above) also arrange deep-sea fishing.

SWIMMING AND SUNNING Most resorts, hotels, condominiums, and cottage colonies are on sandy stretches of beach stocked with chaises, towels, and beach toys (snorkel gear, float boards, Sun- or Sailfish and/or Hobie Cats, all for rent at small fees). All US Virgin Islands beaches are public. Magens Bay, a wide, protected stretch of golden sand thickly edged with palms, is probably best known. In fact, it may be a little too popular on weekends and on cruise ship arrival days, but it is gorgeous. There are changing rooms and a good but tacky-looking snack bar; nominal admission and parking fees.

Sapphire, Morningstar, and Lindbergh Beaches have the same facilities, and are well known and beautiful. But for leisurely picnicking and putting some space between you and the crowds, head for Cowpet Bay or Nazareth Bay, both on the Caribbean side of St. Thomas; on the Atlantic side, try Mandahl Bay, Hull Bay, or Stumpy Bay (axle-fracturing road, but a good beach).

TENNIS Laykold or all-weather courts are the rule; many are lighted for night play and have pro shops and pro instruction.

CHOICE COURTS

Wyndham Sugar Bay This resort may give the *Buccaneer* on St. Croix some competition for the tennis crowd, with the USVI's first stadium tennis court (capacity: 220), plus six additional Laykold lighted courts, lessons under the supervision of Vic Braden, and a pro shop. 6500 Estate Smith Bay (phone: 777-7100; 800-WYNDHAM).

In addition, here's the private court count: *Bluebeard's Castle* (two), *Bolongo Club Everything* (four), *Bolongo Elysian Beach* (one), *Marriott's Frenchman's Reef* (four), *Grand Palazzo* (four), *Limetree Beach* (two), *Point Pleasant* (one), *Sapphire Beach* (four), and *Stouffer Renaissance Grand Beach* (six); see *Checking In* for information on all of the above. *Mahogany Run* (see *Golf,* above) has two courts. The courts at *Cowpet Bay* (Rte. 6; 775-6220), *Watergate* (6222 E. Nazareth St.; phone: 775-2270), *Magens Point,* and *Secret Harbour* (see *Checking In* for the latter two) are for members and hotel guests only. Some condominium complexes limit play to club members, owners, and guests. All hotel courts require players to wear standard whites or clothes designed for the game. Hotel guests are charged no fee (or a very small one) for court use. Non-guests pay a nominal hourly fee to play. In addition, there are two free public courts at Sub Base, available on a first-come, first-served basis.

NIGHTLIFE

On St. Croix, the *Buccaneer* hotel (see *Checking In*) schedules music most nights, limbo shows and reggae at least once a week. In Christiansted, the *Marina Bar* at the *King's Alley* hotel (57 King St.; phone: 773-0103) is the place for sunset and people watching (but no music). There's nightly entertainment at the *Moonraker Lounge* (43-A Queen Cross St.; phone: 773-8492). Softer sounds of "oldies" and guitar selections can be heard nightly at the *Tivoli Gardens* (upstairs at the corner of Queen Cross and Strand Sts.; phone: 773-6782). Just west of town on Northside Road is the *Two Plus Two* disco (phone: 773-3710), with dancing to taped music nightly, plus a live calypso band Fridays and Saturdays, when there's a cover charge. The *Cormorant Beach Club* (see *Checking In*) has steel bands and "moko jumbis" on Thursdays and Sundays and jazz on Fridays. Another Friday night jazz spot is the *Blue Moon* (17 Strand St.; phone: 772-2222). A special treat to watch for is St. Croix's *Quadrille Dancers.* In bright yesteryear costumes, they move to the old plantation-days calls; before the performance ends, you're invited to try a few steps yourself. The amateur group's schedule is erratic, but check *This Week*—and go if they're performing. They also perform for private parties; contact Bradley Christian (phone: 772-2021).

Not a lot is happening on St. John. *Fred's* (Cruz Bay; phone: 776-6363) offers fish fries and live reggae music Wednesdays, Fridays, and occasionally Saturdays; *Sputnik Bar* (Coral Bay; no phone) offers native food and a live reggae/calypso band. The *Caneel* band plays at the *Beach Terrace* at *Caneel Bay* (see *Checking In*). For just hanging out, there's *The Backyard* (Cruz Bay; phone: 693-8886); the new *Bad Art Bar,* complete with velvet Elvis wall hangings and Flintstones pillows (Cruz Bay; phone: 693-8666); and *Skinny Legs,* for darts, horseshoes, and good grilled burgers (Coral Bay; phone: 779-4982).

St. Thomas boasts no star-spangled nightclub shows, no big-deal casinos. *Marriott's Frenchman's Reef* (see *Checking In*) offers nightly dinner-theater featuring off-Broadway shows and musicals by the local *Pistarckle Theatre Company* at its *Top of the Reef* nightclub; at the hotel's *La Terraza* lounge, there's video *karaoke* and a DJ playing top 40 dance music nightly, with occasional live bands. The *Hard Rock Café* (see *Eating Out*) offers rock 'n' roll nightly with a DJ; a live band goes on Mondays through Saturdays about 10:30 PM. Elsewhere, entertainment is simpler. Hotels provide music—songs and a guitar or a small combo—most nights, and many host outdoor barbecues with a steel band and limbo show (usually with a bit of fire-eating or broken-glass walking thrown in) at least one evening a week. If you've never seen a limbo show, check one out, but if you've seen one . . . . Other options: *Bluebeard's* (see *Checking In*) features dancing on Sunday nights; *Barnacle Bill's* at Sub Base (phone: 774-7444) has bands nightly (except Sundays and Tuesdays) and during happy hour Fridays; *Tavern on the Beach* (see *Eating Out*) offers a DJ and a *karaoke* bar. *Agave Terrace* (see *Eating Out*) features steel bands Tuesday and Thursday evenings. *Blackbeard's* (see *Checking In*) offers jazz nightly. At the *Green House* restaurant (see *Eating Out*) a DJ plays oldies Tuesday nights; Wednesdays through Saturdays there's live reggae or rock bands. At *Iggy's,* a *karaoke* bar in the *Bolonga Club Everything* hotel, guests can get up on stage and sing along to their favorite songs; a nightclub with a calypso band and a disco for dancing are upstairs. *The Old Mill* (Upper Constant; phone: 776-3004) features local music, the *East Coast Bar and Grill* is a jazz club with live music Saturday evenings, and *For the Birds* draws a young crowd with its nightly DJ and reggae Friday and Saturday nights (see *Eating Out* for the latter two).

Best on the Islands

CHECKING IN

The US Virgin Islands have just about everything in the way of accommodations except high-rises. Among the nicest properties are condominiums, which, though not inexpensive, can be money savers for families or a few couples sharing an apartment—the usually well-stocked kitchens can really cut down on dining expenses. There are also modest guesthouses and small inns on all three islands. Rates range from as little as $55 for two with breakfast at a 19th-century guesthouse in summer, to $475 and up for two without meals at the *Grand Palazzo* in winter. (A very inexpensive option is pitching a tent at *Cinnamon Bay*'s campgrounds; visitors pay as little as $10 a night for a bare tent site.) In the lists that follow, very expensive is defined as $300 or more per day for a room for two with no meals during the winter season; expensive is $175 to $300; moderate, $125 to $175; and inexpensive, less than $125. Summer rates are 25% to 45% less. Modified American Plan (MAP, which includes breakfast and dinner) is usually available at a $25 to $35 per person per day surcharge. Unless otherwise noted, all hotels listed below feature air conditioning, telephones, TV sets, and private baths. All telephone numbers are in the 809 area code unless otherwise indicated. The central toll-free telephone number for making hotel reservations on St. Croix is 800-524-2026; for St. John and St. Thomas hotel reservations, call 774-6835.

We begin with our favorite havens, followed by recommended hotels listed by price category.

REGAL RESORTS

Caneel Bay, St. John Perfect serenity is the most enticing amenity offered here. This 170-acre resort estate, just a small part of the 7,028 forested acres that Laurance S. Rockefeller gave to the US to become the *Virgin Islands National Park,* is managed by the Rosewood hotel group. The only thing flamboyant on the property is the tree of the same name, and only the colors of the flowers—scarlet hibiscus, yellow trumpet vine, purple morning glories—are loud. Decorated with low-key elegance in Caribbean woods and hand-woven fabrics, the 171 rooms are spacious and airy, with porches just a few steps from the sea; they aren't air conditioned, and there are no TV sets or telephones, but that's part of their appeal—no intrusions from the "real world." There are seven superb beaches, and swimming, basking, snorkeling, and small-boat sailing occupy most days; tranquillity is protected by the national park's ban on water skiing. Just next door is Trunk Bay, with its marked underwater nature trail for snorkeling; more ambitious dive trips are also available, as are ranger-led tours through the park. Amenities also include *Peter Burwash International* tennis. The chic, new *Equator* restaurant offers an enticing menu of "equatorial" cuisine, blending flavors from South America, Thailand, and the Caribbean. There's also elegant dining at the *Turtle Bay* restaurant, with cocktails on the terrace overlooking gardens that sweep down to the sea. The noon buffet on the *Garden Terrace* is a Caneel Bay tradition, but for a change of pace you might want to opt for a picnic at Trunk Bay or a bite at one of Cruz Bay's native restaurants (the hotel offers an EP option). A steel band arrives to play for dinner-dancing several times a week, and there are nightly movies. Otherwise, it is happily, serenely, and early to bed. Caneel Bay (phone: 776-6111; 800-928-8889; fax: 693-8280).

Grand Palazzo, St. Thomas This stunning beachfront resort at Great Bay, on the east end of St. Thomas, is laid out in three sections featuring Italian Renaissance–style architecture. Guests relax among marbled and tiled splendor in 152 upscale rooms and suites. All rooms feature cable TV, hair dryers, and in-room safes, among other amenities. In addition, there is a magnificent 125-foot pool that looks as though it merges with the ocean, a smaller children's pool, a fitness center, *Peter Burwash International* tennis on four lighted courts, and water sports. There are three restaurants, including the romantic *Palm Terrace* (see *Eating Out*), where ceiling fans stir the large palms and guests view the ocean through large windows as they feast on elegantly presented continental specialties. Great Bay (phone: 775-3333; 800-545-0509; fax: 775-4444).

ST. CROIX

CHRISTIANSTED AND ENVIRONS

VERY EXPENSIVE

Buccaneer Sprawling down a hillside outside Christiansted, it has the most extensive facilities on the island—three beaches, an 18-hole golf course, eight highly rated tennis courts, a basketball court, a 2-mile jogging trail, a spa and fitness center, shops, plus a full roster of activities. There's a lot happening, but the atmosphere is easygoing. The 150 recently refurbished rooms, all with private terraces, are large and well appointed; the most popular are the beachside rooms with fieldstone terraces right on the water. The 1653 sugar mill on the property is a popular wedding site. There are also four restaurants; the view of Christiansted from the open-air *Terrace* is unequaled. Estate Shoy (phone: 773-2100; 800-255-3881; fax: 778-8215).

Club St. Croix This stylish beachfront property has 52 studio and one-bedroom units, all with modern decor, rattan furnishings, and ceiling fans (in addition to the air conditioning). The suites also have full kitchens and balconies with sea views. There are three tennis courts, a lap pool, and water sports facilities. The resort launch brings guests to town; day sails can be arranged. The pleasant poolside restaurant/bar overlooks the sea. One mile west of downtown Christiansted (phone: 773-4800; 800-635-1533; fax: 773-4805).

Colony Cove Here are 60 large, good-looking apartments, each with cable TV, a VCR, a full kitchen including a microwave oven and dishwasher, and laundry facilities. The bedrooms are air conditioned; other rooms have ceiling fans. There's a solar-tiled pool (it keeps the water warm for dips after dark) and a good water sports center. The extra-large terraces, all facing the ocean, are especially nice. The property also has a restaurant and two tennis courts. About 10 minutes from Christiansted (phone: 773-1965; 800-828-0746; fax: 773-5397).

Tamarind Reef After being devastated by Hurricane Hugo in 1989, this hotel has been rebuilt and is bigger and better than ever. With Danish architecture and West Indian furnishings, the 46 rooms and one suite are located on the full-service *Green Cay Marina.* Some rooms have kitchenettes; all have cable TV, in-room safes, and air conditioning (at an extra charge). There's a small beach and pool, a beach bar for light fare, and complimentary water sports and continental breakfast. Children under six stay free in their parents' room. 5001 Tamarind Reef (phone: 773-4455; 800-619-0014; fax: 773-3989).

Anchor Inn Here are 31 harborfront rooms in the heart of Christiansted, each with cable TV and refrigerator. There is also a restaurant. Day trips to Buck Island are available. King St. (phone: 773-4000; 800-524-2030; fax: 773-4408).

Caravelle Sitting on the water in Christiansted's historic district, this place has 43 rooms and one suite. A freshwater pool, a variety of water sports, and the *Banana Bay Club,* a harbor-view open-air restaurant, complete the picture. 44A Queen Cross St. (phone: 773-0687; 800-524-0410; fax: 778-7004).

St. Croix by the Sea A pretty, popular spot with 65 rooms with ceiling fans (in addition to air conditioning), a great view of the ocean, a huge saltwater pool, tennis (four courts), and two very good restaurants. Close to downtown (phone: 778-8600; 800-524-5006; fax: 778-8002).

Waves at Cane Bay A small seaside hotel, it's in a beautiful natural setting near the *Westin Carambola Beach* resort. The 11 spacious studios and one villa feature kitchens and balconies with ocean views; some have air conditioning, but none has a telephone. There's a saltwater grotto pool, a small beach area, and superior snorkeling and scuba diving right in front of the property. Beautiful Cane Bay Beach, a golf course, and tennis courts are nearby. There's a restaurant that serves meals on an erratic schedule, and guests may use the grill by the pool. The location is a bit remote; a car is a necessity. Cane Bay (phone: 778-1805; 800-545-0603; fax: 778-1805).

INEXPENSIVE

Danish Manor This lovely, peaceful hotel in the heart of Christiansted offers 34 rooms, all clean and comfortable. A pool and a bar with cafe tables for alfresco lounging are set in the cut-stone courtyard. The hotel is within walking distance of the historic district, duty-free shopping, fine restaurants, and a beach with water sports facilities. The innkeepers are brimming with island hospitality and are happy to share their knowledge of the island. 2 Company St. (phone: 773-1377; 800-524-2069; fax: 773-1913).

Hilty House This small, charming bed and breakfast place is housed in a former 18th-century rum factory. Hugh and Jacquie Hoare-Ward, the owners, take great pains to make their guests feel at home. The building has two-foot-thick outer walls and interior rooms decorated with hand-painted Italian tiles and dark beams. There are five guestrooms and two cottages, tastefully furnished, most with ceiling fans—there's no air conditioning, but the old house is cooled by pleasant breezes. None of the accommodations has a telephone or TV set, but there's a TV and VCR in the main library. There's also a large pool and sun deck. A delicious continental breakfast, prepared with garden-fresh ingredients, is included. No credit cards accepted. Questa Verde Rd., Hermon Hill (phone/fax: 773-2594).

King Christian Its wharfside location in a former historic warehouse couldn't be more convenient. The 39 rooms (25 with ocean views) are basic, but large, with refrigerators and coffee makers; the newer rooms are a bit more refined. The hotel, which draws many repeat visitors, also sports a freshwater pool with a deck. Guests can use *Hotel on the Cay*'s sports facilities for a nominal fee. The *Chart House* restaurant (see *Eating Out*) is on the property. 59 King's Wharf (phone: 773-2285; 800-524-2012; fax: 773-9411).

Pink Fancy Encompassing a restored 18th-century Danish townhouse and its attendant buildings, this small gem is a mosaic of white-shingled, pink-shuttered buildings; walled courtyards; gardens; and terraces on different levels. The 13 large, attractive studios—with living areas and fully stocked kitchenettes—are meant for solid comfort. There's a pretty tiled swimming pool and 24-hour complimentary bar where guests help themselves to continental breakfast and drinks. A five-minute walk from the Christiansted wharf (phone: 773-8460; 800-524-2045; fax: 773-6448).

FREDERIKSTED

Paradise Sunset Beach Drive through a rugged strip of woods to find this pink complex perched above the road. The pool looks like it's hanging over Estate Ham's Bay. One of the few island hotels facing the spectacular sunsets, it has 11 rooms and two cottages with kitchens; all have cable TV, but there are no telephones. On are the grounds are 17th-century sugar mill ruins and a poolside restaurant. On Rte. 63 (phone: 772-2499; fax: 772-0001).

ELSEWHERE ON ST. CROIX

VERY EXPENSIVE

Cormorant Beach Club On a 1,600-foot palm-fringed beach, it has 34 double rooms and four one-bedroom suites, all beautifully furnished and boasting fresh flowers daily and a private patio and/or balcony overlooking the beach. There is a pool, tennis, and snorkeling; also, a restaurant (see *Eating Out*) and a bar. Rates include morning coffee or tea and afternoon tea and pastries; an optional plan includes breakfast, lunch, and all drinks until 5 PM. Adjacent *Cormorant Cove* has six high-rise luxury condominium units, some with marble baths and Jacuzzis, and its own freshwater pool. 4126 La Grande Princesse, 10 minutes west of Christiansted (phone: 778-8920; 800-548-4460; fax: 778-9218).

Westin Carambola Beach Nestled on 28 acres overlooking the Caribbean, this resort's 150 rooms and suites are distributed among several villas around the pristine white sand beach; nearby are a pool and two Jacuzzis. There are two restaurants, as well as tennis courts, snorkeling and scuba facilities, and an 18-hole championship course (see *Golf*), where guests play for reduced greens fees. Davis Bay (phone: 778-3800; 800-333-3333; fax: 778-1682).

Villa Madeleine This stunning resort has 43 villas (three one-bedroom and 40 two-bedroom), each with its own pool, marble baths, and ocean views. The main building, with the restaurant, music room, and gameroom, was built to resemble a sugar plantation greathouse. All villas have kitchens with microwave ovens and TV sets with VCRs. Tennis, golf, horseback riding, and all water sports may be arranged. The beach is within walking distance of units on the lower hill. *The Great House at Villa Madeleine* serves continental and Italian food. Estate Teague Bay, on the east end of the island (phone: 773-8141; 800-548-4461; fax: 773-7518).

MODERATE

Cane Bay Reef Club Surfers and snorkelers like this place's proximity to the beach, while other guests choose to play golf at nearby *Westin Carambola Beach*.

It's small, informal, and friendly; the seven one-bedroom suites have kitchens and balconies with spectacular views of the sea; just two of the suites have air conditioning, and there are no TV sets or telephones. The beach is just down the road; there's a pool on the property. There's also an excellent restaurant. A car is recommended. On the north shore, midway between Christiansted and Frederiksted (phone: 778-2966; 800-253-8534; fax: 778-2966).

Hibiscus Beach Built on the site of the former *Cathy's Fancy,* its 38 immaculate, well-appointed rooms feature a fine ocean view that includes Buck Island, and in-room safes. Guests can walk right onto the beach, and from there to a coral reef; there's also a swimming pool. The open-air restaurant/bar and casual indoor dining room serve good continental fare. Snorkeling equipment is complimentary. An all-inclusive plan is available, featuring all meals (including a dine-around option at several area restaurants), beverages, most sports, a rental car, and admission to local attractions. 4131 La Grande Princesse, 10 minutes west of Christiansted (phone: 773-4042; 800-442-0121; fax: 773-7668).

ST. JOHN

VERY EXPENSIVE

Hyatt Regency St. John This modern, luxury property has 285 rooms, suites, and townhouses perched on 34 acres of lush, tropical hillside. Highlights include a huge pool, an excellent white sand beach, tennis on six lighted courts, water sports, shops, three restaurants (including *Ciao Mein* and *Café Grand;* see *Eating Out*), a bar, a health club, and an airport shuttle to and from St. Thomas. Great Cruz Bay (phone: 693-8000; 800-233-1234; fax: 779-4985).

EXPENSIVE

Estate Zootenvaal An intimate complex of three cottages within 10 minutes of the water's edge, close to the isolated town of Coral Bay. This is a quiet spot with simple, tasteful furnishings, full kitchens, ceiling fans, and a private beach, but no air conditioning, telephones, or TV sets. There's no restaurant, but nearby Coral Bay has a few. Hurricane Hole (phone: 776-6321).

Gallows Point A 60-unit West Indian–influenced condominium complex overlooking Pillsbury Sound and Cruz Bay. The tastefully furnished two-story cottages house one-bedroom suites with no air conditioning (there are ceiling fans) and sea views; some suites have TV sets, but there are no telephones. *Ellington's* restaurant is long on atmosphere, short on service. There's also a pool. Convenient location near town (phone: 776-6434; 800-323-7229; fax: 776-6520).

Harmony Owned by Stanley Selengut of *Maho Bay Camps* (see below), this complex was specially built with the goal of preserving the environment. Nestled above the campgrounds, these eight units in two-story wooden buildings operate solely on sun and wind power; also, much of the furniture was made of recycled material (the plush carpeting was made from plastic bottles, and the floor tiles were made with the glass from crushed light bulbs!). The guestrooms offer kitchenettes with microwaves and magnificent views of St. John's natural beauty. The rooms are air conditioned by "wind scoops" that are engineered to draw hot air out; needless to say, there are no telephones or TV sets. There is also a restaurant. A minimum one-week stay is required; no credit cards accepted. In the *Virgin Islands National Park* (phone: 776-6226 or 776-6240; 800-392-9004; 212-472-9454 in New York).

INEXPENSIVE

Cinnamon Bay Campground For island lovers on a limited budget, or those who prefer to rough it. This place offers tents and cottages with cooking gear, a commissary, a cafeteria, and bathhouses (shared, of course), as well as bare sites on a beachside campground owned by the *National Park Service* and managed by the Rosewood hotel group. Of course, such amenities as air conditioning, telephones, and TV sets aren't an issue here. Extremely popular, so book well in advance. Dive packages, snorkeling instruction, and hikes are available. In the *Virgin Islands National Park* (phone: 776-6330; 800-539-9998; fax: 776-6458).

Maho Bay Camps This ecologically sensitive resort offers a truly laid-back escape from the shoppers and cruise ship passengers. Dotting the 14-acre hillside are 114 tents that serve as small canvas houses, complete with good beds, kitchen areas, refrigerators, and sun decks (but bathrooms are shared with other units and, of course, there are no telephones, TV sets, or air conditioning). The beach, where water sports are available, lies below; the national park, all around. Simple fare is served at an open-air, island-style restaurant. There's live entertainment Friday evenings; a pavilion, with magnificent views and massage facilities, hosts weddings and meetings. A shuttle to Cruz Bay is available. Some units are reserved a year in advance. No credit cards accepted. In the *Virgin Islands National Park* (phone: 776-6226 or 776-6240; 212-472-9454 from New York; 800-392-9004 from elsewhere in the US).

ST. THOMAS

Those who can't find available rooms at the hotels below should check out *Property Management Caribbean,* which handles seven properties that rent condominiums (phone: 800-524-2038).

CHARLOTTE AMALIE AND THE SOUTHERN COAST

VERY EXPENSIVE

Bolongo Club Everything This property incorporates two separate hotels on two beaches; the 230 guestrooms have cable TV. Guests may choose the Breakfast Plan or Club Everything, which includes all meals, drinks, and taxes; both plans include tennis on six courts, water sports (including scuba), a fitness center, three pools, shuttles to the *Bolongo Elysian Beach* (see below), and three tours (a day sail, a sunset cruise, and a snorkeling trip). There are five restaurants, including *Iggy's*, which becomes a *karaoke* bar at night. Calypso, jazz, and reggae bands often perform in the evenings. 50 Estate Bolongo (phone: 779-2844; 800-524-4746; fax: 775-3208).

Bolongo Elysian Beach On the beach at Cowpet Bay (cowpets are baby whales, which sometimes migrate past here), this pretty, pink resort offers 118 stunning condos with kitchens, TV sets with VCRs, and balconies. There's a large freshwater pool with a waterfall and a whirlpool, plus a beach, a fitness center, tennis, day cruises, and water sports. The complex has two restaurants; continental breakfast is included in the rate. Cowpet Bay (phone: 775-1000; 800-524-4746; fax: 775-3208).

Marriott's Frenchman's Reef Set on a cliff overlooking the sea, this huge, very modern resort complex has 421 rooms; most popular are the additional 96 luxurious rooms at the *Morning Star Beach* resort, down the hill at the beach, each with a private entrance, tropical decor, and many special amenities. The resort also offers several restaurant choices, including the open-air *Caesar's Ristorante* and, at *Morning Star*, *Tavern on the Beach* (see *Eating Out* for both); there's also the *Top of the Reef* dinner-theater and *La Terraza* lounge. For sports-minded guests, there is tennis on four lighted courts (with a *Peter Burwash International* program and a pro shop), two freshwater pools, a health club, Jacuzzis, and a beautiful beach. The panoramic ocean view is stunning; the water sports setup is the island's most extensive. Other services include a water taxi into Charlotte Amalie and tour and car rental desks in the lobby. MAP and all-inclusive plans are offered. Ten minutes from town (phone: 776-8500; 800-524-2000 or 800-BEACH-CLUB; fax: 774-6249).

EXPENSIVE

Bluebeard's Castle A historic setting with a terrific view, lush gardens, tennis courts, and 170 rooms. We're sentimentally attached to the old tower (request Room 139 or 140), although a newer building, with 48 rooms and suites and eight condominium units and meeting rooms, has taken away some of the charm here. Not for beach buffs—it has none—but it does provide beach transportation, two night-lighted tennis courts, a freshwater pool, and two restaurants (including the outstanding *Entre Nous*—see *Eating Out*). Near town (phone: 774-1600; 800-524-6599; fax: 774-5134).

Secret Harbour Beach Contemporary and casual, here are 60 suites with expansive sun decks and kitchenettes overlooking Nazareth Bay. Amenities include a pool and a fitness center. Right on the beach with water sports, tennis on two courts, and two restaurants. Complimentary continental breakfast. Five miles east of Charlotte Amalie, on a secluded beach (phone: 775-6550; 800-524-2250; fax: 775-1501).

Secret Harbourview Villas This property has 25 studio and one- and two-bedroom condominium units available for rental. Each unit is attractively furnished and supplied with a full kitchen and balcony with a view of the Caribbean. There are three all-weather tennis courts, a freshwater pool, a Jacuzzi, and a fitness center. On the beach there's a fabulous water sports center, plus a cocktail pavilion and delicious food at the waterfront restaurant/bar. One of the prettiest locations on St. Thomas, just 20 minutes from Charlotte Amalie (phone: 775-2600; 800-874-7897; fax: 775-5901).

MODERATE

Admiral's Inn This small, family-run property offers 16 rooms with ocean or harbor views, all with cable TV. Continental breakfast is included. There's a small beach and pool, an informal restaurant/bar, and the *Chart House* (see *Eating Out*). At Villa Olga in French Town (phone: 774-1376; 800-544-0493; fax: 774-8010).

Blackbeard's Castle Small and intimate, it has 24 rooms and apartments in a restored 17th-century Danish mansion. The watchtower at the center was built in 1679 by Blackbeard so he could spot ships to plunder. The room decor is unassuming, but comfortable. Also on the premises are an Olympic-size pool and an excellent restaurant (see *Eating Out*). There also are great views of Charlotte Amalie and the cruise ship area. Rte. 35 at the top of Blackbeard Hill (phone: 776-1234; 800-344-5771; fax: 776-4321).

Hotel 1829 Long a landmark in historic Charlotte Amalie, this pretty, peach-colored building with the green awning and the wrought-iron gate is small and utterly charming, with lots of ancient tile, stone, and wooden louvers. Everything about it bespeaks graciousness—a shady verandah for daytime reading, a sunny courtyard with a small swimming pool, 15 rooms decorated with taste and imagination, all with refrigerators, and an excellent, popular restaurant where a complimentary continental breakfast is served (see *Eating Out*). A 15-minute drive to the beach. Government Hill (phone: 776-1829; 800-524-2002; fax: 776-4313).

Mafolie A quiet place with a lovely view of the harbor. There are 23 rooms; all of the suites have TV sets, but there are no telephones. There are also two restaurants (including the *Frigate at Mafolie;* see *Eating Out*) and a pool; beach transportation and continental breakfast are included. On Mafolie Hill (phone: 774-2790; 800-225-7035; fax: 809-774-4091).

Ramada Yacht Haven Excellent for sailing buffs, it offers very attractive charter yacht packages from its private 200-slip marina, the largest on St. Thomas. There are 151 rooms and suites with TV sets with VCRs, two pools, three restaurants, and complimentary transportation to the beach. 5400 Long Bay Rd., at the mouth of the cruise ship port (phone: 774-9700; 800-468-3571; fax: 776-3410).

INEXPENSIVE

Danish Chalet A friendly place on a hill overlooking the bay and cruise ship docks, this 15-room bed and breakfast establishment offers a breezy deck and Jacuzzi. Most rooms are air conditioned (the rest have ceiling fans) and have private baths, two have TV sets, and all have phones. Continental breakfast is included in the rate, and there's an honor bar. Five-minute walk to town. Solberg Rd. (phone: 774-5764; 800-635-1531; fax: 777-4886).

NORTHERN COAST

VERY EXPENSIVE

Magens Point On a hill above the famous beach at Magens Bay. The new management has renovated the 44 trim contemporary rooms (ask for one with cathedral ceilings); there's also a pool, two tennis courts, and two restaurants. Close to the *Mahogany Run* golf course (see *Golf*, above). Free transportation to the beach; a nominal charge to Charlotte Amalie (phone: 775-5500; 800-524-2031; fax: 776-5524).

Sapphire Beach On one of the island's loveliest beaches, this huge complex has a 67-slip marina, two restaurants, a pool, and four tennis courts. The 171 suites and villas face either the beach or the marina and have kitchens, microwave ovens, coffee makers, and patios. All water sports are complimentary; lessons cost extra. Children under 12 stay and eat free, and MAP plans are available. On Sapphire Beach (phone: 775-6100; 800-524-2090; fax: 775-4024).

Stouffer Renaissance Grand Beach The architecture here is a departure from that of other island hotels, with wood-shingled dormers, awnings, and French doors. There are 297 rooms and suites, all with cable TV and refrigerators; most have private balconies. There are also two restaurants and lounges, shops, two pools, an activities program for children, and a dock and marina on 34 acres of landscaped grounds. Use of the fitness center, six lighted tennis courts, and water sports center is complimentary. Scuba lessons are also available. Rooms in the Bougainvillea area are conveniently grouped behind the beach and the great beachfront pool, while those in the hillside Hibiscus area have the better view (the resort runs a continuous shuttle up and down the property and a complimentary shuttle to *Coral World*). Whichever area you choose, specify a second-floor or higher room for maximum privacy on your terrace. On an inviting stretch of sand on the island's northeast shore (phone: 775-1510; 800-HOTELS-1; fax: 775-3757).

Point Pleasant A small, secluded, 15-acre ecologically minded world of gardens with great charm, quiet style, and 134 spacious villas overlooking the sea—all with balconies and kitchens. The beach is tiny, but guests may use the beach facilities at the *Stouffer Renaissance Grand Beach* next door. There's also an excellent restaurant and three pools. Included in the rates are a scuba lesson and use of a car (mandatory insurance charge is extra), a tennis court, Sunfish boats, and windsurfing and snorkel gear. The *Agave Terrace* restaurant has a fabulous view and chic clientele (see *Eating Out*). Estate Smith Bay (phone: 775-7200; 800-524-2300; fax: 776-5694).

Wyndham Sugar Bay Recently acquired by the Wyndham hotel chain, this resort sweeps down the hill to the sea near Red Hook. Decorated in elegant plantation style, the hotel's 300 luxury rooms and suites have sea views, ceiling fans (in addition to air conditioning), refrigerators, and private balconies. As part of Wyndham's ambitious renovation program, the beach has recently been enhanced by 1,000 tons of sand shipped over from the British Virgin Islands. The resort also boasts the USVI's first stadium tennis court, in addition to six other lighted courts and a pro shop; there's also an 89-foot trimaran yacht that offers half-day, full-day, and sunset cruises. Other amenities include three connected pools with a waterfall and Jacuzzi, a fitness center, a dive shop, access to golf, two restaurants, a nightclub, and a view of a 1.6-acre historic area with archaeological remains. Rte. 38, Smith Bay Rd. (phone: 777-7100; 800-WYNDHAM; fax:777-7200).

EATING OUT

Menus run from genuine, elegant French and continental fare to casual deli—with Mexican, Italian, Chinese, American steaks and seafood, and a touch of "soul" sandwiched in between. Island fare is limited but good. Staples are delicious fish (red snapper, dolphin, wahoo, yellowtail, grouper) poached or broiled and served with a choice of sauces (we're partial to the hot lime, but creole and spicy West Indian are good, too), and sweet lobster with lemon butter. An alternative main course might be a curry (conch, lamb, or goat), or boiled chicken with vegetables. *Funghi,* dumplings made of okra and cornmeal, are a likely side dish. The best soup around is *callaloo,* thick with greens and bits of ham and crab, spiced with okra and pepper. For dessert: guava or pineapple tart, or soothing soursop ice cream. The *vin du pays* (light Cruzan rum) goes nicely with most everything.

One place to get all this together is at a fish fry, a y'all-come super-picnic with music and dancing, and a favorite island social event. They're held at varying intervals on the beaches of all three islands. Admission, drinks, and food come to about $15 per person, and you really are welcome.

Expect to pay $110 or more for a meal for two (including tip, but not wine or drinks) at a restaurant we list as very expensive. Dinner for two at expensive places costs $75 to $110; moderate places run about $40 to $75; less than $40 at spots we describe as inexpensive. Unless otherwise noted, all restaurants listed below are open for lunch and dinner. All telephone numbers are in the 809 area code unless otherwise indicated. A timely note: Call ahead to be sure the restaurant is open, since some close during the off-season.

ST. CROIX

EXPENSIVE

Cormorant Beach Club This dining spot encompasses two places side by side: an enclosed dinner restaurant and an open-air, more casual restaurant, both beachfront. The menu features such creations as island seafood chowder, chicken Athena (chicken breast filled with spinach, feta cheese, and dried apricots), and filet mignon with mushroom compote. Steel bands play Thursday and Sunday nights, and there's jazz Fridays. Open daily for breakfast, lunch, and dinner; Sunday brunch also is served. Reservations advised. Major credit cards accepted. 4126 La Grande Princesse, 10 minutes west of Christiansted (phone: 778-8920).

Duggan's Reef Overlooking the beach and Buck Island, this informal dining spot serves soups, salads, burgers, and grilled fish at lunch; escargots, rack of lamb, shrimp tempura, and lobster pasta in the evening. Open daily. Reservations advised. Major credit cards accepted. Rte. 82 at Reef Beach (phone: 773-9800).

Indies This restaurant, perhaps St. Croix's best, is set in a partially roofed courtyard surrounded by 18th-century buildings. It's owned and run by acclaimed chef Catherine Diggers, who formerly ran the kitchen at the *Cormorant Beach Club*. The menu features fine West Indian fare, including Caribbean seafood stew and spiced chicken with mango chutney and grilled bananas. Save room for the "tropical trifle" (rum-soaked cake topped with fruit and whipped cream). Open daily; only dinner on weekends. Reservations advised. Major credit cards accepted. 55-56 Company St., Christiansted (phone: 692-9440).

Kendrick's Set in an authentic old Danish home, this establishment offers excellent service and an attractive, antiques-filled decor. Diners enjoy superb angel hair pasta with sun-dried tomatoes, grilled rack of lamb, and enticing appetizers such as baked brie with wild mushrooms. A piano player provides background music nightly in season. Open daily for dinner only; closed Sundays mid-March through mid-November. Reservations advised. Major credit cards accepted. 52 King St., Christiansted (phone: 773-9199).

Top Hat At this cozy eatery set above shops in an 18th-century merchant's home, chef Bent Rasmussen prepares Danish specialties such as meatballs with red cabbage, pâtés, seafood, and Cruzan coffee. Dinner only; closed Sundays and from May through July. Reservations necessary. Major credit cards accepted. 53 Company St., Christiansted (phone: 773-2346).

MODERATE

Dino's This casual Italian eatery serves classic specialties, featuring handmade pasta and prime veal. Entrées include chicken ravioli with a walnut-roast garlic cream sauce and veal saltimbocca with prosciutto, sage, mozzarella, and marsala wine. Save room for the luscious homemade desserts. Open daily for dinner only. Reservations advised. American Express accepted. 4C Hospital St., Christiansted (phone: 778-8005).

Pangaea This funky dining option features an eclectic menu with such delicious entries as chilled mango soup and baked molasses chicken breast with onion rum relish. The restaurant prides itself on using fresh ingredients from local farmers and fishermen. Open daily. Reservations unnecessary. No credit cards accepted. 1103 Queen Cross St., Christiansted (phone: 773-7743).

Sprat Hall Great House Island dishes (pork chops in orange sauce, baked breadfruit, coconut beef) are served by candlelight in the island's oldest continuously lived-in plantation house. The menu changes nightly. Friendly atmosphere; jackets and ties for men and dresses for women are preferred but not mandatory. Dinner only; closed Sundays. Reservations necessary. American Express accepted. On Rte. 63, 1 mile north of Frederiksted (phone: 772-0305).

Tivoli Gardens Prettiest at night, when lights twinkle and greenery ruffles in the harbor breeze. Zesty soups and *coquilles St-Jacques* are fine starters; noteworthy entrées include steak Diane, fresh local fish, and various lobster dishes; the chocolate velvet dessert is superb. Open daily; no lunch on weekends. Reservations advised. Major credit cards accepted. Strand St. and Queen Cross, Christiansted (phone: 773-6782).

Tutto Bene Café One of the newest eateries in Christiansted is this charming Italian bistro that is usually packed with enthusiastic patrons. Its atmosphere is informal; the menu (which changes daily) presents classic dishes such as veal parmigiano, lasagna, and seafood *fra diavolo,* as well as more contemporary specialties, such as grilled mahimahi and crabmeat ravioli. Open daily for dinner. Reservations advised. Major credit cards accepted. 2 Company St., Christiansted (phone: 773-5229).

INEXPENSIVE

Camille's When you're ready to beat the heat, stop in at this air conditioned oasis. Reminiscent of a stateside diner, it features nightly specials such as fresh fish or grilled chicken and ribs. Open daily. Reservations unnecessary. No credit cards accepted. Queen Cross St., Christiansted (phone: 773-2985).

Chart House Part of the US restaurant chain that specializes in historic locations and dishes such as teriyaki chicken, Australian lobster tails, prime ribs, fine steaks, and grilled local fish such as wahoo, tuna, and kingfish, plus an all-you-can-eat salad bar. Open daily for dinner. No reservations. Major credit cards accepted. In the *King Christian Hotel,* 59 King's Wharf, Christiansted (phone: 773-7718).

Jackie's Set in a quiet courtyard, this restaurant serves up excellent local fare such as oxtail soup, curried conch, johnnycakes, and *funghi,* as well as local drinks, including sorrel juice and *mauby,* a refreshing tea made from the bark of a local tree. Open daily. Reservations unnecessary. No credit cards accepted. 46 King St., Christiansted (phone: 773-1955).

ST. JOHN

VERY EXPENSIVE

Ciao Mein This premier restaurant on the top of the *Hyatt Regency St. John* offers a choice of two menus: Italian selections include fried calamari and sambuca shrimp, while Asian dishes feature wok-roasted duck and sizzling yellowtail snapper. Live piano music provides a soothing atmosphere every night. Open daily for dinner. Reservations advised. Major credit cards accepted. Great Cruz Bay (phone: 693-8000).

EXPENSIVE

Café Grand The fare served at this open-air eatery covers a wide range, from burgers to osso buco. Theme nights also are featured. Open daily for breakfast and dinner; Sunday brunch also is served. Reservations advised for dinner. Major credit cards accepted. At the *Hyatt Regency St. John,* Great Cruz Bay (phone: 693-8000).

Château de Bordeaux Set on St. John's highest point, this place is upscale, yet still funky and fun. The food is as fabulous as the view, with menu offerings ranging from fresh fish and lobster to steaks and roasts. Closed Sundays. Reservations necessary. MasterCard and Visa accepted. Coral Bay (phone: 776-6611).

Paradiso An upscale Italian eatery with an extensive wine list. Good menu choices are crab cakes *Paradiso* and seafood *fra diavolo.* Open daily for dinner and cocktails only. Reservations advised. Major credit cards accepted. In *Mongoose Junction,* Cruz Bay (phone: 693-8899).

Sugar Mill A round restaurant at *Caneel Bay's* original sugar mill, it offers a widely varied American and Caribbean-style buffet. Open daily; serves breakfast only to guests, but non-guests are welcome for the buffet lunch and dinner. Reservations advised. Major credit cards accepted. *Caneel Bay* (phone: 776-6111).

Café Roma Italian specialties are featured at this dining spot with a café atmosphere. The menu includes standard pasta dishes, seafood, and pizza. Open daily for dinner. No reservations. Major credit cards accepted. Cruz Bay (phone: 776-6524).

Fish Trap Known for its seafood, especially the island fish chowder and conch fritters. The fresh homemade desserts are also a treat. Dinner only; closed Mondays. Reservations advised for groups of six or more. Major credit cards accepted. At *Raintree Inn,* Cruz Bay (phone: 693-9994).

Lime Inn A casual spot serving salads and sandwiches. The patio is a great place for people watching. Wednesday nights are all-you-can-eat shrimp feasts. Closed Sundays. Reservations advised for dinner (no reservations on Wednesdays). Major credit cards accepted. Cruz Bay (phone: 776-6425 or 779-4199).

Pusser's of the West Indies Informal food in an open-air setting overlooking Cruz Bay that's excellent for viewing the sunset. The *Crow's Nest* (located upstairs) sees lots of action for burgers, steaks, seafood, and drinks. Thursdays are West Indian nights, Fridays are all-you-can-eat Alaskan king crab nights, and Mondays feature live entertainment. Open daily. Reservations advised for parties of six or more. Major credit cards accepted. *Wharfside Village,* Cruz Bay (phone: 693-8489).

Garden of Luscious Licks This tiny coffeehouse serves vegetarian food, including homemade soups and muffins, both for takeout and dining in. It's *the* spot for getting Ben & Jerry's ice cream. Open daily. Reservations unnecessary. No credit cards accepted. Cruz Bay (phone: 776-6070).

Vie's Local to the core, this spot has an ever-changing menu that includes homemade juices, pâté, and tarts, to eat in or take out. Lunch only; closed Sundays, Mondays, and Fridays. Reservations unnecessary. No credit cards accepted. On the fringes of Coral Bay (phone: 693-5033).

ST. THOMAS

Agave Terrace A delightful terrace room opens on one side to reveal a spectacular view of the Caribbean dotted with a dozen Virgin Islands. Wonderful appetizers include lobster Angelina, pasta Palamero, or gazpacho; fresh seafood is prepared according to the diner's choice, with lobster cardinal (sautéed lobster medallions served with plum tomatoes, lobster cream sauce, and angel hair pasta) a highlight. A member of the Chaîne des Rôtisseurs. Live entertainment Tuesday and Thursday nights. Open daily for breakfast and dinner. Reservations advised. Major credit cards accepted. At the *Point Pleasant* resort, Estate Smith Bay (phone: 775-4142).

Baywinds A dining spot that offers fine continental food. Popular dishes include grilled chicken "jerk style" and seared salmon with papaya and pink onions. Don't miss their famous "Fudgesicle" cocktail—a decadent treat made with rum, crème de coconut, crème de banana, and assorted chocolates. There's music Thursday and Saturday evenings. Open daily for breakfast, lunch, and dinner. Reservations advised for dinner. Major credit cards accepted. At the *Stouffer Renaissance Grand Beach* resort (phone: 775-1510).

Café Normandie This small, popular place features French food beautifully presented—beef Wellington, veal, duck, game, local seafood—and a well-chosen wine list. Don't miss the Normandie chocolate fudge pie for dessert. Smoking allowed only at the *Porch Bar.* Open daily for dinner. Reservations advised. Major credit cards accepted. French Town (phone: 774-1622).

Palm Terrace A luxurious dining room with windows overlooking the ocean; there's no air conditioning, but ceiling fans keep things cool. Besides, you'll be too absorbed in feasting upon venison medallions with roasted quince or sautéed fresh Dover sole to notice the temperature. Open daily for dinner. Reservations advised in season. Major credit cards accepted. At *Grand Palazzo,* Great Bay (phone: 775-3333).

EXPENSIVE

Blackbeard's Castle The setting above Government Hill is stunning, with wooden louvers opening to a view of the city and docked cruise ships. Star appetizers include sautéed escargots with sun-dried tomatoes and wild mushrooms, and cheese tortellini with smoked chicken breast and stilton cheese sauce. The poached seafood with vanilla-bean sauce and the sautéed beef tournedos with roasted garlic are outstanding entreés; the richest dessert anywhere must be the flourless chocolate cake with raspberry sauce. Live jazz nightly during high season. Check out the Sunday brunch. Open daily. Reservations advised. Major credit cards accepted. Rte. 35, at the top of Blackbeard Hill (phone: 776-1234).

Craig and Sally's A beautiful mural wraps around the interior of this restaurant, but the real draw here is the inventive cuisine. The eclectic menu features dishes with Caribbean, Italian, Chinese, and Thai flavors; try the shrimp, littleneck clams, or hot Italian sausage over pasta. The fantastic desserts, including an out-of-this-world white chocolate cheesecake, are made on the premises. There's also an excellent wine selection. Open daily for dinner only. Reservations advised. Major credit cards accepted. French Town (phone: 777-9949).

Entre Nous This elegant place is perfect for a romantic dinner. The bill of fare includes Caesar salad, chateaubriand, and fresh local fish prepared in a variety of ways, as well as some lighter items for health-conscious diners. Open daily for dinner. Reservations advised. Major credit cards accepted. In *Bluebeard's Castle* (phone: 776-4050).

L'Escargot Fine French food and a wine cellar to match. Dover sole, herbed rack of lamb, and chocolate mousse remain favorites. Closed Saturday lunch and Sundays. Reservations necessary for dinner. Major credit cards accepted. The Sub Base, near Crown Bay dock (phone: 774-6565).

Frigate at Mafolie A small hotel terrace with a large reputation for charcoal-grilled steaks, lobster, and local seafood, but known especially for its view. *Frigate East,* a spin-off branch with a similar menu, is across from *Red Hook Marina.* Both are open daily for dinner; the hotel branch also serves breakfast to its guests. Reservations advised. Major credit cards accepted. In the *Mafolie Hotel,* Mafolie Rd., Mafolie, overlooking Charlotte Amalie (phone: 774-2790) and at 18-8 Red Hook (phone: 775-6124).

Hotel 1829 The elegant setting—on a verandah with a view of the harbor or inside this handsome old townhouse—complements the fine food. Try the sautéed lobster and salmon crêpe with emerald hollandaise as an appetizer, then flambéed pepper steaks with brandy and mustard-flavored cream sauce. Save room for the award-winning raspberry-chocolate soufflé. Open daily for dinner. Reservations necessary. Major credit cards accepted. Government Hill, Charlotte Amalie (phone: 776-1829).

Tavern on the Beach The current hot spot for "New World" cuisine—chef Eddie Hale's enticing blend of Caribbean, Southwestern, and Oriental flavors. Perched above the pounding surf, this romantic place is ideal for sampling such eclectic dishes as Thai-flavored pork *satay* with crispy noodle salad and lemongrass/coconut sauce, and sautéed local snapper with a Cruzan rum/brown butter, sweet potato salad, and braised endives. There's live Caribbean-style jazz most nights. Open daily for breakfast, Tuesdays through Saturdays for dinner. Reservations advised in season. Major credit cards accepted. At the *Morning Star Beach Club, Marriott's Frenchman's Reef,* 10 minutes from Charlotte Amalie (phone: 776-8500).

Virgilio's This restaurant offers fine Italian cuisine in an intimate, candlelit setting. Specialties include fried calamari, veal marsala, fettuccine Alfredo, and osso buco. Closed Sundays. Reservations advised. Major credit cards accepted. 18 Main St., Charlotte Amalie (phone: 776-4920).

Windjammer The specialties here are fresh seafood and veal dishes. Dolphin, a sautéed seafood platter for two, Wiener schnitzel, and generous-size steaks also are on the menu. Closed Sundays. Reservations advised. MasterCard and Visa accepted. At Compass Point, off Rte. 32 (phone: 775-6194).

Alexander's Café Delicious Austrian/German fare—Wiener schnitzel, roast pork, strudel, plus pasta and seafood—in a café setting. Closed Sundays. Reservations advised. Major credit cards accepted. French Town (phone: 776-4211 or 774-4349).

Café Havensight The food here is served indoors and outdoors, just off the exit from the docked cruise ships. Sandwiches and salads for lunch, Caribbean fare and steaks for dinner; smaller portions are available for kids. Open daily; closed Sunday dinner. Reservations advised for dinner. Major credit cards accepted. At *Havensight Mall* (phone: 774-5818).

Chart House A terrace dining spot featuring an impressive salad bar, beef kebabs, Hawaiian chicken, lobster, prime ribs, fresh fish, shrimp, and sirloin teriyaki. A must-try: the mud pie. Open daily for dinner. Reservations advised. Major credit cards accepted. At the *Admiral's Inn,* Villa Olga, French Town (phone: 774-4262).

Diamond Barrel This eatery is known for its conch and other local fare, plus steaks and seafood (try the fisherman's platter: conch, yellowtail snapper, and shrimp, either fried or broiled). Open daily for breakfast, lunch, and dinner. Reservations advised for parties of more than six. Major credit cards accepted. 18 Norre Gade, Charlotte Amalie (phone: 774-5071).

East Coast Bar & Grill A jazz club featuring choice beef, fresh fish, chicken, and their famous "Coast burgers." Open daily for dinner; brunch Sundays. Live entertainment most nights. No reservations. Major credit cards accepted. Red Hook (phone: 775-1919).

Green House This shady terrace on the waterfront is a great place to cool off when shopping or sightseeing. Burgers, omelettes, salads, and tall frozen drinks are the specialties. A great happy-hour spot with live reggae music and a DJ. Open daily for breakfast, lunch, and dinner. Reservations unnecessary. Major credit cards accepted. On the waterfront, Charlotte Amalie (phone: 774-7998).

Provence At this harborfront restaurant, country-style French cooking is served in a large but intimate dining room decorated with brightly painted murals, crisp tablecloths, and candles. The food is simply superb: Begin with one of the tasty appetizers, such as onion soup au gratin or grilled squid; then move on to the roasted free-range chicken prepared with garlic, the duck cassoulet, or the sautéed shrimp. The wine bar offers 21 vintages by the glass. A fitting end to the meal is the "Chocolate Sin," which lives up to its name. Open daily. Reservations advised. Major credit cards accepted. French Town (phone: 777-5600).

Romano's A popular spot that doesn't advertise, it serves such traditional Italian specialties as veal marsala and osso buco. Dinner only; closed Sundays.

Reservations advised. Major credit cards accepted. On the road to *Coral World* at 97 Smith Bay Rd. (phone: 775-0045).

Victor's New Hideout Extraordinary seafood dishes are turned out with West Indian flair. Lobster Montserrat is served in a white sauce with chunks of pineapple. For meat eaters, the pork chops marinated in ginger sauce are a must. Open daily; closed Sunday lunch. Reservations advised. Major credit cards accepted. 103 Sub Base, near Crown Bay dock (phone: 776-9379).

INEXPENSIVE

Eunice's Terrace This eatery serves some of the best West Indian food on the island. Menu choices, listed on a blackboard, change daily. Locals love the conch soup and *funghi* (okra and cornmeal dumplings); there's also broiled fish or roast chicken with tomatoes accompanied by fried plantains and beans and rice. Don't miss the sweet potato pie if it's available. Open daily; no lunch on Sundays. Reservations unnecessary. Major credit cards accepted. 67 Smith Bay Rd., next to the *Stouffer Renaissance Grand Beach* (phone: 775-3975).

For the Birds Situated on the beach with the pounding surf just steps away, this casual spot features ribs and Tex-Mex specialties. Open daily for lunch, dinner, and after-dinner dancing. Reservations necessary for parties of six or more. Major credit cards accepted. At Scott Beach (phone: 775-6431).

Hard Rock Café Devotees of this international chain will recognize the black Cadillac hanging over the front door; rock memorabilia from such artists as Elvis Presley, Bob Marley, and the *Beatles* decorate the interior. The menu offers solid, casual fare: burgers, sandwiches, French fries. Music is provided by a DJ nightly and a live band Mondays through Saturdays. Open daily. Reservations necessary for parties of 10 or more. Major credit cards accepted. 5144 International Plaza, The Waterfront (phone: 777-5555).

Piccola Marina Café This lively open-air spot, which spills right down to the dock of the *Red Hook Marina,* is a popular stop for boaters. Dinner emphasis is on pasta served with various types of seafood and classic sauces (marinara, pesto, Alfredo). Also good are steaks, fish, and herb-marinated, mesquite-grilled chicken. The lunch menu features salads and sandwiches. Brunch is served Sundays in season. Open daily. Reservations advised. Major credit cards accepted. 16-3 Smith Bay (phone: 775-6350).

Zorba's Chicagoans Jim and Steve Boukas turn out traditional Greek dishes—kebabs, moussaka, lamb specialties—that some consider the best in the islands. The home-baked breads and pastries are also delicious. The decor here recalls the Greek isle of Mykonos. Closed Sundays. Reservations advised. Major credit cards accepted. 1854 Hus, Government Hill (phone: 776-0444).

Venezuela's Caribbean Coast

The string of Caribbean islands known as the Lesser Antilles seems to lead inexorably to Venezuela's 1,750-mile Caribbean coast. The Spanish originally followed that trail to Venezuela in the early 1500s, and that's still the way many tourists come, looking for a new experience after repeated visits to more familiar Caribbean vacation spots. Yet over the past several years, a growing number of first-time Caribbean vacationers have been lured here by super-affordable travel packages, and resorts and hotels have been springing up to meet the surge in interest.

The Spanish first came to Venezuela for gold and pearls, but the coast itself became even more valuable as a convenient pick-up point for the great wealth that poured from Spain's other New World possessions, and as a base from which Spain could protect its Caribbean holdings. Tourists today come primarily for Caracas, Venezuela's cosmopolitan capital city nestled in a mountain valley less than an hour from the coast; Margarita, the country's best-known island possession; and the increasingly popular beach area of Puerto La Cruz.

The first Spanish settlement in the New World was officially founded in 1521 on the site of what is today the town of Cumaná, across from Margarita Island. The coast hardly was enticing: a series of swamps, inlets, jungles, and bays dotted with tiny Indian villages filled with people ravaged by malaria and fever. The Spanish named the country Venezuela—Little Venice—because of the stilt-perched houses of the villages on the shore of Lago Maracaibo (Lake Maracaibo). While the coastal Indians were too sick to fight the Spanish invaders, Venezuela's mountain tribesmen resisted ferociously, and it took 20 years for the Spanish to establish settlements inland.

From the beginning, the Spanish were obsessed with finding gold. They enslaved Indians to work the mines; as the empire grew, they imported African slaves, too. Yet the results were consistently disappointing. Spain also had a voracious appetite for the huge pearls found off Margarita and the mainland coast. So abundant were they that Margarita Island was named for *margarites,* the Greek word for pearl. Indians were forced to dive several times a day off Margarita, Cubagua, and Cumaná, and if they did not bring back enough pearls, they were punished severely. By the 1530s, the oyster beds had been all but depleted and the Spanish abandoned their efforts.

Venezuela participated in the wars of liberation that swept Latin America from the time of the American and French revolutions until Spain gave up

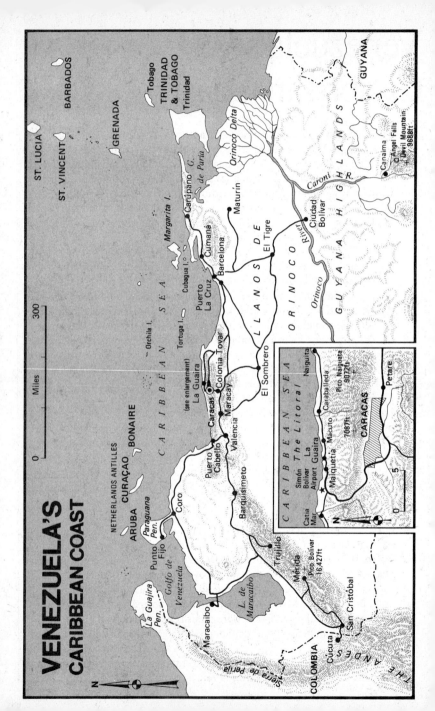

its New World possessions in 1823. Violent slave rebellions always had been a part of Venezuelan life, but by the beginning of the 19th century, the resentment of the dispossessed classes was fed by the frustration of the Creoles, people of pure Spanish blood born in South America and prevented from participating freely in colonial government. Between 1805 and 1811 a Creole man named Francisco de Miranda led two attempts to take over the Spanish government of Venezuela. When he finally was captured, leadership of the revolt passed to a native Venezuelan who came to be known as *El Libertador* (The Liberator)—Simón Bolívar.

Bolívar's wars for the liberation of South America are legendary; he is the Venezuelan equivalent of George Washington. He helped free not only Venezuela, but also Bolivia, Colombia, Ecuador, Peru, and Panama. His dream had been to create a self-governing, democratic republic composed of all those nations—*La República de Gran Colombia* (the Republic of Great Colombia). But this alliance never happened; the revolution succeeded, but the newly independent colonies did nothing but squabble. Bolívar retired to Colombia, where he died penniless and heartbroken.

The next hundred years were violent and difficult for Venezuela; government changed hands by coup, and the country struggled to become a self-supporting entity. Much of this struggle ended earlier this century. When huge stores of oil were discovered at Lago Maracaibo, the political and economic life of the country stabilized. Since 1959, Caracas has been the seat of a democratic government and has become a sophisticated, business-oriented metropolis. However, in recent years, concern about government corruption and the lagging economy has spurred social unrest.

Political troubles began brewing in late 1989, when President Carlos Andrés Pérez introduced an economic austerity program that triggered a series of protest riots. In 1992 he was the target of two unsuccessful coup attempts. Finally, Pérez stepped down in 1993, before completing his term, amid allegations of corruption. (He subsequently was imprisoned on corruption charges.) Elections were held in December, with independent candidate Rafael Caldera winning the mandate. Caldera, a founder of the conservative Social Christian party, had served as president between 1969 and 1974. He took office for his second term vowing to reverse the free-market policies espoused by the Pérez administration.

Oil exportation has made Venezuela a rich country, although falling prices have forced the government to realize it can no longer afford to rely on a single-product economy. The true value of Venezuela isn't in gold or even oil; it lies in the country itself, which, as its cities and economy move toward modernization, struggles to protect its forests from the chainsaw and its beaches from the bulldozer. The perfect introduction to the complex world that is Venezuela is its Caribbean coast, where everything began.

Venezuela's Caribbean Coast
At-a-Glance

FROM THE AIR

The contrasts are startling along Venezuela's 1,750-mile Caribbean coast (the central part is known as El Litoral): sandy beaches, tiny fishing villages, lagoons fed by mountain streams that run down the slopes of the Andes toward the sea, and, just beyond the horizon, uncounted miles of jungle interspersed with open plains. Caracas is in a valley formed by the southern slopes of the coastal range and the northern slopes of the mountains of the Central Highlands. To the west, in the plains beyond a spur of the Sierra Nevada range, lies oil-rich Lago Maracaibo, the source of Venezuela's prosperity.

Inland, south of the Central Highlands (which are parallel to the central section of the Caribbean Coast), lie the *llanos* of the Orinoco, the grassy plains that make up about a third of Venezuela. From here southward the country becomes increasingly mountainous, and patches of jungle begin to mingle with the forests and plains. This area has proven to be rich in gold, diamonds, oil, bauxite, and many other commercially valuable minerals.

Venezuela occupies a central position on South America's northern coast, bordered by Colombia to the west, Guyana and Brazil to the east and south. Its southern border stretches into the Amazon region, and its 352,150 square miles include Pico Bolívar (Bolívar Peak), which rises more than 16,000 feet above sea level, and the 3,212-foot-high Salto Angel (Angel Falls), the tallest waterfall in the world (15 times as high as Niagara Falls).

Caracas shows all the marks of its recent and rapid jump into the 20th century. Large sections of the city have been razed to make way for modern high-rise office buildings, and the installation of the *Metro de Caracas* (subway) has helped alleviate at least some traffic congestion. However, slums of wooden shacks still line dirt roads in the hills above the city. Of the almost 21 million residents of Venezuela, roughly five million live in Caracas; more than half the total population is under the age of 19.

SPECIAL PLACES

Up until the late 1980s, Venezuela's Caribbean coast missed most of the tourist invasion that had already overtaken much of the Caribbean; its development had been inspired primarily by the influx of oil money and international business. As a result, there wasn't the same emphasis on protecting historical landmarks or on developing tourist-oriented amusements as in other Caribbean countries. But Venezuelans have realized that their share of the Caribbean tourism boom can help them recover from a sharp currency devaluation and help pay off the country's hefty foreign debt. Unfortunately, political unrest and mounting crime in Caracas have deterred many visitors, especially those from the United States.

CARACAS Simón Bolívar is Venezuela's greatest hero, and almost all of the city's notable landmarks pay homage to *El Libertador*. In the center of the oldest section of town is the Plaza Bolívar, surrounded by government buildings, many of which are renovated colonial homes. In its time, it was the focus of all activity in the colony, the site of revolts against Spanish rule and of executions of revolutionaries by the Spanish governors. Today, under the watchful eyes of *El Libertador,* who is mounted on horseback in an 1874 statue, *caraqueños* (as residents are called) gather to gossip and discuss the latest news. To the east stands the city's church, a colonial structure granted cathedral status in 1637. The building was nearly demolished by earthquakes early in the 19th century, and large sections were reconstructed in 1876.

A block south and west of Plaza Bolívar is the *Capitolio* (Capitol), easily distinguished by its gold dome. The building was constructed in 114 days in 1874. The interior is filled with paintings of the country's leaders as well as scenes of the Battle of Carabobo on June 24, 1821 (which solidified the country's independence from Spain). At the rear, a formal garden—itself worth a visit—contains a beautiful fountain. The *Capitolio* is closed Mondays and on Wednesday and Thursday afternoons, when Congress is in session. There's no admission charge (phone: 2-562-8011).

Two blocks south of the Plaza Bolívar, at the intersection of San Jacinto and Traposos, is the *Casa Natal del Libertador,* the birthplace of Bolívar. The original adobe dwelling was damaged in an earthquake, rebuilt, abandoned, then rescued by a local patriotic organization in the 1900s and restored. The building houses the font in which Bolívar was baptized, his bed, and many paintings by Venezuelan artists depicting the major military campaigns of the War for Independence and other events of the warrior's life. Closed Mondays. No admission charge (phone: 2-545-7693). Directly next door is the *Museo Bolivariano* (Bolívar Museum), the largest collection of *El Libertador*'s war memorabilia ever assembled, including gifts from the Washington family (the two heroes often are associated in South America). Closed Mondays. No admission charge (phone: 2-545-9828).

The *Panteón Nacional,* or National Pantheon, several blocks north of the Plaza Bolívar, at Plaza Panteón, contains the mortal remains of Bolívar as well as those of other national heroes. There is an open tomb in memory of Francisco de Miranda, whose unsuccessful attempts at freedom gave strength to Bolívar's movement. Miranda died in prison; this resting place awaits the body that was never recovered. (*Note:* Venezuelans have an almost religious attitude toward this monument, so dress respectfully when visiting the tomb. In fact, restrained attire—no shorts or sleeveless shirts— is recommended for visits to most of the national monuments and historic buildings in Caracas, particularly those honoring Bolívar.)

The Caracas Town Council officially conferred the title of *El Libertador* on Simón Bolívar in 1813 in the *Iglesia de San Francisco* (St. Francis Church), which stands at the corner of Avenida Universidad and Calle San Francisco. Most of the building dates from 1574, and many of the paintings and hand-carved wooden altars are from the 17th century.

The *Museo de Arte Colonial* (Colonial Art Museum; Av. Panteón, San Bernardino; phone: 2-518517), in the former residence of the Marqués del Toro (also known as the *Quinta Anauco*), dates from the 17th century and also is highly recommended for its exhibits of original furnishings, ceramics, and other handicrafts from the colonial period. Closed Mondays. Admission charge. The *Museo de Arte Contemporáneo Sofía Imber* (Sofia Imber Museum of Contemporary Art; *Parque Central;* phone: 2-573-0075) is a must stop for modern art; the collection highlights works of Venezuela's top artists as well as works by Pablo Picasso, Marc Chagall, Joan Miró, Henry Moore, and others. Closed Mondays. No admission charge.

Separating Caracas proper from its port town of La Guaira is *El Avila,* the vast, mountainous national park. La Guaira is the working port familiar to any cruise passenger en route to Caracas. However, the beach resort of Caraballeda, east of La Guaira, is more interesting, with its excellent hotels and deluxe resort complexes. The beach facilities of the *Macuto Sheraton* hotel there are open to non-guests (see *Checking In*), and there also are public beaches (for sunning only; the water is polluted).

PUERTO LA CRUZ Dynamic Puerto La Cruz has all the ingredients of paradise— a modern city known for its good service and friendly people; an attractive seaside boulevard with outdoor cafés, handicrafts vendors, and benches for people watching; and a number of beaches, including Playa Colorada and nearby Playa Arapito, a taxi ride away. You can bargain with one of the local fishermen for a boat outing to otherwise inaccessible pristine beaches, book a yacht tour, or dine at a seaside restaurant. If you simply want to laze around, buy a *chinchorro* (hammock) and string it between two trees; beach vendors will soon appear with ice-cold cans of ever-present Polar beer. Puerto La Cruz is the site of several impressive resorts (see *Checking In*), and a cruise ship terminal is under construction.

MARGARITA ISLAND This getaway spot in the Caribbean Sea, about 30 miles north of the coastal town of Cumaná, is popular with *caraqueños* for its shopping bargains and among foreign visitors for its lovely beaches. Most activity centers around the former fishing port of Porlamar on the southeast coast, now a thriving resort where duty-free shops abound. The beaches near town are not the best, but there are several sandy strands not far away, including Playa El Agua (accessible by bus or taxi), and exploring the rest of Margarita is well worth the time. Sip a cool rum drink at an open-air restaurant and stop to chat with the local children; for a small tip, some will recite the history of the area, and even if you don't understand them, the performance is well worth the price. An hour before sunset, hop into your car (or hire a taxi) and head to *Juangriego,* the fort above the bay, to watch the sun dip into the sea. Then enjoy dinner at one of the bayside restaurants.

Margarita is really two little islands joined Siamese-twin fashion by a long, narrow spit of land that forms the north side of a central lagoon, La Restinga. The curvature of the two islands forms the narrow mouth of the lagoon to the south, whose floor was once lined with pearl-bearing oysters. Launches are available for hire by the hour. The lagoon is a bird refuge, but noise from motorized tour boats has driven away the rare, beautiful scarlet ibis, leaving only pelicans and the occasional eagle.

La Asunción, the capital of this island-state, contains several colonial buildings, including two 16th-century churches, the *Catedral de Santa Ana* (St. Anne's Cathedral) and the *Iglesia de Nuestra Señora de la Asunción* (Church of Our Lady of the Assumption).

LOS ROQUES The country's most pristine—and remote—beaches are found in this cluster of tiny cays 100 miles offshore from La Guaira. White sand, turquoise waters, and coral reefs await the intrepid sun worshiper who is willing to get to the cays—which have been designated a national park—by plane, chartered helicopter, or yacht. Don't expect any luxuries in this archipelago; be sure that the charter or package you choose includes all meals and drinks. *Aerotuy* flies daily to the main island of Gran Roque from *Simón Bolívar International Airport* at Maiquetía, Barcelona (near Puerto La Cruz), and Porlamar on Margarita. The flight from Maiquetía takes about 35 minutes; flying time from Barcelona or Porlamar is approximately one hour (see *Plane,* below). *Aerotuy* offers both day trips and overnight stays in small guesthouses with beach and/or fishing excursions. Another option is the floating hotel *Buque Los Roques,* with 36 double cabins and one suite, all with private baths (phone: 95-635093). *Lost World Adventures* arranges cruises to Los Roques, as does *Alpi Tour,* which offers overnight packages on luxury yachts (see *Boating* for both). It's also possible to charter a helicopter to Los Roques from *Helicópteros del Caribe* at Maiquetía (phone: 31-28217).

ELSEWHERE IN VENEZUELA

COLONIA TOVAR Less than two hours from Caracas, the alpine village of Colonia Tovar, built by German immigrants in the 1840s, seems like 19th-century Bavaria. The town is filled with German-style handicrafts and—a surprising sight to those accustomed to seeing darker Latin Venezuelans—a number of blue-eyed, blond residents. Black Forest farmers, carpenters, and masons colonized this area when the Venezuelan government was seeking immigrants to labor in the fields. For more than a hundred years, the villagers here remained isolated; a road finished in 1963 finally linked them to the rest of the country. Much of the traditional German culture brought by these settlers survives today, although it is rapidly being supplanted by an international, modern way of life. For a taste of the old country, try Freiburg or Selva Negra (Black Forest), the local German-style beers, and perhaps some sauerbraten or wurst.

MORROCOY NATIONAL PARK To the west of El Litoral, 85 miles from Caracas, the cays of this park are idyllic for scuba diving, snorkeling, fishing, and bird watching. The drive takes two-and-one-half hours because of the poor condition of the small back roads; for this reason, most visitors prefer to stay here one or more days rather than visiting the park as a day trip. In Tucacas, the best hotel is the 80-room *Manaure*, with a large pool, a bar, and a coffee shop (phone: 42-84611). There are several choices of accommodations in nearby Chichiriviche; the best are the 90-room *Mario*, a full-service hotel with a pool and dining room (on Av. Principal de Chichiriviche between Calles 6 and 7; phone: 42-86114 or 42-86115) and *Náutico*, a 20-room establishment popular with divers and boasting a large pool and a marina (Sector Playa Sur; phone: 42-86301; 2-564-8266 in Caracas). You can rent snorkeling and scuba equipment from Mike Osborn's shop (there's no formal name) at 6 Calle Ayacucho, Tucacas (phone: 42-84082). The park is open daily (no phone).

EXTRA SPECIAL

Those who really want to escape civilization and are willing to endure a little discomfort should consider a trip to *Parque Nacional Canaima* (Canaima National Park) and *Salto Angel* (Angel Falls). Few things in Venezuela, or anywhere else for that matter, match the sight of these falls. They are 3,212 feet high—15 times the height of Niagara Falls and two-and-one-half times as tall as the Empire State Building—and they crash down a sheer drop of 2,648 feet past layers of multicolored rock, then onto the seven lower falls of La Hacha, before creating the calm lagoon that washes the beach. The Gran Sabana, a raised savannah in the jungle with rivers and *tepuís* (flat-topped mountain formations), also is memorable.

Although the outside world did not learn of the falls until 1935, both the falls and the Auyan Tepuí, the tabletop mountain from which they tumble, have been worshipped by area Indians since prehistoric times. Jimmy Angel, the pilot for whom these falls are named, was hired in 1928 to fly a prospector named Robert McCracken into the jungle and back. On his return, McCracken carried 20 pounds of gold estimated to be worth $27,000. It took Angel until 1935 to locate the area again, and although he never found the source of McCracken's gold, he did discover the falls (which had been so shrouded in mist that Angel hadn't seen them when he was first in the area).

The area is inaccessible except by plane, and the landing strip is small. Visitors must fly from Caracas to *Camp Canaima* (run by *Avensa Airlines* within the park grounds) and then travel to the falls by canoe and on foot through virgin forest (not an easy trip). The camp's cabins have electricity, running water, and an open-air restaurant and bar; nearby, a pink sand beach, boats, and jungle walks provide diversion. The falls themselves can be viewed by air on the incoming or departing flight, and are an unforgettable sight. *Aerotuy* also offers flights over Salto Angel as part of day tours or in combination with overnight stays at nearby Kavac in rustic huts owned by Pemón Indians. Bilingual guides accompany tourists on the small propeller planes that fly over the falls. Included are lunch and a hike—with swimming—to the waterfalls and gorge at Kavac Cave. For additional details, see *Natural Wonderlands* in DIVERSIONS. *Aerotuy* flights depart frequently from Caracas's *Simón Bolívar International Airport* at Maiquetía, as well as from Ciudad Bolívar and other points in Venezuela. (See *Plane* below, for details on the airlines mentioned.)

Sources and Resources

TOURIST INFORMATION

In Caracas, the office of *Corpoturismo (Corporación de Turismo de Venezuela)*, the government tourist bureau, is on the 37th floor of *Torre Oeste* in *Parque Central* (phone: 2-574-1513; fax: 2-573-8983). It is closed weekends. There are branch offices open daily at *Simón Bolívar International Airport* in Maiquetía (phone: 31-551060, international terminal; 31-551191, national terminal; fax: 31-552598). Tourism officials will answer questions and provide literature as well as make hotel reservations. For information on Venezuelan tourist offices in the US, see GETTING READY TO GO.

LOCAL COVERAGE Of the 11 daily newspapers, only one, *The Daily Journal,* is published in English and is a handy reference for movies, plays, and musical events. Both *The New York Times* and *The Miami Herald* make their way to newsstands in the larger hotels (usually a day late), as do a number of US news magazines. The biggest local newspapers, *El Diario de Caracas, El Universal,* and *El Nacional,* carry complete coverage of current events.

RADIO AND TELEVISION Some of the larger hotels receive CNN programming.

TELEPHONE When calling from the US, dial 011 (international access code) + 58 (country code) + (city code) + (local number). The city code for Caracas is 2; for Caraballeda, 31; for Puerto La Cruz, 81; and for Margarita Island, 95. To call from elsewhere, the access code may vary, so call the local operator. When dialing from one city to another in Venezuela, you must dial 0 + (city code) + (local number). When calling from within the same city, dial only the local number. Numbers are constantly changing; if you need help, you can dial 103 for information in Caracas (though you probably won't encounter any English-speaking operators), or ask your hotel for assistance. Public telephones operate with coins or phone cards, which can be purchased in phone offices, newspaper kiosks, and some stores. In

Caracas, dial 169 for the police; 545-4545 for an ambulance; elsewhere in the country, dial 103 for a local operator.

ENTRY REQUIREMENTS A passport, tourist card, and return or ongoing ticket are required for US and Canadian citizens entering the country. Tourist cards are issued by the Venezuelan consulate, or by airlines serving Venezuela, upon presentation of a current passport. If you're flying on a Venezuelan airline, it's helpful if your ticket has a *localizador* number assigned to it; this is a computerized number that speeds processing. Often, the *localizador* number is given to you automatically when you make airline reservations; if not, ask for it when you make your reservation. There is an airport departure tax ($12 at press time) payable in US dollars or bolívars for international flights.

CLIMATE AND CLOTHES Although Venezuela is a tropical country, weather in any given place depends almost entirely upon altitude. At about 3,000 feet, Caracas has one of the finest climates in the world, an eternal spring that requires only light wraps in the evening. In the warm zone—from sea level to about 2,000 feet—temperatures range from the upper 70s (20s C) to the 90s (30s C). The rainy season is from May through October; you'll want to keep an umbrella on hand for sudden showers. If you're thinking of traveling into the mountains, regardless of the season, bring raincoats or ponchos and warm sweaters. Otherwise, summer resortwear is acceptable all year. Caracas tends to be fashionable, and women dress smartly for daytime and evening; jackets and ties often are mandatory for men in good restaurants and nightclubs. At resorts, however, life is more casual, and the jacket/tie rule is relaxed.

MONEY The monetary unit is the bolívar, written as a B. The fluctuating exchange rate was nearly 200 Bs to the US dollar at press time. Traveler's checks and major credit cards are accepted by most hotels, restaurants, and stores, but converting traveler's checks to bolívars sometimes involves massive amounts of red tape. ATMs, many of which can draw on American credit card accounts, are found all over Caracas, and credit card advances using the machines (or in banks) are simple. Currency can be changed in banks or *casas de cambio* (exchange houses). Banking hours are weekdays from 8:30 to 11:30 AM and 2 to 4:30 PM. All prices in this chapter are quoted in US dollars.

LANGUAGE Spanish is the official language of the country. However, English generally is understood and spoken in the larger hotels, finer restaurants, and better shops of cities like Caracas, which attracts an international group of travelers. In the rural areas, English is seldom spoken (or understood). With the aid of a phrase book, you should get along okay.

TIME Venezuela is on atlantic standard time, an hour ahead of eastern standard time. When it's noon in New York, it's 1 PM in Caracas. During US daylight saving time, the time in the two cities is the same.

CURRENT Electricity is 110 volts, 60 cycles, AC, the same as in North America. No need for converters.

TIPPING Widespread in Venezuela. A 10% tip usually is included on restaurant bills, but it's customary to add more. Taxi drivers, however, are not tipped unless they help with luggage; bellhops should get about $1 per bag. Attendants who pump gas at service stations should be tipped the equivalent of 50¢ if they wash the windshield, check the oil, etc.

GETTING AROUND

BUS Caracas buses cover the city, but usually are crowded; bus travel requires a basic knowledge of the city and Spanish. *Por puestos* (minibuses) also pick up and discharge passengers along designated routes through Caracas. Bus and minibus fares around the city and its outlying suburbs start at 20 Bs (8¢ US at press time) and depend on distance and type of service. The *por puesto* route from *Simón Bolívar International Airport* at Maiquetía to downtown Caracas takes about 45 minutes, depending on traffic, and costs about 250 Bs ($1.25 at press time). Long-distance buses to destinations outside metropolitan Caracas leave from the *Nuevo Circo* terminal beside *La Hoyada* metro station.

CAR RENTAL The roads in Venezuela are in good condition, and gasoline is incredibly inexpensive. Almost every major rental company is represented here. *Hertz* has offices at *Simón Bolívar International Airport* in Maiquetía (phone: 31-552758, national terminal; 31-551197, international terminal); in Caracas (phone: 2-952-5511); on Margarita Island (at the airport; phone: 95-691274); and in a number of smaller cities. *National* has offices at the *Simón Bolívar International Airport* (phone: 31-522777, national terminal; 31-551183, international terminal); at the hotels *Avila, Tamanaco,* and *Eurobuilding* in Caracas (see *Checking In* for all three); and at the airport on Margarita Island (phone: 95-691171). *Budget Rent-A-Car* has locations in Caracas (50 Av. Luis Roche; phone: 2-283-4333) and on Margarita Island (at the airport; phone: 95-691047). *Fiesta Car Rentals* in Caracas (Av. Venezuela, El Rosal; phone: 2-951-6911) is a reputable local agency. Rental costs vary by agency and make of car; insurance may be included. A credit card will be required. US and Canadian driver's licenses are valid for drivers 18 and over. Avoid rush hours in and around Caracas (7 to 9 AM, noon to 2 PM, and 4 to 7 PM). Also, steer clear of beach traffic on weekends—especially Sunday afternoons. *Note:* Venezuelan driving can be downright hazardous; tourists should be very careful.

FERRY SERVICES The ferry to Margarita Island leaves from Cumaná (a two-hour trip) twice a day and from Puerto La Cruz (four hours) six times a day, depending on demand. The service is run by *Conferry* (Av. Casanova in Sabana Grande, Caracas; phone: 2-782-8544 for a schedule). The firm's other offices are in Porlamar, on Margarita (opposite the *Bella Vista* hotel on Av. Santiago Mariño; phone: 95-619235); in Puerto La Cruz (phone: 81-677847); and in Cumaná (phone: 93-661903).

PLANE Venezuela has some 287 airports, including some small landing strips in the far reaches of the jungle and eight international airports. It's a big country, and all of it is served by the domestic carriers *Avensa,* its subsidiary *Servivensa* (phone for both: 2-561-3366; 800-428-3672), *Aserca* (phone: 2-953-2729), and several regional carriers. An especially interesting package offered by *Avensa* is a two-day excursion to Salto Angel (Angel Falls) and Canaima, available through the airline directly or from most travel agents in Caracas. Due to the easy availability of low-priced fuel, airfares to Margarita and other beach resort areas are inexpensive. The small carrier *Aerotuy* (phone: 2-761-8043) also serves Salto Angel and Kavac, plus Los Roques, Ciudad Bolívar, and several other cities; charters elsewhere in Venezuela and the Caribbean also can be arranged. *American* flies from San Juan, Puerto Rico, to Maiquetía's *Simón Bolívar International Airport; Viasa* (2-576-2611; 800-327-5454; 800-432-9070 in Florida) connects Santo Domingo, in the Dominican Republic, and Caracas.

METRO It's by far the fastest and easiest way to get to the center of Caracas. Fares vary according to the distance traveled, starting at about 35 Bs (20¢ US at press time). Operational between Propatria in the west and Palo Verde in the east, the metro system also has two southbound spurs. The first runs from the downtown area of El Silencio (where it connects to the principal line) south to the *Caricuao Zoo;* the second runs from Plaza Venezuela to the southern suburb of El Valle. The metro system also runs its own buses along routes designated for future subway lines. The metro subway and bus system runs weekdays from 5:30 AM to 11 PM; on weekends metro subway and bus service stops at 9 PM.

SIGHTSEEING BUS TOURS There are many tour operators in Caracas, and most offer similar trips for about the same prices, although each has a favorite or exclusive outing. Let your hotel desk make the arrangements for you, or check tour company ads in *The Daily Journal.*

TAXI More often than not, taxi meters are turned off, so be sure to negotiate the fare before entering the cab. There's a 10% surcharge on Sundays, holidays, and at night. Taxi sightseeing tours with English-speaking drivers are available and are best arranged through your hotel or travel agency. Rates are usually by the hour.

SPECIAL EVENTS

Carnaval takes over parts of Venezuela, with dancing in the streets, costumes, and parades, for the two days and nights before *Ash Wednesday* (February 21 in 1996). Caracas virtually closes down during *Semana Santa* (Holy Week). All of the major Roman Catholic holidays are observed, plus *New Year's Day, Declaration of Independence Day* (April 19), *Labor Day*

(May 1), *Anniversary of the Battle of Carabobo* (June 24), *Independence Day* (July 5), *Bolívar's Birthday* (July 24), and *Día de la Raza* (*Columbus Day;* October 12), now a celebration of all Venezuela's "races" and ethnic groups, rather than just a commemoration of Columbus's arrival. Practically everything shuts down on *New Year's Eve,* a holiday traditionally celebrated with family parties at home.

SHOPPING

The coast's selection of *artesanía* (handicrafts) is wider and less expensive than in Caracas. Margarita Island's duty-free zone has the best buys in liquor, perfume, and gold jewelry. On the coast, also look for fine-quality *chinchorros* (hammocks). Still, Caracas's shopping scene is worth a go-round for the people watching and style sampling in its appealing collection of super-sleek shopping centers. *Centro Comercial Ciudad Tamanaco* (Latin America's largest mall, located in Chuao near *La Carlota Airport*), *Paseo Las Mercedes* in Las Mercedes, and *Centro Comercial Concresa* (just off the *autopista* en route to Prados del Este), boast all the latest Venezuelan/international luxuries, as well as dozens of restaurants and nightspots. In Caracas, the Sabana Grande pedestrian mall, known locally as the *Bulevar* (Boulevard), also offers clothing, leather shoes and bags, music, and jewelry stores galore—plus theaters, clubs, and cafés, including the famous *Gran Café* (phone: 2-719502), a time-honored spot for sipping coffee, people watching, and listening to itinerant street musicians. (But watch out for pickpockets here.)

Venezuela produces fine aged rum (*ron añejo*) and coffee; both make excellent gifts. It is also one of the biggest recording centers on the continent and is a great place to pick up salsa and merengue tapes, as well as South American pop music. If you aren't familiar with the artists, ask the record store attendants to play sample tracks—they'll be happy to do it. In general, Caracas shops are open from 8 AM to 5 PM, with some shops closing between noon and 2 PM; closed Sundays. Caracas shops to explore include the following:

Arte Popular Venezuela Jammed full of folk art and crafts, including weavings by Guajira Indians and wicker basketry from Orinoco regions. Fine-quality hammocks and the famous painted devil masks worn at the *Feast of Corpus Christi* in June are sold. In a building marked Pro-Venezuela in Plaza Venezuela (phone: 2-793-3638).

Audubon Society Store Located at the organization's Venezuelan headquarters, this shop sells books, magazines, and other products that focus on the country's flora and fauna. The best coffee table books (and bird watching guides) are found here. *Paseo Las Mercedes* (phone: 2-913813).

La Francia A nine-story building filled with small jewelry shops—18-karat gold is a specialty. Most jewelry is sold by weight. There are some real buys here.

No credit cards accepted. Off Plaza Bolívar at Esquina Las Monjas (no central phone).

H. Stern Fine gold and precious gems in stylized designs are the attractions here. Look for the intriguing pre-Colombian designs. In the lobbies of the *Caracas Hilton* (phone: 2-571-0520), *Tamanaco Inter-Continental* (phone: 2-927313) and *Eurobuilding* (phone: 2-959-1123). There's also a branch in the international terminal of the *Simón Bolívar International Airport* (phone: 31-552681).

Hannsi The country's largest handicrafts shop, with baskets, hammocks, ceramics, jewelry, and much more. The store likes to boast that 95% of its goods are made in Venezuela; another 3% come from neighboring countries. 12 Calle Bolívar in the Caracas suburb of El Hatillo (phone: 2-963-5577).

SPORTS

BASEBALL The Venezuelan *béisbol* season runs during the US off-season—October through February. Games at the stadium at *Universidad Central,* near Plaza Venezuela in Caracas, generally are played at night, although afternoon games are held some Sundays and Mondays. For information on schedules, either check newspapers or call the tourist office (see *Tourist Information,* above).

BOATING Daylong cruiser tours of the coast are available; they include food and drink. Check *The Daily Journal* ads for packages. For rentals (crewed only), stop by the *Marina Mar* (phone: 31-527097), near the *Macuto Sheraton* hotel in Caraballeda (see *Checking In*); or in Caracas try *Alpi Tour* (phone: 2-283-9837), *Caribbean Nimbus Tours* (phone: 2-310001), or *Lost World Adventures* (phone: 2-717859; 800-999-0558; 404-971-8586 in Georgia).

BULLFIGHTS On occasional Sundays, bullfights are held at the *Plaza de Toros Nuevo Circo* in Caracas (Calles San Martín and San Roques; no phone); call the tourist office for schedules (see *Tourist Information,* above). Tickets, which can be purchased at the bullring at the time of the fight, cost more for seats in the shade; ticket prices also rise if there's a big-name fighter on the bill. The tourist office also has details on bullfights in Maracay, Mérida, and San Cristóbal.

GOLF In Caracas, many hotels can arrange for you to play at the 18-hole courses at the *Junko Golf Club* (Km 18, Carretera El Junkito; phone: 33-21223); the *Lagunita Country Club* (Av. Principal Urbanización Lagunita Country Club, El Hatillo; phone: 2-961-1401); or the *Caracas Country Club* (Av. Principal de Country Club; phone/fax: 2-261-0867). In Guarenas, the 18-hole, members-only *Izcaragua* course also sometimes lets tourists play (Carretera Petare-Guarenas; phone: 36-445954; fax: 36-440743). In Puerto La Cruz, the *Golden Rainbow Maremares* hotel has a golf course (see *Checking In*). Arrangements also can be made at the 18-hole *Puerto La*

Cruz Golf and Country Club (Av. Universidad; phone: 81-667259; fax: 81-681296). Keep in mind that fees for caddies and club rental (if available) are in addition to greens fees, which can be whopping for non-members at all Venezuelan courses. In Caraballeda, the *Macuto Sheraton* and *Meliá Caribe* (see *Checking In* for both) have a standing arrangement that enables guests to play on the 9-hole course at the *Caraballeda Golf Club*. The club's Caracas office is located in *Edificio Venezuela* (Av. Venezuela, El Rosal, Oficina 73; phone: 2-261-2128).

HORSE RACING *La Rinconada* in El Valle, Caracas, holds races weekend afternoons. Evening races are held every Thursday and sometimes on Fridays in Valencia and on Thursdays in Maracaibo. There's no admission charge for races. Check the local papers for details (or call 2-681-3333 in Caracas). Newspaper kiosks also sell weekly magazines with the race schedules at each track. The most popular race guide is *Gaceta Hípica.*

SNORKELING AND SCUBA DIVING For independent dives, the cays of *Morrocoy National Park* (see *Special Places*) provide the best reefs. The *Macuto Sheraton* hotel in Caraballeda (see *Checking In*) rents snorkeling and scuba gear and provides guides, as does the *Marina Mar* beside the *Sheraton* (see *Boating,* above).

SPORT FISHING Fishing charters for up to six people, complete with crew, drinks, lunch, and all the needed gear, are available at the *Marina Mar* (see *Boating*). On Margarita, ask at major Porlamar resort hotels or shop around the waterfront for the best deal. For sport fishing at Los Roques, try *Chapy Tours and Fishing* (phone: 2-781-2108) or *Lost World Adventures* (see *Boating*).

SWIMMING AND SUNNING Venezuela's Caribbean coastline provides fine beaches for swimming and lazing in the sun. El Litoral, as the central coast is called, is just a short drive from Caracas. The beach at Caraballeda, Caracas's favorite weekending place, is not remarkable, nor is the polluted Catia La Mar. But farther jaunts from Caracas lead to lovely, still largely unspoiled Puerto La Cruz to the east (although you'll have to go out of town to swim— its city waterfront, too, is polluted) and Puerto Cabello and *Morrocoy National Park* to the west. Margarita Island, just 30 miles from the coast town of Cumaná, is surrounded by magnificent beaches. A hundred miles offshore from La Guaira are the pristine, undeveloped cays of Los Roques.

TENNIS Non-guests can arrange to play for a nominal fee at the *Caracas Hilton International* and *Tamanaco Inter-Continental* hotels in Caracas, and at the *Macuto Sheraton* and *Meliá Caribe* in Caraballeda (see *Checking In* for all). Hotel guests are given priority.

WINDSURFING On Margarita, most hotels provide water sports facilities for their guests. The *Laguna Mar Beach* hotel (see *Checking In*) provides equipment for non-guests.

NIGHTLIFE

The best thing about Caracas after dark is its restaurants, which are numerous and excellent (see *Eating Out*). A superb range of plays and concerts is offered at the *Teresa Carreño* complex (across from the *Caracas Hilton International,* Av. 25 Sur, El Conde, near *Parque Central;* phone: 2-574-9122). Movies—including week-long foreign film festivals—are cheap and abundant. Check *The Daily Journal* movie guide for listings. *The Daily Journal* also lists local bars, music clubs, and discos; some admit only couples (check with your concierge).

Some of the livelier discos include *Le Club* in *Centro Comercial Chacaito* (Chacaito; phone: 2-952-0807); *1900 Wall Street* in the *CCCT* (near *La Carlota Airport;* phone: 2-959-0441); and *Il Foro Romano* (Av. Principal, Bello Campo; phone: 2-331164). *La Cota 880* offers two orchestras, continuous dancing, and an incredible view (on the top floor of the *Caracas Hilton;* phone: 2-571-0486). After dinner, the *Crystal Club* (Av. Principal in La Castellana; phone: 2-314973) is worth checking out. At the *Juán Sebastián Bar* (Av. Venezuela in El Rosal; phone: 2-951-0595), live jazz starts cooking at about 9:30 PM; from the first note, the place bustles with singles, couples, and jazz lovers in general. At clubs where membership is required, tourists usually can enter by presenting their passports (men should wear jackets and ties).

Current hot spots for a more youthful crowd include *Caffè Ti Amo* (on the corner of Calle Paris and Calle La Trinidad in Las Mercedes; phone: 2-993-7304) for music and a bistro atmosphere; *Iguana Café* (Calle California at Av. Nicolás Copernico, Las Mercedes; phone: 2-916575) for videos, snacks, and beer; and *Weekends* (Av. San Juan Bosco at Second Transversal, Altamira; phone: 2-261-3839) for live bands of every ilk—from rock to reggae.

Best on the Coast

CHECKING IN

Hotel and resort prices in Venezuela are not subject to the seasonal fluctuations that are the rule throughout the rest of the Caribbean. Caracas is primarily a business center, so prices at its best hotels, though not as high as those of the most luxurious Caribbean resorts, can be steep. Reservations are recommended. If you arrive at the airport without lodging, a representative from *Corpoturismo,* the Venezuelan tourist bureau, can assist you (see *Tourist Information*). Expect to pay more than $150 for a double room in hotels listed below as very expensive; $90 to $150 in those listed as expensive; $60 to $90 in those listed as moderate; and less than $60 in inexpensive places. Unless otherwise noted, all hotels listed below have air conditioning, telephones, TV sets, and private baths. Telephone numbers here include both the city code and the local number. When calling within a city, use only the local number. For information about dialing from elsewhere, see *Telephone* earlier in this chapter.

CARACAS

VERY EXPENSIVE

Anauco Hilton The more residential of the Hilton chain's two Caracas properties, this hotel features balconied suites overlooking the city's fine-arts neighborhood. There are 317 suites, some two stories. Other amenities include a pool, two restaurants, a bar, and use of facilities at its sister hotel, the *Caracas Hilton International. Parque Central,* El Conde (phone: 2-573-4111; 800-HILTONS; fax: 2-573-7724).

Caracas Hilton International A very modern 881-room property favored by businesspeople. Features *La Cota 880* nightclub on the top floor and a wide variety of restaurants. There's also a pool, two tennis courts, a gym, a sauna, and lounges on executive floors. Service, however, is spotty. Av. 25 Sur, near *Parque Central,* El Conde (phone: 2-574-1122; 800-HILTONS; fax: 2-575-0024).

Eurobuilding This high-rise, the city's most luxurious, has 800 lavishly decorated rooms and suites and a formal, Old World feel. It also features three restaurants, two coffee shops, three bars, a shopping gallery, a sun deck, a fitness center, a sauna, and a nightclub. Calle La Guairita in Chuao (phone: 2-959-1133; fax: 2-922069).

Tamanaco Inter-Continental One of the best in South America, this 570-room place has both resort and city hotel assets. There's a nightclub, three bars with city views, five restaurants (including a new sushi bar), a pool, four tennis courts, a gym, a sauna, and every hotel service imaginable. Av. Principal in Las Mercedes (phone: 2-914555; 800-327-0200; fax: 2-208-7004).

MODERATE

Avila With only 113 rooms, it's small by the standards of the *Hilton*s or the *Tamanaco,* but pleasantly situated on a hill overlooking the city. This gracious older hotel has a pool, a restaurant, a relaxing piano bar, and plenty of old-fashioned Venezuelan charm. Av. Jorge Washington, San Bernardino (phone: 2-515128; fax: 2-523021).

Lincoln Suites Service is uneven here, but the location can't be beat—the back of the building opens onto the Sabana Grande Boulevard pedestrian mall, and two subway stops are within walking distance. This all-suite hotel offers 128 clean, modern units with refrigerators; ask for a quiet room. There's a restaurant and a bar on the premises. Av. Francisco Solano between Calle Jerónimo and Calle Los Jabillos (phone: 2-762-8576; fax: 2-761-3339).

Paseo Las Mercedes Tucked inside a shopping mall with trendy shops, a nightclub, and restaurants, this 196-room hotel has a pool, a bar, a restaurant, and cordial service. The best rooms offer lovely views of *El Avila* park; ask for a room on an upper floor to escape the street noise. *Paseo Las Mercedes,* Av. Principal in Las Mercedes (phone: 2-910444; fax: 2-921797).

INEXPENSIVE

Continental Altamira Well situated in chic Altamira near pleasant shops, cafés, and restaurants (and not too far from the Caracas business district), it features 82 rooms, a swimming pool, a restaurant, a bar, and room service. Av. San Juan Bosco, Altamira (phone: 2-261-6019; fax: 2-261-0131).

CARABALLEDA

EXPENSIVE

Macuto Sheraton A natural choice for sun worshipers, this 492-room modern resort features two pools, all water sports, and a sandy beach. Other bonuses: four restaurants, a disco, and a nightclub. Service, however, is spotty, and nightly music at the poolside bar can be heard in nearby rooms. On the beach (phone: 31-781-1508 or 31-944300; 800-325-3535; fax: 31-944318).

Meliá Caribe This link in the famous Spanish chain boasts fascinating indoor architecture; much swanker and sleeker, more tropical and original than the *Macuto Sheraton* next door. Set in beautiful gardens, with 290 units (rooms and suites), this property has a pool, water sports, and a sauna, plus tennis courts and golf privileges in the neighborhood. There also are three bars and three restaurants. On the beach at Av. La Playa, Urbanización Caribe (phone: 31-945555; 800-336-3542; fax: 31-941509).

PUERTO LA CRUZ

EXPENSIVE

Doral Beach Villas A massive resort with 1,312 apartments on the coast at Ponzuelo Bay. Facilities include an 18-hole golf course, tennis, water sports, restaurants, and bars. Av. Américo Vespucio, *Complejo Turístico El Morro* (phone: 81-812222; fax: 81-813652).

Golden Rainbow Maremares This 500-room resort offers a range of activities night and day, including golf, two lighted tennis courts, a complete spa program, and water sports. The pool is designed like a lagoon, banked with foliage. Five restaurants, a dinner-theater, three lounges, and a nightclub offer a variety of evening choices. *Complejo Turístico El Morro* (phone: 81-813022; 2-564-6442 in Caracas; 800-472-4626; fax: 81-814561).

Meliá Located on the beach, this deluxe 222-unit property has a bar and four restaurants, a sauna, two tennis courts, a pool, a nightclub, and a disco. All rooms have private balconies. Golf facilities are available nearby. Paseo Colón (phone: 81-691311; 800-336-3542; fax: 81-691241).

Vista Real 112-room hotel, it offers spectacular Caribbean views, a restaurant, and most of the expected luxuries and amenities. *Complejo Turístico El Morro* (phone: 81-811511; 2-284-0484 in Caracas; fax: 2-285-6497).

MODERATE

Rasil Here are 348 luxurious rooms, a pool, several restaurants, a fitness center, a sauna, tennis courts, and a gallery of shops. Calle Monagas at Paseo Colón (phone: 81-672535; fax: 81-673121).

MARGARITA ISLAND

VERY EXPENSIVE

Flamingo Beach A luxury hotel with 163 rooms, two restaurants, two bars, and a disco. The elevated pool gives the impression that it was dropped into the middle of the Caribbean; in fact, a bridge connects the pool area to the sea. There also are facilities for tennis, snorkeling, sailing, and windsurfing. Calle El Cristo, Sector La Caranta in Pampatar (phone: 95-624822 or 95-624750; 800-44U-TELL; fax: 95-622778).

EXPENSIVE

Bella Vista Centrally located, this 321-room property with a view of the sea has a disco, a bar, a restaurant, and a pool. Insist on a room in the newer wing. Breakfast is included. Av. Santiago Mariño in Porlamar (phone: 95-614831; fax: 95-612557).

LagunaMar Beach One of the largest hotels on the island, it has 406 suites, six restaurants, seven pools (including a wave pool and another with a slide), as well as a beach and saltwater lagoon, a spa, and tennis courts. Windsurfers, Sunfish, and water skiing equipment also are available. There is free shuttle service to the airport and to the duty-free shopping areas. Near Porlamar on Vía Pampatar, Sector Apostadero (phone: 95-620711; fax: 95-622173).

Margarita Hilton International On the waterfront, there are 280 rooms and 11 suites, each with a sea view, a balcony or terrace, satellite TV, and a mini-bar. There's also a pool, a fitness center, tennis, water sports facilities, two restaurants, two bars, a nightclub, shops, and all the other amenities generally associated with the chain's name. Calle Los Uveros at Playa Moreno, Porlamar (phone: 95-615882; 800-HILTONS; fax: 95-615387).

MODERATE

Marina Bay A good central location right on the beach and lovely sea views are the pluses at this 170-room property featuring a bar, a restaurant, and a pool. Calle Abancay at Playa Moreno, Porlamar (phone: 95-625211; fax: 95-624110).

EATING OUT

The restaurants in Caracas are excellent, with several superior choices in every culinary category. Expect to pay at least $70 for dinner for two at the restaurants listed below as expensive; from $40 to $70 in our moderate range; and less than $40 at restaurants listed as inexpensive. Prices include a 10% service charge automatically added (it's customary to leave a little extra), but not drinks or wine. Eating outside the capital generally costs less. All are open for lunch and dinner unless otherwise noted. The telephone numbers listed below include both the city code and the local number. When calling within a city, use only the local number.

CARACAS

EXPENSIVE

L'Arbalette A wide variety of fondues is featured at this Swiss restaurant in the lovely colonial town of El Hatillo. The decor is charming, and the luscious desserts, such as chocolate fondue, are a treat. Closed Mondays. Reservations advised. Major credit cards accepted. Calle Santa Rosalía, outside the city in El Hatillo (phone: 2-963-6496).

Arraya Situated in a colonial house, it's one of the few classy restaurants in the city's center and a great favorite with the governmental elite. Traditional criollo (Venezuelan) menu; highlights include *pabellón* (shredded beef with plantains, rice, and black beans), *cazón* (ground shark meat), *natilla* (a cream cheese), *arepas* (corn cakes) with cheese, and the house sangria. Open daily. Reservations advised. Major credit cards accepted. Esquina de San Jacinto at Plaza El Venezolano (phone: 2-545-8235).

Aventino Housed in a gracious villa, this spot features a French kitchen, formal service, and the most extensive wine cellar in the city. The specialty—pressed duck—is considered such an event that every diner who orders it receives a certificate, and his or her meal is recorded in a gold book. Open daily. Reservations necessary. Major credit cards accepted. Av. San Felipe at José Angel Llamas, La Castellana (phone: 2-265-2640).

La Belle Epoque Elegantly French, this dining enclave offers a romantic atmosphere, classic entrées (the trout is especially tasty), and particularly piquant appetizers, all accompanied by music in the evening. Jackets preferred. Closed Sundays. Reservations advised. Major credit cards accepted. In *Edificio Century* on Av. Leonardo da Vinci, Colinas de Bello Monte (phone: 2-752-1342).

El Bogavante Sporting a nautical decor, this spot offers an outstanding seafood menu featuring lobster, crab, shrimp, and fresh fish. The Italian and Spanish wine list is quite good. Open daily. Reservations advised. Major credit cards accepted. Av. Venezuela, El Rosal (phone: 2-952-0146).

Casa Urrutía In a lovely white house, this is undoubtedly the most elegant Spanish restaurant in Caracas. Seafood is the specialty, and the desserts are sumptuous. Closed Sundays. Reservations advised. Major credit cards accepted. Calle Madrid at Calle Monterrey, Las Mercedes (phone: 2-752-4723).

Da Emore This charming family-run eatery offers a very special variety of Italian dishes on a prix fixe menu; the day's selections depend on what's fresh. Open daily. Reservations advised. Major credit cards accepted. In *Centro Comercial Concresa* (phone: 2-979-3242).

Hereford Grill This steakhouse does prime meat to perfection. *Medallón de lomito al oporto* (steak in port) and *pollo deshuasado* Hereford (boned chicken) are special. Open daily. Reservations advised. Major credit cards accepted. Calle Madrid, Las Mercedes (phone: 2-929664).

Lasserre Classic French food is served in elegant surroundings. Of special note is the fine cellar of French wines. Closed Saturday lunch and Sundays. Reservations advised. Major credit cards accepted. Av. 3, between Segunda and Tercera Transversales, Los Palos Grandes (phone: 2-283-4558 or 2-283-3079).

Il Padrino An Italian experience: The place is big, the atmosphere relaxed, the decor intriguing (vaulted ceilings, Italian hardwood, Toledo lamps), and it simmers with music and a festive feeling. The vast menu is worthy of Godfatherly gusto; try the fabulous antipasto—it's almost a meal in itself. Open daily. Reservations advised. Major credit cards accepted. Plaza Altamira Sur (phone: 2-263-3060).

MODERATE

Dama Antañona Housed in a beautifully converted colonial home, its original rooms intact, this spot offers a genuine criollo menu. Best at midday for business lunches. Closed Saturdays. Reservations unnecessary. Major credit cards accepted. 14 Jesuitas at Maturín in Altagracia (phone: 2-563-5639 or 2-837287).

Damasco Kibbe, hummus, tabbouleh, and falafel are just the beginning of the menu at this family-run Middle Eastern restaurant. The fine food is complemented by equally good service. Open daily. Reservations unnecessary. Major credit cards accepted. Calle Guaicaipuro, *Centro Comercial Metropolitano* in Chacao (phone: 2-266-6695).

Lee Hamilton Steak House A US-style steak and potatoes place, it also serves prime ribs and has an impressive salad bar. Good value, agreeable setting. Open daily. Reservations unnecessary. Major credit cards accepted. Av. San Felipe at the corner of Av. El Bosque in La Castellana (phone: 2-263-8429).

El Portón A must on all visitors' restaurant lists, this place is tops for its criollo atmosphere and cookery. Try the *pabellón, lomito con queso* (steak with cheese), or *hallacas* (banana leaves stuffed with a mix of cornmeal, meat, olives, and onions). The Spanish colonial setting is enhanced by Venezuelan music. Open daily. Reservations advised. Major credit cards accepted. 18 Av. Pichincha, El Rosal (phone: 2-952-0027).

ON THE COAST

EXPENSIVE

El Mesón del Faro Perhaps the best restaurant on the central coast, this out-of-the-way lighthouse surrounded by gardens specializes in seafood. Its paella "El Mesón" is a real treat. Open daily. Reservations unnecessary. Major credit cards accepted. Av. Principal de Puerto Viejo, Catia La Mar (phone: 31-511435).

Timotes Tastefully decorated in colonial style, it is famous for fine criollo seafood; the *sancocho* (a sea bass soup) alone is worth the cab ride from Macuto. The service is pleasant as well. Open daily. Reservations unnecessary. Major credit cards accepted. Av. Soublette at Calle Libertador in Maiquetía (phone: 31-22618).

MODERATE

Cookery An informal spot with an international flavor—scampi, pasta, steaks, and French dishes are specialties. There's an air conditioned dining room, with a disco and bar upstairs. Open daily. Reservations unnecessary. Major credit cards accepted. Near the *Macuto Sheraton,* on Av. Principal del Caribe, Caraballeda (phone: 31-944643).

El Portón de Timotes The younger brother of *Timotes* in Maiquetía (see above), this large, colonial-style dining spot offers criollo and international seafood dishes. Open daily. Reservations advised. Major credit cards accepted. Near the *Macuto Sheraton* and *Meliá Caribe* hotels, Av. Principal Urbanización Caribe, Caraballeda (phone: 31-943530).

MARGARITA ISLAND

MODERATE

Da Gaspar This Italian eatery featuring homemade pasta has a loyal following—and no wonder, it's consistently good. It's also the best place in town for seafood. Try the mixed seafood special, a bountiful variety of fish and shellfish in a flavorful broth. Open daily. Reservations unnecessary. Major credit cards accepted. Av. 4 de Mayo (phone: 95-613486).

Martín Pescador Crowded and raucous, this small seafood eatery is nonetheless a great place to sample Margarita's luscious vine-ripe tomatoes; locals say the tomato salad is the best to be had on the island. Open daily. Reservations unnecessary. Major credit cards accepted. Av. 4 de Mayo (phone: 95-611120 or 95-616697).

Diversions

Unexpected Pleasures and Treasures

Few committed sailors, swimmers, or divers can resist the urgent call of the sea, and nowhere in the Western Hemisphere is that voice stronger than in the islands and along the coastal shores of the Caribbean. Traditionally, vacations in the Caribbean are schizophrenic affairs, with periods of the most intense activity—tacking through clusters of tiny land dots in a strong wind; fighting tarpon or, in deeper water, marlin; following the twisting patterns of a coral reef into the depths—relieved by the unabashed luxury of beachside do-nothingism, sipping cool drinks in the hot sun, enjoying the latest best seller unharried by anything more pressing than a date with some suntan oil.

But the islands of the Caribbean are much more than beaches wrapped around volcanoes and dropped into the sea for the convenience of ocean addicts. Their history is a weltering confusion of languages, cultures, and modes of government. The profusion of influences and peoples strewn throughout the area seems almost profligate. An embarrassment of riches, the Caribbean is as lushly endowed with man-made leisure activities as it is with natural ones. When the pleasures of the water begin to pale and even the most devoted sun worshiper has soaked up enough rays for one day, there are a multitude of other distractions—physical and cerebral—with which to pass the time.

What follows are our choices of the best places in the islands in which to enjoy some unexpected pleasures and treasures—from sampling the islands' most splendid natural wonders to discovering the most fascinating historic sites and the most elegant casinos. In each section, arranged alphabetically by island, the emphasis is firmly on the quality of the experience, doing what you want to do in the best possible environment. For more details on each of the areas highlighted here, refer to the individual chapters in THE ISLANDS.

A Few of Our Favorite Things

Though each of the dazzling array of Caribbean islands claims to have the finest accommodations, the most spectacular beaches, the absolute best golf and tennis, we've narrowed down the list to the choicest places that are guaranteed to delight pursuers of a variety of pleasures. Follow our lead; you won't be disappointed.

Each place listed below is described in detail in THE ISLANDS chapter.

REGAL RESORTS, SPECIAL HAVENS, AND ENCHANTED PRIVATE ISLANDS

The following are our special favorites for a stay in the Caribbean. Several are large, self-contained resorts, others are small and intimate, and some even occupy their own islands, but each in its own way offers the highest caliber of service, food, and island ambience.

Cap Juluca, Anguilla *(see page 66)*
Covecastles, Anguilla *(see page 67)*
Malliouhana, Anguilla *(see page 67)*
Curtain Bluff, Antigua *(see page 89)*
Biras Creek, Virgin Gorda, British Virgin Islands *(see page 207)*
Guana Island Club, British Virgin Islands *(see page 207)*
Little Dix Bay, Virgin Gorda, British Virgin Islands *(see page 206)*
Necker Island, British Virgin Islands *(see page 208)*
Peter Island, British Virgin Islands *(see page 208)*
Casa de Campo, Dominican Republic *(see page 327)*
Ciboney Ocho Rios, Jamaica *(see page 423)*
Round Hill, Jamaica *(see pages 424)*
Trident, Jamaica *(see page 424)*
Four Seasons, Nevis *(see page 642)*
El Conquistador, Puerto Rico *(see page 554)*
Horned Dorset Primavera, Puerto Rico *(see page 555)*
Carl Gustaf, St. Barthélemy *(see page 594)*
Les Castelets, St. Barthélemy *(see page 594)*
François Plantation, St. Barthélemy *(see page 594)*
Guanahani, St. Barthélemy *(see page 595)*
Le Toiny, St. Barthélemy *(see page 595)*
Anse Chastanet Beach, St. Lucia *(see page 662)*
Ladera, St. Lucia *(see page 662)*
Oyster Pond, St. Maarten *(see page 691)*
La Belle Créole, St. Martin *(see page 690)*
Le Méridien L'Habitation and Le Domaine, St. Martin *(see page 690)*
La Samanna, St. Martin *(see page 691)*
Cotton House, Mustique, Grenadine Islands *(see page 724)*
Palm Island Beach Club, Grenadine Islands *(see page 724)*
Petit St. Vincent, Grenadine Islands *(see page 725)*
Salt Whistle Bay Club, Mayreau, Grenadine Islands *(see page 725)*
Young Island, Grenadine Islands *(see page 726)*
Caneel Bay, St. John, US Virgin Islands *(see page 798)*
Grand Palazzo, St. Thomas, US Virgin Islands *(see page 799)*

TOP TEE-OFF SPOTS

The Caribbean islands offer some prime challenges for golfers. The courses listed below—our particular favorites—are the inspiration of some of golf's most illustrious architects, such as Robert Trent Jones Sr. and Jr., and Pete Dye. And the views surrounding them are so striking that you may have trouble just keeping your eye on the ball.

Royal Westmoreland Golf & Country Club, Barbados *(see page 134)*
Casa de Campo, Dominican Republic *(see page 321)*
Golf International de St-François, Guadeloupe *(see page 377)*
Tryall, Jamaica *(see page 416)*
El Conquistador, Puerto Rico *(see page 548)*
Hyatt Dorado Beach, Puerto Rico *(see page 548)*
Palmas del Mar, Puerto Rico *(see page 548)*
Four Seasons, Nevis *(see page 639)*
Mount Irvine Golf Club, Tobago *(see page 750)*
Westin Carambola Beach, St. Croix, US Virgin Islands *(see page 790)*
Mahogany Run, St. Thomas, US Virgin Islands *(see page 794)*

CHOICE COURTS

There's something about the islands' gentle sea breezes and warming sunshine that makes the Caribbean a matchless setting for tennis buffs. The resorts below offer all that an ace (or an amateur) could hope for—fine facilities, scenic backdrops, and all the extras.

Curtain Bluff, Antigua *(see page 87)*
Casa de Campo, Dominican Republic *(see page 324)*
Half Moon Golf, Tennis & Beach Club, Jamaica *(see page 420)*
El Conquistador, Puerto Rico *(see page 551)*
Hyatt Regency Cerromar Beach/Hyatt Dorado Beach, Puerto Rico *(see page 551)*
Palmas del Mar, Puerto Rico *(see page 552)*
Four Seasons, Nevis *(see page 640)*
Buccaneer, St. Croix, US Virgin Islands *(see page 792)*
Wyndham Sugar Bay, St. Thomas, US Virgin Islands *(see page 796)*

DREAM BEACHES

Of the seemingly endless miles of sandy shores these islands have to offer, the following strands are guaranteed to deliver the best combination of sun, sand, and endless sea. And as some of these places haven't yet been discovered by the masses, you may even be able to enjoy the much sought-after but often elusive gift of solitude.

West Shoal Bay, Anguilla *(see page 58)*
Cane Garden Bay, Tortola, British Virgin Islands *(see page 204)*
Playa Grande, Dominican Republic *(see page 323)*
Sosúa, Dominican Republic *(see page 323)*
Petite Anse, Marie Galante, Guadeloupe *(see page 378)*
Pointe des Châteaux, Guadeloupe *(see page 378)*

Natural Wonderlands

To most urban dwellers, the island world is one vast natural wonder—a serendipitous embrace of land, sea, and sun that is wide enough to include anyone who ventures into the area. They aren't all that wrong. But even in paradise there are superlatives, and the spots below give a special sense of the islands' splendor.

BARBADOS The *Andromeda Gardens,* overlooking the Atlantic coast, feature an exotic collection of hybrid orchids and other tropical plants in a maze-like, rock garden setting. The 46-acre Turner's Hall Woods are all that remains of the primeval forest that once covered the island. It is part of the *Barbados National Trust,* as is *Welchman Hall Gully,* a botanical garden about 3 miles from the stalagmites and stalactites of Harrison's Cave.

BELIZE *Crooked Tree Wildlife Sanctuary,* just 33 miles northwest of Belize City, is a refuge for thousands of birds and many other varieties of fauna and flora. Visitors may tour the network of lagoons, swamps, and waterways. *Cockscomb Basin Wildlife Sanctuary* in southern Belize was set aside by the government of Belize as the first reserve specifically for the protection and management of jaguars. There are many other species of wild cat here, including the puma, ocelot, margay, and jaguarundi, as well as other wildlife, such as the Central American tapir and the scarlet macaw. *Guanacaste National Park,* near Belmopan, is home to numerous species of birds, including woodcreepers, woodpeckers, tanagers, toucans, wood thrushes, kingfishers, and orioles. *Half Moon Cay Natural Monument,* a sanctuary for the red-footed booby, is located on the southeastern corner of Lighthouse Reef, Belize's outermost coral atoll. Near Half Moon Cay is the famous Blue Hole, formed when the roof of an ancient cave collapsed. *Hol Chan Marine Reserve* covers 5 square miles and is centered around a break in Belize's barrier reef off Ambergris Caye. *Caracol Archaeological Preserve*—a significant Maya excavation site—is located within the *Chiquibul Forest Reserve* of southern Belize. The *Rio Bravo Conservation Area* in northwestern Belize is a part of the proposed three-country "Maya Peace Park." *Las Milpas* is a Maya city within the area that is in the process of being excavated. Information: *Belize Audubon Society,* 12 Fort St., Belize City (phone: 501-2-35004; fax: 501-2-34985).

DOMINICA In Edenesque *Morne Trois Pitons National Park* at the southeast end of the island, giant ferns and bromeliads surround trunks of trees and weave through their limbs, forming latticeworks of foliage that seem to climb to the sky. The Emerald Pool, a water-filled grotto fed by a waterfall and surrounded by beautiful plants, flowers, and ferns, lies hidden deep within the park. So do three remarkable lakes: Boeri, rimmed with volcanic rock; Fresh Water, with sweeping coastal views; and Boiling Crater Lake, kept bubbling by the volcanic heat of the crater in which it is cupped.

Not far from Roseau, in the south-central section of Dominica, are Trafalgar Falls, twin waterfalls surrounded by tree-covered cliffs, which converge in a cluster of rocky ponds fringed with luxurious tropical foliage. Near the falls and the village of Wotton Waven, east of Roseau, are two sulfur springs, hot pools of volcanic mud where the earth bubbles and steams like a huge vat of sorcerer's brew. Information: *Division of Tourism, National Development Corporation,* PO Box 293, Roseau, Dominica (phone: 809-448-2045; fax: 809-448-5840), or the Director of Forestry, *Forestry Division, Botanical Gardens,* Roseau, Dominica (phone: 809-448-2733 or 809-448-2401, ext. 417; fax: 809-448-5200).

GUADELOUPE A day's journey to the *Parc National,* an official national park of France located in the heart of Basse-Terre, is not one you are likely to forget. The tropical rain forests, lakes, waterfalls, natural mountain pools, steaming fumaroles, and well-marked trails make this one of the loveliest hiking spots in the Caribbean.

JAMAICA Off the main road from Kingston to Ocho Rios, on Route A3, a 3-mile stretch of road winds down an old riverbed surrounded by giant ferns. This stretch is called Fern Gully, a deep forest area that offers a taste of cool air and an opportunity to ride beneath the tall ferns—the first complex plant life to populate the island.

While driving along a 2-mile stretch of road in St. Elizabeth Parish, close to Black River, you will suddenly be surrounded by what looks like a soft yellow-green feathery umbrella. This is Bamboo Avenue, a continuous arch of bamboo that seems to appear out of nowhere. To reach it, pass through *Holland Estate,* a former sugar factory.

PUERTO RICO *El Yunque* is a 28,000-acre tropical rain forest and national bird sanctuary, home to 240 different species of native trees, many primeval. While wandering beneath a towering pine or sierra palm you might catch a whiff of white ginger or find a wild orchid as you hear the call of the *coquí,* the tiny tree frog that is Puerto Rico's official mascot. Be on the alert, for there are many delicate, beautifully colored wildflowers that hide behind, beneath, and around the more conspicuous trees and shrubs. Although more than 100 billion gallons of rain fall in the forest annually, the showers are usually short, and shelters dot the trails. The park is about 25 miles east of San Juan via Route 3, then south on Route 191. Information: *Sierra Palm Visitors Center,* Rte. 191 (phone: 809-887-2875 or 809-766-5335).

TRINIDAD Visitors arriving at the *Caroni Bird Sanctuary* at sunset or late afternoon might see a large cluster of bright red feathers swooping through the sky like a gigantic flame. Within moments, hundreds of scarlet ibis (Trinidad's national bird) descend onto the 450-acre sanctuary, where they live and nest amid vast stretches of mangrove trees. In the fall, the sea of red mangroves matches the feathers of the birds they shelter. The sanctuary is about 7 miles south of Port of Spain.

US VIRGIN ISLANDS About two thirds of the island of St. John is a natural haven. In fact, there is little to do on the island but enjoy the scenery, particularly the *Virgin Islands National Park.* Don't hesitate to ask the rangers to fill you in on the flora and fauna that abound in the park—pelicans and sandpipers, mahogany and bay, tamarind, flamboyant, and shower of gold are among the native inhabitants you are likely to run across. Park guides also lead nature walks and give nature talks several times a week (phone: 809-776-6201).

VENEZUELA The highest waterfall (and one of the most beautiful) in the world lies deep in the Venezuelan jungle and is called Salto Angel (Angel Falls), after the American pilot Jimmy Angel, who discovered it in 1935. Approximately 3,212 feet high (15 times as tall as Niagara), steeped in swirling mists and rainbows, the falls tumble down layers of multicolored rock to the jungle floor. The falls are most often seen during a breath-catching flight en route to *Avensa Airlines' Camp Canaima* resort or the Pemón Indian camp operated by *Aerotuy* at Kavac. They also can be reached by a fairly arduous walking-canoeing trip from *Camp Canaima,* a comfortable, simple cottage resort at the edge of Canaima Lagoon—itself fed by a spectacular ring of seven falls. But most guests prefer shorter treks, swimming, or relaxing in the immensely beautiful jungle surroundings.

Testaments in Stone: Historic Sites

With the exception of the ancient Maya and Toltec ruins of Mexico and Belize and scattered Indian relics, most historic sites of the Caribbean and Atlantic islands date from the colonial period after the arrival of Columbus. These sites reflect the course of European colonialism in the New World—the presence and influence of the French, English, Dutch, and Spanish on the islands, and their struggles for control.

ANTIGUA *Nelson's Dockyard* was the major British naval yard in the Caribbean from 1707 until 1899, when ships simply became too large to negotiate the entrance to its harbor. It got its name (and its reputation) from the four-year period (1784–87) when Captain Horatio Nelson was in command. The dockyard area includes the *Admiral's Inn,* a hotel and restaurant made from bricks that came to Antigua as ships' ballast; the *Admiral's House* (now a museum), which never actually housed Admiral Nelson; the *Officers' Quarters Building;* and the *Copper and Lumber Store,* now a hotel.

BARBADOS Some of the finest antique greathouses in the Caribbean can be found on Barbados. *Villa Nova, St. Nicholas Abbey, Francia Plantation, Sam Lord's Castle* (now part of a Marriott hotel), and *Sunbury Plantation House* are all elegantly restored and open to the public. *Porters, Holders House, Mullins Mill,* and *Bay Mansion* are only occasionally open to visitors. *Farley Hill* and the *Morgan Lewis Mill* are other relics of the old plantation days. Information: *Barbados Tourism Authority,* Harbour Rd., Bridgetown, St. Michael, Barbados (phone: 809-427-2623/4) or the *Barbados National Trust,* 2 10th Ave., Belleville, St. Michael, Barbados (phone: 426-2421 or 436-9033).

BELIZE Some of the greatest centers of the once-powerful Maya civilization were found in what is now modern-day Belize. The splendid 2,000-year-old city of *Caracol* still boasts Belize's tallest manmade structure, the 139-foot-high *Caana* (Sky Palace), which is topped with three temples, several pyramids, and a courtyard. The city is hidden deep in the tangled jungle at the foothills of the Maya Mountains and contains more than 4,000 buildings sprinkled across 55 square miles. Guides are required and are available at the site, and scheduled tours are offered. All visitors must obtain a permit (cost: $1), available from the *Forestry Department Station* in the village of Augustine, 30 miles north of *Caracol* (no phone), or from the *Archaeology Commission* in Belmopan (phone: 501-8-22106).

The 1,400-year-old city of *Xunantunich* is one of the best excavated and most popular of Belize's Maya sites. Located about 80 miles southwest of Belize City, near the Guatemalan border, it offers an impressive view of both countries from the top of the 130-foot *El Castillo* pyramid. Only 30 miles north of Belize City is the Maya ceremonial center of *Altun Ha.* The most spectacular find (among many) unearthed here was a carved jade head of the sun god Kinich Ahau. Other sites include the ceremonial center *Nim Li Punit,* the sprawling trading and ceremonial center of *Lamanai, Cuello* (the oldest Maya site yet discovered), *Santa Rita Corozal,* and *Cerros Maya.*

CURAÇAO *Mikve Israel-Emanuel,* the oldest continuously operating synagogue in the Western Hemisphere, is in Willemstad on the corner of Columbusstraat and Kerkstraat. Built in 1732 in the Dutch colonial architectural tradition, the interior is carpeted with a layer of white sand, symbolizing the journey of the Jews across the desert to the Promised Land. Next door is the *Jewish Historical and Cultural Museum,* which served as a rabbi's house and, later, a Chinese laundry, until the remains of an ancient *mikvah* (ritual bath) were uncovered in its courtyard. The museum contains exhibits of centuries-old religious relics, tools, and artifacts. Closed weekends and on all Jewish and public holidays. Admission charge (phone: 5999-611633).

DOMINICAN REPUBLIC As a center of activity in the gold-hunting days, Santo Domingo became a city of elegant living. All along the Calle Las Damas in old Santo Domingo you will find buildings from these gilded days—the

Casa Bastidas (Bastidas House), the *Capilla de los Remedios* (Chapel of Our Lady of Remedies), the *Museo de las Casas Reales* (Museum of the Royal Houses), and others. Also on Calle Las Damas is the *Pantéon Nacional* (National Pantheon), formerly a Jesuit monastery, built between 1714 and 1745.

The oldest cathedral in the Western Hemisphere is the *Catedral de Santa María la Menor,* also in Santo Domingo. Its 450-year-old nave once housed what are said to be the mortal remains of Christopher Columbus, since moved to the *Faro a Colón* (Columbus Lighthouse). The cathedral is on the south side of Parque Colón (Columbus Square).

JAMAICA Across the harbor from Kingston, Port Royal was called "the world's wickedest city" while it served as headquarters for the privateer/pirate Henry Morgan. Although a good part of the town was toppled into the harbor by a treacherous tidal wave and earthquake in 1692, several remnants from those ribald days remain intact, including *St. Peter's Church, Fort Charles, Giddy House* (so named because of the rakish tilt it acquired in a 1907 earthquake), and the old *Naval Hospital* (now a museum of Port Royal relics). All are open daily and have an admission charge.

MARTINIQUE *La Pagerie,* in Les Trois-Ilets, was once a busy plantation and thriving sugar factory. It also was the birthplace of Marie-Josèphe Rose Tascher de la Pagerie, who became the Empress Josephine, wife of Napoleon. Her childhood bed, clothes, and letters are on display in the kitchen, which occupies a separate building beside the crumbled plantation house foundations. Closed Mondays. Admission charge (phone: 596-683455).

Another site worth visiting is the town of St-Pierre, "the Pompeii of the West Indies," which was devastated by a volcano in 1902. All that remains of this once-flourishing city of stately villas, mansions, and gardens are the ruins of the theater and cathedral and the broken walls of the homes.

MEXICO *Chichén Itzá* was a flourishing Maya center that dominated the entire Yucatán Peninsula until 1224. Among those buildings of particular interest are the *Temple of the Warriors,* the *Group of a Thousand Columns,* the *Tzompantiti,* the *Temple of the Chac-Mool,* and the ball court. Bus tours from Cancún and Cozumel visit the site daily. *Tulum,* a walled seaside city-fort, and *Cobá,* a jungle city that is still being excavated, are two other Maya centers near Cancún and Cozumel; a number of tour operators offer excursions to the sites.

PUERTO RICO The seven-block-square area of Old San Juan, in the westernmost part of the city, contains myriad interesting sites dating back to Spanish colonial days, when this harbor was considered essential to Spanish supremacy in the New World. Today, visitors can explore the moats, turrets, and tunnels of *Fuerte San Cristóbal* and *Fuerte San Felipe del Morro,* the two forts that formed part of the wall that protected the city from the likes of Sir Francis Drake. Two blocks from *El Morro*'s exit, at the Plaza de

San José, is the *Iglesia de San José* and, heading west on Calle San Sebastián, you'll find the *Casa Blanca,* the intended home of Juan Ponce de León, which housed his descendants and several Spanish and American military commanders before it was turned into a museum. Nearby is *La Fortaleza,* the Western Hemisphere's oldest continuously occupied executive mansion. Built in 1540 and given palatial additions in the 19th century, it is open to the public for guided tours. *La Casa del Libro,* an 18th-century house, contains thousands of ancient books. Farther on, *La Princesa,* the restored 1837 prison, mounts changing art exhibits.

ST. KITTS The landmark that gave St. Kitts its reputation as "the Gibraltar of the Caribbean" is *Brimstone Hill Fortress.* Atop a 750-foot cliff, this enormous fortress took the British more than a hundred years to build. Although the French captured *Brimstone Hill* in 1782, the fort returned to British hands, as did the island, under the conditions of the Treaty of Versailles in 1783.

US VIRGIN ISLANDS In the heart of Christiansted on St. Croix stands a group of 18th-century buildings that the Danes built after buying St. Croix from the French. The US now maintains this area as a National Historic Site. Pick up a *Walking Tour Guide* at the *Visitors' Information Bureau* in the *Old Scalehouse* near the harborfront. *Fort Christiansvaern,* which contains military treasures, battlements, and dungeons, is one of the area's key attractions.

Sunken and Buried Treasure

It doesn't take too much imagination for a Caribbean vacationer to begin dreaming about discovering sunken or buried treasure. The area is alive with tales and relics of pirates, Spanish gold, sunken ships, and yellowed parchment maps that seem to cry out for some adventurous diver or explorer to dig deeper, look further, dive farther offshore—and discover a wealth of gold and precious stones. Estimates of the number of ships sunk in the Caribbean and western Atlantic are as high as 4,000; in the Anegada Channel of the British Virgin Islands alone, some 134 ships are supposed to have gone down between 1523 and 1833.

The Spanish kept excellent records of the treasure ships transporting the wealth of the New World across the Caribbean and Atlantic. The cargo manifest of a single ship, the *Nôtre Dame de Déliverance,* shows 1,170 pounds of gold bullion (packed into 17 chests), 15,399 gold doubloons, 153 gold snuff boxes weighing six ounces each, more than a million pieces of eight (Spanish coins that equalled eight *reals*), 764 ounces of silver, 31 pounds of silver ore, six pairs of diamond earrings, a diamond ring, and several chests of precious stones.

Most of the ships that went down during this period ran aground, tearing out their hulls on the numerous coral reefs that lie just beneath the surface of the water. A few treasure-laden ships were sent to the bottom by cannon fire, though many ships sunk by enemy fire were warships or light cargo and messenger packets, not treasure galleons. Tides and sifting sands can cover a ship or move the wreck miles from its original site. These same tides can cause lost treasure to rise to the surface, as in the case of the woman who happened upon an estimated $100,000 in gold and diamond jewelry, gold, silver, and platinum on Grand Cayman Island some years ago.

What follows is a list of the best treasure-hunting spots in the Caribbean; we ask only a modest percentage of your findings as recompense.

BELIZE Originally colonized by shipwrecked pirates, with the world's second-longest barrier reef just off its well-traveled coastline, there is every reason to believe that more than one wreck lies among these treacherous shoals. Try the area just beyond Ambergris Reef. Prior permission by the *Archaeology Commission* in Belmopan (phone: 501-8-22106) is required for any excavations.

BRITISH VIRGIN ISLANDS Robert Louis Stevenson's *Treasure Island* is based on activities rumored to have taken place on Norman Island or Dead Chest, both near Tortola, which was a pirate stronghold for quite some time. Also check Anegada and Virgin Gorda, as well as the Anegada Channel between them; the channel is known to be the site of over 130 wrecks. Waters of any of the surrounding isles could hold sunken cargo.

CAYMAN ISLANDS As local legend has it, during a dark night in February 1794, a convoy of British merchant ships was sailing to the east of Grand Cayman. Because of the inaccuracy of the navigational charts in those days—and the coral reefs that lie just beneath the shallow water—this was a particularly hazardous route. The lead ship, the *Cordelia,* struck a reef and raised flags of warning and distress. The other ships misunderstood the signal in the darkness, and nine more ships struck the reef before anything could be done. Many of the passengers were rescued by the residents of the island's East End area. The fluke of an anchor, said to be a relic of what is now known as the "Wreck of the Ten Sails," can be seen today from land, but the reef is known to be infested with sea urchins (which effectively prevent much treasure hunting there). In addition to the jewelry found on the beach here, a platinum bar (dated 1521) was recovered from a shipwreck just off Grand Cayman.

COLOMBIA Henry Morgan would have been one successful pirate if he had really buried treasure on all the islands that claim to be sites of his hidden fortunes. But because it is strategically located between the old Spanish treasure ports of Porto Bello and Cartagena, San Andrés Island is truly a likely possibility. The odds are even better on nearby Providencia Island or on one of the others around San Andrés.

DOMINICAN REPUBLIC In the early days of Spain's presence in the Americas, the city of Santo Domingo was its Caribbean headquarters. Explorers departed from here on their quests for gold and silver, and ships put in here before journeying to Spain. Ships leaving the port city (on the southern crescent of the island) had to pass through the narrow passages at either end of the island on their return trip to Spain. If they passed through the Windward Passage to the west end, they had to skirt the reefs and shallows around the Caicos Islands and pass through the Mouchoir (Silver) Bank (northeast of Hispaniola) before heading for the open sea. Once through the eastern channel (Mona Passage), they were in open waters. Not surprisingly, there have been reports of wrecks near Silver Bank. The wreck of the *Concepción,* discovered here late in 1978, carried about $40 million in silver and antiques. Some of the pieces may be found for sale at Dominican museums and jewelry shops.

JAMAICA On June 7, 1692, an earthquake and tidal wave hit the island of Jamaica, and most of the city of Port Royal literally sank beneath the waves. Long before the city was flooded, it often had been compared with the biblical Sodom, for there was one tavern, alehouse, or winery for every ten people. During the 1960s, divers brought up hundreds of pieces of silver, pewter, and ceramics, and enough ethnographic evidence to prove Port Royal's rightful claim to being the former center of sin in the West Indies. Since then, the remains of this lively city have been picked through by many divers, but something new always is being brought to the surface. There also are reports of several wrecks off Negril, and records show that six ships went down in Montego Bay in 1780. The Seranilla Bank, about 250 miles southeast of Jamaica (nearly halfway between Jamaica and the coast of Honduras), is reputed to be the spot where an entire Spanish treasure fleet went down during a hurricane in 1655.

ST. EUSTATIUS The Dutch pirates were as successful at sea as the Dutch merchants were on land; with financial encouragement from the Dutch West Indies Company (which bought plundered goods for resale), Dutch pirates managed to take a goodly number of Spanish (and other) ships. The entire yield of one successful 1717 expedition, estimated at a million pieces of eight, was placed in a cave on Statia for storage; later, the mouth of the cave was sealed by an earthquake, and the treasure has never been recovered. And the *Zeelander,* a Dutch warship that went down off the northern tip of the island in 1792 carrying 500,000 guilders in gold and silver with it, apparently remains for treasure hunters to find.

ST. MAARTEN/ST. MARTIN The Portuguese galleon *Santissimo Trinidade,* carrying some 2.5 million cruzados in gold, is believed to have been lost off the eastern coast of St. Martin in 1781.

Shopping

There are three distinct kinds of shopping opportunities available in the Caribbean: *duty-free* (or almost), wherein imported goods are offered at relatively low prices because they are not taxed (or taxed at a very low rate) as imports; *in-bond,* where specified goods are sold to tourists as if the merchandise had never entered the vending country and where delivery usually is made to their departing plane or ship; and what can be called *"limited duty-free,"* whereby the island does not tax imports from its mother country, although goods from other countries are charged an import tax. This means that on British islands, English goods will be cheaper than the same brands in the US (which taxes foreign imports); French goods on French islands always represent bargains, and in some cases actually are cheaper than the same goods available in France.

The Caribbean offers fine stores and boutiques that sell imported items and local products. In addition, shopping at native markets is a marvelous way to meet and mingle with local people, absorb atmosphere, tune your ear to the island's patois, bargain for crafts and homemade treats (mango chutney, hot sauce, preserves), and—not incidentally—have a great time. Remember that market dealing in the islands is done on the spot, and you should feel free to haggle a little for the price's sake and for the fun of it. Local vendors enjoy a friendly negotiation, and while they will take your money for the price asked, everyone will have a better time engaging in the good-natured give-and-take of striking a final price.

Imported items to look for in the Caribbean include bone china, crystal, watches, cameras, liquor, perfume, jewelry, silk items, linen, woolens, and cashmere sweaters. Local products include rum and liqueurs, specialty foods, pottery, ceramics, straw work, baskets, rugs, wall hangings, paintings, woodcarvings, shell and coral items, gems, jewelry, resortwear, embroidered clothing, and batik, silk-screened, and Sea Island cotton fabrics.

For detailed information on the best places to shop in the Caribbean, see the *Shopping* entries in the individual island reports in THE ISLANDS. For information on US customs regulations and duty-free allowances, see GETTING READY TO GO.

Horse Races

There are only four places in the whole Caribbean where a bookie stands a chance of making an honest living: Puerto Rico, the Dominican Republic, Venezuela, and Jamaica—all of which schedule flat racing on a regular basis. There's pari-mutuel betting in all four countries; the time-honored British tote-board system also operates at Jamaica's *Caymanas* track. On other islands where racing exists, there are all kinds of formal and informal betting, but it's a long time between meets. And when they are off and running—once a month or four times a year—the scene is much more like a county fair or a big barbecue than the ritualized proceedings at *Belmont* or *Churchill Downs*. Racing fans don't just watch, they *participate*—snacking, tippling, betting, gossiping, and toe tapping to steel band music and calypso (they probably have more fun than the toffs in the boxes). By all means go to the track if you get a kick out of racing, wherever you find it. But if there's island-style racing, go—even if you never follow the ponies back home. Odds are, it'll be a great party.

CONVENTIONAL RACES

DOMINICAN REPUBLIC The *Hipódromo Perla Antillana* in Santo Domingo has races Tuesdays, Thursdays, and Saturdays, and the last Monday of each month. The track is in town on Avenida San Martín near the *Quisqueya* baseball stadium. At press time, a new racetrack, said to be the largest in the Caribbean and Central America, was under construction in Santo Domingo on Avenida las Américas near the airport. Races are slated to start there sometime this year.

JAMAICA There's racing at *Caymanas Race Track,* 7 miles west of the New Kingston area. Races are held every Wednesday, Saturday, and some holidays; check newspapers for times.

PUERTO RICO *El Comandante* racetrack is a modern track 45 minutes east of downtown San Juan on Route 3. It has 18,000 seats and an attractive restaurant. Races are held Wednesdays, Fridays, Sundays, and holidays at 2:30 PM.

VENEZUELA *La Rinconada* in Caracas holds races weekend afternoons. Evening races are held in Valencia every Thursday and sometimes Fridays, and in Maracaibo on Thursdays.

THE PARTIES

BARBADOS The *Barbados Turf Club* holds race meetings on alternating Saturdays during the island's two racing seasons—from January through April and from August through November—on the *Garrison Savannah* outside Bridgetown. Thoroughbred horses are not the only attraction—there also are steel bands, food and drink stands, and a pervasive party atmosphere. Meets usually start at 1 PM and end about 6 PM.

BRITISH VIRGIN ISLANDS There are meets one Sunday a month, on holidays, and during the *BVI Summer Festival* (last week of July, first week of August) at the Tortola track, with informal betting, music, food, and fun. See the *Welcome* guide and the local paper for dates and times.

US VIRGIN ISLANDS The activities at the *Flamboyant Race Track* in Frederiksted on St. Croix usually are flamboyant indeed. Although the event is organized, few horses bear the certified markings or demeanor of a purebred. But the races are always entertaining and amusing, especially when accompanied by lively reggae, rock, soul music, and abundant refreshments. Races are held twice a month, usually on Sundays—check local papers for exact times. Over on St. Thomas, races at the *Estate Nadir Race Track* are similar to those on St. Croix—amusing and lively, with down-home horses, good music, and plenty of food and drink. Check the local paper for the monthly date and time.

Casino Countdown

Island gambling takes one of two forms: action or distraction. The presence of junkets (trips organized to deliver high rollers to the tables by the planeload) and several casinos (rather than just one or two) usually indicates serious play. Otherwise, it's lowercase stuff—something to do with your evenings in town besides eating, dancing, or watching another island floor show.

Only 13 island countries offer casino gambling. In these, certain generalizations apply: Basic games are roulette, craps, and 21 (or blackjack). The minimum bet is $2 (exceptions: baccarat tables, where the stakes are usually *big,* and Colombia, where $1 qualifies), but this can vary slightly (with the designation of certain $5 tables, for example) according to the night, the crowd, and who's in charge. Most islands prohibit their own nationals from gambling, but tourists aren't stopped at the door or charged admission except on the French islands, where they're very serious about rules. (There, you must have identification—with a photograph—that proves you are 21 on Guadeloupe, 18 on Martinique, and there is a 50- to 80-franc admission charge.) Once inside, there may or may not be drinks (which may or may not be free to players).

Judged by breadth of equipment, intensity of action, and the proportion of tourists who list casinos among their prime reasons for choosing a particular destination, Puerto Rico and Aruba are the islands' top gaming spots; Curaçao, St. Maarten, and St. Kitts—all of which attract some junkets—come next; then the French islands, where interest seems to be growing even without junket traffic. These are the best bets:

ANTIGUA There are five casinos: at the *Royal Antiguan* at Deep Bay, at the private *St. James's Club* at Mamora Bay, at *King's Casino* in Heritage Quay, at *Club Antigua* at Jolly Harbour, and at the new *Gabriela Casino* in the *French Quarter* restaurant at Runaway Bay. Slot machines are routinely offered in addition to blackjack, roulette, and craps. Hours: 9 PM to 4 or 5 AM.

ARUBA The island's big tourist parlay is a combination of beaches and casinos at the major Palm Beach hotels: the *Americana Aruba,* the *Aruba Hilton,* the *Aruba Palm Beach,* the *Aruba Sonesta, La Cabaña All-Suite Beach,* the *Holiday Inn,* the *Hyatt Regency Aruba,* and the *Radisson Aruba Caribbean,* several of which have adjacent cabarets in season. There's also the *Alhambra Casino* (part of an entertainment complex), where betting limits are low and the atmosphere pleasantly relaxed. Frequent junkets are available. Drinks are free while you play; people under 18 are not admitted. Hours: 1 PM until 4 AM.

BONAIRE There's a "Barefoot Casino" at the *Divi Flamingo Beach.* More casual fun than real glitter; junkets are not encouraged. Drinks are free for players; no one under 18 admitted. Hours: 4 PM until 3 or 4 AM.

COLOMBIA'S CARIBBEAN COAST The *Casino del Caribe* in Cartagena's *Pierino Gallo* shopping center has one room devoted to slot machines and another for roulette and blackjack. Also in Cartagena is the *Casino Royal.* Minimum table bets are low at both casinos. Casino hours are from early evening to 3 AM. Stakes also start low on San Andrés at the *Casino Internacional* and *Casino El Dorado–Monte Carlo.* The hours are 9 PM to 3 AM.

CURAÇAO The chicest crowds play at the plush-lined *Princess Beach Holiday Inn Crowne Plaza* casino; there also are active gaming rooms in the *Porto Paseo* complex and at the *Coral Cliff,* the *Curaçao Caribbean,* the *Holiday Beach,* the *Holland,* the *Otrabanda,* the *San Marco,* the *Sonesta Beach,* and the *Van der Valk Plaza.* There also is a small casino at the *Las Palmas* hotel. This island is one of the few Caribbean spots where you can lose your blackjack boodle to machines. Junkets are allowed. Players get free drinks. Hours: around midday to 4 AM.

DOMINICAN REPUBLIC *El Embajador,* the *Dominican Fiesta,* the *Hispaniola,* the *Gran Hotel Lina,* the *Jaragua Renaissance,* the *San Gerónimo,* and the *Sheraton* hotels in the capital have casinos, as does *Maunaloa,* a nightclub in the Centro de los Héroes section of Santo Domingo. Casinos at Puerto Plata are in *Jack Tar Village,* the *Playa Dorada,* the *Puerto Plata Beach* resort, and in Punta Cana at the *Bávaro Beach* and *Punta Cana Beach* resorts. Other casinos on the island are at the *Matum* hotel in Santiago and *Decameron Club* in Juan Dolio. US tourists seem to favor *El Embajador, Jaragua,* and the *Sheraton.* There is little junket action. Hours vary from casino to casino, but most are open 4 PM to 4AM.

GUADELOUPE The *Casino de la Marina* at St-François (hours: 9 PM to 3 AM; closed Mondays) is near both the *Méridien* and the *Hamak;* the *Casino Caraïbe Club* (hours: 9 PM to dawn; closed Sundays), on the grounds of the *Arawak* hotel, is handy to Gosier and Bas-du-Fort hotels. Strict French rules apply for admission, and there is an admission charge. No junkets allowed. Players pay for their drinks.

MARTINIQUE The casino at the *Méridien Trois-Ilets* is more accessible than Guadeloupe's casinos. Standard French admission rules apply. Games are roulette and blackjack. Croupiers are European-trained islanders. Admission charge. Hours: 9 PM to 3 AM.

PUERTO RICO The government carefully supervises the casinos at the *Caribe Hilton, Condado Plaza, Dutch Inn, Radisson Ambassador Plaza,* and the new *San Juan Marriott* in the Condado section; *El San Juan, Holiday Inn Crowne Plaza,* and the *Sands* in Isla Verde; the *Palmas del Mar* in Humacao; the *Hyatt* duo—*Dorado Beach* and *Cerromar Beach*—in Dorado; the *El Conquistador* in Las Croabas; the *Ponce Hilton;* and the *Mayagüez Hilton* in Mayagüez. No drinking is allowed at the tables. If asked, you must be able to produce identification that proves you are at least 18. Hours vary, but noon to 4 AM is most common.

ST. KITTS All the action is at the casino of the *Jack Tar Village* at Frigate Bay. There's no charge for admission to the casino, and gamblers are given complimentary drinks at the tables. All the usual games are offered, plus slot machines. Hours: 7 PM to 2 AM.

ST. MAARTEN/ST. MARTIN The Dutch side has the gambling monopoly: at the *Belair Beach, Great Bay Beach, Maho Beach, Mullet Bay, Pelican Beach,* and *Sheraton Port de Plaisance* hotels. There are also in-town casinos—the *Seaview,* the *Coliseum,* and *Rouge et Noir*—as well as the *Atlantis* in Cupecoy Beach and the *Lightning Casino* near the airport. Most casinos open in the afternoon and stay open until 2 AM. Some French-side hotels provide free transport to the Dutch-side casinos. Roulette, 21, craps, and slot machines are all offered; check the rules for slight differences between casinos before playing. Minimum age is 18. Junkets are minor in the overall tourist picture; since gambling is only an incidental reason for most people's trips, the atmosphere is pleasantly relaxed.

ST. VINCENT The *Emerald Valley* hotel has a small gaming room (that resembles a basement rec room more than *Caesar's Palace*) with blackjack, craps, roulette, and slots. Minimum age is 18. Admission charge. Hours: 9 PM to 3 AM; closed Tuesdays.

Climbing and Hiking

Rarely in the islands is there the kind of climbing that is likely to draw a serious mountaineer off the more challenging precipices elsewhere in the world. Many of the islands are of volcanic origin, however, and some of these are still rather threatening—dormant, but hot. And that means extremely interesting climbs are available up, into, and through volcanic craters and bubbling sulfur pits, mud pots, and steam vents to summits that, while hardly high in the eyes of the world, at least provide breathtaking views of the islands. Remember, where there are summits, there are guides. Passing through sulfur pits is a fascinating experience with a guide (a favorite trick is to boil eggs in fuming potholes); without a guide it can be dangerous. See the *Hiking* entries in the individual island reports for details on organized hiking excursions and information on arranging a guide.

Less arduous but no less spectacular scenery is open to hikers who avail themselves of rain forest preserves and parks in the islands. Many islands have some kind of park system, but the rain forests of St. Lucia, Puerto Rico, and Guadeloupe offer an unparalleled sense of the island environment.

Below, our choice of the best hiking and climbing spots in the islands and along the Caribbean coast.

BELIZE The Maya Mountains in the southwest quarter of Belize present a challenging goal to the most avid climbers. Victoria Peak tops the range, at 3,680 feet. As in all the inland areas of this country, which tend to be densely jungled, no expedition should be attempted without a guide. The Chief Forest Officer, *Ministry of Natural Resources,* in Belmopan (phone: 501-8-22333), will help you get in touch with an expert.

DOMINICA The central rain forests, and especially the Emerald Pool in the *Morne Trois Pitons National Park,* provide beautiful day trips; Morne Diablotin (4,747 feet) should not be attempted without a guide—mists the islanders call "liquid sunshine" make it impossible to judge direction near the crest.

GRENADA Hiking along the *Grand Etang National Park*'s trails—all graded and mapped by the government—is a favorite sport of islanders and visitors alike. The tourist board can brief hikers on routes, level of skill required, and—with a day's notice—help arrange expert guides.

GUADELOUPE The lush rain forest scenery (lakes, waterfalls, pools, steaming fumaroles) plus a system of well-marked trails make Basse-Terre's giant *Parc National* exotically beautiful hiking terrain. Information centers, including *La Maison de la Forêt* on La Traversée, display maps of hiking trails through the park. Information: *Organisation des Guides de Montagne, Maison Forestière,* Matouba, St-Claude 97120 (phone: 590-800579).

JAMAICA The 7,402-foot-tall Blue Mountain Peak is a rough climb, even for those in good condition, but it rewards those who achieve it with extraordinary vistas. Climbing, camping, and even cycling excursions are available.

MARTINIQUE For those who wish to stay closer to sea level, there's the peninsula of Presqu'île de la Caravelle, part of the island's *Parc Naturel,* with trails covering a wide range of terrain, but nothing very difficult. Serious climbers should arrange for a guide to take them to the top of Mt. Pelée (the dormant volcano whose 1902 eruption took 30,000 lives), or through the Gorges de la Falaise or the rain forest between Grand' Rivière and Le Prêcheur.

MONTSERRAT Chances Peak, the island's highest point, makes an excellent viewing tower from which to plan island excursions, since almost the entire island can be seen from its 3,002-foot elevation.

ST. LUCIA Rising half a mile from the shore of the Caribbean, with the waves crashing upon their feet, the peaks of the Pitons have been a landmark for mariners since the pirate days. Climbers have been challenging these mountains for just as long. Gros Piton stands 2,619 feet above the sea and Petit Piton just 2,460 feet; the high point of the island is Mt. Gimie—3,145 feet tall. None of these peaks should be attempted without a guide, as the mists and rains that frequently and suddenly cover the island's dense rain forest areas can make visibility a problem. (Petit Piton is closed until further notice because of fire damage caused by climbers.)

ST. VINCENT A climb to the top of St. Vincent's La Soufrière, at 4,049 feet, takes about four hours of walking along steep volcanic ridges androcky streams, through lush rain forests, and over loose volcanic ash. Since its 1979 eruption, new trails have been blazed. A guide is strongly advised for first-time climbers here—if only to get you to the starting point in a four-wheel-drive vehicle. Check the weather forecast before setting out—it's quite a disappointment to reach the crater only to have it, and the magnificent view, obscured by clouds. A canteen of water, a rain poncho, and sturdy shoes are all you'll need for hiking to the volcano's summit. A less strenuous hike is the *Vermont Nature Trail,* with two self-guided loop trails (one taking a half-hour, the other two-and-a-half hours), located near Vermont, a 20-minute drive from Kingstown. The tour winds through tropical rain forest, and there are pre-Columbian stone writings at Buccament Cave.

Glossary

Climate Chart

Average temperatures (in °F)

	January	April	July	October
Anguilla	68–84	68–86	72–90	70–90
Antigua	70–80	72–82	75–85	75–85
Aruba	75–83	76–86	77–87	78–88
Barbados	70–83	72–86	74–86	73–86
Belize	67–81	74–86	75–87	72–86
Bonaire	75–83	76–86	77–87	78–88
British Virgin Islands	72–84	75–84	81–90	77–88
Cayman Islands	68–87	71–89	74–94	72–90
Colombia's Caribbean Coast (for Cartagena)	71–88	74–90	74–92	74–90
Curaçao	75–83	76–86	77–87	78–88
Dominica	71–81	74–85	77–87	75–87
Dominican Republic	66–84	69–85	72–88	72–87
Grenada	62–83	69–92	73–92	71–87
Guadeloupe	70–80	72–82	75–85	75–85
Jamaica	67–86	70–87	73–90	73–88
Martinique	69–83	71–86	74–86	73–87
Mexico's Caribbean Coast (for Cancún)	62–83	69–92	73–92	71–87
Montserrat	73–82	75–86	79–86	79–88
Puerto Rico	70–83	72–85	76–88	75–88
Saba, St. Barthélemy, and St. Eustatius	72–81	73–84	77–86	77–86
St. Kitts and Nevis	73–82	73–84	77–88	77–88
St. Lucia	69–82	71–87	74–87	72–87
St. Maarten/St. Martin	70–82	72–86	75–87	74–87
St. Vincent and the Grenadines	72–85	74–86	76–86	76–86
Trinidad and Tobago	69–87	69–90	71–88	71–89
US Virgin Islands	72–85	74–86	76–88	76–88
Venezuela's Caribbean Coast (for Caracas)	56–75	60–81	61–78	61–79

Weights and Measures

APPROXIMATE EQUIVALENTS

	Metric Unit	Abbreviation	US Equivalent
Length	1 millimeter	mm	.04 inch
	1 meter	m	39.37 inches
	1 kilometer	km	.62 mile
Capacity	1 liter	l	1.057 quarts
Weight	1 gram	g	.035 ounce
	1 kilogram	kg	2.2 pounds
	1 metric ton	MT	1.1 tons
Temperature	0° Celsius	C	32° Fahrenheit

CONVERSION TABLES

METRIC TO US MEASUREMENTS

	Multiply:	by:	to convert to:
Length	millimeters	.04	inches
	meters	3.3	feet
	meters	1.1	yards
	kilometers	.6	miles
Capacity	liters	2.11	pints
(liquid)	liters	1.06	quarts
	liters	.26	gallons
Weight	grams	.04	ounces
	kilograms	2.2	pounds

US TO METRIC MEASUREMENTS

	Multiply:	by:	to convert to:
Length	inches	25.0	millimeters
	feet	.3	meters
	yards	.9	meters
	miles	1.6	kilometers
Capacity	pints	.47	liters
	quarts	.95	liters
	gallons	3.8	liters
Weight	ounces	28.0	grams
	pounds	.45	kilograms

TEMPERATURE

Celsius to Fahrenheit	$(°C \times 9/5) + 32 = °F$
Fahrenheit to Celsius	$(°F - 32) \times 5/9 = °C$

Index